Fodor's

ESSENTIAL SOUTHWEST

Welcome to the Southwest

The American Southwest is known for its rich history, captivating cuisine, and breathtaking natural landscapes. You'll quickly see that it's not all desert, nor barren. Some of the fastest growing cities are here, as are thriving Native American communities. It's a place to explore the great outdoors, test your frontier mettle at a dude ranch, or relax in a luxurious resort spa. The opportunities for exploration in Arizona, New Mexico, Colorado, Utah, and Nevada will thrill and surprise you at every turn. As you plan your travels, please confirm that places are still open and let us know when we need to make updates by writing to us at editors@fodors.com.

TOP REASONS TO GO

★ **Road Trips:** The wide-open spaces of the Southwest dazzle anew with every turn.

★ **Outdoor Activities:** Hiking, biking, horseback riding, and fishing are all excellent.

★ **Great Food:** Great steaks and excellent Mexican and Southwestern flavors will satisfy.

★ **The Grand Canyon:** Whether you hike, raft, or drive it, you shouldn't miss it.

★ **Skiing and Winter Sports:** The best skiing in the U.S. is in the Rocky Mountains.

★ **Native American Heritage:** There's no better place to appreciate these thriving cultures.

Contents

MAPS

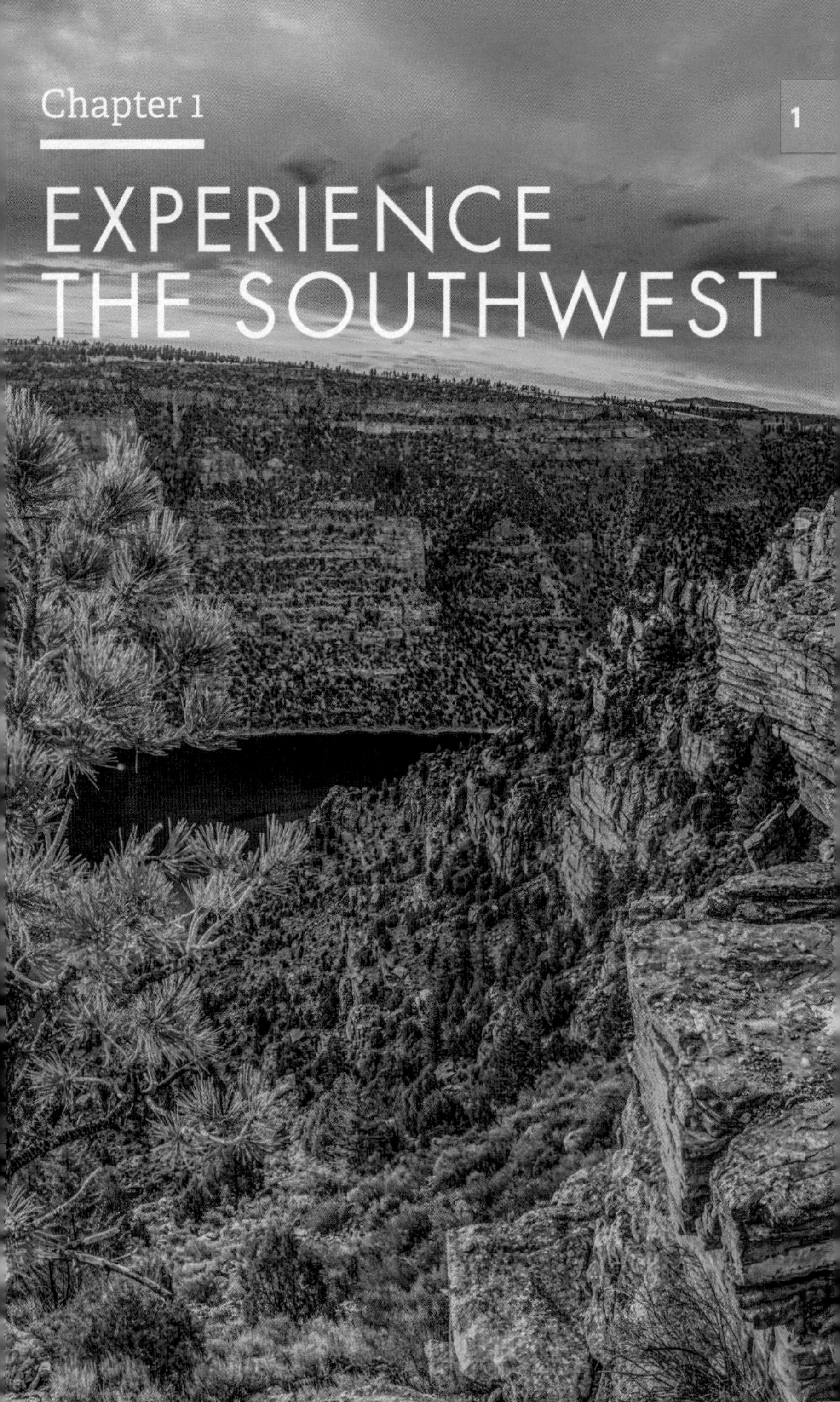

Chapter 1

EXPERIENCE THE SOUTHWEST

25 ULTIMATE EXPERIENCES

The Southwest offers terrific experiences that should be on every traveler's list. Here are Fodor's top picks for a memorable trip.

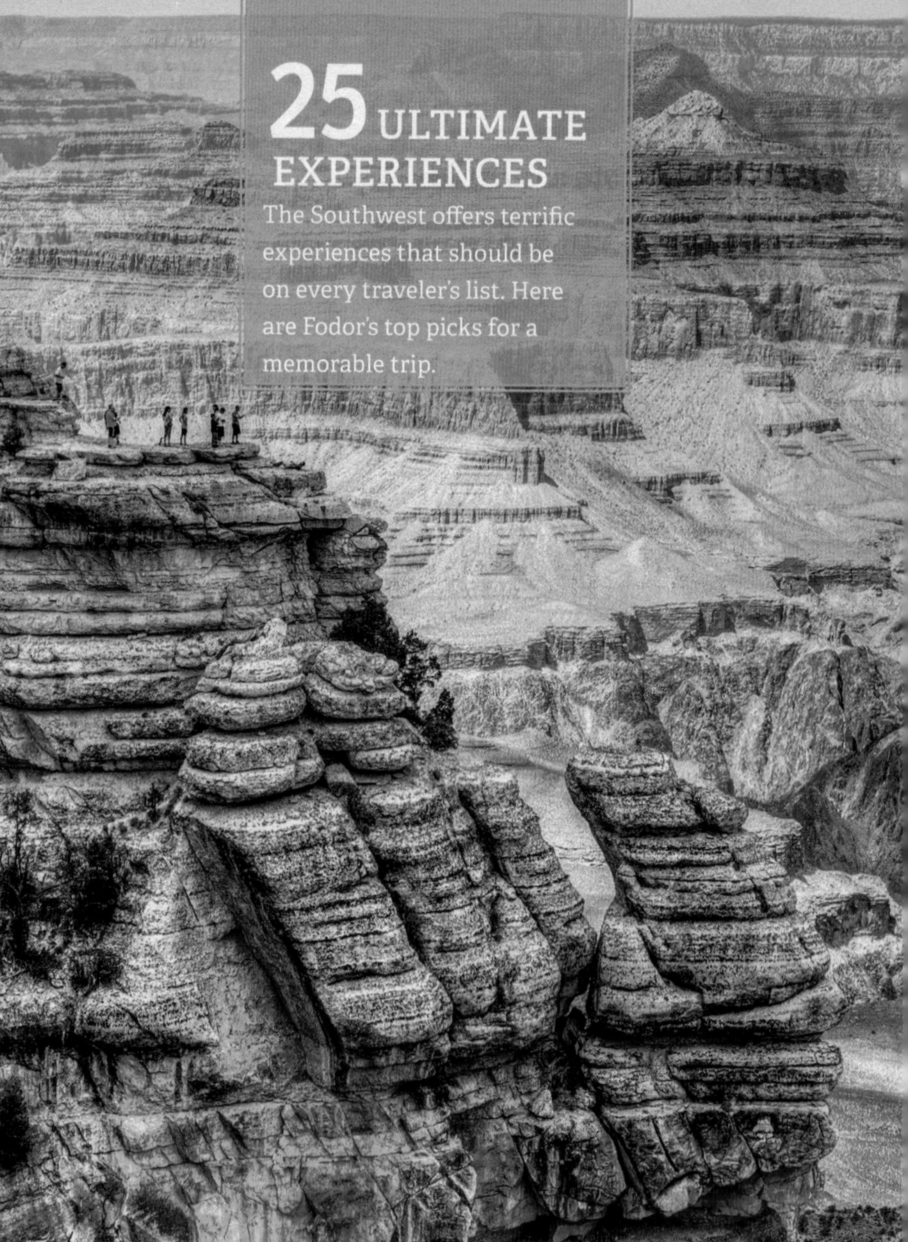

1 Hike the Grand Canyon

Seeing the canyon for the first time is an astounding experience. Witness the sandstone canyon walls, pine and fir forests, mesas, plateaus, volcanic features, and the Colorado River far below. *(Ch. 11)*

2 Scenic drives

Mirror Lake Scenic Byway in Utah is just one of the region's most unforgettable drives. There are many others. *(Ch. 6)*

3 The Strip

There is nowhere on Earth like the Las Vegas Strip. These four neon-bedecked miles of Las Vegas Boulevard South offer endless amusement. *(Ch. 3)*

4 Salt Lake City

At the foot of the Wasatch Mountains, Utah's capital has a stunning setting, Mormon culture, cosmopolitan dining, and easy access to outdoor activities. *(Ch. 5)*

5 Aspen

One of the U.S.'s fabled resort towns, Aspen defines glitz, glamour, and glorious skiing. Top-notch restaurants and high-end shops provide diversions year-round. *(Ch. 17)*

6 Winter sports

Every state in the Southwest has skiing, but Utah and Colorado stand out as among the best ski destinations in the U.S. *(Ch. 5, 6, 15, 16, 17)*

7 Mountain biking

Mountain biking is excellent near Moab, Utah, but bikers will also love Colorado's many trails. *(Ch. 8, 15, 16, 17)*

8 Santa Fe Plaza

Soak up the energy and take in the culture of the city's lively and historic central plaza, which is lined with stellar museums and colorful shops and restaurants. *(Ch. 12)*

9 Discover the beauty of Sedona

With stunning red rock formations—Cathedral Rock, Bear Mountain, Courthouse Rock, Bell Rock—reaching up into an almost-always blue sky, Sedona is a mystical place. *(Ch. 11)*

10 Eat excellent Mexican food

Chimichangas, enchiladas, chilaquiles, tacos, mole, spicy and mild salsas, and, of course, lots of margaritas—a trip to Arizona or New Mexico without indulging is just wrong. *(Ch. 10, 12, 13, 14)*

11 Hot springs

Relax and rejuvenate in one of many mineral hot springs throughout Colorado; among the most popular is Glenwood Springs. *(Ch. 18)*

12 Moab

This countercultural frontier town is a hub of artsy activity and a great base for Arches National Park. It's a must for biking, rock climbing, and rafting as well. *(Ch. 8)*

13 Denver

Colorado's capital boasts historic museums, walkable neighborhoods, parks, breweries, and quaint cafés, as well as live music to rival coastal cities. *(Ch. 15)*

14 The High Road to Taos

For a scenic adventure, drive between Taos and Santa Fe via this breathtaking alpine route through quaint Spanish-colonial villages and past sweeping vistas. *(Ch. 12)*

15 Carlsbad Caverns National Park

The park encompasses more than 100 caves, including its namesake. The Big Room is the largest cavern chamber in North America. *(Ch. 13)*

16 See a show at Red Rocks

Cradled by red sandstone formations that enhance the acoustics, this amphitheater in the foothills southwest of Denver is one of the best concert venues on Earth. *(Ch. 15)*

17 Zion National Park

Angels Landing Trail, with its exhilarating overlooks, and the Narrows Trail, set in a river between dramatic 2,000-foot cliffs, make Zion one of America's top parks. *(Ch. 7)*

18 Pikes Peak

The inspiration for the song "America the Beautiful", Pikes Peak beguiles with its breathtaking views. Take the world's highest cog train all the way to the summit. *(Ch. 16)*

19 Utah Olympic Park

Built for the 2002 Winter Olympic Games, this recreational facility offers fun activities year-round, like tubing, ziplining, and more. *(Ch. 5)*

20 Native American art

The Heard Museum in Phoenix as well as museums in Santa Fe and Denver have some of the premier collections of Native American art in the world. *(Ch. 9)*

21 Marijuana tourism

In Colorado, you can take in a cannabis experience in a controlled setting with cooking classes, guided experiences like "puff and paint" classes, and 420-friendly hotels. *(Ch. 15, 16, 17, 18)*

22 Saguaro National Park

Emblems of the Southwest, these amazing cacti have a life span of up to 200 years and can extend to 60 feet tall. They don't produce their first arm until around age 50. *(Ch. 10)*

23 Get otherworldly in Roswell

Roswell (the site of an alleged flying saucer crash in 1947) is the unabashed epicenter of UFO tourism in the U.S. But extraterrestrial lore is also rich in Area 51 in Nevada. *(Ch. 13)*

24 Rocky Mountain National Park

This premier national park teems with lush forests, alpine lakes, snowcapped peaks, and more than 350 miles of hiking trails filled with bighorn sheep, elk, and mule deer. *(Ch. 15)*

25 Monument Valley

This remote region of Arizona and Utah is impossible to view in a single frame. A scenic 17-mile strip of Valley Drive will have you channeling Ansel Adams. *(Ch. 11)*

WHAT'S WHERE

1 Las Vegas & Vicinity. Sin City is one of the Southwest's most popular destinations.

2 Great Basin National Park. Remote and quiet, the park's caves and backcountry treks are big draws.

3 Salt Lake City. Utah's biggest city provides a central jumping-off point for exploring the region.

4 Park City & Vicinity. Great skiing and mountain beauty draw tourists here year-round.

5 Southwestern Utah. Zion, Bryce Canyon, and Capitol Reef are the major draws to this high-desert region.

6 Moab & Southeastern Utah. Mountain biking and rock climbing are big draws in Moab as well as Arches and Canyonlands.

7 Phoenix, Scottsdale, & Tempe. Arizona's sprawling metropolis is one of the Southwest's fastest-growing cities.

8 Tucson & Southern Arizona. The desert is always near Arizona's second-largest city.

9 Northern Arizona. The Grand Canyon and Sedona are the major draws in this region.

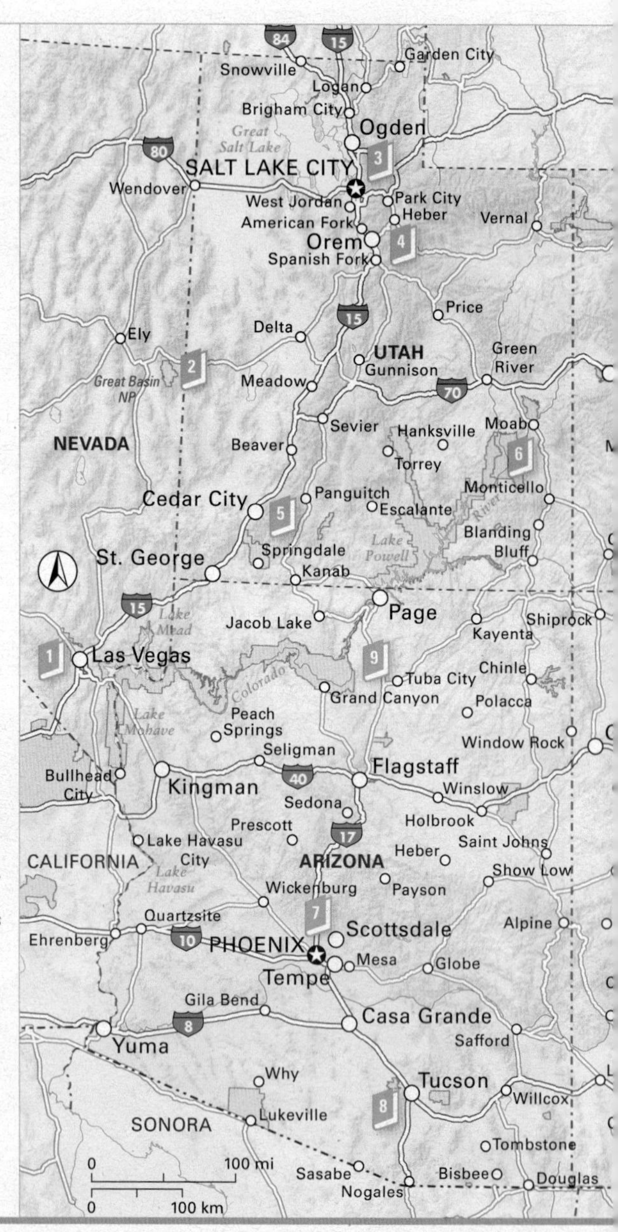

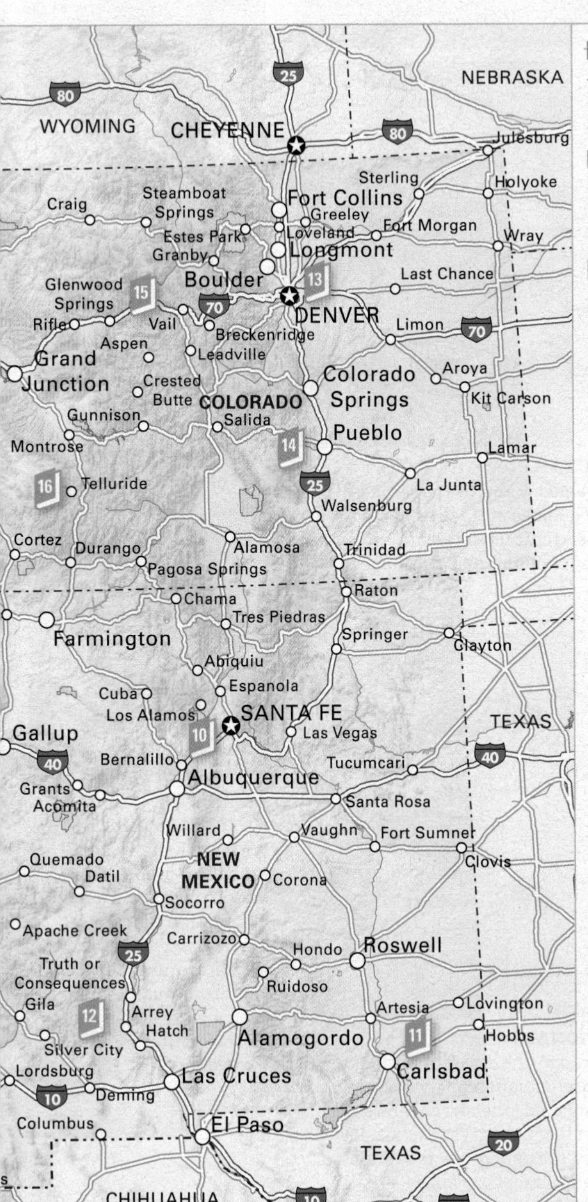

10 Santa Fe, Taos, & Albuquerque. New Mexico's "golden triangle" is its most-visited region.

11 Southeastern New Mexico. Carlsbad Caverns is the major draw in this region.

12 Southwestern New Mexico. From Las Cruces to White Sands National Park, this sparsely populated part of New Mexico is still full of wonders and small towns.

13 Denver, Boulder, & North-Central Colorado. Colorado's largest city is an entry point to the Front Range and Colorado's most popular national park.

14 Colorado Springs & Vicinity. Southeastern Colorado is home to the U.S. Air Force Academy and the magnificent Great Sand Dunes.

15 The Rocky Mountain Ski Resorts. America's premier ski resorts dot the Rocky Mountains from north to south.

16 Western Colorado. Filled with mysterious cliff dwellings and magnificent scenery, western Colorado is a remote but worthy destination.

Best Natural Wonders

MOUNT TIMPANOGOS, UTAH
Mount Timpanogos, nicknamed "Timp," is the second-highest peak in the Wasatch Range at 11,752 feet above sea level, and arguably the most iconic mountain in Utah. It's a destination for hiking and climbing, and also home to Timpanogos Cave National Monument.

PETRIFIED FOREST NATIONAL PARK
More than 200 million years ago, the desert of northeastern Arizona was a much different landscape: wet, lush, and forested. Sediment blanketed fallen trees before they decayed, petrifying them with quartz crystals that slowly supplanted the wood. Today, the park protects countless petrified logs as well as the spectacularly hued Painted Desert.

KARTCHNER CAVERNS STATE PARK, ARIZONA
Discovered in 1974 and kept a secret for 14 years, this cave south of Tucson is one of the best-preserved cave systems in North America.

GREAT SALT LAKE, UTAH
Great is an apt term: This is the largest body of saltwater in the Western Hemisphere and the biggest lake in the U.S. that is not part of the Great Lakes.

ARCHES NATIONAL PARK
With more than 2,000 sandstone arches, this national park and major destination for canyoneering and mountain climbing draws 1.5 million visitors annually, with even more visiting nearby Moab, a center for 2- and 4-wheeling.

GILA WILDERNESS, NEW MEXICO

The first officially designated wilderness area on Earth in 1924, Gila measures nearly 30 miles by 40 miles and is defined by the Mogollon Mountains (topping out at 10,895 feet above sea level) and the Gila River, with numerous trails exploring gorges and forested peaks. The wilderness area's wildlife population is also immense.

BLACK CANYON OF THE GUNNISON NATIONAL PARK, COLORADO

There are bigger, grander canyons, but this 2,000-foot deep canyon is one of the most dramatic, marked by impossibly steep, sheer walls forming a remarkably compact gorge that is only 40 feet wide at its narrowest point.

GREAT SAND DUNES NATIONAL PARK & PRESERVE, COLORADO

The massive dunefield at the foot of the Sangre de Cristo Mountains in Colorado's San Luis Valley is unexpected and otherworldly, with dunes topping out at 750 feet in height (the tallest in North America).

Dinosaur National Monument

LAKE TAHOE, NEVADA

The deep blue lake straddles the Nevada-California state line, with ski areas, lakeside resorts, beaches, and endless scenic views on its eastern shores. It's the largest alpine lake in North America, and the second-deepest lake in the U.S.

DINOSAUR NATIONAL MONUMENT, UTAH/COLORADO

Located along the border between northeastern Utah and northwestern Colorado, the monument was originally designated to protect its renowned Dinosaur Quarry, one of the most productive paleontological sites on the planet, but was later expanded to include the surrounding canyons the Green and Yampa rivers carved over the eons.

GREAT BASIN NATIONAL PARK, NEVADA

Centered on Wheeler Peak in eastern Nevada, this national park isn't a household name yet, so you'll find plenty of peace, quiet, and solitude here, as well as Lehman Caves (open for tours near the base of Wheeler Peak) and groves of bristlecone pines that are thousands of years old.

Best Historic Sights

MESA VERDE NATIONAL PARK, COLORADO
These massive cliff dwellings in southwestern Colorado, built in the 12th and 13th centuries, are some of the best preserved structures once inhabited by the Ancestral Puebloan (also known as Anasazi) people, who suddenly abandoned them.

NEW MEXICO'S HISTORIC PUEBLOS
There are 19 pueblos (Native American settlements with permanent locations) in New Mexico, some of which have existed for more than 1,000 years. The Indian Pueblo Cultural Center in Albuquerque is a good place to start, followed by a trip to Acoma ("Sky City") or Taos Pueblo.

DURANGO AND SILVERTON NARROW GAUGE RAILROAD, COLORADO
This is one of the few moving National Historic Landmarks. The notably narrow (three feet wide) railroad takes passengers on a 45-mile trip full of twists, turns, and stunning mountain scenery from Durango to Silverton.

EXPLORE THE MISSIONS OF NEW MEXICO
Spanish friars established more than 25 missions in what is now New Mexico beginning in the late 1500s and early 1600s to convert Native Americans to Catholicism. Many of them are nicely preserved and still in use as churches, while others were abandoned and are in ruins today. The first, built in 1598 (and rebuilt in the early 1700s), is now part of Pecos National Historical Park near Santa Fe.

CHECK OUT LODO, COLORADO
Short for "Lower Downtown," Denver's historic core features one of the best-preserved collections of historic brick buildings in the West. The LoDo Historic District's establishment in 1988 protected more than 100 remaining buildings. Highlights include Union Station, the Oxford Hotel, and Wynkoop Brewing Company, with modern attractions like Coors Field, the Museum of Contemporary Art Denver, and plenty of nightlife.

TEMPLE SQUARE, UTAH
Brigham Young and the Church of Jesus Christ of Latter-day Saints established this 10-acre plaza at the heart of Salt Lake City in 1847. It now attracts as many as 5 million visitors annually, making it a bigger draw than Utah's national parks and the most popular tourist attraction in the Beehive State. Free tours are available, but the Salt Lake Temple itself is not open to non-Mormons.

Tombstone, Arizona

GOLDEN SPIKE NATIONAL HISTORICAL PARK, UTAH
Named for the last spike in the first official transcontinental railroad across the U.S., this historic site north of the Great Salt Lake on Promontory Summit became part of the country's history books on May 10, 1869. Visitors today can see a pair of replica locomotives, hike on the original railroad grades, go on a scenic drive, and experience railroad-related demonstrations and special events.

TOMBSTONE, ARIZONA
There are few towns that evoke the Wild West like Tombstone. Located about 30 miles north of the U.S.–Mexico border in southeastern Arizona, the town now plays up its history as the site of the legendary Gunfight at the O.K. Corral in 1881 with reenactments, and the Tombstone Historic District features such iconic structures as the Cochise County Courthouse and the Crystal Palace Saloon.

HOVENWEEP NATIONAL MONUMENT, UTAH / COLORADO
Along the Utah-Colorado border, Hovenweep attracted hunter-gatherers for thousands of years before Ancestral Puebloan (or Anasazi) started building elaborate rock castles and other structures about 1,000 years ago.

MONTEZUMA CASTLE NATIONAL MONUMENT, ARIZONA
The Sinagua people built and used these well-preserved cliff dwellings between the 12th and 15th centuries. The high-rise structure is located 90 feet above the ground on a vertical limestone cliff where it was naturally shielded from the elements and accessible only by ladders (to thwart would-be invaders).

Best Outdoor Activities

MOUNTAIN BIKING AT RED ROCK CANYON, NEVADA
Located just west of Las Vegas, this rugged and wild national conservation area protects nearly 200,000 acres. Red Rock Canyon is known for challenging trails like Cowboy—an advanced 7.6-mile loop with 1,325 feet of elevation change—and spectacular desert scenery.

SKI TELLURIDE, COLORADO
Sure, there are bigger ski resorts in Colorado, but none of them can top the superlative scenery and sheer spectacle of Telluride.

SKI UTAH
No state offers better access to the slopes: Salt Lake City International Airport is within an hour of 11 different ski resorts, and it's possible to get a full day of skiing in on the day your flight lands.

FIND YOUR INNER COWBOY AT A DUDE RANCH
If you really want to learn horseback riding, dude ranches are scattered throughout the great wide open spaces of the Southwest, with notable operations in Colorado, Utah, New Mexico, and Arizona.

SUMMIT A 13ER OR A 14ER, COLORADO
There are 96 14ers (mountain peaks that are at least 14,000 feet above sea level) in the U.S.; 53 of them are in Colorado. "Peakbaggers" seek to summit them all; if you want a little more solitude, seek out a 13er (13,000-foot peak), which may have smaller crowds.

SKI TAOS, NEW MEXICO
The late Ernie Blake essentially invented the modern ski vacation when he founded Taos Ski Valley in 1955. The resort remains one of the best places to learn to ski (or snowboard) in the country. In 2014, a new chairlift started ferrying skiers to the top of 12,481-foot Kachina Peak.

FISHING IN LAKE POWELL, ARIZONA/UTAH
Formed by the construction of Glen Canyon Dam, this popular recreational attraction in southern Utah is home to a wide variety of fish, including bass—striped, smallmouth, and largemouth—as well as bluegill and channel catfish.

Ski Telluride

RAFT THE ARKANSAS RIVER, COLORADO
The Arkansas River in south-central Colorado is the most commercially rafted river in the country. It offers a stretch of 125 miles of whitewater for all skill levels, including the popular intermediate run through Browns Canyon and the more difficult route through the Royal Gorge. There are numerous outfitters and river resorts in and around Salida, Buena Vista, and Canon City.

RAFT THE COLORADO RIVER, COLORADO/UTAH/ARIZONA
You'll find plenty of premier paddling on this legendary river as it snakes from its headwaters in north-central Colorado through the Utah and Arizona deserts and the Grand Canyon, where rafting trips are in great demand. There are plenty of other places to more easily experience the river's renowned whitewater, including the upper stretches of the river in Colorado, and Cataract Canyon in Utah.

GOLF PHOENIX-SCOTTSDALE, ARIZONA
With more than 200 courses in and around the metro area, Phoenix-Scottsdale is one of the leading destinations for golf on the planet. Many of them are part of golf resorts with lodging, dining, and other facilities. Thanks to the warm desert weather, this is one of the best places for a winter golfing trip.

What to Eat and Drink in the Southwest

DOWN A PINT OF CRAFT BEER

Colorado's craft brewing industry is nationally known, but the entire Southwest is brimming with standout suds. Colorado has more than 400 breweries, Arizona 125, and there are nearly 100 in New Mexico. Even notoriously teetotaling Utah has more than 40 craft breweries.

POSOLE

What might look to the uninitiated like popcorn soup is actually a sublime marriage of hominy, lime, pork, garlic, and spices. It's a regional staple of Mexico that's become a huge hit in New Mexico.

FRY BREAD

This flat, deep-fried dough is usually served sprinkled with powdered sugar or honey. It can also be an entrée, topped with meat, cheese, and garnish as a Navajo taco.

UTAH CHOCOLATE

Utah has earned a reputation as the country's capital of craft chocolate, thanks largely to the aficionados at Caputo's Market & Deli in Salt Lake City—which is said to carry the largest selection in the U.S.

HIGH DESERT WINE

The high deserts of the Southwest have proven surprisingly fertile for vineyards. Colorado and Arizona are both home to more than 100 wineries, and New Mexico has upwards of 50.

CRAFT SPIRITS

Following the trail blazed by the brewers, about 100 craft distilleries are in operation in Colorado, more than the rest of the Southwest combined.

TASTING LAS VEGAS

Beyond the familiar all-you-can-eat buffets, Sin City is now firmly entrenched in the upper ranks of the country's culinary destinations. The selection runs the gamut from fast food to celebrity chefs, with an ascendent off-Strip scene.

BISON

Compared with beef, bison has less fat, more protein, and fewer calories. It's available in burger, steak, and rib form at restaurants throughout the Southwest, but Colorado stands out: the Centennial State ranks among the top states for bison production, and you'll find it on upscale menus.

GREEN CHILE SAUCE

The mother sauce of the Southwest, green chile sauce makes everything more delicious. Much like salsa, its depth of flavor and heat can vary by chef, but green chile sauce is generally mild and thick, containing chiles, sauteed onions, and spices.

Hatch chiles

SONORAN HOT DOG

It's like no other; this amalgam of Mexican and American flavors is wrapped in bacon, tucked in a *bolillo* (fluffy bun), and topped with condiments like pinto beans, jalapeño salsa, onions, mayo, and mustard. Find them in Phoenix and Tucson.

COLORADO LAMB

Chefs who are in the know prize Colorado lamb. Ranchers breed for meat above all in Colorado, not wool as in New Zealand, and the animals graze in the mountains in summer, giving them a more diverse diet than their lowland counterparts. You'll find Colorado lamb dishes on menus at upscale restaurants throughout the entire Southwest.

HATCH CHILES

You needn't fear the Hatch chile, but you should respect it. These heat-seeking flavor bombs hail from the Hatch Valley of New Mexico, and are the chiles of choice at restaurants throughout the Southwest. Spicy, smoky, and a little sweet, they give a kick to dishes like pozole, salsa, and chili.

The Southwest with Kids

CHOOSING A DESTINATION

The Southwest is full of great places for families to explore: big cities, ski hills, national parks, roadside attractions, and museums and zoos. In Colorado, Denver, Boulder, and Colorado Springs are loaded with kid-friendly attractions, as are the mountain towns and ski resorts in the higher country. Utah is one of the family-friendliest states in the country, and ice cream parlors and playgrounds are the norm. Arizona and New Mexico, likewise, offer both urban and natural destinations that are great for travelers with kids, including Phoenix, Tucson, Albuquerque, and Santa Fe along with Grand Canyon and Carlsbad Caverns national parks.

Then there's Nevada. While its reputation skews towards gambling and other adult vices, Las Vegas has gotten increasingly family-friendly in recent decades, and most resorts offer plenty to keep kids occupied.

CHOOSING A PLACE TO STAY

Most lodgings in the Southwest tend to have rooms for families or else adjoining rooms. Ski-in, ski-out lodging are good picks when you're hitting the slopes with kids: All of the gear and logistics that go with winter sports make for enough tantrum kindling and prolonged transportation can be a spark. Nevada's casino hotels and resorts often have kid-oriented activities and amusements as well as childcare; check when you book. Dude ranches are another good pick for families, as there tends to be a number of horseback riding and other activities for all ages and skill levels, then the clan gets back together for meals.

OUTDOOR ACTIVITIES

National parks—and there are plenty in the Southwest—are terrific destinations for families. Kids not only get a nice dose of the great outdoors, but they have ample opportunities to learn about wildlife, geology, and the interconnected nature of these fragile ecosystems. The parks' Junior Ranger programs allow kids to have some fun as they get a lesson.

But that's just scratching the surface: The region is full of ski areas, state parks, trails to hike, rivers to raft, and more. Many ski areas now feature mountain coasters, tubing hills, and other activities that can break up ski trips when the kiddos need a day off the hill.

INDOOR ACTIVITIES

The major cities are full of attractions that will educate and entertain (and sometimes do both) including a number of top-notch children's and natural history museums, including the Children's Museum of Denver. Major art and history museums have children's exhibits, programs, and events.

ROAD TRIP TIPS

Bring plenty of diversions for the road, but try to keep the kids more engaged in the landscape than they are with their electronic devices. Road bingo is one option, and there are several other games that can cure the kids of boredom. Keep in mind that the Southwest is a vast place with long distances to drive. Plan accordingly; make sure to map out the rest areas on your route and stock plenty of snacks and drinks.

What to Watch and Read

Nevada

CASINO

Martin Scorsese's alternately gritty and glitzy 1995 film captures the rise of Sin City, fueled by organized crime and corporate America in equal measures. The since-demolished Riviera played the part of the fictional Tangiers Casino ran by Sam "Ace" Rothstein (Robert de Niro) in the movie.

THE MONEY AND THE POWER

Published in 2002, this dense history of the rise of Las Vegas by Roger Morris and Sally Denton looks at the intersection of organized crime, corporations, and an increasingly bizarre cast of characters who catalyzed its evolution into the modern mega-destination in the Nevada desert. Of special note is the shadowy story of Howard Hughes and the CIA's involvement in Sin City.

OCEAN'S ELEVEN

Both the Rat Pack-starring original and the George Clooney-Brad Pitt-Matt Damon remake are worthy artifacts of Vegas culture. Featuring Frank Sinatra, Dean Martin, and Sammy Davis, Jr., the 1960 film was shot at the Flamingo, Sands, and other legendary casinos, while the more critically acclaimed 2008 version used the Bellagio as its primary location.

Utah

THE MONKEY WRENCH GANG

Edward Abbey's 1975 cult classic spins a yarn about four ragtag environmentalists fighting development of the desert in Utah and Arizona. As the gang sabotages the projects that they see as spoiling the vast wilderness, their focus shifts to one of the most reviled projects in the region: the Glen Canyon Dam.

MORMON COUNTRY

Part of the acclaimed American Folkways series of the early 1940s, this early work by the great American novelist Wallace Stegner—who was not Mormon but spent part of his formative years in Salt Lake City—engaged in the migration of Mormon settlers to Utah, where they transformed an unforgiving, parched land into a string of bountiful, dynamic communities.

UNDER THE BANNER OF HEAVEN

The fourth book from adventurer and best-selling writer Jon Krakauer came out in 2003 and shines a light—and was the source of some controversy—on the renegade fundamentalist outsider communities that exist in Utah and elsewhere in defiance not only of the mainstream LDS Church but government authorities as well.

Arizona

THE DEVIL'S HIGHWAY: A TRUE STORY

Dubbed the most compelling account of "the absurdity of U.S. border policy" by *The Atlantic,* the book chronicles the 2001 journey of 26 men who traveled north to cross the border in the Arizona desert; only 12 of them made it alive. Writer Luis Alberto Urrea captures the desperation that motivates such crossings and the dangers faced along the way.

LAUGHING BOY

Oliver La Farge's Pulitzer Prize-winning 1929 novel depicts the Navajo people's struggles with assimilation in the early 1900s. The title character has been raised with Navajo traditions, but his relationship with a young woman, Slim Girl, who was educated at boarding schools organized by the U.S. government sets off an illuminating cultural clash.

RIDERS OF THE PURPLE SAGE

Zane Grey's 1912 novel is one of the most iconic Westerns of all time. This classic tale of cowboys and their Old West adventures is one of the primary reasons author Zane Grey is so beloved. His tales of the frontier and adventure helped to shape the narrative of the American cowboy.

New Mexico

BREAKING BAD

Critics regard creator Vince Gilligan's saga of Walter White as one of the great all-time TV series. Not only does the show depict the sordid criminal underbelly of Albuquerque, it also captures the scenery, culture, and feel of Duke City in a way that makes the location something of a supporting character.

THE DAY AFTER ROSWELL

Probing the alleged UFO crash in 1947 near Roswell, New Mexico, authors Col. Philip Corso (retired) and William Birnes make some shocking claims about the infamous event in this 1999 book. Corso, a career military intelligence officer, maintains he handled a program encompassing alien artifacts recovered from the crash site, with far-reaching implications.

THE MAKING OF THE ATOMIC BOMB

Published in 1987, Richard Rhodes' Pulitzer Prize-winning nonfiction epic tells the story of the atomic bomb from pioneering physicists to the horrors of Hiroshima and Nagasaki. A considerable amount of the story takes place in Los Alamos—the home of the top-secret Manhattan Project that developed the world's first atomic weapons—and the Trinity Site near Truth or Consequences, where the bomb was first tested in 1945.

Colorado

CENTENNIAL

James Michener's sprawling work of historical fiction tells a tale of northeastern Colorado from prehistory to the 1970s. First published in 1974 and later adapted into a TV miniseries, the book is rooted in reality, but many of its characters and events are not.

DOWNHILL SLIDE

Hal Clifford examines the diminishing returns on expanding ski resorts by hundreds and thousands of acres in his critical look at the ski industry. The 2003 book covers the toll on the environment and local economies that accompanies the ascent to destination resort, and offers a grassroots path to reclaiming the mountain towns compromised by greed.

SOUTH PARK

Trey Parker and Matt Stone's long-running show on Comedy Central is pure satire, but it often offers an incisive look into the people and places of Colorado. Set in the fictional town of South Park—which many say is modeled after Fairplay in the valley of the same name—the series follows the profane misadventures of four kids as they navigate the fantasies and realities of life in the self-described "redneck mountain town."

Chapter 2

TRAVEL SMART

Updated by
Eric Peterson

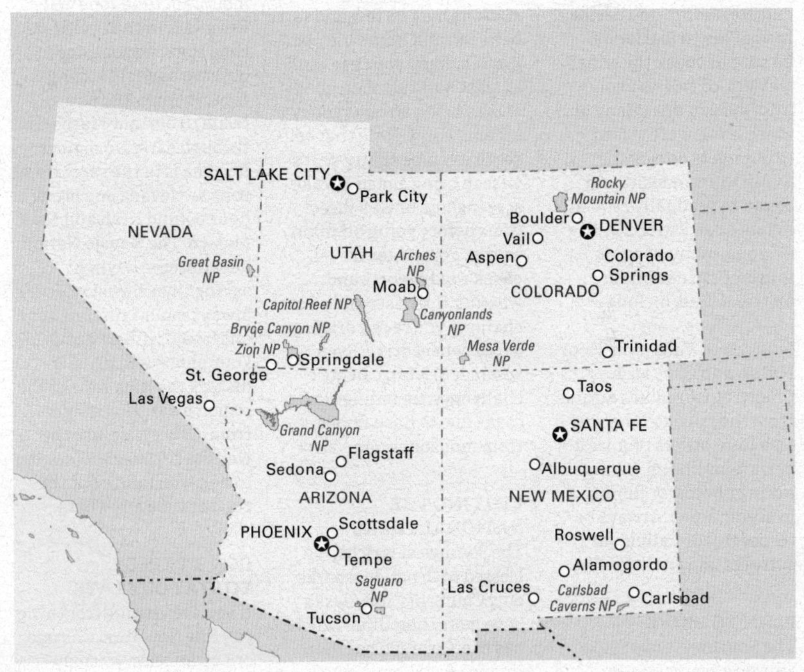

Know Before You Go

As one of the United States's most popular regions, the Southwest has hundreds of notable attractions and can even be a little overwhelming for a first-time visitor. Here are some key tips to help you navigate your trip, whether it's your first time visiting or your twentieth.

PLAN AHEAD FOR VISITS TO TRIBAL LANDS
Arizona has 22 Native American tribes, New Mexico 23, Nevada 32, Utah 8, and Colorado 2, each with its own government and culture. Before you decide to visit any tribal lands, be sure to check the tribe's website, or call its phone information line. Many of these areas were closed to outsiders during the COVID-19 pandemic and began to gradually reopen in mid-2021. Especially in Arizona, many popular tourist destinations are on tribal land, including Antelope Canyon, Monument Valley, the Hopi Mesas, and Canyon de Chelly. Most require a guide from the tribe to take you on a tour; others require a permit for hiking, biking, taking photos, or filming in scenic areas. Always be respectful of individual cultures and traditions.

PLAN TO DRIVE
The Southwest has some amazing scenic drives and you'll need a car to visit most of the popular destinations. Distances can be surprisingly vast. If you aren't driving to the region, make sure you reserve a car that will meet your needs. You'll cover a lot of miles exploring these states. When driving long stretches, keep an eye on the gas gauge, as gas stations may be few and far between and hours may be limited. Keep your gas tank at least half full; it's a good idea to bring an emergency kit and water. Note that cell service can be spotty so it's wise to bring a map or take screenshots of GPS directions before going off main routes. For winter travel, check road reports and weather forecasts and carry chains if you're not driving a four-wheel drive. Even summer driving can pose challenges, including closed roads due to flash floods from monsoons. Stay alert.

VISITING THE NATIONAL PARKS
The Southwest is richly blessed with national parks; only California and Alaska have more than Utah, which has five. Colorado has four, Arizona has three, New Mexico has two, and Nevada has one, and there are dozens of other sites managed by the NPS. With canyons, rock formations, mountains, rivers, exotic flora and fauna, and Native American history, the parks are a delight for outdoor adventurers and photographers. You could spend at least a week just visiting the national parks of Utah, but if you want to see more, you'll need to schedule your trip wisely. Be prepared for crowds in the summer. If you want to stay in any national park lodges, you'll need to book far in advance. Otherwise, you'll usually find lodging in the nearby towns.

BE AWARE OF THE TIME ZONE
Arizona, Utah, Colorado, and New Mexico are in the mountain time zone, but Nevada is in the Pacific time zone. Arizona doesn't observe daylight saving time, though, and as a result, from mid-March through early November Arizona is in the same time zone as Nevada and is one hour behind Utah and New Mexico. The Navajo Nation does observe daylight saving time, however, so it's always mountain time zone on Navajo lands. Confused? Your phone will usually display the time zone of the region it's getting a signal from. Otherwise, use the website 🌐 *Timeanddate.com* to help you figure out the correct time anywhere.

DON'T EXPECT TO STAY OUT LATE
If you are visiting from a big city like New York, Chicago, or Los Angeles, you may be surprised that even in larger cities like Phoenix, Salt Lake City, and Denver, many restaurants close at 9 pm on weeknights (though some may be open until 10

pm on Friday and Saturday). A few places are open later, but they are the exceptions rather than the rule. Eateries in the smaller towns may be shuttered even earlier. Some bars and craft breweries also keep shorter hours, closing by midnight. The one major exception is Las Vegas, where restaurants can be open very late, and some places are open 24 hours a day.

PACK FOR VARYING CLIMATES

From June through August in low-elevation areas, pack lightweight fabrics that are most comfortable in the heat; extend that to April through October in desert areas. (A sweater is handy if the air-conditioning is cranked up, but otherwise you probably won't need it.) This is true in southern Arizona and Mexico, Las Vegas, southwestern Colorado, much of southern Utah, and even Salt Lake City. But in higher elevations, summer temperatures can be considerably cooler. The average daytime summer temperature in Zion National Park (4,000 feet) is 88°; in Bryce Canyon National Park (9,000 feet) it's 74°. Even with the desert extremes, much of the Southwest boasts a mild four-seasons climate because of its altitude. Ski areas but also major cities like Salt Lake and Denver get low temperatures and snow in the winter (considerable as you get into the higher elevations), so bring clothing you can layer, especially for outdoor-oriented trips. In the spring and fall, weather can alternate between cool and wet and warm and dry almost anywhere except the desert areas, which are still mostly warm to hot and dry.

LOOK FOR OFF-SEASON BARGAINS

Winter is high season in much of the desert and in ski areas, but it's low season in Denver, Salt Lake City, and most of the national parks. Even in summer, which is high season in much of the Southwest, there are bargains in hotter places like Las Vegas and Phoenix. In ski areas, you can find bargains in spring and fall, just after and before the ski season.

HIKING SAFETY

There are few real hazards to hiking, but a little preparedness goes a long way. Route out your hike beforehand, and know your limits—make sure the terrain you are about to embark on does not exceed your abilities. It's a good idea to check the elevation change on a trail before you set out—a 1-mile trail might sound easy, until you realize how steep it is—and be careful not to get caught on exposed trails at elevation during afternoon thunderstorms in summer. As a general rule, avoid open terrain above the tree line if it appears a storm is moving in. Bring layers of clothing to accommodate changing weather, and always carry enough drinking water. This is doubly true in desert areas or in the summer in general, when temperatures can be very high across the Southwest. Make sure someone knows where you're going and when to expect your return.

MARIJUANA LAWS

Recreational marijuana use is legal in Colorado. It is important to note that the law varies between residents and visitors, and statutes are subject to change by the year. The industry is highly regulated, and some localities do not allow it. Similarly, recreational marijuana is now legal in New Mexico, Arizona, and Nevada, but also highly restricted. For example, marijuana cannot be consumed in "public" in Nevada, and that includes in hotel rooms. All recreational marijuana is still illegal in Utah under all circumstances.

WATCH THE ALTITUDE

Arizona has the lowest average elevation in the Southwest, with an average of approximately 4,000 feet. The other states rank among the top 10 states in the country for elevation, and most of them have popular ski resorts and other tourist destinations in high-altitude areas. With a mean elevation of 6,800 feet above sea level, however, Colorado has the highest average altitude of any U.S. state, although both Park City, UT, and Santa Fe, NM, sit at over 7,000 feet. Anything above 8,000 feet is considered a high-altitude destination (common in Colorado's Rocky Mountain ski resorts). The three things to consider with high-altitude travel are altitude sickness, dehydration, and sunburn.

Getting Here and Around

Air

The Southwest is easy to access on most major airlines, most of which fly into Denver, Phoenix, Salt Lake City, Albuquerque, and Las Vegas. But there are also a number of secondary airports like Tucson, Colorado Springs, Aspen, and Santa Fe, though you can expect to find fewer flights and higher fares, especially during the high season. However, some of these smaller airports that serve ski resorts and other popular destinations can be easier to navigate and get you closer to your final destination. Unless you are just planning to ski at a specific resort, a car is often a necessity after touching down for a vacation in these places as the major attractions are separated by hundreds of miles of highway.

AIRPORTS

The largest airports in the region are Phoenix Sky Harbor International Airport (PHX) in Arizona; Denver International Airport (DEN) in Colorado; McCarran International Airport (LAS) in Las Vegas, Nevada; Salt Lake City International Airport (SLC) in Utah; and Albuquerque International Sunport (ABQ) in New Mexico. If you have time, it's usually to your advantage to fly into a major air hub and rent a car to drive the rest of the way.

In Utah, flights to smaller, regional, or resort town airports generally connect through Salt Lake. Provo (PVU), Cedar City (CDC), Logan (LGU), Ogden (OGD), and Moab (CNY) all have small airports.

In Colorado, there are also airports in Colorado Springs (COS), Grand Junction (GJT), Durango (DRO), Steamboat Springs (HDN), Gunnison–Crested Butte (GUC), Montrose (MTJ), Telluride (TEX), Aspen (ASE), and Vail (EGE).

In Arizona, Tucson (TUS), Flagstaff (FLG), and Yuma (YUM) also have airports with regular service, but flights are typically less frequent and more expensive than those to Phoenix.

In New Mexico, you can also fly directly to Santa Fe (SAF).

Car

Car travel around the major cities of Salt Lake City, Denver, Las Vegas, Albuquerque, and Phoenix can be congested, particularly on weekday mornings and afternoons. Weekends, too, can have quite a bit of traffic, particularly along major interstates, especially around major metropolitan areas. Once you get off the major interstates (I–40 and I–70 going east–west and I–15 and I–25 going north–south), traffic can be more manageable. Regardless, unless you are visiting a city with good public transportion or just going to ski at a specific resort, you'll need a car to explore the region. It's not practical (or sometimes even possible) to see secondary destinations without one, and the distances are vast. For example, it's 748 miles from Las Vegas to Denver and 855 miles from Las Vegas to Carlsbad Caverns. Seeing just a small portion of the Southwest will take one to two weeks, and you could easily spend three if you want to hit all five states.

CAR RENTALS

Car rentals are widely available around major airports. Though with a scarcity of cars (and high prices) likely to continue well into 2022, make sure to reserve your car in advance, especially around busy travel periods. High taxes on airport rentals can sometimes be offset by lower base rates. You'll usually find better rates by booking by the week and returning your car to your original arrival destination. With drop-off fees, your car rental can actually be almost as expensive as your hotels, so be sure to budget for that if you plan on doing a one-way trip.

PARKING

You'll usually pay for parking in major cities, sometimes even at hotels, especially upscale ones.

WINTER MOUNTAIN DRIVING

Modern highways make mountain driving safe and generally trouble-free even in cold weather. Although winter driving can occasionally present real challenges, road maintenance is good and plowing is prompt. However, in mountain areas tire chains, studs, or snow tires are essential. If you're planning to drive into high elevations, be sure to check the weather forecast and call for road conditions beforehand. Even main highways can close, and some areas have strict rules about tire conditions, use of chains, etc.

It's a good idea to carry an emergency kit and a cellphone, but be aware that the mountains can disrupt service. If you do get stalled by deep snow, do not leave your car. Wait for help, running the engine only if needed, and remember that assistance is never far away. Winter weather isn't confined to winter months in the high country (it's been known to snow in July), so be prepared year-round.

SUMMER DESERT DRIVING

Vehicles and passengers should be well equipped for searing summer heat in the low desert. If you're planning to drive through the desert, make sure you carry plenty of water, a good spare tire, a jack, radiator coolant, a cell phone, and emergency supplies. If you get stranded, stay with your vehicle and wait for help to arrive.

Dust storms are common on the highways and interstates that traverse the open desert. These usually occur from May to mid-September, causing extremely low visibility. If you're on the highway, pull as far off the road as possible, turn on your headlights to stay visible, and wait for the storm to subside.

Warnings about flash floods shouldn't be taken lightly. Sudden downpours send torrents of water racing into low-lying areas so dry that they're unable to absorb such a huge quantity of water quickly. The result can be powerful walls of water suddenly descending upon these low-lying areas, devastating anything in their paths. Major highways are mostly flood-proof, but some smaller roads dip through washes; most roads that traverse these low-lying areas will have flood warning signs, which should be seriously heeded during rainstorms.

Train

Amtrak offers three main train routes across the Southwest. The Southwest Chief passes through both Albuquerque and Flagstaff, offering connecting service to Santa Fe and the Grand Canyon. The Sunset Limited passes through Tucson and Phoenix, as well as Benson and Yuma in Arizona. The California Zephyr runs through the heart of the Rockies, connecting Denver and Salt Lake City as well as Grand Junction, Colorado.

All of these long-distance trains can experience significant delays, so it's better not to plan any specific activity close to your expected time of arrival. Similarly, if you plan on embarking in an intermediate stop, you should allow that the train may be late.

Essentials

Dining

You'll find everything from American diner standards, to prime cuts of beef, to Native American cuisine, to Mexican cuisine throughout the Southwest. All manner of international cuisines are available in major cities like Phoenix, Denver, Salt Lake City, and especially Las Vegas, but beyond those, you'll find the best food is often regionally influenced, with steak houses and Mexican restaurants offering the most upscale (and sometimes the best) options.

DISCOUNTS AND DEALS

If you eat early or late you may be able to take advantage of prix-fixe deals not offered at peak hours. Many upscale restaurants offer great lunch deals with special menus at cut-rate prices designed to give customers a true taste of the place. At high-end restaurants ask for tap water to avoid paying high rates for bottled water.

PAYING

Most restaurants take credit cards, but some smaller places do not. It's worth asking. Waiters expect a 20% tip at high-end restaurants; some add an automatic gratuity for groups of six or more.

RESERVATIONS AND DRESS

Always make a reservation at an upscale restaurant when you can. Some are booked weeks in advance, but some popular restaurants don't accept reservations. As unfair as it seems, the way you look can influence how you're treated—and where you're seated. Generally speaking, jeans and a button-down shirt will suffice at most restaurants in the Southwest, but some pricier restaurants require jackets, and some insist on ties. In reviews, we mention dress only where men are required to wear a jacket or a jacket and tie. If you have doubts, call the restaurant and ask.

MEALS AND MEALTIMES

Many cities in the Southwest have less of an around-the-clock mentality than other big cities, with even upscale restaurants shutting down by 9 or 10 pm. In small towns, it's not unusual for some places to stop serving by 8.

SMOKING

Smoking is banned in all restaurants and bars.

What It Costs

$	$$	$$$	$$$$
AT DINNER			
under $12	$12–$20	$21–$30	over $30

Health and Safety

COVID-19

COVID-19 brought travel to a virtual standstill for most of 2020 and into 2021, but vaccinations have made travel possible and safe again. However, each destination (and each business within that destination) may have its own requirements and regulations. Travelers may expect to continue to wear a mask in public and obey any other rules. Given how abruptly travel was curtailed at the onset of the pandemic, it is wise to consider protecting yourself by purchasing a travel insurance policy that will reimburse you for cancellation costs related to COVID-19. Not all travel insurance policies protect against pandemic-related cancellations, so always read the fine print.

Immunizations

There are no immunization requirements for visitors traveling to the United States for tourism.

Lodging

Accommodations across the Southwest run the gamut from luxurious big-city hotels to small mom-and-pop motels in more out-of-the-way destinations. You'll also find a fair number of self-catering accommodations, and these can be a cost-saving option for larger groups or families that just need more space to spread out. Of course, a share of these are also quite luxurious and expensive as well.

FACILITIES

You can assume that all rooms have private baths, phones, TVs, and air-conditioning, unless otherwise indicated. Breakfast is noted when it is included in the rate, but it's not a typical perk at most Southwest hotels. There are a few hotels with pools, though some are indoors.

PRICES

Rates drop in most Southwest destinations in the summer, when the weather turns hot. Expect lower prices from Easter through early September (and possibly October) in most desert destinations. Ski resorts are typically more expensive in both winter (during ski season) and summer, but may be lower during the shoulder seasons of April through May and October and November.

RESERVATIONS

With some exceptions, you should always make a reservation in big cities and busy resort areas, especially if you are staying a while to explore an area and have specific needs. If you are just driving through and need accommodation for a single night, many places have roadside chain motels and hotels in large numbers, but if you can plan ahead (even by the day), you're more likely to find an accommodation that more readily meets your personal needs.

What It Costs

$	$$	$$$	$$$$
FOR TWO PEOPLE			
under $150	$150–$200	$201–$300	over $300

Passport

All visitors to the United States require a valid passport that is valid for six months beyond your expected period of stay.

Telephones

Cell service is good in major cities, but it can be difficult to find a signal in mountainous regions or in the wide expanses of the desert.

Tipping

Tipping has become increasingly helpful and important to service workers during the COVID-19 pandemic; it's also a nice way to pay it forward to essential service workers once travelers start to hit the road again in larger numbers. Restaurant servers expect at least 15% of the bill (it's more like 20% in large cities like Las Vegas). Don't forget to leave something for your hotel maid; $1 or $2 a day left on the pillow each morning is sufficient, though you may leave more in a luxurious hotel or resort.

U.S. Embassy/Consulate

All foreign governments have embassies in Washington, D.C., and most offer consular services in the embassy building.

Essentials

Tipping Guides for the Southwest

Bartender	\$1–\$5 per round of drinks, depending on the number of drinks
Bellhop	\$1–\$5 per bag, depending on the level of the hotel
Coat Check	\$1–\$2 per coat
Hotel Concierge	\$5 or more, depending on the service
Hotel Doorstaff	\$1–\$5 for help with bags or hailing a cab
Hotel Maid	\$2–\$5 a day (in cash, preferably daily since cleaning staff may be different each day you stay)
Hotel Room Service Waiter	\$1–\$2 per delivery, even if a service charge has been added
Porter at Airport or Train Station	\$1 per bag
Restroom Attendant	\$1 or small change
Skycap at Airport	\$1–\$3 per bag checked
Spa Personnel	15%–20% of the cost of your service
Taxi Driver	15%–20%
Tour Guide	10%–15% of the cost of the tour, per person
Valet Parking Attendant	\$2–\$5, each time your car is brought to you
Waiter	15%–20%, with 20% being the norm at high-end restaurants; nothing additional if a service charge is added to the bill

When to Go

Low Season: The low season depends on the destination. For ski areas, the early part of the season (before mid-Dec.) is typically a shoulder with lower rates, and same goes for late season as the spring thaw progresses towards summer. In the deserts of Arizona or Nevada, the heat turns summer into a low season, but places like Las Vegas have grown increasingly immune to the phenomenon. For national parks, winter is typically the low season, and some become inaccessible or close down during the off-season. Early summer and late fall can often have lower rates and thinner crowds.

Shoulder Season: Spring and fall typically bring the lowest lodging rates to ski resorts and other high-altitude destinations. The catch? The slopes are closed. This dynamic is similar around many national parks that shut down for the winter. The roads can close in spring and fall due to weather, making it a dicier time of year for a trip, but prices can be notably lower.

High Season: In major cities as well as in and around the national parks, summer is high season throughout most of the Southwest. Ski towns have high seasons in both summer and winter, when the week of Christmas commands the highest rates of the year. But many high-altitude towns like Aspen, Crested Butte, and Park City are just as busy in the summer as they are in the winter, if not busier. Winter is also a high season for desert destinations in Arizona and other areas where the mild climate allows for outdoor activities while most of the country shivers.

Contents

 Air

AIRPORTS Albuquerque International Sunport. ✉ *2200 Sunport Blvd. SE, Albuquerque* ☎ *505/244–7700* 🌐 *www.abqsunport.com*. **Aspen/Pitkin County Airport (ASE).** ✉ *233 E. Airport Rd., Aspen* ☎ *970/920–5384* 🌐 *www.aspenairport.com*. **Colorado Springs Airport (COS).** ☎ *719/550–1900* 🌐 *www.coloradosprings.gov/flycos*. **Denver International Airport.** ☎ *303/342–2000* 🌐 *www.flydenver.com*. **Durango–La Plata County Airport (DRO).** ✉ *1000 Airport Rd., Durango* ☎ *970/382–6050* 🌐 *www.flydurango.com*. **Eagle County Airport (EGE).** ✉ *219 Eldon Wilson Rd., Gypsum* ☎ *970/328–2680* 🌐 *www.flyvail.com*. **El Paso International Airport.** ✉ *6701 Convair Dr., El Paso* ☎ *915/212–0330* 🌐 *www.elpasointernationalairport.com*. **Grand Junction Regional Airport.** ✉ *2828 Walker Field Dr., Grand Junction* ☎ *970/244–9100* 🌐 *www.gjairport.com*. **McCarran International Airport (LAS).** ✉ *5757 Wayne Newton Blvd., Las Vegas* ☎ *702/261–5211* 🌐 *www.mccarran.com*. **Montrose Regional Airport (MTJ).** ✉ *2100 Airport Rd., Montrose* ☎ *970/249–3203* 🌐 *www.flymontrose.com*. **Midland International Air and Space Port.** ✉ *9506 La Force Blvd., Midland* ☎ *435/560–2200* 🌐 *www.flymaf.com*. **Phoenix-Mesa Gateway Airport (AZA).** ☎ *480/988–7600* 🌐 *www.gatewayairport.com*. **Phoenix Sky Harbor International.** ☎ *602/273–3300* 🌐 *www.skyharbor.com*. **Pueblo Memorial Airport (PUB).** ☎ *719/553–2760* 🌐 *flypueblo.com*. **Salt Lake City International Airport (SLC).** ✉ *3920 W. Terminal Dr., Salt Lake City* ☎ *801/575–2400* 🌐 *www.slcairport.com*. **Santa Fe Regional Airport (SAF).** ☎ *505/955–2900* 🌐 *www.santafenm.gov/airport*. **St. George Regional Airport.** ✉ *4550 S. Airport Way, St. George* ☎ *435/627–4080* 🌐 *www.flysgu.com*. **Tucson International Airport.** ☎ *520/573–8100* 🌐 *www.flytucson.com*. **Yampa Valley Regional Airport (HDN).** ☎ *970/276–5000* 🌐 *www.flysteamboat.com*. **Yuma International Airport (YUM).** ☎ *928/726–5882* 🌐 *www.yumaairport.com*.

Train

CONTACTS Amtrak. ☎ *800/872–7245* 🌐 *www.amtrak.com*.

Visitor Information

CONTACTS Arizona Office of Tourism. ☎ *866/275–5816, 602/364–3700* 🌐 *www.visitarizona.com*. **Colorado Tourism Office.** ☎ *800/265–6723* 🌐 *www.colorado.com*. **Discover Navajo.** 🌐 *www.discovernavajo.com*. **Hopi Tribe Arts Trail.** ☎ *928/283–4500* 🌐 *www.hopiartstrail.com*. **Indian Pueblo Cultural Center.** ☎ *505/843–7270, 866/855–7902* 🌐 *www.indianpueblo.org*. **Las Vegas Convention and Visitors Authority.** ✉ *3150 Paradise Rd., Paradise Road* ☎ *877/847–4858, 702/892–0711* 🌐 *www.visitlasvegas.com*. **Nevada Commission on Tourism.** ☎ *800/638–2328* 🌐 *travelnevada.com*. **New Mexico Tourism Department Visitor Center.** ✉ *Lamy Bldg., 491 Old Santa Fe Trail, Old Santa Fe Trail and South Capitol* ☎ *505/827–7336* 🌐 *www.newmexico.org*. **Tohono O'odham Nation.** ☎ *520/383–0211* 🌐 *www.tonation-nsn.gov*. **Tourism Santa Fe.** ✉ *Santa Fe Community Convention Center, 201 W. Marcy St., The Plaza* ☎ *505/955–6200, 800/777–2489* 🌐 *www.santafe.org*. **Utah Office of Tourism.** ✉ *Council Hall, Capitol Hill, 300 N. State St., Salt Lake City* ☎ *801/538–1900, 800/200–1160* 🌐 *www.visitutah.com*.

Great Itineraries

Utah's Five Glorious National Parks, 7 Days

DAYS 1 AND 2: ZION NATIONAL PARK

(3 hours from McCarran Airport in Las Vegas)

Start early from Las Vegas, and within three hours you'll be across the most barren stretches of desert and marveling at the bends in the Virgin River gorge. Just past St. George, Utah, on I–15, take the Route 9 exit to **Zion National Park.** Spend your afternoon in the park—if you're visiting in February through November, the National Park Service bus system does the driving for you on Zion Canyon Scenic Drive (in fact, when the bus is running, cars are not allowed on the drive).

For a nice introductory walk, try the short and easy **Weeping Rock Trail.** Follow it along the **Emerald Pools Trail** in Zion Canyon itself, where you might come across wild turkeys and ravens. Before leaving the park, ask the rangers to decide which of Zion's two iconic hikes is right for you the next day—the 1,488-foot elevation gain to **Angel's Landing** or river wading along the improbably steep canyon called the **Narrows.** Overnight at **Zion Lodge** inside the park (book well in advance or call for last-minute cancellations), but venture into the bustling gateway town of **Springdale** for dinner and a peak into an art gallery or boutique. Try **Bit & Spur** for tasty Southwestern food.

Start at dawn the next day to beat the crowds and heat if you're ascending Angel's Landing (allow three to four hours).

DAY 3: BRYCE CANYON NATIONAL PARK

(2 hours from Zion)

It's a long 85 miles from Zion to Bryce via Route 9 (the scenic Zion–Mount Carmel Highway), particularly as traffic must be escorted through a 1.1-mile-long tunnel. Canyon Overlook is a great stopping point, providing views of massive rock formations such as East and West Temples. When you emerge, you are in slickrock country, where huge petrified sandstone dunes have been etched by ancient waters. Stay on Route 9 for 23 miles and then turn north onto U.S. 89 and follow the signs to the entrance of **Bryce Canyon National Park.**

Start at **Sunrise Point.** Check out **Bristlecone Loop Trail** and the **Navajo Loop Trail,** both of which you can easily fit into a day trip and will get you into the heart of the park. Listen for peregrine falcons deep in the side canyons, and keep an eye out for a species of prairie dog that only lives in these parts. If you can't stay in the park (camping or **The Lodge at Bryce Canyon** are your options), overnight at **Ruby's Inn,** near the junction of routes 12 and 63, or the full-featured **Bryce Canyon Grand Hotel** across the street; both are on the park's free shuttle route.

DAY 4: CAPITOL REEF NATIONAL PARK

(2½ hours from Bryce Canyon)

If you can, get up early to see sunrise paint Bryce's hoodoos, then head out on the spectacular Utah Scenic Byway–Route 12. Route 12 winds over and through **Grand Staircase–Escalante National Monument.** Boulder's **Hell's Backbone Grill,** for example, may be the best remote restaurant you'll find in the West, and you don't want to bypass **Fruita's** petroglyphs and bountiful orchards in the late summer and fall.

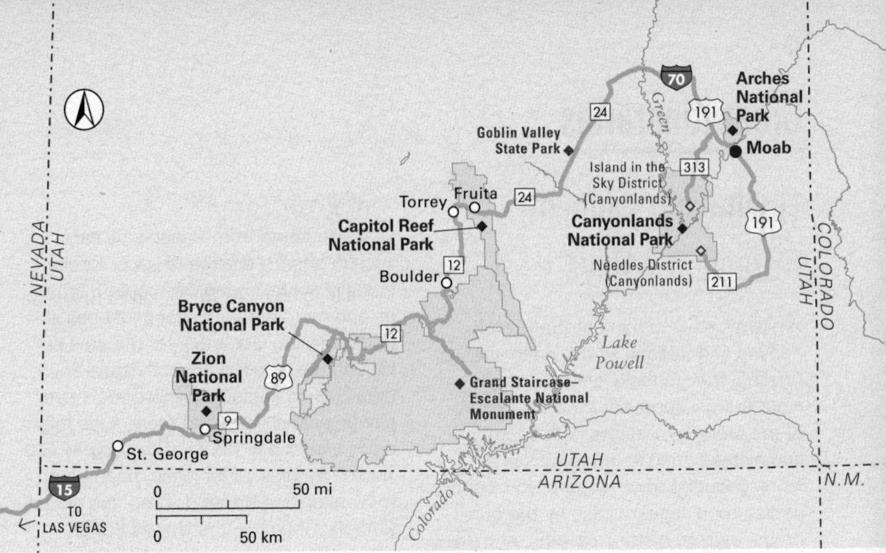

At the intersection of routes 12 and 24, turn east onto Route 24 toward **Capitol Reef National Park.** The crowds are smaller here than at other national parks in the state, and the scenery is stunning. Assuming it's still daylight when you arrive, hike the 1-mile **Hickman Bridge Trail,** stop in at the visitor center, open until 4:30 (later in the spring through fall), and view pioneer and Native American exhibits, talk with rangers about geography or geology, or watch a film. Nearby **Torrey** is your best bet for lodging and you can get a tasty pizza to enjoy with a microbrew and gorgeous red rock views from the **Rim Rock Patio**.

DAYS 5–7: MOAB, ARCHES, AND CANYONLANDS NATIONAL PARKS

(2½ hours from Capitol Reef to Canyonlands)

Explore Capitol Reef more the next morning. An easy way to do this is to drive the 10-mile **Capitol Reef Scenic Drive,** which starts at the park Visitor Center. When you leave, travel east and north for 75 miles on Route 24. If you want a break after about an hour, stop at the small **Goblin Valley State Park.** Continue on Route 24 to I–70 and turn east toward Colorado.

Take Exit 182 south onto U.S. 191, proceeding about 19 miles to Island in the Sky Road. Make sure you have water, food, and gas, as **Canyonlands National Park** offers no services, with the exception of water at The Needles visitor center year-round and the Island in the Sky visitor center seasonally. Be sure to follow the drive out to **Grand View Point** to look down on the convergence of the Colorado and Green rivers. Along the way, **Mesa Arch** is a half-mile walk and offers a sneak preview of what to expect at Arches. More ambitious individuals should hike the mysterious crater at **Upheaval Dome,** which is a steep 1-mile round-trip hike. Whether you plan to explore Canyonlands further the next day or move onto **Arches National Park,** backtrack to U.S. 191 and turn right for the final 12-mile drive into **Moab,** a good base camp for both parks.

Build your Arches itinerary around hikes to **Delicate Arch** (best seen at sunrise to avoid the crowds), **Landscape Arch,** or a guided hike in the **Fiery Furnace.**

You can raft the Colorado River from Moab or bike the **Slickrock Trail.** Or, explore **Needles District** of Canyonlands (about 90 minutes south), viewing petroglyphs on Route 279 (Potash Road), and driving along the Colorado River north of town to **Fisher Towers.**

Great Itineraries

The Best of Southern Arizona in 7 Days

While it's easy to think of the Grand Canyon and Sedona as the go-to sites in Arizona, they're really only the beginning. To truly appreciate the full beauty of the state, bypass the high country and instead head south to Tucson and its neighboring towns. There, you'll see undisturbed saguaro cacti by the hundreds, explore historic caverns, and enjoy quaint artists' communities.

While Tucson does have an international airport, it often isn't as convenient as Phoenix. Typically fares are lower in Phoenix as more flights fly into the city. Plus starting your journey in the Valley gives the perfect opportunity to view the yin and yang of Arizona: urban, sprawling Phoenix and its quiet but charming smaller neighbor to the south, Tucson.

DAYS 1 AND 2: PHOENIX AND THE VALLEY OF THE SUN

Start your trip by immersing yourself in the basics of the desert. First, visit the Heard Museum, regarded as the finest collection of Native American art in the nation. Then head east about 20 minutes and explore the Desert Botanical Garden, where you'll see desert plants in all shapes and colors, and discover that the native landscape is more diverse and beautiful than a thorny cactus. For dinner enjoy a spicy and hearty Mexican meal; be sure to order something filled with machaca beef and covered in green sauce. You won't regret it. In the morning head outdoors for a hike or a balloon ride, or even have a little grown-up playtime at one of Phoenix's many luxurious spas or manicured golf courses. In the evening explore Old Town Scottsdale. Stroll the streets, window-shop for art (you'll be tempted), and then dine at a fine restaurant.

DAY 3: TUCSON

Just two hours from Phoenix by car, Tucson offers a change of pace. Cooler (literally about 10 degrees cooler), smaller, and more natural, Tucson just has a different vibe. Get a feel for the area by visiting the indoor-outdoor Arizona-Sonora Desert Museum, where you'll see plants, animals, art, and more. Kids might enjoy a couple of hours at the nearby Old Tucson Studios. After lunch, head south to Mission San Xavier del Bac, the oldest Catholic Church in the United States.

Logistics: Tucson is about two hours by car from Phoenix. Take Interstate 10 south.

DAY 4: THE WILD WEST

The Old West is alive and well in Southern Arizona. Historic Tombstone, of Wyatt Earp and the O.K. Corral fame, is just an hour outside of Tucson. Visit the Tombstone Historama to get a feel for the town and its history, and then watch a reenactment of the O.K. Corral gunfight. Spend the night in nearby Bisbee, an artists' haven and a great site for shopping, or return to Tucson if metropolitan comforts are more to your liking.

Logistics: Tombstone is about an hour southeast of Tucson. Take Interstate 10 east to AZ 80 to reach Tombstone. Bisbee is farther along AZ 80, just about a half hour outside of Tombstone, and an hour and a half from Tucson.

DAY 5: KARTCHNER CAVERNS STATE PARK

The most impressive cave system in Arizona, and quite possibly the country, was a secret until 1999. Only discovered in 1974 and then kept hidden from the public for some 25 years, Kartchner Caverns State Park is a wet cave system comprising 13,000 feet of passages and two chambers. Reservations are essential, and you'll have to choose between

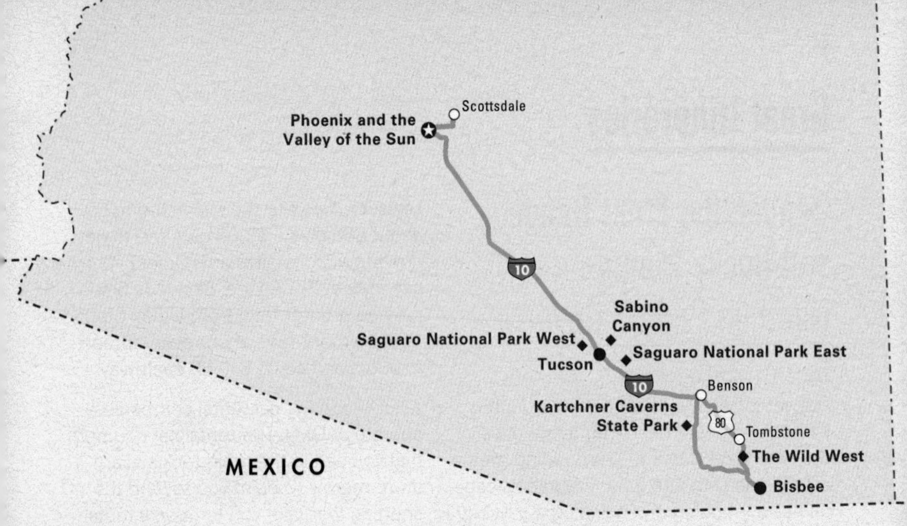

a tour of the Big Room or the Rotunda/Throne Room. There's an on-site café, so don't worry about packing provisions. But plan on making a relatively long drive home—whether that's Tucson or Bisbee—for dinner.

Logistics: To reach Kartchner Caverns State Park, take Interstate 10 to Benson, which is a half hour east of Tucson. Take AZ 90 south for 9 miles to reach the park.

DAY 6: BISBEE

An hour south of Kartchner Caverns is Bisbee, a former mining town that has found new life in its artistic side. You'll find many galleries and some good restaurants and hotels. It's definitely worth spending a night here to enjoy the town's nightlife scene before heading back to Tucson.

Logistics: Bisbee is about an hour south of Kartchner Caverns via AZ 90S. It's about 90 minutes to Saguaro National Park.

DAY 7: SAGUARO NATIONAL PARK OR SABINO CANYON

Before heading back to Phoenix for your departure, visit either Saguaro National Park or Sabino Canyon. If you don't feel like walking, both East and West districts of Saguaro have a scenic drive, and Sabino Canyon has an open-air tram. There you can view one of the densest populations of the iconic saguaro cactus, the most protected and beloved inhabitants of the state; they can reach 50 feet in height and live up to 200 years. Bring food and water for your visit, even if your only plan is to explore by car. Hikes vary from easy to strenuous and will bring you closer to the saguaro-filled hillsides. Allow two hours to return to Phoenix, and two hours to return your rental car and get through the terminal at the airport.

Logistics: Saguaro National Park is split into two halves on either side of Tucson, each about a half hour from the heart of the city. The Tucson Mountain District is west of I–10; the Rincon Mountain District is east of I–10. You'll need about 45 minutes to drive between the two halves of the park, so it may not be practical to see both in a single day. Sabino Canyon is in the northeast corner of Tucson.

Great Itineraries

Denver, the Front Range, and Rocky Mountain National Park, 7 Days

DAYS 1–3: DENVER

Denver is filled with folks who stopped to visit and never left. After a few days in the Mile High City and surrounding metro area it's easy to see why: Colorado's capital has a lot going on, including a thriving cultural scene, restaurants representing every ethnicity, plenty of sunshine, and outdoor options galore, all set beneath a stunning backdrop of snowcapped peaks.

The Old West still holds sway in visitors' imaginations, and there are plenty of throwback trappings to check out, but the reality is that Denver is a modern metropolis that offers cosmopolitan amenities and state-of-the-art amusements.

After you've settled into your hotel, head downtown, or, if you're already staying there—always a good option to explore the city—make your way to Lower Downtown, or **LoDo.** The historic district is home to many of the city's famous brewpubs, art galleries, and **Coors Field,** as well as popular restaurants and some of the area's oldest architecture.

Hop on the free MallRide, the shuttle bus run by RTD, to head up to the 16th Street Mall, a pedestrian-friendly, shopping-oriented strip that runs through the center of downtown. From there you can walk to **Larimer Square** for more shopping and restaurants. You can also visit the **Denver Art Museum, Union Station, the History Colorado Center, the Colorado State Capitol, the Molly Brown House,** and the **U.S. Mint.**

Logistics: Head to the taxi stand to pay about $60 plus a $5.03 gate fee to get downtown, or visit the RTD desk for train schedules. The A-Line, Denver's brand new commuter train from Union Station to the airport, runs about every fifteen minutes and costs $10.50 each way.

All of the major car-rental companies operate at DEN. The rental-car counters that you see in the main terminal are there merely to point you toward the shuttles that take you to the car-rental center. Depending on time of day and traffic, it will take 40 minutes to an hour to reach downtown Denver and another 40 minutes for Boulder and the foothills.

Once in Denver, light-rail is an excellent way to navigate the city. Vending machines at each station for the RTD Light Rail service show destinations and calculate your fare ($3–$5.25 depending on the number of zones crossed). Children under age five ride free when accompanied by a fare-paying adult. RTD buses also provide an excellent way to get around.

DAY 4: RIDE THE RAILS

The former silver-mining era boomtown of **Georgetown** is less than an hour from Denver via I–70. Once there, you can take the Georgetown Loop Railroad to Silver Plume and back in less than two hours, riding in an open-air car in "coach" class (enclosed and heated starting in late fall) or an enclosed parlor car in "first class" (which includes some nonalcoholic drinks and snacks). The trains run several times a day from April through late December; you can add on a visit to the Lebanon Silver Mine and try your hand at some gold-panning. Have lunch at the Alpine Restaurant in Georgetown after your morning train trip. If you

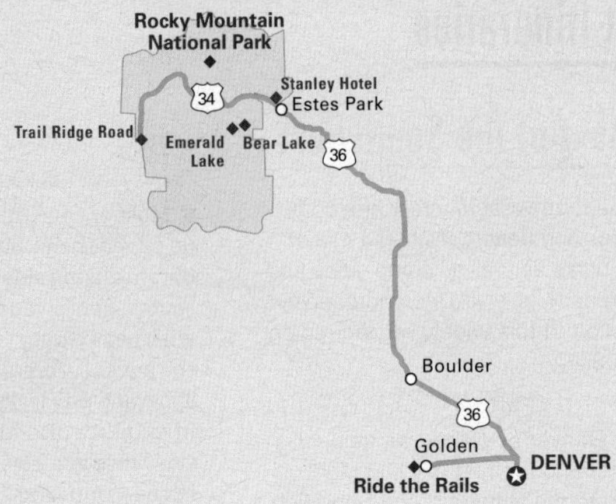

have the time and inclination, there's a spectacular drive south of Georgetown along the **Guanella Pass Scenic Byway** to Grant; the road is now fully paved, so it can be done with any rental car. The drive takes about an hour each way without stops, but you'll have magnificent views of Mount Evans as well as Grays and Torrey's peaks, so you may want to stop frequently. If you skip the drive and get an early start back, you might have time to stop for an afternoon tour at the Coors Brewery in **Golden** on the way back. If you get a late start, you can spend the night in Georgetown at the quaint Hotel Chateau Chamonix.

Logistics: The drive on I–70 is usually less than an hour to Georgetown. The loop railroad takes about 90 minutes, the mine tour adds about 1 hour and 15 minutes to the trip and must be booked in advance.

DAYS 5–7: ROCKY MOUNTAIN NATIONAL PARK

Rocky Mountain National Park (RMNP) is a year-round marvel, a park for every season: hiking in the summer, spotting elk in the fall, snowshoeing in winter, and snapping photos of wildflowers in spring. There are several hikes that shouldn't be missed in the park. For lovely scenery, opt for the one that goes from **Bear Lake to Emerald Lake.** There are some steep sections along the way, but the spectacular mountain views more than make up for it. Also not to be missed is a drive along **Trail Ridge Road,** the world's highest continuous paved highway. You'll enjoy awesome views of waterfalls, lakes, mountain vistas, glaciers, and emerald meadows. Give yourself four hours to complete the drive, and check the weather conditions before you start. Trail Ridge Road is closed in winter.

There are five campgrounds in the park, but those looking for more comfort should opt for **Estes Park.** This picturesque town is the gateway to RMNP and a worthwhile destination itself, a small town swelling to a large one with the tourists who flock to its Western-theme shops and art galleries. The **Stanley Hotel,** the inspiration for Stephen King's novel *The Shining,* provides great lodging in a historic setting.

Logistics: Estes Park is a hop-skip from Denver, about 65 miles northwest via I–25 and then CO–66 and U.S. 36. To get to RMNP, simply take U.S. 34 or U.S. 36 into the park (a 15-minute drive).

Great Itineraries

The Best of the Southwest

The ideal Southwest itinerary hits both mountains and desert, visiting a mix of national parks as well as some cities and resort areas to give you a comprehensive introduction to this widely varying region of the U.S.

DAY 1: DENVER

Arrive in Denver by plane, car, train, or bus and spend the first day and night adjusting to the altitude of the Mile High City. Focus on LoDo and the city center if you have time to explore (the Denver Art Museum, Larimer Square, and Union Station are good places to start). Larimer Square and LoDo have plenty of dining options (try the Wynkoop Brewing Company for a casual meal or Rioja for an upscale one) and there are hotels all over downtown. *(Ch. 16)*

Logistics: Arrive via Denver International Airport, Amtrak, or car. Rent a car if needed. Spend the night downtown.

DAY 2: ROCKY MOUNTAIN NATIONAL PARK

After experiencing Denver, it's time to head to the high country. Northwest of Boulder, Rocky Mountain National Park is just the destination to see (and possibly summit) 14,000-foot peaks and experience alpine tundra above timberline. Depending on your route, you can stay in Estes Park on the east side of Grand Lake on the west side of the park. *(Ch. 16)*

Logistics: From Denver, you can enter through Grand Lake via I–70 and U.S. highways 40 and 34 (102 miles) or Estes Park via I–25 and U.S. 36 through Boulder (65 miles). It's 48 miles through the park on Trail Ridge Road. Stay in either Estes Park or Grand Lake for the night.

Tips

■ Most of this itinerary takes you on paved roads, but there are plenty of tantalizing side trips on unpaved routes. Rent a four-wheel drive car with heavy-duty tires if you are the adventurous sort. While this itinerary was written with summer in mind, it's also nice to have a high-clearance vehicle if you are driving in the mountains in the winter.

■ This itinerary covers a lot of ground in two weeks. While the schedule was designed to minimize distances between stops, some days involve 6 or more hours in the car. Plan accordingly in terms of food, drink, gasoline, and bathroom breaks.

■ The Southwest is a land of extremes, and this itinerary is no exception. Plan to pack a winter coat and long underwear along with shorts and swim suits, even if you are traveling in July or August.

■ This itinerary features stops at 6 national parks. Keep in mind that they can be very busy during peak summer months, and reservations for lodging, dining, and activities might be required months in advance.

DAY 3: GLENWOOD SPRINGS

Get to I–70 via U.S. 40 if you are in Grand Lake or I–25 if you stayed in Estes Park, and head west. Glenwood Springs is a great stopover en route to Utah, featuring the world's largest hot springs pool, a wide variety of restaurants and lodging options, and some great attractions for families. *(Ch. 18)*

Logistics: Glenwood Springs is located 155 miles west of Denver on I-70, with Loveland Pass, the Eisenhower Tunnel, and Vail Pass in between the two. Expect to spend 3 hours en route, more if you stop to gawk at the stellar scenery.

DAY 4: MOAB & ARCHES NATIONAL PARK

This is primarily a day to travel to Utah, but a good jump on the day will give you plenty of time to explore Arches National Park before setting into Moab for the night. The trail to Delicate Arch is 3.4 miles in and out and a good pick for intermediate and advanced hikers. *(Ch. 8)*

Logistics: Moab is 198 miles southwest of Glenwood Springs.

DAY 5: CANYONLANDS NATIONAL PARK

Spend the day in Canyonlands hiking and gawking at some of the best desert scenery in thse Southwest from the overlooks in the park's Island in the Sky district. It is the easiest area of Canyonlands to access in a day from Moab. Plan to take a hike; there are trails here for all skill levels. *(Ch. 8)*

Logistics: From Moab, it's 32 miles on U.S. 191 and Utah Hwy. 313 to the Island in the Sky Visitor Center. Plan to pack a lunch and return to Moab for the night.

DAY 6: BRYCE CANYON NATIONAL PARK

Set your alarm: It's about 250 miles from Moab to Bryce Canyon, and you'll want to make the most of your time there before continuing to Hurricane for the night. In between, plan to spend the afternoon in Bryce Canyon to experience the ornate landscapes of hoodoos from the overlooks. *(Ch. 8)*

Logistics: It's 248 miles from Moab to Bryce Canyon via U.S. 191, I–70, and state highways. From Bryce, Hurricane is 130 miles southwest via I–15 and other roads. Hurricane has a nice selection of lodging and dining.

DAY 7: ZION NATIONAL PARK

Waking up in Hurricane, you're at the doorstep of Zion National Park, so plan a day here to hike and see sights like Zion Canyon and Angels Landing, and the Subway. Plan to return to Hurricane in time for dinner.

Logistics: Pack a lunch to maximize your time in Zion. The park can get very busy; plan any activities well in advance.

Great Itineraries

DAYS 8 AND 9: LAS VEGAS

After five national parks, it's time for a change of pace, and there's no bigger change of pace than a couple of nights in Sin City. Plan to take in a show, hang out at the pool, eat some terrific meals, and otherwise see the sights of this increasingly unbelievable mecca in the desert.

Logistics: From Hurricane, it's a straight shot down I–15 138 miles to Las Vegas. You can easily be people-watching on the Strip by lunchtime.

DAY 10: GRAND CANYON NATIONAL PARK

Don't overdo it on your second night in Vegas: An early start can have you looking at the South Rim by noon. Plan to spend the latter part of the day hiking the Rim Trail or gazing at the panoramas from the many overlooks. Stay the night in Grand Canyon Village or just to the south in Tusayan. *(Ch. 12)*

Logistics: Grand Canyon National Park is 280 miles west of Las Vegas via U.S. 93 and I–40. Kingman and Williams, Arizona, are the best places to stop en route.

DAY 11: MONUMENT VALLEY NAVAJO TRIBAL PARK

From one iconic landscape to another, this day takes you through northeastern Arizona to Monument Valley along the Utah–Arizona border. Take a guided tour and stay at one of the hotels in the park or one of the towns to the east.

Logistics: From Cameron just east of the Grand Canyon, it's a 126-mile drive on U.S. 89 and 160 to Monument Valley. If you stay east of the park, Farmington, New Mexico, has the most options.

DAY 12: SANTA FE

This day involves a good stint in the car to get to Santa Fe, so plan to stay near the Plaza so you can spend the afternoon and evening exploring the galleries and shops on foot. If you stayed in Monument Valley on Day 11, you will want to get an early start, so it could be better to drive a few hours the night before.

Logistics: It takes about 6 hours to cover the 366 miles between Monument Valley and Santa Fe, so plan accordingly. There are several good places to stop on U.S. highways 160, 64, and 550 for gas and fast food, but it's best not to dawdle in order to maximize your time in Santa Fe.

DAY 13: COLORADO SPRINGS

Hit Meow Wolf or another attraction before leaving Santa Fe, then it's a little less than 5 hours north to Colorado Springs. If you time it right, you can drive to the top of Pikes Peak before descending for a night in Manitou Springs or the Broadmoor area.

Logistics: Colorado Springs is 322 miles north of Santa Fe via I–25. Manitou Springs is just 6 miles west of Colorado Springs, and features a wide range of lodgings and restaurants. The Broadmoor is one of the top hotels in the country, and features 10 restaurants and 10 cafés and bars.

DAY 14: DENVER

This closes the loop on two weeks in the American Southwest in all of its glory. Depending on your schedule, you might have time for a short hike in Garden of the Gods before heading north from Colorado Springs to Denver.

Logistics: Denver is 70 miles north of Colorado Springs on I–25. You'll want to give yourself at least 4 hours to get to DIA before your flight if you are traveling by air.

On the Calendar

January

National Western Stock Show And Rodeo (Colorado). Held in Denver for 16 days in January, this is the world's largest livestock show, with more than 15,000 animals in attendance, plus a rodeo extravaganza, with no less than 20 professional events on the docket every year. 🌐 *nationalwestern.com*

Sundance Film Festival (Utah). Organized by Robert Redford's Sundance Institute every January since 1978, the largest film festival in the U.S.A. unspools at theaters in Park City, Salt Lake City, and Sundance Resort near Provo. 🌐 *sundance.org/festival*

February

Cactus League Baseball (Arizona). In February and March, 15 Major League Baseball clubs descend on ballparks in the Phoenix metro area for spring training. It's a great way to see your favorite players swing for the fences, and prices are reasonable. 🌐 *cactusleague.com*

March

National Fiery Foods & BBQ Show. The Fiery Foods show is the Super Bowl for the hot sauce industry. Held in Albuquerque since 1988, the modern event draws more than 1,000 attendees to sample more than 1,000 different products that range from mild to thermonuclear. 🌐 *www.fieryfoodsshow.com*

July

Pioneer Day (Utah). Utahns celebrate this official state holiday every Aug. 24 to mark the day when Brigham Young led a group of Mormon settlers into the Salt Lake Valley in 1847. While it is tied to the LDS church, it has evolved into a semisecular, statewide affair with fireworks, parades, and pioneer-themed activities in most towns and cities.

August

Burning Man (Nevada). This is one of the biggest countercultural events in the U.S. (although countercultural critics say it has gotten too big and too mainstream). For a week before Labor Day in late August in early September, tens of thousands of people create a temporary city celebrating creativity and self-reliance, culminating in a big wooden effigy going up in smoke. 🌐 *burningman.org*

September

Fiesta de Santa Fe (New Mexico). This annual mid-September event marks the retaking of Santa Fe by the Spanish in 1692 after a Pueblo revolt expelled them 12 years earlier. The modern event is marked by arts and crafts booths in the Plaza, parades, and the burning of the 50-foot marionette known as Zozobra. 🌐 *www.santafefiesta.org*

Great American Beer Festival (Colorado). The largest ticketed beer event in the U.S. draws more than 60,000 beer nuts to Denver's Colorado Convention Center every year for three days in late

On the Calendar

September or early October. More than 4,000 beers from 2,300 breweries were available to sample at the 2019 event. 🌐 *greatamericanbeerfestival.com*

October

Albuquerque International Balloon Fiesta (New Mexico). Launched with 13 balloons in 1972, this is now the largest balloon festival in the world. More than 500 hot air balloons of all colors, shapes, and sizes have taken flight from Balloon Fiesta Park at recent events. 🌐 *balloonfiesta.com*

December

Ullr Fest (Colorado). The Norse god of snow, Ullr isn't quite as famous as his stepfather, Thor, except in ski towns like Breckenridge, where locals have celebrated Ullr since 1963. The modern event plays out over 10 zany days, with nightly events like the Ullr Ball, the Ullympics, and a climactic parade and bonfire. 🌐 *gobreck.com/event/ullr-fest/*

Chapter 3

LAS VEGAS AND VICINITY

3

Updated by
Mike Weatherford

Sights ★★★★★ Restaurants ★★★★★ Hotels ★★★★★ Shopping ★★★★★ Nightlife ★★★★★

WELCOME TO LAS VEGAS AND VICINITY

TOP REASONS TO GO

★ **Resorts:** Colossal hotels present exotic themes and over-the-top amenities.

★ **Dining:** Few cities in the world can claim a higher concentration of top restaurants.

★ **Gambling:** Novices and pros alike come to Vegas for legendary casino action.

★ **Shopping:** Lavish malls and bargain outlets provide retail options for every budget.

★ **Nightlife:** Master mixologists serve creative cocktails and famous DJs spin nightly.

★ **Shows:** Cirque du Soleil, top touring concert attractions, and local stars perform day and night.

1 **Las Vegas.** It doesn't matter if you're talking about the world-famous Strip, its re-energized downtown, or shiny new suburbs: Las Vegas is the world's playground for gaming, entertainment, dining, and nightlife.

2 **Hoover Dam.** The Depression-era marvel remains a monument to ingenuity, engineering, and determination.

3 **Lake Mead.** The world's largest man-made reservoir covers 225 square miles. Whether you're water-skiing or enjoying the rugged shoreline from a paddle wheeler, Lake Mead is a refreshing break from the city.

4 **Valley of Fire.** Less than an hour from the Strip, Nevada's first state park is a quick immersion in the stark, colored rock formations that inspired the name.

5 **Area 51.** Pop culture has fueled the popularity of a mysterious military base in a remote pocket of the state. Odds are you won't spot any UFOs, but a visit offers a taste of rural Nevada hospitality.

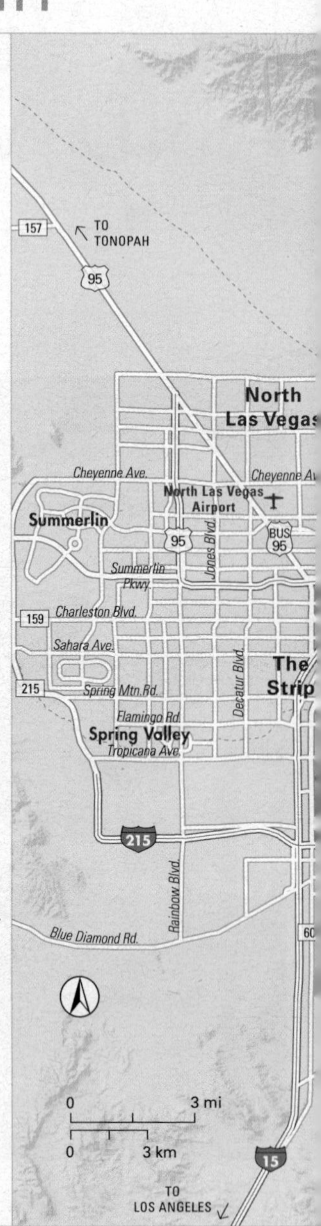

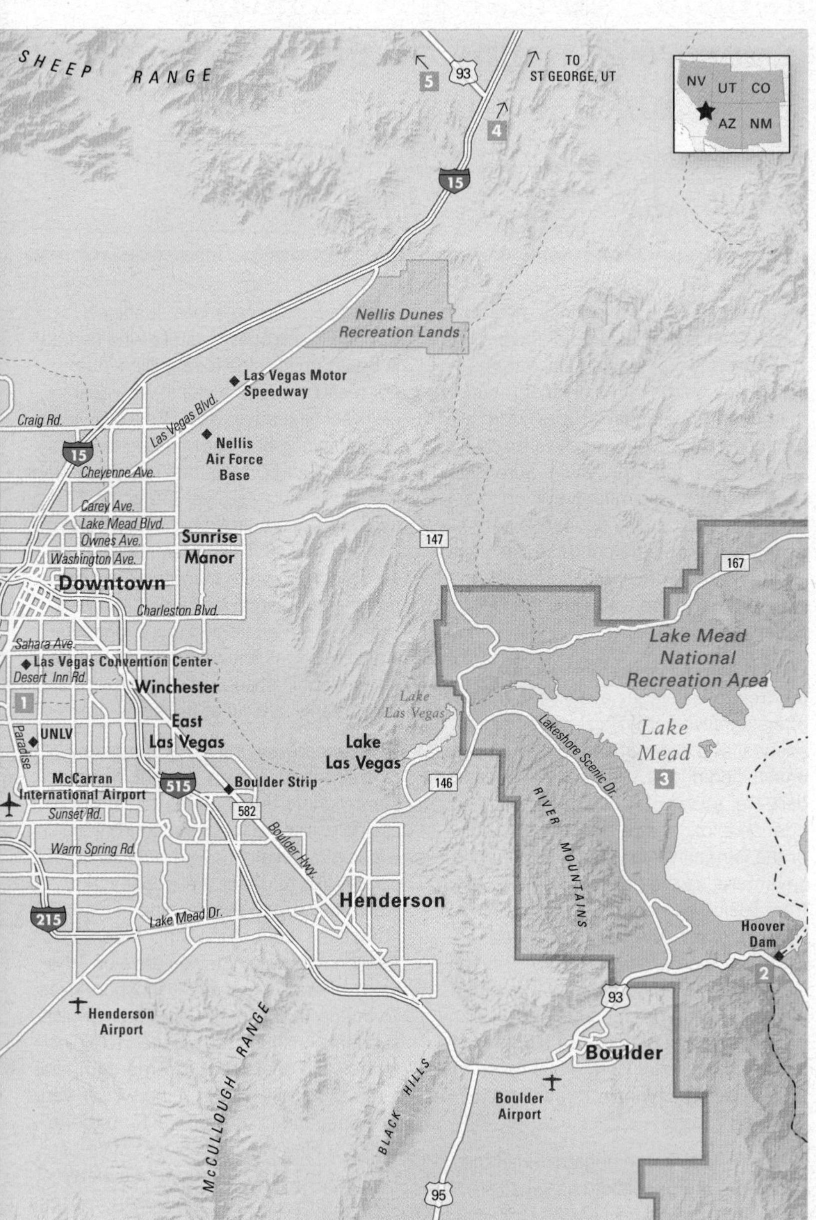

SHEEP RANGE
5
93
TO ST GEORGE, UT
4
15
NV
UT
CO
AZ
NM
Nellis Dunes Recreation Lands
Las Vegas Motor Speedway
Craig Rd.
Las Vegas Blvd.
15
Nellis Air Force Base
Cheyenne Ave.
Carey Ave.
Lake Mead Blvd.
Owens Ave.
Sunrise Manor
Washington Ave.
147
167
Downtown
Charleston Blvd.
Sahara Ave.
Las Vegas Convention Center
Desert Inn Rd.
Winchester
Lake Mead National Recreation Area
1
Lake Las Vegas
East Las Vegas
Lake Las Vegas
Lakeshore Scenic Dr
Lake Mead
UNLV
Paradise
3
McCarran International Airport
515
Boulder Strip
146
582
Sunset Rd.
Boulder Hwy.
RIVER MOUNTAINS
Warm Spring Rd.
Henderson
215
Lake Mead Dr.
Hoover Dam
2
93
Henderson Airport
McCULLOUGH RANGE
Boulder
BLACK HILLS
Boulder Airport
95

Las Vegas knows what everyone wants and casts its net wide. If past eras of its history conjure specific images of hardcore gambling, family fun, or giant nightclubs pulsating to dance music, the city now simply answers "Yes" to all of the above.

Megaresorts fund their dancing waters, fake volcanos, half-size Eiffel Towers, and towering glass pyramids with the collective desires and dollars of more than 30 million annual visitors. From a Wolfgang Puck dinner to a Wolfpack-like adventure on the Strip, you're sure to find your perfect indulgence. Swim up to a blackjack table, chow down at a buffet, or chill out in an ultralounge. A Las Vegas vacation disorients and delights; when you're here, you're all-in, and the "real world" seems far out.

For the millions of visitors who make the trek to Las Vegas every year, the city offers an ever-increasing array of sights, sounds, and experiences to play on their unsatisfied needs. We desire to escape daily life, so we stay in a hotel modeled after an exotic locale, say, the Mirage or the Venetian. We want to experience adventure, so we get an adrenaline jolt from casino games, hiking in Red Rock Canyon, or jet-skiing on Lake Mead. Just for a moment we want to own and consume finer things than we have, so we visit opulent restaurants and visit any of several concentrations of high-end shopping malls, looking to buy items that would be just beyond our reach back in the "real" world.

Beyond and to some degree within the spectacle, the people of Las Vegas are quintessentially American. It shines through in the out-of-staters who settled in Southern Nevada for a million different reasons over the years, who deal blackjack and drive cabs. But also evident is the melting pot; Las Vegas is the city on the hill for both rustbelt retirees and immigrants from all over the world. Miles and miles of suburban housing—most of it built in the 1990s or later, rippling the sunlight from white stucco and red tile roofs—represent a fresh start or a new chapter. For visitors and many locals as well, Las Vegas knows what you want and doles it out in spades. It's both exotic and comfortably familiar at the same time.

Weekenders can still go home bragging about staying up all night, or never stepping into the hot desert sun. But with casino gaming all over the country making it less of a novelty now, more Las Vegas visitors like to offset the indoor action with a day trip to surrounding natural attractions. East of the Strip is Red Rock Canyon, where a one-way drive on "the loop" offers several stops for short hikes. To the north is Mount Charleston, which suddenly changes from desert to alpine terrain, and offers cool summer temperatures and snow skiiing in the winter. Venture about an hour from the Strip to the Valley of Fire, Nevada's oldest state park. Or head to Lake Mead to rent a watercraft or take a ride on the Desert Princess paddlewheeler. Leave time for the Hoover Dam tour or lunch in Boulder City, which retains its historic small-town charm.

Planning

Getting Here and Around

AIR

The gateway to Las Vegas is McCarran International Airport (LAS), immediately east of the southern end of the Strip. The airport, just a few minutes' drive from the Strip, is well served by nonstop and connecting flights from all around the country and a handful of international destinations. The airport is consistently rated among the most passenger-friendly airports in the United States.

CAR

Though you can get around central Las Vegas adequately without a car, the best way to experience the city can be to drive it. A car gives you easy access to all the casinos and attractions; lets you toggle back and forth from the Strip to downtown, and make excursions to Lake Mead, Hoover Dam, and elsewhere at your leisure. Don't forget the sheer fun of cruising the Strip and basking in its neon glow. If you plan to spend most of your time on the Strip, a car probably isn't worth the trouble in the era of ride-sharing services. Self-parking is no longer free at most major resort hotels, so that's also a consideration.

CAR RENTALS

The airport's rental-car companies are off-site at McCarran Rent-a-Car Center, about 3 miles from the main airport complex, and visitors must take the Rental Car Shuttle buses from the center median, located just outside the baggage claim Ground Transportation exits from Level 1 (Terminal 1) and Level Zero (Terminal 3) to get there. The facility reduces congestion in and around the airport, and offers visitors the opportunity to check bags for flights on some airlines without setting foot in the main terminal. Still, the centralized location is far enough away from the airport that it can add anywhere from 15 to 25 minutes to your travel time. The bottom line: If you rent a car, be sure to leave yourself plenty of time to return the vehicle and catch your flight.

Rental Car Rates: The Las Vegas average is anywhere from $35 to upwards of $70 a day for intermediate to full-size cars—usually you can find a car for less than $40 a day (and at very slow times for less than $30), but during very busy times expect sky-high rates, especially at the last minute. Las Vegas has among the highest car-rental taxes and surcharges in the country, however, so be sure to factor in the 8.5% (in Clark County) sales tax, and other fees that will show up before you click the "checkout" button when you book online. Owing to the high demand for rental cars and significant competition, there are many deals to be had at the airport for car rentals. During special events and conventions, rates frequently go up as supply dwindles, but at other times you can find bargains. For the best deals, check with the various online services or your airline, or contact a representative of the hotel where you'll be staying, as many hotels have business relationships with car-rental companies.

Rental Car Requirements: In Nevada you must be 21 to rent a car, and some major car-rental agencies have a minimum age of 25. Those agencies that do rent to people under 25 often assess surcharges to those drivers. There's no upper age limit for renting a car. Non–U.S. residents will need a reservation voucher, a passport, a driver's license, and a travel policy that covers each driver when picking up a car.

TAXI

Taxis aren't allowed to pick up passengers on the street, so you can't hail a cab New York–style. You have to wait in a hotel or other taxi line or call a cab company. If you dine at a restaurant off the Strip, the restaurant will call a cab to take you home.

The fare is $3.50 on the meter when you get in and 23¢ for every 1/12th mile, or $2.76 per mile (there's also a $32.40 per-hour charge for waiting). Taxis are limited by law to carrying a maximum of four passengers, and there's no additional charge per person. No fees are assessed for luggage, but taxis leaving the airport are allowed to add an airport surcharge of $2. There's also a 3% excise tax on all rates and fees.

In response to competition from ride-sharing companies, taxis now have flat-rate "airport zone" rates between the airport and the Strip. Depending on which hotel you are going to, the flat rates range from $19 to $27.

Ride-sharing applications can provide either cheaper or dramatically more expensive service depending on surge pricing.

Hotels

Las Vegas is blessed with a wide variety of lodging choices, from the classic (Caesars Palace, MGM Grand) to the hip and trendy (Cosmopolitan of Las Vegas, Aria) and elegant (Bellagio, The Venetian, Wynn). Boutique hotels-within-hotels such as Nobu and NoMad add another dimension. Family-friendly, non-gaming chain hotels are right off the Strip, and the so-called "locals casinos" in the suburbs offer a budget-friendlier simulation of the Las Vegas experience that's now become familiar in tribal casinos across the country.

Especially on weekends, accommodations in Las Vegas fill up fast. When it's time for a big convention—or a big sporting event—it's not unusual for all of the Las Vegas area's roughly 150,000 hotel rooms to sell out completely. Combine those with three-day holidays, and you can see why it's wise to make lodging arrangements for busy weekends as far ahead as possible.

When business is slow, many hotels reduce rates on rooms in their least desirable sections, sometimes with a buffet breakfast or even a show included. Most "sales" occur from early December to mid-February and in July and August, the coldest and hottest times of the year. The best discounts are always for weekday stays.

Over the last few years, most Strip hotels have clustered "amenities" such as Wi-Fi, fitness center access, and morning newspapers into mandatory resort fees ranging from $30 to $45 *per night*. In addition, most Las Vegas resorts began to charge for parking. **■TIP→ If you book a room through a casino host, request that he or she eliminate resort and parking fees from your folio.**

Restaurants

It's no secret that Las Vegas has become one of the most exciting dining destinations in the world. Less well known is that a few years ago, one survey claimed it surpassed New York as the most expensive dining city in the country.

Reservations at dinner (and occasionally even at lunch) have become a necessity in many cases. Generally, if you have your heart set on dinner at any of the celeb-helmed joints at the bigger Strip casinos, you should book several days, or even a couple of weeks, ahead. On weekends and during other busy times, even at restaurants where reservations aren't absolutely essential, it's still prudent to phone ahead for a table.

You can save money by trying lunch at some of the top eateries, and by checking out the increasingly noteworthy crop of restaurants that have developed off the Strip. Credit cards are almost universally accepted, but it's a good idea to double-check its acceptability when making reservations or before sitting down to eat.

HOTEL AND RESTAURANT PRICES

Hotel prices in the reviews are the lowest cost of a standard double room in high season. Restaurant prices in the reviews are the average cost of a main course at dinner, or if dinner is not served, at lunch.

What It Costs

	$	$$	$$$	$$$$
RESTAURANTS				
	under $12	$12–$20	$21–$30	over $30
HOTELS				
	under $150	$150–$230	$231–$330	over $330

Safety

Few places in the world have tighter security than the casino resorts lining the Strip or clustered together Downtown. Outside of these areas, Las Vegas has the same urban ills as any other big city, but on the whole, violent crime is extremely rare among tourists, and even scams and theft are no more likely here than at other major vacation destinations. Observe the same common-sense rituals you might in any city: stick to populated, well-lighted streets, don't wear flashy jewelry or wave around expensive handbags, keep valuables out of sight (and don't leave them in unattended cars), and be vigilant about what's going on around you.

Tours

Gray Line Tours

BUS TOURS | Gray Line runs tours within Las Vegas and from the city to Hoover Dam and both the south and west rims of the Grand Canyon, the south being the most popular with visitors, the west the one with the suspended, horseshoe-shape glass Skywalk. Various types of vehicles are available for your transport, and some combine water and air elements, even skydiving. ☎ *702/739–7777* 🌐 *www.graylinelasvegas.com.*

Maverick Helicopter

AIR EXCURSIONS | Maverick's selection of Grand Canyon tours includes one in which helicopter passengers land on the floor of the canyon, 3,500 feet below the rim. The company also offers airplane tours to Grand Canyon, combination airplane/helicopter tours, and nighttime 'copter flights over the Las Vegas Strip. ✉ *6075 Las Vegas Blvd. S, Las Vegas* ☎ *702/261–0007* 🌐 *www.maverickhelicopter.com.*

Pink Adventure Tours

BUS TOURS | FAMILY | Pink Adventure Tours specializes in jaunts beyond the glitz and glimmer into the stunning desert landscape that surrounds Las Vegas. Destinations include Red Rock Canyon, Valley of Fire, Death Valley, the Grand Canyon, and Hoover Dam, some in open-air Jeeps, some in climate-controlled vehicles. ☎ *877/998–6089* 🌐 *www.pinkadventuretours.com.*

Las Vegas

The tourist corridor of Las Vegas is easy to navigate, and half the fun is the surprise factor of discovering what's around the next turn or through the next casino entryway. The main action of the Strip falls in a straight, four-mile stretch of Las Vegas Boulevard. The resurgent downtown area, including the Fremont

East and Arts District areas, flow from the original casinos on Fremont Street or pick up where the Strip fades out on the north end of Las Vegas Boulevard. The ability to forget about time and geography only gets tricky if you're trying to get to a certain show or restaurant at a designated hour, especially if it's a concert or sporting event where everyone else is headed as well. Suburban attractions such as Red Rock Canyon are a bit more of a challenge, but bus tours and rental cars make them high-visitation landmarks all the same.

GETTING HERE AND AROUND

Taxis are plentiful and convenient, but ride-shares can be cheaper. Public bus transportation is available via Regional Transportation Commission of Southern Nevada (RTC). Tourist-friendly double-decker buses (dubbed "The Deuce") run up and down the Strip approximately every 15 minutes 24/7—a 24-hour pass is $8; a three-day pass is $20. The fare includes access to the "Strip and Downtown Express" (STX) and all RTC routes, which serve most of the Las Vegas Valley. Stops are near most resort properties, and are marked with signs or shelters. Visitors also can connect to and from McCarran International Airport via a 10-minute ride to the RTC's South Strip Transfer Terminal on Route 109. Buses from there connect to the Deuce, Strip, and Downtown Express, and more.

The Strip and Resort Corridor

Las Vegas Boulevard (known popularly as "The Strip") is where most of the city's famous resort hotels and casinos are located. It is busy with both traffic and pedestrians. Take heed of the weather and any free transportation alternatives when you are moving between hotels. The distances can be surprisingly long. Just to the east of the strip is Paradise Road, where you'll find a few additional major hotels and some non-casino options. A few other places are on the streets in between the Strip and Paradise Road.

Sights

★ Bellagio Conservatory and Botanical Gardens

GARDEN | **FAMILY** | The flowers, trees, and other plants in Bellagio's soaring atrium are fresh and alive, many of them grown in a 5-acre greenhouse. The artistic floral arrangements and ornamental landscaping here is breathtaking and in some cases monumental in scale. Displays change each season, and the holiday displays in December (for Christmas) and January (for Chinese New Year) are particularly dramatic. ✉ *Bellagio Las Vegas, 3600 Las Vegas Blvd. S, Center Strip* ☎ *702/693–7111, 888/987–6667* 🌐 *www.bellagio.com/attractions* 🎟 *Free.*

★ The Big Apple Coaster and Arcade

AMUSEMENT PARK/WATER PARK | **FAMILY** | There are two reasons to ride the Coney Island–style New York–New York roller coaster (aka Manhattan Express): first, with a 144-foot dive and a 360-degree somersault, it's a real scream; and second, it whisks you around the amazing replica of the New York City skyline, giving you fabulous views of the Statue of Liberty, Chrysler Building, and, at night, the Las Vegas lights—you climb to peak heights around 200 feet above the Strip. Get ready to go 67 mph over a dizzying succession of high-banked turns and camelback hills, twirl through a "heartline twist" (like a jet doing a barrel roll), and finally rocket along a 540-degree spiral before pulling back into the station. ✉ *New York–New York, 3790 Las Vegas Blvd. S, South Strip* ☎ *866/815–4365, 702/740–6969* 🌐 *newyorknewyork.mgmresorts.com* 🎟 *From $19.*

★ Fountains of Bellagio

FOUNTAIN | At least once on your visit you should stop in front of Bellagio to view its spectacular water ballet from start to finish. The dazzling fountains stream from more than 1,000 nozzles, accompanied by 4,500 lights, in 27 million gallons of water. Fountain jets shoot 250 feet in the air, tracing undulations you wouldn't have thought possible, in near-perfect time with music ranging from Bocelli and the Beatles to "Billie Jean" and tunes from (DJ) Tiësto. Some of the best views are from the Eiffel Tower's observation deck, directly across the street (unless you've got a north-facing balcony room at the Cosmopolitan). Paris and Planet Hollywood have restaurants with patios on the Strip that also offer good views. ✉ *Bellagio, 3600 Las Vegas Blvd. S, Center Strip* ☎ *888/987–6667, 702/693–7111* 🌐 *www.bellagio.com/attractions.*

High Roller

LOCAL INTEREST | Standing more than 100 feet taller than the London Eye, the High Roller opened in 2014 as the largest observation wheel in the world. The giant Ferris wheel at the east end of the LINQ features 28 glass-enclosed cabins, each of which is equipped to hold up to 40 passengers. One full rotation takes about 30 minutes; along the way, riders are treated to a dynamic video and music show on TV monitors in the pod, as well as one-of-a-kind views of Sin City and the surrounding Las Vegas Valley. The experience begins and ends in a state-of-the-art wheelhouse, where visitors can read about the engineering behind the project as they wait in line, buy drinks to take with them on the ride, or pick up souvenirs commemorating the spin. The best time to ride the wheel is nighttime, when 2,000 LED lights on the wheel itself create an otherworldly vibe. ✉ *3545 Las Vegas Blvd. S, Center Strip* ☎ *855/234–7469* 🌐 *www.caesars.com/linq/high-roller.html* 🎟 *From $21, depending on time of day and options.*

LINQ Promenade

STORE/MALL | **FAMILY** | Yes, the name is confusing, but the LINQ Promenade, the shopping, dining, and entertainment complex between the Flamingo and the LINQ Hotel, is worth the trip. Some of the notable attractions include the two-story I Love Sugar, complete with "candy martini bar"; Purple Zebra, a bar devoted solely to frozen daiquiris; a namesake comedy club for late-night host Jimmy Kimmel (who grew up in Las Vegas); and Brooklyn Bowl, which is one-part bowling alley, one-part live music venue. Of course, there's also a new iteration of O'Shea's, the Irish-theme casino that was razed to create the new streetcape. The big draw, however, is the **High Roller**, a 550-foot-tall observation wheel with spectacular views of the city. ✉ *3545 Las Vegas Blvd. S, Center Strip* ☎ *800/223–7277* 🌐 *www.caesars.com/linq.*

Shark Reef

ZOO | **FAMILY** | Your journey through Mandalay Bay's long-running Shark Reef attraction begins in the mysterious realm of deep water at the ruins of an old Aztec temple. It's tropical and humid for us bipeds, but quite comfy for the golden crocodiles, endangered green sea turtles, and water monitors. Descend through two glass tunnels, which lead you deeper and deeper under the sea (or about 1.6 million gallons of water), where exotic tropical fish and other sea creatures swim all around you. The tour saves the best for last—from the recesses of a sunken galleon, sharks swim below, above, and around the skeleton ship. Elsewhere you'll find a petting zoo for marine life, a Komodo dragon exhibit, and a special jellyfish habitat. If you plan to visit other MGM Resorts attractions you can save with their three-for-$57 promotion. ✉ *Mandalay Bay, 3950 Las Vegas Blvd. S, South Strip* ☎ *702/632–4555* 🌐 *www.sharkreef.com* 🎟 *From $24.*

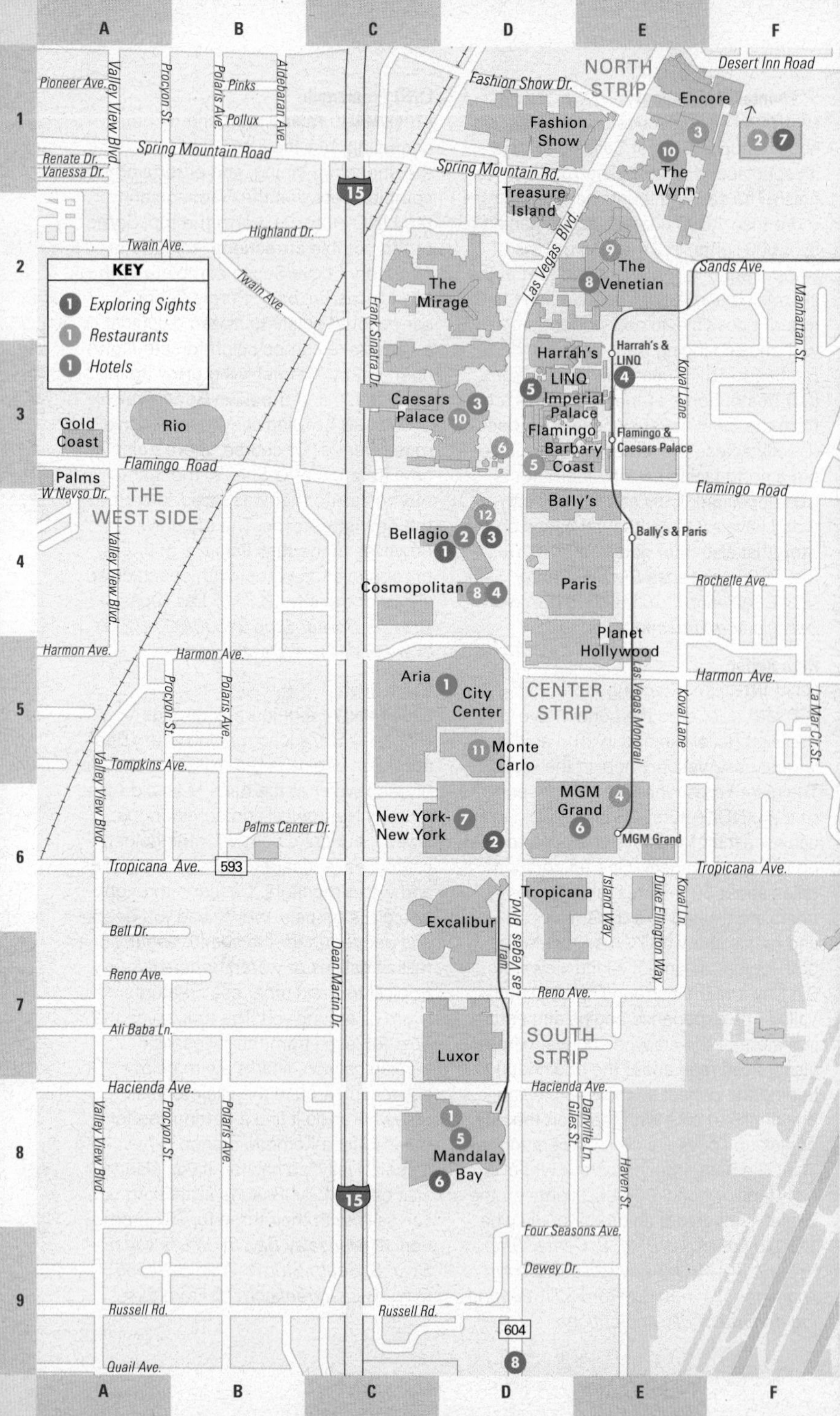

A
B
C
D
E
F
1
2
3
4
5
6
7
8
9
KEY
Exploring Sights
Restaurants
Hotels
NORTH STRIP
CENTER STRIP
SOUTH STRIP
THE WEST SIDE
Fashion Show
Encore
The Wynn
Treasure Island
The Venetian
The Mirage
Harrah's
LINQ
Imperial Palace
Flamingo
Barbary Coast
Caesars Palace
Gold Coast
Rio
Palms
Bally's
Bellagio
Paris
Cosmopolitan
Planet Hollywood
Aria
City Center
Monte Carlo
MGM Grand
New York-New York
Tropicana
Excalibur
Luxor
Mandalay Bay
Harrah's & LINQ
Flamingo & Caesars Palace
Bally's & Paris
MGM Grand
Las Vegas Monorail
Tram
Desert Inn Road
Fashion Show Dr.
Spring Mountain Rd.
Spring Mountain Road
Pioneer Ave.
Pinks
Pollux
Renate Dr.
Vanessa Dr.
Valley View Blvd.
Procyon St.
Polaris Ave.
Aldebaran Ave.
Highland Dr.
Twain Ave.
Frank Sinatra Dr.
Las Vegas Blvd.
Sands Ave.
Manhattan St.
Koval Lane
Flamingo Road
W Nevso Dr.
Rochelle Ave.
Harmon Ave.
Tompkins Ave.
Palms Center Dr.
Tropicana Ave.
593
La Mar Cir.St.
Island Way
Duke Ellington Way
Koval Ln.
Bell Dr.
Reno Ave.
Ali Baba Ln.
Dean Martin Dr.
Hacienda Ave.
Giles St.
Danville Ln.
Haven St.
Four Seasons Ave.
Dewey Dr.
Russell Rd.
Quail Ave.
604
15

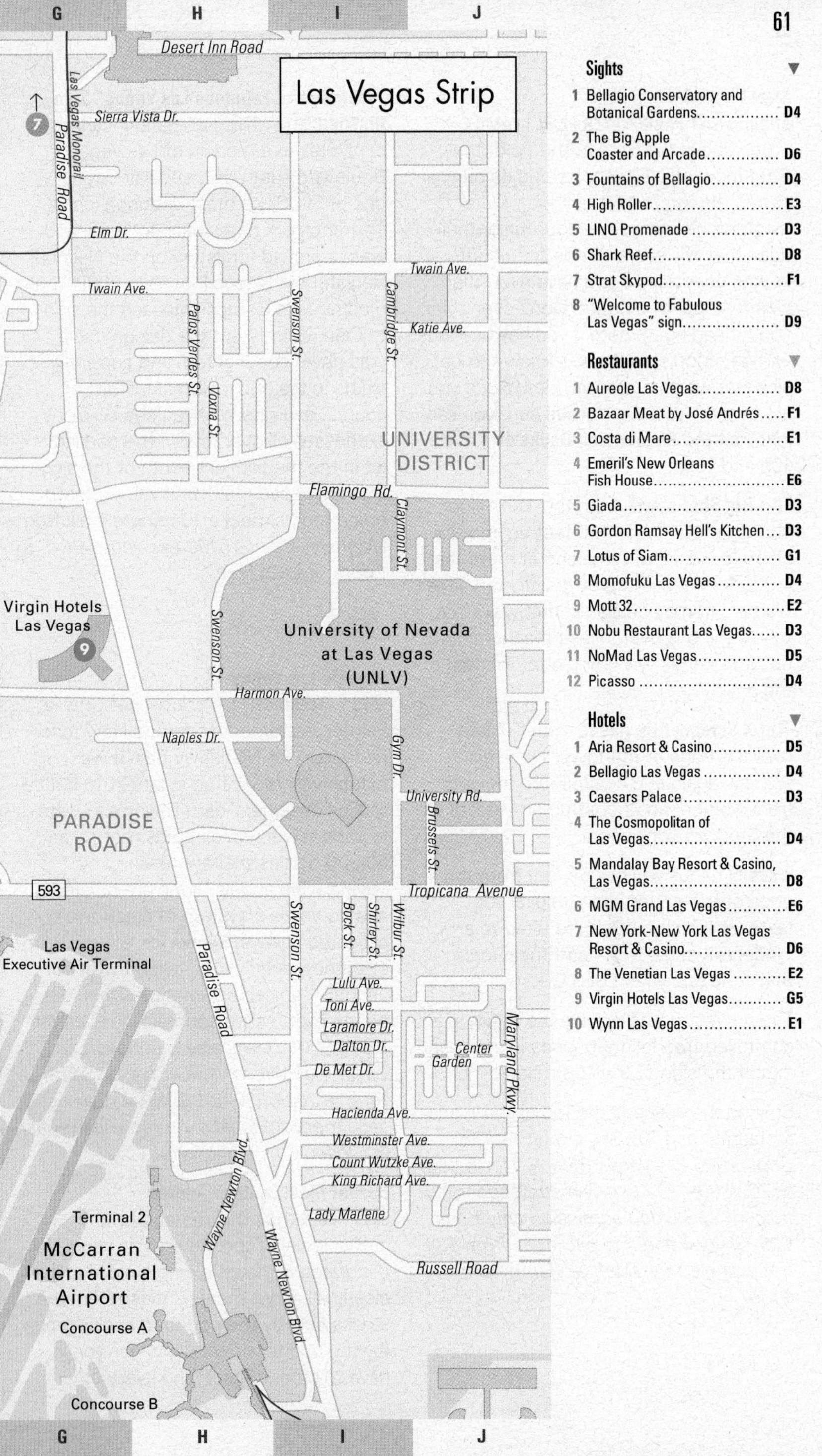

Sights

1 Bellagio Conservatory and Botanical Gardens................ **D4**
2 The Big Apple Coaster and Arcade.............. **D6**
3 Fountains of Bellagio............. **D4**
4 High Roller.......................... **E3**
5 LINQ Promenade **D3**
6 Shark Reef.......................... **D8**
7 Strat Skypod........................ **F1**
8 "Welcome to Fabulous Las Vegas" sign.................. **D9**

Restaurants

1 Aureole Las Vegas................ **D8**
2 Bazaar Meat by José Andrés..... **F1**
3 Costa di Mare....................... **E1**
4 Emeril's New Orleans Fish House.......................... **E6**
5 Giada.............................. **D3**
6 Gordon Ramsay Hell's Kitchen... **D3**
7 Lotus of Siam...................... **G1**
8 Momofuku Las Vegas............ **D4**
9 Mott 32.............................. **E2**
10 Nobu Restaurant Las Vegas...... **D3**
11 NoMad Las Vegas................ **D5**
12 Picasso **D4**

Hotels

1 Aria Resort & Casino............. **D5**
2 Bellagio Las Vegas **D4**
3 Caesars Palace **D3**
4 The Cosmopolitan of Las Vegas......................... **D4**
5 Mandalay Bay Resort & Casino, Las Vegas.......................... **D8**
6 MGM Grand Las Vegas........... **E6**
7 New York-New York Las Vegas Resort & Casino................... **D6**
8 The Venetian Las Vegas **E2**
9 Virgin Hotels Las Vegas........... **G5**
10 Wynn Las Vegas.................... **E1**

Strat Skypod

AMUSEMENT PARK/WATER PARK | FAMILY | High above the Strip at the tip of the Strat (now officially shortening its original name, the Stratosphere Tower, to its longtime nickname) are four major thrill rides that will scare the bejeezus out of you, especially if you have even the slightest fear of heights. Don't even think about heading up here if you have serious vertigo. People have been known to get sick just watching these rides. But if you are of the less adventurous sort, you can just visit the **Observation Decks** on Levels 108 and 109.

The **Big Shot** starts from the 112th floor, shooting four riders 160 feet up into the air at 45 mph and climaxing at more than 1,000 feet above the Strip with very little warning (it may be better that way). The whole thing is over in less than a minute, but your knees will wobble for the rest of the day.

The **X Scream** tips passengers 27 feet over the edge of the tower like a giant seesaw again and again. From the very front, you get an unobstructed view of the Strip, straight down.

Insanity hangs you out 64 feet from the edge of the tower; then it spins you faster and faster, so you're lifted to a 70-degree angle by a centrifugal force that's the equivalent of 3 G-forces.

The newest ride, **SkyJump Las Vegas,** is a controlled free fall that sends you careening off the side of the 108th floor.

Sharing the space is the Top of the World restaurant and 107 Skylounge. ✉ *The Strat, 2000 Las Vegas Blvd. S, North Strip* ☎ *702/380–7777* 🌐 *www.stratospherehotel.com* 🎟 *Skypod admission only from $25; Skypod and ride packages from $34 (for a single thrill ride); Skyjump from $130.*

"Welcome to Fabulous Las Vegas" Sign

HISTORIC SITE | This neon-and-incandescent sign, in a median of Las Vegas Boulevard south of Mandalay Bay, is one of Sin City's most enduring icons. The landmark dates back to 1959, and was approved for listing on the National Register of Historic Places in 2009. Young Electric Sign Company leases the sign to Clark County but the design itself was never copyrighted, and currently exists in the public domain. (This, of course, explains why you see so many likenesses all over town.) The parking lot in the median just south of the sign was expanded in 2015. If you prefer to go on foot, expect a 10-minute walk from Mandalay Bay. ✉ *5100 Las Vegas Blvd. S, South Strip* 🎟 *Free.*

Restaurants

Aureole Las Vegas

$$$$ | AMERICAN | Celebrity-chef Charlie Palmer re-created his famed New York restaurant for Mandalay Bay. It was extensively renovated in late 2016 but retains designer Adam Tihany's four-story wine tower, which holds more than 60,000 bottles that are reached by "flying wine angels," who are hoisted up and down via a system of electronically activated pulleys. **Known for:** Charlie Palmer's innovative cuisine; wine tower with "angels" on cables; windows that look out on picturesque fountain. 💲 *Average main: $50* ✉ *Mandalay Bay Resort & Casino, 3950 Las Vegas Blvd. S, South Strip* ☎ *702/632–7401* 🌐 *www.charliepalmer.com/location/aureole-las-vegas/* 🕓 *Closed Sun. No lunch.*

Bazaar Meat by José Andrés

$$$$ | ECLECTIC | This restaurant, the crown jewel of the Sahara Las Vegas, is decorated in a subtle jungle motif and is clearly all about meat. Choose from the steaks sold by the pound to suckling pig (by the quarter or whole, which you'll have to order ahead), and every other type you can imagine. **Known for:** meat in every form possible; whole suckling pig; jungle-theme atmosphere. *$ Average main: $70 ✉ Sahara Las Vegas, 2535 Las Vegas Blvd. S, North Strip ☎ 702/761–7610 🌐 www.thebazaar.com ⏲ No lunch. Closed Mon.–Wed.*

Costa di Mare

$$$$ | **MEDITERRANEAN** | Longtime Wynn chef Mark LoRusso was given a new showcase in this Mediterranean seafood spot in the space formerly occupied by Bartolotta Ristorante di Mare. Costa continues the tradition of freshly flown-in Mediterranean fish sold by the ounce, plus dishes such as cuttlefish, shrimp, and lobster with cuttlefish-ink pasta, and several raw-fish appetizers. **Known for:** fish flown in daily from Mediterranean; many choices sold by the gram; private cabanas overlooking lagoon. *$ Average main: $60 ✉ The Wynn, 3131 Las Vegas Blvd. S, North Strip ☎ 702/770–3305 🌐 www.wynnlasvegas.com ⏲ No lunch. Closed Sun.–Wed.*

Emeril's New Orleans Fish House

$$$$ | **SOUTHERN** | Chef Emeril Lagasse's first restaurant in Las Vegas dates back to the opening of the MGM Grand, but it's still a popular choice and has been periodically updated. The menu still puts the spotlight on the chef's Creole-inspired cuisine, such as barbecued shrimp, Louisiana-style jambalaya, and oysters on the half shell with watermelon mignonette. **Known for:** Creole and Cajun specialties; lively, family-friendly atmosphere; killer banana cream pie. *$ Average main: $40 ✉ MGM Grand Hotel & Casino, 3799 Las Vegas Blvd. S, South Strip ☎ 702/891–7374 🌐 emerilsrestaurants.com/emerils-new-orleans-fish-house/ ⏲ No lunch.*

Giada

$$$$ | **ITALIAN** | The first restaurant from TV personality and classically trained chef Giada de Laurentiis sits on a prime piece of real estate at the intersection of the Strip and Flamingo Road. The wide expanse of floor-to-ceiling windows provide commanding views, and the food's pretty impressive, too. **Known for:** Giada's first restaurant; expansive view of Strip; huge dessert cart. *$ Average main: $50 ✉ The Cromwell, 3595 Las Vegas Blvd. S, Center Strip ☎ 855/442–3271 🌐 www.caesars.com/cromwell.*

Gordon Ramsay Hell's Kitchen

$$$$ | **BRITISH** | Gordon Ramsay's fifth Las Vegas restaurant is a reflection of his popular Fox TV show, right down to the red and blue teams in the kitchen and TV monitors dotted around. The sprawling restaurant is a lively, noisy place where fire is a frequent motif. **Known for:** beef Wellington; lively, fiery atmosphere that evokes Ramsay himself; innovative bar menu. *$ Average main: $70 ✉ Caesars Palace, 3570 Las Vegas Blvd. S, Center Strip ☎ 702/731–7373 🌐 www.caesars.com.*

★ **Lotus of Siam**

$$$$ | **THAI** | This simple Thai restaurant has attained near-fanatical cult status, leaving some to wonder what all the fuss is about. It's simply that everything is so very good. **Known for:** spicy Issan Thai cuisine; garlic prawns; cult following. *$ Average main: $33 ✉ 953 E. Sahara Ave., Suite A5, East Side ☎ 702/735–3033 phone for both locations 🌐 lotusofsiamlv.com ⏲ No lunch at Flamingo location.*

Momofuku Las Vegas

$$$$ | **ASIAN FUSION** | David Chang's budding New York–based restaurant empire went way west for the first time with this spot at The Cosmopolitan, which offers a mix of Momofuku favorites and only-in-Vegas choices. You can also set up fried chicken and caviar for parties of four to six; other group options are salt-and-pepper lobster and shrimp, or five-spice roasted chicken for three or four. **Known for:** classics honed at New York original; some only-in-Vegas choices; fried chicken and caviar for large parties. *$ Average main: $50 ✉ Cosmopolitan of Las Vegas, 3708 Las Vegas Blvd. S, Center Strip ☎ 877/893–2001 🌐 www.cosmopolitanlasvegas.com.*

★ Mott 32

$$$$ | **CHINESE** | Hong Kong street food comes to life at this lively and architecturally stunning restaurant inside the Palazzo Tower at The Venetian Resort Las Vegas. The eatery, which opened in December 2018, is the first U.S. outpost of a Hong Kong restaurant by the same name. **Known for:** smoked Peking duck; excellent dim sum; lobster ma po tofu. *Average main: $55 The Venetian Las Vegas, 3325 Las Vegas Blvd. S, North Strip 702/607–3232 www.mott32.com/lasvegas No lunch.*

Nobu Restaurant Las Vegas

$$$$ | **SUSHI** | Celebrity chef Nobu Matsuhisa established a foothold in the Vegas market with a namesake restaurant at the Hard Rock Hotel, but later added this modern location at the base of his hotel tower at Caesars Palace. The result: one of the hottest tables in town. **Known for:** Nobu classics like black cod miso; extensive sushi and sashimi list; imported Japanese Wagyu. *Average main: $45 Nobu Hotel Caesars Palace, 3570 Las Vegas Blvd. S, Center Strip 702/785–6628 www.nobuhotels.com No lunch.*

★ NoMad Las Vegas

$$$$ | **ECLECTIC** | Grandiose, spectacular, and heart-stopping are three words to describe the restaurant at NoMad Las Vegas. The restaurant has 40-foot ceilings and is ringed with shelves of real books—a backdrop that creates an intimate and sophisticated vibe. **Known for:** breathtaking atmosphere; delicious communal dishes; jazz brunch in the bar on weekends. *Average main: $43 Park MGM, 3772 Las Vegas Blvd. S, South Strip 702/730–6785 www.thenomadhotel.com/las-vegas.*

★ Picasso

$$$$ | **EUROPEAN** | Adorned with some original works by Picasso, this restaurant raised the city's dining scene a notch when it opened in Bellagio in 1998. Although some say Executive Chef Julian Serrano doesn't change his menu often enough, the artful, innovative cuisine—based on French classics with strong Spanish influences—is consistently outstanding. **Known for:** artworks by the master; Julian Serrano's award-winning food; overlooking Lake Bellagio. *Average main: $135 Bellagio Las Vegas, 3600 Las Vegas Blvd. S, Center Strip 702/693–8865 www.bellagio.com/restaurants No lunch. Closed Mon.–Thurs.*

Hotels

★ ARIA Resort & Casino

$$$$ | **RESORT** | Unlike most casino hotels, ARIA has an abundance of light, even in standard guest rooms, and their modern style makes this one of the Strip's most contemporary-feeling options. **Pros:** high-tech rooms; natural light; excellent restaurants. **Cons:** shower setup soaks the tub; long walk to Strip; end rooms are a very long walk to the single elevator bank. *Rooms from: $540 3730 Las Vegas Blvd. S, Center Strip 702/590–7111, 866/359–7757, 877/580–2742 SkySuites www.aria.com 4004 rooms No meals.*

★ Bellagio Las Vegas

$$$$ | **RESORT** | The Grand Dame of Strip resorts is still as exquisite as ever, with snazzy rooms full of Italian marble and luxurious fabrics. **Pros:** centrally located; posh suites; classy amenities. **Cons:** pricey; can be difficult to grab a quick bite because of crowds; a very long walk out to the Strip. *Rooms from: $699 3600 Las Vegas Blvd. S, Center Strip 702/693–7111, 888/987–6667 www.bellagio.com 3933 rooms No meals.*

Caesars Palace

$$$$ | **RESORT** | Caesars was one of the first properties in town to create rooms so lavish that guests might actually want to spend time in them, and all come standard with marble bathrooms and sumptuous beds. **Pros:** Arctic ice rooms at Qua; Garden of the Gods pool

oasis; storied property. **Cons:** floorplan is difficult to navigate; small casino; limited on-site parking. *Rooms from: $530 3570 Las Vegas Blvd. S, Center Strip 702/731–7110, 866/227–5938 www.caesars.com-caesarspalace 3992 rooms No meals.*

The Cosmopolitan of Las Vegas

$$$$ | RESORT | Balconies make The Cosmopolitan's rooms stand apart: the vast majority have balconies or terraces, the only ones on the Strip. **Pros:** terraces; in-room technology; Yoo-hoo in minibar. **Cons:** kitchenettes seem random; walls paper-thin; queues for Marquee can get annoying. *Rooms from: $540 3708 Las Vegas Blvd. S, Center Strip 702/698–7000 www.cosmopolitanlasvegas.com 2995 rooms No meals.*

★ **Mandalay Bay Resort & Casino, Las Vegas**

$$$ | RESORT | FAMILY | Mandalay Bay remains as swanky as ever, decked out like a South Seas beach resort, complete with cavernous rooms and one of the best pool areas on the Strip. **Pros:** large rooms; ample options for everything; the beach. **Cons:** concerts can be loud; so large it's easy to get lost; nothing comes cheap here, including the resort fee. *Rooms from: $239 3950 Las Vegas Blvd. S, South Strip 702/632–7777, 877/632–7800 www.mandalaybay.com 3209 rooms No meals.*

MGM Grand Las Vegas

$$$ | RESORT | The MGM Grand is one of the largest hotels in the world, with five 30-story towers with rooms in nine different categories. **Pros:** something for everyone; StayWell rooms; fantastic restaurants. **Cons:** easy to get lost; schlep to parking lot; check-in can have very long lines. *Rooms from: $239 3799 Las Vegas Blvd. S, South Strip 702/891–1111, 877/880–0880 www.mgmgrand.com 5044 rooms No meals.*

New York–New York Las Vegas Resort & Casino

$$ | RESORT | The mini-Manhattan skyline is one of our favorite parts of the Strip—there are third-size to half-size re-creations of the Empire State Building, the Statue of Liberty, and the Chrysler Building, as well as the New York Public Library, Grand Central Terminal, and the Brooklyn Bridge. **Pros:** authentic New York experience; art deco lobby; casino floor center bar. **Cons:** layout is somewhat confusing; cramped sports book; mediocre pool. *Rooms from: $179 3790 Las Vegas Blvd. S, South Strip 702/740–6969, 800/689–1797 www.newyorknewyork.com 2024 rooms No meals.*

★ **The Venetian Las Vegas**

$$ | RESORT | It's no secret that this theme hotel re-creates Italy's most romantic city with meticulous reproductions of Venetian landmarks, and the large suites aren't too shabby, either. **Pros:** excellent re-creations of Italian sights; modern amenities; tremendous rooms. **Cons:** sometimes difficult to navigate to rooms; poker room action can be aggressive. *Rooms from: $190 3355 Las Vegas Blvd. S, North Strip 702/414–1000, 866/659–9643 www.venetian.com 4028 suites No meals.*

Virgin Hotels Las Vegas

$$ | RESORT | "Virgin" may be a curious name for Las Vegas, but Sir Richard Branson's brand hopes to sell a completely made-over version of the original Hard Rock Hotel—replacing the guitars and rock memorabilia with a tranquil yet sophisticated desert vibe. **Pros:** tranquil resort atmosphere; great, if pricey, restaurants; no "resort" fee or parking charges for self-parking (yes, that's correct...zero). **Cons:** not directly on the Strip, and the hotel no longer has a Strip shuttle; hotel guests must be 21 (no under-agers allowed, even with their parents); early reopening inconclusive on whether it becomes a convention hotel or if "the party" returns. $ *Rooms from: $200* ✉ *4455 Paradise Rd., Paradise Road* ☎ *702/693–5000, 800/693–7625* 🌐 *www.virginhotelslv.com* 🛏 *1500 rooms* 🍽 *No meals.*

★ Wynn Las Vegas

$$$$ | RESORT | Decked out with replicas of former chairman Steve Wynn's acclaimed art collection, the princely rooms here, averaging a whopping 650 square feet, offer spectacular views through wall-to-wall, floor-to-ceiling windows. **Pros:** opulence throughout casino and hotel; access to gorgeous pool; top-notch restaurant collection. **Cons:** cramped casino walkways; slow elevators; artificial lawns. $ *Rooms from: $842* ✉ *3131 Las Vegas Blvd. S, North Strip* ☎ *702/770–7000* 🌐 *www.wynnlasvegas.com* 🛏 *2716 rooms* 🍽 *No meals.*

Nightlife

BARS AND LOUNGES

★ The Chandelier

BARS/PUBS | True to its name, this swanky lounge sits in a chandelier with 2 million crystal beads, making it the largest chandelier in town (and, perhaps, the world). The bar is separated into three separate levels, and each has a different theme. The ground floor—dubbed "Bottom of The Chandelier," for those of you scoring at home—is dedicated to intricate specialty drinks, the kinds of cocktails you'll find only here. The second floor (non-smoking!) pays homage to molecular gastronomy in cocktail form; spiked sorbets and dehydrated fruits are common in drinks here. Finally, at the top of The Chandelier, everything's coming up floral, with rose and lavender syrups and violet sugar. If you're particularly adventuresome (and you can get a seat on the first floor), try the off-menu Verbena cocktail with a "Szechuan button." This desiccated flower from Africa numbs your mouth to make flavors more potent; it also prompts you to down your cocktail in mere seconds. All three levels offer excellent people-watching opportunities. Open 24/7. ✉ *The Cosmopolitan of Las Vegas, 3708 Las Vegas Blvd. S, South Strip* ☎ *702/698–7000* 🌐 *www.cosmopolitanlasvegas.com/lounges-bars/the-chandelier.*

Mayfair Supper Club

PIANO BARS/LOUNGES | Whatever the name—and past incarnations include Hyde and Fontana Bar—this posh ultralounge is prime real estate inside the Bellagio, famous for its front-and-center view overlooking the Bellagio fountains. As the new name suggests, the latest incarnation hearkens back to an earlier era, with dinner and live entertainment offered in the same room that drips with the chic atmosphere of a black-and-white movie from the 1930s. ✉ *Bellagio, 3600 Las Vegas Blvd. S, Center Strip* ☎ *702/693–8700* 🌐 *www.bellagio.com.*

Skybar

PIANO BARS/LOUNGES | Few views of the Strip are as breathtaking as the one you'll get from this uber-chic lounge on the 23rd floor of the Waldorf Astoria in CityCenter. The room is wrapped with floor-to-ceiling windows, meaning just about every one of the plush banquettes is a winning seat. Mixologists have concocted cocktails themed to southern Nevada ("The Paiute," "The Meadows"), and it's easy to pay a dollar for every floor of that view in a single cocktail. There's also a small menu of bite-size appetizers and "luxurious experiences" that include vodka and caviar pairings. Business-casual dress is recommended. ✉ *Waldorf Astoria, 3452 Las Vegas Blvd. S, Center Strip* ☎ *702/590–8888* 🌐 *www.waldorfastorialasvegas.com.*

107 SkyLounge

PIANO BARS/LOUNGES | The Strat might be downscale compared with other Vegas hotels, but there ain't nothing "down" about the high-in-the-sky experience to be had here. From this sleek, attractive room, the view of Sin City is truly amazing (if slightly remote). For an even bigger thrill, head upstairs and outside (to level 108, of course). ✉ *The Strat, 2000 Las Vegas Blvd. S, North Strip* ☎ *702/380–7777* 🌐 *www.thestrat.com.*

Skyfall Lounge

PIANO BARS/LOUNGES | Head up to the 64th floor of the Delano for the 180-degree views of the city inside Skyfall Lounge. Everything up here is higher, including the prices for craft cocktails. Around sunset the crowds can become unbearable but later in the evening, when live DJs play tunes, the vibe is chill. Be sure to step into the bathrooms for a different view of the city while you relieve yourself. ✉ *Delano Las Vegas, 3940 Las Vegas Blvd. S, South Strip* ☎ *877/632–5400* 🌐 *www.delanolasvegas.com/en/nightlife/skyfall-lounge.html.*

DANCE CLUBS AND NIGHTCLUBS

Drai's

DANCE CLUBS | Victor Drai wants your business day and night, and he nabs it with his multiuse space 11 stories up at The Cromwell. Drai's boasts a rooftop day- and nightclub with pools and cabanas for basking in the sun or dancing to the beats under the moon. It's huge, too, clocking in at 65,000 square feet with a monster-size 7,000-square-foot LED screen and every imaginable seating option. Go ultraswanky at one of 150 VIP tables. ✉ *The Cromwell, 3595 Las Vegas Blvd. S, Center Strip* ☎ *702/777–3800* 🌐 *draislv.com.*

Marquee

DANCE CLUBS | This cavernous joint boasts three different rooms spread across two levels, as well as 50-foot ceilings. In the main area, stadium-style seating surrounds the dance floor, and four-story LED screens and projection walls display light and image shows customized for every performer. For a more intimate experience, check out the Boom Box, a smaller room (usually featuring something other than house music) with windows overlooking the Strip. On the top level, the Library provides a respite from the thumping downstairs with dark wood, books (actual books!), and billiard tables. In spring and summer, the hot spot opens Marquee Dayclub, which features two pools, several bars, a gaming area, and DJs all day long. A dome even permits the pool party to rage on in colder months. ✉ *The Cosmopolitan of Las Vegas, 3708 Las Vegas Blvd. S, Center Strip* ☎ *702/333–9000* 🌐 *marqueelasvegas.com.*

★ XS

DANCE CLUBS | This club backs up onto a pool that converts into one of the most spacious open-air dance floors in town. The Wynn's signature attention to detail shines through with touches such as a chandelier that doubles as a psychedelic disco ball, light fixtures that turn into stripper poles, and walls imprinted with golden body casts (the waitresses modeled for them). At the pool are cabanas, another bar, and outdoor gaming, where the sexiest croupiers in town ply their trade. *Excess* is a pretty good word for all of this. ✉ *Encore, 3121 Las Vegas Blvd. S, North Strip* ☎ *702/770–7300* 🌐 *www.xslasvegas.com.*

Performing Arts

PRODUCTION SHOWS

Absinthe

THEATER | Sometimes it's not the elements but how they are combined. *Absinthe* became one of the most popular shows on the Strip by turning Cirque du Soleil's opulent, dreamlike aesthetic on its head. A downscale, shabby-chic vibe unifies circus acrobatics, raunchy comedy, and saucy burlesque numbers inside a cozy tent in front of Caesars Palace. (At least it's a tentlike structure; once it was decided the show would stick around, fire inspectors insisted on a sturdy, semipermanent pavilion.) The audience surrounds the performances on a small, 9-foot stage. The festive, low-tech atmosphere is furthered along by the host, a shifty insult comic known as the Gazillionaire. This is cheap raunch for a discerning audience. And, like Penn & Teller's show, it's a winking salute to the show-business tradition itself. ✉ *Caesars Palace, 3570 Las Vegas Blvd. S, Center Strip* ☎ *702/534–3419* 🌐 *www.absinthevegas.com* 🎫 *From $99* ☞ *Plays nightly.*

★ Blue Man Group

THEATER | FAMILY | The three bald, blue, and silent characters in utilitarian uniforms have become part of the Las Vegas landscape. The satire of technology and information-overload merges with classic physical comedy and the Blue Man's unique brand of interstellar rock and roll. The group's latest home, a cozy theater at Luxor, brings the Blue dudes closer to their off-Broadway origins: paint splattering, mouth-catching marshmallows, and rollicking percussion jam sessions on PVC pipe contraptions. ✉ *Luxor, 3900 Las Vegas Blvd. S, South Strip* ☎ *702/262–4400, 855/788–6755* 🌐 *www.blueman.com* 🎫 *From $61* ☞ *Usually plays nightly.*

★ KÀ

THEATER | FAMILY | *KÀ*, Cirque du Soleil's biggest Las Vegas production, opened in 2006 and still stands as an amazing monument to the sky's-the-limit mentality that fueled Vegas in the go-go 2000s. The $165-million opus frees the stage itself from gravity, replacing a fixed stage with an 80,000-pound deck, maneuvered by a giant gantry arm into a near-vertical position for the climactic battle. Giant puppets also factor into the bold interpretation of live martial-arts period fantasies like *Crouching Tiger, Hidden Dragon* in the adventures of two separated twins. Though no other Cirque in Las Vegas rivals it for sheer spectacle, those not sitting close enough to see faces can be confused by the story, which is told without dialogue. ✉ *MGM Grand Hotel & Casino, 3805 Las Vegas Blvd. S, South Strip* ☎ *855/788–6755* 🌐 *cirquedusoleil.com/ka* 🎫 *From $75* ☞ *Dark Thurs. and Fri.*

★ LOVE

THEATER | Meet the Beatles again—well, sort of—in a certified home run for Cirque du Soleil. Before he died, George Harrison persuaded the surviving Beatles (and Yoko Ono) to license the group's music to Cirque. The remixed music by the late Beatles producer George Martin and his son Giles is revelatory on 7,000 speakers, often like hearing the songs for the first time. In the summer of 2016, Cirque tweaked the show for its 10th anniversary, dialing down the elegiac version of postwar Liverpool, and punching up the dance elements to emphasize the youth culture of Beatlemania. Cirque also added literal depictions of the Fab Four in videos and projection mapping. It's still a great marriage of sensibilities that explodes with joy. ✉ *Mirage Las Vegas, 3400 Las Vegas Blvd. S, Center Strip* ☎ *702/792–7777, 855/788–6755* 🌐 *www.cirquedusoleil.com* 🎫 *From $87* ☞ *Dark Sun. and Mon.*

★ O

THEATER | FAMILY | More than $70 million was spent on Cirque du Soleil's theater at Bellagio back in 1998, and its liquid stage is the centerpiece of a one-of-a-kind show. It was money well spent: *O* remains one of the best-attended shows on the Strip. The title is taken from the French word for water (*eau*), and water is everywhere—1.5 million gallons of it, 12 million pounds of it, contained by a "stage" that, thanks to hydraulic lifts, can change shape and turn into dry land in no time. The intense and nonstop action by the show's acrobats, aerial gymnasts, trapeze artists, synchronized swimmers, divers, and contortionists make for a stylish spectacle that manages to fashion dreamlike imagery from its acrobatics, with a vague theme about the wellspring of theater and imagination. ✉ *Bellagio Las Vegas, 3600 Las Vegas Blvd. S, Center Strip* ☎ *702/693–8866, 855/788–6755* 🌐 *www.cirquedusoleil.com* 🎫 *From $107* ☞ *Dark Mon. and Tues.*

MAJOR HEADLINERS

David Copperfield

THEATER | FAMILY | The master magician has made Las Vegas a part of his career since the 1980s and now roosts at the MGM Grand for more than 40 weeks per year. At this point, Copperfield is sort of the Rolling Stones of magic; you sense his authority and submit to it from the minute the show opens, and trust him to wow you with illusions such as a recent one involving a T. rex, which take years to perfect. He varies the pace with illusions that can be touching or funny, but most of all they still genuinely fool you. ✉ *MGM Grand Hotel & Casino, 3799 Las Vegas Blvd. S, South Strip* ☎ *800/745–3000, 702/740–7711* 🌐 *www.davidcopperfield.com* 🎫 *From $71* ☞ *Select dates almost year-round.*

★ **Penn & Teller**

THEATER | Eccentric comic magicians Penn & Teller are more popular now than when they settled into the Rio in 2002. Ventures such as their durable TV magic contest *Fool Us* expanded the duo into mainstream culture beyond the Strip. Now they turn up almost everywhere it seems. Back in Las Vegas, their off-kilter humor now seems less jarring as they age gracefully at the Rio. Their magic in a gorgeous 1,500-seat theater is topical and genuinely baffling, pushing the form into new creative directions. And their comedy is satiric, provocative, and thoughtful. The duo used some of their pandemic shutdown time to develop new material for the Rio. ✉ *The Rio, 3700 W. Flamingo Rd., West Side* ☎ *702/777–2782, 855/234–7469* 🌐 *www.pennandteller.com* 🎫 *From $82* ☞ *Dark Thurs. and Fri.*

Shopping

MALLS AND SHOPPING CENTERS

★ **The Forum Shops at Caesars Palace**

SHOPPING CENTERS/MALLS | Amazing ambience, architecture, and design means visitors won't have to drop a single dime to enjoy touring this highly accessible mid-Strip mall. Leave the high heels at home to better roam three levels of restaurants and retail—some paths cobblestoned—that resemble an ancient Roman streetscape, with scattered statuary, immense columns and arches, two central piazzas with ornate fountains, and a cloud-filled ceiling-sky that changes from sunrise to sunset over the course of three hours (to subconsciously spur shoppers to step up their pace of acquisition, perhaps?). ■ **TIP→ The Mitsubishi-designed freestanding Spiral Escalator is a must-ride for the view.**

Of course, shopaholics will rejoice at the selection of designer shops and traditional standbys, from high-end heavy hitters such as Elie Tahari, Brooks Brothers, Gucci, Fendi, Michael Kors, Christian Louboutin, Jimmy Choo, Salvatore Ferragamo, Louis Vuitton, and Balenciaga, to more casual labels like Abercrombie & Fitch, Nike, Guess, and Gap/Gap Kids. Armani fans will find an Exchange for menswear, along with John Varvatos, Hugo Boss, and Canali. Gaze at stunning jewelry, watches, and crystal works at Baccarat, Cartier, Hearts on Fire, Tourneau, Tiffany & Co., Pandora, and David Yurman. Apple offers a whole host of electronics. Cosmetics queens will keep themselves busy at Chanel Beauty, Dior Beauty, and Lush. And don't miss the flagship Victoria's Secret for lingerie and swimwear, or Agent Provocateur and La Perla, for that matter.

When all this walking/shopping brings on the inevitable hunger, head to the renovated The Palm or Carmine's Italian. The Cheesecake Factory is popular, as are Sushi Roku, and Joe's Seafood, Steak & Stone Crab. ✉ *Caesars Palace, 3500 Las Vegas Blvd. S, Center Strip* ☎ *702/893–4800* 🌐 *www.simon.com.*

★ **Fashion Show**

SHOPPING CENTERS/MALLS | The frontage of this fashion-devoted mall is dominated by The Cloud—a giant, oblong disc that looms high above the entrance. Ads and footage of the mall's own fashion events are continuously projected across the expanse of this ovoid screen. Inside, the mall is sleek, spacious, and airy—a nice change from some of the claustrophobic casino malls. The mall delivers on its name: fashion shows are staged in the Great Hall on an 80-foot-long catwalk that rises from the floor (on select weekends, every hour from noon to 5). Although you can find many of the same stores in the casino malls, there's a smattering of different fare, such as Drybar, which specializes in blowouts, and Lolli & Pops, "purveyors of sweetness." Neiman Marcus, Saks Fifth Avenue, Nordstrom, and Dillard's serve as the mall's anchors. Along with an airy food court, dependable chains including Benihana and California Pizza Kitchen offer sit-down dining. ✉ *3200 Las Vegas Blvd. S, North Strip* ☎ *702/784–7000* 🌐 *fslv.com* ☞ *Free valet and self-parking.*

★ Grand Canal Shoppes

SHOPPING CENTERS/MALLS | This is one of the most unforgettable shopping experiences on the Strip. Duck into shops like Field of Dreams, Sephora, or Peter Lik's rustic gallery of fine-art photography. Amble under blue-sky ceilings alongside the Grand Canal. All roads, balustraded bridges, and waterways lead to St. Mark's Square, an enormous open space filled with Italian opera singers and costumed performers. Watch for the living statues, who will intrigue and amuse. If you need to take a load off, hail a gondola.

Closer to The Palazzo, find powerhouse names such as Michael Kors and Tory Burch. Shoe lovers will swoon over the Jimmy Choo boutique. ✉ *The Venetian, 3377 Las Vegas Blvd. S, North Strip* ☎ *702/414–4525* 🌐 *www.grandcanalshoppes.com.*

Downtown

There was a time not so many years ago when Downtown Las Vegas was filled with little more than tired casinos and hotels. Well, that's just not the case any longer. With neon lights—actually, make that a quarter-mile canopy of with 12.5 million synchronized LED modules—single-deck blackjack, legitimately cool bars, and a host of new attractions that spotlight yesteryear (not to mention an influx of new businesses), old Vegas is alive and well Downtown.

This neighborhood revolves around Fremont Street, a covered pedestrian walkway through the heart of the Downtown gambling district. Originally, this attraction was nothing more than a place to stroll; today, however, the canopy sparkles with millions of lights, and outfitters have set up everything from ziplines to band shells on street level down beneath. Use Fremont Street to access resorts such as Circa, the new centerpiece hotel and casino, the Golden Nugget, Four Queens, and the Plaza Hotel and Casino. Just be prepared for sensory overload.

Sights

Downtown Container Park

STORE/MALL | **FAMILY** | It turns out shipping containers—the same kinds you see on cargo ships and tractor trailers—can be pretty versatile. At this open-air mall, for instance, on the outskirts of the Fremont East neighborhood, the structures have been repurposed into food stalls, boutiques (38 of them), offices, and even a three-story "tree house" complete with grown-up-friendly slides. The place also has an amphitheater stage fronted by real grass. Although the tree house is fun (especially with young kids), the highlight of the attraction is the large, fire-spewing praying mantis, which was originally constructed for use at the Burning Man

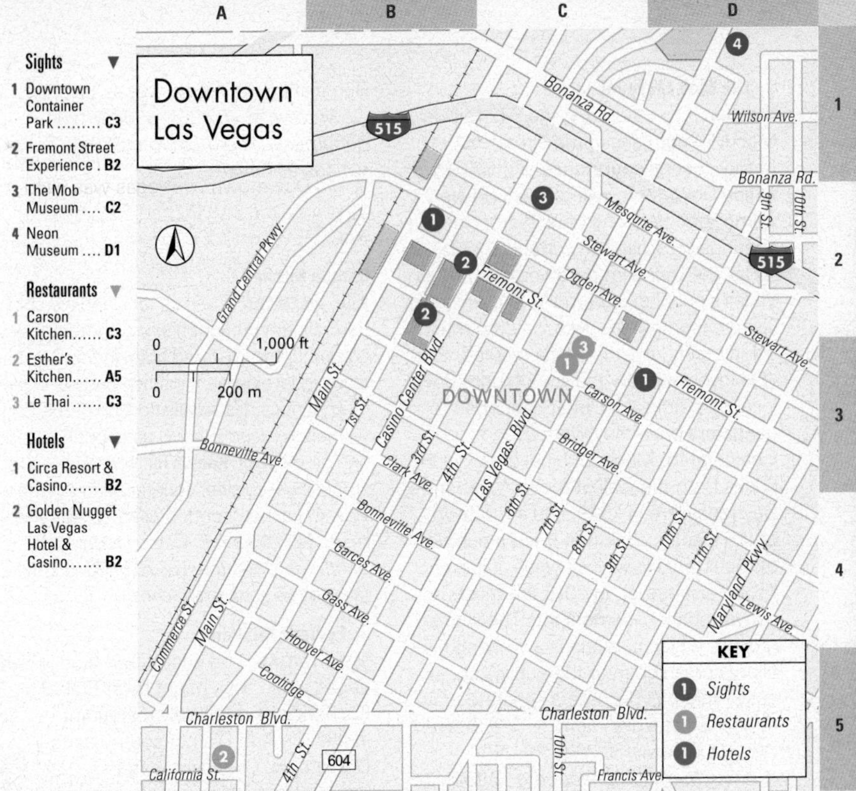

festival in northern Nevada. ✉ *707 E. Fremont St., Downtown* ☎ *702/359–9982* 🌐 *www.downtowncontainerpark.com.*

Fremont Street Experience

PEDESTRIAN MALL | The Experience was originally the name for the 1,450-foot arched canopy that was built 90 feet above "Glitter Gulch," downtown's main drag, to revive its sadly fading epicenter. The plan worked, slowly but spectacularly—now the whole street is an "experience." The Viva Vision synchronized light shows, which run the length of the canopy, got a $32-million makeover in 2019 and now sparkles with LED lights (officially touted as "16.4 million brilliant pixels") to create displays that are seven times brighter and four times sharper than previous versions. The brief shows are themed, such as the salutes to homegrown rockers The Killers, or Las Vegas–based music producer Steve Aoki. They play five to seven times a night, depending on the time of year, and the six-minute presentations change regularly. The upgrades to the overhead show were necessary to keep up with the carnival atmosphere on the street. Costumed characters and street performers vie for attention with the bands playing on two stages, and outdoor bars now line the fronts of the historic casinos, the bartops doubling as stages for dancing showgirls. Thrill-seekers can ride one of two zip lines ($) beneath the length of the canopy; the zips emerge from the face of the world's largest slot machine, appropriately dubbed Slotzilla. ✉ *Fremont St. from Main St. to 4th St., Downtown* 🌐 *www.vegasexperience.com* 🎫 *Free.*

★ **The Mob Museum**

MUSEUM | It's fitting that the $42-million Mob Museum sits in the circa-1933 former federal courthouse and U.S. Post Office Downtown where the Kefauver Committee held one of its historic hearings on organized crime in 1950. Today the museum pays homage to Las Vegas's criminal underbelly, explaining to visitors (sometimes with way too much exhibit text) how the Mafia worked, who was involved, how the law brought down local mobsters, and what happened to gangsters once they were caught and incarcerated. Museum highlights include bricks from the wall of the St. Valentine's Day Massacre in 1929, and a mock-up of the electric chair that killed a number of mobsters (as well as spies Julius and Ethel Rosenberg). In 2018 the museum converted its basement into The Underground, which comprises a working distillery and an open-to-the-public "speakeasy" that has become a separate draw for locals in its own right. ✉ *300 Stewart Ave., Downtown* ☎ *702/229–2734* 🌐 *www.themobmuseum.org* 🎟 *$30.*

★ **Neon Museum**

MUSEUM | **FAMILY** | Consider this Downtown museum the afterlife for old neon signs. The facility, which displays more than 150 signs that date back to the 1930s, opened to the public in 2012. The old La Concha motel's iconic lobby was renovated and now serves as the museum's entry point. The sign collection includes the original signs from the Stardust, the Horseshoe, and other properties. To get up close, visitors must take an educational and informative one-hour guided tour. Daytime tours, especially in summer, can be scorching. For an alternative, try one of the nighttime tours, where you can see four of the signs illuminated the way they were intended to be. In 2018 the museum added "Brilliant," a separate experience in the North Gallery where a laser-light show set to music appears to reanimate some of the signs. The result is, well, illuminating. ✉ *770 Las Vegas Blvd. N, Downtown* ☎ *702/387–6366* 🌐 *www.neonmuseum.org* 🎟 *From $20* ☞ *Reservations essential.*

Restaurants

Carson Kitchen

$$$ | **AMERICAN** | The late rock-and-roll chef Kerry Simon brought his fun, contemporary cuisine to this restored hotel in the Downtown redevelopment district, and his legacy continues. It's small and kind of rustic, with an airy (and kitschy) patio out back and one on the roof. **Known for:** seasonal—and surprising—cuisine; counter seating with a view of kitchen; rooftop patio. [$] *Average main: $25* ✉ *John E. Carson Bldg., 124 S. 6th St., Downtown* ☎ *702/473–9523* 🌐 *www.carsonkitchen.com.*

★ **Esther's Kitchen**

$$$$ | **ITALIAN** | The best Italian food in Las Vegas these days might be at Esther's Kitchen, a hip and lively restaurant in the 18b Arts District southwest of Downtown. Chef James Trees, a Las Vegas native, churns out homemade pastas such as rigatoni carbonara with guanciale, tagliatelle with braised duck, and black fettucine with lobster. **Known for:** homemade pasta; creative cocktails; long wait times for those without reservations. [$] *Average main: $50* ✉ *1130 S. Casino Center Blvd., Downtown* ☎ *702/570–7864* 🌐 *www.esthersIv.com.*

★ **Le Thai**

$$ | **THAI** | **FAMILY** | Noodles are the house specialty at this intimate restaurant in the Fremont East district of Downtown. Although most of the dishes are Thai (try the Awesome Noodles; the name isn't hyperbole), others lean more toward Chinese and Japanese influences. **Known for:** tiny spot with expansive patio; some other Asian influences; Awesome Noodles really are. [$] *Average main: $15* ✉ *523 Fremont St. E, Downtown* ☎ *702/778–0888* 🌐 *www.lethaivegas.com* ⏲ *Closed Tues. No lunch Sun.*

Hotels

Circa Resort & Casino

$$$ | HOTEL | You can debate the aesthetics of a 35-story tower dwarfing all of its Fremont Street neighbors, but you can't argue the statement it makes: Circa, the first ground-up construction on Fremont Street since 1980, is not only the new king of Glitter Gulch, but a formidable competitor to the top Strip resorts as well. **Pros:** party atmosphere; old-Vegas feel with a personal touch; sense of newness combined with a sense of history. **Cons:** parking garage is across the street; everything is vertical, so lots of elevators; lots of togetherness thanks to a small footprint and its newness. *Rooms from: $200* *8 Fremont St., Downtown* *702/247–2258* *www.circalasvegas.com* *777 rooms* *No meals.*

Golden Nugget Las Vegas Hotel & Casino

$ | RESORT | The Golden Nugget has long reigned as Downtown's top property since the mid-1970s, evolving with the times but maintaining classic appeal. **Pros:** legendary Vegas property; one-of-a-kind pool; great poker room. **Cons:** small sports book; table games change frequently; too many room options. *Rooms from: $99* *129 E. Fremont St., Downtown* *702/385–7111, 844/468–4438* *www.goldennugget.com* *2345 rooms* *No meals.*

Nightlife

BARS AND LOUNGES

Commonwealth

BARS/PUBS | As urban renewal continues Downtown, the one-block stretch of Fremont east of Las Vegas Boulevard (dubbed Fremont East) remains the hottest of the hot spots, and Commonwealth arguably is the epicenter. Inside, wrought-iron railings, chandeliers, and a tin ceiling create a feeling of old-school opulence without being excessive. Drink options range from handcrafted cocktails to microbrews; there's also good live music in the evenings. The atmosphere changes as evenings progress, from quiet happy hours conducive to conversation to full-on dance craziness for a younger crowd. Venture upstairs to the rooftop bar, or try to secure an invite to the private Laundry Room speakeasy. It's closed on Monday and Tuesday. *525 Fremont St., Downtown* *702/445–6400* *www.commonwealthlv.com.*

The Suburbs

The explosive growth of Las Vegas began in the 1990s with two master-planned developments. To the west, Summerlin expanded the suburbs nearly to the entry of the once-isolated Red Rock Canyon. To the south, Green Valley kicked off the growth of the once-separate town of Henderson, which is now blended and connected to Las Vegas in a continuous sprawl. For visitors, the chief points of interest may be the "downtown"-style retail and dining developments adjacent to Red Rock Resort in Summerlin, which hosts a state-of the-art minor-league baseball stadium, and Green Valley Ranch in Henderson. If you are headed to Valley of Fire, Hoover Dam, or Lake Mead, you won't have to worry about restroom or food stops, even if the neighborhoods you pass by aren't so different from home.

Sights

★ Red Rock Canyon National Conservation Area

NATURE PRESERVE | FAMILY | Red sandstone cliffs and dramatic desert landscapes await day-trippers and outdoors enthusiasts at Red Rock Canyon National Conservation Area. Operated by the BLM, the 195,819-acre national conservation area features narrow canyons, fantastic rock formations, seasonal waterfalls, desert wildlife, and rock-art sites. The elevated Red Rock Overlook provides a fabulous view of the cream-and-red sandstone cliffs. For a closer look at

Sights ▼

1 Red Rock Canyon National Conservation Area **A3**

Restaurants ▼

1 Grape Street Cafe, Wine Bar, & Grill **B3**

2 Honey Salt **B2**

3 Raku **C3**

4 Todd's Unique Dining **D4**

Hotels ▼

1 Green Valley Ranch Resort, Spa & Casino....... **D4**

2 Red Rock Casino Resort & Spa........ **B2**

the stunning scenery, take the 13-mile, one-way scenic drive through the canyon, open from dawn to dusk. Other activities including hiking, mountain biking, rock climbing, canyoneering, picnicking, and wildlife-watching. A developed campground, 2 miles from the visitor center, has 66 campsites (including RV and group sites), pit toilets, and drinking water for visitors wanting to extend their stay. A modest visitor center, operated by the Red Rock Canyon Interpretive Association and open on weekdays, contains an informative history of the region, as well as a number of exhibits on local flora and fauna. ✉ *1000 Scenic Loop Dr., Summerlin South* ☎ *702/515–5350, 702/515–5367 programs and guided hikes* 🌐 *www.redrockcanyonlv.org* 🎫 *$15 per car, $10 per motorcycle, $5 per individual on bicycle or foot.*

Restaurants

Grape Street Cafe, Wine Bar & Grill

$$$ | **ITALIAN** | This smart neighborhood restaurant that relocated to the downtown Summerlin shopping district serves food intended to coordinate nicely with the restaurant's interesting, affordable, and plentiful (as in, nearly 30 selections by the glass) wine list and craft beer selection. The menu features salads, sandwiches, pizzas, pasta, and seafood, as well as traditional dishes such as short ribs and chicken Parmesan or marsala. **Known for:** varied menu; wines by the glass; romantic dining room. $ *Average main: $30* ✉ *2120 Festival Plaza Dr., #160, Summerlin South* ☎ *702/478–5030* 🌐 *www.grapestreetdowntownsummerlin.com.*

Honey Salt

$$$$ | **AMERICAN** | **FAMILY** | The brainchild of restaurateur Elizabeth Blau and chef Kim Canteenwalla, Honey Salt is, quite simply, a fun place to eat a meal. The atmosphere is convivial, dishes are designed for sharing, and a creative kids' menu encourages diners to bring the whole family. **Known for:** creative kids' menu; weekend brunch; open and festive decor. *Average main: $35 ✉ 1031 S. Rampart Blvd., Summerlin South ☎ 702/445–6100 🌐 www.honeysalt.com.*

★ Raku

$$ | **JAPANESE** | Seating is at a premium in this softly lighted strip-mall *robata*, a favorite of almost every chef in town. At 6 pm sharp every day but Sunday, doors open for small-plate offerings of creamy house-made tofu, fresh sashimi (no sushi), and savory grilled meats, fish, and veggies (cooked over charcoal imported from Japan) that reflect the culinary mastery of its Tokyo-born owner-chef. **Known for:** agedashi tofu, robata foods; daily specials; cozy atmosphere. *Average main: $20 ✉ 5030 W. Spring Mountain Rd., Suite 2, West Side ☎ 702/367–3511 🌐 www.raku-grill.com ⏲ Closed Sun. No lunch.*

Todd's Unique Dining

$$$$ | **AMERICAN** | What's really unique (for Vegas) about this intimate spot a short drive southeast of the airport is that artful, creative contemporary cuisine is served in an easygoing space with an unpretentious vibe. This place, from a former Strip executive chef, used to be something of a sleeper, but it's becoming better known. **Known for:** innovative dishes; former Strip chef; cozy suburban spot. *Average main: $45 ✉ 4350 E. Sunset Rd., Henderson ☎ 702/259–8633 🌐 www.toddsunique.com ⏲ Closed Sun. No lunch.*

Hotels

Green Valley Ranch Resort, Spa & Casino

$$$ | **RESORT** | **FAMILY** | Locals have long known that Green Valley is a low-key, refined resort that prefers style over bustle (the Strip is a 25-minute drive away). **Pros:** sophisticated casino; proximity to malls that offer great shopping; newer sports book. **Cons:** 25 minutes from the Strip; not much in the immediate area; can be overrun with locals. *Rooms from: $235 ✉ 2300 Paseo Verde Pkwy., Henderson ☎ 702/617–7777, 866/782–9487 🌐 greenvalleyranch.com 496 rooms No meals.*

Red Rock Casino Resort & Spa

$$ | **RESORT** | Way out on the western edge of the Las Vegas suburbs, this swanky golden-age Vegas property looks out on the ochre-red Spring Mountains, just a stone's throw from Red Rock National Conservation Area. **Pros:** bowling alley and movie theater on-site; nice, expansive pool area; proximity to Red Rock canyon. **Cons:** waitress service in gaming areas can be slow; long distance from Strip; summertime concerts by pool bring crowds. *Rooms from: $159 ✉ 11011 W. Charleston Blvd., Summerlin South ☎ 702/797–7777, 866/767–7773 🌐 red-rock.sclv.com 813 rooms No meals.*

Hoover Dam

8 miles northeast from Boulder City.

In 1928 Congress authorized $175 million for construction of a dam on the Colorado River to control destructive floods, provide a steady water supply to seven Colorado River basin states, and generate electricity. Considered one of the seven wonders of the industrial world, the art deco Hoover Dam is 726 feet high (the equivalent of a 70-story building) and at the base it's 660 feet thick (more than the length of two football fields). Construction required 4.4 million cubic yards of concrete—enough to build a two-lane highway from San Francisco to New York.

GETTING HERE AND AROUND

Hoover Dam is about a 45-minute drive from Las Vegas via U.S. 93; it's about 15 minutes from Boulder City.

★ Hoover Dam

DAM | FAMILY | Originally referred to as Boulder Dam, this colossal structure, widely considered one of the greatest engineering achievements in history, was later officially named Hoover Dam in recognition of President Herbert Hoover's role in the project. Look for artist Oskar Hansen's plaza sculptures, which include the 30-foot-tall *Winged Figures of the Republic* (the statues and terrazzo floor patterns were copied at the Smith Center for the Performing Arts in Downtown Las Vegas).

The tour itself is a tradition that dates back to 1937, and you can still see the old box office on top of the dam. But now the ticketed tours originate in the modern visitor center (or online), with two options. The cheaper, more popular one is the **Powerplant Tour**, which starts every 15 minutes. It's a half-hour, guided tour that includes a short film and then a 537-foot elevator ride to two points of interest: the chance to stand on top of one of the 30-foot pipes where you can hear and feel the water rushing through to the generators, and the more impressive eight-story room housing still-functional power generators. Self-paced exhibits follow the guided portion, with good interactive museum exhibits and a great indoor/outdoor patio view of the dam from the river side. The more extensive **Hoover Dam Tour** includes everything on the Powerplant Tour but limits the group size to 20 and spends more time inside the dam, including a peek through the air vents. Tours run from 9 to 5 all year, with the last Powerplant tour leaving at 3:45 pm daily, and the last Hoover Dam Tour at 3:30. Visitors for both tours submit to security screening comparable to an airport. January and February are the slowest months, and mornings generally are less busy. The top of the dam is open to pedestrians and vehicles, but you have to remain in your vehicle after sundown. Visitors can still drive over the dam for sightseeing, but cannot continue into Arizona; you have to turn around and come back after the road dead-ends at a scenic lookout (with a snack bar and store) on the Arizona side. **■ TIP→ The dam's High Scaler Café offers fare such as cold drinks, ice cream, and hamburgers.** ✉ *U.S. 93, east of Boulder City, Boulder City* ☎ *323/645–2845, 866/730–9097, 888/248–1259 security, road, and Hoover Dam crossing information* 🌐 *www.usbr.gov/lc/hooverdam* 🎫 *Guided Powerplant Tour $15, Guided Dam Tour $30, self-guided visitor center $10; garage parking $10 (free parking on Arizona-side surface lots).*

RAFTING

Black Canyon, just below Hoover Dam, is the place for river running near Las Vegas. Guided raft trips down the Colorado River are available year-round from the Hoover Dam to Willow Beach. It is the Southwest's only natural water trail and includes views of vertical canyon walls, bighorn sheep on the slopes, peregrine falcons, and feeder streams and waterfalls coming off the bluffs. Transportation to and from Las Vegas is available.

Black Canyon/Willow Beach River Adventures

WHITE-WATER RAFTING | FAMILY | If you're interested in seeing the canyon and Hoover Dam on large motor-assisted rafts, Black Canyon/Willow Beach River Adventures has group excursions launching from the base of the dam for both 3-hour and 90-minute tours. The half-day excursion includes lunch; the shorter "postcard" tour lasts about 90 minutes but includes only 30 minutes on the raft. Round-trip Las Vegas transportation is available. All tours depart from Lake Mead RV Village. ✉ *Lake Mead RV Village, 286 Lakeshore Rd., Boulder City* ☎ *800/455–3490* 🌐 *hooverdamtouradventures.com* 🎫 *From $69.*

Did You Know?

Franklin D. Roosevelt dedicated Hoover Dam on September 30, 1935, and the date is still part of the celestial map found on the dam's terrazzo floor.

Lake Mead

About 4 miles from Hoover Dam.

Lake Mead is actually the Colorado River backed up behind Hoover Dam, making it the nation's largest man-made reservoir: it covers 225 square miles, is 110 miles long, and has an irregular shoreline that extends for 550 miles.

GETTING HERE AND AROUND

From Hoover Dam, travel west on U.S. 93 to the intersection with Lakeshore Drive to reach Alan Bible Visitor Center, which reopened in 2013 with a new welcome film and exhibits after two years and nearly $3 million in renovations. It's open every day, 9 to 4:30. Call ☎ *702/293–8990* for more information.

VISITOR INFORMATION

Alan Bible Visitor Center

The main information center for Lake Mead National Recreation Area is complete with a high-def film about the park, and open seven days a week. Also here are a bookstore, nature exhibits, and a cactus garden. It's at the Lake Mead turnoff from U.S. 93, before you get to the pay booth for park entry. A second, smaller visitor center at the park headquarters is in downtown Boulder City at 601 Nevada Way. ✉ *10 Lakeshore Dr., Boulder City* ☎ *702/293–8990* 🌐 *www.nps.gov/lake.*

Sights

Lake Mead

BODY OF WATER | People come to Lake Mead primarily for boating and fishing. Adjacent marinas offer watercraft rentals, restaurants, and paddle-wheeler cruises; the turn-off for them is just past the entry gate. A few cultivated areas allow for swimming but they are not designated swim beaches, so no lifeguards are on duty. In fact, the National Park Service highly recommends wearing life jackets, as high winds come up fast on the lake making for potentially dangerous swimming conditions. The rocky Boulder Beach swimming area is about 2 miles past the visitor center. ⚠ **A fishing license is required within the states of Nevada and Arizona, so if you plan on fishing Lake Mead, get one.** ✉ *Alan Bible Visitor Center, 10 Lakeshore Dr., Boulder City* ☎ *702/293–8990* 🌐 *www.nps.gov/lake* 🎫 *$25 per vehicle, good for 7 days; lake-use fee $16 for 1st vessel, good for 7 days. Annual pass is $45 per vehicle or $50 per vessel. Regular camping is $20 per site, per night; group camping (12–30 people) is $80 per site, per night.*

Activities

LAKE CRUISES

Lake Mead Cruises

BOATING | At Lake Mead Cruises you can board the 275-passenger *Desert Princess*, an authentic Mississippi-style paddle wheeler that plies a portion of the lake, offering impressive views of Hoover Dam, the bypass bridge, and ancient rock formations such as an extinct volcano called Fortification Hill. Brunch and dinner cruises are available seasonally, while 90-minute sightseeing cruises are offered year-round. Advance tickets are offered online. ✉ *490 Horsepower Cove Rd., Boulder City* ✥ *Just north of Alan Bible Visitor Center, look for signs to Hemenway Harbor* ☎ *866/292–9191* 🌐 *www.lakemeadcruises.com* 🎫 *From $35.*

Valley of Fire

50 miles northeast of Las Vegas.

The 56,000-acre Valley of Fire State Park was dedicated in 1935 as Nevada's first state park. Valley of Fire takes its name from distinctive coloration of its rocky landscape, which ranges from lavender to tangerine to bright red, giving the vistas along the park road an otherworldly appearance.

GETTING HERE AND AROUND

From Las Vegas, take Interstate 15 north about 35 miles to Exit 75–Route 169 and continue 15 miles. If you're coming from the northern Overton Arm of Lake Mead, look for the sign announcing the Valley of Fire and head west onto Valley of Fire Highway for a few miles to the park's visitor center. ■TIP→ **It may also be possible to see some of the remnants of St. Thomas, a settlement within the park that was washed away by the Colorado River after completion of the Hoover Dam, as drought conditions have lowered lake levels dramatically. It's located off unpaved St. Thomas Road north of Overton Beach.**

Sights

Lost City Museum

MUSEUM | FAMILY | The Moapa Valley has one of the finest collections of ancestral Puebloan artifacts in the American Southwest. Lost City, officially known as Pueblo Grande de Nevada, was a major outpost of the ancient culture. The museum's artifacts include baskets, weapons, a restored Basketmaker pit house, reconstructed pueblo houses, and black-and-white photographs of the excavation of Lost City in the 1920s and '30s. To get to the Lost City Museum from Valley of Fire, pass the park's east entrance and head north onto Northshore Drive, which becomes state route 169, toward Overton. ✉ *721 S. Moapa Valley Blvd., Overton* ☎ *702/397–2193* 🌐 *lostcitymuseum.org* 🎫 *$5* ⏲ *Closed Mon. and Tues.*

★ **Valley of Fire State Park**

NATIVE SITE | FAMILY | Valley of Fire's jumbled rock formations are remnants of hardened sand dunes more than 150 million years old. You find petrified trees and one of the park's most photographed features—Elephant Rock—just steps off the main road. Mysterious petroglyphs (carvings etched into the rocks) are believed to be the work of the Basketmaker and early Puebloan people, with their occupation in the area estimated from 300 BC to AD 1150. The easy, essential trail is Mouse's Tank, named for an outlaw who hid out here and managed to find water; so will you in cooler months (but not for drinking). It's a short walk with views of petroglyphs and shaded by steep canyon walls. Sci-fi fans also might recognize Fire Canyon as the alien planet in *Starship Troopers* and several other movies.

The **Valley of Fire Visitor Center** was remodeled in 2011 and has displays on the park's history, ecology, archaeology, and recreation, as well as slide shows and films, and information about the two campgrounds (72 campsites, 20 of them with power and water for RVs) within the park. Campsites at Atlatl Rock and Arch Rock Campgrounds are available on a first-come, first-served basis. The park is open year-round; the best times to visit, especially during the heat of summer, are sunrise and sunset, when the light is truly spectacular. ✉ *29450 Valley of Fire Rd., Overton* ✥ *I–15 N to Exit 75. Merge onto Valley of Fire Hwy. Entrance to park is about 14 miles* ☎ *775/684-2770* 🌐 *parks.nv.gov/parks/valley-of-fire* 🎫 *$10 per vehicle; $15 for non-Nevada vehicles; camping is $20 per vehicle, per night; $25 for non-Nevada vehicles.*

Area 51

148 miles north of Las Vegas.

It's a long way to drive just to buy a T-shirt and take some quirky photos, but for those with Area 51 on their bucket list it can be worth it. It wasn't until 2013 that the CIA, following a Freedom of Information Act request, acknowledged the existence of the restricted Air Force installation, but conspiracy theories have been swirling around the desert facility for years. It's been rumored to contain everything from scientists replicating crashed alien spacecraft to those creating time travel. What we actually do know is the Air Force does, in fact, test top-secret aircraft and related technology here, resulting in many of the strange sights and sounds that have been reported for years. But it's all the mystery and secrecy, wrapped up in a desolate enigma in a locale that looks like the set of a 1950s sci-fi flick. And it's kept folks from around the world driving to the edge of the landmark (also known as Groom Lake and Dreamland) and its closest neighbor, the tiny hamlet of Rachel, Nevada, population about 100.

Keep in mind, it's illegal to get too close to the installation, launch drones in the area, or take photographs in the nearby vicinity. Fines are high, and military police have the authority to use deadly force if necessary. Locals can fill you in on the particulars, or simply heed the posted signs.

GETTING HERE AND AROUND

To get to Rachel, head north from Las Vegas on Interstate 15, then take U.S. 93 north for about 85 miles; you'll pass Alamo and Ash Springs, then go left onto Highway 318 and stay on it for less than a mile before veering left onto Highway 375, Nevada's officially designated "Extraterrestrial Highway." Drive about 40 miles to reach Rachel and the famous Little A'Le'Inn. Little more than a simple roadside diner, it's the main destination for most visitors since places to stop and eat are few and far between. Keep in mind gas stations are also limited in this area, so fuel up before the trip or in Alamo, and look out for cows grazing in the area as they tend to cross the E.T. Highway. The drive from Las Vegas can take 2½ hours.

TOURS

Adventure Tours

DRIVING TOURS | This tour company provides daylong Area 51 photo tours in luxury SUVs, stopping in Rachel and taking in the Air Force installation's guarded perimeter as well as highlights along the way, including ancient petroglyphs and dry lakes associated with UFO lore. The tour includes lunch, unlimited snacks, and pickup at your Las Vegas hotel. It operates regularly on Monday, Wednesday, and Saturday (or other days if you have a group of four or more). ☎ *702/889–8687* 🌐 *www.vegassightseeing.com* 🎟 *From $199.*

Pahranagat National Wildlife Refuge

NATURE PRESERVE | If you're looking for a bookend to your trip to Area 51 that, well, is just more down-to-earth, drop by these spring-fed wetlands, which serve as a stopover for thousands of birds migrating along the Pacific Flyway. The 5,380-acre Pahranagat National Wildlife Refuge is a chain of lakes, marshes, and meadows that provides a convenient stop on the Pacific Flyway for ducks, herons, egrets, eagles, and other species. The Upper Lake is the most accessible, with campsites, picnic tables, and observation points. For a bird list, stop at the refuge headquarters located 4 miles south of Alamo, at milepost 32 off U.S. 93, which also features interactive exhibits, a 15-minute movie and short nature trails. The best times to see more than 230 species of birds are early morning and late evening during the spring and fall migrations. ☎ *775/725–3417* 🌐 *www.fws.gov/refuge/pahranagat* 🎟 *Free.*

Little A'Le'Inn

$ | **AMERICAN** | Even if you aren't hungry for a tasty "alien burger," a pilgrimage to this restaurant/bar is practically a requirement to earn those Area 51 bragging rights. While the food is typical diner fare such as chili and sandwiches, it's very reasonably priced, and the owners put some tender loving care into keeping their oddly famous outpost in top shape. **Known for:** reasonably priced diner fare with pretty good burgers; colorful owners; alien-inspired gifts. 💲 *Average main: $7* ✉ *9631 Old Mill St., Alamo* ✥ *Hwy. 375, about 45 miles northwest of Ash Springs* ☎ *775/729–2515* 🌐 *www.littlealeinn.com.*

Chapter 4

GREAT BASIN NATIONAL PARK

Updated by
Stina Sieg

Camping ★★☆☆☆

Hotels ★☆☆☆☆

Activities ★★★☆☆

Scenery ★★★★☆

Crowds ★☆☆☆☆

WELCOME TO GREAT BASIN NATIONAL PARK

TOP REASONS TO GO

★ **Ancient trees:** The twisting, windswept bristlecone pines in Great Basin can live to be thousands of years old.

★ **Desert skyscraper:** Wheeler Peak rises out of the desert basin with summit temperatures often 20–30 degrees below that of the visitor center.

★ **Rare shields:** Look for hundreds of these unique disk-shape formations inside Lehman Caves.

★ **Gather your pine nuts while you may:** Come in the fall and go a little nutty, as you can gather up to three gunnysacks of pinyon pine nuts, found in abundance throughout the park. They're great on salads.

★ **Celestial show:** Pitch-dark nights make for dazzling stars. Gaze on your own or attend a seasonal nighttime talk, led by a park ranger.

1 **Lehman Caves.** Highlighted by the limestone caverns, this is the primary destination for many Great Basin visitors. It's located next to a popular visitor center and just past the start of Wheeler Peak Scenic Drive.

2 **Wheeler Peak.** This 13,063-footer is the park's centerpiece, and is especially stunning when capped with snow. Hikers can climb the mountain via strenuous, day-use-only trails, which also lead to small alpine lakes, a glacier, and some ancient bristlecone pines.

3 **Snake Creek Canyon.** This is the less crowded, more remote part of an already remote park. Trails follow creeks and cross meadows in the southern parts of the park, and six primitive campgrounds line Snake Creek. A bristlecone pine grove is nearby, though far off any beaten path.

4 **Arch Canyon.** A high-clearance, four-wheel-drive vehicle is recommended, and sturdy boots and sun protection are critical if you want to get to Lexington Arch, which is unusual in that it is formed of limestone, not sandstone as most arches are. This is a day-use-only area.

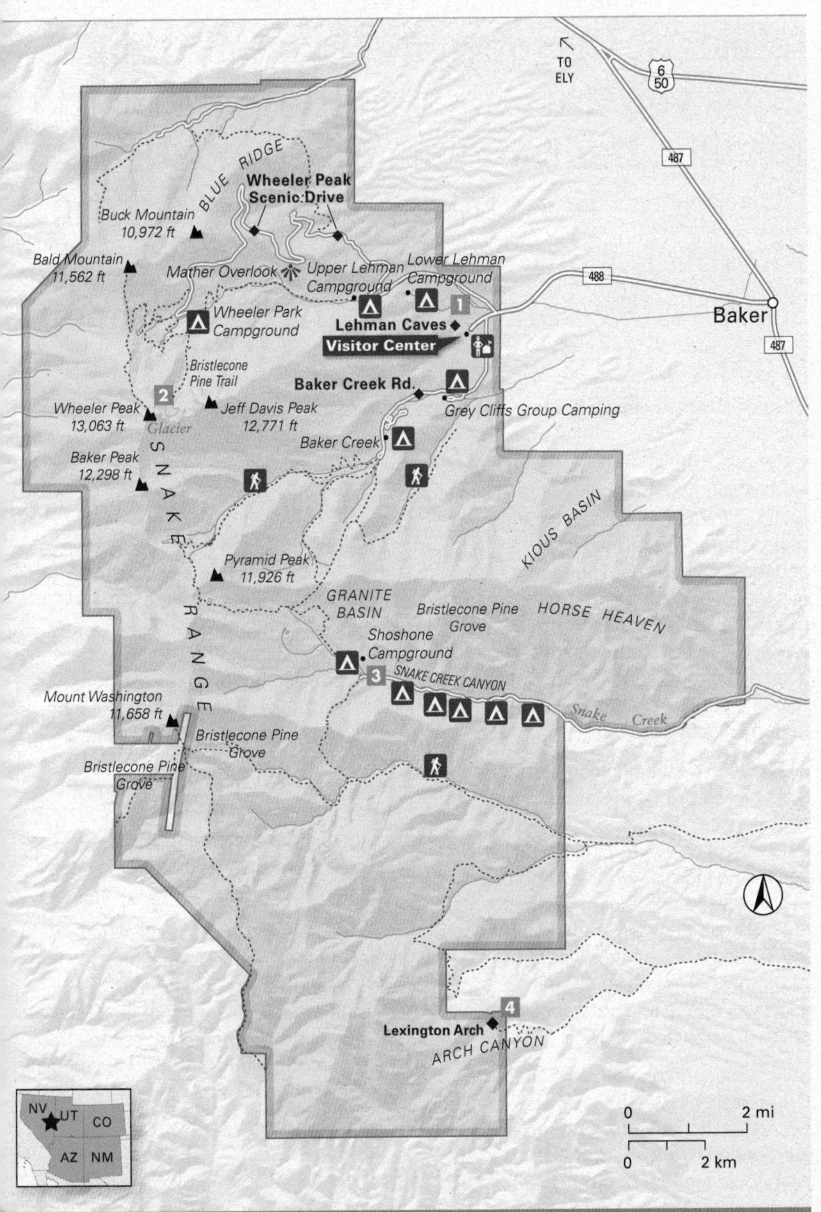
TO ELY
6
50
487
488
487
Baker
BLUE RIDGE
Wheeler Peak Scenic Drive
Buck Mountain 10,972 ft
Bald Mountain 11,562 ft
Mather Overlook
Upper Lehman Campground
Lower Lehman Campground
1
Wheeler Park Campground
Lehman Caves
Visitor Center
Bristlecone Pine Trail
Baker Creek Rd.
2
Wheeler Peak 13,063 ft
Glacier
Jeff Davis Peak 12,771 ft
Grey Cliffs Group Camping
Baker Creek
Baker Peak 12,298 ft
SNAKE RANGE
KIOUS BASIN
Pyramid Peak 11,926 ft
GRANITE BASIN
Bristlecone Pine Grove
HORSE HEAVEN
Shoshone Campground
3
SNAKE CREEK CANYON
Snake Creek
Mount Washington 11,658 ft
Bristlecone Pine Grove
Bristlecone Pine Grove
4
Lexington Arch
ARCH CANYON
NV
UT
CO
AZ
NM
0
2 mi
0
2 km

As you drive from the vast, sagebrush-dotted desert near Great Basin National Park's entrance into the cool alpine forests at the top of its signature scenic drive, you travel only a little more than 10 miles. But the change is so drastic it's like you've been transported to the Rocky Mountains, hundreds of miles away. That's a big part of why this little gem of a park exists.

Created in 1986, it preserves and highlights a sample of the incredible diversity found in the Great Basin, a gigantic arid region that spans almost all of Nevada and reaches into Utah, Oregon, California, Idaho, and Wyoming. The Lehman Caves, located in the heart of the park, went from a private tourist attraction to a national monument in 1922 until being folded into the new national park a few generations later.

Great Basin's founding came after decades of wrangling between the National Park Service, the U.S. Forest Service, local ranchers, White Pine County, and various politicians, whose compromises eventually led to the park being much smaller than originally proposed. At about 77,000 acres, it's just a sliver of the size of better-known parks like Grand Canyon and Yellowstone and gets a much smaller share of visitors, as well.

Still, those who do make the trek to Great Basin—hours from any big city in every direction—find a lot to do while surrounded by the quiet desert. Daily cave tours are one of the biggest draws, especially for families, with tickets so popular they can sell out months in advance. At night, the famously dark skies offset a sea of bright stars, and rangers lead astronomy talks and share telescopes with the public several times a week in the high season (and even host a festival in the fall). Camping and hiking are also huge, with trails to fit pretty much every ability level. Modest walks can get you to alpine lakes or a grove of bristlecone pines, some of the oldest organisms on earth. Longer, more strenuous hikes take you deep into the backcountry or the craggy top of Wheeler Peak. At more than 13,000 feet, it's the second-highest mountain in the state.

Visiting Great Basin is a rustic experience, with few amenities, little cell service, and just a speck of a town nearby. But for those in search of an earthy solitude, it's a much-needed escape from the rest of the world, and draws a certain kind of visitor back year after year.

AVERAGE HIGH/LOW TEMPERATURES					
JAN.	FEB.	MAR.	APR.	MAY	JUNE
41/18	44/21	48/24	56/31	66/40	76/48
JULY	AUG.	SEPT.	OCT.	NOV.	DEC.
86/57	83/56	75/47	62/47	49/26	42/20

Planning

When to Go

Summer is when you'll find the most amenities open and also the most visitors. While Great Basin doesn't get crowded to the extent of larger parks, it has been somewhat "discovered" in recent years, leading to hard-to-find parking and camping spots between around Memorial Day and Labor Day, and sometimes beyond. In these warmer months, you should be comfortable in shorts and T-shirts during the day—though temperatures drop at night, and get colder the higher up you climb, so bring light jackets and pants. Fall and spring can be lovely times to visit, though you should plan for lower temperatures at night and fewer businesses open in Baker, the small town near the park.

A winter visit can be sublime in its solitude, but the hardy visitor must be prepared for the elements, especially if the backcountry is a destination. With temperatures hovering in the low teens, heavy coats, boots, and other appropriate winter gear are necessary. Some roads might be impassable in inclement weather; check ahead with a park ranger. No dining or groceries are available in the park during the winter, and the closest option is several miles away at the year-round Border Inn.

FESTIVALS AND EVENTS

Great Basin Astronomy Festival. In 2016, Great Basin was named a Dark Sky Park by the International Dark Skies Assocation. This festival, spread out over a few days every fall, is a chance to experience these famous nighttime skies, with talks, workshops, and of course, looks at the stars through park telescopes. Be sure to snag a reservation, as it can fill up fast. 🌐 *www.nps.gov/grba/planyourvisit/great-basin-astronomy-festival.htm.*

Silver State Classic Challenge. Twice a year, car enthusiasts of all stripes close a state highway for the country's largest (and most venerable) open-road race for amateur fast-car drivers. The event occurs the third weekend of May and the third weekend of September south of Ely on Route 318, from Lund to Hiko, and is open to just about any four-wheeled vehicle. 🌐 *www.sscc.us.*

White Pine County Fair. Livestock, flower, and vegetable competitions, plus horse races, food booths, dancing, and a barbecue dinner make this fair, held at the White Pine County Fairgrounds in Ely, the real thing. The dates fluctuate every August. 🌐 *www.wpcfair.com.*

Getting Here and Around

AIR

The nearest airport is in Cedar City (142 miles) but will likely be pricey. Salt Lake City (239 miles) and Las Vegas (303 miles) are better bets, though you'll probably get the cheapest fares (and might have the most fun) flying into Vegas.

CAR

The entrance to Great Basin is on Route 488, 5 miles west of its junction with Route 487. From Ely, take U.S. 6/50 to Route 487. From Salt Lake City or Cedar City, Utah, take Interstate 15 South to

Great Basin in One Day

Start your visit with the 90-minute tour of the fascinating limestone caverns of **Lehman Caves**, the park's most famous attraction (advance reservations heavily encouraged, as tours often fill up months in advance). If you have time before or after the tour, hike the short and family-friendly **Mountain View Nature Trail**, near the Lehman Caves Visitor Center, to get your first taste of the area's pinyon-juniper forests. Stop for lunch at the Lehman Caves Cafe (open April through October) or at least plan on a homemade cookie—or have a picnic near the visitor center.

In the afternoon, take a leisurely drive up Wheeler Peak Drive, with fabulous views of **Wheeler Peak**, the park's tallest mountain (and the second highest in Nevada) at just over 13,000 feet. You can stop about halfway along your drive to hike the short **Osceola Ditch Trail**, a remnant of the park's gold-mining days, or, alternatively, just enjoy the views from the two overlooks. If you're feeling energetic, when you reach the top of the winding road hike into the strange beauty of a bristlecone pine grove on the **Bristlecone Pine Trail.**

U.S. 6/50 West; from Las Vegas, drive north on Interstate 15 and then north on Route 93 to access U.S. 6/50. ⚠ **Don't rely on GPS to get to the park, as sometimes it sends people up remote dirt roads. The turnoff to the main section of the park is well marked in the center of Baker.**

In the park, Baker Creek Road and portions of Wheeler Peak Scenic Drive, above Upper Lehman Creek, are closed from November to June. The road to the visitor center and the roads to the developed campgrounds are paved, but two-wheel-drive cars don't do well in winter storms. RVs and trailers over 24 feet aren't allowed above Upper Lehman Creek. With an 8% grade, the road to Wheeler Peak is steep and curvy, but not dangerous if you take it slow. Motorcyclists should watch for gravel on the road's surface.

There are two gas stations located nearby. The tiny Baker Sinclair station is just outside the park entrance, while about 7½ miles farther, the Border Inn has a Phillips 66 station, open 24/7.

Inspiration

Hiking Great Basin National Park, by Bruce Grubbs, will get your Great Basin trip off on the right foot.

Trails to Explore in Great Basin National Park, by Rose Houk, is all about hiking in the park.

Geology of the Great Basin, by Bill Fiero, and *Basin and Range,* by John McPhee, present geological tours of the Great Basin.

Park Essentials

ACCESSIBILITY

Designated accessibility parking spaces are available at both visitor centers. The centers themselves are both on one level, fully accessible to those with impaired mobility, with accessible bathrooms. The park slide show is captioned. The park has two ADA-compliant trails, though both are unpaved: the Island Forest Trail (0.4 mile) at the top of Wheeler Peak Drive and the Shoshone Trail (0.1 mile) at Snake Creek. Baker Creek Campground, Upper Lehman

Creek Campground, and Wheeler Peak Campground are accessible, though the restroom access ramp at Upper Lehman Creek Campground is steep.

PARK FEES AND PERMITS

Admission to the park is free, but if you want to tour Lehman Caves there's a fee ($9–$11, depending on tour length). To fish in Great Basin National Park, those 12 and older need a state fishing license from the Nevada Department of Wildlife (🌐 *www.ndow.org*). The one-day nonresident license is $18, plus $7 for each additional day at time of purchase ($80 for a year). Backcountry hikers do not need permits, but for your own safety you should fill out a form at the visitor center before setting out.

PARK HOURS

The park is open 24/7 year-round; May to August, visitor center hours are 8–4:30; hours may vary from year to year. It's in the Pacific time zone.

CELL PHONE RECEPTION

There's decent coverage close to Lehman Caves; the more remote you get, the spottier it becomes. Some service is available on higher portions of the Wheeler Peak hike.

SHOPS AND GROCERS

While the closest full-service grocery store is an hour away in Ely, the Stargazer Inn in Baker has a small market with some basics, including snacks, beer, and wine. Similar supplies can be found a few miles outside of town at the Border Inn's grocery section.

Hotels

There is no lodging in the park, so plan to arrive early to snag one of its coveted first-come, first-served campsites, or expect to camp in the backcountry. There is a handful of motels in nearby Baker and many more to choose from about an hour away in Ely. *Hotel reviews have been shortened. For full information, visit Fodors.com.*

What It Costs

	$	$$	$$$	$$$$
RESTAURANTS	under $13	$13–$20	$21–$30	over $30
HOTELS	under $101	$101–$150	$151–$200	over $200

Restaurants

Dining in the park itself is limited to basic but tasty breakfast and lunch fare at the Lehman Caves Cafe and Gift Shop. About 5 miles away in Baker, a town of less than 100 people, there are a few good options. Fire grates are available at each campsite in the park's four developed campgrounds for barbecuing. *Restaurant reviews have been shortened. For full information, visit Fodors.com.*

Visitor Information

PARK CONTACT INFORMATION Great Basin National Park. ✉ *Rte. 488, Baker* ☎ *775/234–7331* 🌐 *www.nps.gov/grba.*

Lehman Caves

5½ miles from Baker.

Essentially the gateway to this small park, this area contains an in-depth visitor center and fun gift shop, the park's only restaurant (seasonal), hiking trails, and campgrounds. Perhaps most important, it's home to the Lehman Caves, the park's most well-known attraction. This is a good corner of the park to plan out your adventures or relax with a glass of wine after a day of hiking.

Sights

PICNIC AREAS

Lehman Caves Visitor Center Picnic Area

LOCAL INTEREST | FAMILY | This picnic site, with tables, water, and restrooms (the latter two available during the summer), is a short walk from the visitor center. Summer hours are often extended beyond the standard 8 am–4:30 pm. ✉ *Great Basin National Park* ✣ *Just north of Lehman Caves Visitor Center.*

Pole Canyon Trailhead Picnic Area

LOCAL INTEREST | Inaccessible when Baker Creek Road is closed in the winter, this picnic area at the mouth of a canyon has a handful of tables and fire grills but no water. It does have a restroom. Access is via a narrow, one-lane road. ✉ *Great Basin National Park* ✣ *East of entrance to Grey Cliffs Group Camping site, at mouth of Pole Canyon* ⏲ *Closed Nov.–May.*

Upper Lehman Creek Campground

LOCAL INTEREST | There is a handful of places here where you can sit down for a bite and a breather. A group picnic site requires advance reservations, but areas near the host site and amphitheater are first come, first served. Water is available. ✉ *Great Basin National Park* ✣ *4 miles from Lehman Caves Visitor Center on Wheeler Peak Scenic Dr.*

SCENIC DRIVES

Baker Creek Road

SCENIC DRIVE | Though less popular than the Wheeler Peak Scenic Drive, this gravel road affords gorgeous views of Wheeler Peak, the Baker Creek Drainage, and Snake Valley. Beautiful wildflowers are an extra treat in spring and early summer. The road is closed in the winter, and there are no pull-outs or scenic overlooks. ✣ *½ mile inside park boundary off Rte. 488* ⏲ *Closed Nov.–May.*

SCENIC STOPS

★ Lehman Caves

CAVE | FAMILY | While Indigenous people were the first to explore and use the caves, rancher and miner Absalom Lehman is credited with discovering this underground wonder in 1885. The single limestone and marble cavern is 2½ miles long, with stalactites, stalagmites, helictites, flowstone, popcorn, and other bizarre mineral formations that cover almost every surface. Lehman Caves is one of the best places to see rare shield formations, created when calcite-rich water is forced from tiny cracks in a cave wall, ceiling, or floor. Year-round the cave maintains a constant, damp temperature of 50°F, so wear a light jacket and nonskid shoes. Go for the full 90-minute tour if you have time; during summer, it's offered several times a day, as is the 60-minute tour. Expect daily tours during the winter. Children under age five are not allowed on the 90-minute tours, except during the winter; those under 16 must be accompanied by an adult. Take the 0.3-mile Mountain View Nature Trail beforehand to see the original cave entrance and **Rhodes Cabin,** where black-and-white photographs of the park's earlier days line the walls. ⚠ **Get tickets as far in advance as possible at recreation.gov. Tours can sell out months in advance.** ✉ *Lehman Caves Visitor Center* ☎ *775/234–7331* 🎫 *From $9.*

TRAILS

Baker Lake Trail

TRAIL | This full-day, 12-mile hike can easily be made into a two-day backpacking trip. You'll gain a total of 2,620 feet in elevation on the way to Baker Lake, a jewel-like alpine lake with a backdrop of impressive cliffs. *Difficult.* ✉ *Great Basin National Park* ✣ *Trailhead: Baker Creek Rd., going south from just east of Lehman Caves Visitor Center.*

Lehman Caves: It's amazing what a little water and air can do to a room.

Mountain View Nature Trail

TRAIL | FAMILY | Just past the Rhodes Cabin on the right side of the visitor center, this short and easy trail (0.3 mile) through pinyon pine and juniper trees is marked with signs describing the plants. The path passes the original entrance to Lehman Caves and loops back to the visitor center. It's a great way to spend a half hour or so while you wait for your cave tour to start. *Easy.* ✉ *Great Basin National Park* ✣ *Trailhead: At Lehman Caves Visitor Center.*

VISITOR CENTERS

Great Basin Visitor Center

INFO CENTER | FAMILY | Here you can see exhibits on the flora, fauna, and geology of the park, or ask a ranger to suggest a favorite hike. Books, videos, and souvenirs are for sale. Water is available. ✉ *Rte. 487, just north of Baker* ☎ *775/234–7520* ⏲ *Closed Oct.–late Apr.*

Lehman Caves Visitor Center

INFO CENTER | FAMILY | Regularly scheduled cave tours lasting 60 or 90 minutes depart from here. Mountain View Nature Trail encircles the visitor center and includes Rhodes Cabin and the historic cave entrance. Buy gifts for friends and family back home at the bookstore, or just take in the view with a glass of wine at the adjacent café. There's also a replica of the park's famed caves you can walk through. ✉ *Rte. 488, ½ mile inside park boundary* ☎ *775/234–7331.*

Restaurants

Lehman Caves Cafe and Gift Shop

$ | AMERICAN | This casual spot is a great place to soak in the vast desert view and offers simple breakfasts and lunches. The sandwiches, filled with meats smoked by the owner, are especially good. **Known for:** a nice place to unwind with a beer or glass of wine into the late afternoon; the only restaurant in the park; delicious cookies and other treats, baked by a local pastry chef. $ *Average main: $10* ✉ *Next to visitor center* ☎ *775/234–7200* ⏲ *Closed Nov.–May. No dinner.*

Wheeler Peak

12 miles from the Lehman Caves Visitor Center.

You'll find some of the most dramatic scenery, including panoramic desert views, in this high-elevation section of the park. Here, hiking trails take you to some of Great Basin's most photographed spots: clear alpine lakes, a grove of bristlecone pines, and the top of Nevada's second-highest peak. This area's sole camping area, Wheeler Peak Campground, is one of the most beautiful in the park. The scenic drive that transports you from the desert to the forest is an attraction in itself but, like the campground in this prized section, is open only seasonally.

Sights

SCENIC DRIVES

★ Wheeler Peak Scenic Drive

SCENIC DRIVE | When this stunning seasonable road is open, it's a must for Great Basin visitors. Less than a mile from the visitor center off Route 488, turn onto this paved road that winds its way up to elevations of 10,000 feet. You'll go past pinyon-juniper forest in lower elevations; as you climb, the air cools as much as 20–30 degrees. Along the way, pull off at overlooks for awe-inspiring glimpses of the peaks of the South Snake Range. A short interpretive trail leads to a ditch that once carried water to the historic Osceola mining site. Turn off at Mather Overlook, elevation 9,000 feet, for the best photo ops. Wheeler Overlook is the best place to see Wheeler Peak, as well as fall colors. Allow 1½ hours for the 24-mile round-trip, not including hikes. ✉ *Baker* ✥ *Just inside park boundary, off Rte. 488 about 5 miles west of Baker* 🌐 *www.nps.gov/grba/planyourvisit/wheeler-peak-scenic-drive.htm* ⏲ *Closed Nov.–June.*

TRAILS

Alpine Lakes Trail

TRAIL | This moderate, 2.7-mile trek loops past the beautiful Stella and Teresa lakes from the trailhead near Wheeler Peak Campground. You'll rise and fall about 600 feet in elevation as you pass through subalpine and alpine forest. The views of Wheeler Peak, amid wildflowers (in summer), white fir, shimmering aspens, and towering ponderosa pines, make this a memorable hike. The trailhead is at nearly 10,000 feet, so make sure you're adjusted to the altitude and prepared for changing weather. Allow three hours. *Moderate.* ✉ *Great Basin National Park* ✥ *Trailhead: At Bristlecone parking area, near end of Wheeler Peak Scenic Dr.*

★ Bristlecone Pine Trail

TRAIL | FAMILY | Though the park has several bristlecone pine groves, the only way to see the gnarled, ancient trees up close is to hike this trail. From the parking area to the grove, it's a moderate 2.8-mile hike that takes about an hour each way. Rangers offer informative talks in season; inquire at the visitor center. The Bristlecone Pine Trail also leads to the **Glacier Trail,** which skirts the southernmost permanent ice field on the continent and ends with a view of a small rock glacier, the only one in Nevada. It's less than 3 miles back to the parking lot. Allow three hours for the moderate hike and remember the trailhead is at 9,800 feet above sea level. *Moderate.* ✉ *Great Basin National Park* ✥ *Trailhead: Summit Trail parking area, Wheeler Peak Scenic Dr., 12 miles from Lehman Caves Visitor Center.*

Osceola Ditch Trail

TRAIL | FAMILY | In 1890, at a cost of $108,223, the Osceola Gravel Mining Company constructed an 18-mile-long trench. The ditch was part of an attempt to glean gold from the South Snake Range, but water shortages and the company's failure to find much gold forced the mining operation to shut down in 1905. You can reach portions of the

Plants and Wildlife in Great Basin

Despite the cold, dry conditions in Great Basin, 925 plant species thrive; 13 are considered sensitive species. The region gets less than 10 inches of rain a year, so plants have developed some ingenious methods of dealing with the desert's harshness. For instance, many flowering plants will grow and produce seeds only in a year when there is enough water. Spruces, pines, and junipers have set down roots here, and the bristlecone pine has been doing so for thousands of years.

The park's plants provide a variety of habitats for animals and for more than 230 bird species. In the sagebrush are jackrabbits, ground squirrels, chipmunks, and pronghorn. Mule deer and striped skunks abound in the pygmy forest of pinyon pine and juniper trees. Shrews, ringtail cats, and weasels make their homes around the springs and streams. Mountain lions, bobcats, and sheep live on the rugged slopes and in valleys. The park is also home to coyotes, kit fox, and badgers. Treat the Great Basin rattlesnake with respect. Bites are uncommon and rarely fatal, but if you're bitten, remain calm and call 911.

eastern section of the ditch on foot via the Osceola Ditch Trail, which passes through pine and fir trees and has interpretive signs along the way. Allow 30 minutes for this easy 0.3-mile round-trip hike. *Easy.* ✉ *Great Basin National Park* ⊕ *Trailhead: Wheeler Peak Scenic Dr.*

★ Wheeler Peak Summit Trail
TRAIL | Begin this full-day, 8.6-mile hike early in the day so as to minimize exposure to afternoon storms. Depart and return to Summit Trailhead near the end of Wheeler Peak Scenic Drive. Most of the route follows a ridge up the mountain to the summit. Elevation gain is 2,900 feet to 13,063 feet above sea level, so hikers should have good stamina and watch for altitude sickness and/or hypothermia due to drastic temperature and weather changes. The trail becomes especially steep and challenging, with lots of loose rocks, toward the summit. *Difficult.* ✉ *Great Basin National Park* ⊕ *Trailhead: Wheeler Peak Scenic Dr., Summit Trail parking area.*

Snake Creek Canyon

11 miles from Baker.

Great Basin is already far from pretty much everything, but for those who want to go just a little bit farther, Snake Creek offers true solitude. Free, primitive campsites are shaded by trees, with fire rings and picnic tables but no water or bathrooms. Snake Creek Road is open year-round, but can become snowy or muddy in the winter and spring. High-clearance vehicles are recommended, while RVs and trailers are not. A cluster of trails are at the end of the road, including routes to Johnson and Baker lakes.

Sights

SCENIC SIGHTS

Lexington Arch
NATURE SITE | Tucked far away in the rugged backcountry, Lexington Arch is six stories high, looming over Lexington Creek. While most arches are made of sandstone, this arch is limestone, more often associated with caves. That leads some to believe it was once a passage in

a cave system. The 5.4-mile (round-trip) hike to the arch is challenging, with little to no shade. Hiking boots, sunscreen, water, and snacks are essential. It's one of the few trails in the park where leashed pets are allowed. The arch is actually located south of Snake Creek, outside of the small town of Garrison, Utah. Only high-clearance, four-wheel-drive vehicles are recommended on the dirt road leading to it. ⚠ **Traveling to the arch can be dangerous, as the road becomes rougher the closer you get to the trailhead. Make sure to stop driving before you get in trouble and walk the rest of the way.** ✉ *Baker* ✣ *Drive south from Baker on Rte. 487 until it becomes Utah 21. Pass through Garrison, then past Pruess Lake. Turn right at the sign for Lexington Arch, and take that dirt road about 7 miles until you reach a washed-out section. Take the south fork to reach the trailhead for the arch. Due to road damage, parking will be ½ to 1 mile away from the trailhead.*

Activities

Great Basin National Park is a great place for experienced outdoor adventurers. The closest outdoor store is an hour away in Ely, so bring everything you might need, and be prepared to go it alone. Permits are not required to go off the beaten path, but if you're planning a multiday hike, register with a ranger just in case. The effort is worth it, as the backcountry is pristine and not at all crowded, no matter the time of year. As is the case in all national parks, bicycling is restricted to existing roads, which can get busy with cars, especially Wheeler Peak Scenic Drive. Always be cautious, and consider biking on less popular roads.

BIRD-WATCHING

An impressive list of bird species have been sighted here—238, according to the National Park Service checklist. Some, such as the common raven and American robin, can be seen at most locations. Others, such as the red-naped sapsucker, are more commonly seen near Lehman Creek. In the higher elevations, listen for the loud shriek of Clark's nutcracker, storing nuts.

CAMPING

Great Basin has four developed campgrounds, all easily accessible by car, but only the Lower Lehman Creek Campground is open year-round. All are first come, first served, and can be paid for on-site with cash, check, or credit card. The campgrounds do fill up, so try to snag your spot early.

Primitive campsites around Snake and Strawberry creeks are open year-round and are free; however, snow and rain can make access to the sites difficult. RVs and trailers are not recommended.

Baker Creek Campground. The turnoff is just past the park entrance, on the left as you approach the Lehman Caves Visitor Center. ✉ *2½ miles south of Rte. 488, 3 miles from visitor center in the Lehman Caves section of the park.*

Lower Lehman Creek Campground. Other than Great Basin's primitive sites, this is the only campground in the park that is open year-round. It's the first turnoff past the Lehman Caves Visitor Center. ✉ *2½ miles from visitor center on Wheeler Peak Scenic Dr. in the Lehman Caves section of the park.*

Upper Lehman Creek Campground. About a mile past the Lower Lehman Creek turnoff, this camp fills up quickly in the summer. ✉ *4 miles from visitor center on Wheeler Peak Scenic Dr.in the Lehman Caves section of the park.*

Wheeler Peak Campground. This cool high-elevation campground at the end of Wheeler Peak Scenic Drive has stunning views and is near trailheads. Many consider it the nicest in the park. ✉ *13 miles from Lehman Caves Visitor Center on*

Wheeler Peak Scenic Dr. in the Wheeler Peak section of the park.

Whispering Elms Campground. The largest camping facility close to but not inside the park is also the nearest to offer hookups for RVs. It is open year-round. ✉ *5 miles from the park, 120 Baker Ave., Baker* ☎ *775/234–9900.*

CROSS-COUNTRY SKIING

Lehman Creek Trail

SKIING/SNOWBOARDING | In summer, descend 2,050 feet by hiking Lehman Creek Trail one-way (downhill) from Wheeler Peak campground to Upper Lehman Creek campground. In winter, it is the most popular cross-country skiing trail in the park. You may need snowshoes to reach the skiable upper section, with free rentals available at the Lehman Cave Visitor Center.

EDUCATIONAL OFFERINGS

Junior Ranger Program

TOUR—SIGHT | **FAMILY** | Youngsters answer questions and complete activities related to the park and then are sworn in as Junior Rangers and receive a Great Basin badge. ✉ *Great Basin National Park* ☎ *775/234–7331* 🌐 *www.nps.gov/grba.*

Weekly Astronomy Programs

OBSERVATORY | **FAMILY** | You'll find some of the country's darkest skies—and brightest stars—at Great Basin. Due to its low light pollution, it was even named a Dark Sky Park by the International Dark Sky Association in 2016. As astrotourism has grown, Great Basin has responded by building a brand-new amphitheater for these ranger-led stargazing programs. Expect to be dazzled as you get a chance to see the wild blue yonder through a telescope. It's often crowded, especially during the summer, when the program is held several times a week. It drops down to once a week in shoulder seasons. ✉ *Lehman Caves Visitor Center, Baker* 🌐 *www.nps.gov/grba* ⏲ *Closed Nov.–Mar.*

HIKING

You'll witness beautiful views by driving along the Wheeler Peak Scenic Drive and other park roads, but hiking allows an in-depth experience that just can't be matched. Trails at Great Basin run the gamut from short, wheelchair-accessible paths to multiday backpacking excursions. Destinations include evergreen forest, flowering meadows, and an extremely tall mountain peak. When you pick up a trail map at the visitor center, ask about trail conditions and bring appropriate clothing when you set out from any trailhead.

No matter the trail length, always carry water, and remember that the trails are at high elevations, so pace yourself accordingly. Never enter abandoned mineshafts or tunnels because they are unstable and dangerous. Those headed into the backcountry don't need to obtain a permit, but are encouraged to register at either of the two visitor centers. Regardless of the season, inquire about the weather, as it can be harsh and unpredictable. Since cell reception is spotty at best, a personal locator beacon can be a lifesaver when adventuring on remote trails.

What's Nearby

An hour's drive west of the park, at the intersection of three U.S. highways, **Ely** (population 4,000) is the largest town for hours in every direction. It grew up in the second wave of the early Nevada mining boom, right at the optimistic turn of the 20th century. For 70 years copper kept the town in business, but when it ran out in the early 1980s, Ely declined fast. Then, in 1986, the National Park Service designated Great Basin National Park, and the town got a boost. Ely has since been rebuilt and revitalized, though it's kept a quirky, faded feel. If you want to stay much closer to the park, tiny **Baker** (population roughly 75) has far fewer amenities but is slowly reawakening. The cluster of homes and small businesses on Route 487 is about 5 miles from the Lehman Caves Visitor Center.

Baker

5 miles from the Great Basin Visitor Center.

Located just five miles from the park's entrance, Baker is basically Great Basin's front door. The tiny desert town has a lonesome, funky charm, and is anchored by a few small motels.

Just like much of rural Nevada, Baker has no transportation services and requires a long drive from pretty much everywhere. The first stop for many visitors is the **Great Basin Visitor Center,** which lies about 5 miles northwest.

VISITOR INFORMATION

Great Basin Business and Tourism Council. *www.greatbasinpark.com.*

Restaurants

The Baker's Bean

$ | **BAKERY** | Two professionally trained chefs, who also happen to be twin sisters, make all the sumptuous sweet and savory treats in this compact trailer of a coffee shop in downtown Baker. Their menu is small but excellent, with an emphasis on baked goods. **Known for:** giant and rich ice cream sandwiches; tasty breakfast sandwiches with homemade English muffins; good drip coffee and various espresso drinks. *Average main: $5 40 S. Baker Ave., Baker 719/237-5726 www.saltandsucre.com Closed Nov.–Apr.*

★ Kerouac's

$$ | **AMERICAN** | One of the best restaurants in this corner of rural Nevada can be found in an airy, historic building that resembles an old general store on the edge of town. Expect the same caliber of burgers and artisan pizzas you'd get in a hip urban eatery, as well as incredible cocktails and luscious desserts. **Known for:** everything made from scratch, including the hamburger buns and dough for Neapolitan-style pizzas; the full bar is also a local hangout; friendly, attentive service for dinner and weekend brunch. *Average main: $14 115 S. Baker Ave., Baker 775/234–7323 www.stargazernevada.com/eat-drink Closed mid-Oct.–mid-Apr. No lunch.*

Hotels

The Border Inn

$ | **HOTEL** | Located right on the border between Nevada and Utah on Route 50, the Border Inn is a reliable staple, with air-conditioned rooms, a restaurant, bar, grocery store, gas station, and small casino. **Pros:** open 24/7; low prices, with more amenities and rooms than other Baker motels; family-run business with friendly staff. **Cons:** rooms are simple and rustic; due to remote location, Wi-Fi and cell service can be iffy; a few miles farther from the park than Baker's other motels (though much closer than Ely offerings). *Rooms from: $75 U.S. 6/50, Baker 13 miles northeast of Great Basin National Park 775/234–7300 www.borderinncasino.com 29 rooms No meals.*

★ Hidden Canyon Retreat

$$$ | **B&B/INN** | The most luxurious lodging for hours in any direction, the large rooms here have a modern serenity to them and are surrounded on all sides by hundreds of acres of rugged, high-desert beauty. **Pros:** tucked into a canyon, the setting makes this feel like a true retreat; hot tub and pool are nice for unwinding; features an extensive market, with fresh produce, ready-to-eat meals, alcohol, and more. **Cons:** no cell reception and limited Wi-Fi; far from services and a 30-minute drive to Great Basin National Park; located down a dirt road (but it is well maintained). *Rooms from: $164 2000 Hidden Canyon Pkwy., Baker 775/234–7172*

www.hiddencanyonretreat.com 12 rooms Free Breakfast.

Stargazer Inn

$ | HOTEL | New life has been breathed into this small, quirky roadside motel, with vintage stargazing-theme art and tasteful bedspreads giving the otherwise plain, spotless rooms a rustic elegance. **Pros:** motel and small market are open year-round; great location in downtown Baker, just a few miles from the park; delicious restaurant and popular bar (seasonal). **Cons:** while rooms are comfortable, they are small and older; can fill up far in advance; some of the rooms are located on the other side of the street from motel office, about a 3-minute walk. *Rooms from: $85 115 S. Baker Ave., Baker 775/234–7323 www.stargazernevada.com 10 rooms No meals.*

Ely

66 miles northwest of Great Basin National Park.

Full of rugged Americana charm, Ely is a pleasant place to bed down for the night or even spend a few days. Visitors will find several restaurants and bars to choose from, as well as a large selection of hotels and motels, many with neon signs and low prices. While the community's outskirts look generic, downtown's murals and historic buildings make it a fascinating place to stroll.

Ely prides itself on its remote location, right on the eastern edge of a two-lane highway known as "The Loneliest Road." They only way to get here is to drive, as there's no bus or train service, and the closest airport is hours away.

VISITOR INFORMATION

White Pine County Tourism and Recreation Board. *Bristlecone Convention Center, 150 6th St., Ely 800/496–9350, 775/289–3720 www.elynevada.net.*

Sights

Cave Lake State Park

NATIONAL/STATE PARK | FAMILY | This is an idyllic spot 7,350 feet above sea level in the pine and juniper forest of the big Schell Creek Range that borders Ely to the east. You can spend a day fishing for rainbow and brown trout in the reservoir and a night sleeping under the stars. Arrive early; it gets crowded. Access may be restricted in winter. *15 miles southeast of Ely via U.S. 50/6/93, Great Basin National Park 775/296–1505 parks.nv.gov/parks/cave-lake $5.*

Ely Renaissance Village

MUSEUM VILLAGE | FAMILY | This tiny downtown "village" gives visitors a sense of what Ely looked like more than a 100 years ago. It features a cluster of small restored homes, each representing a different ethnicity of immigrants who came to this desert outpost around the turn of the 20th century. There are also re-creations of a miner's cabin, general store, and barn. The site is open Friday and Saturday (seasonally), and hosts occasional re-enactments and living history presentations. *400 Ely St., Ely www.elynvarts.com Closed late-Sept.–late May and Sun.–Thurs. in season.*

★ Nevada Northern Railway Museum

MUSEUM | FAMILY | The biggest attraction in Ely draws train aficionados from near and far. During the mining boom, the Nevada Northern Railroad connected East Ely, Ruth, and McGill to the transcontinental rail line in the northeast corner of the state. The whole operation is now a museum open year-round and watched over by its famed cat mascot, Dirt, who receives food and gifts from fans across the country. You can tour the depot, offices, warehouses, yard, engine houses, and repair shops. Catch a ride on one of the vintage locomotives, and get history lessons from enthusiastic guides along the way (check website for times). You can even stay overnight in a caboose or bunkhouse. ✉ *1100 Ave. A, Ely* ☎ *866/407–8326* 🌐 *www.nnry.com* 🎟 *$8 for museum, $31 for train ride (museum included)* ⏲ *Closed Tues. Sept.–June.*

U.S. 93 Scenic Byway

SCENIC DRIVE | The 68 miles between the park and Ely make a beautiful drive with diverse views of Nevada's paradoxical geography: dry deserts and lush mountains. You'll catch an occasional glimpse of a snake, perhaps a rattler, slithering on the road's shoulder, or a lizard sunning on a rock. Watch for deer. A straight drive to Ely takes a little more than an hour; if you have the time to take a dirt-road adventure, don't miss the Ward Charcoal Ovens or a peek at Cave Lake.

Restaurants

Cellblock Steakhouse

$$$ | **STEAKHOUSE** | The only fine dining in Ely, this low-lighted spot comes with a big helping of local color. Each table is its own "cell," complete with metal bars and old-timey photos on the wall—a whimsical spot to eat cowboy-size prime rib or bacon-wrapped filet mignon. **Known for:** all your favorite steak-house staples with cute, jail-themed names; crème brûlée and other desserts worth the calories; the fanciest place in Ely for a fun dinner. $ *Average main: $25* ✉ *211 5th St., Ely* ☎ *775/289–3033* 🌐 *www.jailhousecasino.com/dining.php* ⏲ *No lunch.*

Mr. Gino's Restaurant & Bar

$$ | **ITALIAN** | Located right downtown, this spacious spot serves up generous helpings of pasta, pizza, and other Italian favorites. Also offering desserts and a full bar, this is a classy yet casual spot to chill out after the long drive to Ely. **Known for:** local favorite; large portions; expansive menu and full bar. $ *Average main: $17* ✉ *484 Aultman St., Ely* ☎ *775/289–3540.*

Hotels

Hotel Nevada

$ | **HOTEL** | One of the oldest hotels in the state, this six-story local landmark dates from 1929 and towers over Ely's historic downtown. **Pros:** bursting with historic character; in the heart of downtown; updated rooms are light, airy, and comfortable. **Cons:** can fill up quickly during busy times; no pool, hot tub, or gym; older property means small rooms and bathrooms. $ *Rooms from:* ✉ *501 Aultman St., Ely* ☎ *775/289–6665, 888/406–3055* 🌐 *www.hotelnevada.com* *64 rooms* 🍽 *Free Breakfast.*

Jailhouse Motel and Casino

$ | **HOTEL** | This motel at Ely's main intersection was built near the town's old-time jail; the rooms are assigned cell numbers and there are prison bars around the booths at its fancy steak house. **Pros:** location in the center of town; on-site casino, two restaurants, and a bar; good value. **Cons:** smoke can waft from the casino adjacent to registration; not as charming as some historic options in the area; rooms are clean but no frills. $ *Rooms from: $65* ✉ *211 5th St., Ely* ☎ *775/289–3033, 800/841–5430* 🌐 *www.jailhousecasino.com* *60 rooms* 🍽 *No meals.*

Prospector Hotel & Gambling Hall

$ | **HOTEL** | One of the best bets in town, this comfortable hotel walks the line between classy and delightfully kitschy, with Western-theme rooms, on-site gambling, a pool, and a tasty Mexican restaurant. **Pros:** a good value, with quality that far surpasses many other local options; inviting, modern rooms; friendly staff. **Cons:** can book up quickly; not walking distance to downtown; having an in-house casino does not appeal to everyone. $ *Rooms from: $89* ✉ *1501 E. Aultman St., Ely* ☎ *775/289–8900, 800/750–0557* 🌐 *www.prospectorhotel.us* *61 rooms* 🍽 *No meals.*

Chapter 5

SALT LAKE CITY

Updated by
Andrew Collins

Sights ★★★★★ | Restaurants ★★★★★ | Hotels ★★★☆☆ | Shopping ★★★☆☆ | Nightlife ★★★★☆

WELCOME TO SALT LAKE CITY

TOP REASONS TO GO

★ **A downtown renaissance:** Venture into Salt Lake's vibrant downtown, with its respected theater scene, farm-to-table restaurants, craft breweries and coffeehouses, and the impressive City Creek Center retail plaza.

★ **Wander the Wasatch Front:** Lace up your hiking boots and enjoy the dramatic canyons on the city's east side.

★ **Catch the indie spirit:** This region, which has historically embraced chain franchises, has in recent years blossomed with hip independently owned businesses.

★ **Shore adventures:** Explore the city's namesake, the Great Salt Lake, by car, on foot, or by bicycle. If you're here in the summer, try floating off the beaches at Antelope Island—the water is so salty it's impossible to sink.

★ **Pow-pow-powder:** Experience the "greatest snow on earth" within an hour's drive of the airport at one of nine renowned ski resorts.

1 **Temple Square.** The hub of the Church of Jesus Christ of Latter-day Saints is home to both the Salt Lake Temple and Tabernacle.

2 **Downtown and Central City.** Salt Lake City's core is downtown, a quadrant containing most of the city's top hotels, and a slew of theaters, restaurants, and bars.

3 **Capitol Hill and the Avenues.** Surrounding the capitol on all sides are residential areas known for historic houses.

4 **East Side and Sugar House.** This scenic area of the city hugs up against the dramatic Wasatch Range.

5 **Great Salt Lake and West Side.** Great Salt Lake is the remnant of the ancient Bonneville Lake that covered much of the northern half of Utah.

6 **Midvalley and South Valley.** The Midvalley and South Valley suburbs contain mostly bedroom communities.

7 **Little Cottonwood Canyon.** This smaller canyon to the south is arguably even more prestigious among skiers.

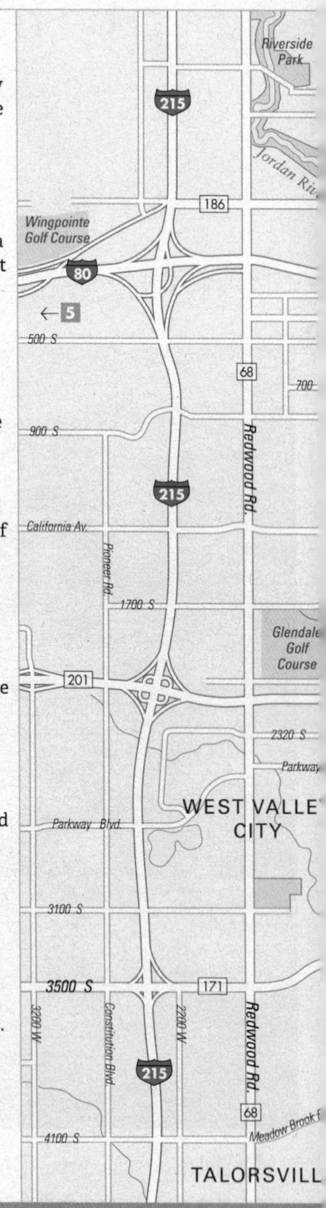

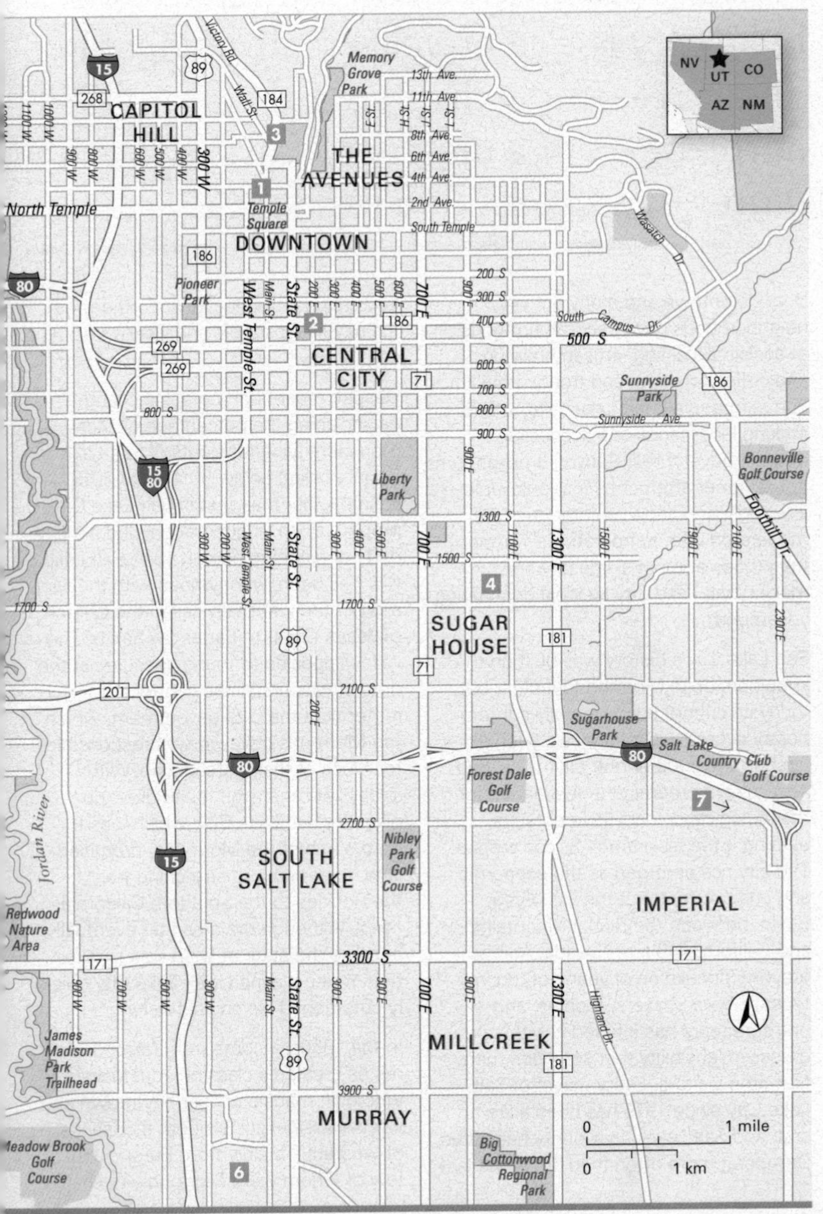
NV
UT
CO
AZ
NM
CAPITOL HILL
THE AVENUES
DOWNTOWN
CENTRAL CITY
SUGAR HOUSE
SOUTH SALT LAKE
IMPERIAL
MILLCREEK
MURRAY
Memory Grove Park
Temple Square
Pioneer Park
Liberty Park
Sunnyside Park
Bonneville Golf Course
Sugarhouse Park
Salt Lake Country Club Golf Course
Forest Dale Golf Course
Nibley Park Golf Course
Redwood Nature Area
James Madison Park Trailhead
Meadow Brook Golf Course
Big Cottonwood Regional Park
Jordan River
Victory Rd.
Wall St.
North Temple
South Temple
13th Ave.
11th Ave.
8th Ave.
6th Ave.
4th Ave.
2nd Ave.
E St.
H St.
West Temple St.
Main St.
State St.
700 E
900 E
1100 E
1300 E
1500 E
1900 E
2100 E
2300 E
300 W
400 W
500 W
600 W
800 W
900 W
1000 W
1100 W
200 E
300 E
400 E
500 E
600 E
200 W
700 W
200 S
300 S
400 S
500 S
600 S
700 S
800 S
900 S
1300 S
1500 S
1700 S
2100 S
2700 S
3300 S
3900 S
South Campus Dr.
Wasatch Dr.
Sunnyside Ave.
Foothill Dr.
Highland Dr.
15
80
89
71
181
171
184
186
201
268
269
1
2
3
4
6
7
0
1 mile
1 km

Nestled at the foot of the rugged Wasatch Mountains and extending to the south shore of the Great Salt Lake, Salt Lake City is a relatively small, navigable, and increasingly diverse and vibrant city at the heart of a metropolitan area with more than 1.25 million residents.

Both downtown and many outlying neighborhoods have become hot beds of acclaimed dining, artisan brewing and coffee-roasting, and trendy retail. The surrounding Salt Lake Valley offers striking landscapes and accessible outdoor adventures. Canyon breezes turn hot summer afternoons into enjoyable evenings, and snowy winter days are moderated with temperatures warmer than those at most ski destinations, making Salt Lake City an ideal destination year-round.

Salt Lake City's history was built on the shoulders of its Mormon founders, but today its culture draws equally contemporary events and influences, such as hosting the 2002 Winter Olympics, and becoming a preeminent destination for technological or innovative pursuits, earning it the nickname "Silicon Slopes." The city has emerged as the economic and cultural center of the vast Great Basin, between the Rocky Mountains and California's Sierra Nevada. And its growing population of young outdoorsy types, artists, makers, foodies, and entrepreneurs has infused it with a progressive sensibility that surprises many first-time visitors. Every mayor of Salt Lake City since 1976 has been a Democrat, and Salt Lake City County has voted Democrat more often than not in the last few presidential elections. Furthermore, the city has a sizable and visible LGBTQ community.

Despite recent demographic changes, including the percentage of Mormon-identifying residents of Salt Lake County falling below 50% as of 2018 (it's far lower than that in Salt Lake City proper), since Brigham Young led his first party of pioneers here in 1847, Salt Lake City has been synonymous with the Mormon Church, formally called the Church of Jesus Christ of Latter-day Saints. The valley appealed to Young because, at the time, it was under the control of Mexico rather than the U.S. government, which the Mormons believed was responsible for much of their persecution. Within days of his arrival, Young drew up plans for Salt Lake City, which was to be the hub of the Mormons' promised land, a vast empire stretching from the Rockies to the Southern California coast. Although the area that eventually became the state of Utah was smaller than Young planned, Salt Lake City quickly outstripped his original vision.

In the 1860s, income from railroads and mines created a class of industrialists who built mansions near downtown and whose businesses brought thousands of workers—mainly from Europe and few of whom were Mormon—to Utah

Territory. By the time Utah became a state in 1896, Salt Lake was a thriving city. Although the majority of the city was members of the Church of Jesus Christ of Latter-day Saints, it claimed a healthy mix of Protestant, Catholic, and Jewish citizens. The Church of Jesus Christ of Latter-day Saints's presence is still evident, as both its headquarters and the Tabernacle, home to the world-famous Tabernacle Choir at Temple Square, call Temple Square home.

Today the city is an important center for business, medicine, education, and technology, and it's a major worldwide hub of Delta Airlines. A growing commitment to the arts from both the public and private sector has led to a booming cultural scene, and sports fans appreciate the presence of two major-league franchises—basketball's Utah Jazz and soccer's Real Salt Lake.

Planning

When to Go

Spring and fall are the best times to visit, as cooler afternoons give way to idyllic breezy evenings. Summertime high temperatures average more than 90° (June–August), with a few days above 100° each month. Winters bring snow, but abundant sunshine melts it quickly in the valley. If your plans include trips to Park City or the Cottonwood Canyons, follow weather forecasts closely, because a fluffy 6-inch snowfall in the city will often be accompanied by 3 to 5 feet "up the hill." Expect larger crowds at the airport and higher rates at hotels and resorts near the ski slopes on winter weekends, particularly around winter holidays, as well as during the Sundance Film Festival.

Getting Here and Around

AIR

For a relatively small city, Salt Lake is served by a large airport, which is one of the major hubs of Delta Airlines, which offers direct flights to most major U.S. cities and a number of international ones. Additionally, most other U.S. airlines and a couple of international ones (AeroMexico, KLM) fly to Salt Lake.

AIRPORT TRANSFERS

Salt Lake City International Airport is just 7 miles northwest of downtown via I–80, or you can take North Temple, which leads to the city center. A taxi or rideshare, such as Uber or Lyft, from the airport to town costs about $21. The Utah Transit Authority (UTA) operates TRAX light-rail to and from the airport in less than 30 minutes for $2.50 each way.

CAR

Although traffic has increased a bit as Salt Lake continues to grow, it's still comparatively less daunting than in most U.S. cities. On the whole, it's an easy city to explore by car. Free or inexpensive parking is easy to find in most neighborhoods, and even downtown garages charge a fraction of what you'll pay in many large cities. Finding your way around Salt Lake City is easy as the city is laid out on an orthogonal grid, but keep in mind that city blocks are longer than in many other cities. You can rent from all the major agencies at the Salt Lake City airport, but because it's a regional hub for travelers to such disparate destinations as Park City and Yellowstone National Park, you do need to reserve a car in advance during the busy summer months and during the winter ski season.

PUBLIC TRANSPORT

Salt Lake has a very workable public transportation system, although it's used more by locals than visitors. One feature that even tourists rely heavily on is the Free Fare Zone for travel by bus within a roughly 36-square-block area downtown and on Capitol Hill.

Hotels

Relatively generic chain hotels in every price range dominate the lodging landscape throughout Salt Lake, and especially in the suburbs beyond, notable exceptions include the historic Peery and Carlton hotels, a smattering of B&Bs, and some distinctive properties out in the ski areas. Hotels here cater to skiers in winter months, and many offer packages that include tickets, transportation, and rentals, as well as knowledgeable staff who often head to the slopes when they're not at work. Most of the hotels are concentrated in the downtown area and near the airport.

Hotel reviews have been shortened. For full information, visit Fodors.com.

What It Costs

$	$$	$$$	$$$$
HOTELS			
under $125	$125–$175	$176–$225	over $225

Restaurants

Ever since the 2002 Winter Olympics cast Salt Lake City in a new, contemporary, more diverse light, growing numbers of hip chef-driven eateries specializing in seasonal, locally sourced fare and myriad varieties of international fare have opened, many of these in the downtown core but increasingly in neighborhoods like 9th and 9th, Sugar House, and Granary/Ballpark. A number of old-school establishments still thrive and enjoy a loyal following among long-time locals, but for the most part, creativity and locavorism rule the scene. And despite Salt Lake's infamously complicated history with drinking laws, the city has come around in recent years, with most newer restaurants offering carefully curated wine lists and a good selection of craft beers and spirits (many of these produced in Utah).

Restaurant reviews have been shortened. For full information, visit Fodors.com.

What It Costs

$	$$	$$$	$$$$
RESTAURANTS			
under $16	$16–$22	$23–$30	over $30

Tours

City Sights (AKA Salt Lake City Tours)
BUS TOURS | A four-hour, 20-mile bus tour of the city includes dozens of major sights and many interesting lesser-known places you wouldn't necessarily find on your own, with a 30-minute organ recital at the Tabernacle and a stop for lunch in Brigham Young's Lion House. A 4½-hour tour also includes a Tabernacle Choir at Temple Square concert or rehearsal. A few other tours cover sights outside the city. ☎ *801/531–1001* 🌐 *www.saltlakecity-tours.org* 🎫 *From $49.*

★ **Preservation Utah**
WALKING TOURS | Tours led by knowledgeable guides from nonprofit Preservation Utah include a walking tour of the Marmalade Historic District, the Kearns Mansion, McCune Mansion, and the City and County Building. It's a good idea to book several days in advance. You can also explore on your own using the organization's app, "Utah Heritage Walks." ✉ *Memory Grove Park, 375 N. Canyon Rd., Capitol Hill* ☎ *801/533–0858* 🌐 *www.preservationutah.org* 🎫 *From $10.*

Visitor Information

CONTACTS Salt Lake Convention and Visitors Bureau. ✉ *90 S. West Temple, Downtown* ☎ *801/534–4900, 800/541–4955* 🌐 *www.visitsaltlake.com.*

Temple Square

When Mormon pioneer and leader Brigham Young first entered the Salt Lake Valley, he chose this spot at the mouth of City Creek Canyon for the headquarters of the Church of Jesus Christ of Latter-day Saints, a role it maintains to this day. The buildings in Temple Square vary in age, from the Tabernacle constructed in the 1860s to the Conference Center constructed in 2000. Perhaps the most striking aspect of the Square is the attention to landscaping, which turns the heart of downtown Salt Lake City into a year-round oasis. The Church takes particular pride in its Christmas decorations, which make a nighttime downtown stroll, or horse-and-buggy ride, a must on December calendars.

The Salt Lake Temple and parts of Temple Square are currently undergoing a four-year renovation and restoration. The Temple and grounds immediately surrounding it will be under construction until 2024.

Sights

Beehive House
HOUSE | Brigham Young's home was constructed in 1854 and is topped with a replica of a beehive, symbolizing industry. Inside are many original furnishings; a tour of the interior will give you a fascinating glimpse of upper-class 19th-century life. ✉ *67 E. South Temple, Temple Square* ☎ *801/240–2681* 🌐 *history.churchofjesuschrist.org* ⏲ *Closed Sun.*

Church of Jesus Christ of Latter-day Saints Conference Center
CONVENTION CENTER | Completed in 2000, this massive center features a 21,000-seat auditorium with a 7,708-pipe organ and a 900-seat theater. Equally impressive are the rooftop gardens landscaped with native plants and streams to mirror the surrounding mountains. Visitors can find flexible tour times that last roughly 45 minutes, but all guests must be accompanied by a guide. The Center is home to the biannual General Conference and regular concerts by the Tabernacle Choir at Temple Square. ✉ *60 W. North Temple, Temple Square* ☎ *801/240–0075* 🌐 *www.templesquare.com/explore.*

Family History Library
LIBRARY | FAMILY | This four-story library houses the world's largest collection of genealogical data, including books, maps, and census information. Mormons and non-Mormons alike come here to research their family history. ✉ *35 N. West Temple, Temple Square* ☎ *801/240–6996* 🌐 *www.familysearch.org/locations* ⏲ *Closed Sun.*

Joseph Smith Memorial Building
HISTORIC SITE | Previously the Hotel Utah, this stately 1911 building is now owned and operated by the Church of Jesus Christ of Latter-day Saints. Inside you can learn how to do genealogical research online at the FamilySearch Center (no charge; volunteers will assist you) or watch an hour-long film about the Church's teaching of how Jesus Christ appeared in the western hemisphere after his resurrection. The center has two restaurants and an elegantly restored lobby. Upstairs is the 1920 census and 70,000 volumes of personal histories of the faithful. ✉ *15 E. South Temple, Temple Square* ☎ *801/531–1000* 🌐 *www.templesquare.com/explore* ⏲ *Closed Sun.*

CAPITOL HILL
TEMPLE SQUARE
Main Street Plaza
DOWNTOWN
Pioneer Park
Washington Square
Library Square
THE GRANARY
CENTRAL NINTH
400 North
300 North
North Temple
South Temple
North Addressing
South Addressing
200 South
300 South
400 South
500 South
600 South
700 South
800 South
900 South
100 South
7th Avenue
4th Avenue
3rd Avenue
2nd Avenue
1st Avenue
A Street
B Street
C Street
600 West
400 West
300 West
200 West
700 West
West Temple
Main Street
State Street
200 East
300 East
400 East
West Addressing
East Addressing
Hubbard Ave.
Belmont Avenue
Williams Ave.
Herbert Avenue
Fremont Ave.
Hampton Ave.
Paxton Avenue
Paxton Ave.
Lucy Avenue
Kelsey Ave.
Edith Avenue
1300 South
Major Street
Roberta Street
15
0
1,000ft
0
200m
KEY
Exploring Sights
Restaurants
Quick Bites
Hotels

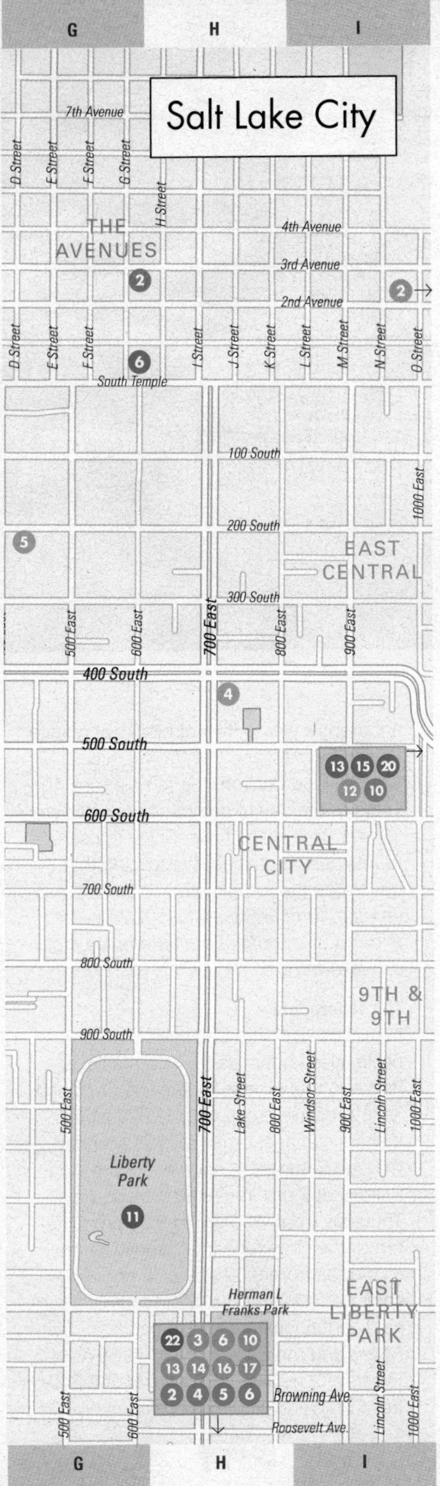

Sights

1 Antelope Island State Park **A1**
2 Beehive House........... **E3**
3 Cathedral of the Madeleine................ **F3**
4 Church of Jesus Christ of Latter-day Saints Conference Center **D2**
5 Family History Library.................... **D2**
6 Governor's Mansion.... **G3**
7 Great Salt Lake State Park **A4**
8 Joseph Smith Memorial Building....... **E3**
9 Land Cruiser Heritage Museum **B5**
10 The Leonardo **F5**
11 Liberty Park............. **G8**
12 Museum of Church History and Art.......... **D2**
13 Natural History Museum of Utah..........**I5**
14 Pioneer Memorial Museum **E1**
15 Red Butte Garden and Arboretum.................**I5**
16 Salt Lake City Public Library **F5**
17 Salt Lake Temple........ **D2**
18 The Tabernacle **D2**
19 Temple Square Visitors' Center.......... **D2**
20 This Is The Place Heritage Park **I5**
21 Utah State Capitol **E1**
22 Wheeler Historic Farm...................... **H9**

Restaurants

1 The Copper Onion **E4**
2 Cucina......................**I2**
3 Feldman's Deli........... **H9**
4 Hires Big H **H5**
5 HSL........................ **G4**
6 Lone Star Taqueria **H9**
7 Nomad Eatery............**C9**
8 Oquirrh.................... **F3**
9 Pretty Bird Chicken...... **E3**
10 Provisions **H9**
11 Red Iguana **A2**
12 Ruth's Diner................**I5**
13 Shallow Shaft **H9**
14 Steak Pit **H9**
15 Sweet Lake Biscuits & Limeade **D9**
16 Swen's **H9**
17 Table X **H9**

Quick Bites

1 Campos Coffee SLC..... **E4**
2 Publik Coffee Roasters **G2**

Hotels

1 AC Hotel by Marriott Salt Lake City Downtown................**C4**
2 Alta Lodge **H9**
3 Carlton Hotel **E3**
4 Castle Creek Inn **H9**
5 Cliff Lodge............... **H9**
6 Hyatt Place Salt Lake City–Cottonwood **H9**
7 Inn on the Hill.............**E2**
8 Kimpton Hotel Monaco Salt Lake City............ **D4**
9 Peery Hotel, Tapestry Collection by Hilton..................... **D4**
10 Salt Lake City Marriott University Park............**I5**

The iconic Salt Lake Temple in Temple Square took 40 years to build.

Museum of Church History and Art

MUSEUM | Here you can view a variety of artifacts and works of art relating to the history and doctrine of the Mormon faith, including personal belongings of church leaders Joseph Smith and Brigham Young. There are also samples of Mormon coins and scrip used as standard currency in Utah during the 1800s, and beautiful examples of quilting, embroidery, and other handicrafts. Upstairs galleries exhibit religious and secular works by Mormon artists from all over the world. ✉ *45 N. West Temple, Temple Square* ☎ *801/240–3310* 🌐 *history.churchofjesuschrist.org* ⏲ *Closed Sun.*

★ Salt Lake Temple

FOUNTAIN | Although the interior is closed as of this writing for renovation through 2024, this centerpiece and spiritual capital of the Church of Jesus Christ of Latter-day Saints is a sacred pilgrimage destination for members of the faith. Brigham Young chose this spot for a temple as soon as he arrived in the Salt Lake Valley in 1847, but work on the building didn't begin for another six years. Built of blocks of granite hauled by oxen and train from Little Cottonwood Canyon, the Temple took 40 years to the day to complete. Its walls are 16 feet thick at the base. Enjoy the serene fountains and pristine landscaping that decorates the Temple area. ✉ *50 N. West Temple, Temple Square* ☎ *801/240–2640* 🌐 *www.churchofjesuschristtemples.org/salt-lake-temple.*

The Tabernacle

RELIGIOUS SITE | The Salt Lake City Tabernacle, also known as the Tabernacle, is home to the famous Tabernacle Choir and its impressive organ with 11,623 pipes. Visitors can hear organ recitals Monday through Saturday at noon and 2 pm, and Sunday at 2 pm. You're also welcome Thursday from 7:30 pm to 9:30 pm to listen to the choir rehearse Sunday hymns, as well as from 9:30 am to 10 am as the choir performs for the world's longest-running continuous network broadcast, *Music and the Spoken Word.* ✉ *50 N. West Temple, Temple Square* ☎ *801/240–2534* 🌐 *www.templesquare.com.*

Temple Square Visitors' Center

INFO CENTER | The history of the Mormon Church and the Mormon pioneers' trek to Utah is outlined in a visitor center on the north side of Temple Square (50 W. North Temple). Diligent missionaries stand by to offer tours and answer questions. ✉ *Temple Sq., Salt Lake City* ☎ *801/240–2534* 🌐 *www.templesquare.com.*

Downtown and Central City

Although businesses and homes stretch in all directions, Downtown's core is a compact, several-block area that contains most of the city's most prominent hotels, plus a good number of high-profile restaurants, historic buildings, theaters, and bars. Although it sounds like it might just be another name for downtown, Central City is a larger quadrant that extends east and south from Downtown, as far as 1300 East and 1300 South. This area contains a mix of residential and commercial pockets and some charming shopping and eating districts, such as Trolley Square and 9th and 9th, and also gracious Liberty Park. Extending south from Downtown along the Main Street and State Street corridor, you'll find some more recently emerging hives of dining as well as craft breweries and distilleries, including the Granary/Ballpark area.

Sights

Land Cruiser Heritage Museum

MUSEUM | Nearly 100 models of Toyota Land Cruisers, some dating back to the early '50s, fill this quirky museum that has something of a cult following among fans of old autos and four-wheel vehicle enthusiasts. In a rugged state like Utah, these rugged SUVs have quite a fan base, but folks come from all over the world, admiring the extensive collection of memorabilia, scale models, artwork, and a very cool 10-by-13-foot 3D map of the state of Utah. ✉ *470 W. 600 S, Salt Lake City* ☎ *505/615–5470* 🌐 *www.landcruiserhm.com* 🎟 *$15* ⏲ *Closed Sun.–Tues.*

The Leonardo

MUSEUM | **FAMILY** | Salt Lake's only museum devoted to the convergence of science, art, and technology hosts large-scale national touring exhibits as well as hands-on permanent exhibits dedicated to inspiring the imaginations of children. In this former library building, you'll be greeted by a main-floor lab space where revolving artists-in-residence offer a variety of free programs where kids can sculpt with clay, draw, design, or write. Head upstairs to the workshop, where volunteers help you build with repurposed household objects and deconstruct electronics. ✉ *209 E. 500 S, Downtown* ☎ *801/531–9800* 🌐 *www.theleonardo.org* 🎟 *$13; more for special exhibits.*

★ **Salt Lake City Public Library**

BUILDING | **FAMILY** | Designed by Moshe Safdie and built in 2003, this spectacular contemporary structure has become the city's cultural center and one of the country's most architecturally noteworthy libraries. Inspired by the Roman Coliseum, it features a six-story walkable wall that serves as both sculpture and function, allowing for great views and a path up the building. From the rooftop garden you get a 360-degree view of the valley and mountains. The on-site branch of Salt Lake Roasting Co. coffeehouse, the Hemingway Cafe, a handful of shops, a writing center, and a public radio station provide ways to spend the entire day here. Kids can fall in love with reading in the Crystal Cave and Treehouse Room in the huge children's section. There are several other libraries in the system, including the Tudor-style Sprague Library that opened in 1928 in the city's popular Sugar House neighborhood. ✉ *210 E. 400 S, Downtown* ☎ *801/524–8200* 🌐 *www.slcpl.org.*

The Salt Lake City Public Library was inspired by the Roman Colosseum.

Restaurants

★ The Copper Onion

$$ | **MODERN AMERICAN** | Celebrated chef-owner Chef Ryan Lowder brings joy with the basics—artful salads, house-made pastas, and charcuterie—and then dazzles with mouthwatering locally sourced dishes, from Cast Iron Mary's Chicken to rainbow trout with charred lemon and Greek yogurt. Stop in at this chic modern downtown bistro before or after a film, gallery tour, or live theater on Salt Lake's Broadway. **Known for:** cavatelli pasta with rich pork ragu; selection of Amari and after-dinner drinks; Valrhona chocolate pudding with sea salt and olive oil. *Average main: $22* *111 E. Broadway, Downtown* *801/355–3282* *www.thecopperonion.com* *No lunch weekdays.*

Hires Big H

$ | **BURGER** | **FAMILY** | A family tradition in Salt Lake since 1959, this old-school burger and shakes joint with curbside car service elevates traditional diner favorites by using fresh, local products prepared in-house. Inside the renovated dining room, root-beer floats are a staple, as are "H" burgers such as the New York H, Canadian H, and Mountain H, all of which pair fresh patties, tasty buns, and the owner's proprietary fry sauce (a Utah staple) with a variety of condiments. **Known for:** retro-style car-side service; frosted root beer mugs; fry sauce. *Average main: $8* *425 S. 700 E, Downtown* *801/364–4582* *www.hiresbigh.com* *Closed Sun.*

★ HSL

$$$$ | **MODERN AMERICAN** | On the east edge of downtown and within a short, pretty stroll of the Avenues and Capitol Hill, this outpost of the original, nationally acclaimed Handle restaurant in Park City turns heads with its stunning plated, locavore-driven cuisine and a fetching interior with marble-top tables, a wood-beam ceiling, and a gleaming, tiled open kitchen. What's served on any given night varies according to what's in season, but you might encounter truffled agnolotti

pasta filled with Swiss chard, corn, and goat's whey cream, or slow-cooked pork shank with carrot-frisee salad, whipped ranch dressing, and apple butter. **Known for:** artful, Instagram-worthy food; exquisitely curated spirits, wine, and beer list; roasted-miso chess pie with lemongrass ice cream. *Average main: $33 ✉ 418 E. 200 S, Salt Lake City ☎ 801/539–9999 🌐 www.hslrestaurant.com ⏲ Closed Sun.–Tues.*

★ Oquirrh

$$$ | **MODERN AMERICAN** | An unprepossessing neighborhood restaurant near the leafy Avenues district, Oquirrh (rhymes with "poker") is named for the snowcapped mountain range west of Downtown and focuses on seasonal fare with locally sourced ingredients. Boldly flavored dishes like spaghetti with butter-poached lobster and curried lamb shank with garam masala–roasted vegetables are presented artfully on handmade stoneware in an intimate, art-filled dining room. **Known for:** beef tartare with fermented vegetables; excellent French- and West Coast–centric wine selection; Sunday brunch. *Average main: $28 ✉ 368 E. 100 S, Salt Lake City ☎ 801/359–0426 🌐 www.oquirrhslc.com ⏲ Closed Mon. and Tues. No lunch.*

Pretty Bird Chicken

$ | **AMERICAN** | As its name hints, this usually packed Downtown fast-casual eatery with counter service and a small seating area specializes in poultry, and the menu couldn't be simpler. Pick your spice level (from medium to the excruciatingly fiery "hot behind"), choose either quarter bird or a boneless-chicken sandwich, and add some sides if you'd like (crinkle-cut fries, cider slaw, pickles). **Known for:** in midst of Downtown shopping and theater scene; astoundingly spicy fried chicken (as requested); day-glo purple cider slaw. *Average main: $12 ✉ 146 S. Regent St., Salt Lake City 🌐 www.prettybirdchicken.com.*

★ Red Iguana

$$ | **MEXICAN** | Visitors are sometimes taken aback to find stunningly authentic, richly flavorful house-made moles, chile verde, carnitas, and other self-described "killer Mexican" dishes in Salt Lake City, and especially in a modest old building on the other side of I–15 from Downtown. But the lines out the door attest to the longstanding adoration of the Red Iguana, which in addition to doling out great food also serves first-rate premium margaritas, good Mexican beers, and delicious and free salsa and chips. **Known for:** chilaquiles for breakfast; richly complex turkey and mole dishes; fried ice cream with shredded coconut and cinnamon-sugar. *Average main: $16 ✉ 736 W. North Temple, Downtown ☎ 801/322–1489 🌐 www.rediguana.com.*

Sweet Lake Biscuits & Limeade

$ | **SOUTHERN** | This super-casual café with a smattering of sidewalk tables serves up heavenly biscuits in an assortment of ways, from blueberry-biscuit pudding French toast to fried chicken biscuit sandwiches with spicy pickles and mustard. Head to the refreshment stand at one end of the dining room to order a refreshing raspberry, habanero, or mint limeade. **Known for:** limeades with rotating seasonal flavors; biscuit-dough breakfast pizzas; strawberry "tall cake" with fresh cream. *Average main: $12 ✉ 54 W. 1700 S, Salt Lake City ☎ 801/953–1978 🌐 www.sweetlakefresh.com ⏲ No dinner.*

Coffee and Quick Bites

★ Campos Coffee SLC

$ | **CAFÉ** | This airy, plant-filled, hipster-approved coffeehouse and daytime eatery tucked down a side street near the Gallivan Center is where you should go when you're seeking an alternative to the lame or overpriced breakfast at your Downtown hotel. The morning menu here is terrific, featuring ginger oatmeal with coconut creme, Idaho trout eggs Benedict, and exceptional coffees and Smith-brand teas. **Known for:** smoked-salmon toast with caper cream cheese; exceptional single-origin coffees; build your own mimosas. *$ Average main: $11 ✉ 228 S. Edison St., Downtown ☎ 801/953–1512 🌐 us.camposcoffee.com ⊗ No dinner.*

Hotels

★ AC Hotel by Marriott Salt Lake City Downtown

$$ | HOTEL | Across from the convention center and Vivint Arena, this dapper midsize property—part of Marriott's hip AC boutique brand—stands out for its smartly designed rooms, each with plush duvets and linens, 55-inch flat-screen TVs, and bathrooms with rainfall showers, as well as a 24-hour gym and a spacious lobby with high ceilings and comfy chairs you can actually enjoy sitting in. **Pros:** many restaurants and bars within walking distance; airy, stylish rooms; nice restaurant and bar on-site. **Cons:** busy downtown location; gym overlooks parking lot; fills up during conventions. *$ Rooms from: $169 ✉ 225 W. 200 S, Downtown ☎ 385/722–9600 🌐 www.marriott.com 🛏 164 rooms 🍽 No meals.*

Carlton Hotel

$ | HOTEL | An absolute steal on the quieter eastern side of Downtown and Temple Square, this atmospheric 1920s hotel with a gorgeous brick exterior has remained resolutely old-fashioned, offering few frills but plenty of value, especially in the spacious suites. **Pros:** excellent Downtown location; friendly service; made-to-order breakfast is quite good. **Cons:** some rooms are small; partly hemmed in by high-rises and a parking garage; no gym. *$ Rooms from: $89 ✉ 140 E. South Temple, Downtown ☎ 801/355–3418 🛏 25 rooms 🍽 Free breakfast.*

★ Kimpton Hotel Monaco Salt Lake City

$$$ | HOTEL | This swank hotel resides in an ornate 14-story former bank tower (built in 1924), distinguished by a sophisticated, eclectic, and upbeat interior design and rooms offering extra touches like big-fringed ottomans, oversize framed mirrors, and lots of pillows. **Pros:** sparkling design, inside and out; exceptional restaurant; short walk to many fun bars and eateries. **Cons:** parking is $26 nightly; in a busy Downtown location; some rooms have street noise. *$ Rooms from: $180 ✉ 15 W. 200 S, Downtown ☎ 801/595–0000, 800/805–1801 🌐 www.monaco-saltlakecity.com 🛏 223 rooms 🍽 No meals.*

Peery Hotel, Tapestry Collection by Hilton

$$$ | HOTEL | Since becoming part of Hilton's indie-spirited Tapestry collection, this elegant 1910 classic hotel with a distinctive gray exterior has undergone a complete top-to-bottom renovation, with a substantial increase in room rates to go with it. **Pros:** well-maintained and charmingly historic; two full-service restaurants on-site; steps from several good bars and eateries. **Cons:** receives noise from traffic and nearby bars; $12 self-parking; quirky heating and AC system. *$ Rooms from: $185 ✉ 110 W. Broadway, Downtown ☎ 801/521–4300 🌐 www.peeryhotel.com 🛏 73 rooms 🍽 No meals.*

Nightlife

BARS AND LOUNGES

★ Beehive Distilling

BARS/PUBS | At the forefront of South Salt Lake's burgeoning spirits and craft brewing scene, this acclaimed small-batch gin and vodka producer has a stylish, post-industrial bar where you can sample expertly crafted cocktails and nibble on tasty apps and sandwiches. Serious enthusiasts might want to book one of Beehive's occasional behind-the-scenes tours. *✉ 2245 S. West Temple ☎ 801/326–3913 🌐 www.beehivedistilling.com ☞ Closed Sun.*

★ Bodega + The Rest

BARS/PUBS | There's more than meets the eye to this modest-looking Downtown bar with pinball machines and cheap drinks. A locked door leads to "the Rest," a basement speakeasy decorated with quirky framed portraits, mounted animals, and odd bric-a-brac. Here you'll discover well-curated menus of creative cocktails and well-prepared modern American food. Reservations are advised for the speakeasy. ✉ *331 S. Main St., Salt Lake City* ☎ *801/532–4042* 🌐 *www.bodegaslc.com* ☞ *Closed Sun. and Mon.*

BREWPUBS AND MICROBREWERIES

★ Fisher Brewing Company

BREWPUBS/BEER GARDENS | Local food trucks dispense tasty eats at this lively craft brewery and beer garden with a dog-friendly patio. The saison and cream ale are among the standout offerings. ✉ *320 W. 800 S* ☎ *801/487–2337* 🌐 *www.fisherbeer.com.*

Squatters Pub Brewery

BREWPUBS/BEER GARDENS | Arguably Utah's most famous microbrewery, Squatters' flagship downtown pub is lined with well-deserved awards from the Great American Beer Festival and World Beer Cup. The pub has friendly staff and an easygoing, casual vibe, although it can get crowded on weekends and when there are conventions in town. ✉ *147 W. Broadway, Downtown* ☎ *801/363–2739* 🌐 *www.squatters.com.*

Shopping

ART GALLERIES

★ Phillips Gallery

ART GALLERIES | The highly respected, longest-running gallery in Utah features three floors of local and regional artists' work, including mixed media, paintings, and sculptures. Check out the sculptures on the rooftop garden. ✉ *444 E. 200 S, Downtown* ☎ *801/364–8284* 🌐 *www.phillips-gallery.com.*

BOOKS

★ Weller Book Works

BOOKS/STATIONERY | The name of this store has been synonymous with independent book sales in Salt Lake City since 1929. Catherine and Tony Weller are the third generation to operate this bookstore, which relocated to the historic former train yard in 2012. Bibliophiles will love the space and the helpful and knowledgeable staff. ✉ *607 Trolley Sq., East Side* ☎ *801/328–2586* 🌐 *www.wellerbookworks.com.*

FOOD

Goodly Cookies

FOOD/CANDY | It's all about the cookie at this delightful little shop whose best sellers include the cobbler-inspired Peachy Keen, the gooey Choc PB Love, and the ethereal White Chocolate Raspberry Delight. But wait, there's more: the store partners with locally renowned Howdy Homemade to produce decadent cookie–ice cream sandwiches. ✉ *432 S. 900 E, Salt Lake City* ☎ *801/784–4848* 🌐 *www.goodlycookies.com.*

Capitol Hill and the Avenues

These picturesque, historic neighborhoods overlook the city from the foothills north of Downtown. Two days after entering the future Salt Lake City, Brigham Young brought his fellow religious leaders to the summit of the most prominent hill here, which he named Ensign Peak, to plan out their new home. New arrivals built sod homes into the hillside of what is now the Avenues. Two-room log cabins and adobe houses dotted the area. Meanwhile, on the western slope of the hill, fruit and nut trees were planted. Some still remain, as does a neighborhood known as Marmalade, with streets named Apricot, Quince, and Almond.

With the coming of the railroad came Victorian homes. The city's rich and prominent families built mansions along South Temple. As the city has grown over the years, wealthy citizens have continued to live close to the city but farther up the hill where the views of the valley are better. Since the early 1970s the lower Avenues has seen an influx of residents interested in restoring the older homes, adding diversity and energy to this evolving community.

The state capitol, for which Capitol Hill is named, was completed in 1915. State offices flank the capitol on three sides. City Creek Canyon forms its eastern boundary. The Avenues denotes the larger neighborhood along the foothills, north of South Temple, extending from Capitol Hill east to the University of Utah.

Sights

Cathedral of the Madeleine

BUILDING | Although the Salt Lake Temple just to the west is Salt Lake's most prominent religious landmark, this 1909 cathedral stands high above the city's north side and is a stunning house of worship in its own right. The exterior sports gargoyles, and its Gothic interior showcases bright frescoes, intricate wood carvings, and a 4,066-pipe organ. The highly regarded Madeleine children's choir gives concerts regularly (especially during the Christmas season). ✉ *331 E. South Temple, The Avenues* ☎ *801/328–8941* 🌐 *www.utcotm.org.*

Governor's Mansion

HISTORIC SITE | Built by silver-mining tycoon Thomas Kearns in 1902, this limestone structure—reminiscent of a French château with all its turrets and balconies—is now the official residence of Utah's governor. In its early days the mansion was visited by President Theodore Roosevelt and other dignitaries from around the world. The mansion was faithfully restored after Christmas lights caused a fire in 1993 that destroyed much of the interior. Free hour-long tours are given by Preservation Utah from June through August and December on Thursday afternoons, by appointment only (call at least 24 hours in advance). ✉ *603 E. South Temple, The Avenues* ☎ *801/533–0858* 🌐 *governor.utah.gov/mansion.*

Pioneer Memorial Museum

MUSEUM | Covering the pioneer era from the departure of the Mormons from Nauvoo, Illinois, to the hammering of the Golden Spike, this massive collection traces the history of pioneer settlers in 38 rooms—plus a carriage house—on four floors. Administered by the Daughters of Utah Pioneers, its displays include clothing, furniture, tools, wagons, and carriages. Be careful with kids—this museum is as cluttered as a westbound covered wagon loaded with all of a family's possessions. ✉ *300 N. Main St., Capitol Hill* ☎ *801/532–6479* 🌐 *www.dup-international.org* 🎟 *Free* 🕒 *Closed Sun.*

★ **Utah State Capitol**

GOVERNMENT BUILDING | The State Capitol, built in 1912, hosts Utah's legislature annually from January to March. The exterior steps offer marvelous views of the Salt Lake Valley. In the rotunda beneath the 165-foot-high dome, a series of murals, commissioned as part of a Works Progress Administration project during the Depression, depicts the state's history. Don't miss the gold-leafed State Reception Room, the original state supreme court, and the Senate gallery. Free guided tours are offered weekdays 9–4 (until 1 pm on Friday), on the hour, except for holidays. ✉ *350 N. State St., Capitol Hill* ☎ *801/538–1800* 🌐 *www.utahstatecapitol.utah.gov* 🕒 *Closed weekends.*

Restaurants

★ Cucina

$$ | MODERN ITALIAN | Foodies flock to this neighborhood café and food market for creative salads and colorful, creative entrées like ahi tuna poke with guajillo chile and mango, or lobster gnocchi in a saffron beurre blanc with dandelion pesto and candied oranges. Also on the menu are house-made soups and generous deli sandwiches. **Known for:** outstanding list of wines by the glass and bottle; hefty deli sandwiches to go; panna cotta with creative rotating preparations. *$ Average main: $22 ✉ 1026 E. 2nd Ave., The Avenues ☎ 801/322–3055 🌐 www.cucinawinebar.com.*

Coffee and Quick Bites

★ Publik Coffee Roasters

$ | CAFÉ | This terrific, uber-cool artisan-coffee purveyor has several locations around town, with this simple, streamlined shop in the Avenues arguably the most inviting, in part because of its handsome wooden tables and for its location along a block of lovely historic homes. Publik sources its fair-trade beans from high-quality farms throughout Latin America and Africa, and always offers an interesting array of seasonal espresso drinks, like the wintertime favorite Sweet Melissa, a honey syrup–infused latte with lemon balm, sage, and sweet mint. **Known for:** artisan toasts; inviting, hip aesthetic; white mochas. *$ Average main: $6 ✉ 502 3rd Ave., Salt Lake City ☎ 385/229–4836 🌐 www.publikcoffee.com.*

Hotels

★ Inn on the Hill

$$$ | B&B/INN | Owned and restored by former *Salt Lake Tribune* publisher Philip McCarthey, this spectacular turn-of-the-20th-century Renaissance Revival mansion makes a striking impression with its red-rock exterior and princely setting on the lower slopes of tony Capitol Hill. **Pros:** short walk from Temple Square and the state capitol; jetted tubs and radiant-heat bathroom floors in every room; exceptionally friendly and helpful staff. **Cons:** lots of steps and no elevator; no kids except in the carriage house; books up fast many weekends. *$ Rooms from: $180 ✉ 225 N. State St., Capitol Hill ☎ 801/328–1466 🌐 www.inn-on-the-hill.com ⇨ 13 rooms 🍴 Free breakfast.*

Nightlife

BARS AND LOUNGES

★ Mountain West Cider

BREWPUBS/BEER GARDENS | One of the state's only craft cider producers, Mountain West uses local ingredients—prickly pear puree, and a wide variety of apples—to create its crisp and refreshing concoctions. In the cheerful tap room and sunny garden, where live bands often perform, you can sample the ciders along with local beers and spirits. *✉ 425 N. 400 W, Salt Lake City ☎ 801/935–4147 🌐 www.mountainwestcider.com.*

Shopping

FOOD

Hatch Family Chocolates

FOOD/CANDY | For a sweet treat, stop by this friendly candy and ice-cream shop. Jerry Hatch uses his mother's secret recipe for creamy caramel, and each piece of chocolate is hand-dipped and sold by weight. They also serve espresso, Italian soda, ice cream, and decadent hot chocolate. *✉ 376 8th Ave., Salt Lake City ☎ 801/532–4912 🌐 www.hatchfamilychocolates.com.*

See emus, parrots, and bald eagles at the Tracy Aviary & Botanical Garden.

East Side and Sugar House

Home to the city's lofty University/Foothill district, the East Side is both a lively urban neighborhood and a scenic slice of nature, with its many trails twisting and turning into the Wasatch Range. Occupying what was once the eastern shoreline of ancient Lake Bonneville, the University of Utah is the state's largest higher-education institution and the oldest university west of the Mississippi. It's the cultural hub of University/Foothill, home to museums, the football stadium that was the site of the opening and closing ceremonies during the 2002 Winter Olympics, a 15,000-seat indoor arena, numerous prominent medical facilities and Research Park, which houses scores of private companies and portions of 30 academic departments in a cooperative enterprise in which research and technology partner to produce marketable products. Near campus, the scenic Red Butte Garden and Arboretum is a great place to learn about plants that thrive in dry climates such as Utah's, and the gleaming copper-colored Natural History Museum of Utah is one of the city's must-see attractions.

A bit south, you'll find the charming Sugar House neighborhood. Utah pioneers tried to produce sugar out of beets at a mill here, and although sugar never made it to their tables, it is a sweet place to find eclectic shops and hip restaurants. The beautiful **Sprague Library** (✉ *2131 S. 1100 E*), in a historic Tudor-style building, is worth a visit. Pick up picnic food and head for tiny Hidden Hollow Park, or cross 1300 East to the expansive Sugar House Park, which hosts the city's most spectacular fireworks and arts festival every July 4.

Sights

★ Liberty Park

NATIONAL/STATE PARK | Salt Lake's oldest park contains a wealth of intriguing amenities, including the Tracy Aviary, the Chase Home Museum, several playgrounds, a large pond, a swimming pool, and a tennis complex on its eight square city blocks. Weekly farmers' markets on Friday nights and the city's biggest Pioneer Day celebration (July 24) mark a busy summer schedule annually. Make a wish and toss a coin into Seven Canyons Fountain, a symbol of the seven major canyons of the Wasatch Front. ✉ *600 E. 900 S, East Side* ☎ *801/521–0962* 🌐 *www.slc.gov/parks.*

★ Natural History Museum of Utah

MUSEUM | FAMILY | Stop and admire the sleek copper and granite form of this contemporary museum on the University of Utah campus before stepping inside to learn about the formation of the region's incredible landscape of parks, mountain ranges, lakes, and basins. Immerse yourself in prehistoric Utah, home to prolific research on dinosaurs and some of the most famous fossil recoveries in history. ✉ *301 Wakara Way, University of Utah* ☎ *801/581–6927* 🌐 *www.nhmu.utah.edu* 🎫 *$15.*

★ Red Butte Garden and Arboretum

GARDEN | With more than 100 acres of gardens and undeveloped acres, this tranquil, mesmerizing nature space provides many enjoyable hours of strolling. Of special interest are the Perennial, Fragrance, and Medicinal gardens, the Daylily Collection, the Water Pavilion, and the Children's Garden. Lectures on everything from bugs to gardening in arid climates, workshops, and concerts are presented regularly. The popular Summer Concert Series attracts well-known musicians from the B-52s to Modest Mouse. The pristine amphitheater seats approximately 3,000 people on its expansive lawn. The Botanic Gift Shop offers books, soaps, sculptures, and fine gifts. ✉ *300 Wakara Way, University of Utah* ☎ *801/585–0556* 🌐 *www.redbuttegarden.org* 🎫 *$14.*

This Is the Place Heritage Park

MUSEUM VILLAGE | FAMILY | Brigham Young and his band of Mormon followers descended into the Salt Lake Valley here. On July 24, 1847 (now a statewide holiday that is bigger than July 4 in many communities), he famously declared that this was the place for the Latter-day Saints to end their cross-country trek. A 60-foot-tall statue of Young, Heber Kimball, and Wilbur Woodruff stands prominently in the park, which includes Heritage Village, a re-created 19th-century community and visitor center. In summer, volunteers dressed in period clothing demonstrate what Mormon pioneer life was like. You can watch artisans at work in historic buildings and take wagon or train rides around the compound. A 20-minute movie depicts the pioneers' trek across America at the visitor center. ✉ *2601 E. Sunnyside Ave., East Side* ☎ *801/582–1847* 🌐 *www.thisistheplace.org* 🎫 *Village: $14 (Sun. $8). Monument: free.*

Restaurants

★ Feldman's Deli

$ | DELI | A bustling space with high ceilings, brick walls, and live music some evenings, this contemporary take on a traditional Jewish deli is in a cheerful neighborhood on the south edge of Sugar House. It's a must for classic dishes—in enormous portions—of Reuben sandwiches, blintzes with fruit compote, matzo ball soup, everything bagels with smoked sockeye salmon and a schmear. **Known for:** plenty of distinctive local beers; authentic boiled bagels baked fresh daily; rugelach pastries. $ *Average main: $14* ✉ *2005 E. 2700 S, Salt Lake City* ☎ *801/906–0369* 🌐 *www.feldmans-deli.com* ⏲ *Closed Sun. and Mon.*

★ Ruth's Diner
$ | AMERICAN | FAMILY | Families love the gussied-up old railcar that serves as Ruth's dining room and the best creek-side patio in the city—you just have to navigate your way up gorgeous Emigration Canyon to find it. Breakfast (served until 4 pm) has been the diner's trademark since 1930, and it starts with 3-inch-high biscuits followed by massive omelets like the King of Hearts (artichokes, garlic, mushrooms, and two cheeses). **Known for:** scenic canyon setting; live music on the patio in summer; long wait times on weekend mornings. *Average main: $14* *4160 Emigration Canyon Rd., East Side* *801/582–5807* *www.ruthsdiner.com.*

★ Table X
$$$ | MODERN AMERICAN | Serving artfully crafted modern American fare in a sceney cathedral-ceilinged restaurant and tall black leather booths, a pair of SLC's most esteemed chefs have created the most alluring dining destination in the Sugar House area. The menu changes frequently and is based on what's in season, but recent offerings have included locally raised lamb shank accompanied by smoked and pickled alliums and saffron lamb jus, and a vegetable "steak" topped with coconut-leek curry, spiced ghee, and garden chili oil. **Known for:** fresh produce grown in the on-site garden; outstanding service; daily-changing selection of house-made ice creams and sorbets. *Average main: $25* *1457 E. 3350 S, Salt Lake City* *385/528–3712* *www.tablexrestaurant.com* *Closed Sun. and Mon. No lunch.*

Salt Lake City Marriott University Park
$$ | HOTEL | Away from the downtown bustle and steps from hiking and biking trails as well as University of Utah attractions, this airy and inviting hotel is popular with business travelers but is actually a great choice if you'd rather be closer to nature and a little away from the bustle of downtown. **Pros:** near Natural History Museum and Red Butte Garden; sweeping Wasatch Mountain views; good on-site restaurant and bar, plus Starbucks. **Cons:** not many businesses within walking distance; expensive breakfast; 10- to 15-minute drive from Downtown. *Rooms from: $132* *480 Wakara Way, University of Utah* *801/581–1000* *www.marriott.com* *218 rooms* *No meals.*

BREWPUBS AND MICROBREWERIES

★ Hopkins Brewing
BREWPUBS/BEER GARDENS | Grab a table in this handsome, brick-walled tap room and try some of the finest and most distinctive craft ales in the city, such as crisp Sauvin Blanc Brut produced with hops and Chardonnay grapes, and a roasty Black Sesame Stout. The kitchen is known for its Thai-style and chipotle-honey wings. *1048 E. 2100 S, Salt Lake City* *385/528–3275* *www.hopkinsbrewingcompany.com.*

Great Salt Lake and West Side

A visit to northern Utah isn't complete without a trip to the Great Salt Lake. The best way to experience this 1,700-square-mile body of water (it's a little smaller than the state of Delaware) is a half-day excursion to Antelope Island. There's no place in the country like this state park, home to millions of waterfowl and hundreds of bison and antelope, and surrounded by some of the saltiest water on earth. Drive the 7-mile narrow causeway that links the shoreline, then explore the historic ranch house and miles of hiking trails, and try a buffalo burger at the small café.

Sights

★ Antelope Island State Park

ISLAND | In the 19th century, settlers grazed sheep and horses on Antelope Island, ferrying them back and forth from the mainland across the waters of the Great Salt Lake. Today, the park is the most developed and scenic spot in which to experience the lake. Hiking and biking trails crisscross the island, and the lack of cover—cottonwood trees provide some of the only shade—gives the place a wide-open feeling and makes for some blistering hot days. You can go saltwater bathing at several beach areas. Since the salinity level of the lake is always greater than that of the ocean, the water is extremely buoyant (and briny smelling). Hot showers at the marina remove the chill and the salt afterward.

The island has historic sites, as well as desert wildlife and birds in their natural habitat. The most popular inhabitants are the members of a herd of more than 700 bison descended from 12 brought here in 1893. Each October at the **Buffalo Roundup** more than 250 volunteers on horseback round up the free-roaming animals and herd them to the island's north end to be counted. The island's **Fielding-Garr House,** built in 1848 and now owned by the state, was the oldest continuously inhabited home in Utah until the last resident moved out in 1981. The house displays assorted ranching artifacts, and guided horseback riding is available from the stables next to the house. Be sure to check out the modern visitor center, and sample a bison burger at the stand that overlooks the lake to the north. If you're lucky, you'll hear coyotes howling in the distance. Access to the island is via a 7½-mile causeway, which is reached from I–15 about a half-hour drive north of Salt Lake City. ✉ *4528 W. 1700 S, Syracuse* ☎ *801/773–2941* 🌐 *stateparks.utah.gov* 🎫 *$15 per vehicle, $3 per pedestrian.*

Great Salt Lake State Park

BEACH—SIGHT | The Great Salt Lake is eight times saltier than the ocean and second only to the Dead Sea in salinity. What makes it so briny? There's no outlet to the ocean, so salts and other minerals carried by rivers and streams become concentrated in this enormous evaporation pond. Ready access to this wonder is possible at this state park on the lake's south shore, 16 miles west of Salt Lake City. A pavilion, souvenir shop, and dance floor honor the park's glory days when ballroom dancing and the lake brought thousands of visitors to its shores.

The state park used to manage the beaches north of the pavilion, but the lake is too shallow here for floating (Antelope Island is better for that). What you can do here is walk down the boat ramp to Great Salt Lake State Marina and stick your legs in the water to experience the unique sensation of floating on water that won't let you sink. Your feet will bob to the surface, and you'll see tiny orange brine shrimp floating with you. You can also rent boats and stand-up paddleboards here, and shower off at the marina. ✉ *13312 W. 1075 S, Magna* ☎ *801/828–0787* 🌐 *www.stateparks.utah.gov* 🎫 *$5 per vehicle.*

Restaurants

Nomad Eatery

$ | **MODERN AMERICAN** | Located in something of a food desert amid the chain hotels southwest of Salt Lake International Airport, there's one terrific gastropub with a rustic-chic vibe, serving elevated comfort fare and creative cocktails. A nice option before or after a flight or on your way to or from Great Salt Lake State Park, Nomad doles out such eclectic dishes as Korean barbecue pulled-pork sandwiches and thin-crust pizzas topped with broccoli rabe, garlic cream, and taleggio cheese. **Known for:** friendly, easy-going staff; ginger-pear-bourbon cocktails; choco-tacos with cinnamon ice cream. [$] *Average* *main: $11* ✉ *1722 Fremont Dr., Salt Lake City* ☎ *801/467–0909* 🌐 *www.nomad-eatery.com* ⏲ *Closed Sun.*

Activities

HIKING

Antelope Island State Park offers plenty of space for the avid hiker to explore, but keep a few things in mind. All trails are also shared by mountain bikers and horseback riders—not to mention the occasional bison. Trees are few and far between on the island, making for high exposure to the elements, so bring (and drink) plenty of water and dress appropriately. In the spring, biting insects make bug repellent a must-have. Pick up a trail map at the visitor center.

Once you're prepared, hiking Antelope Island can be a very enjoyable experience. Trails are fairly level except for a few places, where the hot summer sun makes the climb even more strenuous. Mountain ranges, including the Wasatch Front to the east and the Stansbury Mountains directly to the west, provide beautiful background in every direction, though haze sometimes obscures the view. Aromatic sage plants offer shelter for a variety of wildlife, so don't be startled if your next step flushes a chukar partridge, horned lark, or jackrabbit. A bobcat is a rarely seen island resident that will likely keep its distance.

MOUNTAIN AND ROAD BIKING

Bountiful Bicycle Center

BICYCLING | With two locations north of Salt Lake City, one just Kaysville on the way to Antelope Island, this reputable shop is a great place to pick up rentals to cycle around the state park. ✉ *151 Main St., Layton* ☎ *801/444–2453* 🌐 *www.bountifulbicycle.com.*

Midvalley and South Valley

The swatch of suburban communities south of Salt Lake are divided into the Midvalley and South Valley regions, with more of the notable attractions, eateries, and businesses of interest to visitors in the former, chiefly in the towns of Murray, Millcreek, Holladay, and Cottonwood Heights. In addition to being home to some interesting museums and parks, these areas also have some hotels and dining and nightlife options that are popular with winter skiers and summer hikers and bikers making their way to and from the Cottonwood canyons.

Sights

Wheeler Historic Farm

FARM/RANCH | FAMILY | Now a 75-acre park and living history museum with numerous historic structures and a country store selling snacks, toys, and farm-related gifts, this verdant oasis and still-working farm on Little Cottonwood Creek in suburban Murray was settled in 1898 and is one of the only pioneer-era farmsteads left in the metro area. Activities here include cow-milking, observing the farm animals, tours of the impressive Victorian homestead (which is packed with farming implements and artifacts), and wagon rides and easy hikes on an extensive trail network. A farmers' market is held here on summer Sundays. There's no charge to walk around the property, but tours and various activities have small fees. ✉ *6351 S. 900 E* ☎ *385/468–1755* 🌐 *www.slco.org/wheeler-farm* ⏲ *Closed Sun.*

Restaurants

Lone Star Taqueria

$ | MEXICAN | You can't miss this tiny lime green joint, marked by an old sticker-covered car off Fort Union Boulevard and often packed with skiers from the nearby

Cottonwood canyons. The kitchen serves tasty, inexpensive Mexican food—including house special fish tacos, handmade tamales, burritos, and plenty of chilled Mexican beer. **Known for:** shrimp tacos with cilanto-jalapeño aioli; mammoth burritos; Mexican beers on tap. *Average main: $8 2265 E. Fort Union Blvd., Cottonwood 801/944–2300 www.lstaq.com Closed Sun.*

★ Provisions

$$ | **MODERN AMERICAN** | Renowned for its delicious weekend brunches and a bright and colorful dining room with a lively open kitchen, this modern American bistro with a focus on organic ingredients also turns out flavorful dinner fare. Brunch favorites include slow-roasted pork shoulder with poached eggs and wood-roasted blueberry pancakes, while homemade pappardelle with braised rabbit and smoked bacon stars among the dinner options. **Known for:** shareable, creative small plates; extensive list of artisan spirits; white chocolate–salted yuzu cheesecake. *Average main: $21 3364 S. 2300 E, Salt Lake City 801/410–4046 www.slcprovisions.com No lunch weekdays.*

Hotels

Castle Creek Inn

$$ | **B&B/INN** | Designed like a grand castle, complete with ornate medieval-inspired theme suites (all with jetted tubs and fireplaces), this striking B&B with pretty gardens is popular for celebrating romantic special occasions and being fairly close to skiing in Big and Little Cottonwood canyons. **Pros:** convenient to ski areas; distinctive architecture; extensive breakfast included. **Cons:** small in-room TVs; not suitable for kids; 20 minutes from downtown SLC. *Rooms from: $159 7391 Creek Rd., Cottonwood Heights 801/567–9437 www.castlecreekbb.com 10 rooms Free breakfast.*

★ Hyatt Place Salt Lake City–Cottonwood

$$$ | **HOTEL** | This mid- to upscale pet-welcoming Hyatt mid-rise near the mouth of Big Cottonwood Canyon is a perfect roost for skiers and hikers but also a comfortable base for the metro area, with its access to I–215. **Pros:** outdoor pool and hot tub; nice views of Wasatch Range; convenient to I–215 and ski areas. **Cons:** pleasant but nondescript interior design; not many restaurants within walking distance; 20-minute drive from downtown SLC. *Rooms from: $179 3090 E. 6200 S, Salt Lake City 801/890–1280 www.hyatt.com 124 rooms Free breakfast.*

Activities

GOLF

★ Stonebridge Golf Club

GOLF | One of the state's top public courses is just a five-minute drive from the airport and just 20 minutes from Downtown. The links-style course, designed by Gene Bates and Johnny Miller, offers 27 holes amid beautiful scenery. Water hazards come in the form of lakes and streams, and there are plenty of bunkers, but fairways are wide and generally quite forgiving. *4415 Links Dr., West Valley City 801/957–9000 www.golfstonebridgeutah.com $46 18 holes, 7200 yards, par 36.*

Little Cottonwood Canyon

25 miles from Brighton and Solitude; 20 miles from Salt Lake City.

Skiers have been singing the praises of Little Cottonwood Canyon since 1938, when the Alta Lifts Company pieced together a ski lift using parts from an old mine tram to become the **Alta Ski Resort,** the second such area in North America. With its 550 inches per year of dry, light snow and unparalleled terrain,

Alta, Utah, is a dramatic place to enjoy the slopes or to take in the sights during the off-season.

this canyon is legendary among diehard snow enthusiasts. A mile down the canyon from Alta, **Snowbird Ski and Summer Resort,** which opened in 1971, shares the same mythical snow and terrain quality—the two areas are connected via the Mineral Basin area. You can purchase an Alta Snowbird One Pass that allows you on the lifts at both areas, making this a huge skiing complex.

But skiing isn't all there is to do here. Dazzling mountain-biking and hiking trails access the higher reaches of the Wasatch-Cache National Forest, and the trails over Catherine Pass will put you at the head of Big Cottonwood Canyon at the Brighton Ski Area. Formed by the tireless path of an ancient glacier, Little Cottonwood Canyon cuts a swath through these pristine woodlands. Canyon walls are composed mostly of striated granite, and traditional climbing routes of varied difficulty abound. At Snowbird's base area, modern structures house accommodations, restaurants, and bars. The largest of these buildings, the Cliff Lodge, is an entire ski village under one roof. The resort mounts a variety of entertainment throughout the year, including pop and jazz concerts, and Oktoberfest in fall.

GETTING HERE AND AROUND

To get here, take I–80 East to I–215 South, then hop off the highway at Exit 6 and venture into Little Cottonwood Canyon, following signs for Alta and Snowbird. The canyon's dramatic topography invites very occasional avalanches that block the road, the only entrance and egress.

ESSENTIALS

VISITOR INFORMATION Alta Chamber & Visitors Bureau. *435/633–1394* *www.discoveralta.com.*

Restaurants

★ Shallow Shaft

$$$$ | MODERN AMERICAN | For finely prepared steaks and game dishes—from braised beef ribs with mushroom butter to sea scallops with crispy pork belly—Alta's only sit-down restaurant not in a hotel is the place to go. The small interior is cozy, with a sandy color scheme and walls adorned with 19th-century mining tools found on the mountain. **Known for:** big windows overlooking the mountains; phenomenal wine selection; house-made, daily rotating ice creams. *Average main: $41 ✉ 10199 E. Hwy. 210, Alta ☎ 801/742–2177 🌐 www.shallowshaft.com ⏲ No lunch. Closed Apr.–Nov.*

Steak Pit

$$$$ | **STEAKHOUSE** | Views and food take precedence over interior design at Snowbird's oldest restaurant, with a menu full of well-prepared steak and seafood entrees, including opulent Wagyu New York strip steaks and 16-ounce lobster tails. The dining room is warm and unpretentious, with some wood paneling and an expanse of glass. **Known for:** exceptional steaks with rich sauces; a number of high-ticket bottles on the extensive wine list; signature mud pie dessert. *Average main: $44 ✉ Snowbird Plaza Center, Level 1, Snowbird ☎ 801/933–2222 🌐 www.snowbird.com ⏲ No lunch.*

Swen's

$$$$ | **MODERN AMERICAN** | With its sleek, contemporary vibe, warm lighting and wood accents, open kitchen, and floor-to-ceiling windows overlooking the fantastic ski terrain, this upscale restaurant in the ritzy Snowpine Lodge is Alta's trendiest dining destination. The kitchen takes a farm-to-table approach to its hearty but creative mountain fare, with standout dishes like a warm truffled goat cheese dip with chives and house-made potato chips, and a succulent peppercorn-crusted rib-eye steak with mashed potatoes and Merlot-braised mushrooms. **Known for:** breathaking mountain views; thin-crust pizzas; impressive wine list. *Average main: $32 ✉ 10420 E. Hwy. 210, Alta ☎ 801/742–2000 🌐 www.snowpine.com.*

Hotels

Alta Lodge

$$$$ | **B&B/INN** | Many families have been booking the same week each year for several generations at this low-key 1939 lodge that's home to the famed Sitzmark Club bar as well as saunas and hot pools to help you work out the kinks after a day on the slopes. **Pros:** steps from lift to Alta's steep slopes; magnificent Wasatch Mountain views; breakfast and dinner included during ski season. **Cons:** not many amenities for the price; no TVs in guest rooms; four-night minimum stay in high ski season. *Rooms from: $410 ✉ 10230 E. Hwy. 210, Alta ☎ 801/742–3500, 800/707–2582 🌐 www.altalodge.com ⏲ Closed mid-Apr.–May and early Oct.–mid-Nov. 53 rooms All-inclusive.*

Cliff Lodge

$$$$ | **RESORT** | The stark concrete walls of this 10-story structure, designed to complement the surrounding granite cliffs, enclose a self-contained ski-in, ski-out village with restaurants, bars, shops, and a high-end, two-story spa. **Pros:** central Snowbird ski village location; nice rooftop spa; several eateries and bars on-site. **Cons:** stark, monolithic design isn't to every taste; furnishings are a bit dated; huge property that can feel impersonal. *Rooms from: $510 ✉ 9320 Cliff Lodge Dr., Snowbird ☎ 801/933–2222, 888/205–7322 🌐 www.thecliffflodgeandspasnowbird.com 511 rooms No meals.*

Activities

HIKING

★ Sunset Peak

HIKING/WALKING | The trailhead for the 4-mile out-and-back hike to Sunset Peak starts high in Little Cottonwood Canyon, above Alta Ski Resort, in Albion Basin. This is a popular area for finding wildflowers in July and August. After an initial steep incline, the trail wanders through flat meadows before it climbs again to Catherine Pass at 10,240 feet. From here intermediate hikes continue along the ridge in both directions. Continue up the trail to the summit of Sunset Peak for breathtaking views of the Heber Valley, Park City, Mount Timpanogos, Big and Little Cottonwood Canyons, and even a part of the Salt Lake Valley. You can alter your route by starting in Little Cottonwood Canyon and ending your hike in neighboring Big Cottonwood Canyon, by following the Catherine Pass as it descends along the Brighton Lakes Trail to Brighton Ski Resort (from which it's a nearly an hour's drive back to Alta). ✉ *Cecret Lake/Catherine Pass Trailhead, Albion Basin Rd., Alta.*

SKIING

★ Alta Ski Area

SKIING/SNOWBOARDING | Alta Ski Area has perhaps the best snow anywhere in the world—an average of nearly 550 inches a year, and terrain to match it. Alta is one of the few resorts left in the country that doesn't allow snowboarding. Sprawling across two large basins, Albion and Wildcat, Alta has a good mixture of expert and intermediate terrain, but relatively few beginner runs. Much of the best skiing (for advanced or expert skiers) requires either finding obscure traverses or doing some hiking. It takes some time to get to know this mountain so if you can find a local to show you around you'll be ahead of the game. Albion Basin's lower slopes have a terrific expanse of novice and lower-intermediate terrain. Rolling meadows, wide trails, and light dry snow create one of the best places in the country for less-skilled skiers to learn to ski powder. Two-hour lessons start at $80. In addition to downhill skiing, Alta also has 3 km (2 miles) of groomed track for skating and classic skiing (on a separate ticket), plus a good selection of rental equipment. ✉ *10230 Hwy. 210, Alta* ☎ *801/359–1078, 801/572–3939 snow report* 🌐 *www.alta.com* 🎫 *Lift tickets $125* ☞ *2,020-ft vertical drop; 2,200 skiable acres; 15% novice, 30% intermediate, 55% advanced; 3 high-speed quads, 1 triple chairs, 2 double chairs, 5 surface tows.*

★ Snowbird Resort

SKIING/SNOWBOARDING | For many skiers, this is as close to heaven as you can get. Soar aboard Snowbird's signature 125-passenger tram straight from the base to the resort's highest point, 11,000 feet above sea level, and then descend into a playground of powder-filled chutes, bowls, and meadows—a leg-burning top-to-bottom run of more than 3,000 vertical feet if you choose. The terrain here is weighted more toward experts—35% of Snowbird is rated black diamond—and if there is a drawback to this resort, it's a lack of beginner terrain. The open bowls, such as Little Cloud and Regulator Johnson, are challenging; the Upper Cirque and the Gad Chutes are hair-raising. On deep-powder days—not uncommon at the Bird—these chutes are exhilarating for skiers who like that sense of a cushioned free fall with every turn. With a nod to intermediate skiers, Snowbird opened North America's first skier tunnel in 2006. Skiers and boarders now ride a 600-foot magic carpet through the Peruvian Tunnel, reducing the trek to Mineral Basin. If you're looking for intermediate cruising runs, there's the long, meandering Chip's Run. After a day of powder turns, you can lounge on the 3,000-square-foot deck of Creekside Lodge at the base of Gad Valley. Beginner's lessons start at $120 and include lift ticket, tuition, and rentals. ✉ *Hwy. 210, Snowbird* ☎ *801/933–2222, 801/933–2100 snow report* 🌐 *www.snowbird.com* 🎫 *Lift tickets $130* ☞ *3,240-ft vertical drop; 2,500 skiable acres; 27% novice, 38% intermediate, 35% advanced; 125-passenger tram, 4 quad lifts, 6 double chairs, 1 gondola, and a skier tunnel with surface lift.*

Chapter 6

PARK CITY AND VICINITY

Updated by
Jenie Skoy

Sights ★★★★★ | Restaurants ★★★★★ | Hotels ★★★★★ | Shopping ★★★★★ | Nightlife ★★★★☆

WELCOME TO PARK CITY AND VICINITY

TOP REASONS TO GO

★ **Outdoor fun:** Regardless of the season, Park City is the epicenter of mountain adventure.

★ **Two top-tier resorts:** No place in North America has two world-class and distinct resorts so close to one another, not to mention as expansive, dynamic, luxurious, and unique as Deer Valley and Park City Mountain Resort.

★ **Olympic spirit:** This town seems to contain more Olympians per capita than any town in the country, if not the world.

★ **Old Town Park City:** First laid out by silver miners in the late 1800s, Park City's historic Main Street is especially lively during big events like the Sundance Film Festival and Kimball Arts Festival.

★ **Sundance Resort:** At the base of Mount Timpanogos, Robert Redford's intimate resort pays homage to art and nature.

1 **Park City and the Wasatch Back.** With a high desert climate, you'll smell both sagebrush and pine in this alpine outback. There are rivers, streams, and lakes to fish from and thousands of trails to hike and mountain bike.

2 **Heber Valley.** This valley is what Salt Lake Valley probably looked like 50 years ago. It's still fairly pristine with an agricultural and small-town vibe. A winding river runs through the verdant valley on the west side and horses still clop down the side streets. People come here for the golfing, fishing, and recreational opportunities near Kamas and in the Uinta mountains. Close by is Midway, a Swiss-like village built on the west side where you can find pampered stays at European-like resorts and a dairy farm where you can get ice cream.

3 **Sundance Resort.** Robert Redford bought and preserved this swath of paradise under the snowy head of Mount Timpanogos and shares it with the public. The Provo River is also a famous blue-ribbon fly-fishing destination.

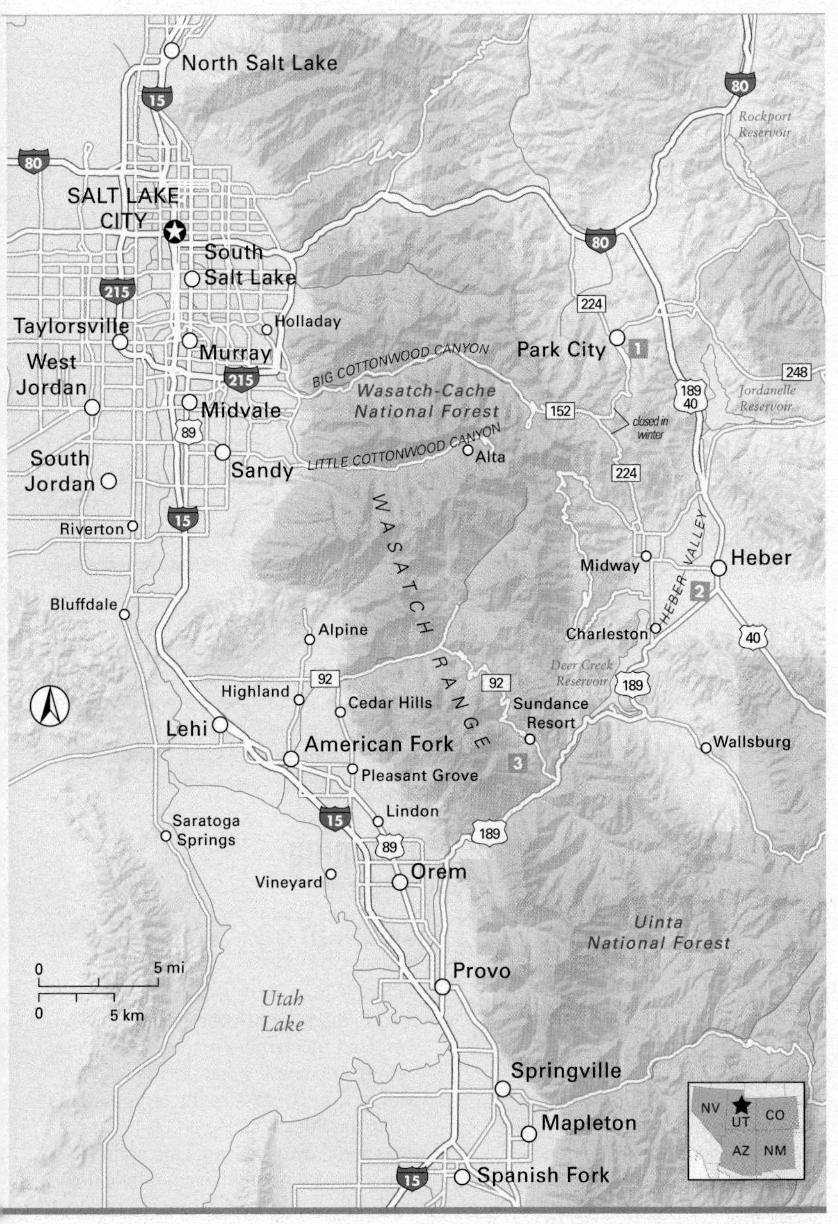
North Salt Lake
15
80
SALT LAKE CITY
South Salt Lake
215
Taylorsville
Holladay
West Jordan
Murray
215
Midvale
89
South Jordan
Sandy
Riverton
15
Bluffdale
BIG COTTONWOOD CANYON
Wasatch-Cache National Forest
LITTLE COTTONWOOD CANYON
Alta
WASATCH RANGE
Alpine
92
Highland
Cedar Hills
Lehi
American Fork
Pleasant Grove
Saratoga Springs
15
Lindon
89
189
Vineyard
Orem
Provo
Utah Lake
Springville
Mapleton
15
Spanish Fork
0
5 mi
0
5 km
80
Rockport Reservoir
80
224
Park City
1
248
189
40
Jordanelle Reservoir
152
closed in winter
224
Midway
HEBER VALLEY
Heber
2
Charleston
40
Deer Creek Reservoir
189
92
Sundance Resort
3
Wallsburg
Uinta National Forest
NV
UT
CO
AZ
NM

The Wasatch Range shares the same desert climate as the Great Basin, which it rims, but these craggy peaks rise to more than 11,000 feet, and stall storms moving in from the Pacific causing massive precipitations. The 160-mile stretch of verdure is home to 2 million people, or three-fourths of all Utahns. Although its landscape is crisscrossed by freeways and dappled by towns large and small, the Wasatch still beckons adventurers with its alpine forests and windswept canyons.

Where three geologically distinct regions—the Rocky Mountains, the Colorado Plateau, and the Basin and Range provinces—converge, the Wasatch Range combines characteristics of each. You'll find broad glacial canyons with towering granite walls, stream-cut gorges through purple, tan, and green shale, and red-rock bluffs and valleys.

Most people associate Park City with its legendary skiing in winter, but this is truly a year-round destination. Bright-blue lakes afford fantastic boating and water sports, and some of the West's best trout streams flow from the high country. Add miles of hiking and biking trails and you have a vacation that's hard to beat.

You can also find cultural activities and entertainment at every turn. The Sundance Film Festival, hosted by Sundance Institute (which was founded by actor-director Robert Redford), attracts movie stars and independent filmmakers from all over. Major recording artists of all types play indoor and outdoor venues, and nightlife abounds in the city and resorts, with an increasing number of nightclubs and music venues.

Planning

When to Go

Winter is long in the mountains (ski resorts buzz from November to mid-April) but much more manageable in the valleys. The snow stops falling in April or May, and a month later the temperatures are in the 80s. In spring and fall, rates drop and crowds lessen. Late spring is also a good time for fishing, rafting on rivers swollen with snowmelt, birding, and wildlife viewing. In summer, watersports enthusiasts of all stripes flock to the region's reservoirs, alpine lakes, rivers, and streams. The Wasatch Mountains draw those seeking respite from the heat of the valley from June through Labor Day. Fall's colors rival those of New England.

Getting Here and Around

AIR

Commercial air traffic flies in and out of Salt Lake International Airport, which is less than an hour from all destinations in the Wasatch and 7 miles northwest of downtown Salt Lake City. The airport is served by Alaska, American, Delta, Southwest, jetBlue, Frontier, United, Air Canada, and KLM.

CAR

Highway travel around the region is quick and easy. The major routes in the area include the transcontinental I–80, which connects Salt Lake City and Park City; and U.S. 40/189, which connects southwest Wyoming, Utah, and northwest Colorado via Park City, Heber City, and Provo. Scenic routes and lookout points are clearly marked, enabling you to slow down and pull over to take in the views. Off the main highways, roads range from well-paved multilane blacktop routes to barely graveled backcountry trails. Watch out for wildlife on the roads just about anywhere in Utah.

SHUTTLE

Shuttles are the best way to travel between the airport and Park City, and fares start at $39 per person one way. A free, efficient Park City transit system operates a reliable network of bus routes, connecting Old Town, the local ski resorts, Kimball Junction, and most neighborhoods.

SHUTTLE CONTACTS Canyon Transportation. ☎ *801/255–1841* 🌐 *www.canyon-transport.com.* **Park City Direct Shuttle.** ☎ *866/655–3010 toll-free, 435/655–3010* 🌐 *www.parkcitydirectshuttle.com.*

Hotels

Chain hotels and motels dot I–15 all along the Wasatch Front and nearly always have availability. Every small town on the back side of the range has at least one good bed-and-breakfast, and most towns have both independent and chain motels. Condominiums dominate Park City lodging, but you also find high-end hotels, luxurious lodges, and well-run bed-and-breakfast inns. All this luxury means prices here tend to be higher than in other areas in the state during the winter. Prices drop significantly in the warmer months, when package deals or special rates are offered. Make reservations well in advance for busy ski holidays like Christmas, Presidents' Day, and Martin Luther King Jr. Day, and during January's Sundance Film Festival. As the mountain country is often on the cool side, lodgings at higher elevations generally don't have air-conditioning. *Hotel reviews have been shortened. For full information, visit Fodors.com.*

Restaurants

American cuisine dominates the Wasatch dining scene, with great steaks, barbecue, and traditional Western fare. There's also an abundance of good seafood, which the busier eateries fly in daily from the west coast. Restaurants range from Swiss to Japanese, French, and Mexican. Hours vary seasonally, so it's a good idea to call ahead. Reservations are essential during winter holiday weekends and the Sundance Film Festival. Park City restaurants offer great deals, such as two-for-one entrées from spring to fall, so check the local newspaper for coupons or ask your concierge which eateries are offering discounts. *Restaurant reviews have been shortened. For full information, visit Fodors.com.*

HOTEL AND RESTAURANT PRICES

Hotel prices in the reviews are the lowest cost of a standard double room in high season. Restaurant prices in the reviews are the average cost of a main course at dinner, or if dinner is not served, at lunch.

What It Costs

	$	$$	$$$	$$$$
RESTAURANTS				
	under $16	$16–$22	$23–$30	over $30
HOTELS				
	under $125	$125–$175	$176–$225	over $225

Visitor Information

CONTACTS Park City Convention and Visitors Bureau. ✉ *1850 Sidewinder Dr., #320, Park City* ☎ *800/453–1360* 🌐 *www.visitparkcity.com.*

Park City

The best-known areas of the Wasatch Mountains lie east of Salt Lake City. Up and over Parley's Canyon via I–80 you'll find the sophisticated mountain town of Park City, with its world-class ski resorts and myriad summer attractions.

After silver was discovered in Park City in 1868, it quickly became a rip-roaring mining town with more than two-dozen saloons and a thriving red-light district. In the process, it earned the nickname "Sin City." A fire destroyed many of the town's buildings in 1898; this, combined with declining mining fortunes in the early 1900s, caused most of the residents to pack up and leave. It wasn't until 1946 that its current livelihood began to take shape in the form of the small Snow Park ski hill, which opened where Deer Valley Resort now sits.

Park City once again profited from the generosity of the mountains as skiing became popular. In 1963 Treasure Mountain Resort began operations with its skier's subway—an underground train and hoist system that ferried skiers to the mountain's summit via old mining tunnels. Facilities were upgraded over time, and Treasure Mountain became the Park City Mountain Resort. Although it has a mind-numbing collection of condominiums, at Park City's heart is a historic downtown that rings with the authenticity of a real town with real roots.

GETTING HERE AND AROUND

If you're arriving via Salt Lake City, a rental car or shuttle bus will get you to Park City in about 35 minutes. Park City has a free transit system running between neighborhoods and to the ski resorts. It operates from roughly 6 am to midnight in summer and winter. The schedule is more limited in fall and spring, so be sure to check schedules at the Transit Center on Swede Alley or on the buses. The Old Town is walkable.

Sights

Park City Farmers Market

MARKET | Held rain or shine each Wednesday from June through October, the Farmers Market is always a good spot to pick up locally sourced bread, fruits and vegetables, flowers, and more. ✉ *Canyons Village, 4000 Canyons Resort Dr., Park City* ☎ *435/671–1455* 🌐 *parkcityfarmersmarket.com.*

Park City Mountain Resort

AMUSEMENT PARK/WATER PARK | **FAMILY** | In the warmer months, the resort transforms itself into a mountain amusement park, with attractions such as the Alpine Slide, ziplines, Alpine Coaster, and a

Park City has been known since its mining heyday as Utah's "Sin City."

climbing wall. Visitors take a chairlift up the mountain to the Alpine Slide, then hop aboard special sleds that carry them down 3,000 feet of winding concrete and fiberglass track at speeds controlled by each rider. Two ziplines offer a high-flying adrenaline rush as riders strap into a harness suspended from a cable. The gravity-propelled Alpine Coaster (which operates year-round) zooms through aspen-lined twists and turns at speeds up to 35 mph. There's also a climbing wall, miniature golf course, trampolines, an adventure zone for younger children, and some of the West's best lift-served mountain biking and hiking. ✉ *1345 Lowell Ave., Park City* ☎ *435/649–8111, 800/222–7275* 🌐 *www.parkcitymountain.com.*

Park City Museum

JAIL | A must-see for history buffs, this museum is housed in the former library, city hall, and the Bell Tower on Main Street. With a two-story scale model of the 19th-century Ontario Mine, a 20th-century gondola hanging overhead, and the old jail below, this is an authentic tribute to Park City's mining and skiing past. Climb aboard a re-created Union Pacific train car, hold on to a quivering and noisy jack drill for a feel of the mining experience, and, if you dare, step inside a jail cell. Tours of historic Main Street also depart from here. ✉ *528 Main St., Park City* ☎ *435/649–7457* 🌐 *www.parkcityhistory.org* 🎟 *$12.*

Park Silly Sunday Market

MARKET | A funky and constantly changing assortment of artisans, entertainers, and culinary vendors transform Old Town into a street festival complete with beer garden and Bloody Mary bar on Sunday, June through September. The Silly Market strives to be a no-waste event with everything recycled or composted. Look for the free bike valet to park your ride while you walk through the crowds. ✉ *Lower Main St., Park City* ☎ *435/714–4036* 🌐 *www.parksillysundaymarket.com.*

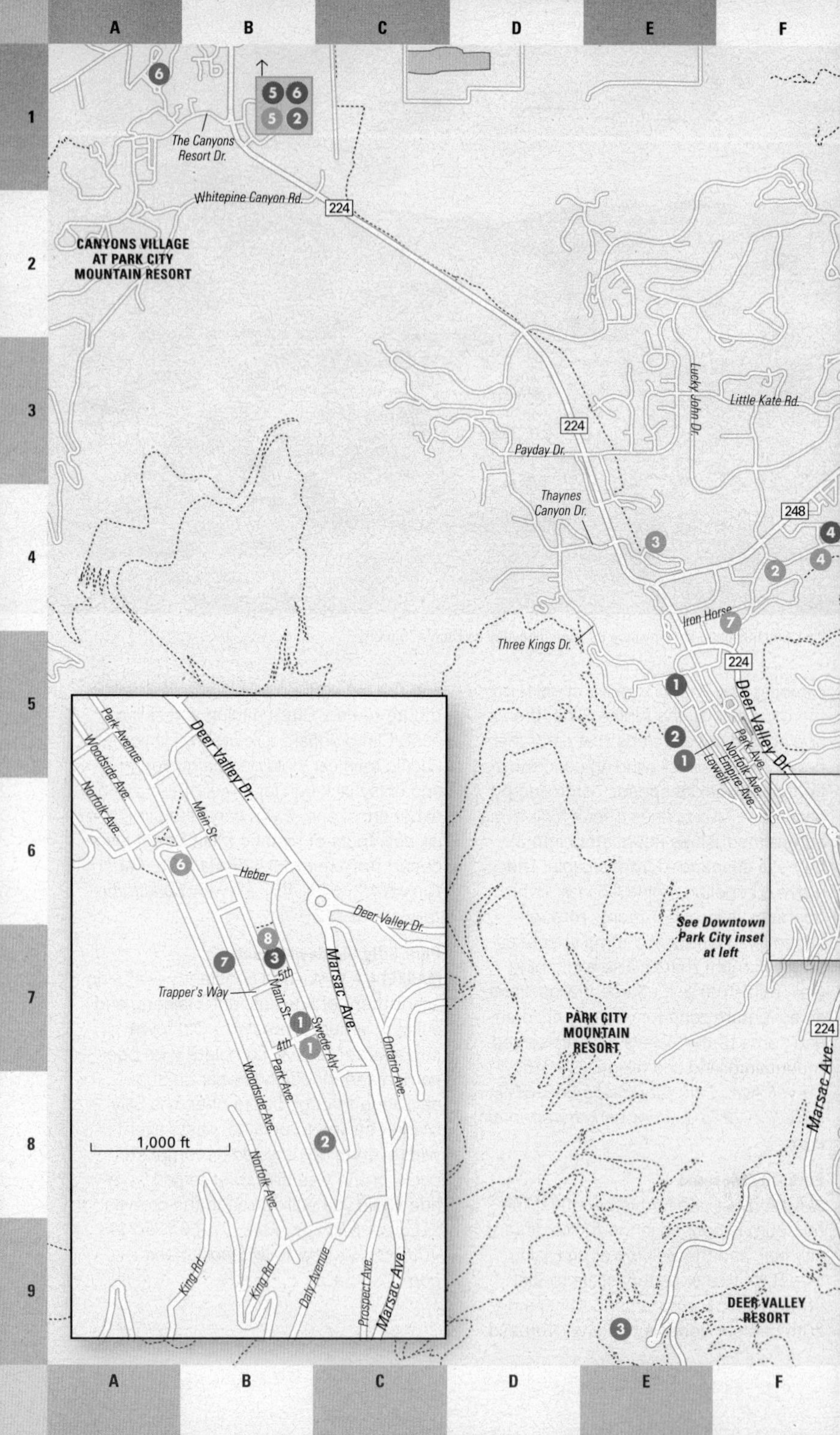

A
B
C
D
E
F
1
2
3
4
5
6
7
8
9
The Canyons Resort Dr.
Whitepine Canyon Rd.
224
CANYONS VILLAGE AT PARK CITY MOUNTAIN RESORT
Lucky John Dr.
Little Kate Rd.
Payday Dr.
Thaynes Canyon Dr.
248
Iron Horse
Three Kings Dr.
Deer Valley Dr.
Park Ave.
Norfolk Ave.
Empire Ave.
Lowell
See Downtown Park City inset at left
PARK CITY MOUNTAIN RESORT
Marsac Ave.
DEER VALLEY RESORT
Park Avenue
Woodside Ave.
Norfolk Ave.
Main St.
Heber
Deer Valley Dr.
Marsac Ave.
5th
Trapper's Way
Main St.
Swede Aly.
4th
Ontario Ave.
Woodside Ave.
Park Ave.
1,000 ft
Norfolk Ave.
King Rd.
King Rd.
Daly Avenue
Prospect Ave.
Marsac Ave.

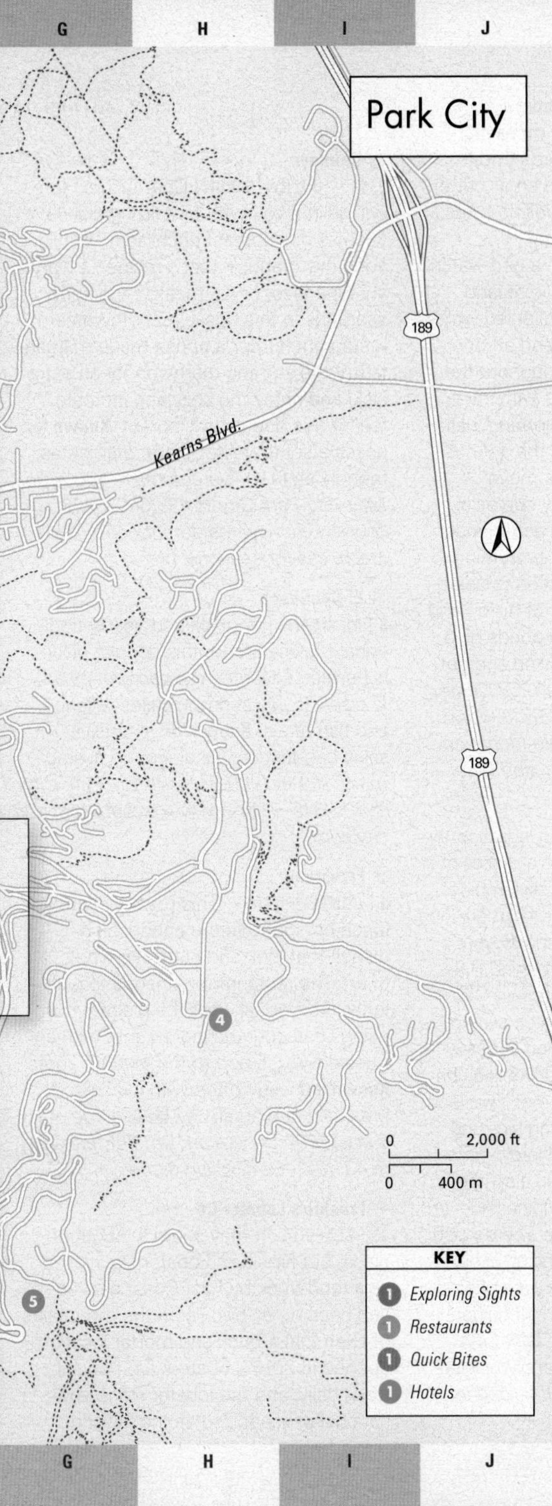

Sights

1 Park City Farmers Market E5
2 Park City Mountain Resort......... E5
3 Park City Museum B7
4 Park Silly Sunday Market.......... F4
5 Swaner Preserve and EcoCenter B1
6 Utah Olympic Park................ B1

Restaurants

1 Chimayo........................... B7
2 El Chubasco....................... F4
3 Five5eeds......................... E4
4 Freshies Lobster Co F4
5 Hearth & Hill...................... B1
6 High West Distillery B6
7 Ritual Cafe & Chocolate Factory F4
8 Riverhorse on Main B7

Quick Bites

1 Java Cow Cafe & Bakery......... B7
2 Riverhorse Provisions............. C8

Hotels

1 Chateau Après...................... F5
2 Holiday Inn Express & Suites Park City.................... B1
3 Montage Deer Valley............... E9
4 The St. Regis Deer Valley......... H7
5 Stein Eriksen Lodge G9
6 Waldorf Astoria Park City......... A1
7 Washington School House B7

Swaner Preserve and EcoCenter

NATURE PRESERVE | Home to more than 100 migratory and native birds (most notably sandhill cranes) and small critters (like the spotted frog), as well as foxes, deer, elk, moose, and coyotes, this 1,200-acre preserve is both a bird-watchers' paradise and an example of land restoration in action. Naturalist-led walks, snowshoe tours in winter, and other events are hosted here throughout the year. The EcoCenter is filled with interactive exhibits, such as a climbing wall with microphones emitting the sounds of the wetlands as climbers move through habitats. The facility serves as an exhibit in itself, given its eco-friendly construction, incorporating everything from recycled denim insulation to solar panels. More than 10 miles of hiking and biking trails and 15 wetland ponds give visitors a great place to unwind and get away from the urban life. ✉ *1258 Center Dr., Newpark* ☎ *435/649–1767* 🌐 *www.swanerecocenter.org* 🎟 *Free (donation appreciated)* ⏲ *Closed Mon. and Tues.*

★ **Utah Olympic Park**

MUSEUM | **FAMILY** | An exciting legacy of the 2002 Winter Olympics, this is a mecca of bobsled, skeleton, luge, and ski jumping. As it is one of the only places in America where you can try these sports, you might have to wait your turn behind U.S. Olympians and aspirants who train here year-round. In summer or winter, screaming down the track in a bobsled at nearly 80 mph with a professional driver is a ride you will never forget. In summer, check out the freestyle ski jumpers doing flips and spins into a splash pool and Nordic jumpers soaring to soft landings on a synthetic outrun. Ride the ziplines or Alpine Slide, or explore the adventure course. There's also an interactive ski museum and an exhibit on the Olympics; guided tours are offered year-round, or you can take a self-guided tour. ✉ *3419 Olympic Pkwy., Park City* ☎ *435/658–4200* 🌐 *www.utaholympiclegacy.com* 🎟 *Museum and self-guided tours free, guided tours $13.*

Restaurants

★ **Chimayo**

$$$$ | **SOUTHWESTERN** | Chef Arturo Flores will delight you with tantalizing dishes such as duck breast enchiladas, tortilla soup (his grandmother's recipe), a giant ahi tuna taco, or his melt-off-the-bone spareribs in this upscale Southwestern restaurant. Order a house-made margarita (try the serrano margarita for an extra kick) and enjoy the cozy and intimate feel of this popular restaurant. **Known for:** upscale southwestern fare; margaritas; friendly staff. [$] *Average main: $40* ✉ *368 Main St., Park City* ☎ *435/649–6222* 🌐 *www.chimayorestaurant.com* ⏲ *No lunch, call for seasonal hrs.*

★ **El Chubasco**

$ | **MEXICAN** | For quick and hearty traditional Mexican food, this popular place is perfect. Favorites are *camarones a la diabla* (spicy shrimp), chiles rellenos, and fish tacos. **Known for:** extensive salsa bar; fast-casual dining. [$] *Average main: $10* ✉ *1890 Bonanza Dr., Park City* ☎ *435/645–9114* 🌐 *www.elchubascoparkcity.com.*

★ **Five5eeds**

$ | **CONTEMPORARY** | This breakfast and lunch hotspot offers up nourishing dishes that look and taste like works of art. The restaurant manages to pull in flavors from all over the globe while using Utah-sourced ingredients with an Aussie twist, a nod to the owners' roots. **Known for:** iced coffee with ice cream; breakfast served all day. [$] *Average main: $14* ✉ *1600 Snow Park Dr., #EF, Park City* ☎ *435/901–8242* ⏲ *No dinner.*

★ **Freshie's Lobster Co**

$$ | **SEAFOOD** | It may seem a bit out of place, but Freshie's Lobster Co started as a food truck by East Coast natives, and became so popular in the mountains of Utah that a brick-and-mortar location opened in 2016. Lobsters are flown in fresh daily, and the lobster roll is now nationally recognized as the "World's

Best Lobster Roll" after taking home the win at a competition in Portland, Maine, in 2017. **Known for:** lobster rolls; casual atmosphere. *Average main: $20 1897 Prospector Ave., Prospector 435/631–9861 www.freshieslobsterco.com.*

★ Hearth & Hill

$$$$ | AMERICAN | Started in 2017 by Brooks Kirchheimer who returned to his Park City hometown, Hearth and Hill—though not in the sexiest neighborhood—has quickly become a hangout for locals in search of comfort food and community. Built with floor-to-ceiling windows inside a modernized industrial space, the restaurant has plenty of elbow room, and the natural lighting and white-tiled open kitchen give the place a distinctive communal vibe. **Known for:** dog-friendly patio; chef-driven menu; inventive cuisine. *Average main: $35 1153 Center Drive, Newpark Retail Center, Park City ✣ Between Jupiter Bowl and Best Buy 435/200–8840 hearth-hill.com.*

★ High West Distillery

$$ | AMERICAN | Touted as the only ski-in, ski-out distillery in the world, High West Saloon sits at the base of the Park City Mountain's Town Lift, serving an eclectically Western, locally focused menu that changes seasonally, and delicious handcrafted cocktails using the distillery's own whiskey and vodka. The family-friendly restaurant and bar, housed in a historical home and livery, is a favorite among locals and visitors alike. **Known for:** whiskey; handcrafted cocktails; lively atmosphere. *Average main: $21 703 Park Ave., Old Town 435/649–8300 www.highwest.com.*

★ Ritual Cafe & Chocolate Factory

$ | AMERICAN | FAMILY | Experience a rush of senses when you visit this fixture in Park City's culinary scene opened in 2015 by Robbie Stout and Anna Davies. Smell just-baked brownies with toasted Peruvian cocoa nibs and watch through an observation window as cocoa beans go into the factory's roll mill as a thick gritty paste then come out smooth and flaky. **Known for:** sustainability; observation window; sipping chocolate. *Average main: $15 1105 Iron Horse, Park City 435/200–8475 www.ritualchocolate.com.*

★ Riverhorse on Main

$$$$ | AMERICAN | With two warehouse loft rooms, exposed wood beams, sleek furnishings, and original art, this award-winning restaurant feels like a big-city supper club where chef-owner Seth Adams pairs imaginative fresh food with a world-class wine list in this elegant—but ski-town relaxed—atmosphere. The menu changes seasonally, but look out for the braised buffalo short rib, pan-roasted tomahawk pork, or signature macadamia-nut-crusted Alaskan halibut. **Known for:** Alaskan halibut; vegan and gluten-free friendly; Sunday brunch. *Average main: $42 540 Main St., Park City 435/649–3536 www.riverhorseparkcity.com No lunch Mon.–Sat.*

Coffee and Quick Bites

Java Cow Cafe & Bakery

$ | DELI | FAMILY | Java Cow has long been a staple on Main Street. Stop in for a panini, a caffeine pick-me-up, or delicious ice cream to satisfy your sweet tooth. **Known for:** excellent coffee; house-made ice cream; quick breakfast or lunch spot. *Average main: $10 402 Main St., Main Street.*

Riverhorse Provisions

$ | CAFÉ | A casual sister to Riverhorse on Main (with the same award-winning chef behind it), Riverhorse Provisions is a café, specialty market, and deli all in one. Come here for one of the few breakfasts served on Main Street, or stop in on your way to an outdoor concert and pick up a signature picnic basket filled with fried chicken, cornbread and peach cobbler, or a chilled lobster salad. **Known for:** signature picnic baskets; gourmet market;

café-style fare. $ *Average main: $12* ✉ *221 Main St., Main Street* ☎ *435/649–0799* 🌐 *www.riverhorseprovisions.com.*

Hotels

Chateau Après

$$ | **B&B/INN** | In one of the most expensive ski towns around, this reasonably priced classic skiers' lodge is a throwback to bygone ski days. **Pros:** comfortable rooms; close to the slopes; longtime local owners. **Cons:** basic accommodations. $ *Rooms from: $145* ✉ *1299 Norfolk Ave., Park City* ☎ *435/649–9372, 800/357–3556* 🌐 *www.chateauapres.com* *32 rooms* *Free breakfast.*

Holiday Inn Express & Suites Park City

$ | **HOTEL** | Just off the main Park City exit near I–80, this chain hotel has a mountain-lodge feel. **Pros:** affordable; walking distance to shops and restaurants; continental breakfast included. **Cons:** you'll need a car or to take free public bus to get to the resorts; close to interstate; rooms are small. $ *Rooms from: $122* ✉ *1501 W. Ute Blvd., Park City* ☎ *435/658–1600, 877/662–6241* 🌐 *www.holidayinn.com* *73 rooms* *Free breakfast.*

★ Montage Deer Valley

$$$$ | **RESORT** | Montage is nestled into Empire Pass at 9,000 feet above the sea like a jewel atop Park City's alpine crown. **Pros:** exquisite location with beautiful views; top-level dining; ample amenities and activities on-site. **Cons:** remote location; car or shuttle required to get to Main Street; can feel cavernous at times. $ *Rooms from: $805* ✉ *9100 Marsac Ave., Park City* ☎ *435/604–1300* 🌐 *www.montagedeervalley.com* *88 rooms, 66 suites* *No meals.*

★ The St. Regis Deer Valley

$$$$ | **RESORT** | A 90-second ride up the funicular will take you to one of the most luxurious hotels at any alpine resort. **Pros:** glitz, glam, and butlers; ski-in, ski-out convenience; award-winning dining on property. **Cons:** additional restaurants are a drive away; layout is confusing, easy to get lost inside; après is popular with locals, get there early. $ *Rooms from: $946* ✉ *2300 Deer Valley Dr. E, Park City* ☎ *435/940–5700, 866/932–7059* 🌐 *www.marriott.com* *115 rooms, 66 suites* *No meals.*

★ Stein Eriksen Lodge

$$$$ | **RESORT** | As enchanting as it gets for a slope-side retreat, this lodge is as perfectly groomed, timelessly gracious, and uniquely charming as its namesake founder, the winner of an Olympic Gold Medal in 1952. **Pros:** award-winning dining on property; service is impeccable and exemplary; only five-star-rated spa in Utah. **Cons:** isolated location means a drive to Main Street and Park City; rooms require a walk outside, which can be cold in the winter; the high-altitude location (8,000-plus feet) can be difficult for some. $ *Rooms from: $900* ✉ *7700 Stein Way, Park City* ☎ *435/649–3700, 800/453–1302* 🌐 *www.steinlodge.com* *180 rooms* *No meals.*

★ Waldorf Astoria Park City

$$$$ | **RESORT** | A sweeping staircase, Baccarat crystal chandelier, and 300-year-old marble fireplace lend grandeur to the first Waldorf Astoria hotel in an alpine location. **Pros:** celebrated restaurant; steps from the gondola; decadent spa. **Cons:** very little within walking distance; gondola nearby is very slow; only one dining option on-site. $ *Rooms from: $740* ✉ *2100 Frostwood Dr., Park City* ☎ *435/647–5500, 866/279–0843* 🌐 *www.waldorfastoriaparkcity.com* *215 rooms* *No meals.*

★ Washington School House

$$$$ | **B&B/INN** | Since 2011, this spectacular boutique hotel has been the hottest "must-stay" destination in Old Town Park City, providing beautifully designed and well-appointed rooms within a National Historic Registry landmark. **Pros:** central location; stellar service (they'll even pack and unpack for you); chefs provide

delicious (included) breakfast and après-ski. **Cons:** not family-friendly; rooms fill up quickly, so book far in advance. *Rooms from: $875 543 Park Ave., Park City 435/649–3800, 800/824–1672 www.washingtonschoolhouse.com 12 rooms Free breakfast.*

 Nightlife

In a state where nearly every town was founded by Mormons who eschewed alcohol and anything associated with it, Park City has always been an exception. Founded by miners with healthy appetites for whiskey and gambling, Park City has been known since its mining heyday as Utah's "Sin City." The miners are gone, but their legacy lives on in this town that has far more bars per capita than any other place in Utah.

Boneyard Saloon and Kitchen

BARS/PUBS | This hot spot is in a somewhat unlikely place—in fact, you might think you're lost as you pull into the industrial-looking area in Prospector. But its off-Main location means it's popular with the locals, and ample parking is a huge plus. TVs lining the wall and a special weekend breakfast menu have made Boneyard the new go-to for Sunday football, and the rooftop deck has stunning views of the mountains. A sister restaurant of No Name on Main Street, Boneyard features beers on tap and an extensive bottle list. Head next door to Wine Dive (same ownership) to find 16 wines on tap and artisan pizza. *1251 Kearns Blvd., Prospector 435/649–0911 www.boneyardsaloon.com.*

★ No Name Saloon

BARS/PUBS | A Park City favorite anchoring Main Street's nightlife, this is a classic wood-backed bar with lots of memorabilia, a shuffleboard table, and a regular local clientele. The upstairs outdoor deck is great for enjoying cool summer nights, but heaters in the winter make this deck comfortable year-round. The eclectic decor looks like everything was purchased at a flea market in the best way possible. If you are looking for some late-night grub, No Name has the best buffalo burgers in town. *447 Main St., Park City 435/649–6667 www.nonamesaloon.net.*

Old Town Cellars

WINE BARS—NIGHTLIFE | The first of its kind in the area, this private label winery opened on Main Street in 2016. Stop in to learn about the urban wine-making process, buy a bottle of their house wine, or enjoy an après-ski tasting in their Bar and Lounge where local beers and spirits are also available. Local meats and chocolate, available on their fare menu, pair perfectly with the experience. *408 Main St., Main Street 435/649–3759 www.otcwines.com.*

The Spur Bar and Grill

MUSIC CLUBS | If you are looking for live music, look no further than The Spur, which hosts bands seven nights a week. A renovation in 2016 more than doubled the size of The Spur, adding two additional bar areas and a Main Street entrance. The front room provides a lively bar atmosphere; head upstairs if you want to hear your conversation. The back room is where you'll find the live music and the dancing. A full kitchen means breakfast, lunch, and dinner are served until 10 pm. *352 Main St., Park City 435/615–1618 www.thespurbarandgrill.com.*

Troll Hallen Lounge

BARS/PUBS | If quiet conversation and a good single-malt scotch or Swiss raclette in front of a fire is your idea of nightlife, this is the place for you. *Stein Eriksen Lodge, 7700 Stein Way, Park City 435/645–6455.*

Within the colorful structures that line Park City's Main Street are a number of clothing boutiques, sporting-goods stores, and gift shops. In recent years, brand-name stores like Lululemon, Patagonia, and Gorsuch have opened their doors along Historic Main Street, but alongside these recognizable names are locally owned boutiques and shops that help preserve the Park City charm.

ART GALLERIES

Park City Gallery Stroll

ART GALLERIES | Main Street is packed with great art galleries, and the best way to see them all is the Park City Gallery Stroll, a free event hosted by the Park City Gallery Association on the last Friday of the month 6–9 pm, sun or snow. ✉ *Park City* 🌐 *www.parkcitygalleryassociation.com.*

BOOKS AND TOYS

Dolly's Bookstore

BOOKS/STATIONERY | **FAMILY** | For many returning visitors, the first stop in town is Dolly's Bookstore to check on the two cats: Dolly and Pippi Longstocking. Oh, and to browse a great selection of regional books as well as national best-sellers. Dolly's also has a uniquely complete selection of children's books and toys. While you are at it, swing through neighboring Rocky Mountain Chocolate Factory to satisfy your sweet tooth. ✉ *510 Main St., Park City* ☎ *435/649–8062.*

J. W. Allen & Sons Toys & Candy

TOYS | **FAMILY** | Jam-packed with classic toys and modern fun, J. W. Allen & Sons rescues parents who forgot to pack toys for their kids on family vacation. Scary dinosaurs, giant stuffed bears, dolls, sleds, scooters, and kites are as irresistible as the candy. ✉ *1675 W. Redstone Center, No. 105, Park City* ☎ *435/575–8697.*

CLOTHING

Indigo Highway

CLOTHING | This eclectic boutique, located in Newpark Town Center, is worth a visit. Here you'll find clothing, gifts, scented candles, Park City keepsakes, and more, all with a modern nomad twist. They sell handmade bags from all over the world (with notes about the women who made them) next to Park City embroidered caps. There's even a full section of small batch, artisanal apothecary items (think body oils, detoxifying bath salts, and more). ✉ *1241 Center Dr. #L170, Newpark* ☎ *435/214–7244* 🌐 *www.indigohighway.com.*

Mary Jane's

CLOTHING | This independently owned boutique has an eclectic selection of trendy clothing and designer jeans, lingerie, statement jewelry, shoes, and handbags. ✉ *613 Main St., Park City* ☎ *435/645–7463* 🌐 *www.maryjanesshoes.com.*

Olive and Tweed

CLOTHING | This artist-driven boutique sells local handmade jewelry, women's clothing accessories, home decor, baby items, and local art. ✉ *608 Main St., Park City* ☎ *435/649–9392* 🌐 *www.oliveandtweed.com.*

FOOD AND CANDY

Rocky Mountain Chocolate Factory

FOOD/CANDY | You'll find a quick fix for your sweet tooth here, and you can watch them make fudge, dozens of different carameled apples, and other scrumptious treats. There's another location at 1385 Lowell Avenue. ✉ *510 Main St., Park City* ☎ *435/649–0997, 435/649–2235.*

BIKING

In 2012, Park City was the first community ever designated a Gold Level Ride Center by the International Mountain Bicycling Association, thanks in large part to the relentless work of the Mountain

Trails Foundation, which oversees and maintains more than 400 miles of area trails. The accolade is based upon bike shops, trail access, variety, and more. Pick up a map at any local bike shop or get details from the Mountain Trails Foundation (☎ *435/649–6839* 🌐 *www.mountaintrails.org*). You can join local road or mountain bikers most nights in the summer for free group rides sponsored by Park City bike shops.

Cole Sport

BICYCLING | Road bikers of all abilities can ride with a pack one evening a week from June to mid-September from this shop. You can rent mountain and road bikes here, too; be ready to ride at 6 pm. ✉ *1615 Park Ave., Park City* ☎ *435/649–4806* 🌐 *www.colesport.com* ☞ *Call in advance for weekly schedule.*

Deer Valley Resort

BICYCLING | Mountain bikers from across the world flock to Deer Valley's single track trails for mountain biking each summer, and it's easy to see why with the variety of terrain and bike offerings available. Nearly 70 miles of trails can be accessed from three chairlifts, spanning all levels of ability, including down-hill flow trails. Bike clinics and lessons, both group and private, are offered through the Deer Valley Mountain Bike School, and rentals are available at the base areas. Trails are open June through September. ✉ *2250 Deer Valley Dr. S, Park City* ☎ *435/649–1000* 🌐 *www.deervalley.com.*

Jans Mountain Outfitters

BICYCLING | When the snow melts, Jans has everything you need to hit the road on two wheels. Whether you're into mountain bikes, road bikes, or cruisers, stop by to rent or demo something new, or to tune your own wheels. ✉ *1600 Park Ave., Park City* ☎ *435/649–4949* 🌐 *www.jans.com.*

Park City Mountain Resort

BICYCLING | Utah's largest ski resort transforms into a summer adventure land for cyclists, with a lift-served bike park at Canyons Village and miles of cross-country and downhill trails across the whole resort. Park City Base Area provides a number of trails accessible directly from the base, or haul your bike up the lift for some downhill riding. Canyons Village is the home of Park City Bike Park, with a dozen downhill flow and jump trails, many of which are accessible to all skill levels. Lessons are available with certified instructors for those who are new to the sport, and cyclists can find bike rentals at both base areas. ✉ *Park City Base Area, 1345 Lowell Ave., Park City* ☎ *435/649–8111* 🌐 *www.parkcitymountain.com.*

Silver Star Ski & Sport

BICYCLING | Look for Azalea, the English bulldog at Silver Star Ski & Sport. While the dog watches the shop, friendly staff help find the best bike or piece of outdoor equipment to suit your needs. In addition to the retail area of the store offering top-of-the-line gear and clothing, Silver Star offers cruiser, road, and mountain bike rentals. ✉ *1825 Three Kings Dr. #85, Park City* ☎ *435/645–7827* 🌐 *www.silverstarskiandsport.com.*

White Pine Touring

BICYCLING | Every Thursday in summer, mountain bikers of all levels gather at 6 pm for a free guided mountain-bike ride. On the last Thursday of June, July, and August, the White Pine guides prepare a barbecue, too. There's also a women-only ride on Tuesday. For both rides, meet at the shop at 6 pm—earlier if you need to rent a bike. Guided road-biking, mountain-biking, climbing, and hiking tours are also available throughout the summer. In the winter, experience their Fat Bike Tours to ride snow-covered singletrack on a bike. ✉ *1790 Bonanza Dr., Park City* ☎ *435/649–8710* 🌐 *www.whitepinetouring.com.*

FLY-FISHING

The mountain-fed waters of the Provo and Weber rivers and several smaller streams near Park City are prime trout habitat.

Jans Mountain Outfitters

FISHING | During the summer, the entire upstairs of this store is dedicated solely to fly-fishing, and knowledgeable staff will help you find the best equipment and gear for your time on the river. Specializing in trout fishing, guides lead fly-fishing excursions year-round in nearby rivers, rent equipment, and provide insight and advice to the local area. Jans also has exclusive access to private waters about the surrounding areas. Guides also give free casting lessons at the Deer Valley ponds on Monday at 5 pm from Memorial Day to Labor Day. ✉ *1600 Park Ave., Park City* ☎ *435/649–4949* 🌐 *www.jans.com.*

Park City Fly Shop and Guide Service

FISHING | See Chris Kunkel, the owner of this shop, for good advice, guide service, and a modest selection of fly-fishing necessities. ✉ *2065 Sidewinder Dr., Park City* ☎ *435/640–2864* 🌐 *www.pcflyshopguideservice.com.*

Trout Bum 2

FISHING | This full-service fly shop can outfit you with everything you need, then guide you to where the fish are. This shop has the largest selection of flies in town, and is the only guide service in all of Park City to have access to the renowned Green River below Flaming Gorge Reservoir. Check the website for fishing reports of the area rivers and streams. ✉ *4343 N. Hwy. 224, Suite 101, Park City* ☎ *435/658–1166, 877/878–2862* 🌐 *www.troutbum2.com.*

GOLF

Within 20 minutes of Park City are 12 golf courses. An equal amount of private and public courses provide a variety of terrain, views, and holes to play.

Canyons Golf

GOLF | The newest course in Park City (opened for play in 2015), this 97-acre course uses the mountainous terrain at the base of the ski resort for a challenging game. Six holes interact with ski runs, with more than 550 feet of elevation change throughout the course. With seven par-3s, the course is not for the faint of heart, but the views alone make it worth checking out no matter your level. ✉ *4000 Canyons Resort Dr., Canyons Resort* ☎ *435/615–4728* 🌐 *www.parkcitymountain.com/golf* 🎫 *$95; rates drop to $70 during off-peak times* 🏌 *18 holes, 6256 yards, par 70.*

Park City Golf Club

GOLF | On this gorgeous and challenging 6,800-yard, par-72 public course, you'll love the views of ski runs, rising peaks, historic Main Street, and an occasional moose. Popular among locals, it's considered one of the best public courses in the area. Everything you need is in the pro shop, in the Hotel Park City right along the course. ✉ *1541 Thaynes Canyon Dr., Park City* ☎ *435/615–5800* 🌐 *www.parkcity.org/departments/park-city-golf-club* 🎫 *$26 for 9 holes, $33 with cart; $52 for 18 holes, $67 with cart* 🏌 *18 holes, 6800 yards, par 72.*

Promontory Club

GOLF | The only private club in the area to make selected tee times available to the general public, Promontory Club welcomes nonmembers on its challenging and sometimes windy Pete Dye–designed course. The club is renowned for extraordinary views and exemplary service. Six sets of tees on this course make for what some call the most level playing field on any course in Utah. ✉ *8758 Promontory Ranch Rd., Park City* ☎ *435/333–4000* 🌐 *www.promontoryclub.com* 🎫 *$250 for nonmembers; check with hotel concierge for better price* 🏌 *18 holes, 7700 yards, par 72.*

Few places in the world can show off such distinct geologic features in an area as small as the 50 to 70 miles along the Wasatch Front.

HIKING

The Wasatch Mountains surrounding Park City offer more than 400 miles of hiking trails, ranging from easy, meandering meadow strolls to strenuous climbs up wind-blown peaks. Getting away from civilization and into the aspens is easy, and lucky hikers might spy foxes, coyotes, moose, elk, deer, and red-tailed hawks. Many of the trails take off from the resort areas, but some of the trailheads are right near Main Street. For beginners, or for those acclimating to the elevation, the Rail Trail is a good place to start. Another alternative is to take the McLeod Creek Trail from behind The Market all the way to the Redstone Center. The Round Valley and Lost Prospector trails are still mellow but slightly more challenging. To really get the blood pumping, head up Spiro or do a lengthy stretch of Mid-Mountain.

For interactive trail maps, up-to-date information about trail conditions and events, and answers to your trail questions, contact the nonprofit Mountain Trails Foundation (🌐 *www.mountaintrails.org*) whose mission is to promote, preserve, advocate for, and maintain Park City's local trail system. Maps detailing trail locations are available at most local gear shops.

HORSEBACK RIDING

Red Pine Adventures

HORSEBACK RIDING | This outfitter leads trail rides through thousands of acres of private land. ✉ *2050 W. White Pine Canyon Rd., Park City* ☎ *435/649–9445* 🌐 *www.redpinetours.com* 🎫 *From $75.*

Rocky Mountain Recreation

HORSEBACK RIDING | Saddle up for a taste and feel of the Old West with guided mountain trail rides, from one hour to all-day or overnight excursions, departing from several locations in the Park City area, complete with fantastic scenery and good cowboy grub. ✉ *Stillman Ranch, Oakley* ☎ *435/645–7256* 🌐 *www.rockymtnrec.com* 🎫 *From $66.*

Wind In Your Hair Riding

HORSEBACK RIDING | Only experienced riders who are looking for a get-up-and-go kind of mountain riding adventure are allowed on these trail rides, so there will be no inexperienced riders to slow you down, and the Paso Fino horses are noted for their smooth ride. Plan to tip the trail leader. Lessons are available for beginners. ✉ *Cherry Canyon Ranch, 46 E. Cherry Canyon Dr., Wanship* ☎ *435/336–4795, 435/901–4644* 🌐 *www.windinyourhair.com* 🎫 *From $150.*

HOT-AIR BALLOONING

Park City Balloon Adventures

BALLOONING | Hour-long scenic sunrise flights are offered daily, weather permitting. Fliers meet at Starbucks in Kimball Junction and are shuttled to the take-off site, which varies from day to day. A champagne or nonalcoholic toast is offered on touchdown. Reservations are required. ✉ *Park City* ☎ *435/645–8787, 800/396–8787* 🎫 *$225 per person.*

RAFTING

Park City Rafting

WHITE-WATER RAFTING | Two-hour, mostly class II rafting adventures are offered, as well as full-day trips that end with a class III splash. Given the Weber's mostly benign water, there are plenty of breaks between plunges to look for moose, deer, beavers, badgers, and feathered friends along the shore. ✉ *1245 Taggart La., Morgan* ☎ *435/655–3800, 866/467–2384* 🌐 *www.parkcityrafting.com* 🎫 *From $49.*

Utah Outdoor Adventures

WHITE-WATER RAFTING | This company specializes in half-day and full-day excursions, all of which are private groups. Tours take place on the Weber River on class II and class III rapids. Perfect for all age groups. ✉ *3310 Mountain La., Park City* ☎ *801/703–3357* 🌐 *www.utahoutdooradventures.com* 🎫 *$60.*

ROCK CLIMBING

White Pine Touring

CLIMBING/MOUNTAINEERING | If you're looking for some hang time on the local rocks but don't know the area, White Pine Touring offers guided climbing tours, equipment rental, and private and group lessons. Reservations are required. ✉ *1790 Bonanza Dr., Park City* ☎ *435/649–8710* 🌐 *www.whitepinetouring.com* 🎫 *From $325.*

SKIING AND SNOWBOARDING

★ Deer Valley Resort

SKIING/SNOWBOARDING | **FAMILY** | Just to the south of downtown Park City, this resort set new standards in the ski industry by providing such amenities as ski valets and slope-side dining of the highest caliber. For such pampering, the resort has drawn rave reviews from virtually every ski and travel magazine, consistently rated #1 Ski Resort in America by *SKI* magazine. The careful layout of runs and the impeccable grooming makes this an intermediate skier's heaven. With the Empire Canyon and Lady Morgan areas, the resort also offers bona fide expert terrain. For many, part of the ski experience includes a two- to three-hour midday interlude of feasting at one of the many world-class dining locations on the mountain and catching major rays on the snow-covered meadow in front of Silver Lake Lodge. The ski experience fits right in with the resort's overall image. With lessons for kids from preschool through teens, Deer Valley's acclaimed children's ski school is sure to please both children and parents. Note: this is one of the only ski resorts in the United States that prohibits snowboards. ✉ *2250 Deer Valley Dr., Park City* ☎ *435/649–1000, 800/424–3337 reservations* 🌐 *www.deervalley.com* 🎫 *Lift ticket $135* ☞ *3,000-ft vertical drop; 2,026 skiable acres; 27% beginner, 41% intermediate, 32% advanced; 101 total runs.*

★ Park City Mountain Resort

SKIING/SNOWBOARDING | FAMILY | Although this has been one of North America's most popular ski and snowboard destinations for quite some time, in 2015 Vail Resorts joined neighboring Canyons Resort to Park City Mountain, creating the largest ski resort in the United States. With more than 330 trails, 17 mountain peaks, 7,300 skiable acres, and 41 lifts, it is almost impossible to ski the entire resort in one day. The trails provide a great mix of beginner, intermediate, and advanced terrain, with Jupiter Peak providing the highest elevation and steepest terrain in town. Three distinct base areas provide a great starting point for the ski day—Park City Base Area has a variety of dining and retail options, along with a stellar après-ski scene. Park City is the only resort with lift access to Historic Main Street with Town Lift, allowing for guests staying near or on Main Street direct access to the slopes. Canyons Village, located on the other side of the mountain, gives ski-in/ski-out access to many of the base area's hotels and lodging properties. The resort is widely acclaimed for being a free-skiing and snowboarding mecca with official Olympic qualifying events each year; you're likely to see Olympic athletes training and playing on the slopes. ✉ *1345 Lowell Ave., Park City* ☎ *435/649–8111* 🌐 *www.parkcitymountain.com* 🎫 *Lift ticket prices change daily; check online for daily rate* ☞ *3,200-ft vertical drop; 7,300 skiable acres; 8% beginner, 42% intermediate, 50% advanced; 41 lifts; 2 halfpipes (including 1 super pipe) and 8 terrain parks.*

Wasatch Powderbird Guides

SKIING/SNOWBOARDING | If you don't mind paying for it, the best way to find untracked Utah powder is with Wasatch Powderbird Guides. A helicopter drops you on the top of the mountain, and a guide leads you back down. Itineraries are always weather dependent. Call to inquire about departures from Snowbird (Little Cottonwood Canyon) or Park City Mountain Resort (Canyons Village). ✉ *3000 Canyons Resort Dr., Park City* ☎ *801/742–2800* 🌐 *www.powderbird.com* 🎫 *From $1260.*

White Pine Nordic Center

SKIING/SNOWBOARDING | Just outside Old Town, White Pine Nordic Center offers around 20 km (12 miles) of set track, in 3-km (2-mile), 5-km (3-mile), and 10-km (6-mile) loops, plus cross-country ski instruction, equipment rentals, and a well-stocked cross-country ski shop. The fee to use the track is $18, or $10 after 3 pm. Reservations are required for their guided backcountry ski and snowshoe tours in the surrounding mountains. ✉ *On Park City Golf Course, 1541 Thaynes Canyon Dr., Park City* ☎ *435/649–6249* 🌐 *www.whitepinetouring.com.*

SKI RENTALS AND EQUIPMENT

Many shops in Park City rent equipment for skiing and other sports. From old-fashioned rental shops that also offer discount lift tickets to luxurious ski-delivery services that will fit you in your room, you have dozens of choices. Prices tend to be slightly lower if you rent in Salt Lake City. **■ TIP→ If you happen to be visiting during holidays, reserve skiing and snowboarding gear in advance.**

Breeze Winter Sports Rentals

SKIING/SNOWBOARDING | You can reserve your equipment online in advance with this company (often for less than day-of rentals), which has two locations in Park City. You'll find them near Canyons Village and at Park City Base Area. They're owned by Vail Resorts, and you can expect good quality and service at a value price. ✉ *4343 N. Hwy. 224, Park City* ☎ *435/655–7066, 888/427–3393* 🌐 *www.skirentals.com.*

Cole Sport

SKIING/SNOWBOARDING | With four locations from Main Street to Deer Valley, Cole Sport carries all of your winter ski, snowboard, and snowshoe rental needs. Come back in summer for bikes, stand-up paddleboards, hiking gear, and more. No matter the season, Cole Sport offers expert fitting and advice with a broad range of equipment. ✉ *1615 Park Ave., Park City* ☎ *435/649–4806, 800/345–2938* 🌐 *www.colesport.com.*

Jans Mountain Outfitters

SKIING/SNOWBOARDING | For almost 40 years, this has been the locals' choice for gear rentals, with ski and snowboard equipment packages and clothing in winter, and bikes and fly-fishing gear in summer. With the most knowledgeable staff around, they'll assist you with any outdoor adventure. There are multiple locations, including the flagship Park Avenue store, Deer Valley, and Park City Mountain Resort. ✉ *1600 Park Ave., Park City* ☎ *435/649–4949* 🌐 *www.jans.com.*

Park City Sport

SKIING/SNOWBOARDING | At the base of Park City Mountain Resort, this is a convenient place to rent ski and snowboard equipment, goggles, and clothing. You can drop off your personal gear at the end of a ski day, and they'll have it tuned and ready for you the next morning with free overnight storage for customers. A second location on Main Street is across from Town Lift. ✉ *1335 Lowell Ave., #104, Park City* ☎ *435/645–7777, 800/523–3922* 🌐 *www.parkcitysport.com.*

Silver Star Ski & Sport

SKIING/SNOWBOARDING | This company rents, tunes, and repairs ski equipment, snowshoes, bike gear, and stand-up paddleboards. It doesn't get much more convenient for winter rentals/gear adjustments, as the shop is located at the base of the Silver Star lift at Park City Mountain Resort. ✉ *1825 Three Kings Dr., #85, Park City* ☎ *435/645–7827* 🌐 *www.silverstarskiandsport.com.*

Ski Butlers

SKIING/SNOWBOARDING | The most prominent of a number of companies offering ski and snowboard delivery, Ski Butlers carries top-of-the-line Rossignol equipment. Their experts will fit you in your hotel room or condo and meet you at any of the resorts should something go wrong. You'll pay a little more, but you'll avoid the hassle of rentals when the snow is falling on your first morning in the mountains. ✉ *Park City* ☎ *877/754–7754* 🌐 *www.skibutlers.com.*

Utah Ski & Golf

SKIING/SNOWBOARDING | Downhill equipment, snowshoes, clothing, and golf-club rental are available here, at Park City Base Area and Town Lift, as well as in downtown Salt Lake City. ✉ *698 Park Ave., Park City* ☎ *435/649–3020* 🌐 *www.utahskigolf.com.*

SKI TOURS

Ski Utah Interconnect Tour

SKIING/SNOWBOARDING | Strong intermediate and advanced skiers can hook up with the Ski Utah Interconnect Tour for a guided alpine ski tour that takes you to as many as six resorts, including Deer Valley and Park City, in a single day, all connected by backcountry ski routes with unparalleled views of the Wasatch Mountains. Guides test your ski ability before departure. The tour includes guide service, lift tickets, lunch, and transportation back to the point of origin. You'll even walk away with a finisher's pin. Reservations are required. ✉ *Park City* ☎ *801/534–1907* 🌐 *www.skiutah.com* 🎫 *$395.*

★ White Pine Touring

SKIING/SNOWBOARDING | Specializing in telemark, cross-country, and alpine touring gear and guided tours, White Pine Touring also has top of the line clothing, as well as mountain bikes, fat bikes, snowshoes, and climbing shoes. ✉ *1790 Bonanza Dr., Park City* ☎ *435/649–8710* 🌐 *www.whitepinetouring.com.*

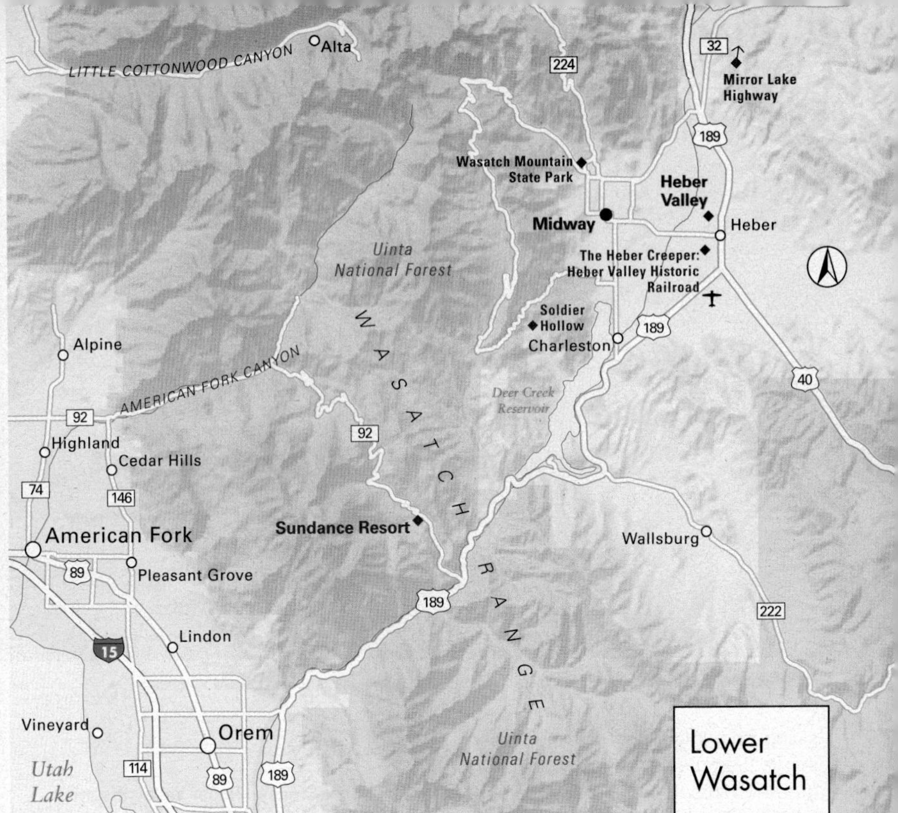

SNOWMOBILING

Red Pine Adventures

SNOW SPORTS | For a winter speed thrill of the machine-powered variety, hop on a snowmobile and follow your guide along private groomed trails adjacent to Park City Mountain Resort. Pick up is in Park City. ✉ *2050 W. White Pine Canyon Rd., Park City* ☎ *435/649–9445* 🌐 *www.redpinetours.com* 🎫 *From $199 single rider, $239 double.*

Thousand Peaks Snowmobile Adventures

SNOW SPORTS | Backcountry snowmobile tours are on one of Utah's largest private mountain ranches, just outside of Park City. Clothing is available to rent. ✉ *Office, 698 Park Ave., Park City* ☎ *888/304–7669* 🌐 *www.powderutah.com* 🎫 *From $169 single rider, $218 double.*

SNOW TUBING

Woodward Park City

SNOW SPORTS | FAMILY | Lift-served snow tubing (with seven lanes) and mini-snowmobile rentals bring families here. ✉ *3863 W. Kilby Rd., Park City* ☎ *435/658–2648* 🌐 *www.woodwardparkcity.com/tickets-passes/tubing* 🎫 *From $40.*

Heber Valley

20 miles south of Park City; 22 miles northeast of Sundance.

Bounded by the Wasatch Mountains on the west and the rolling foothills of the Uinta Mountains on the east, the Heber Valley, including the towns of Heber, Midway, and Charleston, is well-supplied with snow in winter for cross-country

To the west of Heber Valley are the Wasatch Mountains; to the east are the Uinta Mountains.

skiing, snowmobiling, and other snow sports. Summers are mostly cool and green. Events throughout the year entertain locals and visitors alike.

GETTING HERE AND AROUND

From Park City, head east on Highway 40 to enter the Heber Valley. The highway turns into Main Street, which leads straight through Heber City. Turn right on 100 South to reach the Swiss-influenced town of Midway. If you're coming from Sundance, take Highway 92 south then Highway 189 east.

VISITOR INFORMATION

CONTACTS Heber Valley County Chamber of Commerce. ✉ *475 N. Main St., Heber Valley* ☎ *435/654–3666* 🌐 *www.goheber-valley.com.*

Sights

The Heber Creeper: Heber Valley Historic Railroad

TOUR—SIGHT | FAMILY | This steam train takes passengers on a nostalgic trip along a line that first ran in 1899 past the Deer Creek Reservoir and through beautiful Provo Canyon. It continues past Bridal Falls, a veil-like waterfall near snow-capped Mt. Timpanogos. Each car has been restored, and two of the engines are fully operational, steam-powered locomotives. The railroad offers special events including cheese-tasting rides, the local favorite North Pole Christmas Train, Raft 'n Rails (pairing rafting with a train excursion), Reins 'n Trains (with horseback riding), and Wilderness. Lunch is available for an extra cost. **TIP→ There's no climate control in the rail cars, so dress for the weather.** ✉ *450 S. 600 W, Heber* ☎ *435/654–5601* 🌐 *www.hebervalleyrr.org* 🎟 *Provo Canyon $30; Deer Creek $20; call for special event and activity trip prices.*

Mirror Lake Highway
SCENIC DRIVE | East of Park City, this scenic byway winds through aspens and ponderosa pines, skirts alpine lakes and waterfalls, and reaches 11,943-foot Bald Mountain. The ride is good, but getting out of the car is better. A spectacular hike is the 5-mile, five-lake Lofty Lake Loop, which starts at the Pass Lake Trailhead at mile 32. It's also a great place to snowshoe in the winter. Keep an eye out for moose, wildflowers, and changeable weather. Reward yourself with jerky from Samak Smoke House, a typical dry goods store, or a berry shake at Uinta Drive-In, near the Uinta-Wasatch-Cache National Forest's Kamas entrance. ✉ *Kamas* ☎ *435/783–4338* 🌐 *www.fs.fed.us/r4/uwc* 🎟 *$6 per car for 3-day pass* 🕐 *Road closed in winter, depending on snowfall.*

Soldier Hollow
NATIONAL/STATE PARK | On the southern end of the park, this activity center was one site for the 2002 Winter Olympics and still hosts the national championship Nordic ski events and other events, including powwows and sheepdog championships. It's open to the public year-round for hiking, horseback riding, cross-country skiing, tubing, snowshoeing, biathlon, and other events. A beautiful lodge has food concessions, equipment rentals, and a souvenir shop. ✉ *2002 Soldier Hollow La., Midway* ☎ *435/654–2002* 🌐 *www.soldierhollow.com.*

Wasatch Mountain State Park
NATIONAL/STATE PARK | **FAMILY** | This 22,000-acre preserve is 3 miles from Heber City and provides for a number of activities, ranging from serene hikes along winding mountain trails to golfing at one of the four 18-hole courses. Children have their own fishing pond near the visitor center. In winter, hiking turns to snowshoeing, cross-country, or backcountry skiing along the Dutch Hollow, Snake Creek, or Pine Creek trails winding up through stands of Gambel oak, aspen, and maple. ✉ *1281 Warm Springs Rd., Midway* ☎ *435/654–1791, 800/322–3770* 🌐 *stateparks.utah.gov* 🎟 *$7 per car.*

Restaurants

Café Galleria
$ | **PIZZA** | **FAMILY** | This family-friendly restaurant claims to have the best pizza and bagels in the state, and they may not be far off. The wood-fired pizza oven cooks to perfection, and bagel sandwiches, available throughout the day, hit the spot. **Known for:** casual atmosphere; bagels; wood-fired pizza. 💲 *Average main: $11* ✉ *101 W. Main St., Midway* ☎ *435/657–2002* 🌐 *www.thecafegalleria.com.*

★ **Dairy Keen**
$ | **FAST FOOD** | **FAMILY** | A welcome respite from chain fast food, this family-owned drive-in is loved by all the locals and serves the best shakes and burgers for miles around. Railroad artifacts line the walls, and an electric train entertains children as it passes over the booths. **Known for:** signature burgers; vintage vibe. 💲 *Average main: $5* ✉ *199 S. Main St., Heber Valley* ☎ *435/654–5336* 🌐 *www.dairykeen.com.*

Coffee and Quick Bites

The Bagel Den
$ | **AMERICAN** | Locals love this bagel shop, where they can pick up a latte and a New York-style bagel made fresh daily. Try the pumpernickel, French toast, or pretzel bagels and add a schmear like bacon scallion or blueberry cream cheese. **Known for:** New York-style bagels; local favorite; delicious smoothies. 💲 *Average main: $8* ✉ *570 N. Main St., Heber* ☎ *435/654–3193* 🌐 *www.thebagelden.com.*

Hotels

Blue Boar Inn

$$ | **B&B/INN** | Wrought-iron balconies, mountain views, and an antique alpenhorn give this château-style inn a warm, romantic feel. **Pros:** hospitable staff; romantic ambience; full breakfast. **Cons:** not the ideal place for boisterous little ones; 20-plus minutes to the ski resorts; dark decor. *Rooms from: $175 1235 Warm Springs Rd., Midway 435/654–1400, 888/650–1400 www.theblueboarinn.com 12 rooms Free breakfast.*

Homestead Resort

$$ | **HOTEL** | **FAMILY** | Park City silver miners once soaked in the hot springs of this resort, which has been in operation since 1886. **Pros:** a Bruce Summerhays–designed golf course; natural hot springs; family-friendly. **Cons:** far from ski resorts; rooms are basic; a bit sleepy. *Rooms from: $139 700 N. Homestead Dr., Midway 435/654–1102, 800/327–7220 www.homesteadresort.com 147 rooms No meals.*

Zermatt Utah Resort & Spa

$$$ | **RESORT** | **FAMILY** | This charming Swiss-style hotel is a restful retreat tucked into the idyllic countryside. **Pros:** immaculate rooms; stellar views; plenty to do. **Cons:** far from restaurants and ski resorts; expensive resort fee; very quiet. *Rooms from: $215 784 W. Resort Dr., Midway 435/657–0180, 866/840–5087 www.zermattresort.com 427 rooms No meals.*

Activities

GOLF

Homestead Golf Club

GOLF | This incredible course, in the heart of the Heber Valley on the Homestead Resort, offers views of the Wasatch Mountains and plenty of fresh mountain air. GPS-enabled cart paths mean you won't get lost while looking at the scenery. *700 N. Homestead Dr., Midway 435/654–1102, 800/327–7220 playhomesteadgc.com $45 for 18 holes Sun.–Thurs., $49 Fri. and Sat. 18 holes, 7040 yards, par 72 Closed Nov.–Mar.*

Soldier Hollow Golf Course

GOLF | Reflecting the Olympic heritage, the names of the two 18-hole courses are Gold and Silver. While on these greens, golfers enjoy the beauty of both the Heber Valley to the east and the stunning Mount Timpanogos to the west. The Gold course is considered a mountain course, with dramatic elevation changes within each hole. The Silver course is slightly shorter than Gold, but with longer and trickier greens. *1371 W. Soldier Hollow La., Midway 435/654–7442 Gold: $50; Silver: $45 (includes cart) Gold: 18 holes, 7598 yards, par 72; Silver: 18 holes, 7335 yards, par 72.*

★ Wasatch Golf

GOLF | The setting within the Wasatch Mountain State Park is spectacular, particularly at fall foliage time, and with the challenging Mountain Course as well as the gentler Lake Course, this is one of the most popular public courses in the state. The Mountain Course is designed around the natural contours of the surrounding Wasatch mountains, and motorized carts are mandatory. Sometimes you can even see deer and even moose while you golf. The easier Lake Course surrounds eight lakes and ponds, and is a favorite with high, low, and no handicappers. The course's café serves breakfast, lunch, and dinner. *975 W. Golf Course Rd., Midway 435/654–0532 www.wasatchgolfcourse.com $50 (includes cart) Mountain course: 18 holes, 6459 yards, par 71; Lake course: 18 holes, 6942 yards, par 72.*

HIKING

The path connecting the towns of Heber and Midway is an easy walk with spectacular views of the Wasatch Range at a distance and, up close, the Provo River.

Jordanelle State Park

HIKING/WALKING | For a quiet experience, start your hike from the Rock Cliff Nature Center, under tall cottonwoods at the east end of Jordanelle State Park, which lies 10 miles east of Heber City. Hikers often report excellent wildlife viewing along this section of the upper Provo River. No dogs are allowed. ✉ *Hwy. 32, Heber* ☎ *435/782–3030* 🌐 *stateparks.utah.gov.*

Soldier Hollow

BICYCLING | **FAMILY** | Although the trail system here is more exposed than that in the northern end of Wasatch Mountain State Park, hikers will enjoy the stunning view of the east side of Mount Timpanogos as well as the vista of the Uinta Mountains to the east across the Heber Valley. Or, if you'd rather go faster than your feet can take you, rent an electric mountain bike at Soldier Hollow Lodge to zip down the trails. ✉ *2002 Soldier Hollow La., Midway* ☎ *435/654–2002* 🌐 *www.soldierhollow.com* ☞ *To rent an electric bike costs $75 for a half day and $105 for a full day.*

Wasatch Mountain State Park

HIKING/WALKING | Hikers will find lots of foliage and wildlife here, on any number of trails in Dutch Hollow, Pine Canyon, and along Snake Creek. ✉ *1281 Warm Springs Rd., Midway* ☎ *435/654–1791* 🌐 *stateparks.utah.gov.*

HORSEBACK RIDING

Rocky Mountain Outfitters

HORSEBACK RIDING | Visitors can enjoy the spectacular back country of the Wasatch Mountain State Park and surrounding areas on horseback year-round with Rocky Mountain Outfitters. Choose from a variety of ride durations and destinations with the nicest guides in the area. ☎ *435/654–1655* 🌐 *www.rockymtnoutfitters.com* 🎫 *$79 for a 2-hr ride.*

WATER SPORTS

Deer Creek State Park

FISHING | Consistently good fishing, mild canyon winds, and water warmer than you'd expect are responsible for Deer Creek State Park's popularity with windsurfers, sailors, swimmers, and those just kicking back in the mountain sunshine. The park is 5 miles south of Heber City. ✉ *U.S. 189, Heber* ☎ *435/654–0174* 🌐 *stateparks.utah.gov* 🎫 *$10 day-use fee.*

Jordanelle State Park

WATER SPORTS | This park has three recreation areas on a large mountain reservoir. The Hailstone area, 10 miles north of Heber City via U.S. 40, offers day-use areas, boat ramps, playgrounds, and a marina store where water toys (wave runners and the like) can be rented. To the east, across the reservoir on Highway 32, the Rock Cliff area and facilities are near the Provo River. To the north, Ross Creek is where some of the best fishing in the area can be found. ✉ *Hwy. 32, Heber* ☎ *435/649–9540 Hailstone Main Park* 🌐 *stateparks.utah.gov* 🎫 *Hailstone $10 per vehicle, Rock Cliff and Ross Creek $7 per vehicle.*

Sundance Resort

35 miles south of Park City; 12 miles northeast of Provo.

As Thoreau had Walden Pond, so does Redford have Sundance. Lucky for the rest of us, the "Sundance Kid" shares his 5,000-acre bounty. Several miles up a winding mountain lane, Sundance Resort is a full-service ski resort with bustling slopes in winter, except during the Sundance Film Festival. In summer, it's a destination for filmmakers, writers, craftsmen, and artists of all sensibilities. It also caters to visitors looking to relax at spas, shop, or dine.

Fly-fishing on the Provo River is just one activity guests at Sundance Resort can take part in.

GETTING HERE AND AROUND

From Park City, take Highway 40 and 189 south. From Provo, head northeast on Highway 92.

Sights

★ Sundance Resort

RESORT—SIGHT | Set on the eastern slopes of the breathtaking 11,750-foot Mount Timpanogos, the resort came into being when Robert Redford purchased the land in 1969. The 5,000-acre mountain community reflects Redford's commitment to the natural environment, outdoor exploration, and artistic expression. All resort facilities—constructed from materials such as indigenous cedar, fir, and pine, and locally quarried stone—compliment the natural landscape. No matter the season, you'll find plenty of recreational opportunities, including hiking, biking, fly-fishing, horseback riding, alpine and cross-country skiing, snowboarding, snowshoeing, and ziplining. If you're looking for a more indulgent experience, relax with a body treatment in the Spa at Sundance or take one of many creative classes in the Art Studios. Dine in one of on-site restaurants like the cozy Tree Room or the hip western Owl Bar on a night when they play live music. The Sundance Film Festival, based in nearby Park City each January, is an internationally recognized showcase for independent films. Festival screenings and summer workshops are held at the resort. *8841 N. Alpine Loop Rd., Sundance* *866/259–7468, 800/892–1600* *www.sundanceresort.com* *Lift tickets $80* *2,150-ft vertical drop; 450 skiable acres; 35% novice, 45% intermediate, 20% advanced; 3 quad lifts, 1 triple chair, 1 surface lift.*

Restaurants

★ The Foundry Grill

$$$ | **AMERICAN** | Wood-oven pizzas, sizzling steaks, and spit-roasted chicken are among the hearty staples on the menu at this restaurant. Like the rest of Sundance, everything from the food presentation to the interior design is beautiful, and fits right in with the eco-friendly, nature first concept established by Redford. **Known for:** Sunday brunch; open kitchen; wood-burning pizza oven. *Average main: $30 ✉ Sundance Resort, 8841 N. Alpine Loop Rd., Sundance ☎ 866/932–2295 🌐 www.sundanceresort.com.*

★ The Tree Room

$$$$ | AMERICAN | It's easy to imagine that you're a personal guest of Robert Redford at this intimate, rustic restaurant with Western memorabilia from the actor's private collection. With its warm wood interior and natural light, this cozy restaurant is a great place to tuck into for hours to eat delicious food, listen to the creek nearby, and forget about your worries. **Known for:** fine dining; candlelit atmosphere; interesting art. *Average main: $37 ✉ Sundance Resort, 8841 N. Alpine Loop Rd., Sundance ☎ 866/627–8313 🌐 www.sundanceresort.com ⏲ No lunch.*

Hotels

★ Sundance Resort

$$$$ | RESORT | With 11,750-foot Mount Timpanogos serving as a backdrop, Robert Redford's resort is tucked into a 5,000-acre swath of lush wilderness and is a genuine tribute to arts and the natural world. **Pros:** retreat from urban hubbub; glorious scenery; culinary magic. **Cons:** cell reception is spotty; far drive to other restaurants and nightlife; limited ski terrain compared to other Utah resorts. *Rooms from: $285 ✉ 8841 N. Alpine Loop Rd., Sundance ☎ 866/259–7468, 800/892–1600 🌐 www.sundanceresort.com 95 rooms No meals.*

Shopping

General Store

JEWELRY/ACCESSORIES | Step inside the Sundance catalog, which features distinctive home furnishings, clothing, and jewelry reflecting the rustically elegant Sundance style. Ask about many items that are organic or made of recycled materials. *✉ Sundance Resort, 8841 N. Alpine Loop Rd., Sundance ☎ 801/223–4250 🌐 www.sundanceresort.com.*

Sundance Deli

FOOD/CANDY | Selling foods from American cottage farmers and artisans as well as homemade oils, soaps, and bath salts, the Deli also has a juice bar and is a good place to get tea, coffee, shakes, pastries, deli meats, organic produce, and other tasty snacks. Stop here before your hike to pick up a fresh sandwich. *✉ Sundance Resort, 8841 N. Alpine Loop Rd., Sundance ☎ 801/223–4211 🌐 www.sundanceresort.com ⏲ Closed Sun.*

Activities

FLY-FISHING

The Provo River, minutes from Sundance Resort, is a fly-fishing catch-and-release waterway. Access to the rainbow, cutthroat, and German brown trout found in the river is year-round. Tours are provided by Wasatch Guide Service, and include all necessary gear and guides, and some may include drinks and snacks.

Wasatch Guide Service

FISHING | The preferred outfitter of Sundance Resort, Wasatch Guide Service provides access to some of the best fly-fishing in the state. Guides will take you to the world-class Provo River, right near Sundance Resort, or up to the Weber River to help you hook into fun runs of lively cuttroat or brown trout. They can even provide access to private waters and lesser-known streams. One guide to every two guests ensures personalized experiences, and they provide all necessary equipment. Half-day and full-day tours are available year-round, with lunch provided in the full-day tour. *✉ Sundance ☎ 801/830–3316 🌐 www.wasatchguideservice.com From $280 half-day; from $400 full day.*

HIKING

Hiking trails in the Sundance area vary from the easy 1.25-mile Nature Trail and the popular lift-accessed Stewart Falls Trail (3 miles) to the 7½-mile Big Baldy Trail, which leads past a series of waterfalls up steep, rugged terrain. You can access moderate- to expert-level trails from the resort base or chairlift. Select from three routes to summit the 11,000-foot Mount Timpanogos. Guided naturalist hikes are available.

MOUNTAIN BIKING

You'll find more than 25 miles of ski lift–accessed mountain-biking trails at Sundance Resort, extending from the base of Mount Timpanogos to Ray's Summit at 7,250 feet. High-tech gear rentals are available for full or half days, as is individual or group instruction.

Sundance Mountain Outfitters

BICYCLING | Rent all the gear you need for mountain biking, skiing, or snowboarding. ✉ *8841 N. Alpine Loop Rd., Sundance* ☎ *801/223–4121* 🌐 *www.sundanceresort.com.*

SKIING

CROSS-COUNTRY

Enjoy terrain suitable for all skill levels on nearly 10 miles of groomed trails. Six miles of dedicated snowshoeing trails wind through mature aspen groves and pines. Lessons and equipment rentals, including telemark gear, are available for all techniques of cross-country skiing and snowshoeing at the Sundance Nordic Center.

DOWNHILL

Skiers and snowboarders at Sundance Resort will find 44 trails on 450 acres of varied terrain. Services include specialized ski workshops (including ladies' day clinics and personal coaching), a PSIA-certified ski school, and a ski school just for children, with programs that include all-day supervision, lunch, and ski instruction. Children as young as four are eligible for group lessons. Rentals are available for all skill levels. Night skiing is also available four nights a week.

Chapter 7

SOUTHWESTERN UTAH

WITH ZION, BRYCE CANYON, AND CAPITOL REEF NATIONAL PARKS

Updated by Shelley Arenas and Andrew Collins

Sights ★★★★★ | Restaurants ★★★☆☆ | Hotels ★★★★★ | Shopping ★★★★☆ | Nightlife ★★☆☆☆

WELCOME TO SOUTHWESTERN UTAH

TOP REASONS TO GO

★ **Travel through history:** Imagine life during the pioneer days as you explore the historic sites and museums of St. George.

★ **Drive the Scenic Byway:** With its hair-raising twists and turns, spectacular Highway 12 begins just outside Panguitch and continues to Capitol Reef National Park.

★ **Zion:** The park is filled with myriad hikes, breathtaking rock formations, and the widest array of plant life in Utah.

★ **Bryce Canyon:** The boldly colored, gravity-defying limestone tentacles reaching skyward—called hoodoos—are Bryce Canyon's most recognizable attraction.

★ **Capitol Reef:** The main attraction is a 100-mile long fold in the Earth's crust, petroglyphs, and pioneer history.

★ **Shakespeare and more:** Watch productions of the Bard's work in three handsome theaters in Cedar City.

1 **Cedar City.** Home to Southern Utah University.

2 **St. George.** This desert metropolis boasts a slew of diversions.

3 **Springdale.** This gorgeously situated village on the Virgin River is an ideal base for exploring Zion National Park.

4 **Zion National Park.** Beautiful Zion Canyon is the park's main draw.

5 **Kanab.** This funky western hamlet is convenient to Zion, Bryce, and the North Rim of the Grand Canyon.

6 **Panguitch.** You can count on this low-key town in the Sevier River valley for inexpensive, casual lodgings and eateries.

7 **Bryce Canyon National Park.** Columns of eroded limestone called Hoodoos are the main feature of this popular national park.

8 **Escalante.** This picturesque village on Highway 12 has become one of the region's top recreation hubs.

9 **Torrey.** Visitors to Capitol Reef National Park typically eat, stay, and relax here.

10 **Capitol Reef National Park.** The massive Waterpocket Fold is the park's centerpiece.

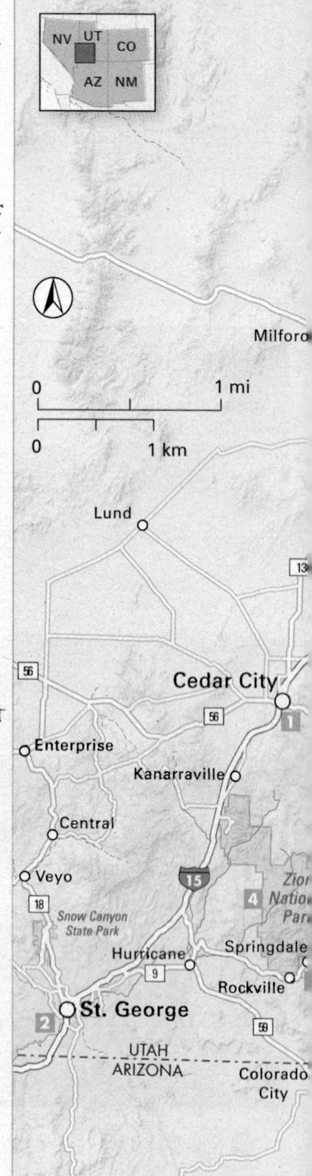

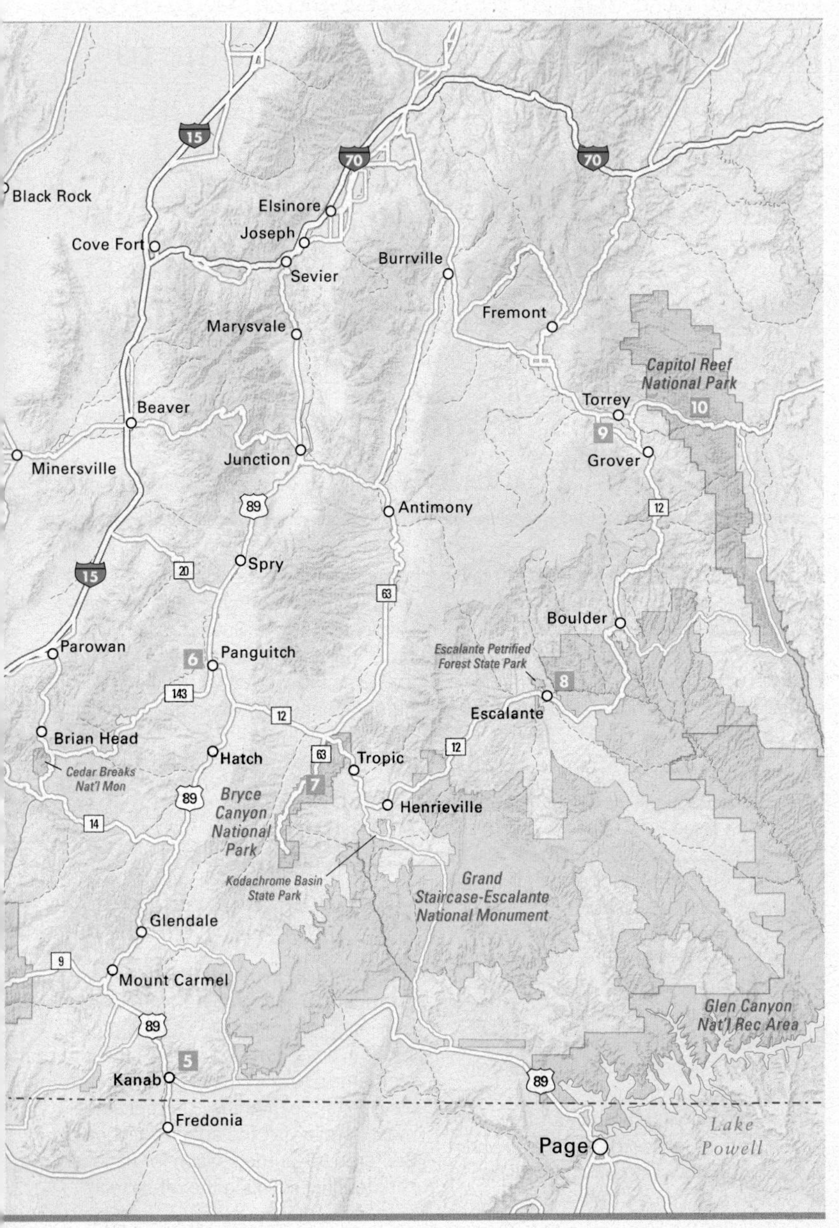

Black Rock
Elsinore
Joseph
Cove Fort
Sevier
Burrville
Fremont
Marysvale
Capitol Reef
National Park
Torrey
10
9
Grover
Beaver
Minersville
Junction
89
Antimony
12
Spry
20
15
63
Boulder
Parowan
Panguitch
6
Escalante Petrified
Forest State Park
8
143
Escalante
12
Brian Head
Hatch
63
Tropic
12
Cedar Breaks
Nat'l Mon
7
89
Bryce
Canyon
National
Park
Henrieville
14
Kodachrome Basin
State Park
Grand
Staircase-Escalante
National Monument
Glendale
9
Mount Carmel
Glen Canyon
Nat'l Rec Area
89
5
Kanab
89
Fredonia
Lake
Powell
Page
70
70
15

Just two hours by desert highway north of the glittering lights of Las Vegas lies one of the most beautiful and distinctive regions of the United States. Home to Zion, Bryce, and Capitol Reef national parks as well as the vast and stunning wilderness of Grand Staircase–Escalante National Monument, this outdoor mecca is anchored by the fast-growing city of St. George, which is itself surrounded by shimmering white and red sandstone and blackened lava formations.

Elsewhere in the region you'll find small recreational base communities—such as Cedar City, Kanab, Escalante, and Torrey—all of which offer plenty of charms, from hip coffeehouses and fine art galleries to breathtaking scenic drives and rugged hikes.

Southwestern Utah is a landscape of both adrenaline thrills and peaceful relaxation—head for one of the swanky spas in St. George for the ultimate rejuvenating getaway. Seasonal fare, like the renowned Utah Shakespeare Festival, and a growing number of noteworthy dining options and one-of-a-kind lodgings make this a region worth slowing down and spending time to discover. You'll find southern Utah's best alpine skiing in Brian Head and opportunities for mountain biking, horseback trail rides, jeep tours, and wildlife viewing throughout the region, and in St. George you'll also find a clutch of renowned golf courses. As you venture to some of the more remote sections of the area, visiting canyons and mesas rich with Native American history and where Butch Cassidy and the Sundance Kid once roamed, it's easy to feel as though you've traveled back in time. And at night, when the dark alpine sky pulses with stars, you can almost imagine you're on another planet.

Planning

When to Go

Year-round, far southwestern Utah is the warmest region in the state. St. George is usually the first city in Utah to break 100°F every summer, and even the winters remain mild at these lower desert elevations. Despite the summer's heat, most people visit the area from June to September—prime season for national park touring—making the off-season winter months preferable if you wish to avoid crowds and sweltering (but arid) heat. If you do decide to brave the heat, wear sunscreen and drink lots of water, regardless of your activity level, but also pack some warmer clothes if you're venturing into the national parks, Brian Head and Dixie National Forest, or the U.S. 89 and Highway 12 corridors, as even in July and August, nights cool down significantly in these high-elevation climates.

Getting Here and Around

AIR

Small, modern, and convenient St. George Regional Airport (SGU) has daily flights to Salt Lake City (Delta), Denver (United), and Phoenix (American). Las Vegas's McCarran International Airport (LAS) is 120 miles south of St. George, and Salt Lake International Airport is 300 miles north. Salt Lake/St. George Express buses make numerous trips per day between McCarran Airport and St. George, and a handful of trips north from St. George to Salt Lake City, with a stop in Cedar City.

CAR

Interstate 15, the main corridor through southwestern Utah, connects St. George and Cedar City with Las Vegas and Salt Lake City and also intersects with Interstate 70 about 75 miles north of Cedar City. It's actually quite pretty for an interstate, but the scenery becomes even more dramatic as you venture onto the region's main two-lane highways, such as Highway 9 through Springdale and Zion National Park, highways 14 and 143 through Brian Head and Dixie National Forest, U.S. 89 through Paria Canyon, Kanab, and Panguitch, and Highway 12 through Bryce City, Tropic, Escalante, and Torrey. ■ TIP→ **If you travel between I–15 and U.S. 89 via Highway 9, you must pay the $35 admission fee to Zion National Park even if you do not plan to stop and visit. If you're planning to visit Zion and at least two other parks, however, you should think about buying an Interagency Annual Pass for $80.**

In winter, Highway 143—the primary access road to Brian Head and Cedar Breaks National Monument—occasionally closes when there's heavy snowfall, and Highway 148 shuts down all winter, typically from mid-November through February. Utah Department of Transportation provides free, up-to-the-minute interactive road conditions. You can also download the app or check conditions online (🌐 *udottraffic.utah.gov)*.

Keep in mind that services are few and far between on back roads in this part of the state, especially as you head east from the Interstate 15 corridor. Cell service can be spotty in these areas, too. It's best to download maps and top off your gas tank before you set out to explore these areas.

Hotels

Budget, midrange, and a handful of upscale chain properties make up the lion's share of lodging options in St. George and the larger towns in the region. *Hotel reviews have been shortened. For full information, visit Fodors.com.*

Restaurants

Cedar City and Springdale offer a number of distinctive options, and perhaps most surprisingly, tiny Kanab now boasting a handful of truly sophisticated destination eateries. In Escalante and Torrey, too, it's become easier to find fair-trade coffee, vegetarian options, and creative dining. Utah has unique wine and liquor laws, but these days, most of the nicer restaurants in bigger communities serve beer, wine, or cocktails. Still, especially in smaller towns, it's a good idea to call ahead and confirm if alcohol is served and also how late dinner is available.

Restaurant reviews have been shortened. For full information, visit Fodors.com.

HOTEL AND RESTAURANT PRICES

Hotel prices in the reviews are the lowest cost of a standard double room in high season. Restaurant prices in the reviews are the average cost of a main course at dinner, or if dinner is not served, at lunch.

What It Costs

$	$$	$$$	$$$$
RESTAURANTS			
under $16	$16–$22	$23–$30	over $30
HOTELS			
under $125	$125–$175	$176–$225	over $225

Cedar City

250 miles southwest of Salt Lake City.

Rich iron-ore deposits captured the attention of Mormon leader Brigham Young. He ordered a Church of Jesus Christ of Latter-day Saints mission be established here in what is now southwestern Utah's second largest community, with a population of about 33,000 (up from just 13,000 in 1990). The first ironworks and foundry opened in 1851 and operated for only eight years; problems with the furnace, flooding, and hostility between settlers and regional Native Americans eventually put out the flame. Residents then turned to ranching and agriculture for their livelihood, and Cedar City has thrived ever since as an agricultural and, since the founding of Southern Utah University in 1897, educational point of the state.

The Southern Utah University campus hosts the city's most popular event, the **Utah Shakespeare Festival** (🌐 *www.bard.org*), with a season that continues to get longer as its reputation grows; it's a major draw for tourists from late June through October. This attractive, youthful city is well situated for exploring the Brian Head area and Cedar Breaks National Monument.

GETTING HERE AND AROUND

Interstate 15 cuts right through Cedar City. Though downtown is walkable, you'll want a car to explore further afield.

VISITOR INFORMATION

CONTACTS Visit Cedar City and Brian Head. ✉ *581 N. Main St.* ☎ *435/586–5124* 🌐 *www.visitcedarcity.com.*

Sights

Dixie National Forest

FOREST | The forest's expansive natural area is divided into four noncontiguous swaths covering a total of nearly 2 million acres. Adjacent to three national parks, two national monuments, and several state parks, the forest has 26 campgrounds with a variety of backdrops, including lakes, mountains, and pine and spruce forests. Hiking, picnicking, horseback riding, and fishing are among the recreational opportunities here. ✉ *Cedar City* ☎ *435/865–3700* 🌐 *www.fs.usda.gov/dixie.*

Frontier Homestead State Park Museum

MUSEUM | **FAMILY** | This interactive living-history museum devoted to the county's early iron industry is home to a number of interesting attractions, including a bullet-scarred stagecoach that ran in the days of Butch Cassidy and the oldest standing home in all of southern Utah, built in 1851. Local artisans demonstrate pioneer crafts, and numerous mining artifacts and tools are on display. ✉ *585 N. Main St.* ☎ *435/586–9290* 🌐 *www.frontierhomestead.org* 🎫 *$4* ⏲ *Closed Sun. in Sept.–May.*

IG Winery

WINERY/DISTILLERY | In a state with few wineries, this popular operation in downtown Cedar City sources grapes from respected vineyards in California's Napa and Sonoma valleys, Washington's Columbia Valley, and Oregon's Rogue Valley. The Bordeaux-style reds are well-crafted, though spendy, while more moderately priced Tempranillo and Sangiovese also have plenty of fans. With exposed brick walls and hardwood floors, the handsome tasting room is hung with local art and warmed by a fireplace in winter. There's also a sunny patio, and live bands perform regularly. ✉ *59 W. Center St.* ☎ *435/867–9463* 🌐 *www.igwinery.com* ⌚ *Closed Sun. and Mon.*

Southern Utah Museum of Art

MUSEUM | Set in a striking modern building designed in 2016 to resemble the region's canyons and rock formations, this excellent regional art museum with a peaceful sculpture garden is part of Southern Utah University's cultural compound, along with the Utah Shakespeare Festival theaters. The galleries feature selections from the museum's permanent collection of some 2,000 works—including pieces by Renoir, Dalí, and Thomas Hart Benton—along with rotating shows that shine a light on emerging regional artists as well as students and faculty. ✉ *13 S. 300 W* ☎ *435/586–5432* 🌐 *www.suu.edu/pva/suma* ⌚ *Closed Sun.*

Restaurants

★ Centro Woodfired Pizzeria

$ | **PIZZA** | You can watch your handmade artisanal pizza being pulled from the fires of the brick oven, then sit back and enjoy a seasonal pie layered with ingredients like house-made fennel sausage and wood-roasted cremini mushrooms. The creamy vanilla gelato layered with a balsamic reduction and sea salt is highly addictive. **Known for:** house-made sausage; good wine and beer list; creative desserts. [$] *Average main: $14* ✉ *50 W. Center St.* ☎ *435/867–8123* 🌐 *www.centropizzeria.com.*

Chef Alfredo's Ristorante Italiano

$$ | **ITALIAN** | With linen tablecloths, a decent wine list, soft background music, and authentic Sicilian-style food, this restaurant tucked away in a strip mall is charmingly old-school. Highlights include fresh-baked bread served with olive oil; traditional antipasto appetizers; specials like butternut ravioli or eggplant Parmesan; and entrées such as linguine in clam sauce or fettuccine primavera, as well as six chicken-breast options—from parmigiana to marsala. **Known for:** romantic atmosphere; flatbread pizzas; tender steaks. [$] *Average main: $22* ✉ *2313 W. 400 N* ☎ *435/586–2693* 🌐 *www.chefalfredos.com* ⌚ *No lunch Fri.–Sun.*

Milt's Stage Stop

$$$ | **STEAKHOUSE** | Cabin decor, friendly service, and canyon views are the hallmarks of this dinner spot 10 minutes southeast of downtown Cedar City by car. Expect traditional, hearty steak house cuisine: rib-eye steaks, prime rib, and seafood dishes, accompanied by loaded baked potatoes, deep-fried zucchini, and similar sides. **Known for:** scenic alpine setting; hefty steaks and seafood; apple crisp à la mode. [$] *Average main: $27* ✉ *3560 E. Hwy. 14* ☎ *435/586–9344* 🌐 *www.miltsstagestop.com* ⌚ *No lunch.*

PorkBelly's Eatery

$ | **AMERICAN** | As the name suggests, this airy contemporary restaurant is a meat-lover's paradise. Starting with tri-tip eggs Benedict and chicken and waffles at breakfast, pulled-pork sandwiches, carne asada nachos, and bacon-mushroom-cheddar burgers follow. **Known for:** mammoth portions of meat-centric fare; smoked baby back ribs on weekends; the chicken bomb (a jalapeño stuffed with cream cheese and sausage and wrapped in chicken and bacon). [$] *Average main: $14* ✉ *565 S. Main St.* ☎ *435/586–5285* www.porkbellyseatery.com Closed Mon. No dinner Sun.

Rusty's Ranch House

$$$ | **STEAKHOUSE** | Locals have long considered the meals at this fun, if a bit touristy, Old West–style roadhouse some of the best in the region. They serve steaks, barbecue brisket and baby back ribs, towering burgers, sweet coconut shrimp, and other classics. **Known for:** extensive cocktail selection; quirky Western vibe; Granny's hot-caramel apple cobbler. *Average main: $25 2275 E. Hwy. 14 435/586–3839 www.rustysranchhouse.com Closed Sun. No lunch.*

Coffee and Quick Bites

Bulloch's Drug Store

$ | **CAFÉ** | **FAMILY** | Built in 1917 and remodeled to retain its historic character, this landmark building in downtown Cedar City contains an old-fashioned drug store, complete with a soda fountain from the 1950s. Enjoy ice cream, shakes, sundaes, and malts, or try one of the uniquely flavored sodas. **Known for:** decadent ice cream sundaes; big selection of penny candies; cool old building. *Average main: $5 91 N. Main St. 435/586–9651 www.bullochdrug.com Closed Sun. No dinner.*

★ **The French Spot**

$$ | **FRENCH** | This tiny takeout patisserie in the center of downtown is a favorite stop for lattes and cold brew; crepes and salads; heartier dinner specials (salmon, filet mignon); and ethereal pastries and sweets, including a rotating selection of chocolate, berry, lemon, and seasonal tarts. Although primarily a to-go option that's perfect for stocking up before a hiking or biking adventure, in warm weather, you can also dine on the cute patio out front. **Known for:** picnic supplies to enjoy before a show at the nearby Utah Shakespeare Festival; scrambled-egg breakfast croissants with ham, bacon, Gruyère, or smoked salmon; colorful macarons. *Average main: $17 5 N. Main St. 347/886–8587 www.thefrenchspotcafe.com.*

Hotels

Abbey Inn Cedar City

$ | **HOTEL** | Just off the interstate and near Southern Utah University, this two-story economical motel has spacious rooms with exterior entrances, fridges, microwaves, and—in the case of suites—kitchens and jetted tubs. **Pros:** 10-minute walk to downtown and festival venues; lots of dining options nearby; nice indoor pool and fitness center. **Cons:** road noise for some rooms; bland setting amid fast-food restaurants and chains; cookie-cutter room decor. *Rooms from: $126 940 W. 200 N 435/586–9966, 800/325–5411 www.abbeyinncedar.com 83 rooms Free breakfast.*

★ **Amid Summer's Inn Bed & Breakfast**

$ | **B&B/INN** | This enchanting 1930s cottage-style inn, set along a quiet tree-lined street close to the Southern Utah University campus, has individually decorated rooms with literary themes, lavish antiques, and fine artwork. **Pros:** friendly, knowledgeable staff; exceptional breakfasts and decadent baked goods; two blocks from Shakespeare Festival and downtown. **Cons:** some rooms are accessible only by a narrow stairway; may be too intimate for some; books up well in advance in summer. *Rooms from: $119 140 S. 100 W 435/586–2600 www.amidsummersinn.com 10 rooms Free breakfast.*

Best Western Town & Country Inn

$ | **HOTEL** | **FAMILY** | In downtown Cedar City, this renovated motel offers spacious rooms, complimentary breakfast, a fitness center, pool, and two on-site eateries. **Pros:** easy to walk to shops and restaurants; great on-site pool; comfortable beds and pillows. **Cons:** breakfast gets mixed reviews; older property; rooms open to outside. *Rooms from: $113 189 N. Main St. 435/586–9900* www.bestwestern.com 145 rooms Free Breakfast.

★ **Iron Gate Inn**

$$ | **B&B/INN** | Set in a grand downtown second-empire Victorian home that underwent an ambitious renovation before becoming a B&B, this gracious lodging has seven large, period-furnished rooms with well-designed modern bathrooms; some have private sitting areas or direct access to verandas and the inn's fragrant gardens. **Pros:** steps from Shakespeare Festival and downtown; impressive gourmet breakfast included; Jacuzzi and firepit in lush back garden. **Cons:** frilly Victorian decor may not suit every taste; friendly cats and dogs live on premises but could be an issue for some; fills up on summer weekends. *Rooms from: $149* *100 N. 200 W* *435/383–5133* *www.theirongateinn.com* *7 rooms* *Free breakfast.*

Activities

RECREATIONAL AREAS

Coal Creek Trail

PARK—SPORTS-OUTDOORS | **FAMILY** | It's easy, even if you're pushing a stroller, to get out into nature in this sunny, mile-high community. Perfect for strolling, jogging, biking, or running, this 3.4-mile paved multipurpose trail starts in Bicentennial Park and cuts in a southeasterly direction right through the center of town, paralleling the scenic creek for which it's named and eventually joining with the similarly paved Cedar Canyon Trail. Other non-paved hiking trails also spur off from the Cedar Creek Trail and into the surrounding foothills. *Bicentennial Park, 660 W. 1045 N* *www.cedarcity.org.*

St. George

50 miles southwest of Cedar City.

Believing the mild year-round climate ideal for growing cotton, Brigham Young dispatched 309 LDS families in 1861 to found St. George. They were to raise cotton and silkworms and to establish a textile industry, to make up for textile shortages resulting from the Civil War.

The fourth fastest-growing metropolitan area in the country, St. George has become the cultural and recreational hub of southern Utah, a favorite place to relocate among both retirees who appreciate the warm winters and younger families and entrepreneurs lured by the high quality of life, stunning scenery, and growing number of restaurants, shops, and other services.

A main draw is the **Dixie Roundup** (*www.stgeorgelions.com*), a three-day rodeo held every September since the 1930s.

GETTING HERE AND AROUND

This burgeoning and increasingly sprawling city is bisected by Interstate 15, and although the very heart of downtown is pedestrian-friendly, you need a car to visit outlying attractions.

VISITOR INFORMATION

CONTACTS Greater Zion Convention & Tourism Office. *20 N. Main St.* *435/634–5747* *www.greaterzion.com.*

Sights

Brigham Young Winter Home

HISTORIC SITE | Mormon leader Brigham Young spent the last seven winters of his life in the warm, sunny climate of St. George. Built of adobe on a sandstone-and-basalt foundation and now a museum, this two-story home, with pretty green and red trim and well-tended gardens, contains a portrait of Young over one fireplace and furnishings from the late 19th century. Visits are by guided tour. ✉ *67 W. 200 N* ☎ *435/673–2517* 🌐 *history.churchofjesuschrist.org/landing/historic-sites* 🎫 *Free.*

Kayenta Art Village

ARTS VENUE | In the heart of an upscale, contemporary planned community in Ivins, not far from Tuacahn Center for the Arts and Red Mountain Resort, this scenic little arts district contains several of southern Utah's top galleries, including Gallery 873, known for jewelry and ceramics; Kayenta Desert Arboretum & Desert Rose Labyrinth, which visitors can freely stroll through; Zia Pottery Studio, a co-op operated by talented local potters; and several others. Set against a red-rock landscape, it's an enchanting neighborhood to stroll through, especially during the Art in Kayenta outdoor festival in mid-October. Also check to see what's on at the Center for the Arts at Kayenta—which presents lectures, movies, theater, and concerts—or grab a bite at the excellent Xetava Gardens Cafe. ✉ *875 Coyote Gulch Ct., Ivins* ☎ *435/688–8535* 🌐 *www.kayentautah.com.*

★ **Red Cliffs Desert Reserve**

NATURE PRESERVE | Encompassing the convergence of the Mojave, Great Basin, and Colorado Plateau desert zones, this pristine 62,000-acre tract of red-rock wilderness begins several miles north of St. George and was established in 2009 to protect the habitat of the desert tortoise. However, countless other flora and fauna—including gila monsters and chuckwallas—thrive in this unique transition zone that can be accessed through miles of designated hiking, mountain-biking, and horseback-riding trails. The best way to start your adventure is by visiting the reserve's contemporary visitor center (open weekdays only) in downtown St. George, where you'll find live animals, interactive exhibits, and staff who can advise you on hikes and other ways to visit. You can pick up trail maps here or download detailed PDF maps from the reserve website. The trail sections closest to St. George include City Creek and Paradise Canyon. Although it adjoins the reserve and is part of the same ecosystem, popular Snow Canyon State Park is administered separately. ✉ *Visitor Center, 10 N. 100 E* ☎ *435/634–5759* 🌐 *www.redcliffsdesertreserve.com.*

★ **Red Hills Desert Garden**

GARDEN | Opened in 2015 as the state's first botanic garden devoted to desert conservation, Red Hills is a beautiful spot for a peaceful stroll as well as a great place to learn about water-efficient plants. More than 5,000 of them—including fragrant mesquite trees, prickly pear cactus, blue agave, Joshua trees, weeping yucca, and desert willows—thrive here, along with a meandering stream that's stocked with desert suckers, Virgin River chub, and other native species. Paths also lead past a number of boulders that preserve the tracks of dinosaurs that roamed here some 200 million years ago. The garden adjoins rugged Pioneer Park, a 52-acre expanse of rock-climbing and hiking terrain, with barbecue pits, picnic pavilions and tables, and both short and long trails. ✉ *375 E. Red Hills Pkwy.* ☎ *435/673–3617* 🌐 *www.redhillsdesertgarden.com.*

★ **Snow Canyon State Park**

NATIONAL/STATE PARK | Named not for winter weather but after a pair of pioneering Utahans named Snow, this gem of a state park—about 10 miles north of St. George—is filled with natural wonders. Hiking trails lead to lava cones, sand dunes, cactus gardens, and high-contrast vistas. From the campground you can scramble up huge sandstone mounds and overlook the entire valley. Park staff lead occasional guided hikes. ✉ *1002 Snow Canyon Dr., Ivins* ☎ *435/628–2255* 🌐 *stateparks.utah.gov/parks/snow-canyon* 🎫 *$15 per vehicle for nonresidents, $10 for Utah residents.*

St. George Art Museum

MUSEUM | FAMILY | The downtown centerpiece of St. George's growing art scene occupies an attractively reimagined former sugar-beet warehouse. The permanent collection celebrates the works of mostly regionally based potters, photographers, and painters, many of them depicting the region's spectacular landscapes. Rotating exhibits highlight local history and lore and showcase emerging contemporary talents. There's also a Family Discovery Center, with materials for kids to create their own works. *47 E. 200 N* *435/627–4525* *www.sgcity.org/artmuseum* *$5* *Closed Sun.*

St. George Dinosaur Discovery Site at Johnson Farm

ARCHAEOLOGICAL SITE | FAMILY | Unearthed in 2000 by property developers, this site preserves and exhibits ancient footprints left by dinosaurs from the Jurassic Period millions of years ago. Fossils unearthed here are also on display in the modern museum, where accurate replicas portray the creatures that left these tantalizing remains and themed displays cover many details of the Jurassic era. There's an interactive area for children and a Dino Park outside the museum with shaded picnic tables and a Walk Through Time exhibit. *2180 E. Riverside Dr.* *435/574–3466* *www.dinosite.org* *$8* *Closed Tues. and Wed.*

St. George Tabernacle

HISTORIC SITE | This is one of the best-preserved pioneer buildings in the entire state, and it is still used for public meetings and programs for the community. Mormon settlers began work on the tabernacle just a few months after the city of St. George was established in June 1863. Upon completion of the sandstone building's 140-foot clock tower 13 years later, Brigham Young formally dedicated the site. You can visit the building by guided tour. *18 S. Main St.* *435/229–8647* *history.churchofjesuschrist.org/landing/historic-sites.*

Restaurants

Benja Thai and Sushi

$ | THAI | In a stone-walled dining room in downtown's charming Ancestor Square, you can dine on authentic hot-and-sour soups, papaya and larb salads, ginger chicken, whole crispy red snapper with spicy basil sauce, and other Thai dishes, as well as offerings from an extensive sushi menu. The room's tapestries, intricate wood carvings, and lilting music give it warmth and tranquility, and large windows provide views of the landscaped courtyard dotted with quaint historic buildings. **Known for:** huge selection of sushi rolls and nigiri; charming setting; mango cheesecake. *Average main: $14* *2 W. St. George Blvd.* *435/628–9538* *benjathai.com* *Closed Sun.*

Cliffside Restaurant

$$ | MODERN AMERICAN | This strikingly situated restaurant beside the Inn on the Cliff Hotel offers dazzling St. George Valley views from both the dining room and patio, making it an especially popular spot for sunset dinners. The kitchen turns out well-prepared modern American fare, with an emphasis on steaks and seafood—consider the seared flat-iron steak with chimichurri sauce or almond-crusted Idaho trout with farro pesto, broccolini, and a beurre blanc sauce. **Known for:** eye-popping views; buttermilk chicken-fried chicken; decadent, seasonally changing desserts. *Average main: $22* *511 S. Tech Ridge Dr.* *435/319–6005* *www.cliffsiderestaurant.com* *Closed Sun.*

Irmita's Casita

$ | MEXICAN | FAMILY | A standby for tasty Mexican-American fare in various locations around town since 1993, this humble spot serves affordable, no-nonsense food that can be quite spicy if requested. Specialties include spicy pork tortas, massive burritos smothered in red or green sauce, and shrimp enchiladas. **Known for:** steak chilaquiles at breakfast;

chicken mole poblano; Mexican soft drinks and juices. *Average main: $12* *95 W. 700 S* *435/703–9162* *No credit cards* *Closed Sun.*

Morty's Cafe

$ | MODERN AMERICAN | FAMILY | At this funky, updated take on a burger joint on the east side of downtown, the brick walls are hung with local art for sale. Creatively topped beef and veggie burgers are offered, plus breakfast burritos, several varieties of quinoa salad, and thick milkshakes. **Known for:** breakfast sandwiches and burritos served all day; three-bean veggie burgers with chipotle mayo; salted peanut-butter milkshakes. *Average main: $8* *702 E. St. George Blvd.* *435/359–4439* *www.mortyscafe.com* *Closed Sun.*

★ Painted Pony

$$$$ | MODERN AMERICAN | Shaded patio dining overlooking Ancestor Square and contemporary Southwestern art on the walls provides a romantic setting for enjoying contemporary American fare with an emphasis on seasonal ingredients, many from the owners' private organic garden. Consider sage-smoked quail with a tamarind glaze, followed by a juniper-brined bone-in pork chop with stuffed pears and smoked-tomato relish, and don't pass up the standout sides that include sweet cornbread pudding, truffle potato chips, and Stilton fritters. **Known for:** knowledgeable servers; one of the best wine lists in town; seasonally changing bread pudding. *Average main: $32* *2 W. St. George Blvd.* *435/634–1700* *www.painted-pony.com* *No lunch Sun.*

★ Wood Ash Rye

$$$ | MODERN AMERICAN | With a white-tile open kitchen, marble tables, and a wood-beam ceiling, this scene-y farm-to-table restaurant and bar in the swanky Advenire Hotel has quickly become St. George's destination for people-watching and deftly crafted seasonal cuisine. The sharing-friendly menu changes regularly but always features a selection of cheeses and charcuterie, and typical offerings include grilled octopus with preserved lemon and smoked olive oil, pan-seared scallops with risotto in Mornay sauce, and duck tacos. **Known for:** innovative cocktails and mocktails; oysters served raw, charbroiled, or fried; rotating selection of house-made ice creams and sorbets. *Average main: $25* *25 W. St. George Blvd.* *435/522–5020* *www.theadvenirehotel.com.*

Coffee and Quick Bites

FeelLove Coffee

$ | CAFÉ | Head to this light-filled, high-ceilinged café just off the east side's Virgin River bike and jogging trail for well-crafted coffees, teas, and lemonades as well as an assortment of tasty, generally healthy, dishes. Start the day with an egg-avocado toast or a turmeric-tofu scramble, and for lunch, try the vegan Greek salad, turkey–Munster cheese baguette, or "nachos" topped with sliced apples, date caramel, almond butter, and pistachios. **Known for:** lots of vegan options; Thai, matcha, and other sweet tea lattes; fresh-baked desserts, including many vegan options. *Average main: $10* *558 E. Riverside Dr.* *435/922–1717* *www.feellovecoffee.com.*

Hotels

The Advenire

$$$ | HOTEL | A strikingly contemporary, upscale hotel that's directly across the street from the buzzy shopping and dining of Ancestor Square, this stylish member of Marriott Bonvoy's indie-spirited Autograph Collection exudes hipness with its hardwood floors, bold-print pillows and chairs, high-tech entertainment centers, and cushy bedding. **Pros:** stylish, cosmopolitan decor; superb on-site restaurant; steps from downtown dining and retail. **Cons:** neighborhood can be crowded and noisy at times; steep cleaning fee if you bring a pet; parking is pricey and valet only unless you find a spot on the street.

$ Rooms from: $184 ✉ 25 W. St. George Blvd. ☎ 435/522–5022 🌐 www.theadvenirehotel.com 🛏 60 rooms 🍽 No meals.

Best Western Coral Hills

$ | HOTEL | FAMILY | This reasonably priced two-story motel set against a back drop of red hills is a handy choice for being a short walk from many restaurants, shops, and downtown attractions, and heated indoor and outdoor pools promise relaxation after a busy day. **Pros:** suites have deep jetted tubs; pool and hot tub set within a red rock grotto; lots of dining options nearby. **Cons:** some issues with street noise; breakfast is basic; kids often congregate around the pools. *$ Rooms from: $108 ✉ 125 E. St. George Blvd. ☎ 435/673–4844 🌐 www.coralhills.com 🛏 98 rooms 🍽 Free breakfast.*

The Inn at Entrada

$$$ | HOTEL | Hikers, spa goers, and—above all—golfers flock to this plush boutique resort set amid the red-rock canyons northwest of downtown, surrounded by a world-class Johnny Miller–designed golf course, and offering a top-notch spa, pool, and fitness facility. **Pros:** adjoins one of the top golf courses in the state; attractive Southwest-inspired contemporary decor; terrific spa. **Cons:** 10- to 15-minute drive from downtown dining; some guests have noted noise from thin walls and construction; can get very expensive depending on time of year. *$ Rooms from: $199 ✉ 2588 W. Singua Trail ☎ 435/634–7100 🌐 www.innatentrada.com 🛏 57 rooms 🍽 No meals.*

★ Inn on the Cliff

$$$ | HOTEL | It's all about the panoramic views at this exceptionally well-maintained midcentury modern boutique hotel set high on a ridge overlooking downtown St. George and the red rocks beyond. **Pros:** reasonable rates for such a nice property; stunning views; continental breakfast delivered to your room. **Cons:** breakfast is a bit meager; too far to walk from downtown; restaurant closed on Sunday. *$ Rooms from: $179 ✉ 511 S. Tech Ridge Dr. ☎ 435/216–5864 🌐 www.innonthecliff.com 🛏 27 rooms 🍽 Free breakfast.*

★ Red Mountain Resort

$$$$ | RESORT | This luxurious red-rock hideaway, with its stunning surroundings near the mouth of Snow Canyon, offers a range of outdoor adventures and fitness and wellness options, from fitness classes, hikes, and yoga sessions to red clay–lavender body wraps and warm Himalayan salt stone massages. **Pros:** world-class spa and fitness facilities; handsome contemporary design fits in with natural surroundings; a range of meal, spa, and activity packages available. **Cons:** caters more to activity-seekers than those looking to relax; 15-minute drive northwest of St. George; all those potential treatment, activity, and meal add-ons can get pricey. *$ Rooms from: $235 ✉ 1275 E. Red Mountain Circle, Ivins ☎ 435/673–4905, 877/246–4453 🌐 www.redmountainresort.com 🛏 106 units 🍽 No meals.*

Shopping

★ Rowley's Red Barn

FOOD/CANDY | FAMILY | Set in a red barn just a 10-minute drive northeast of St. George, this outpost of the legendary family farm and fruitstand in central Utah is a favorite stop for delicious apples, cherries, peaches, pears, and watermelons, along with several items grown out-of-state, including oranges and pineapples. Be sure to sample the fresh-pressed apple juice and cider. The ice cream parlor doles out tasty treats, including shakes and apple-cider slushes. *✉ 25 N. 300 W, Washington ☎ 435/652–6611 🌐 www.rowleysredbarn.com 🕒 Closed Sun.*

Activities

BIKING

Bicycles Unlimited

BICYCLING | A trusted southern Utah biking resource, this shop rents bikes and sells parts and accessories and also offers maps and advice about great rides in the area. ✉ *90 S. 100 E* ☎ *435/673–4492, 888/673–4492* 🌐 *www.bicyclesunlimited.com.*

GOLF

★ **Entrada at Snow Canyon Country Club**

GOLF | Opened in 1996 and surrounded by a spectacular desert landscape, this challenging course designed by Johnny Miller is ranked among the top courses in the Southwest for its perfectly manicured greens and stylish clubhouse. This is a private course, but it is accessible to guests staying at the Inn at Entrada, which offers stay-and-play packages. ✉ *2511 W. Entrada Trail* ☎ *435/986–2200* 🌐 *www.golfentrada.com* *$110–$150* *18 holes, 7062 yards, par 72.*

The Ledges Golf Course

GOLF | Seven miles north of St. George, this state-of-the-art course designed by Matt Dye features meticulously maintained greens and an impressive backdrop of red rock combined with panoramic views of Snow Canyon State Park. The difficult back nine may be a bit intimidating for less experienced golfers. ✉ *1585 Ledges Pkwy.* ☎ *435/634–4640* 🌐 *ledges.com* *$75–$120* *18 holes, 7200 yards, par 72.*

Springdale

40 miles east of St. George.

Although small, this gorgeously situated town of about 600 has more than doubled in population since 1990, thanks in large part to its being directly adjacent to Zion National Park. Hotels, restaurants, and shops continue to pop up, yet the town still manages to maintain its small-town charm.

GETTING HERE AND AROUND

You'll need a car to get to Springdale, via Highway 9, but getting around once you're here is easy. The complimentary canyon-road shuttle bus—from April through October—makes getting from one end of Springdale to the other stress-free, with bus stops throughout town, and connecting service to the free shuttle into Zion National Park. It's also a pleasant town to stroll through, with shops, galleries, and restaurants all in a central district. In winter, when there are fewer crowds, a car is handy for getting around town or visiting the park.

Sights

Grafton

GHOST TOWN | **FAMILY** | A stone school, dusty cemetery, and a few wooden structures are all that remain of the nearby town of Grafton, which is between Springdale and Hurricane, a few miles west of the turnoff onto Bridge Road in Rockville. This ghost town has been featured in films such as *Butch Cassidy and the Sundance Kid.* ✉ *Hwy. 250 S.*

Restaurants

Bit & Spur

$$ | **SOUTHWESTERN** | This laid-back Springdale institution has been delighting locals and tourists since the late 1980s, offering a well-rounded menu that includes fresh fish and pasta dishes, but the emphasis is on creative Southwestern fare, such as roasted-sweet-potato tamales and chili-rubbed rib-eye steak. Craft beers and the popular housemade sangria complement the zesty cuisine. **Known for:** creative margaritas; live music; outdoor dining by a fountain beneath shade trees. *Average main: $20* ✉ *1212 Zion Park Blvd.* ☎ *435/772–3498* 🌐 *www.bitandspur.com* *No lunch. Closed Dec. and Jan.*

★ King's Landing Bistro

$$$ | **MODERN AMERICAN** | Request to be seated on the patio—with dramatic views of the area's red rock monoliths—when dining at this casually stylish bistro at downtown Springdale's popular Driftwood Lodge hotel. The artfully presented cuisine here tends toward creative American—king salmon with saffron couscous, roast chicken with artichoke tapenade—but you'll find some international, mostly Mediterranean, influences in the form of charred Spanish octopus and one or two outstanding pastas. **Known for:** interesting artisanal cocktail list; emphasis on local and seasonal produce and vegetables; rich desserts, including a classic tiramisu. *Average main: $24 ✉ 1515 Zion Park Blvd. ☎ 435/772–7422 🌐 www.klbzion.com ⏲ Closed Sun. No lunch.*

Oscar's Café

$ | **SOUTHWESTERN** | **FAMILY** | Prepare for an active day with a filling breakfast, or reward yourself after a long hike with lunch or dinner at this welcoming Southwestern café with a big, inviting patio offering stunning mountain views. The pork verde breakfast burrito and huevos rancheros are hearty and delicious, and excellent lunch and dinner options include flame-broiled garlic burgers topped with provolone cheese and shrimp tacos with a creamy lime sauce. **Known for:** blue-corn nachos with cheese and guacamole; extensive selection of creative burgers; large heated patio. *Average main: $15 ✉ 948 Zion Park Blvd. ☎ 435/772–3232 🌐 www.oscarscafe.com.*

Park House Cafe

$ | **AMERICAN** | Notable for its big patio with fantastic views into the park and for one of the better selections of vegan and vegetarian dishes in town, this funky little café decorated with colorful artwork serves plenty of tasty meat and egg dishes, too. The grilled ham Benedict has plenty of fans, as do buffalo burgers with havarti cheese and apple-pear-berry salads with organic greens, feta, and walnuts. **Known for:** breakfast served all day; full slate of espresso drinks and smoothies; ice cream sundaes and banana splits. *Average main: $12 ✉ 1880 Zion Park Blvd. ☎ 435/772–0100 ⏲ Closed Tues. No dinner.*

Spotted Dog Café

$$ | **MODERN AMERICAN** | At this upscale, light-filled restaurant with an eclectic menu that typically includes pastas and meat dishes, the staff makes you feel right at home even if you saunter in wearing hiking shoes. The exposed wood beams and large windows that frame the surrounding trees and rock cliffs set a Western mood, with tablecloths and original artworks supplying a dash of refinement. **Known for:** impressive but accessible wine list; lovely patio for alfresco dining; much of the produce is grown on site. *Average main: $22 ✉ Flanigan's Inn, 428 Zion Park Blvd. ☎ 435/772–0700 🌐 www.flanigans.com/dining ⏲ No lunch; no breakfast Oct.–May.*

Zion Pizza & Noodle Co.

$$ | **PIZZA** | **FAMILY** | Creative pizzas and a kickback atmosphere make this a great place to replenish after a trek through the canyon. Meat lovers can dive into the Cholesterol Hiker pizza, topped with pepperoni, Canadian bacon, and Italian sausage, but the Thai chicken and rosemary-garlic pies are also delicious. **Known for:** stone-slate pizzas with creative toppings; lovely garden seating; good craft beer list. *Average main: $16 ✉ 868 Zion Park Blvd. ☎ 435/772–3815 🌐 www.zionpizzanoodle.com ⏲ No lunch. Closed Dec.–Feb.*

Coffee and Quick Bites

★ Deep Creek Coffee Company

$ | **CAFÉ** | Stop by this cheerful coffeehouse with hanging plants and several tables on a spacious side patio to fuel up before your big park adventure or to grab some healthy sustenance for later. Hearty açaí and miso-quinoa bowls, avocado toast with poached eggs, bagels with the requisite schmears, breakfast burritos, and house-made granola are among the tasty offerings. **Known for:** opens at 6 am daily; refreshing house-made cold brew; delicious smoothies. *Average main: $10 932 Zion Park Blvd. 435/669–8849 www.deepcreekcoffee.com No dinner.*

Hotels

★ Cable Mountain Lodge

$$$ | **HOTEL** | This contemporary lodge with a large swimming pool is the closest hotel in Springdale to Zion—it's a scenic five-minute walk over a footbridge across the Virgin River. **Pros:** steps from Zion National Park's south entrance; many suites have full kitchens; beautiful picnic area along river with gas grills and tables. **Cons:** no breakfast (but a coffeehouse and market steps away); not all rooms have park views; no pets. *Rooms from: $189 147 Zion Park Blvd. 435/772–3366, 877/712–3366 www.cablemountainlodge.com 52 rooms No meals.*

Cliffrose Springdale, Curio Collection by Hilton

$$$$ | **HOTEL** | The canyon views, acres of lush lawns and flowers, and pool and two-tier waterfall hot tubs at this stylish riverside hotel make it more than a place to rest your head, and you could throw a rock across the river and hit Zion National Park. **Pros:** close to Zion's south entrance; enchanting grounds and views; good restaurant serving breakfast and dinner. **Cons:** steep rates; lots of foot and car traffic nearby; no elevator. *Rooms from: $336 281 Zion Park Blvd. 435/772–3234 www.cliffroselodge.com 52 rooms No meals.*

★ Desert Pearl Inn

$$$$ | **HOTEL** | Offering spacious rooms with vaulted ceilings, oversize windows, sitting areas, small kitchens with wet bars and dishwashers, and a pleasing contemporary decor, this riverside lodge is special. **Pros:** spacious, smartly designed rooms; walking distance to restaurants; rooms facing river have balconies or terraces. **Cons:** often books up well in advance spring through fall; breakfast not included; pets not permitted. *Rooms from: $289 707 Zion Park Blvd. 435/772–8888, 888/828–0898 www.desertpearl.com 73 rooms No meals.*

Driftwood Lodge

$$$ | **HOTEL** | The rooms at this friendly roadside lodge are among the most reasonably priced in town, even for the premium units, which have balconies or patios along with great views of the Virgin River and surrounding canyons. **Pros:** excellent value; superb restaurant; attractive pool and picnic area. **Cons:** least expensive rooms have no view or balcony; breakfast not included; limited pet reservations must be booked by phone. *Rooms from: $189 1515 Zion Park Blvd., Springville 435/772–3262 www.driftwoodlodge.net 63 rooms No meals.*

Flanigan's Inn

$$ | **HOTEL** | A tranquil, nicely landscaped inn with canyon views and a small pool, Flanigan's has big, comfortable accommodations, including two private villas and suites that sleep six; some units have a patio or a deck. **Pros:** easy shuttle ride or pleasant walk to Zion Canyon Visitor Center; a meditation maze on the hilltop; great seasonal on-site café. **Cons:** not all rooms have views; smaller property that tends to book up quickly; breakfast, though discounted, isn't complimentary (and is unavailable in winter). *Rooms from: $159 450 Zion Park Blvd. 435/772–3244 www.flanigans.com 34 rooms No meals.*

Shopping

David J. West Gallery

ART GALLERIES | The radiant photography of artist David West captures Zion's natural setting in its full grandeur, along with Bryce, Cedar Breaks, Arches, and other stunning spots throughout Utah and the Southwest. The gallery also stocks contemporary landscape paintings by Michelle Condrat and geologically inspired pottery by Bill Campbell. ✉ *801 Zion Park Blvd.* ☎ *435/772–3510* 🌐 *www.davidjwest.com.*

Sol Foods Supermarket

FOOD/CANDY | Stop by this market specializing in healthy, organic foods for sandwiches, salads, and vegetarian snacks or box lunches for your adventures into the park. Also be sure to poke around the affiliated and well-stocked hardware and camping store next door. A few blocks closer to the park entrance, the owners also operate Hoodoos General Store, which dispenses espresso drinks, ice cream, pizza, and more gourmet goodies. ✉ *995 Zion Park Blvd.* ☎ *435/772–3100* 🌐 *www.solfoods.com.*

★ Worthington Gallery

ART GALLERIES | The emphasis at this superb gallery set inside an 1880s pioneer home is on regional art, including pottery, works in glass, jewelry, beguiling copper wind sculptures by Lyman Whitaker, and paintings that capture the dramatic beauty of southern Utah. ✉ *789 Zion Park Blvd.* ☎ *435/772–3446* 🌐 *www.worthingtongallery.com.*

Zion National Park

The walls of Zion Canyon soar more than 2,000 feet above the valley. Bands of limestone, sandstone, and lava in the strata point to the distant past. Greenery high in the cliff walls indicate the presence of water seepage or a spring. Erosion has left behind a collection of domes, fins, and blocky massifs bearing the names of cathedrals and temples, prophets and angels.

Trails lead deep into side canyons and up narrow ledges to waterfalls, serene spring-fed pools, and shaded spots of solitude. So diverse is this place that 85% of Utah's flora and fauna species are found here. Some, like the tiny Zion snail, appear nowhere else in the world.

The Colorado River helped create the Grand Canyon, while the Virgin River—the Colorado's muddy progeny—carved Zion's features. Because of the park's unique topography, distant storms and spring runoff can transform a tranquil slot canyon into a sluice, and flood damage does sometimes result in extended trail closures, as happened in summer 2018 to three trails near the Grotto and Zion Lodge sections of Zion Canyon.

GETTING HERE AND AROUND

Zion National Park lies east of Interstate 15 in southwestern Utah. From the interstate, head east on Highway 9. After 21 miles you'll reach Springdale, which abuts the main entrance.

From February through November, you can drive on Zion Canyon Scenic Drive only if you have reservations at the Zion Lodge. Otherwise, you must park your car in Springdale or at the Zion Canyon Visitor Center and take the shuttle. There are no car restrictions in December and January. You can avoid parking heartburn by leaving your car in Springdale and riding the shuttle to the park entrance.

PARK ESSENTIALS

PARK FEES AND PERMITS

Entrance to Zion National Park costs $35 per vehicle for a seven-day pass. People entering on foot or by bicycle pay $20 per person for a seven-day pass; those on motorcycle pay $30.

Permits are required for backcountry camping and overnight hikes (from $15). Depending on which parts of the trails you intend to explore, you'll need a special permit for the Narrows and Kolob Creek or the Subway slot canyon. Climbing and canyoneering parties need a permit before using technical equipment.

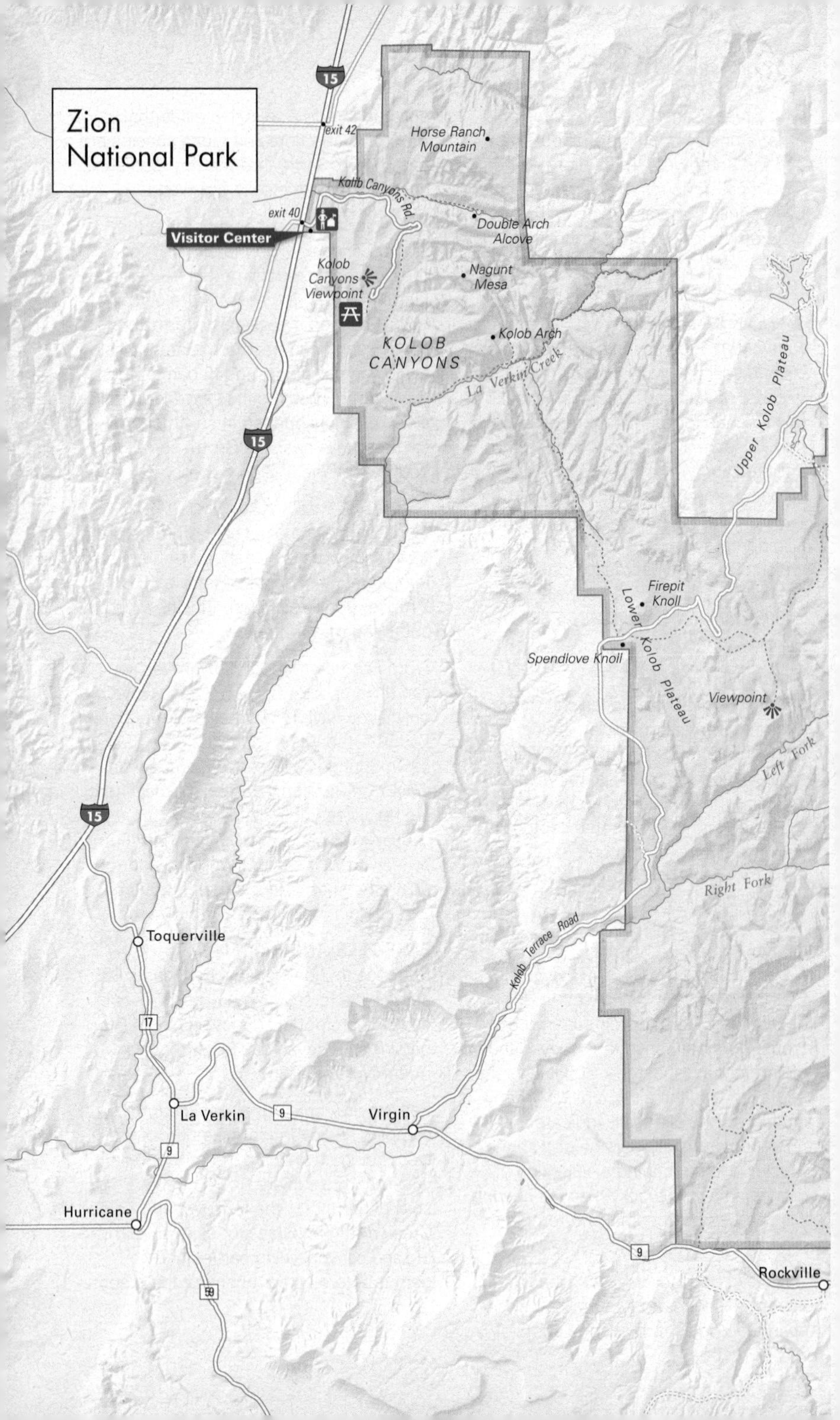
Zion
National Park
15
exit 42
Horse Ranch
Mountain
Kolob Canyons Rd.
exit 40
Visitor Center
Double Arch
Alcove
Kolob
Canyons
Viewpoint
Nagunt
Mesa
KOLOB
CANYONS
Kolob Arch
La Verkin Creek
Upper Kolob Plateau
15
Firepit
Knoll
Lower Kolob Plateau
Spendlove Knoll
Viewpoint
Left Fork
15
Right Fork
Kolob Terrace Road
Toquerville
17
La Verkin
9
Virgin
9
Hurricane
9
Rockville
59

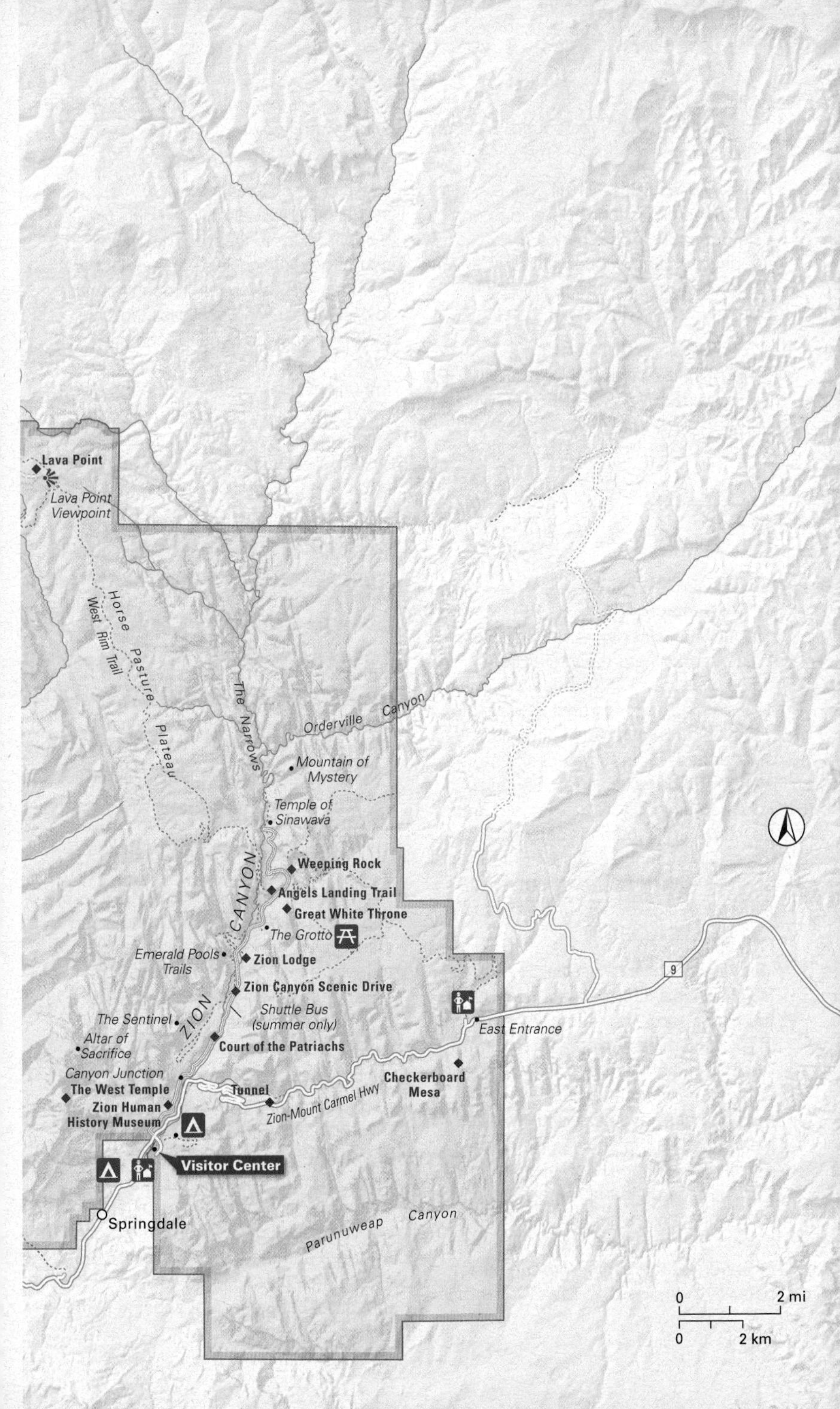

Lava Point
Lava Point Viewpoint
Horse Pasture Plateau
West Rim Trail
The Narrows
Orderville Canyon
Mountain of Mystery
Temple of Sinawava
ZION CANYON
Weeping Rock
Angels Landing Trail
Great White Throne
The Grotto
Emerald Pools Trails
Zion Lodge
Zion Canyon Scenic Drive
Shuttle Bus (summer only)
The Sentinel
Altar of Sacrifice
Court of the Patriachs
Canyon Junction
The West Temple
Zion Human History Museum
Tunnel
Zion-Mount Carmel Hwy
Checkerboard Mesa
East Entrance
9
Visitor Center
Springdale
Parunuweap Canyon
0
2 mi
0
2 km

PARK HOURS

The park, open daily year-round, 24 hours a day, is in the mountain time zone.

CELL PHONE RECEPTION

Cell phone reception is good in Springdale but spotty in the park. Public telephones can be found at Zion Canyon Visitor Center, Zion Lodge, and Zion Human History Museum.

VISITOR INFORMATION

CONTACTS Zion National Park. ✉ *Hwy. 9, Springdale* ☎ *435/772–3256* 🌐 *www.nps.gov/zion.*

Zion Canyon

GEOLOGICAL LANDMARKS

★ The Narrows

NATURE SITE | This sinuous, 16-mile crack in the earth where the Virgin River flows over gravel and boulders is one of the world's most stunning gorges. If you hike through it, you'll find yourself surrounded—sometimes nearly boxed in—by smooth walls stretching high into the heavens. Plan to get wet, and beware that flash floods can occur here, especially in spring and summer. Check on the weather before you enter. ✉ *Zion National Park* ✣ *Begins at Riverside Walk.*

HISTORIC SIGHTS

Zion Human History Museum

MUSEUM | This informative museum tells the park's story from the perspective of its human inhabitants, among them Ancestral Puebloans and early Mormon settlers. Permanent exhibits illustrate how humans have dealt with wildlife, plants, and natural forces. Temporary exhibits have touched on everything from vintage park-employee photography to the history of Union Pacific Railroad hotels. Don't miss the incredible view of Towers of the Virgin from the back patio. ✉ *Zion Canyon Scenic Dr., ½ mile north of south entrance* ☎ *435/772–3256* 🌐 *www.nps.gov/zion* 💵 *Free.*

SCENIC DRIVES

★ Zion Canyon Scenic Drive

SCENIC DRIVE | Vividly colored cliffs tower 2,000 feet above the road that meanders north from Springdale along the floor of Zion Canyon. As you roll through the narrow, steep canyon, you'll pass the Court of the Patriarchs, the Sentinel, and the Great White Throne, among other imposing rock formations. From February through November, unless you're staying at the lodge, Zion Canyon Scenic Drive is accessed only by park shuttle. You can drive it yourself at other times. ✉ *Off Hwy. 9.*

Zion–Mt. Carmel Highway and Tunnels

SCENIC DRIVE | Two narrow tunnels as old as the park itself lie between the east entrance and Zion Canyon on this breathtaking 12-mile stretch of Highway 9. One was once the longest man-made tunnel in the world. As you travel the (1.1-mile) passage through solid rock, five arched portals along one side provide fleeting glimpses of cliffs and canyons. When you emerge you'll find that the landscape has changed dramatically. Large vehicles require traffic control and a $15 permit, available at the park entrance, and have restricted hours of travel. This includes nearly all RVs, trailers, dual-wheel trucks, and campers. The Canyon Overlook Trail starts from a parking area between the tunnels. ✉ *Hwy. 9, 5 miles east of Canyon Junction* 🌐 *www.nps.gov/zion/planyourvisit/the-zion-mount-carmel-tunnel.htm.*

SCENIC STOPS

Checkerboard Mesa

NATURE SITE | It's well worth stopping at the pull-out 1 mile west of Zion's east entrance to observe the distinctive waffle patterns on this huge white mound of sandstone. The stunning crosshatch effect visible today is the result of eons of freeze-and-thaw cycles that caused vertical fractures, combined with erosion that produced horizontal bedding planes. ✉ *Zion–Mt. Carmel Hwy.*

Court of the Patriarchs

NATURE SITE | This trio of peaks bears the names of, from left to right, Abraham, Isaac, and Jacob. Mount Moroni is the reddish peak on the far right that partially blocks the view of Jacob. Hike the trail that leaves from the Court of the Patriarchs Viewpoint, 1½ miles north of Canyon Junction, to get a much better view of the sandstone prophets. ✉ *Zion Canyon Scenic Dr.*

Great White Throne

NATURE SITE | Dominating the Grotto picnic area near Zion Lodge, this massive Navajo sandstone peak juts 2,000 feet above the valley floor. The popular formation lies about 3 miles north of Canyon Junction. ✉ *Zion Canyon Scenic Dr.*

Weeping Rock

NATURE SITE | Surface water from the rim of Echo Canyon spends several thousand years seeping down through the porous sandstone before exiting at this picturesque alcove 4½ miles north of Canyon Junction. A paved walkway climbs ¼ mile to this flowing rock face where wildflowers and delicate ferns grow. In fall, the maples and cottonwoods burst with color, and lizards point the way down the path, which is too steep for wheelchairs or strollers. A major rockslide closed the Weeping Rock Trail in summer 2019; check with the visitor center to see if it has reopened. ✉ *Zion Canyon Scenic Dr.*

TRAILS

★ Angels Landing Trail

TRAIL | As much a trial as a trail, this path beneath the Great White Throne, which you access from the Lower West Rim Trail, is one of the park's most challenging hikes. Early on, you work your way through Walter's Wiggles, a series of 21 switchbacks built out of sandstone blocks. From there you traverse sheer cliffs that have chains bolted into the rock face to serve as handrails in some (but not all) places. In spite of its hair-raising nature, this trail is popular. Allow 2½ hours round trip if you stop at Scout's Lookout (2 miles), and 4 hours if you keep going to where the angels (and birds of prey) play. The trail is 5 miles round trip and is not appropriate for children or those who are uneasy about heights. *Difficult.* ✉ *Zion National Park* ✥ *Trailhead: Off Zion Canyon Scenic Dr. at the Grotto.*

★ Canyon Overlook Trail

TRAIL | FAMILY | The parking area just east of Zion–Mt. Carmel Tunnel leads to this popular trail, which is about 1 mile round trip and takes about an hour to finish. From the breathtaking overlook at the trail's end, you can see the West and East temples, the Towers of the Virgin, the Streaked Wall, and other Zion Canyon cliffs and peaks. The elevation change is 160 feet. There's no shuttle to this trail, and the parking area often fills up—try to come very early or late in the day to avoid crowds. *Moderate.* ✉ *Zion National Park* ✥ *Trailhead: Off Hwy. 9 just east of Zion–Mt. Carmel Tunnel.*

Emerald Pools Trail

TRAIL | FAMILY | Multiple waterfalls cascade (or drip, in dry weather) into algae-filled pools along this trail, about 3 miles north of Canyon Junction. The path leading to the lower pool is paved and appropriate for strollers and wheelchairs. If you've got any energy left, keep going past the lower pool. The ¼ mile from there to the middle pool becomes rocky and somewhat steep but offers increasingly scenic views. A less crowded and exceptionally enjoyable return route follows the Kayenta Trail, connecting to the Grotto Trail. Allow 50 minutes for the 1¼-mile round-trip hike to the lower pool, and an hour more each round trip to the middle (2 miles) and upper pools (3 miles). *Lower, easy. Upper, moderate.* ✉ *Zion National Park* ✥ *Trailhead: Off Zion Canyon Scenic Dr., at Zion Lodge or the Grotto.*

Grotto Trail

TRAIL | **FAMILY** | This flat trail takes you from Zion Lodge, about 3 miles north of Canyon Junction, to the Grotto picnic area, traveling for the most part along the park road. Allow 20 minutes or less for the walk along the ½-mile trail. If you are up for a longer hike and have two or three hours, connect with the Kayenta Trail after you cross the footbridge, and head for the Emerald Pools. You will begin gaining elevation, and it's a steady, steep climb to the pools, which you will begin to see after about 1 mile. *Easy.* ✉ *Zion National Park* ✣ *Trailhead: Off Zion Canyon Scenic Dr. at the Grotto.*

Hidden Canyon Trail

TRAIL | This steep, 2-mile round-trip hike takes you up 850 feet in elevation. Not too crowded, the trail is paved all the way to Hidden Canyon. Allow about three hours for the round-trip hike. A massive rockfall in summer 2019 resulted in the closure of this trail—check with the visitor center for updates. *Moderate–Difficult.* ✉ *Zion National Park* ✣ *Trailhead: Off Zion Canyon Scenic Dr. at Weeping Rock.*

★ The Narrows Trail

TRAIL | After leaving the paved ease of the Gateway to the Narrows trail behind, walk on the riverbed itself. You'll find a pebbly shingle or dry sandbar path, but when the walls of the canyon close in, you'll be forced into the chilly waters of the Virgin River. A walking stick and good shoes are a must. Be prepared to swim, as chest-deep holes may occur even when water levels are low. Check with park rangers about the likelihood of flash floods. A day trip up the lower section of the Narrows is 6 miles one-way to the turnaround point. Allow at least five hours round-trip. *Difficult.* ✉ *Zion National Park* ✣ *Trailhead: Off Zion Canyon Scenic Dr., at the end of Riverside Walk.*

Pa'rus Trail

TRAIL | **FAMILY** | An approximately 1¾-mile, relatively flat, paved walking and biking path, Pa'rus parallels and occasionally crosses the Virgin River. Starting at South Campground, ½ mile north of the South Entrance, the walk proceeds north along the river to the beginning of Zion Canyon Scenic Drive. Along the way you'll take in great views of the Watchman, the Sentinel, the East and West temples, and the Towers of the Virgin. Leashed dogs are allowed on this trail. Wheelchair users may need assistance. *Easy.* ✉ *Zion National Park* ✣ *Trailhead: At Canyon Junction.*

Riverside Walk

TRAIL | **FAMILY** | This 2.2-mile round-trip hike shadows the Virgin River. In spring, wildflowers bloom on the opposite canyon wall in lovely hanging gardens. The trail, which begins 6½ miles north of Canyon Junction at the end of Zion Canyon Scenic Drive, is the park's most visited, so be prepared for crowds in high season. Riverside Walk is paved and suitable for strollers and wheelchairs, though some wheelchair users may need assistance. Round-trip it takes about 90 minutes. At the end, the much more challenging Narrows Trail begins. *Easy.* ✉ *Zion National Park* ✣ *Trailhead: Off Zion Canyon Scenic Dr. at the Temple of Sinawava.*

Watchman Trail

TRAIL | For a dramatic view of Springdale and a look at lower Zion Creek Canyon and Towers of the Virgin, this strenuous hike begins on a service road east of Watchman Campground. Some springs seep out of the sandstone, nourishing the hanging gardens and attracting wildlife. There are a few sheer cliff edges, so supervise children carefully. Plan on two hours for this 3.3-mile round-trip hike that has a 368-foot elevation change. *Moderate.* ✉ *Zion National Park* ✣ *Trailhead: At Zion Canyon Visitor Center.*

Take a shuttle or scenic horseback ride within the walls of Zion Canyon.

VISITOR CENTERS

Zion Canyon Visitor Center

INFO CENTER | Learn about the area's geology, flora, and fauna at an outdoor exhibit next to a gurgling stream. Inside, a large shop sells everything from field guides to souvenirs. Zion Canyon shuttle buses leave regularly from the center and make several stops along the canyon's beautiful Scenic Drive; ranger-guided shuttle tours depart once a day from Memorial Day to late September. ✉ *Zion Park Blvd. at south entrance, Springdale* ☎ *435/772–3256* 🌐 *www.nps.gov/zion.*

Restaurants

Red Rock Grill

$$ | AMERICAN | The dinner fare at this restaurant in Zion Lodge includes steaks, seafood, and Western specialties, such as pecan-encrusted trout and jalapeño-topped bison cheeseburgers; salads, sandwiches, and hearty burgers are lunch highlights; and, for breakfast, you can partake of the plentiful buffet or order off the menu. Photos showcasing the surrounding landscape adorn the walls of the spacious dining room; enormous windows and a large patio take in the actual landscape. **Known for:** dinner reservations necessary in summer; astounding views inside and out; only full-service restaurant in the park. [$] *Average main: $19* ✉ *Zion Lodge, Zion Canyon Scenic Dr.* ☎ *435/772–7760* 🌐 *www.zionlodge.com/dining/red-rock-grill.*

Hotels

★ Zion Lodge

$$$$ | HOTEL | For a dramatic location inside the park, you'd be hard-pressed to improve on a stay at the historic Zion Lodge: the canyon's jaw-dropping beauty surrounds you, access to trailheads is easy, and guests can drive their cars on the lower half of Zion Park Scenic Drive year-round. **Pros:** handsome hotel in the tradition of historic park properties; incredible views; bike rentals on-site. **Cons:** pathways are dimly lit (bring a flashlight); spotty Wi-Fi, poor cell service; books up months ahead. [$] *Rooms* *from: $229* ✉ *Zion Canyon Scenic Dr.* ☎ *888/297–2757 reservations only, 435/772–7700* 🌐 *www.zionlodge.com* 🛏 *122 rooms* 🍽 *No meals.*

Kolob Canyons

Sights

SCENIC DRIVES

Kolob Canyons Road

SCENIC DRIVE | Kolob Canyons Road is a 5-mile immersion into red rock canyons that extend east-to-west along three forks of Taylor Creek and La Verkin Creek. The beauty starts modestly at the junction with Interstate 15, but as you move along this 5-mile road, the red walls of the Kolob finger canyons rise suddenly and spectacularly. With the crowds left behind at Zion Canyon, this drive offers the chance to take in incredible vistas at your leisure. Trails include the short but rugged Middle Fork of Taylor Creek Trail, which passes two 1930s homestead cabins, culminating 2¾ miles later in the Double Arch Alcove. At the end of the drive, take the short hike to the Kolob Canyons Viewpoint to see Nagunt Mesa, Shuntavi Butte, and Gregory Butte, each rising to nearly 8,000 feet above sea level. During heavy snowfall Kolob Canyons Road may be closed. ✉ *I–15, Exit 40.*

Kolob Terrace Road

SCENIC DRIVE | Hundreds of miles of scenic desert roads crisscross the Southwest, and Kolob Terrace Road will remind you of many of them. Sprawling as much as 4,000 feet above the floor of Zion Canyon, and without the benefit of the canyon's breezes and shade, the landscape along it is arid—browns and grays and ambers—but not without rugged beauty. The 21-mile stretch begins 15 miles west of Springdale at Virgin and winds north. As you travel along, peaks and knolls emerge from the high plateau, birds circle overhead, and you might not see more than a half-dozen cars. The drive meanders in and out of the park boundaries, crossing several important trailheads, all the while overlooking the cliffs of North Creek. A popular day-use trail (permit required) leads past fossilized dinosaur tracks to the Subway, a stretch of the stream where the walls of the slot canyon close in so tightly as to form a near tunnel. Farther along the road is the Wildcat Canyon trailhead, which connects to the path overlooking the North Guardian Angel. The road terminates at the Kolob Reservoir, beneath 8,933-foot Kolob Peak. Although paved, this narrow, twisting road is not recommended for RVs. Because of limited winter plowing, the road is closed from November or December through April or May. ✉ *Zion National Park* ✣ *Begins in Virgin at Hwy. 9.*

SCENIC STOPS

Lava Point

VIEWPOINT | Infrequently visited, this area has a primitive campground and two nearby reservoirs that offer the only significant fishing opportunities in the park. Lava Point Overlook, one of the park's highest viewpoints, provides vistas of Zion Canyon from the north. The higher elevation here makes it much cooler than the Zion Canyon area. Park visitors looking for a respite from crowds and heat find the campground a nice change of pace, though the six sites fill up quickly and are only open May through September. ✉ *Zion National Park* ✣ *Kolob Terrace Rd. to Lava Point Rd., then turn right.*

Kolob Canyons Viewpoint

LOCAL INTEREST | FAMILY | Nearly 100% of travelers along Interstate 15 from Las Vegas to Salt Lake overlook this short drive a few hundred yards from the highway. The reward is a beautiful view of Kolob's "finger" canyons from about six picnic tables spread out beneath the trees. The parking lot has plenty of space, a pit toilet, and an overlook with a display pointing out canyon features. Restrooms and drinking water are available 5 miles away at the Kolob Canyons Visitor Center.

✉ *Zion National Park* ✣ *On Timber Creek Trail at the end of Kolob Canyons Rd.*

TRAILS

Taylor Creek Trail

TRAIL | This trail in the Kolob Canyons area descends parallel to Taylor Creek, sometimes crossing it, sometimes shortcutting benches beside it. The historic Larson Cabin precedes the entrance to the canyon of the Middle Fork, where the trail becomes rougher. After the old Fife Cabin, the canyon bends to the right into Double Arch Alcove, a large, colorful grotto with a high blind arch (or arch "embryo") towering above. To Double Arch it's 2½ miles one-way—about four hours round-trip. The elevation change is 450 feet. *Moderate.* ✉ *Zion National Park* ✣ *Trailhead: At Kolob Canyons Rd., about 1½ miles east of Kolob Canyons Visitor Center.*

VISITOR CENTERS

Kolob Canyons Visitor Center

INFO CENTER | Make this your first stop as you enter this remote section of the park. There are books and maps, a small gift shop, and clean restrooms here, and rangers are on hand to answer questions about Kolob Canyons exploration. ✉ *3752 E. Kolob Canyons Rd., Exit 40 off I–15* ☎ *435/772–3256* 🌐 *www.nps.gov/zion.*

Activities

BIKING

Zion Cycles

BICYCLING | This shop just outside the park rents bikes by the hour or longer, sells parts, and has a full-time mechanic on duty. You can pick up trail tips and other advice from the staff here. They also offer guided road-biking treks in the park and mountain-biking excursions elsewhere in southern Utah. ✉ *868 Zion Park Blvd., Springdale* ☎ *435/772–0400* 🌐 *www.zioncycles.com* 💵 *Guided tours from $175; bike rentals from $40/day.*

CAMPING

South Campground. All the sites here are under big cottonwood trees that provide some relief from the summer sun. The campground operates on a reservation system. ✉ *Hwy. 9, ½ mile north of south entrance* ☎ *435/772–3256, 877/444–6777* 🌐 *www.recreation.gov.*

Watchman Campground. This large campground on the Virgin River operates on a reservation system between March and November, but you do not get to choose your site. ✉ *Access road off Zion Canyon Visitor Center parking lot* ☎ *435/772–3256, 877/444–6777* 🌐 *www.recreation.gov.*

HORSEBACK RIDING

Canyon Trail Rides

HORSEBACK RIDING | **FAMILY** | Easygoing, one-hour and half-day guided rides are available (minimum age 7 and 10 years, respectively). These friendly folks have been around for years and are the only outfitter for trail rides inside the park. Reservations are recommended and can be made online. The maximum weight is 220 pounds, and the season runs from March through October. ✉ *Across from Zion Lodge* ☎ *435/679–8665* 🌐 *www.canyonrides.com* 💵 *From $45.*

Kanab

43 miles southeast of Springdale.

Since the 1920s, Kanab has been Hollywood's vision of the American West. Soaring vermilion sandstone cliffs and sagebrush flats with endless vistas have lured filmmakers to this area, which has appeared in more than 170 movies and TV shows, including *Stagecoach, My Friend Flicka, Fort Apache, The Outlaw Josey Wales, Maverick,* and many others. Abandoned film sets have become tourist attractions, and old movie posters or still photographs are a decorating staple at local businesses, but this town of about 5,000 has prospered more recently because it's a perfect base for visiting three of the nation's top national parks: Zion, Bryce Canyon, and the Grand Canyon (North Rim). It's also an excellent base for visiting Grand Staircase–Escalante and Pipe Spring national monuments as well as the mesmerizing landscapes of the Paria Canyon–Vermilion Cliffs Wilderness. As adventurers from all over the world continue to visit, Kanab has developed a relatively new crop of hip boutique hotels and casually stylish eateries.

GETTING HERE AND AROUND

U.S. 89 is the main route into town, along with U.S. 89A from due south. You can walk to many hotels and restaurants within town, but a car is a must for exploring the area.

TOURS

★ Dreamland Safari Tours

EXCURSIONS | This long-respected Kanab-based outfitter with around 10 super-knowledgeable full-time guides offers myriad half- and full-day excursions throughout the surrounding countryside, from slot canyon and sunset photography trips near town to adventures a bit farther afield. Tours take place in the Paria Canyon Wildneress and Vermilion Cliffs National Monument, in Grand Staircase–Escalante National Monument, and around the North Rim of the Grand Canyon and nearby Marble Canyon. Multiday "desert safari" and photography tours are offered as well. ✉ *Kanab* ☎ *435/677–5967* 🌐 *www.dreamlandtours.net* 🎫 *From $90.*

★ Paria Outpost & Outfitters

GUIDED TOURS | Husband-and-wife owners Steve and Susan Dodson and their small team of guides are among the best experts on Paria Canyon–Vermilion Cliffs Wilderness and Grand Staircase–Escalante National Monument (especially the southern sections). The company offers photo workshops and guided tours of all of the key destinations in these wilderness areas, including the Wave, as well as shuttle services if you're doing a one-way hike through Buckskin Gulch or Paria Canyon. Tours leave from the office on U.S. 89, about 42 miles east of Kanab, which also has a single-room overnight accommodation and a barbecue restaurant that's open only for groups by advance reservation. Note that all services are cash only. ✉ *U.S. 89, between mile makers 21 and 22, Paria* ☎ *928/691–1047* 🌐 *www.paria.com* 🎫 *From $125.*

VISITOR INFORMATION

CONTACTS Big Water BLM Visitor Center. ✉ *100 Upper Revolution Way, Big Water* ☎ *435/675–3200* 🌐 *www.blm.gov.* **Kanab BLM Visitor Center.** ✉ *745 E. U.S. 89* ☎ *435/644–1300* 🌐 *www.blm.gov.*

Sights

★ Best Friends Animal Sanctuary

NATURE PRESERVE | FAMILY | On a typical day, this 3,700-acre compound 7 miles north of town houses some 1,600 rescued animals, mostly dogs and cats but also horses, rabbits, farm animals, and even wildlife in need of shelter. They receive dozens of visitors who come to take one of the free 90-minute tours (offered four times daily), or a special tour of the Dogtown, Cat World Headquarters, Bunny House, Parrot Garden, or one of the other animal-specific areas of the sanctuary, a walk through the animal cemetery, or even a guided one-hour hike of adjacent Angel Canyon (offered Sunday and Thursday mornings). Founded in 1984 and with several other adoption centers and offices around the country, Best Friends is the largest animal sanctuary in the country and one of the world's most successful and influential no-kill animal rescue advocacy organizations. It's a rewarding visit if you love animals, and if have the time and interest, you and your family can volunteer for a day at this amazing place. The organization also operates the Best Friends Roadhouse & Mercantile, a unique pet-centric hotel and gift shop. All tours should be booked online or by phone, even if same day. ✉ *5001 Angel Canyon Rd.* ☎ *435/644–2001* 🌐 *www.bestfriends.org.*

Coral Pink Sand Dunes State Park

NATIONAL/STATE PARK | Visitors to this sweeping expanse of pink sand about 20 miles west of Kanab enjoy a slice of nature produced by eroding sandstone. Funneled through a notch in the rock, wind picks up speed and carries grains of sand into the area—the undulating formations can move as much as 50 feet per year. Once the wind slows down, the sand is deposited, creating this giant playground for dune buggies, ATVs, and dirt bikes. A small area is fenced off for walking, but the sound of wheeled toys is always with you. Children love to play in the sand, but check the surface temperature; it can get very hot. ✉ *Coral Sand Dunes Rd. (Hwy. 43)* ✣ *11 miles west of U.S. 89* ☎ *435/648–2800* 🌐 *stateparks.utah.gov* 🎟 *$10 per vehicle.*

Kanab Heritage House Museum

HOUSE | One of the most stately residences in southern Utah, this 1890s redbrick gingerbread Victorian home in the center of town is surrounded by herb and flowers gardens and contains many of the original owners' furnishings. Guided tours are offered throughout the day, and historical demonstrations are presented from time to time. A visit provides an interesting look at pioneer life in the Southwest. ✉ *115 S. Main St.* ☎ *435/644–3506* 🌐 *www.kanabheritagehouse.com* ⏲ *Closed Sun., and Mon.–Thurs. in Oct.–mid-May.*

Maynard Dixon Living History Museum and Gallery

MUSEUM | Two miles north of Mount Carmel Junction, you can tour the final summer residence of the famous painter of Western life and landscapes. Dixon lived from 1875 to 1946 and was married to the renowned WPA photographer Dorothea Lange, and, following their divorce, to San Francisco muralist Edith Hamlin. He and Hamlin summered on this property from 1939 until his death; shortly after his death, she scattered his ashes on a ridge behind the property, which consists of the original log cabin structure and an exceptional Western Art gallery, both of which are maintained by the nonprofit Thunderbird Foundation for the Arts. From March through November, self-guided and docent-led tours (by appointment only) are offered. The gallery and gift shop are open daily year-round. ✉ *2200 S. State St. (U.S. 89), Mount Carmel* ☎ *435/648–2653* 🌐 *www.thunderbirdfoundation.com* 🎟 *Gallery free, self-guided tours $10, guided tours $20.*

Old Paria Townsite and Movie Set

GHOST TOWN | Surrounded by stunning striated bluffs and rock formations, here in this remote valley you can visit two ghost towns at once at the Paria (sometimes called Pahreah) Townsite and movie set, one settled by hardy pioneers and one built by Hollywood but lost in 1998, briefly rebuilt, and then lost to a fire in 2006. In fact, floods also caused the demise of the original settlements along the Pahreah River, with the original town fully abandoned by around 1930. Films shot here include the 1962 Rat Pack comedy *Sergeants 3*, the Gregory Peck film *Mackenna's Gold*, and the famous Clint Eastwood Civil War western, *The Outlaw Josey Wales*, which was wrapped up filming in 1976, making it the last of the site's movie productions. The area is reached by driving 33 miles east of Kanab on U.S. 89, turning left—shortly after milemarker 31—at the Paria Townsite sign, and following the unpaved road about 4.5 miles north to the parking area and wooden restroom. ✉ *Paria Valley Rd., Paria.*

★ Paria Canyon–Vermilion Cliffs Wilderness

NATURE SITE | In this extremely remote 112,500-acre expanse of otherworldly canyons, cliffs, and mesas that straddles the Utah–Arizona border south of Grand Staircase–Escalante National

Monument and along the Arizona border, you'll find the subjects of some of the most famous and photographed rock formations in the Southwest, including "the Wave," an oceanlike landscape of waves frozen in striated red, orange, and yellow sandstone that can be accessed by permit only. The area has a number of other spectacular features, several of them a bit easier to access, such as the moderately easy 3.7-mile Wire Pass Trail, which leads to the longest slot canyon in the world, 13-mile Buckskin Gulch. For any visits to this wilderness, part of which falls within Vermilion Cliffs National Monument, it's essential that you check with the area's BLM ranger offices in Kanab or Big Water (near Lake Powell) for guidance and conditions (deadly flash floods can occur with little warning in some of these slot canyons), and for permit information if you want to visit the Wave or Coyote Buttes. Or consider visiting the area on tour through one of the reputable outfitters in Kanab or Escalante, such as Dreamland Safari Tours, Forever Adventure Tours, and Paria Outpost & Outfitters. The parking lot for the Wire Pass Trailhead, a good place to start your explorations of the area, is 45 miles east of Kanab via U.S. 89 (turn right onto House Rock Valley Road shortly after milemarker 26, and continue 8.5 miles down the unpaved road). *Only 20 people are granted permits to visit the Wave each day, and all are awarded by lottery (10 online, 10 in person at the BLM visitor center in Kanab). The chances of winning a permit are about 2% in high season. Visit www.blm.gov/node/7605 for details.* ✉ *Wire Pass Trailhead parking lot, House Rock Valley Rd., Paria* ☎ *435/644–1300 Kanab BLM Visitor Center* 🌐 *www.blm.gov/visit/paria-canyon-vermilion-cliffs-wilderness-area* 🎫 *$6 day use; reservations and permits required for some hikes.*

Restaurants

Rocking V Cafe

$$$ | **SOUTHWESTERN** | Serving creative specialties like jalapeño lime chicken and fish tacos, this popular eatery inside the town's former post office focuses on slow-cooked meals made from scratch, such as the Kanab-A-Dabba-A-Doo burger, a half-pound patty topped with Hatch chiles, bacon, cheddar, and avocado, and char-grilled bison tenderloin with a fig demi-glace. Rocking V stays busy even on weeknights. **Known for:** excellent margaritas; attractive seasonal patio; bread pudding with rotating preparations. $ *Average main: $24* ✉ *97 W. Center St.* ☎ *435/644–8001* 🌐 *www.rockingvcafe.com* ⏲ *Closed Tues. and Wed.*

★ Sego

$$ | **MODERN AMERICAN** | Folks have been known to drive for an hour or more to partake of the outstanding modern American and Asian fare served in this charmingly intimate dining room just off the lobby of the romantic Canyons Boutique Hotel in Kanab. The small-plates-focused menu here changes often according to what's fresh, but recent standouts have included a pork belly and watermelon salad, foraged mushrooms with artichokes and goat cheese, and seared duck-breast lo mein with sambal and jalapeño cream. **Known for:** creative, globally inspired cooking; stellar wine and cocktail list; romantic yet unfussy vibe. $ *Average main: $20* ✉ *190 N. 300 W* ☎ *435/644–5680* 🌐 *www.segokanab.com* ⏲ *Closed Sun. No lunch.*

★ Vermillion 45

$$$ | **MEDITERRANEAN** | The sophisticated contemporary Mediterranean fare served in this snazzy bistro with a cathedral ceiling and an open kitchen would hold its own in any big city. Start off your evening with escargot with herbed garlic butter or French onion soup, before graduating to gnocchi with sautéed lobster tail or pan-seared duck breast with a cherry

reduction and truffle-dusted potatoes. **Known for:** charcuterie and cheese boards; outstanding wine and cocktail selection; house-made gelato. *Average main: $23 210 S. 100 E 435/644–3300 www.vermillion45.com Closed Mon. and Tues.*

Wild Thyme Cafe

$$ | **MODERN AMERICAN** | Using herbs and produce from the on-site organic garden and sourcing meat and seafood from top-quality purveyors, the kitchen at this contemporary neighborhood bistro serves up delicious regional American fare, often with Southwestern and Louisiana influences. Cajun-spiced, fire-grilled Idaho trout and slow-braised, char-grilled cowboy pork ribs with barbecue sauce and an agave-mustard vinaigrette are a couple of house specialties, and there's also a nice selection of bowls featuring sesame tofu, shredded chicken verde, Jamaican-spiced pork, and other tasty proteins. **Known for:** pretty deck with red rock views; one of the best craft cocktail lists in southern Utah; flourless dark chocolate cake. *Average main: $20 198 S. 100 E 435/644–2848 www.wildthymekanab.com.*

Coffee and Quick Bites

★ Kanab Creek Bakery

$ | **CAFÉ** | Drop by this urbane little bakery-café with an expansive patio for some of the tastiest breakfast and lunch fare for miles, as well as fine espresso drinks, teas, raw juice blends, and a small but well-chosen selection of beer and wine. The Belgian–French-inspired menu features sweet (crepes with jam and delectable pastries) and savory dishes, with croque monsieur, salade Nicoise, and avocado-hummus-tomato panini standing out among the latter. **Known for:** cheerful patio (but limited indoor) seating; heavenly croissants, Belgian chocolate chip cookies, and other sweet treats; fantastic breakfasts. *Average main: $10 238 W. Center St. 435/644–5689 www.kanabcreekbakery.com Closed Mon.*

Hotels

★ Best Friends Roadhouse & Mercantile

$$$ | **HOTEL** | The Best Friends Animal Society, a nationally renowned Kanab-based animal rescue organization, runs this smartly designed, pet-centric motel that offers a slew of amenities for travelers with four-legged friends, including a fenced dog park and water feature, pet treats and beds, built-in cubbies for snuggling and napping, and dog-walking and pet-visit services. **Pros:** hip, modern design; an absolute oasis for travelers with pets; staying here supports a great cause. **Cons:** not a great fit if you're not a fan of pets; on a busy road; a bit pricey. *Rooms from: $189 30 N. 300 W 435/644–3400 www.bestfriends-roadhouse.org 40 rooms Free breakfast.*

Best Western East Zion Thunderbird Lodge

$$ | **HOTEL** | About 13 miles beyond the east entrance of Zion National Park, this low-slung motel with clean, spacious rooms decorated with rustic lodge-style furniture is a good option if you also want to be within an hour's drive of Bryce Canyon National Park. **Pros:** restaurant serves delicious pies; outdoor heated pool, hot tub; well-manicured grounds. **Cons:** no elevator; 20-minute drive to Kanab restaurants; breakfast not included. *Rooms from: $159 4530 State St. (U.S. 89), Mount Carmel Junction 435/648–2203 hotel direct, 800/780–7234 reservations www.bestwestern.com 61 rooms No meals.*

★ Canyon's Lodge

$ | **HOTEL** | With cattle-print throw pillows, papier-mâché mounted deer heads, log walls, and custom beds with rattan headboards or carved-wood headboards, the playful vibe at this quirky 16-room boutique inn sets it apart from the usual budget-friendly lodgings in the Zion and

Bryce area. **Pros:** fun and quirky ambience; good base for Zion, Bryce, and the North Rim of the Grand Canyon; there's a small pool. **Cons:** the least expensive rooms are tiny; complimentary breakfast is at nearby sister property; some road noise. *Rooms from: $99 ✉ 236 N. 300 W ☎ 435/644–3069 🌐 www.canyonslodge.com ⇆ 16 rooms 🍴 Free breakfast.*

Parry Lodge

$$ | HOTEL | Constructed in 1929, this landmark lodge hosted dozens of movie stars during Kanab's movie location heyday and is now a fun and simple, well-located base for budget-minded parks visitors. **Pros:** fascinating "old Hollywood" ambience; large pool; reasonably priced. **Cons:** some rooms are quite small; no elevator; breakfast costs extra. *Rooms from: $139 ✉ 89 E. Center St. ☎ 435/644–2601 🌐 www.parrylodge.com ⇆ 89 rooms 🍴 No meals.*

Zion Mountain Ranch

$$$$ | RESORT | This peaceful ranch-style resort with more than 50 handsomely furnished cabins and lodge-style vacation homes that sleep from two to 15 guests lies a mere 4 miles from the east entrance of Zion National Park and offers a variety of activities, including horseback riding, jeep tours, and guided hikes. **Pros:** rustic-chic aesthetic; spectacularly scenic surroundings; exceptional farm-to-table restaurant. **Cons:** limited Wi-Fi and no TV reception; expensive; half-hour drive to Kanab. *Rooms from: $235 ✉ 9065 W. Hwy. 9, Orderville ☎ 435/648–2555, 866/648–2555 🌐 www.zmr.com ⇆ 53 cabins 🍴 No meals.*

Zion Ponderosa Ranch Resort

$$$$ | RESORT | FAMILY | Just a few miles beyond Zion National Park's east entrance and about 16 miles northwest of Mount Carmel Junction, this scenic, 4,000-acre ranch offers a varied lineup of lodgings and a dizzying array of activities. **Pros:** lots of family-friendly activities; tranquil setting near Zion's east entrance; off-season packages include breakfast and Jeep tours. **Cons:** pool gets crowded in summer; very kid-centric; not many dining options nearby. *Rooms from: $249 ✉ Twin Knolls Rd., Orderville ☎ 435/648–2700, 800/293–5444 🌐 www.zionponderosa.com ⇆ 31 cabins 🍴 No meals.*

Activities

HIKING

★ Squaw Trail

HIKING/WALKING | FAMILY | With a trailhead right on the north side of downtown, this rugged 3-mile round-trip hike offers tremendous views of Kanab Valley and the surrounding high-desert landscape. Although a bit steep in places, the total elevation gain of about 800 feet is manageable for most and the trail is very well-maintained—and the eye-popping scenery is worth the effort, especially considering how much less crowded this hike is than those at nearby national parks. *✉ N. 100 E at W. 600 N 🌐 www.trailskanab.com.*

Bryce Canyon National Park

A land that captures the imagination and the heart, Bryce is a favorite among the Southwest's national parks. Although its splendor had been well known for decades, Bryce Canyon wasn't designated a national park until 1928. Bryce Canyon is famous for its fanciful hoodoos, best viewed at sunrise or sunset, when the light plays off the red rock.

In geological terms, Bryce is actually an amphitheater, not a canyon. The hoodoos in the amphitheater took on their unusual shapes because the top layer of rock—cap rock—is harder than the layers below it. If erosion undercuts the soft rock beneath the cap too much, the hoodoo will tumble. Bryce continues to evolve today, but the hoodoos are a permanent feature; old ones may die, but new ones are constantly forming as the amphitheater rim recedes.

GETTING HERE AND AROUND

The closest major cities to Bryce Canyon are Salt Lake City and Las Vegas, each about 270 miles away. You reach the park via Highway 63, just off of Highway 12, which connects U.S. 89 just south of Panguitch with Torrey, near Capitol Reef National Park. You can see the park's highlights by driving along the well-maintained road running the length of the main scenic area. Bryce has no restrictions on automobiles on the main road, but from spring through fall you may encounter heavy traffic and full parking lots—it's advisable to take the shuttle bus at this time.

A shuttle bus system operates in Bryce Canyon from mid-April through mid-October. Buses start at 8 am and run every 10 to 15 minutes until 8 pm in summer and 6 pm in early spring and October; they're free once you pay park admission. The route begins at the Shuttle Station north of the park, where parking is available (visitors can also park at Ruby's Inn or Ruby's Campground outside the park entrance and catch the shuttle there). It stops at the visitor center, lodge, campgrounds, and all the main overlooks and trailheads.

PARK ESSENTIALS

PARK FEES

The entrance fee is $35 per vehicle for a seven-day pass and $20 for pedestrians or bicyclists, and includes unlimited use of the park shuttle. An annual Bryce Canyon park pass, good for one year from the date of purchase, costs $40. If you leave your private vehicle outside the park at the shuttle staging area or Ruby's Inn or Campground, the one-time entrance fee is $35 per party and includes transportation on the shuttle.

A $5 backcountry permit, available from the visitor center, is required for camping in the park's interior, allowed only on Under-the-Rim Trail and Rigg's Spring Loop, both south of Bryce Point. Campfires are not permitted.

PARK HOURS

The park is open 24/7, year-round. It's in the mountain time zone.

CELL PHONE RECEPTION

Cell phone reception is hit-or-miss in the park, with some of the higher points along the main road your best bet. The lodge and visitor center have limited (it can be slow during busy periods) Wi-Fi, and there are pay phones at a few key spots in the park, but these are gradually being removed.

TOURS

Bryce Canyon Airlines & Helicopters

AIR EXCURSIONS | For a bird's-eye view of Bryce Canyon National Park, take a dramatic helicopter ride or airplane tour over the fantastic sandstone formations. Longer full-canyon tours and added excursions to sites such as the Grand Canyon, Monument Valley, and Zion are also offered. Flights last from 35 minutes to four hours. ☎ *435/834–8060* 🌐 *www.rubysinn.com/scenic-flights* 🎫 *From $110.*

VISITOR INFORMATION

PARK CONTACT INFORMATION Bryce Canyon National Park. ☎ *435/834–5322* 🌐 *www.nps.gov/brca.*

Bryce Canyon North

Bryce Ampitheater is the central part of the park. Here you'll find the visitor center, lodge, campgrounds, and many of the most popular trails and viewpoints. A convenient free shuttle runs a loop through this area, stopping at eight main spots where you can get out and explore. It also runs through the nearby town of Bryce Canyon City, so you don't need to bring your vehicle if you're staying at one of the hotels just outside the park.

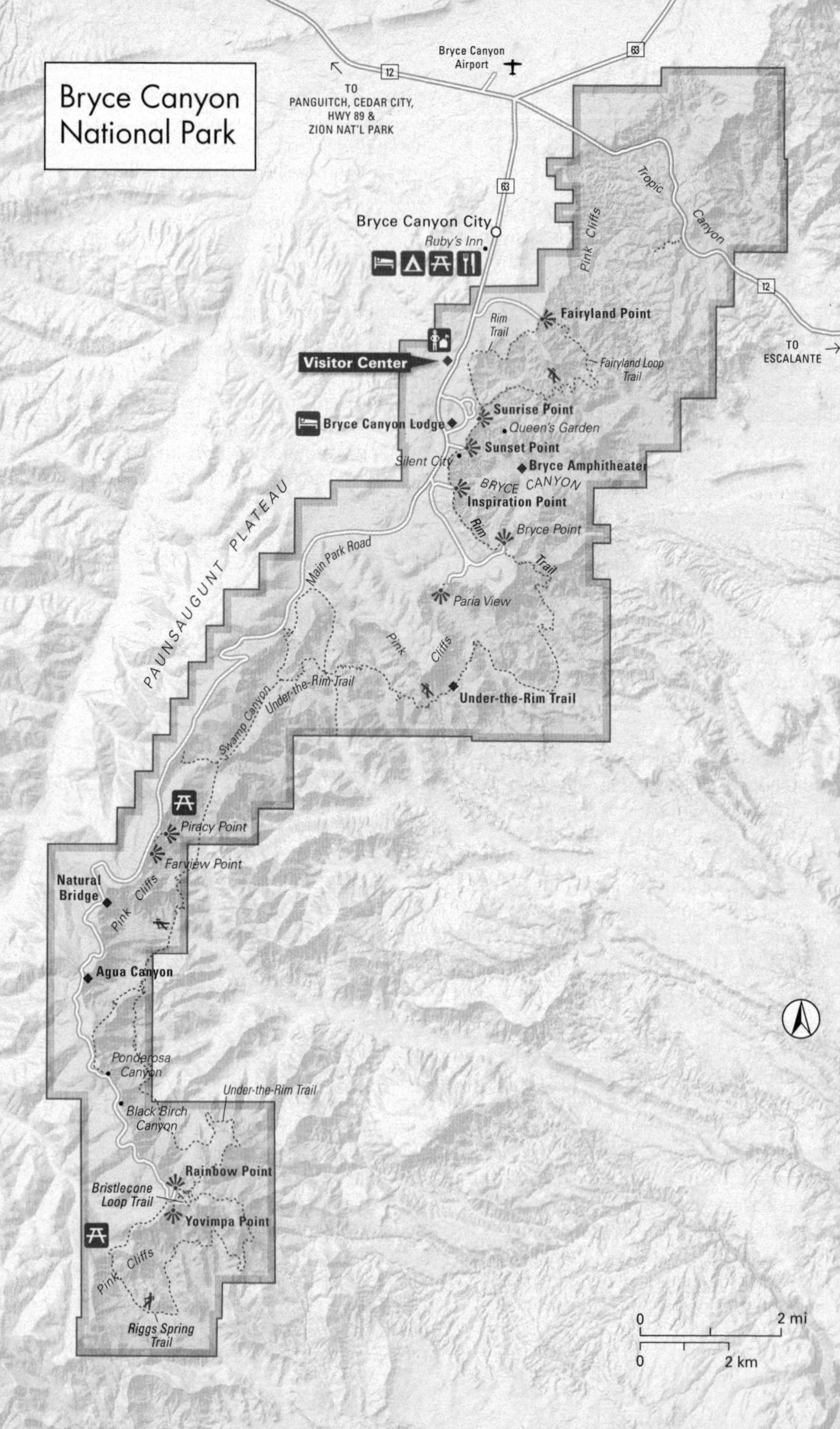

Bryce Canyon National Park
TO PANGUITCH, CEDAR CITY, HWY 89 & ZION NAT'L PARK
12
Bryce Canyon Airport
63
Bryce Canyon City
Ruby's Inn
Tropic Canyon
Pink Cliffs
TO ESCALANTE
Fairyland Point
Rim Trail
Fairyland Loop Trail
Visitor Center
Sunrise Point
Bryce Canyon Lodge
Queen's Garden
Sunset Point
Silent City
Bryce Amphitheater
BRYCE CANYON
Inspiration Point
Bryce Point
Rim Trail
Main Park Road
Paria View
PAUNSAUGUNT PLATEAU
Pink Cliffs
Under-the-Rim Trail
Swamp Canyon
Piracy Point
Farview Point
Natural Bridge
Agua Canyon
Ponderosa Canyon
Under-the-Rim Trail
Black Birch Canyon
Rainbow Point
Bristlecone Loop Trail
Yovimpa Point
Riggs Spring Trail
0
2 mi
2 km

Bryce Canyon's longest trail leads backpackers under the rim of the park's plateau that edges the natural amphitheater. Hiking the full 23-mile Under the Rim Trail will require an overnight stay, though there are some shorter trails to access parts of this area on day hikes. On clear nights, the stargazing can be amazing.

Sights

HISTORICAL SIGHTS

Bryce Canyon Lodge

BUILDING | The lodge's architect, Gilbert Stanley Underwood, was a national park specialist, having designed lodges at Zion and the Grand Canyon before turning his T square to Bryce in 1924. The results are worth a visit as this National Historic Landmark has been faithfully restored, right down to the lobby's huge limestone fireplace and log and wrought-iron chandelier. Inside the historic building, the only remaining hotel built by the Grand Circle Utah Parks Company, are a restaurant and gift shop, as well as information on park activities. The lodge operation includes several historic log cabins and two motels nearby on the wooded grounds, just a short walk from the rim trail. Everything but the Sunset Lodge (which is open early March–early January) shuts down from early November through late March. ✉ *Off Hwy. 63* ☎ *435/834–8700* 🌐 *www.brycecanyonforever.com.*

SCENIC DRIVES

★ Main Park Road

SCENIC DRIVE | Following miles of canyon rim, this thoroughfare gives access to more than a dozen scenic overlooks between the park entrance and Rainbow Point. Major overlooks are rarely more than a few minutes' walk from the parking areas, and many let you see more than 100 miles on clear days. Remember that all overlooks lie east of the road. To keep things simple, proceed to the southern end of the park and stop at the overlooks on your northbound return; they will all be on the right side of the road. Allow two to three hours to travel the entire 36-mile round-trip. The road is open year-round, but may close temporarily after heavy snowfalls. Keep your eyes open for wildlife as you drive. Trailers are not allowed at Bryce Point and Paria View, but you can park them at the parking lot across the road from the visitor center. RVs can drive throughout the park (with limited parking options spring through fall), but vehicles longer than 25 feet are not allowed at Paria View. ✉ *Bryce Canyon National Park.*

SCENIC STOPS

Agua Canyon

VIEWPOINT | This overlook in the southern section of the park, 12 miles south of the park entrance, has a nice view of several standout hoodoos. Look for the top-heavy formation called the Hunter, which actually has a few small hardy trees growing on its cap. As the rock erodes, the park evolves; snap a picture because the Hunter may look different the next time you visit. ✉ *Bryce Canyon National Park* 🌐 *www.nps.gov/brca/planyourvisit/aguacanyon.htm.*

Bryce Point

VIEWPOINT | After absorbing views of the Black Mountains and Navajo Mountain, you can follow the Under-the-Rim Trail and go exploring beyond Bryce Amphitheater to the cluster of top-heavy hoodoos known collectively as the Hat Shop. Or, take a left off the Under-the-Rim Trail and hike the challenging Peekaboo Loop Trail with its geological highlight, the Wall of Windows. Openings carved into a wall of rock illustrate the drama of erosion that formed Bryce Canyon. ✉ *Inspiration Point Rd., 5½ miles south of park entrance.*

Fairyland Point

VIEWPOINT | Best visited as you exit the park, this scenic overlook adjacent to Boat Mesa, ½ mile north of the visitor center and a mile off the main park road, has splendid views of Fairyland

Amphitheater and its delicate, fanciful forms. The Sinking Ship and other formations stand before the grand backdrop of the Aquarius Plateau and distant Navajo Mountain. Nearby is the Fairyland Loop trailhead—it's a stunning five-hour hike in summer and a favorite of snowshoers in winter. ✉ *Off Hwy. 63.*

★ Inspiration Point

VIEWPOINT | Not far (1½ miles) east along the Rim Trail from Bryce Point is Inspiration Point, site of a wonderful vista on the main amphitheater and one of the best places in the park to see the sunset. (You will have plenty of company and hear a variety of languages as the sun goes down.) ✉ *Inspiration Point Rd.* 🌐 *www.nps.gov/brca/planyourvisit/inspiration.htm.*

Natural Bridge

VIEWPOINT | Formed over millions of years by wind, water, and chemical erosion, this 85-foot rusty-orange arch formation—one of several rock arches in the park—is an essential photo op. Beyond the parking lot lies a rare stand of aspen trees, their leaves twinkling in the wind. Watch out for distracted drivers at this stunning viewpoint. ✉ *Main park road, 11 miles south of park entrance* 🌐 *www.nps.gov/brca/planyourvisit/naturalbridge.htm.*

North Campground Viewpoint

VIEWPOINT | **FAMILY** | Across the road and slightly east of the Bryce Canyon Visitor Center, this popular campground has a couple of scenic picnic areas plus a general store and easy trail access. ✉ *Main park road* ✣ *½ mile south of visitor center.*

★ Sunrise Point

VIEWPOINT | Named for its stunning views at dawn, this overlook a short walk from Bryce Canyon Lodge is one of the park's most popular stops. It's also the trailhead for the Queen's Garden Trail and the Fairyland Loop Trail. You have to descend the Queen's Garden Trail to get a glimpse of the regal Queen Victoria, a hoodoo that appears to sport a crown and glorious full skirt. The trail is popular and marked clearly, but a bit challenging with 350 feet of elevation change. ✉ *Off Hwy. 63.*

Sunset Point

VIEWPOINT | Watch the late-day sun paint the hoodoos here. You can see Thor's Hammer, a delicate formation similar to a balanced rock, from the rim, but when you hike 550 feet down into the amphitheater on the Navajo Loop Trail, you can walk through the famous and very popular Wall Street—a deep, shady "slot" canyon. The point is near Bryce Canyon Lodge. ✉ *Bryce Canyon National Park* 🌐 *www.nps.gov/brca/planyourvisit/sunset.htm.*

TRAILS

Fairyland Loop Trail

TRAIL | Hike into whimsical Fairyland Canyon on this trail that gets more strenuous and less crowded as you progress along its 8 miles. It winds around hoodoos, across trickles of water, and finally to a natural window in the rock at Tower Bridge, 1½ miles from Sunrise Point and 4 miles from Fairyland Point. The pink-and-white badlands and hoodoos surround you the whole way. Don't feel like you have to go the whole distance to make it worthwhile. But if you do, allow at least five hours round-trip with 1,700 feet of elevation change. *Difficult.* ✉ *Bryce Canyon National Park* ✣ *Trailheads: At Fairyland Point and Sunrise Point* 🌐 *www.nps.gov/brca/planyourvisit/fairylandloop.htm.*

Hat Shop Trail

TRAIL | The sedimentary haberdashery sits 2 miles from the trailhead. Hard gray caps balance precariously atop narrow pedestals of softer, rust-color rock. Allow three to four hours to travel this somewhat strenuous but rewarding 4-mile round-trip trail, the first part of the longer Under-the-Rim Trail. *Moderate.* ✉ *Bryce Canyon National Park* ✣ *Trailhead: At Bryce Point, 5½ miles south of park* *entrance* 🌐 *www.nps.gov/brca/planyourvisit/hatshop.htm.*

Navajo Loop Trail

TRAIL | FAMILY | One of Bryce's most popular and dramatic attractions is this steep descent via a series of switchbacks leading to Wall Street, a slightly claustrophobic hallway of rock only 20 feet wide in places, with walls 100 feet high. After a walk through the Silent City, the northern end of the trail brings Thor's Hammer into view. A well-marked intersection offers a shorter way back via Two Bridges Trail or continuing on the Queen's Garden Trail to Sunrise Point. For the short version allow at least an hour on this 1½-mile trail with 550 feet of elevation change. *Moderate.* ✉ *Bryce Canyon National Park* ✣ *Trailhead: At Sunset Point, near Bryce Canyon Lodge* 🌐 *www.nps.gov/brca/planyourvisit/navajotrail.htm.*

★ Navajo/Queen's Garden Combination Loop

TRAIL | FAMILY | By walking this extended 3-mile loop, you can see some of the best of Bryce; it takes a little more than two hours. The route passes fantastic formations and an open forest of pine and juniper on the amphitheater floor. Descend into the amphitheater from Sunrise Point on the Queen's Garden Trail and ascend via the Navajo Loop Trail; return to your starting point via the Rim Trail. *Moderate.* ✉ *Bryce Canyon National Park* ✣ *Trailheads: At Sunset and Sunrise Points, 2 miles south of park entrance* 🌐 *www.nps.gov/brca/planyourvisit/qgnavajocombo.htm.*

★ Queen's Garden Trail

TRAIL | FAMILY | This hike is the easiest way down into the amphitheater, with 350 feet of elevation change leading to a short tunnel, quirky hoodoos, and lots of like-minded hikers. It's the essential Bryce "sampler." Allow two hours total to hike the 1½-mile trail plus the ½-mile rim-side path and back. *Easy.* ✉ *Bryce Canyon National Park* ✣ *Trailhead: At Sunrise Point, 2 miles south of park entrance* 🌐 *www.nps.gov/brca/planyourvisit/queensgarden.htm.*

Under-the-Rim Trail

TRAIL | Starting at Bryce Point, the trail travels 23 miles to Rainbow Point, passing through the Pink Cliffs, traversing Agua Canyon and Ponderosa Canyon, and taking you by several springs. Most of the hike is on the amphitheater floor, characterized by up-and-down terrain among stands of ponderosa pine; the elevation change totals about 1,500 feet. It's the park's longest trail, but four trailheads along the main park road allow you to connect to the Under-the-Rim Trail and cover its length as a series of day hikes. Allow at least two days to hike the route in its entirety, and although it's not a hoodoo-heavy hike, there's plenty to see to make it a more leisurely three-day affair. *Difficult.* ✉ *Bryce Canyon National Park* ✣ *Trailheads: At Bryce Point, Swamp Canyon, Ponderosa Canyon, and Rainbow Point.*

VISITOR CENTERS

★ Bryce Canyon Visitor Center

INFO CENTER | FAMILY | Even if you're anxious to hit the hoodoos, the visitor center—just to your right after the park entrance station—is the best place to start if you want to know what you're looking at and how it got there. Rangers staff a counter where you can ask questions or let them map out an itinerary of "must-sees" based on your time and physical abilities. There are also multimedia exhibits, Wi-Fi, books, maps, backcountry camping permits for sale, and the Bryce Canyon Natural History Association gift shop, whose proceeds help to support park programs and conservation. ✉ *Hwy. 63* ☎ *435/834–5322* 🌐 *www.nps.gov/brca.*

Yovimpa Point looks to the south of Bryce Canyon, offering a spectacular view.

Restaurants

★ Bryce Canyon Lodge Restaurant

$$$ | **AMERICAN** | With a high-beam ceiling, tall windows, and a massive stone fireplace, the dining room at this historic lodge set among towering pines abounds with rustic western charm. The kitchen serves three meals a day (reservations aren't accepted, so be prepared for a wait), and the dishes—highlights of which include buffalo sirloin steak, burgundy-braised bison stew, and almond-and-panko-crusted trout—feature organic or sustainable ingredients whenever possible. **Known for:** good selection of local craft beers; delicious desserts, including a fudge-brownie sundae and six-layer carrot cake; hearty breakfasts. *Average main: $28 Off Hwy. 63 435/834–8700 www.brycecanyonforever.com/dining Closed early Nov.–late Mar.*

Hotels

★ Bryce Canyon Lodge

$$$ | **HOTEL** | This historic, rugged stone-and-wood lodge close to the amphitheater's rim offers western-style rooms with semi-private balconies or porches in two motel buildings; suites in the historic inn; and cozy, beautifully designed lodge-pole pine-and-stone cabins, some with cathedral ceilings and gas fireplaces. **Pros:** close to canyon rim and trails; lodge is steeped in history and has loads of personality; cabins have fireplaces and exude rustic charm. **Cons:** closed in winter; books up fast; no TVs or air-conditioning. *Rooms from: $223 Off Hwy. 63 435/834–8700, 877/386–4383 www.brycecanyonforever.com Closed Jan.–early Mar. 113 rooms No meals.*

Bryce Canyon South

Heading south from park entrance, this is as far as you can drive on the 18-mile park road. The area includes a short, easy trail through the forest as well as a longer difficult trail. The viewpoints at Rainbow and Yovimpa look to the north and south, so you'll want to visit both. Many visitors like to drive to this part of the park first, then drive back north.

Sights

SCENIC DRIVES AND OVERLOOKS

★ Rainbow and Yovimpa Points

VIEWPOINT | Separated by less than half a mile, Rainbow and Yovimpa points offer two fine panoramas facing opposite directions. Rainbow Point's best view is to the north overlooking the southern rim of the amphitheater and giving a glimpse of Grand Staircase–Escalante National Monument; Yovimpa Point's vista spreads out to the south. On an especially clear day you can see all the way to Arizona's highest point, Humphreys Peak, 150 miles away. Yovimpa Point also has a shady and quiet picnic area with tables and restrooms. You can hike between them on the easy Bristlecone Loop Trail or tackle the more strenuous 9-mile Riggs Spring Loop Trail, which passes the tallest point in the park. This is the outermost auto stop on the main road, so visitors often drive here first and make it their starting point, then work their way back to the park entrance. ✉ *End of main park road, 18 miles south of park entrance.*

TRAILS

Bristlecone Loop Trail

TRAIL | This 1-mile trail with a modest 200 feet of elevation gain lets you see the park from its highest points of more than 9,000 feet, alternating between spruce and fir forest and wide-open vistas out over Grand Staircase–Escalante National Monument and beyond. You might see yellow-bellied marmots and dusky grouse, critters not found at lower elevations in the park. Plan on 45 minutes to an hour. *Easy.* ✉ *Bryce Canyon National Park* ✣ *Trailhead: At Rainbow Point parking lot, 18 miles south of park entrance* 🌐 *www.nps.gov/brca/planyourvisit/bristleconeloop.htm.*

Bryce Canyon City

Right outside the park, this village has several lodging and dining options, shops, gas, tourist attractions, and other helpful amenities for park visitors. The park shuttle bus makes several stops in the town.

Sights

Bryce Wildlife Adventure

MUSEUM | **FAMILY** | Imagine a zoo frozen in time: this 14,000-square-foot private museum contains more than 1,600 butterflies and 1,000 taxidermy animals in tableaux mimicking actual terrain and animal behavior. The animals and birds come from all parts of the world. An African room has baboons, bush pigs, Cape buffalo, and a lion. There's also a collection of living deer that kids delight in feeding, and ATV and bike rentals for touring scenic Highway 12 and the Paunsaugunt Plateau. ✉ *1945 W. Hwy. 12, Bryce Canyon City* ☎ *435/834–5555* 🌐 *www.brycewildlifeadventure.com* 🎫 *$8* 🕒 *Closed mid-Nov.–Mar.*

U.S. 89/Utah's Heritage Highway

SCENIC DRIVE | Winding north from the Arizona border all the way to Spanish Fork Canyon, an hour south of Salt Lake City, U.S. 89 is known as the Heritage Highway for its role in shaping Utah history. At its southern end, Kanab is known as "Little Hollywood," having provided the backdrop for many famous Western movies and TV commercials. Other towns north along this famous road may not have the same notoriety in these parts, but they do offer eye-popping scenery as well as some lodging and dining options relatively close to Bryce Canyon.

Restaurants

Bryce Canyon Pines Restaurant

$$ | **AMERICAN** | Inside the Bryce Canyon Pines Motel, about 6 miles northwest of Bryce Canyon National Park, this down-home, family-friendly roadhouse decorated with Old West photos and memorabilia serves reliably good stick-to-your-ribs breakfasts, hefty elk burgers, rib-eye steaks, and Utah rainbow trout. But the top draw here is homemade pie, which comes in a vast assortment of flavors, from banana-blueberry cream to boysenberry. **Known for:** delectable pies; friendly staff; plenty of kids' options. *Average main: $16 Hwy. 12, mile marker 10, Bryce Canyon City 435/834–5441 www.brycecanyonrestaurant.com.*

Hotels

Best Western Bryce Canyon Grand Hotel

$$$ | **HOTEL** | If you appreciate creature comforts but can do without much in the way of local personality, this four-story hotel just outside the park fits the bill—rooms are relatively posh, with comfortable mattresses, pillows, and bedding, spacious bathrooms, and modern appliances, and there's an outdoor pool and pleasant patio. **Pros:** clean, spacious rooms; lots of amenities and activities; short drive or free shuttle ride from Bryce Canyon. **Cons:** no pets allowed; pricey during busy times; standard chain ambience. *Rooms from: $220 30 N. 100 E, Bryce Canyon City 866/866–6634, 435/834–5700 www.brycecanyongrand.com 164 rooms Free breakfast.*

Best Western Plus Ruby's Inn

$$$ | **HOTEL** | **FAMILY** | This bustling Southwestern-themed hotel has expanded over the years to include various wings with rooms that vary widely in terms of size and character. **Pros:** lots of services and amenities; short drive or free shuttle ride into the park; nice indoor pool. **Cons:** can get very busy, especially when the big tour buses roll in; too big for charm or a quiet getaway; uneven quality of restaurants. *Rooms from: $190 26 S. Main St., Bryce Canyon City 435/834–5341, 866/866–6616 www.rubysinn.com 368 rooms Free breakfast.*

Bryce Canyon Pines Motel

$$ | **HOTEL** | Most rooms in this motel complex tucked into the woods 6 miles southwest of the park entrance have excellent mountain views. **Pros:** guided horseback rides; outdoor pool and hot tub; lively restaurant famed for homemade pies. **Cons:** thin walls; room quality varies widely; furnishings are a bit dated. *Rooms from: $125 Hwy. 12, mile marker 10, Bryce Canyon City 435/834–5441 www.brycecanyonmotel.com 46 rooms No meals.*

Shopping

Ruby's General Store

CONVENIENCE/GENERAL STORES | It may not be one of the area's geological wonders, but this giant mercantile center almost has to be seen to be believed. On a busy evening, it bustles with tourists plucking through souvenirs that range from sweatshirts to wind chimes. There are also selections of Western wear, children's toys, holiday gifts, and groceries. Even the camping equipment is in ample supply. Need a folding stove, sleeping bag, or fishing gear? You will find it at Ruby's. You can also cross Main Street to where this ever-expanding complex has added a line of shops trimmed like an Old West town, complete with candy store and rock shop. *26 S. Main St. 435/834–5484 www.rubysinn.com/rubys-inn-store.*

Activities

Most visitors explore Bryce Canyon by car, but the hiking trails are far more rewarding. At these elevations, you'll have to stop to catch your breath more often if you're used to being closer to sea level. It gets warm in summer but rarely uncomfortably hot, so hiking farther into the depths of the park is not difficult, so long as you don't pick a hike that is beyond your abilities.

CAMPING

The two campgrounds in Bryce Canyon National Park fill up fast, especially in summer, and are family-friendly. All are drive-in, except for the handful of backcountry sites that only backpackers and gung-ho day hikers ever see.

North Campground. A cool, shady retreat in a forest of ponderosa pines, this is a great home base for campers visiting Bryce Canyon. You're near the general store, The Lodge, trailheads, and the visitor center. Reservations are accepted for some RV sites; for the rest it's first-come, first-served, and the campground usually fills by early afternoon in July, August, and September. Just be aware that some sites feel crowded and not private. ✉ *Main park road, ½ mile south of visitor center* ☎ *435/834–5322.*

Sunset Campground. This serene alpine campground is within walking distance of Bryce Canyon Lodge and many trailheads. Most of the 100 or so sites are filled on a first-come, first-served basis, but 20 tent sites can be reserved up to six months in advance. The campground fills by early afternoon in July though September, so secure your campsite before you sightsee. Reservations are required for the group site. As one of the most accessible hiking areas of the park, it can be crowded. ✉ *Main park road, 2 miles south of visitor center* ☎ *435/834–5322.*

HIKING

To get up close and personal with the park's hoodoos, set aside a half day to hike into the amphitheater. Remember, after you descend below the rim you'll have to get back up. The air gets warmer the lower you go, and the altitude will have you huffing and puffing unless you're very fit. The uneven terrain calls for lace-up shoes on even the well-trodden, high-traffic trails and sturdy hiking boots for the more challenging ones. No below-rim trails are paved. For trail maps, information, and ranger recommendations, stop at the visitor center. Bathrooms are at most trailheads but not down in the amphitheater. ⇨ *For more information on hiking trails, see the Sights sections, above.*

HORSEBACK RIDING

Many of the park's hiking trails were first formed beneath the hooves of cattle wranglers. Today, hikers and riders share the trails. A number of outfitters can set you up with a gentle mount and lead you to the park's best sights. Not only can you cover more ground than you would walking, but equine traffic has the right-of-way at all times. Call ahead to the stables for reservations to find a trip that's right for you, from 90 minutes to all day. The biggest outfitters have more than 100 horses and mules to choose from. People under the age of seven or who weigh more than 220 pounds are prohibited from riding.

Canyon Trail Rides

HORSEBACK RIDING | FAMILY | Descend to the floor of the Bryce Canyon Amphitheater via horse or mule—most visitors have no riding experience, so don't hesitate to join in. A two-hour ride (children as young as 7 can participate) ambles along the amphitheater floor through the Queen's Garden before returning to Sunrise Point. The three-hour expedition (children must be at least 10 years old) follows Peekaboo Loop Trail, winds past the Fairy Castle, and passes the Wall of

Windows before returning to Sunrise Point. For either ride, the weight limit is 220 pounds. Two rides a day of each type leave in the morning and early afternoon. There are no rides from November through March. ✉ *Bryce Canyon Lodge, Off Hwy. 63* ☎ *435/679–8665, 435/834–5500 Bryce Canyon reservations* 🌐 *www.canyonrides.com* 🎫 *From $65.*

Ruby's Horseback Adventures

HORSEBACK RIDING | FAMILY | Ride to the rim of Bryce Canyon, venture through narrow slot canyons in Grand Staircase–Escalante National Monument, or even retrace the trails taken by outlaw Butch Cassidy more than a century ago. Rides last from 90 minutes to all day. Kids must be 7 or older to ride, in some cases 10. Wagon rides to the rim of Bryce Canyon are available for all ages, as are sleigh rides in winter. ✉ *Bryce Canyon National Park* ☎ *866/782–0002* 🌐 *www.horserides.net* 🎫 *From $68.*

Escalante

38 miles east of Tropic.

Though the Dominguez and Escalante expedition of 1776 came nowhere near this area, the town's name does honor the Spanish explorer. It was bestowed nearly a century later by a member of a survey party led by John Wesley Powell, charged with mapping this remote area. Today, this friendly little town is home to a steadily growing crop of lodgings, eateries, and tour operators. Escalante is the northern gateway to Grand Staircase–Escalante National Monument, an amazing 1.9-million acre wilderness that earned monument status in September 1996.

Unlike parks and monuments operated by the national park service, Grand Staircase–Escalante is administered by the Bureau of Land Management (BLM), and visiting its key attractions requires a bit more research and effort than, for example, Bryce or Capitol Reef, which are relatively more compact and accessible. A good way to plan your visit is to stop by one of the several visitor centers in the area, such as the Escalante Interagency office right in town or the BLM Visitor Center in Cannonville. If you're entering the monument from the south, you might also want to check out the BLM visitor centers in Kanab and Big Water. Given that many of this enormous national monument's top attractions are in remote areas with limited signage and accessed via unpaved roads, it may be worth hiring one of the many experienced outfitters and guides in the area, especially if it's your first time in the area. You'll find more details about some of the monument's top attractions—including Calf Creek Falls and the several sites on or just off of Hole-in-the-Rock Road—in this section.

GETTING HERE AND AROUND

Escalante is accessible by Highway 12, one of the prettiest drives in the state, especially the stretch that runs north to Boulder. You can explore the vast Grand Staircase–Escalante National Monument via unpaved roads and sometimes pretty rough roads, ideally with a four-wheel-drive vehicle, although in dry weather, a passenger car can handle some areas. Most access points are off of Highway 12. It costs nothing to enter the park, but fees apply for camping and backcountry permits.

TOURS

Escape Goats

SPECIAL-INTEREST | This noted family-owned operation offers a variety of day and evening hikes, multiday backpacking trips, and photo and artist tours, which can be customized to any ability or age. The company provides shuttle services, too. ✉ *Escalante* ☎ *435/826–4652* 🌐 *www.escalantecanyonguides.com* 🎫 *From $150.*

Excursions of Escalante

ADVENTURE TOURS | Hiking, backpacking, photography, and canyoneering tours in the Escalante region are custom-fit to your needs and abilities by experienced guides. Canyoneers will be taken into the slot canyons to move through slot chutes or rappel down walls and other obstacles. All gear and provisions are provided whether it's a day hike or multiday adventure. ✉ *125 E. Main St.* ☎ *800/839–7567, 435/826–4714* 🌐 *www.excursionsofescalante.com* 🎫 *From $165.*

★ **Utah Canyon Outdoors**

SPECIAL-INTEREST | Run by a young husband and wife team with extensive experience in Utah as naturalists and guides, this stellar outfitter operates an outdoor gear shop and coffeehouse in a charming little converted house in downtown Escalante. In addition to full-day hikes through slot canyons and the area's other dramatic features, the company also offers Escalante yoga experiences. ✉ *325 W. Main St.* ☎ *435/826–4967* 🌐 *www.utahcanyonoutdoors.com* 🎫 *From $140.*

VISITOR INFORMATION

CONTACTS Cannonville BLM Visitor Center. ✉ *10 Center St., Cannonville* ☎ *435/826–5640* 🌐 *www.blm.gov/visit/cannonville-visitor-center.* **Escalante Interagency Visitor Center.** ✉ *755 W. Main St.* ☎ *435/826–5499* 🌐 *www.blm.gov/visit/escalante-interagency-visitor-center.*

Sights

★ **Calf Creek Falls Recreation Area**

NATIONAL/STATE PARK | FAMILY | One of the more easily accessible and rewarding adventures in the area, this picturesque canyon rife with oak trees and cacti and sandstone pictographs is reached via a 6-mile round-trip hike that starts at Calf Creek Campground, which is just 15 miles east of Escalante and 12 miles south of Boulder along scenic Highway 12. The big payoff, and it's especially pleasing on warm days, is a 126-foot spring-fed waterfall. The pool at the base is a beautiful spot for a swim or picnic. ✉ *Hwy. 12* ☎ *435/826–5499* 🌐 *www.blm.gov/visit/calf-creek-recreation-area-day-use-site* 🎫 *$5 per vehicle.*

Escalante Petrified Forest State Park

NATIONAL/STATE PARK | FAMILY | This park just 2 miles outside Escalante protects a huge repository of petrified wood, easily spotted along two short but moderately taxing hiking trails (the shorter and steeper of the two, the Sleeping Rainbows Trail, requires some scrambling over boulders). Of equal interest is the park's Wide Hollow Reservoir, which has a swimming beach and is popular for kayaking, standup paddling, trout fishing, and birding. ✉ *710 N. Reservoir Rd.* ☎ *435/826–4466* 🌐 *stateparks.utah.gov/parks/escalante-petrified-forest* 🎫 *$8 per vehicle.*

★ **Hell's Backbone Road**

SCENIC DRIVE | For a scenic, topsy-turvy backcountry drive or a challenging mountain-bike ride, follow 35-mile Hell's Backbone Road (aka Forest Road 153) from Escalante, where it begins as Posey Lake Road, to Boulder. Built by the Civilian Conservation Corps in the early 1930s, it's a gravel-surface alternate route that's arguably even more spectacular than scenic Highway 12. You can make the drive with an ordinary passenger car in summer (it's impassable in winter), assuming dry conditions, but a four-wheel-drive vehicle is more comfortable. Allow about two hours to drive it. ✉ *Hell's Backbone Rd.*

★ **Highway 12 Scenic Byway**

SCENIC DRIVE | Keep your camera handy and steering wheel steady along this entrancing 123-mile route between Escalante and Torrey, just west of Capitol Reef National Park. Though the highway starts at the intersection of U.S. 89, west of Bryce Canyon National Park, the stretch that begins in Escalante is one of the most spectacular. Be sure to stop at the scenic overlooks; almost every one will give you an eye-popping view, and information panels let you know what you're looking at. Pay attention while driving, though; the paved road is twisting and steep, and at times climbs over a hogback with sheer drop-offs on both sides. ✉ *Hwy. 12.*

Hole-in-the-Rock Road

SCENIC DRIVE | On the way to southeastern Utah in 1879, Mormon pioneers chipped and blasted a narrow passageway in solid rock, through which they lowered their wagons. The Hole-in-the-Rock Trail, now a very rugged 60-mile unpaved washboard road (aka BLM 200), leads south from Highway 12, 5 miles east of Escalante, to the actual hole-in-the-rock site in Glen Canyon Recreation Area. The original passageway ends where the canyon has been flooded by the waters of Lake Powell—you can hike the half-mile from the end of the road to a dramatic viewpoint overlooking the lake. Just keep in mind that it can take up to three hours to drive to the end of the road, and high-clearance vehicles are best (and a requirement when muddy—check with the Escalante BLM visitor center before setting out). However, there are some amazing hiking spots located off the road, including Zebra Slot Canyon (at mile 8.5), Devil's Garden (at mile 12), Peekaboo Gulch (off Dry Fork Road, at mile 26), and Dance Hall Rock (at mile 36). ✉ *Hole-in-the-Rock Road* ☎ *435/826–5499* 🌐 *www.nps.gov/glca/learn/historyculture/holeintherock.htm.*

★ **Kodachrome Basin State Park**

NATIONAL/STATE PARK | **FAMILY** | Yes, it is named after the old-fashioned color photo film, and once you see it you'll understand why the National Geographic Society gave it the name. The stone spires known as "sand pipes" cannot be found anywhere else in the world. Hike any of the trails to spot some of the 67 pipes in and around the park. The short Angels Palace Trail takes you quickly into the park's interior, up, over, and around some of the badlands. Note that the oft-photographed Shakespeare Arch collapsed in April 2019, although the trail leading to it is still open. ✉ *Off Cottonwood Canyon Rd., Cannonville* ☎ *435/679–8562* 🌐 *stateparks.utah.gov/parks/kodachrome-basin* 🎫 *$10 per vehicle.*

Restaurants

★ **Escalante Outfitters Restaurant**

$ | **MODERN AMERICAN** | This warm and inviting log cabin–style restaurant—operated by a popular tour operator that also runs a camp store and cabin and camping compound—is a great place to sit back and relax after a day of hiking, fly-fishing, or road-tripping. Try one of the creatively topped pizzas, a veggie sandwich, or an apple-pecan-arugula salad, or drop in for one of the best cups of (Fair Trade) coffee in the region and a light breakfast to kick off the day. **Known for:** one of the better craft beer selections in the region; lively and fun dining room; fine coffees, quiches, and pastries in the morning. $ *Average main: $12* ✉ *310 W. Main St.* ☎ *435/826–4266* 🌐 *www.escalanteoutfitters.com* ⏲ *Closed Dec.–Feb.*

Coffee and Quick Bites

★ **Kiva Koffeehouse**

$ | **CAFÉ** | This fun stop along scenic Highway 12 at mile marker 73.86, 13 miles east of Escalante, was constructed by the late artist and inventor Bradshaw Bowman, who began building it when he was in his eighties and spent two years finding and transporting the 13 Douglas-fir logs surrounding the structure. The distinctive eatery with amazing views serves homemade soups, bagel sandwiches, salads, and desserts, and an array of espresso drinks. **Known for:** breathtaking canyon views; breakfast sandwiches and bagels; housemade pies and cupcakes. $ *Average main: $10* ✉ *Escalante* ✣ *Hwy. 12 between mileposts 73 and 74* ☎ *435/826–4550* *www.kivakoffeehouse.com No credit cards Closed Nov.–Feb. and Mon.–Tues. No dinner.*

Hotels

Canyon Country Lodge

$$$ | **HOTEL** | **FAMILY** | A boutique hotel on the outskirts of town, just off Highway 12, Canyon Country Lodge contains 28 spacious rooms—many of them with northerly views toward Escalante Canyon—comfortably outfitted with smart TVs, microwaves, refrigerators, and modern tile bathrooms. **Pros:** stylishly decorated; nice indoor pool and hot tub; close to but just outside downtown. **Cons:** 15-minute walk to most dining options; on-site restaurant gets mixed reviews; no elevator. *Rooms from: $199 760 E. Hwy. 12 435/826–4545, 844/367–3080 www.canyoncountrylodge.com 28 rooms Free breakfast.*

Circle D Motel

$ | **HOTEL** | Although there's nothing fancy about this low-slung adobe motel on the edge of downtown Escalante, the simple rooms have all the basics you need for a comfortable night or two—microwaves, fridges, coffeemakers, HDTVs, climate control—and one larger suite with a kitchenette sleeps six. **Pros:** short walk from downtown businesses; casual restaurant with a pleasant patio; among the lowest rates in the area. **Cons:** standard rooms are small; no pool or gym; no breakfast. *Rooms from: $86 475 W. Main St. 435/826–4297 www.escalantecircledmotel.com 22 rooms No meals.*

★ Entrada Escalante Lodge

$$ | **HOTEL** | Each of the eight rooms in this smart, contemporary lodge in Escalante has a patio with grand views of the surrounding mountains, plus plenty of cushy perks like French presses and fresh-ground coffee, plush bedding, and 50-inch smart TVs. **Pros:** stunning views of Grand Staircase–Escalante National Monument; spacious rooms; pets are welcome in some rooms and the property is horse friendly, too. **Cons:** books up well ahead many weekends; in a very secluded, small town; no gym or pool. *Rooms from: $139 480 W. Main St. 435/826–4000 www.entradaescalante.com Closed Jan. and Feb. 8 rooms No meals.*

★ Slot Canyons Inn B&B

$$ | **B&B/INN** | Set in a dramatic, New Mexico adobe–style building, this upscale inn with spacious rooms and lots of big windows is 5 miles west of town—at the mouth of a canyon on the edge of the national monument—and has hikes right outside its door, as well as hosts who can provide guidance on regional treks. **Pros:** utterly peaceful and enchanting setting; within a short hike of petroglyphs and dramatic cliffs; many rooms have jetted soaking tubs. **Cons:** very remote setting; the one economically priced room is a little small; not within walking distance of town. *Rooms from: $125 3680 Hwy. 12 435/826–4901 www.slotcanyonsinn.com 11 rooms Free breakfast.*

Torrey

36 miles north of Boulder.

Torrey, just west the Capitol Reef National Park, has lots of personality and charm. The town dates back to the 1880s, when Mormon settlers first arrived. Giant cottonwood trees alongside a narrow canal make it a shady spot, and its altitude of 6,830 feet keeps it a cool in the height of the summer. The townspeople, numbering just under 250, are friendly and accommodating. There are plenty of places to eat and stay, making this an ideal base for exploring Capitol Reef.

GETTING HERE AND AROUND

Highway 24 passes right through Torrey, where it joins scenic Highway 12, which leads south to Boulder and Escalante.

TOURS

Hondoo Rivers & Trails
GUIDED TOURS | This tour company has been providing high-quality backcountry trips into Capitol Reef National Park, Escalante Canyons, and the High Plateaus since the mid-1970s. From April to October, they offer hiking, horseback-riding, and Jeep day tours. Trips are designed to explore the geologic landforms in the area, seek out wildflowers in season, and to encounter free-roaming mustangs, bison, and bighorn sheep when possible. Multiday horseback inn-to-inn and camping excursions are also available. ✉ *90 E. Main St., Torrey* ☎ *435/425–3519* 🌐 *www.hondoo.com* *From $120.*

Restaurants

Capitol Reef Café
$$ | **AMERICAN** | Known for its varied selection of reliably good and healthy fare, this unpretentious eatery has a laid-back vibe and is attached to a gift shop that stocks an eclectic selection of Native American and Southwestern books and artwork. Favorites dishes include huevos rancheros in the morning, and smoked-trout salad, wild-mushroom lasagna, and charbroiled New York steaks later in the day. **Known for:** hearty breakfasts; nice mix of vegetarian options; good beer and wine selection. *$ Average main: $17* ✉ *360 W. Main St. (Hwy. 24), Torrey* ☎ *435/425–3271* 🌐 *www.capitolreefinn.com* *Closed late Oct.–mid-Mar.*

Slacker's Burger Joint
$ | **BURGER** | **FAMILY** | After a long day of hiking, this friendly '50s-style burger joint decorated with old license plates is a welcome sight, with its two-fisted burgers, stick-to-your-ribs buffalo chili, and soft-serve ice cream and sundaes. Burgers come in a variety of styles, from classic double-bacon cheeseburgers to pastrami-and-Swiss, and there's a nice range of sides, including traditional and sweet potato fries, onion rings, and fried green beans. **Known for:** covered outdoor seating; the fiery-hot Outlaw burger with ghost-pepper cheese and jalapeños; seasonal fruit cobblers. *$ Average main: $10* ✉ *165 E. Main St., Torrey* ☎ *435/425–3710* 🌐 *www.slackersburgerjoint.com* *Closed Sun.*

★ Torrey Grill & BBQ
$$ | **BARBECUE** | **FAMILY** | Located a little west of town in the middle of Thousand Lakes RV Park, this festive barbecue joint offers chuckwagon-style indoor and outdoor seating around firepits. Think elevated comfort food, with dishes like dry-rub smoked pork spare ribs, spiced-rubbed grilled salmon, and char-grilled rib-eye steaks packed with flavor, and delicious side dishes and desserts, too. **Known for:** corn muffins with pecan-honey butter; slow-smoked half chicken; make your own s'mores. *$ Average main: $21* ✉ *1110 Hwy. 24, Torrey* ☎ *435/609–6997* 🌐 *www.torreygrillandbbq.com* *Closed Sun. No lunch.*

Coffee and Quick Bites

Wild Rabbit Cafe
$ | **CAFÉ** | Torrey's best little source of fair-trade organic coffee and fresh-baked pastries is a terrific go-to for breakfast or lunch before you head to the Capitol Reef. Consider pancakes with fresh fruit, French toast with maple syrup, and bagels with smoked trout and capers. **Known for:** biscuits with sausage gravy; lavender vanilla lattes; fruit-and-granola parfaits. *$ Average main: $7* ✉ *135 E. Main St., Torrey* ☎ *435/425–3074* 🌐 *www.thewildrabbitcafe.com* *Closed Mon.–Wed.*

Hotels

Austin's Chuck Wagon Motel
$ | **HOTEL** | **FAMILY** | Foremost at this pleasant complex are friendly service and immaculate rooms, including standard-size in the motel-style lodge or stand-alone cabins that sleep up to six. **Pros:** bargain rates; several restaurants and

shops within walking distance; large outdoor pool. **Cons:** family atmosphere might not please solitary travelers; handful of original rooms are a bit rustic; breakfast not included. *Rooms from: $82 ✉ 12 W. Main St., Torrey ☎ 435/425–3335, 800/863–3288 🌐 www.austinschuckwagonmotel.com ⏲ Closed Nov.–Mar. 28 rooms No meals.*

Capitol Reef Resort

$$ | HOTEL | FAMILY | A relaxing and well-kept home base with excellent amenities and a wide range of accommodations—from traditional hotel rooms to luxurious cabins to authentically designed tents and Conestoga wagons—this hilltop lodging lies just a few miles west of the Capitol Reef's western border, and many rooms have patios and balconies overlook the not-so-distant sandstone cliffs. **Pros:** good restaurant and gift shop; astounding Capitol Reef views; nice gym and outdoor pool. **Cons:** breakfast not included in rates; sometimes books up with weddings; pets not allowed. *Rooms from: $152 ✉ 2600 E. Hwy. 24, Torrey ☎ 435/425–3761 🌐 www.capitolreefresort.com 149 rooms No meals.*

Cowboy Homestead Cabins

$ | B&B/INN | Perfect if you want to be near the restaurants and services of Torrey but on a quiet, picturesque property a bit outside of town, this relaxing hideaway comprises four custom-built contemporary cabins minimally stocked kitchenettes, comfy bedding, front porches, and charcoal grills. **Pros:** peaceful location; dramatic views of red rock cliffs; friendly dogs to play with. **Cons:** not within walking distance of town; cabins are right next to one another; no common spaces or amenities. *Rooms from: $119 ✉ 2345 Cowboy Rd., Torrey ✣ off Hwy. 12 ☎ 435/425–3414 🌐 www.cowboyhomesteadcabins.com 4 cabins No meals.*

Rim Rock Inn

$ | HOTEL | On a bluff with outstanding views into the desert, this motel with clean, basic, and reasonably priced rooms (a basic breakfast is included) is one of the closest to the western entrance of Capitol Reef National Park. **Pros:** two distinctive dining options on-site; very affordable; set on 10 rugged acres. **Cons:** a bit removed from town; rooms lack personality; very rudimentary breakfast. *Rooms from: $89 ✉ 2523 E. Hwy. 24, Torrey ☎ 435/425–3398 🌐 www.therimrock.net ⏲ Closed Nov.–Mar. 19 rooms Free breakfast.*

Shopping

ART GALLERIES

Gallery 24

ART GALLERIES | This attractive gallery next to Slacker's Burger Joint sells contemporary fine art from Southern Utah–based artists that includes paintings, photography, ceramics, and sculpture. *✉ 135 E. Main St., Torrey ☎ 435/425–2124 🌐 www.gallery24.biz.*

★ Torrey Gallery

ART GALLERIES | In a pioneer home off Main Street, this handsome gallery specializes in regional art. Its offerings include paintings, sculpture, and photographs, as well as antique and contemporary Navajo rugs discovered by the longtime collectors who own the gallery. *✉ 160 W. Main St., Torrey ☎ 435/425–3909 🌐 www.torreygallery.com.*

CRAFTS

Torrey Trading Post

CRAFTS | Come here for Native American jewelry and pottery, T-shirts, wood carvings, stone figures, gifts for children, and more. The trading post also rents out a handful of deluxe and camping cabins. *✉ 25 W. Main St., Torrey ☎ 435/425–3716 🌐 www.torreytradingpost.com.*

Capitol Reef National Park

Capitol Reef National Park is a natural kaleidoscopic feast for the eyes, with colors more dramatic than anywhere else in the West. The Moenkopi rock formation is a rich, red-chocolate hue; deep blue-green juniper and pinyon stand out against it. Sunset brings out the colors in an explosion of copper, platinum, and orange, then dusk turns the cliffs purple and blue.

The park, established in 1971, preserves the Waterpocket Fold, a giant wrinkle in the earth that extends 100 miles between Thousand Lake Mountain and Lake Powell. When you climb high onto the rocks or into the mountains, you can see this remarkable geologic wonder and the jumble of colorful cliffs, massive domes, soaring spires, and twisting canyons that surround it. It's no wonder early pioneers called this part of the country the "land of the sleeping rainbow."

Beyond incredible sights, the fragrance of pine and sage rises from the earth, and canyon wrens serenade you as you sit by the water. Flowing across the heart of Capitol Reef is the Fremont River, a narrow little creek that can turn into a swollen, raging torrent during desert flash floods. The river sustains cottonwoods, wildlife, and verdant valleys rich with fruit. During the harvest, your sensory experience is complete when you bite into a perfect ripe peach or apple from the park's orchards. Your soul, too, will be gratified here. You can walk the trails in relative solitude and—except during busier periods—enjoy the beauty without confronting significant crowds on the roads or paths. All around you are signs of those who came before: ancient Native Americans of the Fremont culture, Mormon pioneers who settled the land, and other courageous explorers who traveled the canyons.

GETTING HERE AND AROUND

You can approach Capitol Reef country from several routes, including highways 24 and 72 from Interstate 70 (and Moab), Highway 12 from Bryce Canyon National Park, and Highway 20 to U.S. 89 to Highway 62 from Interstate 15. All are well-maintained, safe roads that bisect rich agricultural communities steeped in Mormon history (especially in the nearby towns of Bicknell and Loa). Highway 24 runs across the middle of Capitol Reef National Park, offering scenic views the entire way.

PARK ESSENTIALS

PARK FEES AND PERMITS

There is no fee to enter the park, but it's $20 per vehicle (or $10 per bicycle and $15 per motorcycle) to travel on Scenic Drive beyond Fruita Campground; this fee is good for one week, paid via the "honor system" at a drop box versus a staffed entry gate. Backcountry camping permits are free; pick them up at the visitor center. An annual pass that allows unlimited access to Scenic Drive is $35.

PARK HOURS

The park is open 24/7 year-round. It's in the mountain time zone.

CELL PHONE RECEPTION

Cell phone reception is nearly nonexistent in the park, although you may pick up a weak signal in a few spots. Pay phones are at the visitor center and at Fruita Campground.

VISITOR INFORMATION

CONTACTS Capitol Reef National Park. ✉ *Off Hwy. 24* ☎ *435/425–3791* 🌐 *www.nps.gov/care.*

Fruita

In the 1880s, Nels Johnson became the first homesteader in the Fremont River Valley, building his home near the confluence of Sulphur Creek and the Fremont River. Other Mormon settlers followed and established small farms and orchards, creating the village of Junction.

Did You Know?

The 3.5-mile round-trip trek up to Chimney Rock has some steep switchbacks, but the journey yields panoramic views. The trailhead is 3 miles from the park visitor center, near the entrance. It is forbidden to rock climb on it.

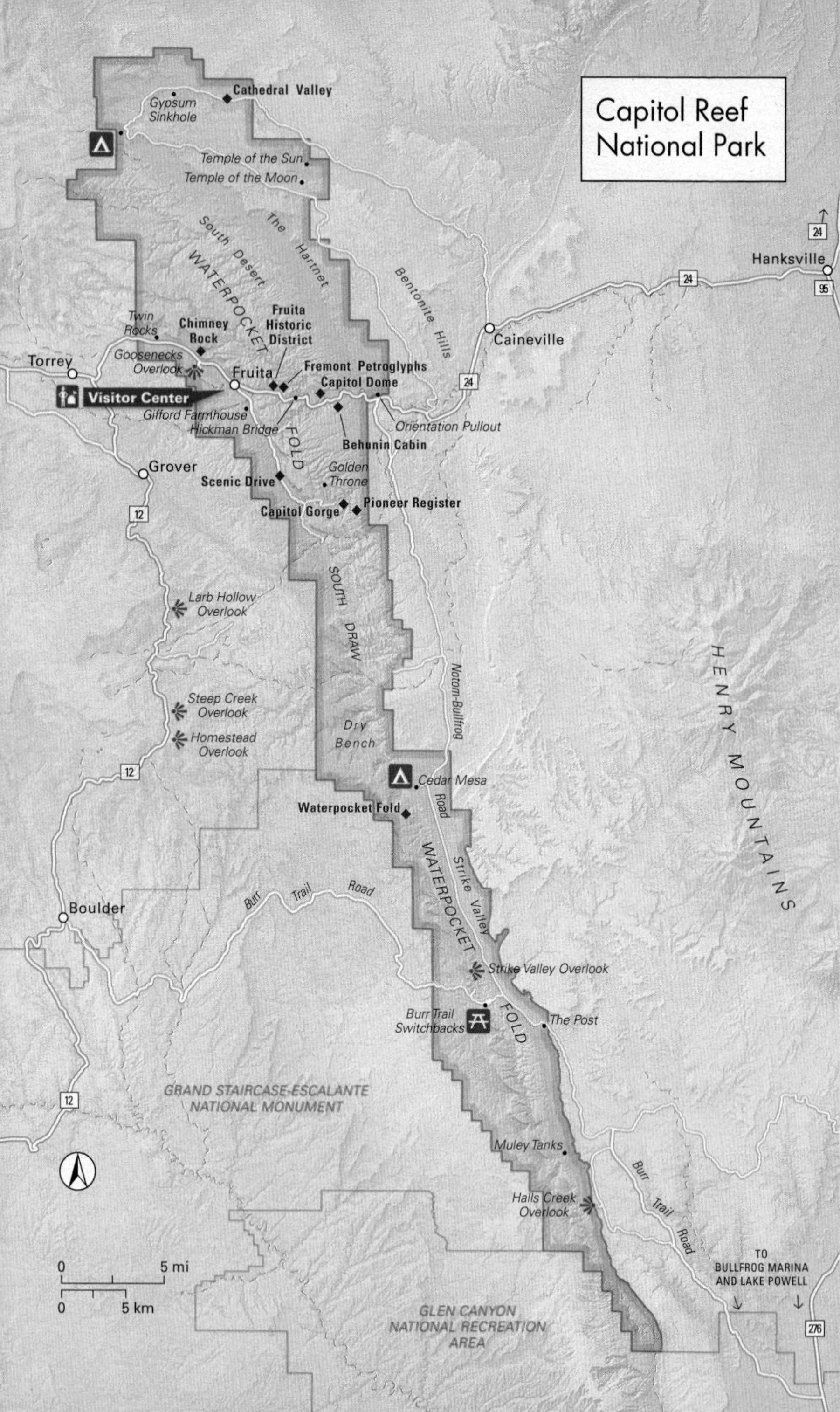

Capitol Reef National Park
Cathedral Valley
Gypsum Sinkhole
Temple of the Sun
Temple of the Moon
South Desert
The Hartnet
WATERPOCKET
Bentonite Hills
Hanksville
24
95
Caineville
Twin Rocks
Chimney Rock
Fruita Historic District
Goosenecks Overlook
Torrey
Fruita
Fremont Petroglyphs
Capitol Dome
Visitor Center
Gifford Farmhouse
Hickman Bridge
FOLD
Orientation Pullout
Behunin Cabin
Grover
Golden Throne
Scenic Drive
Pioneer Register
Capitol Gorge
12
SOUTH DRAW
Larb Hollow Overlook
Notom-Bullfrog
Steep Creek Overlook
Homestead Overlook
Dry Bench
HENRY MOUNTAINS
Cedar Mesa
Road
Waterpocket Fold
Strike Valley
Boulder
Burr Trail Road
Strike Valley Overlook
Burr Trail Switchbacks
The Post
GRAND STAIRCASE-ESCALANTE NATIONAL MONUMENT
Muley Tanks
Halls Creek Overlook
0
5 mi
5 km
TO BULLFROG MARINA AND LAKE POWELL
GLEN CANYON NATIONAL RECREATION AREA
276

The orchards thrived, and by 1900 the name was changed to Fruita. The orchards, less than a mile from the visitor center, are preserved and protected as a Rural Historic District.

Sights

GEOLOGICAL LANDMARKS

Capitol Dome

NATURE SITE | One of the rock formations that gave the park its name, this giant sandstone dome is visible in the vicinity of the Hickman Bridge trailhead, 1.9 miles east of the visitor center. ✉ *Hwy. 24.*

Chimney Rock

NATURE SITE | Even in a landscape of spires, cliffs, and knobs, this deep-red landform, 3.9 miles west of the visitor center, is unmistakable. ✉ *Hwy. 24.*

HISTORIC SIGHTS

Behunin Cabin

BUILDING | **FAMILY** | Elijah Cutler Behunin used blocks of sandstone to build this cabin in 1882. Floods in the lowlands made life too difficult, and he moved before the turn of that century. The house, 5.9 miles east of the visitor center, is empty, but you can peek through the window to see the interior. ✉ *Hwy. 24.*

Fremont Petroglyphs

NATIVE SITE | Between AD 300 and 1300, the Capitol Reef area was occupied by Native Americans who were eventually referred to by archaeologists as the Fremont, named after the Fremont River that flows through the park. A nice stroll along a boardwalk bridge, 1.1 miles east of the visitor center, allows close-up views of ancient rock art, which can be identified by the large trapezoidal figures often depicted wearing headdresses and ear baubles. ✉ *Hwy. 24.*

TRAILS

★ Chimney Rock Trail

TRAIL | You're almost sure to see ravens drifting on thermal winds around the deep-red Mummy Cliff that rings the base of this trail. This loop trail begins with a steep climb to a rim above dramatic Chimney Rock. The trail is 3.6 miles round-trip, with a 590-foot elevation change. No shade. Use caution during monsoon storms due to lightning hazards. Allow three to four hours. *Moderate–Difficult.* ✉ *Capitol Reef National Park* ✣ *Trailhead: Hwy. 24, about 3 miles west of visitor center.*

Fremont River Trail

TRAIL | What starts as a quiet little stroll beside the river turns into an adventure. The first ½ mile of the trail wanders past orchards next to the Fremont River. After you pass through a narrow gate, the trail changes personality and you're in for a steep climb on an exposed ledge with drop-offs. The views at the top of the 480-foot ascent are worth it. It's 2 miles round-trip; allow two hours. *Moderate.* ✉ *Capitol Reef National Park* ✣ *Trailhead: Near amphitheater off Loop C of Fruita Campground, about 1 mile from visitor center.*

Goosenecks Trail

TRAIL | This nice little walk gives you a good introduction to the land surrounding Capitol Reef. You'll enjoy the dizzying views from the overlook. It's only 0.2 miles round-trip to the overlook and a very easy walk. *Easy.* ✉ *Hwy. 24, about 3 miles west of visitor center.*

Hickman Bridge Trail

TRAIL | This trail leads to a natural bridge of Kayenta sandstone, with a 133-foot opening carved by intermittent flash floods. Early on, the route climbs a set of steps along the Fremont River. The trail splits, leading along the right-hand branch to a strenuous uphill climb to the Rim Overlook and Navajo Knobs. Stay to your left to see the bridge, and you'll encounter a moderate up-and-down trail. Up the wash on your way to the bridge is a Fremont granary on the right side of the small canyon. Allow about two hours for the 1.8-mile round-trip. Expect lots of company. *Moderate.* ✉ *Capitol Reef National Park* ✣ *Trailhead: Hwy. 24, 2 miles east of visitor center.*

Sunset Point Trail

TRAIL | The trail starts from the same parking lot as the Goosenecks Trail, on your way into the park about 3.3 miles west of the visitor center. Benches along this easy, 0.8-mile round-trip invite you to sit and meditate surrounded by the colorful desert. At the trail's end, you will be rewarded with broad vistas into the park; it's even better at sunset. *Easy.* ✉ *Hwy. 24.*

SCENIC DRIVES

★ Utah Scenic Byway 24

SCENIC DRIVE | For 75 miles between Loa and Hanksville, you'll cut right through Capitol Reef National Park. Colorful rock formations in all their hues of red, cream, pink, gold, and deep purple extend from one end of the route to the other. The closer you get to the park the more colorful the landscape becomes. The vibrant rock finally gives way to lush green hills and the mountains west of Loa.

VISITOR CENTERS

Capitol Reef Visitor Center

INFO CENTER | **FAMILY** | Watch a park movie, talk with rangers, or peruse the many books, maps, and materials for sale in the bookstore. Towering over the center (11 miles east of Torrey) is the Castle, one of the park's most prominent rock formations. ✉ *Scenic Dr. at Hwy. 24* ☎ *435/425–3791* 🌐 *www.nps.gov/care.*

Scenic Drive

This 8-mile road, simply called Scenic Drive, starts at the visitor center and winds its way through the Fruita Historic District and colorful sandstone cliffs into Capitol Gorge; a side road, Grand Wash Road, provides access into the canyon. At Capitol Gorge, the canyon walls become steep and impressive but the route becomes unpaved for about the last 2 miles, and road conditions may vary due to weather and usage. Check with the visitor center before setting out.

GEOLOGICAL LANDMARKS

The Waterpocket Fold

NATURE SITE | A giant wrinkle in the earth extends almost 100 miles between Thousand Lake Mountain and Lake Powell. You can glimpse the fold by driving south on Scenic Drive after it branches off Highway 24, past the Fruita Historic District. For complete immersion enter the park via the 36-mile Burr Trail from Boulder. Roads through the southernmost reaches of the park are largely unpaved. The area is accessible to most vehicles during dry weather, but check with the visitor center for current road conditions. ✉ *Capitol Reef National Park.*

HISTORIC SIGHTS

Gifford House Store and Museum

NATIONAL/STATE PARK | One mile south of the visitor center in a grassy meadow with the Fremont River flowing by, this is an idyllic shady spot in the Fruita Historic District for a sack lunch, complete with tables, drinking water, grills, and a convenient restroom. The store sells reproductions of pioneer tools and items made by local craftspeople; there's also locally made fruit pies and ice cream to enjoy with your picnic. ✉ *Scenic Dr.*

Pioneer Register

HISTORIC SITE | Travelers passing through Capitol Gorge in the 19th and early 20th centuries etched the canyon wall with their names and the date. Directly across the canyon from the Pioneer Register and about 50 feet up are signatures etched into the canyon wall by an early United States Geologic Survey crew. Though it's illegal to write or scratch on the canyon walls today, plenty of damage has been done by vandals over the years. You can reach the register via an easy hike from the sheltered trailhead at the end of Capitol Gorge Road, 10.3 miles south of the visitor center; the register is about 10 minutes along the hike to the sandstone "tanks." ✉ *Off Scenic Dr.*

SCENIC DRIVES

★ Capitol Gorge

SCENIC DRIVE | Eight miles south of the visitor center, Scenic Drive ends, at which point you can drive an unpaved spur road into Capitol Gorge. The narrow, twisting road on the floor of the gorge was a route for pioneer wagons traversing this part of Utah starting in the 1860s. After every flash flood, pioneers would laboriously clear the route so wagons could continue to go through. The gorge became the main automobile route in the area until 1962, when Highway 24 was built. The short drive to the end of the road has striking views of the surrounding cliffs and leads to one of the park's most popular walks: the hiking trail to the water-holding "tanks" eroded into the sandstone. ✉ *Scenic Dr.*

TRAILS

★ Capitol Gorge Trail and the Tanks

NATIONAL/STATE PARK | Starting at the Pioneer Register, about a ½ mile from the Capitol Gorge parking lot, is a ½-mile trail that climbs to the Tanks—holes in the sandstone, formed by erosion, that hold water after it rains. After a scramble up about ¼ mile of steep trail with cliff drop-offs, you can look down into the Tanks and see a natural bridge below the lower tank. Including the walk to the Pioneer Register, allow an hour or more for this interesting hike, one of the park's most popular. *Moderate.* ✉ *Capitol Reef National Park* ✣ *Trailhead: At end of Scenic Dr., 10 miles south of visitor center.*

Cohab Canyon Trail

TRAIL | Find rock wrens and Western pipistrelles (canyon bats) on this trail. One end is directly across from the Fruita Campground on Scenic Drive; the other is across from the Hickman Bridge parking lot. The first ¼ mile from Fruita is strenuous, but the walk becomes easier except for turnoffs to the overlooks, which are short. You'll find miniature arches, skinny side canyons, and honeycombed patterns on canyon walls where the wrens make nests. The trail is 3.2 miles round-trip to the Hickman Bridge parking lot (two to three hours). The Overlook Trail adds 1 mile. Allow two hours to overlooks and back. *Moderate.* ✉ *Capitol Reef National Park* ✣ *Trailheads: Scenic Dr., about 1 mile south of visitor center, or Hwy. 24, about 2 miles east of visitor center.*

Grand Wash Trail

TRAIL | At the end of unpaved Grand Wash Road you can continue on foot through the canyon to its end at Highway 24. This flat hike takes you through a wide wash between canyon walls, and is an excellent place to study the geology up close. The round-trip hike is 4.4 miles; allow two to three hours for your walk. Check at the ranger station for flash-flood warnings before entering the wash. *Easy.* ✉ *Capitol Reef National Park* ✣ *Trailhead: At Hwy. 24, east of Hickman Bridge parking lot, or at end of Grand Wash Rd., off Scenic Dr. about 5 miles from visitor center.*

Cathedral Valley

This primitive, rugged area was named for its sandstone geological features that are reminiscent of Gothic cathedrals. Visiting is quite the backroad adventure, so not many people make the effort to drive on roads that some have called brutal. But if you have the right vehicle and an adventurous spirit, the rewards of seeing ancient natural wonders should be worth it. The selenite crystals of Glass Mountain attract rockhounds for a closer look, but no collecting is allowed. Sunset and sunrise at the Temple of the Sun and Temple of the Moon monoliths are especially colorful and photogenic.

SCENIC DRIVES

Cathedral Valley/North District Loop

TRAIL | The north end of Capitol Reef, along this backcountry road, is filled with towering monoliths, panoramic vistas, water crossings, and a stark desert landscape. The area is remote and the road through it unpaved, so do not enter without a suitable mountain bike or high-clearance vehicle, some planning, and a cell phone (although reception is virtually nonexistent). The trail through the valley is a 58-mile loop that you can begin at River Ford Road, 11¾ miles east of the visitor center off Highway 24; allow half a day. If your time is limited, you can tour only the Caineville Wash Road, which takes about two hours by ATV or four-wheel drive vehicle. If you are planning a multiday trip, there's a primitive campground about halfway through the loop. Pick up a self-guided tour brochure at the visitor center. ✉ *River Ford Rd., off Hwy. 24.*

Activities

BIKING

Bicycles are allowed only on established roads in the park. Highway 24 is a state highway and receives a substantial amount of through traffic, so it's not the best place to pedal. Scenic Drive is better, but the road is narrow, and you have to contend with drivers dazed by the beautiful surroundings. In fact, it's a good idea to traverse it in the morning or evening when traffic is reduced, or in the off-season. Four-wheel-drive roads are certainly less traveled, but they are often sandy, rocky, and steep. The Cathedral Valley/North District Loop is popular with mountain bikers (but also with four-wheelers). You cannot ride your bicycle in washes or on hiking trails.

South Draw Road

BICYCLING | This is a very strenuous but picturesque ride that traverses dirt, sand, and rocky surfaces, and crosses several creeks that may be muddy. It's not recommended in winter or spring because of deep snow at higher elevations. The route starts at an elevation of 8,500 feet on Boulder Mountain, 13 miles south of Torrey, and ends 15¾ miles later at 5,500 feet in the Pleasant Creek parking area at the end of Scenic Drive. ✉ *Bowns Reservoir Rd. and Hwy. 12.*

CAMPING

Campgrounds—both the highly convenient Fruita Campground and the backcountry sites—in Capitol Reef fill up fast between March and October. Most of the area's state parks have camping facilities, and the region's two national forests offer many wonderful sites.

Cathedral Valley Campground. This small (just six sites), basic (no water, pit toilet), no-fee campground in the park's remote northern district touts sprawling views, but the bumpy road there is hard to navigate. ✉ *Hartnet Junction, on Caineville Wash Rd.* ☎ *435/425–3791.*

Cedar Mesa Campground. Wonderful views of the Waterpocket Fold and Henry Mountains surround this primitive (pit toilet, no water), no-fee campground with five sites in the park's southern district. ✉ *Notom-Bullfrog Rd., 22 miles south of Hwy. 24* ☎ *435/425–3791.*

Fruita Campground. Near the orchards and the Fremont River, the park's developed (flush toilets, running water), shady campground is a great place to call home for a few days. The sites require a $20 nightly fee, and those nearest the Fremont River or the orchards are the most coveted. ✉ *Scenic Dr., about 1 mile south of visitor center* ☎ *435/425–3791* 🌐 *www.recreation.gov.*

HIKING

Many park trails in Capitol Reef include steep climbs, but there are a few easy-to-moderate hikes. A short drive from the visitor center takes you to a dozen trails near the Fruita Historic District, but there are more challenging hikes in the other areas.

Chapter 8

MOAB AND SOUTHEASTERN UTAH

WITH ARCHES AND CANYONLANDS NATIONAL PARKS

Updated by
Stina Sieg

Sights	Restaurants	Hotels	Shopping	Nightlife
★★★★★	★★★☆☆	★★★☆☆	★★☆☆☆	★☆☆☆☆

WELCOME TO MOAB AND SOUTHEASTERN UTAH

TOP REASONS TO GO

★ **Get out and play:** Mountain and road biking, rafting, rock climbing, hiking, four-wheeling, and cross-country skiing are all wildly popular.

★ **Creature Comforts:** Though remote, southeastern Utah—and Moab, in particular—has an array of lodging and dining options, including elegant bistros, fancy hotels, and quaint bed-and-breakfasts.

★ **Festivals:** Especially in the spring and summer months, this area is chock-full of gatherings focused on art, music, and recreation.

★ **Arches National Park:** Nowhere in the world has as large an array or quantity of natural arches.

★ **Canyonlands National Park:** The view from Island in the Sky stretches for miles as you look out over millennia of sculpting by wind and rain.

1 **Moab.** This increasingly busy heart of the area is full of shops, restaurants, and hotels.

2 **Arches National Park.** A park with almost unimaginable rock formations.

3 **Canyonlands National Park.** Amazing canyons and untouched wilderness.

4 **Green River.** This small town right off the interstate is a place to stock up on supplies and gas before heading off on farther-flung adventures.

5 **Blanding.** This tiny place isn't a huge draw on its own but is close to several natural wonders and two Native American reservations.

6 **Bluff.** A small, arty town with a big personality, Bluff has a few great places to stay and eat and many historic buildings that are fun to stroll past.

7 **Natural Bridges National Monument.** The remote park features three of its namesake spans of red rock, including the Sipapu Bridge, one of the largest natural bridges in the world.

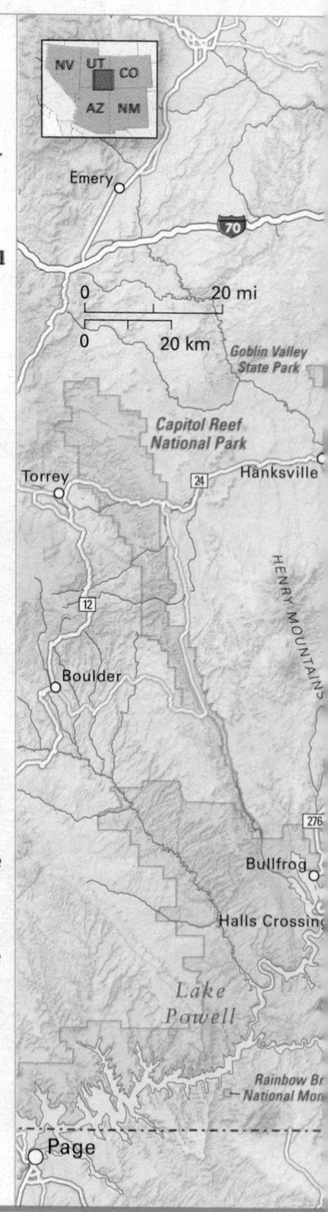

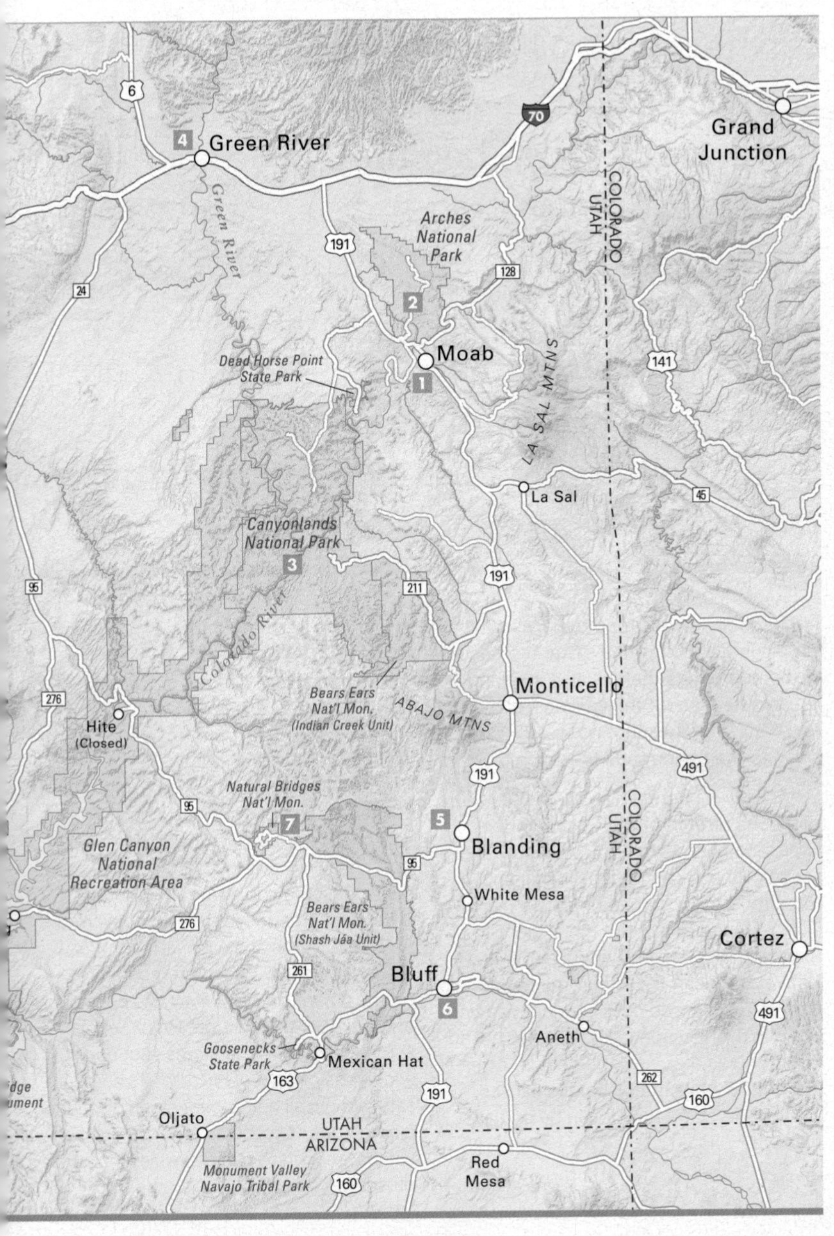
6
70
4
Green River
Grand Junction
Green River
Arches National Park
191
128
24
2
Moab
Dead Horse Point State Park
1
LA SAL MTNS
141
COLORADO
UTAH
La Sal
45
Canyonlands National Park
3
Colorado River
191
211
95
Bears Ears Nat'l Mon. (Indian Creek Unit)
ABAJO MTNS
Monticello
276
Hite (Closed)
491
191
Natural Bridges Nat'l Mon.
95
7
5
Blanding
COLORADO
UTAH
Glen Canyon National Recreation Area
95
White Mesa
276
Bears Ears Nat'l Mon. (Shash Jáa Unit)
Cortez
261
Bluff
6
491
Aneth
Goosenecks State Park
Mexican Hat
163
191
262
160
Oljato
UTAH
ARIZONA
Red Mesa
Monument Valley Navajo Tribal Park
160

Southeastern Utah, especially Moab, is full of converts, and not so much in a religious sense. These are people formerly from suburbs or cities who came here long ago for vacation and never truly left. They may have spent just a few days surrounded by the vast desert and the clean, welcoming rivers, but in that short time, the land became a part of them. Moab has a certain kind of magic to it, as anyone who has ever visited will tell you, and many stay for the empty beauty of the region.

Although the towns tend to be visually simple in this part of the state, the beauty that surrounds them is awe-inspiring. You can hear about the canyons, arches, and natural bridges, but no words come close to their enormous presence.

Ostensibly, visitors arrive to run the gorgeous stretch of the Colorado River near Moab or to explore the unique landscape of the area's national parks and monuments. Or perhaps they are history buffs, excited to explore the ancient ruins and rock art left behind by various Native American tribes. For the most part, tourists come out of curiosity to find out if this landscape is just as special and disarming as they have heard it is. After just a little while in this unique canvas, you'll understand how it can be so hard to leave.

Planning

When to Go

The most enjoyable times to be in this part of Utah are the beginning and end of high season, March and October, respectively. April and May have the best weather—and the biggest crowds. May to September is the best time to hit the river, but is also when the towns and national parks are filled with people, and the temperatures can be downright fiery. From the beginning of November through the end of February some restaurants and stores shut down, and things can get eerily quiet. To compensate, almost all hotels offer steep discounts (sometimes as much as 40% off high-season prices), which can make visiting in the off-season a steal.

Getting Here and Around

AIR

The nearest large airport to southeastern Utah is Walker Field Airport in Grand Junction, Colorado, 110 miles from Moab, but you can catch a regional flight directly to Moab. Rental cars are now available at the Moab Airport; advance reservations are highly recommended.

CAR

To reach southeastern Utah from Salt Lake City, take I–15 to U.S. 6 and then U.S. 191 south. From Colorado or more eastern locations, use I–70 or U.S. 491. Take U.S. 191 from either Wyoming or Arizona. Most roads are well-maintained two-lane highways, though snow can be a factor during winter travel. Be sure your car is in good working order and keep the gas tank topped off, as there are long stretches of empty road between towns.

TRAIN

The *California Zephyr*, operated by Amtrak (🌐 *www.amtrak.com*), stops daily in Green River, about 50 miles northwest of Moab.

Hotels

Every type of lodging is available in southeastern Utah, from economy chain motels, to B&Bs and high-end, high-adventure resorts to rental condos. There are 26 BLM (Bureau of Land Management) campgrounds in the area, all for $20, all first-come, first-served. *Hotel reviews have been shortened. For full information, visit Fodors.com.*

Restaurants

Including a few surprising twists, Moab-area restaurants have anything you might crave. The other smaller towns in southeastern Utah don't have quite the culinary kaleidoscope, and focus on all-American cuisine. Though not the best destination for vegetarians or those with a restricted diet, the comfort food will satisfy after a day of activity. *Restaurant reviews have been shortened. For full information, visit Fodors.com.*

HOTEL AND RESTAURANT PRICES

Hotel prices in the reviews are the lowest cost of a standard double room in high season. Restaurant prices in the reviews are the average cost of a main course at dinner, or if dinner is not served, at lunch.

What It Costs

	$	$$	$$$	$$$$
RESTAURANTS	under $16	$16–$22	$23–$30	over $30
HOTELS	under $125	$125–$175	$176–$225	over $225

Moab

When you first drive down crowded Main Street (Moab's commercial, downtown strip), you might not get the town's appeal right away. The wide thoroughfare is lined with T-shirt shops and touristy restaurants. But don't let Moab's impersonal exterior fool you; take a few walks, visit some of the town's locally owned stores and eateries, and talk to some of the residents, and you'll realize this is a town centered on community. Local theater, local radio, and local art rule. At its core, this is a frontier outpost, where people have had to create their own livelihoods for more than 100 years. In the late 1880s, it was settled as a farming and ranching community. By the 1950s it became a center for uranium mining after Charlie Steen found a huge deposit of the stuff outside town. After about a decade of unbelievable monetary success, there was a massive downturn in the mining industry, and Moab plunged into an economic free fall. Then came tourism. Moab was able to rebuild itself with the dollars of sightseers, four-wheelers, bikers, and boaters. Today the town is dealing with environmental and development issues while becoming more and more popular with tourists and second-homeowners from around the world. No matter how it changes, though, one thing never will: this town has a different flavor from any other found in the state.

GETTING HERE AND AROUND

Although Moab is friendly to bikes and pedestrians, the only practical way to reach it is by car. If you're coming from the south, U.S. 191 runs straight into Moab. If you're arriving from Salt Lake City, travel 50 miles via I–15, then go 150 miles southeast via U.S. 6, and finally 30 miles south via U.S. 191. Signs for Moab will be obvious past Green River. **TIP→ If you are approaching from the east on I–70, take Exit 214 into the ghost town of Cisco, and then drive down Colorado River Scenic Byway—Route 128 into Moab. The views of the river, rocks, and mesas are second to none.**

TOURS

Canyonlands by Night & Day

BOAT TOURS | Since 1963 this outfitter has been known for its Sound and Light Show Jet Boat Tour, a two-hour, after-dark boat ride on the Colorado River (March–October). While illuminating the canyon walls with 40,000 watts, the trip includes music and narration highlighting Moab's history, Native American legends, and geologic formations along the river. A dutch oven dinner is included, though you can exclude it and save $10. Daytime jet boat tours are offered, too, as well as tours by Hummer, airplane, and helicopter (land and air tours are offered year-round). *1861 U.S. 191* *435/259–2628, 800/394–9978* *www.canyonlandsbynight.com* *Boat tour with dinner from $79.*

VISITOR INFORMATION

CONTACTS Discover Moab Information Center. *25 E. Center St.* *435/259–8825* *www.discovermoab.com.*

Sights

★ Colorado River Scenic Byway—Highway 128

SCENIC DRIVE | One of the most scenic drives in the Four Corners region, Highway 128 intersects U.S. 191, 3 miles south of Arches. The 44-mile highway runs along the Colorado River with 2,000-foot red rock cliffs rising on both sides. This gorgeous river corridor is home to a winery, orchards, and a couple of luxury lodging options. It also offers a spectacular view of world-class climbing destination Fisher Towers before winding north to Interstate 70. Give yourself an hour to 90 minutes to drive it. *Hwy. 128.*

Colorado River Scenic Byway—Highway 279

SCENIC DRIVE | If you're interested in Native American rock art, Highway 279 northwest of Moab is a perfect place to spend a couple of hours immersed in the past.

To get there, go north on U.S. 191 for about 3½ miles and turn left onto Highway 279. If you start late in the afternoon, the cliffs will be glowing orange as the sun sets. Along the first part of the route you'll see signs reading "Indian Writings." Park only in designated areas to view the petroglyphs on the cliff side of the road. At the 18-mile marker you'll see Jug Handle Arch. A few miles beyond this point the road turns to four-wheel-drive only, and takes you into the Island in the Sky District of Canyonlands. Do not continue onto the Island in the Sky unless you are in a high-clearance four-wheel-drive vehicle with a full gas tank and plenty of water. Allow about two hours round-trip for the Scenic Byway drive. **TIP→ If you happen to be in Moab during a heavy rainstorm, Highway 279 is also a good option for viewing the**

amazing waterfalls caused by rain pouring off the cliffs on both sides of the Colorado River. ✉ *Hwy. 279.*

★ Dead Horse Point State Park

NATIONAL/STATE PARK | **FAMILY** | One of the gems of Utah's state park system, right at the edge of the Island in the Sky section of Canyonlands, this park overlooks a sweeping oxbow of the Colorado River some 2,000 feet below. Dead Horse Point itself is a small peninsula connected to the main mesa by a narrow neck of land. As the story goes, cowboys used to drive wild mustangs onto the point and pen them there with a brush fence. There's a modern visitor center with a coffee shop and museum. The park's Intrepid trail system is popular with mountain bikers and hikers alike. Be sure to walk the 4-mile rim trail loop and drive to the park's eponymous point if it's a nice day. ✉ *Hwy. 313, Canyonlands National Park* ☎ *435/259–2614, 800/322–3770 camping reservations* 🌐 *stateparks.utah.gov* 🎫 *$20 per vehicle.*

Moab Museum

MUSEUM | **FAMILY** | Exhibits on the history, geology, and paleontology of the Moab area include settler-era antiques, and ancient and historic Native Americans are remembered in displays of baskets, pottery, sandals, and other artifacts. Displays also chronicle early Spanish expeditions into the area, regional dinosaur finds, and the history of uranium discovery. ✉ *118 E. Center St.* ☎ *435/259–7985* 🌐 *www.moabmuseum.org* 🎫 *$5* 🕑 *Closed Sun.*

Scott and Norma Matheson Wetlands Preserve

NATURE PRESERVE | **FAMILY** | Owned and operated by the Nature Conservancy, this is the best place in the Moab area for bird-watching. The 894-acre oasis is home to more than 200 species, including such treasures as the pied-billed grebe, the cinnamon teal, and the northern flicker. It's also a great place to spot beavers and muskrats playing in the water. Hear a big "Slap!" on the water? That's a beaver warning you that you're too close. Always remember to respect the wildlife preserved in these areas, and enjoy the nature you find here. An information kiosk greets visitors just inside the preserve and a boardwalk winds through the property to a viewing shelter. To reach the preserve, turn northwest off U.S. 191 at Kane Creek Boulevard and continue northwest approximately 2 miles. ✉ *934 W. Kane Creek Blvd.* ☎ *435/259–4629* 🌐 *www.nature.org* 🎫 *Free.*

Restaurants

From juicy steaks and fresh sushi to rich Mexican and savory Thai, there are enough menu options in Moab to keep you satiated.

Antica Forma

$ | **ITALIAN** | Moab's best pizza joint, which has a wildly popular original location in the northeastern Utah town of Vernal, offers an extensive list of thin-crust wood-fired pizzas with a variety of toppings, plus plenty of classic antipasto (mussels in white wine, homemade burrata, arancini) and pasta options. Have a seat at one of the granite-top tables under high ceilings in the dining room, peruse the carefully chosen wine and beer list, and tuck into one of the specialty pies, perhaps the white pie with pistachio pesto, Italian sausage, homemade mozzarella, pecorino romano, basil, and olive oil. **Known for:** delicious thin crusts (both traditional and gluten-free); extensive craft beer selection; creative pizza toppings. $ *Average main: $15* ✉ *267 N. Main St.* ☎ *435/355–0167* 🌐 *www.anticaforma.com.*

Miguel's Baja Grill

$ | **MEXICAN** | This isn't the cheapest Mexican menu around, but it's definitely the best. Not your standard south-of-the-border fare, the food here comes from the culinary spirit of Baja, California, which means some excellent seafood dishes like ceviche, a tangy blend of raw fish,

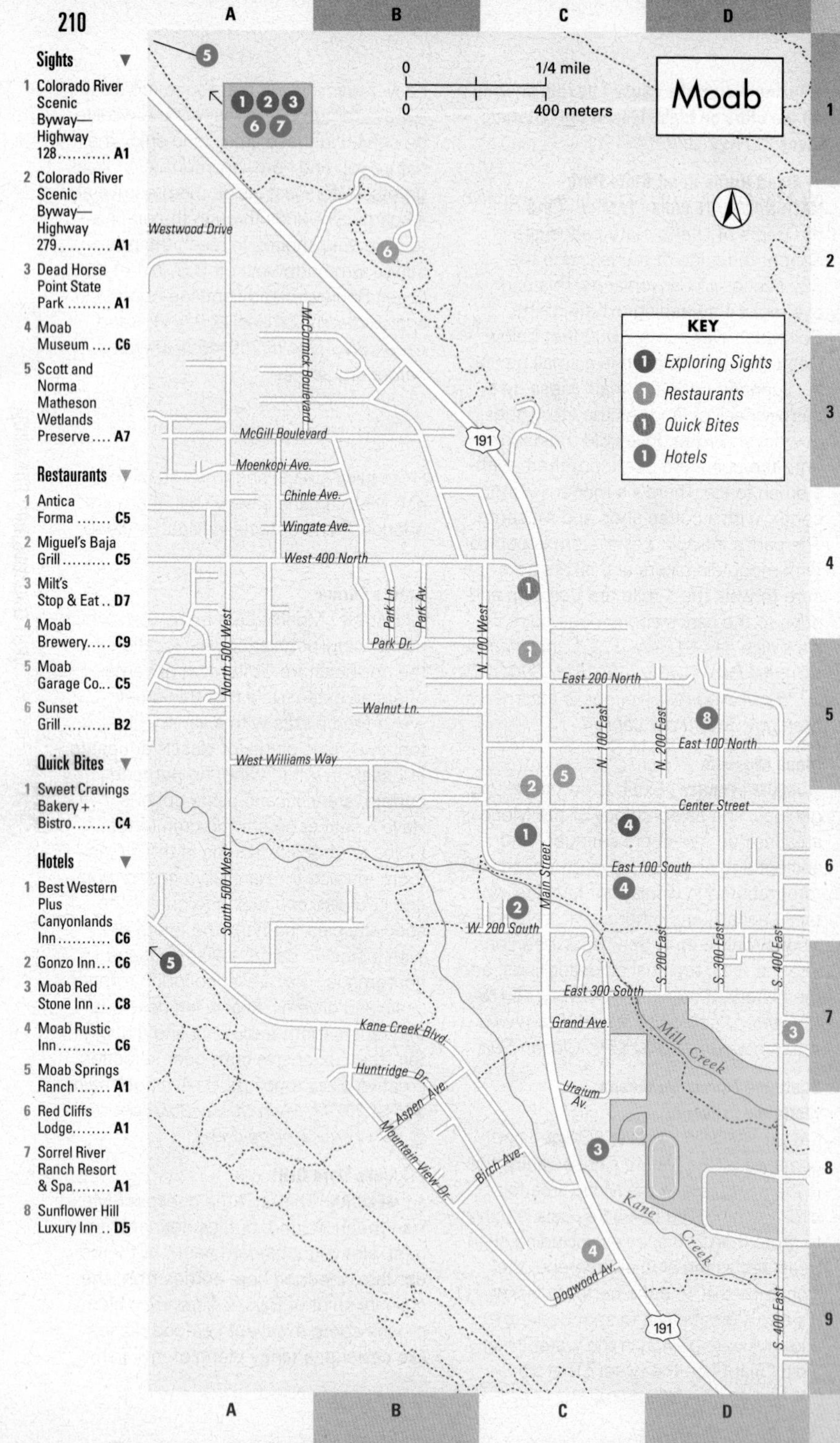
Sights
1 Colorado River Scenic Byway—Highway 128 .... A1
2 Colorado River Scenic Byway—Highway 279 .... A1
3 Dead Horse Point State Park A1
4 Moab Museum C6
5 Scott and Norma Matheson Wetlands Preserve A7
Restaurants
1 Antica Forma C5
2 Miguel's Baja Grill C5
3 Milt's Stop & Eat .. D7
4 Moab Brewery..... C9
5 Moab Garage Co... C5
6 Sunset Grill B2
Quick Bites
1 Sweet Cravings Bakery + Bistro C4
Hotels
1 Best Western Plus Canyonlands Inn C6
2 Gonzo Inn ... C6
3 Moab Red Stone Inn ... C8
4 Moab Rustic Inn C6
5 Moab Springs Ranch A1
6 Red Cliffs Lodge........ A1
7 Sorrel River Ranch Resort & Spa........ A1
8 Sunflower Hill Luxury Inn .. D5
A
B
C
D
1
2
3
4
5
6
7
8
9
Moab
0
1/4 mile
0
400 meters
KEY
Exploring Sights
Restaurants
Quick Bites
Hotels
Westwood Drive
McCormick Boulevard
McGill Boulevard
Moenkopi Ave.
Chinle Ave.
Wingate Ave.
West 400 North
191
Park Ln.
Park Av.
Park Dr.
N. 100 West
North 500 West
East 200 North
Walnut Ln.
N. 100 East
N. 200 East
East 100 North
West Williams Way
Center Street
Main Street
East 100 South
South 500 West
W. 200 South
S. 200 East
S. 300 East
S. 400 East
East 300 South
Grand Ave.
Mill Creek
Kane Creek Blvd.
Huntridge Dr.
Aspen Ave.
Mountain View Dr.
Uraium Av.
Birch Ave.
Kane Creek
Dogwood Av.

onions, tomatoes, and spices. **Known for:** house-made margaritas; big portions; fresh seafood (despite desert locale). *Average main: $15 51 N. Main St. 435/259–6546 Closed Dec.–Feb. No lunch.*

Milt's Stop and Eat

$ | **FAST FOOD** | **FAMILY** | Since 1954, Milt's has offered delicious burgers and shakes from an unassuming, off-Main Street drive-up stand. About all that's changed is that the Buffalo Burger is now nearly as popular as the beef version. **Known for:** tasty burgers and shakes; local institution; friendly, vintage feel. *Average main: $6 356 Millcreek Dr. 435/259–7424 www.miltsstopandeat.com.*

Moab Brewery

$ | **AMERICAN** | Moab's first microbrewery is known for its Scorpion Pale Ale, Squeaky Bike Nut Brown Ale, and an assortment of other brews from light to dark. The on-site restaurant is spacious and comfortable and decorated with kayaks, bikes, and other adventure paraphernalia. **Known for:** lively crowd; house-made gelato; very good craft beer. *Average main: $14 686 S. Main St. 435/259–6333 www.themoabbrewery.com.*

★ Moab Garage Co.

$ | **ECLECTIC** | Set in a vintage redbrick storefront on downtown Moab's busiest block, this urbane café and ice-cream shop also offers enough hearty savory dishes throughout the day—plus a well-curated selection of beer and wine—to serve as a legit breakfast, lunch, or dinner option. Consider the Liege-style waffles with fresh berries or avocado toast early in the day, or a veggie "meatball" or fancy grilled cheese sandwich (the preparation of the latter changes daily), Cobb salad, or street tacos later in the day. **Known for:** nitro-infused ice cream; superb coffee; cool, centrally located hangout. *Average main: $9 78 N. Main St. 435/554–8467 moabgarageco.com Closed Tues.*

Sunset Grill

$$$ | **AMERICAN** | This cliffside home of former uranium kingpin Charlie Steen offers the best views of any restaurant in town, especially at sunset—the dining room's big windows take in the Colorado River and surrounding red rocks. The traditional American fare—including filet mignon, prime rib, sautéed Idaho trout, and shrimp scampi—is generally well-prepared if not especially inventive. **Known for:** historical setting; stunning view; slow-roasted prime rib. *Average main: $25 900 N. Main St. 435/259–7146 www.moabsunsetgrill.com Closed Sun. No lunch.*

Coffee and Quick Bites

★ Sweet Cravings Bakery + Bistro

$ | **BAKERY** | **FAMILY** | In addition to doling out some of the largest and most delicious cookies and cinnamon rolls you've ever tried, this cheerful and informal bakery café presents a terrific roster of breakfast and lunch panini, wraps, and sandwiches, and daily comfort foods like potpies and soups. Baked goods are all from scratch, gluten-free options abound, produce is local, meats are preservative-free, and coffee is 100% Rainforest Alliance and organic. **Known for:** hefty cinnamon rolls; many gluten-free options; local produce and ingredients. *Average main: $10 397 N. Main St. 435/259–8983 www.cravemoab.com No dinner.*

Hotels

★ Best Western Plus Canyonlands Inn

$$$ | **HOTEL** | **FAMILY** | The confluence of Main and Center streets is the epicenter of Moab, and this comfortable, contemporary, impeccably clean hotel anchors the intersection, providing a perfect base for families. **Pros:** steps from many restaurants; sparkling, contemporary rooms; complimentary breakfast alfresco on outdoor patio. **Cons:** central location

can feel a bit crowded at busy times; books up far in advance; pool is closed in winter (but hot tub is open year-round). *Rooms from: $199* *16 S. Main St.* *435/259–2300* *www.bestwestern.com* *80 rooms* *Free breakfast.*

Gonzo Inn

$$$ | **HOTEL** | This eclectic inn stands out for its fun design, brightly colored walls, desert-inspired art, and varnished adobe construction. **Pros:** unique, spotless, and hip; steps to Main Street; pool and hot tub. **Cons:** interior hallways can be dark; no elevator; not all rooms have a good view. *Rooms from: $209* *100 W. 200 S* *435/259–2515* *www.gonzoinn.com* *43 rooms* *Free breakfast.*

Moab Red Stone Inn

$$ | **HOTEL** | One of the best bargains in town, this timber-frame motel offers small, clean rooms at the south end of the Moab strip near restaurants and shops. **Pros:** walking distance to many restaurants and shops; the price is right; all rooms have small kitchenettes. **Cons:** pool is at sister property across busy Main Street; no frills; rooms close to the road are noisy. *Rooms from: $139* *535 S. Main St.* *435/259–3500, 800/772–1972* *www.moabredstone.com* *52 rooms* *No meals.*

Moab Rustic Inn

$ | **HOTEL** | One of the best values amid Moab's increasingly pricey lodging landscape, this homey downtown sister property to Red Cliffs Lodge is, as the name suggests, rustic, but the 35 rooms are all clean and comfortable, and provide ample room for families or friends traveling together. **Pros:** most rooms sleep at least four guests; terrific value; nice pool and barbecue area. **Cons:** simple (but comfortable) furnishings; downtown location is busy at times; can book up months in advance, especially the apartments. *Rooms from: $100* *120 E. 100 S* *435/259–6177* *www.moabrusticinn.com* *35 rooms* *Free breakfast.*

Moab Springs Ranch

$$$$ | **RENTAL** | **FAMILY** | First developed by William Grandstaff in the late 19th century, this 18-acre property about 3 miles from Arches and 1 mile from downtown Moab features spacious, studio-style bungalows (completed in 2019) and town houses, set by a meandering spring and decades-old sycamores, mulberries, and cottonwoods. **Pros:** scenic setting is a respite; boutique accomodations; features hiking trails and sits on a bike path into town. **Cons:** about a 30-minute walk from downtown; some U.S. 191 traffic noise; most units have two-night minimum stays. *Rooms from: $235* *1266 N. Highway 191* *435/259–7891* *www.moabspringsranch.com* *35 units* *No meals.*

Red Cliffs Lodge

$$$$ | **RESORT** | Discovered in the late 1940s by director John Ford, this former ranch was the setting for several 1950s Westerns, and you can feel transported into one as you gaze onto the Colorado River and high canyon walls from your simple but elegant room. **Pros:** beautiful spot, with peaceful canyon and river views; many luxury amenities and great restaurant; private cabins are woodsy but modern. **Cons:** drive to town can be long during busy season; spotty cell service; not all rooms have river or creek views. *Rooms from: $289* *Hwy. 128, mile marker 14* *435/259–2002, 866/812–2002* *www.redcliffslodge.com* *110 rooms* *No meals.*

Sorrel River Ranch Resort & Spa

$$$$ | **RESORT** | One of the premier luxury resorts in the Southwest, this lodge on the banks of the Colorado River, 17 miles north of Moab, is the ultimate destination for a relaxing and plush getaway, especially if you enjoy spa treatments. **Pros:** swanky spa and restaurant; luxurious rooms; red rock setting along the Colorado River. **Cons:** drive to town is long during the busy season; steep rates; breakfast not included. *Rooms from:*

$599 ✉ *Hwy. 128* ✣ *Mile marker 17.5* ☎ *435/259–4642* 🌐 *www.sorrelriver.com* *59 rooms* 🍴 *No meals.*

★ Sunflower Hill Luxury Inn
$$$ | B&B/INN | Near the heart of old downtown Moab, this thriving turn-of-the-20th-century inn is all about comfort and the guest experience, with elegant interiors and lush surroundings. **Pros:** just blocks from town; beautifully appointed rooms; friendly hosts. **Cons:** children younger than 10 not allowed; some rooms are a bit dark; not ideal if you prefer a larger property. $ *Rooms from: $219* ✉ *185 N. 300 E* ☎ *435/259–2974, 800/662–2786* 🌐 *www.sunflowerhill.com* *12 rooms* 🍴 *Free breakfast.*

 Shopping

Shopping opportunities are plentiful in Moab, with art galleries, jewelry stores, and shops carrying T-shirts and souvenirs throughout Main Street.

ART GALLERIES

Lema's Kokopelli Gallery
ART GALLERIES | The Lema family has built a reputation for fair prices on a large selection of Native American and Southwest-themed jewelry, art, pottery, rugs, and more. Everything sold here is authentic. ✉ *70 N. Main St.* ☎ *435/259–5055* 🌐 *www.kokopellioutlet.com.*

Moab Art Walk
Moab galleries and shops celebrate the perfect weather of spring and fall with a series of exhibits. Art Walks are held the second Saturday of the month from April through June and September through November. Stroll the streets (5–8 pm) to see and purchase original works by Moab and regional artists. ✉ *Moab* ☎ *435/259–6272.*

Tom Till Gallery
ART GALLERIES | Moab photographer Tom Till is internationally known for his stunning original photographs of the Arches and Canyonlands areas, as well as other regions of the world. The gallery features mostly images of southeastern Utah, but also other gorgeous remote places to fuel your wanderlust. ✉ *61 N. Main St.* ☎ *435/259–9808* 🌐 *tomtill.com.*

BOOKS

Back of Beyond Books
BOOKS/STATIONERY | FAMILY | A Main Street treasure, this comprehensive shop features books on the American West, environmental studies, Native American cultures, water issues, and Western history, as well as rare antiquarian books on the Southwest. There's also a nice nook for kids. ✉ *83 N. Main St.* ☎ *435/259–5154, 800/700–2859* 🌐 *www.backofbeyondbooks.com.*

SUPPLIES

Dave's Corner Market
CONVENIENCE/GENERAL STORES | You can get most anything you may need here for your travels, including some of the best cappuccino and Colombian coffee in town. The store is also the heartbeat of the local community, where everyone gossips, discusses local politics, and swaps info on the best hiking and adventure spots. ✉ *401 Mill Creek Dr.* ☎ *435/259–6999.*

GearHeads
SPECIALTY STORES | If you forget anything for your camping, climbing, hiking, or other outdoor adventure, you can get a replacement here. GearHeads is packed with essentials, and fun extras like booties and packs for your dog, water filtration straws, and cool souvenirs. The store's owners invented a high-end LED flashlight that has become very popular with the U.S. military, available at the store. ✉ *1040 S. Main St.* ☎ *435/259–4327* 🌐 *www.moabgear.com.*

Activities

Moab's towering cliffs and deep canyons can be intimidating, and some are unreachable without the help of a guide. Fortunately, guide services are abundant in Moab. Whether you are interested in a 4x4 expedition into the rugged backcountry, a river-rafting trip, a jet-boat tour on calm water, bicycle tours, rock-art tours, or a scenic flight, you can find the pro to help you on your way. It's always best to make reservations. Book the Fiery Furnace tour in Arches National Park at least one month in advance; you can book as early as six months in advance.

SHUTTLES

If you need a ride to or from your trailhead or river trip put-in point, a couple of Moab companies provide the service (and also provide airport shuttle service by reservation), with vehicles large enough to handle most groups. Coyote's website is worth checking out for trail and river conditions and other information. Inquiries for Roadrunner are handled by Dual Sport, under the same ownership.

Coyote Shuttle

BICYCLING | ✉ *55 W. 300 S* ☎ *435/260–2097* 🌐 *www.coyoteshuttle.com.*

Roadrunner Shuttle

BOATING | ✉ *Deal Sport Utah, 197 W. Center St.* ☎ *435/259–9402* 🌐 *www.roadrunnershuttle.com.*

FOUR-WHEELING

There are thousands of miles of four-wheel-drive roads in and around Moab suitable for all levels of drivers. Seasoned 4x4 drivers might tackle the daunting Moab Rim, Elephant Hill, or Poison Spider Mesa. Novices will be happier touring Long Canyon, Hurrah Pass. If you're not afraid of precipitous cliff edges, the famous Shafer Trail may be a good option for you. Expect to pay around $75 for a half-day tour and $120 for a full day; multiday safaris usually start at around $600. Almost all of Moab's river-running companies also offer four-wheeling excursions.

Coyote Land Tours

FOUR-WHEELING | FAMILY | Imposing Mercedes-Benz Unimog trucks (which dwarf Hummers) take you to parts of the backcountry where you could never wander on your own. Technical tours challenge drivers with imposing rock formations, washes, and assorted obstacles, and there are tamer sunset excursions and camp-style ride-and-dine trips. They stand by their money-back "great time" guarantee. ✉ *Moab* ☎ *435/260–6056* 🌐 *www.coyotelandtours.com* 🎫 *From $59.*

Dual Sport Utah

FOUR-WHEELING | If you're into dirt biking, this is the only outfitter in Moab specializing in street-legal, off-road dirt-bike tours and rentals. New in 2020, you can also rent pedal-assist, electric bikes. Follow the Klondike Bluffs trail to Arches, or negotiate the White Rim Trail in Canyonlands in a fraction of the time you would spend on a mountain bike. ✉ *197 W. Center. St.* ☎ *435/260–2724* 🌐 *www.dualsportutah.com* 🎫 *$300 for rentals.*

High Point Hummer & ATV

FOUR-WHEELING | FAMILY | You can rent vehicles, including ATVs, UTVs, and Jeeps, or get a guided tour of the backcountry in open-air Hummer vehicles or ATVs, or dune buggy–like "side-by-sides" that seat up to six people. The enthusiastic owners love families and small, intimate groups, and offer hiking and canyoneering as well. ✉ *301 S. Main St.* ☎ *435/259–2972, 877/486–6833* 🌐 *www.highpointhummer.com* 🎫 *From $69.*

HIKING

For a great view of the Moab Valley and surrounding red-rock country, hike up the steep **Moab Rim Trail.** For something a little less taxing, hike the shady, cool path of **Grandstaff Canyon,** which is off Route Highway 129. At the end of the trail you'll find giant Morning Glory Arch towering over a serene pool created by a natural spring. If you want to take a stroll through the heart of Moab, hop on the **Mill Creek Parkway,** which winds along the creek from one side of town to the other. It's paved and perfect for bicycles, strollers, or joggers. For a taste of slick-rock hiking that feels like the backcountry but is easy to access, try the **Corona Arch Trail** off Highway 279. You'll be rewarded with two large arches hidden from view of the highway. The Moab Information Center carries a free hiking trail guide.

MOUNTAIN BIKING

Mountain biking originated in Moab, and the region has earned the well-deserved reputation as the mountain-biking capital of the world. Riders of all ages and skill levels are drawn to the many rugged roads and trails found here. One of the most popular routes is the **Slickrock Trail,** a stunning area of steep Navajo Sandstone dunes a few miles east of Moab. ■ TIP→ **Beginners should master the 2⅓-mile practice loop before attempting the longer, and very challenging, 10-mile loop.** More moderate rides can be found on the **Gemini Bridges** or **Monitor and Merrimac** trails, both found off U.S. 191 north of Moab. **Klondike Bluffs,** north of Moab, is an excellent novice ride, as are sections of the newer trails in the Klonzo trail system. The Moab Information Center carries a free biking trail guide. Mountain-bike rentals range from $40 for a good bike to $75 for a top-of-the-line workhorse. If you want to go on a guided ride, expect to pay between $120 and $135 per person for a half-day, and $155 to $190 for a full day, including the cost of the bike rental. You can save money by joining a larger group to keep the per-person rates down; even a party of two will save drastically over a single rider. Several companies offer shuttles to and from the trailheads.

Chile Pepper Bike Shop
BICYCLING | For mountain bike rentals, sales, service, and gear, plus espresso, stop here before you set out. ✉ *702 S. Main St.* ☎ *435/259–4688* 🌐 *www.chilebikes.com.*

★ **Poison Spider Bicycles**
BICYCLING | In a town of great bike shops, this fully loaded shop is one of the best. Poison Spider serves the thriving road-cycling community as well as mountain bikers. Rent, buy, or service your bike here. You can also arrange for shuttle and guide services and purchase merchandise. Want to ship your bike to Moab for your adventure? Poison Spider will store it until you arrive and the staff will reassemble it for you and make sure everything is in perfect working order. ✉ *497 N. Main St.* ☎ *435/259–7882, 800/635–1792* 🌐 *www.poisonspiderbicycles.com.*

Rim Tours
BICYCLING | Reliable, friendly, and professional, Rim Tours has been taking guests on guided one-day or multiday mountain-bike tours, including Klondike Bluffs (which enters Arches) and the White Rim Trail (inside Canyonlands) since 1985. Road-bike tours as well as bike rentals are also available. Bike skills a little rusty? Rim Tours also offers mountain-bike instructional tours. For all tours, the larger the group, the cheaper the price per person. ✉ *1233 S. U.S. 191* ☎ *435/259–5223* 🌐 *www.rimtours.com* 🎫 *Tours start at $155 for a solo rider.*

Western Spirit Cycling Adventures
BICYCLING | Head here for fully supported, go-at-your-own-pace, multiday mountain-bike and road-bike tours throughout the western states, including trips to Canyonlands, Bears Ears, and the 140-mile Kokopelli Trail, which runs from Grand Junction, Colorado, to Moab. Guides versed in the geologic wonders of the area cook up meals worthy of the

scenery each night. Ask about family rides, and road bike trips, too. Electric bicycles are available. ✉ *478 S. Mill Creek Dr.* ☎ *435/259–8732, 800/845–2453* 🌐 *www.westernspirit.com* 🎫 *From $995.*

MULTISPORT

Outdoor lovers wear many hats in Moab: boaters, bikers, and even Jeep-drivers. Here are a few companies that cater to a range of adventure seekers.

Adrift Adventures

BOATING | FAMILY | This outfitter takes pride in well-trained guides who can take you via foot, raft, kayak, 4x4, jet boat, stand-up paddleboard, and more, all over the Moab area, including the Colorado and Green rivers and Arches Jeep and hiking adventures. They also offer history, movie, and rock-art tours. They've been in business since 1977 and have a great reputation around town. ✉ *378 N. Main St.* ☎ *435/259–8594, 800/874–4483* 🌐 *www.adrift.net* 🎫 *From $49.*

Moab Adventure Center

BOATING | FAMILY | At the prominent storefront on Main Street you can schedule most any type of local adventure experience you want, including rafting, 4x4 tours, scenic flights, hikes, balloon rides, and a couple of excellent bus overview tours of Arches highlights. You can also purchase clothing and outdoor gear for your visit. ✉ *225 S. Main St.* ☎ *435/259–7019, 866/904–1163* 🌐 *www.moabadventurecenter.com* 🎫 *From $89.*

NAVTEC

BOATING | FAMILY | Doc Williams was the first doctor in Moab in 1896, and some of his descendants never left, sharing his love for the area through this rafting, canyoneering, and 4x4 company. Whether you want to explore the region by boat, boots, or wheels, you'll find a multitude of one-day and multiday options here. ✉ *321 N. Main St.* ☎ *435/259–7983, 800/833–1278* 🌐 *www.navtec.com* 🎫 *From $69.*

Oars

WHITE-WATER RAFTING | FAMILY | This well-regarded outfitter can take you for several days of rafting the Colorado, Green, and San Juan rivers. Hiking/interpretive trips are available in Canyonlands and Arches. ✉ *Moab* ☎ *435/259–5865, 800/346–6277* 🌐 *www.oars.com/utah* 🎫 *From $109.*

RIVER EXPEDITIONS

On the Colorado River northeast of Arches and very near Moab, you can take one of America's most scenic—but not intimidating—river-raft rides. The river rolls by the red Fisher Towers as they rise into the sky in front of the La Sal Mountains. A day trip on this stretch of the river will take you about 15 miles. Outfitters offer full, half, or multiday adventures here. Upriver, in narrow, winding Westwater Canyon near the Utah–Colorado border, the Colorado River cuts through the oldest exposed geologic layer on Earth. Most outfitters offer this trip as a one-day getaway, but you may also take as long as three days to complete the journey. A permit is required from the Bureau of Land Management (BLM) in Moab to run Westwater Canyon.

★ Canyon Voyages Adventure Co.

BOATING | FAMILY | This is an excellent choice for rafting or kayaking adventures on the Colorado River—including the Fisher Towers section—or Green River. Don and Denise Oblak run a friendly, professional company with a retail store and rental shop that's open year-round. Most customers take one-day trips, but they also offer multiday itineraries, guided tours, and rentals. They also operate a great kayak school. Ask about stand-up paddleboarding, biking, and horseback riding, too. ✉ *211 N. Main St.* ☎ *435/241–3846,* 🌐 *www.canyonvoyages.com* 🎫 *From $65.*

Holiday River Expeditions

BOATING | FAMILY | Since 1966, this outfitter has offered one-day and multiday trips on the San Juan, Green, and Colorado rivers, including inside Canyonlands National Park. They also offer multisport trips, women's retreats, and bike adventures, including the White Rim Trail. ✉ *2075 E. Main St., Green River* ☎ *435/564–3273, 800/624–6323* 🌐 *www.bikeraft.com* 🎫 *From $210.*

Sheri Griffith Expeditions

BOATING | FAMILY | In addition to trips through the white water of Cataract, Westwater, and Desolation canyons, on the Colorado and Green rivers, this company also offers specialty expeditions for women, writers, photographers, and families. One of their more luxurious expeditions features dinners cooked by a professional chef and served on linen-covered tables. Cots and other sleeping amenities also make roughing it a little more comfortable. ✉ *2231 S. U.S. 191* ☎ *435/259–8229, 800/332–2439* 🌐 *www.griffithexp.com* 🎫 *From $185.*

ROCK CLIMBING

Rock climbing is an integral part of Moab culture. The area's rock walls and towers bring climbers from around the world, and a surprising number end up sticking around. Moab offers some of the best climbing challenges in the country, and any enthusiast will find bliss here.

Desert Highlights

CLIMBING/MOUNTAINEERING | This guide company takes adventurous types on descents and ascents through canyons (with the help of ropes), including those found in the Fiery Furnace at Arches National Park. Full-day and multiday canyoneering treks are available to destinations both in and near the national parks. ✉ *16 S. 100 E* ☎ *435/259–4433* 🌐 *www.deserthighlights.com* 🎫 *From $105.*

★ Moab Cliffs & Canyons

CLIMBING/MOUNTAINEERING | In a town where everyone seems to offer rafting and 4x4 expeditions, Moab Cliffs & Canyons focuses on canyoneering, climbing, and rappelling—for novice and veteran adventurers. Prices vary according to how many people sign up. This is the outfitter that provided technical assistance to the crew on the movie *127 Hours*. ✉ *253 N. Main St.* ☎ *435/259–3317, 877/641–5271* 🌐 *www.cliffsandcanyons.com* 🎫 *From $175.*

Pagan Mountaineering

CLIMBING/MOUNTAINEERING | Climbers in need of gear and advice on local terrain should speak with the knowledgeable staff here, who can help plot your adventure. ✉ *59 S. Main St., No. 2* ☎ *435/259–1117* 🌐 *paganclimber.com.*

Arches National Park

More than 1.5 million visitors come to Arches annually, drawn by the red rock landscape and its wind- and water-carved rock formations. The park is named for the 2,000-plus sandstone arches that frame horizons, cast precious shade, and are in a perpetual state of gradual transformation, the result of constant erosion.

Fancifully named attractions like Three Penguins, Queen Nefertiti, and Tower of Babel stir curiosity, beckoning visitors to stop and marvel. Immerse yourself in this spectacular landscape, but don't lose yourself entirely—summer temperatures frequently exceed 100°F, and water is hard to come by inside the park boundaries.

It's easy to spot some of the arches from your car, but take the time to step outside and walk beneath the spans and giant walls of orange rock. This gives you a much better idea of their proportion. You may feel as writer Edward Abbey did when he awoke on his first day as a park ranger in Arches: that you're walking in the most beautiful place on Earth.

It's especially worthwhile to visit as the sun goes down. At sunset, the rock formations glow, and you'll often find photographers behind their tripods waiting for magnificent rays to descend on Delicate Arch or other popular sites. The Fiery Furnace earns its name as its narrow fins glow red just before the sun dips below the horizon. Full-moon nights

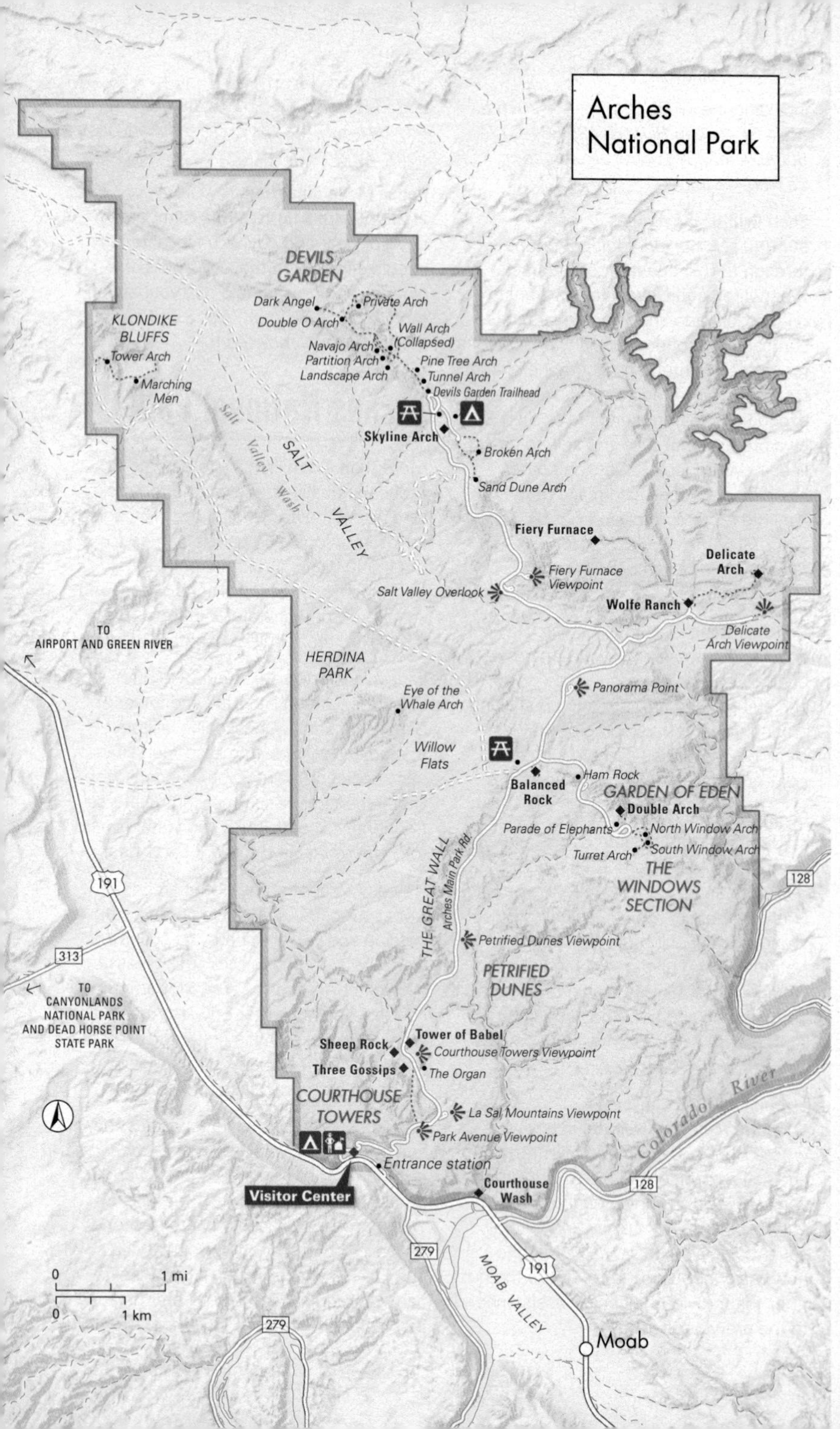

Arches National Park
DEVILS GARDEN
KLONDIKE BLUFFS
Dark Angel
Private Arch
Double O Arch
Wall Arch (Collapsed)
Navajo Arch
Partition Arch
Pine Tree Arch
Landscape Arch
Tunnel Arch
Devils Garden Trailhead
Tower Arch
Marching Men
Skyline Arch
Broken Arch
Sand Dune Arch
Salt Valley Wash
SALT VALLEY
Fiery Furnace
Fiery Furnace Viewpoint
Delicate Arch
Salt Valley Overlook
Wolfe Ranch
Delicate Arch Viewpoint
TO AIRPORT AND GREEN RIVER
HERDINA PARK
Eye of the Whale Arch
Panorama Point
Willow Flats
Balanced Rock
Ham Rock
GARDEN OF EDEN
Double Arch
Parade of Elephants
North Window Arch
South Window Arch
Turret Arch
THE WINDOWS SECTION
THE GREAT WALL
Arches Main Park Rd.
191
128
313
Petrified Dunes Viewpoint
PETRIFIED DUNES
TO CANYONLANDS NATIONAL PARK AND DEAD HORSE POINT STATE PARK
Tower of Babel
Sheep Rock
Courthouse Towers Viewpoint
Three Gossips
The Organ
COURTHOUSE TOWERS
La Sal Mountains Viewpoint
Park Avenue Viewpoint
Colorado River
Entrance station
Visitor Center
Courthouse Wash
128
279
191
MOAB VALLEY
0
1 mi
0
1 km
279
Moab

are particularly dramatic in Arches as the creamy white Navajo sandstone reflects light, and eerie silhouettes are created by towering fins and formations.

GETTING HERE AND AROUND

The park entrance is just off U.S. 191 on the north side of downtown Moab, 28 miles south of Interstate 70 and 130 miles north of the Arizona border. Arches is also about 30 miles from the Island in the Sky section and 80 miles from the Needles District of Canyonlands National Park. If you're driving to Arches from points east on Interstate 70, consider taking Exit 214 in Utah (about 50 miles west of Grand Junction), and continuing south on picturesque Highway 128, the Colorado River Scenic Byway, about 50 miles to Moab. Bear in mind that services can be sparse on even major roads in these parts.

Branching off the main 18-mile park road—officially known as Arches Scenic Road—are two spurs, one 2½ miles to the Windows section and one 1.6 miles to Delicate Arch trailhead and viewpoint. There are several four-wheel-drive roads in the park; always check at the visitor center for conditions before attempting to traverse them. The entrance road into the park can back up midmorning to early afternoon during busy periods. You'll encounter less traffic early in the morning or at sunset.

PARK ESSENTIALS

PARK FEES AND PERMITS

Admission to the park is $30 per vehicle, $25 per motorcycle, and $15 per person entering on foot or bicycle, valid for seven days. To encourage visitation to the park during less busy times, a $50 local park pass grants you admission to both Arches and Canyonlands parks as well as Natural Bridges and Hovenweep national monuments for one year.

PARK HOURS

Arches National Park is open year-round, seven days a week, around the clock. It's in the mountain time zone.

CELL PHONE RECEPTION

Cell phone reception is spotty in the park and in general is strongest whenever the La Sal mountains are visible. There are pay phones outside the visitor center.

VISITOR INFORMATION

CONTACTS Arches National Park. ✉ *N. U.S. 191* ☎ *435/719–2299* 🌐 *www.nps.gov/arch.*

Devils Garden

18 miles north of the visitor center.

At the end of the paved road in Arches, Devils Garden is the most developed area of the park, with the park's only campground and drinking water. It's also the site of the busiest trailheads.

GEOLOGICAL FORMATIONS

Skyline Arch

NATURE SITE | **FAMILY** | A quick walk from the parking lot at Skyline Arch, 16½ miles from the park entrance, gives you closer views and better photos. The short trail is less than a ½ mile round-trip and takes only a few minutes to travel. ✉ *Devils Garden Rd.*

SCENIC DRIVES

★ Arches Main Park Road

SCENIC DRIVE | The main park road and its two short spurs are extremely scenic and allow you to enjoy many park sights from your car. The main road leads through Courthouse Towers, where you can see Sheep Rock and the Three Gossips, then alongside the Great Wall, the Petrified Dunes, and Balanced Rock. A drive to the Windows section takes you to attractions like Double Arch, and you can see Skyline Arch along the roadside as you approach the Devils Garden campground. The road to Delicate Arch allows hiking access to one of the park's main features. Allow about two hours to drive the 45-mile round-trip, more if you explore the spurs and their features and stop at viewpoints along the way. ✉ *Arches National Park.*

TRAILS

Broken Arch Trail

TRAIL | An easy walk across open grassland, this loop trail passes Broken Arch, which is also visible from the road. The arch gets its name because it appears to be cracked in the middle, but it's not really broken. The trail is 1¼ miles round-trip, but you can extend your adventure to about 2 miles round-trip by continuing north past Tapestry Arch and through Devils Garden Campground. *Easy.* ✉ *Arches National Park* ✣ *Trailhead: Off Devils Garden Rd., 16½ miles from park entrance.*

★ Devils Garden Trail

TRAIL | Landscape Arch is a highlight of this trail but is just one of several arches within reach, depending on your ambitions. It's an easy ¾-mile one-way (mostly gravel, relatively flat) trip to Landscape Arch, one of the longest stone spans in the world. Beyond Landscape Arch the scenery changes dramatically and the hike becomes more strenuous, as you must climb and straddle slickrock fins and negotiate some short, steep inclines. Finally, around a sharp bend, the stacked spans that compose Double O Arch come suddenly into view. Allow up to three hours for this round-trip hike of just over 4 miles. For a still longer (about a 7-mile round-trip) and more rigorous trek, venture on to see a formation called Dark Angel and then return to the trailhead on the primitive loop, making the short side hike to Private Arch. The hike to Dark Angel is a difficult route through fins. Other possible (and worthwhile) detours lead to Navajo Arch, Partition Arch, Tunnel Arch, and Pine Tree Arch. Allow about five hours for this adventure, take plenty of water, and watch your route carefully. Pick up the park's useful guide to Devils Garden, or download it from the website before you go. *Moderate–Difficult.* ✉ *Arches National Park* ✣ *Trailhead: On Devils Garden Rd., end of main road, 18 miles from park entrance.*

Landscape Arch

TRAIL | This natural rock opening, which measures 306 feet from base to base and looks like a delicate ribbon of rock bending over the horizon, is the longest geologic span in North America. In 1991, a slab of rock about 60 feet long, 11 feet wide, and 4 feet thick fell from the underside, leaving it even thinner. You reach it via a rolling, gravel, 1.6-mile-long trail. *Easy–Moderate.* ✉ *Arches National Park* ✣ *Trailhead: At Devils Garden Rd., at end of main road, 18 miles north of park entrance.*

Tower Arch Trail

TRAIL | Check with park rangers before attempting the dirt road through Salt Valley to Klondike Bluffs parking area. If rains haven't washed out the road, a trip to this seldom-visited area provides a solitude-filled hike culminating in a giant rock opening. Allow from two to three hours for this 3½-mile round-trip hike, not including the drive. *Moderate.* ✉ *Arches National Park* ✣ *Trailhead: At Klondike Bluffs parking area, 24½ miles from park entrance, 7¾ miles off main road.*

Fiery Furnace

14 miles north of the park entrance.

Fewer than 10% of the park's visitors ever descend into the chasms and washes of Fiery Furnace (a permit or a ranger-led hike is the only way to go), but you can gain an appreciation for this twisted, unyielding landscape from the Overlook. At sunset, the rocks glow a vibrant flamelike red, which gives the formation its daunting moniker.

"I happened to catch this beautiful light on the back side of Pine Tree Arch on the Devils Garden Trail." —photo by Merryl Edelstein, Fodors.com member

Sights

TRAILS

Fiery Furnace

TRAIL | This area of the park has taken on a near-mythical lure for park visitors, who are drawn to challenging yet breathtaking terrain. Rangers strongly discourage inexperienced hikers from entering here—in fact, you can't enter without watching a video about how to help protect this very special section of the park and obtaining a permit ($6). Reservations can be made up to six months in advance to get a spot on the 2-mile round-trip ranger-led hikes ($16), offered mid-April–September, through this unique formation. A hike through these rugged rocks and sandy washes is challenging but fascinating. Hikers will need to use their hands at times to scramble up and through narrow cracks and along vertigo-inducing ledges above drop-offs, and there are no trail markings. If you're not familiar with the Furnace you can easily get lost or cause damage, so watch your step and use great caution. For information about reservations, see Ranger Programs Overview above. The less intrepid can view Fiery Furnace from the Overlook off the main road. *Difficult.* ⊠ *Arches National Park* ✣ *Trailhead: Off main road, about 14 miles from park entrance.*

Sand Dune Arch Trail

TRAIL | FAMILY | You may return to the car with shoes full of bright red sand from this giant sandbox in the desert—it's fun exploring in and around the rock. Set aside five minutes for this shady, 530-yard walk and plenty of time if you have kids, who will love playing amid this dramatic landscape. Never climb on this or any other arch in the park, no matter how tempting—it's illegal, and it could result in damage to the fragile geology or personal injury. The trail intersects with the Broken Arch Trail—you can visit both arches with an easy 1½-mile round-trip walk. *Easy.* ⊠ *Arches National Park* ✣ *Trailhead: Off Arches Scenic Dr., about 16½ miles from park entrance.*

Delicate Arch/Wolfe Ranch

13 miles north of the park entrance.

The iconic symbol of the park and the state (it appears on many of Utah's license plates), Delicate Arch is tall and prominent compared with many of the spans in the park—it's big enough that it could shelter a four-story building. The arch is a remnant of an Entrada Sandstone fin; the rest of the rock has eroded and it now frames La Sal Mountains in the background. Drive 2.2 miles off the main road to the viewpoint to see the arch from a distance, or hike right up to it from the trailhead that starts near Wolfe Ranch. The trail, 1.2 miles off the main road, is a moderately strenuous 3-mile round-trip hike with no shade or access to water. It's especially picturesque shortly after sunrise or before sunset.

Sights

HISTORIC SIGHTS

Wolfe Ranch

HISTORIC SITE | Civil War veteran John Wesley Wolfe and his son started a small ranch here in 1888. He added a cabin in 1906 when his daughter Esther and her family came west to live. Built out of Fremont cottonwoods, the rustic one-room cabin still stands on the site. Look for remains of a root cellar and a corral as well. Even older than these structures is the nearby Ute rock-art panel by the Delicate Arch trailhead. About 150 feet past the footbridge and before the trail starts to climb, you can see images of bighorn sheep and figures on horseback, as well as some smaller images believed to be dogs. ✉ *Off Delicate Arch Rd.*

TRAILS

★ Delicate Arch Trail

TRAIL | To see the park's most famous freestanding arch up close takes effort and won't offer you much solitude—but it's worth every step. The 3-mile round-trip trail ascends via steep slickrock, sandy paths, and along one narrow ledge (at the very end) that might give pause to anyone afraid of heights. Plus, there's almost no shade. First-timers should start early to avoid the midday heat in summer. Still, at sunrise, sunset, and every hour in between, it's the park's busiest trail. Bring plenty of water, especially in the warmer months, as heatstroke and dehydration are very real possibilities. Allow two to three hours, depending on your fitness level and how long you care to linger at the arch. If you go at sunset or sunrise, bring a headlamp or flashlight. Don't miss Wolfe Ranch and some ancient rock art near the trailhead. *Moderate–Difficult.* ✉ *Arches National Park* ✣ *Trailhead: On Delicate Arch Rd., 13 miles from park entrance.*

The Windows

11¾ miles north of the park entrance.

As you head north from the park entrance, turn right at Balanced Rock to find this concentration of natural windows, caves, and needles. Stretch your legs on the easy paths that wind between the arches and soak in a variety of geological formations.

Sights

GEOLOGICAL FORMATIONS

Double Arch

NATURE SITE | In the Windows section of the park, 11¾ miles from the park entrance, Double Arch has appeared in several Hollywood movies, including *Indiana Jones and the Last Crusade.* From the parking lot you can also take the short and easy Window Trail to view North Window, South Window, and Turret Arch. ✉ *The Windows Rd.*

TRAILS

Double Arch Trail

TRAIL | **FAMILY** | If it's not too hot, it's a simple walk to here from Windows Trail. This relatively flat trek leads to two massive arches that make for great photo opportunities. The ½-mile round-trip gives you a good taste of desert flora and fauna. *Easy.* ✉ *Arches National Park* ✣ *Trailhead: 2½ miles from main road, on Windows Section spur road.*

The Windows

TRAIL | FAMILY | An early stop for many visitors to the park, a trek through the Windows gives you an opportunity to get out and enjoy the desert air. Here you'll see three giant openings in the rock and walk on a trail that leads right through the holes. Allow about an hour on this gently inclined, 1-mile round-trip hike. As most visitors don't follow the "primitive" trail around the backside of the two windows, take advantage if you want some desert solitude. The primitive trail adds an extra half hour to the hike. *Easy.* ✉ *Arches National Park* ✣ *Trailhead: On the Windows Rd., 12 miles from park entrance.*

Balanced Rock

9¼ miles north of the park entrance.

One of the park's favorite sights, this rock is visible for several minutes as you approach—and just gets more impressive and mysterious as you get closer. The formation's total height is 128 feet, with the huge balanced rock rising 55 feet above the pedestal. Be sure to hop out of the car and walk the short (⅓-mile) loop around the base.

Sights

TRAILS

Balanced Rock Trail

TRAIL | FAMILY | You'll want to stop at Balanced Rock for photo ops, so you may as well walk the easy, partially paved trail around the famous landmark. This is one of the most accessible trails in the park and is suitable even for small children. The 15-minute stroll is only about ⅓ mile round-trip. *Easy.* ✉ *Arches National Park* ✣ *Trailhead: Approximately 9¼ miles from park entrance.*

Park Avenue Trail

TRAIL | The first named trail that park visitors encounter, this is a relatively easy, 2-mile round-trip walk (with only one small hill but a somewhat steep descent into the canyon) amid walls and towers that vaguely resemble a New York City skyline. You'll walk under the gaze of Queen Nefertiti, a giant rock formation that some observers think has Egyptian-looking features. If you are traveling with companions, make it a one-way, 1-mile downhill trek by having them pick you up at the Courthouse Towers Viewpoint. Allow about 45 minutes for the one-way journey. *Easy–Moderate.* ✉ *Arches National Park* ✣ *Trailhead: 2 miles from park entrance on main park road.*

VISITOR CENTERS

Arches Visitor Center

INFO CENTER | FAMILY | With well-designed hands-on exhibits about the park's geology, wildlife, and history; helpful rangers; a water station; and a bookstore; the center is a great way to start your park visit. It also has picnic tables and something that's rare in the park: cell service for many carriers. ✉ *N. U.S. 191* ☎ *435/719–2299* 🌐 *nps.gov/arch.*

Petrified Dunes

5 miles north of the visitor center.

Sights

Petrified Dunes

NATURE SITE | FAMILY | Just a tiny pull-out, this memorable stop features acres upon acres of reddish-gold, petrified sand dunes. There's no trail here, so roam as you like while keeping track of where you are. If you do lose your way, heading west will take you back to the main road. ✉ *Arches National Park* ✣ *6 miles from park entrance.*

Courthouse Towers

3 miles north of the visitor center.

This collection of towering rock formations looks unreal from a distance and even more breathtaking up close. The Three Gossips does indeed resemble a gaggle of wildly tall people sharing some kind of secret. Sheep Rock is right below, with the massive Tower of Babel just a bit north. Enter this section of the park 3 miles past the visitor center. The extremely popular Park Avenue Trail winds through the area.

Sights

SCENIC STOPS

Courthouse Wash

NATURE SITE | Although this rock-art panel fell victim to an unusual case of vandalism in 1980, when someone scoured the petroglyphs and pictographs that had been left by four cultures, you can still see ancient images if you take a short walk from the parking area on the left-hand side of the road, heading south. ✉ *U.S. 191, about 2 miles south of Arches entrance.*

Activities

Arches lies in the middle of one of the adventure capitals of the United States. Deep canyons and towering walls are everywhere you look. Thousand-foot sandstone walls draw rock climbers from across the globe. Hikers can choose from shady canyons or red rock ridges that put you in the company of the West's big sky. The Colorado River forms the southeast boundary of the park and can give you every grade of white-water adventure. Moab-based outfitters can set you up for just about any sport you may have a desire to try: mountain biking, ATVs, dirt bikes, four-wheel-drive vehicles, kayaking, climbing, stand-up paddleboarding, and even skydiving. Within the park, it's best to stick with basics such as hiking, sightseeing, and photography. Climbers and other adventure seekers should always inquire at the visitor center about restrictions, which can also be seen on the park's website.

CAMPING

Campgrounds in and around Arches range from sprawling RV parks with myriad amenities to quaint, shady retreats near a babbling brook. The Devils Garden Campground in the park is a wonderful spot to call home for a few days, though it is often full and lacks an RV dump station. More than 350 campsites are operated in the vicinity by the Bureau of Land Management—their sites on the Colorado River and near the Slickrock Trail are some of the nicest (and most affordable, at just $20/night) in the area. The most centrally located campgrounds in Moab generally accommodate RVs.

Devils Garden Campground. This campground is one of the most unusual—and gorgeous—in the West, and in the national park system, for that matter. ✉ *End of main road, 18 miles from park entrance* ☎ *435/719–2299, 877/444–6777 for reservations* 🌐 *www.recreation.gov.*

HIKING

Getting out on any one of the park trails will surely cause you to fall in love with this Mars-like landscape. But remember, you are hiking in a desert environment and approximately 1 mile above sea level. Many people succumb to heat and dehydration because they do not drink enough water. Park rangers recommend a gallon of water per day per person, plus electrolytes.

★ Fiery Furnace Walk

HIKING/WALKING | Join a park ranger on a 2½-hour scramble through a labyrinth of rock fins and narrow sandstone canyons. You'll see arches and other eye-popping formations that can't be viewed from the road. You should be very fit and not afraid of heights or confined spaces for this moderately strenuous experience. Wear sturdy hiking shoes, sunscreen, and a hat, and bring at least a liter of water. Guided walks into the Fiery Furnace are offered mid-April through September, usually a few times a day (hours vary), and leave from Fiery Furnace Viewpoint, about 15 miles from the park visitor center. Tickets for the morning walks must be reserved (at 🌐 *www.recreation.gov*) and are available beginning six months in advance and up to four days before the day of the tour. Tickets for afternoon Fiery Furnace walks must be purchased in person at the park visitor center, ideally as soon as you arrive in Moab and as far ahead as seven days before your hike. Children ages 5–12 are charged half price; kids under 5 are not allowed. Book early as the program usually fills months prior to each walk. ✉ *Arches National Park* ✣ *Trailhead: On Arches Scenic Dr.* 🎫 *$16* 🕒 *Guided hikes not offered Oct.–mid-April.*

ROCK CLIMBING AND CANYONEERING

Rock climbers travel from across the country to scale the sheer red rock walls of Arches National Park and surrounding areas. Most climbing routes in the park require advanced techniques. Permits are not required, but climbers are encouraged to register for a free permit, either online or at a kiosk outside the visitor center. Climbers are responsible for knowing park regulations, temporary route closures, and restricted routes. Two popular routes ascend Owl Rock in the Garden of Eden (about 10 miles from the visitor center); the well-worn route has a difficulty of 5.8, while a more challenging option is 5.11 on a scale that goes up to 5.13-plus. Many climbing routes are available in the Park Avenue area, about 2.2 miles from the visitor center. These routes are also extremely difficult climbs. No commercial outfitters are allowed to lead rock-climbing excursions in the park, but guided canyoneering (which involves ropes, rappelling, and some basic climbing) is allowed, and permits are required for canyoneering. Before climbing, it's imperative that you stop at the visitor center and check with a ranger about climbing regulations.

Desert Highlights

CLIMBING/MOUNTAINEERING | This guide company takes adventurous types on descents and ascents through canyons (with the help of ropes), including those found in the Fiery Furnace at Arches National Park. Full-day and multiday canyoneering treks are available to destinations both in and near the national parks. ✉ *16 S. 100 E, Moab* ☎ *435/259–4433* 🌐 *www.deserthighlights.com* 🎫 *From $105.*

Canyonlands National Park

Canyonlands is truly four parks in one, but the majority of visitors drive through the panoramic vistas of Island in the Sky and barely venture anywhere else. Plan a day to explore the Needles district and see the park from the bottom up. Float down the Green and Colorado rivers on a family-friendly rafting trip, or take on the white water in the legendary Cataract Canyon.

GETTING HERE AND AROUND

Off U.S. 191, Canyonlands' Island in the Sky Visitor Center is 29 miles from Arches National Park and 32 miles from Moab on Highway 313 west of U.S. 191; the Needles District is 80 miles from Moab and reached via Highway 211, 34 miles west of U.S. 191.

Before starting a journey to any of Canyonlands' three districts, make sure your gas tank is topped off, as there are no services inside the large park. The Maze is especially remote, 135 miles from Moab, and actually a bit closer (100 miles) to Capitol Reef National Park. In the Island in the Sky District, it's about 12 miles from the entrance station to Grand View Point, with a 5-mile spur to

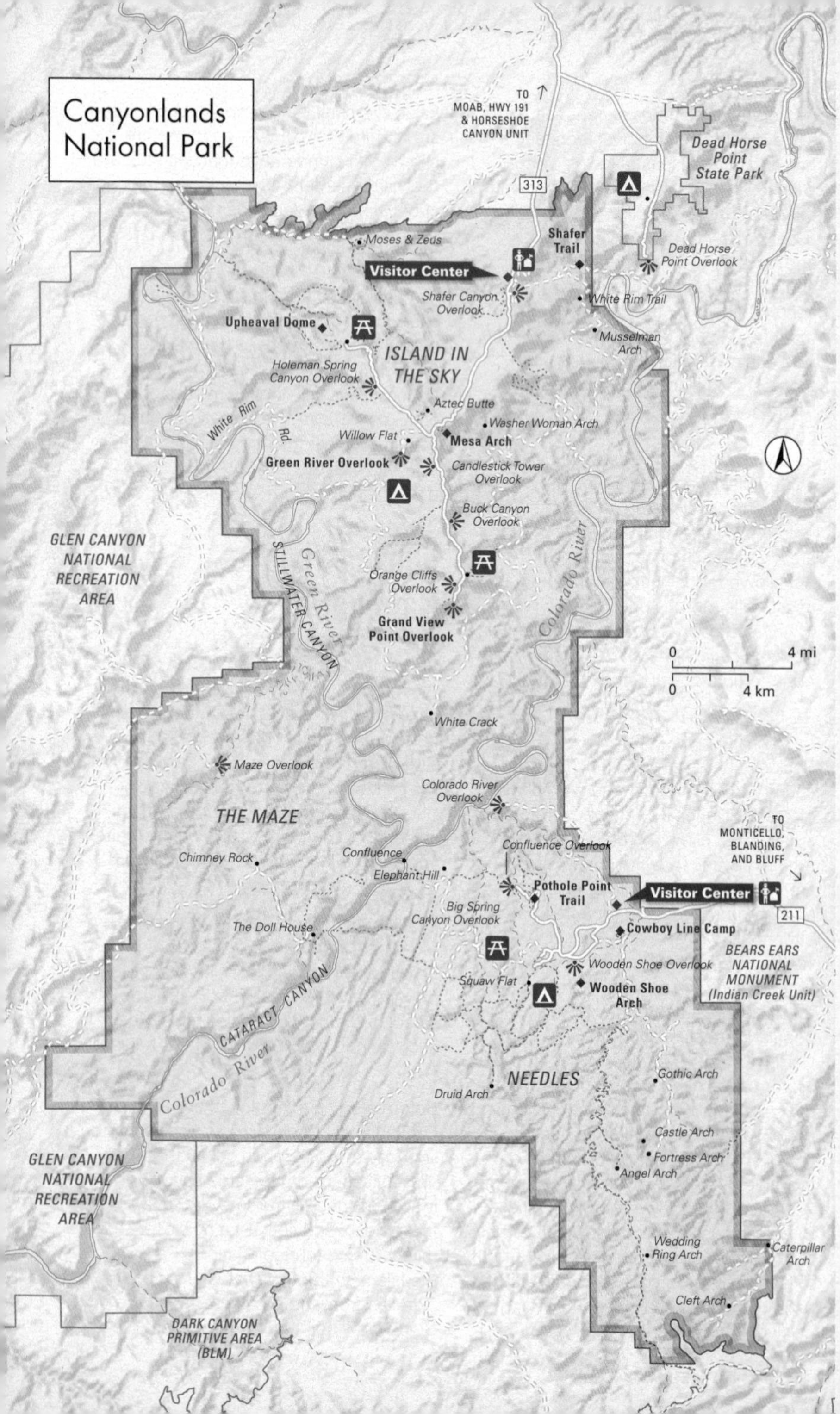

Canyonlands National Park
TO MOAB, HWY 191 & HORSESHOE CANYON UNIT
313
Dead Horse Point State Park
Shafer Trail
Moses & Zeus
Visitor Center
Dead Horse Point Overlook
Shafer Canyon Overlook
White Rim Trail
Upheaval Dome
Musselman Arch
ISLAND IN THE SKY
Holeman Spring Canyon Overlook
Aztec Butte
White Rim Rd.
Washer Woman Arch
Willow Flat
Mesa Arch
Green River Overlook
Candlestick Tower Overlook
Buck Canyon Overlook
GLEN CANYON NATIONAL RECREATION AREA
STILLWATER CANYON
Green River
Colorado River
Orange Cliffs Overlook
Grand View Point Overlook
0 4 mi
0 4 km
White Crack
Maze Overlook
Colorado River Overlook
THE MAZE
TO MONTICELLO, BLANDING, AND BLUFF
Confluence Overlook
Chimney Rock
Confluence
Elephant Hill
Pothole Point Trail
Visitor Center
211
Big Spring Canyon Overlook
The Doll House
Cowboy Line Camp
BEARS EARS NATIONAL MONUMENT (Indian Creek Unit)
Wooden Shoe Overlook
Squaw Flat
Wooden Shoe Arch
CATARACT CANYON
Colorado River
NEEDLES
Gothic Arch
Druid Arch
Castle Arch
Fortress Arch
GLEN CANYON NATIONAL RECREATION AREA
Angel Arch
Wedding Ring Arch
Caterpillar Arch
Cleft Arch
DARK CANYON PRIMITIVE AREA (BLM)

Upheaval Dome. The Needles scenic drive is 10 miles from the entrance station, with two spurs, about 3 miles each. Roads in the Maze—suitable only for high-clearance, four-wheel-drive vehicles—wind for hundreds of miles through the rugged canyons. Within the parks, it's critical that you park only in designated pull-outs or parking areas.

PARK ESSENTIALS

PARK FEES AND PERMITS

Admission is $30 per vehicle, $15 per person on foot or bicycle, and $25 per motorcycle, good for seven days. Your Canyonlands pass is good for all the park's districts. There's no entrance fee to the Maze District of Canyonlands. A $55 local park pass grants you admission to both Arches and Canyonlands as well as Natural Bridges and Hovenweep national monuments for one year.

You need a permit for overnight backpacking, four-wheel-drive camping, river trips, and mountain-bike camping. Online reservations can be made four months in advance on the park website (🌐 *www.nps.gov/cany*). Four-wheel-drive day use in Salt, Horse, and Lavender canyons and all motorized vehicles and bicycles on the Elephant Hill and White Rim trails also require a permit, which you can obtain online up to 24 hours before your trip or in person at visitor centers.

PARK HOURS

Canyonlands National Park is open 24 hours a day, seven days a week, year-round. It is in the mountain time zone.

CELL PHONE RECEPTION

Cell phone reception may be available in some parts of the park, but not reliably so. Public telephones are at the park's visitor centers.

TOURS

Redtail Air Adventures

AIR EXCURSIONS | This company's daily, regional tours give you an eagle's-eye view of the park, and you'll walk away with new respect and understanding of the word "wilderness." The Canyonlands Tour, one of several flightseeing options, lasts for one hour. A two-person minimum applies. ✉ *Canyonlands Field Airport, 94 W. Aviation Way, Moab* ✣ *Off U.S. 191* ☎ *435/259–7421* 🌐 *flyredtail.com* 🎫 *From $184 per person.*

VISITOR INFORMATION

CONTACTS Canyonlands National Park. ☎ *435/719–2313* 🌐 *www.nps.gov/cany.*

Island in the Sky

Standing at one of the overlooks at Island in the Sky, it's hard to fully take in what looks like an oil painting a thousand feet below. Rivers and rain have eroded the desert floor for millennia, creating mesas, towers, and the park's famously deep canyons, all with an earthy red hue. While the view alone is worth the trip, getting onto one of the district's hiking trails or four-wheel roads will get you up close with its rough beauty. While it's still a shade over 30 miles from Moab, this is the most accessible—and far most visited—section of the park.

SCENIC DRIVES

Island in the Sky Park Road

SCENIC DRIVE | This 12-mile-long main road inside the park is bisected by a 5-mile side road to the Upheaval Dome area. To enjoy dramatic views, including the Green and Colorado river basins, stop at the overlooks and take the short walks. Once you get to the park, allow at least two hours—and ideally four—to explore. ✉ *Island in the Sky.*

SCENIC STOPS

Green River Overlook

VIEWPOINT | From the road it's just 100 yards to this stunning view of the Green River to the south and west. It's not far from Island in the Sky (Willow Flat) campground. ✉ *About 1 mile off Upheaval*

Dome Rd., Island in the Sky ⊕ 7 miles from visitor center.

White Rim Overlook Trail

VIEWPOINT | The cliffs fall away on three sides at the end of this 1-mile level hike until you get a dramatic view of the White Rim and Monument Basin. There are restrooms at the trailhead. ✉ *Grand View Point, Island in the Sky.*

TRAILS

Aztec Butte Trail

TRAIL | The highlight of the 2-mile round-trip hike is the chance to see Ancestral Pueblo granaries. The view into Taylor Canyon is also nice. *Moderate.* ✉ *Island in the Sky ⊕ Trailhead: Upheaval Dome Rd., about 7 miles from visitor center.*

★ Grand View Point Trail

TRAIL | This 360-degree view is the main event for many visitors to Island in the Sky. Look down on the deep canyons of the Colorado and Green rivers, which have been carved by water and erosion over the millennia. Many people just stop at the paved overlook and drive on, but you'll gain breathtaking perspective by strolling along this 2-mile round-trip, flat cliffside trail. On a clear day you can see up to 100 miles to the Maze and Needles districts of the park and each of Utah's major laccolithic mountain ranges: the Henrys, Abajos, and La Sals. *Easy.* ✉ *End of main park road, Island in the Sky ⊕ 12 miles from visitor center.*

★ Mesa Arch Trail

TRAIL | If you don't have time for the 2,000 arches in nearby Arches National Park, you should take the easy, ½-mile round-trip walk to Mesa Arch. After the overlooks this is the most popular trail in the park. The arch is above a cliff that drops 800 feet to the canyon bottom. Through the arch, views of Washerwoman Arch and surrounding buttes, spires, and canyons make this a favorite photo opportunity. *Easy.* ✉ *Off main park road, Island in the Sky ⊕ 6 miles from visitor center.*

★ Upheaval Dome Trail

TRAIL | This mysterious crater is one of the wonders of Island in the Sky. Some geologists believe it's an eroded salt dome, but others think it was made by a meteorite. Either way, it's worth the steep hike to see it and decide for yourself. The moderate hike to the first overlook is about a ½-mile; energetic visitors can continue another ½-mile to the second overlook for an even better perspective. The trail is steeper and rougher after the first overlook. Round-trip to the second overlook is 2 miles. The trailhead has restrooms and a picnic area. *Moderate.* ✉ *End of Upheaval Dome Rd., Island in the Sky ⊕ 11 miles from visitor center.*

Whale Rock Trail

TRAIL | If you've been hankering to walk across some of that pavement-smooth stuff they call slickrock, the hike to Whale Rock will make your feet happy. This 1-mile round-trip adventure, which culminates with a tough final 100-foot climb and features some potentially dangerous dropoffs, takes you to the very top of the whale's back. Once you get there, you are rewarded with great views of Upheaval Dome and Trail Canyon. *Moderate.* ✉ *Island in the Sky ⊕ Trailhead: Upheaval Dome Rd., 10 miles from visitor center.*

VISITOR CENTERS

★ Island in the Sky Visitor Center

INFO CENTER | The gateway to the world-famous White Rim Trail, this visitor center 21 miles from U.S. 191 draws a mix of mountain bikers, hikers, and tourists. Enjoy the orientation film, then browse the bookstore for information about the region. Exhibits help explain animal adaptations as well as some of the history of the park. Check the website or at the center for a daily schedule of ranger-led programs. ✉ *Off Hwy. 313, Island in the Sky* ☎ *435/259–4712* ⊙ *Closed late Dec.–early Mar.*

Needles

Lower in elevation than Island in the Sky, Needles is more about on-the-ground exploration than far-off vistas, but it's an especially good area for long-distance hiking, mountain biking, and four-wheel driving. The district is named for its massive sandstone spires, with hundreds of the formations poking up toward the sky. There are also several striking examples of Native American rock art here, well worth the hikes to reach them. With relatively few visitors, Needles makes for a quiet place to set up camp and recharge for a few days before returning to busy nearby Moab.

Sights

HISTORIC SIGHTS

Cowboy Camp

HISTORIC SITE | FAMILY | This fascinating stop on the 0.6-mile round-trip **Cave Spring Trail** is an authentic example of cowboy life more than a century ago. You do not need to complete the entire trail (which includes two short ladders and some rocky hiking) to see the 19th-century artifacts at Cowboy Camp. ✉ *End of Cave Springs Rd., Needles* ✢ *2.3 miles from visitor center.*

SCENIC DRIVES

Needles District Park Road

SCENIC DRIVE | You'll feel like you've driven into a Hollywood Western as you roll along the park road in the Needles District. Red mesas and buttes rise against the horizon, blue mountain ranges interrupt the rangelands, and the colorful red-and-white needles stand like soldiers on the far side of grassy meadows. Definitely hop out of the car at a few of the marked roadside stops, including both overlooks at Pothole Point. Allow at least two hours in this less-traveled section of the park. ✉ *Needles.*

SCENIC STOPS

Wooden Shoe Arch Overlook

VIEWPOINT | FAMILY | Kids enjoy looking for the tiny window in the rock that looks like a wooden shoe with a turned-up toe. If you can't find it on your own, there's a marker to help you. ✉ *Off main park road, Needles* ✢ *2 miles from visitor center.*

TRAILS

★ **Cave Spring Trail**

TRAIL | One of the best, most interesting trails in the park takes you past a historic cowboy camp, precontact rock art, and great views. Two wooden ladders and one short, steep stretch may make this a little daunting for the extremely young or old, but it's also a short hike (0.6 mile round-trip), features some shade, and has many notable features. *Moderate.* ✉ *Needles* ✢ *Trailhead: End of Cave Springs Rd., 2.3 miles from visitor center.*

Pothole Point Trail

TRAIL | Microscopic creatures lie dormant in pools that fill only after rare rainstorms. When the rains do come, some eggs hatch within hours and life becomes visible. If you're lucky, you'll hit Pothole Point after a storm. The dramatic views of the Needles and Six Shooter Peak make this easy, 0.6-mile round-trip worthwhile. Plan for about 45 minutes. There's no shade, so wear a hat and take plenty of water. ✉ *Off main road, Needles* ✢ *5 miles from visitor center.*

Slickrock Trail

TRAIL | Wear a hat and carry plenty of water if you're on this trail—you won't find any shade along the 2.4-mile round-trip trek. This is the rare frontcountry site where you might spot one of the few remaining native herds of bighorn sheep in the national park system. Nice panoramic views. *Easy.* ✉ *Needles* ✢ *Trailhead: Main park road, 6 miles from visitor center.*

VISITOR CENTERS

Needles District Visitor Center

INFO CENTER | This gorgeous building is 34 miles from U.S. 191 via Highway 211, near the park entrance. Needles is remote, so it's worth stopping to inquire about road, weather, and park conditions. You can also watch the interesting orientation film, refill water bottles, and get books, trail maps, and other information. ✉ *Off Hwy. 211, Needles* ☎ *435/259–4711* ⏲ *Closed late Nov.–early Mar.*

Maze

The most remote district of the park, the Maze is hours away from any town and is accessible only via high-clearance, four-wheel-drive vehicles. A trip here should not be taken lightly. Many of the hikes are considered some of the most dangerous in the world, and self-sufficiency is critical. But the few who do choose to visit this wild tangle of rock and desert are handsomely rewarded with unforgettable views and a silent solitude that's hard to find anywhere else. Plan to spend at least several days here, and bring all the water, food, and gas you'll need.

VISITOR CENTER

Hans Flat Ranger Station

INFO CENTER | Only experienced and intrepid visitors will likely ever visit this remote outpost—on a dirt road 46 miles east of Highway 24 in Hanksville. The office is a trove of books, maps, and other documents about the unforgiving Maze District of Canyonlands, but rangers will strongly dissuade any inexperienced off-road drivers and backpackers to proceed into this truly rugged wilderness. There's a pit toilet, but no water, food, or services of any kind. If you're headed for the backcountry, permits cost $30 per group for up to 14 days. Rangers offer guided hikes in Horseshoe Canyon on most weekends in spring and fall. ■ **TIP→ Call the ranger station for road conditions leading to Horseshoe Canyon/Hans Flat, as rain can make travel difficult.** ✉ *Jct. of Recreation Rds. 777 and 633, Maze* ☎ *435/259–2652.*

Horseshoe Canyon

Remote Horseshoe Canyon is not contiguous with the rest of Canyonlands National Park. Added to the park in 1971, it has what may be America's most significant surviving examples of rock art. While the canyon can usually be accessed by two-wheel drive vehicles via a graded dirt road, it's still 2½ hours from Moab. And the road conditions can change abruptly, so visitors without a four-wheel drive vehicle should always consult the park's road conditions hotline before departing. Rangers lead hikes here in the spring and fall.

Horseshoe Canyon Trail

TRAIL | This remote region of the park is accessible by dirt road, and only in good weather. Park at the lip of the canyon and hike 7 miles round trip to the Great Gallery, considered by some to be the most significant rock-art panel in North America. Ghostly life-size figures in the Barrier Canyon style populate the amazing panel. The hike is moderately strenuous, with a 700-foot descent. Allow at least six hours for the trip and take a gallon of water per person. There's no camping allowed in the canyon, although you can camp on top near the parking lot. *Difficult.* ■ **TIP→ Call Hans Flat Ranger Station before heading out, because rain can make the access road a muddy mess.** ✉ *Horseshoe Canyon* ✥ *Trailhead: 32 miles east of Hwy. 24.*

Serious mountain bikers traverse all 100 miles of White Rim Road.

Activities

BIKING

Mountain bikers from all over the world like to brag that they've conquered the 100 miles of White Rim Road. The trail's fame is well deserved: it traverses steep roads, broken rock, and dramatic ledges, as well as long stretches that wind through the canyons and look down onto others. If you're biking White Rim without an outfitter, you'll need careful planning, vehicle support, and much sought-after backcountry reservations. Permits are available no more than four months, and no less than two days, prior to permit start date. There is a 15-person, three-vehicle limit for groups. Day-use permits are also required and can be obtained at the Island in the Sky visitor center or reserved 24 hours in advance through the park's website. Follow the turn-off about 1 mile from the entrance, then 11 miles farther along Shafer Trail in Island in the Sky.

In addition to the company listed below, **Rim Tours** and **Western Spirit Cycling Adventures** offer tours in both Arches and Canyonlands.

Magpie Cycling

BICYCLING | Professional guides and mountain biking instructors lead groups (or lone riders) on daylong and multiday bike trips exploring the Moab region's most memorable terrain, including the White Rim, Needles, and the Maze. If you need to rent a bike, Magpie can meet you at its preferred shop, Poison Spider Bicycles (☎ *800/635–1792* 🌐 *poisonspiderbicycles.com*). ✉ *Moab* ☎ *435/259–4464* 🌐 *www.magpiecycling.com* 🎫 *Day tours from $150, multiday from $875.*

CAMPING

Canyonlands campgrounds are some of the most beautiful in the national park system. At the Needles District, campers will enjoy fairly private campsites tucked against red rock walls and dotted with pinyon and juniper trees. At Island in the Sky, starry nights and spectacular vistas make the small campground an intimate treasure. Hookups are not available in either of the park's campgrounds; however, some sites are long enough to accommodate units up to 28 feet long.

Needles Campground. The defining features of the camp sites at Squaw Flat are house-size red rock formations, which provide some shade, offer privacy from adjacent campers, and make this one of the more unique campgrounds in the national park system. ✉ *Off main road, about 3 miles from park entrance, Needles* ☎ *435/259–4711.*

Willow Flat Campground. From this little campground on a mesa top, you can walk to spectacular views of the Green River. Most sites have a bit of shade from juniper trees. ✉ *Off main park road, about 7 miles from park entrance, Island in the Sky* ☎ *435/259–4712.*

FOUR-WHEELING

Nearly 200 miles of challenging backcountry roads lead to campsites, trailheads, and natural and cultural features in Canyonlands. All of the roads require high-clearance, four-wheel-drive vehicles, and many are inappropriate for inexperienced drivers. The 100-mile White Rim Trail, for example, can be extremely challenging, so make sure that your four-wheel-drive skills are well honed and that you are capable of making basic vehicle repairs. Carry at least one full-size spare tire, extra gas, extra water, a shovel, a high-lift jack, and—October through April—chains for all four tires. Double-check to see that your vehicle is in top-notch condition, for you definitely don't want to break down in the interior of the park: towing expenses can exceed $1,000.

Day-use permits, available at the park visitor centers or 24 hours in advance through the park website, are required for motorized and bicycle trips on the Elephant Hill and White Rim trails. For overnight four-wheeling trips, you must purchase a $30 permit, which you can reserve no more than four months and no fewer than two days in advance by contacting the Backcountry Reservations Office (☎ *435/259–4351*). Cyclists share all roads, so be aware and cautious of their presence. Vehicular traffic traveling uphill has the right-of-way. Check at the visitor center for current road conditions before taking off into the backcountry. You must carry a washable, reusable toilet with you in the Maze District and carry out all waste.

HIKING

At Canyonlands National Park you can immerse yourself in the intoxicating colors, smells, and textures of the desert. ⚠ **Make sure to bring water and electrolytes, as dehydration is the number-one cause of search-and-rescue calls here.**

Island in the Sky has several easy and moderate hikes that are popular with day-trippers, including the **Aztec Butte Trail, Grand View Point Trail, Upheaval Dome Trail,** and **Whale Rock Trail.** If you're up for a strenuous day of hiking, try the 8-mile **Syncline Loop Trail,** which follows the canyons around Upheaval Dome.

Green River

70 miles west of the Colorado state line and about 50 miles northwest of Moab.

The town of **Green River** and the namesake river that runs through it are historically important. Early Native Americans used the river for centuries; the Old Spanish Trail crossed it, and the Denver and Rio Grande Railroad bridged it in 1883. Some say the "green" refers to the color of the water; others claim it's named for the plants along the riverbank. And yet another story gives the credit to a mysterious trapper named Green. Whatever the etymology, Green River remains a sleepy little town, and a nice break from some of the more "hip" tourist communities in southern Utah.

Green River has some less expensive—but also less noteworthy—dining and lodging options, and the excellent John Wesley Powell River History Museum. Each September the fragrance of fresh cantaloupe, watermelon, and honeydew fills the air, especially during Melon Days, a family-fun harvest celebration held annually on the third weekend of the month. As Moab hotels have become more expensive and crowded spring through fall, many park visitors have taken to staying farther south in the small southeastern Utah towns of **Blanding** and **Bluff,** and even 110 miles away up in **Grand Junction, Colorado,** a city of about 63,000 that's come into its own in recent years with a quaint, historic downtown and close proximity to gorgeous Colorado National Monument.

GETTING HERE AND AROUND

Reaching Green River is as easy as finding I–70. The town is 180 miles southeast of Salt Lake City, 100 miles west of Grand Junction, Colorado, and 50 miles northwest of Moab.

Sights

★ Goblin Valley State Park
NATURE SITE | FAMILY | Strange-looking "hoodoos" rise up from the desert landscape 12 miles north of Hanksville, making Goblin Valley home to hundreds of strange goblin-like rock formations with a dramatic orange hue. Short, easy trails wind through the goblins making it a fun walk for kids and adults. ✉ *Hwy. 24* ☎ *435/275–4584* 🌐 *stateparks.utah.gov* 🎫 *$15 per vehicle.*

Green River State Park
NATIONAL/STATE PARK | A shady respite on the banks of the Green River, this park is best known for its golf course. It's also the starting point for boaters drifting along the river through Labyrinth and Stillwater canyons. Fishing and bird-watching are favorite pastimes here. ✉ *450 S. Green River Rd.* ☎ *435/564–3633, 800/322–3770 for campground reservations* 🌐 *stateparks.utah.gov* 🎫 *$5 per vehicle.*

★ John Wesley Powell River History Museum
MUSEUM | FAMILY | Learn what it was like to travel down the Green and Colorado rivers in the 1800s in wooden boats. A series of displays tracks the Powell Party's arduous, dangerous 1869 journey, and visitors can watch the award-winning film *Journey Into the Unknown* for a cinematic taste of the white-water adventure. The center also houses the River Runner's Hall of Fame, a tribute to those who have followed in Powell's wake. River-themed art occupies a gallery and there's a dinosaur exhibit on the lower level. ✉ *1765 E. Main St.* ☎ *435/564–3427* 🌐 *www.johnwesleypowell.com* 🎫 *$6* ⏲ *Closed Mon. in winter.*

Sego Canyon Rock Art Interpretive Site
ARCHAEOLOGICAL SITE | Sego is one of the most dramatic and mystifying rock-art sites in the entire state. Large, ghostlike rock-art figures painted and etched by Native Americans approximately 4,000 years ago cover these canyon walls. There's also art left by the Ute from the 19th century. Distinctive for their large anthropomorphic figures, and for horses, buffalo, and shields painted with red-and-white pigment, these rare drawings are a must-see. ✉ *I–70, Exit 187, Thompson Springs* ✣ *25 miles east of Green River on I–70, at Exit 187 go north onto Hwy. 94 through Thompson Springs* ☎ *435/259–2100 Bureau of Land Management Office in Moab* 🌐 *www.blm.gov.*

Restaurants

Ray's Tavern
$ | AMERICAN | In little downtown Green River, Ray's is something of a Western legend and a favorite hangout for river runners. The bar that runs the length of this 1940s restaurant reminds you this is still a tavern and a serious watering

hole—but all the photos and rafting memorabilia make it comfortable for families as well. **Known for:** legendary burgers; great people-watching; homemade apple pie. $ *Average main: $12* ✉ *25 S. Broadway* ☎ *435/564–3511.*

Tamarisk Restaurant

$ | **AMERICAN** | Views of the Green River make this no-frills restaurant a nice stop after a long drive. Though the interior has gotten hipper in recent years, the breakfast, lunch, and dinner menus are filled with the same classic diner favorites the spot has been serving up for decades. **Known for:** great river view; Navajo tacos; salad bar. $ *Average main: $12* ✉ *1710 E. Main St.* 🌐 *www.tamariskrestaurant.com.*

Hotels

River Terrace Hotel

$$ | **HOTEL** | The peaceful setting, on the bank of the Green River, is conducive to a good night's rest, and this nicely maintained hotel is conveniently less than 2 miles off Interstate 70, although nearly an hour's drive from Arches. **Pros:** shady riverside location (be sure to request a river-view room); reasonable rates; on-site restaurant. **Cons:** in a sleepy town with few attractions; not within distance of downtown Green River; about 50 miles north of Moab. $ *Rooms from: $141* ✉ *1740 E. Main St.* ☎ *435/564–3401, 877/564–3401* 🌐 *www.river-terrace.com* *50 rooms* *Free breakfast.*

Activities

RIVER FLOAT TRIPS

Bearing little resemblance to its name, Desolation Canyon acquaints those who venture down the Green River with some of the last true American wilderness: a lush, verdant canyon, where the rapids promise more laughter than fear. It's a favorite destination of canoe paddlers, kayakers, and novice rafters. May through September, raft trips can be arranged by outfitters in Green River or Moab. South of town the river drifts at a lazier pace through Labyrinth and Stillwater canyons, and the stretch south to Mineral Bottom in Canyonlands is best suited to canoes and motor boats.

For river-trip outfitters, see the Moab Activities section.

Blanding

126 miles south of Green River.

For nearly the first 20 years of its history, this small town near the base of the Abajo and Henry mountains was known as Grayson. This changed when wealthy Thomas Bicknell offered a huge library of books to any town willing to take his name. In the end, another town got the name, and Blanding was honored with Bicknell's wife's maiden name, as well as a share of the book bounty.

There is famously little to do around here, yet many residents love it for its peaceful quality. As the biggest town in San Juan County and the gateway to several national monuments, state parks, and two Native American reservations, it remains vital in its own way.

GETTING HERE AND AROUND

The town is about 90 minutes from Moab traveling south on U.S. 191.

VISITOR INFORMATION

CONTACTS Blanding Visitor Center. ✉ *12 N. Grayson Pkwy.* ☎ *435/678–3662* 🌐 *www.blanding-ut.gov.*

Sights

Dinosaur Museum

MUSEUM | **FAMILY** | Skeletons, fossils, footprints, and reconstructed dinosaur skins are all on display at this small museum. Hallways hold a collection of movie posters featuring Godzilla and other monsters dating back to the 1930s. ✉ *754 S. 200 W* ☎ *435/678–3454* 🌐 *www.dinosaur-museum.org* *$5* *Closed mid-Oct.–mid-Apr.*

★ Edge of the Cedars State Park Museum

MUSEUM | FAMILY | Behind what is one of the nation's foremost museums dedicated to the Ancestral Puebloan culture, an interpretive trail leads to an ancient village that they once inhabited. Portions have been partially excavated, and visitors can climb down a ladder into a 1,000-year-old ceremonial room called a kiva. The museum displays a variety of pots, baskets, spear points, and rare artifacts—even a pair of sandals said to date back 1,500 years. ✉ *660 W. 400 N* ☎ *435/678–2238* 🌐 *stateparks.utah.gov* 🎟 *$5* ⏲ *Closed Sun.*

Hovenweep National Monument

NATIONAL/STATE PARK | The best place in southeast Utah to see ancient tower ruins dotting the scenic cliffs, if you're headed south from Canyonlands and have an interest in Ancestral Puebloan culture, a visit to this monument is a must. Park rangers strongly advise following printed maps and signs from U.S. 191 near Blanding, Utah, or County Road G from Cortez, Colorado. GPS is not reliable here. Once you get there, you'll find unusual tower structures (which may have been used for astronomical observation) and ancient dwellings. ✉ *Hovenweep Rd.* ☎ *970/562–4282* 🌐 *www.nps.gov/hove.*

Newspaper Rock State Historic Monument

NATIVE SITE | FAMILY | One of the West's most famous rock-art sites, about 15 miles west of U.S. 191, this site contains Native American designs engraved on the rock over the course of 2,000 years. Early pioneers and explorers to the region named the site Newspaper Rock because they believed the rock, crowded with drawings, constituted a written language with which early people communicated. Archaeologists now agree that the petroglyphs do not represent language. ✉ *Hwy. 211.*

Restaurants

Homestead Steak House

$ | AMERICAN | The folks here specialize in authentic Navajo frybread and Navajo tacos. At lunch the popular—and massive—sheepherder's sandwich is made with frybread, and comes with your choice of beef, turkey, or ham, and all the trimmings. **Known for:** homemade soups; Friday night seafood; banana pudding. $ *Average main: $14* ✉ *121 E. Center St.* ☎ *435/678–3456* 🌐 *www.homesteadsteakhouseut.com* ⏲ *Closed Sun.*

Hotels

Inn at the Canyons

$ | HOTEL | One of the largest properties in Monticello, which is just under an hour from Needles District Visitor Center, this is also one of the comfiest, with a heated indoor pool and a hot tub that's just what the doctor ordered for soaking adventure-weary bodies. **Pros:** close to Needles district of Canyonlands; year-round indoor pool and hot tub; pets allowed on request. **Cons:** sits near the main road through town, so might be noisy; in a sleepy town; rooms are clean not memorable. $ *Rooms from: $115* ✉ *533 N. Main St., Monticello* ☎ *435/587–2458* 🌐 *www.monticellocanyonlandsinn.com* 🔑 *43 rooms* 🍽 *Free breakfast.*

Stone Lizard Lodge

$$ | HOTEL | This rustic yet classy spot stands out from the local hotel chains and motor lodges with its individually decorated rooms, all with local art on the walls and Navajo-style rugs on the hardwood floors. **Pros:** one of the most comfortable lodgings around; hearty continental breakfast, with several hot items and homemade baked goods; calming garden area. **Cons:** smallish rooms (due to being built in the 1940s); more expensive than most other lodgings in the area; a limited number of pet-friendly rooms (and only dogs are allowed). $ *Rooms from: $134* ✉ *88 W. Center St.* ☎ *435/678–3323* *www.stonelizardlodge.com* *17 rooms* *Free breakfast.*

Bluff

25 miles south of Blanding via U.S. 191.

Bluff is a tiny but unexpectedly cool town that's built a reputation for fun events. Like Moab, it doesn't have a palpable Mormon feel, and it remains a mini–melting pot of Navajos, river rats, hippies, and old-time Utahans. Surrounded by red-rock mesas, its cell phone service is spotty at best.

Settled in 1880, Bluff is one of southeastern Utah's oldest towns. Mormon pioneers from the original Hole in the Rock journey built a ranching empire that made the town, at one time, the richest per capita in the state. Although this early period of affluence passed, several historic Victorian-style homes remain. Pick up the free brochure "Historic Bluff by Bicycle and on Foot" at any business in town. Most of the original homes from the 1880 town-site of Bluff City are part of the Bluff Historic District. In a dozen or so blocks, there are 42 historic structures, most built between about 1890 and 1905.

GETTING HERE AND AROUND

Bluff is just under two hours from Moab south on U.S. 191.

Sights

Four Corners Monument

LOCAL INTEREST | The Navajo Nation manages this interesting landmark about 65 miles southeast of Bluff and 6 miles north of Teec Nos Pos, Arizona. Primarily a photo-op spot, you'll also find Navajo and Ute artisans selling authentic jewelry and crafts, as well as traditional foods. It's the only place in the United States where four states meet at one single point. Surveyors now believe the monument—a stone and metal marker sitting at the intersection of Colorado, Arizona, Utah, and New Mexico—is at least 1,800 feet east of the correct spot. The small entry fee of $5 per person is cash-only, so be sure to get money prior to heading out. *Four Corners Monument Rd., off U.S. 160.*

Sand Island Recreation Site

NATIVE SITE | Three miles southwest of Bluff you'll find a large panel of Ancestral Puebloan rock art. The panel includes several large images of Kokopelli, the mischief-maker from Puebloan lore. *U.S. 191* *435/587–1500 Monticello BLM office.*

★ Valley of the Gods

SCENIC DRIVE | A red fairyland of slender spires and buttes, the Valley of the Gods is a smaller version of Monument Valley. Approximately 15 miles west of Bluff, you can take a pretty drive through this relatively unvisited area on the 17-mile-long Valley of the Gods Road, which begins on U.S. 163 and ends on Highway 261. **TIP→ The road is unpaved but should be drivable as long as it's dry.** *Mexican Hat* *435/587–1500* *www.bluffutah.org/valley-of-the-gods.*

Restaurants

Comb Ridge Eat and Drink

$ | AMERICAN | Get a feel for the local color at one of the best restaurants in the area, with big wooden posts breaking up the barn-like space, and works by local artists on the walls. The menu is filled with burgers, pizzas, and salads, all with creative flairs. **Known for:** large portions; vegetarian options; excellent coffee and desserts. *Average main: $15* *680 S. U.S. 191* *435/485–5555* *www.combridgeeatanddrink.com* *Closed Sun.*

Cottonwood Steakhouse

$$$ | STEAKHOUSE | The ribs served here will blow your mind, and the charming Old West theme begins when you drive up to the rustic, false-front exterior. Inside, animal pelts, guns, and other memorabilia of the era adorn the walls.

Natural Bridges National Monument preserves several natural bridges made from eroded sandstone, including beautiful Owachomo.

Known for: outstanding barbecue ribs; decadent homemade desserts; old-timey look, in and out. Ⓢ *Average main: $23* ✉ *409 W. Main St.* ☎ *435/672–2282* 🌐 *www.cottonwoodsteakhouse.com* ⏲ *Closed Nov.–Mar. No lunch.*

Twin Rocks Cafe
$ | **SOUTHWESTERN** | Part of the appeal of eating at this colorful diner-style spot in tiny Bluff is that the restaurant sits beneath a striking pair of 150-foot-tall rock spires. There's also an outstanding Navajo trading post inside, and the kitchen turns out tasty and hearty Native American and Southwestern fare, from Navajo frybread French toast with local peaches in the morning to burgers, beef stew, and chili at lunch and dinner. **Known for:** Navajo frybread; locally crafted jewelry and weavings in the trading post; delicious and filling breakfasts. Ⓢ *Average main: $13* ✉ *913 E. Navajo Twins Dr.* ☎ *435/672–2341* 🌐 *www.facebook.com/twinrockscafe* ⏲ *No dinner Sun.–Thurs. during winter.*

Hotels

★ Desert Rose Inn and Cabins
$$ | **HOTEL** | Bluff's largest and most upscale hotel, which also contains two of the region's best restaurants, is an attractive, wood-sided lodge with a huge two-story front porch. **Pros:** rustic-elegant room furnishings; fitness center in adjacent building; pool and hot tub. **Cons:** nearly two-hour drive to Needles District; remote town without many amenities; a bit spendy for the area. Ⓢ *Rooms from: $169* ✉ *701 W. Main St.* ☎ *435/672–2303* 🌐 *www.desertroseinn.com* *53 rooms* 🍴 *No meals.*

Recapture Lodge
$ | **HOTEL** | Rooms at this family-operated inn are basic and clean, mostly with wood paneling; there's also a playground and pool. **Pros:** set on shady grounds with riverside chairs and walking trails; pool and hot tub; pets and horses welcome. **Cons:** nearly two-hour drive to Needles District; older property with small rooms and basic amenities; pool not close

to rooms. $ *Rooms from: $98* ✉ *250 E. Main St.* ☎ *435/672–2281* 🌐 *www.recapturelodge.com* 🛏 *26 rooms* 🍽 *Free breakfast.*

Activities

RIVER EXPEDITIONS

While somewhat calmer than the Colorado, the San Juan River offers some truly exceptional scenery and abundant opportunities to visit archaeological sites. It can be run in two sections: from Bluff to Mexican Hat, or from Mexican Hat to Lake Powell. Near Bluff (3 miles southwest on U.S. 191), the Sand Island Recreation Site is the launch site for most river trips. You'll find a primitive campground there as well. Permits from the Bureau of Land Management are required for floating on the San Juan River.

Wild River Expeditions

BOATING | FAMILY | The San Juan River is one of the prettiest floats in the region, and this reliable outfitter can take you on one- to seven-day trips. They are known for educational adventures that emphasize the geology, natural history, and archaeological wonders of the area. ✉ *2625 S. U.S. 191* ☎ *435/672–2244* 🌐 *www.riversandruins.com* 🎟 *From $199.*

Natural Bridges National Monument

The scenery and rock formations found in this national monument must be seen to be believed.

Sights

Natural Bridges National Monument

NATIONAL/STATE PARK | FAMILY | Stunning natural bridges, ancient Native American ruins, and magnificent scenery throughout make Natural Bridges National Monument a must-see if you have time to make the trip. Sipapu is one of the largest natural bridges in the world, spanning 268 feet and standing 220 feet tall. You can take in the Sipapu, Owachomo, and Kachina bridges via an 8.6-mile round-trip hike that meanders around and under them. A 13-site primitive campground is an optimal spot for stargazing. The national monument is 40 miles from Blanding. ✉ *Hwy. 275, off Hwy. 95* ☎ *435/692–1234* 🌐 *www.nps.gov/nabr* 🎟 *$20 per vehicle.*

Chapter 9

PHOENIX, SCOTTSDALE, AND TEMPE

Updated by
Elise Riley

Sights	Restaurants	Hotels	Shopping	Nightlife
★★★★☆	★★★★★	★★★★★	★★★★★	★★★★☆

WELCOME TO PHOENIX, SCOTTSDALE, AND TEMPE

TOP REASONS TO GO

★ **Resorts:** If you are looking for a gorgeous desert getaway within a metro area, Phoenix should be at the top of your list.

★ **Shops and restaurants:** Boutiques, art galleries, and gift shops throughout Scottsdale and along the Camelback Corridor offer yet another way to retreat and relax in the Valley of the Sun. A thriving restaurant scene provides a perfect end to a day of retail therapy.

★ **The Heard Museum:** This small but world-renowned museum elegantly celebrates Native American people, culture, art, and history.

★ **The great outdoors:** Sure there's urban sprawl, but Phoenix also has cool and accessible places to get away from it all, like the Desert Botanical Garden, Papago Park, Tempe Town Lake, and mountain and desert preserves.

★ **Golf:** All year long, links lovers can take their pick of top-rated public and private courses—many with incredibly spectacular views.

1 **Phoenix.** Downtown Phoenix used to be strictly for business. Nowadays it's home to some of the Valley's major museums, galleries, performance venues and sports arenas, plenty of high-rise homeowners, and a light-rail system that's changing the face of the city. Greater Phoenix offers an unusual mix of attractions that includes historic neighborhoods, acres of mountain preserves, and cultural centers.

2 **Scottsdale.** Scottsdale is a bastion of high-end and specialty shopping, historic sites, elite resorts, restaurants, spas, and golf greens next to desert views.

3 **Tempe, Mesa, and Chandler.** Known collectively as part of the East Valley, these three small cities make up much of the eastern half of metro Phoenix.

4 **Side Trips Near Phoenix.** Venture an hour and a half outside the city to get an authentic taste of the West with dude ranches, villages trapped in time, artists' havens, and luxury retreats.

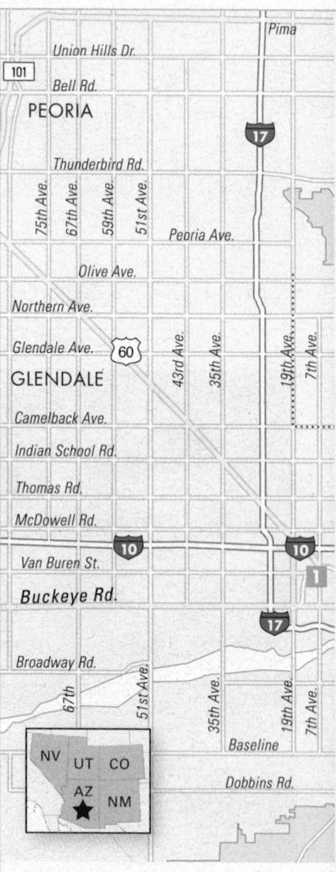

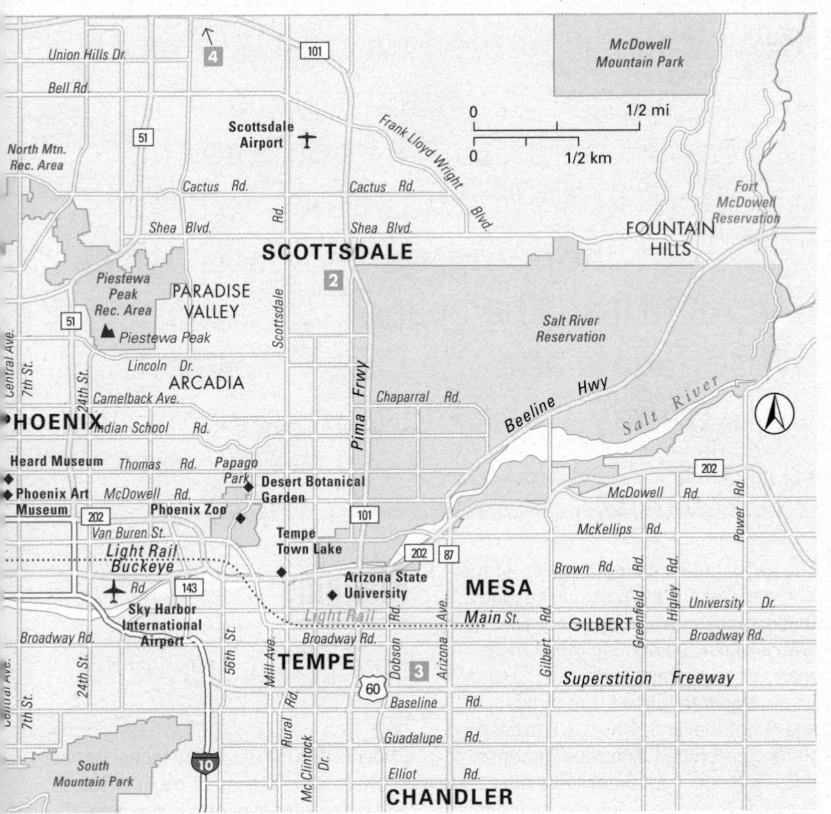
McDowell Mountain Park
Union Hills Dr.
Bell Rd.
101
4
51
Scottsdale Airport
North Mtn. Rec. Area
Frank Lloyd Wright Blvd.
0
1/2 mi
0
1/2 km
Cactus Rd.
Cactus Rd.
Shea Blvd.
Shea Blvd.
Scottsdale Rd.
SCOTTSDALE
2
Fort McDowell Reservation
FOUNTAIN HILLS
Piestewa Peak Rec. Area
PARADISE VALLEY
51
Piestewa Peak
Salt River Reservation
Lincoln Dr.
ARCADIA
Central Ave.
7th St.
24th St.
Camelback Ave.
Pima Frwy
Chaparral Rd.
Beeline Hwy
Salt River
PHOENIX
Indian School Rd.
Heard Museum
Thomas Rd.
Papago Park
Desert Botanical Garden
Phoenix Art Museum
McDowell Rd.
202
McDowell Rd.
Phoenix Zoo
202
101
McKellips Rd.
Power Rd.
Van Buren St.
Tempe Town Lake
Light Rail
Buckeye Rd.
202
87
Brown Rd.
Arizona State University
MESA
143
Sky Harbor International Airport
Light Rail
Main St.
GILBERT
University Dr.
Broadway Rd.
Broadway Rd.
Broadway Rd.
56th St.
Mill Ave.
TEMPE
Dobson Rd.
Arizona Ave.
Gilbert Rd.
Greenfield Rd.
Higley Rd.
3
Superstition Freeway
60
Rural Rd.
Baseline Rd.
Guadalupe Rd.
South Mountain Park
10
Mc Clintock Dr.
Elliot Rd.
CHANDLER

The Valley of the Sun, otherwise known as metro Phoenix (i.e., Phoenix and all its suburbs, including Tempe and Scottsdale), is named for its 325-plus days of sunshine each year. Although many come to Phoenix for the golf and the weather, the Valley has much to offer by way of shopping, outdoor activities, and nightlife. The best of the latter is in Scottsdale and the East Valley with their trendy clubs, old-time saloons, and upscale wine bars.

The Valley marks the northern tip of the Sonoran Desert, a prehistoric seabed that extends into northwestern Mexico with a landscape offering much more than just cacti. Palo verde and mesquite trees, creosote bushes, brittle bush, and agave dot the land, which is accustomed to being scorched by temperatures in excess of 100°F for weeks at a time. Late summer brings precious rain as monsoon storms illuminate the sky with lightning shows and the desert exudes the scent of creosote. Spring sets the Valley blooming, and the giant saguaros are crowned with white flowers for a short time in May—in the evening and cool early mornings—and masses of vibrant wildflowers fill desert crevices and span mountain landscapes.

Planning

Getting Here and Around

AIR

Phoenix Sky Harbor International Airport (PHX) is served by most major airlines and is the largest airport in the area. The Phoenix airport is a 15-minute drive from Downtown Phoenix or Tempe, and 30 minutes from North Scottsdale. Phoenix-Mesa Gateway Airport (AZA) is smaller and serves regional carriers. It's about a 45-minute drive to either Downtown Phoenix or North Scottsdale. SuperShuttle vans service both airports and take up to seven passengers to different destinations. One-way fares from either airport range from about $15 to $50.

CAR

To get around Phoenix, *you will need a car.* Only the major downtown areas of Phoenix, Scottsdale, and Tempe are pedestrian-friendly. Don't expect to nab a rental car without a reservation, especially from January to April.

PUBLIC TRANSPORTATION

The Valley's light-rail system is convenient for exploring Downtown Phoenix museums or the area near Arizona State University. The fare is $4 per day, and multiday passes are available. Phoenix runs a free Downtown Area Shuttle (DASH).

TAXI AND RIDE SHARE

Taxi fares are unregulated in Phoenix, except at the airport. The 800-square-mile metro area is so large that one-way fares in excess of $50 are not uncommon. Except within a compact area, travel by taxi isn't recommended. Taxis charge about $5 for the first mile and $3 per mile thereafter, not including tips. Ride-share services such as Uber and Lyft are widely available and can be cheaper than taxis (or dramtically more expensive during surge periods).

Hotels

With more than 60,000 hotel rooms in the metro area, you can take your pick of anything from a luxurious resort to a guest ranch to an extended-stay hotel.

Resort fees are common, ranging from $20 to $30 per day and covering such amenities as parking, in-room Wi-Fi, daily newspapers, in-room coffee/tea, fitness centers, pools, and more.

Restaurants

Phoenix and its surroundings have metamorphosed into a melting pot for every type of cuisine imaginable: Northern to Tuscan Italian; mom-and-pop to Mexico City Mexican; low-key Cuban to high-end French- and Greek-inspired Southwestern; Japanese- to Spanish-style tapas; and kosher to American classics with subtle ethnic twists.

Many of the best restaurants in the Valley are in resorts, camouflaged behind courtyard walls, or tucked away in shopping malls. Newer, upscale eateries are clustered along the Camelback Corridor—a veritable restaurant row, running west to east from Phoenix to Scottsdale—and in Scottsdale itself. Great Mexican food can be found throughout the Valley, but the most authentic spots are in North Central and South Phoenix.

Show up without a reservation during tourist season (November through mid-March), and you may have to head for a fast-food drive-through window to avoid an hour-long wait for a table.

Hotel and restaurant reviews have been shortened. For full information, visit Fodors.com.

HOTEL AND RESTAURANT PRICES

Hotel prices in the reviews are the lowest cost of a standard double room in high season. Restaurant prices in the reviews are the average cost of a main course at dinner, or if dinner is not served, at lunch.

What It Costs

$	$$	$$$	$$$$
RESTAURANTS			
Under $13	$13–$20	$21–$30	Over $30
HOTELS			
Under $151	$151–$225	$226–$350	Over $350

Tours

Open Road Tours

GUIDED TOURS | This operator offers excursions to Sedona and the Grand Canyon, Phoenix city tours, and Native

American–culture trips to the Salt River Pima–Maricopa Indian Reservation. ☎ *602/997–6474, 855/563–8830* 🌐 *open-roadtoursusa.com* 🎫 *From $79.*

Vaughan's Southwest Tours

GUIDED TOURS | This 4½-hour city tour stops at the Pueblo Grande Museum, Mummy Mountain, and Old Town Scottsdale. Vaughan's tours use custom vans and accommodate groups of up to 11 passengers. The company will also take you east to the Apache Trail, or on day trips north to Sedona or the Grand Canyon. ☎ *602/971–1381, 800/513–1381* 🌐 *www.southwesttours.com* 🎫 *From $70.*

Visitor Information

CONTACTS Experience Scottsdale. ✉ *Scottsdale Fashion Square, 7014 E. Camelback Rd., Camelback Corridor* ✣ *Near food court* ☎ *800/782–1117, 480/421–1004* 🌐 *www.experiencescottsdale.com.* **Greater Phoenix Convention & Visitors Bureau.** ✉ *Phoenix Convention Center West Building, 125 N. 2nd St., Suite 120, Downtown Phoenix* ☎ *877/225–5749, 602/254–6500* 🌐 *www.visitphoenix.com.* **Tempe Tourism.** ✉ *222 S. Mill Ave., Suite 120, Tempe* ☎ *800/283–6734, 480/894–8158* 🌐 *www.tempetourism.com.*

Phoenix

113 miles north of Tucson, 144 miles south of Flagstaff.

The nation's fifth-largest city is a bustling metropolis, still growing past its boundaries. Warm weather, stunning sunsets, year-round golf and sports, and delicious cuisine have beckoned visitors to Phoenix for generations. Despite the modern urban sprawl, the city, particularly its historic central corridor, still retains its charm. Visit a museum or hit the links, enjoy a meal or a drink on a patio, and take in the sunshine. There's a reason it's called the Valley of the Sun.

GETTING HERE AND AROUND

There are lots of parking options in Downtown Phoenix, and they're listed on the free map provided by Downtown Phoenix Partnership, available in many local restaurants (🌐 *www.downtownphoenix.com*). Many Downtown Phoenix sites are served by the light-rail system or the free DASH (Downtown Area Shuttle) bus service. Beyond Downtown Phoenix, you'll really need a car to get around.

Downtown Phoenix

Sights

While Downtown Phoenix used to be a sleepy area that shut down after 5 pm, today it is humming long past midnight year-round. There are restaurants and bars; apartments and loft spaces; cultural and sports facilities, including Jefferson Street's Chase Field and Talking Stick Resort Arena; and large areas for conventions and trade shows. It's retained a mix of past and present, too, as restored homes in Heritage Square, from the original townsite, give an idea of how far the city has come since its inception around the turn of the 20th century.

Arizona Science Center

MUSEUM | **FAMILY** | With more than 300 hands-on exhibits, this is the venue for science-related exploration. You can pilot a simulated airplane flight, travel through the human body, navigate your way through the solar system in the Dorrance Planetarium, and watch a movie in a giant, five-story IMAX theater. ✉ *600 E. Washington St., Downtown Phoenix* ☎ *602/716–2000* 🌐 *www.azscience.org* 🎫 *Museum $20; museum, IMAX, planetarium, and exhibition $44.*

Rosson House Museum

HOUSE | This 1895 Queen Anne Victorian is the queen of Heritage Square. Built by a physician who served a brief term as mayor, it's the sole survivor among fewer than two dozen Victorians erected in Phoenix. It was bought and restored by the city in 1974. ✉ *113 N. 6th St., Downtown Phoenix* ☎ *602/262–5070* 🌐 *www.heritagesquarephx.org* 🎫 *$12* ⏲ *Closed Mon.–Thurs.*

Restaurants

The Arrogant Butcher

$$$ | MODERN AMERICAN | The attention-grabbing name is intentional, as is the in-your-face decor and cuisine of this Downtown Phoenix not-quite-bar, not-quite-restaurant. It's noisy, but that's part of the charm: you'll sit next to couples on their first date, bachelorette parties, families having a reunion, and concertgoers who are prepping their vocal cords for an upcoming show. **Known for:** shareable appetizers; party atmosphere; attentive service. $ *Average main: $23* ✉ *2 E. Jefferson St., Downtown Phoenix* ☎ *602/324–8502* 🌐 *www.foxrc.com/restaurants/the-arrogant-butcher.*

★ Matt's Big Breakfast

$ | AMERICAN | Fresh, filling, and simply fantastic, the food at this itty-bitty, retro cool diner is a great way to start any day, especially when you have time to walk or sleep it off afterward. Ingredients like hearty bacon strips, jams, and whole-grain breads come from local sources, and each one is of the highest quality. **Known for:** extra-thick pancakes; a worthwhile wait for a table; making otherwise simple breakfast food extraordinary. $ *Average main: $11* ✉ *825 N. 1st St., Downtown Phoenix* ☎ *602/254–1074* 🌐 *mattsbigbreakfast.com* ⏲ *No dinner.*

Hotels

★ Kimpton Hotel Palomar Phoenix

$$$$ | HOTEL | Hip and unabashedly quirky, this urban hotel has kicked up Phoenix's cool factor a few notches and offers a compelling reason to stay in Downtown. **Pros:** modern and luxurious furnishings; great Downtown views; attentive staff; evening wine reception; pets welcome. **Cons:** costly parking; rowdy atmosphere could be tiresome; missing the luxe amenities of nearby, grand resorts. $ *Rooms from: $369* ✉ *2 E. Jefferson St., Downtown Phoenix* ☎ *602/253–6633, 877/488–1908* 🌐 *www.hotelpalomar-phoenix.com* 🛏 *242 rooms* 🍽 *No meals.*

Sheraton Phoenix Downtown

$$$ | HOTEL | The grande dame of Downtown Phoenix hotels has positioned itself as the go-to residence of convention goers, but its service and proximity to sports and arts venues make it desirable for leisure travelers as well. **Pros:** can't-beat location within walking distance of almost everything desirable in Downtown; great lobby for lounging or meeting people; high level of personal attention for such a large property. **Cons:** long and impersonal hallways; expensive parking; limited outdoor space. $ *Rooms from: $299* ✉ *340 N. 3rd St., Downtown Phoenix* ☎ *602/262–2500, 866/837–4213* 🌐 *www.sheratonphoenixdowntown.com* 🛏 *1,003 rooms* 🍽 *No meals.*

Nightlife

Fez

BARS/PUBS | This place is a stylish restaurant by day and a LGBTQ+ hot spot by night. The sleek interior and fancy drinks make you feel uptown, while the happy-hour prices and location keep this place grounded. ✉ *105 W. Portland St., Downtown Phoenix* ☎ *602/287–8700* 🌐 *www.fezoncentral.com.*

A
B
C
D
E
F
1
2
3
4
5
6
7
8
9
35th Ave.
19th Ave.
15th Ave.
7th St.
16th St.
Cave Creek Rd.
32nd St.
Tatum Blvd.
Hayden Rhodes Aqueduct
Bell Rd.
Greenway Rd.
Thunderbird Rd.
Cactus Rd.
Peoria Rd.
Dunlap Ave.
Northern Ave.
Glendale Ave.
Bethany Home Rd.
Camelback Rd.
Indian School Rd.
Thomas Rd.
McDowell Rd.
Buckeye Rd.
Lower Buckeye Rd.
Broadway Rd.
Southern Ave.
Baseline Rd.
Dobbins Rd.
Guadalupe Rd.
Lookout Mountain Preserve
Scottsdale Municipal Airport
Black Canyon Fwy.
40th St.
59th St.
64th St.(Invergordon Rd.)
Scottsdale Rd.
Shea Blvd.
Doubletree Ranch Rd.
Piestewa Peak Recreational Area
PARADISE VALLEY
Lincoln Dr.
McDonald Dr.
Central Ave.
Piestewa Peak Freeway
Grand Ave.
24th St.
44th St.
Papago Fwy.
Red Mountain Fwy.
Van Buren St.
DOWNTOWN
Light Rail
Sky Harbor International Airport
Priest Dr.
Mill Ave.
Rural Rd.
Salt River
SOUTH PHOENIX
48th St.
0
2 mi
0
2 km

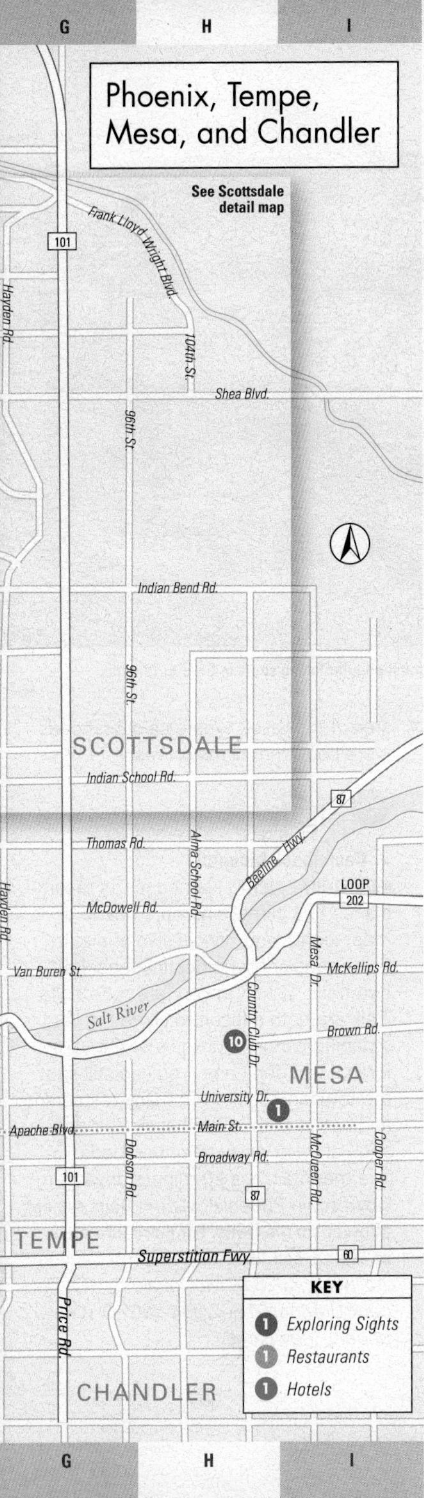

Sights

1 Arizona Museum of Natural History H7
2 Arizona Science Center B7
3 Arizona State University Art Museum F7
4 Camelback Mountain ... E5
5 Deer Valley Petroglyph Preserve A1
6 Desert Botanical Garden F6
7 Hall of Flame E7
8 Heard Museum B6
9 LEGOLAND Discovery Center Arizona E8
10 Mesa Grande Cultural Park H7
11 Mystery Castle C9
12 Phoenix Art Museum... B6
13 Phoenix Zoo F7
14 Pueblo Grande Museum and Archaeological Park E7
15 Rosson House Museum B7
16 South Mountain Park... B9

Restaurants

1 The Arrogant Butcher B7
2 Carolina's Mexican Food C2
3 Chelsea's Kitchen D5
4 Haji Baba F8
5 House of Tricks F7
6 J&G Steakhouse F5
7 Kai E9
8 Lon's at The Hermosa D5
9 Los Dos Molinos B9
10 Matt's Big Breakfast.... B6
11 Pane Bianco B5
12 Richardson's Cuisine of New Mexico C4
13 T. Cook's at the Royal Palms E5

Hotels

1 Arizona Biltmore Resort & Spa D4
2 Arizona Grand Resort ... E9
3 Hermosa Inn D5
4 Hilton Phoenix Resort at the Peak C4
5 JW Marriott Phoenix Desert Ridge Resort & Spa E1
6 Kimpton Hotel Palomar Phoenix B7
7 The Phoenician E5
8 Royal Palms Resort and Spa E5
9 Sanctuary on Camelback Mountain Resort & Spa E4
10 Sheraton Grand at Wild Horse Pass E9
11 Sheraton Phoenix Downtown B6
12 Tempe Mission Palms... F7

The sun rises over Camelback Mountain, one of the most popular hiking spots in Greater Phoenix.

Lux Central

CAFES—NIGHTLIFE | Decorated with local art and retro furniture, Lux is an eclectic gathering place where artists, architects, and Downtown businesspeople enjoy excellent classic European espresso drinks. ✉ *4400 N. Central Ave., Downtown Phoenix* ☎ *602/327–1396* 🌐 *www.luxcoffee.com.*

Majerle's Sports Grill

BARS/PUBS | Operated by former Phoenix Suns basketball player Dan Majerle, this sports bar offers a comprehensive menu for pre- and postgame celebrations as well as some of the best people-watching potential in town. ✉ *24 N. 2nd St., Downtown Phoenix* ☎ *602/253–0118* 🌐 *majerles.com.*

Camelback Corridor

A hub of boutique retail stores, fine dining establishments, and upscale resorts, the Camelback Corridor stretches from North Central Phoenix into Arcadia, Paradise Valley, and Scottsdale. This is a more mature area of the Valley, where neighborhoods were born from citrus groves.

Sights

★ **Camelback Mountain**

MOUNTAIN—SIGHT | Named for its resemblance to a camel's hump, Phoenix's most iconic landmark is also one of its most popular hiking destinations. Its two trails, Echo Canyon Trail and Cholla Trail, are both difficult to climb but lead to stunning panoramic views of the Valley. Even if you don't hike, you can still spot the towering peak from many restaurants and hotels in the Camelback Corridor and Paradise Valley neighborhoods. The mountain is a 20-minute drive from Downtown Phoenix. **TIP→ Dogs are not allowed on the trails. For more information on hiking, see Activities.** ✉ *Echo Canyon Trailhead, 4925 E. McDonald Dr., Camelback Corridor* ☎ *602/534-5867* 🌐 *www.phoenix.gov/parks.*

Restaurants

★ Chelsea's Kitchen

$$$ | **AMERICAN** | With its hip, Pacific Northwest–chic interior and a patio that feels more like a secret garden, Chelsea's Kitchen can easily make you forget you're dining in the desert. Expect a wait on the weekends but don't fret: it's an opportunity to grab a drink on the patio bar. **Known for:** delightfully rowdy patio dining; weekend brunch; changing specials. *Average main: $30* ✉ *5040 N. 40th St., Camelback Corridor* ☎ *602/957–2555* 🌐 *www.chelseaskitchenaz.com.*

★ J&G Steakhouse

$$$$ | **STEAKHOUSE** | This is more than a steak house; it's an experience. The menu changes seasonally, but if you're lucky enough to be here when the sweet-corn ravioli is available, stop, order, and savor. **Known for:** its balcony, one of the most romantic spots in town; fast, quiet service; extensive wine list. *Average main: $47* ✉ *The Phoenician, 6000 E. Camelback Rd., Camelback Corridor* ☎ *480/214–8000* 🌐 *www.jgsteakhousescottsdale.com* ⏲ *No lunch.*

★ T. Cook's at the Royal Palms

$$$$ | **MEDITERRANEAN** | One of the finest restaurants in the Valley, T. Cook's exudes romance, from the floor-to-ceiling windows with dramatic views of Camelback Mountain to its 1930s-style Spanish-colonial architecture and decor. **Known for:** palm trees in dining room that extend through the ceiling; one of the nicest brunches in town; diverse Mediterranean-inspired menu. *Average main: $47* ✉ *Royal Palms Resort & Spa, 5200 E. Camelback Rd., Camelback Corridor* ☎ *602/808–0766* 🌐 *royalpalmshotel.com/tcooks.*

Hotels

Arizona Biltmore Resort & Spa

$$$$ | **RESORT** | Designed by Frank Lloyd Wright's colleague Albert Chase McArthur, the Biltmore has been Phoenix's premier resort since it opened in 1929. **Pros:** centrally located; stately; historic charm. **Cons:** finding a parking spot near your room can be a headache; hard to find lounge chairs at some pools; low ceilings in the resort's more-historic areas. *Rooms from: $519* ✉ *2400 E. Missouri Ave., Camelback Corridor* ☎ *602/955–6600, 800/950–0086* 🌐 *www.arizonabiltmore.com* *738 rooms* *No meals.*

★ The Phoenician

$$$$ | **RESORT** | **FAMILY** | In a town where luxurious, expensive resorts are the rule, the Phoenician still stands apart, primarily in the realm of service. **Pros:** has everything you'd expect from a luxury resort, and then some; highest industry standards; fantastic pools. **Cons:** high prices, even in the off-season; casual, comfortable decor can feel a little skimpy for the price; elevators can be confusing. *Rooms from: $819* ✉ *6000 E. Camelback Rd., Camelback Corridor* ☎ *480/941–8200, 800/888–8234* 🌐 *www.thephoenician.com* *645 rooms* *No meals.*

★ Royal Palms Resort and Spa

$$$$ | **RESORT** | Once the home of Cunard Steamship executive Delos T. Cooke, this Mediterranean-style resort has a stately row of the namesake palms at its entrance, courtyards with fountains, and individually designed rooms that feel more like mini casitas than basic hotel rooms. **Pros:** great for romantic getaways; houses a cozy cigar lounge, renowned restaurant, and open-air spa; impeccable service. **Cons:** expensive; only one pool, and it's small; it's really easy to miss the entrance off of busy Camelback Road. *Rooms from: $499* ✉ *5200 E. Camelback Rd., Camelback Corridor* ☎ *602/840–3610, 800/672–6011* 🌐 *www.royalpalmshotel.com* *119 rooms* *No meals.*

Shopping

Biltmore Fashion Park

SHOPPING CENTERS/MALLS | Macy's, Saks Fifth Avenue, and Ralph Lauren anchor more than 70 stores and upscale boutiques in this posh, parklike setting. It's accessible from the Camelback Esplanade and The Camby hotel by a pedestrian tunnel that runs beneath Camelback Road. ✉ *2502 E. Camelback Rd., Camelback Corridor* ☎ *602/955–8400* 🌐 *www.shopbiltmore.com.*

Cornelia Park

GIFTS/SOUVENIRS | If Alice in Wonderland decided to open a store, this would be it. An eclectic mix of home furnishings, gifts, and touches of whimsy, this boutique is one of the best places in the Valley to find a treasure or a gift. ✉ *Biltmore Fashion Park, 2502 E. Camelback Rd., Camelback Corridor* ☎ *602/955–3195* 🌐 *www.corneliapark.com.*

North Central Phoenix

One of the oldest and most traditional areas of Phoenix, the North Central corridor is located just north of Downtown Phoenix. Decades ago, this was the area Downtown's workers called home. Now that millions call Phoenix home, North Central has a bit of a "frozen in time" quality. Seventh Avenue is a hub for shopping—particularly resale home furnishings and decor. Seventh Street, meanwhile, has emerged as the go-to area for dining. This might be "old Phoenix," but it's thriving.

Sights

Deer Valley Petroglyph Preserve

NATIVE SITE | FAMILY | Any visit to Arizona requires a viewing of petroglyphs, and the Deer Valley Rock Art Center is one of the best in the state. Its proximity to the Valley makes it a no-brainer stop, and it's the largest concentration of ancient petroglyphs in the metropolitan Phoenix area. Some 1,500 of the cryptic symbols are here, left behind by Native American cultures that lived in the Valley (or passed through) during the last 1,000 years. After watching a video about the petroglyphs, pick up a pair of binoculars ($1) and an informative trail map and set out on the ¼-mile path. Telescopes point to some of the most skillful petroglyphs; they range from human and animal forms to more abstract figures. ✉ *3711 W. Deer Valley Rd., Phoenix* ☎ *623/582–8007* 🌐 *shesc.asu.edu/dvpp* 💵 *$9* ⏲ *Closed May–Sept. Closed Sun. and Mon.*

★ **Heard Museum**

MUSEUM | FAMILY | Pioneer settlers Dwight and Maie Heard built a Spanish colonial-style building on their property to house their collection of Southwestern art. Today the staggering collection includes such exhibits as a Navajo hogan dwelling and rooms filled with art, pottery, jewelry, kachinas, and textiles. The Heard also actively supports contemporary Native American artists and displays their work. Annual events include the World Championship Hoop Dance Contest in February and the Indian Fair & Market in March. Children enjoy the interactive art-making exhibits. ■ **TIP→ The museum also has an incredible gift shop with authentic, high-quality goods purchased directly from Native American artists.** ✉ *2301 N. Central Ave., North Central Phoenix* ☎ *602/252–8840* 🌐 *www.heard.org* 💵 *$20* ⏲ *Closed Mon.*

Phoenix Art Museum

MUSEUM | FAMILY | This museum is one of the most visually appealing pieces of architecture in the Southwest. Basking in natural light, the museum makes great use of its modern, open space by tastefully fitting more than 17,000 works of art from around the world—including sculptures by Frederic Remington and paintings by Georgia O'Keeffe, Thomas Moran, and Maxfield Parrish—within its soaring concrete walls. The museum hosts more than 20 significant exhibitions annually and has one of the most acclaimed fashion collections in the country. ✉ *1625 N. Central Ave., North Central Phoenix* ☎ *602/257–1222* 🌐 *www.phxart.org* 🎫 *$25; free Wed. 3–7, 1st Fri. of month 3–7* ⏲ *Closed Mon. and Tues.*

Restaurants

Carolina's Mexican Food
$ | **MEXICAN** | This small, nondescript restaurant in North Phoenix makes the most delicious, thin-as-air flour tortillas imaginable. In-the-know locals have been lining up at Carolina's for years to partake of the homey, inexpensive Mexican food, so it makes sense that she expanded from the original Downtown Phoenix location to let a little more of the Valley in on the action. **Known for:** lines out the door; paper-plate, no-silverware service; one of the most efficient kitchens in town. Ⓢ *Average main: $6* ✉ *2126 E. Cactus Rd., North Central Phoenix* ☎ *602/275–8231* 🌐 *www.carolinasmexicanfood.com* ⏲ *Closed Sun.*

★ **Pane Bianco**
$$ | **ITALIAN** | Chef-owner Chris Bianco is known for his pizza-making skills, but it turns out he creates to-die-for sandwiches, too. This no-frills eatery offers three sandwiches and just as many salads, but don't let the small menu fool you: they're all delicious. **Known for:** walk-in and walk-out brown-bagging; some of the best bread in the city; mozzarella sandwich. Ⓢ *Average main: $14* ✉ *4404 N. Central Ave., North Central Phoenix* ☎ *602/234–2100* 🌐 *www.pizzeriabianco.com* ⏲ *No dinner. Closed Sun.*

★ **Richardson's Cuisine of New Mexico**
$$$$ | **SOUTHWESTERN** | Richardson's lures back locals with heat-filled dishes that test the limits of your palate—but not in a threatening way. This is fine New Mexican cuisine, which means everything (including heat and quality) is ratcheted up about three notches. **Known for:** small, cozy booths; prickly pear margaritas; beef-tenderloin chile relleno. Ⓢ *Average main: $36* ✉ *6335 N. 16th St., North Central Phoenix* ☎ *602/287–8900* 🌐 *richardsonsnm.com.*

Hotels

★ **Hilton Phoenix Resort at the Peak**
$$$ | **RESORT** | **FAMILY** | The highlight of this family-oriented, all-suite hotel is the 9-acre River Ranch Water Park; it has swimming pools with waterfalls, a 130-foot waterslide, and a 1,000-foot "river" that winds past a miniature golf course, tennis courts, and artificial buttes. **Pros:** adjacent to the Phoenix Mountain Preserve, making it an ideal base for hiking and biking trips; affordable alternative to luxury resorts nearby; family-friendly. **Cons:** finding a parking spot can be a challenge; rooms near lobby are noisy; buildings are so spread out, it can be a hike to get a meal. Ⓢ *Rooms from: $229* ✉ *7677 N. 16th St., North Central Phoenix* ☎ *602/997–2626, 800/947–9784* 🌐 *www.hiltonphoenixresortatthepeak.com* *563 units* *No meals.*

Shopping

★ **The Heard Museum Shop**
CRAFTS | The shop at the Heard Museum is hands-down the best place in town for Southwestern Native American and other crafts, both traditional and modern. Prices tend to be high, but quality is assured, with many one-of-a-kind items among the collection of rugs, kachina dolls, pottery, and other crafts; there's also a wide selection of lower-priced gifts. ✉ *2301 N. Central Ave., North Central Phoenix* ☎ *602/252–8840* 🌐 *www.heard.org.*

North Phoenix

Desert Ridge is a bustling area on the far northern edge of Phoenix and Scottsdale. The area developed around 2000, and it's now home to thousands of Valley residents. It's where you'll find the Mayo

Did You Know?

The Heard Museum is a great stop for more than just artifacts and exhibitions. Events, like the Indian Fair & Market, and shopping also showcase Native American art and culture.

Clinic, the Musical Instrument Museum, and Paradise Valley's JW Marriott Desert Ridge Resort & Spa.

JW Marriott Desert Ridge Resort & Spa
$$$$ | **RESORT** | **FAMILY** | Arizona's largest resort has an immense entryway with floor-to-ceiling windows that allow the sandstone lobby, the Sonoran Desert, and the resort's amazing water features to meld together perfectly. **Pros:** perfect for luxuriating with family or groups; close to north Valley restaurants, entertainment, and attractions; so many amenities, there's no need to leave the property. **Cons:** large size makes it a bit impersonal; lots of walking and stairs required to get anywhere; on-site dining has a steep price tag. *Rooms from: $399 ✉ 5350 E. Marriott Dr., North Phoenix ☎ 480/293–5000, 800/835–6206 ⊕ www.jwdesertridgeresort.com 950 rooms No meals.*

Paradise Valley

One of the smallest communities in the Valley of the Sun, Paradise Valley is known to locals as one of the premier places to live. For visitors, it's equally luxurious. Many of the area's finest resorts and restaurants are located here.

Lon's at the Hermosa
$$$$ | **AMERICAN** | In an adobe hacienda hand-built by cowboy artist Lon Megargee, this romantic spot has sweeping vistas of Camelback Mountain and the perfect patio for after-dinner drinks under the stars. Megargee's art and cowboy memorabilia decorate the dining room. **Known for:** quiet, intimate setting; cowboy candy bar dessert; weekend brunch. *Average main: $41 ✉ Hermosa Inn, 5532 N. Palo Cristi Dr., Paradise Valley ☎ 602/955–7878 ⊕ www.hermosainn.com/lons.*

Hermosa Inn
$$$$ | **HOTEL** | On 6 acres of lushly landscaped desert, the Hermosa is a blessedly peaceful alternative to some of the larger resorts nearby. **Pros:** luxurious but cozy; pet-friendly; fantastic restaurant. **Cons:** neighborhood location means you'll have to drive to get anywhere; lacks some luxury amenities of larger resorts nearby; although delicious, only one restaurant. *Rooms from: $399 ✉ 5532 N. Palo Cristi Rd., Paradise Valley ☎ 602/955–8614, 800/241–1210 ⊕ www.hermosainn.com 43 casitas No meals.*

★ **Sanctuary on Camelback Mountain Resort & Spa**
$$$$ | **HOTEL** | This luxurious boutique hotel is the only resort on the north slope of Camelback Mountain; secluded mountain casitas have chic modern furnishings, which contrast with the breathtaking views of Camelback Mountain, the Praying Monk (from some vantages), and the setting western sun. **Pros:** secluded location in one of the most bustling areas of Phoenix; unparalleled views of Camelback's Praying Monk rock; great restaurant, pool, and spa. **Cons:** walking between buildings can mean conquering slopes or flights of stairs; not kid-friendly; grounds very dark at night. *Rooms from: $659 ✉ 5700 E. McDonald Dr., Paradise Valley ☎ 480/948–2100, 800/245–2051 ⊕ www.sanctuaryoncamelback.com 116 rooms No meals.*

Shopping

★ **Cosanti Originals**
CRAFTS | This is the studio where architect Paolo Soleri's famous bronze and ceramic wind chimes are made and sold. You can watch the craftspeople at work, then pick out your own—prices are surprisingly reasonable. *✉ 6433 Doubletree Ranch*

Rd., Paradise Valley ☎ *800/752–3187, 480/948–6145* 🌐 *www.cosanti.com.*

Papago Park

A historic and cultural hub for the Valley, Papago Park showcases the history—and the exceptional urban planning—of the Valley of the Sun. It's home to the tomb of George W. P. Hunt, Arizona's first governor, as well as one of the city's largest parks, the Phoenix Zoo, the Desert Botanical Garden, and hundreds of acres for recreation.

Sights

★ Desert Botanical Garden

GARDEN | FAMILY | Opened in 1939 to conserve and showcase the ecology of the desert, these 150 acres contain more than 4,000 different species of cacti, succulents, trees, and flowers. A stroll along the ½-mile "Plants and People of the Sonoran Desert" trail is a fascinating lesson in environmental adaptations. Kid-centric activity areas encourage tactile play and exploration. Specialized tours are available at an extra cost; check online for times and prices. **■ TIP→ The Desert Botanical Garden stays open late, to 8 pm year-round, and it's particularly lovely when lighted by the setting sun or by moonlight. You can plan for a cool, late visit after a full day of activities.** ✉ *1201 N. Galvin Pkwy., Phoenix* ☎ *480/941–1225* 🌐 *www.dbg.org* 🎫 *$15.*

Hall of Flame

MUSEUM | FAMILY | Retired firefighters lead tours through nearly 100 restored fire engines and tell harrowing tales of the "world's most dangerous profession." The museum has the world's largest collection of firefighting equipment, and children can climb on a 1916 engine, operate alarm systems, and learn fire safety from the pros. Helmets, badges, and other firefighting-related articles from as far back as 1725 are on display. ✉ *6101 E. Van Buren St., Phoenix* ☎ *602/275–3473* 🌐 *www.hallofflame.org* 🎫 *$10* ⏲ *Closed Sun. and Mon.*

Phoenix Zoo

ZOO | FAMILY | Four designated trails wind through this 125-acre zoo, replicating such habitats as an African savanna and a tropical rain forest. Meerkats, warthogs, desert bighorn sheep, and the endangered Arabian oryx are among the species here. The zoo is full of interactive stops for kids of all sizes. Harmony Farm introduces youngsters to small mammals, and a stop at the Big Red Barn petting zoo provides a chance to interact with goats, cows, and more. **■ TIP→ In December the zoo stays open late (until 10) for the popular "ZooLights" exhibit, which transforms the area into an enchanted forest of more than 225 million twinkling lights, many in the shape of the zoo's residents.** Starry Safari Friday Nights in summer are fun, too. ✉ *455 N. Galvin Pkwy., Phoenix* ☎ *602/273–1341* 🌐 *www.phoenixzoo.org* 🎫 *$25.*

South Phoenix

Although Phoenix has grown well outside its municipal borders, there still are plenty of historical sites to visit close to Downtown Phoenix and near Phoenix Sky Harbor airport.

Sights

Mystery Castle

HOUSE | FAMILY | At the foot of South Mountain lies a curious dwelling built from desert rocks by Boyce Gulley, who came to Arizona to cure his tuberculosis. Full of fascinating oddities, the castle has 18 rooms with 13 fireplaces, a downstairs grotto tavern, and a quirky collection of Southwestern antiques. The pump organ belonged to Elsie, the "Widow of Tombstone," who buried six husbands under suspicious circumstances. ✉ *800 E. Mineral Rd., South Phoenix*

The Mystery Castle in South Phoenix is full of quirky, unusual artifacts.

☎ 602/268–1581 ⊕ www.mymystery-castle.com 🎫 $10 ⏲ Closed June–Sept. Closed Mon.–Wed.

Pueblo Grande Museum and Archaeological Park

ARCHAEOLOGICAL SITE | FAMILY | Phoenix's only national landmark, this park was once the site of a 500-acre Hohokam village supporting about 1,000 people and containing homes, storage rooms, cemeteries, and ball courts. Three exhibition galleries hold displays on the Hohokam culture and archaeological methods. View the 10-minute orientation video before heading out on the ½-mile Ruin Trail past excavated sites that give a hint of Hohokam savvy: there's a building whose corner doorway was perfectly placed for watching the summer-solstice sunrise. Children especially like the hands-on interactive learning center. Guided tours by appointment only. *✉ 4619 E. Washington St., South Phoenix ☎ 602/495–0900 ⊕ phoenix.gov/parks/arts-culture-history/pueblo-grande 🎫 $6 ⏲ May–Sept. closed Sun. and Mon.*

South Mountain Park

NATIONAL/STATE PARK | The world's largest city park (almost 17,000 acres) offers a wilderness of mountain-desert trails for hikers, bikers, and horseback riders—and a great place to view sunsets. The Environmental Center has a model of the park as well as displays detailing its history, from the time of the ancient Hohokam people to gold seekers. Roads climb past picnic ramadas constructed by the Civilian Conservation Corps, winding through desert flora to the trailheads. Look for ancient petroglyphs, try to spot a desert cottontail rabbit or chuckwalla lizard, or simply stroll among the desert vegetation. Maps of all scenic drives as well as hiking, mountain biking, and horseback trails are available at the Gatehouse Entrance just inside the park boundary. *✉ 10919 S. Central Ave., South Phoenix ☎ 602/495–5458 ⊕ www.phoenix.gov/parks 🎫 Free.*

Restaurants

Just a few minutes from Downtown Phoenix, South Phoenix includes one of the most heralded Mexican restaurants in Los Dos Molinos.

Los Dos Molinos

$$ | **MEXICAN** | This fun restaurant is a must-do dining experience if you want true New Mexican–style food. New Mexico chiles form the backbone and fiery breath of the dishes here. **Known for:** "You order it, you own it" menu warning; La Rosa margaritas to cool your mouth; hacienda setting with outdoor seating. *Average main: $14 ⊠ 8646 S. Central Ave., South Phoenix ☎ 602/243–9113 ⊕ losdosmolinosphoenix.com ⊙ Closed Sun. and Mon.*

Hotels

Arizona Grand Resort

$$$$ | **RESORT** | **FAMILY** | This beautiful all-suites resort next to South Mountain Park is home to Oasis, one of the largest water parks in the country, and one of the Valley's more challenging golf courses. **Pros:** great family or large-group location; all rooms are suites; plenty of activities to entertain you. **Cons:** huge property can be overwhelming; freeway noise could be a problem in some rooms; lacking in luxury. *Rooms from: $369 ⊠ 8000 S. Arizona Grand Pkwy., South Phoenix ☎ 602/438–9000, 866/267–1321 ⊕ www.arizonagrandresort.com 744 suites No meals.*

Activities

The mountains surrounding the Valley of the Sun are among its greatest assets, and outdoors enthusiasts have plenty of options within the city limits to pursue hiking, bird-watching, or mountain-biking passions. Piestewa Peak, north of Downtown Phoenix, is popular with hikers, and Camelback Mountain and the Papago Peaks are landmarks between Phoenix and the East Valley. South of Downtown are the much less lofty peaks of South Mountain Park, which separates the Valley from the rest of the Sonoran Desert.

Central Arizona's dry desert heat imposes particular restraints on outdoor endeavors—even in winter, hikers and cyclists should wear lightweight opaque clothing, a hat or visor, and high UV–rated sunglasses, and should carry a quart of water for each hour of activity. The intensity of the sun makes strong sunscreen (SPF 30 or higher) a must, and don't forget to apply it to your hands and feet. **TIP→ From May 1 to October 1 you shouldn't jog or hike from one hour after sunrise until a half hour before sunset.** During these times the air is so hot and dry that your body will lose moisture at a dangerous, potentially lethal rate. And keep your eyes peeled in natural desert areas; rattlesnakes and scorpions could be on the prowl.

BALLOONING

A sunrise or sunset hot-air-balloon ascent is a remarkable desert sightseeing experience. The average fee is $200 per person, and hotel pickup is usually included. Because flight paths and landing sites vary with wind speed and direction, a roving land crew follows each balloon in flight. Time in the air is generally between 1 and 1½ hours, but allow 3 hours for the total excursion.

★ Hot Air Expeditions

BALLOONING | This is the best ballooning in Phoenix. Flights are long, the staff are charming, and the gourmet snacks, catered by the acclaimed Vincent restaurant, are out of this world. *⊠ Phoenix ☎ 480/502–6999, 800/831–7610 ⊕ www.hotairexpeditions.com From $179.*

FOUR-WHEELING

Taking a jeep through the backcountry has become a popular way to experience the desert's saguaro-covered mountains and curious rock formations.

Baseball's Spring Training

For dyed-in-the-wool baseball fans there's no better place than the Valley of the Sun. Baseball has become nearly a year-round activity in the Phoenix area, beginning with spring training in late February and continuing through the Arizona Fall League championships in mid-November.

Spring

Today the Cactus League consists of 15 Major League teams that play at stadiums across the Valley. Ticket prices are reasonable, around $15 for bleacher seats and $20 to $30 for reserved seats. Many stadiums have lawn-seating areas in the outfield where you can spread a blanket and bring a picnic. Cactus League stadiums are more intimate than big-league parks, and players often come right up to the stands to say hello and to sign autographs.

Tickets for some teams go on sale as early as December. Brochures listing game schedules and ticket information are available from the **Cactus League**'s website (*www.cactusleague.com*).

Summer

During the regular Major League season, the hometown Arizona Diamondbacks (*www.azdiamondbacks.com*) play on natural grass at Chase Field in the heart of Downtown Phoenix. The stadium is a technological wonder; if the weather's a little too warm outside, they close the roof and turn on gigantic air-conditioners. You can tour the stadium except on afternoon-game days and holidays.

Fall

At the conclusion of the regular season, the Arizona Fall League runs until the week before Thanksgiving. Each major-league team sends six of its most talented young prospects to compete with other young promising players—180 players in all. There are six teams in the league, broken down into two divisions. It's a great way to see future Hall of Famers in their early years. Tickets for Fall League games are $8.

Call **Scottsdale Stadium** (*480/312–2586*), one of the league's host sites, for ticket information.

Desert Dog Offroad Adventures

FOUR-WHEELING | This operator heads out on half- and full-day Humvee, dune buggy, and ATV tours to the Four Peaks Wilderness Area in Tonto National Forest and the Sonoran Desert. *480/837–3966* *www.azadventures.com* *From $145.*

Wild West Jeep Tours

FOUR-WHEELING | Special permits allow Wild West Jeep Tours to conduct four-wheel excursions in Tonto National Forest, which, in addition to a wild ride, lets you also visit 1,000-year-old Native American sites. *480/922–0144* *www.wildwestjeeptours.com* *From $99.*

GOLF

Arizona has more golf courses per capita than any other state west of the Mississippi River, making it one of the most popular golf destinations in the United States. The sport is also one of Arizona's major industries, and greens fees can run from $35 at a public course to more than $500 at some of the premier golfing spots. Pricing can vary greatly—online reservation systems automatically adjust pricing by demand, day of the week, hour, and even the weather. New courses seem to pop up routinely: there are more than 200 in the Valley (some lighted at night), and the PGA's Southwest section has its headquarters here.

PUBLIC COURSES

Hillcrest Golf Club

GOLF | With 18 holes on 179 acres of well-designed turf, Hillcrest Golf Club is the best course in the Sun Cities. ✉ *20002 Star Ridge Dr., Sun City West* ☎ *623/584–1500* 🌐 *www.hillcrestgolfclub.com* 🎫 *$70* ⛳ *18 holes, 7002 yards, par 72.*

RESORT COURSES

Arizona Biltmore Country Club

GOLF | The granddaddy of Valley golf courses, Arizona Biltmore Country Club has two 18-hole PGA championship courses, lessons, and clinics. ✉ *Arizona Biltmore Resort & Spa, 24th St. and Missouri Ave., Camelback Corridor* ☎ *602/955–9655* 🌐 *www.arizonabiltmore.com* 🎫 *$159* ⛳ *Adobe: 18 holes, 6430 yards, par 71; Links: 18 holes, 6300 yards, par 71.*

Camelback Golf Club

GOLF | Challenging water holes and layouts make the two 18-hole courses at the JW Marriott's Camelback Golf Club among the best in the area. ✉ *JW Marriott Camelback Inn, 7847 N. Mockingbird La., Paradise Valley* ☎ *480/948–1700* 🌐 *www.camelbackinn.com* 🎫 *Padre $259, Ambiente $299* ⛳ *Padre: 18 holes, 6903 yards, par 72; Ambiente: 18 holes, 7221 yards, par 72.*

★ The Phoenician Golf Club

GOLF | Set at the base of Camelback Mountain, the Phoenician's Phil Smith-designed course debuted in 2018 and is one of the most aesthetically beautiful courses in the Valley. ✉ *The Phoenician, 6000 E. Camelback Rd., Camelback Corridor* ☎ *480/941–8200* 🌐 *www.thephoenician.com* 🎫 *$250* ⛳ *18 holes, 6518 yards, par 71.*

HIKING

One of the best ways to see the beauty of the Valley of the Sun is from above, so hikers of all calibers seek a vantage point in the mountains surrounding the flat Valley. A short drive from Downtown Phoenix, South Mountain Park is the jewel of the city's mountain park preserves, with more than 60 miles of marked trails for hikers, horseback riders, and mountain bikers. **■ TIP→ No matter the season, be sure to bring sunscreen, a hat, plenty of water, and a camera to capture a dazzling sunset. It's always a good idea to tell someone where you'll be and when you plan to return.**

Piestewa Peak

HIKING/WALKING | Just north of Lincoln Drive, Piestewa Peak has a series of trails for all levels of hikers. It's a great place to get views of Downtown Phoenix. Allow about 1½ hours for each direction. *Moderate.* ✉ *2701 E. Piestewa Peak Dr., North Central Phoenix* ☎ *602/262–6862* 🌐 *www.phoenix.gov/parks.*

HORSEBACK RIDING

More than two dozen stables and equestrian-tour outfitters in the Valley attest to the saddle's enduring importance in Arizona—even in this auto-dominated metropolis. Stables offer rides for an hour, a whole day, and even overnight adventures. Some local resorts can arrange for lessons on-site or at nearby stables.

Ponderosa Stables

HORSEBACK RIDING | Enjoy your South Mountain experience from a higher perch by renting horses at this nearby stable. The private company rents its land from the City of Phoenix, and will take you on an excursion or send you on one of your own. ✉ *10215 S. Central Ave., South Phoenix* ☎ *602/268–1261* 🌐 *www.arizona-horses.com* 🎫 *From $40.*

Scottsdale

Scottsdale is 12 miles (19 km) northeast of Phoenix.

Reveling in its reputation as the "West's Most Western Town," Scottsdale prides itself in its roots—dude ranches, cowboy-boot outfitters, and horseback riding. But don't fool yourself: this is a luxury traveler's paradise. Fine resorts, world-class dining, manicured golf courses, a thriving arts community, and some of the best (and most expensive) shopping in the state make Scottsdale an adult's playground.

Nationally known art galleries, souvenir shops, and a funky Old Town fill downtown Scottsdale. Visit Native American jewelry and crafts stores, or hobnob with the international art set at galleries and interior-design shops.

GETTING HERE AND AROUND

Although your tour of the downtown area can easily be completed on foot, there's a regular, free trolley service (☎ *480/312–3111* 🌐 *www.scottsdaleaz.gov/trolley*).

Central Scottsdale

The West's Most Western Town earned its nickname largely because of central Scottsdale, a collection of art galleries, cowboy hat and boot outfitters, and some of the finest dining in the Valley of the Sun.

Restaurants

Chez Vous

$ | **BISTRO** | An authentic French creperie tucked into a Scottsdale shopping center, Chez Vous transports just enough Paris to make diners say "Merci" instead of "Thank you" throughout the meal. Owners Richard and Isabelle Horvath make and serve the food, and their accents are undeniably legit. **Known for:** locals trying to speak French with the owners; rubbernecking to see what other diners ordered; crepes, quiche, and tartes. $ *Average main: $11* ✉ *8787 N. Scottsdale Rd., Central Scottsdale* ☎ *480/433–2575* ⏲ *Closed Mon. No dinner.*

Rancho Pinot

$$$$ | **ECLECTIC** | The attention to quality here makes this one of the town's most lauded dining spots. The minimalist cowboy decor and almost secret-handshake location are forgotten upon the first bite of food and replaced with tastebud heaven. **Known for:** seeing your meal prepared in the open kitchen; neighborhood vibe, despite its Valley-wide draw; locally grown ingredients. $ *Average main: $31* ✉ *6208 N. Scottsdale Rd., Central Scottsdale* ✣ *Northwest of Trader Joe's in Lincoln Village Shops* ☎ *480/367–8030* 🌐 *www.ranchopinot.com* ⏲ *Closed Sun. and Mon. May–Sept., and 1st 2 wks of July. No lunch.*

Hotels

★ **Hyatt Regency Scottsdale Resort and Spa at Gainey Ranch**

$$$$ | **RESORT** | **FAMILY** | While staying here, it's easy to imagine that you're relaxing at an oceanside resort instead of in the desert; shaded by towering palms and with manicured gardens and paths, the property has water everywhere—a large pool area has a beach, three-story waterslide, waterfalls, and a lagoon. **Pros:** gondola rides at night; oasis atmosphere; live entertainment in the lobby bar. **Cons:** if you're early to bed, avoid a room near the lobby; it's enormous; frustrating parking lot logistics. $ *Rooms from: $379* ✉ *7500 E. Doubletree Ranch Rd., Central Scottsdale* ☎ *480/444–1234* 🌐 *scottsdale.regency.hyatt.com* *493 rooms* *No meals.*

Shopping

Scottsdale Marketplace

ANTIQUES/COLLECTIBLES | One of the largest antiques stores in the Valley, this marketplace has more than three dozen privately run booths that feature Asian and French antiques, furnishings, housewares, and a large selection of Western goods. ✉ *6310 N. Scottsdale Rd., Central Scottsdale* ☎ *480/368–5720* 🌐 *scottsdalemarketplace.com.*

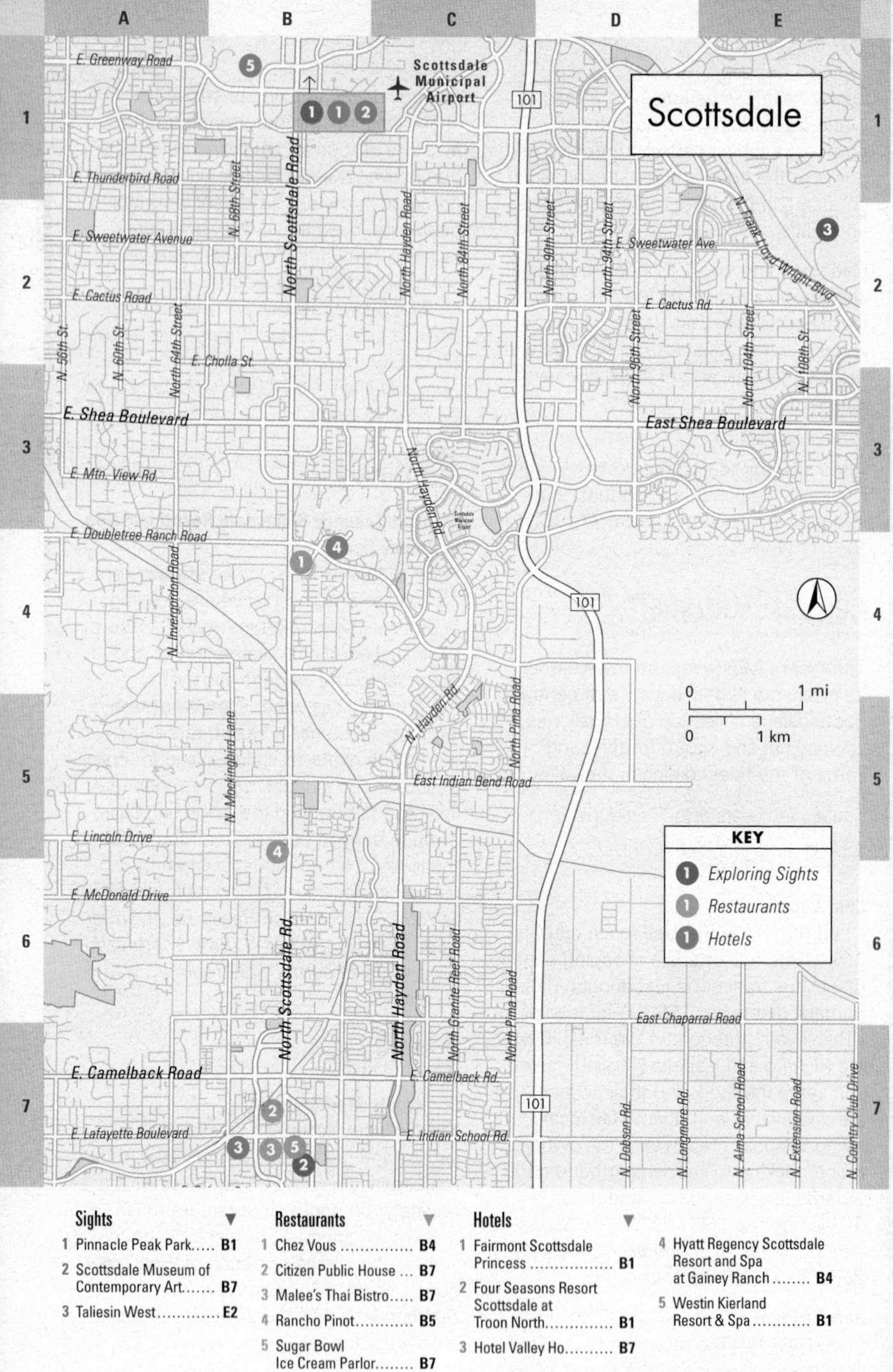

Sights

1 Pinnacle Peak Park..... **B1**

2 Scottsdale Museum of Contemporary Art....... **B7**

3 Taliesin West............. **E2**

Restaurants

1 Chez Vous **B4**

2 Citizen Public House ... **B7**

3 Malee's Thai Bistro..... **B7**

4 Rancho Pinot............ **B5**

5 Sugar Bowl Ice Cream Parlor........ **B7**

Hotels

1 Fairmont Scottsdale Princess **B1**

2 Four Seasons Resort Scottsdale at Troon North.............. **B1**

3 Hotel Valley Ho.......... **B7**

4 Hyatt Regency Scottsdale Resort and Spa at Gainey Ranch **B4**

5 Westin Kierland Resort & Spa **B1**

North Scottsdale

Away from the bustle of Old Town and the city center, North Scottsdale is a haven for hikers and adventure seekers as well as those who value luxury. It's home to some of the area's finest restaurants and, unsurprisingly, the priciest real estate around.

Sights

★ Pinnacle Peak Park

TRAIL | This popular trailhead with jaw-dropping views of the Valley is a good spot to picnic, rock climb, bike, or hike in a beautiful desert environment. The moderately difficult trail is 3.5 miles out and back, winding up a mountain strewn with boulders and towering saguaro cacti. **TIP→ Dogs are not allowed on the trail. For more information on hiking, see Activities.** ✉ *26802 N. 102nd Way, North Scottsdale* ☎ *480/312–0990* 🌐 *www.scottsdaleaz.gov/parks.*

★ Taliesin West

HOUSE | Ten years after visiting Arizona in 1927 to consult on designs for the Biltmore hotel, architect Frank Lloyd Wright chose 600 acres of rugged Sonoran Desert at the foothills of the McDowell Mountains as the site for his permanent winter residence. Today it's a National Historic Landmark. Wright and apprentices constructed a desert camp here using organic architecture to integrate the buildings with their natural surroundings. In addition to the living quarters, drafting studio, and small apartments of the Apprentice Court, Taliesin West has two theaters, a music pavilion, and the Sun Trap—sleeping spaces surrounding an open patio and fireplace. Five guided tours are offered, ranging from a 90-minute "insights" tour to a three-hour behind-the-scenes tour, with other tours offered seasonally; all visitors must be accompanied by a guide. **TIP→ Wear comfortable shoes for walking.** To reach Taliesin West, drive north on the 101 Freeway to Frank Lloyd Wright Boulevard. Follow Frank Lloyd Wright Boulevard for a few miles to the entrance at the corner of Cactus Road. ✉ *12621 Frank Lloyd Wright Blvd., North Scottsdale* ☎ *888/516–0811, 480/860–2700* 🌐 *franklloydwright.org/taliesin-west* 🎫 *$38–$75.*

Hotels

Fairmont Scottsdale Princess

$$$$ | **RESORT** | **FAMILY** | Home of the Tournament Players Club Stadium golf course and the Phoenix Open, this resort covers 450 breathtakingly landscaped acres of desert. **Pros:** upscale favorite, especially for families; excellent spa and rooftop pool; some of the city's best restaurants are here. **Cons:** sprawling campus can be difficult to navigate; a bit far from popular Scottsdale attractions; shade is a limited commodity around pools and paths. $ *Rooms from: $699* ✉ *7575 E. Princess Dr., North Scottsdale* ☎ *480/585–4848* 🌐 *www.scottsdaleprincess.com* *750 rooms* *No meals.*

★ Four Seasons Resort Scottsdale at Troon North

$$$$ | **RESORT** | A resort in every sense of the word, Four Seasons Scottsdale is tucked in the shadows of Pinnacle Peak, near the popular hiking trail, and features large, casita-style rooms with separate sitting and sleeping areas as well as fireplaces and balconies or patios. **Pros:** amazing service; breathtaking views; peaceful, calm atmosphere. **Cons:** far from everything; awkward parking situation necessitates valet service; very dark at night. $ *Rooms from: $680* ✉ *10600 E. Crescent Moon Dr., North Scottsdale* ☎ *480/515–5700, 866/207–9696* 🌐 *www.fourseasons.com/scottsdale* *210 rooms* *No meals.*

★ Westin Kierland Resort & Spa

$$$$ | **RESORT** | **FAMILY** | Original artwork by Arizona artists is displayed throughout the public spaces of the Westin Kierland,

Frank Lloyd Wright's Taliesin West

More than just an artist's retreat and workshop, Taliesin West and the surrounding desert still inspire both visitors and architects who study here. Frank Lloyd Wright once said, "The desert abhors the straight, hard line." Though much of Wright's most famed work is based on such lines, this sprawling compound takes its environment into consideration as few desert structures do. Taliesin West mirrors the jagged shapes and earthen colors of its mountain backdrop and desert surroundings. Even Wright's interior pieces of "origami" furniture assume the mountain's unpredictable shapes.

Arizona Inspiration

Wright first came to Phoenix from Wisconsin in 1927 to act as a consultant to architect Albert Chase McArthur on the now famed Arizona Biltmore. Later Wright was also hired to design a new hotel in what is currently Phoenix South Mountain Park. Wright and his working entourage returned to the Valley and, instead of residing in apartments, they built a camp of asymmetrical cabins with canvas roofs that maximized but pleasantly diffused light, and blended into the rugged mountain backdrop.

When the hotel project failed due to the stock market crash of 1929, Wright and his crew returned to Taliesin, his Wisconsin home and site of his architectural fellowship, and the camp was disassembled and carted away. But the concept of his humble worker village would remain in Wright's creative consciousness, and a decade later the renowned architect found an appropriate plot of land north of Scottsdale.

Natural Construction

Built upon foundations of caliche, known as nature's own concrete, and painted in crimson and amber hues that highlight the "desert masonry," the buildings seem to adhere naturally to the landscape. The asymmetrical roofs resemble those of Wright's South Mountain camp and were covered with canvas for many years before Wright added glass. Supported by painted-steel-and-redwood beams, they face the sun-filled sky like the hard shell of a desert animal that seems to be comfortable here despite all the odds against its survival.

Architectural Legacy

The more-than-80-year-old property and its structures, which Wright envisioned as a "little fleet of ships," are perhaps some of the best nonnative examples of organic architecture. They also serve as desert building blocks for future generations of Wright protégés—some perhaps schooled on these very grounds—to balance man and Mother Nature.

and the spacious rooms have balconies or patios with views of the mountains or the resort's water park and tubing river. **Pros:** on-site Scotch library; walking distance to Kierland Commons boutiques and restaurants; fantastic children's programs. **Cons:** rooms lack personality; adults' pool very close to kids' area; steep parking prices. $ *Rooms from: $409* ✉ *6902 E. Greenway Pkwy., North Scottsdale* ☎ *480/624–1000, 800/354–5892* 🌐 *www.kierlandresort.com* *732 rooms* *No meals.*

Taliesin West was Frank Lloyd Wright's winter residence. The original Taliesin in Wisconsin was his summer home.

Old Town

One of the most pedestrian-friendly areas of the Valley, Old Town Scottsdale is great for travelers. Stroll by (or through) art galleries and souvenir shops, saddle up to a bar, or feast on some of the area's most beloved cuisine.

Sights

Scottsdale Museum of Contemporary Art
MUSEUM | SMoCA, the Scottsdale Museum of Contemporary Art is often referred to as a "museum without walls." There's a good museum store here for unusual jewelry and stationery, posters, and art books. New installations are planned every few months, with an emphasis on contemporary art, architecture, and design. *7374 E. 2nd St., Old Town 480/874–4666 smoca.org $10, free Thurs. and second Sat. each month Closed Mon.*

Restaurants

Citizen Public House
$$$$ | MODERN AMERICAN | With its hip Scottsdale address, central see-and-be-seen bar, and—most important—its menu of modern twists on traditional favorites, this place is the epitome of "cool." While the entrées are finger-licking good, you can enjoy one of the best meals of your life by simply ordering a series of appetizers to share. Don't-miss items include the pork belly spätzle and the mac 'n' cheese with gorgonzola and Emmental. **Known for:** bacon-fat popcorn; a libations menu that goes well beyond cosmos and Manhattans; chopped salad with a side of Phoenix culinary history. *Average main: $35 711 E. 5th Ave., Old Town 480/398–4208 www.citizenpublichouse.com No lunch.*

Malee's Thai Bistro
$$ | THAI | This cozy but fashionable eatery in the heart of Scottsdale's Main Street Arts District serves sophisticated, Thai-inspired fare. Try the crispy *pla*: flash-fried

whitefish fillets with fresh cilantro and sweet jalapeño garlic sauce. **Known for:** a Valley institution for nearly 30 years; often the first stop in a night of reveling in Old Town; Arizona heat-wave red curry. *Average main: $19 7131 E. Main St., Old Town 480/947–6042 www.maleesonmain.com Closed Sun.*

★ Sugar Bowl Ice Cream Parlor
$ | **DINER** | **FAMILY** | This iconic Scottsdale destination transports you back in time to a 1950s malt shop, complete with great burgers and lots of yummy ice-cream confections. **Known for:** iconic Family Circus cartoons on the walls; the "Spectacular Banana Bowl," which children try in vain to conquer; being one of the few spots that hasn't changed in decades. *Average main: $9 4005 N. Scottsdale Rd., Old Town 480/946–0051 www.sugarbowlscottsdale.com.*

Hotels

Hotel Valley Ho
$$$ | **HOTEL** | When it originally opened in 1956, this hotel was a hangout for celebrities, including Natalie Wood, Robert Wagner, and Tony Curtis, but it remains a hot spot today, especially the main pool. **Pros:** retro decor; great history; trendy, youthful style. **Cons:** busy location; occasionally rowdy weekend crowd; the retro vibe can feel a bit dated, too. *Rooms from: $299 6850 E. Main St., Old Town 480/248–2000, 866/882–4484 www.hotelvalley-ho.com 241 rooms No meals.*

Nightlife

Salty Senorita
BARS/PUBS | This spot is known more for its extensive margarita selection and lively patio crowd than for its food. The restaurant-bar touts 51 different margaritas—with some recipes so secret they won't tell you what goes in them. Try the El Presidente or the Chupacabra. *3748 N. Scottsdale Rd., Old Town 480/947–2116 www.saltysenorita.com.*

Shopping

Main Street Arts District
SHOPPING NEIGHBORHOODS | Gallery after gallery displays artwork in myriad styles—contemporary, Western realism, Native American, and traditional. Several antiques shops are also here; specialties include porcelain and china, jewelry, and Oriental rugs. *Old Town Bounded by Main St. and 1st Ave., Scottsdale Rd. and 69th St.*

★ Wilde Meyer Gallery
ART GALLERIES | With locations in Scottsdale and Tucson, this is the place to go for the true colors of the Southwest. In addition to one-of-a-kind paintings, the galleries also feature rustic, fine-art imports from around the state and the world, including furniture, sculptures, and jewelry. *4142 N. Marshall Way, Old Town 480/945–2323 wildemeyer.com.*

Activities

GOLF

Tournament Players Club of Scottsdale
GOLF | This 36-hole course is the site of the PGA Waste Management Phoenix Open, which takes place in January/February. *Fairmont Scottsdale Princess Resort, 17020 N. Hayden Rd., North Scottsdale 480/585–4334, 888/400–4001 www.tpc.com Stadium $300, Champions $175 Stadium: 18 holes, 7261 yards, par 71; Champions: 18 holes, 7115 yards, par 71.*

★ Troon North
GOLF | Long considered one of the finest golf courses in the country, a visit to Troon North is a must for any golfer that wants to experience a desert course. The multimillion-dollar views add to the experience at this perfectly maintained 36-hole course. *10320 E. Dynamite Blvd., North Scottsdale 480/585–7700 www.troonnorthgolf.com $275 Monument: 18 holes, 7039 yards, par 72; Pinnacle: 18 holes, 7009 yards, par 71.*

Old Town Scottsdale's waterfront is lined with shops and restaurants.

HIKING

Lost Dog Wash Trail

HIKING/WALKING | Part of the continually expanding McDowell Sonoran Preserve (🌐 *www.mcdowellsonoran.org*), Lost Dog Wash Trail is a mostly gentle 4½-mile round trip that will get you away from the bustle of the city in a hurry. The trailhead has restrooms and a map that shows a series of trails for varying skill levels. *Easy.* ✉ *12601 N. 124th St., north of Shea Blvd., North Scottsdale* ☎ *480/312–7013* 🌐 *www.scottsdaleaz.gov/preserve.*

★ Pinnacle Peak Trail

HIKING/WALKING | This is a well-maintained trail offering a moderately challenging 3½-mile round-trip hike—or a horseback experience for those who care to round one up at the local stables. Interpretive programs and trail signs along the way describe the geology, flora, fauna, and cultural history of the area. *Moderate.* ✉ *26802 N. 102nd Way, North Scottsdale* ✣ *1 mile south of Dynamite and Alma School Rds.* ☎ *480/312–0990* 🌐 *www.scottsdaleaz.gov/parks/pinnacle-peak-park.*

Tempe, Mesa, and Chandler

Tempe is 11 miles (18 km) southeast of Phoenix.

Tempe, Mesa, and Chandler are part of the East Valley, a term for the collection of suburbs located east of Phoenix. Because of their close proximity and similarities, it helps to think of them as one area. The East Valley is a great destination for families traveling with children. It has excellent museums and cultural centers—and also happens to be home to the finest restaurant in the state.

Most notably, Tempe is the home of Arizona State University's main campus and a thriving student population. A 20-minute drive from Phoenix, tree- and brick-lined Mill Avenue is the main drag, filled with student hangouts, bookstores, boutiques, eateries, and a repertory movie house. There are always things to do or see, and plenty of music venues and fun, casual dining spots.

The banks of the Rio Salado in Tempe are the site of a commercial and entertainment district, and Tempe Town Lake—a 2-mile-long waterway created by inflatable dams in a flood-control channel—which is open for boating. There are biking and jogging paths on the perimeter.

Mesa, Arizona's third-largest city, has long been considered Phoenix's underachieving sibling. Today, it's making a name for itself. An arts center—reachable by the Valley's light-rail system—showcases theatre, dance, singers and comedians nightly. And its museums offer a closer look into Arizona and its ancient history.

Chandler, another suburb of the East Valley, is home to the annual Ostrich Festival, casinos, and fine restaurants.

GETTING HERE AND AROUND

Street parking is hard to find, especially amid all the construction, but there are plenty of public parking garages. Some merchants validate parking for reduced parking charges. The Orbit free shuttle does a loop around Arizona State University, with stops at Mill Avenue and Sun Devil Stadium. The light rail also stops at 3rd Street and Mill Avenue.

Sights

Arizona State University and nearby Mill Avenue are the heart of Tempe. Stroll along Mill, and you'll see Tempe in a nutshell: students, galleries, clubs and bars, and independent shops. It's also the location of some of the Valley's most inspired architecture. The inverted pyramid that is Tempe City Hall, on 5th Street, one block east of Mill Avenue, was constructed by local architects Rolf Osland and Michael Goodwin not just to win design awards (which they have), but also to shield city workers from the desert sun. The pyramid is built mainly of bronzed glass and stainless steel, and the point disappears in a sunken courtyard lushly landscaped with jacaranda, ivy, and flowers, out of which the pyramid widens to the sky; stand underneath and gaze up for a weird fish-eye perspective.

Arizona Museum of Natural History

MUSEUM | FAMILY | Kids young and old get a thrill out of the largest collection of dinosaur fossils in the state. You can also pan for gold and see changing exhibits from around the world. ✉ *53 N. Macdonald St., Mesa* ☎ *480/644–2230* 🌐 *arizonamuseumofnaturalhistory.org* 🎫 *$12* 🕑 *Closed Mon.*

Arizona State University Art Museum

MUSEUM | This museum is in the gray-purple stucco Nelson Fine Arts Center, just north of Gammage Auditorium on the Arizona State campus. For a relatively small museum, it has an extensive collection, including 19th- and 20th-century paintings and sculptures by masters such as Winslow Homer, Edward Hopper, Georgia O'Keeffe, and Rockwell Kent. Works by faculty and student artists are also on display, and there's a gift shop. ✉ *Nelson Fine Arts Center, Mill Ave. and 10th St., Tempe* ☎ *480/965–2787* 🌐 *asuartmuseum.asu.edu* 🎫 *Free* 🕑 *Closed Sun. and Mon.*

LEGOLAND Discovery Center Arizona

AMUSEMENT PARK/WATER PARK | FAMILY | Imagine thousands of square feet full of LEGO bricks, and not having to clean up any of them. No, it's not a dream—it's LEGOLAND. Kids can see giant LEGO creations as well as play, build, and watch. ■ **TIP→ Buy a dual ticket with the adjoining Sea Life Arizona Aquarium and save on admission.** ✉ *Arizona Mills, 5000 Arizona Mills Cir., Tempe* ☎ *855/450–0558* 🌐 *arizona.legolanddiscoverycenter.com* 🎫 *$25.*

Mesa Grande Cultural Park

ARCHAEOLOGICAL SITE | FAMILY | Unpreserved in the middle of the city for years, this amazing, six-acre historic site features a group of Hohokam structures dating to 1400–1100 BC. Once protected only by locals and the occasional landowner, it's now operated by the Arizona Museum of Natural History. ✉ *1000 N. Date St., Mesa* ☎ *480/644–3075* 🌐 *arizonamuseumofnaturalhistory.org* 🎟 *$5* ⏲ *Closed mid-May–mid-Oct. Closed Mon. and Tues.*

Restaurants

Home to Arizona State University, Tempe is synonymous with college energy. Mill Avenue is a hub of clubs, movie theaters, and restaurants. Nearby Chandler is home to one of the best restaurants in the Greater Phoenix area.

Haji Baba

$ | **MIDDLE EASTERN** | This casual treasure is a hole-in-the-wall Middle Eastern favorite that gets consistent rave reviews. The reasonably priced menu includes hummus, *lebni* (fresh cheese made from yogurt), fabulous falafel, gyros, shawarma, and kebab plates, all served by a friendly and efficient staff. **Known for:** feeding a decent percentage of ASU faculty; the grocery store, almost as busy as the restaurant; hearty servings of chicken shawarma. 💲 *Average main: $10* ✉ *1513 E. Apache Blvd., Tempe* ☎ *480/894–1905* ⏲ *No dinner Sun.*

★ House of Tricks

$$$ | **CONTEMPORARY** | There's nothing up the sleeves of Robert and Robin Trick, who work magic on their ever-changing eclectic menu. One of the Valley's most unusual dining venues, the restaurant encompasses an utterly charming 1920s home and a separate brick-and-adobe-style house originally built in 1903, adjoined by an intimate wooden deck and outdoor patio shaded by a canopy of grapevines and trees. **Known for:** idyllic location in the middle of a college campus; outdoor patio dining under twinkling lights; menu that adapts to the season and the whims of the chef. 💲 *Average main: $27* ✉ *114 E. 7th St., Tempe* ☎ *480/968–1114* 🌐 *www.houseoftricks.com* ⏲ *Closed Sun.*

★ Kai

$$$$ | **SOUTHWESTERN** | One of the finest restaurants in all of the Valley, the prestigious Kai ("seed" in the Pima language) uses indigenous ingredients from local tribal farms to create innovative Southwestern cuisine. The seasonal menu reflects the restaurant's natural setting on the Gila River Indian Community. **Known for:** unparalleled, orchestrated service that's worth a drive to Chandler; a "dinner and a show" experience with every meal; huge windows that show off mountain and desert views at sunset. 💲 *Average main: $53* ✉ *Sheraton Grand at Wild Horse Pass, 5594 W. Wild Horse Pass Blvd., Chandler* ☎ *602/225–0100* 🌐 *www.wildhorsepass.com* ⏲ *Closed Sun.–Tues. No lunch.*

Hotels

Sheraton Grand at Wild Horse Pass

$$$$ | **RESORT** | **FAMILY** | The culture and heritage of the Pima and Maricopa tribes are reflected in every aspect of this tranquil property on the grounds of the Gila River Indian community, 11 miles south of Sky Harbor Airport. **Pros:** great views and service; peaceful; good for families and older travelers looking to escape urban chaos. **Cons:** conferences can sometimes overrun the place; beautiful hand-hewn guest-room doors are loud when they slam shut; long walk to reach most guest rooms from the lobby. 💲 *Rooms from: $379* ✉ *5594 W. Wild Horse Pass Blvd., Chandler* ☎ *602/225–0100* 🌐 *www.wildhorsepass.com* *500 rooms* *No meals.*

Tempe Mission Palms

$$$$ | **HOTEL** | A handsome, casual lobby and an energetic young staff set the tone at this three-story courtyard hotel with comfortable, Southwestern-style rooms. **Pros:** nice hotel with friendly service and a rooftop pool; right at the center of ASU

and Mill Avenue activity; mere minutes from the airport. **Cons:** all that activity can be bad for light sleepers; a bit dated overall; few amenities. *Rooms from: $359* ✉ *60 E. 5th St., Tempe* ☎ *480/894–1400, 800/547–8705* 🌐 *www.destinationhotels.com/tempe-mission-palms* *303 rooms* *No meals.*

Saba's Western Wear

CLOTHING | For nearly 100 years, the Saba family has outfitted Arizonans and visitors alike with authentic Western wear. Just a single store remains, in downtown Chandler, but it's worth a drive if you're searching for boots and authentic cowboy garb including jeans, shirts, and belts. If you can't find a boot here, you're just not made for them. ✉ *67 W. Boston St., Chandler* ☎ *480/963–4496* 🌐 *www.sabasofchandler.com.*

GOLF

Ocotillo Golf Club

GOLF | There's water in play on nearly all 27 holes at Ocotillo Golf Club, which was designed around 95 acres of man-made lakes. ✉ *3751 S. Clubhouse Dr., Chandler* ☎ *480/917–6660* 🌐 *www.ocotillogolf.com* *$119* *Blue/Gold: 18 holes, 7016 yards, par 72; White/Gold: 18 holes, 6804 yards, par 71; Blue/White: 18 holes, 6782 yards, par 71.*

HORSEBACK RIDING

★ **OK Corral Stables**

HORSEBACK RIDING | Half-, one-, two-, and four-hour horseback trail rides and steak cookouts are available from this company, which also runs one- to three-day horse-packing trips. They have the oldest pack station in the history of the Superstition Mountains, and all their guides are U.S. Forest Service–licensed. ✉ *5470 E Apache Trail, Apache Junction* ☎ *480/982–4040* 🌐 *www.okcorrals.com* *From $40.*

Side Trips Near Phoenix

There are a number of interesting sights within a 1- to 1½-hour drive of Phoenix. To the north, the thriving artist communities of Carefree and Cave Creek are popular Western attractions. Arcosanti and Wickenburg are half- or full-day trips from Phoenix. Stop along the way to visit the petroglyphs of Deer Valley Rock Art Center and the reenactments of Arizona territorial life at the Pioneer Living History Village. You also might consider Arcosanti and Wickenburg as stopovers on the way to or from Flagstaff, Prescott, or Sedona.

South of Phoenix, an hour's drive takes you back to prehistoric times and the site of Arizona's first known civilization at Casa Grande Ruins National Monument, a vivid reminder of the Hohokam who began farming this area more than 1,500 years ago.

Pioneer Living History Village

25 miles north of Downtown Phoenix.

It's easy to wonder what places in Arizona were like 100 years ago or more. A trip to the Pioneer Living History Village provides an answer. Here you can get a glimpse at 19th-century desert living.

GETTING HERE AND AROUND

Take Interstate 17 north from Downtown Phoenix for 25 miles. Just north of Carefree Highway (AZ 74), take Exit 225, and turn left on Pioneer Road to get to the entrance.

Pioneer Living History Museum

MUSEUM VILLAGE | FAMILY | This museum contains 28 original and reconstructed buildings from throughout territorial Arizona. Costumed guides filter through the bank, schoolhouse, jail, and print shop, as well as the Pioneer Opera House, where classic melodramas are performed

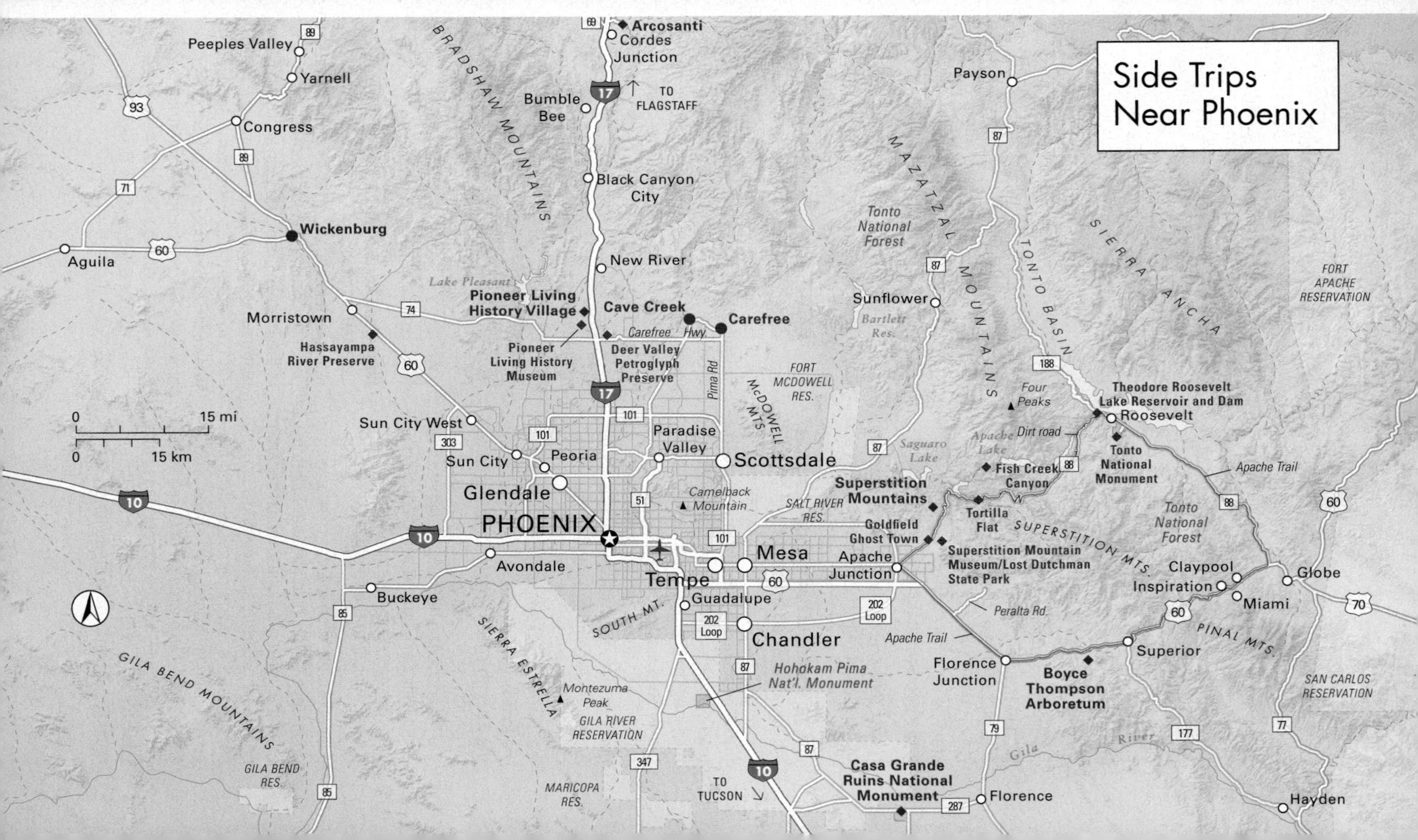

Side Trips Near Phoenix
Arcosanti
Cordes Junction
TO FLAGSTAFF
Peeples Valley
Yarnell
Congress
Bumble Bee
Black Canyon City
BRADSHAW MOUNTAINS
Wickenburg
Aguila
New River
Lake Pleasant
Pioneer Living History Village
Cave Creek
Carefree
Carefree Hwy.
Morristown
Hassayampa River Preserve
Pioneer Living History Museum
Deer Valley Petroglyph Preserve
Pima Rd
FORT McDOWELL RES.
McDOWELL MTS
Sun City West
Sun City
Peoria
Paradise Valley
Scottsdale
Glendale
Camelback Mountain
PHOENIX
Avondale
Mesa
Tempe
Guadalupe
Chandler
Buckeye
SOUTH MT.
SALT RIVER RES.
SIERRA ESTRELLA
Montezuma Peak
GILA RIVER RESERVATION
Hohokam Pima Nat'l. Monument
GILA BEND MOUNTAINS
GILA BEND RES.
MARICOPA RES.
TO TUCSON
Casa Grande Ruins National Monument
Florence
Florence Junction
Boyce Thompson Arboretum
Superior
Apache Junction
Apache Trail
Peralta Rd.
Goldfield Ghost Town
Superstition Mountains
Superstition Mountain Museum/Lost Dutchman State Park
SUPERSTITION MTS.
Tortilla Flat
Fish Creek Canyon
Saguaro Lake
Apache Lake
Dirt road
Four Peaks
Sunflower
Bartlett Res.
Tonto National Forest
MAZATZAL MOUNTAINS
Payson
TONTO BASIN
SIERRA ANCHA
Theodore Roosevelt Lake Reservoir and Dam
Roosevelt
Tonto National Monument
Tonto National Forest
Claypool
Inspiration
Miami
Globe
PINAL MTS.
FORT APACHE RESERVATION
SAN CARLOS RESERVATION
Hayden
Gila River
0 15 mi
0 15 km

daily. It's popular with the grade-school field-trip set, and it's your lucky day if you can tag along for their tour of the site. ✉ *3901 W. Pioneer Rd., Pioneer* ☎ *623/465–1052* 🌐 *www.pioneeraz.org* *$10* ⏱ *Closed Mon. and Tues.*

Cave Creek and Carefree

30 miles north of Downtown Phoenix.

Some 30 miles north of Phoenix, resting high in the Sonoran Desert at an elevation of 2,500 feet, the towns of Cave Creek and Carefree hearken back to a lifestyle far different from that of their more populous neighbors to the south.

Cave Creek got its start with the discovery of gold in the region. When the mines and claims "played out," the cattlemen arrived, and the sounds of horse hooves and lowing cattle replaced those of miners' picks. The area grew slowly and independently from Phoenix to the south, until a paved road connected the two in 1952. Today the mile-long main stretch of town on Cave Creek Road is a great spot to have some hot chili and cold beer, try on Western duds, or learn the two-step in a "cowboy" bar. You're likely to run into folks dressed in cowboy hats, boots, and bold belt buckles. Horseback riders and horse-drawn wagons have the right of way here, and the 25 mph speed limit is strictly enforced by county deputies. You can amble up the hill and rent a horse for a trip into the Tonto National Forest in search of some long-forgotten native petroglyphs, or take a jeep tour out to the forest.

Just about the time the dirt-road era ended in Cave Creek, planners were sketching out a new community, which became neighboring Carefree. The world's largest sundial, at the town's center, is surrounded by galleries, artists' workshops, and cafés. Today Cave Creek and Carefree sit cheek by jowl—but the former has beans, beef, biscuits, and beer, while the latter doesn't hesitate to flaunt its luxury.

GETTING HERE AND AROUND

Follow Interstate 17 north of Downtown Phoenix for 15 miles. Exit at Carefree Highway (AZ 74) and turn right, then go 12 miles. Turn left onto Cave Creek Road and go 3 miles to downtown Cave Creek, then another 4 miles on Cave Creek Road to Carefree. Pick up maps and information about the area at the Chamber of Commerce.

VISITOR INFORMATION

CONTACTS Carefree–Cave Creek Chamber of Commerce. ✉ *748 Easy St., Carefree* ☎ *480/488–3381* 🌐 *www.carefree-cavecreek.org.*

Sights

Cave Creek Museum

MUSEUM | Exhibits at the Cave Creek Museum depict pioneer living, mining, and ranching. See an original 1920s tuberculosis cabin and a collection of artifacts from the Hohokam and Yavapai tribes. ✉ *6140 E. Skyline Dr., Cave Creek* ☎ *480/488–2764* 🌐 *www.cavecreekmuseum.org* *$7* ⏱ *Closed June–Sept. Closed Sat.–Tues.*

Frontier Town

NEIGHBORHOOD | **FAMILY** | The pseudo-Western Frontier Town has wooden sidewalks, ramshackle buildings, and souvenir shops. ✉ *6245 E. Cave Creek Rd., Cave Creek* *Free.*

Restaurants

Horny Toad Restaurant

$$$ | **AMERICAN** | Cave Creek's oldest restaurant is a rustic spot for barbecued pork ribs and steak, but the real star is the fried chicken. The quirky menu features a range of fare from soup "de joor" to Icelandic cod and carne asada. **Known for:** kid-friendly environment; a bit of a Cave Creek–meets–Woodstock feel; homemade barbecue sauce. $ *Average main: $22* ✉ *6738 E. Cave Creek Rd.,*

Cave Creek ☎ 480/488–9542 🌐 www.thehornytoad.com.

Hotels

★ Boulders Resort & Spa

$$$$ | RESORT | One of the country's top resorts hides amid hill-size, 12-million-year-old granite boulders and the picturesque Sonoran Desert. **Pros:** remote desert getaway; even standard accommodations are luxurious; exceptional service, spa, and golfing. **Cons:** on-site dining is priced above average; minimum 45-minute drive to Phoenix attractions; few non-pool-related dining options for a resort of its caliber. *Rooms from: $429 ✉ 34631 N. Tom Darlington Dr., Carefree ☎ 480/488–9009, 888/579–2631 🌐 www.theboulders.com 218 units No meals.*

Activities

The Boulders Golf Club

GOLF | There are two championship 18-hole courses at this club, which has one of the most unique settings in the Valley. The Jay Morrish–designed courses wind around the granite boulders for which the resort is named. *✉ Boulders Resort & Spa, 34631 N. Tom Darlington Dr., Carefree ☎ 480/488–9009, 888/579–2631 🌐 www.theboulders.com $259 North Course: 18 holes, 6959 yards, par 72; South Course: 18 holes, 6917 yards, par 71.*

Spur Cross Stables

HORSEBACK RIDING | FAMILY | Well-cared-for horses will take you on one- to six-hour rides to the high Sonoran Desert of the Spur Cross Preserve and the Tonto National Forest. Some rides include visits to petroglyph sites and a saddlebag lunch. *✉ 44029 Spur Cross Rd., Cave Creek ☎ 480/488–9117, 800/758–9530 🌐 arizonahorsebackadventures.com From $50.*

Wickenburg

70 miles northwest of Downtown Phoenix.

This town, land of guest ranches and tall tales, is named for Henry Wickenburg, whose nearby Vulture Mine was the richest gold strike in the Arizona Territory. In the late 1800s Wickenburg was a booming mining town on the banks of the Hassayampa River, with a seemingly endless supply of gold, copper, and silver. Nowadays Wickenburg's Old West history attracts visitors hoping to awaken their inner cowboy to its guest ranches.

GETTING HERE AND AROUND

Follow Interstate 17 north from Phoenix for about 15 miles to the Carefree Highway (AZ 74) junction. About 30 miles west on AZ 74, take U.S. 89/93 north and go another 10 miles to Wickenburg.

Maps for self-guided walking tours of the town's historic buildings are available at the Wickenburg Chamber of Commerce, in the town's old Santa Fe Depot.

VISITOR INFORMATION

CONTACTS Wickenburg Chamber of Commerce. *✉ 216 N. Frontier St., Wickenburg ☎ 928/684–5479 🌐 www.wickenburg-chamber.com.*

Sights

Desert Caballeros Western Museum

MUSEUM | FAMILY | One of the best collections of Western art in the nation includes paintings and sculpture by Frederic Remington, Albert Bierstadt, Joe Beeler (founder of the Cowboy Artists of America), and others. Kids enjoy the re-creation of a turn-of-the-20th-century Main Street that includes a general store, period clothing, and a large collection of cowboy gear. *✉ 21 N. Frontier St., Wickenburg ☎ 928/684–2272 🌐 www.westernmuseum.org $12 Closed Mon. June–Aug.*

The Superstition Mountains are dotted with scrub as well as soaring saguaro cactus.

Hassayampa River Preserve

NATURE PRESERVE | Self-guided trails wind through lush cottonwood-willow forests, mesquite trees, and around a 4-acre, spring-fed pond and marsh habitat. Waterfowl, herons, and Arizona's rarest raptors shelter here. ✉ *49614 U.S. 60, Wickenburg* ✣ *3 miles southeast of Wickenburg* ☎ *928/684–2772* 🌐 *maricopacountyparks.net* 🎟 *$5* 🕒 *Closed Mon.–Wed.*

Jail Tree

JAIL | Prisoners were chained to this now 200-year-old mesquite tree on the northeast corner of Wickenburg Way and Tegner Street. The desert heat sometimes finished them off before their sentences were served. ✉ *Wickenburg.*

Restaurants

Anita's Cocina

$$ | **MEXICAN** | A favorite for locals or those just passing through, Anita's Cocina serves reliable Mexican fare including fresh tamales for lunch or dinner and warm, sugary *sopapillas* (piping-hot, fried pastry pillows) for dessert. **Known for:** the spot for dinner in Wickenburg; charming Western decor; tamales. $ *Average main: $13* ✉ *57 N. Valentine St., Wickenburg* ☎ *928/684–5777* 🌐 *www.anitascocina.com.*

Hotels

★ Rancho de los Caballeros

$$$$ | **RESORT** | **FAMILY** | This 20,000-acre property combines the guest-ranch experience with first-class amenities. **Pros:** large rooms, casitas, and suites; abundant activity roster; a great place for family gatherings. **Cons:** remote location; long hikes to rooms; might not interest those who don't like golf or horseback riding. $ *Rooms from: $495* ✉ *1551 S. Vulture Mine Rd., Wickenburg* ☎ *928/684–5484, 800/684–5030* 🌐 *www.ranchodeloscaballeros.com* 🕒 *Closed mid-May–early Oct.* 🛏 *79 rooms* 🍽 *All meals.*

Arcosanti

65 miles north of Downtown Phoenix.

Off the beaten path near Cordes Junction is the unusual community started by Italian architect Paolo Soleri, Arcosanti. Tourists visit partially to stretch their legs and see the grounds, but mostly to buy a sought-after wind chime.

GETTING HERE AND AROUND
From Phoenix, take Interstate 17 north 65 miles to Exit 262 (Cordes Junction). Follow the partly paved road 2½ miles northeast to the community.

Sights

Arcosanti
TOWN | The evolving complex and community of Arcosanti was masterminded by Italian architect Paolo Soleri to be a self-sustaining habitat in which architecture and ecology function in symbiosis. Building began in 1970, but Arcosanti hasn't quite achieved Soleri's original vision. It's still worth a stop to take a tour, have a bite at the café, and purchase one of the hand-cast bronze wind bells made on-site. ✉ *Arcosanti* ✥ *2 miles off I–17 and Exit 263 (Arcosanti Rd.)* ☎ *928/632–7135* 🌐 *www.arcosanti.org* 🎫 *Tour $15.*

Casa Grande Ruins National Monument

36 miles southeast of Downtown Phoenix.

Visitors have been fascinated by Casa Grande Ruins for more than 300 years, and it's no wonder. The buildings are a marvel of not just architecture, but also ancient astronomy.

GETTING HERE AND AROUND
Take U.S. 60 (Superstition Freeway) east to Florence Junction (U.S. 60 and AZ 89), and head south 16 miles on AZ 89 to Florence. Casa Grande is 9 miles west of Florence on AZ 287 or, from Interstate 10, 16 miles east on AZ 387 and AZ 87. Note: follow signs to the ruins, not to the town of Casa Grande. When leaving the ruins, take AZ 87 north 35 miles back to U.S. 60.

Sights

Casa Grande Ruins National Monument
ARCHAEOLOGICAL SITE | This site, whose original purpose still eludes archaeologists, was unknown to European explorers until Father Kino, a Jesuit missionary, first recorded the site's existence in 1694. The area was set aside as federal land in 1892 and named a national monument in 1918. Although only a few prehistoric sites can be viewed, more than 60 are in the monument area, including the 35-foot-tall—that's four stories—Casa Grande (Big House). The tallest known Hohokam building, Casa Grande was built in the early 14th century and is believed by some to have been an ancient astronomical observatory or a center of government, religion, trade, or education. Allow an hour to explore the site, longer if park rangers are giving a talk or leading a tour. On your way out, cross the parking lot by the covered picnic grounds and climb the platform for a view of a ball court and two platform mounds, said to date from the 1100s. ✉ *1100 W. Ruins Dr., Coolidge* ☎ *520/723–3172* 🌐 *www.nps.gov/cagr* 🎫 *Free.*

Superstition Mountains

30 miles east of Downtown Phoenix.

Folklore abounds in the Superstition Mountains, where visitors have sought treasure from the Lost Dutchman Mine for generations.

GETTING HERE AND AROUND
From Phoenix, take Interstate 10 and then U.S. 60 (the Superstition Freeway) east through the suburbs of Tempe, Mesa, and Apache Junction.

Sights

Goldfield Ghost Town

GHOST TOWN | FAMILY | Goldfield became an instant town of about 4,000 residents after a gold strike in 1892; it dried up five years later when the gold mine flooded. Today the Goldfield Ghost Town is an interesting place to grab a cool drink, pan for gold, go for a mine tour, or take a desert jeep ride or horseback tour of the area. The ghost town's shops and saloon are open daily and gunfights are held on weekends. ✉ *4650 N. Mammoth Mine Rd., Goldfield* ✥ *4 miles northeast of Apache Junction on AZ 188* ☎ *480/983–0333* 🌐 *goldfieldghosttown.com* 🎫 *Free.*

Lost Dutchman State Park

MOUNTAIN—SIGHT | As the Phoenix metro area gives way to cactus- and creosote-dotted desert, the massive escarpment of the Superstition Mountains heaves into view and slides by to the north. The Superstitions are supposedly where the legendary Lost Dutchman Mine is, the location—not to mention the existence—of which has been hotly debated since pioneer days. ✉ *5470 N. Apache Trail, Apache Junction* 🌐 *azstateparks.com/lost-dutchman* 🎫 *$7 per vehicle.*

Superstition Mountain Museum

MUSEUM | FAMILY | The best place to learn about the "Dutchman" Jacob Waltz and the Lost Dutchman Mine is at Superstition Mountain Museum. Exhibits include a collection of mining tools, historical maps, and artifacts relating to the "gold" age of the Superstition Mountains. ✉ *4087 N. Apache Trail (AZ 188), Apache Junction* ☎ *480/983–4888* 🌐 *superstitionmountainmuseum.org* 🎫 *$5.*

Activities

Peralta Trail

HIKING/WALKING | The 4-mile round-trip Peralta Trail winds 1,400 feet up a small valley for a spectacular view of **Weaver's Needle,** a monolithic rock formation that is one of Arizona's more famous sights. Allow a few hours for this rugged and challenging hike, bring plenty of water, sunscreen, a hat, and a snack or lunch. Don't hike it in the middle of the day in summer. *Moderate.* ✉ *Goldfield.*

Boyce Thompson Arboretum

60 miles east of Downtown Phoenix, 30 miles southeast of the Peralta Trail.

If all that cacti get overwhelming, take a trip about an hour outside of Phoenix to the Boyce Thompson Arboretum, where you'll find a wonderland of exotic plants. Desert plants and tropical birds make this oasis worth the visit.

GETTING HERE AND AROUND

From Florence Junction, take U.S. 60 east for 12 miles.

Sights

Boyce Thompson Arboretum

GARDEN | At the foot of Picketpost Mountain in Superior, the Boyce Thompson Arboretum is often called an oasis in the desert: the arid rocky expanse gives way to lush riparian glades home to 3,200 different desert plants and more than 230 bird and 72 terrestrial species. The arboretum offers a living album of the world's desert and semiarid region plants, including exotic species such as Canary Islands date palms and Australian eucalyptus. Trails offer breathtaking scenery in the gardens and the exhibits, especially during the spring wildflower season. A variety of tours are offered year-round. Benches with built-in misters offer relief from the heat. Bring along a picnic and enjoy the beauty. ✉ *37615 U.S. 60, mile marker 223, Superior* ☎ *520/689–2723* 🌐 *www.btarboretum.org* 🎫 *$15.*

Chapter 10

TUCSON AND SOUTHERN ARIZONA

Updated by
Mara Levin

Sights ★★★★☆ Restaurants ★★★★☆ Hotels ★★★★☆ Shopping ★★★☆☆ Nightlife ★★★☆☆

WELCOME TO TUCSON AND SOUTHERN ARIZONA

TOP REASONS TO GO

★ **Towering Saguaro:** Unique to this region, the saguaro is the quintessential symbol of the Southwest. See them at Sabino Canyon and Saguaro National Park.

★ **Mexican Food:** Tucson boasts that it's the "Mexican Food Capital of the United States," and you won't be disappointed at any of the authentic restaurants.

★ **Arizona-Sonora Desert Museum:** Anyone who thinks that museums are boring hasn't been here, where you can learn about the region's animals, plants, and geology up close in a gorgeous, mostly outdoor setting.

★ **Hiking in the Chirachuas:** Stunning "upsidedown" rock formations, flourishing wildlife, and relatively easy trails make for great hiking in this unspoiled region.

★ **Bisbee:** Board the Queen Mine train and venture into the life of a copper miner at the turn of the last century. Afterward check out the narrow, hilly town's Victorian houses and thriving shops.

1 **Tucson.** Arizona's second-largest city is both a bustling center of business and development and a laid-back university and resort town, with abundant hiking trails and nature preserves.

2 **Saguaro National Park.** Hillsides of stately saguaro cacti dominate the land in the East and West sections of this National Park; the West district also has petroglyphs.

3 **Side Trips Near Tucson.** The ASARCO Mineral Discovery Center, Titan Missile Museum, artist colony of Tubac, Madera Canyon, and Tumacácori National Historic Park are easy excursions.

4 **Tombstone.** Channel your inner cowboy in this well-preserved western town with saloons, stagecoach rides, and a courthouse.

5 **Bisbee.** A picturesque mining town-turned-artist-colony, Bisbee is brimming with history and architecture, as well as shopping and nightlife.

6 **Chiracahua National Monument.** Stunning rock formations and abundant wildlife are a draw for hikers and birders in this remote southeast region.

7 **Texas Canyon.** These rocky hillsides, where the Apaches and their leader, Cochise, reigned, can be explored by foot or on horseback.

8 **Karchner Caverns.** Touring one of the only living cave systems in the world is a unique experience.

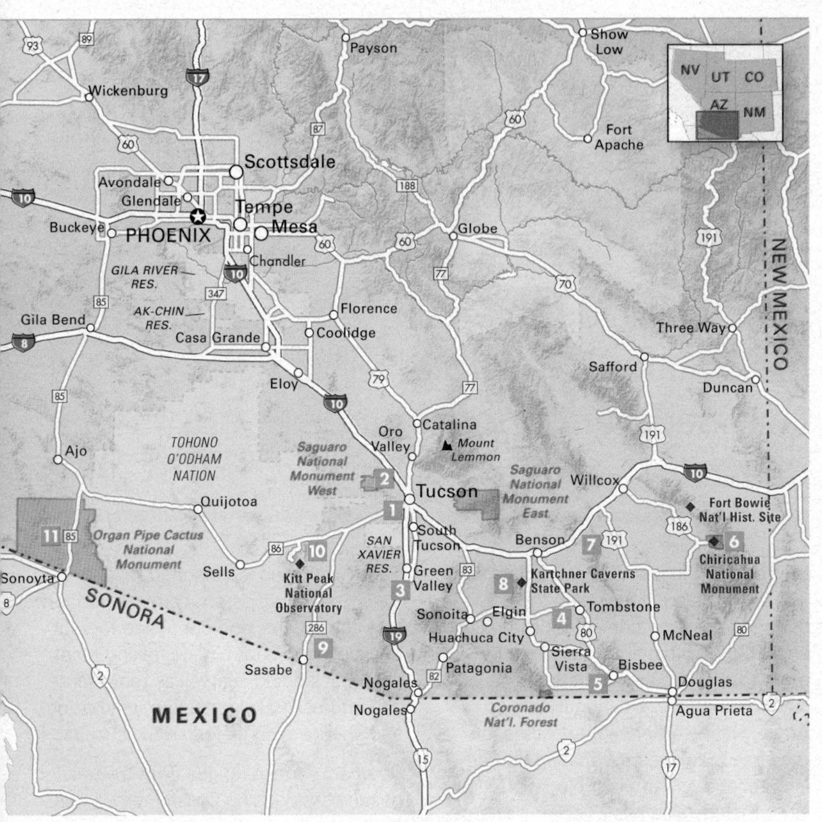

9 Buenos Aires National Wildlife Refuge. You won't have much human company while birding and hiking in this tranquil spot.

10 Kitt Peak National Observatory. Stargaze with telescopes used by top astronomers on this isolated peak on the Tohono O'odham nation.

11 Organ Pipe Cactus National Monument. Rare and beautiful Organ Pipe cacti are copious in this isolated area near the Mexican border.

12 Yuma. Halfway between the Phoenix and the California coast, Yuma (aka "The Lettuce Capital") is a pleasant city on the Colorado River.

13 Imperial National Wildlife Refuge. Hiking, birding, fishing, and hunting are popular in this refuge north of Yuma.

The "Old Pueblo," as Tucson is affectionately known, is built upon a deep Native American, Spanish, Mexican, and Old West foundation, and you can find elements of these influences in the city's architecture, restaurants, and friendly, relaxed vibe. The rest of southern Arizona can do little to escape its cliché-ridden image as a landscape of cow skulls, tumbleweeds, dried-up riverbeds, and mother lodes—but it doesn't need to.

Metropolitan Tucson has more than 850,000 residents, including thousands of snowbirds who flee colder climes to enjoy the sun that shines on the city more than 340 days out of 365. The city's tricultural population (Hispanic, Anglo, Native American) offers visitors the chance to see how these cultures interact and to sample their flavorful cuisine. The city also has a youthful energy, largely due to the population of students attending the University of Arizona.

The metropolitan area covers more than 500 square miles in a valley ringed by mountains—the Santa Catalinas to the north, the Santa Ritas to the south, the Rincons to the east, and the Tucson Mountains to the west. Saguaro National Park bookends Tucson, with one section on the far east side and the other out west near the Arizona–Sonora Desert Museum.

South of Tucson, abandoned mining towns, sleepy Western hamlets, rugged rock formations, and deep pine forests beckon visitors for birding, hiking, and horseback riding, as well as more tame adventures like wine-tasting, stargazing, and shopping on historic main streets.

Southern Arizona ranges from the searing deserts surrounding Organ Pipe Cactus National Monument and the town of Yuma in the southwest to the soaring "Sky Islands"—steep hills that rise from the desert floor into the clouds—and rolling grasslands in the southeast. Rich veins of copper and silver were mined in the 19th century, when Fort Yuma was established in the state's far-western corner. The Tohono O'odham people, known for a long time as the Papago, were deeded a large portion of their ancestral homeland by the U.S. Bureau of Indian Affairs, and you'll traverse their vast reservation if you travel to Organ Pipe Cactus National Monument and Kitt Peak Observatory.

Planning

When to Go

Winter is high season in the southern desert. Summer lodging rates (late May to September) are hugely discounted, even at many of the resorts, but there's a good reason: summer in Tucson is hot! Swimming and indoor activities like visiting museums (and spa treatments) are doable; but only the hardiest hikers and golfers stay out past noon in summer.

Tucson averages only 12 inches of rain a year. Winter temperatures hover around 65°F during the day and 38°F at night. Summers are unquestionably hot—July averages 104°F during the day and 75°F at night—but, as Tucsonans are fond of saying, "It's a dry heat."

Getting Here and Around

AIR

You can fly to Tucson International Airport (TUS), which is 8½ miles south of Downtown, off the Valencia exit of Interstate 10, but cheaper, nonstop flights into Phoenix—a two-hour drive away on Interstate 10—are often easier to find. Once in town, a car is essential to get to the outlying tourist sights, and that's doubly true if you want to explore beyond the Tucson metropolitan area. Tucson is the major starting point for exploring the southern portions the state, but the area is vast. Yuma is a long three-hour drive west of Tucson.

Many Tucson hotels have a courtesy airport shuttle; otherwise, taxis and ride-shares are abundant at the airport. The Tucson Stagecoach Express shuttle will carry you between the airport and all parts of Tucson and outlying areas.

CONTACTS Tucson Stagecoach Express. ☎ *520/889–1000* 🌐 *www.stagecoachexpressshuttle.com.*

CAR

You'll need a car to get around Tucson and the rest of southern Arizona, and it makes sense to rent at the airport; all the major car-rental agencies are represented. If you are spending a few days in Tucson, a few rental agencies have additional locations in Central Tucson, and the larger resorts arrange rental-car pickups on-site.

The intricate network of highways in the San Pedro Valley provides looping access to the many scenic vistas and Old West communities, which makes the drive an integral part of the adventure. In stark contrast, a drive through the southwestern portion of the state is filled with long stretches of desert broken infrequently with tiny towns and intermittent gas stations. If you're heading west, pack a lunch, a few games, and plenty of music for entertainment along the way.

TRAIN

Amtrak serves the city with westbound trains (to Los Angeles, CA) and eastbound trains daily. The train station is in the downtown district. Within Arizona, trains connect Tucson to Benson and Yuma.

Hotels

If you like being able to walk to sights, shops, and restaurants, plan on staying in either the Downtown or University neighborhood. For a quieter but equally convenient base, opt for one of the charming B&Bs near the U of A campus. The posh resorts, primarily situated in the Catalina Foothills and Northwest areas, although farther away from town, have many activities on-site, as well as some of Tucson's top-rated restaurants, golf courses, and spas; resort staff can arrange transportation to shopping and sights. There are even a few dude ranches on the outskirts.

Beyond Tucson, you'll find mostly chain hotels, especially along the interstate highways, but some destinations have historic hotels, rustic casitas at working cattle ranches, or even homey bed-and-breakfasts. There are a few scattered dude ranches in the sweeping grasslands to the south. It's usually not hard to find a room any time of the year, but keep in mind that prices tend to go up in high season (winter and spring) and down in low season (summer through early fall) throughout the region, and especially in Tucson itself.

Restaurants

Tucson boldly proclaims itself to be the "Mexican Food Capital of the United States," and most of the Mexican food in town is Sonoran-style. This means prolific use of cheese, mild peppers, corn tortillas, pinto beans, and beef or chicken. It's the birthplace of the *chimichanga* (Spanish for "whatchamacallit"), a flour tortilla filled with meat or cheese, rolled, and deep-fried. The best Mexican restaurants are concentrated in South Tucson and Downtown, although some favorites have additional locations around town.

In the rest of Southern Arizona, cowboy fare is more common than haute cuisine. There are exceptions, though, especially in the artsy town of Bisbee, both popular for weekend outings from Tucson. And, as one would expect, Mexican food dominates menus.

HOTEL AND RESTAURANT PRICES

Hotel prices in the reviews are the lowest cost of a standard double room in high season. Restaurant prices in the reviews are the average cost of a main course at dinner, or if dinner is not served, at lunch.

What It Costs

	$	$$	$$$	$$$$
RESTAURANTS				
	Under $12	$12–$20	$21–$30	Over $30
HOTELS				
	Under $150	$150–$175	$176–$250	Over $250

Tucson

The metropolitan area covers more than 500 square miles in a valley ringed by mountains—the Santa Catalinas to the north, the Santa Ritas to the south, the Rincons to the east, and the Tucson Mountains to the west. Saguaro National Park bookends Tucson, with one section on the far east side and the other out west near the Arizona–Sonora Desert Museum.

The central portion of the city has most of the shops, restaurants, and businesses, but not many tourist sites. It is roughly bounded by Craycroft Road to the east, Oracle Road to the west, River Road to the north, and 22nd Street to the south. The Downtown section, east of Interstate 10 off the Broadway-Congress exit, is smaller and easy to navigate on foot.

Up north in the Catalina Foothills are first-class resorts, restaurants, and hiking trails, most with spectacular views of the entire valley.

Downtown streets don't run on any sort of grid, however, and many are one way, so it's best to get a good, detailed map. The city's Westside area is the vast region west of interstates 10 and 19, which includes the western section of Saguaro National Park and the San Xavier Mission.

Downtown Tucson is known for its colorful adobe houses and shops.

Downtown Tucson

The area bordered by Franklin Street on the north, Cushing Street on the south, Church Avenue on the east, and Main Avenue on the west contains more than two centuries of Tucson's history, dating from the original walled fortress, El Presidio de Tucson, built by the Spanish in 1776, when Arizona was still part of New Spain. A good deal of the city's history was destroyed in the 1960s, when large sections of Downtown's barrio were bulldozed to make way for the Tucson Convention Center, high-rises, and parking lots.

Nevertheless, within the area's three small historic districts it's still possible to explore Tucson's cultural and architectural past. Adobe—brick made of mud and straw, cured in the hot sun—was used widely as a building material in early Tucson because it provides natural insulation from the heat and cold and because it's durable in Tucson's dry climate. When these buildings are properly made and maintained, they can last for centuries. Driving around Downtown Tucson, you'll see adobe houses painted in vibrant hues such as bright pink and canary yellow.

Sights

"A" Mountain

MOUNTAIN—SIGHT | The original name of this mountain, Sentinel Peak, west of Downtown, came from its function as a lookout point for the Spanish, though the Pima village and cultivated fields that once lay at the base of the peak are long gone. In 1915 fans of the University of Arizona football team whitewashed a large "A" on its side to celebrate a victory, and the tradition has been kept up ever since—the permanent "A" is now red, white, and blue. During the day, the peak's a great place to get an overview of the town's layout; at night the city lights below form a dazzling carpet, but the teenage hangout scene may make some uncomfortable. ✉ *Congress St. on Sentinel Peak Rd., Downtown.*

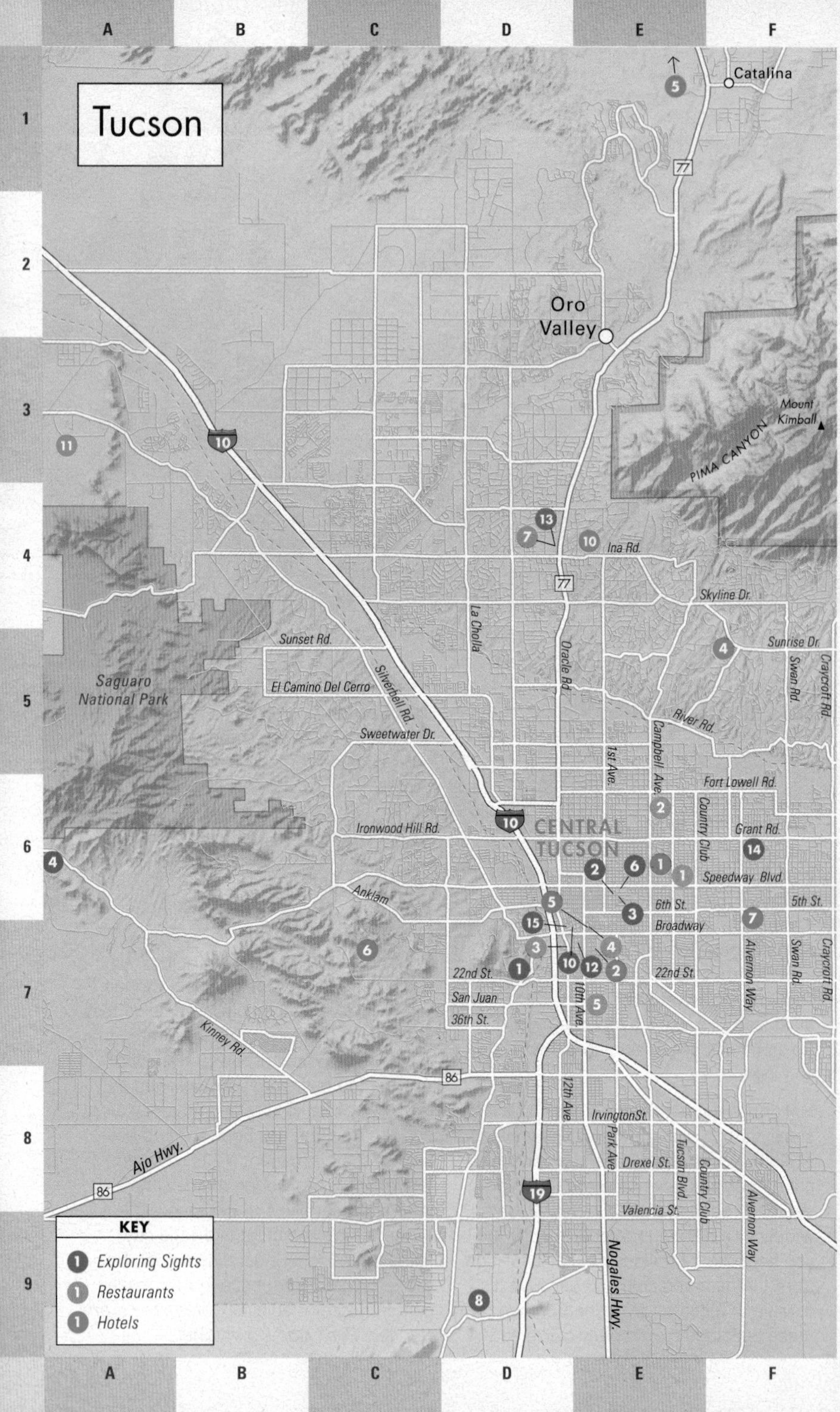
Tucson
A
B
C
D
E
F
1
2
3
4
5
6
7
8
9
Catalina
Oro Valley
Mount Kimball
PIMA CANYON
Ina Rd.
Skyline Dr.
Sunrise Dr.
Sunset Rd.
El Camino Del Cerro
Saguaro National Park
La Cholla
Oracle Rd
Silverbell Rd.
Sweetwater Dr.
River Rd.
Swan Rd.
Craycroft Rd
1st Ave.
Campbell Ave.
Fort Lowell Rd.
Country Club
Grant Rd.
Ironwood Hill Rd.
CENTRAL TUCSON
Speedway Blvd.
6th St.
5th St.
Broadway
Anklam
22nd St.
San Juan
36th St.
10th Ave.
Alvernon Way
Kinney Rd.
12th Ave
IrvingtonSt.
Park Ave.
Drexel St.
Tucson Blvd.
Valencia St.
Nogales Hwy.
Ajo Hwy.
KEY
Exploring Sights
Restaurants
Hotels

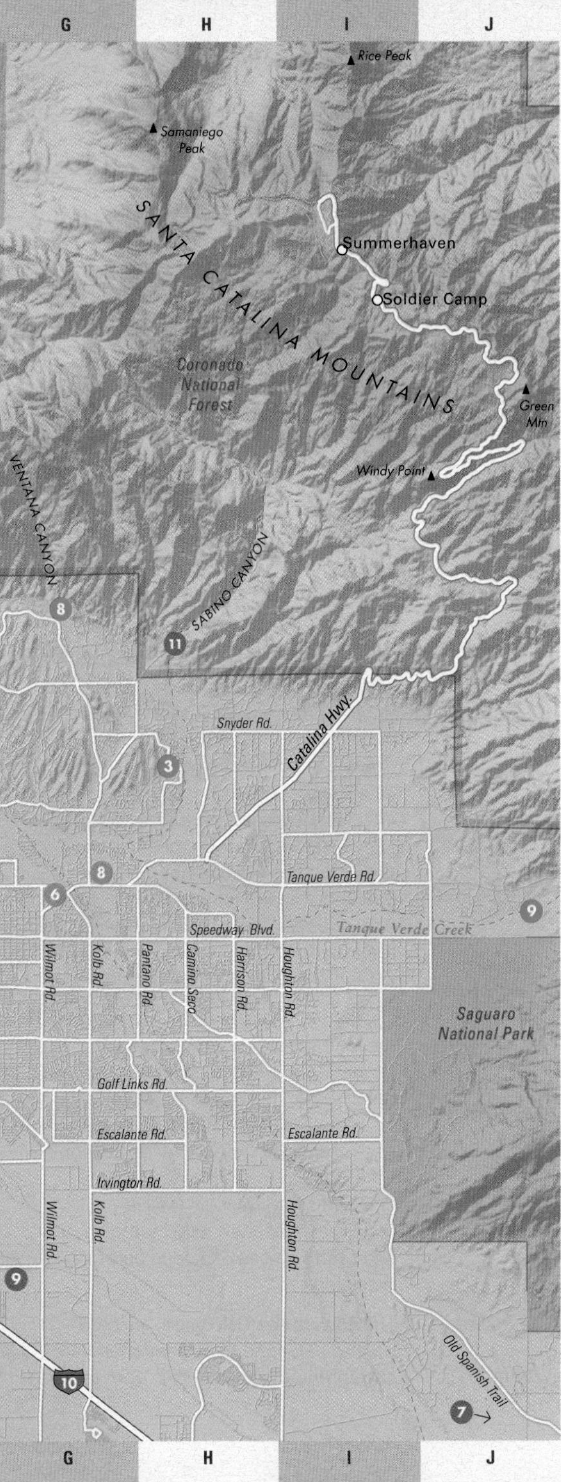

Sights

1 "A" Mountain D7
2 Arizona History Museum E6
3 Arizona State Museum............ E6
4 Arizona-Sonora Desert Museum.. .... A6
5 Biosphere 2.......................... E1
6 Center for Creative Photography.............. E6
7 Colossal Cave Mountain Park..... J9
8 Mission San Xavier del Bac...... D9
9 Pima Air and Space Museum.... G8
10 Pima County Courthouse D7
11 Sabino Canyon...................... H4
12 St. Augustine Cathedral........... E7
13 Tohono Chul Park.................. D4
14 Tucson Botanical Gardens F6
15 Tucson Museum of Art and Historic Block D7

Restaurants

1 Bangkok Cafe E6
2 Beyond Bread........................ E6
3 El Minuto Café D7
4 Maynards............................. E7
5 Mi Nidito.............................. E7
6 Pinnacle Peak Steakhouse....... G6
7 Tohono Chul Garden Bistro....... D4
8 Tucson Tamale Company G6

Hotels

1 Arizona Inn E6
2 Armory Park Inn D7
3 Canyon Ranch........................ H5
4 Hacienda del Sol Guest Ranch Resort................ F5
5 Hotel Congress....................... E7
6 JW Marriott Starr Pass C7
7 Lodge on the Desert................ F6
8 Loews Ventana Canyon Resort.............................. G4
9 Tanque Verde Ranch J6
10 Westward Look Wyndham Grand Resort........................ E4
11 White Stallion Ranch.............. A3

Pima County Courthouse

GOVERNMENT BUILDING | This pink Spanish colonial–style building with a mosaic-tile dome is among Tucson's most beautiful historic structures. Still in use, it was built in 1927 on the site of the original single-story adobe court of 1869; a portion of the old presidio wall can be seen in the south wing of the courthouse's second floor. The first floor now houses the Tucson Visitor Center and the University of Arizona Gem and Mineral Museum. At the side of the building is a diorama depicting the area's early days. ✉ *115 N. Church Ave., Downtown* ✥ *Between Alameda and Pennington Sts.* 🌐 *www.sc.pima.gov* 🎫 *Free* ⏲ *Closed Sun.*

St. Augustine Cathedral

RELIGIOUS SITE | Although the imposing white-and-beige, late-19th-century, Spanish-style building was modeled after the Cathedral of Queretaro in Mexico, a number of its details reflect the desert setting. For instance, above the entryway, next to a bronze statue of St. Augustine, are carvings of local desert scenes with saguaro cacti, yucca, and prickly pears—look closely and you'll find the horned toad. Compared with the magnificent facade, the modernized interior is a bit disappointing. ■ **TIP→ For a distinctly Southwestern experience, attend the mariachi Mass celebrated Sunday at 8 am.** ✉ *192 S. Stone Ave., Downtown* ☎ *520/623–6351* 🌐 *cathedral-staugustine.org* 🎫 *Free.*

Tucson Museum of Art and Historic Block

MUSEUM | The museum consists of a modern building housing superb collections of Latin American Art and Western Art, and five adjacent historic buildings on Main Avenue that are listed in the National Register of Historic Places. You can tour four of the historic houses, La Casa Cordova, the Stevens Home, the J. Knox Corbett House, and the Edward Nye Fish House, though each have different hours. The fifth, the Romero House, believed to incorporate a section of the presidio wall, is now used for the museum's ceramics education program. Visitors enter through the main museum on Alameda Street. The Latin American Art wing includes ancient Andean and Incan sculpture and Spanish-Colonial art as well as contemporary Latin works. The Art of the American West exhibits showcase Western and indigenous Southwestern art.

La Casa Cordova, one of the oldest buildings in Tucson and one of the best local examples of a Sonoran row house has a Spanish-style design adapted to adobe construction. The oldest section of La Casa Cordova, constructed around 1848, is only open November to January to display El Nacimiento, the largest nativity scene in the Southwest.

The **Stevens Home** was where the wealthy politician and cattle rancher Hiram Stevens and his wife, Petra Santa Cruz, entertained many of Tucson's leaders during the 1800s. A drought brought the Stevens' cattle ranching to a halt in 1893, and Stevens killed himself in despair after unsuccessfully attempting to shoot his wife (the bullet was deflected by the comb she wore in her hair). The 1865 house was restored in 1980 and now houses Café à la C'Art, a delightful restaurant.

The **J. Knox Corbett House** was built in 1906–07 and occupied by members of the Corbett family until 1963. J. Knox Corbett was a successful businessman, postmaster, and mayor of Tucson, and his wife, Elizabeth Hughes Corbett, an accomplished musician and daughter of Tucson pioneer Sam Hughes. The two-story, Mission Revival–style residence has been furnished with Arts and Crafts pieces. It's open only on weekends.

The **Edward Nye Fish House,** an 1868 adobe that belonged to an early merchant, entrepreneur, and politician and his wife, is notable for its 15-foot beamed ceilings and saguaro cactus–rib supports.

Admission to the museum and all four homes is free on the second Sunday and the first Thursday evening of every month, and there are free docent tours daily. ✉ *140 N. Main Ave., Downtown* ☎ *520/624–2333* 🌐 *www.tucsonmuseumofart.org* 🎟 *$12* 🕒 *Closed Mon.*

Restaurants

El Minuto Café

$$ | **MEXICAN** | Popular with local families and the business crowd at lunch, this bustling restaurant in Tucson's Barrio Historico neighborhood has been serving *topopo* salads (a crispy tortilla shell heaped with beans, guacamole, and many other ingredients), huge burritos, and green-corn tamales (in season) made just right for over 50 years. The spicy *menudo* (tripe soup) is reputed to be a great hangover remedy. **Known for:** consistent, tasty Sonoran food; good value; cheese crisps (cheese and veggies melted on tortillas). 💲 *Average main: $12* ✉ *354 S. Main Ave., Downtown* ☎ *520/882–4145* 🌐 *www.elminutotucson.com* 🕒 *Closed Mon.*

★ **Maynards**

$$$ | **FRENCH** | An anchor in the downtown district, this French-inspired bistro, bar, and gourmet market takes up part of Tucson's historic train depot. Clever thematic touches—a dining room fashioned long and narrow like a train car, with wheel-like divider walls and lamps made from rail spikes—and the attentive yet relaxed service evoke the romance of a largely bygone era. **Known for:** romantic dining; great patio (especially for train-watching); one of the city's best restaurants. 💲 *Average main: $27* ✉ *400 N. Toole Ave., Downtown* ☎ *520/545–0577* 🌐 *www.maynardstucson.com* 🕒 *No lunch Mon.–Sat. in restaurant (only at The Market).*

Hotels

Armory Park Inn

$$$$ | **B&B/INN** | Historic charm meets modern luxury in this beautifully renovated 1875 adobe home, walking distance to Downtown sights, dining, and nightlife. **Pros:** gorgeous historic property; plentiful common spaces for relaxing; full breakfasts and evening cocktails. **Cons:** pricey; street parking; some rooms are on second floor (stairs only). 💲 *Rooms from: $259* ✉ *438 S. 3rd Ave., Downtown* ☎ *520/838–0535* 🌐 *armoryparkinn.com* 🛏 *7 rooms* 🍽 *Free breakfast.*

★ **Hotel Congress**

$ | **HOTEL** | This hotel, built in 1919, has been artfully restored to its original Western version of art deco; it's now the center of Tucson's hippest scene and a great place for younger and adventurous travelers to stay. **Pros:** prime location; good restaurant and bars; historic, funky, and fun. **Cons:** no elevator to guest rooms; no TVs in rooms (only in common areas); noise from nightclub in some rooms. 💲 *Rooms from: $119* ✉ *311 E. Congress St., Downtown* ☎ *520/622–8848, 800/722–8848* 🌐 *www.hotelcongress.com* 🛏 *40 rooms* 🍽 *No meals.*

Shopping

★ **Etherton Gallery**

ART GALLERIES | This gallery specializes in vintage, classic, and contemporary photography but also represents artists in other media. ✉ *135 S. 6th Ave., Downtown* ☎ *520/624–7370* 🌐 *www.ethertongallery.com* 🕒 *Closed Sun. and Mon.*

★ **Philabaum Glass Gallery and Studio**

CERAMICS/GLASSWARE | Magnificent hand-blown glass pieces by Tom Philabaum and others, including vases, artwork, table settings, and jewelry, are sold at this gallery at the southern edge of Downtown. ✉ *711 S. 6th Ave., Downtown* ☎ *520/884–7404* 🌐 *www.philabaumglass.com.*

The University of Arizona's lush campus and museums are worth a visit.

The University of Arizona

The U of A (as opposed to rival ASU, in Tempe) is a major economic influence in Tucson, with a student population of more than 40,000. The land for the university was "donated" by a couple of gamblers and a saloon owner in 1891—their benevolence reputedly inspired by a bad hand of cards—and $25,000 of territorial money (Arizona was still a territory back then) was used to build Old Main, the original building, and to hire six faculty members.

The university's flora is impressive—it represents a collection of plants from arid and semiarid regions around the world. An extremely rare mutated, or "crested," saguaro grows at the northeast corner of the Old Main building. The long, grassy mall in the heart of campus—itself once a vast cactus garden—sits atop a huge underground student activity center, and makes for a pleasant stroll on a balmy evening.

Sights

Arizona History Museum

MUSEUM | **FAMILY** | The museum has exhibits exploring the history of Southern Arizona, starting with the indigenous Hohokam Tribe and the Spanish explorers. The harrowing "Life on the Edge: A History of Medicine in Arizona" exhibit promotes a new appreciation of modern drugstores in present-day Tucson. Children enjoy the exhibit on copper mining (with an atmospheric replica of a mine shaft and camp) and the stagecoaches in the transportation area.

The library has an extensive collection of historic Arizona photographs and sells inexpensive reprints. Park in the garage at the corner of 2nd and Euclid streets and get a free parking pass in the museum. ✉ *949 E. 2nd St., University* ☎ *520/628–5774* 🌐 *www.arizonahistoricalsociety.org/tucson* 🎟 *$10* 🕑 *Closed Sun. and Mon.*

Arizona State Museum

MUSEUM | FAMILY | Inside the main gate of the university is Arizona's oldest museum, dating from territorial days (1893) and a preeminent resource for the study of Southwestern cultures. Exhibits include the largest collections of Southwest Native American pottery and basketry, as well as *Paths of Life: American Indians of the Southwest*—a permanent exhibit that explores the cultural traditions, origins, and contemporary lives of 10 native tribes of Arizona and Sonora, Mexico. *1013 E. University Blvd., at Park Ave., University* *520/621–6302* *www.statemuseum.arizona.edu* *$8* *Closed Sun.*

Center for Creative Photography

MUSEUM | Ansel Adams conceived the idea of a photographer's archive and donated the majority of his negatives to this museum. In addition to its superb collection of his work, the center houses the David Hume Kennerly Archive and works by other major photographers, including Paul Strand, W. Eugene Smith, Edward Weston, and Louise Dahl-Wolfe. Changing exhibits in the main gallery display selected pieces from the collection. *1030 N. Olive Rd., north of 2nd St., University* *520/621–7968* *ccp.arizona.edu* *Free* *Closed Sun. and Mon.*

Hotels

★ Arizona Inn

$$$$ | HOTEL | Although near the university and many sights, the beautifully landscaped lawns and gardens of this 1930 inn seem far from the hustle and bustle. **Pros:** unique historical property; emphasis on service; gorgeous gardens and common areas. **Cons:** rooms may not be modern enough for some; close to University Medical Center but long walk (1½ miles) from the main campus; too sedate and posh for some. *Rooms from: $359* *2200 E. Elm St., University* *520/325–1541, 800/933–1093* *www.arizonainn.com* *94 rooms* *No meals.*

Nightlife

Tap and Bottle

BARS/PUBS | Known for its huge selection of beers—especially local craft beers—and convivial atmosphere, this popular pub sits two blocks off 4th Avenue. It's a pleasant alternative to the rowdier college hangouts and dive bars nearby. *403 N. 6th Ave., University* *520/344–8999* *thetapandbottle.com.*

Shopping

Antigone Books

BOOKS/STATIONERY | This lovely independent bookstore on 4th Avenue specializes in books by and about women, and sells creative cards, gifts, and T-shirts as well as a broad range of books. *411 N. 4th Ave., University* *520/792–3715* *www.antigonebooks.com.*

★ Popcycle

CRAFTS | This unique and fun store sells affordable art and gifts, ranging from the funky to the divine, all made by local artists using recycled materials. *422 N. 4th Ave., University* *520/622–3297* *www.popcycleshop.com.*

Central Tucson

Tucson expanded north and east from the university during the 1950s and '60s, and currently continues to spread southeast. The east–west thoroughfares of Broadway, Speedway, and Grant are lined with small and large businesses and eateries, mostly in unattractive strip malls. Sights worth seeing in this area include the Reid Park Zoo, the Tucson Botanical Gardens, and a couple of eccentric museums.

Sights

Tucson Botanical Gardens

GARDEN | Five acres of gardens are home to a variety of experiences: a tropical greenhouse; a sensory garden, where you can touch and smell the plants and listen to the abundant bird life; historical gardens that display the Mediterranean landscaping the property's original owners planted in the 1930s; a garden designed to attract birds; and a cactus garden. Other gardens showcase wildflowers, Australian plants, and Native American crops and herbs. From October through April, interact with butterflies from all over the world in their own greenhouse. A delightful café is open for breakfast and lunch daily. All paths are wheelchair accessible. ✉ *2150 N. Alvernon Way, Central* ☎ *520/326–9686* 🌐 *www.tucsonbotanical.org* 🎟 *$15.*

Restaurants

Bangkok Cafe

$$ | THAI | Easily the best Thai food in town, this bright, spacious café serves favorite Thai dishes and has pleasant service. The Thoong Tong appetizer of fried veggie-filled pouches is blissfully good, as are the curries and soups. **Known for:** top-notch Thai; weekend crowds; lunch specials. $ *Average main: $15* ✉ *2511 E. Speedway Blvd., Central* ☎ *520/323–6555* 🌐 *www.bangkokcafe.net* ⏲ *No lunch Sun.*

Beyond Bread

$ | CAFÉ | Twenty-seven varieties of bread are made at this bustling bakery with Central, Eastside, and Northwest locations, and highlights from the menu of generous sandwiches include Annie's Addiction (hummus, tomato, sprouts, red onion, and cucumber) and Brad's Beef (roast beef, provolone, onion, green chiles, and Russian dressing); soups, salads, and desserts are equally scrumptious. Eat inside or on the patio, or order takeout, but either way, splurge on one of the incredible desserts. **Known for:** stellar breads and pastries; large portions; friendliness. $ *Average main: $10* ✉ *3026 N. Campbell Ave., Central* ☎ *520/322–9965* 🌐 *www.beyondbread.com* ⏲ *No dinner Sun.*

Hotels

Lodge on the Desert

$$ | HOTEL | A charming hacienda-style hotel built in the 1930s offers modern comfort in an old-world setting. **Pros:** quiet, garden setting with attractive pool area; central location; excellent breakfast included. **Cons:** short drive but long walk to shops and restaurants; located just off busy thoroughfare; some plumbing issues in older historic rooms. $ *Rooms from: $195* ✉ *306 N. Alvernon Way, Central* ☎ *520/320–2000* 🌐 *www.lodgeonthedesert.com* *103 rooms* 🍽 *Free breakfast.*

Nightlife

The Shelter

MUSIC CLUBS | Sip a martini or a local brew and go totally retro at the Shelter, a former bomb shelter decked out in plastic 1960s kitsch, lava lamps, and JFK memorabilia. Watch Elvis videos and listen to the music of Burt Bacharach, as well as current alternative rock. ✉ *4155 E. Grant Rd., Central* ☎ *520/326–1345.*

Shopping

The Lost Barrio Tucson

SHOPPING CENTERS/MALLS | Located in an old warehouse district southeast of Downtown, the Lost Barrio is a cluster of shops with Southwestern art, furniture, and funky gifts (both antique and modern). ✉ *228 S. Park Ave., south of Broadway, Central* ☎ *520/628–4764* 🌐 *www.thelostbarriotucson.com.*

★ Native Seeds/SEARCH

LOCAL SPECIALTIES | Dedicated to preserving native crops and traditional farming methods, Native Seeds/SEARCH sells 350 kinds of seeds as well as an excellent selection of Native American foods, baking mixes, woven baskets, and other regional crafts. ✉ *3061 N. Campbell Ave., Central* ☎ *520/622–5561* 🌐 *www.nativeseeds.org.*

Colorful murals can be seen all over Tucson, especially Downtown and South Tucson.

Activities

★ Randolph-North Course

GOLF | A longtime LPGA Tour host and the flagship of Tucson's municipal courses, Randolph North is also the longest municipal course, with great mountain views and tall trees lining the fairways. ✉ *600 S. Alvernon Way, Central* ☎ *520/791–4653* 🌐 *www.tucsoncitygolf.com* 🎟 *$36 for 9 holes, $56 for 18 holes* ⛳ *18 holes, 6863 yards, par 72.*

Eastside

The sprawling Eastside of Tucson is mostly residential, but there are a few gems on the southeastern outskirts that are well worth the journey: the Pima Air and Space Museum, Colossal Cave, and Saguaro National Park's east district.

Sights

Colossal Cave Mountain Park

CAVE | **FAMILY** | This limestone grotto 20 miles southeast of Tucson is the largest dry cavern in the world. Guides discuss the fascinating crystal formations and relate the many romantic tales surrounding the cave, including the legend that an enormous sum of money stolen in a stagecoach robbery is hidden here.

Forty-five-minute cave tours begin every hour on the hour and require a ½-mile walk and a climb of 363 steps. The park includes a ranch area with trail rides through saguaro forests (from $38), hiking trails, a gemstone-sluicing area, a petting zoo, a gift shop, and a café. ✉ *16721 E. Old Spanish Trail, Eastside* ☎ *520/647–7275* 🌐 *www.colossalcave.com* 🎟 *$18.*

Pima Air and Space Museum

MUSEUM | **FAMILY** | This huge facility ranks among the largest private collections of aircraft in the world. More than 300 airplanes are on display in hangars and outside, including a presidential plane used by both John F. Kennedy and Lyndon B. Johnson; a full-scale replica of the Wright brothers' 1903 Wright Flyer; the SR-71 reconnaissance jet; and a mock-up of the X-15, the world's fastest aircraft. World War II planes are particularly well represented.

Meander on your own (even leashed pets are allowed) or take a free walking tour led by volunteer docents. The open-air tram tour (an additional $6 fee) narrates all outside aircraft. A two-hour tour of Aerospace Maintenance and Regeneration Group (AMARG)—affectionately nicknamed "The Boneyard"—provides an eerie glimpse of hundreds of mothballed aircraft lined up in rows on a vast tract of desert. This $10 AMARG tour, available only on weekdays by reservation, is a photographer's delight. An on-site restaurant, The Flight Grill, is open daily. *6000 E. Valencia Rd., Eastside* *Off I–10, Exit 267* *520/574–0462* *www.pimaair.org* *$17.*

Restaurants

Pinnacle Peak Steakhouse

$$ | **STEAKHOUSE** | **FAMILY** | Anybody caught eating newfangled foods like fish tacos here would probably get a glare, and city slickers' ties would be snipped. This cowboy steak house is part of the family-friendly Trail Dust Town, a re-creation of a turn-of-the-20th-century town, complete with a working antique carousel, a narrow-gauge train, and Western stunt shows staged outside Wednesday through Sunday at 7 and 8 ($5). **Known for:** basic steaks and ribs; kitschy cowboy fun; good for large groups. *Average main: $20* *6541 E. Tanque Verde Rd., Eastside* *520/296–0911* *www.traildusttown.com* *No lunch.*

Tucson Tamale Company

$ | **MODERN MEXICAN** | A good homemade tamale is special, and a restaurant that prepares and serves them fresh every day with all sorts of creative fillings is a find indeed. Carnivores can indulge in beef, pork, or chicken tamales, while vegetarians can opt for traditional, cheese-filled green-corn tamales or numerous vegan choices like the Austin, with a spinach and mushroom filling. **Known for:** tamales with creative fillings; an abundance of gluten-free fare; tasty vegan options. *Average main: $9* *7159 E. Tanque Verde Rd., Eastside* *520/298–8404* *tucsontamale.com* *Closed Mon.*

Hotels

Tanque Verde Ranch

$$$ | **RESORT** | **FAMILY** | The most upscale of Tucson's guest ranches and one of the oldest in the country, the Tanque Verde sits on 640 beautiful acres in the Rincon Mountains next to Saguaro National Park East. **Pros:** authentic Western experience, including great riding; loads of all-inclusive activities; bed-and-breakfast-only is an economical option. **Cons:** at the eastern edge of town; all-inclusive package excludes alcohol. *Rooms from: $250* *14301 E. Speedway Blvd., Eastside* *520/296–6275, 800/234–3833* *www.tanqueverderanch.com* *74 rooms* *Free breakfast.*

Activities

Arizona National Golf Club

GOLF | This is a gorgeous Robert Trent Jones Jr.–designed course at the base of the Santa Catalina Mountains on the northeastern edge of town. You won't need to go to Saguaro National Park after playing here—the saguaro-studded hillsides around the course are as magnificent and plentiful. *9777 E. Sabino Greens Dr., Eastside* *520/749–4089* *www.arizonanationalgolfclub.com* *$65* *18 holes, 6776 yards, par 71.*

Balloon America

BALLOONING | Passengers can soar above Sabino Canyon and the Santa Catalinas in a hot-air balloon. Two-hour tours (includes a film of your flight and a Champagne

Sabino Canyon, with its inviting swimming holes and trails, is one of Tucson's most popular hiking areas.

breakfast) depart from the Eastside of Tucson, October through mid-May. ✉ *1501 N. Houghton Rd.* ☎ *520/299–7744* 🎫 *From $249.*

Saguaro Stables

HORSEBACK RIDING | This reliable operator offers one-hour and longer rides into Saguaro National Park East. ✉ *7151 S. Camino Loma Alta, Eastside* ☎ *520/298–8980* 🌐 *www.allaroundtrailhorses.com/saguaro-stables.*

Catalina Foothills

Considered by some to be the "Beverly Hills of Tucson," the Catalina Foothills area is home to posh resorts and upscale shopping. Because the neighborhood abuts the beautiful Santa Catalina Mountains, it also has an abundance of hiking trails.

Sights

★ Sabino Canyon

NATURE PRESERVE | Year-round, but especially in summer, locals flock to Coronado National Forest to hike, picnic, and enjoy the waterfalls, streams, swimming holes, saguaros, and shade trees. No cars are allowed, but a narrated tram ride (about 45 minutes round-trip) takes you up a WPA-built road to the top of the canyon; you can hop off and on at any of the nine stops or hike any of the numerous trails.

There's also a shorter tram ride (or you can walk) to adjacent Bear Canyon, where a rigorous but rewarding hike leads to the popular Seven Falls (it'll take about 1½ to 2 hours each way from the drop-off point, so carry plenty of water). **■ TIP→ If you're in Tucson near a full moon between April and November, take the special night tram and watch the desert come alive with nocturnal critters.** ✉ *Sabino Canyon Rd. at Sunrise Dr., Foothills* ☎ *520/749–8700 for visitor center and* *recorded tram info* 🌐 *www.fs.usda.gov/coronado* 🎫 *$8 per vehicle, tram $6–$12.*

Hotels

★ Canyon Ranch

$$$$ | **RESORT** | This award-winning resort draws an international crowd of well-to-do health seekers to its superb spa facilities on 70 acres in the desert foothills. **Pros:** a stay here can be a life-changing experience; gorgeous setting; all-inclusive activities are varied and engaging. **Cons:** very pricey; not family-friendly; vast property means greater distances between activities. *Rooms from: $1050* ✉ *8600 E. Rockcliff Rd., Foothills* ☎ *520/749–9000, 855/376–1056* 🌐 *www.canyonranch.com* *240 rooms* 🍴 *All-inclusive.*

Hacienda del Sol Guest Ranch Resort

$$$ | **RESORT** | This 32-acre hideaway in the Santa Catalina Foothills is a charming and more intimate alternative to the larger resorts, combining luxury with Southwestern character. **Pros:** outstanding restaurant and bar; historic and stunningly beautiful property; quieter than the larger resorts. **Cons:** golfers must be shuttled to a nearby course; some historic rooms are smaller; may feel too posh for some. *Rooms from: $225* ✉ *5501 N. Hacienda Del Sol Rd., Foothills* ☎ *520/299–1501, 800/728–6514* 🌐 *www.haciendadelsol.com* *59 rooms* 🍴 *No meals.*

★ Loews Ventana Canyon Resort

$$$ | **RESORT** | **FAMILY** | This is one of the most luxurious and prettiest of the big resorts, with dramatic stone architecture and an 80-foot waterfall cascading down the mountains. **Pros:** many activities including great golf; excellent full spa and amenities; spectacular setting close to hiking. **Cons:** some rooms overlook the parking lot; not for those who don't like a posh atmosphere; at the eastern edge of the foothills. *Rooms from: $269* ✉ *7000 N. Resort Dr., Foothills* ☎ *520/299–2020, 800/234–5117* 🌐 *www.loewshotels.com/Ventana-Canyon* *398 rooms* 🍴 *No meals.*

Shopping

Bahti Indian Arts

CRAFTS | This shop is owned and run by the knowledgeable Mark Bahti, whose father, Tom, literally wrote the book on Native American art, including an early definitive work on katsinas. The store sells high-quality jewelry, pottery, rugs, art, and more. ✉ *St. Philip's Plaza, 4330 N. Campbell Ave., Foothills* ☎ *520/577–0290* 🌐 *mark-bahti-btof.squarespace.com.*

Activities

★ Bear Canyon Trail

Also known as Seven Falls Trail, this favorite route in Sabino Canyon is a three- to four-hour, 7.8-mile round-trip that is moderate and fun, crossing the stream several times on the way up the canyon. Kids enjoy the boulder-hopping, and all hikers are rewarded with pools and waterfalls as well as views at the top. The trailhead can be reached from the parking area by either taking a five-minute Bear Canyon Tram ride ($6) or walking the 1.8-mile tram route. *Moderate.* ✉ *Sabino Canyon Rd., at Sunrise Dr., Foothills* ☎ *520/749–2861* 🌐 *www.fs.usda.gov/coronado.*

Northwest Tucson

Once a vast, open space dotted with horse ranches, Northwest Tucson is now a rapidly growing residential area encompassing the townships of Oro Valley and Marana. Families and retirees are moving here in droves, and the traffic congestion proves the point. You'll also find first-rate golf resorts and restaurants, a popular outlet store mall, and the oases of Tohono Chul Park and Catalina State Park, which calm the senses.

Sights

Biosphere 2

GARDEN | In the town of Oracle, about 30 minutes northwest of Tucson, this unique, self-contained cluster of ecosystems opened in 1991 as a facility to test nature technology and human interaction with it. Now managed by the University of Arizona, the biomes include tropical rain forest, savanna, desert, thorn scrub, marsh, and ocean areas. The newest biome, the Landscape Evolutionary Observatory, tracks rainfall in simulated desert environments to study the effects of climate change on water sources and plant life in this region.

Guided walking tours take you inside the biomes, and a brief film gives an overview of Biosphere projects, from the original "human missions"—where scientists literally ate, slept, and breathed their work in a closed system—to current research. A snack bar overlooks the Santa Catalina Mountains. ✉ *32540 S. Biosphere Rd., Northwest* ✣ *Off AZ 77 at mile marker 96.5* ☎ *520/838–6200* 🌐 *www.biosphere2.org* 🎫 *$20.*

Tohono Chul Park

NATIONAL/STATE PARK | A 48-acre desert garden retreat designed to promote the conservation of arid regions, Tohono Chul—"desert corner" in the language of the Tohono O'odham—uses demonstration gardens, a greenhouse, and a geology wall to explain this unique desert area. Nature trails, a small art gallery, gift shops (including folk art, prickly pear products, and a great selection of desert plants), and a bistro can all be found at this peaceful spot. **■ TIP→ You can visit the restaurant and outstanding gift shops without paying admission.** ✉ *7366 N. Paseo del Norte, Northwest* ☎ *520/742–6455* 🌐 *tohonochul.org* 🎫 *$15.*

Restaurants

Tohono Chul Garden Bistro

$$ | SOUTHWESTERN | FAMILY | The food at Tohono Chul Garden Bistro is fine, but what many come for is the location inside a wildlife sanctuary, surrounded by flowering desert gardens. The Southwestern interior has Mexican tile, light wood, and a cobblestone courtyard, but the back patio, where you can watch hummingbirds and butterflies, is the place to be. **Known for:** beautiful patio dining; popular weekend brunch; prickly pear chicken salad. $ *Average main: $15* ✉ *Tohono Chul Park, 7366 N. Paseo del Norte, Northwest* ☎ *520/742–6455* 🌐 *www.tohonochul.org* ⏲ *No dinner; Closed Mon.–Wed.*

Hotels

Westward Look Wyndham Grand Resort

$$ | RESORT | FAMILY | Originally the 1912 homestead of William and Mary Watson, this laid-back lodging with gorgeous city views and desert gardens has Southwestern character and all the amenities you expect at a major resort. **Pros:** great tennis, horseback riding, and nature trails; convenient yet feels like a retreat; you can actually park near your room. **Cons:** no golf (privileges at private club 4 miles away); rather plain pool areas; less plush than neighboring resorts. $ *Rooms from: $159* ✉ *245 E. Ina Rd., Northwest* ☎ *520/297–1151, 800/722–2500* 🌐 *www.westwardlook.com* 🛏 *244 rooms* 🍽 *No meals.*

★ White Stallion Ranch

$$$$ | RESORT | FAMILY | A 3,000-acre working cattle ranch run by the hospitable True family since 1965, this place is the real deal, satisfying for families as well as singles or couples. **Pros:** solid dude-ranch experience with exceptional riding program; plentiful ranch activities and evening entertainment; charming hosts. **Cons:** no TV in rooms; alcohol not included in the rate—pay extra or bring

Walk through rain forest, savanna, and desert habitats at Biosphere 2, an Earth Science research center north of Tucson.

your own; rustic, rather than luxurious. $ *Rooms from: $468* ✉ *9251 W. Twin Peaks Rd., Northwest* ☎ *520/297–0252* 🌐 *www.whitestallion.com* *41 rooms, 1 house* *All-inclusive.*

Activities

Fleur de Tucson Balloon Tours

BALLOONING | Operating out of Northwest Tucson from October through April, this company flies over the Tucson Mountains and Saguaro National Park West. Flights include photos as well as a continental champagne brunch after you arrive back on the ground. ✉ *Northwest* ☎ *520/403–8547* 🌐 *www.fleurdetucson.net* *From $250.*

Westside

The Westside is far less developed than other areas of Tucson, and beautiful vistas of saguaro-studded hills are around every bend. Saguaro National Park West, the Arizona–Sonora Desert Museum, Old Tucson Studios, and the San Xavier Mission are all in this section of town. If you're interested in the flora and fauna of the Sonoran Desert—as well as some of its appearances in the cinema—heed the same advice given the pioneers: go west.

Sights

★ **Arizona–Sonora Desert Museum**

MUSEUM | **FAMILY** | The name "museum" is a bit misleading, since this delightful site is actually a zoo, aquarium, and botanical garden featuring the animals, plants, and even fish of the Sonoran Desert. Hummingbirds, coatis, rattlesnakes, scorpions, bighorn sheep, bobcats, and Mexican wolves all busy themselves in ingeniously designed habitats.

An Earth Sciences Center has an artificial limestone cave to climb through and an excellent mineral display. The coyote and javelina (a wild, piglike mammal with an oddly oversize head) exhibits have "invisible" fencing that separates humans from animals, and at the Raptor Free Flight show (October through April, daily at 10 and 2), you can see the powerful birds soar and dive, untethered, inches above your head.

The restaurants are above average, and the gift shop, which carries books, jewelry, and crafts, is outstanding. **■ TIP→ June through August, the museum stays open until 10 pm every Saturday, which provides a great opportunity to see nocturnal critters.** ✉ *2021 N. Kinney Rd., Westside* ☎ *520/883–2702* 🌐 *www.desertmuseum.org* 🎫 *$22.*

★ Mission San Xavier del Bac

RELIGIOUS SITE | The oldest Catholic church in the United States still serving the community for which it was built, San Xavier was founded in 1692 by Father Eusebio Francisco Kino, who established 22 missions in northern Mexico and Southern Arizona. The current structure was made out of native materials by Franciscan missionaries between 1777 and 1797, and is owned by the Tohono O'odham tribe.

The beauty of the mission, with elements of Spanish, baroque, and Moorish architectural styles, is highlighted by the stark landscape against which it is set, inspiring an early-20th-century poet to dub it the White Dove of the Desert.

Inside, there's a wealth of painted statues, carvings, and frescoes. Paul Schwartzbaum, who helped restore Michelangelo's masterwork in Rome, supervised Tohono O'odham artisans in the restoration of the mission's artwork, completed in 1997; Schwartzbaum has called the mission the Sistine Chapel of the United States.

Across the parking lot from the mission, San Xavier Plaza has a couple of crafts shops selling the handiwork of the Tohono O'odham tribe, including jewelry, pottery, friendship bowls, and woven baskets with man-in-the-maze designs. ✉ *1950 W. San Xavier Rd., Westside* ✣ *9 miles southwest of Tucson on I–19* ☎ *520/294–2624* 🌐 *www.sanxaviermission.org* 🎫 *Free.*

★ JW Marriott Starr Pass

$$$$ | **RESORT** | Set amid saguaro forests and mesquite groves in the Tucson Mountains (yet only 15 minutes from Downtown), the city's largest resort has massive sun-bleached stone walls that blend rather than compete with the natural surroundings and stunning views from the interior dining areas and lounges. **Pros:** posh and beautiful; excellent spa and golf; great walking/hiking paths. **Cons:** expensive; parking is far from lobby areas and guest rooms; setting may feel too isolated for some. Ⓢ *Rooms from: $339* ✉ *3800 W. Starr Pass Blvd., Westside* ☎ *520/792–3500* 🌐 *www.jwmarriottstarrpass.com* *575 rooms* 🍽 *No meals.*

Activities

★ Starr Pass Golf Club

GOLF | With 27 magnificent holes in the Tucson Mountains, Starr Pass has become a favorite of visiting pros; playing its No. 15 signature hole has been likened to threading a moving needle. Guests at the JW Marriott Starr Pass Resort have privileges (and pay lower greens fees) here. ✉ *3645 W. Starr Pass Blvd., Westside* ☎ *520/791–6270* 🌐 *www.jwmarriottstarrpass.com* 🎫 *$100 for 9 holes, $179 for 18 holes* *27 holes, 6731 yards, par 71.*

South Tucson

This 1-square-mile district directly south of Downtown is a city in its own right, with its own mayor, close-knit neighborhoods, and abundance of Mexican eateries, ranging from legendary restaurants to tiny taquerias. Everyone you ask will have their own favorite spot to recommend, but you really can't go wrong at any of them.

The main streets of South Tucson, 6th Avenue and 4th Avenue, run parallel to each other. You can drive down 6th Avenue to see some classic mid-century modern buildings like the KY Market; then you'll probably want to head over to 4th Avenue, between 22nd Street and 36th Street, where most restaurants are located.

Restaurants

★ Mi Nidito

$$ | **MEXICAN** | A perennial favorite among locals (the wait is worth it), Mi Nidito ("my little nest") has also hosted its share of visiting celebrities: following President Clinton's lunch here, the rather hefty Presidential Plate (bean tostada, taco with barbecued meat, chiles rellenos, chicken enchilada, and beef tamale with rice and beans) was added to the menu. Top that off with the mango chimichangas for dessert, and you're talkin' executive privilege. **Known for:** reliably delicious Mexican food; festive atmosphere; great margaritas. *Average main: $12* ✉ *1813 S. 4th Ave., South* ☎ *520/622–5081* 🌐 *www.miniditorestaurant.com* ⊗ *Closed Mon. and Tues.*

Saguaro National Park

Saguaro National Park West: 14 miles west of Central Tucson; Saguaro National Park East: 12 miles east of Central Tucson.

Saguaro National Park's two distinct sections flank the city of Tucson. Perhaps the most familiar emblem of the Southwest, the towering saguaros are found only in the Sonoran Desert. Saguaro National Park preserves some of the densest stands of these massive cacti.

Known for their height (often 50 feet) and arms reaching out in weird configurations, these slow-growing giants can take 15 years to grow a foot high and up to 75 years to grow their first arm. The cacti can live up to 200 years and weigh up to 2 tons. In late spring (usually May), the succulent's top is covered with tiny white blooms—the Arizona state flower. The cacti are protected by state and federal laws, so don't disturb them.

WHEN TO GO

Saguaro never gets crowded. Nevertheless, most people visit in milder weather, October through May. December through February can be cool and are likely to see gentle rain showers. The spring days of March through May are bright and sunny with wildflowers and cacti in bloom. Because of high temperatures, from June through September it's best to visit the park in the early morning or late afternoon. Cooler temperatures return in October and November, providing perfect weather for hiking and camping throughout the park.

GETTING HERE AND AROUND

Both districts are about a half-hour drive from Central Tucson. To reach the Rincon Mountain District (East section) from Interstate 10, take Exit 275, then go north on Houghton Road for 10 miles. Turn right on Escalante and left onto Old Spanish Trail, and the park will be on the right side. If you're coming from town, go east on Speedway Boulevard to Houghton Road. Turn right on Houghton and left onto Old Spanish Trail.

To reach the Tucson Mountain District (West section) from Interstate 10, take Exit 242 or Exit 257, then go west on Speedway Boulevard (the name will change to Gates Pass Road), follow it to Kinney Road, and turn right.

As there's no public transportation to or within Saguaro, a car is a necessity. In the western section, Bajada Loop Drive takes you through the park and to various trailheads; Cactus Forest Drive does the same for the eastern section.

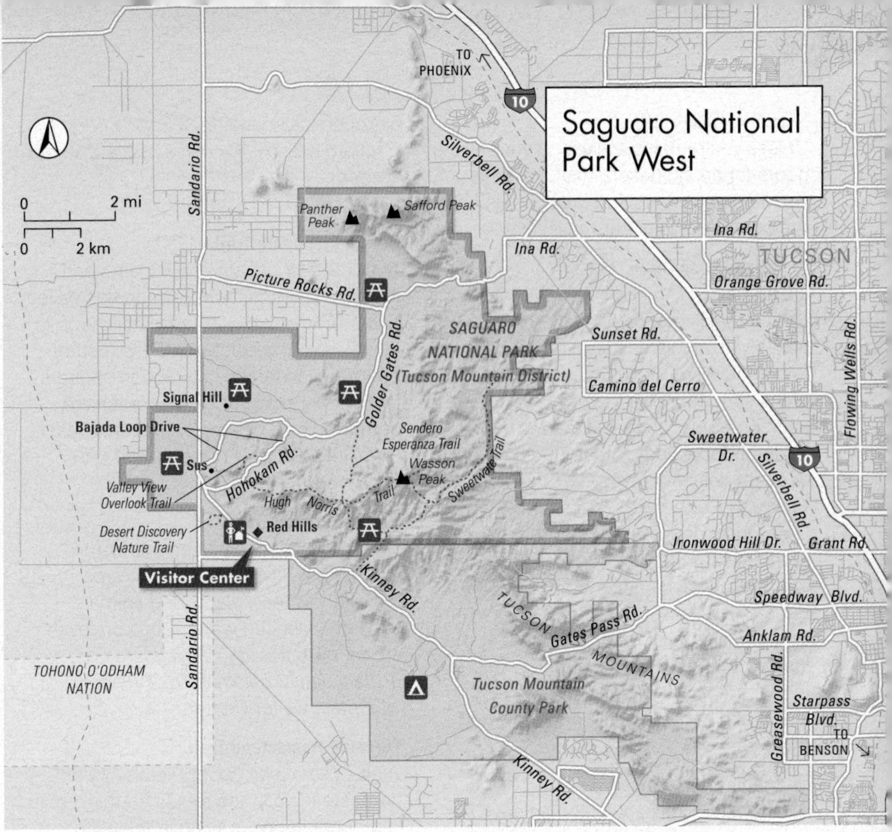

Saguaro National Park West

PARK ESSENTIALS

In the western section, the Red Hills Visitor Center and two nearby nature trails are wheelchair accessible. The eastern district's visitor center is accessible, as are the paved Desert Ecology and Cactus Garden Trails.

Admission to Saguaro is $25 per vehicle and $15 for individuals on foot or bicycle; it's good for seven days from purchase at both park districts. Annual passes cost $45. For hike-in camping at one of the primitive campsites in the eastern district (the closest campsite is 6 miles from the trailhead), obtain a required backcountry permit ($8 per night) up to three months in advance. 🌐 *www.recreation.gov*

VISITOR INFORMATION

PARK CONTACT INFORMATION Saguaro National Park. ✉ *3693 S. Old Spanish Trail, Tucson* ☎ *520/733–5158 for Saguaro West, 520/733–5153 for Saguaro East* 🌐 *www.nps.gov/sagu.*

Sights

HISTORIC SIGHTS

Manning Camp

HOUSE | The summer home of Levi Manning, onetime Tucson mayor, was a popular gathering spot for the city's elite in the early 1900s. The cabin can be reached only on foot or horseback via one of several challenging high-country trails: Douglas Spring Trail to Cow Head Saddle Trail (12 miles), Turkey Creek Trail (7.5 miles), or Tanque Verde Ridge Trail (15.4 miles). The cabin itself is not open for viewing. ✉ *Saguaro East* ✥ *Douglas Spring Trail (6 miles) to Cow Head Saddle Trail (6 miles).*

SCENIC DRIVES

Unless you're ready to lace up your hiking boots for a long desert hike, the best way to see Saguaro National Park is from the comfort of your car.

★ Bajada Loop Drive

SCENIC DRIVE | This 6-mile drive winds through thick stands of saguaros and past two picnic areas and trailheads to a few short hikes, including one to a petroglyph site. Although the road is unpaved and somewhat bumpy, it's a worthwhile trade-off for access to some of the park's densest desert growth. It's one-way between Hugh Norris Trail and Golden Gate Road, so if you want to make the complete circuit, travel counterclockwise. The road is susceptible to flash floods during the monsoon season (July and August), so check road conditions at the visitor center before proceeding. This loop route is also popular among bicyclists, and dogs on leash are permitted along the road. ✉ *Saguaro West.*

★ Cactus Forest Drive

SCENIC DRIVE | This paved 8-mile drive provides a great overview of all Saguaro East has to offer. The one-way road, which circles clockwise, has several turnouts with roadside displays that make it easy to pull over and admire the scenery; you can also stop at two picnic areas and three easy nature trails. This is a good bicycling route, but watch out for snakes and javelinas crossing in front of you. ✉ *Cactus Forest Dr., Saguaro East.*

SCENIC STOPS

Signal Hill

ARCHAEOLOGICAL SITE | **FAMILY** | The most impressive petroglyphs, and the only ones with explanatory signs, are on the Bajada Loop Drive in Saguaro West. An easy five-minute stroll from the signposted parking area takes you to one of the largest concentrations of rock carvings in the Southwest. You'll have a close-up view of the designs left by the Hohokam people between AD 900 and 1200, including large spirals some believe are astronomical markers. ✉ *Bajada Loop Dr., Saguaro West* ✣ *4½ miles north of visitor center.*

TRAILS

Desert Discovery Trail

TRAIL | **FAMILY** | Learn about plants and animals native to the region on this paved path in Saguaro West. The ½-mile loop is wheelchair accessible, and has resting benches and ramadas (wooden shelters that supply shade). Dogs on leash are permitted here. *Easy.* ✉ *Saguaro West* ✣ *Trailhead: 1 mile north of Red Hills Visitor Center.*

Desert Ecology Trail

TRAIL | **FAMILY** | Exhibits on this ¼-mile loop near the Mica View picnic area explain how local plants and animals subsist on limited water. Dogs on leash are permitted. *Easy.* ✉ *Saguaro East* ✣ *Trailhead: 2 miles north of Rincon Mountain Visitor Center.*

Freeman Homestead Trail

TRAIL | Learn a bit about the history of homesteading in the region on this 1-mile loop. Look for owls living in the cliffs above as you make your way through the lowland vegetation. *Easy.* ✉ *Saguaro East* ✣ *Trailhead: Next to Javelina picnic area, 2 miles south of Rincon Mountain Visitor Center.*

★ Signal Hill Trail

TRAIL | **FAMILY** | This ¼-mile trail in Saguaro West is a simple, rewarding ascent to ancient petroglyphs carved a millennium ago by the Hohokam people. *Easy.* ✉ *Saguaro West* ✣ *Trailhead: 4½ miles north of Red Hills Visitor Center on Bajada Loop Dr.*

VISITOR CENTERS

Red Hills Visitor Center

INFO CENTER | Take in gorgeous views of nearby mountains and the surrounding desert from the center's large windows and shaded outdoor terrace. A spacious gallery is filled with educational exhibits, and a lifelike display simulates the flora and fauna of the region. A 15-minute

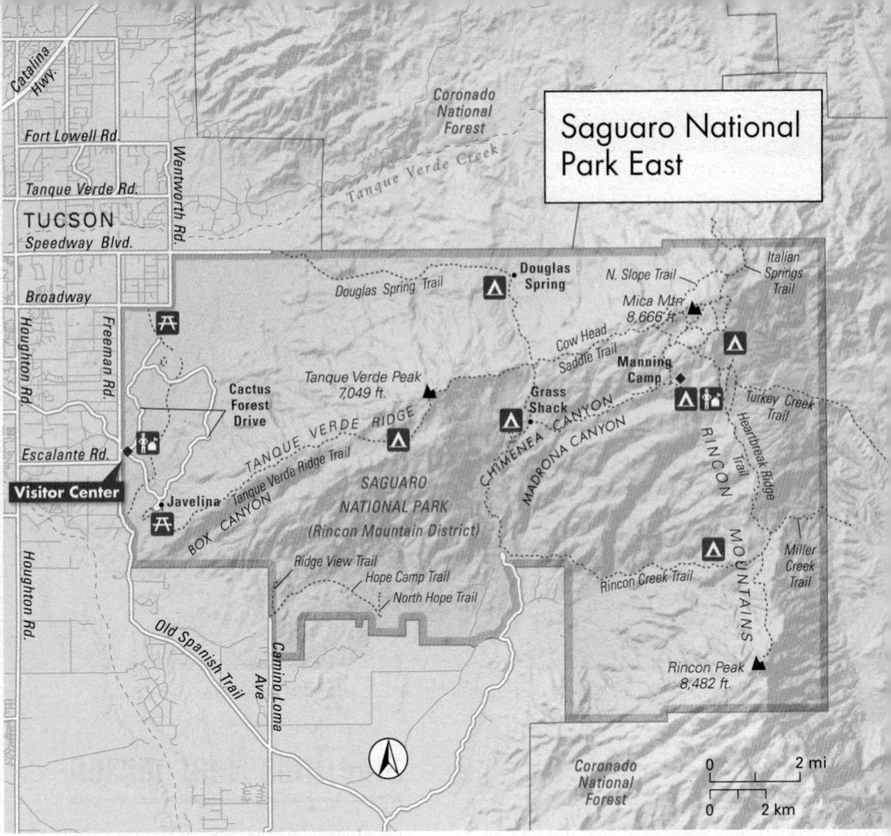

Saguaro National Park East

slide show, "Voices of the Desert," provides a poetic, Native American perspective on the Saguaro. Park rangers and volunteers hand out maps and suggest hikes to suit your interests. The bookstore sells books, trinkets, a few local items like honey and prickly pear jellies, and reusable water bottles that you can fill at water stations outside. ✉ *2700 N. Kinney Rd., Saguaro West* ☎ *520/733–5158* 🌐 *www.nps.gov/sagu.*

Rincon Mountain Visitor Center

INFO CENTER | Stop here to pick up free maps and printed materials on various aspects of the park, including maps of hiking trails and backcountry camping permits. Exhibits at the center are comprehensive, and a relief map of the park lays out the complexities of this protected landscape. Two 20-minute slide shows explain the botanical and cultural history of the region, and there is a short self-guided nature walk along the paved Cactus Garden Trail. A select variety of books and other gift items, along with energy bars, beef jerky, and refillable water bottles, are sold here. ✉ *3693 S. Old Spanish Trail, Saguaro East* ☎ *520/733–5153* 🌐 *www.nps.gov/sagu.*

Activities

BIKING

Scenic drives in the park—Bajada Loop in the West and Cactus Forest Drive in the East section—are popular among cyclists, though you'll have to share the roads with cars. Bajada Loop Drive is a gravel and dirt road, so it's quite bumpy and only suitable for mountain bikers; Cactus Forest Drive is paved. In the East section, Cactus Forest Trail (2.5 miles) is a great unpaved path for both beginning

A massive, open-pit copper mine lies just south of Tucson at the ASARCO Mineral Discovery Center.

and experienced mountain bikers who don't mind sharing the trail with hikers and the occasional horse; Hope Camp Trail is also open to mountain bikes.

HIKING

The park has more than 100 miles of trails. The shorter hikes, such as the **Desert Discovery** and **Desert Ecology** trails, are perfect for those looking to learn about the desert ecosystem without expending too much energy. The **Hope Camp Trail, Hugh Norris Trail,** and **Signal Hill Trail** are also excellent for hiking. For more information see the trail listings under ⇨ *Sights.*

■TIP→ Rattlesnakes are commonly seen on trails; so are coyotes, javelinas, roadrunners, Gambel's quail, and desert spiny lizards. Hikers should keep their distance from all wildlife.

Side Trips Near Tucson

Interstate 19 heads south from Tucson through Tubac to Nogales at the border of Mexico, carrying with it history buffs, bird-watchers, hikers, art enthusiasts, duffers, and shoppers. The road roughly follows the Camino Real (King's Road), which the conquistadors and missionaries traveled from Mexico up to what was once the northernmost portion of New Spain.

The ASARCO Mineral Discovery Center

15 miles south of Tucson off I–19.

The American Smelting and Refining Company (abbreviated as ASARCO) gives visitors a glimpse not only of a vast, open-pit mine but also of the complex processes involved in extracting minerals like copper from the earth.

From Interstate 19 south take Exit 80. Turn right (west) onto Pima Mine Road, and the entrance will be almost immediately on your left.

Sights

ASARCO Mineral Discovery Center

MINE | This mining operations center elucidates the importance of mining to everyday life. Indoor exhibits include a walk-through model of an ore crusher, video stations that explain refining processes, and a film about how minerals are actually extracted. Outside, you can see some of the actual equipment, including a few gargantuan trucks used for hauling the stuff. The big draw, though, is the yawning open pit of the Mission Mine, some 2 miles long and 1¾ miles wide because so much earth has to be torn up to extract the 1% that is copper. It's impressive, but doesn't bolster the case the center tries to make about how environmentally conscious mining has become. Tours of the pit take a little over an hour; the last one starts at 3:30. From May to September, pit mine tours are only offered on Saturday. *✉ 1421 W. Pima Mine Rd. ☎ 520/625–7513 🌐 www.asarco.com 🎫 Mine tour $10 (Discovery Center is free) 🕒 Closed Sun. and Mon.*

Titan Missile Museum

25 miles south of Tucson.

The Titan Missile Museum houses one of the 54 missile silos built around the country during the Cold War in case the United States needed to deploy nuclear bombs. A guided tour gives you a sense of the military mindset during this era.

From Interstate 19, take Exit 69 (Duval Mine Road) approximately 1 mile west to the museum.

Sights

Titan Missile Museum

MILITARY SITE | Now a National Historic Landmark, the Titan Missile Museum makes for a sobering visit. During the Cold War, Tucson was ringed by 18 of the 54 Titan II missiles maintained in the United States. After the SALT II treaty with the Soviet Union was signed in 1979, this was the only missile-launch site left intact.

Guided one-hour tours, which must be reserved in advance, take you down 55 steps into the command post, where a ground crew of four lived and waited. Among the sights is the 103-foot, 165-ton, two-stage liquid-fuel rocket. Now empty, it originally held a nuclear warhead with 214 times the explosive power of the bomb that destroyed Hiroshima. *✉ 1580 W. Duval Mine Rd., off I–19, Exit 69, Green Valley ☎ 520/625–7736 🌐 www.titanmissilemuseum.org 🎫 $13.*

Madera Canyon

61½ miles southeast of Tucson.

This prime hiking and birding area south of Tucson is where the Coronado National Forest meets the Santa Rita Mountains. Higher elevations and thick pine cover make it especially popular with Tucsonans looking to escape the summer heat.

From Interstate 19, take Exit 63 (Continental Road) east for about a mile, then turn right (southeast) on White House Canyon Road for 12½ miles (it turns into Madera Canyon Road).

Sights

Madera Canyon

NATURE PRESERVE | With approximately 200 miles of scenic trails, the recreation area of Madera Canyon—which includes Mount Wrightson, the highest peak in Southern Arizona, at 9,453 feet—is a

Colorful ceramic pottery is sold at local markets in the artist colony of Tubac.

haven for hikers and birders. Trails vary from a steep trek up Mount Baldy to a paved, wheelchair-accessible path along the creek. Birders flock here year-round; about 400 avian species have been spotted in the area.

There are picnic tables and ramadas near the parking areas, and camping is available. The Santa Rita Lodge (🌐 *santaritalodge.com*), with charming cabins, has numerous bird feeders and a gift shop. Friends of Madera Canyon (🌐 *friendsofmaderacanyon.org*) operates an information station here on the weekends. ✉ *Madera Canyon Rd., Madera Canyon* ☎ *520/281–2296 for Nogales Ranger District office* 🌐 *www.fs.usda.gov/coronado* 🎟 *$8.*

Tubac

45 miles south of Tucson at Exit 40 off I–19.

Established in 1726, Tubac is the site of the first European settlement in Arizona. A year after the Pima uprising in 1751, a military garrison was established here to protect Spanish settlers, missionaries, and peaceful Native American converts of the nearby Tumacácori Mission. It was from here that Juan Bautista de Anza led 240 colonists across the desert—the expedition resulted in the founding of San Francisco in 1776. In 1860 Tubac was the largest town in Arizona. Today the quiet little town is a popular art colony. More than 80 shops sell such crafts as carved wooden furniture, hand-thrown pottery, delicately painted tiles, and silkscreen fabrics (many shops are closed Monday). You can also find Mexican pottery and trinkets without having to cross the border. The annual **Tubac Festival of the Arts** has been held in February for more than 50 years.

When you exit Interstate 19 at Tubac Road, signs will point you east into Tubac village. There's plenty of free parking, and you can pick up a free map of the village at most of the shops.

VISITOR INFORMATION Tubac Chamber of Commerce. ☎ *520/398–2704* 🌐 *tubacaz.com.*

Sights

Tubac Presidio State Historic Park

NATIONAL/STATE PARK | There's an archaeological display of portions of the original 1752 fort at this museum, as well as artifacts and detailed exhibits on the history of the early colony. The park includes picnic areas, gardens, an adobe rowhouse built in 1897, and Tubac's well-preserved 1885 schoolhouse. ✉ *1 Burruel St., Tubac* ☎ *520/398–2252* 🌐 *www.tubacpresidio.org* 🎫 *$7* 🕒 *Closed Mon. and Tues.*

Restaurants

★ Elvira's

$$ | **MEXICAN** | This colorful and deservedly popular restaurant serves delicious Sonoran classics in Tubac village. Try one of the five chicken moles, ranging from sweet to nutty to spicy, and you'll know why chef Ruben has such a devoted following. **Known for:** delicious Sonoran classics with a contemporary twist; weekend nightlife; striking dining room. $ *Average main: $19* ✉ *2221 E. Frontage Rd., Tubac* ☎ *520/398–9421* 🌐 *elvirasrestaurant.com* 🕒 *Closed Mon. No dinner Sun.*

Tubac Deli & Coffee Co.

$ | **AMERICAN** | With freshly roasted coffee, breakfast pastries, and generous sandwiches, salads, and soups, this pleasant little eatery smack in the middle of Tubac village is a very convenient and friendly place to "set awhile" with the locals. **Known for:** homemade breads and pastries; inexpensive lunch break while shopping; hearty breakfasts. $ *Average main: $9* ✉ *6 Plaza Rd., Tubac* ☎ *520/398–3330* 🌐 *tubacdeli.com.*

Activities

Juan Bautista de Anza National Historic Trail

HIKING/WALKING | **FAMILY** | You can tread the same road as the conquistadors: the first 4½ miles of the Juan Bautista de Anza National Historic Trail—which stretches all the way from Nogales, Arizona, to Bautista's end point in San Francisco—lead from Tumacácori to Tubac. You'll have to cross the Santa Cruz River—which is usually low—three times to complete the hike, and the path is rather sandy, but it's a pleasant journey along the tree-shaded banks of the river. *Moderate.* ☎ *415/623–2344* 🌐 *www.anzahistorictrail.org, www.nps.gov/juba.*

Tumacácori National Historic Park

3 miles south of Tubac.

Father Kino established the Tumacácori Mission in 1791, but the Jesuits didn't build a church here until 60 years later. Walk through the mission ruins and visit the main attraction, the pretty Mission of San José de Tumacácori, built by the Franciscans around 1799–1803. The historic Anza Trail runs through the park.

Take Exit 29 off Interstate 19 and follow signs half a mile to the park (from Tucson, go under the highway to East Frontage Road and turn left).

Sights

Santa Cruz Chili & Spice Co.

STORE/MALL | Across the street from the Tumacácori National Historic Park, the Santa Cruz Spice Factory packs and sells 240 varieties of herbs and spices, including the owner's home-grown chili powders and pastes. A little museum, tasting area, and store are open Monday through Saturday. ✉ *1868 E. Frontage Rd., Tumacácori* ☎ *520/398–2591* 🌐 *www.santacruzchili.com* ⊙ *Closed Sun.*

Tumacácori National Historic Park
NATIONAL/STATE PARK | FAMILY | Encompassing mission ruins, the church of San José de Tumacácori, and a portion of the Juan Bautista de Anza National Historic Trail, this park became a national monument in 1908. Guided tours of the beautiful church and grounds are available daily at 11 and 2, January through March, and information on both the mission and the historic trail is available at the visitor center. A small museum displays some of the mission's artifacts, and often during winter and spring months fresh tortillas are made on a wood-fire stove in the courtyard. Creative educational programs, such as full-moon tours, bird walks, and a Junior Ranger Program, are offered throughout the year. An annual fiesta the first weekend of December has arts and crafts and food booths. ✉ *1891 E. Frontage Rd., Tumacácori* ✥ *Off I–19, Exit 29* ☎ *520/377–5060* 🌐 *www.nps.gov/tuma* 🎫 *$10.*

Tombstone

70 miles southeast of Tucson, 24 miles south of Benson via AZ 80, 28 miles northeast of Sierra Vista via AZ 90.

When prospector Ed Schieffelin headed out in 1877 to seek his fortune along the arid washes of San Pedro Valley, a patrolling soldier warned that all he'd find was his tombstone. Against all odds, his luck held out: he evaded bands of Apaches, braved the harsh desert terrain, and eventually stumbled across a ledge of silver ore. The town of Tombstone was named after the soldier's offhand comment.

The rich silver lodes from the area's mines attracted a wide mix of fortune seekers ranging from prospectors to prostitutes and gamblers to gunmen. But as the riches continued to pour in, wealthy citizens began importing the best entertainment and culture that silver could purchase. Even though saloons and gambling halls made up two out of every three businesses on Allen Street, the town also claimed the Cochise County seat, a cultural center, and fancy French restaurants. By the early 1880s the notorious boomtown was touted as the most cultivated city west of the Mississippi.

In 1881 a shoot-out between the Earp brothers and the Clanton gang ended with three of the "cowboys" (Billy Clanton and Tom and Frank McLaury) dead and two of the Earps (Virgil and Morgan) and Doc Holliday wounded. The infamous "gunfight at the O.K. Corral" and the ensuing feud between the Earp brothers and the Clanton gang firmly cemented Tombstone's place in the Wild West—even though the actual course of events is still debated by historians.

All in all, Tombstone's heyday lasted only a decade, but the colorful characters attached to the town's history live on—immortalized on the silver screen in such famous flicks as *Gunfight at the O.K. Corral, Tombstone,* and *Wyatt Earp.* The town's tourist industry parallels Hollywood hype. As a result, the main drag on Allen Street looks and feels like a movie set (even though most of the buildings are original), complete with gunning desperados, satin-bedecked saloon girls, and leather-clad cowboys. Today the kitschy "Town Too Tough to Die" attracts a mix of rough-and-tumble bikers, European tourists, and pulp-fiction thrill seekers looking to walk the boardwalks of Tombstone's infamous past.

GETTING HERE AND AROUND

Start your tour of this tiny town and pick up a free map at the visitor center. As you drive into Tombstone on U.S. 80, historic Allen Street, closed to cars, parallels the highway one block west. The visitor center sits in the middle, on the corner of Allen and 4th streets. Park along any side street or at the free lot on 6th Street.

VISITOR INFORMATION

CONTACTS City of Tombstone Visitor Center. ✉ *395 E. Allen St., at 4th St., Tombstone* ☎ *520/457–3929.*

Sights

The Bird Cage Theater

LOCAL INTEREST | A Tombstone institution, known as the wildest, wickedest night spot between Basin Street and the Barbary Coast, the Bird Cage Theater is a former music hall where Enrico Caruso, Sarah Bernhardt, and Lillian Russell, among others, performed. It was also the site of the longest continuous poker game recorded: the game started when the Bird Cage opened in 1881 and lasted eight years, five months, and three days. Some of the better-known players included Diamond Jim Brady, Adolphus Busch (of brewery fame), and William Randolph Hearst's father. The cards were dealt round the clock; players had to give a 20-minute notice when they were planning to vacate their seats, because there was always a waiting list of at least 10 people ready to shell out $1,000 (the equivalent of about $30,000 today) to get in. In all, some $10 million changed hands.

When the mines closed in 1889, the Bird Cage was abandoned, but the building has remained in the hands of the same family, who threw nothing out. You can walk on the stage visited by some of the top traveling performers of the time, see

The Legend of Wyatt Earp

Popularized in dime novels and on the silver screen, the legend of Wyatt Earp follows the American tradition of the tall tale. This larger-than-life hero of the Wild West is cloaked with romance and derring-do. Stripped of the glamour, though, Earp emerges as a man with a checkered past who switched from fugitive to lawman several times during his long life.

Born in 1848, Wyatt Berry Stapp Earp earned renown as the assistant city marshal of Dodge City. Wyatt and his brothers James, Virgil, and Morgan moved to Tombstone in 1879, and it was here that they, along with Wyatt's friend Doc Holliday, made their mark in history. Wyatt ran a gambling concession at the Oriental Saloon, and Virgil became Tombstone's city marshal. When trouble began to brew with the Clanton gang, Virgil recruited Wyatt and Morgan as deputy policemen. The escalating animosity between the "cowboys" and the Earps peaked on October 26, 1881, at the O.K. Corral—a 30-second gunfight that left three of the Clanton gang dead and Morgan and Virgil wounded. Doc Holliday was grazed, but Wyatt walked away from the fight uninjured. And then the real trouble for the Earps began.

In December Virgil was shot and crippled by unknown assailants, and on March 18, 1882, Morgan was shot to death in a pool hall. In retribution, Wyatt went on a bloody vendetta. After the smoke settled, the remaining "cowboys" were dead and Wyatt had left Tombstone for good. He made the rounds of mining camps in the West and up into Alaska, and then settled in California. He died on January 13, 1929. His legend lives on in movies such as *Tombstone* and *Wyatt Earp*.

the faro table once touched by the legendary gambler Doc Holliday, and pass by the hearse that carried Tombstone's deceased to Boot Hill. The basement, which served as an upscale bordello and gambling hall, still has all the original furnishings and fixtures intact, and you can see the personal belongings left behind by the ladies of the night when the mines closed and they, and their clients, headed for California. Nightly 90-minute ghost tours ($25) are also popular. ✉ *535 E. Allen St., at 6th St., Tombstone* ☎ *520/457–3421* 🌐 *www.tombstonebirdcage.com* 🎫 *$14.*

Boot Hill Graveyard
CEMETERY | This graveyard, where the victims of the O.K. Corral shoot-out are buried, is on the northwest corner of town, facing U.S. 80. Chinese names in one section of the "bone orchard" bear testament to the laundry and restaurant workers who came from San Francisco during the height of Tombstone's mining fever. One of the more amusing epitaphs at the cemetery, however, is engraved on the headstone of Wells Fargo agent Lester Moore; it poetically lists the cause of his untimely demise: "Here lies Lester Moore, four slugs from a.44, no les [sic], no more." If you're put off by the commercialism of the place—you enter through a gift shop that sells novelty items in the shape of tombstones—remember that Tombstone itself is the result of crass acquisition. ✉ *408 U.S. 80, Tombstone* ☎ *520/457–2540* 🌐 *tombstoneboothillgiftshop.com* 🎫 *$3, no credit cards.*

O.K. Corral and Tombstone Historama
MUSEUM | **FAMILY** | Vincent Price narrates the dramatic version of the town's fascinating past in the "Historama"—a

26-minute multimedia presentation that provides a solid overview. At the adjoining, authentic **O.K. Corral,** the actual spot where the 1881 shootout took place, a recorded voiceover details the gunfight, while life-size figures of the participants stand poised to shoot. A reenactment of the gunfight at the O.K. Corral is held daily at 11, noon, 2, and 3:30. Photographer C. S. Fly, whose studio was next door to the corral, didn't record this bit of history, but Geronimo and his pursuers were among the historic figures he did capture with his camera. Many of his fascinating Old West images and his equipment may be viewed at the **Fly Exhibition Gallery & Studio.** ✉ *326 Allen St., between 3rd and 4th Sts., Tombstone* ☎ *520/457–3456* 🌐 *www.ok-corral.com* 🎫 *$10 ($6 without gunfight reenactment).*

Rose Tree Inn Museum

MUSEUM | The museum might not look like much from the outside, but the collectibles and tree make this one of the best places to visit in town. Originally a boardinghouse for the Vizina Mining Company and later a popular hotel, the Rose Tree Inn Museum has 1880s period rooms and—its main attraction—a humongous rose tree (hence the name). Covering more than 8,600 square feet, the Lady Banksia rose tree, planted by a homesick bride in 1885, is reported to be the largest of its kind in the world. The best time to see the tree is from mid-March to May, when its tiny white roses bloom. Romantics can purchase a healthy clipping from the tree to plant in their own yards. ✉ *118 S. 4th St., at Toughnut St., Tombstone* ☎ *520/457–3326* 🌐 *tombstonerosetree.com* 🎫 *$5.*

★ Tombstone Courthouse State Historic Park

MUSEUM | For an introduction to the town's—and the area's—past, visit the Tombstone Courthouse State Historic Park. This redbrick 1882 county courthouse offers exhibits on the area's mining and ranching history and a collection of Wyatt Earp's letters; you can also see the restored 1904 courtroom and district attorney's office. The two-story building housed the Cochise County jail, a courtroom, and public offices until the county seat was moved to Bisbee in 1929. The stately building became the cornerstone of Tombstone's historic-preservation efforts in the 1950s, and was Arizona's first operational state park. ✉ *219 E. Toughnut St., at 3rd St., Tombstone* ☎ *520/457–3311* 🌐 *azstateparks.com/tombstone* 🎫 *$7.*

Tombstone Epitaph Museum

MUSEUM | You can see the original printing presses for the town's newspaper and watch a video about the production process at the Tombstone Epitaph Museum. The newspaper was founded in 1880 by John P. Clum, a colorful character in his own right, and is still publishing today. You can purchase one of the newspaper's special editions—*The Life and Times of Wyatt Earp, The Life and Times of Doc Holliday,* or *Tombstone's Pioneering Prostitutes.* ✉ *11 S. 5th St., Tombstone* ☎ *520/457–2211* 🌐 *www.tombstoneepitaph.com* 🎫 *Free.*

Restaurants

Crystal Palace Saloon

$$ | **AMERICAN** | If you're looking to wet your whistle or fill up on satisfying portions of steak, salmon, or pizza, stop by the Crystal Palace, where a beautiful mirrored mahogany bar, wrought-iron chandeliers, and tinwork ceilings date back to Tombstone's heyday. Locals come here on weekends to dance to live country-and-western music. **Known for:** historic building; somewhat bawdy saloon atmosphere; burgers and milkshakes. 💲 *Average main: $12* ✉ *436 E. Allen St., at 5th St., Tombstone* ☎ *520/457–3611* 🌐 *www.crystalpalacesaloon.com.*

Longhorn Restaurant

$$ | **AMERICAN** | **FAMILY** | You won't find anything fancy at this friendly eatery just down the street from Big Nose

Kate's Saloon, but you will find generous helpings of basic American and Mexican food at decent prices. The menu covers everything from breakfast to dinner with such entrées as omelets, burgers, steaks, tacos, and enchiladas. **Known for:** American and Mexican favorites; kid-friendly menu; hearty breakfasts. $ *Average main: $12* ✉ *501 E. Allen St., Tombstone* ☎ *520/457–3405* 🌐 *thelonghornrestaurant.com.*

Bisbee

24 miles southeast of Tombstone on AZ 80.

Like Tombstone, Bisbee was a mining boomtown, but its wealth was in copper, not silver, and its success continued much longer. The gnarled Mule Mountains aren't as impressive as some of the other mountain ranges in Southern Arizona, but their rocky canyons concealed one of the richest mineral sites in the world.

Jack Dunn, a scout with Company C from Fort Huachuca, first discovered an outcropping of rich ore here while chasing the Apaches in 1877. By 1900 more than 20,000 people lived in the crowded canyons around the Bisbee mines. Phelps Dodge purchased all the major mines by the Great Depression, and mining continued until 1975, when the mines were closed for good. In less than 100 years of mining, the area surrounding Bisbee yielded more than $6.1 billion of mineral wealth.

Once known as the Queen of the Copper Camps, Bisbee was rediscovered in the 1980s by burned-out city dwellers, and the cool but scruffy vibe, hilly terrain, and Victorian architecture conjure up a sort of 1960s San Francisco scene. The locals are an interesting mix of retired miners and their families, aging hippie jewelry makers, and enterprising restaurateurs and boutique owners from all over the country. Milder temperatures (about 10 to 15 degrees lower than Tucson), plentiful lodging (quaint inns, cottage rentals, and vintage trailers), and the town's history and natural beauty make for a rewarding visit.

GETTING HERE AND AROUND

If you want to head straight into town from AZ 80, get off at the Brewery Gulch interchange. You can cross under the highway, taking Main, Commerce, or Brewery Gulch streets, all of which intersect at the large, free public parking lot. Most restaurants and shops are in an easily navigated 4-to 5-block area. This includes Main Street, lined with appealing art galleries, antiques stores, crafts shops, boutiques, and restaurants—many in well-preserved turn-of-the-20th-century brick buildings. To reach the Lavender Pit Mine, drive a half mile south on AZ 80. A little farther south, at the roundabout, take the turnoff for the Warren district to see where the mining managers built beautiful mansions.

TOURS

Lavender Jeep Tours

DRIVING TOURS | Run by Bisbee natives, these tours range from a one-hour ride around greater Bisbee to a six-hour tour that includes neighboring ghost towns. Driver guides regale visitors with fascinating tales while winding through the hills of historic Bisbee and the surrounding region. ✉ *Copper Queen Hotel, 11 Howell Ave., Bisbee* ☎ *520/432–5369* 🌐 *www.lavenderjeeptours.com* 🎟 *From $50.*

VISITOR INFORMATION

CONTACTS Bisbee Visitor Center. ✉ *5 Copper Queen Plaza, Bisbee* ✥ *south side of the Bisbee Mining and Historical Museum* ☎ *520/432–3554* 🌐 *www.discoverbisbee.com.*

Sights

Bisbee Mining and Historical Museum

MUSEUM | The redbrick structure this museum is housed in was built in 1897 to serve as the Copper Queen Consolidated Mining Offices. The rooms today are filled with colorful exhibits, photographs, and artifacts that offer a glimpse into the everyday life of Bisbee's early mining community. The exhibit *Bisbee: Urban Outpost on the Frontier* paints a fascinating portrait of how this "Shady Lady" of a mining town transformed into a true mini urban center. Upstairs, the *Digging In* exhibit shows you everything you ever wanted to know about copper mining, including what it felt and sounded like in a mining car. This was the first rural museum in the United States to become a member of the Smithsonian Institution Affiliations Program, and it tells a story you can take with you as you wander through Bisbee's funky streets. ⊠ *5 Copper Queen Plaza, Bisbee* ☎ *520/432–7071* ⊕ *bisbeemuseum.org* 🎫 *$8.*

Brewery Gulch

HISTORIC SITE | A short street running north–south, Brewery Gulch is adjacent to the Copper Queen Hotel. In the old days the brewery housed here allowed the dregs of the beer that was being brewed to flow down the street and into the gutter. Nowadays this narrow road is home to Bisbee's nightlife. ⊠ *Bisbee.*

Copper Queen Hotel

BUILDING | Built a century ago and still in operation, the Copper Queen Hotel has hosted some famous people over the years; General John "Black Jack" Pershing, John Wayne, Theodore Roosevelt, and mining executives from all over the world made this their home away from home. Though the restaurant fare is basic, the outdoor bar area is a great spot for enjoying a margarita and people-watching. The hotel also allegedly hosts three resident ghosts; the journal at the front desk contains descriptions of guests' encounters. ⊠ *11 Howell Ave., Bisbee* ✣ *behind the Mining and Historical Museum* ☎ *520/432–2216* ⊕ *www.copperqueen.com.*

Copper Queen Mine Underground Tour

MINE | **FAMILY** | For a lesson in mining history, take a tour led by Bisbee's retired copper miners, who are wont to embellish their spiel with tales from their mining days. The 60-minute tours (you can't enter the mine at any other time) go into the shaft via a small open train, like those the miners rode when the mine was active. Before you climb aboard, you're outfitted in miner's garb—a safety vest and a hard hat with a light that runs off a battery pack. You'll travel thousands of feet into the mine, up a grade of 30 feet (not down, as many visitors expect). The mine is less than ½ mile to the east of the Lavender Pit, across AZ 80 from downtown at the Brewery Gulch interchange. Reservations are suggested. ⊠ *478 N. Dart Rd., Bisbee* ☎ *520/432–2071, 866/432–2071* ⊕ *www.queenminetour.com* 🎫 *$14.*

Lavender Pit Mine

MINE | About ¼ mile after AZ 80 intersects with AZ 92, you can pull off the highway into a gravel parking lot for a view of the Lavender Pit Mine, a huge hole left by the copper miners. Though the piles of "tailings," or waste, are lavender-hued, the pit's namesake is actually Harrison (Harry) Lavender, the engineer largely responsible for transforming Bisbee's rock into commercial copper ore. Arizona's largest pit mine yielded some 94 million tons of ore before mining activity came to a halt. ⊠ *AZ 80, Bisbee.*

Restaurants

Bisbee's Table

$$ | **AMERICAN** | You might not expect diversity at a place with a reputation for having the best burger in town, but this restaurant delivers with salads, sandwiches, pasta, salmon, steaks, and ribs. The dining room, built to resemble an old train depot, fills up fast on weekends. **Known for:** healthy comfort food; gluten-free options; vibrant atmosphere. $ *Average main: $17* ✉ *2 Copper Queen Plaza, Bisbee* ☎ *520/432–6788* 🌐 *www.bisbeetable.com.*

★ Café Roka

$$$ | MODERN AMERICAN | This is the deserved darling of both the hip Bisbee crowd and foodies from all over. The constantly changing, locally sourced evening menu is not extensive, but whatever you order—wild yellow fin tuna, roasted duck, rack of lamb—will be wonderful. **Known for:** best dining in the region; excellent wine list; sophisticated yet relaxed vibe. $ *Average main: $26* ✉ *35 Main St., Bisbee* ☎ *520/432–5153* 🌐 *caferoka.com* ⏲ *Closed Mon.–Wed. No lunch.*

Hotels

Canyon Rose Suites

$ | HOTEL | Steps from the heart of downtown, this all-suites inn includes seven pretty and spacious units of varying size, all with hardwood floors, 10-foot ceilings, and fully equipped kitchens. **Pros:** quiet, yet just off Main Street; well-equipped, attractive suites; easy parking behind building. **Cons:** no common area; no elevator (guest rooms are on second floor); some street noise. $ *Rooms from: $129* ✉ *27 Subway St., Bisbee* ☎ *520/432–5098* 🌐 *www.canyonrose.com* *7 rooms* *No meals.*

★ Shady Dell Trailer Court

$ | RENTAL | For a blast from the past, stay in one of the funky vintage aluminum trailers at this trailer park south of town, where accommodations range from a 1952 10-foot homemade unit to a 1951 33-foot Royal Mansion. **Pros:** unique and fun (how many hip vintage trailer-park hotels are there?); cheap; Dot's Diner (on-site) is great for a quick bite. **Cons:** no children under 12, except with prior approval; walking to the public restrooms in the middle of the night (some trailers don't have a toilet; some have toilet but no shower); drive into town. $ *Rooms from: $75* ✉ *1 Douglas Rd., Bisbee* ☎ *520/432–3567* 🌐 *www.theshadydell.com* *10 trailers* *No meals.*

Shopping

Belleza Gallery

ART GALLERIES | This fine-art gallery is owned and operated by Bisbee's Women's Transition Project, which aids homeless women and their children. Belleza features the work of local and national artists, as well as a line of wood Adirondack furniture made by women receiving assistance from the program. The gallery's commission from furniture sales goes directly into funding the Transition Project. ✉ *23 Main St., Bisbee* ☎ *520/432–5877.*

55 Main Gallery

ART GALLERIES | Although many artist studios, galleries, and boutiques in historic buildings line Main Street, which runs though Tombstone Canyon, 55 Main Gallery is one of several noteworthy galleries selling contemporary work at a range of prices along the main drag. ✉ *55 Main St., Bisbee* ☎ *520/432–4694.*

Killer Bee Guy

FOOD/CANDY | A trip to Bisbee wouldn't be complete without a stop at the tiny shop of beekeeper Reed Booth. Sample his amazing array of honeys, honey butters, and mustards, and pick up some killer honey recipes. ✉ *20 Main St., Bisbee* ☎ *520/432–8016* 🌐 *www.killerbeeguy.com.*

★ Óptimo Custom Panama Hatworks

JEWELRY/ACCESSORIES | Custom, handwoven Panama hats, as well as works of beaver, hare, and rabbit fur-felt, are what this nationally renowned shop is known for. It's also where people get their historical hats cleaned and restored.

Chiricahua National Monument is filled with dramatic "upside-down" or "standing-up" volcanic rocks.

47 Main St., Bisbee 520/432–4544 www.optimohatworks.com.

Chiricahua National Monument

65 miles northeast of Sierra Vista on AZ 90 to I–10 to AZ 186, 58 miles northeast of Douglas on U.S. 191 to AZ 181, 36 miles southeast of Willcox.

With its "upside-down" rock formations and abundant wildlife, the Chiricahua National Monument is well worth the two-hour drive from Tucson. You'll be rewarded with unique, stunning scenery and unspoiled wilderness for birding, hiking, and camping.

GETTING HERE AND AROUND

Though a little more remote than other sights in southeastern Arizona, Chiricahua National Monument is just more than a half-hour drive from Willcox. You might combine a trip to this area with a Willcox wine tasting. The nearest gas stations are in Willcox or Sunizona, so be sure to fill your tank first.

Sights

★ **Chiricahua National Monument**

NATIONAL/STATE PARK | FAMILY | Vast fields of desert grass are suddenly transformed into a landscape of forest, mountains, and striking rock formations as you enter the 12,000-acre Chiricahua National Monument. The Chiricahua Apache—who lived in the mountains for centuries and, led by Cochise and Geronimo, tried for 25 years to prevent white pioneers from settling here—dubbed it "the Land of the Standing-Up Rocks." Enormous outcroppings of volcanic rock have been worn by erosion and fractured by uplift into strange pinnacles and spires. Because of the particular balance of sunshine and rain in the area, April and May see brown, yellow, and red leaves coexisting with new green foliage. Summer in Chiricahua National Monument is exceptionally wet: from July through September there are thunderstorms nearly every afternoon.

Geronimo: No Bullet Shall Pass

The fearless Apache war shaman Geronimo, known among his people as "the one who yawns," fought to the very end in the Apache Wars. His surrender to General Nelson Miles on September 5, 1886, marked the end of the Indian Wars in the West. Geronimo's fleetness in evading the massed troops of the U.S. Army and his legendary immunity to bullets made him the darling of sensationalistic journalists, and he became the most famous outlaw in America.

When the combined forces of the U.S. Army and Mexican troops failed to rout the powerful shaman from his territory straddling Arizona and Mexico, General Miles sent his officer Lieutenant Gatewood and relatives of Geronimo's renegade band of warriors to persuade Geronimo to parley with Miles near the mouth of Skeleton Canyon, at the edge of the Peloncillo Mountains. After several days of talks, Geronimo and his warriors agreed to the presented treaty and surrendered their arms.

Geronimo related the scene years later: "We stood between his troopers and my warriors. We placed a large stone on the blanket before us. Our treaty was made by this stone, as it was to last until the stone should crumble to dust; so we made the treaty, and bound each other with an oath." Nevertheless, the political promises quickly unraveled, and the most feared among Apache medicine men spent his next 23 years in exile as a prisoner of war. He died on February 17, 1909, never having returned to his beloved homeland, and was buried in the Apache cemetery in Fort Sill, Oklahoma.

In 1934 a stone monument was built on State Route 80 in Apache, Arizona, as a reminder of Geronimo's surrender in 1886. The 16-foot-tall monument lies 10 miles northwest of the actual surrender site in Skeleton Canyon, where an unobtrusive sign and a pile of rocks mark the place where the last stone was cast.

Few other areas in the United States have such varied plant, bird, and animal life. Deer, coatimundi, peccaries, and lizards live among the aspen, ponderosa pine, Douglas fir, oak, and cypress trees—to name just a few.

Chiricahua National Monument is an excellent area for bird-watchers, and hikers have more than 17 miles of scenic trails. Hiking-trail maps and advice are available at the visitor center. A popular and rewarding hike is the moderately easy **Echo Canyon Loop Trail**, a 3½-mile path that winds through cavelike grottos, brilliant rock formations, and a wooded canyon. Birds and other wildlife are abundant. ✉ *AZ 181, Chiricahua National Monument* ✥ *36 miles southeast of Willcox* ☎ *520/824–3560* 🌐 *www.nps.gov/chir* 🎫 *Free.*

Hotels

Lodging is a bit of a challenge in this remote area. Campsites in Bonita Canyon Campground, within the monument, can be reserved in advance (☎ *877/444–6777* or 🌐 *www.recreation.gov*). For those preferring to sleep indoors, the closest accommodations are about a half-hour drive, either north to one of several decent chain hotels in Willcox or to a B&B south of the monument.

Dreamcatcher Bed and Breakfast

$ | **B&B/INN** | Twelve miles south of Chiricahua National Monument, this 27-acre property has plenty of wildlife, from deer to Mexican blue jays, and a U-shaped hacienda with five rooms, all with large walk-in showers, ceiling fans, and private entrances that open onto a flower-filled courtyard. **Pros:** excellent value; tranquil; convenient to Chiricahuas. **Cons:** isolated; no services nearby (though dinner is offered for an extra charge). *$ Rooms from: $105 ✉ 13097 S. AZ 181, Pearce ☎ 520/824–3127 🌐 www.dreamcatcherb-nb.com 5 rooms Free breakfast.*

Texas Canyon

16 miles southwest of Willcox off I–10.

A dramatic change of scenery along Interstate 10 will signal that you're entering Texas Canyon. The rock formations here are exceptional—huge boulders appear to be delicately balanced against each other. It's worth a stop for a picnic, a short hike, and some photo opportunities.

GETTING HERE AND AROUND

Get off Interstate 10 at Exit 318, and then turn right onto Dragoon Road. The Amerind Foundation is a mile down on the left, and Triangle T Guest Ranch, with lodging and a restaurant, is next door.

Sights

The Amerind Foundation

MUSEUM | Texas Canyon is the home of the Amerind Foundation (a contraction of "American" and "Indian"), founded by amateur archaeologist William Fulton in 1937 to foster understanding about Native American cultures. The research facility and museum are housed in a Spanish colonial–style structure designed by noted Tucson architect H. M. Starkweather. The museum's rotating displays of archaeological materials, crafts, and photographs give an overview of Native American cultures of the Southwest and Mexico.

The adjacent Fulton–Hayden Memorial Art Gallery displays an assortment of art collected by William Fulton. Permanent exhibits include the work of Tohono O'odham women potters, an exquisite collection of Hopi kachina dolls, prized paintings by acclaimed Hopi artists, Pueblo pottery ranging from prehistoric pieces to modern ceramics, and archaeological exhibits on the indigenous cultures of the prehistoric Southwest. The museum's gift shop has a superlative selection of Native American art, crafts, and jewelry. Beautiful picnic areas among the boulders can accommodate large and small groups. *✉ 2100 N. Amerind Rd., Dragoon ✣ 1 mile southeast of I–10, Exit 318 ☎ 520/586–3666 🌐 www.amerind.org $10 Closed Mon.*

Hotels

Triangle T Guest Ranch

$$$ | **B&B/INN** | Enjoy the romance of the Old West at this historic ranch on 160 acres of prime real estate in Texas Canyon. **Pros:** horseback riding (fee) and hiking trails; restaurant and bar with live country and Western music; good base for exploring the region. **Cons:** isolated; rustic; less authentic feel than some guest ranches. *$ Rooms from: $179 ✉ 4190 Dragoon Rd., off I–10, Exit 318, Dragoon ☎ 520/586–7533 🌐 www.azretreatcenter.com 11 casitas Free breakfast.*

Kartchner Caverns State Park

9 miles south of Benson on AZ 90.

Kartchner Caverns is a large and beautifully maintained cave system where visitors can walk through the fantastic stalactites and stalagmites while learning about the unique and fragile ecosystem. It's a wet, "live" cave, meaning that water still rises up from the surface to continually add to the multicolor calcium carbonate formations already visible. Amateur cavers discovered Kartchner Caverns in 1974, and it opened to the public in 1999.

GETTING HERE AND AROUND

From Exit 302 off Interstate 10, take AZ 90 for 9 miles.

The closest place to stay to the caverns is Benson, a small town 12 miles west of Texas Canyon and 50 miles southeast of Tucson via I–10. Amtrak runs trains from Tucson to Benson three times a week. You likely won't linger in Benson on your way to the caverns, but it's a good place to grab a meal and fill your gas tank.

Sights

★ Kartchner Caverns

CAVE | FAMILY | The publicity that surrounded the official opening of Kartchner Caverns in 1999 was in marked contrast to the secrecy that shrouded their discovery 25 years earlier and concealed their existence for 14 years. The two young spelunkers, Gary Tenen and Randy Tufts, who stumbled into what is now considered one of the most spectacular cave systems anywhere, played a fundamental role in its protection and eventual development. Great precautions have been taken to protect the wet-cave system—which comprises 13,000 feet of passages and two chambers as long as football fields—from damage by light and dryness.

The Discovery Center introduces visitors to the cave and its formations, and guided Rotunda/Throne Room tours take small groups into the upper cave. Spectacular formations include the longest soda straw stalactite in the United States at 21 feet and 2 inches. The Big Room is viewed on a separate tour for ages 7 and up: it holds the world's most extensive formation of brushite moonmilk, the first reported occurrence of turnip shields, and the first noted occurrence of birds-nest needle formations. Other funky and fabulous formations include brilliant red flowstone, rippling multihued stalactites, delicate white helictites, translucent orange bacon, and expansive mudflats. It's also the nursery roost for female cave myotis bats from mid-April through mid-October, during which time this lower cave is closed.

The total cavern size is 2.4 miles long, but the explored areas cover only 1,600 feet by 1,100 feet. The average relative humidity inside is 99%, so visitors are often graced with "cave kisses," water droplets from above. Because the climate outside the caves is so dry, it is estimated that if air got inside, it could deplete the moisture in only a few days, halting the growth of the speleothems that decorate its walls. To prevent this, there are 22 environmental monitoring stations that measure air and soil temperature, relative humidity, evaporation rates, air trace gases, and airflow inside the caverns. ■ **TIP→ Tour reservations are strongly recommended, especially during winter months. If you're here and didn't make a reservation, go ahead and check: sometimes same-day reservations are available (call or arrive early in the day for these).** Hiking trails, picnic areas, and campsites are available on the park's 550 acres, and the Bat Cave Café, open daily, serves pizza, hot dogs, salads, and sandwiches. ✉ *AZ 90, Benson* ✢ *9 miles south of I–10, Exit 302* ☎ *520/586–4100 info and tour reservations* 🌐 *azstateparks.com/kartchner* 🎫 *Park admission $7 per vehicle up to 4 people, $3 each additional person (fees waived for those with cave tour reservations). Rotunda/Throne Room tour or Big Room tour $23.*

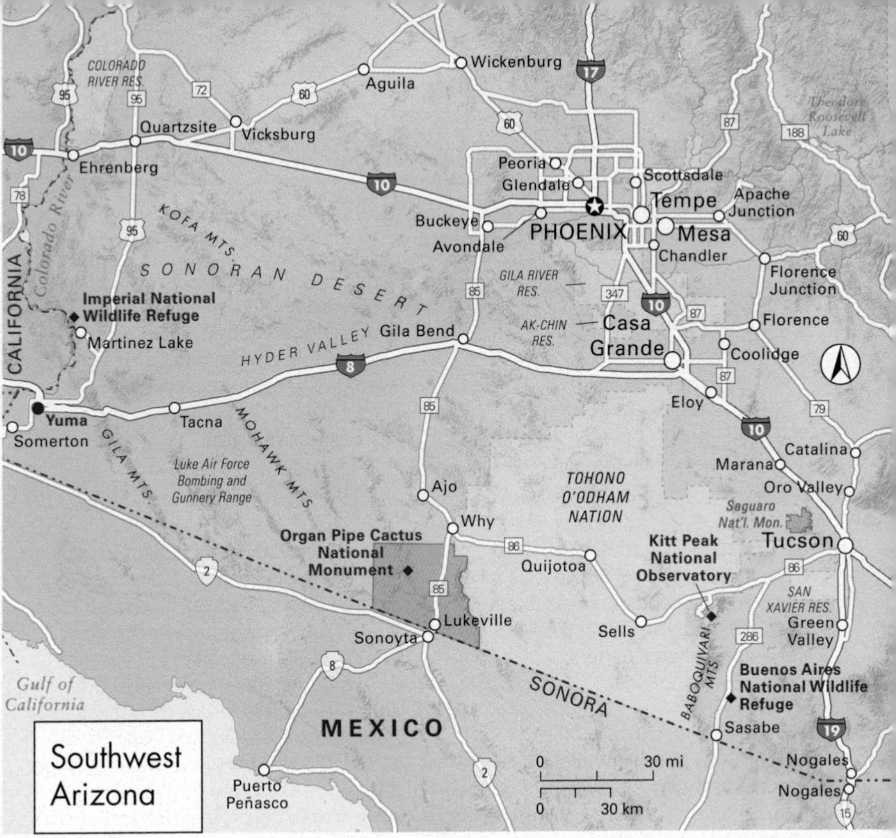

Southwest Arizona

Hotels

Comfort Inn Benson

$ | **HOTEL** | The closest lodging to Kartchner Caverns State Park, this modern motel just off Interstate 10 at the "Kartchner Corridor," a few miles west of Benson, has the comfort and amenities you'd expect, but with a bit of Southwestern elegance rarely found in properties around the area. **Pros:** convenient location; friendly; bountiful breakfast included. **Cons:** just off the highway; not particularly serene or scenic; generic. *$ Rooms from: $105 ✉ 630 S. Village Loop, Benson ☎ 520/586–8800 🌐 www.choicehotels.com ⇨ 62 rooms 🍽 Free breakfast.*

Buenos Aires National Wildlife Refuge

66 miles southwest of Tucson.

Encircled by seven mountain ranges in the Altar Valley, remote Buenos Aires National Wildlife Refuge is the only place in the United States where the Sonoran-savanna grasslands that once pervaded this region can still be seen. The U.S. Fish and Wildlife Service oversees this 115,000-acre preserve, managing programs to restore native grasses and protect endangered species such as the masked bobwhite quail. Birding and wildlife-viewing are popular here.

Border Town Safety: Nogales, Mexico

Nogales used to draw tourists and locals who would park on the American side and walk across the border. Though shopping bargains and cheap bars are enticing, safety issues have changed in recent years.

■ TIP→ **Drug-related violence in Mexico—especially near the U.S. border—has increased to the point that the U.S. government strongly discourages travel in and around Mexico border towns. Check travel.state.gov for updates and details.**

If you decide to cross, bring your passport (it's required), remain alert, and stay in the central area on Avenida Obregón, which begins a few blocks west of the border entrance and runs north–south.

GETTING HERE AND AROUND

From Tucson, take AZ 86 west 22 miles to AZ 286; go south 40 miles to mile marker 8, and it's another 3 miles east to the preserve headquarters.

Sights

Buenos Aires National Wildlife Refuge

NATURE PRESERVE | Bird-watchers consider Buenos Aires National Wildlife Refuge unique because it's the only place in the United States where they can see a "grand slam" (four species) of quail: Montezuma quail, Gambel's quail, scaled quail, and masked bobwhite. If it rains, the 100-acre Aguirre Lake, 1½ miles north of the headquarters, attracts wading birds, shorebirds, and waterfowl—in all, more than 320 avian species have been spotted here. The quail share the turf with deer, coati, badgers, bobcats, and mountain lions. Touring options include a 10-mile auto tour; nature trails; a 3¾-mile guided hike in Brown Canyon (second and fourth Saturdays, November–April, or call to arrange other dates for private groups); a boardwalk through the marshes at Arivaca Cienega; and guided bird walks, also at Arivaca Cienega (November–April, first Saturday at 8). Admission and guided bird walks are free; Brown Canyon hikes cost $5. Pick up maps at the visitor center. ✉ *AZ 286, at mile marker 7.5, Sasabe* ✣ *Turn off AZ 286 at mile marker 7.5, and drive into the refuge for 3 miles to Refuge Headquarters and Visitor Center* ☎ *520/823–4251* 🌐 *www.fws.gov/refuge/buenos_aires* 🎫 *Free* ⏲ *Visitor center open limited hours Apr.–Oct. (call ahead).*

Hotels

Rancho de la Osa

$$ | **ALL-INCLUSIVE** | **FAMILY** | Set on 250 eucalyptus-shaded acres near the Mexican border and Buenos Aires Wildlife Refuge, this tranquil late 19th-century ranch with adobe buildings offers guests plenty of activities like horseback riding, hiking, biking, and archery. **Pros:** excellent ranch activities; good food and extensive wine list; historic setting. **Cons:** somewhat isolated; about an hour and a half drive from Tucson. $ *Rooms from: $169* ✉ *41480 S. Sasabe Hwy., Sasabe* ☎ *520/339–1086* 🌐 *www.ranchodelaosa.com* 🛏 *18 rooms* 🍽 *Free breakfast.*

Kitt Peak National Observatory

70 miles northwest of Buenos Aires National Wildlife Refuge on AZ 286 to AZ 86, 56 miles southwest of Tucson.

Funded by the National Science Foundation and managed by a group of more than 20 universities, Kitt Peak National Observatory is on the Tohono O'odham Reservation. Kitt Peak scientists use the high-powered telescopes here to conduct vital solar research and observe distant galaxies; visitors can tour the facilities by day and view stellar happenings at the evening observation program.

GETTING HERE AND AROUND

To reach Kitt Peak from Tucson, take Interstate 10 to Interstate 19 south, and then AZ 86. After 44 miles on AZ 86, turn left at the AZ 386 junction and follow the winding mountain road 12 miles up to the observatory. In inclement weather, contact the highway department to confirm that the road is open. To get to Sells (for the nearest food and gas) from the base of the mountain, it's 20 miles west on AZ 86.

 Sights

Kitt Peak National Observatory

OBSERVATORY | After much discussion back in the late 1950s, tribal leaders of the Tohono O'odham nation agreed to share a small section of their 4,400-square-mile reservation with the National Science Foundation to house sophisticated research telescopes. Among these is the McMath-Pierce, the world's largest solar telescope, which uses piped-in liquid coolant. From the visitors' gallery you can see into the telescope's light-path tunnel, which goes down hundreds of feet into the mountain.

The visitor center has exhibits on astronomy, information about the telescopes, and hour-long guided tours ($11 per person) that depart daily at 10, 11:30, and 1:30. Complimentary brochures enable you to take self-guided tours of the grounds, and there are picnic areas outside and below the observatory. The observatory sells snacks and drinks, which is good to know, because there are no restaurants (or gas stations, for that matter) within 20 miles of Kitt Peak. The observatory offers an outstanding nightly program for ages eight and older ($55 per person); reservations are necessary. ✉ *AZ 386, Pan Tak* ☎ *520/318–8726* 🌐 *www.noao.edu/kpno* 🎫 *Free; tours and observatory programs extra.*

Organ Pipe Cactus National Monument

32 miles southwest of Ajo on AZ 86 to AZ 85.

The largest habitat north of the border for organ pipe cacti (the beautiful multi-armed cousins of the saguaro) is off the beaten path unless you're driving to Puerto Penasco, Mexico. But it's a worthwhile destination to view large groves of this desert flora, fairly common in Mexico but rare in the United States.

GETTING HERE AND AROUND

From Ajo, drive to Why and take AZ 85 south for 22 miles to reach the visitor center.

SAFETY AND PRECAUTIONS

Be aware that Organ Pipe continues to be an illegal-border-crossing hot spot where some people cross from Mexico under the cover of darkness. You probably won't encounter this type of situation, but it is possible, even with the copious fencing along the U.S.–Mexico border. Park officials emphasize that tourists only occasionally have been the victims of isolated property crimes—primarily theft of personal items from parked cars. Visitors are advised by rangers to keep valuables locked and out of plain view and not to initiate contact with groups of strangers whom they may encounter on hiking trails.

Sights

Organ Pipe Cactus National Monument
NATIONAL/STATE PARK | This designated part of the Sonoran Desert preserves more than two dozen species of cacti, including the park's namesake, as well as other desert plants and animals. Because organ pipe cactus tend to grow on the warmer, usually south-facing slopes, you'll get the best views by taking either the 21-mile scenic loop **Ajo Mountain Drive** (a one-way, partly dirt road) or **Puerto Blanco Drive,** a 45-mile loop road (4-wheel drive vehicles are recommended). Ranger-led talks and guided van tours are offered January through April. Check with rangers for the schedule of "trailhead drops," which enable hikers to leave their cars in more populated areas. ✉ *10 Organ Pipe Dr., Ajo* ☎ *520/387–6849* 🌐 *www.nps.gov/orpi* 🎟 *$25 per vehicle.*

Yuma

232 miles northwest of Organ Pipe Cactus National Monument, 170 miles northwest of Ajo.

Today many people think of Yuma as a convenient stop for gas and a meal between Phoenix or Tucson and San Diego. Although this is surely true, the town boasts some historical sites and agricultural tours (Yuma is the lettuce capital of the U.S.) that may prompt you to pause here a bit longer.

It's difficult to imagine the lower Colorado River, now dammed and bridged, as either a barrier or a means of transportation, but until the early part of the 20th century this section of the great waterway was a force to contend with. Records show that since at least 1540 the Spanish were using Yuma (then the home of the indigenous Quechan tribe) as a ford across a relatively shallow stretch of the Colorado.

Three centuries later, the advent of the shallow-draft steamboat made the settlement a point of entry for fortune seekers heading through the Gulf of California to mining sites in Eastern Arizona. Fort Yuma was established in 1850 to guard against Indian attacks, and by 1873 the town was a county seat, a U.S. port of entry, and an army depot.

During World War II, the Yuma Proving Ground was used to train bomber pilots, and General Patton readied some of his desert war forces for battle at secret areas in the city. Many who served here during the war returned to Yuma to retire, and the city's population swells during the winter months with retirees from cold climates who park their homes on wheels at one of the many RV communities. One fact may explain this: according to National Weather Service statistics, Yuma is the sunniest city in the United States.

GETTING HERE AND AROUND

AZ 8 runs through Yuma, which is approximately halfway between Casa Grande and the California coast. Most of the interesting historical sites are at the north end of town. Stop in at the Yuma Visitor Center, on the grounds of Colorado River State Historic Park, and pick up a visitor guide. You can also rent bikes here to ride along the riverfront.

Yuma is accessible by air through American Airlines, which has several direct flights daily between Yuma and Phoenix.

Amtrak trains run three times a week from Tucson west to Yuma (get your ticket or make a reservation beforehand as there's no kiosk or ticket window).

VISITOR INFORMATION

CONTACTS Yuma Visitor Center. ✉ *201 N 4th Ave., Yuma* ☎ *928/783–0071* 🌐 *www.visityuma.com.*

Sights

Colorado River State Historic Park

NATIONAL/STATE PARK | On the other side of the river from Fort Yuma, the Civil War–period quartermaster depot resupplied army posts to the north and east and served as a distribution point for steamboat freight headed overland to Arizona forts. The 1853 home of riverboat captain G. A. Johnson is the depot's earliest building and the centerpiece of this park. The residence also served as a weather bureau and home for customs agents, among other functions, and the self-guided tour through the house provides a complete history. Also on display are antique surreys and more "modern" modes of transportation like a 1931 Model A Ford pickup. You can visit a re-creation of the Commanding Officer's Quarters, complete with period furnishings. The Yuma Visitor Center and a pie shop are also here. ✉ *201 N. 4th Ave., between 1st St. and I–8, Yuma* ☎ *928/783–0071* 🌐 *azstateparks.com* 🎫 *$6* 🕒 *Closed Mon. June–Sept.*

Yuma Territorial Prison State Historic Park

JAIL | FAMILY | The most notorious tourist sight in town is now an Arizona state historic park, but it was built for the most part by the convicts who were incarcerated here from 1876 until 1909, when the prison outgrew its location. The hilly site on the Colorado River, chosen for security purposes, precluded further expansion.

Visitors gazing today at the tiny cells that held six inmates each, often in 115°F heat, are likely to be appalled, but the prison—dubbed "the Country Club of the Colorado" by locals—was considered a model of enlightenment by turn-of-the-20th-century standards: in an era when beatings were common, the only punishments meted out here were solitary confinement and assignment to a dark cell. The complex housed a hospital as well as Yuma's only public library, where the 25¢ that visitors paid for a prison tour financed the acquisition of new books.

The 3,069 prisoners who served time at what was then the territory's only prison included men and women from 21 different countries. They came from all social classes and were sent up for everything from armed robbery and murder to polygamy. R. L. McDonald, incarcerated for forgery, had been the superintendent of the Phoenix public school system. Chosen as the prison bookkeeper, he absconded with $130 of the inmates' money when he was released.

The mess hall opened as a museum in 1940, and the entire prison complex was designated a state historic park in 1961. ✉ *220 N. Prison Hill Rd., off I–8, Exit 1, Yuma* ☎ *928/783–4771* 🌐 *www.yumaprison.org* 🎫 *$8* 🕒 *Closed Tues. and Wed. June–Sept.*

Restaurants

La Fonda

$ | MEXICAN | A Yuma institution, La Fonda opened as a tortilla factory in 1940, then added a colorful restaurant onto the original building in 1982; locals have been enjoying the carne asada, pollo asado, and chiles rellenos here ever since. Only canola oil is used (not lard), and all the sauces and marinades are made fresh, as are the corn tortillas, which many say are the best in town. **Known for:** classic Mexican; chipotle corn tortillas; best place to buy fresh tortillas. 💲 *Average main: $11* ✉ *1095 S. 3rd Ave., Yuma* ☎ *928/783–6902* 🌐 *www.lafondarestaurantyumaaz.com* 🕒 *Closed Sun.*

★ Lutes Casino

$ | SOUTHWESTERN | Packed with locals at lunchtime, this large, funky restaurant and bar claims to be the oldest pool hall and domino parlor in Arizona. It's a great place for a burger or tacos and a brew. **Known for:** the "Especial" cheeseburger–hot dog combo; friendly atmosphere; great bar. 💲 *Average main: $10* ✉ *221 S.*

Main St., Yuma ☎ 928/782–2192 🌐 www.lutescasino.com.

River City Grill

$$$ | **AMERICAN** | This hip downtown restaurant is a favorite dining spot for locals and visitors, and though it gets a bit loud on weekend nights, the camaraderie of diners is well worth it. Owners Nan and Tony Bain dish out a medley of flavors drawing on Mediterranean, Pacific Rim, Indian, and Caribbean influences. **Known for:** best upscale dining in Yuma; large, eclectic menu; vegan and gluten-free selections. *$ Average main: $24 ✉ 600 W. 3rd St., Yuma ☎ 928/782–7988 🌐 www.rivercitygrill.com ⏲ No lunch Sun.*

Hotels

★ Coronado Motor Hotel

$ | **HOTEL** | Built in 1938, this Spanish tile–roofed motor hotel has been well cared for and was where Bob Hope used to stay during World War II, when he entertained the gunnery troops training in Yuma. **Pros:** convenient location near AZ 8 and a short walk from the historic downtown area; great retro property; full breakfast at neighboring restaurant. **Cons:** some highway and street noise; older property might not appeal to some; rooms are somewhat small. *$ Rooms from: $99 ✉ 233 S. 4th Ave., Yuma ☎ 928/783–4453, 877/234–5567 🌐 coronadomotorhotel.com ⇆ 86 rooms 🍽 Free breakfast.*

Hilton Garden Inn Yuma-Pivot Point

$ | **HOTEL** | One of the newer hotels in town, the Hilton Garden Inn Yuma caters to families and business travelers equally, with well-equipped rooms, an on-site restaurant, a pleasant pool area, and convenience to historic sights and the highway. **Pros:** comfortable rooms; pool, hot tub, and gym; easy walk to riverfront park and historic area. **Cons:** generic property; higher rates on weekdays. *$ Rooms from: $109 ✉ 310 N. Madison Ave., Yuma ☎ 928/783–1500 🌐 www.hiltongarden-inn.com ⇆ 150 rooms 🍽 No meals.*

Imperial National Wildlife Refuge

30 miles north of Yuma on U.S. 95.

Something of an anomaly, this 25,765-acre wildlife refuge, created when the Imperial Dam was built, is home both to marshy-river species and creatures that inhabit the adjacent Sonoran Desert—coyotes, bobcats, desert tortoises, and bighorn sheep. Mostly, though, it's a major bird habitat, with waterfowl and shorebirds year-round and masses of migrating flocks during spring and fall.

GETTING HERE AND AROUND

From Yuma, take U.S. 95 north and follow the signs to the refuge; it's about a 40-minute drive. Between January and March look for army paratroopers taking practice jumps as you pass the Yuma Proving Ground.

Sights

Imperial National Wildlife Refuge

NATURE PRESERVE | **FAMILY** | A guided, volunteer-led tour is a good way to visit this wildlife refuge and birder's paradise. The peak seasons for bird-watching are spring and fall, when you can expect to see everything from pelicans and cormorants to Canada geese, snowy egrets, and some rarer species. Mid-October through May is the most pleasant time to visit, as it's cooler and the ever-present mosquitoes are least active.

Kids especially enjoy the 1¼-mile Painted Desert Trail, which winds through the different levels of the Sonoran Desert. From an observation tower at the visitor center, you can see the river as well as the fields where migrating birds like to feed. You can sign up for guided walks from November through March. *✉ 12812 Wildlife Way, Yuma ☎ 928/783–3371 🌐 www.fws.gov/refuge/Imperial 🎟 Free ⏲ Visitor center closed weekdays Apr.–mid-Nov.*

Chapter 11

NORTHERN ARIZONA

WITH SEDONA, THE GRAND CANYON, AND MONUMENT VALLEY

Updated by
Teresa Bitler, Mara Levin, and Elise Riley

Sights ★★★★★ | Restaurants ★★★★☆ | Hotels ★★★★☆ | Shopping ★★★★★ | Nightlife ★★★☆☆

WELCOME TO NORTHERN ARIZONA

TOP REASONS TO GO

★ **Mother Nature:** Stunning red rocks, snowcapped mountains, and crisp country air rejuvenate the most cynical city dwellers.

★ **Father Time:** Ancient Native American sites show life before Columbus "discovered" America.

★ **Free spirits:** The energy of Sedona is delightful; even skeptics might be tempted to get their aura read.

★ **The Grand Canyon:** One of America's most breathtaking wonders stretches across northern Arizona.

★ **See Canyon de Chelly and Antelope Canyon:** Visit two of the most spectacular natural wonders in the Southwest. Both are musts for photography buffs.

★ **Take a jeep tour through Monument Valley:** See firsthand the landscape depicted in iconic Western films.

1 **Flagstaff.** College-town spirit and high-country charm make this one of Arizona's most outdoors-friendly towns.

2 **East of Flagstaff.** East of Flagstaff are craters and volcanoes, Native American archaeology, and architecture.

3 **Sedona and Oak Creek Canyon.** You'll enjoy breathtaking red rock views, fantastic cuisine, and New Age whimsy.

4 **Grand Canyon National Park.** A magnificent canyon carved by the Colorado River.

5 **Glenn Canyon and Lake Powell.** A geological wonderland of waterways, arches, and slot canyons best explored by boat.

6 **Monument Valley.** These ancient lands appear in everything from classic Westerns to Ansel Adams photos.

7 **The Hopi Mesas.** A tribal land home to the Hopi Arts Trail, the 1,000-year-old village of Oraibi, and trading posts.

8 **Petrified Forest National Park.** The Petrified Forest is rich with with fossils that show the plant and animal life of an ancient ecosystem.

9 **Canyon de Chelly.** National Monument with some of the most spectacular panoramas in the Southwest.

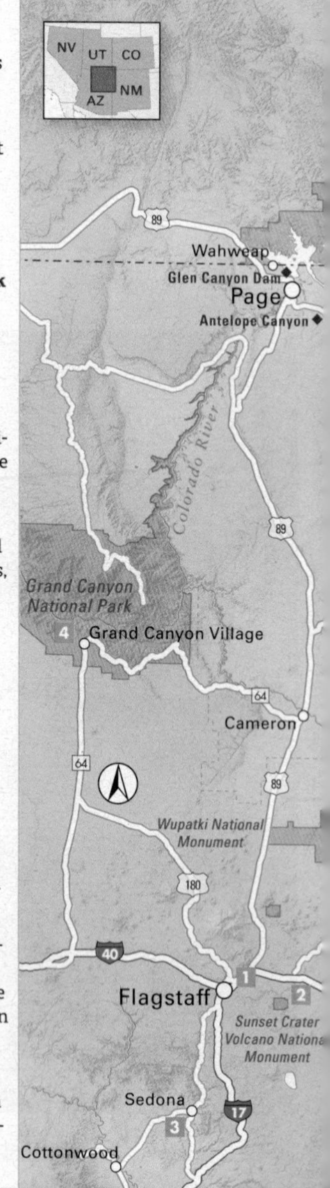

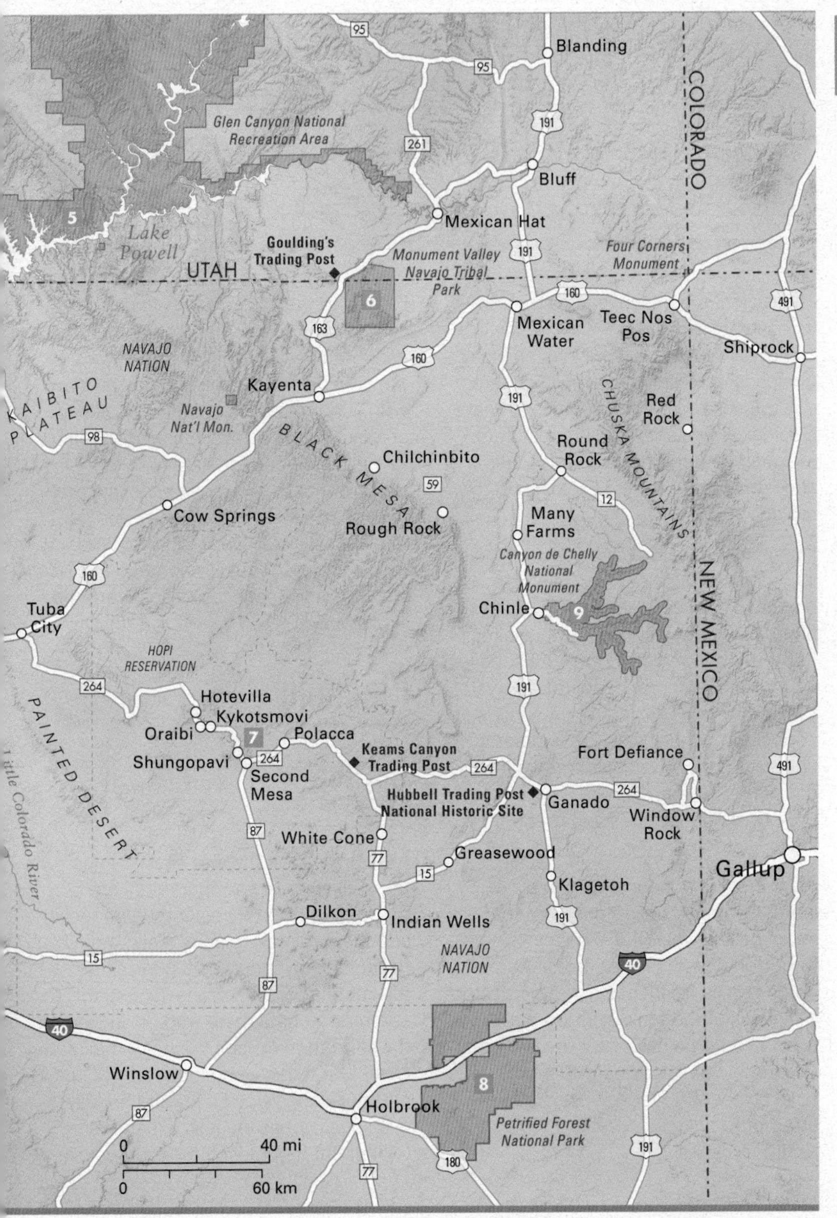
Blanding
COLORADO
Glen Canyon National Recreation Area
Bluff
Mexican Hat
Lake Powell
Goulding's Trading Post
Monument Valley Navajo Tribal Park
Four Corners Monument
UTAH
Mexican Water
Teec Nos Pos
Shiprock
NAVAJO NATION
KAIBITO PLATEAU
Kayenta
Navajo Nat'l Mon.
CHUSKA MOUNTAINS
Red Rock
Round Rock
BLACK MESA
Chilchinbito
Cow Springs
Rough Rock
Many Farms
Canyon de Chelly National Monument
Chinle
NEW MEXICO
Tuba City
HOPI RESERVATION
Hotevilla
Kykotsmovi
Oraibi
Polacca
Keams Canyon Trading Post
Shungopavi
Second Mesa
Fort Defiance
PAINTED DESERT
Little Colorado River
Hubbell Trading Post National Historic Site
Ganado
Window Rock
White Cone
Greasewood
Gallup
Klagetoh
Dilkon
Indian Wells
NAVAJO NATION
Winslow
Holbrook
Petrified Forest National Park
0 40 mi
0 60 km

Red rock buttes ablaze in the light of late afternoon, majestic mountains tipped white from a fresh snowfall, pine forests clad in dark green needles—northern Arizona is rich in natural beauty, a landscape of vast plateaus punctuated by steep ridges and canyons.

The region is also rich in artifacts from its earliest inhabitants—well-preserved cliff dwellings and petroglyphs provide glimpses into Native American cultures dating back more than a thousand years. Geological wonders, like huge craters formed by meteorites and volcanoes, add yet another layer to exploring in the region.

Down in Sedona, the average age and income rises considerably. This was once a hidden hamlet used by Western filmmakers, but New Age enthusiasts flocked to the region in the 1980s, believing it was the center of spiritual powers. Well-off executives and retirees followed soon after. Sophisticated restaurants, upscale shops, luxe accommodations, and New Age entrepreneurs cater to both these populations and to the thriving tourist trade.

Pioneers and miners are now part of North-Central Arizona's past, but the wild and woolly days of the Old West aren't forgotten. The preserved fort at Camp Verde recalls frontier life, and the decrepit facades of the funky former mining town of Jerome have their own charm. The jumble of saloons and Victorian houses in temperate Prescott attests to the attempt to bring "civilization" to Arizona's territorial capital.

Farther to the east is a vast and magnificent land of lofty buttes, towering cliffs, and turquoise skies. Most of the land in the area belongs to the Navajo and Hopi, who adhere to ancient traditions based on spiritual values, kinship, and an affinity for nature. Spend time at some of the region's most spectacular sites, such as Canyon de Chelly, Lake Powell and surrounding Glen Canyon, and Monument Valley, and you'll quickly come to appreciate why indigenous locals so revere the landscape.

Planning

Getting Here and Around

WHEN TO GO

Autumn—when the wet season ends, the stifling desert temperatures are moderate (it's 20°F cooler than Phoenix), and the mountain aspens reach their full golden splendor—is a great time to visit this part of Arizona. During the summer months many Phoenix residents travel north to escape the heat, meaning excessive traffic along Interstate 17 just north of Phoenix on Friday and Sunday evenings. Hotels are less expensive in winter, but mountain temperatures dip below zero, and snowstorms can occur weekly, especially near Flagstaff.

Sedona has springlike temperatures even in January, when it's snowing in Flagstaff, but summer temperatures above 90°F are common.

AIR

Don't plan on flying into Flagstaff; commercial flights are limited. Plus the scenery on the two-hour drive from Phoenix is gorgeous. There's no air access at all to northeastern Arizona. The Grand Canyon's north rim is actually closer to Las Vegas than Phoenix.

CAR

It makes sense to rent a car in this region, since trails and monuments stretch miles past city limits and many area towns can't be reached by the major bus companies. The major rental agencies have offices in Flagstaff, Prescott, and Sedona. Avoid interstates when possible; the back ways can be more direct and have the best views of the stunning landscape. Instead of Interstate 17, take AZ 89A through Verde Valley and Oak Creek Canyon. Weekend traffic around Sedona can be heavy, so leave early and allow extra time.

Hotels

In northern Arizona, Flagstaff has the more affordable lodging options, with lots of comfortable motels and B&Bs, but no real luxury. The opposite is true in Sedona, which is filled with opulent resorts and hideaways—just don't expect a bargain. Reservations are essential for Sedona and suggested for Flagstaff in summer. Make reservations at the Grand Canyon as far in advance as possible regardless of the season. Page has northeast Arizona's greatest concentration of lodgings, most of them fairly standard chain motels and hotels, but this base camp for exploring Lake Powell also has houseboat rental. You'll find a handful of well-maintained chains in the Navajo Nation and in Tuba City.

Restaurants

You'll find lots of American comfort food in this part of the country: barbecue restaurants, steak houses, and burger joints predominate. If you're looking for something different, Sedona and Flagstaff have the majority of good, multiethnic restaurants in the area, and if you're craving Mexican, you're sure to find something authentic and delicious (note that burritos are often called "burros" around here). Some area restaurants close in the slower months of January and February, so call ahead. Reservations are suggested April through October.

HOTEL AND RESTAURANT PRICES

Hotel prices in the reviews are the lowest cost of a standard double room in high season. Restaurant prices in the reviews are the average cost of a main course at dinner, or if dinner is not served, at lunch.

What It Costs

	$	$$	$$$	$$$$
RESTAURANTS	Under $13	$13–$20	$21–$30	Over $30
HOTELS	Under $121	$121–$175	$176–$250	Over $250

Flagstaff

146 miles northwest of Phoenix, 27 miles north of Sedona via Oak Creek Canyon.

Few travelers slow down long enough to explore Flagstaff, a city of 72,000 known locally as "Flag"; most stop only to spend the night at one of the town's many motels before making the last leg of the trip to the Grand Canyon, 80 miles north. Flag makes a good base for day trips to ancient Native American sites and the Navajo and Hopi reservations, as well as to Petrified Forest National Park and the Painted Desert, but the city is a worthwhile destination in its own right. Set against a lovely backdrop of pine forests and the snowcapped San Francisco Peaks, Flagstaff is a laid-back college town with a frontier flavor.

In summer Phoenix residents head here seeking relief from the desert heat, because at any time of the year temperatures in Flagstaff are about 20°F cooler than in Phoenix. They also come to Flagstaff in winter to ski at the Arizona Snowbowl, about 15 miles northeast of town among the San Francisco Peaks.

GETTING HERE AND AROUND

Flagstaff lies at the intersection of Interstate 40 (east–west) and Interstate 17 (running south from Flagstaff), 146 miles north of Phoenix via Interstate 17. If you're driving from Sedona to Flagstaff or the Grand Canyon, head north on AZ 89A through the wooded Oak Creek Canyon: it's the most scenic route.

Flagstaff Airport is 3 miles south of town off Interstate 17 at Exit 337. American flies from Phoenix to Flagstaff, and United has direct flights to Denver and Dallas. A taxi from Flagstaff Airport to downtown should cost about $15. Cabs aren't regulated; some, but not all, have meters, so it's wise to agree on a rate before you leave for your destination. Amtrak comes into the downtown Flagstaff station twice daily.

VISITOR INFORMATION

CONTACTS Flagstaff Visitor Center. ✉ *Santa Fe Depot, 1 E. Rte. 66, Downtown* ☎ *928/213–2951, 800/842–7293* 🌐 *www.flagstaffarizona.org.*

Sights

Arizona Snowbowl

VIEWPOINT | FAMILY | Although the Arizona Snowbowl is still one of Flagstaff's biggest attractions, snowy slopes can be a luxury in times of drought. Fortunately visitors can enjoy the beauty of the area year-round, with or without the fluffy white stuff. The chairlift climbs the San Francisco Peaks to a height of 10,800 feet, and doubles as a 30-minute scenic gondola ride in summer. From this vantage point you can see up to 70 miles; views may even include Sedona's red rocks and the Grand Canyon. There's a lodge at the base with a restaurant, bar, and ski school. To reach the ski area, take U.S. 180 north from Flagstaff; it's 7 miles from the Snowbowl exit to the skyride entrance. ✉ *Snowbowl Rd., North Flagstaff* ☎ *928/779–1951* 🌐 *www.snowbowl.ski* 🎫 *Varies.*

Historic Downtown District

NEIGHBORHOOD | Storied Route 66 runs right through the heart of downtown Flagstaff. The late Victorian, Tudor Revival, and early art deco architecture in this district recall the town's heyday as a logging and railroad center. The **Santa Fe Depot** now houses the visitor center. The 1927 **Hotel Monte Vista**, built after a community drive raised $200,000 in 60 days, is one of the art deco highlights of the district; today it houses a restaurant and a combination coffeehouse and cocktail bar. Across the street, the 1888 **Babbitt Brothers Building** was constructed as a building-supply store and then turned into a department store by David Babbitt, the mastermind of the Babbitt empire. (The Babbitts are one of Flagstaff's wealthiest founding families.) The Weatherford Hotel, built in 1900, hosted many celebrities; Western author Zane Grey wrote *The Call of the Canyon* here. Most of the area's first businesses were saloons catering to railroad construction workers, which was the case with the 1888 **Vail Building**. Nowadays, downtown

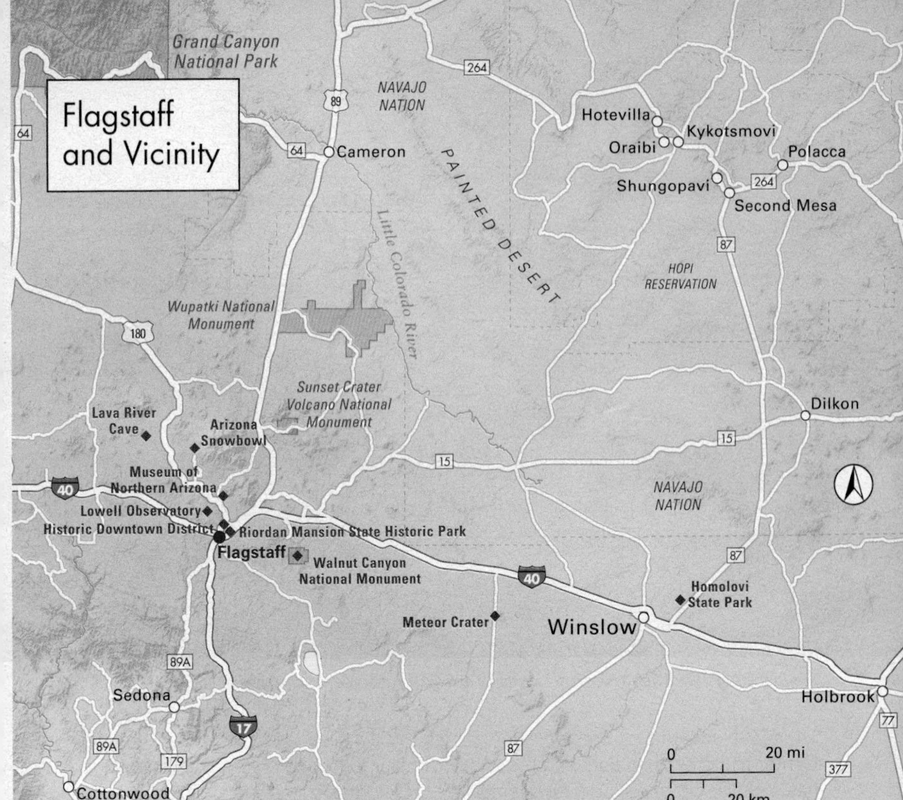

is a bustling dining and retail district, with restaurants, bakeries, and alluring shops. Across the railroad tracks, the revitalized Southside is home to popular eateries and craft breweries. ✉ *Rte. 66 north to Birch Ave., and Beaver St. east to Agassiz St., Downtown.*

Lava River Cave

CAVE | FAMILY | Subterranean lava flow formed this mile-long cave roughly 700,000 years ago. Once you descend into its boulder-strewn maw, the cave is spacious, with 40-foot ceilings, but claustrophobes take heed: about halfway through, the cave tapers to a 4-foot-high squeeze that can be a bit unnerving. A 40°F chill pervades the cave throughout the year so take warm clothing.

To reach the turnoff for the cave, go approximately 9 miles north of Flagstaff on U.S. 180, then turn west onto Forest Road (FR) 245. Turn left at the intersection of FR 171 and look for the sign to the cave. Note: these forest roads are closed from mid-November to March due to snow. The trip is approximately 45 minutes from Flagstaff. Although the cave is on Coconino National Forest Service property, there are no rangers on-site; the only thing here is an interpretive sign, so it's definitely something you tackle at your own risk. **■ TIP→ Pack a flashlight (or two).** ✉ *FR 171B, Flagstaff* 🌐 *fs.usda.gov/coconino.*

★ Lowell Observatory

OBSERVATORY | FAMILY | In 1894 Boston businessman, author, and scientist Percival Lowell founded this observatory from which he studied Mars. His theories of the existence of a ninth planet sowed the seeds for the discovery of Pluto at Lowell in 1930 by Clyde Tombaugh.

The tunnels of Lava River Cave were formed by lava flow hundreds of thousands of years ago.

The 6,500-square-foot Steele Visitor Center hosts exhibits and lectures and has a stellar gift shop. Several interactive exhibits—among them Pluto Walk, a scale model of the solar system—appeal to children. Visitors can peer through several telescopes at the Giovale Open Deck Observatory, including the 24-inch Clark telescope and the McAllister, a 16-inch reflector telescope. ■ **TIP→ The observatory is open and unheated, so dress for the outdoors.** ✉ *1400 W. Mars Hill Rd., West Flagstaff* ☎ *928/774–3358, 928/233–3212 for recorded info* 🌐 *www.lowell.edu* 🎟 *from $30.*

Museum of Northern Arizona

MUSEUM | **FAMILY** | This institution, founded in 1928, is respected worldwide for its research and for its collections centering on the natural and cultural history of the Colorado Plateau. Among the permanent exhibitions are an extensive collection of Navajo rugs and a Hopi *kiva* (men's ceremonial chamber).

A gallery devoted to area geology is usually a hit with children: it includes a life-size model dilophosaurus, a carnivorous dinosaur that once roamed northern Arizona. Outdoors a life-zone exhibit shows the changing vegetation from the bottom of the Grand Canyon to the highest peak in Flagstaff. A nature trail, open only in summer, heads down across a small stream into a canyon and up into an aspen grove. Also in summer the museum hosts exhibits and the works of Native American artists, whose wares are sold in the well-stocked museum gift shop. ✉ *3101 N. Fort Valley Rd., North Flagstaff* ☎ *928/774–5213* 🌐 *musnaz.org* 🎟 *$12.*

Riordan Mansion State Historic Park

HOUSE | This artifact of Flagstaff's logging heyday is near Northern Arizona University. The centerpiece is a mansion built in 1904 for Michael and Timothy Riordan, lumber-baron brothers who married two sisters. The 13,300-square-foot, 40-room log-and-stone structure—designed by Charles Whittlesley, who was also responsible for El Tovar Hotel at the Grand Canyon—contains furniture by Gustav Stickley, father of the American

Arts and Crafts design movement. One room holds "Paul Bunyan's shoes," a 2-foot-long pair of boots made by Timothy in his workshop. Everything on display is original to the house. The inside of the mansion may be explored only by guided tour (hourly on the hour); reservations are suggested. ✉ *409 W. Riordan Rd., University* ☎ *928/779–4395* 🌐 *www.arizonahistoricalsociety.org* 🎟 *$12* 🕓 *Closed Tues. and Wed. Nov.–Apr.*

Restaurants

Beaver Street Brewery

$$ | **AMERICAN** | **FAMILY** | This restaurant and microbrewery is a popular, casual, and family-friendly place with a pleasant patio. Wood-fired pizzas include the Enchanted Forest—with Brie, Portobello mushrooms, roasted red peppers, spinach, and artichoke pesto. **Known for:** crowd-pleasing pizza and pub fare; excellent craft beers; late hours. [$] *Average main: $16* ✉ *11 S. Beaver St., Downtown* ☎ *928/779–0079* 🌐 *beaverstreetbrewery.com.*

★ **Brix Restaurant & Wine Bar**

$$$ | **AMERICAN** | A redbrick carriage house, built around 1910 as a garage for one of the first automobiles in Flagstaff, is home to one of the city's most sophisticated restaurants. With a seasonally updated menu, the chef pairs locally raised pork, beef, and roasted duck with wines from a list of almost 200 bottles (Brix refers to the sugar content of grapes at harvest). **Known for:** consistently delicious, locally sourced food; extensive wine list; commitment to sustainability. [$] *Average main: $29* ✉ *413 N. San Francisco St., Downtown* ☎ *928/213–1021* 🌐 *www.brixflagstaff.com* 🕓 *Closed Sun. and Mon. No lunch.*

Diablo Burger

$ | **AMERICAN** | With juicy burgers made from locally sourced, antibiotic- and hormone-free beef, this is arguably the best burger joint in the Southwest. Freshly cut french fries lightly dusted with herbs, veggie burgers, grilled cheese sandwiches, and organic salads round out the menu. **Known for:** best (and locally sourced) burgers; English muffin buns; crowds at lunchtime. [$] *Average main: $12* ✉ *Heritage Square, 120 Leroux St., Downtown* ☎ *928/774–3274* 🌐 *www.diabloburger.com.*

Salsa Brava

$$ | **MEXICAN** | **FAMILY** | This cheerful Mexican restaurant, with light-wood booths and colorful designs, eschews heavy Sonoran-style fare in favor of the grilled dishes found in Guadalajara. It's considered the best Mexican food in town. **Known for:** unpretentious, fresh Mexican food; plenty of gluten-free dishes; appearance on Food Network's Diners, Drive-Ins and Dives. [$] *Average main: $14* ✉ *2220 E. Rte. 66, East Flagstaff* ☎ *928/779–5293* 🌐 *www.salsabravaflagstaff.com.*

Tourist Home All Day Cafe

$ | **AMERICAN** | **FAMILY** | The creative team that owns Tinderbox Kitchen and Annex Cocktail Lounge reclaimed the decaying building next door and turned it into the trendiest breakfast and lunch spot around. Breakfast burritos, eggs Benedict, salads, and sandwiches all get a modern spin, and the quinoa falafel makes a great burger or vegan "hashbowl." Decadent desserts and a selection of daytime cocktails are equally alluring. **Known for:** breakfast served all day; fresh salads, sandwiches, and desserts; best patio dining. [$] *Average main: $12* ✉ *52 S. San Francisco St., Downtown* ☎ *928/779–2811* 🌐 *touristhomecafe.com* 🕓 *No dinner.*

Hotels

Trains pass through the downtown area along Route 66 about every 15 minutes throughout the day and night. Light sleepers may prefer to stay in the south or east section of town to avoid hearing trains rumbling through; at least the whistles are no longer blown within the downtown district.

Drury Inn & Suites

$$$ | **HOTEL** | So clean it sparkles, the Drury Inn sits at the edge of Northern Arizona University's campus and packs in the amenities, like happy hour dinner and drinks, an indoor pool, and comfy lounge areas with mountain views. **Pros:** plenty of extras; great location (walk to campus and historic district); spacious and well-equipped rooms. **Cons:** large-scale property; generic-looking rooms; the parking garage is a bit of a trek. *Rooms from: $179 ✉ 300 S. Milton Rd., Downtown ☎ 928/773–4900 🌐 www.druryhotels.com 160 rooms 🍴 Free breakfast.*

The Inn at 410

$$$ | **B&B/INN** | This downtown B&B in a beautifully restored 1907 residence—an inviting alternative to Flagstaff's chain motels—has spacious suites with private baths and fireplaces, some with two-person Jacuzzi tubs. **Pros:** convenient downtown location; romantic; complimentary cookies and cocktails every afternoon. **Cons:** some rooms are upstairs (no elevator); no children allowed; two-night minimum stay during high season. *Rooms from: $220 ✉ 410 N. Leroux St., Downtown ☎ 928/774–0088, 800/774–2008 🌐 www.inn410.com 10 suites 🍴 Free breakfast.*

Little America Hotel Flagstaff

$$$ | **HOTEL** | **FAMILY** | This deservedly popular hotel is a little distance from the roar of the trains, the grounds are surrounded by evergreen forests, and it's one of the few places in Flagstaff with room service. **Pros:** large, clean rooms; many amenities, including restaurant, gym, pool, and store; walking trails through the forested grounds. **Cons:** large-scale property; a few miles east of the shopping and dining district; some highway noise outside (but rooms are quiet). *Rooms from: $214 ✉ 2515 E. Butler Ave., Downtown ☎ 928/779–7900, 800/865–1401 🌐 flagstaff.littleamerica.com 247 rooms 🍴 No meals.*

Shopping

The Artists' Gallery

CRAFTS | For fine arts and crafts—everything from ceramics and stained glass to weaving and painting—visit the Artists' Gallery, a local artists' cooperative. *✉ 17 N. San Francisco St., Downtown ☎ 928/773–0958 🌐 www.flagstaffartistsgallery.com.*

Babbitt's Backcountry Outfitters

SPORTING GOODS | Just about all your sporting-goods needs can be met at Babbitt's Backcountry Outfitters. *✉ 12 E. Aspen Ave., Downtown ☎ 928/774–4775 🌐 babbittsbackcountry.com.*

Museum of Northern Arizona Gift Shop

GIFTS/SOUVENIRS | High-quality Native American art, jewelry, and crafts can be found at the Museum of Northern Arizona Gift Shop. *✉ 3101 N. Fort Valley Rd., North Flagstaff ☎ 928/774–5213 🌐 musnaz.org.*

Activities

HIKING

You can explore Arizona's alpine tundra in the San Francisco Peaks, part of the Coconino National Forest, where more than 80 species of plants grow on the upper elevations. The habitat is fragile, so hikers are asked to stay on established trails (there are lots of them). ■ **TIP→ Flatlanders should give themselves a day or two to adjust to the altitude before lengthy or strenuous hiking.** The altitude here will make even the hardiest hikers breathe a little harder, so anyone with cardiac or respiratory problems should be cautious about overexertion. Note that most of the forest trails aren't accessible during winter due to snow.

Coconino National Forest–Flagstaff Ranger District

HIKING/WALKING | The rangers of the Coconino National Forest maintain many of the region's trails and can provide you with details on hiking in the area.

Excellent maps of the Flagstaff trails are sold here for $12. Both the forest's main office in West Flagstaff and the ranger station in East Flagstaff (5075 N. U.S. 89) are open weekdays 8–4. ✉ *1824 S. Thompson St., West Flagstaff* ☎ *928/527–3600 for main office, West Flagstaff, 928/526–0866 for East Flagstaff office* 🌐 *fs.usda.gov/coconino.*

Kachina Trail

HIKING/WALKING | Those who don't want a long hike can do just the first mile or two of the 5-mile-long Kachina Trail; gently rolling, this route is surrounded by huge stands of aspen and offers fantastic vistas. In fall, changing leaves paint the landscape shades of yellow, russet, and amber. *Moderate.* ✉ *Flagstaff* ✣ *Trailhead: Snowbowl Rd., 7 miles north of U.S. 180.*

MOUNTAIN BIKING

With more than 50 miles of urban bike trails and more than 30 miles of challenging forest and mountain trails a short ride from town, it was inevitable that one of Flagstaff's best-kept secrets would leak out. The mountain biking on Mount Elden is on par with that of more celebrated trails in Colorado and Utah. Although there isn't a concise loop trail such as those in Moab, Utah, experienced bikers can create one by connecting Schultz Creek Trail, Sunset Trail, and Elden Lookout Road. Beginners (as well as those looking for rewarding scenery with less of an incline) may want to start with Lower Fort Valley and Campbell Mesa. Local bike-shop staff can help with advice and planning. Pick up a FUTS (Flagstaff Urban Trails System) map at the visitor center detailing low- and no-traffic bike routes around town.

EQUIPMENT AND RENTALS

Absolute Bikes

BICYCLING | You can rent mountain bikes, get good advice and gear, and purchase trail maps here. ✉ *202 E. Rte. 66, Downtown* ☎ *928/779–5969* 🌐 *www.absolutebikes.net.*

SKIING AND SNOWBOARDING

The ski season usually starts in mid-December and ends in mid-April.

Arizona Snowbowl

SKIING/SNOWBOARDING | **FAMILY** | Seven miles north of Flagstaff off U.S. 180, the Arizona Snowbowl, on the western slope of Mount Humphreys, has 55 downhill runs, eight lifts, and a vertical drop of 2,800 feet. The eight-person Agassiz Lift gondolas whisk skiers 2,000 feet up in seven minutes, affording a fabulous view of the Grand Canyon in the distance. There are two restaurants, an equipment-rental and retail shop, and a SKIwee center for ages four to seven.

All-day adult lift tickets are $99, and children 10 and under can ski for free all season. (Prices can vary based on dates and demand.) The closest lodging to the ski area is Snowbowl's Ski Lift Lodge, with cabins and a restaurant at the base of the mountain. Some Flagstaff motels have ski packages that include transportation to Snowbowl. ✉ *Snowbowl Rd., North Flagstaff* ☎ *928/779–1951, 928/779–4577 for snow report* 🌐 *www.snowbowl.ski.*

East of Flagstaff

Within an hour's drive east of Flagstaff, you'll find plenty of natural and cultural attractions, from craters and volcanoes to Native American art and architecture. After exploring sites like Walnut Canyon and Homolovi State Park, you can take a break by "standing on a corner in Winslow, Arizona," and then tour the beautifully restored La Posada Hotel.

GETTING HERE AND AROUND

From Flagstaff, follow Interstate 40 a few miles east to Exit 204 for Walnut Canyon National Monument. Continue east along the highway for Meteor Crater off Exit 233, a 45-minute drive. Continue east on Interstate 40, to the town of Winslow, about 50 miles from Flagstaff; head 4 miles northeast to see the Hopi pueblos at Homolovi State Park.

Sights

Homolovi State Park

ARCHAEOLOGICAL SITE | *Homolovi* is a Hopi word meaning "place of the little hills." The pueblo sites here are thought to have been occupied between AD 1200 and 1425, and include 40 ceremonial kivas and two pueblos containing more than 1,000 rooms each. The Hopi believe their immediate ancestors inhabited this place, and they consider the site sacred. Many rooms have been excavated and recovered for protection. The Homolovi Visitor Center has a small museum with Hopi pottery and Ancestral Pueblo artifacts; it also hosts workshops on native art, ethnobotany, and traditional foods. Campsites with water and hookups are nearby. ✉ *AZ 87, Winslow* ⊕ *4 miles northeast of Winslow* ☎ *928/289–4106, 877/697–2757 for camping reservations* 🌐 *azstateparks.com/homolovi* 🎫 *$7 per vehicle.*

Meteor Crater

NATURE SITE | **FAMILY** | A natural phenomenon in a privately owned park 43 miles east of Flagstaff, Meteor Crater is impressive if for no other reason than its sheer size. A hole in the ground 600 feet deep, nearly 1 mile across, and more than 3 miles in circumference, Meteor Crater is large enough to accommodate the Washington Monument or 20 football fields. It was created by a meteorite crash 49,000 years ago.

You can't descend into the crater because of the efforts of its owners to maintain its condition—scientists consider this to be the best-preserved crater on Earth—but guided rim tours give useful background information, and telescopes along the rim offer you a closer look. There's a restaurant on-site, and the gift shop sells specimens from the area and jewelry made from native stones. ✉ *I–40, Exit 233, Winslow* ☎ *928/289–5898* 🌐 *meteorcrater.com* 🎫 *$22.*

★ **Walnut Canyon National Monument**

ARCHAEOLOGICAL SITE | The group of cliff dwellings that make up Walnut Canyon National Monument were constructed by the Sinagua people, who lived and farmed in and around the canyon starting around AD 700. The more than 300 dwellings here were built between 1080 and 1250, and abandoned, like those at so many other settlements in Arizona and New Mexico, around 1300. The Sinagua traded far and wide with other indigenous groups, including people at Wupatki. Even macaw feathers, which would have come from tribes in what is now Mexico, have been excavated in the canyon. Early Flagstaff settlers looted the site for pots and "treasure"; Woodrow Wilson declared this a national monument in 1915, which began a 30-year process of stabilizing the site.

Part of the fascination of Walnut Canyon is the opportunity to enter the dwellings, stepping back in time to an ancient way of life. Some of the Sinagua homes are in near-perfect condition in spite of all the looting, because of the dry, hot climate and the protection of overhanging cliffs. You can reach them by descending 185 feet on the 1-mile, 240-stair, stepped **Island Trail,** which starts at the visitor center. As you follow the trail, look across the canyon for other dwellings not accessible on the path. Island Trail takes about an hour to complete at a normal pace. Those with health concerns should opt for the easier 0.5-mile **Rim Trail,** which has overlooks from which dwellings, as well as an excavated, reconstructed pit house, can be viewed. ■ **TIP→ Do not rely on GPS to get here; stick to Interstate 40.** ✉ *Walnut Canyon Rd., Winona* ⊕ *3 miles south of I–40, Exit 204* ☎ *928/526–3367* 🌐 *www.nps.gov/waca* 🎫 *$15.*

A visit to Meteor Crater complements Arizona's many observatories for a different look at the impact of the heavens.

Sedona and Oak Creek Canyon

27 miles south of Flagstaff on AZ 89A; 114 miles north of Phoenix, I–17 to AZ 179 to AZ 89A; 60 miles northeast of Prescott, U.S. 89 to AZ 89A.

It's easy to see what draws so many people to Sedona. Red rock buttes—Cathedral Rock, Bear Mountain, Courthouse Rock, and Bell Rock, among others—reach up into an almost-always blue sky, and both colors are intensified by dark-green pine forests. Surrealist Max Ernst, writer Zane Grey, and many filmmakers drew inspiration from these vistas—more than 80 Westerns were shot in the area in the 1940s and '50s alone.

These days, Sedona lures enterprising restaurateurs and gallery owners from the East and West coasts. New Age followers, who believe that the area contains some of Earth's more important vortexes (energy centers), also come in great numbers, seeking a "vibe" that confers a sense of balance and well-being and enhances creativity.

Expansion since the early 1980s has been rapid, and lack of planning has taken its toll in the form of unattractive developments and increased traffic.

The city of Sedona is young, and there are few historic sites; as many visitors conclude, you don't come to Sedona to tour the town itself. The main downtown activity is shopping, mostly for Southwestern-style paintings, clothing, rugs, and jewelry. Just beyond the shops and restaurants, however, canyons, creeks, ancient dwellings, and the red rocks beckon. The area is relatively easy to hike and bike, or you can take a jeep tour into the hills.

GETTING HERE AND AROUND

Sedona stretches along AZ 89A, its main east-west thoroughfare, and AZ 179, which winds south to the Village of Oak Creek. Uptown, the section with most of the shops and restaurants, is at the east

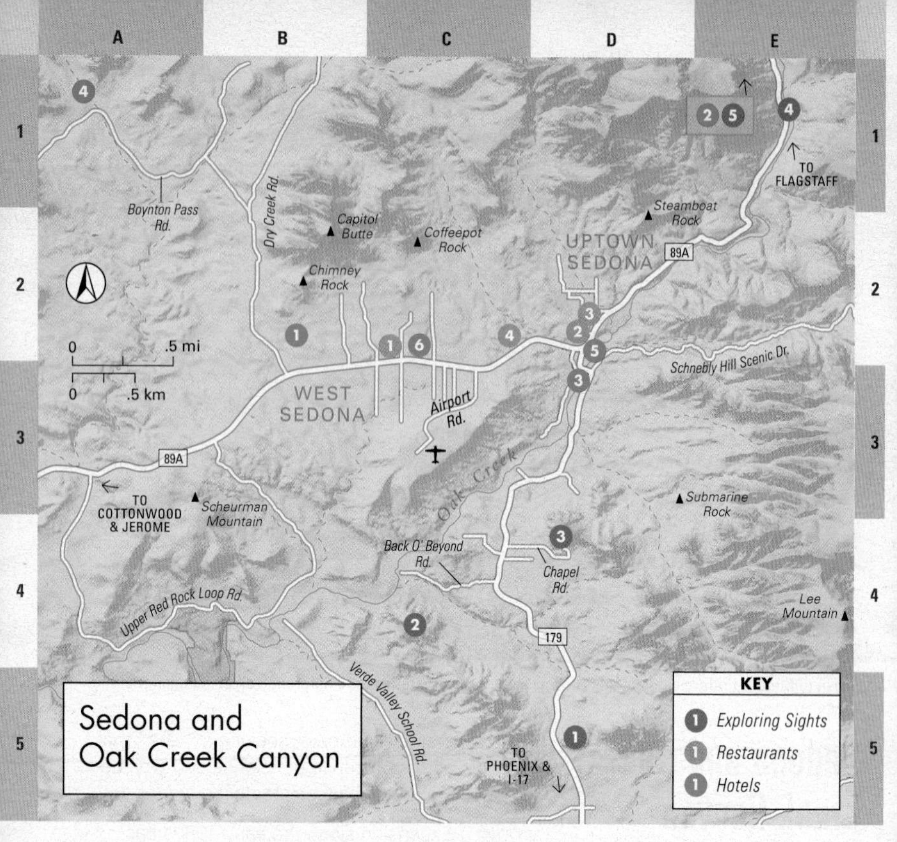

Sights

1 Bell Rock D5
2 Cathedral Rock C4
3 Chapel of the Holy Cross D4
4 Oak Creek Canyon E1
5 Slide Rock State Park ... E1

Restaurants

1 Coffee Pot Restaurant C2
2 Cowboy Club D2
3 Elote Café D2
4 Mariposa C2

Hotels

1 Alma de Sedona Bed and Breakfast Inn B2
2 The Canyon Wren E1
3 El Portal Sedona Hotel D3
4 Enchantment Resort ... A1
5 L'Auberge de Sedona D2
6 Sugar Loaf Lodge C2

In addition to panoramic views, the Airport Vortex is said to have spirals of energy that strengthen focus.

end of AZ 89A. There is metered parking here, or park all day in the free public lot off Jordan Road. Free parking is much more plentiful in West Sedona and the Village of Oak Creek.

Sedona Trolley offers two types of daily orientation tours, both departing from the main bus stop in Uptown and lasting less than an hour. One goes along AZ 179 to the Chapel of the Holy Cross; the other passes through West Sedona to Boynton Canyon (Enchantment Resort). Rates are $20 for one or $30 for both.

VISITOR INFORMATION

CONTACTS Sedona Visitor Center. ✉ *331 Forest Rd., Uptown* ✥ *Just off AZ 89A* ☎ *928/282–7722, 800/288–7336* 🌐 *visit-sedona.com.*

Sights

Bell Rock

NATURE SITE | With its distinctive shape right out of your favorite Western film and its proximity to the main drag, this popular butte ensures a steady flow of admirers, so you may want to arrive early in the day. The parking lot next to the Bell Rock Pathway often fills by midmorning, even midweek. The views from here are good, but an easy and fairly accessible path follows mostly gentle terrain for 1 mile to the base of the butte. Mountain bikers, parents with all-terrain baby strollers, and not-so-avid hikers should have little problem getting there. No official paths climb the rock itself, but many forge their own routes (at their own risk). ✉ *AZ 179, Big Park* ✥ *Several hundred yards north of Bell Rock Blvd.*

Cathedral Rock

NATURE SITE | It's almost impossible not to be drawn to this butte's towering, variegated spires. The approximately 1,200-foot-high Cathedral Rock looms dramatically over town. When you emerge from the narrow gorge of Oak Creek Canyon, this is the first recognizable formation you'll spot. The butte is best seen toward dusk from a distance. Hikers may want to drive to the Airport Mesa and then hike the rugged but generally flat path that loops around the airfield. The trail is ½ mile up Airport Road off AZ 89A in West Sedona; the reward is a panoramic view of Cathedral Rock without the crowds. **■ TIP→ Those not hiking should drive through the Village of Oak Creek and 5 miles west on Verde Valley School Road to its end, where you can view Cathedral Rock from a beautiful streamside vantage point and take a dip in Oak Creek if you wish.** ✉ *Big Park* ✥ *5 miles to end of Verde Valley School Rd., west off AZ 179.*

Chapel of the Holy Cross

RELIGIOUS SITE | You needn't be religious to be inspired by the setting and the architecture here. Built in 1956 by Marguerite Brunwig Staude, a student of Frank Lloyd Wright, this modern landmark, with a huge cross on the facade, rises between two red rock peaks. Vistas of the town and the surrounding area are spectacular. Though there is only one regular service—a beautiful Taizé service of prayer and song on Monday at 5 pm—all are welcome for quiet meditation.

A small gift shop sells religious artifacts and books. A trail east of the chapel leads you—after a 20-minute walk over occasional loose-rock surfaces—to a seat surrounded by voluptuous red-limestone walls, worlds away from the bustle and commerce around the chapel. ✉ *Chapel Rd., off AZ 179, Big Park* ☎ *928/282–4069* 🌐 *www.chapeloftheholycross.com* 🎫 *Free.*

Oak Creek Canyon

CANYON | Whether you want to swim, hike, picnic, or enjoy beautiful scenery framed through a car window, head north through the wooded Oak Creek Canyon. It's the most scenic route to Flagstaff and the Grand Canyon, and worth a drive-through even if you're not heading north. The road winds through a steep-walled canyon, where you crane your neck for views of the dramatic rock formations above. Although the forest is primarily evergreen, the fall foliage is glorious. Oak Creek, which runs along the bottom, is lined with tent campgrounds, fishing camps, cabins, motels, and restaurants. ✉ *AZ 89A, Oak Creek Canyon* ✥ *Beginning 1 mile north of Sedona.*

Slide Rock State Park

NATIONAL/STATE PARK | **FAMILY** | A good place for a picnic, Slide Rock is 7 miles north of Sedona. On a hot day you can plunge down a natural rock slide into a swimming hole (bring an extra pair of jeans or a sturdy bathing suit and river shoes to wear on the slide). The site started as an early-20th-century apple orchard, and the natural beauty attracted Hollywood—a number of John Wayne and Jimmy Stewart movies were filmed here.

A few easy hikes run along the rim of the gorge. One downside is the traffic, particularly on summer weekends; you might have to wait to get into the park after midmorning. Unfortunately the popularity of the stream has led to the occasional midsummer closing due to *E. coli*–bacteria infestations; the water is tested daily, and there is a water-quality hotline at ☎ *602/542–0202.* ✉ *6871 N. AZ 89A, Oak Creek Canyon* ☎ *928/282–3034* 🌐 *azstateparks.com/slide-rock* 🎫 *Mid-May–Oct.: $20 per vehicle Mon.–Thurs., $30 per vehicle Fri.–Sun. Mar.–mid-May: $20 per vehicle. Nov.–Feb.: $10 per vehicle.*

Restaurants

Some Sedona restaurants close in January and February, so call before you go; if you're planning a visit in high season (April through October), make reservations.

Coffee Pot Restaurant

$ | **AMERICAN** | Locals and tourists alike swarm to this spacious, old-school eatery for scrumptious breakfast (served all day) and lunch, served by a friendly waitstaff. One hundred and one omelet options are the stars of the show and include such concoctions as a basic ham and cheese and the quirky peanut butter, jelly, and banana, purportedly Elvis Presley's order back in the day. **Known for:** big omelets;

Sedona's striking red rocks are often named after their shape, such as Coffee Pot Rock, shown here on the far right.

unpretentious all-day breakfast and lunch; family-friendly place. $ *Average main: $10* ✉ *2050 W. AZ 89A, West* ☎ *928/282–6626* 🌐 *www.coffeepotsedona.com* ⏲ *No dinner.*

Cowboy Club

$$$ | STEAKHOUSE | At this restaurant catering to carnivores, you can hang out in the casual Cowboy Club or dine in the more formal Silver Saddle Room, where suede booths are surrounded by cowboy art and a pair of large cattle horns. High-quality cuts of beef are the specialty, but the burgers, grilled trout, and vegetable pot pies are delicious, too. **Known for:** steaks, burgers, and even rattlesnake; old-fashioned Western ambience; institution status. $ *Average main: $25* ✉ *241 N. AZ 89A, Uptown* ☎ *928/282–4200* 🌐 *www.cowboyclub.com.*

★ Elote Café

$$$ | MEXICAN | Traditional Mexican recipes get a creative and tasty update at this deservedly popular restaurant. Start with the namesake *elote*, roasted corn on a stick; this Mexican street-food favorite is transformed into an addictive dip of grilled corn kernels, Cotija cheese, lime, and chiles. **Known for:** great creative Mexican food; being one of Sedona's top restaurants; taking reservations. $ *Average main: $27* ✉ *350 Jordan Rd., Uptown* ☎ *928/203–0105* 🌐 *www.elotecafe.com* ⏲ *Closed Sun. and Mon. No lunch.*

★ Mariposa

$$$$ | LATIN AMERICAN | At this Latin-inspired restaurant in one of Sedona's most picturesque spots, chef-owner Lisa Dahl proves her fourth restaurant in town is another culinary masterpiece. Enjoy tapas, empanadas, and grilled selections with your view, either on the expansive patio or in the more formal, romantic dining room; the experience is worth the splurge. **Known for:** tapas and South American dishes; outstanding wine list; stunning red rock views. $ *Average main: $36* ✉ *700 AZ 89A, West* ☎ *928/862–4444* 🌐 *mariposasedona.com* ⏲ *Closed Tues. and Wed.*

Hotels

Alma de Sedona Bed and Breakfast Inn
$$$ | **B&B/INN** | This romantic B&B with spectacular views and ultracomfortable beds was built well off the main drag and in the shadow of the buttes for views and privacy. **Pros:** spacious and private rooms; all rooms have deck or patio with excellent views; peaceful vibe. **Cons:** most rooms only accommodate two; some rooms require climbing stairs; decor could use updating in some rooms. *Rooms from: $199 50 Hozoni Dr., West 928/282–2737 www.almadesedona.com 12 rooms Free breakfast.*

The Canyon Wren
$$ | **B&B/INN** | The best value in the Oak Creek Canyon area, this small and serene B&B across the road from the creek has four private cabins, all with kitchens, decks, and views of the canyon walls. **Pros:** romantic yet homey; wonderful hosts and breakfast; foresty feel, with private decks. **Cons:** some cabins close to road; added cleaning fee per stay; some may find the space a little too cozy. *Rooms from: $165 6425 N. AZ 89A, Oak Creek Canyon 928/282–6900, 800/437–9736 www.canyonwrencabins.com 4 cabins Free breakfast.*

★ **El Portal Sedona Hotel**
$$$$ | **B&B/INN** | This stunning hacienda, one of the most beautifully designed boutique hotels in the Southwest, has decor accents including authentic Tiffany and Roycroft pieces, French doors leading to balconies or a grassy central courtyard, stained-glass windows and ceiling panels, river-rock or tile fireplaces, and huge custom-designed beds. **Pros:** attractive rooms and grounds; next to Tlaquepaque shops and restaurants; pet-friendly rooms have private outdoor spaces and no extra fee. **Cons:** location not as secluded as some; pricey (but luxurious); fewer amenities than a resort. *Rooms from: $299 95 Portal La., Central 928/203–9405, 800/313–0017 www.elportalsedona.com 12 rooms No meals.*

★ **Enchantment Resort**
$$$$ | **RESORT** | A few miles outside town, gorgeous Boynton Canyon is the setting for this luxurious resort and its world-class destination spa, Mii amo. **Pros:** gorgeous setting next to great hiking trails; state-of-the-art spa; numerous on-site activities. **Cons:** 20-minute drive into town; world-class luxury comes at a price; property is spread out. *Rooms from: $425 525 Boynton Canyon Rd., West 928/282–2900, 888/250–1699 www.enchantmentresort.com 118 rooms No meals.*

★ **L'Auberge de Sedona**
$$$$ | **RESORT** | This elegant resort consists of private hillside units with spectacular views and cozy cottages in the woods along Oak Creek. **Pros:** luxurious rooms and cabins; secluded setting yet close to town; excellent restaurant and bar for romantic creekside dining. **Cons:** in-house restaurant is the most expensive in Sedona; at the upper price point for Sedona lodging; may feel too exclusive for some. *Rooms from: $499 301 L'Auberge La., Uptown 928/282–1661, 855/905–5745 www.lauberge.com 89 units No meals.*

Sugar Loaf Lodge
$ | **HOTEL** | Though it may be hard to believe, there are still bargains in Sedona, and this one-story, no-frills, family-run motel delivers. **Pros:** cheap and clean; walk to restaurants and shops in West Sedona; pool and hot tub. **Cons:** older, basic furnishings; smallish rooms; some traffic noise in rooms closer to the road. *Rooms from: $105 1870 W. AZ 89A, West 928/282–9451, 877/282–0632 www.sedonasugarloaf.com 15 rooms Free breakfast.*

Shopping

With a few exceptions, most of the stores in Uptown Sedona north of the "Y" (running along AZ 89A to the east of its intersection with AZ 179) cater to the tour-bus trade with New Age souvenirs and jewelry made by Native American artists. If this isn't your style, the largest concentration of stores and galleries is along AZ 179, just south of the "Y," with plenty of offerings for serious shoppers.

ARTS AND CRAFTS

Garland's Navajo Rugs

HOUSEHOLD ITEMS/FURNITURE | There's a huge collection of new and antique rugs here, as well as Native American kachina dolls, pottery, and baskets. ✉ *411 AZ 179, Uptown* ☎ *928/282–4070* 🌐 *www.garlandsjewelry.com.*

James Ratliff Gallery

ART GALLERIES | Fun and functional pieces by up-and-coming artists are exhibited here. ✉ *Hillside Sedona, 671 AZ 179, A1 and A2, Uptown* ☎ *928/282–1404* 🌐 *www.jamesratliffgallery.com.*

SHOPPING CENTERS

Hillside Sedona

ART GALLERIES | Half a dozen galleries and two popular restaurants, The Hudson and Javelina Cantina, are housed in the Hillside Sedona complex. ✉ *671 AZ 179, Uptown* ☎ *928/282–4500* 🌐 *www.hillsidesedona.net.*

★ **Tlaquepaque Arts & Crafts Village**

SHOPPING CENTERS/MALLS | Home to more than 55 shops and galleries and several restaurants, Tlaquepaque Arts & Crafts Village remains one of the best places for travelers to find mementos from their trip to Sedona. The complex of clay tile–roofed buildings arranged around a series of courtyards shares its name and architectural style with a crafts village just outside Guadalajara. It's a lovely place to browse, but beware: prices tend to be high, and locals joke that it's pronounced "to-lock-your-pocket." ✉ *AZ 179, just south of "Y,," Uptown* ☎ *928/282–4838* 🌐 *www.tlaq.com.*

Activities

A Red Rock Pass is required to park in the Coconino National Forest from Oak Creek Canyon through Sedona and the Village of Oak Creek. Passes cost $5 for the day, $15 for the week, or $20 for an entire year, and can be purchased online and at the **Coconino Forest Service Red Rock Ranger Station** (✉ *8375 AZ 179, just south of Village of Oak Creek* ☎ *928/203–7500* 🌐 *www.redrockcountry.org*), which is open daily and has copious information on regional outdoor activities. Passes are also available from vending machines at popular trailheads—including Boynton Canyon and Bell Rock—and at the Sedona Chamber of Commerce, Circle K stores, grocery stores, and many Sedona hotels.

HIKING AND BACKPACKING

Among the most popular hikes in Sedona are West Fork Trail (traversing Oak Creek Canyon), Doe Mountain Trail (an easy ascent with many switchbacks), and Cathedral Rock Trail (with panoramic views). Backpacking in the **Red Rock–Secret Mountain Wilderness** near Sedona guarantees stunning vistas, otherworldly rock formations, and Zen-like serenity, but little water, so pack a good supply. ■ TIP→ **Plan your trip for spring or fall: summer brings 100°F heat and sudden thunderstorms that flood canyons without warning.** Most individual trails in the wilderness are too short for anything longer than an overnighter, but several trails can be linked up to form a memorable multiday trip. Contact Coconino National Forest's Red Rock Ranger District in Sedona for hiking and backpacking details.

JEEP TOURS

Several jeep-tour operators headquartered along Sedona's main Uptown drag conduct excursions, some focusing on geology, some on astronomy, some on

Jeep tours get you close to Sedona's red rocks while someone else does the driving.

vortexes, some on all three. You can even find a combination jeep tour and horseback ride. Prices start at about $60 per person for two hours and go upward of $100 per person for four hours. Although all the excursions are safe, many aren't for those who dislike heights or bumps.

A Day in the West

TOUR—SPORTS | With this tour operator, you can go to all the prime spots and combine a jeep tour with a horseback ride or local wine tasting. ☎ *928/282–4320, 800/973–3662* 🌐 *www.adayinthewest.com* 🎫 *From $75.*

Pink Adventure Tours

TOUR—SPORTS | The ubiquitous Pink jeeps are a popular choice for driving through the red rocks. Off-road tours range from 1 to 4 hours; paved-road tours are offered for those seeking a smoother adventure. ✉ *204 N. AZ 89A, Uptown* ☎ *800/873–3662, 928/282–5000* 🌐 *www.pinkadventuretours.com* 🎫 *From $65.*

Grand Canyon National Park

Grand Canyon South Rim is 79 miles north of Flagstaff.

When it comes to the Grand Canyon, there are statistics, and there are sensations. While the former are impressive—the canyon measures an average width of 10 miles, length of 277 river miles, and depth of 1 mile—they don't truly prepare you for that first impression. Viewing the canyon for the first time is an astounding experience. Actually, it's more than an experience: it's an emotion, one that only just begins to be captured with the word "Grand," the name bestowed upon the canyon by John Wesley Powell, an explorer of the American West, as he led his expedition down the Colorado River in 1869.

When President Teddy Roosevelt declared it a National Monument in 1908, he called it "the one great sight every American should see." Though many visitors do just that—stand at the rim and marvel in awe—there are manifold ways to soak up the canyon's magnificence. Hike or ride a trusty mule down into the canyon, bike or ramble along its rim, fly over, or raft through on the Colorado River.

Roughly 6 million visitors come to the park each year. You can access the canyon via two main points—the South Rim and the North Rim—but the South Rim is much easier to get to and therefore much more visited. The width from the North Rim to the South Rim varies from 600 feet to 18 miles, but traveling between rims by road requires a 215-mile drive. Hiking arduous trails from rim to rim is a steep and strenuous trek of at least 21 miles, but it's well worth the effort. You'll travel through five of North America's seven life zones. (To do this any other way, you'd have to journey from the Mexican desert to the Canadian woods.) West of Grand Canyon National Park, the tribal lands of the Hualapai and the Havasupai lie along the so-called West Rim of the canyon, where you'll find the impressive glass Skywalk.

Planning

GETTING HERE AND AROUND

The best route into the park from the east or south is from Flagstaff. Take U.S. 180 northwest to the park's southern entrance and Grand Canyon Visitor Center. From the west on Interstate 40, the most direct route to the South Rim is taking Highway 64 from Williams to U.S. 180.

The South Rim is open to car traffic year-round, though access to Hermits Rest is limited to **shuttle buses** during summer months. There are four free shuttle routes that run from one hour before sunrise until one hour after sunset, every 15 to 30 minutes: the **Hermits Rest Route** operates March through November, between Grand Canyon Village and Hermits Rest. The **Village Route** operates year-round in the village area, stopping at lodgings, the general store, and the Grand Canyon Visitor Center. The **Kaibab Rim Route** goes from the visitor center to five viewpoints, including the Yavapai Geology Museum and Yaki Point (where cars are not permitted). The **Tusayan Route** travels between the village and the town of Tusayan from March through September. A fifth route, the **Hiker's Express,** shuttles hikers from the village to the South Kaibab Trailhead twice each morning. ■ TIP→ **In summer, South Rim roads are congested and it's easier, and sometimes required, to park your car and take the free shuttle.**

PARK ESSENTIALS

A fee of $35 per vehicle or $20 per person for pedestrians and cyclists is good for one week's access at both rims.

The South Rim is open continuously every day of the year (weather permitting), while the North Rim is open mid-May through October. Because Arizona does not observe daylight saving time, the park is in the same time zone as California and Nevada from mid-March to early November, and in the mountain time zone the rest of the year. Just to the east of the park, the Navajo Nation observes daylight saving time.

Cell phone coverage can be spotty at both the South Rim and North Rim—though Verizon customers report better reception at the South Rim. Don't expect a strong signal anywhere in the park, but Grand Canyon Village is usually the best bet.

TOURS

Xanterra Motorcoach Tours

GUIDED TOURS | Narrated by knowledgeable guides, tours include the Hermits Rest Tour, which travels along the old wagon road built by the Santa Fe Railway; the Desert View Tour, which glimpses the Colorado River's rapids and stops at Lipan Point; Sunrise and Sunset Tours; and combination tours. ☎ *303/297–2757, 888/297–2757* 🌐 *www.grandcanyonlodges.com* 🎫 *From $40.*

VISITOR INFORMATION

Grand Canyon National Park

Before you go, you can view and print the complimentary *Pocket Map and Service Guide,* updated regularly, from the Grand Canyon National Park website. You can also pick up a copy at the entrance stations and the visitor centers. ☎ *928/638–7888* 🌐 *www.nps.gov/grca.*

Grand Canyon South Rim

Visitors to the canyon converge mostly on the South Rim, and mostly in summer. Grand Canyon Village is here, with a majority of the park's lodging and camping, trailheads, restaurants, stores, and museums, along with a nearby airport and railroad depot. Believe it or not, the average stay in the park is a mere half day or so; this is not advised! You need to spend several days to truly appreciate this marvelous place, but at the very least, give it a full day. Hike down into the canyon, or along the rim, to get away from the crowds and experience nature at its finest.

Sights

HISTORIC SIGHTS

Tusayan Ruin and Museum

ARCHAEOLOGICAL SITE | This museum offers a quick orientation to the prehistoric and modern indigenous populations of the Grand Canyon and the Colorado Plateau, including an excavation of an 800-year-old Pueblo site. Of special interest are split-twig figurines dating back 2,000 to 4,000 years and other artifacts left behind by ancient cultures. A ranger leads daily interpretive tours of the Ancestral Pueblo village. ✉ *Grand Canyon National Park* ⊕ *About 20 miles east of Grand Canyon Village on E. Rim Dr.* ☎ *928/638–7888* 🎫 *Free.*

SCENIC DRIVES

Desert View Drive

SCENIC DRIVE | This heavily traveled 25-mile stretch of road follows the rim from the east entrance to Grand Canyon Village. Starting from the less-congested entry near Desert View, road warriors can get their first glimpse of the canyon from the 70-foot-tall watchtower, the top of which provides the highest viewpoint on the South Rim. Six developed canyon viewpoints in addition to unmarked pullouts, the remains of an Ancestral Puebloan dwelling at the Tusayan Ruin and Museum, and the secluded and lovely Buggeln picnic area make for great stops along the South Rim. The Kaibab Rim Route shuttle bus travels a short section of Desert View Drive and takes 50 minutes to ride round-trip without getting off at any of the stops: Grand Canyon Visitor Center, South Kaibab Trailhead, Yaki Point, Pipe Creek Vista, Mather Point, and Yavapai Geology Museum. ✉ *Grand Canyon National Park.*

SCENIC STOPS

★ Hopi Point

VIEWPOINT | From this elevation of 7,071 feet, you can see a large section of the Colorado River; although it appears as a thin line, the river is nearly 350 feet wide. The overlook extends farther into the canyon than any other point on Hermit Road. The incredible unobstructed views make this a popular place to watch the sunset.

Across the canyon to the north is Shiva Temple. In 1937 Harold Anthony of the American Museum of Natural History led an expedition to the rock formation in the belief that it supported life that

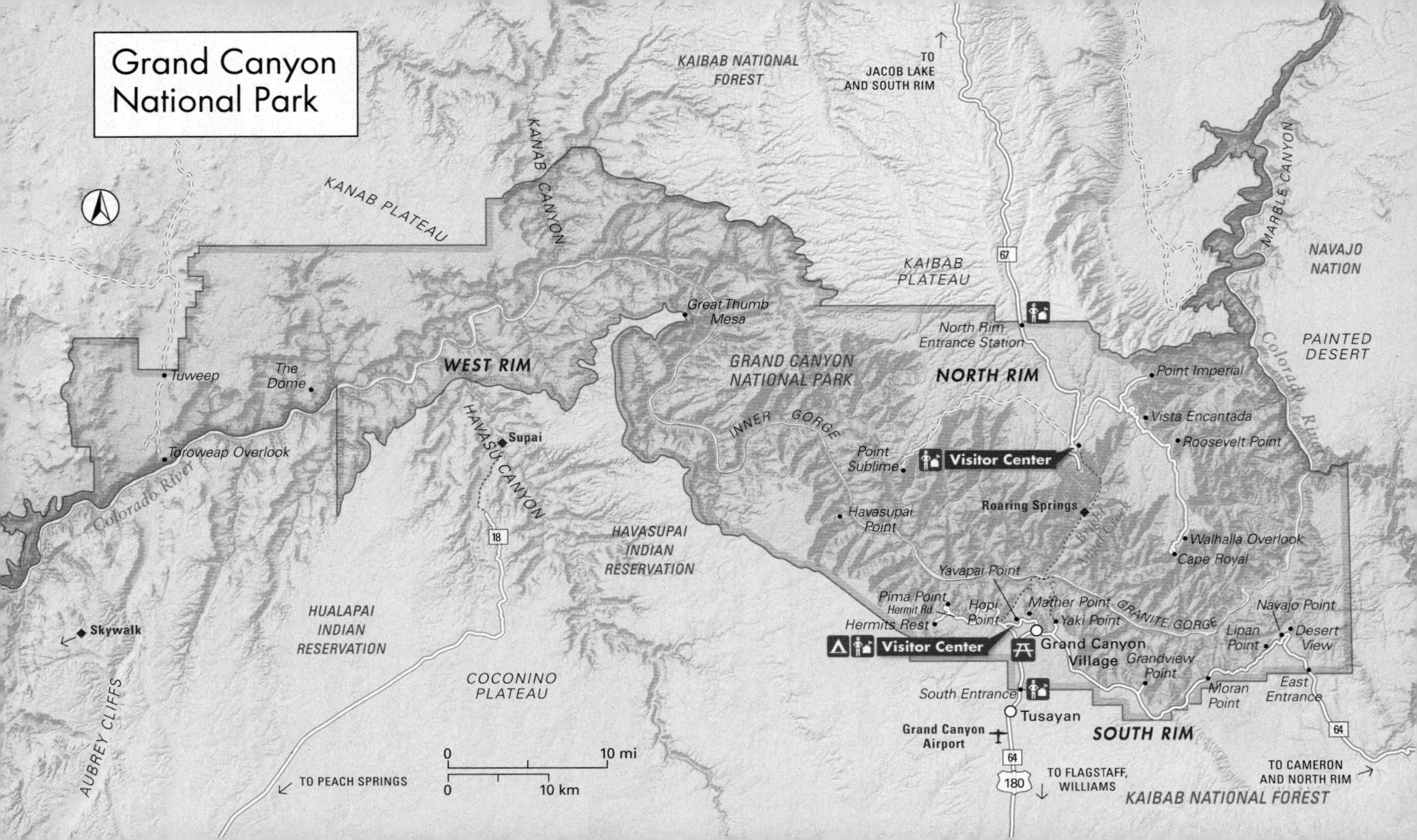
Grand Canyon National Park
KAIBAB NATIONAL FOREST
TO JACOB LAKE AND SOUTH RIM
KANAB CANYON
KANAB PLATEAU
KAIBAB PLATEAU
67
MARBLE CANYON
NAVAJO NATION
PAINTED DESERT
Colorado River
Great Thumb Mesa
North Rim Entrance Station
GRAND CANYON NATIONAL PARK
NORTH RIM
WEST RIM
Tuweep
The Dome
Point Imperial
Vista Encantada
Roosevelt Point
INNER GORGE
Point Sublime
Visitor Center
Supai
HAVASU CANYON
Toroweap Overlook
Colorado River
Roaring Springs
Bright Angel Creek
Havasupai Point
18
HAVASUPAI INDIAN RESERVATION
Walhalla Overlook
Cape Royal
Yavapai Point
Pima Point
Hermit Rd.
Hopi Point
Mather Point
Yaki Point
GRANITE GORGE
Navajo Point
Lipan Point
Desert View
Hermits Rest
Visitor Center
Grand Canyon Village
Grandview Point
HUALAPAI INDIAN RESERVATION
Skywalk
South Entrance
Moran Point
East Entrance
Tusayan
COCONINO PLATEAU
Grand Canyon Airport
SOUTH RIM
64
AUBREY CLIFFS
0
10 mi
0
10 km
TO PEACH SPRINGS
64
180
TO FLAGSTAFF, WILLIAMS
TO CAMERON AND NORTH RIM
KAIBAB NATIONAL FOREST

had been cut off from the rest of the canyon. Imagine the expedition members' surprise when they found an empty Kodak film box on top of the temple—it had been left behind by Emery Kolb, who felt slighted for not having been invited to join Anthony's tour.

Directly below Hopi Point lies Dana Butte, named for a prominent 19th-century geologist. In 1919 an entrepreneur proposed connecting Hopi Point, Dana Butte, and the Tower of Set across the river with an aerial tramway, a technically feasible plan that fortunately has not been realized. ✉ *Grand Canyon National Park* ⤧ *About 4 miles west of Hermit Rd. Junction on Hermit Rd.*

★ Mather Point

VIEWPOINT | You'll likely get your first glimpse of the canyon from this viewpoint, one of the most impressive and accessible (next to the main visitor center plaza) on the South Rim. Named for the National Park Service's first director, Stephen Mather, this spot yields extraordinary views of the Grand Canyon, including deep into the inner gorge and numerous buttes: Wotans Throne, Brahma Temple, and Zoroaster Temple, among others. The Grand Canyon Lodge, on the North Rim, is almost directly north from Mather Point and only 10 miles away—yet you have to drive 215 miles to get from one spot to the other. ✉ *Near Grand Canyon Visitor Center, Grand Canyon National Park* ☎ *928/638–7888* 🌐 *www.nps.gov/grca.*

Trailview Overlook

VIEWPOINT | Look down on a dramatic view of the Bright Angel and Plateau Point trails as they zigzag down the canyon. In the deep gorge to the north flows Bright Angel Creek, one of the region's few permanent tributary streams of the Colorado River. Toward the south is an unobstructed view of the distant San Francisco Peaks, as well as Bill Williams Mountain (on the horizon) and Red Butte (about 15 miles south of the canyon rim). ✉ *Grand Canyon National Park* ⤧ *About 2 miles west of Hermit Rd. Junction on Hermit Rd.*

Yaki Point

VIEWPOINT | Stop here for an exceptional view of Wotans Throne, a flat-top butte named by François Matthes, a U.S. Geological Survey scientist who developed the first topographical map of the Grand Canyon. The overlook juts out over the canyon, providing unobstructed views of inner-canyon rock formations, South Rim cliffs, and Clear Creek Canyon. About a mile south of Yaki Point is the trailhead for the South Kaibab Trail. **■ TIP→ The point is one of the best places on the South Rim to watch the sunrise and the sunset.** ✉ *Grand Canyon National Park* ⤧ *4 miles east of Grand Canyon Village on Desert View Dr.*

★ Yavapai Point

MUSEUM | Dominated by the Yavapai Geology Museum and Observation Station, this point displays panoramic views of the mighty gorge through a wall of windows. Exhibits at the museum include videos of the canyon floor and the Colorado River, a scaled diorama of the canyon with national park boundaries, fossils, and rock fragments used to re-create the complex layers of the canyon walls, and a display on the natural forces used to carve the chasm. Dig even deeper into Grand Canyon geology with free daily ranger programs. This point is also a good location to watch the sunset. ✉ *Grand Canyon Village* ⤧ *1 mile east of Market Plaza.*

TRAILS

★ Bright Angel Trail

TRAIL | This well-maintained trail is one of the most scenic (and busiest) hiking paths from the South Rim to the bottom of the canyon (9.6 miles each way). Rest houses are equipped with water at the 1½- and 3-mile points from May through September, and at Indian Garden (4 miles) year-round. Water is also available at Bright Angel Campground, 9¼ miles below the trailhead. Plateau Point, on a spur trail about 1½ miles below Indian Garden, is as far as you should attempt to go on a day hike; the round-trip will take six to nine hours.

Bright Angel Trail is the easiest of all the footpaths into the canyon, but because the climb out from the bottom is an ascent of 5,510 feet, the trip should be attempted only by those in good physical condition and should be avoided in midsummer due to extreme heat. The top of the trail can be icy in winter. Originally a bighorn sheep path and later used by the Havasupai, the trail was widened late in the 19th century for prospectors and is now used for both mule and foot traffic. Also note that mule trains have the right-of-way—and sometimes leave unpleasant surprises in your path. *Moderate.* ✉ *Grand Canyon National Park* ✢ *Trailhead: Kolb Studio, Hermit Rd.*

★ Rim Trail

TRAIL | The South Rim's most popular walking path is the 12.8-mile (one-way) Rim Trail, which runs along the edge of the canyon from Pipe Creek Vista (the first overlook on Desert View Drive) to Hermits Rest. This walk, which is paved to Maricopa Point and for the last 1½ miles to Hermits Rest, visits several of the South Rim's historic landmarks. Allow anywhere from 15 minutes to a full day, depending on how much of the trail you want to cover; the Rim Trail is an ideal day hike, as it varies only a few hundred feet in elevation from Mather Point (7,120 feet) to the trailhead at Hermits Rest (6,650 feet). The trail also can be accessed from several spots in Grand Canyon Village and from the major viewpoints along Hermit Road, which are serviced by shuttle buses during the busy summer months. On the Rim Trail, water is available only in the Grand Canyon Village area and at Hermits Rest. *Easy.* ✉ *Grand Canyon National Park.*

VISITOR CENTERS

Desert View Information Center

INFO CENTER | Near the watchtower, at Desert View Point, this nonprofit Grand Canyon Association store and information center has a nice selection of books, park pamphlets, gifts, and educational materials. It's also a handy place to pick up maps and info if you enter the park at the Eastern entrance. All sales from the association stores go to support the park programs. ✉ *Eastern entrance, Grand Canyon National Park* ☎ *800/858–2808, 928/638–7888.*

Grand Canyon Verkamp's Visitor Center

INFO CENTER | This small visitor center is named for the Verkamp family, who operated a curios shop on the South Rim for more than a hundred years. The building serves as an official visitor center, ranger station (get your Junior Ranger badges here), bookstore, and museum, with compelling exhibits on the Verkamps and other pioneers in this region. ✉ *Desert View Dr., Grand Canyon Village* ✢ *Across from El Tovar Hotel* ☎ *928/638–7146.*

Grand Canyon Visitor Center

INFO CENTER | The park's main orientation center provides pamphlets and resources to help plan your visit. It also holds engaging interpretive exhibits on the park. Rangers are on hand to answer questions and aid in planning canyon excursions. A daily schedule of ranger-led hikes and evening lectures is available, and a 20-minute film about the history, geology, and wildlife of the canyon plays every 30 minutes in the theater. The bicycle rental office, a small café, and a huge gift store are also in this complex. It's a 5-minute walk from here to Mather Point, or a short ride on the shuttle bus, which can take you into Grand Canyon Village. The visitor center is also accessible from the village via a leisurely 2-mile walk on the Greenway Trail, a paved pathway that meanders through the forest. ✉ *East side of Grand Canyon Village, 450 Hwy. 64, Grand Canyon* ☎ *928/638–7888.*

Yavapai Geology Museum

INFO CENTER | Learn about the geology of the canyon at this Grand Canyon Association museum and bookstore that doubles as a visitor center. You can also catch the park shuttle bus or pick up information for the Rim Trail here. The views of the canyon and Phantom Ranch from inside this historic building are stupendous. ✉ *1 mile east of Market Plaza, Grand Canyon Village* ☎ *928/638–7890.*

Restaurants

All Grand Canyon lodges have casual dining. Fred Harvey Burger, at Bright Angel Lodge, is busy all day long. There's a popular food court at Maswick Lodge and a cafeteria-style restaurant at Yavapai Lodge.

Arizona Steakhouse

$$$ | **STEAKHOUSE** | The canyon views from this casual Southwestern-style steak house are the best of any restaurant at the South Rim. The dinner menu leans toward steakhouse dishes, while lunch is primarily salads and sandwiches with a Southwestern twist. **Known for:** views of the Grand Canyon; Southwestern fare; local craft beers and wines. 💲 *Average main: $28* ✉ *Bright Angel Lodge, 9 N. Village Loop Dr., Grand Canyon Village* ☎ *928/638–2631* 🌐 *www.grandcanyonlodges.com.*

★ El Tovar Dining Room

$$$ | **SOUTHWESTERN** | Even at the edge of the Grand Canyon it's possible to find gourmet dining. This cozy room of dark wood beams and stone, nestled in the historic El Tovar Lodge, dates to 1905. **Known for:** historic setting with canyon views; local and organic ingredients; fine dining that's worth the splurge. 💲 *Average main: $28* ✉ *El Tovar Hotel, 1 El Tovar Rd., Grand Canyon Village* ☎ *928/638–2631* 🌐 *www.grandcanyonlodges.com.*

Hotels

South Rim accommodations include three "historic-rustic" facilities and four motel-style lodges, all of which have undergone significant upgrades over the past decade. Outside El Tovar Hotel, the canyon's architectural highlight, accommodations are relatively basic but comfortable, and the most sought-after rooms have canyon views. Rates vary widely, but most rooms fall in the $175 to $250 range, though the most basic units on the South Rim are cheaper.

Bright Angel Lodge

$$ | **HOTEL** | Famed architect Mary Jane Colter designed this 1935 log-and-stone structure, which sits within a few yards of the canyon rim and blends superbly with the canyon walls; its location is similar to El Tovar's but for about half the price. **Pros:** good value for the amazing location; charming rooms and cabins steps from the rim; on-site Internet kiosks and transportation desk for the mule ride. **Cons:** popular lobby is always packed; parking is a bit of a hike; only some rooms have canyon views. 💲 *Rooms from: $150* ✉ *9 N. Village Loop Dr., Grand Canyon Village* ☎ *888/297–2757 reservations only, 928/638–2631* 🌐 *www.grandcanyonlodges.com* *105 units* *No meals.*

★ El Tovar Hotel

$$$$ | **HOTEL** | The hotel's proximity to all of the canyon's facilities, European hunting-lodge atmosphere, attractively updated rooms and tile baths, and renowned dining room make it the best place to stay on the South Rim. A registered National Historic Landmark, the "architectural crown jewel of the Grand Canyon" was built in 1905 of Oregon pine logs and native stone. **Pros:** historic lodging just steps from the South Rim; fabulous lounge with outdoor seating and canyon views; best in-park dining on-site. **Cons:** books up quickly; priciest lodging in the park; rooms are comfortable,

not luxurious. $ *Rooms from: $275* ✉ *1 El Tovar Rd., Grand Canyon Village* ☎ *888/297–2757 reservations only, 928/638–2631* 🌐 *www.grandcanyonlodges.com* 78 rooms 🍽 *No meals.*

Maswik Lodge

$$ | HOTEL | FAMILY | Far from the noisy crowds, Maswik accommodations are in two-story, contemporary motel-style buildings nestled in a shady ponderosa pine forest. **Pros:** units are modern, spacious, and well equipped; good for families; affordable dining options. **Cons:** rooms lack historic charm; tucked away from the rim in the forest; no elevators for second-floor rooms. $ *Rooms from: $170* ✉ *Grand Canyon Village* ☎ *888/297–2757 reservations only, 928/638–2631* 🌐 *www.grandcanyonlodges.com* *278 rooms* 🍽 *No meals.*

Phantom Ranch

$ | B&B/INN | In a grove of cottonwood trees on the canyon floor, Phantom Ranch is accessible only to hikers, river rafters, and mule trekkers; there are 40 dormitory bunk beds and 14 beds in cabins, all with shared baths (though cabins have toilets and sinks). **Pros:** only inner-canyon lodging option; fabulous canyon views; remote access limits crowds. **Cons:** reservations are booked more than a year in advance; few amenities; shared bathrooms. $ *Rooms from: $65* ✉ *On canyon floor, Grand Canyon National Park* ✣ *At intersection of Bright Angel and Kaibab trails* ☎ *303/297–2757, 888/297–2757* 🌐 *www.grandcanyonlodges.com* *54 beds* 🍽 *No meals.*

Activities

CAMPING

Within the national park, there are two developed campgrounds on the South Rim and one on the North Rim. All campgrounds charge nightly camping fees in addition to the general park entrance fee; some accept reservations up to six months in advance (☎ *877/444–6777* 🌐 *www.recreation.gov*) and others are first-come, first-served.

Camping anywhere outside a developed rim campground, including in the canyon, requires a permit from the Backcountry Information Center, which also serves as your reservation. Permits can be requested by mail or fax only; applying well in advance is recommended. Call ☎ *928/638–7875* between 1 pm and 5 pm weekdays for information.

Bright Angel Campground. This backcountry campground is near Phantom Ranch at the bottom of the canyon. There are toilet facilities and running water, but no showers. ✉ *Intersection of South and North Kaibab trails, South Rim* ☎ *928/638–7875.*

Desert View Campground. Popular for spectacular views of the canyon from the nearby watchtower, this developed campground near the east entrance doesn't take reservations; show up before noon, as it fills up fast in summer. Open mid-May through mid-October, these sites have no hookups. ✉ *Desert View Dr., 23 miles east of Grand Canyon Village off Hwy. 64, South Rim.*

Indian Garden. Halfway down the canyon is this campground, en route to Phantom Ranch on the Bright Angel Trail. Running water and toilet facilities are available, but not showers. A backcountry permit, which serves as a reservation, is required. You can book up to four months in advance. ✉ *Bright Angel Trail* ☎ *928/638–7875, 928/638–2125*

Mather Campground. The largest developed campground in the park is set in a forested area near Grand Canyon Village. Open all year, Mather takes reservations from March to November and has water and toilet facilities, as well as showers and laundry (for an extra fee). There is a cofee bar/deli on-site, and the park shuttle stops here. ✉ *Grand Canyon Village* ☎ *877/444–6777* 🌐 *www.recreation.gov*

Trailer Village. This campground in Grand Canyon Village has RV sites—but no tent-camping sites—with full hookups and bathroom facilities, though the bathrooms are ½ mile from the campground. The facility is very busy in spring and summer, so make reservations ahead of time. The dump station is closed in winter. ✉ *Grand Canyon Village* ☎ *303/297–2757, 888/297–2757 reservations only, 303/297–3175 reservations only* 🌐 *www.visitgrandcanyon.com*

HIKING

Although permits are not required for day hikes, you must have a backcountry permit for longer trips (⇨ *see Park Fees and Permits*). Some of the more popular trails are listed under ⇨ *Sights*, including **Bright Angel Trail** and **Rim Trail**; more detailed information and maps can be obtained from the Backcountry Information centers. Also, rangers can help design a trip to suit your abilities.

■ TIP→ **Under no circumstances should you attempt a day hike from the rim to the river and back.** Remember that when it's 85°F on the South Rim, it's 110°F on the canyon floor. Allow two to four days if you want to hike rim to rim (it's easier to descend from the North Rim, as it's more than 1,000 feet higher than the South Rim). Hiking steep trails from rim to rim is a strenuous trek of at least 21 miles and should be attempted only by experienced canyon hikers.

HORSEBACK RIDING

Mule rides provide an intimate glimpse into the canyon for those who have the time, but not the stamina, to see the canyon on foot. ■ TIP→ **Reservations are essential and are accepted up to 13 months in advance.**

These trips have been conducted since the early 1900s. A comforting fact as you ride the narrow trail: no one's ever been killed while riding a mule that fell off a cliff. (Nevertheless, the treks are not for the faint of heart or people in questionable health.)

★ **Xanterra Parks & Resorts Mule Rides**

TOUR—SPORTS | These trips delve either into the canyon from the South Rim to Phantom Ranch, or east along the canyon's rim. Riders must be at least nine years old and 57 inches tall, weigh less than 200 pounds for the Phantom Ranch ride or less than 225 pounds for the rim ride, and understand English. Children under 18 must be accompanied by an adult. Riders must be in fairly good physical condition, and pregnant women are advised not to take these trips.

The two-hour ride along the rim costs $155. An overnight mule ride with a stay in a cabin at Phantom Ranch at the bottom of the canyon, with meals included, is $705 ($1,226 for two riders). Package prices vary since a cabin at Phantom Ranch can accommodate up to four people. From November through March, you can stay for up to two nights at Phantom Ranch. Reservations are a must, but you can check at the Bright Angel Transportation Desk to see if there's last-minute availability. ☎ *888/297–2757, 303/297–2757* 🌐 *www.grandcanyonlodges.com* ✍ *Reservations essential.*

JEEP TOURS

Jeep rides can be rough; if you have had back injuries, check with your doctor before taking a 4x4 tour. It's a good idea to book a week or two ahead, and even longer if you're visiting in summer or on busy weekends.

Buck Wild Hummer Tours

DRIVING TOURS | With this tour company, you can see majestic rim views in Grand Canyon National Park and learn about the history, geology, and wildlife of the canyon from the comfort of a 13-passenger Hummer. Daily tours run either in the morning or at sunset. ✉ *469 AZ 64, Grand Canyon* ☎ *928/362–5940* 🌐 *buckwildhummertours.com* 🎟 *From $99.*

Did You Know?

Sure-footed mules take riders along the rim for half-day trips and down into the canyon for longer excursions. Two-day trips include an overnight stay at Phantom Ranch on the canyon floor.

SCENIC FLIGHTS

Flights by plane and helicopter over the canyon are offered by a number of companies, departing from the Grand Canyon Airport at the south end of Tusayan. Though the noise and disruption of so many aircraft buzzing around the canyon is controversial, flightseeing remains a popular, if expensive, option. You'll have more visibility from a helicopter, but they're louder and more expensive than the fixed-wing planes. Prices and lengths of tours vary, but you can expect to pay about $159 per adult for short plane trips and approximately $300 for helicopter tours. These companies often have significant discounts in winter—check the company websites to find the best deals.

Grand Canyon Airlines

FLYING/SKYDIVING/SOARING | This company offers a variety of plane tours, from a 45-minute fixed-wing tour of the eastern edge of the Grand Canyon, the North Rim, and the Kaibab Plateau to an all-day tour that combines "flightseeing" with four-wheel-drive tours of Antelope Canyon and float trips on the Colorado River. ✉ *Grand Canyon Airport, Tusayan* ☎ *702/835–8484, 866/235–9422* 🌐 *www.grandcanyonairlines.com* 🎫 *From $159.*

Grand Canyon West

186 miles northwest of Williams, 70 miles north of Kingman.

The plateau-dwelling Hualapai ("people of the tall pines") acquired a larger chunk of traditional Pai lands with the creation of their reservation in 1883. Hualapai tribal lands include diverse habitats ranging from rolling grasslands to rugged canyons, and travel from elevations of 1,500 feet at the Colorado River to more than 7,300 feet at Aubrey Cliffs. In recent years, the Hualapai have been attempting to foster tourism on the West Rim—most notably with the spectacular Skywalk, a glass walkway suspended 70 feet over the edge of the canyon rim. Not hampered by the regulations in place at Grand Canyon National Park, Grand Canyon West offers helicopter flights down into the bottom of the canyon, horseback rides to rim viewpoints, ziplining, and rafting trips on the Colorado River.

The Hualapai Reservation encompasses a million acres in the Grand Canyon, along 108 miles of the Colorado River, with two main areas open to tourists. The West Rim has the Skywalk, Hualapai cultural exhibits and dancing, horseback riding, ziplining, and helicopter rides. Peach Springs, a two-hour drive from the West Rim on historic Route 66, is the tribal capital and the launch site for raft trips on this stretch of the river. Lodging is available both on the rim, at Hualapai Ranch, and in Peach Springs, at the Hualapai Lodge. Although increasingly popular, the West Rim is still relatively remote and visited by far fewer people than the South Rim—keep in mind that it's more than 120 miles away from the nearest interstate highways.

The West Rim is a five-hour drive from the South Rim of Grand Canyon National Park or a 2½-hour drive from Las Vegas. From Kingman, drive north 30 miles on U.S. 93, and then turn right onto Pierce Ferry Road and follow it for 28 miles. (A more scenic but slightly longer alternative is to drive 42 miles north on Stockton Hill Road, turning right onto Pierce Ferry Road for 7 miles.) Turn right (east) onto Diamond Bar Road and follow it for 21 miles to Grand Canyon West entrance.

Visitors aren't allowed to travel in their own vehicles to the viewpoints once they reach Grand Canyon West, and must purchase a tour package—which can range from day use to horseback or helicopter rides to lodging and meals—either online (🌐 *grandcanyonwest.com*) or in person from Hualapai Tourism.

In addition to the exploring options provided by the Hualapai tribe, more than 30 tour and transportation companies service Grand Canyon West from Las Vegas, Phoenix, and Sedona by airplane, helicopter, coach, SUV, and Hummer. Perhaps the easiest way to visit the West Rim from Vegas is with a tour.

Bighorn Wild West Tours

GUIDED TOURS | This full-day tour takes you to Grand Canyon West in the comfort of a Hummer. Admission fees and lunch are included, as is a stop for photos at Hoover Dam. *702/385–4676 www.bighorntours.com From $277.*

CONTACTS Grand Canyon West. *888/868–9378, 928/769–2636 www.grandcanyonwest.com.*

Sights

SCENIC SPOTS

★ Grand Canyon Skywalk

VIEWPOINT | This cantilevered glass terrace is suspended nearly 4,000 feet above the Colorado River and extends 70 feet from the edge of the Grand Canyon. Approximately 10 feet wide, the bridge's deck, made of tempered glass several inches thick, has 5-foot glass railings on each side creating an unobstructed open-air platform. Admission to the skywalk is an add-on to the basic Grand Canyon West admission. Visitors must store personal items, including cameras, cell phones, and video cameras, in lockers before entering. A professional photographer takes photographs of visitors, which can be purchased from the gift shop. *www.grandcanyonwest.com $23.*

Hotels

The Cabins at Grand Canyon West

$$$ | **B&B/INN** | **FAMILY** | The only lodging on the West Rim, the comfortable cabins at Hualapai Ranch are clean and neat, but also small and unassuming. **Pros:** front porches with nice desert views; rustlers tell tall tales while you roast s'mores at the campfire; dining room and "saloon" serve all day long. **Cons:** no phones or TVs; no Internet; remote setting. *Rooms from: $199 Quartermaster Point Rd., Grand Canyon West 928/769–2636, 888/868–9378 www.grandcanyonwest.com 26 cabins Free breakfast.*

Activities

BOATING AND RAFTING

Hualapai River Runners

TOUR—SPORTS | One-, two- and five-day river trips are offered by the Hualapai Tribe through the Hualapai River Runners from mid-March through October. The trips leave from Peach Springs (a two-hour drive from the West Rim) and include rafting, hiking, and transport. Meals, snacks, and beverages are provided. Children must be at least 8 to take the one-day trip and 12 for the overnight trips; the rapids here are rated as Class III–VII, depending on the river flow. *5001 Buck N. Doe Rd., Peach Springs 928/769–2636, 888/868–9378 www.grandcanyonwest.com From $325.*

Grand Canyon North Rim

The North Rim stands 1,000 feet higher than the South Rim and has a more alpine climate, with twice as much annual precipitation. Here, in the deep forests of the Kaibab Plateau, the crowds are thinner, the facilities fewer, and the views even more spectacular. Due to snow, the North Rim is off-limits in winter. The buildings and concessions are closed mid-October through mid-May. The road and entrance gate close when the snow makes them impassable—usually by the end of November.

Lodgings are limited in this more remote park, with only one historic lodge (with cabins and hotel-type rooms as well as a restaurant) and a single campground. Dining options have opened up a little with a deli and a coffeehouse/saloon next door to the lodge. Your best bet may be to pack your camping gear and hiking boots and take several days to explore the lush Kaibab Forest. The canyon's highest, most dramatic rim views can also be enjoyed on two wheels (via primitive dirt access roads) and on four legs (courtesy of a trusty mule).

Sights

HISTORIC SIGHTS

Grand Canyon Lodge

HISTORIC SITE | Built in 1937 by the Union Pacific Railroad (replacing the original 1928 building, which burned in a fire), this massive stone structure is listed on the National Register of Historic Places. Its huge sunroom has hardwood floors, high-beamed ceilings, and a marvelous view of the canyon through plate-glass windows. On warm days, visitors sit in the sun and drink in the surrounding beauty on an outdoor viewing deck, where National Park Service employees deliver free lectures on geology and history. The dining room serves breakfast, lunch, and dinner; the Roughrider Saloon is a bar by night and a coffee shop in the morning. ✉ *Grand Canyon National Park* ✣ *Off Hwy. 67 near Bright Angel Point* ☎ *928/638–2611 May.–Oct., 877/386–4383 reservations* 🌐 *www.grandcanyonforever.com* ⏲ *Closed mid-Oct.–mid-May.*

SCENIC STOPS

★ Bright Angel Point

TRAIL | Bright Angel Point is one of the most awe-inspiring overlooks on either rim. To get to it, follow the trail that starts on the grounds of the Grand Canyon Lodge and runs along the crest of a point of rocks that juts into the canyon for several hundred yards. The walk is only ½ mile round-trip, but it's an exciting trek accented by sheer drops on each side of the trail. In a few spots where the route is extremely narrow, metal railings ensure visitors' safety. The temptation to clamber out on precarious perches to have your picture taken should be resisted at all costs. ✉ *North Rim Dr., Grand Canyon National Park* ✣ *Near Grand Canyon Lodge.*

Cape Royal

TRAIL | A popular sunset destination, Cape Royal showcases the canyon's jagged landscape; you'll also get a glimpse of the Colorado River, framed by a natural stone arch called Angels Window. In autumn, the aspens turn a beautiful gold, adding even more color to an already magnificent scene of the forested surroundings. The easy and rewarding 1-mile round-trip hike along **Cliff Springs Trail** starts here; it takes you through a forested ravine and terminates at Cliff Springs, where the forest opens to another impressive view of the canyon walls. ✉ *Cape Royal Scenic Dr., Grand Canyon National Park* ✣ *23 miles southeast of Grand Canyon Lodge.*

★ Point Sublime

VIEWPOINT | You can camp within feet of the canyon's edge at this awe-inspiring site. Sunrises and sunsets are spectacular. The winding road, through gorgeous high country, is only 17 miles, but it will take you at least two hours one-way. The road is intended only for vehicles with high road clearance (pickups and four-wheel-drive vehicles). It is also necessary to be properly equipped for wilderness road travel. Check with a park ranger or at the information desk at Grand Canyon Lodge before taking this journey. You may camp here only with a permit from the Backcountry Information Center. ✉ *North Rim Dr., Grand Canyon National Park* ✣ *About 20 miles west of North Rim Visitor Center.*

TRAILS

Cape Final Trail

TRAIL | This 4-mile (round-trip) gravel path follows an old jeep trail through a ponderosa pine forest to the canyon overlook at Cape Final with panoramic views of the northern canyon, the Palisades of the Desert, and the impressive spectacle of Juno Temple. *Easy.* ✉ *Grand Canyon National Park* ✣ *Trailhead: dirt* *parking lot 5 miles south of Roosevelt Point on Cape Royal Rd.*

Roosevelt Point Trail

TRAIL | FAMILY | This easy 0.2-mile round-trip trail loops through the forest to the scenic viewpoint. Allow 20 minutes for this relaxed, secluded hike. *Easy.* ✉ *Grand Canyon National Park* ✢ *Trailhead: Cape Royal Rd.*

Transept Trail

TRAIL | FAMILY | This 3-mile round-trip, 1½-hour trail begins near the Grand Canyon Lodge at 8,255 feet. Well maintained and well marked, it has little elevation change, sticking near the rim before reaching a dramatic view of a large stream through Bright Angel Canyon. The trail leads to Transept Canyon, which geologist Clarence Dutton named in 1882, declaring it "far grander than Yosemite." Check the posted schedule to find a ranger talk along this trail; it's also a great place to view fall foliage. Flash floods can occur any time of the year, especially June through September when thunderstorms develop rapidly. *Easy.* ✉ *Grand Canyon National Park* ✢ *Trailhead: near Grand Canyon Lodge east patio.*

VISITOR CENTER

North Rim Visitor Center

View exhibits, peruse the bookstore, and pick up useful maps and brochures at this visitor center. Interpretive programs are often scheduled in summer. If you're craving refreshments, it's a short walk from here to the Roughrider Saloon at the Grand Canyon Lodge. ✉ *Near Grand Canyon Lodge at North Rim, Grand Canyon National Park* ☎ *928/638–7864* 🌐 *www.nps.gov/grca.*

★ **Grand Canyon Lodge Dining Room**

$$$ | SOUTHWESTERN | The high wood-beamed ceilings, stone walls, and spectacular views in this spacious, historic room are perhaps the biggest draw for the lodge's main restaurant. Dinner includes southwestern steak-house fare that would make any cowboy feel at home, including selections such as bison and venison. **Known for:** incredible views; charming, historic room; steaks, fish, game, and vegetarian selections. [$] *Average main: $25* ✉ *Grand Canyon Lodge, Bright Angel Point, North Rim* ☎ *928/638–8562* 🌐 *www.grandcanyonforever.com* ⏲ *Closed mid-Oct.–mid-May.*

★ **Grand Canyon Lodge**

$$$ | HOTEL | This historic property, constructed mainly in the 1920s and '30s, is the only lodging on the North Rim. The main building has locally quarried limestone walls and timbered ceilings. **Pros:** steps away from gorgeous North Rim views; close to several easy hiking trails; historic lodge building a national landmark. **Cons:** fills up fast; limited amenities; most cabins far from main lodge building. [$] *Rooms from: $200* ✉ *Hwy. 67, North Rim* ☎ *877/386–4383 reservations, 928/638–2611 May–Oct.* 🌐 *www.grandcanyonforever.com* ⏲ *Closed mid-Oct.–mid-May* 🛏 *218 rooms* 🍴 *No meals.*

CAMPING

North Rim Campground. The only designated campground at the North Rim of Grand Canyon National Park sits in a pine forest 3 miles north of the rim, and has 84 RV and tent sites (no hookups). Reserve in advance. ✉ *Hwy. 67, North Rim* ☎ *877/444–6777* 🌐 *www.recreation.gov.*

HORSEBACK RIDING

Canyon Trail Rides

TOUR—SPORTS | FAMILY | This company leads mule rides along the easier trails of the North Rim. Options include one- and three-hour rides along the rim or a three-hour ride down into the canyon (minimum age 7 for one-hour rides, 10 for three-hour rides). The one-hour ride is $50, and the three-hour rides are $100. Weight limits are 200 pounds for canyon rides and 220 pounds for the rim rides. Available daily from May 15 to October 15, these excursions are popular, so make reservations in advance. *435/679–8665 www.canyonrides.com From $50.*

Glen Canyon Dam and Lake Powell

1 mile north of Page on U.S. 89.

Lake Powell is the heart of the huge Glen Canyon National Recreation Area, which at about 1.25 million acres is roughly the size of Grand Canyon National Park. Created by the barrier of Glen Canyon Dam in the Colorado River, Lake Powell is ringed by red cliffs that twist off into 96 major canyons and countless inlets (most accessible only by boat) with huge, red-sandstone buttes randomly jutting from the sapphire waters. It extends through terrain so rugged it was the last major area of the United States to be mapped. In the 1990s, the Sierra Club and Glen Canyon Institute started a movement to drain the lake to restore water-filled Glen Canyon, which some believe was more spectacular than the Grand Canyon, but these efforts failed to gain significant momentum, and the lake is likely to be around for years to come. The remote lakefront and rock formations are best visited by tour boat or houseboat. **TIP→ For restaurants and hotels near Glen Canyon Dam and Lake Powell, see Page or Wahweap marina, the area's closest access points.**

GETTING HERE AND AROUND

Just off the highway at the north end of the bridge is the **Carl Hayden Visitor Center,** where you can learn about the controversial creation of Glen Canyon Dam and Lake Powell, enjoy panoramic views of both, and take guided tours of the dam ($5).

Page is an all-around practical base with plenty of dining and lodging. Wahweap is the main marina.

Sights

★ Glen Canyon Dam National Recreation Area

DAM | FAMILY | Once you leave the Page business district heading northwest, the Glen Canyon Dam National Recreation Area and Lake Powell behind it immediately become visible. This concrete-arch dam—all 5 million cubic feet of it—was completed in September 1963, its power plant an engineering feat that rivaled the Hoover Dam. The dam's crest is 1,560 feet across and rises 710 feet from bedrock and 583 feet above the waters of the Colorado River. When Lake Powell is full, it's 560 feet deep at the dam. The plant generates some 1.3 million kilowatts of electricity when each generator's 40-ton shaft is producing nearly 200,000 horsepower. Power from the dam serves a five-state grid consisting of Colorado, Arizona, Utah, California, and New Mexico, and provides energy for more than 1.5 million users.

With only 8 inches of annual rainfall, the Lake Powell area enjoys blue skies nearly year-round. Summer temperatures range from the 60s to the 90s. Fall and spring are usually balmy, with daytime temperatures often in the 70s and 80s, but chilly weather can set in. Nights are cool even in summer, and in winter the risk of a cold spell increases, but all-weather houseboats and tour boats make for year-round cruising. Boaters and campers should note that regulations require the use of portable toilets on the lake and lakeshore to prevent water pollution. *U.S. 89, Page ⊕ 2 miles northwest of town 928/608–6200 www.nps.gov/glca $30 per vehicle or $15 per person*

Houseboats are a unique lodging option; they're also great for exploring Lake Powell's almost 2,000 miles of shoreline.

(entering on foot or by bicycle), good for up to 7 days; boating fee $30 up to 7 days.

Lake Powell

BODY OF WATER | You could spend 30 years exploring the lake's 2,000 miles of shoreline within Glen Canyon National Recreation Area and still not experience everything there is to see. Most of us have only a few days or a week, but that's still plenty of time for recreation in the second-largest reservoir in the nation. Every water sport imaginable awaits you, from waterskiing to fishing. Renting a houseboat and camping are popular within Lake Powell, though small communities around marinas in Page and Wahweap have hotels, restaurants, and shops where you can restock vital supplies.

South of Lake Powell the landscape gives way to **Echo Cliffs,** orange-sandstone formations rising 1,000 feet and more above the highway in places. At **Bitter Springs** the road ascends the cliffs and provides a spectacular view of the 9,000-square-mile Arizona Strip to the west and the 3,000-foot Vermilion Cliffs to the northwest. ✉ *Page* ✣ *2 miles northwest of Page via S Lake Powell Blvd. and US-89* 🌐 *www.lakepowell.com.*

Activities

Dam Overlook

HIKING/WALKING | This hike, a short walk from the parking lot down a flight of uneven rock steps, takes you to a viewpoint on the canyon rim high above the Colorado River, and provides fantastic views of the Colorado as it flows through Glen Canyon. *Easy.* ✉ *Off U.S. 89, Page* ✣ *To reach parking lot, turn west on Scenic View Dr., 1½ miles south of Carl Hayden Visitor Center.*

Page

90 miles west of the Navajo National Monument, 136 miles north of Flagstaff on U.S. 89.

Built in 1957 as a Glen Canyon Dam construction camp, Page is now a tourist spot and a popular base for day trips to Lake Powell; it's also become a major point of entry to Horseshoe Bend Trail and Navajo Nation's Antelope Canyon. At the nearby Vermilion Cliffs, the endangered California condor has been successfully reintroduced into the wild. The town's human population of about 7,600 makes it the largest community in far-northern Arizona, and each year more than 3 million people come to play at Lake Powell.

Most of the motels, restaurants, and shopping centers are concentrated along Lake Powell Boulevard, the name given to U.S. 89 as it loops through the business district.

CONTACTS Page/Lake Powell Tourism Bureau. ✉ *Powell Museum, 6 N. Lake Powell Blvd., Page* ☎ *928/645–9496* 🌐 *www.visitpagelakepowell.com.*

Restaurants

Big John's Texas BBQ
$$ | **BARBECUE** | Hungry carnivores queue under a blanket of smoke for fall-off-the-bone-tender pork ribs, Texas-style low-and-slow-cooked brisket, and hot corn bread muffins drizzled with honey. Seating is inside a repurposed gas station or at picnic tables under the covered space where the pumps used to be. **Known for:** some of the best Texas-style barbecue in the state; live country music and line dancing; covered outdoor patio. $ *Average main: $15* ✉ *153 S. Lake Powell Blvd.* ☎ *928/645–3300* 🌐 *www.bigjohnstexasbbq.com* ⊗ *Closed Dec. and Jan.*

BirdHouse
$ | **FAST FOOD** | Fried chicken is elevated to an art form at this repurposed Sonic Drive-In with a walk-up counter and covered patio dining. Choose from three crispy coating flavors (original, very spicy, or honey butter) and sides like crinkle-cut fries and broccoli salad. **Known for:** fast fried chicken; outdoor dining; Arizona-brewed beer. $ *Average main: $10* ✉ *707 N. Navajo Dr., Page* ☎ *928/645-4087* ⊗ *Closed Wed.*

Hotels

Best Western View of Lake Powell
$$ | **HOTEL** | On a bluff at the northern end of Page, this ordinary though reliable motel has large rooms with beige and burnt-orange walls, queen-size beds, and simple furnishings, not to mention some of the best views of Lake Powell, just 2 miles away, in the area. **Pros:** panoramic views with lake in the distance; renovated rooms; fine dining restaurant next door. **Cons:** pricey for what you get; few amenities; mediocre breakfast. $ *Rooms from: $150* ✉ *716 Rimview Dr., Page* ☎ *928/645–8868, 800/780–7234* 🌐 *www.bestwestern.com* *102 rooms* *Free breakfast.*

Activities

For water sports on Lake Powell, see Wahweap.

BOATING

★ Colorado River Discovery
TOUR—SPORTS | **FAMILY** | This respected outfitter offers waterborne tours, including a 4½-hour guided rafting excursion down a calm portion of the Colorado River on comfortable, motorized pontoon boats. The scenery—multicolor-sandstone cliffs adorned with Native American petroglyphs—is spectacular. The company also offers full-day rowing trips along the river, using smaller boats maneuvered by well-trained guides. These trips are quieter and more low-key,

and provide a more intimate brush with this magnificent body of water. ✉ *6900 Townsend Winona Rd., Flagstaff* ☎ *800/637–7238* 🌐 *outdoorsunlimited.com/colorado-river-discovery.html* 🎫 *From $87.*

HIKING

★ Horseshoe Bend Trail

HIKING/WALKING | The views along this hike are well worth the steep up-and-down paths and the bit of deep sand to maneuver. The trail leads up to a bird's-eye view of Glen Canyon and the Colorado River downstream from Glen Canyon Dam. There are some sheer drop-offs here, so watch children. To reach the trail, drive 4 miles south of Page on U.S. 89 and turn west (right) onto a blacktop road just south of mile marker 545. It's a ¾-mile hike from the parking area to the top of the canyon, and the entire round-trip hike can easily be done in an hour. ■ **TIP→ No parking on U.S. 89.** *Difficult.* ✉ *Off U.S. 89, Page* 🌐 *cityofpage.org/hsb* 🎫 *$10 per car.*

Antelope Canyon

4 miles east of Page in the Navajo Nation, on AZ 98.

It's saying a lot that in the beautiful swath of Northeast Arizona, Antelope Canyon is arguably the favorite destination of both professional and amateur photographers. Accessible only if accompanied by a licensed Navajo guide, Antelope Canyon is a narrow, red-sandstone slot canyon famous for the mesmerizing way sunlight filters through it.

Access to Antelope Canyon is restricted by the Navajo tribe to licensed tour operators. The tribe charges an $8 per-person fee, included in the price of tours offered by the licensed concessionaires in Page. The easiest way to book a tour is in town at the John Wesley Powell Memorial Museum Visitor Center. Most companies offer 1- to 1½-hour sightseeing tours for about $60 to $80. ■ **TIP→ The best time to see the canyon is between 8 am and 2 pm. Note that photography tours of Upper Antelope Canyon (the most popular one) are no longer allowed due to crowds. You are allowed to take photos on a regular tour but without a monopod or tripod.**

Antelope Canyon Navajo Tours

GUIDED TOURS | One-hour sightseeing tours are available at Antelope Canyon. The canyon's $8 admission fee is included. ☎ *928/310–9458, 928/691–0244* 🌐 *navajotours.com* 🎫 *$80.*

Antelope Canyon Tours

GUIDED TOURS | Several tours are offered daily, from 8 am to 4:30 pm, each running 90 minutes. The company also offers all-day Vermilion Cliff tour options. ✉ *22 S. Lake Powell Blvd., Page* ☎ *855/574–9102* 🌐 *www.antelopecanyon.com* 🎫 *From $57.*

Sights

★ Antelope Canyon

CANYON | You've probably seen dozens of photographs of Antelope Canyon, a narrow, red-sandstone slot canyon with convoluted corkscrew formations, dramatically illuminated by light streaming down from above. And you're likely to see assorted shutterbugs waiting patiently for just the right shot of these colorful, photogenic rocks, which are actually petrified sand dunes. The best photos are taken at high noon, when light filters through the slot in the canyon surface. Be prepared to protect your camera equipment against blowing dust and leave your tripod and monopod at home. Navajo Nation and Recreation no longer permits photography tours of the canyon, and while regular tours permit you to take photos, you won't be able to set up your tripod or monopod during your visit. ✉ *AZ 98, Page* ↔ *3 miles east of Page* ☎ *928/871–6647* 🌐 *navajonationparks.org* 🎫 *$8.*

Midday light on Antelope Canyon's sandstone walls is a favorite shot for many photographers.

Wahweap

5 miles north of Glen Canyon Dam on U.S. 89.

Most waterborne recreational activity on the Arizona side of Lake Powell is centered on this vacation village, where everything needed for a lakeside holiday is available: tour boats, fishing, boat rentals, dinner cruises, and more. The Lake Powell Resorts have excellent views of the lake area, and you can take a boat tour from the Wahweap Marina.

Wahweap has two well-marked entrance roads off U.S. 89, one just north of Glen Canyon Dam, and the other about 3½ miles north and more direct if arriving from Utah. Keep in mind that you must pay the Glen Canyon National Recreation Area entry fee on entering Wahweap—this is true even if you're just passing through or having a meal at Lake Powell Resorts (although the fee collection stations are often closed in winter, meaning you can pass through freely).

Sights

Rainbow Bridge National Monument

NATURE SITE | The 290-foot red-sandstone arch is the world's largest natural bridge; it can be reached by boat or strenuous hike and can also be viewed by air. A boat tour to the monument ($126) is a great way to see not only the monument but also the enormity of the lake and its incredible, rugged beauty. The lake level is down, however, due to the prolonged drought throughout the region, so expect a 1-mile (or more) hike from the boat dock to the monument. To the Navajos this is a sacred area with deep religious and spiritual significance, so outsiders are asked not to hike underneath the arch itself. ✉ *Wahweap* ☎ *928/608–6200, 888/896–3829 boat tour info* 🌐 *www.nps.gov/rabr* 🎫 *Free.*

Hotels

Lake Powell Resorts & Marinas
$$$ | RESORT | FAMILY | This sprawling property consisting of several one- and two-story buildings, run by Aramark, sits on a promontory above Lake Powell and serves as the center for recreational activities in the area—guests can relax beside two seasonal swimming pools. **Pros:** stunning lake setting; couldn't be closer to the water; all rooms have patios or balconies. **Cons:** can be a long way from your room to the restaurant and lobby; property in need of a refresh; only reliable Internet is in the lobby. *$ Rooms from: $225 ✉ 100 Lake Shore Dr., off U.S. 89, Page ✣ 7 miles north of Page ☎ 888/896–3829 🌐 www.lakepowell.com 🛏 348 rooms 🍽 No meals.*

HOUSEBOATS

Without a doubt, the most popular and fun way to vacation on Lake Powell is to rent a houseboat. Houseboats, ranging in size from 46 to 75 feet and sleeping 6 to 16 people, come complete with marine radios, fully equipped kitchens, and bathrooms with hot showers; you need only bring sheets and towels. The larger, luxury boats are a good choice in hot summer months, since they have air-conditioning.

Lake Powell Resorts & Marinas
Houseboat rentals at this marina—the only concessionaire that rents boats on Lake Powell—range widely in size, amenities, and price, depending on season. A smaller, more basic houseboat that sleeps up to 12 runs from $3,800 for a week in winter to about $6,000 for a week during the summer peak. At the other end of the spectrum, 75-foot luxury houseboats, some of which can sleep up to 16, cost as much as $15,000 in high season for seven nights. You receive hands-on instruction before you leave the marina. You may want to rent a powerboat or personal watercraft along with a houseboat to explore the many narrow canyons and waterways on the lake. A 19-foot powerboat for eight passengers starts at $360 and goes to $500 per day from June through mid-August. Kayaks rent for $50 per day, and wakeboards, water skis, stand-up paddleboards, and Jet Skis are also available. There are many vacation packages available. *✉ 100 Lakeshore Dr. ☎ 928/645–2433, 888/896–3829 🌐 www.lakepowell.com.*

Activities

BOATING

One of the most scenic lakes of the American West, Lake Powell has 185 miles of clear sapphire waters edged with vast canyons of red and orange rock. Ninety-six major side canyons intricately twist and turn into the main channel of Lake Powell, into what was once the main artery of the Colorado River through Glen Canyon. In some places the lake is 500 feet deep, and by June the lake's waters begin to warm and stay that way well into October.

Monument Valley

The magnificent Monument Valley stretches to the northeast of Kayenta into Utah. At a base altitude of about 5,500 feet, the sprawling, arid expanse was once populated by Ancestral Puebloan people (more popularly known by the Navajo word "Anasazi," which means both "ancient ones" and "ancient enemies") and in the last few centuries has been home to generations of Navajo farmers. The soaring red buttes, eroded mesas, deep canyons, and naturally sculpted rock formations of Monument Valley are easy to enjoy on a leisurely drive.

At U.S. 163 and the Monument Valley entrance is a street of disheveled buildings called Vendor Village. Here you can purchase trinkets and souvenirs; bartering is perfectly acceptable and expected.

Kayenta

75 miles northeast of Tuba City, on U.S. 160, 22 miles south of Monument Valley.

Kayenta, a small and rather dusty town with a couple of convenience stores, three hotels, and a hospital, is a good base for exploring nearby Monument Valley Navajo Tribal Park and the Navajo National Monument. The Burger King in town has an excellent "Navajo Code Talker" exhibit, with lots of memorabilia relating to this heroic World War II marine group.

Kayenta is the first sizable Arizona community you reach if driving to the Navajo Nation via the Four Corners on U.S. 160 or U.S. 163.

Sights

Navajo Cultural Center of Kayenta

MUSEUM | FAMILY | Take a self-guided walking tour through the Navajo Cultural Center of Kayenta, which includes the small Shadehouse Museum and a 2-acre outdoor cultural park. The museum is designed to resemble an authentic shadehouse (these wood-frame, rather crude structures are used to shelter sheepherders in the region's often unforgiving high-desert sun). Inside, visitors will find an extensive collection of Navajo code talkers memorabilia and local artwork, as well as exhibits on the beliefs and traditions that have shaped North America's largest Native American tribe. As you walk through the grounds of the cultural park, note the different types of traditional hogans and sweat lodges. *✉ U.S. 160, Kayenta ✥ Between Hampton Inn and Burger King ☎ 928/697–3170 Hampton Inn 🎫 Free ⏲ Museum closed Nov.–Feb.*

Restaurants

Amigo Cafe

$ | SOUTHWESTERN | The tables are packed with locals who frequent this small establishment, where everything is made from scratch. The delicious frybread is the real draw. **Known for:** made-from-scratch Mexican dishes; some of the best fry bread in northeast Arizona; adobe-walled patio. *$ Average main: $10 ✉ U.S. 163, just north of U.S. 160, Kayenta ☎ 928/697–8448 🌐 www.amigocafekayenta.com ⏲ Closed Sun.*

Hotels

★ Hampton Inn of Kayenta

$$ | HOTEL | FAMILY | This warm and inviting hotel is the best accommodation in Kayenta, although it's much like any other hotel in the chain except for its unusually good restaurant and Navajo-inspired design. **Pros:** clean, updated rooms; welcoming staff; excellent restaurant and quality gift shop. **Cons:** books up many weeks in advance in summer; Internet can be spotty; on busy, unattractive stretch of road. *$ Rooms from: $169 ✉ U.S. 160, Kayenta ☎ 928/697–3170 🌐 www.hamptoninn.hilton.com 73 rooms 🍽 Free breakfast.*

Monument Valley Navajo Tribal Park

24 miles northeast of Kayenta, off U.S. 163.

Even first-time visitors to Monument Valley typically recognize the otherworldly landscape—it has appeared in countless Hollywood feature films. Straddling the Arizona/Utah border, the Monument Valley Navajo Tribal Park contains a 17-mile drive through this dramatic scenery as well as one of the most beautifully situated hotels in Arizona.

It's impossible not to drive slowly on this park's bumpy roads, which are best conquered with an SUV or all-wheel-drive vehicle (especially during rainy times of year), but if you take your time and exercise caution, you can make the entire drive in a conventional car. If in doubt, inquire at the drive's entrance gate. Call ahead for road conditions in winter.

Sights

★ Monument Valley Navajo Tribal Park
NATIONAL/STATE PARK | FAMILY | For generations, the Navajo have grown crops and herded sheep in Monument Valley, considered to be one of the most scenic and mesmerizing destinations in the Navajo Nation. Within Monument Valley lies the 30,000-acre Monument Valley Navajo Tribal Park, home as well to the View Hotel, where eons of wind and rain have carved the mammoth red-sandstone monoliths into memorable formations. The monoliths, which jut hundreds of feet above the desert floor, stand on the horizon like sentinels, frozen in time and unencumbered by electric wires, telephone poles, or fences—a scene virtually unchanged for centuries. These are the very same nostalgic images so familiar to movie buffs who recall the early Western films of John Wayne. A 17-mile self-guided driving tour on an extremely rough dirt road (there's only one road, so you can't get lost) passes the memorable **Mittens** and **Totem Pole** formations, among others. **■ TIP→ Be sure to walk (15 minutes round-trip) from North Window around the end of Cly Butte for the views.** ✉ *Monument Valley Rd.* ✣ *Off U.S. 163, just north of Arizona/Utah border* ☎ *435/727–5874 visitor center* 🌐 *navajonationparks.org* 🎫 *$10 per person or $20 per vehicle (up to 4 people).*

Monument Valley Visitor Center
INFO CENTER | FAMILY | The handsome center contains an extensive crafts shop and exhibits devoted to ancient and modern Native American history, including a display on the World War II Navajo code talkers. Most of the independent guided group tours, necessary to go deep into the valley, leave from the center. You can generally find Navajo guides—who will escort you to places that you are not allowed to visit on your own—in the center or at the booths in the parking lot. The center adjoins the stunning View Hotel (and restaurant), which sits on a gradual rise overlooking the valley and its magnificent red rock monoliths, with big-sky views in every direction. ✉ *Monument Valley Rd., off U.S. 163* ☎ *435/727–5874* 🌐 *navajonationparks.org.*

Hotels

★ View Hotel
$$$ | HOTEL | The Navajo tribe operates this sleek pink-stucco hotel, the only lodging inside Monument Valley Navajo Tribal Park and one of the most spectacularly situated hotels in the Southwest, with astounding vistas that lend the hotel its name. **Pros:** only hotel in the park; design reflects the surroundings and Navajo culture; unbelievable panoramas from every room; eco-conscious bath products, appliances, and buildings standards; rates are similar to or less than run-of-the-mill hotels nearby. **Cons:** books up weeks in advance in summer; Wi-Fi doesn't reach all rooms; on-site dining is mediocre. 💲 *Rooms from: $219* ✉ *Monument Valley Rd., off U.S. 163, Monument Valley Navajo Tribal Park* ☎ *435/727–5555* 🌐 *monumentvalleyview.com* 🛏 *96 rooms* 🍽 *No meals.*

Activities

Monument Valley Tours
TOUR—SPORTS | Some of the jeep tours on offer include entertainment and outdoor barbecues, and custom hikes into the valley as well. The all-day, 60-mile Monument Valley and Mystery Valley tour, which includes lunch, is especially

popular. ☎ *435/727–3313* 🌐 *www.monumentvalleytours.net* *From $70.*

Roy Black's Guided Tours

TOUR—SPORTS | A wide variety of tour options—from jeep and horseback adventures to hiking—are available with this respected tour operator. You can also book an overnight stay in a Navajo hogan. ✉ *Monument Valley* ☎ *505/701–9609* 🌐 *royblacksguidedtours.com* *From $85.*

Sacred Monument Tours

TOUR—SPORTS | Native guides lead hiking, jeep, and horseback-riding tours into Monument Valley. ✉ *Monument Valley* ☎ *435/727–3218, 435/459–2501 mobile/text* 🌐 *toursacred.com* *From $65.*

Simpson's Trailhandler Tours

TOUR—SPORTS | This operator offers four-wheel-drive jeep trips, photography tours, and guided hikes, plus the chance to stay overnight in a traditional Navajo hogan. If you don't have time or interest in one of the several-hour hiking tours, Simpson's can also customize a fairly easy hour-long guided hike, tailored to your interest and skill level. ✉ *Monument Valley* ☎ *435/727–3362, 888/723–6236* 🌐 *emonumentvalley.com* *From $75.*

Goulding's Trading Post

2 miles west of entrance road to Monument Valley Navajo Tribal Park, off U.S. 163 on Indian Hwy. 42.

Established in 1924 by Harry Goulding and his wife "Mike," this trading post provided a place where Navajos could exchange livestock and handmade goods for necessities. Goulding's is probably best known, though, for being used as a headquarters by director John Ford when he filmed the Western classic *Stagecoach.* Today the compound has a lodge, restaurant, museum, gift shop, grocery store, and campground. The Goulding Museum displays Native American artifacts and Goulding family memorabilia, as well as an excellent multimedia show about Monument Valley.

Hotels

★ Goulding's Lodge

$$$ | **HOTEL** | Nestled beneath a massive red rock monolith, this two-level property affords spectacular views of Monument Valley from each room's private balcony. **Pros:** incredible views; very peaceful; indoor pool open all year. **Cons:** remote location; not cheap; books up weeks in advance in summer. *Rooms from: $222* ✉ *1000 Gouldings Trading Post Rd.* ✣ *U.S. 163 to Monument Valley Rd. (24 miles north of Kayenta), left on Gouldings Trading Post Rd.* ☎ *866/313-9769* 🌐 *www.gouldings.com* *159 rooms* *No meals.*

The Hopi Mesas

The Hopi occupy 12 villages in regions referred to as First Mesa, Second Mesa, and Third Mesa. Although these areas have similar languages and traditions, each has its own individual features. Generations of Hopitu, "the peaceful people," much like their Puebloan ancestors, have lived in these largely agrarian settlements of stone-and-adobe houses, which blend in with the earth so well that they appear to be natural formations. Television antennae, satellite dishes, and automobiles notwithstanding, these Hopi villages still exude the air of another time.

Descendants of the ancient Hisatsinom, the number of Hopi living among the villages today is about 7,000. Their culture can be traced back more than 2,000 years, making them one of the oldest known tribes in North America. They successfully developed "dry farming," and grow many kinds of vegetables and corn (called maize) as their basic food—in fact the Hopi are often called the "corn people." They incorporate nature's cycles into most of their religious rituals. In

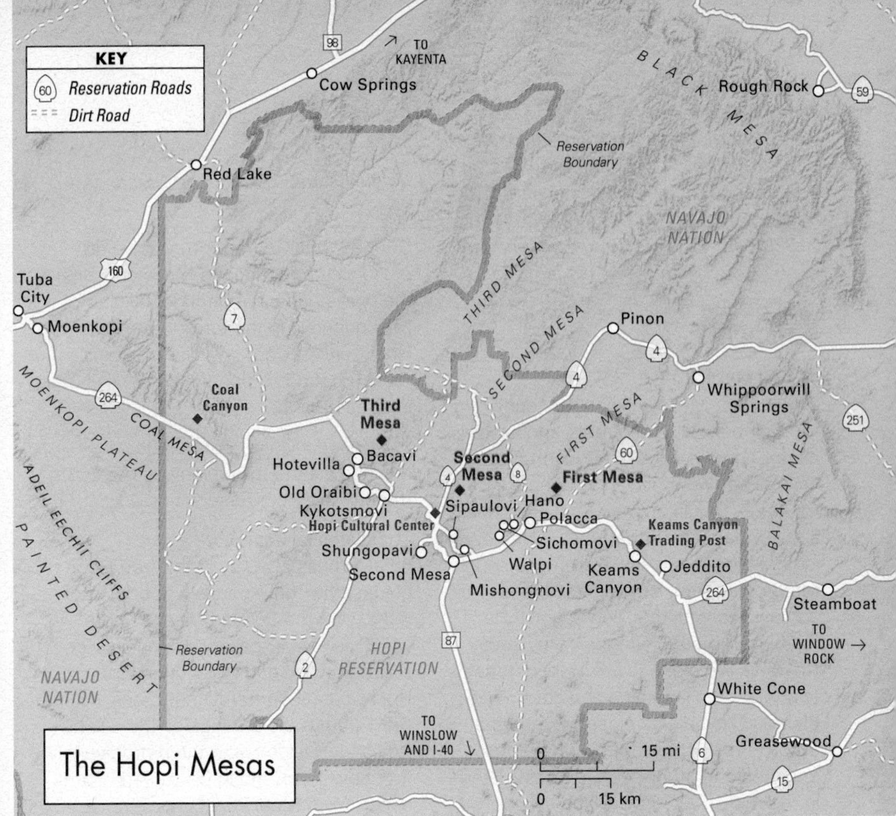

the celebrated Snake Dance ceremony, dancers carry venomous snakes in their mouths to appease the gods and to bring rain. In addition to farming the land, the Hopi create fine pottery and basketwork and excel at carving wooden kachina dolls.

First Mesa

11 miles west of Keams Canyon, on AZ 264.

The easternmost of the three main Hopi Mesas, First Mesa comprises several centuries-old communities acclaimed for polychrome pottery and kachina-doll carving. Hano, Sichomovi, and Walpi—with its dramatic setting beneath sheer cliffs—are the key communities at First Mesa.

The first village that you approach is Polacca; the older and more impressive villages of Hano, Sichomovi, and Walpi are at the top of the sweeping mesa. From Polacca, a paved road (off AZ 264) angles up to a parking lot near the village of Sichomovi and to the Punsi Hall Visitor Center. **■ TIP→ You must get permission to take the guided walking tour of Hano, Sichomovi, and Walpi. Tour times vary; call ahead to the Moenkopi Legacy Inn in Tuba City for more information.**

Hopi Tribe
Staff at the Hopi Tribe offices can answer basic questions and provide guidance for visiting the Hopi Mesas. ☎ *928/734–3202* 🌐 *www.hopi-nsn.gov.*

Moenkopi Legacy Inn
Although the Hopi Tribe offices can provide basic information to travelers, the staff at the Moenkopi Legacy Inn in

Tuba City has become the tribe's de facto visitor information center and best overall tourism resource. The staff here can also arrange tours led by Hopi-certified guides. ✉ *AZ 164 at U.S. 160, Tuba City* ☎ *928/283–4500* 🌐 *www.experiencehopi.com.*

Sights

★ First Mesa

TOWN | First Mesa villages are renowned for their polychrome pottery and kachina-doll carvings. The older Hopi villages have structures built of rock and adobe mortar in simple architectural style. **Hano** actually belongs to the Tewa, a New Mexico Pueblo tribe. In 1696 the Tewa sought refuge with the Hopi on First Mesa after an unsuccessful rebellion against the Spanish in the Rio Grande Valley. Today the Tewa live close to the Hopi but maintain their own language and ceremonies. **Sichomovi** is built so close to Hano that only the residents can tell where one ends and the other begins. Constructed in the mid-1600s, this village is believed to have been built to ease overcrowding at Walpi, the highest point on the mesa. **Walpi,** built on solid rock and surrounded by steep cliffs, frequently hosts ceremonial dances. It's the most pristine of the Hopi villages, with cliff-edge houses and vast scenic vistas. Inhabited for more than 1,100 years (dating back to 900 AD), Walpi's cliff-edge houses seem to grow out of the nearby terrain. Today only about 10 residents occupy this settlement, which has neither electricity nor running water; one-hour guided tours of the village are available daily, except when certain ceremonies are taking place (call for hours). Note that Walpi's steep terrain makes it a less than ideal destination for acrophobes. ✉ *Punsi Hall Visitor Center, AZ 264, at milepost 392, First Mesa* ☎ *928/737–2670* 🌐 *www.experiencehopi.com/walpi-village* 🎫 *Guided tours $20.*

Second Mesa

8 miles southwest of First Mesa, on AZ 264.

Dubbed the "Center of the Universe" of Hopi culture, Second Mesa contains the communities of Shungopavi and Mishongnovi; in the former, you'll find the Hopi Cultural Center, which contains a museum, trading post, and no-frills hotel and restaurant.

The Second Mesa communities are reached via the main highway (AZ 264) through the Hopi Reservation.

★ Experience Hopi Tour

GUIDED TOURS | Led by authorized Hopi guides, this tour spends a good part of the day on the Second Mesa, where you'll visit an art gallery, watch a silversmith at work, and have lunch at the Hopi Cultural Center. Other stops include the 1,000-year-old village of Old Oraibi, Coalmine Canyon, and the petroglyphs at Prophecy Rock and in Dawa Park. Tours depart from Moenkopi Legacy Inn at 8:30 am and end at approximately 4 pm. ✉ *AZ 164 at U.S. 160, Tuba City* ☎ *928/283–4500 schedule through front desk* 🌐 *experiencehopi.com/tours* 🎫 *$145 per person, two-person minimum.*

Sights

Hopi Cultural Center

INFO CENTER | Here you can stop for the night, learn about the people and their communities, and eat authentic Hopi cuisine. The center's museum is dedicated to preserving Hopi traditions and to presenting those traditions to non-Hopi visitors; hours vary. A gift shop sells works by local Hopi artisans at reasonable prices, and a modest picnic area on the west side of the building is a pleasant spot for lunch with a view of the San Francisco Peaks. ✉ *AZ 264, Second Mesa* ☎ *928/734–2401* 🎫 *Museum $3.*

Second Mesa

TOWN | The Mesas are the Hopi universe, and Second Mesa is the "Center of the Universe." **Shungopavi,** the largest and oldest village on Second Mesa, which was founded by the Bear Clan, is reached by a paved road angling south off AZ 264, between the junction of AZ 87 and the Hopi Cultural Center. The villagers here make silver overlay jewelry and coil plaques. Coil plaques are woven from galleta grass and yucca and are adorned with designs of kachinas, animals, and corn. The art of making the plaques has been passed from mother to daughter for generations, and fine coil plaques have become highly sought-after collector's items. The famous Hopi snake dances (closed to the public) are held here in August during even-numbered years. Two smaller villages are off a paved road that runs north from AZ 264, about 2 miles east of the Hopi Cultural Center. **Mishongnovi,** the easternmost settlement, was established in the late 1600s. ✉ *Second Mesa.*

Restaurants

Hopi Cultural Center Restaurant

$ | **SOUTHWESTERN** | The restaurant at the Hopi Cultural Center is an attractive, light-filled room where you can sample traditional tribal fare. Authentic dishes include traditional tacos, Hopi blue-corn pancakes, *piki* (paper-thin, blue-corn bread), fry bread (delicious with honey or salsa), and *nok qui vi* (a tasty stew made with tender bits of lamb, hominy, and mild green chiles). **Known for:** Hopi crafts for sale in the gift shop; authentic Hopi dishes; one of the few Hopi restaurants on tribal lands. $ *Average main: $11* ✉ *AZ 264, Second Mesa* ✣ *5 miles west of AZ 87* ☎ *928/734–2401* 🌐 *hopiculturalcenter.com.*

Hotels

Hopi Cultural Center Inn

$ | **HOTEL** | This small Hopi-run motel, the only place to eat or sleep in the immediate area, occupies an attractive adobe building with a reddish-brown exterior. **Pros:** adjacent to cultural center; only place to stay for miles in either direction; peaceful setting. **Cons:** remote unless you are here to explore Hopi culture; Wi-Fi in rooms can be slow and unreliable; basic accommodations are not for everybody. $ *Rooms from: $115* ✉ *AZ 264, Second Mesa* ✣ *5 miles west of AZ 87* ☎ *928/734–2401* *34 rooms* *No meals.*

Shopping

Hopi Cultural Center

CRAFTS | This collection of shops carries work by local artists and artisans, including pottery, baskets, and dolls. ✉ *AZ 264, Second Mesa* ☎ *928/734–2401.*

Tsa-Kursh-Ovi

CRAFTS | At this small shop, 1½ miles east of the Hopi Cultural Center, Hopi come to buy bundles of sweetgrass and sage, deer hooves with which to make rattles, and ceremonial belts adorned with seashells. Proprietors Joseph and Janice Day (she is a renowned Hopi basket maker) are a font of information on local artwork, and the shop has one of the largest collections of Hopi baskets in the Southwest. It's also where you'll find the popular "Don't Worry Be Hopi" novelty T-shirts. ✉ *AZ 264, Second Mesa* ☎ *928/734–2478* ⏲ *Closed Sun.*

Third Mesa

12 miles northwest of Second Mesa, on AZ 264.

Home to a number of studios in which artisans create weavings, wicker baskets, and jewelry, the Hopi tribe's Third Mesa has four main communities: Kykotsmovi, Old Oraibi, Hotevilla, and Bacavi.

The Third Mesa communities are the closest to Tuba City, about 50 miles away along AZ 264.

Ancient Pathways Tours
GUIDED TOURS | A knowledgeable guide and member of a Hopi clan from Old Oraibi, Bertram "Tsaava" Tsavadawa leads one-, three-, and six-hour tours of the Third Mesa area, including trips to see the Taawa petroglyphs, symbols of the people who have resided here for more than 1,000 years. ☎ *928/797–8145* *From $15.*

Third Mesa
TOWN | Third Mesa villages are known for their agricultural accomplishments, textile weaving, wicker baskets, silver overlay, and plaques. You'll find crafts shops and art galleries, as well as occasional roadside vendors, along AZ 264.

At the eastern base of Third Mesa, **Kykotsmovi,** literally "ruins on the hills," is named for the sites on the valley floor and in the surrounding hills. Present-day Kykotsmovi was established by Hopi people from nearby Oraibi who either converted to Christianity or wished to attend school and be educated. Kykotsmovi is the seat of the Hopi Tribal Government.

Old Oraibi, a few miles west and on top of Third Mesa at about 7,200 feet in elevation, is believed to be the oldest continuously inhabited community in the United States, dating from around AD 1150. It was also the site of a rare, bloodless conflict between two groups of the Hopi people; in 1906, a dispute, settled uniquely by a "push of war" (a pushing contest), sent the losers off to establish the town of Hotevilla. Oraibi is a dusty spot and, as a courtesy, tourists are asked to park their cars outside and approach the village on foot.

Hotevilla and **Bacavi** are about 4 miles west of Oraibi, and their inhabitants are descended from the former residents of that village. The men of Hotevilla continue to plant crops and beautiful gardens along the mesa slopes. ✉ *Moenkopi Legacy Inn & Suites, U.S. 160, at AZ 264, Tuba City* ☎ *928/283–4500* 🌐 *www.experiencehopi.com.*

Petrified Forest National Park

Northern Entrance: 110 miles northwest of Springerville-Eagar on U.S. 191 and I–40, 27 miles east of Holbrook on I–40. Southern Entrance: 66 miles northwest of Springerville-Eagar on U.S. 191 and U.S. 180, 18 miles east of Holbrook on U.S. 180.

Only about 1½ hours from Show Low and the lush, verdant forests of the White Mountains, Arizona's diverse and dramatic landscape changes from pine-crested mountains to sunbaked terrain. Inside the lunar landscape of the Painted Desert is the Petrified Forest.

There are few places where the span of geologic and human history is as wide or apparent as it is at Petrified Forest National Park. Fossilized trees and countless other fossils date back to the Triassic Period, while a stretch of the famed Route 66 of more modern lore is protected within park boundaries. Ancestors of the Hopi, Zuni, and Navajo left petroglyphs, pottery, and even structures built of petrified wood. Nine park sites are on the National Register of Historic Places;

The petroglyphs on Newspaper Rock are among many that are preserved in Petrified Forest National Park.

one, the Painted Desert Inn, is one of only 3% of such sites that are also listed as National Historic Landmarks.

The good thing is that most of Petrified Forest's treasures can easily be viewed without a great amount of athletic conditioning. Much can be seen by driving along the main road, from which historic sites are readily accessible. By combining a drive along the park road with a short hike here and there and a visit to one of the park's landmarks, you can see most of the sights in as little as half a day.

GETTING HERE AND AROUND

Holbrook, the nearest large town with services such as gas or food, is on U.S. 40, 27 miles from the park's north entrance and 18 miles from its south entrance.

Parking is free, and there's ample space at all trailheads, as well as at the visitor center and the museum. The main park road extends 28 miles from the Painted Desert Visitor Center (north entrance) to the Rainbow Forest Museum (south entrance). For park road conditions, call ☎ *928/524–6228.*

PARK ESSENTIALS

PARK FEES AND PERMITS

Entrance fees are $25 per car for seven consecutive days or $15 per person on foot or bicycle, or $20 per motorcycle. Backcountry hiking and camping permits are free (15-day limit) at the Painted Desert Visitor Center or the Rainbow Forest Museum before 4 pm.

PARK HOURS

It's a good idea to call ahead or check the website, because the park's hours vary so much; as a rule of thumb, the park is open daily from sunrise to sunset or approximately 8 am–5 pm. Keep in mind that the area does not observe daylight saving time.

VISITOR INFORMATION

CONTACTS Petrified Forest National Park. ✉ *1 Park Rd., Petrified Forest National Park* ☎ *928/524–6228* 🌐 *www.nps.gov/pefo.*

One of the most commonly asked questions about the Petrified Forest is, "Can I touch the wood?" Yes! Feel comfortable to touch anything, pick it up, inspect it . . . just make sure you put it back where you found it. It's illegal to remove even a small sliver of fossilized wood from the park.

HISTORIC SIGHTS

Agate House

ARCHAEOLOGICAL SITE | This eight-room pueblo is thought to have been built entirely of petrified wood 700 years ago. Researchers believe it might have been used as a temporary dwelling by seasonal farmers or traders from one of the area tribes. ✉ *Rainbow Forest Museum parking area, Petrified Forest National Park.*

Newspaper Rock

ARCHAEOLOGICAL SITE | See huge boulders covered with petroglyphs believed to have been carved by the Pueblo people more than 500 years ago. ■ **TIP→ Look through the binoculars that are provided here—you'll be surprised at what the naked eye misses.** ✉ *Main park road, Petrified Forest National Park* ✣ *6 miles south of Painted Desert Visitor Center.*

Painted Desert Inn National Historic Landmark

MUSEUM | A nice place to stop and rest in the shade, this site offers vast views of the Painted Desert from several lookouts. Inside, cultural history exhibits, murals, and Native American crafts are on display. ✉ *Main park road, Petrified Forest National Park* ✣ *2 miles north of Painted Desert Visitor Center.*

SCENIC DRIVES

Painted Desert Scenic Drive

SCENIC DRIVE | A 28-mile scenic drive takes you through the park from one entrance to the other. If you begin at the north end, the first 5 miles take you along the edge of a high mesa, with spectacular views of the Painted Desert. Beyond lies the desolate Painted Desert Wilderness Area. After the 5-mile point, the road crosses Interstate 40, then swings south toward the Puerco River across a landscape covered with sagebrush, saltbrush, sunflowers, and Apache plume. Past the river, the road climbs onto a narrow mesa leading to Newspaper Rock, a panel of Pueblo rock art. Then the road bends southeast, enters a barren stretch, and passes tepee-shape buttes in the distance. Next you come to Blue Mesa, roughly the park's midpoint and a good place to stop for views of petrified logs. The next stop on the drive is Agate Bridge, really a 100-foot log over a wide wash. The remaining overlooks are Jasper and Crystal forests, where you can get further glimpses of the accumulated petrified wood. On your way out of the park, stop at the Rainbow Forest Museum for a rest and to shop for a memento. ✉ *Begins at Painted Desert Visitor Center, Petrified Forest National Park.*

SCENIC SPOTS

Agate Bridge

NATURE SITE | Here you'll see a 100-foot log spanning a 40-foot-wide wash. ✉ *Main park road, Petrified Forest National Park* ✣ *19 miles south of Painted Desert Visitor Center.*

Crystal Forest

NATURE SITE | The fragments of petrified wood strewn here once held clear quartz and amethyst crystals. ✉ *Main park road, Petrified Forest National Park* ✣ *20 miles south of Painted Desert Visitor Center.*

Giant Logs Interpretive Loop Trail

NATURE SITE | A short walk leads you past the park's largest log, known as Old Faithful. It's considered the largest because of its diameter (9 feet 9 inches), as well as how tall it once was. ✉ *Main park road, Petrified Forest National Park* ✣ *28 miles south of Painted Desert Visitor Center.*

Some of the cliff walls of Canyon de Chelly are 1,000 feet tall.

VISITOR CENTERS

Painted Desert Inn National Historic Landmark

INFO CENTER | This visitor center isn't as large as the other two, but here you can get information as well as view cultural history exhibits. ✉ *Main park road, Petrified Forest National Park* ⊕ *2 miles north of Painted Desert Visitor Center* ☎ *928/524–6228.*

Painted Desert Visitor Center

INFO CENTER | This is the place to go for general park information and an informative 20-minute film. Proceeds from books purchased here will fund continued research and interpretive activities for the park. ✉ *North entrance, Petrified Forest National Park* ⊕ *Off I–40, 27 miles east of Holbrook* ☎ *928/524–6228.*

Rainbow Forest Museum and Visitor Center

INFO CENTER | View displays of prehistoric animals, watch an orientation video, and—perhaps most important—use the restroom facilities at this visitor center at the southern end of the park. ✉ *South entrance, Petrified Forest National Park* ⊕ *Off U.S. 180, 18 miles southeast of Holbrook* ☎ *928/524–6228.*

Canyon de Chelly

30 miles west of Window Rock on AZ 264, then 25 miles north on U.S. 191.

Comprising two long canyons, each one more than 1,000 feet deep, Canyon de Chelly is one of the major sites in the Four Corners region. It's somewhat overshadowed by the Grand Canyon and some of southern Utah's national parks, and you can only venture into the canyons with an authorized guide, but visitors with just a little time can experience Canyon de Chelly's dramatic viewing areas along two park roads (there's no admission fee) that snake along the canyon rims.

GETTING HERE AND AROUND

U.S. 191 runs north–south through Chinle, the closest town to the Canyon de Chelly entrance.

Guided tours allow visits directly into the canyons, not just the park drives high above them; jeep tours even have the option of camping overnight. Each kind of tour has its pros and cons: you'll cover the most ground in a jeep; horseback trips get you close to one of the park's most notable geological formations, Spider Rock; and guided walks provide the most leisurely pace and an excellent opportunity to interact with your guide and ask questions. You can also plan custom treks lasting several days.

VISITOR INFORMATION

CONTACTS Canyon de Chelly Visitor Center. ✉ *Indian Hwy. 7, Chinle ✣ 3 miles east of U.S. 191 ☎ 928/674–5500 🌐 www.nps.gov/cach.*

Sights

★ Canyon de Chelly

ARCHAEOLOGICAL SITE | Home to Ancestral Pueblo from AD 350 to 1300, the nearly 84,000-acre Canyon de Chelly (pronounced d'*shay*) is one of the most spectacular natural wonders in the Southwest. On a smaller scale, it rivals the Grand Canyon for beauty. Its main gorges—the 26-mile-long Canyon de Chelly ("canyon in the rock") and the adjoining 35-mile-long Canyon del Muerto ("canyon of the dead")—comprise sheer, heavily eroded sandstone walls that rise to 1,100 feet over dramatic valleys. Ancient pictographs and petroglyphs decorate some of the cliffs, and within the canyon complex there are more than 7,000 archaeological sites. Stone walls rise hundreds of feet above streams, hogans, tilled fields, and sheep-grazing lands.

You can view prehistoric sites near the base of cliffs and perched on high, sheltering ledges, some of which you can access from the park's two main drives along the canyon rims. The dwellings and cultivated fields of the present-day Navajo lie in the flatlands between the cliffs, and those who inhabit the canyon today farm much the way their ancestors did. Most residents leave the canyon in winter but return in early spring to farm.

Canyon de Chelly's South Rim Drive (37 miles round-trip with seven overlooks) starts at the visitor center and ends at **Spider Rock Overlook,** where cliffs plunge nearly 1,000 feet to the canyon floor. The view here is of two pinnacles, Speaking Rock and Spider Rock. Other highlights on the South Rim Drive are Junction Overlook, where Canyon del Muerto joins Canyon de Chelly; White House Overlook, from which a 2½-mile round-trip trail leads to the **White House Ruin,** with remains of nearly 60 rooms and several kivas; and Sliding House Overlook, where you can see dwellings on a narrow, sloped ledge across the canyon. The carved and sometimes narrow trail down the canyon side to White House Ruin is the only access into Canyon de Chelly without a guide—if you have a fear of heights, this may not be the hike for you.

The only slightly less breathtaking **North Rim Drive** (34 miles round-trip with three overlooks) of Canyon del Muerto also begins at the visitor center and continues northeast on Indian Highway 64 toward the town of Tsaile. Major stops include **Antelope House Overlook,** a large site named for the animals painted on an adjacent cliff; **Mummy Cave Overlook,** where two mummies were found inside a remarkably unspoiled pueblo dwelling; and **Massacre Case Overlook,** which marks the spot where an estimated 115 Navajo were killed by the Spanish in 1805. (The rock walls of the cave are still pockmarked by the Spaniards' ricocheting bullets.) ✉ *Indian Hwy. 7, Chinle ✣ 3 miles east of U.S. 191 ☎ 928/674–5500 visitor center 🌐 www.nps.gov/cach 🎫 Free.*

Restaurants

Chinle is the closest town to Canyon de Chelly. There are lodgings with basic restaurants, as well as a supermarket and a campground. Be aware that you may be approached by panhandlers in the grocery store parking lot.

Garcia's Restaurant

$$ | **AMERICAN** | The lobby restaurant at Chinle's Holiday Inn is low-key, a bit lacking in natural light, and rather ordinary, but people come here because it is one of the area's only non–fast food dining options. You can count on well-prepared Navajo and American fare, such as frybread topped with chili and cheese, but be prepared for slow service and no alcohol. **Known for:** reliable food; Southwestern decor; limited hours in the winter. *Average main: $13* *Indian Hwy. 7, Chinle* *928/674–5000 hotel* *www.holidayinn.com* *No lunch Nov.–Mar.*

Hotels

Thunderbird Lodge

$ | **HOTEL** | **FAMILY** | Ideally located within the national monument's borders, this pleasant, if basic, establishment owned by the Navajo Nation hosts Native American dance performances weekends August through October. **Pros:** only hotel inside park borders; summer performances by Native American dancers; tours offered right from hotel. **Cons:** small, rustic rooms not for everyone; spotty area cell phone service; a distance from other restaurants and services. *Rooms from: $99* *Indian Hwy. 7, Chinle* *928/674–5842, 800/679–2473* *thunderbirdlodge.com* *70 rooms* *No meals.*

Activities

HIKING

From about late May through early September, free three-hour ranger hikes depart most weekend mornings from the Canyon de Chelly Visitor Center—call ahead for times and to reserve a spot. Only one hike within Canyon de Chelly National Monument—the **White House Ruin Trail** on the South Rim Drive—can be undertaken without an authorized guide. The trail starts near White House Overlook and runs along sheer walls that drop about 550 feet. If you have concerns about heights, be aware that the path gets narrow and requires careful footing. The hike is 2½ miles round-trip, and hikers should carry their own drinking water.

TOURS

Ancient Canyon Tours

TOUR—SPORTS | This Navajo-owned tour company offers both day-hiking and overnight-camping excursions into the park's two canyons, de Chelly and del Muerto. The moderately difficult day hikes venture into some of the park's most spectacular backcountry and can last from three to four hours, if covering the lower parts of the canyons, and as long as nine hours for excursions into the higher terrain. The cost is $40 per hour (three-hour minimum) for up to 10 hikers; there are additional $30 per guide and $50 per night land-use fees for overnight trips. Private 4x4 tours into the canyons are also available. *Chinle* *928/349–6185* *www.ancientcanyontours.com* *From $40/hr.*

Canyon de Chelly Tours

TOUR—SPORTS | Book a private jeep tour into Canyon de Chelly or choose from group tours, late-afternoon and evening tours, and bus tours along South Rim Drive. Entertainment such as storytellers, music, and Navajo legends can be arranged with an advance reservation.

✉ *Best Western Canyon de Chelly Inn, 100 Main St., Chinle* ☎ *928/349–1600* 🌐 *www.canyondechellytours.com* 🎫 *From $88.*

Thunderbird Lodge Canyon Tours

TOUR—SPORTS | Treks in six-wheel-drive Pinzgauer army troop vehicles are available from late spring to late fall. Choose a half-day tour or an all-day tour with lunch. ✉ *Indian Hwy. 7, Chinle* ☎ *928/674–5842, 800/679–2473* 🌐 *www.thunderbirdlodge.com/tours* 🎫 *From $70.*

HORSEBACK RIDING

Justin's Horse Rental

HORSEBACK RIDING | FAMILY | Located just past the visitor center on Indian Route 7, this outfitter guides riders on horseback tours, ranging from a 2-hour, round-trip ride to First Ruins to a 10-hour journey to Massacre Cave. Overnight adventures are available as well. ✉ *Indian Rte. 7, Chinle* ☎ *928/675–5575* 🌐 *www.justinshorserental.com.*

Chapter 12

SANTA FE, TAOS, AND ALBUQUERQUE

Updated by
Lynne Arany, Yvonne Pesquera, Eric Peterson, and Zibby Wilder

Sights	Restaurants	Hotels	Shopping	Nightlife
★★★★☆	★★★★★	★★★★☆	★★★★☆	★★★☆☆

WELCOME TO SANTA FE, TAOS, AND ALBUQUERQUE

TOP REASONS TO GO

★ **Santa Fe Plaza:** This is one of the most historic places in the U.S., laid out in 1610 and the center of one of the Southwest's most dynamic cities ever since.

★ **Taos Ski Valley:** With 110 trails on 1,294 acres (and 300 inches of annual snowfall), this is the premier winter sports destination in New Mexico.

★ **Meow Wolf:** The permanent "immersive art installation" *House of Eternal Return* has quickly become one of Santa Fe's leading attractions.

★ **Taos Art Museum at Fechin House:** The collection of about 600 works includes paintings by founders of the original Taos Society of Artists.

★ **Indian Pueblo Cultural Center:** This Albuquerque attraction is the perfect starting point to explore the history and culture of New Mexico's Pueblo people.

1 **Santa Fe.** At the foot of the Sangre de Cristo Mountains— 7,000 feet above sea level— New Mexico's state capital reflects four centuries of history.

2 **Kasha-Katuwe Tent Rocks National Monument.** The otherworldly sandstone formations make for a great day trip from Santa Fe.

3 **Bandelier National Monument.** The monument preserves petroglyphs and cave dwellings of the Ancestral Puebloan people.

4 **Taos.** Steeped in history, the town is synonymous with art and skiing.

5 **Albuquerque.** New Mexico's largest city with almost 600,000 residents is home to a vibrant arts scene and plenty of great restaurants.

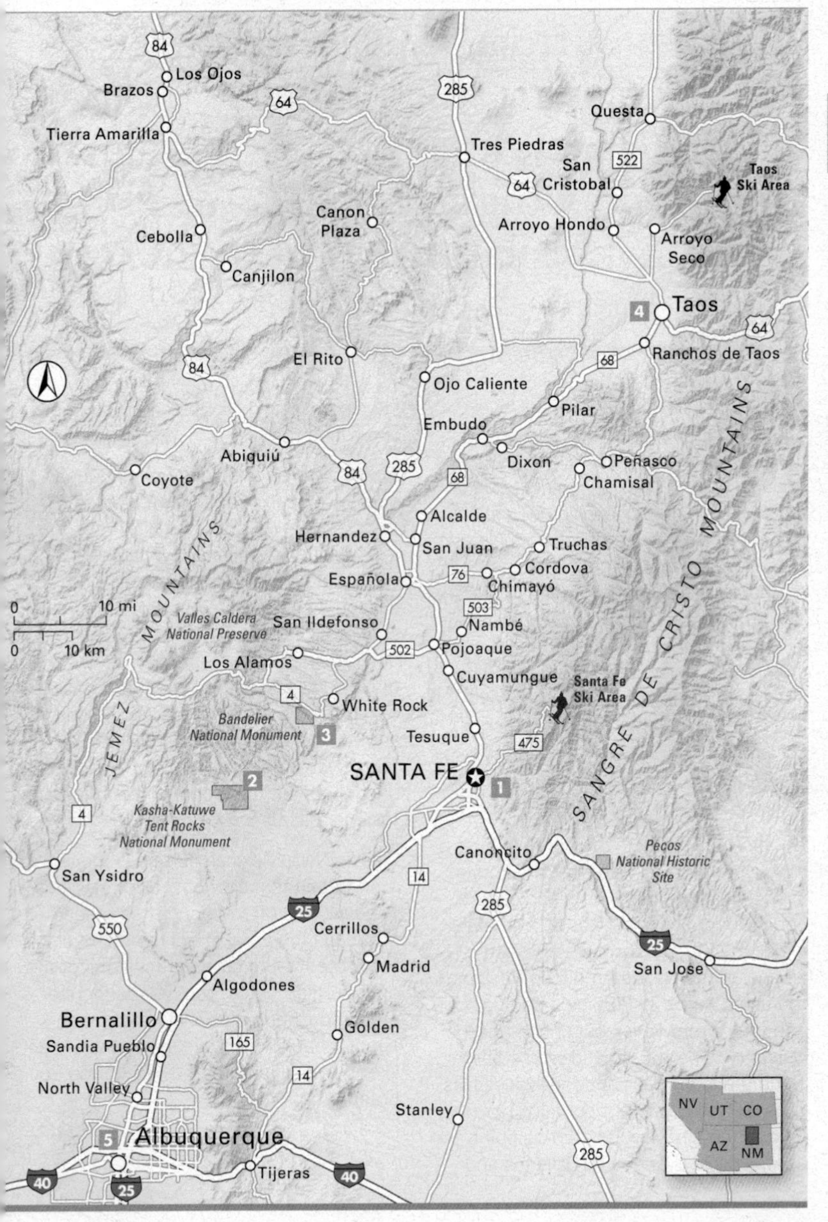
Los Ojos
Brazos
Tierra Amarilla
Questa
Tres Piedras
San Cristobal
Taos Ski Area
Canon Plaza
Arroyo Hondo
Arroyo Seco
Cebolla
Canjilon
Taos
Ranchos de Taos
El Rito
Ojo Caliente
Pilar
Embudo
Abiquiú
Dixon
Peñasco
Chamisal
Coyote
Alcalde
Hernandez
San Juan
Truchas
Cordova
Española
Chimayó
Nambé
San Ildefonso
Pojoaque
Valles Caldera National Preserve
Los Alamos
Cuyamungue
Santa Fe Ski Area
White Rock
Bandelier National Monument
Tesuque
SANTA FE
JEMEZ MOUNTAINS
SANGRE DE CRISTO MOUNTAINS
Kasha-Katuwe Tent Rocks National Monument
Canoncito
Pecos National Historic Site
San Ysidro
Cerrillos
Madrid
San Jose
Algodones
Bernalillo
Sandia Pueblo
Golden
North Valley
Stanley
Albuquerque
Tijeras
0 10 mi
0 10 km
NV
UT
CO
AZ
NM

In north-central New Mexico, these three distinctive communities showcase the evolution of the region over a millennium, from Native American Pueblos that are still thriving to the modern city of Albuquerque. The allures are many, but the spicy cuisine and superlative visual arts are at the top of the list.

Perched at 7,199 feet above sea level, Santa Fe is the highest state capital in the U.S. It's also the oldest (founded as a Spanish colony in 1610), giving it one of the most fascinating back stories of any city in the country, centered on a historic plaza that has been a center of commerce and trade for more than 400 years. The many museums here run the gamut from folk art to cutting-edge, and the shopping is legendary, especially when it comes to Native American art and jewelry. Beyond city limits, the Sangre De Cristo Mountains present a bounty of recreational opportunities, most notably hiking and downhill skiing.

About 70 miles north of Santa Fe, Taos (pop. about 6,000) also offers visitors a strong dose of history, arts and culture, and outdoor activities, but on a smaller, more intimate scale. Established alongside the Native American Pueblo of the same name in 1795 as a trading post and fort, the town is best known for the artists who have lived and worked here since the late 1800s and the world-class Taos Ski Valley in the mountains northeast of the city. A good starting point, the central plaza is ringed by galleries and shops, but don't skip the art museums and hiking trails.

Also known as the Duke City, Albuquerque, with nearly 600,000 residents, is the state's most populous city, but it has a long history beginning with its founding in 1706. Old Town Albuquerque encompasses the original townsite. Just to the east of Old Town is the more modern downtown. Farther east, the University of New Mexico is the largest four-year college in the state. Keep heading east and you'll end up in the Sandia Mountains, with a popular tramway (the second-longest in the world) and numerous trails for hiking and biking.

Classic New Mexican cuisine is the common thread that connects all three cities. The flavorful, often fiery dishes that are staples in the Land of Enchantment are the rooted in the culinary traditions of the entire region. When you're ordering, be prepared for the official state question about what kind of chile sauce you'd like your meal smothered with: "Red or green?"

Planning

Getting Here and Around

AIR

Most visitors to the area fly into Albuquerque, home of the region's main airport, but Santa Fe also has a charmingly small and handily located airport with daily nonstop service to a few key hubs. From Albuquerque, ground transportation is available to both Santa Fe (65 miles away) and Taos (130 miles), although most visitors rent a car.

All the major car-rental agencies are represented at Albuquerque's airport, and several of them have branches at Santa Fe airport (Avis and Hertz) or in downtown Santa Fe (Avis, Budget, Enterprise, Hertz).

CAR

A car is a basic necessity in New Mexico, as even the few cities are challenging to get around solely using public transportation. Distances are considerable, but you can make excellent time on long stretches of interstate and other four-lane highways with speed limits of up to 75 mph. If you wander off major thoroughfares, slow down. Speed limits here generally are only 55 mph, and for good reason. Many such roadways have no shoulders; on many twisting and turning mountain roads speed limits dip to 25 mph. For the most part, the scenery on rural highways makes the drive a form of sightseeing in itself.

U.S. and state highways connect Santa Fe, Albuquerque, and Taos with a number of key towns elsewhere in New Mexico and in neighboring states. Many of these highways, including large stretches of U.S. 285 and U.S. 550, have four lanes and high speed limits. You can make nearly as good time on these roads as you can on interstates. Throughout the region, you're likely to encounter some unpaved surface streets. Santa Fe has a higher percentage of dirt roads than any other state capital in the nation.

TAXI

Santa Fe has no taxi company, but the city is well served by Lyft and Uber, which are also widely available in Taos and Albuquerque.

TRAIN

Amtrak's *Southwest Chief,* from Chicago to Los Angeles via Kansas City, stops in Las Vegas, Lamy (near Santa Fe), and Albuquerque.

The state's commuter train line, the *New Mexico Rail Runner Express,* runs from Santa Fe south through Bernalillo and into the city of Albuquerque, continuing south through Los Lunas to the suburb of Belén, covering a distance of about 100 miles and stopping at 15 stations. The Rail Runner offers a very inexpensive and scenic alternative to getting to and from the Albuquerque airport to Santa Fe (shuttle buses run from the airport to the *Rail Runner* stop in downtown Albuquerque).

Hotels

Although New Mexico itself has relatively affordable hotel prices, tourist-driven Santa Fe (and to a slightly lesser extent Taos) can be fairly pricey, especially during high season from spring through fall, with rates particularly high during major Santa Fe festivals (such as the Indian and Spanish markets). Generally, you'll pay the most at hotels within walking distance of the Plaza and those located in some of the more scenic and mountainous areas north and east of the city; B&Bs usually cost a bit less, and you can find some especially reasonable deals on Airbnb, which has extensive listings throughout the region.

Performing Arts

Few small cities in America can claim an arts scene as thriving as Santa Fe's—with opera, symphony, and theater in splendid abundance. The music acts here tend to be high caliber, but rather sporadic. A wonderful eight-week series of music on the Plaza bandstand runs through the summer with performances four nights a week. Gallery openings, poetry readings, plays, and dance concerts take place year-round, not to mention the city's famed opera and chamber-music festivals. Check the arts and entertainment listings in Santa Fe's daily newspaper, the *New Mexican* (🌐 *www.santafenewmexican.com*), particularly on Friday, when the arts and entertainment section, "Pasatiempo," is included, or check the weekly *Santa Fe Reporter* (🌐 *www.sfreporter.com*) for shows and events. As you might suspect, activities peak in the summer.

Restaurants

Dining out is a major pastime in Santa Fe as well as in Taos, Albuquerque, and even many of the small towns throughout the region. Although Santa Fe in particular has a reputation for upscale dining at restaurants with several high-profile chefs where dinner for two can easily set you back more than $200, the region also offers plenty of low-key, affordable spots, from mom-and-pop taquerias and diners to hip coffeehouses and gastropubs.

Reservations for dinner at the better restaurants are a must in summer and on weekends the rest of the year. In cities like Santa Fe and Albuquerque, some restaurants stay open until 10 or 11. In smaller communities, including Taos, many kitchens stop serving around 8 pm.

HOTEL AND RESTAURANT PRICES

Hotel prices in the reviews are the lowest cost of a standard double room in high season. Restaurant prices in the reviews are the average cost of a main course at dinner, or if dinner is not served, at lunch.

What It Costs

$	$$	$$$	$$$$
RESTAURANTS			
under $16	$16–$22	$23–$30	over $30
HOTELS			
under $120	$121–$180	$181–$240	over $240

Tours

BIKE TOURS

★ Routes Bicycle Tours

BICYCLE TOURS | Based in Albuquerque's Old Town and with a satellite location at Santa Fe's La Fonda Hotel, this full-service repair and rental shop offers a wide range of guided bike tours. In Santa Fe, excursions are offered March through November and include daily two-hour treks focused on the city's art and history as well as weekly tours geared around food and brewpubs. ✉ *Albuquerque* ☎ *505/933–5667* 🌐 *www.routesrentals.com.*

GUIDED TOURS

Food Tour New Mexico

GUIDED TOURS | Savor some of the tastiest posole, blue-corn enchiladas, margaritas, craft beers, and sweets on lunch and dinner excursions—some offered with wine pairings—in Santa Fe and Albuquerque, which make four to five stops at locally revered hot spots. ☎ *505/465–9474* 🌐 *www.foodtournewmexico.com.*

★ Heritage Inspirations

GUIDED TOURS | This team of highly knowledgeable, friendly guides offers nearly two dozen engaging, culturally immersive driving, walking, and hiking tours throughout northern New Mexico. Excursions include hikes through Bandelier and Kasha-Katuwe Tent Rocks, a highly popular Santa Fe architecture and wine walk, Taos and Chaco Canyon glamping trips, and agricultural adventures in Albuquerque's Rio Grande Valley. ☎ *888/344–8687* 🌐 *www.heritageinspirations.com.*

Historic Walks of Santa Fe
WALKING TOURS | Get to know the fascinating stories behind many of Santa Fe's most storied landmarks on these engaging strolls through Downtown and along Canyon Road. Other walks focus on ghosts, galleries, shopping, and food; Bandelier, Chimayó, and Taos excursions are also offered. ☎ *505/986–8388* 🌐 *www.historicwalksofsantafe.com.*

Santa Fe

64 miles northeast of Albuquerque, 70 miles southwest of Taos.

With its crisp, clear air and bright, sunny weather, Santa Fe couldn't be more welcoming or more unique. On a plateau at the base of the Sangre de Cristo Mountains—at an elevation of 7,000 feet—the city is brimming with reminders of nearly four centuries of Spanish and Mexican rule, and of the Pueblo cultures that have been here for hundreds more. The town's placid central Plaza, which dates from the early 17th century, has been the site of bullfights, public floggings, gunfights, political rallies, promenades, and public markets over the years. A one-of-a-kind destination, Santa Fe is fabled for its rows of chic art galleries, superb restaurants, and diverse shops selling everything from Southwestern furnishings and cowboy gear, to Tibetan textiles and Moroccan jewelry.

VISITOR INFORMATION

CONTACTS Indian Pueblo Cultural Center. ☎ *505/843–7270, 866/855–7902* 🌐 *www.indianpueblo.org.* **Tourism Santa Fe.** ✉ *Santa Fe Community Convention Center, 201 W. Marcy St., The Plaza* ☎ *505/955–6200, 800/777–2489* 🌐 *www.santafe.org.*

The Plaza and Downtown

Much of the history of Santa Fe, New Mexico, the Southwest, and even the West has some association with Santa Fe's central Plaza, which New Mexico governor Don Pedro de Peralta laid out in 1610. The Plaza was already well established by the time of the Pueblo revolt in 1680. Freight wagons unloaded here after completing their arduous journey across the Santa Fe Trail. The American flag was raised over the Plaza in 1846, during the Mexican War, which resulted in Mexico's loss of all its territories in the present Southwestern United States. For a time the Plaza was a tree-shaded park with a white picket fence. In the 1890s it was an expanse of lawn where uniformed bands played in an ornate gazebo. Particularly festive times on the Plaza are the weekend after Labor Day, during Las Fiestas de Santa Fe, on Indigenous Peoples Day in October (which brings dance celebrations), and during the winter holidays, when all the trees are filled with lights and rooftops are outlined with *farolitos,* votive candles lit within paper-bag lanterns.

With its eclectic mix of museums, shops, galleries, restaurants, and more, downtown Santa Fe can take days to explore thoroughly. A good way to plan for a visit is to start in the historic central Plaza and work your way out from there or, plan one day for museums, another for sights, and another for shopping. Downtown Santa Fe is lively both day and night so it's easy to start exploring in the morning and still be going as night falls. To ensure you get a real "taste" of the area, make reservations for dinner as restaurants tend to fill up quickly with both locals and visitors—one of the reasons some call Santa Fe "the city that never stops eating."

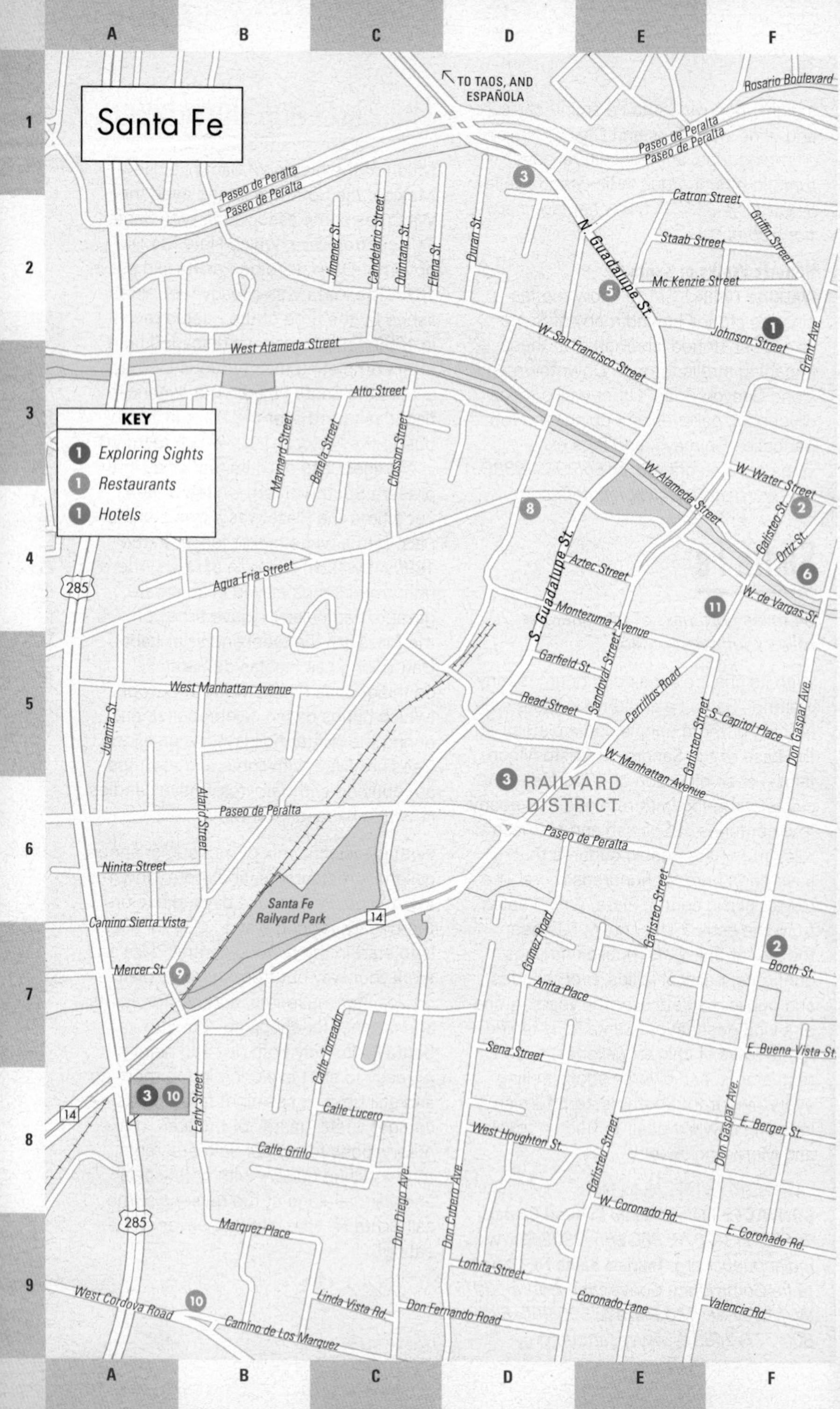
Santa Fe
KEY
Exploring Sights
Restaurants
Hotels
TO TAOS, AND ESPAÑOLA
Rosario Boulevard
Paseo de Peralta
Catron Street
Griffin Street
Staab Street
Mc Kenzie Street
Johnson Street
Grant Ave.
N. Guadalupe St.
W. San Francisco Street
Jimenez St.
Candelario Street
Quintana St.
Elena St.
Duran St.
West Alameda Street
Alto Street
Maynard Street
Barela Street
Closson Street
W. Alameda Street
W. Water Street
Galisteo St.
Ortiz St.
W. de Vargas St.
Aztec Street
S. Guadalupe St.
Agua Fria Street
Montezuma Avenue
Garfield St.
Sandoval Street
Cerrillos Road
Read Street
West Manhattan Avenue
Juanita St.
Galisteo Street
S. Capitol Place
Don Gaspar Ave.
W. Manhattan Avenue
RAILYARD DISTRICT
Alarid Street
Ninita Street
Camino Sierra Vista
Santa Fe Railyard Park
Mercer St.
Gomez Road
Booth St.
Anita Place
Calle Torreador
Sena Street
E. Buena Vista St.
Early Street
Calle Lucero
E. Berger St.
West Houghton St.
Calle Grillo
W. Coronado Rd.
E. Coronado Rd.
Don Diego Ave.
Don Cubero Ave.
Marquez Place
Lomita Street
West Cordova Road
Linda Vista Rd.
Don Fernando Road
Coronado Lane
Valencia Rd.
Camino de Los Marquez
285
14

Sights

1 Georgia O'Keeffe Museum F2
2 IAIA Museum of Contemporary Native Arts (MoCNA)........................ H3
3 Meow Wolf........................ A8
4 Museum of International Folk Art (MOIFA) I9
5 New Mexico History Museum ... G3
6 New Mexico Museum of Art..... G3
7 New Mexico State Capitol....... G6
8 San Miguel Mission G5

Restaurants

1 Cafe Pasqual's G4
2 Coyote Cafe F4
3 Dolina Cafe & Bakery D1
4 El Mesón Restaurant & Tapas Bar........................... H2
5 Fire & Hops.......................... E2
6 Geronimo J5
7 Harry's Roadhouse H9
8 Joseph's Culinary Pub............ D4
9 La Choza B7
10 Paper Dosa.......................... B9
11 Plaza Café Downtown............ G3
12 Sazón.................................. G4
13 The Shed............................. H3

Hotels

1 Bobcat Inn........................... H9
2 Casa Culinaria....................... F7
3 Hotel Santa Fe D5
4 Inn and Spa at Loretto H4
5 The Inn of the Five Graces........ G5
6 Inn of the Governors F4
7 Inn of the Turquoise Bear......... G8
8 Inn on the Alameda................ I4
9 La Fonda on the Plaza............ G4
10 Ojo Santa Fe........................ A8
11 Old Santa Fe Inn F4
12 Rosewood Inn of the Anasazi.... H3

Dozens of restaurants and shops surround the city's historic Plaza.

Sights

★ Georgia O'Keeffe Museum

MUSEUM | One of many East Coast artists who visited New Mexico in the first half of the 20th century, Georgia O'Keeffe, today known as the "Mother of American Modernism," returned to live and paint in northern New Mexico for the last half of her life, eventually emerging as the demigoddess of Southwestern art. At this museum dedicated to her work, you'll find how O'Keeffe's innovative view of the landscape is captured in *From the Plains,* inspired by her memory of the Texas plains, and in *Jimson Weed,* a study of one of her favorite plants; additional highlights include selections from O'Keeffe's early days as an illustrator, abstract pieces from her time in New York City, and iconic works featuring floating skulls, flowers, and bones. Special exhibitions with O'Keeffe's modernist peers, as well as contemporary artists, are on view throughout the year—many of these are exceptional, and just as interesting as the museum's permanent collection, which numbers some 3,000 works. The museum also manages a visitor center and tours of O'Keeffe's famous home and studio in Abiquiú, about an hour north of Santa Fe. ✉ *217 Johnson St., The Plaza* ☎ *505/946–1000* 🌐 *www.okeeffemuseum.org* 🎫 *$20* 🕐 *Closed Tues. and Wed.*

IAIA Museum of Contemporary Native Arts (MoCNA)

MUSEUM | This fascinating museum that's part of the esteemed Institute of American Indian Arts (IAIA) is just a block from the Plaza and contains the largest collection—some 7,500 works—of contemporary Native American art in the United States. The collection of paintings, photography, sculptures, prints, and traditional crafts was created by past and present students and teachers. In the 1960s and 1970s it blossomed into the nation's premier center for Native American arts and its alumni represent almost 600 tribes around the country. The museum continues to showcase the cultural and artistic vibrancy of indigenous people and expands what is still an often limited public perception of what "Indian" art is and can be. Be sure to step out back to the beautiful sculpture garden. Artist Fritz Scholder taught here, as did sculptor Allan Houser. Among their disciples were the painter T. C. Cannon and sculptor and painter Dan Namingha. ✉ *108 Cathedral Pl., The Plaza* ☎ *505/983–8900, 888/922–4242* 🌐 *www.iaia.edu* 🎟 *$10* ⏲ *Closed Tues.*

★ New Mexico History Museum

MUSEUM | **FAMILY** | This impressive, modern museum anchors a campus that encompasses the **Palace of the Governors,** the **Palace Print Shop & Bindery,** the **Fray Angélico Chávez History Library,** and **Photo Archives** (an assemblage of more than 1 million images dating from the 1850s). Behind the palace on Lincoln Avenue, the museum thoroughly explores the early history of indigenous people, Spanish colonization, the Mexican Period, and travel and commerce on the legendary Santa Fe Trail. Inside are changing and permanent exhibits. By appointment, visitors can tour the comprehensive Fray Angélico Chávez History Library and its rare maps, manuscripts, and photographs (more than 120,000 prints and negatives). The Palace Print Shop & Bindery, which prints books, pamphlets, and cards on antique presses, also hosts bookbinding demonstrations, lectures, and slide shows. The Palace of the Governors is a humble one-story neo-Pueblo adobe on the north side of the Plaza, and is the oldest public building in the United States. Its rooms contain period furnishings and exhibits illustrating the building's many functions over the past four centuries. Built at the same time as the Plaza, circa 1610, it was the seat of four regional governments—those of Spain, Mexico, the Confederacy, and the U.S. territory that preceded New Mexico's statehood, which was achieved in 1912. It served as the residence for 100 Spanish, Mexican, and American governors, including Governor Lew Wallace, who wrote his epic *Ben Hur* in its then drafty rooms, all the while complaining of the dust and mud that fell from its earthen ceiling.

Dozens of Native American vendors gather daily under the portal of the Palace of the Governors to sell pottery, jewelry, bread, and other goods. With few exceptions, the more than 500 artists and craftspeople registered to sell here are Pueblo or Navajo Indians. The merchandise for sale is required to meet strict standards. Prices tend to reflect the high quality of the merchandise but are often significantly less than what you'd pay in a shop. Please remember not to take photographs without permission. ✉ *Palace Ave., north side of Plaza, 113 Lincoln Ave., The Plaza* ☎ *505/476–5200* 🌐 *www.nmhistorymuseum.org* 🎟 *$7* ⏲ *Closed Nov.–Apr., closed Mon.*

★ New Mexico Museum of Art

MUSEUM | Designed by Isaac Hamilton Rapp in 1917, the museum contains one of America's finest regional collections. It's also one of Santa Fe's earliest Pueblo Revival structures, inspired by the adobe structures at Acoma Pueblo. Split-cedar *latillas* (branches set in a crosshatch pattern) and hand-hewn vigas form the ceilings. The 20,000-piece permanent collection, of which only a fraction is exhibited at any given time, emphasizes the work of regional and nationally renowned artists, including Georgia O'Keeffe; realist Robert Henri; the Cinco Pintores (five painters) of Santa Fe (including Fremont Ellis and Will Shuster, the creative mind behind Zozóbra); members of the Taos Society of Artists (Ernest L. Blumenschein, Bert G. Phillips, Joseph H. Sharp, and E. Irving Couse, among others); and the works of noted 20th-century photographers of the Southwest, including Laura Gilpin, Ansel Adams, and Dorothea Lange. Rotating exhibits are staged throughout the year. Many excellent examples of Spanish-colonial-style furniture are on display. Other highlights include an interior *placita* (small plaza) with fountains, WPA

The interior of San Miguel Mission, the oldest church in America, still reflects its 1610 origins.

murals, and sculpture, and the St. Francis Auditorium, where concerts and lectures are often held. ✉ *107 W. Palace Ave., The Plaza* ☎ *505/476–5072* 🌐 *www.nmartmuseum.org* 🎫 *$12* ⏲ *Closed Nov.–Apr. and Mon.*

New Mexico State Capitol

GOVERNMENT BUILDING | **FAMILY** | The symbol of the Zía Pueblo, which represents the Circle of Life, was the inspiration for the state's capitol building, also known as the Roundhouse. Doorways at opposing sides of the 1966 structure symbolize the four times of day, the four directions, the four stages of life, and the four seasons. Throughout the building are artworks from the outstanding 600-work collection of the Capitol Art Foundation, historical and cultural displays, and handcrafted furniture—it's a superb and somewhat overlooked array of fine art. The Governor's Gallery hosts temporary exhibits. Six acres of imaginatively landscaped gardens shelter outstanding sculptures. ✉ *490 Old Santa Fe Trail, Old Santa Fe Trail and South Capitol* ☎ *505/986–4589* 🌐 *www.nmlegis.gov/visitors* 🎫 *Free* ⏲ *Closed Sun. year-round and Sat. Sept.–late May.*

★ **San Miguel Mission**

RELIGIOUS SITE | **FAMILY** | Believed to be the oldest church still in use in the United States, this simple earth-hewn adobe structure was built around 1610 by the Tlaxcalan Indians of Mexico, who came to New Mexico as servants of the Spanish. Badly damaged in the 1680 Pueblo Revolt, the structure was restored and enlarged in 1710. On display in the chapel are priceless statues and paintings and the San José Bell, weighing nearly 800 pounds, which is believed to have been cast in Spain in 1356. In winter the church sometimes closes before its official closing hour. Latin mass is held daily at 2 pm, and new mass is on Sunday at 5 pm. ✉ *401 Old Santa Fe Trail, Old Santa Fe Trail and South Capitol* ☎ *505/983–3974* 🌐 *www.sanmiguelchapel.org.*

Restaurants

★ Cafe Pasqual's

$$$ | **SOUTHWESTERN** | A perennial favorite, this cheerful cubbyhole dishes up Nuevo Latino and occasional Asian specialties for breakfast, lunch, and dinner. The culinary muse behind Pasqual's is James Beard Award–winning chef and cookbook author Katharine Kagel, who champions organic, local ingredients, and whose expert kitchen staff produces mouthwatering breakfast and lunch specialties like *huevos motuleños* (eggs in a tangy tomatillo salsa with black beans and fried bananas) and the sublime grilled free-range chicken sandwich on toasted-chile corn bread. **Known for:** smoked-trout hash with tomatillo salsa and mole enchiladas; colorful folk art and murals; long waits with reservations only available for dinner. *Average main: $30 ✉ 121 Don Gaspar Ave., The Plaza ☎ 505/983–9340 ⊕ www.pasquals.com.*

Coyote Cafe

$$$$ | **SOUTHWESTERN** | A Santa Fe hot spot since it opened in 1987, this pioneer of contemporary Southwestern cuisine is enjoying a bit of a renaissance under the guidance of new-ish (since 2017) owner and long-time bartender/manager Quinn Stephenson. The spot serves some of the most extravagant and delicious cuisine in the city. **Known for:** tellicherry peppered elk tenderloin; Frito pies in the less expensive Coyote Cantina next-door; creative agave and tequila cocktails. *Average main: $39 ✉ 132 W. Water St., The Plaza ☎ 505/983–1615 ⊕ www.coyotecafe.com ⏲ No lunch.*

★ Dolina Cafe & Bakery

$ | **CAFÉ** | Slovakian transplant Annamaria O'Brien's bustling bakery and brunch spot is as bright and crisp as her food. The menu borrows a bit from the chef's Eastern European roots with favorites such as paprikash, langos, and goulash, but also features regional American dishes like cornmeal waffles with buttermilk fried chicken and a surprising bone broth "morning soup". **Known for:** Eastern European pastries; eclectic and hearty breakfast-brunch fare; farm-fresh local ingredients. *Average main: $12 ✉ 402 N. Guadalupe St., West of the Plaza ☎ 505/982–9394 ⊕ www.dolinasantafe.com ⏲ No dinner.*

El Mesón Restaurant & Tapas Bar

$$$ | **SPANISH** | This place is as fun for having drinks and late-night tapas or catching live music (from tango nights to Sephardic music) as it is for enjoying a full meal. The lively tapas bar feels like a Spanish *taberna*, with a menu that includes dishes like classic Tortilla Española with aioli or fried artichoke hearts stuffed with Spanish goat cheese over *romesco* sauce. **Known for:** live jazz, Flamenco, and Tango Tuesdays; paella à la Valenciana with seafood, chorizo, and chicken; nice selection of Spanish wines, including Jerez sherries. *Average main: $25 ✉ 213 Washington Ave., The Plaza ☎ 505/983–6756 ⊕ www.elmeson-santafe.com ⏲ Closed Sun. and Mon. No lunch.*

★ Fire & Hops

$ | **ECLECTIC** | Tucked inside a cozy house on busy Guadalupe Street, Fire & Hops turns out some of the most flavorful, local, seasonal, and affordable gastropub-style food in Santa Fe while also offering a stellar list of craft beers from regional breweries such as Bosque, Bow & Arrow, Le Cumbre, Marble, and Ex Novo. Fire & Hops also features an extensive wine and cider list, and reserves a tap for hard kombucha crafted by celebrated local producer HoneyMoon Brewery. **Known for:** upscale pub food with an Asian flair; small plates like crispy fried Brussels sprouts; house-made ice cream in unusual flavors. *Average main: $14 ✉ 222 N. Guadalupe St., West of the Plaza ☎ 505/954–1635 ⊕ www.fireandhopsgastropub.com ⏲ No lunch.*

Plaza Café Downtown

$$ | **SOUTHWESTERN** | **FAMILY** | Run with homespun care by the Razatos family since 1947, this café has been a fixture on the Plaza since 1905. The food runs

the gamut, from cashew mole enchiladas to New Mexico meat loaf to chile-smothered burritos to a handful of Greek favorites, but the ingredients tend toward Southwestern. **Known for:** chicken-fried steak and excellent tortilla soup; retro diner charm; breakfast all day. *Average main: $17 54 Lincoln Ave., The Plaza 505/982–1664 www.plazacafesantafe.com.*

★ Sazón

$$$$ | MODERN MEXICAN | The realm of Mexico City–born chef Fernando Olea, who's been working his culinary magic at different Santa Fe restaurants since 1991, Sazón offers an upscale take on regional Mexican fare, complete with an exhaustive list of artisan tequilas and mezcals. Within the handsome dining room warmed by a kiva fireplace and filled with Frida Kahlo and Day of the Dead–inspired artwork, the focus is on one of Mexico's greatest dishes, mole. **Known for:** house-made mole sauces; chapulines (baby grasshoppers) on corn taquitos; encyclopedic selection of artisan mezcals. *Average main: $37 221 Shelby St., The Plaza 505/983–8604 www.sazonsantafe.com Closed Sun. No lunch.*

★ The Shed

$ | SOUTHWESTERN | FAMILY | The lines at lunch attest to the status of this downtown eatery that's been family operated since 1953, serving some of the most flavorful New Mexican food, and margaritas, around. Even if you're a devoted green-chile sauce fan, consider trying the locally grown red chile the place is famous for; it is rich and perfectly spicy. **Known for:** red-chile enchiladas and posole; potent margaritas; historic adobe setting dating from 1692. *Average main: $14 113½ E. Palace Ave., The Plaza 505/982–9030 www.sfshed.com Closed Sun.*

Hotels

Casa Culinaria

$$$ | B&B/INN | Known as the "Gourmet Inn," this is one of the city's most charming little finds, an exquisitely landscaped and attractively decorated compound on a pretty residential street a half-mile south of the Plaza. **Pros:** some units have fully equipped kitchens; the owners offer superb breakfasts and cooking classes; lush gardens. **Cons:** occasional noise from nearby elementary school; about a 10-minute walk from downtown; not too much to do in the immediate vicinity. *Rooms from: $217 617 Don Gaspar Ave., Old Santa Fe Trail and South Capitol 505/986–8664, 888/986–8664 www.ccsantafe.com 12 rooms Free Breakfast.*

★ Inn and Spa at Loretto

$$ | HOTEL | FAMILY | This plush, oft-photographed, pueblo-inspired property attracts a loyal clientele, many of whom swear by the friendly staff and high decorating standards. **Pros:** ideal location; gorgeous grounds and pool; distinctive architecture. **Cons:** expensive parking and resort fees; bathrooms feel a bit ordinary, small, and dated, and they also lack counter space; some rooms can have noise from the road. *Rooms from: $170 211 Old Santa Fe Trail, The Plaza 505/988–5531 www.hotelloretto.com 134 rooms No meals.*

★ The Inn of the Five Graces

$$$$ | B&B/INN | There isn't another property in Santa Fe to compare to this sumptuous yet relaxed inn with an unmistakable East-meets-West feel. **Pros:** tucked into a quiet, ancient neighborhood; loads of cushy perks and in-room amenities; fantastic staff—attentive but not overbearing. **Cons:** very steep rates; a short walk to downtown; can hear faint city noise from certain rooms. *Rooms from: $675 150 E. DeVargas St., Old Santa Fe Trail and South Capitol 505/992–0957, 866/992–0957 www.fivegraces.com 26 rooms Free Breakfast.*

★ Inn of the Governors

$$ | HOTEL | FAMILY | This rambling, reasonably priced hotel by the Santa Fe River is staffed by a polite, enthusiastic bunch. **Pros:** close to Plaza; year-round, heated pool; free parking (unusual for downtown). **Cons:** standard rooms are a bit small; some rooms view parking lot; some traffic noise. *Rooms from: $179 ✉ 101 W. Alameda St., The Plaza ☎ 505/982–4333, 800/234–4534 ⊕ www.innofthegovernors.com 100 rooms No Free Breakfast.*

★ Inn of the Turquoise Bear

$$$ | B&B/INN | In the 1920s, poet Witter Bynner played host to an eccentric circle of artists and intellectuals, as well as some wild parties in his mid-19th-century Spanish–Pueblo Revival home, which is now a superb bed-and-breakfast with a great location a few blocks from the capitol; in sum, it's the quintessential Santa Fe inn. **Pros:** gorgeous grounds and a house steeped in local history; gracious, knowledgeable staff; generous gourmet breakfasts. **Cons:** no pool or hot tub on-site; quirky layout of some rooms isn't for everyone; about a 15-minute walk to the Plaza. *Rooms from: $220 ✉ 342 E. Buena Vista, Old Santa Fe Trail and South Capitol ☎ 505/983–0798, 800/396–4104 ⊕ www.turquoisebear.com 9 rooms Free Breakfast.*

★ La Fonda on the Plaza

$$$$ | HOTEL | FAMILY | This venerable downtown landmark comes with modern amenities but still retains a warm, artful design—including whimsical painted headboards and handcrafted furniture—that's faithful to the vision of Mary Elizabeth Jane Colter, the vaunted architect responsible for the hotel's elegant Southwestern aesthetic. **Pros:** iconic building steeped in history; Plaza is right outside the door; excellent restaurant, bars, and pool. **Cons:** lobby often packed with tourists and nonguests; fitness facilities are modest for an upscale hotel; busy downtown location means some noise. *Rooms from: $269 ✉ 100 E. San Francisco St., The Plaza ☎ 505/982–5511, 800/523–5002 ⊕ www.lafondasantafe.com 180 rooms No meals.*

★ Rosewood Inn of the Anasazi

$$$$ | HOTEL | This intimate and artfully designed boutique hotel steps from the Plaza is one of Santa Fe's finest, with superb architectural detail, top-notch service, and a much-celebrated restaurant, bar, and lounge. **Pros:** thoughtful luxurious touches throughout; superb restaurant and charming bar; beautiful, lodgelike public spaces that are ideal for conversation or curling up with a book. **Cons:** standard rooms are a bit small for the price; only a few rooms have balconies; no hot tub or pool. *Rooms from: $450 ✉ 113 Washington Ave., The Plaza ☎ 505/988–3030, 888/767–3966 ⊕ www.rosewoodhotels.com 58 rooms No meals.*

The East Side with Canyon Road and Museum Hill

The historic neighborhoods of the East Side are infinitely walkable and a slow stroll makes for a great way to experience Santa Fe's famous pueblo revival architecture.

While most buildings in the city are required to adhere to this style, it is in the East Side neighborhoods where you will find true historic adobe homes, made of earthen bricks, versus newer concrete and stucco finishes. Even where facades are crumbling, a peek of adobe just adds to the charm. Topping these East Side neighborhoods, Museum Hill has spectacular vistas and, of course, is a culture haven thanks to its impressive museums; it also serves as a gateway to the many walking and hiking trails that line the foothills of the Sangre de Christos.

The East Side is anchored by Canyon Road. Once a trail used by indigenous people to access water and the lush

The famed Inn at Loretto has a partnership with tour company Heritage Inspirations, offering guided tours around the area.

forest in the foothills east of town, then a route for Hispanic woodcutters and their burros, and for most of the 20th century a prosaic residential street with only a gas station and a general store, Canyon Road today is lined with nearly 100 mostly upscale art galleries along with a handful of shops and restaurants.

Sights

★ Museum of International Folk Art (MOIFA)

MUSEUM | **FAMILY** | A delight for adults and children alike, this museum is the best institution of its kind in the world, with a permanent collection of more than 130,000 objects from about 100 countries. In the Girard Wing, you'll find thousands of amazingly inventive handmade objects, like a tin Madonna, a devil made from bread dough, dolls from around the world, and miniature village scenes. The Hispanic Heritage Wing rotates exhibitions of art from throughout Latin America, dating from New Mexico's Spanish-colonial period (1598–1821) to the present. The exhibits in the Neutrogena Wing rotate, showing subjects ranging from outsider art to the magnificent quilts of Gee's Bend. Lloyd's Treasure Chest, the wing's innovative basement section, provides a behind-the-scenes look at the museum's permanent collection and explores the question of what exactly constitutes folk art. The innovative Gallery of Conscience explores topics at the intersection of folk art and social justice. Each exhibition also includes educational activities for both kids and adults. Allow time to visit the outstanding gift shop and bookstore. ✉ *706 Camino Lejo, Museum Hill* ☎ *505/476–1200* 🌐 *www.internationalfolkart.org* 🎟 *$12* 🕓 *Closed Mon. in Nov.–Apr.*

Restaurants

★ Geronimo

$$$$ | **MODERN AMERICAN** | This bastion of dazzling, sophisticated contemporary cuisine occupies the historic Borrego House, built in 1756 by Geronimo Lopez, a massive-walled Canyon Road adobe with intimate white dining rooms, beamed ceilings, wood floors, fireplaces, and cushioned *bancos* (banquettes). It's one of the loveliest venues in New Mexico for a special meal, perhaps local rack of lamb with roasted leeks and a Merlot–natural jus reduction or mesquite grilled Maine lobster tails with a creamy garlic chile sauce. **Known for:** complex and sophisticated contemporary fare; setting in beautiful 18th-century Canyon Road adobe; sublime service. *$ Average main: $42 ✉ 724 Canyon Rd., East Side and Canyon Road ☎ 505/982–1500 🌐 www.geronimorestaurant.com ⏲ No lunch.*

Hotels

★ Inn on the Alameda

$$$ | **HOTEL** | Within an easy walk of both the Plaza and Canyon Road, this midpriced charmer with spacious Southwest-style rooms is one of the city's best small hotels. **Pros:** the solicitous staff is first-rate; excellent, expansive breakfast buffet and afternoon snacks and wine; free parking. **Cons:** rooms closest to Alameda can be a bit noisy; no pool; grounds can be a challenge for strollers or wheelchairs. *$ Rooms from: $189 ✉ 303 E. Alameda St., East Side and Canyon Road ☎ 505/984–2121, 888/984–2121 🌐 www.innonthealameda.com 72 rooms Free Breakfast.*

Activities

HIKING

Hiking around Santa Fe can take you into high-altitude alpine country or into lunaresque high desert as you head south and west to lower elevations. For winter hiking, the gentler climates to the south are less likely to be snow packed, while the alpine areas tend to require snowshoes or cross-country skis. In summer, wildflowers bloom in the high country, and the temperature is generally at least 10 degrees cooler than in town. The mountain trails accessible at the base of the Ski Santa Fe area and at nearby Hyde Memorial State Park (near the end of NM 475) stay cool on even the hottest summer days. Weather can change with one gust of wind, so be prepared with extra clothing, rain gear, food, and lots of water. Keep in mind that the sun at 10,000 feet is very powerful, even with a hat and sunscreen.

★ Atalaya Trail

HIKING/WALKING | Spurring off the Dale Ball Trail system, the steep but rewarding (and dog-friendly) Atalaya Trail runs from the visitor parking lot of St. John's College, up a winding, ponderosa pine–studded trail to the peak of Mt. Atalaya, which affords incredible 270-degree views of Santa Fe. The nearly 6-mile round-trip hike climbs almost 2,000 feet (to an elevation of 9,121 feet), so pace yourself. The good news: the return to the parking area is nearly all downhill. *✉ 1160 Camino de Cruz Blanca, East Side and Canyon Road.*

The Railyard District

The most significant development in Santa Fe in recent years has taken place in the Railyard District, a neighborhood just south of the Plaza that was for years called the Guadalupe District (and is occasionally still known by that name).

Comprising a few easily walked blocks along Guadalupe Street between Agua Fria and Paseo de Peralta, the district has been revitalized with a snazzy park and outdoor performance space, a permanent indoor–outdoor home for the farmers' market, and quite a few notable restaurants, shops, and galleries.

A central feature of the district's redevelopment is Railyard Park, at the corner of Cerrillos Road and Guadalupe Street, which was designed to highlight native plants and provide citizens with a lush, urban space. On weekends, the Railyard District is a lively spot thanks to the

A weekly Santa Fe Farmers' Market is one of the Railyard District's biggest draws.

ever-popular Santa Fe Farmers' Market and the Sunday Artisan Market.

Restaurants

★ Joseph's Culinary Pub

$$$ | MODERN AMERICAN | Chef-restauranteur Joseph Wrede has garnered countless accolades since the 1990s at various restaurants in Taos and then Santa Fe, and his current eatery—a stylish gastropub set in a vintage adobe with low beamed ceilings, slate floors, and a cozy patio—continues to showcase his considerable talents, featuring a menu of deliciously updated comfort fare. Dishes you're already familiar with receive novel twists, including caviar-topped duck fat-fried potato chips with crème fraîche, pickled onion, and cured egg yolk; and posole verde with chicken, a farm egg, tomatillos, and avocado. **Known for:** duck fat fries; excellent steak au poivre; stellar beer and wine selection. *$ Average main: $30 ✉ 428 Agua Fria St., Railyard District ☎ 505/982–1272 🌐 www.josephsofsantafe.com ⏲ No lunch.*

★ La Choza

$ | SOUTHWESTERN | FAMILY | The off-the-beaten-path and less expensive sister to the Shed located downtown, La Choza (which means "the shed" in Spanish), serves supertasty, supertraditional New Mexican fare. It's hard to go wrong here: chicken or pork *carne adovada* (marinated in red chile and slow-cooked until tender) burritos, white clam chowder spiced with green chiles, green chile stew, and the classic huevos rancheros are exceptional. **Known for:** stuffed sopaipilla; outstanding and extensive margarita and premium-tequila list; long waits unless you make a reservation. *$ Average main: $14 ✉ 905 Alarid St., Railyard District ☎ 505/982–0909 🌐 www.lachozasf.com ⏲ Closed Sun.*

Hotels

★ Hotel Santa Fe

$$$$ | HOTEL | Picurís Pueblo has controlling interest in this handsome Pueblo-style three-story hotel on the Railyard District's edge and a 15-minute walk from the Plaza. **Pros:** lots of amenities, including spa and pool; easy access to Railyard District's trendy shopping and dining; interesting focus on Native American history and culture. **Cons:** standard rooms are a bit small; room rates vary greatly; a bit far from downtown. *Rooms from: $250 1501 Paseo de Peralta, Railyard District 855/825–9876 www.hotelsantafe.com 158 rooms No meals.*

★ **Old Santa Fe Inn**

$$ | **HOTEL** | This contemporary motor court–style inn looks from the outside like an attractive, if fairly ordinary, adobe motel, but it has stunning and spotless rooms with elegant Southwestern decor. **Pros:** rooms are more inviting than several more-expensive downtown hotels; short walk to the Plaza; free parking. **Cons:** rooms set around parking lot; noise from other rooms; decor can be a bit drab in places. *Rooms from: $139 201 Montezuma Ave., Railyard District 505/995–0800 www.oldsantafeinn.com 58 rooms Free Breakfast.*

Greater Santa Fe

Beyond Santa Fe's commercial core, you'll find a bevy of other notable attractions, restaurants, shops, and inns around the easy-to-access north, west, and south sides of town.

Sights

Meow Wolf

ARTS VENUE | **FAMILY** | Both the name of an ambitious visual and musical arts collective and of the dazzling multimillion-dollar arts complex the group created out of a former bowling alley (with much of the funding coming from Santa Fe–based *Game of Thrones* author George R. R. Martin), visitors now flock to the arts complex's first permanent exhibition, the self-billed "immersive art installation" *House of Eternal Return*, which has become one of the city's leading attractions. Give yourself at least a couple of hours to tour this sci-fi-inspired, 20,000-square-foot interactive exhibit in which you'll encounter hidden doorways, mysterious corridors, ambient music, and clever, surrealistic, and often slyly humorous artistic renderings. It's a strange, almost impossible to describe, experience, but it is absolutely family-friendly, and although wildly imaginative and occasionally eerie, the subject matter isn't at all frightening. Tickets are good throughout the day—you can leave and reenter the installation, and perhaps break up the experience by enjoying a light bite and craft beer at the lobby bar/café. Be aware that the experience is highly sensory and can be a little overstimulating for those who are sensitive to noise, changing lighting, and crowds. Meow Wolf is open until 8 most evenings and 10 on Friday and Saturday. The collective also presents concerts and other events both at the Meow Wolf arts complex and at other venues around the city. *1352 Rufina Cir., South Side 505/395–6369 www.meowwolf.com $35 Closed Tues.–Thurs.*

Restaurants

★ **Harry's Roadhouse**

$ | **ECLECTIC** | **FAMILY** | This busy, friendly, art-filled compound 6 miles southeast of downtown consists of several inviting rooms, from a diner-style space with counter seating to a cozier nook with a fireplace, and an enchanting courtyard out back with juniper trees and flower gardens. The varied menu of contemporary diner favorites, pizzas, New Mexican fare, and bountiful salads is supplemented by a long list of daily specials, which often include delicious international dishes and an array of scrumptious homemade desserts. **Known for:** friendly neighborhood hangout; stellar margaritas; house-made desserts. *Average main: $13 96-B Old Las Vegas Hwy., 1 mile east of Old Pecos Trail exit off I–25, East*

Side and Canyon Road *505/989–4629* *www.harrysroadhousesantafe.com.*

★ Paper Dosa

$$ | **MODERN INDIAN** | **FAMILY** | Begun as a catering business that threw occasional pop-up dinners, Paper Dosa became so beloved for its boldly flavored southern Indian cuisine that the owners opened what has become a tremendously popular brick-and-mortar restaurant. Dosas (large, thin crepes made with fermented rice and lentils and stuffed with different fillings) are the specialty here and come in about 10 varieties, from paneer and peas to a locally inspired version with green chile and three cheeses. **Known for:** dosas with interesting fillings; chile-dusted mango salad; a thoughtful, diverse wine list. *Average main: $17* *551 W. Cordova Rd., Old Santa Fe Trail and South Capitol* *505/930–5521* *www.paper-dosa.com* *Closed Mon.*

Hotels

Bobcat Inn

$$ | **B&B/INN** | A delightful, affordable, country hacienda that's a 15-minute drive southeast of the Plaza, this adobe bed-and-breakfast sits amid 10 secluded acres of piñon and ponderosa pine, with grand views of the Ortiz Mountains and the area's high-desert mesas. **Pros:** gracious inn and secluded location; wonderful hosts; spectacular views. **Cons:** located outside of town; small bathrooms in some rooms; breakfast not served until 8:30 am. *Rooms from: $165* *442 Old Las Vegas Hwy., South Side* *505/988–9239* *www.bobcatinn.com* *8 rooms* *Free Breakfast.*

★ Ojo Santa Fe

$$$$ | **RESORT** | This tranquil 70-acre resort offers 32 rooms overlooking verdant gardens and 20 casitas with gas fireplaces and secluded patios, plus a first-rate spa focused on energy healing and integrative medicine, a variety of open-air soaking tubs, a large outdoor pool, yoga and fitness studios, a sweat lodge, and an outstanding restaurant—Blue Heron—serving healthy, locally sourced contemporary fare. **Pros:** great restaurant using organic vegetables and herbs grown on-site; unbelievably soothing cottonwood-shaded soaking tubs; superb spa with an extensive list of treatments (including playing with puppies!). **Cons:** 20-minute drive away from downtown; located in very rural setting; property size requires a lot of walking. *Rooms from: $270* *242 Los Pinos Rd., South Side* *877/977–8212* *ojosantafe.ojospa.com* *52 rooms* *No meals.*

Performing Arts

★ Santa Fe Opera

MUSIC | To watch opera in this strikingly modern structure—a 2,128-seat, indoor–outdoor amphitheater with excellent acoustics and sight lines—is a memorable visual and auditory experience. Carved into the natural curves of a hillside 7 miles north of the Plaza, the opera overlooks mountains, mesas, and sky. Add some of the most acclaimed operatic talents from Europe and the United States, and you begin to understand the excitement that builds every June. This world-renowned company presents five works in repertory each summer—a blend of seasoned classics, neglected masterpieces, and world premieres. Many evenings sell out far in advance, but less expensive standing-room tickets are often available on the day of the performance. A favorite pre-opera pastime is tailgating in the parking lot before the evening performance—many guests set up elaborate picnics of their own, but you can also preorder picnic meals at the opera website by calling 24 hours in advance or ordering a take-out meal from one of the many local restaurants that offer opera meals. In the off-season, the opera house hosts shows by contemporary artists such as Bonnie Raitt, St. Vincent, The Shins, and The National. *301*

Opera Dr., North Side ☎ *505/986–5900, 800/280–4654* 🌐 *www.santafeopera.org.*

Shopping

★ Jackalope

ANTIQUES/COLLECTIBLES | FAMILY | You could easily spend a couple of hours wandering through this legendary indoor–outdoor bazaar, which sprawls over 7 acres, incorporating pottery barns, a furniture store, endless aisles of knickknacks from Latin America and Asia, and a glassblowing studio. There's also an area where craftspeople, artisans, and others sell their wares—sort of a mini–flea market. ✉ *2820 Cerrillos Rd., South Side* ☎ *505/471–8539* 🌐 *www.jackalope.com.*

Activities

HIKING

★ Aspen Vista

HIKING/WALKING | FAMILY | Especially in autumn, when golden aspens shimmer on the mountainside, this trail up near Santa Fe's ski area makes for a lovely hike. After walking a few miles through thick aspen groves you come to panoramic views of Santa Fe. The path, which is well marked and gradually inclines toward Tesuque Peak, becomes steeper with elevation—also note that snow has been reported on the upper portions of the trail as late as July. In winter, after heavy snows, the trail is great for intermediate–advanced cross-country skiing. The full hike to the peak makes for a long, rigorous day—it's 12 miles round-trip and sees an elevation gain of 2,000 feet, but it's just 3½ miles to the spectacular overlook. Note that the Aspen Vista Picnic Site is also the trailhead for the Alamo Vista Trail, which leads to the summit of the ski area. ✉ *Hyde Park Rd. (NM 475), 2 miles before ski area, North Side* ✥ *Parking lot at Aspen Vista Picnic Site.*

SKIING

Ski Santa Fe

SKIING/SNOWBOARDING | FAMILY | Open roughly from late November through early April, this is a somewhat underrated, midsize ski and snowboard operation that receives an average of 225 inches of snow a year and plenty of sunshine. It's one of America's highest ski areas—the 12,075-foot summit has unbelievable views and a varied terrain which make its 1,725 feet of vertical rise and 660 acres seem even bigger. There are some great powder stashes, tough bump runs, and many wide, gentle cruising runs. The 87 trails are ranked 20% beginner, 40% intermediate, and 40% advanced; there are seven lifts: one quad, two triples, two doubles, and two surface lifts. Chipmunk Corner provides day care and supervised kids' skiing. The ski school is excellent. Rentals, a ski shop, and a good restaurant round out the amenities at bright and modern La Casa Lodge base-camp, and Totemoff's Bar and Grill is a welcome midmountain option with frequent live music during the season. While Ski Santa Fe doesn't offer cross-country skiing, there are many Nordic trails available off of Hyde Park Road just before the downhill ski area. Ski Santa Fe is also fun for hiking during the summer months and the Super Chief Quad Chair operates from late August through mid-October, catering to hikers and shutterbugs eager to view the high-mountain fall foliage, including acres of shimmering golden aspens. ✉ *End of NM 475, 18 miles northeast of Downtown, North Side* ☎ *505/982–4429 general info, 505/983–9155 snow report* 🌐 *www.skisantafe.com.*

Kasha-Katuwe Tent Rocks National Monument

36 miles west of Santa Fe.

Hoodoos and slot canyons form an enchanted hiking getaway that can be accessed from Interstate 25 on the drive between Albuquerque and Santa Fe. If you have time for just one hike, this is an excellent choice. The national monument was established by President Clinton in 2001 in order to protect the remarkable volcanic rock formations that are shaped like tents. The monument is managed in cooperation with Cochiti Pueblo, whose people call the area Kasha-Katuwe.

★ **Kasha-Katuwe Tent Rocks National Monument**

NATURE SITE | FAMILY | The sandstone rock formations here are a visual marvel, resembling stacked tents in a stark, water- and wind-eroded box canyon. Tent Rocks offers superb hiking year-round, although it can get hot in summer, when you should bring extra water. The drive to this magical landscape offers its own delights, as the road heads west toward Cochiti Dam and through the cottonwood groves around the pueblo. It's a good hike for kids. The round-trip hiking distance is only 2 miles, about 1½ leisurely hours, but it's the kind of place where you'll want to hang out for a while. Take a camera, but leave your pets at home—no dogs are allowed. There are no facilities here, just a small parking area with a posted trail map and a self-pay admission box; you can get gas and pick up picnic supplies and bottled water (along with some locally made Pueblo items) at Pueblo de Cochiti Convenience Store. ✉ *Cochiti Pueblo, Indian Service Rte. 92, Cochiti Lake* ✣ *Follow signs to Kasha-Katuwe Tent Rocks National Monument* ☎ *505/331–6259* 🌐 *www.blm.gov/visit/kktr* 🎫 *$5 per vehicle.*

Bandelier National Monument

40 miles west of Santa Fe.

Seven centuries before the Declaration of Independence was signed, compact city-states existed in the Southwest. Remnants of one of the most impressive examples can be seen at Frijoles Canyon in Bandelier National Monument. At the canyon's base, near a gurgling stream, the remains of cave dwellings, ancient ceremonial kivas, and other stone structures stretch out for more than a mile beneath the sheer walls of the canyon's tree-fringed rim. For hundreds of years the Ancestral Puebloan people, relatives of today's Rio Grande Pueblo Indians, thrived on wild game, corn, and beans. Suddenly, for reasons still undetermined, the settlements were abandoned.

★ **Bandelier National Monument**

ARCHAEOLOGICAL SITE | A fascinating trip back in time, Bandelier National Monument is home to a stunning collection of preserved petroglyphs and cave dwellings of the Ancestral Puebloan people. Along a paved, self-guided trail, steep wooden ladders and narrow doorways lead to a series of cave dwellings and cell-like rooms. There is one kiva in the cliff wall that is large, and tall enough to stand in. Bandelier National Monument, named after author and ethnologist Adolph Bandelier (his novel *The Delight Makers* is set in Frijoles Canyon), contains 33,000 acres of backcountry wilderness, waterfalls, and wildlife. Some 70 miles of trails traverse the park; the short Pueblo Loop Trail is an easy, self-guided walk. Pick up the $2 trail guide at the monument's main building to read about the 21 numbered sites along the trail. A small museum in the visitor center focuses on the area's prehistoric and contemporary Native American cultures, with displays of artifacts from 1200 to modern times.

Note that from mid-May to mid-October, visitors arriving by car between 9 am and 3 pm must park at the White Rock Visitor Center 10 miles east on NM 4 and take a free shuttle bus into the park. ✉ *15 Entrance Rd., Los Alamos* ☎ *505/672–3861* 🌐 *www.nps.gov/band* 🎫 *$15 on foot or bicycle; $25 per car.*

Taos

70 miles northeast of Santa Fe.

Taos casts a lingering spell. Set on an undulating mesa at the base of the Sangre de Cristo Mountains, it's a place of piercing light and spectacular views, where the desert palette changes almost hourly as the sun moves across the sky.

Adobe buildings—some of them centuries old—lie nestled amid pine trees and scrub, some in the shadow of majestic Wheeler Peak, the state's highest point, at just over 13,000 feet. The smell of piñon-wood smoke rises from the valley from early autumn through late spring; during the warmer months, the air smells of fragrant sage.

The earliest residents, members of the Taos-Tiwa tribe, have inhabited this breathtaking valley for more than a millennium; about 2,000 of their descendants still live and maintain a traditional way of life at Taos Pueblo, a 95,000-acre reserve 4 miles northeast of Taos Plaza. Spanish settlers arrived in the 1500s, bringing both farming and Catholicism to the area; their influence remains most pronounced in the diminutive village of Ranchos de Taos, 4 miles south of town, where the massive adobe walls and *camposanto* (graveyard) of San Francisco de Asís Church have been attracting photographers for generations.

In the early 20th century, another population—artists—discovered Taos and began making the pilgrimage here to write, paint, and take photographs. The early adopters of this movement, painters Bert Phillips and Ernest Blumenschein, stopped here in 1898 quite by chance to repair a wagon wheel while en route from Denver to Mexico in 1898. Enthralled with the earthy beauty of the region, they abandoned their intended plan, settled near the plaza, and in 1915 formed the Taos Society of Artists. In later years, many illustrious artists—including Georgia O'Keeffe, Ansel Adams, and D. H. Lawrence—frequented the area, helping cement a vaunted arts tradition that thrives to this day. The steadily emerging bohemian spirit has continued to attract hippies, counterculturalists, New Agers, the LGBTQ community, and free spirits. Downtown, along with some outlying villages to the south and north, such as Ranchos de Taos and Arroyo Seco, now support a rich abundance of galleries and design-driven shops. Whereas Santa Fe, Aspen, Scottsdale, and other gallery hubs in the West tend toward pricey work, much of it by artists living elsewhere, Taos remains very much an ardent hub of local arts and crafts production and sales. A half dozen excellent museums here also document the town's esteemed artistic history.

About 5,800 people live year-round within Taos town limits, but another 28,000 reside in the surrounding county, much of which is unincorporated, and quite a few others live here seasonally. This means that in summer and, to a lesser extent, during the winter ski season, the town can feel much larger and busier than you might expect, with a considerable supply of shops, restaurants, and accommodations. Still, overall, the valley and soaring mountains of Taos enjoy relative isolation, low population density, and magnificent scenery, parts of which you can access by visiting Rio Grande del Norte National Monument. These elements combine to make Taos an ideal retreat for those aiming to escape, slow down, and embrace a distinct regional blend of art, cuisine, outdoor recreation, and natural beauty.

GETTING HERE AND AROUND

A car is your most practical means both for reaching and getting around Taos. The main route from Santa Fe is via U.S. 285 north to NM 68 north, also known as the Low Road, which winds between the Rio Grande and red-rock cliffs before rising to a sweeping view of the mesa and river gorge. You can also take the spectacular and vertiginous High Road to Taos, which takes longer but offers a wonderfully scenic ride—many visitors come to Taos via the Low Road, which is more dramatic when driven south to north, and then return to Santa Fe via the High Road, which has better views as you drive south. From Denver, it's a five-hour drive south via Interstate 25, U.S. 160 west (at Walsenburg), and CO 159 to NM 522—the stretch from Walsenburg into Taos is quite scenic.

VISITOR INFORMATION

CONTACTS Taos Visitor Center. ✉ *1139 Paseo del Pueblo Sur, Taos* ☎ *800/732–8267* 🌐 *www.taos.org.*

Historic Downtown Taos

The historic Taos Plaza is the central focal point of Taos. Established in 1796, the plaza began as a quadrangle for a Spanish fortlike settlement. Merchants and traders traveled from all over the West to display their wares on the plaza. Today, Taos Plaza continues to be a gathering place for the local community and visitors. Dozens of independent shops and galleries, along with several notable restaurants, hotels, and museums, thrive here. The plaza itself is a bit overrun with mediocre souvenir shops, but you only need to walk a block in any direction—especially north and east—to find better offerings.

Sights

★ Harwood Museum of Art

MUSEUM | The Pueblo Revival former home of Burritt Elihu "Burt" Harwood, a dedicated painter who studied in France before moving to Taos in 1916, is adjacent to a museum dedicated to the works of local artists. Traditional Hispanic northern New Mexican artists, early art-colony painters, post–World War II modernists, and contemporary artists such as Larry Bell, Agnes Martin, Ken Price, and Earl Stroh are represented. Mabel Dodge Luhan, a major arts patron, bequeathed many of the 19th- and early-20th-century works in the Harwood's collection, including *retablos* (painted wood representations of Catholic saints) and *bultos* (three-dimensional carvings of the saints). In the Hispanic Traditions Gallery upstairs are 19th-century tinwork, furniture, and sculpture. Downstairs, among early-20th-century art-colony holdings, look for E. Martin Hennings's *Chamisa in Bloom,* which captures the Taos landscape particularly beautifully. A tour of the ground-floor galleries shows that Taos painters of the era, notably Oscar Berninghaus, Ernest Blumenschein, Victor Higgins, Walter Ufer, Marsden Hartley, and John Marin, were fascinated by the land and the people linked to it. ✉ *238 Ledoux St., Plaza and Vicinity* ✣ *One block south of Historic Taos Plaza* ☎ *575/758–9826* 🌐 *www.harwoodmuseum.org* 🎟 *$10* 🕑 *Closed Mon.*

★ Historic Taos Plaza

PLAZA | **FAMILY** | The first European explorers of the Taos Valley came here with Captain Hernando de Alvarado, a member of Francisco Vásquez de Coronado's expedition of 1540. Basque explorer Don Juan de Oñate arrived in Taos in July 1598 and established a mission and trading arrangements with residents of Taos Pueblo. The settlement developed into two plazas: the plaza at the heart of the town became a thriving business district for the early colony, and a walled residential plaza was constructed a few hundred yards behind. It remains active today, home to a throng of schlocky gift shops, plus a few more noteworthy galleries and boutiques. On any given day you can stumble upon Aztec dancers pounding traditional beats with ankle bells, flamenco dancers sharpening their performance, and buskers strumming an Americana tune. In the summer, the plaza hosts a farmers' market and a lively concert season, which turns the plaza into an open-air dance floor. On the southeastern corner is the Hotel La Fonda de Taos. Nine infamous erotic paintings by D. H. Lawrence that were naughty in his day but are quite tame by present standards can be viewed in a small gallery in the hotel. ✉ *Plaza and Vicinity* 🌐 *www.taos.org/what-to-do/landmark-sites/taos-plaza.*

Taos Art Museum at Fechin House

MUSEUM | The interior of this extraordinary adobe house, built between 1927 and 1933 by Russian émigré and artist Nicolai Fechin, is a marvel of carved Russian-style woodwork and furniture. Fechin constructed it to showcase his daringly colorful paintings, intricate wood carvings and cabinetry, and coppersmith work on fixtures. The house now contains the Taos Art Museum, which showcases a rotating collection of some 600 paintings by more than 50 Taos artists, including founders of the original Taos Society of Artists, among them Joseph Sharp, Ernest Blumenschein, Bert Phillips, E. I. Couse, and Oscar Berninghaus. ✉ *227 Paseo del Pueblo Norte, Plaza and Vicinity* ☎ *575/758–2690* 🌐 *www.taosart-museum.org* 🎫 *$10* ⊙ *Closed Mon.*

Restaurants

Doc Martin's

$$$ | **SOUTHWESTERN** | The old-world restaurant of the Historic Taos Inn takes its name from the building's original owner, a local physician who saw patients in the rooms that are now the dining areas. The creative menu hews toward innovative takes on comforting classics, with an emphasis on sustainable ingredients—a favorite is the relleno platter comprising a pair of blue corn–beer battered Anaheim chiles, green chile, pumpkin seeds, and goat cheese cream. **Known for:** authentic chiles rellenos; fresh, local ingredients; some of the best margaritas in town. 💲 *Average main: $25* ✉ *Historic Taos Inn, 125 Paseo del Pueblo Norte, Plaza and Vicinity* ☎ *575/758–2233* 🌐 *www.taosinn.com/doc-martins.*

Donabe Asian Kitchen

$$ | **ASIAN** | Chef-owner Marshall Thompson has long had a following in Taos, overseeing some top kitchens as well as a popular noodle cart, and Donabe is his own Asian-cuisine restaurant that serves delightful and satisfying food. The kitchen whips out an impressive array of Japanese, Korean, Chinese, Thai, and Vietnamese dishes, with various meats (including yak), fish, chicken, pork, and vegetarian options. **Known for:** unique yak dishes; impressive range of Asian continent dishes; historic building. 💲 *Average main: $20* ✉ *133 Paseo del Pueblo Norte, Plaza and Vicinity* ☎ *575/751–9700* 🌐 *www.donabetaos.com* ⊙ *Closed Tues.*

★ **Lambert's of Taos**

$$$ | **CONTEMPORARY** | Superb service, creative cuisine, and an utterly romantic setting inside a historic adobe house a short walk north of the plaza define this Taos landmark that's been a go-to for special meals since the mid-1990s (it was previously located a few blocks away). The rich fare here fuses regional and Mediterranean recipes and ingredients and includes such standouts as red-beet

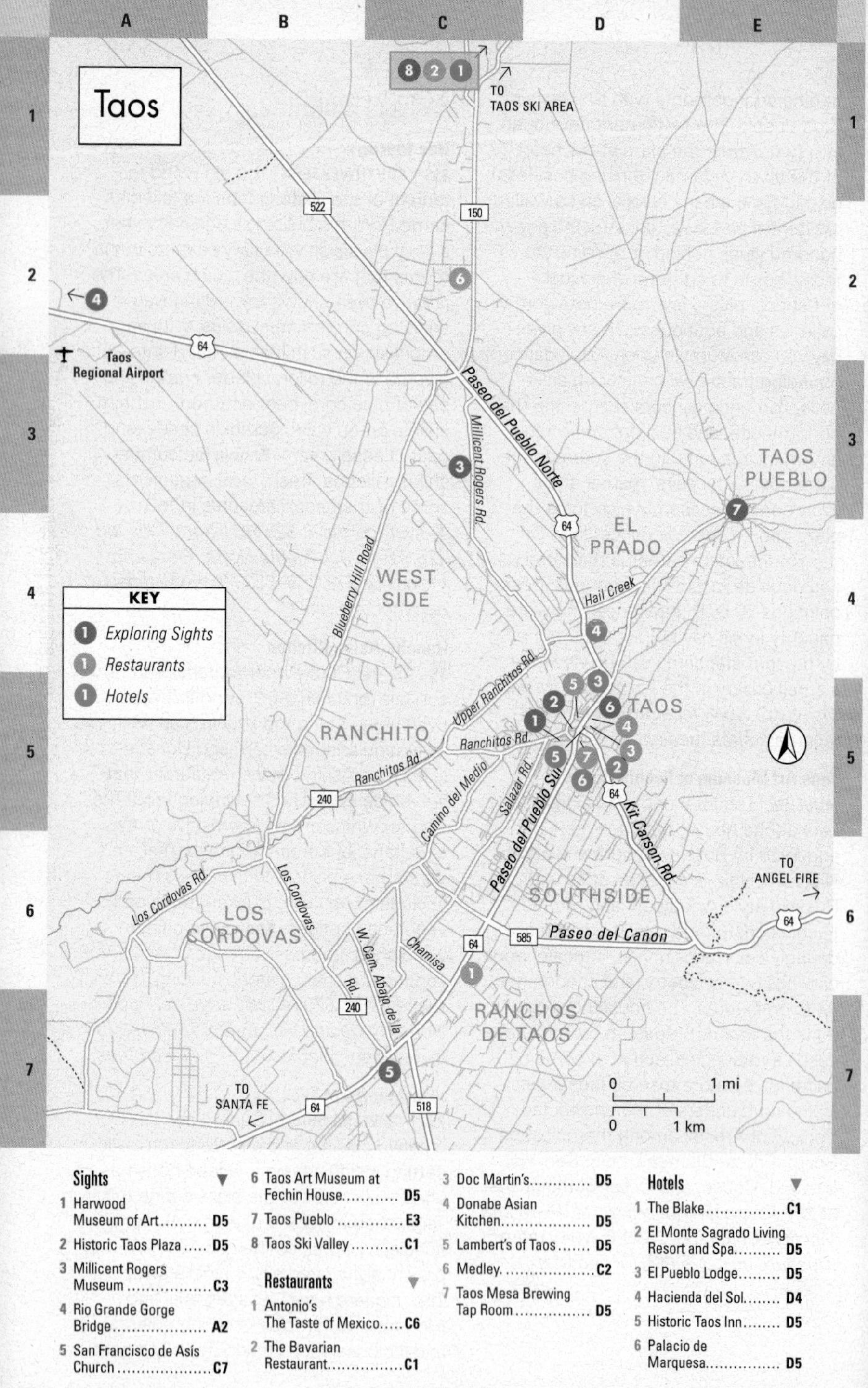

Taos
A
B
C
D
E
1
2
3
4
5
6
7
TO TAOS SKI AREA
522
150
64
Taos Regional Airport
Paseo del Pueblo Norte
Millicent Rogers Rd.
TAOS PUEBLO
EL PRADO
WEST SIDE
Blueberry Hill Road
Hail Creek
KEY
Exploring Sights
Restaurants
Hotels
Upper Ranchitos Rd.
TAOS
RANCHITO
Ranchitos Rd.
240
Camino del Medio
Salazar Rd.
Paseo del Pueblo Sur
Kit Carson Rd.
TO ANGEL FIRE
SOUTHSIDE
Los Cordovas Rd.
LOS CORDOVAS
Los Cordovas Rd.
W. Cam. Abajo de la
Chamisa
585
Paseo del Canon
RANCHOS DE TAOS
TO SANTA FE
518
0
1 mi
1 km
Sights
1 Harwood Museum of Art.......... D5
2 Historic Taos Plaza D5
3 Millicent Rogers Museum C3
4 Rio Grande Gorge Bridge..................... A2
5 San Francisco de Asís Church C7
6 Taos Art Museum at Fechin House............ D5
7 Taos Pueblo E3
8 Taos Ski Valley C1
Restaurants
1 Antonio's The Taste of Mexico..... C6
2 The Bavarian Restaurant................ C1
3 Doc Martin's............. D5
4 Donabe Asian Kitchen.................... D5
5 Lambert's of Taos D5
6 Medley. C2
7 Taos Mesa Brewing Tap Room D5
Hotels
1 The Blake.................C1
2 El Monte Sagrado Living Resort and Spa.......... D5
3 El Pueblo Lodge......... D5
4 Hacienda del Sol........ D4
5 Historic Taos Inn........ D5
6 Palacio de Marquesa................ D5

risotto with chèvre and watercress, and braised Colorado lamb shank with black eye pea–root veggie ragout, au jus, and turmeric raita. **Known for:** elegant dining experience; casual yet refined bar lounge upstairs; great wine list. *Average main: $30* *123 Bent St., Plaza and Vicinity* *575/758–1009* *www.lambertsoftaos.com.*

Taos Mesa Brewing Tap Room
$ | **PIZZA** | You don't have to be a craft-beer fan to enjoy this convivial taproom a five-minute walk south of the plaza, although it is a terrific place to sample a crisp Take A Knee IPA or a ruby-red Amarillo Rojo red ale. Pizza lovers also appreciate this spot, which serves delicious, generously topped pies—the inferno, with chorizo, chiles, taleggio and mozzarella cheese, and hot honey has a devoted following. **Known for:** locally brewed beers; easy, no-fuss pub pizza menu; large space with different seating areas. *Average main: $10* *201 Paseo del Pueblo Sur, Plaza and Vicinity* *575/758–1900* *www.taosmesabrewing.com.*

Hotels

★ **El Monte Sagrado Living Resort and Spa**
$$$ | **RESORT** | This posh, eco-minded, and decidedly quirky boutique resort—part of New Mexico's stylish Heritage Hotels & Resorts brand—has some of the swankiest rooms in town as well as a fabulous spa. **Pros:** luxurious resort experience; blend of Southwestern architecture and stunning natural landscaping; excellent spa offering restorative treatments. **Cons:** art and decor can be bold in some spots; service doesn't always measure up to premium rates; half-mile walk to the plaza includes a slight uphill. *Rooms from: $190* *317 Kit Carson Rd., Plaza and Vicinity* *855/846–8267 reservations* *www.elmontesagrado.com* *84 rooms* *No meals.*

El Pueblo Lodge
$$ | **HOTEL** | **FAMILY** | Among the budget-oriented properties in town, this well-maintained adobe-style hotel with a fun retro sign out front and the vibe of an old-school Route 66 motel is a real gem. **Pros:** terrific value for its central location; short walk north of the plaza; fun decor. **Cons:** nothing fancy; located on a busy section of the main road; Southwestern retro design may feel tacky to some. *Rooms from: $125* *412 Paseo del Pueblo Norte, Plaza and Vicinity* *575/758–8700, 800/433–9612* *www.elpueblolodge.com* *50 rooms* *Free Breakfast.*

★ **Hacienda del Sol**
$$ | **B&B/INN** | Art patron Mabel Dodge Luhan bought this house about a mile north of Taos Plaza in the 1920s and lived here with her husband, Tony Luhan, while building their main house. **Pros:** stunning mountain views; private retreat setting; some excellent restaurants within walking distance. **Cons:** traffic noise from the main road; some rooms are less private than others; 1-mile walk to the plaza. *Rooms from: $180* *109 Mabel Dodge La., Historic Downtown* *575/758–0287, 866/333–4459* *www.taoshaciendadelsol.com* *12 rooms* *Free Breakfast.*

Historic Taos Inn
$$ | **B&B/INN** | A 10-minute walk north of Taos Plaza, this celebrated property is a local landmark, with some devotees having been regulars here for decades. **Pros:** legendary bar and excellent restaurant; authentic Southwestern character and rich history; unbeatable location in the heart of Historic Downtown Taos. **Cons:** highly active social scene not for everyone; some rooms are very small; noise from traffic on the main road. *Rooms from: $125* *125 Paseo del Pueblo Norte, Plaza and Vicinity* *575/758–2233* *www.taosinn.com* *45 rooms* *No meals.*

Palacio de Marquesa

$$ | **B&B/INN** | Tile hearths, French doors, and traditional viga ceilings grace this luxury boutique hotel whose rooms stand out from the pack for their clean, uncluttered looks, posh linens, and decor inspired by female artists of local acclaim, from modernist Agnes Martin to transplanted British aristocrat Dorothy Brett. **Pros:** tranquil and secluded setting; sophisticated, contemporary rooms with lots of luxury touches; walking distance from plaza. **Cons:** a little pricey; noise from nearby main road; walk to plaza is slightly uphill. *Rooms from: $175* *405 Cordoba La., Plaza and Vicinity* *855/997–8230* *www.marquesataos.com* *8 rooms* *No meals.*

The Southside and Ranchos de Taos

The first Spanish settlers were agrarian, and many families continue to till the fertile land south of Taos, an area anchored by tine Ranchos de Taos, which is home to iconic San Francisco de Asis Church, memorialized by Georgia O'Keeffe and photographer Ansel Adams. The main approach road into Taos from the south, NM 68, is lined with gas stations, convenience stores, and chain motels, but there are a few lovely hotels and eateries too.

Sights

★ **San Francisco de Asís Church**

RELIGIOUS SITE | A National Historic Landmark, this is a beloved destination among the faithful, as well as for artists, photographers, and architectural buffs. The active Catholic church regularly celebrates Mass, contains numerous Hispanic religious artifacts, and is open to the public for visiting. Be sure to show respect for house of worship norms. The building's shape is a surprise with rounded, sculpted buttresses. Construction began in 1772 and today its mud-and-straw adobe walls are replastered by hand every year in an annual event. The "Ranchos Church" has a spiritual simplicity that inspired Georgia O'Keeffe to include it in a series of paintings and Ansel Adams to photograph it many times. *60 St. Francis Pl., Ranchos de Taos* *575/758–2754* *www.sfranchos.org.*

Restaurants

Antonio's The Taste of Mexico

$ | **MEXICAN** | Chef Antonio Matus has been delighting diners in the Taos area for many years with his authentic, boldly flavorful, and beautifully plated regional Mexican cuisine. In this intimate art-filled restaurant with a slate courtyard, Matus focuses more on regional Mexican than New Mexican fare. **Known for:** red-chile pork posole; chile en nogada; tres leches (three milks) cake. *Average main: $15* *1379 Paseo del Pueblo Sur, Southside* *575/758–2599* *Closed weekends.*

El Prado

As you drive north from Taos toward Arroyo Seco and points north or west, you'll first take the main thoroughfare, Paseo del Pueblo Norte (U.S. 64) through the small village of El Prado, a mostly agrarian area that's notable for having several of the area's best restaurants, bed-and-breakfasts, and shops.

Sights

★ **Millicent Rogers Museum**

MUSEUM | More than 7,000 pieces of spectacular Native American and Hispanic art, many of them from the private collection of the late Standard Oil heiress Millicent Rogers, are on display here. Among the pieces are baskets, blankets, rugs, kachina dolls, carvings, tinwork, paintings, rare religious artifacts, and, most significantly, jewelry (Rogers, a fashion icon in her day, was one of the first Americans to appreciate the turquoise-and-silver artistry of Native American jewelers). Other important works include the pottery and ceramics of Maria Martinez and other potters from San Ildefonso Pueblo (north of Santa Fe). Docents conduct guided tours by appointment, and the museum hosts lectures, films, workshops, and demonstrations. The two-room gift shop has exceptional jewelry, rugs, books, and pottery. ✉ *1504 Millicent Rogers Rd., off Paseo del Pueblo Norte, just south of junction with NM 150, El Prado* ☎ *575/758–2462* 🌐 *www.millicentrogers.org* 🎟 *$10* 🕒 *Closed Mon. Nov.–Mar.*

Restaurants

★ Medley

$$$ | MODERN AMERICAN | Set in a rustic-chic roadhouse on the scenic road between El Prado and Arroyo Seco that adjoins one of the area's best wineshops (it often hosts wine tastings), Medley strikes a happy balance between gastropub and special-night-out restaurant. You could make a meal of a few shareable small plates—tuna tartare tostadas, mac-and-cheese with roasted Hatch chiles, crispy-chicken sliders with sriracha mayo—or dive into one of the more substantial entrée offerings, such as mango-tamari-glazed salmon or a 10-ounce porterhouse steak with Brussels sprouts hash and house-made apple-bacon jam. **Known for:** elaborate and satisfying small plates; terrific mountain views from courtyard; extensive wine list. $ *Average main: $23* ✉ *100 NM 150, El Prado* ☎ *575/776–5656* 🌐 *www.medleytaos.com* 🕒 *Closed Sun. and Mon.*

Taos Pueblo

The Pueblo is the ancient beating heart of the entire valley, the historic and architectural basis for everything that Taos has become. A small, unmemorable casino aside, this area a short drive northeast of the plaza has been spared commercial development and remains a neighborhood of modest homes and farms. The Pueblo itself is the sole draw for visitors and worth a visit.

Sights

★ Taos Pueblo

BUILDING | FAMILY | For nearly 1,000 years the mud-and-straw adobe walls of Taos Pueblo have sheltered Tiwa-speaking Native Americans. A United Nations World Heritage Site, this is the largest collection of multistory pueblo dwellings in the United States. The pueblo's main buildings, Hlauuma (north house) and Hlaukwima (south house), are separated by a creek. These structures are believed to be of a similar age, probably built between 1000 and 1450. The dwellings have common walls but no connecting doorways—the Tiwas gained access only from the top, via ladders that were retrieved after entering. Small buildings and corrals are scattered about.

The pueblo today appears much as it did when the first Spanish explorers arrived in New Mexico in 1540. The adobe walls glistening with mica caused the conquistadors to believe they had discovered one of the fabled Seven Cities of Gold. The outside surfaces are continuously maintained by replastering with thin layers of mud, and the interior walls are frequently coated with thin washes of white clay. Some walls are several feet thick in places. The roofs of each of the five-story structures are supported by large timbers, or *vigas,* hauled down from the mountain forests. Pine or aspen *latillas* (smaller pieces of wood) are

Parts of Taos Pueblo (a UNESCO World Heritage Site) may be more than 1,000 years old.

placed side by side between the vigas; the entire roof is then packed with dirt.

Even after 400 years of Spanish and Anglo presence in Taos, inside the pueblo the traditional Native American way of life has endured. Tribal custom allows no electricity or running water in Hlauuma and Hlaukwima, where varying numbers (roughly 150) of Taos Native Americans live full time. About 1,900 others live in conventional homes on the pueblo's 95,000 acres. The crystal-clear Rio Pueblo de Taos, originating high above in the mountains at the sacred Blue Lake, is the primary source of water for drinking and irrigating. Bread is still baked in *hornos* (outdoor domed ovens). Artisans of the Taos Pueblo produce and sell (tax-free) traditionally handcrafted wares, such as mica-flecked pottery and silver jewelry. Great hunters, the Taos Native Americans are also known for their work with animal skins and their excellent moccasins, boots, and drums.

Although the population is predominantly Catholic, the people of Taos Pueblo, like most Pueblo Native Americans, also maintain their original religious traditions. At Christmas and other sacred holidays, for instance, immediately after mass, dancers dressed in seasonal sacred garb proceed down the aisle of St. Jerome Chapel, drums beating and rattles shaking, to begin other religious rites.

The pueblo **Church of San Geronimo,** or St. Jerome, the patron saint of Taos Pueblo, was completed in 1850 to replace the one destroyed by the U.S. Army in 1847 during the Mexican War. With its smooth symmetry, stepped portal, and twin bell towers, the church is a popular subject for photographers and artists.

The public is invited to certain ceremonial dances held throughout the year (a full list of these is posted on the pueblo website's Events page): highlights include the Feast of Santa Cruz (May 3); Taos Pueblo Pow Wow (mid-July); Santiago and Santa Ana Feast Days (July 25 and 26); San Geronimo Days (September 29 and 30); Procession of the Virgin Mary (December 24); and Deer Dance or Matachines Dance (December 25). While you're at the pueblo, respect all rules and customs, which are posted prominently. There are some restrictions, which are posted, on personal photography. Guided tours are available daily and are the way to start your visit. Tours are typically led by Taos Pueblo college students, and provide insight into the history of the Pueblo and the native traditions that continue into the present day. ✉ *120 Veterans Hwy., Taos Pueblo* ☎ *575/758–1028* 🌐 *www.taospueblo.com* 🎫 *$16.*

The Mesa

Taos is hemmed in by the Sangre de Cristo Mountains on the east, but to the west, extending from downtown clear across the precipitously deep Rio Grande Gorge (and the famous bridge that crosses it), the landscape is dominated by sweeping, high-desert scrub and wide-open spaces. The west side of the city (also called the Mesa) is mostly residential and makes for a scenic shortcut around the sometimes traffic-clogged plaza (from Ranchos de Taos, just follow NM 240 to Blueberry Hill Road to complete this bypass).

Sights

★ Rio Grande Gorge Bridge

BRIDGE/TUNNEL | It's a dizzying experience to see the Rio Grande 650 feet underfoot, where it flows at the bottom of an immense, steep rock canyon. In summer the reddish rocks dotted with green scrub contrast brilliantly with the blue sky, where you might see a hawk lazily floating in circles. The bridge is the second-highest suspension bridge in the country. Hold on to your camera and eyeglasses when looking down. Many days just after daybreak, hot-air balloons fly above and even inside the gorge. There's a campground with picnic shelters and basic restrooms on the west side of the bridge. ✉ *U.S. 64, 8 miles west of junction NM 522 and 150, El Prado.*

Nightlife

★ Taos Mesa Brewing

BARS/PUBS | It's worth the 15-minute drive northwest of Taos Plaza to reach this fabulously bizarre-looking pub and microbrewery near the airport, just a few miles east of the Rio Grande Gorge Bridge. In a high-ceilinged, eco-friendly building with soaring windows, sample exceptionally well-crafted Scottish Ale, Black Widow Porter, and Kolsch 45. Live music and entertainment is presented on indoor and outdoor stages—the latter has amazing mountain and mesa views. Tasty tapas and bar snacks are served, too. You can also sip the same beers and eat outstanding pizza at the Taos Mesa Brewing Tap Room, near the plaza, and there's another branch up at Taos Ski Valley. ✉ *20 ABC Mesa Rd., Mesa* ☎ *575/758–1900* 🌐 *www.taosmesabrewing.com.*

Taos Ski Valley

Skiers and snowboarders travel to this legendary ski area from all over the world for the thrill of its steep slopes. But it's not just for expert skiers; all of its services are geared toward families, helping to create a fun and light-hearted vibe. For summer visitors, Taos Ski Valley offers hiking, biking, and scenic chairlift rides. There's also an active calendar of events, including ski competitions, guest lectures, outdoor parties, and fireworks shows.

Sights

★ Taos Ski Valley

SKIING/SNOWBOARDING | **FAMILY** | With 110 runs—just under half of them for experts—and an average of more than 320 inches of annual snowfall, Taos Ski Valley ranks among the country's most respected, and challenging, resorts. The slopes, which cover a 2,600-foot vertical gain of lift-served terrain and another 700 feet of hike-in skiing, tend to be narrow and demanding (note the ridge chutes,

Al's Run, Inferno), but about a quarter of them (e.g., Honeysuckle) are for intermediate skiers, and another quarter (e.g., Bambi, Porcupine) are for beginners. Taos Ski Valley is justly famous for its outstanding ski school, which is one of the best in the country. ✉ *116 Sutton Pl., Taos Ski Valley* ☎ *888/388–8457, 800/776–1111* 🌐 *www.skitaos.com* 🎫 *Lift ticket from $90.*

Restaurants

The Bavarian Restaurant

$$$ | GERMAN | The restaurant inside the romantic, magically situated alpine lodge, which also offers Taos Ski Valley's most luxurious accommodations, serves outstanding contemporary Bavarian-inspired cuisine, such as baked artichokes and Gruyère, and braised local lamb shank with mashed potatoes and red wine–roasted garlic-thyme jus. Lunch is more casual and less expensive, with burgers and salads available. **Known for:** large deck facing Kachina Peak; authentic German dishes; imported German beers. $ *Average main: $26* ✉ *100 Kachina Rd., Taos Ski Valley* ☎ *575/776–8020* 🌐 *www.skitaos.com/things-to-do/bavarian.*

Hotels

The Blake

$$$$ | RESORT | This luxury boutique hotel just steps from the resort's lifts has quickly developed a reputation as the swankiest accommodation in the Taos region. **Pros:** steps from the main lift; sizable rooms and plenty of amenities; beautiful views of the mountain. **Cons:** a 30-minute drive from Taos; feeling of remoteness if you're not outdoorsy; lobby is only modestly sized. $ *Rooms from: $306* ✉ *116 Sutton Pl., Taos Ski Valley* ☎ *575/776–5335 reception, 855/208-4988 reservations* 🌐 *www.skitaos.com/theblake* 🛏 *80 rooms* 🍽 *No meals.*

Activities

HIKING

Williams Lake Trail

HIKING/WALKING | This is a popular trail with visitors and locals alike. Before hiking, contact the Carson National Forest Office for information on the latest trail conditions; they rank this trail as "easy to intermediate" in difficulty level. It's important to note that the Williams Lake Trail and its surrounding forest is not a park, but a federally designated wilderness area and is not staffed with rangers or facilities. Natural hazards, debris, and wildlife exist. The well-trodden hiking trail is two miles (one-way) and climbs from 10,200 feet to 11,100 feet in elevation. It leads you to a remote alpine lake that is not huge, but is quite lovely. The body of water is snow melt from the surrounding mountains so when you dip your toe in, the water is likely to be very cold even in the summer. Throughout the hike, the trail mostly follows under the shade of tree canopy and passes some large and interesting boulder fields, usually filled with the chirping of marmots. Upon arrival at the lake, you'll find people resting on the grassy slopes around its perimeter. Most hikers pack a picnic lunch while hike in with tents and plan to spend the night. Towering above Williams Lake is Wheeler Peak, the highest peak in New Mexico. Consult with the Forest Office or a local outfitter to inquire about recommended footwear, provisions, and appropriate clothing for the hike. It is advisable to stay hydrated, practice skin protection, and adjust your level of activity if necessary. ✉ *Taos Ski Valley* ✣ *Near end of Kachina Rd. Trailhead parking lot is well-signed* ☎ *575/758–6200 Carson National Forest Office* 🌐 *www.fs.usda.gov.*

Albuquerque

64 miles southwest of Santa Fe.

Perfectly set as the gateway to other New Mexico wonders like Chaco Canyon, the Four Corners area, and the Gila Wilderness, Albuquerque's own rich history and dramatic terrain—desert volcanoes, unique cottonwood bosque along the broad banks of the river that flows through its very center, and a striking confluence of mountain ranges—have long captured the imagination of folks en route from here to there.

Today's smart traveler knows something special is afoot in this wonderfully diverse and charmingly quirky historic town halved by the Rio Grande. You'll want to plan on spending at least a day or more before venturing beyond. Vibrant art galleries, growers' markets, a coffee and microbrewery scene, and world-class museums as well as superb nature trails and spectacular topography—and, of course, the seemingly endless blue sky and the joyous hot-air balloons that decorate it—make it a worthy destination of its own.

Centuries-old traces of Native American populations past and present abound throughout the Rio Grande Valley, and Albuquerque is no exception. Their trade routes are what drew the Spanish here; sections of what became their Camino Real are still intact. The little farming settlement was proclaimed "Alburquerque," after the Viceroy of New Spain—the 10th Duke of Alburquerque—in 1706. By the time Anglo traders arrived in the 1800s, that first "r" had been dropped, but that settlement, now known as Old Town, was still the heart of town. By the 1880s, with the railroad in place, the center of town moved east to meet it, in the Downtown we know today. Remnants of all linger still—and may readily be seen in the soft aging adobes in the North and South Valley, or the old Rail Yard buildings in Barelas.

In the spirit of one of the earliest local proponents of preserving the area's natural heritage, Aldo Leopold, Albuquerque is committed to protecting its exquisite bosque lands—and the waterfowl, porcupines, and other wildlife that call them home. A network of bicycle trails has been extended from there throughout the city. A noted Public Art program, a developing innovation economy, a remarkably diverse population, and a surprisingly eclectic range of architecture further set this city apart.

A bit of quiet attention reveals Albuquerque's subtle beauty—a flock of sandhill cranes overhead; a hot-air balloon, seemingly within reach; vintage art deco buildings and motel signs along old Route 66; Pueblo Revival details on the university campus; the fabulous facade of the KiMo theater; a sudden glimpse across the western desert to a 100-mile-distant snowcapped Mt. Taylor; and the Sandia Mountains lit pink by the fading sun.

Albuquerque's terrain is diverse, too. Along the river in the North and South valleys, the elevation hovers at about 4,800 feet. East of the river, the land rises gently to the foothills of the Sandia Mountains, which climb to more than 6,000 feet; the 10,378-foot summit is a grand spot from which to view the city below. West of the Rio Grande, where Albuquerque is growing most aggressively, the terrain rises abruptly in a string of mesas topped by five volcanic cones. The changes in elevation from one part of the city to another result in corresponding changes in temperature, as much as 10°F at any time. It's not uncommon for snow or rain to fall on one part of town but for it to remain dry and sunny in another, and because temperatures can shift considerably throughout the day and evening, it's a good idea to bring along a couple of layers when exploring.

GETTING HERE AND AROUND

The major gateway to New Mexico is Albuquerque International Sunport, a well-designed and attractive art-filled facility that's just 5 miles southeast of downtown and 3 miles south of UNM/Nob Hill. The city's ABQ Ride bus service runs a shuttle from the airport to downtown's Alvarado Transportation Center, where you can connect with local bus routes as well as the Rail Runner Express train service to Santa Fe.

TOURS

Abq Tours

Abq Tours offers guided history and ghost-centric walking strolls around Old Town. The standard tour lasts about 75 minutes and is offered four times daily. Longer ghost-hunting and moonlight tours are also offered on occasion—check the website for times. ✉ *303 Romero St. NW, Plaza Don Luis N-120, Albuquerque* ☎ *505/246–8687* 🌐 *www.abqtours.fun.*

ABQ Trolley Co.

(*AT&SF*) Narrated 100-minute open-air trolley trips are the feature here—join them on a Best of ABQ City Tour (film shoot locations—including some *Breaking Bad* and *Better Call Saul* sites—are always included) or a brew cruise ride. There's also a 2½-hour Duke City Pedaler version and a 3½-house Hopper for those looking for a deeper look into Albuquerque's lively microbrew scene. Their Albucreepy Ghost Walk tour takes a different view of the spirit scene downtown. Tour trollies depart year-round from Hotel Albuquerque (Old Town) while brew excursions start from downtown (*330 Tijeras Ave. NW*). ✉ *Hotel Albuquerque, 800 Rio Grande NW, Albuquerque* ☎ *505/200–2642* 🌐 *www.tourabq.com.*

VISITOR INFORMATION

CONTACTS Visit Albuquerque. ✉ *Downtown* ☎ *505/842–9918, 800/284–2282* 🌐 *www.visitalbuquerque.org.*

Old Town

Albuquerque's social and commercial anchor since the settlement was established in 1706, Old Town and its surrounding blocks contain the wealth of the city's top cultural attractions, including several excellent museums, as well as scads of restaurants, galleries, and shops.

Sights

★ ABQ BioPark

ZOO | FAMILY | The city's foremost outdoor attraction and nature center, the park comprises Tingley Beach (and its trout-stocked ponds) as well as three distinct attractions: Aquarium, Botanic Garden, and Zoo. The garden and aquarium are located together (admission gets you into both facilities), just west of Old Town, off Central Avenue; the zoo is a short drive southeast, off 10th Street. You can also ride the scenic Rio Line vintage narrow-gauge railroad between the zoo and gardens and the aquarium complex; rides are free if you purchase a combination ticket to all of the park's facilities. ✉ *903 10th St. SW, Old Town* ☎ *505/768–2000* 🌐 *www.abqbiopark.com* 🎫 *Tingley Beach and grounds free; Aquarium and Botanic Garden $15; Zoo $15; Zoo train ticket $3; combination ticket for all attractions, including unlimited train tickets, $22.*

★ Albuquerque Museum

MUSEUM | FAMILY | In a modern, light-filled space, the Albuquerque Museum serves up a brilliantly curated selection of contemporary art from the museum's own Southwestern artists–centric collections and world-class touring shows; it also presents illuminating shows with regionally topical, historical, and cultural themes. "Trinity: Reflections on the Bomb," "Jim Henson: Imagination Unlimited," "Making Africa: A Continent of Contemporary Design," and Patrick Nagatani's "Excavations" are but a few that have drawn crowds. The Common Ground galleries represent an important permanent collection of primarily 20th-century paintings, all by world-renowned artists with a New Mexico connection. A changing rotation of 19th- and 20th-century photographs from the museum's extensive local archive lines the museum's walkway halls; other spaces dig even deeper into compelling aspects of Albuquerque and regional history. The Sculpture Garden contains more than 50 contemporary works by an internationally known roster of artists that includes Basia Irland, Tom Waldron, Ed Haddaway, and Fritz Scholder; Nora Naranjo-Morse's spiral land-art piece resonates deeply for a city—and a museum—that recognizes that water and land issues define Albuquerque's history and its future. Visitors may pick up a self-guided Sculpture Garden map or come for the free (with admission) docent-led tours at 11 am Wednesday and Saturday (March through November); docent-led tours of the galleries, also free, are held daily at 2 pm, year-round. The museum's innovative children's activity room always ties in to current exhibits and is an instant magnet for kids. Slate at the Museum, a casual eatery operated by downtown's Slate Street Cafe, serves soups, salads, espresso drinks, desserts, and other tasty light fare. ✉ *2000 Mountain Rd. NW, Old Town* ☎ *505/243–7255 museum, 505/242–0434 shop, 505/242–5316 café* 🌐 *www.cabq.gov/museum* 🎫 *$4; free Sun. 9–1 and all day 1st Wed. each month* ⊗ *Closed Mon.*

American International Rattlesnake Museum

MUSEUM | **FAMILY** | Included in the largest collection of different species of living rattlers in the world are such rare and unusual specimens as an albino western diamondback and a melanistic (solid black) diamondback. From the outside the museum looks like just a plain old shop—aside from the friendly crew of tortoises who are usually there to greet you—but inside, the museum's exhibits, its engaging staff, and explanatory videos supply visitors with the lowdown on these venomous creatures. Did you know that they can't hear their own rattles and that the human death rate from rattlesnake bites is less than 1%? The mission here is to educate the public on the many positive benefits of rattlesnakes, and to contribute to their conservation. ✉ *202 San Felipe St. NW, just off southeast corner of Plaza, Old Town* ☎ *505/242–6569* 🌐 *www.rattlesnakes.com* 🎫 *$6.*

Indian Pueblo Cultural Center

MUSEUM | **FAMILY** | The multilevel semicircular layout of this museum was inspired by Pueblo Bonito, the prehistoric ruin in northwestern New Mexico. Start by visiting their permanent exhibit space "We Are of This Place: The Pueblo Story," which interprets the Pueblo people's legacy through carried-down traditions and remarkable pieces from their renowned holdings of fine Native American pottery, textiles, baskets, and other masterworks. Changing exhibits may feature close-ups of a particular artist, such as the gorgeously composed and colorful copper-plate prints of Santa Clara Pueblo painter Helen Hardin. Mural Discovery Tours are offered on Friday at 1 pm and ceremonial dances are performed year-round on weekends; there are often arts-and-crafts demonstrations as well. The museum gift shop provides a fine overview of current Pueblo arts. Its **Indian Pueblo Kitchen** restaurant is a tasty spot for breakfast, lunch, or dinner. Note that the museum lies a bit northeast of Old Town, in the Los Duranes neighborhood—a five-minute drive away. ✉ *2401 12th St. NW, Los Duranes* ☎ *505/843–7270, 866/855–7902* 🌐 *www.indianpueblo.org* 🎫 *$9.*

Old Town Plaza

PLAZA | **FAMILY** | Tranquil, with the lovely 1793 San Felipe de Neri Catholic Church still presiding along the north side, Old Town Plaza is a pleasant place to sit on wrought-iron benches under shade trees. Roughly 200 shops, restaurants, cafés, galleries, and several cultural sites in *placitas* (small plazas) and lanes surround the plaza. During fiestas Old

A
B
C
D
E
F
1
2
3
4
5
6
7
8
9
Towner Ave. N.W.
Prospect Ave. N.W.
Indian School Rd. N.W.
Menaul Boulevard N.W.
12th Street N.W.
Towner Ave. N.W.
Prospect Ave. N.W.
Apache Ave. N.W.
Cutler Ave. N.W.
4th Street Northwest
2nd Street Northwest
40
Rio Grande Blvd. N.W.
Aspen Ave. N.W.
Zearing Avenue N.W.
Bellamah Avenue N.W.
20th St. N.W.
8th Street Northwest
7th Street Northwest
Haines Ave. N.W.
Aspen Ave. N.W.
Aspen Ave. N.W.
Sawmill Rd. N.W.
Romero St.
Mountain Road N.W.
OLD TOWN
Dora Ave. N.W.
Edna Ave. N.W.
Hollywood Ave. N.W.
Soto Ave. N.W.
San Felipe St.
Old Town Rd. N.W.
12th Street N.W.
Constitution Ave. N.W.
Kinley Ave. N.W.
Summer Ave. N.W.
Mountain Rd. N.W.
Granite Ave. N.W.
Marble Ave. N.W.
Orchard Place N.W.
15th Street N.W.
Forrester Avenue N.W.
7th St. N.W.
Los Tomases Dr. N.W.
6th Street Northwest
5th Street N.W.
4th Street Northwest
3rd Street Northwest
2nd Street Northwest
1st Street Northwest
Lomas Boulevard Northwest
Lomas Boulevard N.W.
San Pasquale Ave. S.W.
14th Street N.W.
13th Street N.W.
12th Street N.W.
11th Street N.W.
Keleher Avenue N.W.
8th Street N.W.
7th Street N.W.
Tingley Dr. S.W.
Laguna Boulevard Southwest
Central Avenue
Tijeras Ave. N.W.
Roma Ave. N.W.
Marquette Ave.
Tijeras Ave.
Park Ave. S.W.
14th St. S.W.
13th St. S.W.
12th St. S.W.
11th St. S.W.
10th St. S.W.
9th St. S.W.
8th St. S.W.
DOWNTOWN
Lead Avenue Southwest
Coal Avenue Southwest
Iron Avenue Southwest
Stover Avenue Southwest
2nd Street S.W.
Broadway Blvd. S.E.
Iron Avenu
1st Street S.W.
3rd Street Southwest
4th Street Southwest
Rio Grande
Tingley Drive Southwest
8th St. S.W.
Hazeldi
Edith Boulevard S.E.
Arno Street S.E.
Broadway Boulevard S.E.
BARELAS
Bridge Boulevard S.E.
0
1,000 ft
0
200 m
Dan Ave. S.E

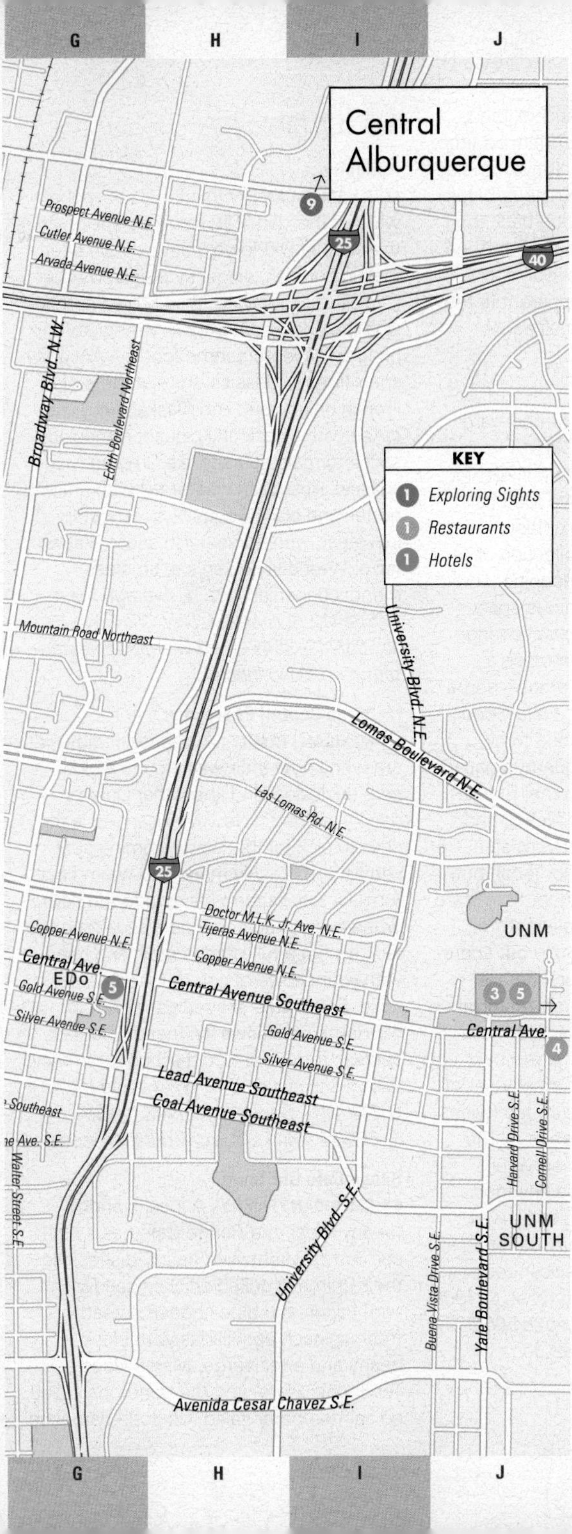

Central Alburquerque

KEY
Exploring Sights
Restaurants
Hotels

Prospect Avenue N.E.
Cutler Avenue N.E.
Arvada Avenue N.E.
Broadway Blvd. N.W.
Edith Boulevard Northeast
Mountain Road Northeast
University Blvd. N.E.
Lomas Boulevard N.E.
Las Lomas Rd. N.E.
Doctor M.L.K. Jr. Ave. N.E.
Tijeras Avenue N.E.
Copper Avenue N.E.
Copper Avenue N.E.
Central Ave.
EDo
Gold Avenue S.E.
Silver Avenue S.E.
Central Avenue Southeast
Gold Avenue S.E.
Silver Avenue S.E.
UNM
Central Ave.
Lead Avenue Southeast
Coal Avenue Southeast
Southeast
ne Ave. S.E.
Walter Street S.E.
Harvard Drive S.E.
Cornell Drive S.E.
University Blvd. S.E.
UNM SOUTH
Buena Vista Drive S.E.
Yale Boulevard S.E.
Avenida Cesar Chavez S.E.

Sights

1	ABQ BioPark	C7
2	Albuquerque Museum	B3
3	American International Rattlesnake Museum	B4
4	516 Arts	E6
5	Indian Pueblo Cultural Center	D1
6	Old Town Plaza	B4
7	Open Space Visitor Center	A2
8	Petroglyph National Monument	A2
9	Sandia Peak Aerial Tramway	I1
10	Sawmill Market	B3

Restaurants

1	Antiquity	B4
2	Duran Central Pharmacy	B4
3	Flying Star Cafe	J7
4	Frontier Restaurant	J7
5	Frenchish	J7
6	Range Café Old Town	B2
7	Vinaigrette	B5

Hotels

1	Casas de Sueños	B4
2	El Vado Motel	A4
3	Hotel Albuquerque at Old Town	B3
4	Hotel Chaco	B3
5	Hotel Parq Central	G6
6	Los Poblanos Historic Inn & Organic Farm	A1
7	Painted Lady Bed & Brew	D3

Town comes alive with mariachi bands and dancing señoritas; at Christmas time it is lit with luminarias (the votive candles in paper bag lanterns known as *farolitos* up in Santa Fe). Mostly dating back to the late 1800s, styles from Queen Anne to Territorial and Pueblo Revival, and even Mediterranean, are apparent in the one- and two-story (almost all adobe) structures. ✉ *Old Town.*

★ Sawmill Market

MARKET | **FAMILY** | A former lumber-yard building located by the old AT&SF Railway line in the city's Sawmill district has been turned into a grand food hall that captures a true sense of history and place. A carefully honed collection of some two-dozen dining, shopping, and drinking vendors inhabit unique spaces from which they offer an eclectic range of high-quality wares. All embrace a definitively fresh and local ethos—some by way of Santa Fe, like Dr. Field Goods (an established spot with food-truck roots); some already Albuquerque-based (like Eldora Chocolate, Spurline, Estella Flowers, Naruto, Neko and Neko); and others talented transplants from afar (like Blue Door Patisserie and Flor Taco), but all with the same commitment to in-state growers, makers, and suppliers. Stroll around a bit and you can't help but appreciate the original architectural details (just gaze up at the fabulously restored wooden ceiling). Paxton's taproom has a seasonal rotation of New Mexico–brewed beers, as well as a steady set of the state's best craft beers on tap (wines lean local as well as international). The cool Mobile Bar is ready to serve out on their grassy patio, where any food bought inside may be enjoyed as well; more formal dine-in fare may be found at Flora, where traditional Mexican recipes are revisited with a modern twist. ✉ *1909 Bellamah Ave. NW, Old Town* ☎ *505/563–4470* 🌐 *www.sawmillmarket.com.*

Restaurants

Antiquity

$$$$ | **AMERICAN** | Within the thick adobe walls of this darkly lit, romantic space off the plaza in Old Town, patrons have been feasting on rich, elegantly prepared American classics for more than 50 years. This isn't the edgy, contemporary restaurant to bring an adventuresome foodie—Antiquity specializes in classics, from starters of French onion soup and Alaskan King crab cakes with a perfectly piquant remoulade sauce to main courses like Chicken Madagascar, Australian lobster tail with drawn butter, and black Angus New York strip-loin steak with horseradish sauce. **Known for:** old-world-style service; timeless menu; congenial buzz. $ *Average main: $45* ✉ *112 Romero St. NW, Old Town* ☎ *505/247–3545* 🌐 *www.antiquityrestaurant.com* ⏲ *No lunch.*

★ Duran Central Pharmacy

$ | **MEXICAN** | **FAMILY** | A favorite of old-timers who know their way around a blue-corn enchilada (and know that Duran's deeply authentic New Mexican red is the chile to pick for it), this welcoming spot serves fine, freshly made and warm flour tortillas, too. Duran's harkens to the days when every drugstore had a soda fountain; it's got a full kitchen now (and beer), with your choice of counter stools, cozy table, or the little shaded patio right off old Route 66. **Known for:** friendly but fast service; retro charm; old-school pharmacy still on-site since 1942. $ *Average main: $11* ✉ *1815 Central Ave. NW, Old Town* ☎ *505/247–4141* 🌐 *www.duransrx.com.*

Range Café Old Town

$ | **AMERICAN** | **FAMILY** | A local standby for any meal, the Range Café has a high comfort quotient with hearty dishes like their Chimayó grilled-chicken sandwich with bacon and blue-cheese spread, fresh-spinach enchiladas with black beans and arroz verde, Matt's Hoosier Tenderloin Plate, and the generously plated salmon-berry salad. Chipotle barbecue beer-battered onion rings work great as a side, whether supporting burgers or standard New Mexican plates. **Known for:** exemplary New Mexican classics; colorful, funky decor; strong local roots. $ *Average main: $13 ✉ 1050 Rio Grande Blvd. NW, Old Town ☎ 505/508–2640 🌐 www.rangecafe.com.*

Vinaigrette

$$ | AMERICAN | Salads are the thing at Vinaigrette, just as they are at owner Erin Wade's popular original outpost in Santa Fe. Fresh, local greens are featured, but heartier add-ons (from seared tuna and panko-crusted goat cheese to hibiscus-cured duck confit and flank steak) will satisfy the hungriest in your party. **Known for:** bright and inviting contemporary space; robust servings; patio dining in season. $ *Average main: $18 ✉ 1828 Central Ave. SW, Old Town ☎ 505/842–5507 🌐 www.vinaigretteonline.com.*

Hotels

Casas de Sueños

$$ | B&B/INN | This historic compound (it's a National Register property) of 1930s- and '40s-era adobe casitas is perfect if you're seeking seclusion and quiet, yet desire proximity to museums, restaurants, and shops. **Pros:** charming, quirky, and tucked away; some private patios; free parking. **Cons:** units vary in ambience and age—some are more enchanting than others; some high beds, claw baths, and tall steps—ask about accessibility; decor not for everyone. $ *Rooms from: $139 ✉ 310 Rio Grande Blvd. SW, on the south side of Central Ave., Old Town ☎ 505/767–1000 🌐 www.casasdesuenos.com ⇆ 21 casitas 🍴 Free Breakfast.*

El Vado Motel

$$ | HOTEL | Back in the day, El Vado was a prime Route 66 stay-over for those driving west (or back east), and now the 1937 vintage former motor court has been transformed into a destination-worthy, fully modern motel, with a decor that winningly embraces midcentury modernism. **Pros:** gorgeous decor; outdoor lounging by the pool; small shops and dining spots on-site. **Cons:** limited parking, so guests may have to find spots on local streets; spillover sound travels from events on the plaza; pool on the small side. $ *Rooms from: $150 ✉ 2500 Central Ave. SW, Old Town ☎ 505/361–1667 🌐 www.elvadoabq.com ⇆ 22 rooms 🍴 No meals.*

Hotel Albuquerque at Old Town

$$$ | HOTEL | This 11-story Heritage Hotels & Resorts property overlooking Old Town has historic Territorial-style touches across its inviting facade, and attention is paid throughout its public spaces to New Mexican artisan craftwork, from Nambe Pueblo–designed metalwork to Navajo rugs. **Pros:** warmly appointed, Southwestern-style decor; lovely gardens and pool; mountain views available. **Cons:** air-conditioning units can be loud; in-room furnishing sufficient but spare; amenity fee. $ *Rooms from: $189 ✉ 800 Rio Grande Blvd. NW, Old Town ☎ 505/843–6300, 866/505–7829 🌐 www.hotelabq.com ⇆ 188 rooms 🍴 No meals.*

Hotel Chaco

$$$$ | HOTEL | A special commitment to New Mexico shines through in this fastidious study of Chaco Canyon as an inspiration for one of Albuquerque's most popular hotels; it uses materials meant to evoke the fine stone chinking that comprise most of the 9th- to 12th-century structures found at that not-to be-missed ancient Puebloan site. **Pros:** contemplative outdoor lounge space; hip Sawmill location; 24/7 fitness center. **Cons:** fortress-like entrance; $30 resort fee (includes parking); joint-use pool is on adjacent Hotel Albuquerque site. $ *Rooms from: $259 ✉ 2000 Bellamah Ave. NW, Old Town ☎ 505/246–9989, 855/997–8208 reservations only 🌐 www.hotelchaco.com ⇆ 118 rooms 🍴 No meals.*

Painted Lady Bed & Brew

$$ | **B&B/INN** | On a quiet side street on the fringe of Albuquerque's Sawmill-Wells Park districts, a particular personality is revealed in this low-slung historic adobe: while it decidedly favors fans of the ever-growing craft brew scene, it also offers comfortably appointed suites that have been thoughtfully modernized from their original early 1900s construction. **Pros:** locally crafted metalwork and murals enhance garden areas; cool history; daily happy hour focused on local beers. **Cons:** furnishings might feel quirky and mismatched; monthly on-site beer garden events get noisy; no breakfast. *Rooms from: $170 ✉ 1100 Bellamah Ave. NW, Old Town ☎ 505/200–3999 🌐 www.breakfastisoverrated.com 2 suites No meals.*

Downtown and EDo

You may visit Downtown for its anchoring arts and brews scene, events at the Pueblo Deco dazzler KiMo Theatre, or a stroll through the Downtown Growers' Market, but this neighborhood rewards those who take a closer look. Along Central Avenue and the parallel Gold Avenue, there's a prime trail of architectural detail, from the midcentury landmark Simms Building to the Venetian Gothic Revival Occidental Insurance Building along with the old federal courthouse's Spanish Mission pile. Hints of Albuquerque's 1880s railroad-era and Route 66 past abound.

Sights

★ 516 Arts

MUSEUM | World-class contemporary art dominates the changing shows at this multilevel nonprofit that holds a special place in the New Mexico art scene. Visually compelling collaborations with an international set of museums and artists cross media boundaries, and often explore issues that are not only dear to the hearts and minds of this multicultural, environmentally diverse state, but resonate globally. The installations here are always top-notch, the works displayed are of the highest quality, the ideas—whether expressed in video, prints, sculpture, diodes, or paint—provocative. *✉ 516 Central Ave. SW, Downtown ☎ 505/242–1445 🌐 www.516arts.org ⏲ Closed Sun. and Mon.*

Hotels

★ Hotel Parq Central

$$ | **HOTEL** | A decidedly imaginative adaptation of a disused building, the landmark Parq Central occupies a striking Moravian tile–trimmed three-story former AT& SF Railroad employees' hospital that dates to 1926. **Pros:** wonderfully landscaped, historic building; smartly designed rooms with sound-blocking windows; free shuttle to airport and within 3 miles of hotel. **Cons:** desks in rooms are quite small (though hotel will provide a larger one on request); parking (free) can be sparse when Apothecary Lounge is hopping; noise might travel to rooms nearest the Lounge. *Rooms from: $150 ✉ 806 Central Ave. SE, Downtown ☎ 505/242–0040 🌐 www.hotelparqcentral.com 74 rooms Free Breakfast.*

UNM and Nob Hill

Established in 1889, the University of New Mexico (UNM) is the state's leading institution of higher education. Its outstanding galleries and museums are open to the public free of charge. The university's predominately Pueblo Revival–style architecture is noteworthy, particularly the beautifully preserved 1938 west wing of Zimmerman Library, and the Alumni Chapel, both designed by John Gaw Meem, a Santa Fe–based architect. Federico Muelas's mesmerizing 2012 "Blue Flower/Flor Azul" artwork, the 900-square-foot LED-and-sound installation on the west end of George Pearl Hall, is best seen at night. Stop at the campus Welcome Center (☎ *505/277–1989* 🌐 *www.unm.edu*) to pick up self-guided campus art and architecture tour maps.

The campus's easterly spread leads directly into the heart of Nob Hill and a quintessential assortment of Route 66 and art deco–influenced buildings. The vintage motels and gas stations with neon signage have housed a shifting landscape of galleries, microbreweries, cafés, upscale furnishing shops, and more.

Restaurants

Flying Star Cafe
$ | **CAFÉ** | A staple in the city, each outpost of this locally owned order-at-the-counter-first café suits its neighborhood (some have patios and allow pets). At the original spot in Nob Hill, the university crowd crunches into a snug space to dig into a mix of creative American and New Mexican dishes (plus several types of wine and beer). **Known for:** late-night dessert; bottomless coffee and Wi-Fi; creative menu with solid basics at heart. *$ Average main: $13 ✉ 3416 Central Ave. SE, Nob Hill ☎ 505/255–6633 🌐 www.flyingstarcafe.com.*

Frenchish
$$$ | **BISTRO** | Innovative, flavorful, fun, and, indeed, French-ish, the renowned culinary team of Nelle Bauer and James Beard award semifinalist Jennifer James shines at this coolly modern spot with a refreshing bistro menu. There's the perfectly turned grilled beef rib eye, but also a winter squash–and–sautéed greens buckwheat crepe, rocket salad (with hazelnuts and pear), a french onion burger (of course), ruby trout filet, their now famous devilish egg, and a very popular carrot dog. **Known for:** twists on French classics; reservations recommended; walk-ins may sit at congenial chef's counter. *$ Average main: $27 ✉ 3509 Central Ave. NE, Nob Hill ☎ 505/433–5911 🌐 www.frenchish.co ⏲ Closed Sun. and Mon. No lunch.*

Frontier Restaurant
$ | **CAFÉ** | **FAMILY** | This definitive student hangout—it's directly across from UNM—is open seven days from 5 am till the wee hours, and hits the spot for inexpensive diner-style American and New Mexican chow. A notch up from a fast-food joint, the chile's good (vegetarian and non), the breakfast burritos are fine (the burgers are, too), and who can resist a hot, melty oversize Frontier sweet roll? **Known for:** hours to suit both early birds and night owls; succulent cinnamon buns; roadside attraction–style decor. *$ Average main: $7 ✉ 2400 Central Ave. SE, at Cornell Dr. SE, University of New Mexico ☎ 505/266–0550 🌐 www.frontierrestaurant.com.*

Uptown and Northeast Heights

In the Northeast Heights you are approaching the foothills of the Sandia Mountains, with upscale neighborhoods that surprise with the sudden appearance of piñon and ponderosa. Trips to this area can easily be combined with more north-central venues. The Uptown area is closer to the center of town, and shopping and restaurants are its main attractions.

Sights

★ Sandia Peak Aerial Tramway
VIEWPOINT | **FAMILY** | One of the world's longest aerial tramways, here tramway cars climb nearly three miles up the steep western face of the Sandias, giving you a dazzling close-up view (whatever the season) of the imposing rock formations and wind-blown wilderness. From the observation deck at the 10,378-foot summit you can see Santa Fe to the northeast and Los Alamos to the northwest: about 11,000 square miles of spectacular scenery. You may also see graceful hawks

or eagles soaring above or mountain lions roaming the cliff sides. An exhibit room at the top surveys the wildlife and landscape of the mountain; a few steps away is **Ten 3,** where a lounge and cliffside dining await. You can also use the tram as a way to reach the Sandia Peak ski and mountain-biking area. **■ TIP→ It's much colder and windier at the summit than at the tram's base, so pack a jacket.** Tram cars leave from the base at regular intervals for the 15-minute ride to the top. Purchase tickets (all round-trip) up to 24 hours ahead online; parking fee is included. ✉ *10 Tramway Loop NE, Far Northeast Heights* ☎ *505/856–7325, 505/856–1532, 505/764–8363 Ten 3 restaurant* 🌐 *www.sandiapeak.com* 🎟 *$25; $3 parking fee.*

East Side and West Side

South of Interstate 40 and the Northeast Heights, the East Side bridges the older and historic parts of Route 66 with pockets of strip-shopping centers (especially along Eubank Boulevard) and some newer development of an upscale nature. Farther west, the fastest-growing part of Albuquerque lies on a broad mesa high above the Rio Grande Valley. The West Side is primarily the domain of new suburban housing developments and strip malls, some designed more attractively than others.

★ Open Space Visitor Center

MUSEUM | FAMILY | Sandhill cranes make their winter home here or stop for a snack en route to the Bosque del Apache, just south in Socorro. Albuquerque is right in their flyway, and the Open Space Center, which is replete with trails heading down to the shores of the Rio Grande, provides a most hospitable setting for them. The outdoor viewing station opens onto the site's expansive field, which faces out to the Sandia Mountains; the hush—aside from the occasional flock circling above—is restorative. Complementing the experience inside are changing art and photography exhibits, an interpretative display on the adjacent 14th- to 15th-century Piedras Marcadas Pueblo ruins, and well-informed guides. A native garden interspersed with mosaics and sculptures fills the patio at the center's entryway; the latter theme is introduced when you make the turn-off from busy Coors Boulevard—Robert Wilson's large-scale public art installation "Flyway" is at the northeast corner as you approach. Ongoing family activities, occasional live music, and educational and other special programming are on tap year-round. ✉ *500 Coors Blvd. NW, West Side* ☎ *505/897–8831* 🌐 *www.cabq.gov/openspace* 🕓 *Closed Sun. and Mon.*

Petroglyph National Monument

ARCHAEOLOGICAL SITE | FAMILY | Beneath the stumps of five extinct volcanoes, this park encompasses more than 25,000 ancient Native American rock drawings inscribed on the 17-mile-long West Mesa escarpment overlooking the Rio Grande Valley. For centuries, Native American hunting parties camped at the base, chipping and scribbling away. Archaeologists believe most of the petroglyphs were carved on the lava formations between 1100 and 1600, but some images at the park may date back as far as 1000 BC. A paved trail at **Boca Negra Canyon** (north of the information center on Unser Boulevard, beyond Montaño Road) leads past several dozen petroglyphs. A tad more remote is the sandy **Piedras Marcadas Canyon** trail, a few miles farther north. The trail at **Rinconada Canyon** (south of the information center on Unser) is unpaved. The rangers at the small information center will supply maps and help you determine which trail is best for the time you have. ✉ *Visitor center, 6001 Unser Blvd. NW, at Western Trail Rd., 3 miles north of I–40 Exit 154, West Side* ☎ *505/899–0205* 🌐 *www.nps.gov/petr* 🎟 *Free; parking $1 for Boca Negra trail, free for the Piedras Marcadas and Rinconada trails.*

Chapter 13

SOUTHEASTERN NEW MEXICO

WITH CARLSBAD CAVERNS

Updated by
Eric Peterson and
Andrew Collins

Sights	Restaurants	Hotels	Shopping	Nightlife
★★★☆☆	★★★☆☆	★★☆☆☆	★★☆☆☆	★★☆☆☆

WELCOME TO SOUTHEASTERN NEW MEXICO

TOP REASONS TO GO

★ **Carlsbad Caverns National Park:** The cave system here includes the largest subterranean chamber in North America (the aptly named Big Room) and hundreds of thousands of bats.

★ **Roswell:** An alleged UFO crash in 1947 is now a big draw for this small city, and the locals have embraced extraterrestrial-driven tourism in a big way.

★ **The Blue Hole:** The crystalline azure waters of this natural pool attracts scuba divers and swimmers from near and far.

★ **Lincoln Historic Site:** Experience the Wild West with this nicely preserved town that's rife with lore about Billy the Kid and other outlaws. Modern visitors can explore a number of historic buildings and museums.

★ **Ski Apache:** With 11 lifts (including a gondola) and 55 trails for all skill levels, this is the premiere ski area in southern New Mexico, centered on the 11,981-foot peak of Sierra Blanca.

1 **Roswell.** The city of about 50,000 is the UFO capital of the Southwest, with a fertile arts scene.

2 **Santa Rosa.** Here you'll find an unlikely scuba-diving destination in the Blue Hole.

3 **Lincoln.** This state-owned historic site encompasses Lincoln, known for the notorious Lincoln County War of the 1870s and 1880s.

4 **Ruidoso.** Nestled in the Sierra Blanca Mountains, Ruidoso is known for world-class horse racing as well as year-round outdoor recreation.

5 **Cloudcroft.** This touristy town is located high above the desert below, making it a place to escape the heat in summer and a skiing destination in winter.

6 **Carlsbad.** The gateway town to Carlsbad Caverns National Park has some unique attractions aboveground as well.

7 **Carlsbad Caverns National Park.** The park includes more than 100 caves, including its namesake Carlsbad Cavern.

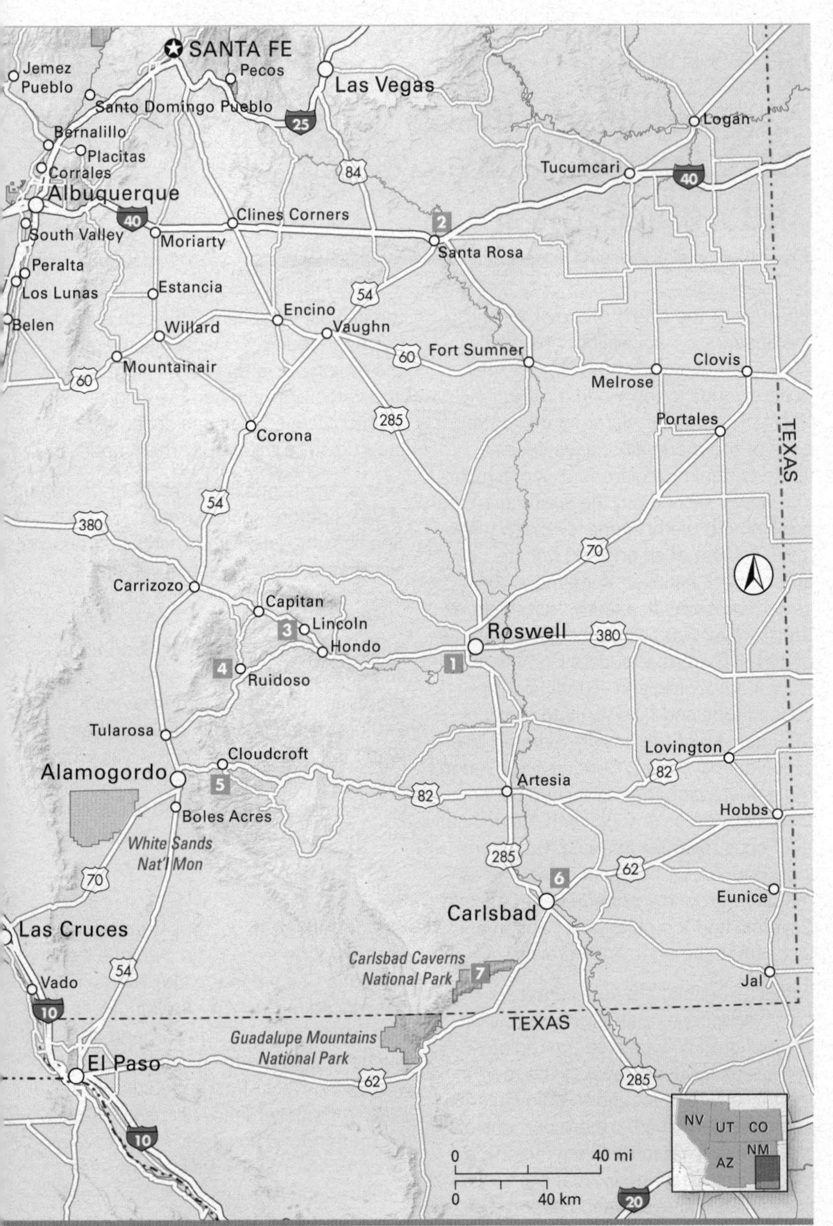
SANTA FE
Jemez Pueblo
Pecos
Las Vegas
Santo Domingo Pueblo
25
Logan
Bernalillo
Placitas
84
Tucumcari
Corrales
40
Albuquerque
40
Clines Corners
2
South Valley
Moriarty
Santa Rosa
Peralta
Estancia
Los Lunas
54
Encino
Belen
Willard
Vaughn
60
Fort Sumner
Clovis
Mountainair
60
Melrose
285
Portales
Corona
TEXAS
54
380
70
Carrizozo
Capitan
3
Lincoln
Roswell
380
Hondo
1
4
Ruidoso
Tularosa
Lovington
Cloudcroft
Alamogordo
82
5
Artesia
82
Hobbs
Boles Acres
White Sands Nat'l Mon
285
62
6
70
Eunice
Carlsbad
Las Cruces
Carlsbad Caverns National Park
7
54
Vado
Jal
10
TEXAS
Guadalupe Mountains National Park
El Paso
62
285
10
NV
UT
CO
NM
AZ
0
40 mi
0
40 km
20

Southeastern New Mexico retains a delicious feeling of wildness. The nearest interstate is generally as far as 200 miles away, and with few lights from strip malls and no urban sprawl, the stargazing here is a treat for the expert and novice alike.

Because of the clarity of the skies and the absence of typical light pollution, Cloudcroft has one of the largest solar observatories in the world, the National Solar Observatory. Alamogordo, at the base of the mountains, uses special lights to minimize glare for optimal night-sky views. Of course, the area's seeming proximity to the heavens is what's made it the subject of an ongoing debate among UFO believers for almost 60 years: what was it, exactly, that fell from the sky over Roswell that night in July of 1947? Drive to Cloudcroft (8,675 feet) from Alamogordo and you will double your altitude and take you into the cool mountain air of the heavily forested Lincoln National Forest. Curious, large-eared mule deer wander amid the juniper and pines, as well as among sand dunes near the Pecos River farther east. The seemingly endless Chihuahuan Desert holds the underground wonderland of Carlsbad Caverns, and the hulking El Capitan peak just across the state line in Texas.

For all its beauty, the area can seem a harsh landscape to strangers. Spanish settlers quickly bypassed the region in the late 1500s, in favor of the more friendly environs around the Rio Grande in the western and northern portions of New Mexico. Yet in this very region—at Black Water Draw near what is now Portales and Clovis—evidence of some of the earliest inhabitants of North America has been found. Artifacts discovered in the region prove that primitive hunters and gatherers lived here as long as 11,000 years ago, alongside fantastic creatures like the woolly mammoth.

Native Americans lived here for hundreds of years before encroachment by the Spanish, and later the Americans. Though Hispanic settlers had established a few scattered communities, the area was primarily the homeland of Mescalero Apaches. In the mid-1800s Fort Sumner and Fort Stanton were erected to offer protection for miners and American settlers during intensified skirmishes with local tribes. Near Ruidoso, in what is left of their traditional homeland in the Sacramento Mountains, the Mescalero Apaches now own a luxury resort and ski area that attract tens of thousands of visitors annually.

The grasslands in southeastern New Mexico came to be ruled by cattle kings like John Chisum in the late 1800s. The baby-faced outlaw Billy the Kid (Henry McCarty) became a living legend here during the infamous Lincoln County War, waged by rival entrepreneurs in 1872. He wasn't the only outlaw to make his mark on the territory, however; in the now-vanished town of Seven Rivers, between Carlsbad and Artesia, shoot-outs were said to be so common around the turn of the 20th century that it was claimed "you could read your newspaper by the light of the gunfire." Things calmed down—a bit—once the discovery of oil and other valuable minerals brought miners to the area in the early 1900s.

Planning

Getting Here and Around

AIR

Southeastern New Mexico has no regular air service. The closest major airports are actually in El Paso and Midland, both in Texas. El Paso is 150 miles from Carlsbad Caverns, while Midland is 160 miles away. The closest airport in New Mexico with commercial service is in Albuquerque, which is 380 miles north of Carlsbad Caverns and 295 miles north of Roswell. In Carlsbad, the Cavern City Air Terminal offers charter service.

CAR

The quality of the roadways in southeastern New Mexico varies widely, particularly in remote rural areas. Drive with caution on the region's narrow highways, which particularly in mountainous areas have no shoulders. On minor roadways, even if paved, be alert for curves, dips, and steep drop-offs. You can rent a car at El Paso International Airport and Albuquerque International Sunport. Some auto dealerships in some southeastern New Mexico cities rent cars. Your best bet for finding car rentals in smaller communities, such as Roswell and Carlsbad, is at municipal airports. Both Enterprise and Budget rent cars at the Roswell airport.

Hotels

You'll find generally reliable chain motels to choose from if that's what suits you, but you can also choose from a luxury resort, numerous quaint cabins, and several charming and beautiful bed-and-breakfasts in the Sacramento Mountains. These private facilities serve some of the tastiest food in the region and can offer amenities like therapeutic massage, horseback riding, and guided fishing and hiking tours.

Restaurants

Leave the fancy duds at home—you're unlikely to find a formal dining room to strut into. Casual dress reigns supreme in this part of the world. Although much of southeastern New Mexico is cowboy country, where thick steaks and barbecue make the meal, good Mexican food can be found, too. Food tends to lean heavily toward the old-fashioned American meat-and-potatoes style—often with the addition of mild chiles. There are a few standout restaurants, and we've noted them.

HOTEL AND RESTAURANT PRICES

Hotel prices in the reviews are the lowest cost of a standard double room in high season. Restaurant prices in the reviews are the average cost of a main course at dinner, or if dinner is not served, at lunch.

What It Costs

	$	$$	$$$	$$$$
RESTAURANTS				
	under $16	$16–$22	$23–$30	over $30
HOTELS				
	under $120	$120–$180	$181–$240	over $240

Roswell

40 miles north of Artesia on U.S. 285; 205 miles southeast of Albuquerque, south on I–25 and east on U.S. 380; 78 miles southwest of Fort Sumner, via NM 20 and U.S. 285.

The true character of Roswell has been largely obscured over the last few decades by the brouhaha over UFOs. Rather than a hotbed of extraterrestrial activity, Roswell is in reality a simple, conservative city with an economy based on manufacturing, agriculture, oil, and gas. The population of around 50,000 grew out of a farming community founded in the fertile Pecos Valley about a century ago; artesian wells still provide the water used to irrigate crops like alfalfa, hay, and cotton. Residents may sigh over the fact that visitors only come here in search of spaceships—but they've also learned to have fun with it, and they are happy to cash in on the tourist trade.

GETTING HERE

You can reach Roswell by heading south from Interstate 40 or north from Interstate 10 (in Texas) on U.S. 285. From Interstate 25, take U.S. 70 at Las Cruces, or U.S. 380 at Carrizozo. Public transport doesn't exist out here. You're best off renting a car at El Paso or Albuquerque.

VISITOR INFORMATION

Roswell Chamber of Commerce
✉ *131 W. 2nd St.* ☎ *575/623–5695, 877/849–7679* 🌐 *www.roswellnm.org.*

Sights

★ Anderson Museum of Contemporary Art
MUSEUM | The Anderson Museum of Contemporary Art, which started as a personal collection evolving from founder late Don Anderson's patronage of artists, since the 1960s has become an important showcase of contemporary art. This 22,000-square-foot, salon-style museum exhibits sculpture, painting, print, and textiles, and it continues to evolve. Among the 500-plus pieces is an impressive collection of the dramatic, large-scale fiberglass sculptures by the late El Paso artist Luis Jiménez. The remarkable and competitive Roswell Artist-in-Residence program, whose participants' work feeds the ongoing collection, is operated by the museum's foundation and provides a home, studio, supplies and a stipend to participating artists. ✉ *409 E. College Blvd.* ☎ *575/623–5600* 🌐 *www.rair.org* 🎟 *Free.*

Bottomless Lakes State Park
BODY OF WATER | FAMILY | The lakes at Bottomless Lakes State Park were created when an ancient sea that covered the area 240 million years ago evaporated, leaving behind salt and gypsum deposits. Those deposits then slowly dissolved with accumulations of rain, and ceilings collapsed into sinkholes. Scuba divers, boaters, and swimmers now take advantage of the crystal-clear, spring-fed water. The main Lea Lake facility has a bathhouse with modern showers and restrooms; paddleboards can be rented from late May to early September. ✉ *545 A Bottomless Lakes Rd.* ✣ *12 miles east of Roswell off U.S. 380, turn south on NM 409 and continue 3 miles* ☎ *575/988–3638* 🌐 *www.emnrd.state.nm.us/SPD/bottomlesslakesstatepark.html* 🎟 *$5 per vehicle.*

Bitter Lake National Wildlife Refuge
NATURE PRESERVE | From the viewing platforms along the 8½-mile self-guided tour at the Bitter Lake National Wildlife Refuge, you can watch for snow geese, sandhill cranes, and other exotic birds, along with more-familiar species. ✉ *4200 E. Pine Lodge Rd., from Roswell, head north on U.S. 285, then turn east on Pine Lodge Rd. for 7 miles* ☎ *575/625–4011* 🌐 *www.fws.gov/refuge/bitter_lake* 🎟 *Free.*

★ International UFO Museum and Research Center

MUSEUM | FAMILY | Depending on your point of view, the International UFO Museum and Research Center will either seem like a display of only-in-America kitsch or a real opportunity to examine UFO documentation and other phenomena involving extraterrestrials. This homespun nonprofit facility is surprisingly low-tech—some of the displays look like they've seen previous duty on B-movie sets (the museum is, coincidentally, inside an old movie house). The blowups of newspaper stories about the 1947 Roswell crash, its fallout, and 1950s UFO mania make interesting reading, and you can view the videotaped recollections of residents who say they saw the crash firsthand. The gift shop sells all manner of souvenirs depicting wide-eyed extraterrestrials, along with books and videos. Though some of the exhibits are whimsical, the portion of the museum devoted to research accumulates serious written collections and investigations of reported UFOs. The city hosts **AlienFest** (🌐 *www.ufofestivalroswell.com* ☎ *575/914–8017*) over the first weekend of July each year. ✉ *114 N. Main St.* ☎ *575/625–9495, 575/625–1907* 🌐 *www.roswellufomuseum.com* 🎟 *$5.*

★ Roswell Museum and Art Center

MUSEUM | The impressive Roswell Museum and Art Center often gets overlooked in favor of alien hoopla, but it contains a very good collection of Southwestern artists, including works by Georgia O'Keeffe, Henriette Wyeth, Peter Hurd, plus early modernist pieces from members of the early Taos and Santa Fe art colonies. The extensive Rogers and Mary Ellen Aston Collection of the American West has displays of Plains Indian artifacts and Spanish armor. Robert H. Goddard's collection exhibits the inventions and journals of the rocketry genius, who conducted some of his early experiments near Roswell. The **Robert H. Goddard Planetarium,** which is part of the museum, is open only occasionally, generally on holiday weekends and for celestial events—call ahead for the schedule. ✉ *Roswell Convention Center, 100 W. 11th St.* ☎ *575/624–6744* 🌐 *www.roswellmuseum.org* 🎟 *$10* 🕒 *Closed Sun.*

Restaurants

Cattle Baron

$$ | STEAKHOUSE | FAMILY | You'll find the standard array of grilled meats and seafood at this centrally located restaurant, which is part of a regional chain. While the food and service is merely adequate, the extensive and fresh salad bar is a relief if you're hankering for a big plate of fresh veggies with lots of toppings and tasty dressings. **Known for:** hearty fare, with an emphasis on beef; reliable eatery with a long history in town; good for families. 💲 *Average main: $19* ✉ *1113 N. Main St.* ☎ *575/622–2465* 🌐 *www.cattlebaron.com.*

El Toro Bravo

$ | MEXICAN | Next to the International UFO Museum and Research Center, this Mexican restaurant achieves a kitschy flair with matador paintings, piñatas, and wrought-iron wall lamps. The kitchen uses family recipes in the preparation of ethnic favorites such as fajitas, enchiladas, tacos, and burritos. **Known for:** spicy red and green chile; tasty Mexican combination plates; hearty fare. 💲 *Average main: $15* ✉ *102 S. Main St.* ☎ *575/622–9280* 🌐 *eltorobravorestaurant.business.site* 🕒 *No dinner Sun.*

Hotels

Hampton Inn & Suites Roswell

$ | HOTEL | FAMILY | This contemporary hotel stands out even among the reliable Hampton Inn chain properties. **Pros:** friendly, professional staff; exceptionally clean rooms; walking distance to several reliable chain restaurants. **Cons:** 2 miles from downtown; no real restaurant

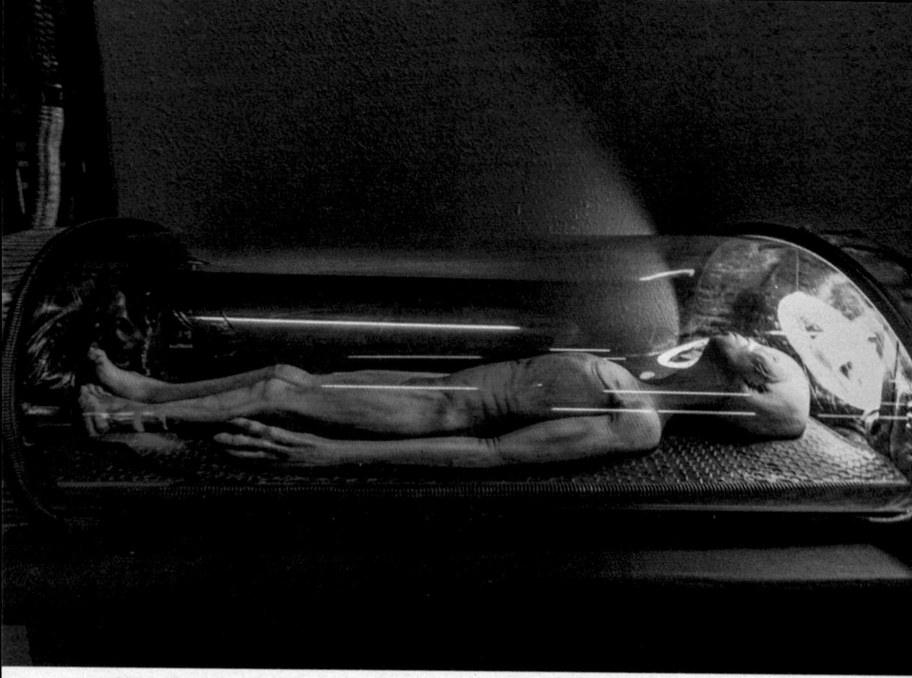

You'll see all manner of UFO-related ephemera and displays (yes, some kitschy) at Roswell's International UFO Museum and Research Center.

on-site; typical chain hotel (though nice). *Rooms from: $102* *3607 N. Main St.* *575/623–5151* *www.roswellsuites.hamptoninn.com* *70 rooms* *Free Breakfast.*

Activities

CAMPING

Lea Lake Campground. At 90 feet deep, this is the only lake in Bottomless Lakes State Park where swimming is allowed. In summer, you can rent paddleboards and paddleboats for a small fee. The lakes stand in stark contrast to the hot, unshaded surroundings, although the campgrounds do have sheltered picnic tables. Rainbow trout are stocked in Devil's Inkwell during the winter months. There are tent sites and sites for RVs with electric hookups, but there's no food service in the park. At $10 per night, rates are very reasonably priced. *Off U.S. 380, 12 miles east of Roswell; turn south on NM 409 and continue 3 miles* *877/664–7787* *www.reserveamerica.com* *32 RV sites, 27 tent sites*

Santa Rosa

32 miles north of Fort Sumner on U.S. 84, at I–40; 117 miles east of Albuquerque on I–40.

A visually charming little town loaded with history, Santa Rosa also has the only body of water in the state—the Blue Hole—where divers can obtain deep water certification. That spot, along with the Pecos River and other natural bodies of water, were created by ancient sinkholes in the bedrock that drew early peoples and animals as far back as the time of woolly mammoths.

GETTING HERE

Santa Rosa is right along Interstate 40, 117 miles east of Albuquerque; it's 133 miles north of Roswell via U.S. 285 and U.S. 54. Like most smaller towns in New Mexico, this isn't a place to point yourself if you don't have a car because public transport just doesn't exist.

VISITOR INFORMATION

Santa Rosa Visitor Information Center
1085 Blue Hole Rd. *575/472–3763* *www.santarosanm.org.*

Sights

★ Blue Hole
BODY OF WATER | FAMILY | About 8,000 diving permits are issued per year for folks who strap on tanks and plunge into the 80-foot-deep artesian spring–fed pool at the Blue Hole, which is also open for public swimming during daylight hours (no fee). Cliff diving is great fun here, as is snorkeling and coming face to face with the many koi and goldfish that have been deposited here over the years.

Stella Salazar runs the **dive shop** (*575/472–3370*) adjacent to the Blue Hole; hours are generally restricted to the weekends, although the pool is open seven days a week. Tanks, air, weight belts, and a few other basics are available there. Weekly dive permits are $20; annual permits are $50. *1085 Blue Hole Rd.* *turn south off Rte. 66 onto Lake Dr.; turn left onto Blue Hole Rd. just past Park Lake* *575/472–3763* *www.santarosabluehole.com* *Free.*

Puerto de Luna
TOWN | Spanish explorer Francisco Vásquez de Coronado is said to have settled the quaint village of Puerto de Luna, 10 miles south of Santa Rosa on NM 91, back in 1541, and the area has been a crossroads of settlers, travelers, and the railroad ever since. The bypassing of Santa Rosa, when Route 66 was replaced by I–40, has clearly impacted the town, although it maintains more vitality and economic activity than many of the towns along the route in this part of the state. There is a real pride among Santa Rosa's residents, and traditions of the town's deep Hispanic roots are still apparent. *Santa Rosa* *10 miles south of Santa Rosa on NM 91.*

Hotels

La Quinta Inn & Suites by Wyndham Santa Rosa
$ | HOTEL | Perched on a high point in Santa Rosa, this motel is a good option for a night or two in town, and the wonderful views of the surrounding Pecos River Valley are a treat. **Pros:** the free breakfast is large and offers lots of choices; great view; helpful staff. **Cons:** not within walking distance of the Blue Hole or the historic Downtown; no dining on-site (other than the included breakfast); split bathrooms (sink section is in the room). *Rooms from: $104* *2277 Historic Rte. 66* *575/339–2826* *www.wyndhamhotels.com* *60 rooms* *Free Breakfast.*

Lincoln

12 miles east of Capitan on U.S. 380; 47 miles west of Roswell on U.S. 70/380 to Hondo, then 10 miles northwest on U.S. 380 to Lincoln.

It may not be as well-known as Tombstone, Arizona, or Deadwood, South Dakota, but Lincoln ranks right up there with the toughest of the tough old towns of the Old West. Mellowing with age, the notorious one-street town has become a National Historic Landmark and a state monument. A single ticket ($5) still grants entry to all attractions (you can purchase the ticket at Historic Lincoln Center, Tunstall Store Museum, or Lincoln County Courthouse Museum).

The violent, gang-style Lincoln County War consumed this region between 1878 and 1881, as two factions, the Tunstall-McSween and the Murphy-Dolan groups, clashed over lucrative government contracts to provide food for the U.S. Army at Fort Stanton and area Native American reservations. The local conflict made national news, and President Hayes ordered Lew Wallace, governor of

New Mexico, to settle the conflict. One of the more infamous figures to emerge from the bloodshed was a short, slight, sallow young man with buckteeth, startling blue eyes, and curly reddish-brown hair called Billy the Kid.

He is said to have killed 21 men (probably an exaggeration), including Lincoln County's sheriff William Brady—for whose murder he was convicted in 1881 and sentenced to hang. Billy managed to elude the gallows. On April 28, 1881, though manacled and shackled, he made a daring escape from the old Lincoln County Courthouse, gunning down two men and receiving cheers from townspeople who supported his group, the Tunstall-McSweens. Three months later a posse led by Sheriff Pat Garrett tracked down Billy at a home in Fort Sumner, surprised him in the dark, and finished him off with two clean shots. One of the West's most notorious gunmen, and ultimately one of its best-known folk legends, was dead at age 21.

GETTING HERE

Getting to Lincoln is part of any sightseeing adventure, as it's a very scenic drive. Take U.S. 380, heading east out of Carrizozo for 32 miles, or heading west 56 miles from Roswell. It's an easy day trip from Ruidoso, via NM 48 or back on U.S. 70 to U.S. 380.

VISITOR INFORMATION

The Historic Lincoln Center, on the eastern end of town, serves as an information center for the Lincoln Historic Site. There's a 12-minute video about Lincoln and exhibits devoted to Billy the Kid, the Lincoln County War, cowboys, Apaches, and Buffalo Soldiers, African-American cavalry troops who earned a sterling reputation as fierce protectors of Western frontiers. The center's guides and attendants dress in period costumes and lead a walking tour through town on the hour, vividly describing each building's role as a setting in the Lincoln County War.

Sights

Dr. Woods House

HOUSE | Now part of Lincoln Historic Site, Dr. Woods House was once occupied by a country doctor specializing in treatments for chest ailments. The doctor's house is filled with pre-1920s furnishings along with books, instruments, and pharmaceutical supplies from his era. ✉ *Main St. (U.S. 380)* ✣ *north side of highway, midway between Historic Lincoln Center and Tunstall Store Museum* 💵 *$5 to access all of the Lincoln historic sites* 🕑 *Closed Tues. and Wed.*

Historic Lincoln Center

The Historic Lincoln Center, on the eastern end of town, serves as an information center for the Lincoln Historic Site. There's a 12-minute video about Lincoln and exhibits devoted to Billy the Kid, the Lincoln County War, cowboys, Apaches, and Buffalo Soldiers, African-American cavalry troops who earned a sterling reputation as fierce protectors of Western frontiers. The center's guides and attendants dress in period costumes and lead a walking tour through town on the hour, vividly describing each building's role as a setting in the Lincoln County War. You can also buy a ticket to access the town's historic sites here. ✉ *Main St. (U.S. 380)* ✣ *far eastern end of Lincoln, on south side of road* ☎ *575/653–4025* 🌐 *www.nmhistoricsites.org.*

Iglesia de San Juan Bautista

RELIGIOUS SITE | When church services, weddings, funerals, and other regularly scheduled functions are not taking place here, Lincoln's historic Iglesia de San Juan Bautista, originally built in 1887, can be viewed free. The tiny church was built and restored entirely from local materials. Roof beams and other wood elements including *latillas* (small branches laid on top of larger, rounded wood beams known as vigas) were dragged by oxcart from the nearby Capitan Mountains. ✉ *Main St. (U.S. 380)* ✣ *south side of highway* *between Montaño Store and Lincoln County Courthouse Museum* 🎫 *Free.*

Lincoln County Courthouse Museum
MUSEUM | FAMILY | The Lincoln County Courthouse Museum is the building from which Billy the Kid made his famous escape. You can walk in the room where Billy was imprisoned and view a hole in the wall that just might have been caused by the gun he fired during his escape. Display cases contain historical documents, including one of Billy's handwritten, eloquent letters to Governor Lew Wallace, defending his reputation. ✉ *Main St. (U.S. 380)* ✣ *far west side of town, south side of highway* 🎫 *$5 to access all of the Lincoln historic sites* ⏲ *Closed Tues. and Wed.*

Montaño Store
HISTORIC SITE | José Montaño ran a saloon and boardinghouse within his Montaño Store for more than 30 years after the Civil War. Governor Lew Wallace stayed here when trying to arrange a meeting with Billy the Kid. Today, displayed writings in both English and Spanish describe the history of the site. ✉ *Main St. (U.S. 380)* ✣ *east end of town, south side of road* 🎫 *$5 to access all of the Lincoln historic sites* ⏲ *Closed Tues. and Wed.*

Torreon
MILITARY SITE | Lincoln was first settled by Spanish settlers in the 1840s. The short, round Torreon fortress served as protection from Apache raids in those days; it came in handy during the Lincoln County War, too. Crews restored it in the 1930s. ✉ *Main St. (US 380)* 🎫 *$5 to access all of the Lincoln historic sites* ⏲ *Closed Tues. and Wed.*

Tunstall Store Museum
MUSEUM | FAMILY | Nothing has changed much at the Tunstall Store Museum since the days of the Old West. When the state of New Mexico purchased the store in 1957, boxes of stock dating from the late 19th and early 20th centuries were discovered here, still unused. The clothes, hardware, butter churns, kerosene lamps, and other items are displayed in the store's original cases. ✉ *Main St. (U.S. 380)* ✣ *about midway through town on north side of road* 🎫 *$5 to access all of the Lincoln historic sites* ⏲ *Closed Tues. and Wed.*

Restaurants

Tinnie Silver Dollar
$$$ | AMERICAN | Just 2 miles east of the U.S. 70 turnoff to Ruidoso is the little town of Tinnie and this real find of a restaurant. With a menu of traditional favorites like chicken-fried steak, rib eye steaks, and salmon meuniere, the food at the Silver Dollar is more than worth the drive, and if you're in need of a place to stay, they have two well-appointed guest suites ($100 per night and up). **Known for:** historic ambience; heart American fare; slick guest suites. 💲 *Average main: $24* ✉ *U.S. 70, 28842 U.S.70* ✣ *17 miles southeast of Lincoln.* ☎ *575/653–4425* 🌐 *www.tinniesilverdollar.com.*

Ruidoso

20 miles west of San Patricio on U.S. 70.

A year-round mountain resort town on the eastern slopes of the pine-covered Sacramento Mountains, Ruidoso retains a certain rustic charm. Shops, antiques stores, bars, and restaurants line its main street, and in winter, skiers flock to nearby Ski Apache. In summer, Ruidoso is a paradise for outdoors lovers and Texans seeking respite from the blazing heat of lower elevations.

The general quality of lodging and dining options in town is very good, and service is friendly and laid-back, as are most patrons. Cuisine tends toward basic American and Americanized Mexican, but a handful of restaurants serve fresher and more updated variations on this theme.

One of the big draws is the annual **All American Cowboy Fest** (🌐 *www.cowboysymposium.org*). Formerly the Lincoln County Cowboy Symposium, this legendary gathering of cowboy poets, musicians, chuckwagon cooks, artists, craftspeople, and—of course—cowboys takes place in late September and early October at Ruidoso Downs racetrack. The three-day event includes the Chuckwagon Competition, in which participants cook Old West–style food in full regalia. Horsemanship skills, blacksmithing, and all sorts of activities for kids are part of this fun weekend. Concerts on Friday and Saturday night are a big hit with people of all ages, and there's a new rodeo on Saturday as well.

GETTING HERE

Whichever direction you're coming from, east or west, Ruidoso is easy to find—and a real pleasure after leaving the heat from the valleys below. From 13 miles north of Alamogordo, in Tularosa, you'll turn east and head up U.S. 70 for 33 miles. From Roswell, head west on U.S. 70/380 for 70 miles, just past the even smaller village of Ruidoso Downs. You then head north NM 48, also called Sudderth Drive, dropping you immediately into Ruidoso.

VISITOR INFORMATION

Ruidoso Valley Chamber & Visitor Center
✉ *720 Sudderth Dr.* ☎ *575/257–7395, 877/784–3676* 🌐 *www.experienceruidoso.com.*

Sights

★ Hubbard Museum of the American West
MUSEUM | FAMILY | The museum, a Smithsonian affiliate, houses the Anne C. Stradling Collection of more than 10,000 artworks and objects related to the horse—paintings, drawings, and bronzes by master artists; saddles from Mexico, China, and the Pony Express; carriages and wagons; a horse-drawn grain thresher; and clothing worn by Native Americans and cowboys. An indoor children's exhibit offers kids the chance to climb and touch an adobe home, a tepee, a wagon, as well as lots of other hands-on activities. ✉ *26301 U.S. 70, Ruidoso Downs* ☎ *575/378–4142* 🎫 *$6.*

Mescalero Apache Reservation
NATIVE SITE | The bordering Ruidoso to the west, is inhabited by more than 3,000 Mescalero Apache, most of whom work for the tribal government or for the tribally owned **Inn of the Mountain Gods,** one of the state's most elegant resorts and a major destination for visitors from all over the country and Mexico. Also on the reservation are a general store, a trading post, and a museum where a 12-minute video about life on the reservation is screened. Regular talks are also given on the history and culture of the Mescalero Apache. There are campsites here (with hook-ups at Silver and Eagle lakes only) and picnic areas. The July 4th weekend dances, which include a rodeo, powwow, and demonstration dances of young women going through puberty rites, are open to the public. ✉ *Tribal Office:, 106 Central Mescalero Ave., off U.S. 70, Mescalero* ☎ *575/671–4494* 🌐 *www.mescaleroapachetribe.com* 🎫 *Free.*

Ruidoso Downs Racetrack & Casino
SPORTS VENUE | The self-proclaimed home of the world's richest quarter-horse race, has a fabulous mountain vista as the setting for cheering the ponies. On Labor Day the track is the site of the All-American Quarter Horse Futurity, with a total purse of as much as $3 million. Revenues from the **Billy the Kid Casino,** which has some 300 slot machines, funds the races. Casino gambling allowed at horse-racing tracks is credited with reviving the sport in New Mexico by attracting quality horses and competition. The casino is decorated with murals suggesting nearby historic Lincoln, where Billy the Kid once hung out. The facility offers year-round, full-card simulcasting from the nation's largest tracks. ✉ *26225 U.S.*

70, Ruidoso Downs ☎ *575/378–4431* 🌐 *www.raceruidoso.com* 🎫 *Racetrack open seating is free, reserved seating $5 and up; Turf Club $10, higher on special weekends.*

Smokey Bear Historical Park

HISTORIC SITE | FAMILY | Capitan is famous as the birthplace and resting place of Smokey Bear, the nation's symbol of wildfire prevention. The original bear concept was created in 1944, and the poster bear is still seen in public service announcements issued by the Ad Council. After a devastating 1950 forest fire in the Capitan Mountains, a bear cub was found badly burned and clinging to a tree. Named Smokey after the poster bear, he lived in the National Zoo in Washington until his death in 1976, when he was returned home for burial. Displays at the Smokey Bear Historical Park visitor center explain forest-fire prevention and fire ecology. A theater with informational films is offered at the 3-acre park, which also contains a picnic area. Capitan's original train depot is adjacent to the museum and gift shop. The site hosts special events for youngsters, such as an Easter egg hunt, Halloween night, and Smokey's Christmas at the Park. ✉ *118 Smokey Bear Blvd., off NM 380, Capitan* ✣ *22 miles north of Ruidoso* ☎ *575/354–2748* 🌐 *www.emnrd.state.nm.us/SFD/SmokeyBear/SmokeyBearPark.html* 🎫 *$2.*

Restaurants

Lincoln County Grill

$ | AMERICAN | This little cabinlike place on a hill is known for quick service and good inexpensive food. Step up to the counter to order hearty Texas chili, old-fashioned hamburgers, or the local favorite green-chile chicken-fried steak. **Known for:** big cinnamon rolls; tasty Mexican food; big burgers. 💲 *Average main: $10* ✉ *2717 Sudderth Dr.* ☎ *575/257–7669* 🌐 *www.lcgrill.com.*

★ **Village Buttery**

$ | AMERICAN | A long-time local favorite for lunch (they're only open from 10:30 until 2:30), the Buttery serves savory soups, creative sandwiches, daily-changing quiches, and delectable desserts. Soups, like the tomato basil or the chunky cream of broccoli, are main-course worthy—add a fresh salad and a slice of buttermilk pie, and you're good to go. **Known for:** closing early (at 2:30 pm); nice outdoor patio; good pies. 💲 *Average main: $9* ✉ *2107 Sudderth Dr.* ☎ *575/257–9251* 🌐 *www.thevillagebuttery.com* ⏲ *Closed Sun. No dinner.*

Coffee and Quick Bites

Sacred Grounds Coffee & Tea House

$ | AMERICAN | Sacred Grounds Coffee & Tea House is a locally owned place with great organic coffee, an impressive variety of exotic teas, plus homemade pastries, muffins, and cookies, a variety of quiches (try the green-chile-chicken), and tasty sandwiches. The space is cozy, but the patio out front is a great spot to enjoy the mountain air. **Known for:** the best coffee; fresh pastries; free Wi-Fi. 💲 *Average main: $8* ✉ *2825 Sudderth* ☎ *575/257–2273* 🌐 *www.sacredgrounds-coffee-and-tea-house.com* ⏲ *Closed Tues. and Wed.*

Hotels

★ **Inn of the Mountain Gods**

$$ | HOTEL | There is nothing run-of-the-mill about this beautifully designed hotel and resort with luxurious rooms and common areas that are decorated with contemporary Southwestern flourishes and nods to the inn's Mescalero Apache ownership. **Pros:** luxury and a great staff; great location with access to outdoor activities; large casino. **Cons:** lingering smell of cigarette smoke in the public areas; if you don't like the casino scene, this is probably not the place for you; service is sometimes unhelpful. 💲 *Rooms* *from: $129 ✉ 287 Carrizo Canyon Rd. ☎ 575/464–7059, 800/545–9011 🌐 www.innofthemountaingods.com ⇆ 273 rooms 🍽 No meals.*

MCM Elegante Lodge and Resort

$$ | HOTEL | This comfortable hotel is next door to a top-rated New Mexico golf course (the Links at Sierra Blanca) and to the Ruidoso Convention Center. **Pros:** a good pick for golfers; extensive facilities: dining, pool, lounge, massage, fitness center; good location. **Cons:** more expensive than some other options; geared towards golfers; a bit cookie-cutter. *$ Rooms from: $139 ✉ 107 Sierra Blanca Dr. ☎ 575/258–5500, 866/211–7727 🌐 www.mcmeleganteruidoso.com ⇆ 117 rooms 🍽 Free Breakfast.*

Ruidoso Lodge Cabins

$ | RENTAL | FAMILY | In the heart of Ruidoso's gorgeous, tree-filled Upper Canyon, owners Judy and Kurt Wilkie oversee a placid retreat of renovated 1920s, knotty-pine abodes. **Pros:** great for families; all cabins nonsmoking; quiet riverside location. **Cons:** no pets allowed; smoking is allowed on cabin porches, so it can drift; property doesn't have an ice machine. *$ Rooms from: $119 ✉ 300 Main St. ✥ take Sudderth Dr. north from U.S. 70 through Downtown Ruidoso; continue west through Upper Canyon, where Sudderth turns into Main St. ☎ 575/257–2510, 800/950–2510 🌐 www.ruidosocabins.com ⇆ 10 cabins 🍽 No meals.*

Shadow Mountain Lodge

$$ | RENTAL | Designed for couples, this lodge in the Upper Canyon has king suites with fireplaces and furnished kitchens in the lodge, and cabins with queen beds, two-person whirlpools, and two-sided fireplaces opening into the living room and bedroom. **Pros:** lodge is within easy walking distance of Downtown restaurants and shops; nicely landscaped grounds; solid in-room amenities. **Cons:** not geared towards families; rooms and cabins are double-occupancy only; minimum stays often required. *$ Rooms from: $125 ✉ 107 Main Rd. ☎ 575/257–4886, 877/361–4103 🌐 www.shadowmountainlodge.com ⇆ 19 suites, 4 cabins.*

Activities

SKIING

Ski Apache

SKIING/SNOWBOARDING | Run by the Mescalero Apaches on 11,981-foot Sierra Blanca, **Ski Apache** has powder skiing for all skill levels on 55 trails and 750 acres. One of Ski Apache's distinctions is its high mountain elevation surrounded by desert. This unique climate can produce heavy snowfall (averaging more than 15 feet each winter) followed by days of pleasant, sunny weather. With the largest lift capacity in New Mexico, this good-sized resort can transport more than 5,000 people hourly. Ski Apache also has the state's only gondola. The season typically runs from Thanksgiving through Easter, and the snowmaking system is able to cover a third of the trails. Lift operations are open daily from 9 to 4; the ski area charges adults $85 to $110 for full-day lift tickets. Slightly higher fees apply for certain dates, including the week between December 26 and January 1, and special weekends in January and February. Snowboarding is allowed on all trails. Although there are no overnight accommodations at the resort, day lodges have cafeterias, snack bars, and outdoor grills. From Ruidoso take NM 48 for 6 miles, and turn west on NM 532 for 12 miles. *✉ 1286 Ski Run Rd. ☎ 575/464–3600, 575/257–9001 snow report 🌐 www.skiapache.com.*

Cloudcroft

19 miles east of Alamogordo on U.S. 82.

Cloudcroft was established in 1898 when the El Paso–Northeastern Railroad crew laid out the route for the Cloud Climbing Railroad. The natural beauty and business possibilities for creating a getaway from the blistering summer heat in the valley below were obvious, and plans were quickly made for a mountaintop resort. You can still see the Mexican Canyon trestle from this era as you drive NM 82 to the west of town. This incredibly steep, twisty, and scenic drive links Cloudcroft to the desert basin below and gains 4,700 feet in elevation during the steepest 16-mile stretch. Be sure to pull off the road and take a look.

One way this little mountain town promotes itself these days is with the slogan "9,000 feet above stress level," and from its perch high above the Tularosa desert valley the town lives up to the claim. Flowers and ponderosa and other greenery give the air an incredible mountain fragrance, and the boardwalks lining the main street, Burro Avenue, lend the town a kitschy Old West atmosphere that's a bit contrived, though still charming. Despite a significant influx of retirees and big-city expats over the past few years, the town has held onto its country friendliness.

There are two festivals that bookend the warm season here, and a number of others in between. Mayfest happens over Memorial Day and Aspencade is held the first weekend of October. The July Jamboree, and a Labor Day weekend fiesta are two more events held, along with street dances and the melodramas that most of the residents seem to participate in. Festivals typically include arts-and-crafts booths and all sorts of calorie-laden munchies.

Cloudcroft has the southernmost ski area in the United States, although it's a very small operation and only open during years when snow is abundant (snowfall is about 120 inches a year on average). It's a nice place for beginner skiers to get their snow legs. Contact the Chamber of Commerce for season info and ticket prices.

It is well worth getting off the boardwalks of the main village and getting into the forest to explore the countless trails and canyons, either on foot or on a mountain bike. There are trails for every level of fitness—don't miss having a hike in the clean, cool mountain air before you head back down to the heat below.

GETTING HERE

Despite its remote-seeming location, Cloudcroft is a fairly short (about 20 miles) drive up the hill from Alamogordo, via U.S. 82. From Artesia, it's 89 miles west on U.S. 82. It's a gorgeous drive from Ruidoso; 10 miles southwest on U.S. 70 then south again for 29 winding, beautiful miles on NM 244.

VISITOR INFORMATION

Cloudcroft Chamber of Commerce
INFO CENTER | ✉ *1001 James Canyon Hwy.* ☎ *575/682–2733* 🌐 *www.coolcloudcroft.com.*

Sights

★ **Bridal Veil Falls and Grand View Trail**
TRAIL | If you have time for just one hike around Cloudcroft, make it this 7.7-mile loop, which takes in a 45-foot waterfall, a restored railroad trestle, and a steep desert landscape that offers a rugged contrast to the dune hikes down at White Sands. The trail is just off scenic U.S. 82 between Alamogordo and Cloudcroft. Farther up the hill in Cloudcroft, at the Mexican Canyon Trestle Overlook, you can get a better look at the old railroad tracks—and impressive wooden trestle—that from 1898 to 1945 carried trains up the canyon and across the chasm. The 32-mile trip from Alamogordo to Cloudcroft entails a dizzying elevation gain of about 4,700 feet. *Moderate.* ✉ *County Rd. A60, off U.S. 82 in High Rolls.*

★ National Solar Observatory–Sacramento Peak

OBSERVATORY | **FAMILY** | The National Solar Observatory–Sacramento Peak, 20 miles south of Cloudcroft on the Sunspot Highway at an elevation of 9,200 feet, is designated for observations of the Sun. The observatory, established in 1947, has four telescopes, including a 329-foot Vacuum Tower that resembles a pyramid. One observation point has a majestic view of White Sands and the Tularosa Basin. During the day you can inspect the telescopes on a self-guided tour and watch live, filtered television views of the Sun. Interactive displays at the visitor center allow you to, among other activities, make infrared fingerprints. The community of Sunspot, home of the observatory, is an actual working community of scientists—not a tourist attraction—so you should stay within areas designated for visitors. ✉ *3010 Coronal Loop, off Sunspot Hwy., Sunspot* ☎ *575/434–7000, 575/434–7190 Visitor Center* 🌐 *nsosp.nso.edu* 🎫 *$5 per vehicle.*

Nelson Canyon Vista Trail

TRAIL | Five miles south of Cloudcroft on Highway 6563, take Forest Road 64 (paved) to Nelson Canyon Vista Trail for a well-marked walking trail with absolutely breathtaking views of White Sands. This ¼-mile walk among the shade of tall trees is made all the more sweet if you've recently spent time down in the blazing summer heat of the Tularosa desert. ✉ *Forest Road 64.*

 Restaurants

★ Big Daddy's Diner

$ | **AMERICAN** | **FAMILY** | You'll catch a whiff of Big Daddy's tasty food as you turn off U.S. 82 into Cloudcroft. There's something for everyone at this homey joint, where the staff seems to know darned near everyone by first name. **Known for:** fun, family-friendly atmosphere; creative takes on classics; local favorite. Ⓢ *Average main: $10* ✉ *1705 James Canyon (U.S. 82)* ☎ *575/682–1224* 🌐 *www.bigdaddysdinercloudcroft.com.*

★ Cloudcroft Brewing Company

$ | **AMERICAN** | Superb wood-fired pizzas and craft beer are the draw at this friendly, rustic brewery with reclaimed-wood walls, high ceilings, and a large side patio. The Zia Pie with chorizo, green chiles, and sharp cheddar is a local favorite, best enjoyed with a pint of Trainwreck IPA. **Known for:** cheerful, social vibe; rotating seasonal taps; pizzas with creative toppings. Ⓢ *Average main: $14* ✉ *1301 Burro Ave.* ☎ *575/682–2337* 🌐 *www.cloudcroftbrewing.com* ⏲ *Closed Tues.*

★ Mad Jack's Mountaintop Barbecue

$ | **BARBECUE** | **FAMILY** | This down-home joint set amid the pine-scented air of Cloudcroft is revered for its Texas-style brisket, which is best enjoyed at the outside picnic tables. The extra-cooked burnt ends get raves from people who know their barbecue, which explains the often long lines snaking around the building, especially on weekends. **Known for:** slow-smoked brisket, pulled pork, and turkey; jalapeño-cheddar sausage; fresh berry cobbler. Ⓢ *Average main: $12* ✉ *105 James Canyon Hwy.* ☎ *575/682–7577* ⏲ *Closed Mon.–Wed. No dinner.*

Western Bar & Cafe

$ | **AMERICAN** | Locals jokingly refer to the regular morning gatherings here as "the old men's club," where all the latest happenings in Cloudcroft are discussed at great length, and sometimes with great passion. Come in as you are (this place is casual personified) and get ready for great big helpings of local favorites such as chicken-fried steak. **Known for:** vintage decor; hearty food; store inside restaurant. Ⓢ *Average main: $12* ✉ *304 Burro Ave.* ☎ *575/682–2445* 🌐 *www.westernbarandcafe.net* 💳 *No credit cards.*

Coffee and Quick Bites

Black Bear Coffee Shop

$ | **CAFÉ** | Serving the best coffee in town, this cozy café is an ideal place to kick off a day of hiking and exploring. Drinks are made with locally roasted beans, and there's a light menu of breakfast pastries, including gluten-free and vegetarian options. **Known for:** lavender lattes; tasty pastries; quick and friendly service. *Average main: $5 200 Burro Ave. 575/682–1239 www.mybbcoffee.com Closed Mon. and Tues. No dinner.*

Hotels

The Cabins at Cloudcroft

$ | **RENTAL** | You can rent these utilitarian, one- to four-bedroom cabins and be in the heart of the forest. **Pros:** woodsy decor that is fitting for the location; close to Ski Cloudcrooft; forested grounds with deer and wildlife. **Cons:** two-night minimum; a bit dated; often booked in advance. *Rooms from: $109 1008 Coyote Ave. 575/682–2396, 800/248–7967 www.cabinsatcloudcroft.com 15 cabins No meals.*

★ **The Lodge Resort and Spa**

$$ | **HOTEL** | Extensive renovations completed in 2021 expanded the size of many rooms and added plush bedding, heated bathroom floors, and other comforts to most of the rooms and suites in this historic—reputedly haunted—Bavarian-style grand dame situated at 9,000 feet in elevation, high in the piney, rarefied air of Cloudcroft. **Pros:** exudes historic charm; full-service spa, outdoor pool, and seasonal 9-hole golf course; atmospheric restaurant. **Cons:** chilly and sometimes closed due to snow in winter; 45-minute drive from White Sands; a bit old-fashioned for some tastes. *Rooms from: $135 601 Corona Pl. 800/395–6343 www.thelodgeresort.com 59 rooms No meals.*

Carlsbad

25 miles north of Carlsbad Caverns National Park, 52 miles north of Guadalupe Mountains National Park.

With a few notable attractions of its own, this small city with about 29,300 residents is part–oil boom town, part–Old West, with a decided Mexican-American accent.

GETTING HERE AND AROUND

Carlsbad lies in the southeastern corner of New Mexico at the junction of U.S. 62 and 180. It's a remote part of the world, and a car is a must for getting around. The nearest good-size cities are El Paso and Lubbock, Texas, both of which are about a 2½-hour drive. It takes about 4½ hours to drive to Albuquerque.

CONTACTS Carlsbad Chamber of Commerce. *302 S. Canal St., Carlsbad 575/887–6516 www.carlsbadchamber.com.*

Sights

Carlsbad Museum and Arts Center

MUSEUM | Pueblo pottery, Native American artifacts, and early cowboy and ranch memorabilia fill this downtown cultural center, along with contemporary art shows and an exhibit on Carlsbad's bats. The real treasure, though, is the McAdoo Collection, with works by painters of the Taos Society of Artists. *418 W. Fox St., Carlsbad 575/887–0276 www.cityofcarlsbadnm.com Closed Sun. and Mon.*

★ **Living Desert Zoo and Gardens State Park**

GARDEN | **FAMILY** | More preserve than traditional zoo, this park contains an impressive collection of plants and animals native to the Chihuahuan Desert. The Desert Arboretum has hundreds of exotic cacti and succulents, and the Living Desert Zoo is home to mountain lions, javelinas, deer, elk, bobcats, bison, and a black bear. Nocturnal exhibits let you view the area's nighttime wildlife, a walk-through aviary houses birds of prey, and there's a reptile exhibit. The park also sponsors some great educational events. Though there are shaded rest areas, restrooms, and water fountains, in summer it's more comfortable to visit in the morning before the desert oven heats up. The expansive view from here is the best in town. ✉ *1504 Miehls Dr. N, Carlsbad* ☎ *575/887–5516* 🌐 *www.livingdesertnm.org* 🎫 *$5.*

Restaurants

Blue House Bakery & Cafe

$ | **BAKERY** | This breakfast nook housed in a charming historic bungalow is a favorite of locals and a treat for travelers weary of so many generic coffee shops. Freshly squeezed juices, inventive breakfast sandwiches, homemade pastries, and arguably the best coffee in town start the day off right. **Known for:** spacious, umbrella-shaded outdoor patio; gooey cinnamon rolls; breakfast croissants filled with sausage, potatoes, and green chile. 💲 *Average main: $7* ✉ *609 N. Canyon St., Carlsbad* ☎ *575/628–0555* 🕑 *Closed Sun. No dinner.*

Carniceria San Juan de Los Lagos

$ | **MEXICAN** | Equal parts butcher, bakery, and short-order restaurant, this spacious and colorfully decorated compound turns out some of the most authentic Mexican food in this corner of the state, from burritos and tacos to *chicharrón*. There's a long menu, and although alcohol isn't available, there is a selection of Mexican soft drinks and sweets. **Known for:** carnitas-stuffed tacos and tortas; breakfast burritos; traditional house-baked Mexican pastries. 💲 *Average main: $9* ✉ *1200 N. Pate St., Carlsbad* ☎ *575/887–0034.*

Lucky Bull

$$ | **SOUTHWESTERN** | Set inside the city's historic former city hall, this casual tavern serves tasty pub grub, including roasted green chile queso blanco, mammoth burgers with a range of interesting toppings, and hand-cut rib-eye steaks. An upstairs tap room carries a fine selection of craft beers, with an emphasis on New Mexico brewers. **Known for:** Pecos Valley poutine (fries topped with green chile gravy and cheddar); country-fried steak; impressive craft-beer selection. 💲 *Average main: $17* ✉ *220 W. Fox St., Carlsbad* ☎ *575/725–5444* 🌐 *www.luckybullcarlsbad.com* 🕑 *Closed Sun.*

★ Red Chimney Pit Bar-B-Q

$ | **BARBECUE** | **FAMILY** | If you hanker for sweet-and-tangy pecan wood–smoked barbecue, this homey, log-cabin-style spot serves up consistently tasty fare at reasonable prices. Sauce from an old family recipe is slathered on chicken, pork, beef brisket, turkey, and ham. **Known for:** sides of smoked mac-and-cheese and seasoned corn; charbroiled burgers; spicy jalapeño sausage. 💲 *Average main: $14* ✉ *817 N. Canal St., Carlsbad* ☎ *575/885–8744* 🌐 *www.redchimneybbq.com* 🕑 *Closed Sun. and Mon.*

★ Trinity Hotel

$$ | **ITALIAN** | The region's top pick for a romantic, elegant meal, this handsome dining room with vaulted ceilings, tall windows, and a long old-fashioned bar is set inside the beautifully restored 1892 Trinity Hotel. The kitchen turns out hearty and flavorful Italian fare, from traditional pastas to halibut with lemon-caper sauce, and a signature dish, chicken bolloco—essentially fettuccine Alfredo with fresh green chilies added. **Known for:** local goat cheese with blackberries and habañero sauce; an excellent selection of acclaimed New Mexico wines; biscuits and gravy at brunch. 💲 *Average main: $18* ✉ *201 S. Canal St., Carlsbad* ☎ *575/234–9891* 🌐 *www.thetrinityhotel.com.*

YellowBrix

$$ | **MODERN AMERICAN** | This attractive restaurant set in a former 1920s home has several different dining rooms as well as a breezy courtyard patio where local acoustic musicians sometimes perform. The kitchen serves eclectic fare with sophisticated flourishes, including poached-pear salads, sashimi tuna with a

spicy wasabi-soy sauce, pressed Cuban sandwiches, and an extensive selection of steaks. **Known for:** Brix bacon-wrapped meat loaf; friendly and efficient service; chocolate lava cake. *Average main: $22 ✉ 201 N. Canal St., Carlsbad ☎ 575/941–2749 ⊕ www.yellowbrixrestaurant.com.*

Hotels

Hampton Inn and Suites
$$ | **HOTEL** | On the south side of downtown leading to the Carlsbad Caverns, this well-maintained chain property lies within walking distance of a few restaurants, a gas station, and a Walmart. **Pros:** friendly staff; clean, well-kept amenities; convenient location. **Cons:** thin walls; cookie-cutter decor; on a busy road. *Rooms from: $160 ✉ 120 Esperanza Circle, Carlsbad ☎ 575/725–5700 ⊕ www.hilton.com 85 rooms Free Breakfast.*

Hyatt House Carlsbad
$$$ | **HOTEL** | This sleek, contemporary newcomer to Carlsbad's growing hotel scene has smartly appointed rooms, some with kitchens, and all furnished with large flat-screen TVs, individual climate control, laptop safes, and blackout curtains. **Pros:** stylish, contemporary design; pool and well-equipped gym; decent bar and restaurant on-site; good base for exploring Carlsbad Caverns. **Cons:** not much in the way of local ambience; on a busy road. *Rooms from: $189 ✉ 4019 National Parks Hwy., Carlsbad ☎ 575/689–6700 ⊕ www.hyatt.com 97 rooms Free Breakfast.*

TownePlace Suites by Marriott Carlsbad
$$$$ | **HOTEL** | **FAMILY** | This attractive, contemporary outpost of Marriott's extended-stay-oriented TownPlace Suites brand has large and nicely equipped accommodations. **Pros:** convenient location; smartly designed rooms; in-room kitchens. **Cons:** it looks like any other TownePlace Suites property; can be very expensive when demand soars; on a busy road. *Rooms from: $309 ✉ 311 Pompa St., Carlsbad ☎ 575/689–8850 ⊕ www.marriott.com 94 rooms Free Breakfast.*

★ **Trinity Hotel**
$$ | **B&B/INN** | The region's most elegant and atmospheric lodging option occupies a graceful 1892 redbrick former bank building with nine luxuriously appointed rooms with high ceilings, plush beds with pillow-top mattresses, hidden flat-screen TVs, and spacious bathrooms with glass walk-in showers. **Pros:** steps from several good restaurants; reasonable rates; terrific bar and restaurant. **Cons:** no elevator; no interior access to the lobby; no pets allowed. *Rooms from: $159 ✉ 201 S. Canal St., Carlsbad ☎ 575/234–9891 ⊕ www.thetrinityhotel.com 9 rooms Free Breakfast.*

Nightlife

★ **Milton's Taproom and Brewery**
BREWPUBS/BEER GARDENS | This first-rate downtown craft brewery has rapidly become one of the top beer makers in southern New Mexico. There's often live music. *✉ 213 W. Mermod St., Carlsbad ☎ 575/725–5779 ⊕ www.miltonsbrewing.com.*

Carlsbad Caverns National Park

25 miles south of Carlsbad, 146 miles southeast of Cloudcroft, 96 miles south of Roswell.

On the surface, Carlsbad Caverns National Park looks deceptively like the rest of southeastern New Mexico's high desert—but all bets are off once visitors set foot in the elevator, which plunges 75 stories underground into a massive cavern, part of a network of formations located within a massive reef that formed 265 million years ago when this area was covered by a vast inland sea.

Indeed, Carlsbad Caverns offers a pretty remarkable illustration of the adage "there's more than meets the eye." Wherever you go within the park's 46,766 acres, whether driving or hiking aboveground or touring subterranean areas open to visitors, it's impossible to fully grasp the sheer wonder and immensity of the area's unique geology. You'll never see more than a tiny fraction of the park from any given vantage point.

Carlsbad Cavern, whose 14-acre Big Room is the park's definitive must-see attraction, and one that you'll want to set aside at least three hours to explore. This eerie world beneath the surface is part silky darkness, part subterranean hallucination—its hundreds of formations alternately resemble cakes, ocean waves, and the face of a mountain troll. Explorer Jim White began exploring the caves in the 1890s, and in 1930 both the main cavern and a vast tract of aboveground canyons and mesas were designated Carlsbad Caverns National Park.

Remarkably, the main Carlsbad Cavern is but one of more than 110 limestone caves that have been identified within the park's boundaries. Most of them, including the largest and deepest (at 1,604 feet belowground), Lechuguilla, aren't open to the general public. Scientists only discovered Lechuguilla's huge network of rooms in 1986. So far they've mapped more than 145 miles of passages—and their work continues.

If you spend most of your first visit to the park exploring its subterranean caverns, you may be surprised to learn how much terrain there is to cover aboveground. Hikers can trek for miles across cactus-studded ridges and through wildlife-rich canyons—there's even a lush little oasis of cottonwood trees, Rattlesnake Springs, in the park's western section, which you reach by taking an entirely different road into the park.

GETTING HERE AND AROUND

The nearest full-service airports are in the Texas cities of El Paso (150 miles away) and Midland (160 miles away). Cavern City Air Terminal, between Carlsbad and the park, is served by a small regional carrier, Boutique Air, with regularly scheduled service to both Albuquerque and Dallas/Fort Worth.

The park entrance is 21 miles southwest of Carlsbad, New Mexico, and 32 miles north of Guadalupe Mountains National Park via U.S. 62/180. The ascending 7-mile Carlsbad Cavern Highway from the turnoff at Whites City (which has a gas station) is paved with pull-outs that allow scenic vistas. Be alert for wildlife crossing roadways, especially in the early morning and at night.

PARK ESSENTIALS

ACCESSIBILITY

Though the park covers a huge expanse aboveground (with key areas reached by paved roads), most of the parts you'll want to see are below the surface. Trails through the most-visited portion of the main cavern are paved and well maintained, and portions of the paved Big Room trail in Carlsbad Cavern is accessible to wheelchairs. Individuals who have difficulty walking should access the Big Room via elevator. Strollers are not permitted on any trails.

PARK FEES AND PERMITS

No fee is charged to enter the aboveground portion of the park. It costs $15 to descend into Carlsbad Caverns either by elevator or through the Natural Entrance (admission is free for kids 15 and under). Costs for guided tours of other parts of the main cavern or the other cavern in the park, Slaughter Canyon Cave, range from $7 to $20 plus general admission. For guided-tour reservations go to 🌐 *www.recreation.gov* or call ☎ *877/444–6777*.

Those planning overnight hikes must obtain a free backcountry permit, and all hikers are advised to stop at the visitor center information desk for trail and park road conditions. Trails are marked by cairns (rock piles) and in some places can be tricky to follow; download or carry a good topographic map. Dogs are not allowed in the park, but a kennel is available at the park visitor center for a fee.

PARK HOURS
The park is open year-round, except Christmas Day, New Year's Day, and Thanksgiving. From Memorial Day weekend through Labor Day, access to the cavern is from 8:30 to 5; entrance tickets are sold until 4:45, with the last entry via the Natural Entrance at 4. After Labor Day until Memorial Day weekend, cavern access is from 8:30 to 3:30; entrance tickets are sold until 3:15, and the last entry via the Natural Entrance is at 2:30. Last-ticket times do sometimes change throughout the year due to maintenance and other causes—always confirm hours on the website before you arrive. Carlsbad Caverns is in the mountain time zone.

TOURS
Carlsbad Caverns is famous for the beauty and breadth of its inky depths, as well as for the accessibility of some of its largest caves. All cave tours, except for the self-guided Natural Entrance and Big Room, are ranger-led, so you can count on a safe experience, even in remote caves. Depending on the difficulty of your cave selection (the Hall of the White Giant cavern is hardest to navigate), you'll need sturdy pants, hiking boots with ankle support, and some water. The fee for the Natural Entrance and Big Room is $15 and is good for three days. Guided tours have an additional fee of $7 to $20.

VISITOR INFORMATION
CONTACTS Carlsbad Caverns National Park. ✉ *Park Visitor Center, 727 Carlsbad Caverns Hwy., Carlsbad* ☎ *575/785–2232, 575/875–3012 bat flight schedule* 🌐 *www.nps.gov/cave.*

Carlsbad Cavern Aboveground

7 miles west of White City, 25 miles southwest of Carlsbad.

The eastern half of Carlsbad Caverns National Park, reached from U.S. 62/180 at Whites City via Carlsbad Caverns Highway, is where you'll find most of the key attractions, including the visitor center, which sits directly above the main cavern for which the park is named. This section of the park also contains several worthwhile hiking trails, some accessed from the visitor center and others from Walnut Canyon Desert Drive, a scenic unpaved loop road with several overlooks.

SCENIC DRIVES
Walnut Canyon Desert Drive
SCENIC DRIVE | This scenic drive (labeled as Reef Top Cir. on some maps) begins a ½ mile from the visitor center and travels 9½ miles along the top of a ridge to the edge of Rattlesnake Canyon—which you can access via a marked trail—and sinks back down through upper Walnut Canyon to the main entrance road. The backcountry scenery on this one-way gravel loop is stunning; go late in the afternoon or early in the morning to enjoy the full spectrum of changing light and dancing colors. Along the way, you'll see Big Hill Seep's trickling water, the tall, flowing ridges of the Guadalupe mountain range, and maybe even some robust mule deer. The scenic road is not for RVs or trailers. ✉ *Off Carlsbad Caverns Hwy., Carlsbad Caverns National Park* ✣ *Just before entrance to visitor center parking lot.*

SCENIC STOPS
Bat Flight
CAVE | The 400,000-member Brazilian free-tailed bat colony here snatches up 3 tons of bugs a night. Watch them leave at dusk from the park amphitheater at

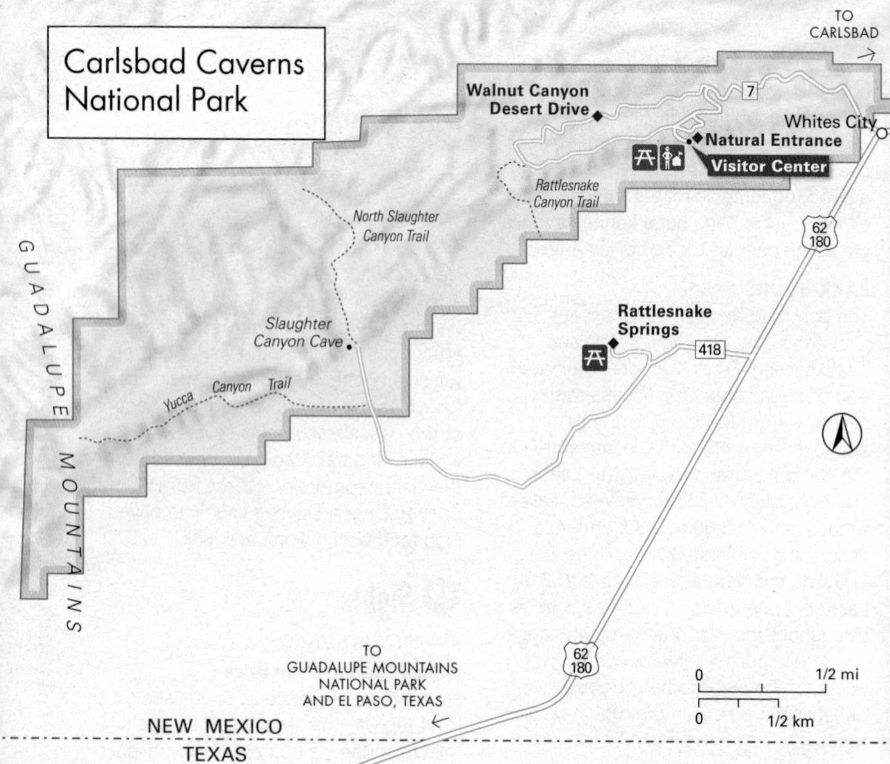

the Natural Entrance, where a ranger discusses these intriguing creatures. The bats aren't on any predictable schedule, so times can be a little iffy. Ideally, viewers will first hear the bats preparing to exit, followed by a vortex of black specks swirling out of the cave mouth in search of dinner against the darkening sky. When conditions are favorable, hundreds of thousands of bats will soar off over the span of half an hour or longer. ✉ *727 Carlsbad Caverns Hwy., Carlsbad Caverns National Park.*

TRAILS

Chihuahuan Desert Nature Trail

TRAIL | **FAMILY** | While waiting for the evening bat-flight program, take this ½-mile self-guided loop hike that begins just east of the visitor center. The tagged and identified flowers and plants make this a good place to get acquainted with local desert flora. Part of the trail is an easy stroll even for the littlest ones, and part is wheelchair accessible. The payoff is great for everyone, too: a sweeping, vivid view of the desert basin. *Easy.* ✉ *Carlsbad Caverns National Park* ✣ *Trailhead: Just east of visitor center.*

Old Guano Road Trail

TRAIL | Meandering a little more than 3½ miles one-way on steadily descending terrain (elevation gain is about 750 feet), the trail dips sharply toward its end at Whites City campground. Give yourself two to three hours to complete the walk. The high desert sun can make this hike a bit taxing any time of year, especially in summer. *Moderate.* ✉ *Carlsbad Caverns National Park* ✣ *Trailhead: Bat Flight Amphitheater.*

★ **Rattlesnake Canyon Trail**

TRAIL | Small cairns guide you along this picturesque trail, which winds 600 feet into the canyon—it's especially lush with greenery from spring through fall. Allow half a day to trek down into the canyon and make the somewhat strenuous climb out; the total trip is about 6 miles. For a look into the canyon, you can make the ¼-mile stroll to an overlook. *Moderate.* ✉ *Carlsbad Caverns National Park* ✣ *Trailhead: Interpretive marker 9, Walnut Canyon Desert Dr.*

VISITOR CENTERS

★ **Carlsbad Caverns Visitor Center**

INFO CENTER | **FAMILY** | Within this spacious, modern facility at the top of an escarpment, a 75-seat theater offers engrossing films and ranger programs about the different types of caves. Exhibits offer a primer on bats, geology, wildlife, and the early tribes and settlers who once lived in and passed through the area. There's also an excellent exhibit on Lechuguilla, the country's deepest limestone cave, which scientists began mapping in 1986 and have located some 145 miles (it's on the park's northern border and isn't open to the general public). Friendly rangers staff an information desk, where maps are distributed and cavern tickets are sold. There's also an extensive gift shop and bookstore, and restaurant. ✉ *727 Carlsbad Caverns Hwy., Carlsbad Caverns National Park* ☎ *575/785–2232* 🌐 *www.nps.gov/cave.*

Carlsbad Caverns Restaurant

$ | **AMERICAN** | This comfy, cafeteria-style restaurant in the visitor center serves basic food—hamburgers, sandwiches, some Mexican dishes—and is fine in a pinch. There are also packaged takeout items. **Known for:** close proximity to the main cavern; no alcohol; takeout options. Ⓢ *Average main: $9* ✉ *727 Carlsbad Caverns Hwy., Carlsbad Caverns National Park* ☎ *575/785–2281* 🌐 *www.carlsbadcavernstradingco.com* ⏲ *No dinner.*

Whites City Cavern Inn

$ | **HOTEL** | This bland but economical two-story motel just outside the entrance to the national park has spacious rooms that have recently undergone a remodel. **Pros:** closest lodging to Carlsbad Caverns; water park is a welcome splash in summer; cheap rates. **Cons:** rooms and service are very bare-bones; often books well ahead, especially on summer weekends; few dining options nearby. Ⓢ *Rooms from: $91* ✉ *6 Carlsbad Caverns Hwy., Whites City* ☎ *575/361–2687* 🌐 *www.whitescitynm.com* *60 rooms* *Free Breakfast.*

Carlsbad Cavern Belowground

Directly beneath Carlsbad Caverns Visitor Center.

With a floor space equal to about 14 football fields, this subterranean focal point of Carlsbad Cavern clues visitors in to just how large the cavern really is. The White House could fit in one corner of the Big Room, and wouldn't come close to grazing the 230-foot ceiling. Once you buy a $15 ticket at the visitor center, you can enter the cavern by elevator or through the Natural Entrance via a 1¼-mile descending trail. Either way, at 750 feet below the surface you will connect with the self-guided 1¼-mile Big Room loop. Even in summer, long pants and long-sleeved shirts are advised for cave temperatures in the mid-50s. The main cavern also accesses the King's Palace, Left Hand Tunnel, and Hall of the White Giant caves, which can be visited only by guided tour (these all depart from the visitor center). As of this writing, tentative plans are underway to renovate and redesign some of the cavern's trails. These projects may result in the temporary closure of some portions of the cavern; check the park website for the latest advisories.

The Big Room is a limestone chamber in Carlsbad Caverns.

Sights

GEOLOGICAL SITES

★ The Big Room

CAVE | FAMILY | A relatively level (it has some steps), paved pathway leads through these almost hallucinatory wonders of various formations and decorations. Exhibits and signage also provide a layman's lesson on how the cavern was carved (for even more details, rent an audio guide from the visitor center for $5). ✉ *Visitor Center, Carlsbad Caverns National Park* 🎫 *$15.*

Hall of the White Giant

SPELUNKING | Plan to squirm—and even crawl on your belly—through some tight passages for long distances to access a very remote chamber, where you'll see towering, glistening white formations that explain the name. This strenuous, ranger-led tour lasts about four hours. Steep climbs and sharp drop-offs might elate you—or make you queasy. Wear sturdy hiking shoes. No kids under 12. ✉ *Carlsbad Caverns National Park* ☎ *877/444–6777 reservations* 🌐 *www.recreation.gov* 🎫 *$20* ✍ *Reservations essential.*

★ King's Palace

SPELUNKING | FAMILY | Throughout this regal room, stunningly handsome and indeed fit for a king, you'll see leggy "soda straws" large enough for a giant to sip, plus bizarre formations that defy reality. The tour also winds through the Queen's Chamber, dressed in ladylike, multitiered curtains of stone. The mile-long walk is on a paved trail, but there's one steep hill toward the end. This ranger-guided tour lasts about 1½ hours and gives you a "look" at the natural essence of a cave—a complete blackout, when artificial lights (and sound) are extinguished. While advance reservations are highly recommended, this is the one tour you might be able to sign up for on the spot. Children younger than four aren't permitted. ✉ *Carlsbad Caverns National Park* ☎ *877/444–6777 reservations* 🌐 *www.recreation.gov* 🎫 *$8.*

Left Hand Tunnel

SPELUNKING | FAMILY | Lantern light illuminates the easy ½-mile walk on this detour in the main Carlsbad Cavern, which leads to Permian Age fossils—indicating that these caves were hollowed from the Permian Reef that still underlies the Guadalupe Mountain range above. The guided tour over a packed dirt trail lasts about two hours. It's a moderate trek that older kids can easily negotiate, but children under six aren't allowed. ✉ *Carlsbad Caverns National Park* ☎ *877/444–6777 reservations* 🌐 *www.recreation.gov* 🎟 *$7.*

Lower Cave

SPELUNKING | Fifty-foot vertical ladders and a dirt path lead you into undeveloped portions of Carlsbad Cavern. It takes about three hours to negotiate this moderately strenuous side trip led by a knowledgeable ranger. No children under 12. ✉ *Carlsbad Caverns National Park* ☎ *877/444–6777 reservations* 🌐 *www.recreation.gov* 🎟 *$20* ✍ *Reservations essential.*

★ **Natural Entrance**

CAVE | FAMILY | As natural daylight recedes, a self-guided, paved trail twists and turns downward from the yawning mouth of the main cavern, about 100 yards east of the visitor center. The route is winding and sometimes slick from water seepage aboveground. A steep descent of about 750 feet, much of it secured by hand rails, takes you about a mile through the main corridor and past dramatic features such as the Bat Cave and the Boneyard. (Despite its eerie name, the formations here don't look much like femurs and fibulae; they're more like spongy bone insides.) Iceberg Rock is a massive boulder that dropped from the cave ceiling millennia ago. After about a mile, you'll link up underground with the Big Room Trail and can return to the surface via elevator or by hiking back out. Footware with a good grip is recommended. ✉ *727 Carlsbad Cavern Hwy., Carlsbad Caverns National Park* 🎟 *$15.*

Restaurants

Underground Lunchroom

$ | FAST FOOD | At 750 feet underground, near the elevator and entrance to the Big Room, you can grab a snack, soft drink, or club sandwich at this handy snack bar. Service is quick, even when there's a crowd, and although the food doesn't stand out, it's fun dining in this otherworldly setting. **Known for:** unusual cavern setting; quick service; convenience. 💲 *Average main: $7* ✉ *727 Carlsbad Caverns Hwy., Carlsbad Caverns National Park* ☎ *575/785–2232* 🌐 *www.carlsbadcavernstradingco.com* ⏲ *No dinner.*

Rattlesnake Springs and Slaughter Canyon

16 miles south of Carlsbad Caverns Visitor Center, 29 miles southwest of Carlsbad.

Accessed from U.S. 62/180 via Highway 418, the secluded western half of the park contains a handful of notable wilderness features, including the lush and small Rattlesnake Springs area and the visually striking Slaughter Canyon, which contains some terrific hiking trails and a popular but challenging cave accessible only by guided tour. Enormous cottonwood trees shade Rattlesnake Springs, a cool, tranquil oasis near the Black River. The rare desert wetland harbors butterflies, mammals, and reptiles, as well as 90% of the park's 357 bird species. This oasis also has a shaded picnic area, potable water, and permanent toilets, but camping and overnight parking are not allowed.

Sights

GEOLOGICAL SITES

Slaughter Canyon Cave

CAVE | Discovered in the 1930s by a local goatherd, this cave is one of the most popular secondary sites in the park, about a 40-minute drive southwest of the visitor center (you'll follow a ranger in your own vehicle to get there). Both the hike to the cave mouth and the tour will take about half a day, but it's worth it to view the deep cavern darkness as it's penetrated only by flashlights and sometimes headlamps. From the Slaughter Canyon parking area, it takes about 45 minutes to make the steep ½-mile climb up a trail leading to the mouth of the cave. You'll find that the cave consists primarily of a single corridor, 1,140 feet long, with numerous side passages.

You can take some worthwhile pictures of this cave. Wear hiking shoes with ankle support, and carry plenty of water. No kids under eight. It's a great adventure if you're in shape and love caving. ✉ *End of Hwy. 418, Carlsbad Caverns National Park* ☎ *877/444–6777 reservations* 🌐 *www.recreation.gov* 🎫 *$15* ✍ *Reservations essential.*

SCENIC SPOTS

★ Rattlesnake Springs

NATURE PRESERVE | **FAMILY** | Enormous old-growth cottonwood trees shade the recreation area at this cool, secluded oasis near Black River. The rare desert wetland harbors butterflies, mammals, and reptiles, as well as 90% of the park's 357 bird species. Because southern New Mexico is in the northernmost region of the Chihuahuan Desert, you're likely to see birds largely unseen anywhere else in the United States outside extreme southern Texas and Arizona. If you see a flash of crimson, you might have spotted a vermilion flycatcher. Wild turkeys also flap around this oasis. Don't let the name scare you; there may be rattlesnakes here, but no more than at any similar site in the Southwest. Restroom facilities are available, but camping and overnight parking are not allowed. ✉ *Hwy. 418, Carlsbad Caverns National Park* ✣ *8½ miles southwest of Whites City.*

TRAILS

Slaughter Canyon Trail

TRAIL | Beginning at the Slaughter Canyon Cave parking lot (four-wheel-drive or high-clearance vehicles are recommended; check with visitor center for road conditions before setting out), the trail traverses a heavily vegetated canyon bottom into a remote part of the park. As you begin hiking, look off to the east (to your right) to see the dun-colored ridges and wrinkles of the Elephant Back formation, the first of many dramatic limestone formations visible from the trail. The route travels 5½ miles one-way, the last 3 miles steeply climbing onto a limestone ridge escarpment. Allow a full day for the round-trip, and prepare for an elevation gain of 1,850 feet. *Difficult.* ✉ *Carlsbad Caverns National Park* ✣ *Trailhead: At Slaughter Canyon Cave parking lot, Hwy. 418, 10 miles west of U.S. 62/180.*

Chapter 14

SOUTHWESTERN NEW MEXICO

WITH WHITE SANDS NATIONAL PARK

Updated by
Eric Peterson and
Andrew Collins

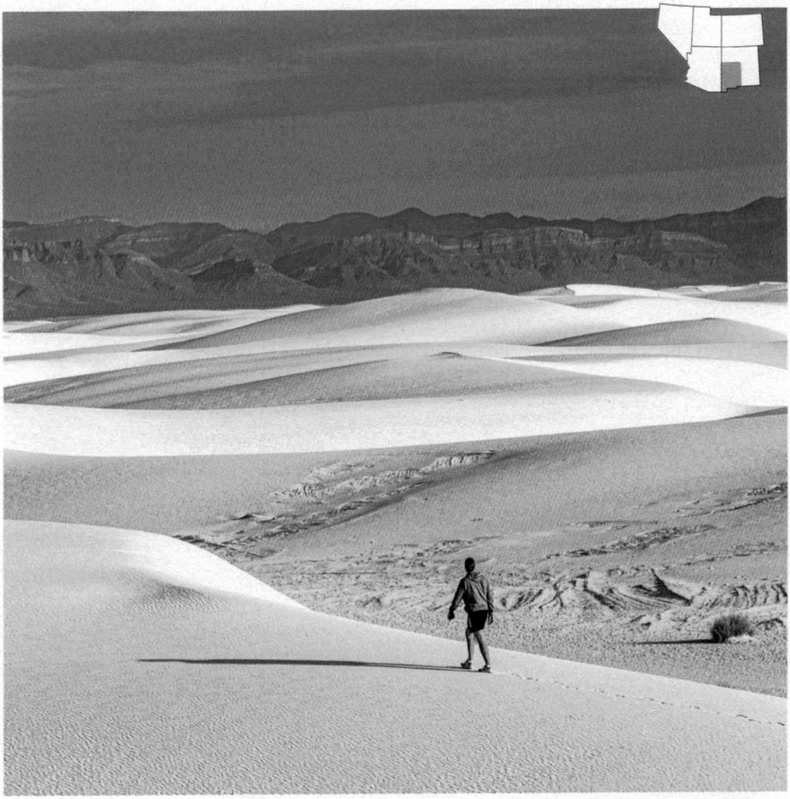

Sights	Restaurants	Hotels	Shopping	Nightlife
★★★☆☆	★★★★☆	★★★☆☆	★★☆☆☆	★★☆☆☆

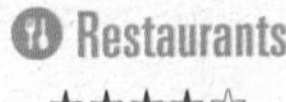

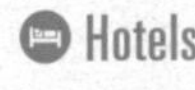

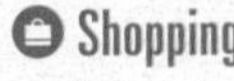

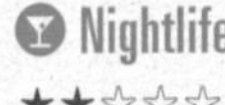

WELCOME TO SOUTHWESTERN NEW MEXICO

TOP REASONS TO GO

★ **Explore the Gila Wilderness:** The oldest official wilderness area in the U.S. (and one of the largest) has endless trails to hike, and remains a bit undiscovered.

★ **Visit White Sands National Park:** One of the newest national parks in the system is centered on iconic gypsum sand dunes in a desert wilderness.

★ **See the plaza at Old Mesilla:** The historic stage stop just outside Las Cruces features a lively landscape of shops and eateries on its historic plaza.

★ **Revisit the Old West:** Silver City is firmly entrenched in Western lore as the hometown of Billy the Kid, and the area has a rich history.

★ **Visit the Very Large Array:** The massive facility, with 27 glistening-white 80-foot radio-telescopes, is an epicenter for space research.

1 **U.S. 60 Corridor.** Pass through tiny hamlets and interesting scenery all the way to Arizona.

2 **Hatch.** Hatch is synonymous with the chile peppers that bear its name and which are used to make spicy dishes throughout the Southwest.

3 **Alamogordo.** This military-driven city of about 30,000 provides a good base for exploring the area.

4 **White Sands National Park.** The 275-square-mile park protects the biggest gypsum dunefield on Earth.

5 **Las Cruces.** This booming college town sits just northwest of the Texas–New Mexico state line, offering history, hiking, and other lures.

6 **Old Mesilla.** Just two miles from Las Cruces, Mesilla Plaza is one of the best-preserved sites of its kind in the Southwest.

7 **Silver City.** The historic town, rife with stories of the Wild West, offers a great jumping-off point to the surrounding great outdoors.

8 **Gila National Forest.** The forest is home to the Gila Wilderness, the first official wilderness area in the U.S.

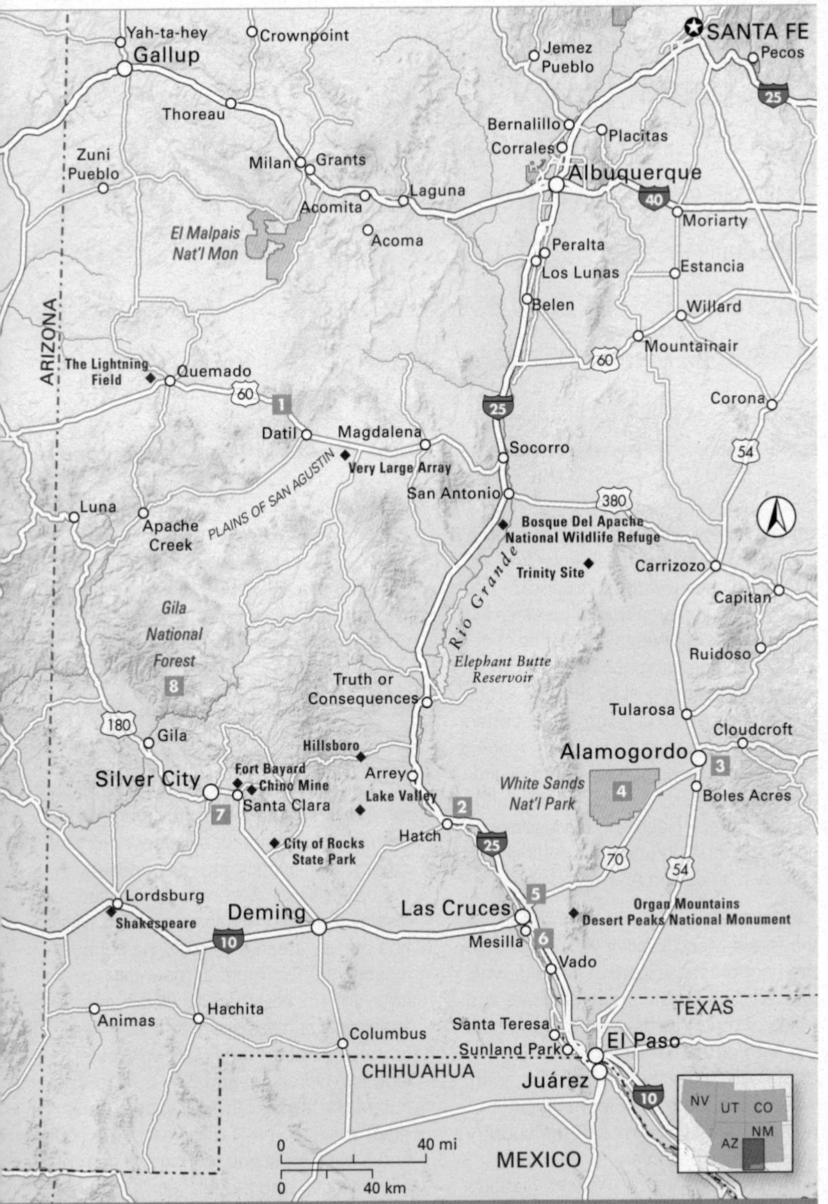
SANTA FE
Pecos
Yah-ta-hey
Crownpoint
Gallup
Jemez Pueblo
Thoreau
Bernalillo
Placitas
Corrales
Zuni Pueblo
Milan
Grants
Albuquerque
Laguna
Acomita
Moriarty
El Malpais Nat'l Mon
Acoma
Peralta
Los Lunas
Estancia
Belen
Willard
Mountainair
ARIZONA
The Lightning Field
Quemado
Corona
Datil
Magdalena
Socorro
Very Large Array
PLAINS OF SAN AGUSTIN
San Antonio
Luna
Apache Creek
Bosque Del Apache National Wildlife Refuge
Trinity Site
Carrizozo
Capitan
Rio Grande
Gila National Forest
Ruidoso
Elephant Butte Reservoir
Truth or Consequences
Tularosa
Cloudcroft
Gila
Hillsboro
Alamogordo
Fort Bayard
Arrey
Silver City
Chino Mine
White Sands Nat'l Park
Santa Clara
Lake Valley
Boles Acres
Hatch
City of Rocks State Park
Lordsburg
Organ Mountains Desert Peaks National Monument
Shakespeare
Deming
Las Cruces
Mesilla
Vado
TEXAS
Hachita
Animas
Santa Teresa
Columbus
El Paso
Sunland Park
CHIHUAHUA
Juárez
NV
UT
CO
AZ
NM
0
40 mi
0
40 km
MEXICO

Calling southwestern New Mexico a borderland may seem a bit obvious, but it is one in the broadest possible sense. The proximity of Mexico is inescapable as you travel through the region, but so is the delightful blend of the people whose cultures have met and mingled in this area since long before there was a border. Southwestern New Mexico is a trove of diversity, from the scenery, to the people and their cultures, to the food.

Both Albuquerque and El Paso are convenient gateways, but the hub of southern New Mexico is Las Cruces (the Crosses, so named because of the number of people buried in the area due to hardship and Apache attacks). With a population of about 75,000 (and growing quickly), Las Cruces is bordered to the east by the jagged and beautiful Organ Mountains. Sunset often colors the jagged peaks a brilliant magenta, called "Las Cruces purple," and they are depicted endlessly by local painters and photographers. Nearby, Old Mesilla once served as the Confederate territorial capital of New Mexico and Arizona.

The incredible, irrigated lushness in the fertile Mesilla Valley would surprise the hard-pressed Spanish settlers who passed through the area 400 years ago. Miles of green fields and orchards track the path of the Rio Grande from north of El Paso to north of Las Cruces, with water from the huge Elephant Butte reservoir irrigating some of the country's most prolific pecan and chile pepper farms. The Bosque del Apache National Wildlife Refuge is a resting place for millions of migrating birds each year. Whether you're a bird enthusiast or not, it is quite a treat to witness the sky fill up with enormous varieties of birds taking off or landing in the marshy area.

Outdoors enthusiasts from all over head to the Gila (pronounced *hee*-la) National Forest and Gila Wilderness areas for access to fantastic camping and hiking and natural hot springs. Old mining towns remind you of the thousands who came here on their quest for silver, copper, and other minerals once found abundantly in the ore-rich hills. Several small museums display the region's minerals, along with fine pottery created by early indigenous inhabitants. This rugged, mountainous area, with its breathtaking vistas and seemingly endless span of trees, was home at different times to two Western legends: Geronimo and Billy the Kid. The hub of the area is Silver City, one of the great small towns of the West. Here you'll find a lively art scene, numerous community festivals, and friendly locals.

Planning

Getting Here and Around

AIR

The nearest commercial airports are in Albuquerque and El Paso, Texas; however, the tiny airport near Silver City has commuter service from Albuquerque.

CAR

Two major interstates travel through southwestern New Mexico, I–10 from west to east and I–25 from north to south. U.S. 70 connects Las Cruces to Alamogordo and the southeast. From Albuquerque, the drive is about two hours to Truth or Consequences, three hours to Las Cruces. Silver City can be accessed from minor highways leading off I–10 and I–25. From Las Cruces, I–10 leads south to El Paso.

The quality of the region's roadways varies widely, particularly in remote rural areas. Drive with caution on the narrow highways, which particularly in mountainous areas have no shoulders. On minor roadways, even if paved, be alert for curves, dips, and steep drop-offs. If you veer too far into unexplored territory with primitive, unpaved roads, make sure you have a vehicle with high clearance and four-wheel drive, such as an SUV.

You can rent a car from one of the national agencies at either Albuquerque International Sunport or El Paso International Airport. Avis, Hertz, and Enterprise have rental locations in Las Cruces. Auto dealerships in some communities rent cars.

TRAIN

Amtrak services El Paso, Texas, and Lordsburg and Deming, New Mexico, on the Sunset Limited, which operates between Los Angeles and New Orleans.

Hotels

Whether they're historic lodgings or chain hotels, you'll find many of the accommodations in this part of the state incorporate Spanish influences in their architecture. Haciendas, mission-style buildings with tile roofs, and courtyards with fountains and gardens are everywhere here—evidence of the style first introduced by Spanish colonists more than four centuries ago.

Restaurants

The cost of a meal in this area is extremely reasonable, although the food options are limited compared to what you'll find farther north. Mexican food is an almost sure bet in this area, especially if you're a fan of the locally grown green chiles. You won't get far before you realize that barbecue joints and steak houses are almost as numerous as the Mexican restaurants. Las Cruces has several tasty ethnic-food restaurants in the university district; again, generally at very reasonable prices and Old Mesilla is a dining destination.

HOTEL AND RESTAURANT PRICES

Hotel prices in the reviews are the lowest cost of a standard double room in high season. Restaurant prices in the reviews are the average cost of a main course at dinner, or if dinner is not served, at lunch.

What It Costs

$	$$	$$$	$$$$
RESTAURANTS			
under $15	$15–$22	$23–$30	over $30
HOTELS			
under $110	$110–$200	$201–$300	over $300

Tours

WolfHorse Outfitters
WolfHorse Outfitters is a Native American guide service offering superb horseback expeditions into the heart of Gila country. Most are led by owner Joe Saenz, who is of Warm Springs Apache ancestry, and convey an especially rich appreciation of the land and its history. ☎ *575/534–1379* 🌐 *www.wolfhorseoutfitters.com.*

U.S. 60 Corridor

Socorro is 76 miles southwest of Albuquerque via I–25.

Maybe you're a traveler who prefers to stay off the beaten path, and venture to places you've never even heard of. If you're in the mood to take the slow road and encounter an authentic Western America decades removed from today's franchise operations, head west on old U.S. 60 out of Socorro and keep going—as far as the Arizona border if you like (this is also a popular "scenic route" for travelers headed from Tucson and Phoenix to Albuquerque and points north). The speed limit is mostly 65 mph, there's not a chain restaurant for 200 miles, and the stunning scenery hasn't changed much for 50 years.

This long, often lonely highway opened in 1926 as the first numbered auto route to cross the United States. Called the Ocean to Ocean Highway, U.S. 60 eventually ran from Norfolk, Virginia, to Los Angeles. Earlier in the 20th century this stretch of it was a "hoof highway," the route of cattle drives from Springerville, Arizona, to Magdalena, New Mexico. Walk into any café along this dusty roadside and you're still likely to be greeted by a cowboy in spurs fresh from tending to ranch business.

People really ranch here, much the way they have for more than 100 years—prior to the era of homesteaders and ranchers, the Apaches ruled and weren't much inclined to allow ranching or settlements of any kind. Livestock production and timber are still the leading industries. U.S. 60 takes you through the heart of Catron County, New Mexico's largest county by area, and least populated by square mile. Notoriously politically incorrect and proud of it, this is a place where Confederate flags fly and animal trophies are considered high art.

After you've headed as far west as Quemado, you can head 7 miles south on NM 32 and find yourself at the northern gateway to the Gila National Forest, or make an interesting and scenic loop by continuing north on NM 36 to NM 117, which skirts the east side of El Malpais National Monument, eventually hooking up with I–40 east of Grants. To get to Albuquerque take I–40 east.

Sights

From the town of Socorro, you can follow scenic and solitary U.S. 60 all the way into Arizona. From the western edge of the White Sands Missle Range, the route pass through a handful of small, quirky villages. Gape at expansive mountains, and marvel at the giant antennae at the Very Large Array. Touring this immutable area often feels like a trip through the Old West.

★ Bosque del Apache National Wildlife Refuge
NATURE PRESERVE | FAMILY | Hundreds of different types of birds, including snow geese, cranes, herons, and eagles, can be spotted from viewing platforms and directly through your car window at the popular Bosque del Apache National Wildlife Refuge. Besides serving as a rest stop for migrating birds, the Bosque del Apache also shelters mule deer, turkeys, quail, and other wildlife. Photo

opportunities abound on the 12-mile auto loop tour; you can also hike through arid shrub land or bike through the refuge or take a van tour. October and November are the months the cottonwoods show their colors. In winter months, the refuge echoes with the haunting cries of whooping cranes flocking for the evening. Snow geese are so thick on lakes at times that shores are white with feathers washed ashore. Whether you're a bird-watcher or not, it is well worth bringing binoculars or a spotting scope to get some idea of how many varieties of birds land here (nearly 400 species have been spotted since 1940). The Festival of the Cranes (🌐 *www.friendsofbosquedelapache.org*) in mid-November draws thousands of people. ✉ *1001 NM 1, San Antonio* ☎ *575/835–1828* 🌐 *www.fws.gov/refuge/Bosque_del_Apache* 🎟 *$5 per vehicle.*

★ Lightning Field

PUBLIC ART | The sculptor Walter De Maria created *Lightning Field,* a work of land art composed of 400 stainless-steel poles of varying heights (the average is about 20 feet, although they create a horizontal plane) arranged in a rectangular grid over 1 mile by ½ mile of flat, isolated terrain, and installed in 1977. Groups of up to six people are permitted to stay overnight from May through October—the only way you can experience the artwork—at a rustic on-site 1930s cabin. Fees include dinner and breakfast, and range from $600 (May to June, September to October) to $1,000 (July to August) per group; additional people incur extra fees. Dia Art Foundation administers *Lightning Field,* shuttling visitors from Quemado to the sculpture, which is on private land 45 minutes to the northeast. Thunder-and-lightning storms are most common from July to mid-September; book way ahead for visits during this time. If you're lucky, you'll see flashes you'll never forget (though lightning isn't required for the sculpture to be stunning in effect). ✉ *Quemado* ✣ *It is a 45-minute shuttle ride from Quemado to Lighting Field; you may not take your own vehicle.* ☎ *505/898–3335 reservations* 🌐 *www.lightningfield.org* ✍ *Reservations essential.*

★ Trinity Site

HISTORIC SITE | Only a monument remains at Trinity Site, where the world's first atomic bomb exploded, on July 16, 1945. The resulting crater has been filled in, but the test site and monument are open for public viewing and self-guided tours two days of the year (the first Satudays in April and October). The McDonald ranch house, where the first plutonium core for the bomb was assembled, can be toured on those days. Picnic tables are available. It's wheelchair-accessible. **■ TIP→ There are no vehicle services or gas at the site, and visitors must bring their own food and water.** ✉ *Socorro* ✣ *Off I–25, 34 miles southeast of Socorro; Exit 139 (10 miles south of Socorro), at San Antonio, and go 12 miles east on U.S. 380 and turn south onto paved road, NM 525 (there is a large sign for Trinity Site), for 5 miles until route reaches Stallion Range Center gate; visitors (everyone over age 16 must present photo ID) will be met at the gate and escorted 17 miles east to site* ☎ *575/678–1134* 🌐 *www.wsmr.army.mil* 🎟 *Free.*

★ Very Large Array

OBSERVATORY | With its 27 glistening-white 80-foot radio-telescope antennae arranged in patterns (their configuration is altered every four months or so), the Very Large Array is a startling sight when spotted along the Plains of San Augustin. The complex's dish-shaped "ears," each weighing 230 tons, are tuned in to the cosmos. The array is part of a series of facilities that compose the National Radio Astronomy Observatory. The antennas, which provided an impressive backdrop for the movie *Contact,* based on the Carl Sagan book, form the largest, most advanced radio telescope in the world. The telescope chronicles the birth and death of stars and galaxies from 10 to

12 billion light-years away. Hundreds of scientists from around the world travel to this windy, remote spot to research black holes, colliding galaxies, and exploding stars, as well as to chart the movements of planets. Visitors are permitted to stroll right up to the array on a self-guided walking tour that begins at the unstaffed visitor center. Staff members emphasize that their work does *not* involve a search for life on other planets. ✉ *NM 52, south off U.S. 60, Magdalena* ✣ *23 miles west of Magdalena* ☎ *575/835–7410* 🌐 *www.nrao.edu* 🎫 *$6 per adult.*

Hatch

109 miles south of Socorro, 40 miles north of Las Cruces on NM 185 or I–25.

Hatch bills itself the Chile Capital of the World. And although chiles are grown elsewhere in the state—and some might argue taste just as good—Hatch is still considered *the* source for the headily aromatic, highly addictive, metabolism-firing, not always killer-hot state vegetable (it actually shares this honor with *frijoles,* aka pinto beans, and it's technically a fruit rather than a vegetable). Come here in the fall when the roasters are firing, and you'll immediately understand the allure of this otherwise rather indistinct small town. If you need additional tempting, consider Hatch's enviable location on the lovely NM 185/187, a two-lane river-valley road that parallels I–25 and makes for an enchanting scenic drive between Las Cruces and Truth or Consequences.

The famed **Hatch Chile Fest** (🌐 *www.hatchchilefest.com*) has been held in August since the early 1970s. Show that you're not a chile rube and mingle with aficionados who know their NuMex 6-4s (an heirloom variety regenerated from 1960s seeds) from their Big Jims (a medium-hot chile, cultivated locally). Between tastes (don't worry, some varieties are no hotter than a standard bell pepper), check out the Chile Festival Parade, play some horseshoes, or sign up for the chile-eating contest (if you dare).

GETTING HERE

From Socorro, Hatch is about 90 minutes via I–25. From Las Cruces, Hatch is a 40-mile drive north along I–25 (the drive takes 35 minutes) or NM 185, which takes more like an hour, with its slower speeds and curving path.

Sights

Hatch Museum

MUSEUM | In the tradition of classic small-town museums, the modest Hatch Museum brims with odd memorabilia of local, historic interest. Witness: A corset, World War I and II military uniforms, household items, and a lot of odds and ends. ✉ *149 W. Hall St., Hatch* ☎ *575/267–3638* 🎫 *Donation requested.*

Fort Selden Historic Site

MILITARY SITE | Fort Selden was established in 1865 to protect Mesilla Valley settlers and travelers. The adobe ruins at Fort Selden are arranged around a drill field. Several units of buffalo soldiers were stationed here. These were the acclaimed African-American cavalry troops noted for their bravery and crucial role in helping protect frontier settlers from Native American attacks and desperadoes. Native Americans thought the soldiers' hair resembled that of a buffalo and gave the regiments their name. Knowing the respect the Apaches held for the animals, the soldiers did not take offense. Buffalo soldiers were also stationed at Fort Bayard, near Silver City, and Fort Stanton, in Lincoln County, to shield miners and travelers from attacks by Apaches.

In the early 1880s Captain Arthur MacArthur was appointed post commander of Fort Selden. His young son spent several years on the post and grew up to become World War II hero General Douglas MacArthur. Exhibits in the visitor cover the fort's compelling history. ✉ *1280 Fort Selden Rd., Hatch* ✥ *Off I–25 at Radium Springs Exit (Exit 19), 25 miles south of Hatch* ☎ *575/526–8911* 🌐 *www.nmmonuments.org* 🎫 *$5.*

Restaurants

Pepper Pot

$ | **MEXICAN** | The exterior isn't much, but once inside you're given the chance to sample some serious local heat. This is Hatch, after all, and if you're game, you can tuck into some tasty authentic Mexican and New Mexican fare—enchiladas, rellenos, *chilaquiles*—here, produced with chiles grown in the area. **Known for:** local chiles; Mexican specialties; good breakfast. *Average main: $9* ✉ *207 W. Hall St., Hatch* ☎ *575/267–3822* ⏲ *No dinner.*

Alamogordo

15 miles northeast White Sands National Park, 90 miles north of El Paso, Texas, 208 miles southeast of Albuquerque.

Defense-related activities are vital to small city of Alamogordo (population 32,000) and surrounding Otero County, which covers much of the Tularosa Basin desert and White Sands National Park.

GETTING HERE AND AROUND

Located at the junction of U.S. 70, 54, and 82, this crossroads community of south-central New Mexico is just a 15-minute drive from White Sands National Park. Alamogordo is suburban in character, and a car is needed to get around.

VISITOR INFORMATION

CONTACTS Alamogordo Chamber of Commerce. ✉ *1301 N. White Sands Blvd., Alamogordo* ☎ *575/437–6120* 🌐 *www.alamogordo.com.*

Sights

McGinn's Pistachioland

STORE/MALL | **FAMILY** | This working pistachio farm a little north of Alamogordo doubles as an old-fashioned, if endearingly kitschy, roadside attraction—complete with an ice cream parlor, koi pond, wine tastings, and a mechanical talking cowboy named Pappy. Take a farm tour and graze the pistachio tasting bar, snap a photo of yourself beneath a sculpture billed as the world's largest pistachio, and enjoy a dish of pistachio ice cream. ✉ *7320 U.S. 54/70, Alamogordo* ☎ *800/368–3081* 🌐 *www.pistachioland.com* 🎫 *$2.*

New Mexico Museum of Space History

MUSEUM | **FAMILY** | The exhibits at this museum in the foothills on Alamogordo's east side highlight southern New Mexico's extensive and ongoing history of rocket launches, test flights, and space exploration. On the way in, check out the various rockets and other craft in the adjacent John P. Stapp Air & Space Park, and pay your respects to the gravesite of Ham the chimpanzee, who became the first hominid in space in 1961 and is now buried under a plaque dedicated to the "world's first astrochimp." The museum's highlights include the International Space Hall of Fame, a planetarium and dome theater, and a simulated Martian landscape. ✉ *3198 Hwy. 2001, Alamogordo* ☎ *575/437–2840* 🌐 *www.nmspacemuseum.org* 🎫 *$8* ⏲ *Closed Tues.*

Oliver Lee Memorial State Park

NATIONAL/STATE PARK | Just south of Alamogordo at the base of the Sacramento Mountains, this 640-acre expanse of Chihuahuan Desert offers both a short ½-mile hike along the Riparian Nature Trail and a strenuous 10-mile round-trip climb up through steep but stunning Dog Canyon—give yourself the better part of the day, as the elevation gain of about 3,500 feet is demanding. Even along the shorter trail, however, you'll be treated to good views back across the Tularosa Basin and White Sands National Park. ✉ *409 Dog Canyon Rd., Alamogordo* ☎ *575/437–8284* 🎟 *$5 per vehicle.*

Restaurants

Brown Bag Deli

$ | **DELI** | You'll find generous sandwiches with coleslaw and dill pickles on the side at this simple deli on the east side of downtown. Stop here on your way to the park for the fixings for a picnic-style lunch on the dunes. **Known for:** good soups and salads; green-chile chicken sandwiches; red-velvet cake. 💲 *Average main: $8* ✉ *900 Washington Ave., Alamogordo* ☎ *575/437–9751.*

★ **Nuckleweed Place**

$$$$ | **AMERICAN** | It takes a little effort to get to what's quite possibly the best restaurant in the region—it's set in a cheerfully decorated prefab house deep in La Borcita Canyon, about midway between Alamogordo and Cloudcroft. Open for dinner as well as weekend brunch, this quirky spot with a friendly staff turns out delicious biscuits and gravy and eggs Benedict for brunch, and choice steaks and grilled seafood at night. **Known for:** sticky pecan cinnamon rolls; tranquil, out-of-the-way setting; steak verde (with green chiles and havarti cheese). 💲 *Average main: $34* ✉ *526 LaBorcita Canyon Rd., Alamogordo* ☎ *575/434–0000* ⏲ *Closed Mon.–Wed. No lunch.*

★ **Waffle and Pancake Shoppe**

$ | **AMERICAN** | This bustling restaurant is on the short list of locals and visitors in the know for tasty, and big, breakfasts and early lunches (they close at 1). Aside from fluffy waffles and pancakes (which can come loaded with all sorts of toppings), they serve very good Mexican breakfasts and lunches—the chile verde plate for breakfast is great, as are the chicken enchiladas for lunch. **Known for:** friendly down-home service; huge portions; strawberry French toast. 💲 *Average main: $8* ✉ *950 S. White Sands Blvd., Alamogordo* ☎ *575/437–0433* ⏲ *No dinner.*

Hotels

Holiday Inn Express

$ | **HOTEL** | The most pleasant and contemporary of Alamogordo's several chain hotels, this centrally located mid-rise offers friendly, professional service, immaculate grounds and interior spaces, and spacious, comfortable rooms. **Pros:** close to several restaurants; generous breakfast included; good proximity to White Sands National Park. **Cons:** looks like any other Holiday Inn Express; overlooks parking lot; on busy road. 💲 *Rooms from: $115* ✉ *100 Kerry Ave., Alamogordo* ☎ *575/434–9773* 🌐 *www.ihg.com* *80 rooms* 🍽 *Free Breakfast.*

White Sands National Park

Stretching across a 275-square-mile swath of the Tularosa Basin, half of it protected within the national park, this surreal landscape is the largest gypsum dunefield on earth. Located in the northern tip of the Chihuahuan Desert and framed by dramatic mountain ranges, White Sands National Park shimmers beneath the big, blue southern New Mexico sky. A wonderland for photographers, it's also a playground for outdoors lovers who come for dune-sledding, hiking, and picnicking—you can even pitch a tent and camp beneath the region's dark, starry canopy.

Indigenous tribes began farming in the Tularosa Basin following the end of the last Ice Age some 11,000 years ago, and European Americans arrived in the late 19th century. By the 1940s, the U.S. military had discovered a new use for this isolated landscape: testing weapons. On July 16, 1945, scientists from New

Mexico's Los Alamos National Laboratory detonated the first atomic bomb in a lonely, arid patch of desert about 75 miles north of the park, now known as the Trinity Site. The site is part of the vast White Sands Missile Range, which forms the park's western border and still conducts missile tests that result in the temporary closure of both the park and a stretch U.S. 70—these pauses usually take place for about an hour or two, up to twice a week. Holloman Air Force Base is just beyond the range.

As the region's military importance grew, so too did the reputation of its astounding white dunes, which began to draw tourists from far and near. The dunes also drew commercial interest, as mining companies saw the potential value in extracting the vast stores of gypsum sand, the primary ingredient in plaster and wallboard. Conservationists ultimately convinced the federal government of the need to protect this unique natural resource, and in 1933, President Herbert Hoover designed White Sands National Monument. In December 2019, White Sands achieved full national park status.

Visitors who spend even a couple of hours exploring the undulating white-sand dunes often come away transformed by the experience. Beyond the sheer grandeur of the endless dunes, one of the park's most amazing attributes is that it supports a habitat of plants and animals that can be found only here. These flora and fauna have thrived through ingenious adaptation—sand verbena that spread its seeds quickly, shrubs with dense root systems that take hold in the sand, and lizards and mice whose light coloring both camouflage and cool them down amid the shifting white dunes. As enormous as it is, White Sands is a relatively straightforward park to visit, as the portion of it accessible to the public is relatively small and can be fully experienced in a full day. A single 8-mile park road leads through the heart of the park, which has only a handful of marked trails and no lodgings or restaurants—just a gift shop that also sells a few snacks. You will find an impressive visitor center, however, that's noteworthy both for its historic Pueblo Revival design and the engaging exhibits in its museum.

GETTING HERE AND AROUND

The nearest major airport to the park is in El Paso, about 100 miles south, and it's served by all major airlines and car rental companies. Another option is Albuquerque, 225 miles north.

The entrance to White Sands is along a well-traveled four-lane highway, U.S. 70, about an hour's drive northeast of Las Cruces and a 20-minute drive southwest of Alamogordo, which is also where you'll find the nearest gas stations and other services.

PARK ESSENTIALS

The park's gift shop and visitor center are fully accessible for wheelchairs, and there are several accessible tables and vault toilets at the three designated picnic areas. Most importantly, the outstanding Interdune Boardwalk Trail is fully accessible and provides an up-close view of some of the park's biggest dunes.

The park fee of $25 per vehicle, $20 per motorcycle, and $15 per pedestrian or cyclist is good for one week and payable at the entrance station to Dunes Drive; there's no fee just to enter the visitor center and see its exhibits. Backcountry camping is $3 nightly per person.

The park is open year-round except on Christmas Day, and the gate opens each morning at 7. It closes in the evening generally between 6 and 9 pm, depending on the season (later in summer, earlier in winter). Visitor center hours are 9–5 most of the year, but until 6 pm from Memorial Day to early September. The park is in the Mountain time zone.

Boardwalks allow you to walk across the gypsum dunes at White Sands National Park.

VISITOR INFORMATION

CONTACTS White Sands National Park. ✉ *19955 U.S. 70 W, Alamogordo* ☎ *575/479–6124* 🌐 *www.nps.gov/whsa.*

Sights

The park's 8-mile loop drive, Dunes Drive, provides access to all of the park's attractions, from the visitor center at the start of the road to several hiking trails and three picnic areas. Just making your way along this road, which has a hard-packed white-sand surface along the section in the heart of the park, is great fun and yields astonishing views.

SCENIC DRIVES

★ Dunes Drive

SCENIC DRIVE | FAMILY | This gorgeous drive through the heart of White Sands accesses virtually every part of the park that's accessible to visitors, including all of the trails and picnic areas. It's an 8-mile drive from the visitor center and entrance gate to the one-way loop at the end. The first 5 miles are paved, and as you make your way from the park entrance, the landscape becomes steadily more dominated by higher and whiter dunes, until you reach the final 3 miles, which are unpaved along smooth, hard-packed gypsum. This is where the experience starts to feel truly surreal, as it's easy to feel as though you're driving through a winter wonderland—the gypsum really does look like snow (which feels particularly odd if you're driving this route on a hot summer day). You'll come to the Primrose and Roadrunner picnic areas, on the right, as you enter the one-way loop portion of Dunes Drive, and you'll come to several larger parking areas that access some of the park's biggest dunes as the road curves back around at the Alkali Flat Trailhead. It takes only about 45 minutes to drive the entire route, round-trip, but you'll want to stop and explore the dunes on foot. Part of the fun is watching park visitors, especially kids, riding sleds down the dunes. Groups of friends and families also regularly come and set up tents and umbrellas on the dunes nearest the parking areas and bask in the sun all day. It's quite a sight. Do obey speed limits, which are 45 mph as you enter but drop to 15 mph along the unpaved loop in areas with lots of pedestrian traffic. It may look tempting to zip around, but the sand can get slippery, and the road curves in places, limiting visibility. ✉ *Alamogordo.*

SCENIC STOPS

Native Plant Garden

GARDEN | FAMILY | Located in front of the park visitor center, which is outside the entrance station (and thus free of charge), this small garden that's especially colorful and fragrant from mid-March through November (even more so after it rains) provides an up-close look at plant life—including soaptree yucca, ocotillos, myriad wildflowers, and cottonwood trees (which have beautiful foliage in autumn)—that's native to the Chihuahuan Desert. You can download a plant guide from the park website or pick one up in the visitor center. ✉ *White Sands Visitor Center, Alamogordo* ☎ *505/479–6124.*

TRAILS

★ Alkali Flat Trail

TRAIL | The park's most ambitious trail is arguably its most rewarding, too, as it crosses an ancient lakebed now piled high with dunes, and once you're about a mile into it, it can feel as though you're on another planet, as you'll see almost nothing but white sand. Despite the name, it's actually an undulating 5-mile round-trip route over sometimes quite steep dunes. It's not the distance that makes it challenging but those hills, and that walking on dunes is slower going, and more taxing—especially in summer—than over conventional terrain. Along the way, you'll cross ridges and pinnacles, and see some of the biggest dunes in the park. Pack lots of water, hike with at least one buddy, and keep an eye out for the bright red trail markers—it can be easy to get disoriented if there's a lot of wind (common in spring), which can greatly reduce visibility. *Difficult.* ✉ *Alamogordo* ✣ *Trailhead: Just past the 8-mile mark of Dunes Dr.*

★ Dune Life Nature Trail

TRAIL | FAMILY | Give yourself about an hour to complete this 1-mile self-guided loop trail that, while short, does climb over a couple of pretty tall dunes. This hike offers an interesting contrast with other parts of the park, as there's quite a lot of flora along it—you can really learn about the unusual plants that thrive in this harsh environment. Keep an eye out for the series of 14 interpretive signs that discuss the foxes, birds, reptiles, and other wildlife that live in the park. *Easy–Moderate.* ✉ *Alamogordo* ✣ *Trailhead: 2.3 miles north of entrance station on Dunes Dr.*

★ Interdune Boardwalk

TRAIL | FAMILY | Along this easy 0.4-mile boardwalk trail, the only one in the park fully accessible to wheelchairs and strollers, you can read about the park's fascinating geology and ecosystem at 10 different signed interpretive stations along the route. The trail provides a fun and simple way to observe the dunes up close without having to walk through the sand itself. *Easy.* ✉ *Alamogordo* ✣ *Trailhead: Just before the end of the paved section of Dune Dr.*

Playa Trail

TRAIL | FAMILY | This short and level ½-mile round-trip ramble is the first one you'll come to along Dunes Drive after passing through the entrance station. It's not as exciting as some of the other park trails, although it is interesting in summer when the otherwise dry lake bed it leads to usually fills with rain water. *Easy.* ✉ *Alamogordo* ✣ *Trailhead: About 2 miles past entrance station on Dunes Dr.*

VISITOR CENTERS

★ White Sands Visitor Center

BUILDING | FAMILY | The centerpiece of the small White Sands Historic District, a complex of park buildings constructed by the WPA in New Mexico's distinctive

Spanish–Pueblo Revival style in the mid-1930s, the park's only visitor center is built of thick adobe (mud and straw) bricks and has a traditional *viga* (beam) and *savina* (also called latilla) aspen-pole ceiling and architectural details typical of the period and style, like punched-tin light fixtures and hand-carved wooden benches. Inside you'll find an info desk and an array of excellent, modern, interactive exhibits as well as a small theater that shows a short film about the dunes. Walk out back to reach the park gift shop, which has books, souvenirs, water, a very limited assortment of snacks, and sleds with which to careen down the park's dunes. The district's other seven buildings include a visitor restroom, ranger residences, and various utility buildings. ✉ *19955 U.S. 70W, Alamogordo* ☎ *575/479–6124* 🌐 *www.nps.gov/whsa.*

Activities

CAMPING

Although there are no campgrounds inside the park, you can set up a tent at one of the primitive sites along the short backcountry camping loop trail just off Dunes Drive (about 6 miles from the entrance station). You must obtain a permit—the cost is $3 per person per night—at the entrance station.

HIKING

Although there are only a few marked trails in the park, you can easily hike short distances over any dunefield adjoining the several parking areas along Dunes Drive. Traipsing through this strangely gorgeous landscape can take some getting used to, however, and despite the fact that the park's gently rolling dunes look about as threatening as a big sandbox, this terrain is deceptively dangerous, and you should take its potential hazards seriously. Because the dunes shift constantly and are sometimes buffeted by high winds (especially in spring), which can severely reduce visibility, it's relatively easy to get lost. Take it slow, bring lots of water, and always have a compass and a charged cell phone with you (cell service is a little uneven but it generally works on and near Dunes Drive). Although the park is in a broad basin, it's still at a lofty elevation of 4,235 feet. It's also completely unshaded, and temperatures can exceed 100 degrees in summer—it's rare, but visitors have been injured and even died from heat exhaustion after becoming disoriented. Unless you're on a marked trail, always stay within view of Dunes Drive, or at the very least other people. The good news: you don't have to scamper far from Dunes Drive to encounter mesmerizing views of seemingly endless dunes framed against majestic mountain peaks. Also, the white gypsum sand is cool to the touch, which makes it pleasant to walk barefoot through even on hot days. However, if hiking more than a few hundred feet, and especially on the longer Alkali Flat Trail, wear hiking boots, as your feet will appreciate the extra support after a mile or so of trekking over sometimes steep dunes.

SLEDDING

Further contributing to the sensation at times that you've entered an enormous landscape of snow rather than white sand, as you make your way along Dunes Drive into the heart of the park, you'll see kids and adults sledding down the dunes on plastic sleds, or snow saucers, which—if you don't have your own—you can buy at the gift shop attached to the visitor center for about $20, plus a couple of bucks for wax, which you'll need to coat your sled for it to work on the sand. Used sleds cost less but aren't always available; you can also return your new sled for $5 when you're finished. Park staffers are great with tips on how to sled on gypsum sand and also the best areas to do it, but a good place to start are the dunes adjacent either to the Interdune Boardwalk or beside the Alkali Flat Trailhead parking lot. There's also a good "how to" video on the park website.

Las Cruces

323 mi south of Albuquerque and 40 miles south of Hatch on I–25; 45 miles northwest of El Paso on I–10.

The Mesilla Valley has been populated for centuries. The Spanish passed through the region first in 1598 and continued to use the route to reach the northern territories around Santa Fe. Though the Spanish could not maintain settlements in the region at all during the 1700s, by the early 1800s people were able to move in and create hamlets that grew to become Doña Ana and, eventually, Las Cruces.

In 1848 the Treaty of Guadalupe Hidalgo ended the Mexican-American War, but rendered uncertain the sovereignty of Las Cruces. The Mesilla Valley ended up split between two nations, with the town of Mesilla on the west of the Rio Grande belonging to Mexico and Las Cruces, on the eastern banks of the river, belonging to the United States. The Gadsden Purchase in 1853 made the whole area U.S. territory and Las Cruces began its ascent as the area's power center. The railroad, irrigation, agriculture, and local ranching drove the city's growth. Much of the new city was built in the Territorial and Victorian styles popular at the time. Las Cruces College was founded in 1888 and eventually became New Mexico State University.

With growth spurred by retirees looking for sun and mild winters, the defense and commercial business at White Sands Missile Range, the increasing strength of New Mexico State University, and its proximity to the business on the border with Mexico, this city of about 100,000 people *is* growing. Las Cruces is following the lead of many U.S. cities by pushing a major revitalization of its historic downtown. The district and its surrounding residential neighborhoods date back more than a century, and a casual walk around will show all sorts of renovation—from simple painting and planting to the restabilization of entire buildings. Despite the revitalization, greater Las Cruces tends to be a bit sterile, as its historical district is surrounded by ever-expanding rings of strip malls and cookie-cutter subdivisions.

GETTING HERE

Las Cruces is at the crossroads of I-25 (north-south) and I-10 (east-west). Note that at the south end of town, I-25 merges into I-10—which then carries on south to El Paso and other points in south Texas. If that's confusing, not to worry, it's actually very easy to navigate around the rather gridlike town itself. Also note that it is U.S. 70—from I-25 exit 6, at the north end of town—that will get you to wonders near (Organ Mountains and Aguirre Springs) and far (White Sands and beyond).

VISITOR INFORMATION

CONTACTS Las Cruces Convention & Visitors Bureau. ✉ *336 S. Main St., Las Cruces* ☎ *575/541–2444* 🌐 *www.lascrucescvb.org.*

Sights

Many artists (painters, sculptors, actors, writers, metalsmiths) make their homes here not just because the surrounding area offers a perpetually inspiring palette, but also because the arts community is supportive and the town an affordable alternative to chic and expensive Santa Fe. Museums, a performing arts center, a renovated movie theater, and new shops and some cafés are draws. A farmers' market on the weekends makes for a fun way to spend a Saturday morning.

The Hispanic population in Las Cruces comprises descendants from the Spanish settlers as well as many Mexican immigrants; both influences add unique cultural elements to the community as well as some seriously spicy food. The

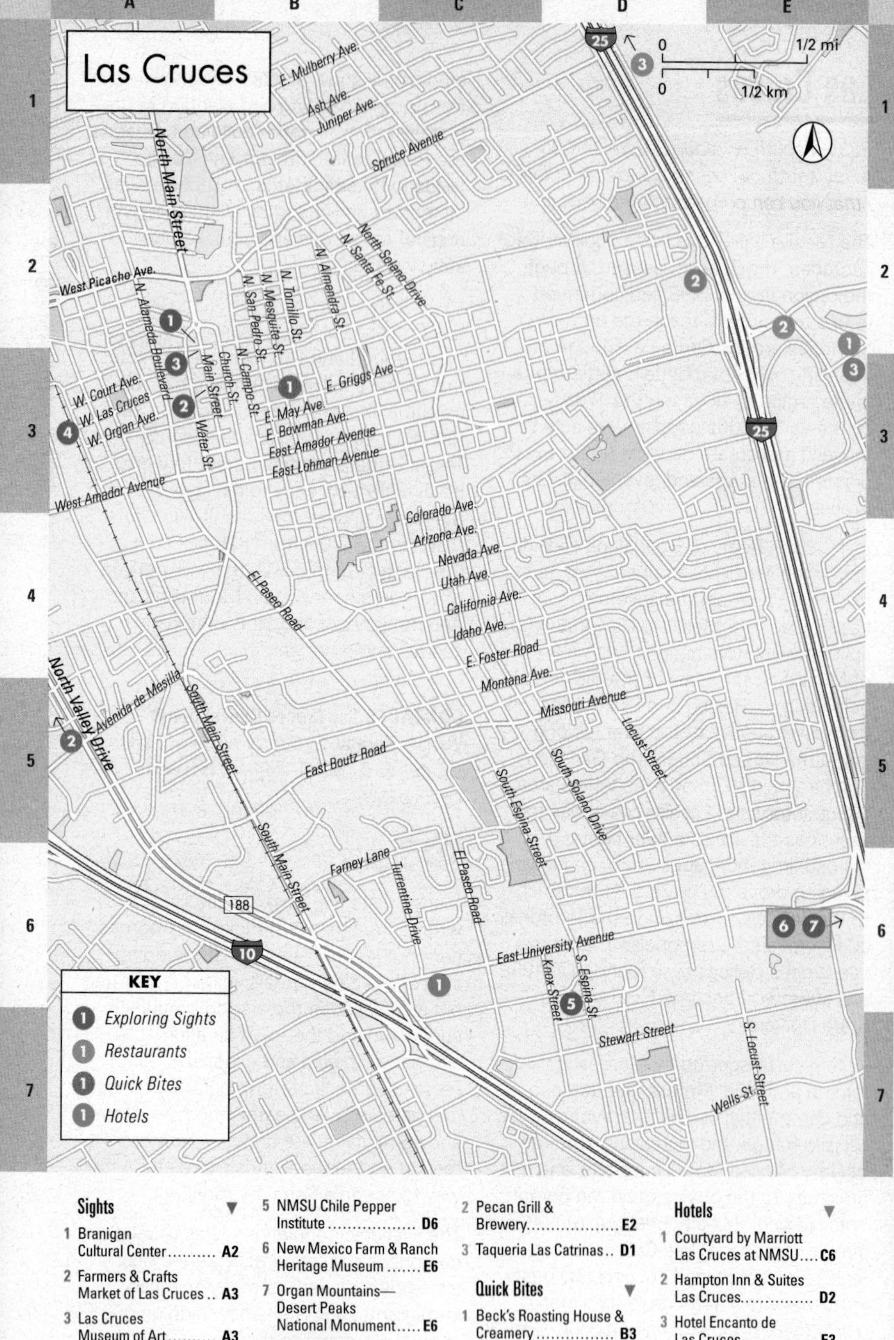

Sights

1 Branigan Cultural Center **A2**

2 Farmers & Crafts Market of Las Cruces .. **A3**

3 Las Cruces Museum of Art **A3**

4 Las Cruces Railroad Museum **A3**

5 NMSU Chile Pepper Institute **D6**

6 New Mexico Farm & Ranch Heritage Museum **E6**

7 Organ Mountains—Desert Peaks National Monument **E6**

Restaurants

1 Farley's Food, Fun & Pub **E2**

2 Pecan Grill & Brewery **E2**

3 Taqueria Las Catrinas .. **D1**

Quick Bites

1 Beck's Roasting House & Creamery **B3**

2 Caliche's Frozen Custard **A5**

Hotels

1 Courtyard by Marriott Las Cruces at NMSU **C6**

2 Hampton Inn & Suites Las Cruces **D2**

3 Hotel Encanto de Las Cruces **E3**

emphasis on family is strong here, and kids are welcome just about everywhere.

Although Old Mesilla is listed separately in this chapter, it's so close to Las Cruces that you can comfortably go back and forth to eat, shop, or enjoy a night out.

★ Branigan Cultural Center

MUSEUM | The Branigan Cultural Center, in a striking 1935 Pueblo Revival building embellished inside with murals by Tom Lea, offers compelling programs covering such topics as the 1942–1964 Bracero Program (a Mexican guest workers initiative), or a reflection on Frida Kahlo's later years through rarely seen photographs, along with rotating exhibits covering local history and culture.The city-run Branigan is a focal point—along with the Las Cruces Museum of Art next door—of the revitalized downtown. ✉ *501 N. Main St., , Downtown Mall, Las Cruces* ☎ *575/541–2154* 🌐 *www.las-cruces.org/museums* 🎫 *Free* ⏲ *Closed Sun. and Mon.*

★ Farmers & Crafts Market of Las Cruces

MARKET | If you're in town on a Wednesday or Saturday, don't miss one of the Southwest's largest and most impressive farmers markets, where some 300 vendors sell produce, handcrafted items, baked goods, and even geodes and fossils along a lively seven-block stretch of the city's lively downtown. Mingle with the locals and enjoy the scene, which is open between 8:30 am and 1 pm. ✉ *Main St., Las Cruces* ✥ *Along 7 blocks of Main St. from 500 North to 200 South.* 🌐 *www.farmersandcraftsmarketoflascruces.com.*

Las Cruces Museum of Art

MUSEUM | Across an open courtyard from the Branigan Cultural Center, the Las Cruces Museum of Art shows the eclectic, contemporary works of regional artists. Subjects covered include life in the borderlands as well as landscapes of the Organ Mountains and nearby ghost towns. ✉ *491 N. Main St., Las Cruces* ☎ *575/541–2137* 🌐 *www.las-cruces.org/museums* 🎫 *Free* ⏲ *Closed Sun. and Mon.*

Las Cruces Railroad Museum

MUSEUM | **FAMILY** | Inside the historic (1910) Atchison, Topeka, & Santa Fe Railway Depot, the Las Cruces Railroad Museum uses photos and ephemera to tell the story of early regional railroad history, and a model-train room and train table entertain kids especially. Temporary shows, such as one built around train travel advertisements from the last century, rotate throughout the year. Outside is a 1918 wooden caboose you can tour. The museum is several blocks west of the Cultural Center, by way of the Alameda Historic District. ✉ *351 N. Mesilla St., Las Cruces* ☎ *575/528–3444* 🌐 *www.las-cruces.org/museums* 🎫 *Free* ⏲ *Closed Sun. and Mon.*

★ New Mexico Farm & Ranch Heritage Museum

MUSEUM | **FAMILY** | This handsomely designed museum east of town, near the Organ Mountains, documents 3,000 years of agriculture in New Mexico and the Southwest. Visit a re-creation of a 1,200-year-old Mogollon farmhouse, based on styles built by some of the first nonnomadic people to live in what is now New Mexico. Longhorn cattle, Churro sheep, and dairy cows are among the heritage breeds—descendants of animals the Spanish brought from Mexico—raised at the museum. At milking times, you can learn about the history of dairy farming in New Mexico, or take a look in the "beef barn" where six different breeds of beef cattle are housed. A span of the historic Green Bridge, which used to span the Hondo River, has been reassembled over the arroyo on the grounds. Chuck-wagon cooking demonstrations are offered during special events. ✉ *4100 Dripping Springs Rd., Las Cruces* ☎ *575/522–4100* 🌐 *www.nmfarmandranchmuseum.org* 🎫 *$5* ⏲ *Closed Sun.*

The Mesilla Valley around Las Cruces is a favorite area for artists because if its immense beauty (and also its affordability).

NMSU Chile Pepper Institute

COLLEGE | *Capsicum* matters greatly to New Mexicans, and much of the research into this invaluable agricultural product takes place at NMSU's Chile Pepper Institute, where visitors can explore the Hall of Flame and the gift shop as well as the outdoor research garden. Guided tours are available by appointment. ✉ *New Mexico State University, Gerald Thomas Hall, 945 College Ave., Las Cruces* ☎ *575/646–3028* 🌐 *cpi.nmsu.edu* 🎟 *Free* ⏲ *Closed weekends. Garden closed Nov.–June.*

★ Organ Mountains–Desert Peaks National Monument

NATIONAL/STATE PARK | Established as a national monument in 2014 on the outskirts of Las Cruces, this dramatic 496,330-acre expanse of jagged spirelike peaks—which in the distance resembles a giant pipe organ—is one of the region's natural treasures. Although it receives relatively few visitors, especially compared with the more famous White Sands, it's laced with more than 15 well-marked trails, ranging from the relatively easy 3-mile round-trip trek around Dripping Springs waterfall to longer and more strenuous hikes that traverse the mountain range's spiny backbone and offer dazzling views in every direction. The eastern part of the park in the Organ Mountains has two main sections, **Dripping Springs,** is on the western slope, closer to Las Cruces, also has a visitor center with exhibits about the park's vast trove of archaeological sites; the site is an abandoned mountain resort built in the 1870s and converted decades later into a sanatorium for tuberculosis patients.

✉ *15000 Dripping Springs Rd., Las Cruces* ☎ *575/525–4300* 🌐 *www.organmountains.org* 🎟 *$5 per vehicle.*

Restaurants

Farley's Food, Fun & Pub

$ | **AMERICAN** | **FAMILY** | For a family evening out with no worries about the kids being loud or throwing their peanut shells on the floor, Farley's is the place.

Choose from a huge menu of basic pub victuals: popcorn shrimp, burgers and sandwiches, salads, wood-fired pizzas, all sorts of appetizers, and, of course, beer. **Known for:** good burgers; wood-fired pizzas; pool and arcade games. *Average main: $12 3499 Foothills Rd., Las Cruces 575/522–0466 www.farleyspub.com.*

Pecan Grill & Brewery

$$ | **AMERICAN** | Craft beers and classic comfort fare that favors locally grown ingredients are the draws at this bustling spot with a smart layout, excellent service, and inviting outdoor dining—complete with a view over the Mesilla Valley. Pecan wood is used for grilling steak and chicken, and burgers and rib-eyes come smothered with green chile and Amber Ale–grilled onions. **Known for:** craft beer brewed on site; local flavor; green chiles. *Average main: $18 500 S. Telshor Blvd., Las Cruces 575/521–1099 www.pecangrill.com.*

Taqueria Las Catrinas

$ | **MEXICAN** | **FAMILY** | This inexpensive and festively decorated Mexican restaurant opened inside a former gas station on U.S. 70 several miles east of town, making it one of the last and best dining options en route to White Sands and the Aguirre Springs side of Organ Mountains–Desert Peaks National Monument. The specialty is tacos al pastor, made with tender pork marinated with a recipe from the restaurant's original sister location in Michoacán, Mexico, but you can also savor sirloin steak quesadillas and chicken flautas. **Known for:** fresh house-made tortillas; volcán-style (topped with gooey cheese) tacos al pastor tostadas; jamaica (hibiscus) and horchata agua frescas. *Average main: $8 5580 Bataan Memorial Hwy., Las Cruces 575/382–5641 www.lascatrinastacos.com Closed Mon.*

Coffee and Quick Bites

Beck's Roasting House & Creamery

$ | **RESTAURANT—SIGHT** | |**RESTAURANT—SIGHT** | Kick off your morning with a single-origin pour-over or dirty vanilla chai latte at this cheery café and roastery set in a stone-and-adobe house in a historic residential neighborhood a few blocks from Main Street. Artisan ice cream and a range of baked goods are available, too. *130 N. Mesquite St., Las Cruces 575/556–9850 www.beckscoffeelc.com No dinner.*

Caliche's Frozen Custard

$ | **CAFÉ** | This beloved local joint—it opened as Scoopy's in the 1990s and longtime fans still call it that—offers all kinds of mix-ins (such as regional faves, salted and unsalted pecans) and toppings to embellish the luscious custard-style ice cream. Chili dogs are among the savory treats. **Known for:** neon and nostalgia; custard-style ice cream; hot dogs. *Average main: $6 590 S. Valley Dr., Las Cruces 575/647–5066 www.caliches.com.*

Hotels

Courtyard by Marriott Las Cruces at NMSU

$$ | **HOTEL** | A short way from the attractive campus and museums of New Mexico State University, this contemporary low-rise opened in 2019 and offers some of the comfiest rooms in the city, plus a good-size pool and a patio with a firepit. **Pros:** sleek, modern design; well-equipped 24-hour gym; quiet but convenient location. **Cons:** not within walking distance of downtown or Old Mesilla; a chain hotel without a ton of character; can get crowded during college weekends. *Rooms from: $156 456 E. University Ave., Las Cruces 575/526–1722 www.marriott.com 126 rooms No meals.*

Hampton Inn & Suites Las Cruces

$ | **HOTEL** | This well-kept chain property is a highlight among Las Cruces accommodations—extra clean, with great service, a logical layout, and plenty of handy amenities (free Internet, a lap-style pool, and fitness center, plus microwaves and refrigerators in rooms). **Pros:** big breakfast included; unobtrusive contemporary decor; rooms have ample desks and ergonomic seating. **Cons:** most restaurants are at least a five-minute drive away. *Rooms from: $95 2350 E. Griggs Ave., Las Cruces 575/527–8777 www.hilton.com 73 rooms Free Breakfast.*

Hotel Encanto de Las Cruces

$$ | **HOTEL** | A striking, contemporary hotel high on a bluff on the east side of town channels a gracious hacienda with its colorful common spaces and restaurants. **Pros:** reasonable prices; nice pool and good dining options; good base for visiting Organ Mountains and White Sands. **Cons:** rooms are a little dark; perfunctory bathrooms; on a busy road next to a shopping center. *Rooms from: $130 705 S. Telshor Blvd., Las Cruces 575/522–4300, 866/383–0443 www.hotelencanto.com 210 rooms No meals.*

Broken Spoke Taphouse

BREWPUBS/BEER GARDENS | More than 60 beers are on tap, many of them local, at this lively downtown ale house with an expansive beer garden that often features live music. There's good pub food, too. *302 S. Main St., Las Cruces 575/323–8051 www.thebrokenspoketaphouse.com Closed Sun. and Mon.*

Azul Ultra Lounge

BARS/PUBS | Small plates and inventive cocktails are the draw at this slick hotel lounge. *Hotel Encanto, 705 S. Telshor Blvd., Las Cruces 575/522–4300 www.hotelencanto.com.*

HIKING

The area's best hiking is in **Organ Mountains Desert Peaks National Monument,** about 10 miles northeast of Las Cruces. The site encompasses two natural areas that were set aside for their distinct beauty. There are also several good trails. The 3-mile Dripping Springs Trail passes through the ruins of a 19th-century health resort and has picnic tables, but hikers must register at the park visitor center. The 4-mile Pine Tree Trail, which runs thorugh beautiful ponderosa pines, and the 6-mile Baylor Pass Trail, which affords great mountain views, both leave from Aguirre Springs, the furthest and part of the park from Las Cruces.

GOLF

New Mexico State University Golf Course

GOLF | An 18-hole course that hosts men's and women's NCAA championships also has a full-service bar and grill in addition to the pro shop, driving range, and practice green. Greens fees are $37 on weekends ($51 with cart). *3000 Herb Wimberley Dr., Las Cruces 575/646–3219 www.nmsugolf.com.*

OUTDOOR RECREATION

Leasburg Dam State Park

PARK—SPORTS-OUTDOORS | Built in 1908, Leasburg Dam retains irrigation water for Mesilla Valley farmland and recreational water for this reservoir. Kayakers and anglers enjoy boating and fishing here, and on hot days the cool water draws dozens of swimmers. *12712 State Park Rd., Las Cruces 13 mi north of Las Cruces, take I–25 to Exit 19 575/524–4068 www.emnrd.state.nm.us/SPD/leasburgdamstatepark.html Day use $5 per vehicle.*

Old Mesilla

2 miles southwest of Las Cruces on NM 28.

Historians disagree about the origins of Mesilla (called both Mesilla and Old Mesilla), which in Spanish means "Little Table." Some say the town occupies the exact spot that Don Juan de Oñate declared "the first pueblo of this kingdom."

Many of the sturdy adobe structures abundant in this community date back as far as 150 years and are still in use today. The thick walls of the adobes in this area not only helped keep the interiors cool and comfortable during hot days, but also helped defend against attacks by Apaches, who were none too excited about the influx of people into their territory.

Mesilla was established by a group of lifetime Mexican residents when the territory of New Mexico was acquired by the United States in 1848. Wishing to remain Mexican, they left Las Cruces, moved a few miles west across the new border of the Rio Grande, and established their village in Mexican territory. All this effort was for naught, because the Rio Grande not only changed its path in 1865, putting both Las Cruces and Mesilla east of the river, but the whole area had already been annexed by the United States in 1854. Mesilla had established itself well and was the largest station between El Paso and Los Angeles on the Butterfield Stage Line, and for a time served as the Confederate territorial capital, an area that covered Arizona and western New Mexico. In 1881 the Santa Fe Railroad extended its line into Las Cruces, bypassing Mesilla and establishing Las Cruces as the area's major hub of commerce and transportation.

Mesilla has seen celebrations, weddings, bloody political battles, and the milestone trial of Billy the Kid. A Mesilla jury convicted the Kid for the murder of Matthew Brady, the sheriff of Lincoln County. The Kid was transferred to the Lincoln County Courthouse to be hanged for the crime but briefly staved off the inevitable by escaping.

Head south from Mesilla on NM 28, and you'll find a rural countryside with pecan trees reaching overhead, and onions, chiles, and vineyards filling the fields. This is where you'll also find New Mexico's largest wine-making region. All **Mesilla Valley Wine Trail** wineries have tasting rooms, tours, and are usually closed midweek. The Las Cruces CVB (🌐 *www.lascrucescvb.org*) has information on all the wineries you can visit.

GETTING HERE

Old Mesilla is effectively a community within greater Las Cruces. It lies just a couple of miles southwest of Las Cruces, a short drive on NM 28, which is also locally signed as Avenida de Mesilla.

VISITOR INFORMATION

CONTACTS J. Paul Taylor Visitor Center. ✉ *2231 Avenida de Mesilla [NM 28], Mesilla* ✥ *In Mesilla Town Hall* ☎ *575/524–3262 ext. 117* 🌐 *www.oldmesilla.org.*

Sights

Touristy shops, galleries, and restaurants line the cobbled streets of Old Mesilla. With a Mexican-style plaza and gazebo where many weddings and fiestas take place, the village retains the charm of bygone days. It is well worth parking your car and strolling around the village and the surrounding neighborhoods, where many of the adobe homes are lovingly maintained.

Basilica of San Albino

RELIGIOUS SITE | On the north side of the plaza is the Basilica of San Albino, an impressive 1908 Romanesque brick-and-stained-glass building that is supported by the foundation of the adobe church, built in 1856, that originally stood here. ✉ *2070 Calle de Santiago, Old Mesilla*

Plaza, Mesilla ☎ *575/526–9349* 🌐 *www.sanalbino.org.*

La Viña Winery

WINERY/DISTILLERY | New Mexico's oldest winery—established in 1977—La Viña Winery is now run by proprietors Denise and Ken Stark. La Viña hosts a popular wine festivals in October and April. A wide variety of wines is produced here—from a crisp Viognier, to Pinot Noir, to White Zinfandel. ✉ *4201 S. NM 28, La Union* ✥ *25 miles south of Mesilla* ☎ *575/882–7632* 🌐 *lavina.wolfep.com.*

Rio Grande Vineyard & Winery

WINERY/DISTILLERY | Rio Grande Vineyard & Winery, just over 4 miles south of Old Mesilla, is worth a look. The comfortably appointed tasting room has a fine view of the Organ Mountains, and proprietor Gordon Steel is congenial and informed. ✉ *5321 NM 28, 4 miles south of Mesilla, at mile marker 25, Mesilla* ☎ *575/524–3985* 🌐 *www.riograndewinery.com.*

Zin Valle Vineyards

WINERY/DISTILLERY | In the Mesilla Valley, you may not notice, but you will have crossed into Texas and the town of Canutillo, home of the newest winery in the bunch, Zin Valle Vineyards. They favor sweet wines, such as Gewürztraminer made from grapes grown on-site. ✉ *7315 S. NM 28, Canutillo* ✥ *36 miles south of Mesilla* ☎ *915/877–4544* 🌐 *www.zinvalle.com.*

Restaurants

★ Chope's Bar & Cafe

$ | **MEXICAN** | Pronounced *cho-pez*, it looks like a run-of-the-mill adobe building from the outside, but inside the 150-year-old former Benavidez homestead you'll find happy locals and many turistas eating well-seasoned Mexican food and drinking ice-cold beer and tasty margaritas. Bikers join the convivial crowd in the bar next door; like the restaurant, it's still owned by the Benavidez family. **Known for:** local favorite; homemade rellenos; history (est. 1909). $ *Average main: $8* ✉ *16145 S. NM 28, La Mesa* ☎ *575/233–3420 restaurant, 575/233–3420 bar.*

★ Double Eagle

$$$$ | **EUROPEAN** | Chandeliers, century-old wall tapestries, and gold-leaf ceilings set the scene at this elegant restaurant inside an 1848 mansion on Old Mesilla's plaza. Some say ghosts, including one of a young man who incurred his mother's wrath by falling in love with a servant girl, haunt the property. **Known for:** margaritas; tableside preparation; historic ambience. $ *Average main: $35* ✉ *2355 Calle de Guadalupe, Mesilla* ☎ *575/523–6700* 🌐 *www.doubleeagleonline.com.*

La Posta

$ | **MEXICAN** | Once a way station for the Butterfield Overland Mail and Wells Fargo stagecoaches, this restaurant in an old adobe structure has hosted many celebrities through the years, including Bob Hope and Mexican revolutionary Pancho Villa. Some of the Mexican recipes here date back more than a century; among the best menu choices are *tostadas compuestas* (red or green chile, meat, and pinto beans in tortilla shells), and enchiladas with red or green chile. **Known for:** spicy Mexican food; historic ambiance; unique atrium with plants and birds. $ *Average main: $13* ✉ *2410 Calle de San Albino, Mesilla* ☎ *575/524–3524* 🌐 *www.lapostademesilla.com.*

★ Luna Rossa Winery & Pizzeria

$$ | **ITALIAN** | Skeptics are sometimes surprised by the high quality of southern New Mexico wines, with Mimbres Valley's Luna Rossa among the region's most impressive vintners, specializing in estate-grown, mostly Italian and Spanish, varietals like Dolcetto and Tempranillo. Here at the winery's casual restaurant in Mesilla, you can sample the wines while enjoying terrific pizzas, pastas, panini sandwiches, and house-made gelato. **Known for:** romantic enclosed patio; extensive selection of local wines; green chile-prosciutto pizzas. $ *Average main: $15* ✉ *1321 Ave. de*

Mesilla, Mesilla ☎ 575/526–2484 🌐 www.lunarossawinery.com.

★ **Salud! de Mesilla**

$$ | **BISTRO** | Close to Old Mesilla Plaza, this stylish neighborhood bistro is filled with local art for sale and has several different dining areas, including a lively little bar and a covered patio. Known for its all-day, everyday brunch menu (try the French toast with berry compote, perhaps with a Prosecco mimosa) as well as a selection of international tapas, it's a welcoming venue for a leisurely meal. **Known for:** market selling local wines, gourmet snacks, and gifts; build-your-own Benedicts with creative toppings; crème brûlée. *$ Average main: $19 ✉ 1800 Ave. de Mesilla, Mesilla ☎ 575/323–3548 🌐 www.saludmesilla.com ⏲ Closed Mon. and Tues.*

Performing Arts

The Fountain Theatre

THEATER | The Fountain Theatre, which still has its original 1870s facade and vintage murals from the 1910s and 1920s inside, was bought in 1905 by the prominent Fountain family, who began showing movies here in 1912. Now under the aegis of the Mesilla Valley Film Society, the oldest continuously operating theater in New Mexico presents independent films, amateur theater, and some chamber music concerts. *✉ 2469 Calle de Guadalupe, ½ block south of Old Mesilla Plaza, Mesilla ☎ 575/524–8287 🌐 www.mesillavalleyfilm.org.*

Nightlife

El Patio

MUSIC CLUBS | Head over to El Patio, in the plaza in Old Mesilla, for some of the area's best live music. Established in 1934, this unassuming little adobe cantina touts itself as the oldest bar in New Mexico. The cantina is open seven days a week, live music happens Wednesday through Saturday. *✉ 2171 Calle de Parian, Mesilla ☎ 575/526–9943.*

Shopping

ART GALLERIES

Mesilla Valley Fine Arts Gallery

ART GALLERIES | The oldest artist co-op in the Las Cruces area, the Mesilla Valley Fine Arts Gallery has a broad range of art by 30 juried artists. *✉ 2470A Calle de Guadalupe, southeast corner of Old Mesilla Plaza, Mesilla ☎ 575/522–2933 🌐 www.mesillavalleyfinearts.com.*

SHOPPING NEIGHBORHOODS

Old Mesilla Plaza

SHOPPING NEIGHBORHOODS | High-quality Native American jewelry and crafts are sold at surprisingly good prices in the adobe shops of Old Mesilla Plaza if you have the patience to weed through multitudes of cheesy ceramic Native American dolls with feathered headdresses (not what the locals wore) and other various and sundry tourist tchotchkes. The al fresco **Farmers Market** offers homegrown produce such as watermelons and green chiles (in season), as well as handcrafted souvenirs and jewelry, on the plaza noon to 4 Sunday and 11 to 4 Friday year-round. In mid-afternoon on Sunday from September to early November, you can enjoy live mariachi music here, too. *✉ Mesilla.*

Silver City

235 miles southwest of Albuquerque on I–25 to NM 152; 115 miles northwest of Las Cruces, west on I–10 and northwest on U.S. 180; 152 miles south of Quemado/U.S. 60 via NM 32/12 to U.S. 180.

Silver City began as a tough and lawless mining camp in 1870, and struggled for a long time to become a more respectable—and permanent—settlement. Henry McCarty spent part of his boyhood here, perhaps learning some of the ruthlessness that led to his later infamy under his nickname—Billy the Kid. Other mining towns in the area sparked briefly and then died, but Silver City eventually flourished and became the area's most populated city. Today, even though it has about 10,000 residents, Silver City retains a sense of remote wildness—largely due to the nearby Gila National Forest and vast Gila Wilderness.

GETTING HERE

Most travelers come to Silver City either from Las Cruces via U.S. 180, which turns into Silver Heights Boulevard within the city limits and intersects Hudson Street; or from Albuquerque via I–25 south, then either turning west onto U.S. 60, and south along the western extent of the Gila National Forest via NM32/12 and U.S. 180, or, exiting I-25 onto NM 152 (part of the Geronimo Trail Scenic Byway). If you're headed here from southern Arizona on I–10, you'll want to turn north on NM 90 at Lordsburg. ■ **TIP→ NM 152 is a spectacular (and very slow) ride, but seasonal snow and ice can make for treacherous driving.** If the weather has become dicey, continue on I-25 south to Hatch, then proceed west on NM 26 to U.S. 180. Call ahead for road conditions.

VISITOR INFORMATION

CONTACTS Silver City/Grant County Chamber of Commerce. ✉ *201 N. Hudson St., Silver City* ☎ *575/538–3785, 575/538–5555* 🌐 *www.visitsilvercity.org.*

Sights

Since the area's copper ore is now close to depleted and the huge mine nearby all but officially closed, the town's traditional population of miners is being replaced by artists, outdoors enthusiasts, and retirees looking for a more bohemian community than, say, Las Cruces. Thanks to efforts of preservationists, though, Silver City's origins are evident in the many distinctive houses and storefronts of the downtown area, making it ideal for exploring by foot. The characterless strip-style development of the surrounding town belies the charm of the compact, walkable historic downtown.

A stroll through the historic downtown district will take you by many of the town's dozen or so art galleries, several tasty cafés, and antiques stores. Silver City's arts scene couldn't be more different from the one in Santa Fe. A local artist once said, "Silver City is where art is for *the* people, not *some* people."

City of Rocks State Park

NATIONAL/STATE PARK | **FAMILY** | One look at the spires here and you'll figure out how the area came by its name. The unusual rock formations were spewed from an ancient volcano and have been eroded over the centuries by wind and rain into the marvelous shapes there today—some more than 40 feet tall. You've got to walk through the city to fully appreciate the place—and it's a great, easy adventure to have with kids (make sure you wear tennis shoes or hiking shoes). The park has a visitor center, and a large developed campground ($10 to $14) with 9 RV sites with water and electric hookups, 41 camping sites, picnic tables, grills, flush toilets, and showers. This is a great spot to camp, with sites nestled amongst the huge rocks. An on-site observatory regularly hosts star parties. ✉ *327 NM 61, Faywood* ✣ *From Silver City, follow U.S. 180 southeast for 26 miles; then NM 61 northeast for 4 miles* ☎ *575/536–2800* 🌐 *www.emnrd.state.nm.us/SPD/cityofrocksstatepark.html* 🎟 *Day use $5 per vehicle.*

El Chino Mine

MINE | The wrenching 1954 movie *Salt of the Earth* chronicled the Empire Zinc Mine strike that took place less than 1 mile away, in Hanover, and while that mine is long gone, the ups and downs of the El Chino Mine reveal a similar and compelling story about economy, race, and politics in Grant County. Now owned by Freeport-McMoRan Copper & Gold, the vast, open-pit mine—commonly referred to as the Santa Rita Mine, for the little village that was founded here in 1803, and was literally swallowed as the pit expanded in the mid-20th century—is 1,500-feet-deep and 1½ miles across. It cuts back or ceases operation when the price of copper falls too low. Copper mining in the region dates back centuries, and began in tunnels that were labored over first by indigenous populations, then by the Spanish and Mexicans. The observation point offers interpretative signage. ✉ *NM 152, Hanover* ✥ *15 miles east of Silver City, just west of mile marker 6* ☎ *575/537–3327 or 800/548–9378* 🎫 *Observation point free.*

Fort Bayard

HISTORIC SITE | Established in 1866, Fort Bayard was built by the U.S. Army when it became clear that conflict between homeland Apaches and early Anglo and Spanish settlers would not easily abate. Company B of the 125th U.S. Colored Infantry was first in command, and hundreds of African-American enlisted men, or buffalo soldiers, made their mark here. A huge Fort Bayard Days celebration takes place annually, on the third weekend of September, and visitors can watch re-enactors and learn about this national historic landmark's later life as a groundbreaking tuberculosis research facility; bimonthly tours (reservations essential) are offered. ✉ *U.S. 180, Bayard* ✥ *10 miles east of Silver City* ☎ *575/388–4477* 🌐 *www.fortbayard.org* 🎫 *Donations accepted.*

Geronimo Trail Scenic Byway

SCENIC DRIVE | One of the most visually dramatic ways to reach Silver City is via NM 152, which forms the southern prong of the backward-C-shaped Geronimo Trail Scenic Byway (the northern prong is NM 52, leading into Winston and Chloride). As you're heading south down I–25 from Albuquerque and Truth or Consequences, take exit 63, and follow NM 152 west. It's about an 80-mi drive to Silver City, and you should allow two to four hours, depending on how much you stop to look around—and weather conditions.

This twisting byway provides an exciting link to the Wild West. The remote drive (there are no gas stations) follows part of the route taken by the Kingston Lake Valley Stage Line, which operated when this region was terrorized by Apache leaders like Geronimo and outlaw bands led by the likes of Butch Cassidy. Heading west on NM 152, after about 25 miles you'll come to the mining-era boomtown, **Hillsboro,** where gold was discovered as well as silver (about $6 million worth of the two ores was extracted). The town, slowly coming back to life with the artists and retirees who've moved in, has a small museum, some shops, restaurants, and galleries.

From Hillsboro, you might consider a brief detour south down NM 27, known as the Lake Valley Back Country Byway. A landmark, west of NM 27, is Cooke's Peak, where the first wagon road through the Southwest to California was opened in 1846. Not much is going on these days in the old silver mining town of **Lake Valley**—the last residents departed in the mid-1990s—but it once was home to 4,000 people. The mine produced 2.5 million ounces of pure silver and gave up one nugget weighing several hundred pounds. Visit the schoolhouse (which later served as a saloon), walk around the chapel, the railroad depot, and some of the few remaining old homes. ✉ *Silver City* 🌐 *www.geronimotrail.com.*

Percha Bank Museum

MUSEUM | Back on NM 152, continue 10 miles west to reach another vintage mining town, Kingston, home to the **Percha Bank Museum,** which is just a skip away from the Black Range Lodge and is well worth a visit. It was built in 1885 to handle the enormous wealth that so suddenly, and so briefly, transformed this town when a massive silver lode was discovered. All that remains intact of that era is the building itself, which is beautifully preserved, with the original vault and teller windows still in place. Photos of the town during its heyday in the late 1880s are fascinating. From Kingston, it's another 50 mi to Silver City on NM 152, which joins U.S. 180 just east of town. ✉ *46 Main St., Kingston* ☎ *575/895–5652* 🎫 *Donations accepted.*

Shakespeare Ghost Town

GHOST TOWN | FAMILY | If you're heading southwest from Silver City (or west toward Arizona from Las Cruces), this is a fun stop. Portions of this settlement in the heart of a working ranch just outside the sleepy town of Lordsburg have been preserved as they were in the town's heyday as a gold and silver mining town in the late 1800s. Founded in 1856, the ghost town has been designated a National Historic Site, and original structures such as homes, saloons, and stables still stand. You'll find no snack shops or other tourist amenities in Shakespeare, as owner Janaloo Hill (who grew up on the ranch, and died in May 2005) vowed not to compromise the authenticity of this genuine piece of the Old West. Shakespeare is about 50 miles from Silver City via NM 90 through Lordsburg. ✉ *Lordsburg* ✣ *2½ miles southwest of Lordsburg, south of I–10 at Exit 22* ☎ *575/542–9034* 🌐 *www.shakespearehostown.com* 🎫 *$5 monthly scheduled tour, $7 private tours.*

Silver City Museum

MUSEUM | The unusual mansard-roof Italianate-style Henry B. Ailman House, built in 1881, serves as headquarters for the Silver City Museum, whose main gallery mural of the mining and ranching community circa 1882 provides a good overview of the area's colorful history. Displays include pottery and other relics from the area's ancient (and now extinct) Mimbres and Mogollon cultures, as well as a nice lot of items from the heyday of the mining era. From the museum's tower you can catch a grand view of the eclectic architecture around town. The store carries Southwest-themed books and gifts, and the museum also has a local-history research library. ✉ *312 W. Broadway, Silver City* ☎ *575/538–5921* 🌐 *www.silvercitymuseum.org* 🎫 *$5 suggested donation.*

Western New Mexico University Museum (WNMU)

MUSEUM | The Western New Mexico University Museum (WNMU) contains the world's largest permanent display of distinctive black-on-white Mimbres pottery (it's especially notable for its crisply painted animal forms). The Mimbres collection—which the museum bought for a remarkable $1,000 from the family of the man who procured most of the pieces by illicit pot hunting—fills the main floor of this 1917 Trost & Trost building that once housed WNMU's science classes and gym. Town history exhibits are displayed downstairs, including a period classroom and the original gym floor. Set on a hill on the west end of town, WNMU's campus offers a nice view of the surrounding mountains and the valley below; the museum's topmost floor is window-lined, and visitors can enjoy the broader view from that vantage point, as well as historic photos and other university memorabilia. Mimbres designs are reproduced on mugs and more in the gift shop. ✉ *Fleming Hall, 1000 W. College Ave., on campus at west end of 10th St., Silver City* ☎ *575/538–6386* 🌐 *museum.wnmu.edu* 🎫 *Donations accepted; tours $10 per person suggested* ⏲ *Closed Sun.*

Restaurants

Diane's Restaurant

$$ | AMERICAN | Fresh flowers grace the wooden tables and light streams through the large windows at this cheerful bakery and eatery. Owner Diane Barrett's menu includes Hatch-green-chile Benedict, "Grandma's" spaghetti, steaks, and a deftly prepared lemon-caper chicken. **Known for:** house-baked bread and desserts; quality ingredients; eclectic menu.

$ *Average main: $20* ✉ *510 N. Bullard St., Silver City* ☎ *575/538-8722* 🌐 *www.dianesrestaurant.com* ⏲ *No dinner Sun.*

Jalisco Cafe

$ | **MEXICAN** | The Mesa family serves up hunger-busting traditional Mexican food here, all based on old family recipes. Enchiladas and chiles rellenos (ask for the green chile on the rellenos—strangely, they charge extra for it, but it's worth it) satisfy big appetites in the cheerful dining rooms decorated with art from local artists and packed with families. **Known for:** spicy green chile; local favorite; rellenos. $ *Average main: $12* ✉ *103 S. Bullard St., Silver City* ☎ *575/388-2060* ⏲ *Closed Sun.*

Coffee and Quick Bites

Javalina Coffee House

$ | **CAFÉ** | Although the food menu is scant at this quirky java spot, the coffees are good and the space comfortable for spreading out and sipping. There's free Wi-Fi. $ *Average main: $3* ✉ *200 N. Bullard St., Silver City* ☎ *575/388-1350.*

Hotels

Bear Mountain Lodge

$$ | **B&B/INNHOTEL** | Once owned and operated by the Nature Conservancy, this serene 1928 haven was restored in 2010, and reopened to great acclaim in the hands of new owners, Linda Brewer and John Rohovec, who continue to offer luxury accommodations for bird-watchers and nature lovers. **Pros:** quiet, distinctive hideaway; range of activities beyond bird-watching; separate cottages good for groups. **Cons:** a 10- to 15-minute drive to Silver City dining and shopping; it can be quiet here... too quiet for some; restaurant doesn't serve dinner except on request. $ *Rooms from: $170* ✉ *60 Bear Mountain Ranch Rd., 3 miles north of Silver City via Alabama St., which becomes Cottage San Rd., Silver City* ☎ *575/538-2538* 🌐 *www.bearmountainlodge.com* *11 rooms* 🍽 *Free Breakfast.*

Black Range Lodge

$ | **B&B/INN** | **FAMILY** | This getaway in the old mining ghost town of Kingston, along the Geronimo Trail Scenic Byway (NM 152), has sturdy log-beam ceilings, massive stone walls, an interesting history, and an informal, rustic atmosphere that makes it nice for families, but the charm here owes a lot to the care and tending, and presence, of the proprietors. **Pros:** great for a group retreat or family reunion; in a genuine near-ghost town; some rooms have fantastic views. **Cons:** no restaurants for miles; Silver City is about an hour away; only breakfast is prepared for guests. $ *Rooms from: $99* ✉ *119 Main St. (NM 152), Kingston* ☎ *575/895-5652* 🌐 *www.blackrangelodge.com* *8 rooms* 🍽 *Free Breakfast.*

Palace Hotel

$ | **HOTEL** | This grand two-story building was built in 1882 as a bank, but it was reinvented as a hotel in 1900. **Pros:** located downtown; steeped in history; free Wi-Fi. **Cons:** no a/c, which is okay most of the time at this elevation, but it can get downright hot; no restaurant in the hotel (just breakfast); rooms and bathrooms are period-small. $ *Rooms from: $62* ✉ *106 W. Broadway, Silver City* ☎ *575/388-1811* *19 rooms* 🍽 *Free Breakfast.*

Shopping

Shops, galleries, cafés, parks, and all sorts of building renovation make walking Silver City's Downtown district a super way to explore this great little town.

Silver City Trading Co.'s Antique Mall

ANTIQUES/COLLECTIBLES | Vendors at the Silver City Trading Co.'s Antique Mall stock antiques, collectibles, and various and sundry treasures and trinkets. There are some real finds in this filled-to-the-rafters space, for a lot less than you'll see in many areas. Take some time to look in the nooks and crannies. ✉ *205 W. Broadway, Silver City* ☎ *505/388–8989* 🌐 *www.silvercitytrading.com.*

★ **Syzygy Tileworks**

CERAMICS/GLASSWARE | For folks drawn to the unique warmth and hand-crafted look of decorative tiles, Syzygy Tileworks is a must-stop. The founders of Syzygy create their own art tiles inspired by the famed Moravian tile works in Doylestown, Pennsylvania; the results are a refreshing complement to traditional Southwestern styles. ✉ *106 N. Bullard St., Silver City* ☎ *575/388–5472* 🌐 *www.syzygytile.com.*

★ **Wild West Weaving**

TEXTILES/SEWING | Hosana Eilert, the proprietor of Wild West Weaving learned her craft in Chimayó, with the masters of the Rio Grande weaving style, the Trujillos of Centinela Traditional Arts. Eilert's skills are comparable but her special sense of color and design are hers alone. She uses mostly natural dyes and handspun wool for her work, which may be used either as tapestry or rug. ✉ *211D Texas St., Silver City* ☎ *575/313–1032* 🌐 *www.wildwestweaving.com.*

Gila National Forest

8 miles northeast of Silver City via NM 15 to Pinos Altos range and Gila Cliff Dwellings portion of Gila National Forest; 60 miles northwest of Silver City via U.S. 180 to western portions of forest; 6 miles southwest of U.S. 60 at Quemado via NM 32 to northern forest areas. The eastern edge of forest can be accessed via NM 152, the Geronimo Trail Scenic Byway, which spans about 80 miles between Silver City and I–25 near Caballo Lake (which is between Truth of Consequences and Las Cruces).

The Gila, as it's called, covers 3.3 million acres—that's 65 miles by 100 miles—and includes the first land in the nation to be set aside as a protected "wilderness" by the U.S. Forest Service back in 1924. The area is vast and continues to feel like a great, relatively undiscovered treasure. You are unlikely to come across any crowds, even in peak summer months. Whether you're backpacking or doing day hikes, you have hundreds of miles of incredibly diverse trails to explore. Open camping is permitted throughout the forest, although there are 18 developed campgrounds (all with toilets and seven with potable water). The Gila is an outdoors-lover's paradise: with seemingly endless trails to explore on mountain bikes, white-water rafting (the season usually starts in April), and fishing in rivers, lakes (three of them), and streams.

The **Trail of the Mountain Spirits Scenic Byway** (also referred to as the **Inner Loop Scenic Drive**) snakes through 93 miles of some of the most gorgeous and scenic forest in the wilderness. The roads are paved but the sharp, narrow, and steep turns make it inadvisable for large RVs. From Silver City, take NM 15 north to Gila Cliff Dwellings National Monument. From the monument backtrack on NM 15 to NM 35 heading southeast to NM 152, which leads west back to Silver City. ■ **TIP→ Remember: these forest roads are slow—double your travel time estimates. And don't pass up an opportunity to fill-up your tank—gas stations beyond Silver City can be scarce.**

VISITOR INFORMATION

All area Forest Service offices are open 8 am to 4:30 pm, Monday through Friday, and can provide maps, trail information, and travel conditions. (🌐 *fs.usda.gov/gila*)

CONTACTS Silver City Ranger District. ✉ *3005 E. Camino del Bosque, Silver City* ☎ *575/388–8201.* **Wilderness Ranger District.** ✉ *3697 NM 35,* ✣ *11 miles north of NM 152* ☎ *575/536–2250.* **Glenwood Ranger District.** ✉ *18 Ranger Station Rd., Glenwood* ☎ *575/539–2481.*

Catwalk National Recreation Trail

TRAIL | A primary destination here is the splendid Catwalk National Recreation Trail, a 250-foot-long metal walkway drilled into the sides of the massive rock cliffs of the breathtaking Whitewater Canyon—which is only 20 feet wide in places. This is one of the most verdant, beautiful canyons in the state, with the creek and tumbling waterfalls surrounded by gorgeous rocks and shade trees. The Catwalk, first installed as an access route for water lines critical to local gold- and silver-mining operations in the late 1800s, was rebuilt in 1935 for recreation purposes, and rebuilt again after a 2012 flood. A number of famous outlaws, including Butch Cassidy and the Wild Bunch, have used the canyon as a hideout because of its remote, and almost inaccessible, location. You need to be in reasonably good physical condition to scramble up some stone stairways, but the 2.2-mile round-trip trail is well-maintained and worth the effort; there is a nice alternate route that is wheelchair accessible. Bring your bathing suit so you can enjoy standing under the waterfalls and splashing in the creek. Admission is $3. ✉ *Catwalk Rd. [NM 174], Glenwood* ✢ *turn east from U.S. 180 and proceed 5 miles.*

★ Gila Cliff Dwellings National Monument
NATIVE SITE | FAMILY | At **Gila Cliff Dwellings National Monument** the mystery of the Mogollon (*muh*-gee-yohn) people's short-lived occupation of the deeply recessed caves high above the canyon floor may never be resolved. But the finely detailed stone dwellings they left behind stand in silent testimony to the challenges as well as the beauty of the surrounding Gila Wilderness. Built and inhabited for a span of barely two generations, from 1280 to the early 1300s AD, its 42 rooms are tucked into six natural caves that are reached via a rugged one-mile loop trail that ascends 180 feet from the trail head. Constructed from the same pale volcanic stone as the cliffs themselves, the rooms are all but camouflaged until you are about a half-mile along the trail. You can contemplate, from a rare close-up vantage point, the keyhole doorways that punctuate the dwelling walls and gaze out upon a ponderosa pine- and cottonwood-forested terrain that looks much like the one the Mogollon people inhabited seven centuries ago. The wealth of pottery, yucca sandals, tools, and other artifacts buried here were picked clean by the late 1800s—dispersed to private collectors. But the visitor center has a small museum with books and other materials about the wilderness, its trails, and the Mogollon. It's a 2-mile drive from the visitor center to the Dwellings trail head (and other nearby trails); there are interesting pictographs to be seen on the wheelchair-accessible **Trail to the Past.**

■ TIP→ Allow a good 2 hours from Silver City to the Cliff Dwellings via NM 15 or via NM 35; though longer in mileage, the NM 35 route is an easier ride. If you can spare the time, spend the night at one of the mountain inns close to the dwellings to maximize your time in the park. ✉ *26 Big Jim Bradford Trail* ✢ *44 miles north of Silver City* ☎ *575/536–9461, 575/536–9344* 🌐 *www.nps.gov/gicl* 🎫 *Free.*

Whitewater Canyon
GHOST TOWN | U.S. 180 leads northwest about 50 mi from Silver City to Glenwood and Whitewater Canyon—the gateway to the western reaches of the Gila. Return to U.S. 180, and go north 3 miles (just before the very little town of Alma, where you can get some snacks at the **Alma Grill** or Trading Post), and turn east onto NM 159. Your rewarding destination, about 45 minutes in, on a sometimes one-lane dirt road, is **Mogollon** (muh-gee-yohn). The gold-mining town, established in the 1880s, was a ghost town for many years but has been revived in the last few decades by a dozen or so residents who live there year-round. A small museum, an antique shop, and a café operate on the weekends. Book a stay at the Silver Creek Inn (🌐 *www.silvercreekinn.com*) and you can spend the weekend exploring this interesting relic of the American West, as well as the breathtaking, and huge, Gila National Forest bordering it. 🎫 *Free*

Restaurants

Along the western reaches of the Gila, your best bets for dining and lodging are in the towns of Gila, Glenwood, Alma, Mogollon, and Reserve—all on (or just off) U.S. 180/NM 12. If you're venturing up to the Cliff Dwellings, consider spots in Pinos Altos or Gila Hot Springs, both along NM 15.

★ Buckhorn Saloon & Opera House

$$ | **STEAKHOUSE** | Come here to see 1860s Western decor and stay for the food—including some of the best steak and seafood in the region. The bar is a friendly place to gather; the dining rooms are cozy, the tablecloths white, and the walls replete with photos from the last 140 years of the area's history. **Known for:** historic ambience; hearty fare; live music. *Average main: $19 32 Main St., off NM 15, 7 miles north of Silver City, Pinos Altos 575/538–9911 www.buckhornsaloonandoperahouse.com Closed Sun. No lunch.*

Carmen's

$ | **MEXICAN** | Here's a great little place to stop on NM 12 in the northwestern reaches of the Gila National Forest. Not just because of the spicy enchiladas and chicken-fried steak, but because once you leave the hamlet of Reserve, New Mexico (population about 500), dinner options are scarce—Quemado is about 55 miles to the north. **Known for:** spicy Mexican food; local favorite; very reasonable prices. *Average main: $9 110 Main St., Reserve 575/533–6999.*

Hotels

★ Bear Creek Motel & Cabins

$$ | **RENTAL** | **FAMILY** | A ponderosa pine forest surrounds the silvered wood-and-stone, two-story cabins, half of which have kitchens with cookware, and fireplaces. **Pros:** just 7 miles north of Silver City, but appealingly remote; en route to Gila Cliff Dwellings; plenty of nearby activities. **Cons:** dining choices nearby are limited; no food service on site, but you do have a kitchen; rustic but inviting. *Rooms from: $119 88 Main St. (NM 15), 7 miles north of Silver City, Pinos Altos 575/388–4501, 888/388–4515 www.bearcreekcabins.com 15 cabins No meals.*

★ Casitas de Gila

$$ | **RENTAL** | On the western edge of the Gila Wilderness are five well-appointed private casitas ("little houses" in Spanish) overlooking Bear Creek, nestled on 260 gorgeous acres. **Pros:** peace and quiet; mountain vistas and the brightest stars you've ever seen; trails right on property. **Cons:** access is by a winding, slow (with some gravel) road for the last 4 miles; the nearest town of Gila doesn't offer much; property has only one shared hot tub. *Rooms from: $170 50 Casita Flats Rd., off Hooker Loop, 30 miles northwest of Silver City 575/535–4455 www.casitasdegila.com 5 casitas Free Breakfast.*

Chapter 15

DENVER AND NORTH-CENTRAL COLORADO

WITH ROCKY MOUNTAIN NATIONAL PARK

Updated by
Lindsey Gallowa,
Aimee Heckel, and
Kyle Wagner

Sights	Restaurants	Hotels	Shopping	Nightlife
★★★★★	★★★★★	★★★★★	★★★★☆	★★★★☆

WELCOME TO DENVER AND NORTH-CENTRAL COLORADO

TOP REASONS TO GO

★ **LoDo:** Lower downtown's appeal lies in its proximity to Coors Field. Shops and galleries are busy during the day, and it's also a hot spot at night.

★ **Red Rocks Park and Amphitheatre:** Even if you aren't attending a concert, the awe-inspiring red rocks of this formation-turned-venue are worth a look, and there are hiking trails nearby.

★ **Tour the Coors Brewery:** An entertaining (and free) tour ends with an informal tasting.

★ **Ride the Georgetown Loop Railroad:** The vintage train ride from Georgetown to Silverplume provides an eye-opening lesson in 1800s transportation.

★ **Gorgeous scenery:** Rocky Mountain National Park has more than 100 lakes, majestic mountain peaks, lush wetlands, pine-scented woods, forests of spruce and fir, and alpine tundra.

1 **Denver.** Colorado's capital city is a thriving metropolis on a high plateau east of the Rockies.

2 **Greater Denver.** A collection of neighborhoods east, west, north, and south of the city center, including Cherry Creek and the Central Platte Valley.

3 **Golden.** Once the territorial capital of Colorado and home to Coors Brewery.

4 **Georgetown.** A one-time silver mining boom town.

5 **Estes Park.** The main gateway to Rocky Mountain Nationl Park may be best known for the majestic Stanley Hotel.

6 **Rocky Mountain National Park.** Known for its scenery, hiking, wildlife-watching, camping, and snowshoeing.

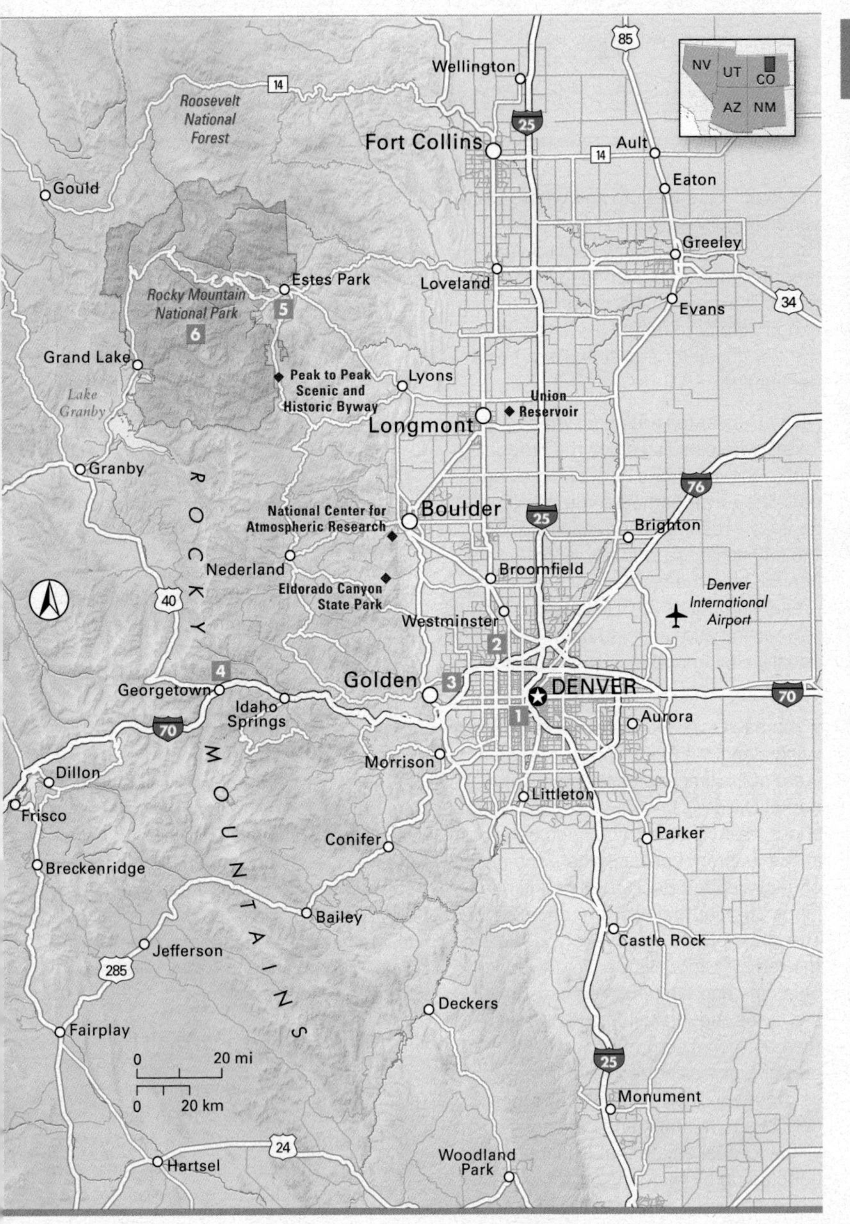

Wellington
Roosevelt National Forest
Fort Collins
Ault
Gould
Eaton
Greeley
Estes Park
Loveland
Rocky Mountain National Park
Evans
Grand Lake
Peak to Peak Scenic and Historic Byway
Lyons
Union Reservoir
Lake Granby
Longmont
Granby
ROCKY MOUNTAINS
National Center for Atmospheric Research
Boulder
Brighton
Nederland
Broomfield
Eldorado Canyon State Park
Denver International Airport
Westminster
Golden
Georgetown
Idaho Springs
DENVER
Aurora
Dillon
Morrison
Frisco
Littleton
Conifer
Parker
Breckenridge
Bailey
Castle Rock
Jefferson
Deckers
Fairplay
0
20 mi
20 km
Monument
Hartsel
Woodland Park
NV
UT
CO
AZ
NM

You can tell from its skyline alone that Denver is a major metropolis, with a Major League Baseball stadium at one end of downtown and the State Capitol building at the other.

But look to the west to see where Denver distinguishes itself in the majestic Rocky Mountains, snow-peaked and breathtakingly huge, looming in the distance. This combination of urban sprawl and proximity to nature is what gives the city character and sets it apart as a destination.

Many Denverites are unabashed nature lovers who can also enjoy the outdoors within the city limits by walking along the park-lined river paths downtown. (Perhaps as a result of their active lifestyle, the city is named annually as one of the healthiest in the nation.) For Denverites, preserving the environment and the city's rich mining and ranching heritage are of equally vital importance to the quality of life.

If you have ever wondered why folks living along the Front Range—as the area west of Denver and east of the Continental Divide is known—continually brag about their lifestyles, you need only look at the western horizon, where the peaks of snowcapped Rocky Mountains rise just a 35-minute drive from downtown. The allure of this area, which rises from the red-rock foothills cloaked in lodgepole pine and white-barked aspens to the steep mountainsides draped with the occasional summer snowfields, has brought increasing recreational pressures as mountain bikers, equestrians, hikers, dog lovers, hunters, and conservationists all vie for real estate that is increasingly gobbled up by McMansion sprawl.

Farther north, the scenery is even more spectacular and the climate equally appealing. Rocky Mountain National Park is one of the nation's most popular outdoor areas, with hiking, rock climbing, biking, skiing, and kayaking.

Planning

When to Go

Denver weather defies easy weather predictions. Although the blizzards are infamous, snowstorms are often followed by beautiful spring weather just a day or two later. Arts and music festivals start up in May and continue through September, with a rock-concert slate and films on the big screen at nearby Red Rocks Park and Amphitheatre in the summer. Perhaps the best times to visit, though, are spring and fall, when the heat isn't so intense, the snow isn't so plentiful, and crowds are relatively thin. Ski resorts are still as scenic, but less expensive. Since summers are hot in the cities, locals tend to escape to the higher elevations of the Front Range, and the heavy weekend traffic bears that out.

More than 80% of Rocky Mountain National Park's annual 4.7 million visitors come in summer and fall. For thinner high-season crowds, come in early June or September. But there is a good reason to put up with summer crowds: only from late May to mid-October will you get the chance to make the unforgettable drive over Trail Ridge Road (note that the road may still be closed during those months if the weather turns bad). Spring is capricious—75°F one day and a blizzard the next (March sees the most snow).

Getting Here and Around

AIR

Denver International Airport (DEN) is 15 miles northeast of downtown, but it usually takes about a half hour to 45 minutes to travel between them, depending on the time of day. It's served by most major domestic carriers and many international ones. Arrive at the airport with plenty of time before your flight, preferably two hours; the airport's check-in and security-check lines are particularly long.

AIRPORT TRANSFERS

Between the airport and downtown Denver, Super Shuttle makes door-to-door trips. The region's public bus service, Regional Transportation District (RTD), runs SkyRide to and from the airport; the trip takes 50 minutes, and the fare is $9–$26 each way. There's a transportation center in the airport just outside baggage claim. A taxi ride to downtown costs $60–$70.

Estes Park Shuttle (reservations essential) serves Estes Park and Rocky Mountain National Park from Denver and Denver International Airport.

CONTACTS Estes Park Shuttle. ☎ *970/586–5151* 🌐 *www.estesparkshuttle.com.* **Regional Transportation District/SkyRide.** ☎ *303/299–6000 for route and schedule information* 🌐 *www.rtd-denver.com.* **Super Shuttle.** ☎ *303/370–1300* 🌐 *www.supershuttle.com.*

BUS

In downtown Denver, a free shuttle-bus service, called the Free MallRide, operates about every 10 minutes from 5 am weekdays (5:30 am Saturday; 6:30 am Sunday and holidays) until 1:19 am, running the length of the 16th Street Mall (which bisects downtown) and stopping at one-block intervals. In addition, the Free MetroRide offers weekday rush-hour service between Union Station and Civic Center Station, making limited stops along 18th and 19th streets. If you plan to spend much time outside downtown, a car is advised, although Denver has one of the best city bus systems in the country.

The region's public bus service, RTD, is comprehensive, with routes throughout the metropolitan area. The service also links Denver to outlying towns such as Boulder, Longmont, and Nederland. You can buy bus tokens at grocery stores or pay with exact change on the bus. Fares vary according to time and zone. Within the city limits, buses cost $2.80.

CONTACTS RTD. ☎ *303/299–6000, 800/366–7433* 🌐 *www.rtd-denver.com.*

CAR

Rental-car companies all have airport and downtown representatives.

Reaching Denver by car is fairly easy, except during rush hour. Interstate highways 70 and 25 intersect near downtown; an entrance to I–70 is just outside the airport. Try to avoid driving in the area during rush hour, when traffic gets heavy. Interstates 25 and 225 are particularly slow during those times; although the Transportation Expansion Project (T-REX) added extra lanes, a light-rail system along the highways, bicycle lanes, and other improvements, expansion in the metro area outpaced the project.

Interstate 25, the most direct route from Denver to Fort Collins, is the north–south artery that connects the cities in the urban corridor along the Front Range. From Denver, U.S. 36 runs through Boulder, Lyons, and Estes Park to Rocky Mountain National Park. If you're driving directly to Estes Park and Rocky Mountain National Park from Denver International Airport, take the E–470 tollway to

I-25. U.S. 36 between Boulder and Estes Park is heavily traveled, while highways 119, 72, and 7 have much less traffic.

CONTACTS

TAXI AND RIDE SHARE

Within Denver, taxis can be costly and difficult to simply flag down compared to some some major metropolitan areas; instead, you usually must call ahead to arrange for one. Cabs are $2.50–$3.50 minimum and $2.25–$2.80 per mile, depending on the company. However, at peak times—during major events, and at 2 am when the bars close—taxis are very hard to come by. Ride Share services like Uber and Lyft can be considerably cheaper and faster.

CONTACTS Metro Taxi. ☎ *303/333–3333* 🌐 *www.metrotransportationdenver.com.* **Yellow Cab.** ☎ *303/777–7777* 🌐 *www.denveryellowcab.com.*

TRAIN

Denver's historic Union Station in the heart of downtown has undergone extensive redevelopment and features an open-air train hall behind the refurbished historic building, where passengers once again can hop aboard the California Zephyr as it stops in Denver on its runs between Chicago and San Francisco.

RTD's Light Rail service's eleven lines and 113 miles of track links southeast, southwest, west, and east Denver to downtown, including service from Union Station. The peak fare is $3 within the city limits.

CONTACTS Amtrak. ✉ *Union Station, 1701 Wynkoop St., Denver* ☎ *800/872–7245* 🌐 *www.amtrak.com.* **RTD Light Rail.** ☎ *303/299–6000* 🌐 *www.rtd-denver.com.*

Hotels

Denver's lodging choices include the stately Brown Palace, bed-and-breakfasts, and business hotels. Unless you're planning a quick escape to the mountains, consider staying in or around downtown, where most of the city's attractions are within walking distance. Many of the hotels cater to business travelers, with accordingly lower rates on weekends—many establishments slash their rates in half on Friday and Saturday. The hotels in the vicinity of Cherry Creek are about a 10- to 15-minute drive from downtown.

In summertime, out-of-state and regional visitors flock to Georgetown to explore the rustic ambience, tour a mine, and hike or mountain bike on trails that thread the mountainsides; or to Golden to tour the Coors Brewery.

Restaurants

As befits such a diverse crossroads, Denver lays out a dizzying range of eateries. Head for LoDo, the Highland District, the RiNo Art District, or south of the city for the more inventive kitchens. Try Federal Street for cheap international eats—especially Mexican and Vietnamese—and expect authentic takes on classic Italian, French, and Asian cuisines. Throughout Denver, menus at trendy restaurants focus on locally sourced, organic, and healthier options; Denver's top chefs continue to gain the attention of national food magazines and win culinary competitions, but between the increased exposure and the rapid influx of residents, prices have skyrocketed to match or exceed those of larger cities.

Front Range dining draws primarily from the Denver metro area; you'll find standard chains, mom-and-pop restaurants, upscale dining, and good international food choices like Mexican and Thai, with the occasional Middle Eastern restaurant thrown in.

HOTEL AND RESTAURANT PRICES

Restaurant and hotel reviews have been shortened. For full information, visit Fodors.com. Restaurant prices are the average cost of a main course at dinner or, if dinner is not served, at lunch. Hotel prices are the lowest cost of a standard double room in high season, excluding service charges and 5.75%–14.85% tax.

What It Costs

$	$$	$$$	$$$$
RESTAURANTS			
under $15	$15–$22	$23–$30	over $30
HOTELS			
under $125	$125–$200	$201–$300	over $300

Tours

Denver History Tours
BUS TOURS | FAMILY | Personalized, guided tours of historic Denver are available, as are tours to select surrounding areas along the Front Range, in buses (for groups only) and on walking tours for a minimum of two people; prices and times vary according to the tour. Guides are knowledgeable locals eager to tailor the tour to individual tastes and interests, and work to accommodate varying fitness levels within a group. Trains, the Old West, the Art District on Santa Fe, and "haunted" Denver are particular specialties. ✉ *Denver* ☎ *720/234–7929* 🌐 *www.denverhistorytours.com* 🎫 *From $20.*

Denver Microbrew Tour
WALKING TOURS | This guided walking tour in LoDo includes beer sampling at several microbreweries and a comprehensive history of local beer making as well as Denver's history; a swing through Coors Field is also included. The fee covers the samples along the way and a voucher for a full pint, as well. A newer tour on Sundays through the hip arts district RiNo (River North) includes cider tastings, too (but not Coors Field). The guides are all beer enthusiasts who thoroughly enjoy sharing beer trivia, and can recommend anything beer-related in Denver. ✉ *Denver* ☎ *303/578–9548* 🌐 *www.denvermicrobrewtour.com* 🎫 *From $50.*

Visitor Information

CONTACTS Lower Downtown District, Inc. ☎ *303/605–3510* 🌐 *www.lodo.org.* **VISIT Denver, The Convention and Visitors Bureau.** ✉ *1575 California St., LoDo* ☎ *303/892–1505, 800/233–6837* 🌐 *www.denver.org.*

Denver

LoDo, a business-and-shopping area, buzzes with jazz clubs, restaurants, and art galleries housed in carefully restored century-old buildings; more recently, the up-and-coming RiNo (the River North Arts District) has begun to rival LoDo with its contemporary art galleries, food halls, brewpubs, and concert venues. The culturally diverse populace avidly supports the Denver Art Museum, the Denver Museum of Nature & Science, the Museo de las Americas, and the History Colorado Center. The Denver Performing Arts Complex is the nation's second-largest theatrical venue, bested in capacity only by New York's Lincoln Center. An excellent public transportation system, including a popular, growing light-rail system and 85 miles of bike paths, makes getting around easy.

Central Business District

Downtown Denver is really made up of two distinct neighborhoods: hip LoDo, and the more business-minded Central Business District. With a more traditional "downtown" look thanks to its many skyscrapers, the CBD has less to offer in terms of restaurants and bars, but it does have a few key sights (like the popular 16th Street Mall) along with the city's highest concentration of hotels.

Sights

Daniels & Fisher Tower

BUILDING | This 330-foot-high, 20-floor structure emulates the Campanile of St. Mark's Square in Venice, and it was the tallest building west of the Mississippi when it was built in 1909. William Cooke Daniels originally commissioned the tower to stand adjacent to his five-story department store. Today it's an office building with a cabaret in the basement as well as the city's most convenient clock tower. It's particularly striking—the clock is 16 feet high—when viewed in concert with the fountains in the adjacent Skyline Park. ✉ *1601 Arapahoe St., at 16th St., LoDo* ☎ *303/877–0742* 🌐 *www.clocktowerevents.com.*

Denver Firefighters Museum

MUSEUM | **FAMILY** | Denver's first firehouse was built in 1909 and now serves as a museum where original items of the trade are on view, including uniforms, nets, fire carts and trucks, bells, and switchboards. Artifacts and photos document the progression of firefighting machinery from horses and carriages in the early 1900s to the flashy red-and-white trucks of today. ✉ *1326 Tremont Pl., LoDo* ☎ *303/892–1436* 🌐 *www.denverfirefightersmuseum.org* 🎫 *$9.*

★ 16th Street Mall

COMMERCIAL CENTER | Outdoor cafés and tempting shops line this pedestrian-only 18-block, 1¼-mile thoroughfare, shaded by red-oak and locust trees. The mall's businesses run the entire socioeconomic range. There are popular meeting spots for business types at places like the Yard House in the Sheraton Hotel; a front-row view of the many street performers and goings-on from restaurants' sidewalk patios; and plenty of fast-food chains. Although some Denverites swear by the higher-end Cherry Creek Shopping District, the 16th Street Mall covers every retail area and is a more affordable, diverse experience. You can find Denver's best people-watching here. Catch one of the free shuttle buses at any corner that run the length of downtown. Pay attention when you're wandering across the street, as the walking area and bus lanes are the same color and are hard to distinguish. ✉ *From Broadway to Chestnut Pl., LoDo* 🌐 *16thstreetmalldenver.com.*

Restaurants

The Nickel

$$ | **MODERN AMERICAN** | A basic contemporary American menu offers classics done well at the Nickel, the restaurant located in the Hotel Teatro. Enjoy a top-notch burger, a vegetarian take on Wellington using beets instead of beef, or Mediterranean-style salmon, all while kicking back in sumptuous leather wing chairs. **Known for:** tasty steak frites; pre- and post-theater dining; barrel-aged cocktails. 💲 *Average main: $17* ✉ *1100 14th St., Downtown* ☎ *720/889–2128* 🌐 *www.thenickeldenver.com.*

Sam's No. 3

$ | **DINER** | **FAMILY** | Greek immigrant Sam Armatas opened his first eatery in Denver in 1927, and his three sons use the same recipes their father did in their updated version of his all-American diner, from the famous red and green chilies to the Coney Island–style hot dogs and creamy rice pudding. The retro diner resembles a fancy Denny's, and the bar is crowded with theatergoers and hipsters after dark. **Known for:** heavenly milkshakes; all-day breakfast;

old-school horseshoe counter. $ *Average main: $14 ✉ 1500 Curtis St., Downtown ☎ 303/534–1927 🌐 samsno3.com.*

Hotels

★ Brown Palace

$$$ | HOTEL | This grande dame of Colorado lodging has hosted public figures from President Eisenhower to the Beatles since it first opened its doors in 1892, and the details are exquisite: a dramatic nine-story lobby is topped with a glorious stained-glass ceiling, and the Victorian rooms have sophisticated wainscoting and art deco fixtures. **Pros:** sleeping here feels like being part of history; spacious and comfortable rooms; beautiful full-service spa. **Cons:** restaurants feel dated; parking is expensive and not included; lobby can be chaotic. $ *Rooms from: $254 ✉ 321 17th St., Downtown ☎ 303/297–3111, 800/321–2599 🌐 www.brownpalace.com ⇆ 241 rooms 🍴 No meals.*

★ The Curtis—A Doubletree by Hilton Hotel

$$ | HOTEL | FAMILY | Each floor here has a pop-culture theme, from classic cars to TV to science fiction, and the rooms are spacious and groovy, with speakers for your music and comfy, mod furnishings. **Pros:** across the street from Denver Performing Arts Complex; pet- and kid-friendly; unique and fun decor. **Cons:** can be noisy; high-traffic area; some of the rooms feel small. $ *Rooms from: $199 ✉ 1405 Curtis St., Downtown ☎ 303/571–0300, 800/525–6651 🌐 www.thecurtis.com ⇆ 338 rooms 🍴 No meals.*

★ Kimpton Hotel Monaco

$$$ | HOTEL | Celebrities and business travelers check into this hip property, which occupies the historic 1917 Railway Exchange Building and the 1937 art moderne Title Building, for the modern perks and art deco–meets–classic French style. **Pros:** one of the pet-friendliest hotels in town; welcoming complimentary wine hour; central location. **Cons:** may be too pet-friendly; hotel has decidedly business rather than romantic feel; popular with partiers. $ *Rooms from: $260 ✉ 1717 Champa St., Downtown ☎ 303/296–1717, 800/990–1303 🌐 www.monaco-denver.com ⇆ 189 rooms 🍴 No meals.*

Queen Anne Inn

$$ | B&B/INN | Just north of downtown in the regentrified Clements historic district (some of the neighboring blocks have yet to be reclaimed), this inn made up of adjacent Victorians is a delightful, romantic getaway. **Pros:** lovely rooms; daily wine tastings; hearty breakfast. **Cons:** not right downtown; neighborhood can be noisy; thin walls. $ *Rooms from: $165 ✉ 2147 Tremont Pl., Downtown ☎ 303/296–6666, 800/432–4667 🌐 www.queenannebnb.com ⇆ 13 rooms 🍴 Free Breakfast.*

Nightlife

Dazzle at Baur's

MUSIC CLUBS | This is a cozy, casual spot for live jazz and blues six nights a week downtown. *Downbeat* magazine has named it one of the 100 best jazz clubs in the world. The location, in the historic Baur's Building, offers a classy setting and exceptional acoustics as well as updated takes on classic comfort food before and during shows. ✉ *1512 Curtis St., Downtown ☎ 303/839–5100 🌐 dazzledenver.com.*

LoDo and Five Points

Officially, the Lower Downtown Historic District, the 25-plus square-block area that was the site of the original 1858 settlement of Denver City, is nicknamed LoDo. It's home to art galleries, chic shops, nightclubs, and restaurants ranging from Denver's most upscale to its most down-home. This part of town was once the city's thriving retail center, then it fell into disuse. Since the early 1990s LoDo has been transformed into the city's cultural center, thanks to its resident artists, retailers, and loft dwellers

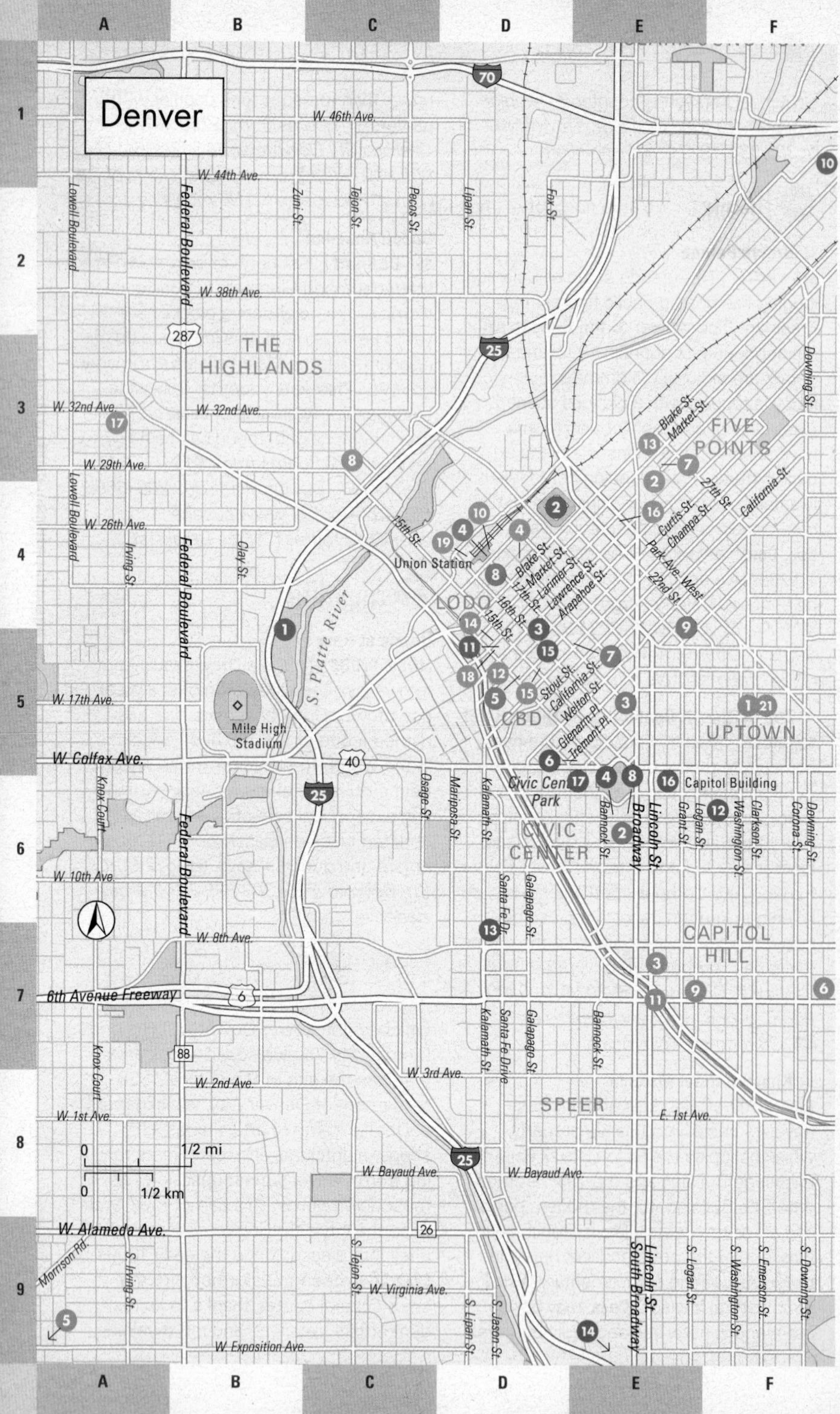

Denver
A
B
C
D
E
F
1
2
3
4
5
6
7
8
9
W. 46th Ave.
W. 44th Ave.
W. 38th Ave.
W. 32nd Ave.
W. 29th Ave.
W. 26th Ave.
W. 17th Ave.
W. Colfax Ave.
W. 10th Ave.
W. 8th Ave.
6th Avenue Freeway
W. 3rd Ave.
W. 2nd Ave.
W. 1st Ave.
E. 1st Ave.
W. Bayaud Ave.
W. Alameda Ave.
W. Virginia Ave.
W. Exposition Ave.
Lowell Boulevard
Federal Boulevard
Zuni St.
Tejon St.
Pecos St.
Lipan St.
Fox St.
Irving St.
Clay St.
Knox Court
Osage St.
Mariposa St.
Kalamath St.
Santa Fe Dr.
Santa Fe Drive
Galapago St.
Bannock St.
Broadway
Lincoln St.
Grant St.
Logan St.
Washington St.
Clarkson St.
Corona St.
Downing St.
Morrison Rd.
S. Irving St.
S. Tejon St.
S. Lipan St.
S. Jason St.
Lincoln St.
South Broadway
S. Logan St.
S. Washington St.
S. Emerson St.
S. Downing St.
Blake St.
Market St.
Larimer St.
Lawrence St.
Arapahoe St.
Curtis St.
Champa St.
Stout St.
California St.
Welton St.
Glenarm Pl.
Tremont Pl.
15th St.
16th St.
17th St.
22nd St.
27th St.
Park Ave. West
THE HIGHLANDS
FIVE POINTS
LODO
CBD
UPTOWN
CIVIC CENTER
CAPITOL HILL
SPEER
Union Station
S. Platte River
Mile High Stadium
Civic Center Park
Capitol Building
70
25
287
40
6
88
26
0
1/2 mi
1/2 km

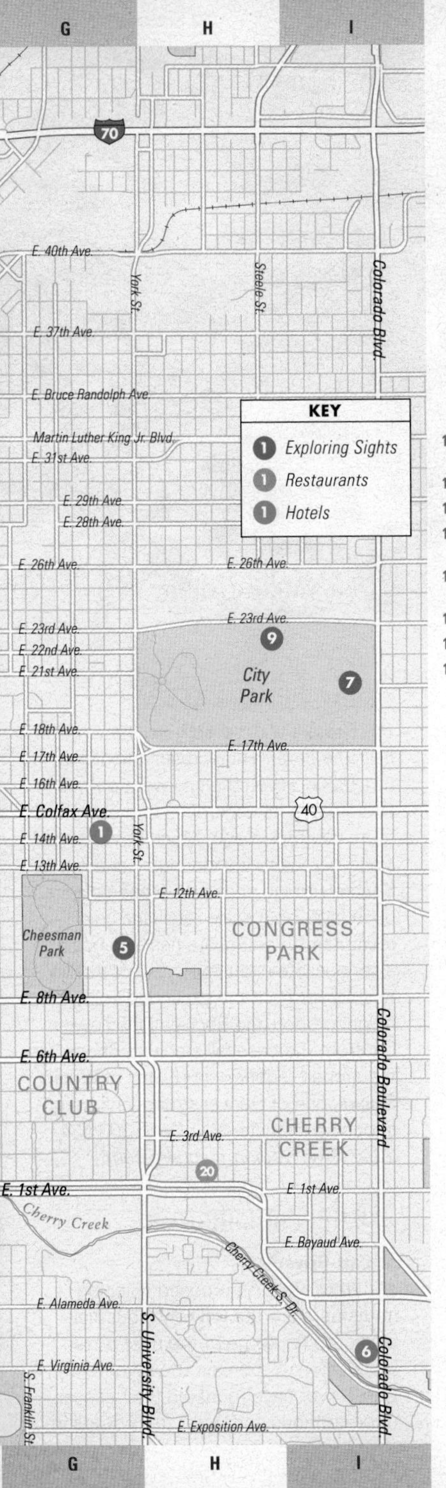

Sights

1 Children's Museum of Denver B4
2 Coors Field.............. D4
3 Daniels & Fisher Tower D5
4 Denver Art Museum..... E6
5 Denver Botanic Gardens........ G6
6 Denver Firefighters Museum D5
7 Denver Museum of Nature & Science I5
8 Denver Public Library's Central Library E6
9 Denver Zoo H4
10 Forney Museum of Transportation............ F1
11 Larimer Square D5
12 Molly Brown House F6
13 Museo de las Americas D7
14 Red Rocks Amphitheatre............ E9
15 16th Street Mall......... D5
16 State Capitol............. E6
17 U. S. Mint E6

Restaurants

1 Beast + Bottle............ F5
2 Cart-Driver................ E4
3 City Cafe E7
4 Denver Milk Market.... D4
5 The Fort Restaurant A9
6 Fruition.................... F7
7 Il Posto..................... E3
8 Lola Denver............... C3
9 Luca E7
10 Mercantile Dining & Provisions D4
11 Mizuna E7
12 The Nickel D5
13 Osaka Ramen E3
14 Rioja D5
15 Sam's No. 3.............. D5
16 Snooze E4
17 Tacos Tequila Whiskey.................. A3
18 Tamayo.................... D5
19 Tavernetta D4
20 True Food Kitchen H8
21 WaterCourse Foods..... F5

Hotels

1 Adagio Bed & Breakfast........ G6
2 The ART Hotel............ E6
3 Brown Palace............ E5
4 The Crawford Hotel..... D4
5 The Curtis—a DoubleTree by Hilton Hotel.............. D5
6 DoubleTree by Hilton Denver Cherry Creek.....I9
7 Kimpton Hotel Monaco.................. E5
8 Oxford Hotel............. D4
9 Queen Anne Inn.......... E4

Built in 1892, Brown Palace is Denver's most historic hotel.

who have taken over the old warehouses and redbricks.

Also nearby, the city's newest revitalized area, RiNo (River North Art District), comprises the historic neighborhoods of Globeville, Elyria-Swansea, Five Points, and Cole and has established itself as a solid option for galleries and restaurants.

Sights

★ Coors Field

BASEBALL/SOFTBALL | The Colorado Rockies, Denver's National League baseball team, play April through October in Coors Field. Because it's set in high altitude and thin air, the park is among the best in the major leagues for home-run hitters—and likewise, one of the worst for pitchers. ✉ *2001 Blake St., LoDo* ☎ *303/292–0200, 800/388–7625* 🌐 *www.coloradorockies.com.*

★ Larimer Square

COMMERCIAL CENTER | This square, on the oldest street in the city, was immortalized by Jack Kerouac in his seminal book *On the Road*. It was saved from the wrecker's ball by a determined preservationist in the 1960s, when the city went demolition-crazy in its eagerness to present a more youthful image. Much has changed since Kerouac's wanderings: Larimer Square's rough edges have been cleaned up in favor of upscale retail and chic restaurants. The Square has also become a serious late-night party district thanks to spillover from the expanded LoDo neighborhood and Rockies fans flowing out from the baseball stadium. Shops line the arched redbrick courtyards of **Writer Square**, one of Denver's most charming shopping districts. ✉ *LoDo* ☎ *303/534–2367* 🌐 *www.larimersquare.com.*

Restaurants

★ Cart-Driver

$$ | **PIZZA** | Two repurposed shipping containers are the unlikely industrial backdrop for some of the best pizza and oysters in Denver. The owners of Cart-Driver have modeled their casual, unpretentious spot after truck stops in

Legalized Marijuana in Denver

How to Purchase

On January 1, 2014, Colorado became the first state to allow legal recreational marijuana sales for any purpose to anyone over 21. Purchasing marijuana in Colorado at a licensed recreational shop is as simple as walking into the store, showing your ID, and buying it in the desired form. Some dispensaries are medical-only, however, and require a doctor-issued medical card for entry, while some buildings are designated as offering medical and recreational.

The amount a person is legally allowed to purchase is no longer dependent on residency; anyone over the age of 21 with a valid ID may buy up to one ounce of marijuana per day. No personal information is collected, and your ID is used only for proof of age.

Recreational marijuana stores are located in cities and towns around the state, but the vast majority of the licenses are held in Denver. Some counties have banned recreational stores. In addition, many cities limit store hours (in Denver, for instance, they can't be open past 10 pm). Call ahead to find out if a shop takes credit or debit cards, as many are still cash-only. *The Denver Post's The Cannabist* and the weekly *Westword* publish online guides that list shops, as well as reviews and information on the latest marijuana products.

Where to Consume

Where to smoke marijuana is considerably more restricted. Marijuana products cannot be consumed on-site at a retail outlet, nor can they be smoked in public spaces, including ski areas or national parks (both of which are on federal lands, where getting caught can result in jail time or hefty fines, as marijuana possession is still illegal under federal law). Under Colorado's Clean Indoor Air Act, weed smoking is banned anywhere that cigarette smoking is also banned. A handful of private cannabis social lounges have opened with membership fees, and some hotels advertise as "cannabis-friendly," meaning they allow consumption in designated smoking areas on-property. References to "420"—a once-obscure, insider allusion to all things marijuana-related—are meant as an indication of an establishment's openness to assisting clientele in procurement or consumption. In 2018, the first public-consumption cannabis café opened in the Lincoln Park neighborhood.

You can drive legally while possessing marijuana in a vehicle the same way you can with alcohol: it just needs to be sealed. Driving stoned is against the law, and legal limits have been established for the amount of THC a driver can have in his or her system. Taking marijuana on a plane is illegal, as is transporting it to another state, even to a state where it's also legal.

Several tour groups offer marijuana-based services that include airport transfers, tours of marijuana-growing operations, transport to recreational shops, and enough time in party-style buses to smoke, consume edible marijuana products and visit local eateries, explore museums and other cultural events, and then get dropped off for a stay at a "cannabis-friendly" hotel.

Historic Larimer Square is now one of Denver's best places to drink and dine.

Italy—the Autogrills that focus on putting out simple, easily worked menus that focus on high quality—and the result is crusts that hold their crisp all the way to the center of each pie and briny-fresh oysters, satiny mousses of tuna and chicken liver, and an odd but intriguing roster of canned beers. **Known for:** raucous atmosphere with long waits for a table; clam pizza; house-made chocolate pudding. $ *Average main: $17* ✉ *2500 Larimer St., Suite 100, RiNo* ☎ *303/292–3553* 🌐 *www.cart-driver.com.*

★ Denver Milk Market

$ | ITALIAN | As if chef and restaurateur Frank Bonanno didn't have enough on his plate with nine other eateries—including Mizuna, Luca, and Osteria Marco—he opened this market hall containing three bars and 13 food counters. Among the offerings: a reworking of a former Bonanno eatery, Lou's Hot and Naked, and its Nashville-style fried chicken; fresh seafood at Albina by the Sea; wood-fired pizza at Bonanno Brothers Pizzeria; handmade pasta from Mano Pastaria; and boozy milkshakes and freshly crafted soft-serve at Cornicello Gelato. **Known for:** wide variety of vendors; pizza until 3 am; locally sourced food. $ *Average main: $14* ✉ *1800 Wazee St., LoDo* ☎ *303/792–8242* 🌐 *www.denvermilkmarket.com.*

Il Posto

$$ | MODERN ITALIAN | The menu, written on a chalkboard on the wall, changes daily at Il Posto (The Place), where chef/owner Andrea Frizzi cooks intricately layered Italian dishes based on what's fresh, often from local farms. Get anything with foie gras, nasturtiums, or fennel—all of which can be easily paired with the eatery's focused and well-priced Italian-only wine list. **Known for:** savvy sommeliers; great people-watching; lively communal table. $ *Average main: $20* ✉ *2601 Larimer St., RiNo* ☎ *303/394–0100* 🌐 *www.ilpostodenver.com.*

★ Mercantile Dining & Provisions

$$$ | MODERN AMERICAN | Brought to you by the same James Beard award–winning chef Alex Seidel of Fruition, Mercantile features the same ingredients from their farm and creamery as well as the emphasis on fresh and local. The pretty space, with its powder-blue upholstery and milky-white walls, calms and invites lingering, ideal for a menu that includes starters doubling as small plates—the bone marrow brûlée has become legendary, and the "provisions" platter pulls from the farm's cheeses and pickles that are also available at the on-site market. **Known for:** the very essence of seasonal dining with farm-fresh ingredients; bone marrow brûlée; creative cocktails and unique wines. *Average main: $28 ✉ 1701 Wynkoop St., Suite 155, LoDo ☎ 720/460–3733 🌐 www.mercantiledenver.com.*

Osaka Ramen

$ | **JAPANESE** | This spot makes some of the best ramen in town, including a solid shoyu—complete with pork shoulder and a soft egg—and a top-notch *tonkotsu,* with the richness of the pork belly cut with pickled ginger. Although on the small side, the space is casual and comfortable, but it fills up fast. **Known for:** fast service; dessert doughnuts served with salted butter; half-price happy hour. *Average main: $14 ✉ 2611 Walnut St. ☎ 303/955–7938 🌐 www.osakaramendenver.com.*

★ **Rioja**

$$$ | **MEDITERRANEAN** | The restaurant is hip and artsy, with exposed brick and blown-glass lighting, arched doorways, and textured draperies. Chef Jennifer Jasinski's intense attention to detail is evident in her tribute to Mediterranean food with contemporary flair. **Known for:** classy atmosphere; Rioja-focused wine list; hearty portions. *Average main: $30 ✉ 1431 Larimer St., Larimer Square ☎ 303/820–2282 🌐 www.riojadenver.com ⊗ No lunch Mon. and Tues.*

Snooze

$ | **AMERICAN** | The line for this Ballpark neighborhood joint starts just before the 6:30 am weekday opening and sometimes an hour before it opens on weekends, because the lavish breakfasts are well worth the wait. The hollandaise-smothered creations alone—for instance, the Bella!, with Taleggio cheese and prosciutto on toasted ciabatta—are a must-try, and the pineapple upside-down pancakes, with vanilla crème anglaise and cinnamon butter, are exquisite. **Known for:** huge crowds and long waits; filling breakfasts; sugar-bomb French toast. *Average main: $13 ✉ 2262 Larimer St., Five Points ☎ 303/297–0700 🌐 www.snoozeeatery.com.*

Tamayo

$$$ | **MEXICAN** | Chef-owner Richard Sandoval brought his popular concept of modern, upscale Mexican cuisine from New York to Denver, and it's just as welcome here. The food is classic Mexican with a twist, such as seafood tacos, *huitlacoche* (edible fungus) dumpling soup, and elaborate moles. **Known for:** tequila flights; mountain views from the patio; bottomless drinks at brunch. *Average main: $24 ✉ 1400 Larimer St., Larimer Square ☎ 720/946–1433 🌐 www.eattamayo.com.*

★ **Tavernetta**

$$$ | **FRIULIAN** | The modern and elegant Tavernetta features inventive takes on classic Italian dishes (specifically, from the Friuli region) such as homemade pastas, house-cured meats and cheeses, rabbit, quail, and lamb. The appealing, well-varied (and not surprisingly, Italian-heavy) wine list is curated by the multiple sommeliers on staff. **Known for:** impeccable service; perfect lobster tagliatelle; extensive Amari roster. *Average main: $24 ✉ 1889 16th St., LoDo ☎ 720/605–1889 🌐 www.tavernettadenver.com.*

Hotels

★ **The Crawford Hotel**

$$$ | **HOTEL** | The lobby here—which guests can view from each floor—is the impressively renovated Union Station, a retro delight of desks with chain-pull lamps, long wooden benches, and constant bustle; the nostalgic sense of

being on a train journey is carried elegantly into the 112 rooms, each of which offers a unique layout and design. **Pros:** centralized location; never have to leave Union Station; large choice of excellent restaurants. **Cons:** on the pricey side; lobby chaos at peak times can be jarring; trains whistle constantly. *Rooms from: $225* ✉ *1701 Wynkoop St., LoDo* ☎ *720/460–3700, 844/432–9374* 🌐 *www.thecrawfordhotel.com* *112 rooms* *No meals.*

★ Oxford Hotel

$$$ | HOTEL | During the Victorian era this hotel was an elegant fixture on the Denver landscape; its comfortable rooms are furnished with French and English period antiques, and civilized touches like complimentary shoe shines, afternoon sherry, and morning coffee remain. **Pros:** prime LoDo location; gorgeous historic setting; great restaurants on-site and nearby. **Cons:** noisy ballpark crowds in season turn LoDo area into a big party; one of the pricier hotels in town; some rooms are tiny. *Rooms from: $260* ✉ *1600 17th St., LoDo* ☎ *303/628–5400, 833/524–0368* 🌐 *www.theoxfordhotel.com* *88 rooms* *No meals.*

Nightlife

Herb's Bar

MUSIC CLUBS | Hidden in the back of a parking lot, the hipster favorite Herb's Bar, known locally by its previous name, Herb's Hideout, is a gloriously nostalgic bar with dim lighting, comfortable booths, and inexpensive cocktails. ✉ *2057 Larimer St., LoDo* ☎ *303/299–9555* 🌐 *www.herbsbar.com.*

★ Wynkoop Brewing Company

BREWPUBS/BEER GARDENS | One of the city's best-known bars has anchored LoDo since it was a pre–Coors Field warehouse district. The Wynkoop Brewing Company is now more famous for its founder—former Denver mayor and Colorado governor and current senator John Hickenlooper—than for its brews, food, or ambience, but it remains a relaxing, slightly upscale, two-story joint filled with halfway-decent bar food, the usual pool tables, and games and beers of all types. ✉ *1634 18th St., LoDo* ☎ *303/297–2700* 🌐 *www.wynkoop.com.*

Shopping

David Cook Fine Art

ART GALLERIES | Historic Native American art and regional paintings, particularly Santa Fe modernists, are David Cook's specialty. ✉ *1637 Wazee St., LoDo* ☎ *303/623–8181* 🌐 *www.davidcookgalleries.com.*

Native American Trading Company

ART GALLERIES | The collection of crafts, jewelry, and regional paintings here is outstanding. ✉ *213 W. 13th Ave., Golden Triangle* ☎ *303/534–0771* 🌐 *www.nativeamericantradingco.com.*

Capitol Hill and Civic Center

These two seperate but adjacent neighborhoods both offer a nice taste of Denver's history and culture. Capitol Hill surrounds the gold-domed Colorado State Capitol building and features plenty of bars and restaurants along with historic mansions turned museums. The Civic Center and its vibrant Golden Triangle Arts District has plenty of art galleries and museums, including the Denver Museum of Art.

Sights

★ Denver Art Museum

MUSEUM | FAMILY | Unique displays of Asian, pre-Columbian, Spanish Colonial, and Native American art are the hallmarks of this model of museum design. Among the museum's regular holdings are John DeAndrea's life-size polyvinyl painting *Linda* (1983); Claude Monet's dreamy flowerscape *Le Bassin aux*

The Denver Art Museum features a wide array of exhibits.

Nympheas (1904); and Charles Deas's red-cowboy-on-horseback *Long Jakes, The Rocky Mountain Man* (1844). The works are thoughtfully lighted, though dazzling mountain views through hallway windows sometimes steal your attention. Imaginative hands-on exhibits, game- and puzzle-filled Family Backpacks, and video corners will appeal to children; the Adventures in Art Center has hands-on art classes and exploration for children and adults. The museum doubled in size with the 2007 opening of the Frederic C. Hamilton building, a 146,000-square-foot addition designed by architect Daniel Libeskind that has prompted debate: some say the glass and titanium design has ruined the view, while others think the building is a work of art in its own right. To the east of the museum is an outdoor plaza—you'll know it by the huge orange metal sculpture—that leads to the Denver Public Library next door. ✉ *100 W. 14th Ave. Pkwy., Civic Center* ☎ *720/913–0130* 🌐 *www.denverartmuseum.org* 🎫 *$13.*

★ Denver Public Library's Central Library
LIBRARY | **FAMILY** | A life-size horse on a 20-foot-tall chair and other sculptures decorate the expansive lawn of this sprawling complex with round towers and tall, oblong windows. The map and manuscript rooms, Gates Western History Reading Room (with amazing views of the mountains), and Schlessman Hall (with its three-story atrium) merit a visit. Built in the mid-'50s, the library houses a world-renowned collection of books, photographs, and newspapers that chronicle the American West, as well as original paintings by Remington, Russell, Audubon, and Bierstadt. The children's library is notable for its captivating design and its unique, child-friendly multimedia computer catalog. ✉ *10 W. 14th Ave. Pkwy., Civic Center* ☎ *720/865–1111* 🌐 *www.denverlibrary.org.*

Molly Brown House
HOUSE | This Victorian celebrates the life and times of the scandalous, "unsinkable" Molly Brown. The heroine of the *Titanic* courageously saved several lives

and continued to provide assistance to survivors back on terra firma. Costumed guides and period furnishings in the museum, including flamboyant gilt-edge wallpaper, lace curtains, tile fireplaces, and tapestries, evoke bygone days. The museum collects and displays artifacts that belonged to Brown, as well as period items dating to 1894–1912, when the Browns lived in the house. Tours run every half hour; you won't need much more than that to see the whole place. A bit of trivia: Margaret Tobin Brown was known as Maggie, not Molly—allegedly a Hollywood invention that Brown did not like—during her lifetime. ✉ *1340 Pennsylvania St., Capitol Hill* ☎ *303/832–4092* 🌐 *www.mollybrown.org* 🎫 *$14.*

Museo de las Americas

MUSEUM | The region's first museum dedicated to the achievements of Latinx in the Americas has a permanent collection as well as rotating exhibits that cover everything from Latin Americans in the state legislature to Latin American female artists in the 20th century. Among the more than 3,300 permanent pieces are the oil painting *Virgin of Solitude* (circa 1730) and a Mayan polychrome jar (circa 650–950), as well as contemporary works. In addition to the regular hours, the museum is open (with free admission) the first Friday evening of each month from 5 to 9. ✉ *861 Santa Fe Dr., Lincoln Park* ☎ *303/571–4401* 🌐 *www.museo.org* 🎫 *$8* ⏲ *Closed Sun. and Mon.*

★ State Capitol

GOVERNMENT BUILDING | Built in 1886, the capitol was constructed mostly of materials indigenous to Colorado, including marble, granite, and rose onyx. Especially inspiring is the gold-leaf dome, a reminder of the state's mining heritage. The dome is open for tours weekdays by appointment on the hour and 30 people at a time can go to the top (using a 99-step staircase from the third floor) to take in the 360-degree view of the Rockies. Historical tours and a legislative tour are available. Outside, a marker on the 13th step indicates where the elevation is exactly 1 mile high (above sea level). The legislature is generally in session from January through May, and visitors are welcome to sit in third-floor viewing galleries above the House and Senate chambers. ✉ *200 E. Colfax Ave., Capitol Hill* ☎ *303/866–2604 dome tours* 🌐 *capitol.colorado.gov* 🎫 *Free.*

U.S. Mint

GOVERNMENT BUILDING | Tour this facility to catch a glimpse of the coin-making process, as presses spit out thousands of coins a minute. There are also exhibits on the history of money and a restored version of Denver's original mint prior to numerous expansions. More than 14 billion coins are minted yearly, and the nation's second-largest hoard of gold is stashed away here. To schedule a 45-minute tour and prepare for your visit (there are strict security guidelines), visit the Mint's website. Reservations are required for all tours, which are guided (Monday to Thursday from 8:00 to 3:30), free, and available to visitors age seven and older. The gift shop, which sells authentic coins and currency, is in the Tremont Center, across Colfax Avenue from the Mint. ✉ *320 W. Colfax Ave., Civic Center* ☎ *303/405–4761* 🌐 *www.usmint.gov/mint_tours* 🎫 *Free.*

Restaurants

Beast + Bottle

$$ | **MODERN AMERICAN** | A cozy space that's just right for couples and small get-togethers, this Uptown eatery is aptly named for its constantly rotating roster of small plates and handful of entrées that focus on a fish, a couple of meat options, and always one or two vegetarian dishes. The kitchen proclaims a focus on "using the whole animal," with an attempt to introduce diners to new cuts or unusual preparations—they make all the broths and sauces from scraps and bones and offer organ meats in delectable ways.

Known for: precision cooking; root beer–braised short ribs; unique wine list. *Average main: $22* *719 E. 17th Ave., Capitol Hill* *303/623–3223* *www.beastandbottle.com* *Closed Mon. No lunch Tues.–Fri.*

City Cafe

$ | **AMERICAN** | **FAMILY** | Everything is made from scratch at this charming little bakery and café, including the stocks for the French onion soup and other daily restoratives offered alongside the stacked-high sandwiches. Freshly baked for more than a hundred local restaurants, the dozens of varieties of breads are also available to take home or eat at a booth in the light-filled space. **Known for:** excellent baked goods; Christmas stollen (a fruit bread); delicious French dip. *Average main: $9* *726 Lincoln St., Downtown* *303/861–0809* *www.citycafedenver.com* *Closed Sun. No dinner.*

★ **Fruition**

$$$$ | **MODERN AMERICAN** | Well-crafted, elegant comfort food made from seasonal ingredients is served in compelling combinations, like roasted pork with fennel, sausage-stuffed squash blossoms, and Colorado lamb loin served with ricotta tortellini. The bonus is that the cheese is made from sheep's milk at chef/owner Alex Seidel's own farm. **Known for:** intimate atmosphere; farm-raised ingredients; potato-wrapped oysters Rockefeller. *Average main: $31* *1313 E. 6th Ave., City Park* *303/831–1962* *www.fruitionrestaurant.com* *No lunch.*

Luca

$$$ | **ITALIAN** | The restaurant's steel-gray, orange-and-red contemporary decor belies the fact that it's one of the most authentic Italian restaurants in the city. Chef-owner Frank Bonanno summons the memory of his Italian grandmother to re-create small-town Italy through wild boar with pappardelle, goat-stuffed *caramelle* (pasta shaped like candy wrappers), and house-cured capocollo and homemade cheeses. **Known for:** Italian-focused wine list; perfect tiramisu; house-cured meats and cheeses. *Average main: $26* *711 Grant St., Capitol Hill* *303/832–6600* *www.lucadenver.com* *Closed Mon. and Tues. No lunch.*

★ **Mizuna**

$$$$ | **MODERN AMERICAN** | Chef-owner Frank Bonanno knows how to transform butter and cream into comforting masterpieces at this cozy eatery with warm colors and intimate seating. His menu is reminiscent of California's French Laundry—witness the foie gras torchon—but his Italian heritage has given him the ability to work wonders with house-made pastas and gnocchi, and he often offers a ragout or other long-stewed sauce. **Known for:** fine French dining; rotating menu; butter-poached lobster. *Average main: $42* *225 E. 7th Ave., Capitol Hill* *303/832–4778* *www.mizunadenver.com* *Closed Sun. and Mon. No lunch.*

WaterCourse Foods

$ | **VEGETARIAN** | In a town known for its beef, WaterCourse stands out as a devoted vegan eatery in spacious digs uptown. This casual, low-key place serves herbivores three meals a day, most of which are based on fruits, vegetables, whole grains, and meat-like soy substitutes. **Known for:** clever meat substitutes; vegan baked goods; organic wine and local kombucha. *Average main: $14* *837 E. 17th Ave., Capitol Hill* *303/832–7313* *www.watercoursefoods.com.*

Hotels

★ **Adagio Bed & Breakfast**

$$ | **B&B/INN** | After converting to a "Bud + Breakfast" B&B experience, this striking property became famous as a good place to stay if you love music and marijuana, as the Adagio and its sister B&B in Silverthorne are committed to making sure guests can enjoy cannabis during a visit by providing the necessary paraphernalia and a place to use it (note that it is 21-and-over only). **Pros:** pretty,

cozy rooms; within driving distance of major attractions; full-meal-plan option available. **Cons:** not within walking distance of downtown or Cherry Creek; limited amenities due to size; overpriced. *Rooms from: $199* *1430 Race St., Capitol Hill* *303/370–6911, 800/533–4640* *www.adagiodenverbb.com* *6 rooms* *Free Breakfast.*

★ The ART Hotel

$$$$ | HOTEL | Each floor of rooms in this nine-story building is dedicated to a different artist, with original art in every room by the artist, as well—you can't miss the entry-level greeting *Wall Drawing #397* by Sol LeWitt or the video art in the elevators that signal this is going to be a unique lodging experience. **Pros:** compelling art collection; comfortable, stylish rooms; incredible views. **Cons:** one of the most expensive hotels in Denver; restaurant still working out the kinks; conventions sometimes overcrowd the hotel. *Rooms from: $375* *1201 Broadway, Civic Center* *303/572–8000* *www.thearthotel.com* *145 rooms* *No meals.*

Nightlife

Charlie's Denver

BARS/PUBS | Charlie's has country-western atmosphere, music, and dancing, and a drag show at least one night a week. *900 E. Colfax Ave., Capitol Hill* *303/839–8890* *www.charliesdenver.com.*

★ The Church

DANCE CLUBS | Multiple rooms on three floors in a decommissioned church host DJ-spun Goth, indie, and industrial dance music on Sunday nights, as well as progressive trance, hip-hop, and global on Friday, and bachata, reggaeton, salsa, cumbia, and Latin house music on Saturday. *1160 Lincoln St., Capitol Hill* *303/832–2383* *www.coclubs.com/the-church.*

Hi-Dive

MUSIC CLUBS | This energetic, hip club located in the Baker neighborhood just south of Capitol Hill books a diverse and eclectic range of talented indie rockers. The crowd is young, likes Red Bull, and tends to revel in the discovery of obscure underground music. *7 S. Broadway, Capitol Hill* *303/733–0230* *www.hi-dive.com.*

Shopping

★ Tattered Cover Book Store

BOOKS/STATIONERY | A must for all bibliophiles, the Tattered Cover may be the best bookstore in the United States, not only for the near-endless selection (more than 400,000 books on two floors at the Colfax Avenue location and 300,000 in a new location in McGregor Square near Coors Field, along with much smaller versions of the stores at Union Station and Denver International Airport) and helpful, knowledgeable staff, but also for the incomparably refined atmosphere. Treat yourself to the overstuffed armchairs, reading nooks, and afternoon readings and lectures, and stop by the café for an espresso drink and bakery treat at the Capitol Hill site in the renovated historic Lowenstein Theater. *2526 E. Colfax Ave., Capitol Hill* *303/322–7727* *www.tatteredcover.com.*

City Park and Around

Acquired by the city in 1881, City Park, Denver's largest public space (330 acres), contains rose gardens, lakes, a golf course, tennis courts, and a huge playground. A shuttle runs between two of the city's most popular attractions: the Denver Zoo and the Denver Museum of Nature & Science, both on the site. City Park is east of downtown Denver, and runs from East 17th Avenue to East 26th Avenue, between York Street and Colorado Boulevard.

Sights

★ Denver Botanic Gardens

GARDEN | FAMILY | More than 15,000 plant species from Australia, South Africa, the Himalayas, and especially the western United States compose the horticultural displays in the thoughtfully laid-out theme gardens here. They are at their peak in July and August, when garden enthusiasts could spend half a day here; the tropical conservatory alone is worth an hour's visit in the off-season. Spring brings a brilliant display of wildflowers to the world-renowned rock alpine garden, primarily in late May and early June. The OmniGlobe simulates the climate and atmospheric changes on Earth; other environmental attractions include a "green roof" atop the café and an extensive interactive children's garden that covers part of the parking structure. Tea ceremonies take place some summer weekends in the tranquil Japanese garden, and artists such as singer-songwriter Melissa Etheridge, jazz musician Herbie Hancock, and blues legend Buddy Guy have performed as part of the summer concert series. ✉ *1007 York St., Cheesman Park* ☎ *720/865–3500* 🌐 *www.botanicgardens.org* 🎟 *$15.*

★ Denver Museum of Nature & Science

MUSEUM | FAMILY | Founded in 1900, the museum has amassed more than 775,000 objects, making it the largest natural history museum in the western United States. It houses a rich combination of traditional collections—dinosaur remains, animal dioramas, a mineralogy display, an Egyptology wing—and intriguing hands-on exhibits. In Expedition Health you can test your health and fitness on a variety of contraptions and receive a personalized health profile. The Prehistoric Journey exhibit covers the seven stages of Earth's development. The massive complex also includes an IMAX movie theater and a planetarium, where the Space Odyssey exhibit simulates a trip to Mars. An impressive eating-and-relaxation area has a full-window panoramic view of the Rocky Mountains. ✉ *2001 Colorado Blvd., City Park* ☎ *303/370–6000, 800/925–2250* 🌐 *www.dmns.org* 🎟 *Museum $16.95, IMAX $10.95, planetarium $23.95; $23.95–$29.95 for combined pass (any two or all three).*

Denver Zoo

ZOO | FAMILY | The state's most popular cultural attraction, this easily navigated property's best-known exhibit showcases man-eating Komodo dragons in a lush re-creation of a cavernous riverbank. Another popular exhibit is The Edge, a series of overhead yards and bridges that allow the Amur (Siberian) tigers to roam 12 feet above visitors. The 10-acre Toyota Elephant Passage houses elephants, gibbons, rhinos, clouded leopards, and tapirs, along with other animals from the Asian continent. The Conservation Carousel ($2) rotates in the center of the 80-acre zoo, with hand-crafted endangered species as mounts. A 7-acre Primate Panorama houses 31 species of primates in state-of-the-art environments that simulate the animals' natural habitats. Other highlights include a nursery for baby animals; seal shows; the electric Safari Shuttle, which snakes through the property as you are treated to a lesson on the zoo's inhabitants; and the usual lions, tigers, bears, giraffes, and monkeys. The exhibits are spaced far apart along sprawling concrete paths, so build in plenty of time to visit. ✉ *2300 Steele St., City Park* ☎ *720/337–1400* 🌐 *www.denverzoo.org* 🎟 *Nov.–Feb. $15, Mar.–May $17, Jun.–Oct. $20.*

Nightlife

Bluebird Theater

MUSIC CLUBS | Of Denver's numerous old-school music hangouts, the most popular is the regally restored Bluebird Theater, which showcases local and national acts, emphasizing rock, hip-hop, Americana, and ambient genres. ✉ 3317

E. Colfax Ave., City Park ☎ 303/377–1666, 888/929–7849 tickets 🌐 www.bluebirdtheater.net.

Lion's Lair

MUSIC CLUBS | The Lion's Lair is a dive where punk-rock bands and occasional name acts—the Black Keys played here a couple of times years ago, as did British rocker Graham Parker—squeeze onto a tiny stage just above a huge, square, central bar. ✉ *2022 E. Colfax Ave., Cheesman Park* ☎ *303/320–9200* 🌐 *www.lionslairco.com.*

Greater Denver

Where neighborhoods have gentrified—Highland, for instance—residents struggle to retain the area's historical significance and original allure in the face of a seemingly unstoppable surge of development. Meanwhile, older sections, such as Washington Park and Cherry Creek, sport the awkward look of lush old-growth foliage interspersed with the constant presence of construction cranes that often afflict the affluent areas of a city in the midst of a boom.

Less than a mile west of downtown is the booming Central Platte Valley, with the Highlands neighborhood at its center. Once the cluttered heart of Denver's railroad system, it's now overflowing with attractions. The imposing glass facade of the Broncos' home, Empower Field at Mile High, the stately Ball Arena sports arena (formerly the Pepsi Center), the Downtown Aquarium, and the flagship REI outdoors store are four of the biggest attractions. Hip restaurants, a couple of coffeehouses, and a few small, locally owned shops, including a wine boutique, make it appealing to wander around.

The South Platte River valley concrete path, which extends several miles from downtown to the east and west, snakes along the water through out-of-the-way parks and trails. The 15th Street Bridge is particularly cyclist- and pedestrian-friendly, connecting LoDo with sprawling northwest Denver in a seamless way.

Sights

★ Children's Museum of Denver

MUSEUM | FAMILY | This is one of the finest museums of its kind in North America, with constantly changing hands-on exhibits that engage children up to about age 10 in discovery. A three-and-a-half-story climbing structure soars through the center of the museum, complete with a bridge and gondola, along with a water area featuring geysers, pumps, and a 30-gallon structure that replicates a toilet flushing. Also among the six indoor playscapes and an outdoor area are a teaching kitchen where kids can cook real food; an art studio staffed by artists in residence; a camping area with a faux fire; a car assembly plant; and Fire Station No. 1, a real fire hall with a pole and kitchen. One of the biggest attractions is the Center for the Young Child, a 3,700-square-foot playscape aimed at newborns and toddlers and their caregivers; or little ones can enter Bubbles Playscape, where science and soap collide in kid-made bubbles up to 6 feet long. ✉ *2121 Children's Museum Dr., off Exit 211 of I–25, Jefferson Park* ☎ *303/433–7444* 🌐 *www.mychildsmuseum.org* 🎟 *$14.*

Forney Museum of Transportation

MUSEUM | Inside a converted warehouse are an 1898 Renault coupe, Amelia Earhart's immaculately maintained "Goldbug," and a Big Boy steam locomotive, among other historic vehicles. Other exhibits in this eccentric museum consist of antique bicycles, cable cars, and even experimental car-planes. This trivia-laden showcase is outside of the downtown loop: Go north on Brighton Boulevard; the museum is adjacent to the Denver Coliseum on the south side of I–70. ✉ *4303 Brighton Blvd., Globeville* ☎ *303/297–1113* 🌐 *www.forneymuseum.org* 🎟 *$10.*

★ Red Rocks Amphitheatre

CONCERTS | The exquisite 9,000-seat Red Rocks Amphitheatre, amid majestic geological formations in nearby Morrison, is renowned for its natural acoustics, which have awed the likes of Leopold Stokowski and the Beatles. Although Red Rocks is one of the best places in the country to hear live music, be sure to leave extra time when visiting—parking is sparse, crowds are thick, paths are long and extremely uphill, and seating is usually general admission. ✉ *18300 W. Alameda Pkwy., Morrison* ✣ *Off U.S. 285 or I–70* ☎ *720/865–2494* 🌐 *www.redrocksonline.com.*

Restaurants

★ The Fort Restaurant

$$$$ | STEAKHOUSE | This adobe structure near Red Rocks Amphitheatre, complete with flickering luminarias and a pinyon-pine bonfire in the courtyard, is a perfect reproduction of Bent's Fort, a Colorado fur-trade center. Buffalo meat and game are the specialties. **Known for:** authentic Old West atmosphere complete with costumed characters; gun-powder cocktails; buffalo steaks and Rocky Mountain oysters. $ *Average main: $46* ✉ *19192 Hwy. 8, Morrison* ☎ *303/697–4771* 🌐 *www.thefort.com* ⏲ *No lunch.*

★ Lola Denver

$$ | MEXICAN | This casual, modern Mexican eatery with valet parking brings in a young, hip clientele and provides a spectacular view of the city skyline from most of the sunny dining room, bar, and patio. More than 90 tequilas, superior margaritas, and a clever, glass-lined bar area are just a few of the reasons the lovely Lola remains a locals' hangout. **Known for:** Mexican-style weekend brunch; tableside guacamole; heated patio. $ *Average main: $22* ✉ *1575 Boulder St., Highland* ☎ *720/570–8686* 🌐 *www.loladenver.com* ⏲ *No lunch.*

Tacos Tequila Whiskey

$ | MODERN MEXICAN | Originally a food truck, the name of this taqueria showcases exactly what it specializes in: *queso a la plancha* tacos and seared ahi tuna tacos, with house-made salsas and tangy margaritas. Get to know your fellow diners at the communal tables or the long bar, or sit on the patio that opens from the dining area through the garage door. **Known for:** street-style tacos; festive patio; tequila cocktails. $ *Average main: $8* ✉ *3300 W. 32nd Ave., Highland* ☎ *720/502–4608* 🌐 *www.tacostequilawhiskey.com* ⏲ *No lunch Mon.*

Hotels

DoubleTree by Hilton Denver Cherry Creek

$$ | HOTEL | The Cherry Creek shopping district is 4 miles away, and the major museums and the zoo are a five-minute drive from this bustling hotel, which provides coveted mountain views from many of its rooms. **Pros:** good for business travelers; location bridges gap for folks who want both museums and downtown; free shuttle on weekdays. **Cons:** not walking distance to any attractions; far from downtown; can be noisy. $ *Rooms from: $139* ✉ *455 S. Colorado Blvd., Cherry Creek* ☎ *303/388–5561, 800/388–6129* 🌐 *www.hilton.com* ⇨ *269 rooms* 🍽 *No meals.*

Golden

15 miles west of Denver via I–70 or U.S. 6 (W. 6th Ave.).

Golden was once the territorial capital of Colorado. City residents have smarted ever since losing that distinction to Denver by "dubious" vote in 1867, but in 1994 then-Governor Roy Romer restored "ceremonial" territorial-capital status to Golden. While the growth boosted by the high-tech industry as well as the original Coors Brewery and the Colorado School of Mines has slowed down, it remains a top draw for outdoors and history enthusiasts. Locals love to kayak along Clear Creek as it runs through Golden; there's even a racecourse and a white-water park on the water.

GETTING HERE AND AROUND

Golden is a 30-minute drive from downtown Denver via U.S. 6. Downtown Golden is compact and easily walkable. You may want to drive to the Colorado School of Mines area of town; it's about a mile away from the downtown area, and you'll want a car to reach the Buffalo Bill Museum, which is several miles away. The parking area for the Coors tours is within walking distance of downtown.

TIMING

You can explore downtown and tour the Coors Brewery in three hours or so.

VISITOR INFORMATION Greater Golden Chamber of Commerce. ✉ *1010 Washington Ave.* ☎ *303/279–3113* 🌐 *www.goldenchamber.org.*

Sights

★ Buffalo Bill Museum and Grave

MUSEUM | FAMILY | The drive up **Lookout Mountain** to the Buffalo Bill Museum and Grave provides a sensational panoramic view of Denver that alone is worth the price of admission. It was this view that encouraged Bill Cody—Pony Express rider, cavalry scout, and tireless promoter of the West—to request Lookout Mountain as his burial site. Adjacent to the grave is a small museum with art and artifacts detailing Cody's life and times, as well as a souvenir shop. The grave is 100 yards past the gift shop on a paved walkway. ✉ *987½ Lookout Mountain Rd.* ✣ *Rte. 5 off I–70 Exit 256, or 19th Ave. out of Golden* ☎ *303/526–0744* 🌐 *www.buffalobill.org* 🎫 *$5.*

Colorado Railroad Museum

MUSEUM | FAMILY | Just outside Golden is the Colorado Railroad Museum, a must-visit for any train lover. More than 100 vintage locomotives and cars are displayed outside the museum. Inside the replica-1880 masonry depot are historical photos and memorabilia of Puffing Billy (the nickname for steam trains), along with an astounding model train set that steams through a miniature-scale version of Golden. In the Roundhouse you can witness a train's restoration in progress, and in winter, the popular tale of *The Polar Express* is theatrically performed. ✉ *17155 W. 44th Ave.* ☎ *800/365–6263* 🌐 *www.coloradorailroadmuseum.org* 🎫 *$10.*

★ Coors Brewery

WINERY/DISTILLERY | Thousands of beer lovers make the pilgrimage to the venerable Coors Brewery (formerly the MillerCoors Brewery) each year. Founded in 1873 by Adolph Coors, a 21-year-old German stowaway, today it's the largest single-site brewery in the world and part of Molson Coors. The free self-paced tour explains the malting, brewing, and packaging processes. Informal tastings are held at the end of the tour, and you can buy souvenirs in the gift shop. A free shuttle runs from the parking lot to the brewery. ✉ *13th and Ford Sts.* ☎ *303/277–2337, 866/812–2337* 🌐 *www.coorsbrewerytour.com* ⊗ *Closed Sun. in winter* ☞ *Children under 18 must be accompanied by an adult.*

Golden History Museum & Park

HISTORIC SITE | FAMILY | Two properties—the Golden History Center, and Clear Creek Golden History Park (formerly Clear Creek History Park)—have combined under the name of Golden History Museum & Park. The park interprets the Golden area circa 1843–1900 via restored structures and reproductions, including a teepee, prospector's camp, one-room schoolhouse, and cabins. It is also populated with live chickens and bees. On select days, guides in period clothing lead 45-minute tours, but you can stroll the park and peek into the buildings anytime. There's also a research center and an interactive area for kids. ✉ *11th and*

Arapahoe Sts. 303/278–3557 www.goldenhistory.org Free Museum closed Tues.

Restaurants

★ **Woody's Wood Fired Pizza**
$$ | PIZZA | FAMILY | Woody's has a full menu, with pastas, chicken, calzones, and burgers, but it's the pizza, with its smoky, wood-charred crust, that's the big draw. Woody's is so popular that the pies are always just out of the oven. **Known for:** honey dip for the crust; beer cheese soup; lots of crowds. *Average main: $17 1305 Washington Ave. 303/277–0443 www.woodysgolden.com.*

Georgetown

50 miles west of Denver via I–70.

Georgetown rode the crest of the silver boom during the second half of the 19th century. Most of the impeccably maintained brick buildings that make up the town's historic district date from that period. Georgetown hasn't been tarted up, so it provides a true sense of what living was like in those rough-and-tumble times. It's a popular tourist stop in the summertime. Be sure to keep an eye out for the state's largest herd of rare bighorn sheep that often grazes alongside I–70 in this region.

GETTING HERE AND AROUND

Just west of where I–70 and U.S. 40 intersect, the downtown historic area is just a few blocks long and a few blocks wide, so park and start walking.

VISITOR INFORMATION

CONTACTS Georgetown. *Georgetown City Hall, 404 6th St. 303/569–2405 georgetown-colorado.org.*

Sights

★ **Georgetown Loop Railroad**
TRANSPORTATION SITE (AIRPORT/BUS/FERRY/TRAIN) | FAMILY | This 1920s narrow-gauge train connects Georgetown with the equally historic community of Silver Plume. The 6-mile round-trip excursion takes about 70 minutes, and winds through vast stands of pine and fir before crossing the 95-foot-high Devil's Gate Bridge, where the track actually loops back over itself as it gains elevation. You can add on a tour of the **Lebanon Silver Mill and Mine,** which is a separate stop between the two towns, as well as meals in the dining car. In fall and around the holidays, special trains run, including popular rides with Santa. *646 Loop Dr. 888/456–6777 www.georgetownlooprr.com $27.95 for train; $37.95 with mine tour.*

Guanella Pass Scenic Byway
VIEWPOINT | South of Georgetown, the Guanella Pass Scenic Byway treats you to marvelous views of the Mount Evans Wilderness Area. Along the way—while negotiating some tight curves, especially as you head down to Grant—you'll get close views of Mount Evans as well as Grays and Torrey's peaks—two Fourteeners. It takes about 40 minutes to cross the 22-mile fully paved road. *Hwy. 381.*

Hotel de Paris
HOTEL—SIGHT | The elaborate Hotel de Paris, built almost single-handedly by Frenchman Louis Dupuy in 1878, was one of the Old West's preeminent hostelries. Now a museum, the hotel depicts how luxuriously the rich were accommodated: Tiffany fixtures, lace curtains, and hand-carved furniture re-create an era of opulence. *409 6th St. 303/569–2311 www.hoteldeparismuseum.org $8.*

The historic Georgetown Loop Railroad crosses the 95-foot-high Devil's Gate Bridge.

Restaurants

The Alpine Restaurant and Bar

$ | **PIZZA** | **FAMILY** | The thin-crust brick-oven pizzas and ingredient-packed stromboli and calzones draw families and groups to the casual, bustling Alpine, which serves lunch and dinner and offers live music Thursday to Saturday. Kids love the operating model train that winds around the restaurant overhead, and adults love the cozy bar. **Known for:** Wednesday-night trivia; warm cookie à la mode; extensive beer roster. *Average main: $14* *1106 Rose St.* *303/569–0200* *alpinerestaurantgeorgetown.com* *Closed Tues.*

Hotels

Hotel Chateau Chamonix

$$ | **B&B/INN** | With its log exterior and green roof, this hotel doesn't look exceptional for the region outside, but inside it's a lovely property put together with care by local owners. **Pros:** some rooms overlook a stream and have a two-person hot tub on a porch; rooms have espresso-cappuccino machines; owners often greet you with a glass of wine. **Cons:** on a busy main street; not within easy walking distance to downtown; thin walls and noisy overhead floors. *Rooms from: $180* *1414 Argentine St.* *303/569–1109, 888/569–1109* *www.hotelchateauchamonix.com* *10 rooms* *Free Breakfast.*

Estes Park

2 miles east of Rocky Mountain National Park via U.S. 36E.

The vast scenery on the U.S. 36 approach to Estes Park gives little hint of the grandeur to come, but if ever there was a classic picture-postcard Rockies view, Estes Park has it. The town sits at an altitude of more than 7,500 feet, at the foot of a stunning backdrop of 14,259-foot Longs Peak, the majestic Stanley Hotel, and surrounding mountains.

GETTING HERE AND AROUND

To get to Estes Park from Boulder, take U.S. 36 north through Lyons and the town of Pinewood Springs (about 38 miles). You can also reach Estes Park via the Peak to Peak Scenic and Historic Byway. To reach the byway from Boulder, take Highway 119 west to Nederland and turn right (north) onto Highway 72, or follow Sunshine Canyon Drive/Gold Hill Road into Ward, and pick up Highway 72 there.

Estes Park's main downtown area is walkable, which is good news on summer weekends, when traffic can be heavy (and parking can be challenging). Keep an eye out for parking signs throughout town, as the public lots are your best chance for a close-in spot.

The National Park Service operates a free bus service in and around Estes Park and between Estes Park and Rocky Mountain National Park. Buses operate daily from early June to Labor Day, then on weekends until the end of September.

VISITOR INFORMATION Estes Park Visitor Center. ✉ *500 Big Thompson Ave., Estes Park* ☎ *970/577–9900, 800/443–7837* 🌐 *www.visitestespark.com.*

Hiking the Continental Divide

The Continental Divide, that iconic geographic division that sends raindrops to either the Atlantic or Pacific Ocean, makes a worthy pilgrimage for day hikers and backpackers alike in summer. The easiest way to reach the divide is to drive up U.S. 6 over Loveland Pass at the Eisenhower Tunnel on I–70 and park on top of the divide. Hiking trails lead both east and west along the divide. Bring cash or a check for the $5 parking fee, and carpool if you can—parking is limited and tight during nice weather.

Sights

Estes Park Museum

MUSEUM | The museum showcases Ute and pioneer artifacts, displays on the founding of Rocky Mountain National Park, and changing exhibits. It also publishes a self-guided walking tour of historic sites, which are mostly clustered along Elkhorn Avenue downtown. ✉ *200 4th St., Estes Park* ☎ *970/586–6256* 🌐 *www.estes.org/museum* 🎫 *Free.*

MacGregor Ranch Museum

HISTORIC SITE | This working ranch, homesteaded in 1873, is on the National Register of Historic Places and provides a well-preserved record of typical ranch life. Take a guided tour of the 1896 ranch house, then explore the outbuildings and machinery on your own as you take in views of the Twin Owls and Longs Peak. ✉ *180 MacGregor La., Estes Park* ✣ *1½ miles north of town on U.S. 34. Turn right on MacGregor La., a dirt road* ☎ *970/586–3749* 🌐 *www.macgregor-ranch.org* 🎫 *$7.*

Restaurants

Bighorn Restaurant

$ | AMERICAN | FAMILY | An Estes Park staple since 1972, this family-run outfit is where the locals go for breakfast. Try a double-cheese omelet, huevos rancheros, or grits before heading into the park in the morning. **Known for:** hearty breakfast; huge portions; picnic lunches to-go. 💲 *Average main: $12* ✉ *401 W. Elkhorn Ave., Estes Park* ☎ *970/586–2792* 🌐 *www.estesparkbighorn.com.*

Ed's Cantina & Grill

$ | MEXICAN | FAMILY | The fajitas and well-stocked bar make this lively Mexican restaurant popular with locals and visitors alike. The decor is bright, with light woods and large windows. *$ Average main: $13 ✉ 390 E. Elkhorn Ave., Estes Park ☎ 970/586–2919.*

Estes Park Brewery

$ | **AMERICAN** | If you want to sample some local brews, check out the Estes Park Brewery, which has been crafting beer since 1993. The food is no-frills (beer chili is the specialty), and the menu includes things like pizza, burgers, sandwiches, and house-made bratwurst. **Known for:** local beer; pool tables; laid-back atmosphere. *$ Average main: $11 ✉ 470 Prospect Village Dr., Estes Park ☎ 970/586–5421 🌐 www.epbrewery.com.*

Mama Rose's

$$ | **ITALIAN** | **FAMILY** | An Estes Park institution since 1989, Mama Rose's consistently serves no-nonsense Italian meals, including the house specialty: hearty lasagna concocted with house-made meatballs and sausage. There are also plenty of lighter options, including vegetarian and gluten-free entrées, as well as build-your-own pasta from three noodles, six sauces, and nine meats and vegetables. *$ Average main: $16 ✉ 338 E. Elkhorn Ave., Estes Park ☎ 970/586–3330 🌐 www.mamarosesrestaurant.com ⏲ Closed Jan. No lunch.*

Poppy's Pizza & Grill

$ | **PIZZA** | **FAMILY** | This casual riverside eatery serves creative signature pizzas. Try the spinach, artichoke, and feta pie made with sun-dried tomato pesto. **Known for:** create-your-own pizza; riverfront patio; vegan- and gluten-free-friendly. *$ Average main: $10 ✉ 342 E. Elkhorn Ave., Estes Park ☎ 970/586–8282 🌐 www.poppyspizzaandgrill.com ⏲ Closed Jan.*

★ Seasoned

$$$ | **AMERICAN** | With a menu that changes monthly, Seasoned takes its name to heart with its always-changing ingredients from local farms. The creative dishes, created by chef-owner and Michelin-star veteran Rob Corey, reflect influences from North, South, and Central America and feature Colorado specialties like lamb, trout, and bass. **Known for:** creative cuisine; Colorado lamb, trout, and bass; attentive service. *$ Average main: $30 ✉ 205 Park La., Estes Park ☎ 970/586–9000 🌐 seasonedbistro.com ⏲ Closed Mon.*

Hotels

Boulder Brook

$$$ | **HOTEL** | Watch elk stroll past your spacious luxury suite at this smart, secluded spot on the river amid towering pines. **Pros:** scenic location; quiet area; attractive grounds. **Cons:** not within walking distance of attractions; no nearby dining. *$ Rooms from: $250 ✉ 1900 Fall River Rd., Estes Park ☎ 970/586–0910, 800/238–0910 🌐 www.boulderbrook.com ⇨ 20 suites 🍽 No meals.*

Glacier Lodge

$$ | **RESORT** | **FAMILY** | Families are the specialty at this secluded, 22-acre guest resort on the banks of the Big Thompson River. **Pros:** great place for families; attractive grounds on the river; on free bus route. **Cons:** not within walking distance of attractions; along rather busy road. *$ Rooms from: $160 ✉ 2166 Hwy. 66, Estes Park ☎ 800/523–3920 🌐 www.glacierlodgeonline.com ⏲ Closed Nov.–Apr. ⇨ 30 cabins 🍽 No meals.*

★ The Maxwell Inn

$$ | **HOTEL** | Within walking distance of downtown, this family-run spot features small but comfortable rooms decorated with arts and crafts–style furnishings and locally built custom wood furniture. **Pros:** walking distance to downtown; relatively affordable for Estes Park; clean and comfortable. **Cons:** rooms are small; fairly basic accommodations. *$ Rooms from: $145 ✉ 553 W. Elkhorn Ave., Estes Park ☎ 970/586-2833 🌐 www.themaxwellinn.com ⏲ Closed Jan. and Feb. ⇨ 21 rooms 🍽 Free breakfast.*

★ Stanley Hotel
$$$ | **HOTEL** | Perched regally on a hill, with a commanding view of town, the Stanley is one of Colorado's great old hotels, featuring Georgian colonial–style architecture and a storied, haunted history, inspiring Stephen King's novel *The Shining* and daily "ghost" tours. **Pros:** historic hotel; many rooms have been updated; good restaurant. **Cons:** some rooms are small and tight; building is old; no air-conditioning. *Rooms from: $299 333 Wonderview Ave., Estes Park 970/577–4000, 800/976–1377 www.stanleyhotel.com 140 rooms No meals.*

Taharaa Mountain Lodge
$$$ | **B&B/INN** | Every room at this luxury B&B has its own balcony and views of the High Rockies and Estes Valley and is decorated with an individual theme. **Pros:** beautiful mountain views; friendly hosts. **Cons:** not within walking distance of attractions or on bus route; no young children allowed; two-day minimum stay (three-day minimum for summer and holidays). *Rooms from: $289 3110 S. St. Vrain Ave., Estes Park 4 miles south of downtown Estes Park 970/577–0098, 800/597–0098 www.taharaa.com 9 rooms, 9 suites Free breakfast.*

YMCA of the Rockies–Estes Park Center
$$ | **RESORT** | **FAMILY** | Surrounded on three sides by Rocky Mountain National Park, this 860-acre family-friendly property has attractive, clean lodge rooms (with either queen, full, or bunk beds), simple cabins for two to four people, and larger cabins that can sleep as many as 88 people. **Pros:** good value for large groups and longer stays; lots of family-oriented activities and amenities; stunning scenery. **Cons:** very large, busy, and crowded property; fills fast; location requires vehicle to visit town or the national park. *Rooms from: $169 2515 Tunnel Rd., Estes Park 970/586–3341, 888/613–9622 family reservations, 800/777–9622 group reservations www.ymcarockies.org 770 rooms No meals.*

Shopping

Shopping in Estes Park focuses around several T-shirt and souvenir shops, a labyrinth of sweets shops (taffy, caramel corn, and chocolate, oh my!), plus a number of more upscale gift shops and art galleries.

CRAFTS AND ART GALLERIES

Earthwood Collections
ART GALLERIES | This fine art and handicrafts shop sells a wide assortment of art, including ceramics, frames, jewelry, oil paintings, and more. *141 E. Elkhorn Ave., Estes Park 970/577–8100 www.earthwoodcollections.com.*

Images of Rocky Mountain National Park
ART GALLERIES | This shop showcases photographer Erik Stensland's stunning images of the park—a must-see collection of local photography. *203 Park La., Estes Park 970/586–4352 www.imagesofrmnp.com.*

Patterson Glassworks of Estes Park
ART GALLERIES | Watch glassblowing in action and browse a wide variety of glass creations. *323 W. Elkhorn Ave., Estes Park 970/586–8619 www.glassworksofestespark.com.*

Wild Spirits Gallery
ART GALLERIES | Shop for limited-edition prints, photographs, and paintings of the West and Rocky Mountain National Park. Custom framing and shipping are also available. *148 W. Elkhorn Ave., Estes Park 970/586–4392 wildspiritsgalleryestespark.com.*

Rocky Mountain National Park

With its towering mountains, active and abundant wildlife, and crystal clear lakes and rivers, Rocky Mountain attracts nearly 5 million visitors per year, trailing only the Grand Canyon and the Great Smoky Mountains in the country's most visited national parks. Established as the 10th National Park in 1915, the picturesque land has attracted humans since at least 11,000 years ago, based on the archaeological artifacts like shelters and speartips that have been found throughout the park.

These ancient people used the very same trail as today's visitors: the 48-mile Trail Ridge Road. With an apex of 12,183 feet, the road travels from the east-side Estes Park entrance, across the Continental Divide, to the west-side Grand Lake entrance, giving even nonhikers a close look at the Montane, Supalpine, and Alpine ecosystems found at different areas of the park.

Those who do hike have their pick of more than 355 miles of trails, with paths suited for every ability level. The park's high altitude—the lowest elevation starts at 7,000 feet above sea level—often affects out-of-towners, but a good night's sleep and healthy hydration go a long way. The park is famous for its robust elk population, especially active in "Elk-tober" when the elk come to lower elevations for their annual mating season. Moose are more common on the west side near the Kawuneeche Visitor Center and near rivers and lakes, while bighorn sheep are best spotted in late spring and early summer at the appropriately named Sheeps Lake in Horseshoe Park.

Rocky Mountain has more than 1,000 archaeological sites and 150 buildings of historic significance; 47 of the buildings are listed in the National Register of Historic Places. Most buildings at Rocky Mountain are done in the rustic style, which strives to incorporate nature into man-made structures.

Though the park has year-round access and activities, most visitors come between late spring and mid-autumn when Trail Ridge Road remains open. In the high summer months, the east side entrance and lower elevation trails can become quite congested, so beat the crowds by using the west entrance or arriving before 8 am. *In 2020, a pair of devastating fires swept across approximately 30,000 acres, around 9 percent of the park, primarily in the west and far north part of the park, so check the latest conditions and closures on the park's website before setting off.*

GETTING HERE AND AROUND

Estes Park and Grand Lake are the Rocky Mountains' gateway communities; from these you can enter the park via U.S. 34 or 36 (Estes Park) or U.S. 34 (Grand Lake). U.S. 36 runs from Denver through Boulder, Lyons, and Estes Park to the park; the portion between Boulder and Estes Park is heavily traveled—especially on summer weekends. Though less direct, Colorado Routes 119, 72, and 7 have much less traffic (and better scenery). If you're driving directly to Rocky Mountain from the airport, take the E–470 tollway from Peña Boulevard to Interstate 25.

Rocky Mountain has limited parking, but offers three free shuttle buses, which operate daily from 7 am to 8 pm, late May to early October. All three shuttles can be accessed from a large Park & Ride located within the park, 7 miles from the Beaver Meadows entrance. Visitors who don't want to drive into the park at all can hop on the Hiker Shuttle at the Estes Park Visitor Center. The shuttle, which runs every half hour during peak times, makes stops at the Beaver Meadows Visitor Center and the Park & Ride, where visitors can switch to one of the other two shuttles, which head to various trailheads. The Moraine Park Route shuttle runs every 30 minutes and stops at the Moraine Park Visitor Center and then continues on to the Fern Lake Trailhead. The Bear Lake Route shuttle runs every 10 to 15 minutes from the Park & Ride to the Bear Lake Trailhead.

WITHIN THE PARK

The main thoroughfare in the park is Trail Ridge Road (U.S. 34); in winter, it's closed from the first storm in the fall (typically in October) through the spring (depending on snowpack, this could be at any time between May and June). During that time, it's plowed only up to Many Parks Curve on the east side and the Colorado River trailhead on the west side. (For current road information: ☎ *970/586–1222* 🌐 *www.codot.gov.*)

The spectacular Old Fall River Road runs one-way between the Endovalley Picnic Area on the eastern edge of the park and the Alpine Visitor Center at the summit of Trail Ridge Road, on the western side. It is typically open from July to September, depending on snowfall. It's a steep, narrow road (no wider than 14 feet), and trailers and vehicles longer than 25 feet are prohibited, but a trip on this 100-year-old thoroughfare is well worth the effort. For information on road closures, contact the park: ☎ *970/586–1206* 🌐 *www.nps.gov/romo.*

PARK ESSENTIALS

PARK FEES AND PERMITS

Entrance fees are $25 per automobile for a one-day pass or $35 for a seven-day pass. Those who enter via foot or bicycle can get a seven-day pass for $20. Motorcyclists can get a seven-day pass for $30. An annual pass to Rocky Mountain costs $70, while the National Parks' America The Beautiful pass costs $80 and grants admission to more than 2,000 sites across the U.S.

Wilderness camping requires a permit that's $30 per party from May through October, and free the rest of the year. Visit 🌐 *www.nps.gov/romo/planyourvisit/wilderness-camping.htm* before you go for a planning guide to backcountry camping. You can get your permit online, by phone (☎ *970/586–1242*), or in person. In person, you can get a day-of-trip permit year-round at one of the park's two backcountry offices, located next to the Beaver Meadows Visitor Center and in the Kawuneeche Visitor Center.

PARK HOURS

The park is open 24/7 year-round; some roads close in winter. It is in the mountain time zone.

CELL PHONE RECEPTION

Cell phones work in some sections of the park, and free Wi-Fi can be accessed in and around the Beaver Meadows Visitor Center, Fall River, and the Kawuneeche Visitor Center.

TOURS

Green Jeep Tours

ADVENTURE TOURS | FAMILY | From the back of an open-air, neon-green Jeep on these tours, you can enjoy the majestic scenery while your experienced guide points out wildlife along the way. Green Jeep Tours also offers a three-hour tour in September and October that focuses on finding elk. Admission includes the cost of the one-day pass into the park. ✉ *157 Moraine Ave., Estes Park* ☎ *970/577–0034* 🎫 *From $90.*

Wildside 4x4 Tours

DRIVING TOURS | This company's most popular tour, the "Top of the World," takes visitors in an open-top vehicle all the way to Old Fall River Road and back down Trail Ridge. A waterfall tour and sunset valley tour offer great wildlife spottings at lower elevations. ✉ *212 E. Elkhorn Ave., Estes Park* ☎ *970/586–8687* 🌐 *www.wildside4x4tours.com* 🎫 *From $80.*

★ Yellow Wood Guiding

ADVENTURE TOURS | Guided photo safaris, offered year-round, ensure visitors leave the Rocky Mountain National Park with more than just memories. Customized for either beginners or experts, the tours offer the use of professional digital cameras for visitors who don't have their own. ✉ *404 Driftwood Ave., Estes Park* ☎ *303/775–5484* 🌐 *www.ywguiding.com* 🎫 *From $175.*

VISITOR INFORMATION

CONTACTS Rocky Mountain National Park. ✉ *1000 U.S. 36, Estes Park* ☎ *970/586–1206* 🌐 *www.nps.gov/romo.*

Moraine Park

The starting point for most first-timers, the easternmost part of the park is easy to access via car or park shuttle. A number of popular trailheads originate here, particularly suited for half-day hikes, and a large campground accommodates those who want to stay overnight. It's also where you'll find the Beaver Meadows Visitor Center.

Sights

TRAILS

Cub Lake Trail

TRAIL | This 4.6-mile, three-hour (round-trip) hike takes you through meadows and stands of aspen trees and up 540 feet in elevation to a lake with water lilies. *Moderate.* ✉ *Rocky Mountain National Park* ✣ *Trailhead: At Cub Lake, about 1¾ miles from Moraine Park Campground.*

Deer Mountain Trail

TRAIL | This 6-mile round-trip trek to the top of 10,083-foot Deer Mountain is a great way for hikers who don't mind a bit of a climb to enjoy the views from the summit of a more manageable peak. You'll gain more than 1,000 feet in elevation as you follow the switchbacking trail through ponderosa pine, aspen, and fir trees. The reward at the top is a panoramic view of the park's eastern mountains. *Difficult.* ✉ *Rocky Mountain National Park* ✣ *Trailhead: At Deer Ridge Junction, about 4 miles west of Moraine Park Visitor Center, U.S. 34 at U.S. 36.*

Fern Lake Trail

TRAIL | Heading to Odessa Lake from the north involves a steep hike, but on most days you'll encounter fewer other hikers than if you had begun the trip at Bear Lake. Along the way, you'll come to the Arch Rocks; the Pool, an eroded formation in the Big Thompson River; two waterfalls; and Fern Lake (3.8 miles from your starting point). Less than a mile farther, Odessa Lake itself lies at the foot of Tourmaline Gorge, below the craggy summits of Gabletop Mountain, Little Matterhorn, Knobtop Mountain, and Notchtop Mountain. For a full day of spectacular scenery, continue past Odessa to Bear Lake (9 miles total), where you can pick up the shuttle back to the Fern Lake Trailhead. *Moderate.* ✉ *Rocky Mountain National Park* ✣ *Trailhead: Off Fern Lake Rd., about 2½ miles south of Moraine Park Visitor Center.*

Sprague Lake

TRAIL | With virtually no elevation gain, this ½-mile, pine-lined looped path near a popular backcountry campground is wheelchair accessible and provides views of Hallet Peak and Flattop Mountain. *Easy.* ✉ *Rocky Mountain National Park* ✣ *Trailhead: At Sprague Lake, Bear Lake Rd., 4½ miles southwest of Moraine Park Visitor Center.*

Restaurants

Café at Trail Ridge

$ | **AMERICAN** | The park's only source for food, this small café offers snacks, sandwiches, hot dogs, and soups. A coffee bar also serves fair-trade coffee, espresso drinks, and tea, plus water, juice, and salads. **Known for:** quick bite; fair-trade coffee; no-frills food. [$] *Average main: $7*

One of the easiest trails in the park is the loop around stunning Bear Lake.

✉ Trail Ridge Rd., at Alpine Visitor Center ☎ 970/586–3097 🌐 www.trailridgegiftstore.com ⏲ Closed mid-Oct.–late May. No dinner.

Shopping

Trail Ridge Store

CLOTHING | This is the park's only official store (though you'll find a small selection of park souvenirs and books at the visitor centers). Trail Ridge stocks sweatshirts and jackets, postcards, and assorted craft items. *✉ Trail Ridge Rd., adjacent to Alpine Visitor Center 🌐 www.trailridgegiftstore.com.*

Bear Lake

Thanks to its picturesque location, easy accessibility, and the good hiking trails nearby, this small lake below Flattop Mountain and Hallett Peak is one of the park's most popular destinations.

Sights

SCENIC DRIVES

Bear Lake Road

SCENIC DRIVE | This 23-mile round-trip drive offers superlative views of Longs Peak (14,259-foot summit) and the glaciers surrounding Bear Lake, winding past shimmering waterfalls shrouded with rainbows. You can either drive the road yourself (open year-round) or hop on one of the park's free shuttle buses. *✉ Runs from the Beaver Meadow Entrance Station to Bear Lake.*

SCENIC STOPS

Farview Curve Overlook

VIEWPOINT | At an elevation of 10,120 feet, this lookout affords a panoramic view of the Colorado River near its origin and the Grand Ditch, a water diversion project dating from 1890 that's still in use today. You can also see the once-volcanic peaks of Never Summer Range along the park's western boundary. *✉ Trail Ridge Rd., about 14 miles north of Kawuneeche Visitor Center.*

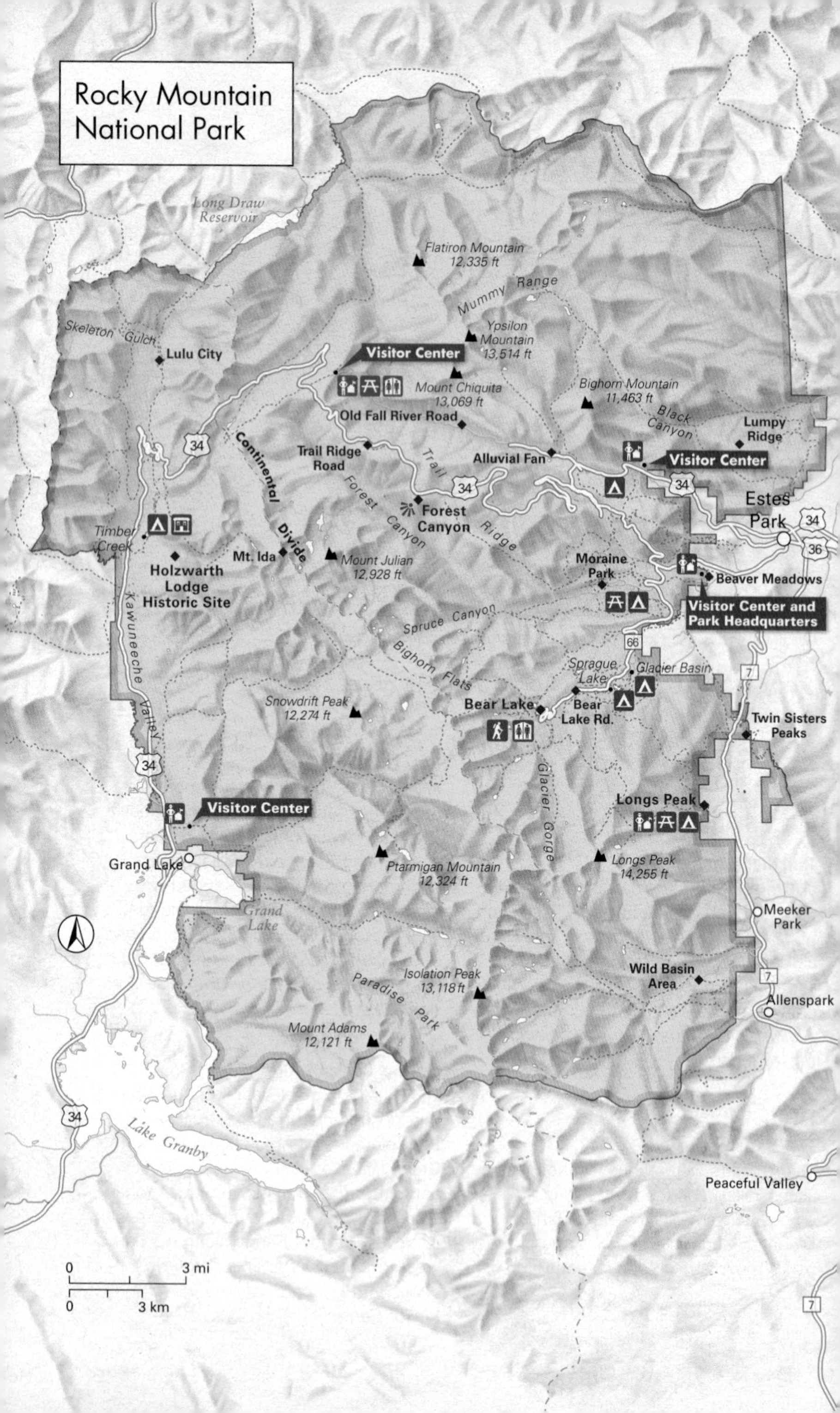

Rocky Mountain National Park
Long Draw Reservoir
Flatiron Mountain 12,335 ft
Mummy Range
Ypsilon Mountain 13,514 ft
Skeleton Gulch
Lulu City
Visitor Center
Mount Chiquita 13,069 ft
Bighorn Mountain 11,463 ft
Old Fall River Road
Black Canyon
Lumpy Ridge
34
Continental Divide
Trail Ridge Road
Trail Ridge
Alluvial Fan
Visitor Center
34
Forest Canyon
Forest Canyon
Estes Park
34
36
Timber Creek
Holzwarth Lodge Historic Site
Mt. Ida
Mount Julian 12,928 ft
Moraine Park
Beaver Meadows
Visitor Center and Park Headquarters
Kawuneeche Valley
Spruce Canyon
Bighorn Flats
66
Sprague Lake
Glacier Basin
7
Snowdrift Peak 12,274 ft
Bear Lake
Bear Lake Rd.
Twin Sisters Peaks
34
Glacier Gorge
Longs Peak
Visitor Center
Grand Lake
Ptarmigan Mountain 12,324 ft
Longs Peak 14,255 ft
Grand Lake
Meeker Park
Isolation Peak 13,118 ft
Paradise Park
Wild Basin Area
7
Allenspark
Mount Adams 12,121 ft
34
Lake Granby
Peaceful Valley
0
3 mi
0
3 km
7

Forest Canyon Overlook

VIEWPOINT | Park at a dedicated lot to disembark on a wildflower-rich, 0.2-mile trail. Easy to access for all skill levels, this glacial valley overlook offers views of ice-blue pools (the Gorge Lakes) framed by ragged peaks. ✉ *Trail Ridge Rd., 6 miles east of Alpine Visitor Center.*

TRAILS

Bear Lake Trail

TRAIL | The virtually flat nature trail around Bear Lake is an easy, 0.6-mile loop that's wheelchair and stroller accessible. Sharing the route with you will likely be plenty of other hikers as well as songbirds and chipmunks. *Easy.* ✉ *Rocky Mountain National Park* ✥ *Trailhead: At Bear Lake, Bear Lake Rd.*

★ **Bear Lake to Emerald Lake**

TRAIL | This scenic, calorie-burning hike begins with a moderately level, ½-mile journey to **Nymph Lake.** From here, the trail gets steeper, with a 425-foot elevation gain, as it winds around for 0.6 miles to **Dream Lake.** The last stretch is the most arduous part of the hike, an almost all-uphill 0.7-mile trek to lovely **Emerald Lake,** where you can perch on a boulder and enjoy the view. All told, the hike is 3.6 miles, with an elevation gain of 605 feet. Allow two hours or more. *Moderate.* ✉ *Rocky Mountain National Park* ✥ *Trailhead: At Bear Lake, off Bear Lake Rd., 8 miles southwest of the Moraine Park Visitor Center.*

★ **Glacier Gorge Trail**

TRAIL | The 2.8-mile hike to **Mills Lake** can be crowded, but the reward is one of the park's prettiest lakes, set against the breathtaking backdrop of Longs Peak, Pagoda Mountain, and the Keyboard of the Winds. There's a modest elevation gain of 750 feet. On the way, about 1 mile in, you pass **Alberta Falls,** a popular destination in and of itself. The hike travels along Glacier Creek, under the shade of a subalpine forest. Give yourself at least four hours for hiking and lingering. *Easy.* ✉ *Rocky Mountain National Park* ✥ *Trailhead: Off Bear Lake Rd., about 1 mile southeast of Bear Lake.*

Mills Lake

TRAIL | From this popular spot, you can admire the Keyboard of the Winds, a jagged ridge connecting Pagoda and Longs Peaks that looks like the top of a spiny reptile's back. The 5.6-mile hike gains 750 feet in elevation as it takes you past Alberta Falls and Glacier Falls en route to the shimmering lake at the mouth of Glacier Gorge. *Moderate.* ✉ *Rocky Mountain National Park* ✥ *Trailhead: At Glacier Gorge Junction, about 1 mile from Bear Lake.*

Longs Peak

At 14,259 feet above sea level, Longs Peak has long fascinated explorers to the region. Longs Peak is the northernmost of the Fourteeners—the 53 mountains in Colorado that reach above the 14,000-foot mark—and one of more than 114 named mountains in the park that are higher than 10,000 feet. The peak, in the park's southeast quadrant, has a distinctive flat-topped, rectangular summit that is visible from many spots on the park's east side and on Trail Ridge Road.

Explorer and author Isabella L. Bird wrote of it: "It is one of the noblest of mountains, but in one's imagination it grows to be much more than a mountain. It becomes invested with a personality." It was named after Major Stephen H. Long, who led an expedition in 1820 up the Platte River to the base of the Rockies. Long never ascended the mountain—in fact, he didn't even get within 40 miles of it—but a few decades later, in 1868, the one-armed Civil War veteran John Wesley Powell climbed to its summit.

The ambitious climb to Longs summit is recommended only for those who are strong climbers and well acclimated to the altitude. If you're up for the 10- to 15-hour climb, begin before dawn so that

The Glacier Gorge Trail takes you past pretty Alberta Falls.

you're down from the summit prior to typical afternoon thunderstorms.

Sights

TRAILS

Chasm Lake Trail

TRAIL | Nestled in the shadow of Longs Peak and Mount Meeker, Chasm Lake offers one of Colorado's most impressive backdrops, which also means you can expect to encounter plenty of other hikers on the way. The 4.2-mile Chasm Lake Trail, reached via the Longs Peak Trail, has a 2,360-foot elevation gain. Just before the lake, you'll need to climb a small rock ledge, which can be a bit of a challenge for the less sure-footed; follow the cairns for the most straightforward route. Once atop the ledge, you'll catch your first memorable view of the lake. *Difficult.* ✉ *Rocky Mountain National Park* ✥ *Trailhead: At Longs Peak Ranger Station, off Rte. 7, 10 miles from the Beaver Meadows Visitor Center.*

Longs Peak Trail

TRAIL | Climbing this 14,259-foot mountain (one of 53 "Fourteeners" in Colorado) is an ambitious goal for almost anyone—but only those who are very fit and acclimated to the altitude should attempt it. The 16-mile round-trip climb requires a predawn start (3 am is ideal), so that you're off the summit before the typical summer afternoon thunderstorm hits. Also, the last 2 miles or so of the trail are very exposed—you have to traverse narrow ledges with vertigo-inducing drop-offs. That said, summiting Longs can be one of the most rewarding experiences you'll ever have. The Keyhole route is the most popular means of ascent, and the number of people going up it on a summer day can be astounding, given the rigors of the climb. Though just as scenic, the Loft route, between Longs and Mount Meeker from Chasm Lake, is less crowded but not as clearly marked and therefore more difficult to navigate. *Difficult.* ✉ *Rocky Mountain National Park* ✥ *Trailhead: At Longs Peak Ranger*

Station, off Rte. 7, 10 miles from Beaver Meadows Visitor Center.

Trail Ridge Road

The park's star attraction and the world's highest continuous paved highway (topping out at 12,183 feet), this 48-mile road connects the park's gateways of Estes Park and Grand Lake. The views around each bend—of moraines and glaciers, and craggy hills framing emerald meadows carpeted with columbine—are truly awesome. As it passes through three ecosystems—montane, subalpine, and arctic tundra—the road climbs 4,300 feet. You can complete a one-way trip across the park on Trail Ridge Road in two hours, but it's best to give yourself three or four hours to allow for leisurely breaks at the overlooks. Note that the middle part of the road closes with the first big snow (typically by mid-October) and most often reopens around Memorial Day, though you can still drive up about 10 miles from the west and 8 miles from the east.

Sights

HISTORIC SIGHTS

Lulu City

ARCHAEOLOGICAL SITE | The remains of a few cabins are all that's left of this onetime silver-mining town, established around 1880. Reach it by hiking the 3.6-mile Colorado River Trail. Look for wagon ruts from the old Stewart Toll Road and mine tailings in nearby Shipler Park (this is also a good place to spot moose). ✉ *Off Trail Ridge Rd., 9½ miles north of Grand Lake Entrance Station.*

SCENIC DRIVES

Old Fall River Road

SCENIC DRIVE | More than 100 years old and never more than 14 feet wide, this road stretches from the park's east side to the Fall River Pass (11,796 feet above sea level) on the west. The drive provides a few white-knuckle moments, as the road is steep, serpentine, and lacking in guardrails. Start at West Horseshoe Park, which has the park's largest concentrations of sheep and elk, and head up the gravel road, passing Chasm Falls. ✉ *Runs north of and roughly parallel to Trail Ridge Road, starting near Endovalley Campground (on east) and ending at Fall River Pass/Alpine Visitor Center (on west).*

TRAILS

Chapin Pass

TRAIL | This is a tough hike, but it comes with great views of the park's eastern lower valleys. It's about 3½ miles one way, including a 2,874-foot gain in elevation to the summit of Ypsilon Mountain (elevation 13,514 feet); you pass the summits of Mount Chapin and Mount Chiquita on the way. From the trailhead, the path heads downhill to Chapin Creek. For a short distance after leaving the trailhead, keep a sharp eye out to the right for a less obvious trail that heads uphill to the tree line and disappears. From here head up along the steep ridge to the summit of Mount Chapin. Chiquita and Ypsilon are to the left, and the distance between each peak is about 1 mile and involves a descent of about 400 feet to the saddle and an ascent of 1,000 feet along the ridge to Chiquita. From Ypsilon's summit you'll look down 2,000 feet at Spectacle Lakes. You may wish to bring a topo map and compass. *Difficult.* ✉ *Rocky Mountain National Park* ✣ *Trailhead: At Chapin Pass, off Old Fall River Rd., about 6½ miles from the Endovalley Picnic Area.*

Timber Creek

Located along the Colorado River, the west part of the park attracts fewer people and more wildlife in its valleys, especially moose. The towering mountain vistas are fewer here than in the east, but the expansive meadows, rivers, and lakes offer their own peaceful beauty. Unfortunately, wildfires in 2020 destroyed many acres of forest and damaged trails here, so check conditions and closures before setting off.

Sights

HISTORIC SITES

Holzwarth Historic Site

ARCHAEOLOGICAL SITE | FAMILY | A scenic ½-mile interpretive trail leads you over the Colorado River to the original dude ranch that the Holzwarth family, some of the park's original homesteaders, ran between the 1920s and 1950s. Allow about an hour to view the buildings—including a dozen small guest cabins—and chat with a ranger. Though the site is open year-round, the inside of the buildings can be seen only June through early September. ✉ *Off U.S. 34, about 8 miles north of Kawuneeche Visitor Center, Estes Park.*

TRAILS

Colorado River Trail

TRAIL | This walk to the ghost town of Lulu City on the west side of the park is excellent for looking for the bighorn sheep, elk, and moose that reside in the area. Part of the former stagecoach route that went from Granby to Walden, the 3.7-mile trail parallels the infant Colorado River to the meadow where Lulu City once stood. The elevation gain is 350 feet. *Moderate.* ✉ *Rocky Mountain National Park* ⊕ *Trailhead: At Colorado River, off Trail Ridge Rd., 1¾ miles north of the Timber Creek Campground.*

Continental Divide National Scenic Trail

TRAIL | This 3,100-mile corridor, which extends from Montana's Canadian border to the southern edge of New Mexico, enters Rocky Mountain National Park in two places, at trailheads only about 4 miles apart and located on either side of the Kawuneeche Visitor Center on Trail Ridge Road, at the park's southwestern end. Within the park, it covers about 30 miles of spectacular montane and subalpine terrain and follows the existing Green Mountain, Tonahutu Creek, North Inlet, and East Shore Trails. *Moderate.* ✉ *Rocky Mountain National Park* ⊕ *Trailheads: At Harbison Meadows Picnic Area, off Trail Ridge Rd., about 1 mile inside park from Grand Lake Entrance, and at East Shore Trailhead, just south of Grand Lake.*

East Inlet Trail

TRAIL | An easy hike of 0.3 miles from East Inlet trailhead, just outside the park in Grand Lake, will get you to **Adams Falls** in about 15 minutes. The area around the falls is often packed with visitors, so if you have time, continue east to enjoy more solitude, see wildlife, and catch views of **Mount Craig** from near the East Meadow campground. Note, however, that the trail beyond the falls has an elevation gain of between 1,500 and 1,900 feet, making it a more challenging hike. *Easy.* ✉ *Grand Lake* ⊕ *Trailhead: At East Inlet, end of W. Portal Rd. (CO 278) in Grand Lake.*

Wild Basin

This section in the southeast region of the park consists of lovely expanses of subalpine forest punctuated by streams and lakes. The area's high peaks, along the Continental Divide, are not as easily accessible as those in the vicinity of Bear Lake; hiking to the base of the divide and back makes for a long day. Nonetheless, a visit here is worth the drive south from Estes Park, and because the Wild Basin trailhead is set apart from the park hub, crowding isn't a problem.

Elk are some of the park's most famous residents.

Sights

TRAILS

Copeland Falls

TRAIL | FAMILY | The 0.3-mile hike to these Wild Basin Area falls is a good option for families, as the terrain is relatively flat (there's only a 15-foot elevation gain). *Easy.* ✉ *Rocky Mountain National Park* ✣ *Trailhead: At Wild Basin Ranger Station.*

Activities

CAMPING

The park's five campgrounds accommodate campers looking to stay in a tent, trailer, or RV (only three campgrounds accept reservations—up to six months in advance at 🌐 *www.recreation.gov* or 🌐 *www.reserveamerica.com*; the others fill up on a first-come, first-served basis).

Aspenglen Campground. This quiet, east-side spot near the north entrance is set in open pine woodland along Fall River. There are a few excellent walk-in sites for those who want to pitch a tent away from the crowds but still be close to the car. Reservations are recommended in summer. ✉ *Drive past Fall River Visitor Center on U.S. 34 and turn left at the campground road.*

Glacier Basin Campground. This spot offers expansive views of the Continental Divide, easy access to the free summer shuttles to Bear Lake and Estes Park, and ranger-led evening programs in the summer. Reservations are essential. ✉ *5 miles south on Bear Lake Rd. from U.S. 36* ☎ *877/444–6777.*

Longs Peak Campground. Open May to November, this campgound is only a short walk from the Longs Peak trailhead, making it a favorite among hikers looking to get an early start there. The tent-only sites, which are first come, first served, are limited to eight people; firewood, lighting fluid, and charcoal are sold in summer. ✉ *9 miles south of Estes Park on Rte. 7.*

Moraine Park Campground. The only campground in Rocky Mountain open year-round, this spot connects to many hiking trails and has easy access to the free summer shuttles. Rangers lead evening programs in the summer. You'll hear elk bugling if you camp here in September or October. Reservations are essential from mid-May to late September. ✉ *Drive south on Bear Lake Rd. from U.S. 36, 1 mile to campground entrance.*

Timber Creek Campground. Anglers love this spot on the Colorado River, 10 miles from Grand Lake village and the only east-side campground. In the evening you can sit in on ranger-led campfire programs. The 98 campsites are first come, first served. ✉ *1 Trail Ridge Rd., 2 miles west of Alpine Visitor Center.*

Wilderness Camping, Rocky Mountain National Park. Experienced hikers can camp at one of the park's many designated backcountry sites with advance reservations or a day-of-trip permit (which comes with a $30 fee in May through October). Contact the Wilderness Office before starting out to get a sense of current conditions. ✉ *Beaver Meadows Visitor Center, Kawuneeche Visitor Center* ☎ *970/586–1242.*

FISHING

Rocky Mountain is a wonderful place to fish, especially for trout—German brown, brook, rainbow, cutthroat, and greenback cutthroat—but check at a visitor center about regulations and closures. No fishing is allowed at Bear Lake. To avoid the crowds, rangers recommend angling in the more-remote backcountry. To fish in the park, anyone 16 and older must have a valid Colorado fishing license, which you can obtain at local sporting-goods stores. See 🌐 *cpw.state.co.us* for details.

Estes Angler

FISHING | This popular fishing guide arranges fly-fishing trips from two to eight hours into the park's quieter regions, year-round. The best times for fishing are generally from April to mid-November. Equipment is also available for rent. ✉ *338 W. Riverside Dr., Estes Park* ☎ *970/586–2110, 800/586–2110* 🌐 *www.estesangler.com* 🎟 *From $149.*

Kirks Fly Shop

CAMPING—SPORTS-OUTDOORS | This Estes Park outfitter offers various guided fly-fishing trips, as well as backpacking, horseback, and llama pack trips. The store also carries fishing and backpacking gear. ✉ *230 E. Elkhorn Ave., Estes Park* ☎ *970/577–0790, 877/669–1859* 🌐 *www.kirksflyshop.com* 🎟 *From $149.*

Scot's Sporting Goods

FISHING | This shop rents and sells fishing gear, and provides instruction trips daily from May through mid-October. Clinics, geared toward first-timers, focus on casting, reading the water, identifying insects for flies, and properly presenting natural and artificial flies to the fish. ✉ *870 Moraine Ave., Estes Park* ☎ *970/586–2877 May–Sept., 970/443–4932 Oct.–Apr.* 🌐 *www.scotssportinggoods.com* 🎟 *From $220.*

HIKING

Rocky Mountain National Park contains more than 355 miles of hiking trails, so you could theoretically wander the park for weeks. Most visitors explore just a small portion of these trails—those that are closest to the roads and visitor centers—which means that some of the park's most accessible and scenic paths can resemble a backcountry highway on busy summer days. The high-alpine terrain around Bear Lake is the park's most popular hiking area, and although it's well worth exploring, you'll get a more frontierlike experience by hiking one of the trails in the less-explored sections of the park, such as the far northern end or in the Wild Basin area to the south.

Keep in mind that trails at higher elevations may have some snow on them, even in late summer. And because of afternoon thunderstorms on most summer days, an early morning start is highly recommended: the last place you want to be when a storm approaches is on a peak or anywhere above the tree line.

HORSEBACK RIDING

Horses and riders can access 260 miles of trails in Rocky Mountain National Park.

Glacier Creek Stable

HORSEBACK RIDING | FAMILY | Located within the park near Sprague Lake, Glacier Creek Stable offers 2- to 10-hour rides to Glacier Basin, Odessa Lake, and Storm Pass. ✉ *Glacier Creek Campground, off Bear Lake Rd. near Sprague Lake* ☎ *970/586–3244 stables, 970/586–4577 off-season reservations* 🌐 *rockymountainhorserides.com* 🎫 *From $70.*

Moraine Park Stable

HORSEBACK RIDING | FAMILY | Located inside the park just before the Cub Lake Trailhead, Moraine Park Stable offers two- to eight-hour trips to Beaver Meadows, Fern Lake, and Tourmaline Gorge. ✉ *549 Fern Lake Rd.* ☎ *970/586–2327 stables, 970/586–4577 off-season reservations* 🌐 *www.sombrero.com* 🎫 *From $70.*

National Park Gateway Stables

HORSEBACK RIDING | FAMILY | Guided trips into the national park range from two-hour rides to Little Horseshoe Park to half-day rides to Endo Valley and Fall River. The six-hour ride to the summit of Deer Mountain is a favorite. Preschool-aged children can take a 10- or 30-minute pony ride on nearby trails. ✉ *4600 Fall River Rd., Estes Park* ☎ *970/586–5269* 🌐 *www.skhorses.com* 🎫 *From $80.*

ROCK CLIMBING

Experts as well as novices can try hundreds of classic and big-wall climbs here (there's also ample opportunity for bouldering and mountaineering). The burgeoning sport of ice climbing also thrives in the park. The Diamond, Lumpy Ridge, and Petit Grepon are the places for serious rock climbing, while well-known ice-climbing spots include Hidden Falls, Loch Vale, and Emerald and Black lakes.

★ Colorado Mountain School

CLIMBING/MOUNTAINEERING | FAMILY | Guiding climbers since 1877, Colorado Mountain School is the park's only official provider of technical climbing services. They can teach you rock climbing, mountaineering, ice climbing, avalanche survival, and many other skills. Take introductory half-day and one- to five-day courses on climbing and rappelling technique, or sign up for guided introductory trips, full-day climbs, and longer expeditions. Make reservations a month in advance for summer climbs. ✉ *341 Moraine Ave., Estes Park* ☎ *720/387–8944, 303/447–2804* 🌐 *coloradomountainschool.com* 🎫 *From $199.*

WINTER ACTIVITIES

Each winter, the popularity of snowshoeing in the park increases. It's a wonderful way to experience Rocky Mountain's majestic winter side, when the jagged peaks are softened with a blanket of snow and the summer hordes are nonexistent. You can snowshoe any of the summer hiking trails that are accessible by road; many of them also become well-traveled cross-country ski trails. Two trails to try are Tonahutu Creek Trail (near Kawuneeche Visitor Center) and the Colorado River Trail to Lulu City (start at the Timber Creek Campground).

Estes Park Mountain Shop

CLIMBING/MOUNTAINEERING | You can rent or buy snowshoes and skis here, as well as fishing, hiking, and climbing equipment. The store is open year-round and gives four-, six-, and eight-hour guided snowshoeing, fly-fishing, and climbing trips to areas in and around Rocky Mountain National Park. ✉ *2050 Big Thompson Ave., Estes Park* ☎ *970/586–6548, 866/303–6548* 🌐 *www.estesparkmountainshop.com* 🎫 *From $95.*

Never Summer Mountain Products

CAMPING—SPORTS-OUTDOORS | This well-stocked shop sells and rents all sorts of outdoor equipment, including cross-country skis, hiking gear, kayaks, and camping supplies. ✉ *919 Grand Ave., Grand Lake* ☎ *970/627–3642* 🌐 *www.neversummermtn.com.*

Chapter 16

COLORADO SPRINGS AND VICINITY

WITH GREAT SAND DUNES NATIONAL PARK

Updated by
Whitney Bryen

Sights ★★★★☆ | Restaurants ★★★☆☆ | Hotels ★★★☆☆ | Shopping ★★★☆☆ | Nightlife ★★★☆☆

WELCOME TO COLORADO SPRINGS AND VICINITY

TOP REASONS TO GO

★ **Hike a Fourteener:** Coloradans collect hikes to the summit of Fourteeners—mountains that top 14,000 feet above sea level—like trophies.

★ **Play on the Sand Dunes:** At Great Sand Dunes, one of nature's most spectacular sandboxes, you'll feel like a kid again as you hike up a 750-foot dune then roll down (or sandboard) the other side.

★ **Raft on the Arkansas:** The Arkansas River is one of the most popular rivers for rafting and kayaking—from gentle floats to Class V rapids—in the United States.

★ **Ride Up Pikes Peak:** Katharine Bates wrote "America the Beautiful" after riding to the top of Pikes Peak. Ride the Pikes Peak shuttle to the top for the same see-forever views.

★ **Visit the U.S. Air Force Academy:** Here you can learn more about the academy that trains future Air Force leaders and visit the stunning, nondenominational Cadet Chapel.

1 **Colorado Springs.** The second-largest city in the state and a major cultural hub and outdoor mecca.

2 **Cripple Creek.** A former mining and current gambling town.

3 **Florissant Fossil Beds.** A haven for dinosaur enthusiasts.

4 **Palmer Lake.** An artsy town with great hiking.

5 **Royal Gorge Region and Cañon City.** A dramatic canyon and its gateway city.

6 **Buena Vista.** A small community surrounded by the Collegiate Peaks.

7 **Salida.** A mountain town dominated by Mount Shavano.

8 **Pueblo.** A historical trading post.

9 **La Junta.** A small town with the fascinating Koshare Indian Museum.

10 **Trinidad.** A historic charming town.

11 **Cuchara Valley.** A true rural setting, home to San Isabel National Forest.

12 **Great Sand Dunes National Park and Preserve.** Colorado's unforgettable sand dunes.

13 **Alamosa.** The main city of San Luis Valley.

14 **San Luis and Fort Garland Loop.** A road trip or scenic railway ride.

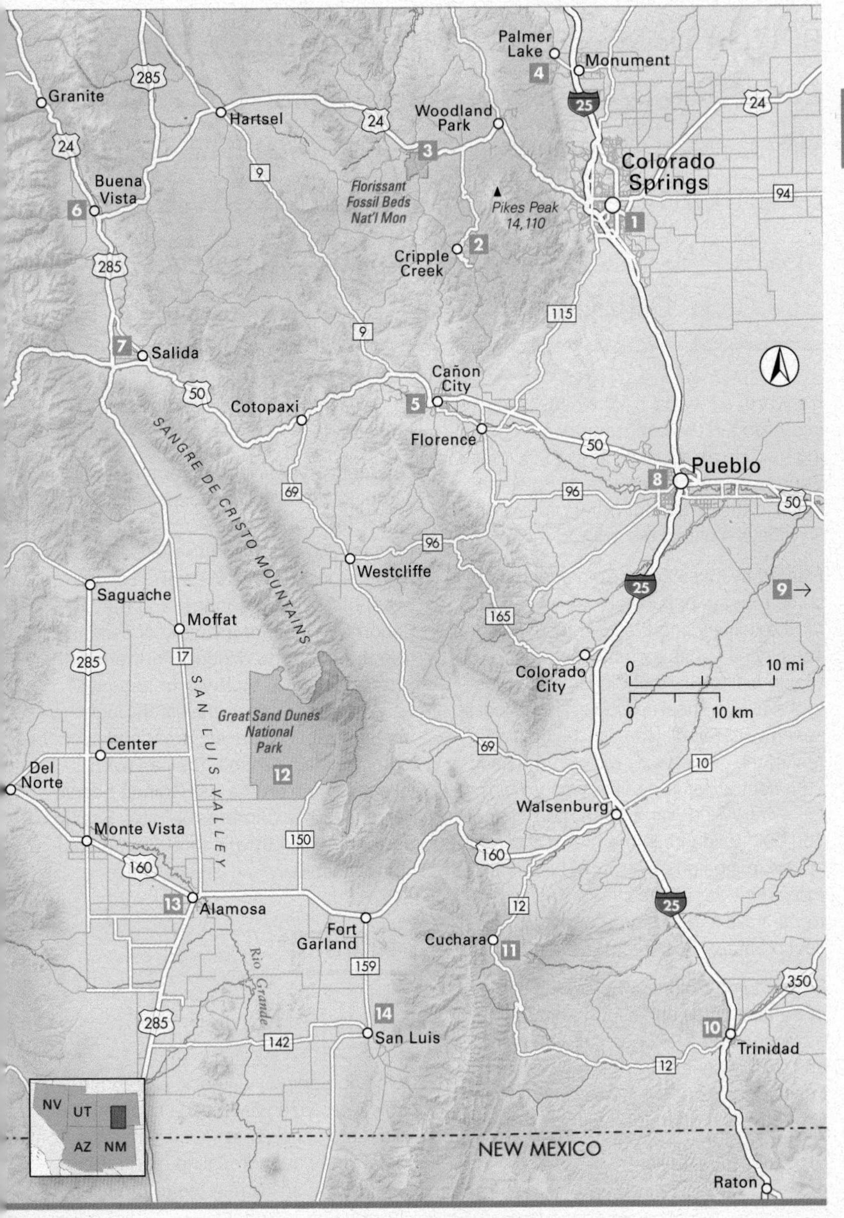
Palmer Lake
Monument
Granite
Hartsel
Woodland Park
Colorado Springs
Buena Vista
Florissant Fossil Beds Nat'l Mon
Pikes Peak 14,110
Cripple Creek
Salida
Cañon City
Cotopaxi
Florence
Pueblo
SANGRE DE CRISTO MOUNTAINS
Westcliffe
Saguache
Moffat
SAN LUIS VALLEY
Great Sand Dunes National Park
Colorado City
0 10 mi
0 10 km
Center
Del Norte
Monte Vista
Walsenburg
Alamosa
Fort Garland
Cucharа
Rio Grande
San Luis
Trinidad
NV UT AZ NM
NEW MEXICO
Raton

Stretching from majestic mountains into rugged, high desert plains, south central Colorado has plenty of 14,000-foot peaks, astounding natural hot springs, striking red-rock outcroppings, rivers that roll with white-water rapids in spring, and even the incongruous sight of towering sand dunes dwarfed by a mountain range at their back.

It's worth a few days for white-water rafting, hiking in the backcountry, and exploring historic gold-mining towns. Colorado Springs is one of the fastest growing cities in the West, but other parts of the area have a barely discovered feel.

Framed by Pikes Peak, Colorado Springs is the region's population center and a hub for the military and the high-tech industry. The city has been a destination for out-of-towners since its founding in 1870, due to the alleged healing power of the local spring water and clean air. The gold rush fueled the city's boom through the early 20th century, as the military boom did following World War II. With more than 700,000 residents in the metro area, Colorado Springs offers a mix of history and modernity, as well as incredible access to the trails and red-rock scenery in this section of the Rockies.

Surrounding Colorado Springs is a ring of smaller cities and alluring natural attractions. To the west, between alpine and desert scenery, are the Florissant Fossil Beds, the Royal Gorge, and Cripple Creek, which offers gambling in casinos housed in historic buildings. You can go rafting near Cañon City, while Pueblo has a dash of public art and history museums.

Outdoorsy types love the entire area: camping and hiking are especially superb in the San Isabel and Pike national forests. Climbers head to the Collegiate Peaks around Buena Vista and Salida (west of Colorado Springs) and the Cañon City area for a variety of ascents from moderate to difficult. Farther south, you can take the Highway of Legends Scenic Byway, which travels through the San Isabel National Forest and over high mountain passes. You can even take a day trip on the Rio Grande Scenic Railroad or the Cumbres & Toltec Scenic Railroad, which travels through regions not reachable by car.

Planning

When to Go

Colorado Springs is a good year-round choice because winters are relatively mild. Late spring or early summer is best if you want adrenaline-rush rafting, because the snowmelt feeds the rivers.

Summer is tourist season everywhere in south central Colorado. Early fall is another good time to visit, especially when the aspen leaves are turning gold. Some of the lodging properties in the smaller towns are closed in winter, although there are always some open for the cross-country skiers who enjoy staying in the small high-mountain towns.

Getting Here and Around

AIR

Colorado Springs Airport (COS) is the major airport in the region, with more than a dozen nonstop destinations. Most south central residents south of Colorado Springs drive to this city to fly out.

Alternatively, you can choose to fly to Denver International Airport (DEN), which has a lot more nonstop flights from other major cities to Colorado. It's a 70-mile drive from Denver to the Springs, but during rush hour it might take a solid two hours, whether you're in your own car or in one of the Denver–Colorado Springs shuttles. It's fastest to take the E–470 toll road. Another option is Pueblo Memorial Airport (PUB), which has direct flights to Denver.

CAR

In Colorado Springs (whose airport has the typical lineup of car-rental agencies), the main north–south roads are I–25, Academy Boulevard, Nevada Avenue, and Powers Boulevard, and each will get you where you want to go in good time; east–west routes along Woodmen Road (far north), Austin Bluffs Parkway (north central), and Platte Boulevard (south central) can get backed up.

Running north–south from Wyoming to New Mexico, I–25 bisects Colorado and is the major artery into the area.

TRAIN

Amtrak's *Southwest Chief* stops in Trinidad and La Junta three days a week.

Hotels

The lodging star is the Broadmoor resort in Colorado Springs, built from the booty of the late 19th-century gold-rush days, but there are also predictable boxy-bed motel rooms awaiting travelers at the junctions of major highways throughout the region. Interspersed are quaint mom-and-pop motels, as well as bed-and-breakfasts and rustic lodges in tourist districts.

Restaurants

Many restaurants serve regional trout and game, as well as locally grown fruits and vegetables. In summer, look for cantaloupe from the town of Rocky Ford, the self-proclaimed "Sweet Melon Capital." Colorado Springs offers unique Colorado cuisine that zings taste buds without zapping budgets.

HOTEL AND RESTAURANT PRICES

Restaurant and hotel reviews have been shortened. For full information, visit Fodors.com. Restaurant prices are for a main course at dinner, excluding 7.4% tax. Hotel prices are for two people in a standard double room in high season, excluding service charges and 9.4%–11.7% tax.

What It Costs

$	$$	$$$	$$$$
RESTAURANTS			
under $15	$15–$22	$23–$30	over $30
HOTELS			
under $125	$125–$200	$201–$300	over $300

Colorado Springs

The contented residents of the Colorado Springs area believe they live in an ideal location, and it's hard to argue with them. To the west the Rockies form a majestic backdrop. To the east the plains stretch for miles. Taken together, the setting ensures a mild, sunny climate year-round, and makes skiing and golfing on the same day feasible with no more than a two- or three-hour drive. You don't have to choose between adventures here: you can climb the Collegiate Peaks one day and go white-water rafting on the Arkansas River the next.

The state's second-largest city has a strong cultural scene, between the outstanding Colorado Springs Fine Arts Center, the Colorado Springs Philharmonic, and the variety of plays and musicals offered at several independent theaters.

The region abounds in natural and man-made wonders, from the red sandstone monoliths of the Garden of the Gods to the space-age architecture of the U.S. Air Force Academy's Cadet Chapel. The most indelible landmark is unquestionably Pikes Peak (14,115 feet), which is a constant reminder that this contemporary city is still close to nature. Purple in the early morning, snow-packed after winter storms, capped with clouds on windy days, the mountain is a landmark for directions and, when needed, a focus of contemplation.

GETTING HERE AND AROUND

It's easiest to explore this region in a private car because the attractions are spread out; rent a car at the Denver Airport upon arrival, or you can take the Colorado Springs Shuttle. If you're staying in the heart of town and don't intend to head out to Pikes Peak, the Air Force Academy, or other attractions farther away, you could grab a taxi.

VISITOR INFORMATION

CONTACTS Visit Colorado Springs Information Center. ✉ *515 S. Cascade Ave., Colorado Springs* ☎ *719/635–7506, 800/888–4748* 🌐 *www.visitcos.com.*

★ Cave of the Winds

CAVE | FAMILY | Discovered by two boys in 1880, the cave has been exploited as a tourist sensation ever since. The only way to enter the site is by purchasing a tour, but once inside the cave you'll forget the hype and commercialism of the gimmicky entrance. The cave contains examples of every major sort of limestone formation, from icicle-shaped stalactites and stump-like stalagmites to delicate anthodite crystals (or cave flowers), flowstone (or frozen waterfalls), and cave popcorn. Enthusiastic guides host easy 45-minute walking tours, adventurous cave expeditions, and lantern tours that last 1½ hours. An outdoor ropes course and rides like the Terror-dactyl, which swings riders off a 200-foot cliff, offer more fun outside of the cave. ✉ *100 Cave of the Winds Rd., off U.S. 24, Manitou Springs* ☎ *719/685–5444* 🌐 *www.caveofthewinds.com* 🎫 *Tours start at $23.*

Cheyenne Mountain Zoo

ZOO | FAMILY | America's only mountain zoo, at 6,700 feet, has more than 750 animals housed amid mossy boulders and ponderosa pines. You can hand-feed the giraffe herd in the zoo's African Rift Valley and check out the animals living in Primate World, Rocky Mountain Wild, or the Asian Highlands. ✉ *4250 Cheyenne Mountain Zoo Rd., Colorado Springs* ☎ *719/633–9925* 🌐 *www.cmzoo.org* 🎫 *$29.75, includes same-day admission to Will Rogers Shrine.*

Colorado Springs Fine Arts Center

ARTS VENUE | This regional museum has a fine permanent collection of modern art and excellent rotating exhibits. Some highlight the cultural contributions of regional artists; others focus on famous artists such as the glassmaker Dale Chihuly and American pop artist Andy Warhol. Enjoy the view of Pikes Peak and the mountains from the patio in the summer. ✉ *30 W. Dale St., Colorado Springs* ☎ *719/634–5581* 🌐 *fac.coloradocollege.edu* 🎫 *$10* ⏲ *Closed Mon.*

★ **Garden of the Gods**

NATURE SITE | These magnificent, eroded red-sandstone formations—from gnarled jutting spires to sensuously abstract monoliths—were sculpted more than 300 million years ago. Follow the road as it loops past such oddities as the Three Graces, the Siamese Twins, and the Kissing Camels or get an up-close look at the rocks with a guided climbing expedition booked at the visitor center. High Point, near the south entrance, provides camera hounds with the ultimate photo op: a formation known as Balanced Rock and jagged formations that frame Pikes Peak. The visitor center has maps of the trails and several geological, historical, and interactive hands-on displays, as well as a café. It's a short, paved hike into the park from the parking lot. ✉ *Visitor and Nature Center, 1805 N. 30th St., Colorado Springs* ☎ *719/634–6666* 🌐 *www.gardenofgods.com* 🎫 *Free.*

Ghost Town

GHOST TOWN | **FAMILY** | You can see and hear a real player piano and a nickelodeon at this Western town with a sheriff's office, general store, saloon, and smithy. There's also gold panning in the summer. ✉ *400 S. 21st St., Colorado Springs* ☎ *719/634–0696* 🌐 *www.ghosttownmuseum.com* 🎫 *$7.50.*

Manitou Cliff Dwellings

NATIVE SITE | Some Ancestral Pueblo cliff dwellings that date back nearly 1,000 years have been moved from other sites in southern Colorado to this museum. Two rooms of artifacts in the museum offer information on the history of the dwellings. Smartphone codes provide a free audio tour through the space. ✉ *10 Cliff Rd., off U.S. 24, Manitou Springs* ☎ *719/685–5242, 800/354–9971* 🌐 *www.cliffdwellingsmuseum.com* 🎫 *$12.*

Manitou Springs Mineral Springs

LOCAL INTEREST | The town grew around the springs, so there are eight mineral springs open to the public in or near downtown. Competitions to design the fountains that bring the spring water to the public ensured that each fountain design is unique. It's a bring-your-own-cup affair; the water (frequently tested) is potable and free. The chamber of commerce publishes a free guide to the springs and the Mineral Springs Foundation offers tours. ✉ *Manitou Springs* ☎ *719/685–5089* 🌐 *www.visitcos.com/areas/manitou-springs/manitou-mineral-springs* 🎫 *Free.*

Miramont Castle Museum

MUSEUM | Commissioned in 1895 as the private home of French priest Jean-Baptiste Francolon, this museum in Manitou Springs is still decorated, in part, as if a family lived here. More than 30 rooms in this 14,000-square-foot space offer a wide variety of displays and furnishings primarily from the Victorian era. You can also have lunch or high tea in the Queens Parlour Tea Room (reservations required). ✉ *9 Capitol Hill Ave., Manitou Springs* ☎ *719/685–1011* 🌐 *www.miramontcastle.org* 🎫 *$12* ⏲ *Closed Mon. in winter.*

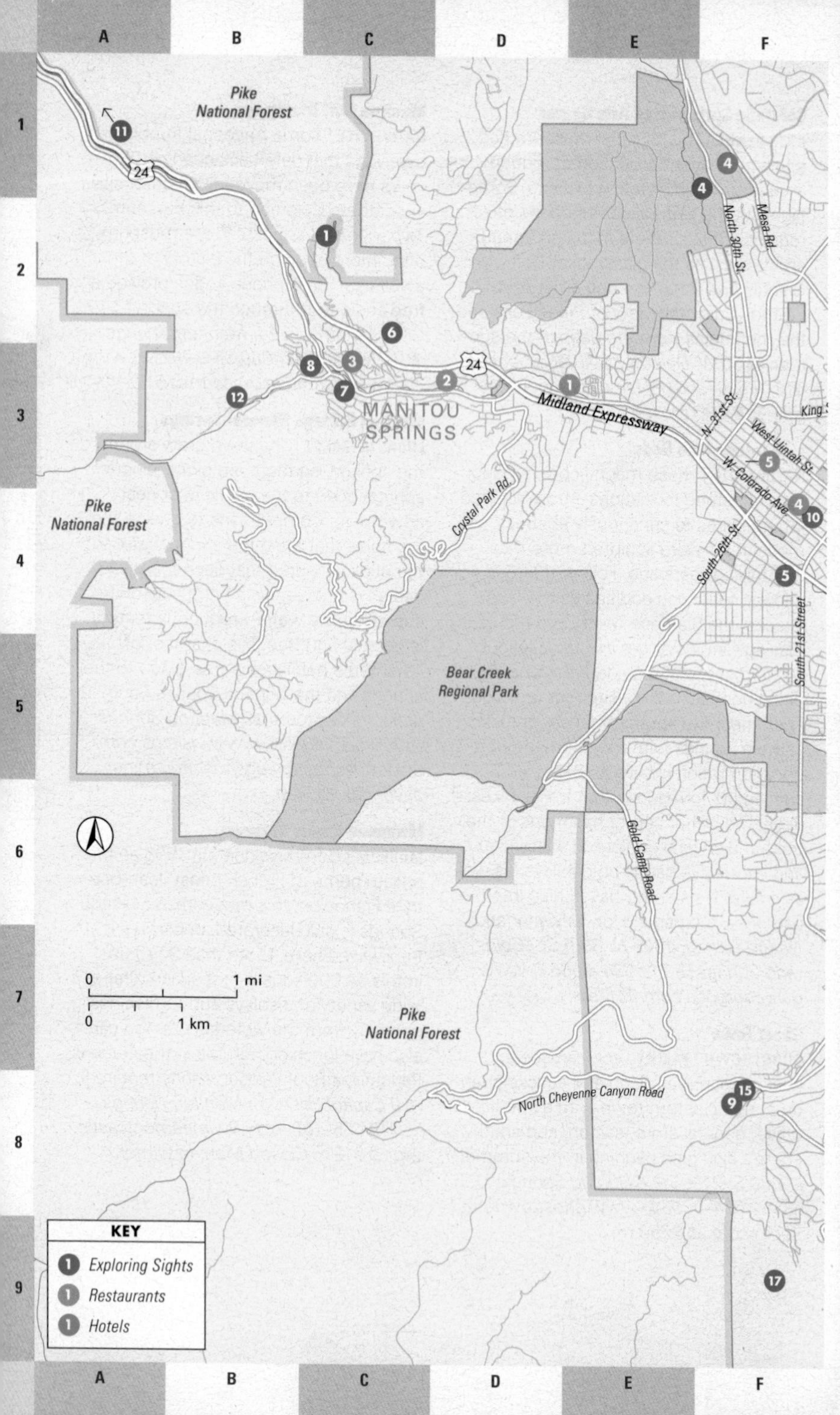

A
B
C
D
E
F
1
2
3
4
5
6
7
8
9
Pike
National Forest
11
24
1
4
4
North 30th St.
Mesa Rd.
6
8
3
24
2
1
7
12
MANITOU
SPRINGS
Midland Expressway
N. 31st St.
King S
West Uintah St.
5
W. Colorado Ave.
4
10
Pike
National Forest
Crystal Park Rd.
South 26th St.
5
South 21st Street
Bear Creek
Regional Park
Gold Camp Road
0
1 mi
0
1 km
Pike
National Forest
North Cheyenne Canyon Road
15
9
KEY
Exploring Sights
Restaurants
Hotels
17

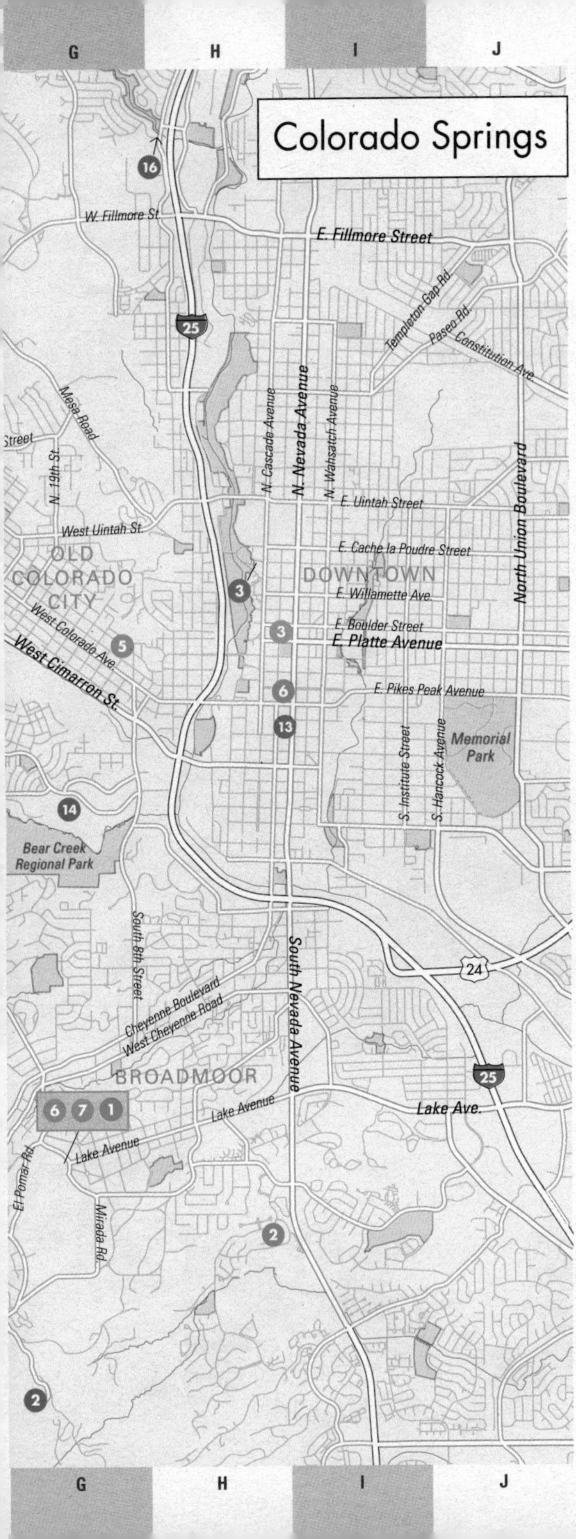

Colorado Springs

Sights

1 Cave of the Winds C2
2 Cheyenne Mountain Zoo G9
3 Colorado Springs Fine Arts Center H4
4 Garden of the Gods F1
5 Ghost Town F4
6 Manitou Cliff Dwellings C2
7 Manitou Springs Mineral Springs C3
8 Miramont Castle Museum C3
9 North Cheyenne Cañon Park F8
10 Old Colorado City F4
11 Pikes Peak A1
12 Pikes Peak Cog Railway B3
13 Pioneers Museum H5
14 Seven Falls G5
15 Starsmore Visitor and Nature Center F8
16 U.S. Air Force Academy H1
17 Will Rogers Shrine of the Sun F9

Restaurants

1 Adam's Mountain Café E3
2 Briarhurst Manor D3
3 Four by Brother Luck H4
4 Front Range Barbeque F4
5 Paravicini's Italian Bistro F3
6 Penrose Room at the Broadmoor G8
7 Ristorante Del Lago at the Broadmoor G8

Hotels

1 The Broadmoor G8
2 Cheyenne Mountain Resort H8
3 Cliff House C3
4 Garden of the Gods Club and Resort F1
5 Holden House G4
6 The Mining Exchange I5

Did You Know?

The famous Garden of the Gods is home to a large population of bighorn sheep.

North Cheyenne Cañon Park

NATIONAL/STATE PARK | **FAMILY** | The 1,600 acres of this city park, which is open year-round, manifest nature and natural history without a hint of commercialism—or charge. The canyon's moderate hikes include the Lower Columbine and Mount Cutler trails, each less than a 3-mile round-trip. Both afford a view of the city and a sense of accomplishment. ✉ *2120 S. Cheyenne Canyon Rd., Colorado Springs* ☎ *719/385–5940* 🌐 *coloradosprings.gov/page/north-cheyenne-canon* 🎫 *Free.*

★ Pikes Peak

MOUNTAIN—SIGHT | **FAMILY** | If you want to see the view from the top of Pikes Peak, head up this 14,115-foot-high mountain by shuttle or in a pair of hiking boots if you've got the stamina. (The Pikes Peak Cog Railway, which opened in 1891, has just undergone a major renovation and reopened in May 2021.) To prevent congestion on the Pikes Peak Highway, those visiting the summit are required to take a complimentary shuttle instead of driving. Exceptions to this rule are vehicles with more than six passengers, child safety seats, or people with disabilities ($15 per person or $50 per car).

Two shuttle options are available including a 32-mile round-trip that takes about 15 minutes to get to the top, or a 14-mile round-trip that takes about 30 minutes to the summit. Once at the top, stop for a doughnut at the Pikes Peak Summit House café and trading post. Whichever route you choose to take up the prominent peak, you'll understand why the pioneers heading West via wagon train used to say: "Pikes Peak or Bust." ✉ *U.S. 24, Colorado Springs* ✣ *5 miles west of Manitou Springs* ☎ *719/385–7325* 🌐 *www.coloradosprings.gov/pikes-peak-americas-mountain* 🎫 *$15 per person, $50 per vehicle; summit shuttle is free.*

Pikes Peak Cog Railway

MOUNTAIN—SIGHT | **FAMILY** | The world's highest cog train departs from Manitou Springs and follows a frolicking stream up a steep canyon, through stands of quaking aspen and towering lodgepole pines, before reaching the timberline, where you can see far into the plains until arriving at the summit. Advance reservations are recommended in summer and on weekends, as this three-hour trip sells out regularly. ✉ *515 Ruxton Ave., Colorado Springs* ☎ *719/685–5401* 🌐 *www.cograilway.com* 🎫 *$37* ✍ *Reservations essential.*

Pioneers Museum

MUSEUM | Once the Old El Paso County Courthouse, this repository has artifacts relating to the entire Pikes Peak area. The historic courtroom is absolutely elegant, and so perfectly appointed that it looks as if a judge will walk in any minute to start a trial. It's most notable for the special exhibits the museum puts together or receives on loan from other museums and institutions. ✉ *215 S. Tejon St., Colorado Springs* ☎ *719/385–5990* 🌐 *www.cspm.org* 🎫 *Free.*

Starsmore Visitor and Nature Center

MUSEUM | At the mouth of the canyon off Cheyenne Boulevard, this center is chock-full of nature exhibits. ✉ *2120 S. Cheyenne Cañon Rd., Colorado Springs* ☎ *719/385–6086* 🌐 *coloradosprings.gov/parks/page/starsmore-visitor-and-nature-center* ⏲ *Closed Mon. Labor Day–Memorial Day.*

Seven Falls

BODY OF WATER | Surrounded by towering red-rock canyon walls, these seven steep waterfalls plummet 181 feet into a tiny emerald pool that shimmers below. Hiking the steep 224 steps to the top of the falls is worth it for the view but you can also take an elevator to the Eagle's Nest look-out. Parking is free at the Penrose Equestrian Center where a

The Will Rogers Shrine of the Sun is dedicated to America's favorite cowboy.

shuttle will take passengers to and from the site. Guides at Soaring Adventures sail patrons across the nearby canyon on 10 ziplines and lead those daring enough to make the trip across rope bridges and on rappelling adventures that feature views of the falls. Restaurant 1858 serves Southern comfort food like shrimp and grits, roasted game, and local trout (Cajun style, barbecued, and fried) that is best enjoyed out on the patio overlooking the falls. ✉ *1045 Lower Gold Camp Rd., Colorado Springs* ☎ *855/923–7272* 🌐 *www.broadmoor.com/broadmoor-adventures/seven-falls* 🎫 *$16.*

★ U.S. Air Force Academy

MILITARY SITE | The academy, which set up camp in 1954, is one of the most popular attractions in Colorado. Highlights include the futuristic design, 18,500 beautiful acres of land, and antique and historic aircraft displays. At the visitor center you'll find photo exhibits, a model of a cadet's room, a gift shop, a snack bar in the summer, and a film highlighting the history and bravery of the Air Force. Other stops on the self-guided tour include a B-52 display, sports facilities, and the chapel. Some days you can catch the impressive cadet lunch formation that begins between 11:30 and noon. The Air Force chapel, which can accommodate simultaneous Catholic, Jewish, and Protestant services, is easily recognized by its unconventional design, which features 17 spires that resemble airplane wings. Don't miss the smaller chapels, including the Buddhist room. Visitors can enter only through the North and South gates. ✉ *N. Gate Blvd., off I–25, Exit 156, Colorado Springs* ☎ *719/333–2025* 🌐 *www.usafa.edu/visitors* 🎫 *Free.*

★ Will Rogers Shrine of the Sun

MEMORIAL | **FAMILY** | This five-story tower was dedicated in 1937, after the tragic plane crash that claimed Rogers's life. Its interior is painted with all manner of Western murals in which Colorado Springs benefactor Spencer Penrose figures prominently, and is plastered with photos and homespun sayings of Rogers, America's favorite cowboy. In the chapel are 15th- and 16th-century European artworks. ✉ *4250 Cheyenne Mountain Zoo Rd., Colorado Springs* ☎ *719/578–5367* 🌐 *www.cmzoo.org/visit/will-rogers-shrine-of-the-sun* 🎫 *$29.75, includes same-day admission to Cheyenne Mountain Zoo.*

 Restaurants

Adam's Mountain Café

$$ | **CAFÉ** | Join the locals sitting at mismatched tables, viewing drawings by regional artists, and mingling at the community table. The food has an organic bent, with many vegetarian options. **Known for:** famous huevos rancheros; plenty of vegetarian and vegan options; local charm. 💲 *Average main: $15* ✉ *26 Manitou Ave., Colorado Springs* ☎ *719/685–1430* 🌐 *adamsmountaincafe.com* 🕒 *No dinner Sun. and Mon.*

Briarhurst Manor

$$$$ | **MODERN EUROPEAN** | One of the most exquisitely romantic restaurants in Colorado, Briarhurst Manor has several dining rooms, each with its own look and mood like the book-lined library or the drawing room with an ornate chandelier. The menu regularly features lamb, poultry, fish, and wild game dishes, which change as the chef adds a seasonal flair. **Known for:** intimate atmosphere; historic estate; meat and wild game. 💲 *Average main: $32* ✉ *404 Manitou Ave., Colorado Springs* ☎ *719/685–1864* 🌐 *www.briarhurst.com* 🕒 *Closed Mon. and Tues. No lunch.*

Four by Brother Luck

$$$$ | **MODERN AMERICAN** | With a focus on the historical cuisine of the Four Corners region where Utah, Arizona, New Mexico, and Colorado touch borders, chef Brother Luck's restaurant serves up creative tasting-style menus sure to impress his *Top Chef* fan base. Along with the Four Corners significance, the number four represents Luck's four key sources of ingredients—hunters, gatherers, farmers, and fishermen; the four seasonal menus; and the fact that Luck is the fourth generation in his family to have the name Brother Luck. **Known for:** lively atmosphere perfect for modern foodies; dirty farro creole dish inspired by the chef's father; chef's table. 💲 *Average main: $47* ✉ *321 N. Tejon St., Colorado Springs* ☎ *719/434–2741* 🌐 *www.fourbybrotherluck.com* 🕒 *No dinner Sun.*

Front Range Barbeque

$$ | **BARBECUE** | **FAMILY** | Tunes, brews, and barbecue attract visitors and locals to the outdoor patio at this causal smokehouse in Old Colorado City. Guests can be overheard arguing about which homemade sauce is best and singing along to the music of live acts from across the country that can be heard throughout the block. **Known for:** dry ribs; century-old pecan pie recipe; lively atmosphere. 💲 *Average main: $15* ✉ *2330 W. Colorado Ave., Colorado Springs* ☎ *719/632–2596* 🌐 *www.frbbq.com* 🕒 *Closed Mon. and Tues.*

Paravicini's Italian Bistro

$$ | **ITALIAN** | Named for the proprietor's grandmother, Paravicini lives up to its Italian name, which translates to "for the neighborhood." Locals of all ages gather in the colorful and well-lit space that provides a balance of fun and romance to sip glasses of wine and share the family-style salad, fresh bread, and heaping piles of noodles. Pasta reigns on this traditional Italian menu highlighting classic and surf-and-turf options. **Known for:** great spaghetti and meatballs; authentic Italian; perfect date-night setting. 💲 *Average main: $20* ✉ *2802 W. Colorado Ave., Colorado Springs* ☎ *719/471–8200* 🌐 *paravicinis.com* 💳 *No credit cards.*

Penrose Room at the Broadmoor

$$$$ | **MODERN AMERICAN** | Whatever number of courses you choose from the prix-fixe menu, you're guaranteed a memorable culinary experience at the award-winning Penrose Room where seasonal seafood, poultry, and red meat are served with French flair. Chef de

cuisine Luis Young brings his background in American and French cuisine to the always evolving seasonal dishes. **Known for:** mountain and city views from the penthouse tower; smoked duck foie gras; chef's tasting menu with wine pairings. *$ Average main: $90 ✉ The Broadmoor South, 1 Lake Circle, Colorado Springs ☎ 719/577–5733, 844/727–8730 🌐 www.broadmoor.com/dining/penrose-room ⊗ Closed Sun. and Mon. No lunch 👔 Jacket required.*

Ristorante Del Lago at the Broadmoor

$$$$ | **ITALIAN** | With stunning views of Cheyenne Lake and the main hotel, this "restaurant of the lake" features an open kitchen and cozy lounge. Smaller portions allow guests to try a variety of authentic Italian dishes from antipasti and wood-fired pizzas to lasagne and house-made sausage. **Known for:** patio with lake view; imported Italian meats and cheese; impressive wine list. *$ Average main: $40 ✉ 1 Lake Ave., Colorado Springs ☎ 719/577–5774, 866/381–8432 🌐 www.broadmoor.com/ristorante-del-lago ⊗ Closed Tues. No lunch.*

Hotels

★ The Broadmoor

$$$$ | **HOTEL** | With its old-world ambience that emits pure luxury—including the signature pink building with the Mediterranean-style towers—the Broadmoor continues to redefine itself with settings where guests can unwind and be pampered. **Pros:** thoroughly pampering atmosphere; many excellent dining options; you won't need to leave the property with so many amenities available. **Cons:** very expensive; formal style might not be everyone's preference; rooms (especially with a view) book quickly. *$ Rooms from: $445 ✉ 1 Lake Circle, Colorado Springs ☎ 719/634–7711, 844/727–8730 🌐 www.broadmoor.com 🛏 784 rooms 🍽 No meals.*

Cheyenne Mountain Resort

$$$ | **RESORT** | At this 217-acre resort on the slopes of Cheyenne Mountain, superb swimming facilities (including an Olympic-size pool), a variety of tennis courts, and a Pete Dye championship golf course tempt you to remain on-property, despite the easy access to the high country. **Pros:** resort ambience; outstanding views; large fitness center and spa. **Cons:** you must walk outside to get to the main lodge; can get crowded for conferences; few dining options nearby. *$ Rooms from: $249 ✉ 3225 Broadmoor Valley Rd., Colorado Springs ☎ 719/538–4000, 800/588–0250 🌐 www.cheyennemountain.com 🛏 316 rooms 🍽 No meals.*

Cliff House

$$ | **HOTEL** | This Victorian-era jewel was built in 1873 as a stagecoach stop between Colorado Springs and Leadville, and can name crown princes, presidents, and entertainers as past guests; their names live on as monikers for several distinctly different and extremely attractive suites: the Katharine Bates, the Teddy Roosevelt, and the Clark Gable are a few. **Pros:** convenient location; old-fashioned charm; luxurious amenities. **Cons:** might be a little too old-fashioned for some; price excludes resort fees; charge for valet parking with few other options. *$ Rooms from: $200 ✉ 306 Cañon Ave., Manitou Springs ☎ 719/685–3000, 888/212–7000 🌐 www.thecliffhouse.com 🛏 54 rooms 🍽 Free Breakfast.*

Garden of the Gods Club and Resort

$$$$ | **RESORT** | The views are spectacular from this longtime private club overlooking the red rocks in the Garden of the Gods. **Pros:** great views; access to great golf on the Kissing Camels course; guests have exclusive access to the fitness center and infinity pool. **Cons:** a car is needed to get downtown; expensive; events and public amenities bring daytime traffic to the property. *$ Rooms from: $320 ✉ 3320 Mesa Rd., Colorado Springs ☎ 719/632–5541, 800/923–8838*

www.gardenofthegodsclub.com 56 rooms No meals.

Holden House

$$ | B&B/INN | Innkeepers Sallie and Welling Clark realized their dream when they restored this 1902 home and transformed it into a B&B. **Pros:** good choice for travelers who want something homey; excellent breakfasts; friendly staff and owners. **Cons:** old-fashioned ambience may not suit all tastes; not suitable for young children; few on-site amenities. *Rooms from: $175* *1102 W. Pikes Peak Ave., Colorado Springs* *719/471–3980, 888/565–3980* *www.holdenhouse.com* *6 rooms* *Free Breakfast.*

The Mining Exchange

$$$ | HOTEL | Built as a stock exchange for local mining companies in 1902, this downtown hotel merges historic details, like an old vault and antique piano in the lobby, with modern amenities. **Pros:** historic charm; walkable, downtown location; lovely hotel courtyard. **Cons:** sometimes noisy from downtown crowds and traffic; mazelike hallways are difficult to navigate; some rooms are small. *Rooms from: $219* *8 S. Nevada Ave., Colorado Springs* *719/323–2000, 877/999–3223 for reservations only* *www.wyndhamhotels.com* *117 rooms* *No meals.*

Nightlife

BARS AND CLUBS

Cowboys

BARS/PUBS | This is a favorite hangout for country music lovers and two-steppers. *25 N. Tejon St., Colorado Springs* *719/596–1212* *www.csnightclubs.com/cowboys.*

Golden Bee

BARS/PUBS | Remnants of a 19th-century English pub were discovered in a warehouse in New York City in the 1950s and moved to the Broadmoor site where the original mahogany bar, wood carvings, mirrors, and tin ceilings still define the Golden Bee's charm. The old-fashioned bar features a piano player leading singalongs. Watch out for the bees—as part of a long-standing tradition, they flick bee stickers into the audience during the show. *International Center at the Broadmoor, 1 Lake Circle, Colorado Springs* *719/634–7711* *www.broadmoor.com/dining/golden-bee.*

BREWPUBS

★ Ivywild School

BARS/PUBS | Student art still lingers on the bathroom walls of this historic elementary school turned hipster haunt. On one end of the 1916 school, Bristol Brewing Company schools patrons with its microbrews while creative libations are shaken and stirred down the hall at The Principal's Office. Trendy locals flock to the historic site with large patios and lots of charm for the tastiest cafeteria grub around served up by Ivywild School Kitchen lining the art-covered hallway between the two bars. Axe and The Oak Whiskey House serve up spirits distilled from local grain at this popular hangout. *1604 S. Cascade Ave., Colorado Springs* *719/368–6100* *ivywildschool.com.*

Phantom Canyon Brewing Co.

BREWPUBS/BEER GARDENS | In a century-old brick building, this noted brewpub has shuffleboard and billiards in an upstairs hall. There's great pub grub, plus hop-infused desserts. *2 E. Pikes Peak Ave., Colorado Springs* *719/635–2800* *www.phantomcanyon.com.*

Shopping

Colorado Springs has a mix of upscale boutiques and chain stores. Many boutiques and galleries cluster in Old Colorado City and the posh Broadmoor One Lake Avenue Shopping Arcade.

Manitou Springs, a small town between Garden of the Gods and Pikes Peak, has a historic district, and large artists' population. Walk along Manitou Avenue and Ruxton Avenue, where you'll find a mix of galleries, quaint shops, and stores selling souvenirs.

ANTIQUES AND COLLECTIBLES

Ruxton's Trading Post

ANTIQUES/COLLECTIBLES | Look here for cowboy-era antiques and collectibles, Native American art, and nostalgia items from old TV programs and movies. ✉ *22 Ruxton Ave., Manitou Springs* ☎ *719/685–9024* 🌐 *www.ruxtons.com.*

CRAFT AND ART GALLERIES

Commonwheel Artists Co-Op

ART GALLERIES | This longtime co-op gallery is packed with art in various mediums, jewelry, paintings, sculpture, fiber, clay, and glass art. ✉ *102 Cañon Ave., Manitou Springs* ☎ *719/685–1008* 🌐 *www.commonwheel.com.*

Gallery 113

ART GALLERIES | Rotating exhibits by local artists keep visitors coming back to this popular co-op gallery on Tejon Street. Members display a variety of mediums, but vibrant paintings often dominate the gallery walls and space. You will also find locally created jewelry, pottery, and sculptures throughout. ✉ *125½ N. Tejon St., Colorado Springs* ☎ *719/634–5299* 🌐 *www.gallery113cos.com.*

Sculpture by Michael Garman

ART GALLERIES | This gallery in Old Colorado City carries the contemporary sculptures of renowned artist Michael Garman, including Western-themed pieces and a firefighter series. ✉ *2418 W. Colorado Ave., Colorado Springs* ☎ *719/471–9391* 🌐 *www.michaelgarman.com.*

Activities

A number of activities are available within an hour or two of Colorado Springs, including hot-air ballooning, white-water rafting, and all-access Jeep tours. Riding in a Jeep is one way to view the backcountry; a horseback ride on trails through meadows and along mountainsides is another.

Some of the best choices for hiking in this region are the Barr Trail, which heads up Pikes Peak (and is for hardy, well-conditioned hikers), and the array of trails in North Cheyenne Cañon Park.

ADVENTURE TOURS

Adventures Out West

TOUR—SPORTS | This outfitter offers Jeep tours of Colorado Springs and Manitou Springs covering local sites like Garden of the Gods, Pike National Forest, and North Cheyenne Cañon Park. It can also arrange other activities, such as ballooning, horseback riding, ziplining, and climbing. ✉ *1680 S. 21st St., Colorado Springs* ☎ *719/578–0935* 🌐 *advoutwest.com.*

HIKING

Barr Trail

MOUNTAIN—SIGHT | The 12-mile hike up Barr Trail gains nearly 8,000 feet in elevation before you reach the summit. About halfway up the steep trail is Barr Camp, where many hikers spend the night. Many of the trail's parking lots charge a fee. ✉ *Colorado Springs* 🌐 *www.visitcos.com/directory/barr-trail-pikes-peak.*

The Manitou Incline

TRAIL | Nearly 3,000 stairs stand between hikers at the bottom of this heart-pounding feat and the spectacular views above. Once a cable car track, now nearly a mile of steep steps and a 2,000 feet of elevation gain make this an advanced trail with rewarding views of Manitou and Colorado Springs. ✉ *10 Old*

Mans Trail, Manitou Springs ✣ Park at Hiawatha Gardens where a shuttle takes hikers to the trailhead ☎ 719/385–5940 ⊕ www.coloradosprings.gov/parks/page/manitou-incline.

Pikes Peak Greenway Trail

HIKING/WALKING | The Pikes Peak Greenway offers 16 miles of multisurface hiking and biking trails running from Palmer Lake to the town of Fountain. On the north end, the trail connects with the Santa Fe Trail, which runs from Palmer Lake to the beautifully forested grounds of the U.S. Air Force Academy. For a scenic tour of the city, start at America the Beautiful Park in the heart of downtown and ride north to the Air Force Academy on 10 miles of open trail. You can also take the route west from the park for a 6-mile ride into Manitou Springs. ✉ *126 Cimino Dr., Colorado Springs* ☎ *719/385–5940* ⊕ *www.trailsandopenspaces.org/trails/pikes-peak-greenwaysanta-fefountain-creekfront-range-trail.*

HORSEBACK RIDING

Academy Riding Stables

HORSEBACK RIDING | Year-round trail rides, most notably through the Garden of the Gods, are offered here. ✉ *4 El Paso Blvd., Colorado Springs* ☎ *719/633–5667* ⊕ *www.academyridingstables.com.*

MOUNTAIN BIKING

Challenge Unlimited

BICYCLING | For nearly 30 years this outfitter has been leading bike tours throughout Colorado, including the daily 20-mile bike tour down Pikes Peak from May through mid-October. The tours include helmets and bikes, and breakfast and lunch. Other trips combine biking and ziplining. ✉ *204 S. 24th St., Colorado Springs* ☎ *800/798–5954* ⊕ *www.pikespeakbybike.co.*

Pikes Peak Mountain Bike Tours

BICYCLING | The guides with this company will take you to the top of Pikes Peak, then let you ride all the way down on one of their lightweight mountain bikes. An alternative tour is the 20-mile tour on Upper Gold Camp Road, which is a self-paced downhill ride along an old railroad tract converted to a hiking–bicycling trail that cuts through the mountains. Another option allows you to saddle up and pedal down, a partnership with the Stables at the Broadmoor. ✉ *306 S. 25th St., Colorado Springs* ☎ *719/337—5311* ⊕ *www.bikepikespeak.com.*

Cripple Creek

46 miles west of Colorado Springs via U.S. 24 and Hwy. 67.

One of Colorado's three legalized gambling towns, Cripple Creek once had the most lucrative mines in the state—and 10,000 boozing, brawling, bawdy citizens. Today the old-timey main street is lined with casinos housed in quaint Victorian buildings. Outside the central area, old mining structures and the stupendous curtain of the Collegiate Peaks are marred by slag heaps and parking lots.

Miners gathered around card games in most of the nearly 100 saloons in Cripple Creek, which opened during the wild years after Bob Womack discovered gold in the late 1800s. Today there's a lineup of casinos set into storefronts and buildings with exteriors retaining the aura they had a century ago. But today the casinos are chock-full of slot machines, video and live poker tables, roulette, craps, and blackjack tables.

Most of the casinos on East Bennett Avenue house predictable (albeit inexpensive) restaurants. Beef is the common denominator across all the menus. Some casinos also have hotel rooms.

GETTING HERE AND AROUND

The town is tiny, though a bit hilly off the main drag, so it's easy to walk around and explore. Drive here in a private car, or hitch a ride on one of the Ramblin'

Express casino shuttles from Colorado Springs to Cripple Creek.

CONTACTS Ramblin' Express. ☎ *303/572–8687* 🌐 *www.casinoshuttle.com.*

VISITOR INFORMATION

CONTACTS Cripple Creek Heritage and Information Center. ✉ *9283 S. Hwy. 67, Cripple Creek* ☎ *877/858–4653, 719/689–3461* 🌐 *www.visitcripplecreek.com.*

Sights

Bronco Billy's

CASINO—SIGHT | This longtime casino embodies the atmosphere of Cripple Creek's main drag with its Western theme and friendly staff. Known for its customer service, Bronco Billy's is a favorite among locals and tourists, with hotel rooms upstairs and restaurants on-site. ✉ *233 E. Bennett Ave., Cripple Creek* ☎ *719/689–2142, 866/689–0353* 🌐 *www.broncobillyscasino.com.*

Cripple Creek District Museum

MUSEUM | The museum set in five historic buildings—including a vintage railway depot—contains a vast collection of artifacts, photos, and exhibits that provide a glimpse into mining life at the turn of the 20th century. ✉ *510 Bennett Ave., Cripple Creek* ☎ *719/689–9540* 🌐 *cripplecreek-museum.com* 🎫 *$8* ⏲ *Closed weekdays Labor Day–Memorial Day.*

Mollie Kathleen Gold Mine Tour

MINE | Descending 100 stories, the Mollie Kathleen Gold Mine Tour tours a mine that operated continuously from 1891 to 1961. The tours are fascinating, sometimes led by a former miner, and definitely not for the claustrophobic. Tours depart about every 30 minutes. ✉ *9388 Hwy. 67, northeast of town, Cripple Creek* ☎ *719/689–2466* 🌐 *www.goldminetours.com* 🎫 *$25.*

Florissant Fossil Beds

35 miles west of Colorado Springs via U.S. 24.

Florissant Fossil beds is an excellent place to explore the nicely preserved fossils from the area.

GETTING HERE AND AROUND

From Colorado Springs, take U.S. 24 W. It's about 37 miles from town.

Sights

Florissant Fossil Beds National Monument

NATURE SITE | Once a temperate subtropical climate, Florissant Fossil Beds National Monument was perfectly preserved by volcanic ash and mud flow 34 million years ago. This little-known site is a haven for paleontologists. The visitor center offers a daily guided walk and ranger talks in the amphitheater in summer, or you can follow the more than 15 miles of well-marked hiking trails and lose yourself in the remnants of petrified redwoods from the Eocene epoch. ✉ *15807 Teller County Rd. 1, Florissant* ☎ *719/748–3253* 🌐 *www.nps.gov/flfo* 🎫 *$10.*

Royal Gorge Region and Cañon City

45 miles southwest of Colorado Springs via Hwy. 115 and U.S. 50.

From the glut of adventure tours that line U.S. 50 west of the city and the nearby Royal Gorge—a dramatic crack that plunges more than 1,000 feet into the earth—to the strip mall veneer and juxtaposed revitalization of historic downtown buildings of Cañon City, the region is undeniably quirky. The Royal Gorge Region encompasses all of Fremont County, which is an outdoor adventure haven for some, but more commonly dubbed "Colorado's Correctional Capital" by others. In Cañon City and nearby Florence (also the "Antique Capital of Colorado") there are more than a dozen prisons, including ADX, the country's only federal supermax prison. Despite the prisons having pumped millions of dollars into the local economy, the prisons are not exactly a source of town pride, but locals hope a host of new hiking and biking trails, and local businesses aimed at tourists, will overshadow the city's reputation as a prison town.

GETTING HERE AND AROUND

The route from Colorado Springs to Cañon City (on Highway 115 and U.S. 50) goes through Red Rock Canyon, with lovely views. You'll need a car to get to Cañon City, where there are limited transportation options.

VISITOR INFORMATION Cañon City Chamber of Commerce. ✉ *424 Main St., Cañon City* ☎ *719/275–2331, 800/876–7922* 🌐 *www.canoncitycolorado.com.*

Sights

Museum of Colorado Prisons

JAIL | Introduce yourself to life behind bars at the Museum of Colorado Prisons, which formerly housed the Women's State Correctional Facility and where many of the exhibits are housed in cells. The museum exhaustively documents prison life in Colorado through old photos and newspaper accounts, as well as with inmates' confiscated weapons and contraband. The gas chamber sits in the courtyard. While an important window into prison life, past and present, the museum can be disturbing for young kids and those with loved ones in the prison system. ✉ *201 N. 1st St., Cañon City* ☎ *719/269–3015* 🌐 *www.prisonmuseum.org* 🎫 *$10* 🕙 *Closed Mon. and Tues. in winter.*

Royal Gorge Bridge and Park

CITY PARK | Carved by the Arkansas River more than 3 million years ago, the Royal Gorge canyon walls tower up to 1,200 feet high. The site is known for the 1877 Royal Gorge War between the Denver & Rio Grand and Santa Fe railroads over the right-of-way through the canyon. Rival crews laid tracks during the day and would dynamite each other's work at night until the Denver & Rio Grande eventually prevailed. Today, a private company runs the Royal Gorge Bridge and Park featuring the highest **suspension bridge** in the country, constructed in 1929 as a tourist attraction. The 956-foot-high bridge sways on gusty afternoons and the river can be seen clearly between gaps in the boards, adding to the thrill of a crossing. You can cross the suspension bridge and ride the astonishing **aerial tram** (2,400 feet long and more than 1,000 feet above the canyon floor) or experience the Cloudscraper, America's highest zipline. Renovations to the park following a devastating wildfire in 2013 brought a Children's Playland with a playground, carousel, maze, and splash pad to the site. A ride on the **Royal Rush Skycoaster** ensures an adrenaline rush—you'll swing from a free-fall tower and momentarily hang over the gorge. Also on hand are outdoor musical entertainment in summer, and the usual assortment of food and gift shops. ✉ *4218 Fremont County Rd. 3A, Cañon City* ☎ *719/275–7507, 888/333–5597* 🌐 *www.royalgorgebridge.com* 🎫 *$29.*

Royal Gorge Route Railroad

TRANSPORTATION SITE (AIRPORT/BUS/FERRY/TRAIN) | **FAMILY** | A ride on the Royal Gorge Route Railroad takes you under the bridge and through one of the most dramatic parts of the canyon. From the Santa Fe depot in Cañon City, the train leaves several times a day for the two-hour ride. The breakfast, lunch, and dinner rides are pleasant, and the food is good, although not exactly "gourmet" as advertised. Seasonal rides like the Oktoberfest train and Santa Express offer additional entertainment. For an extra fee you can ride in the cab with the engineer. ✉ *330 Royal Gorge Blvd., Cañon City* ☎ *719/274–4000* 🌐 *www.royalgorgeroute.com* 🎫 *From $44.*

Westcliffe

SCENIC DRIVE | In a joint effort with neighboring Silver Cliff, this remote town at the base of the Sangre de Cristo Mountains became the state's first International Dark Sky Community in 2015. Nestled in quiet Custer County, mountains shade the town from light pollution to the east preserving the dark nights that provide a perfect backdrop for stargazing year-round. Once a mining town, Westcliffe's 600 residents now thrive mostly on agriculture and ranching, but spring and summer festivals attract tourists from around the world to the charming Main Street. ✣ *55 miles west of Pueblo via Hwy. 96 and 50 miles southwest of Cañon City via scenic Hwys. 50 and 69.*

Winery at Holy Cross Abbey

WINERY/DISTILLERY | The Benedictine monks once cloistered at Holy Cross Abbey came to Cañon City for spiritual repose. But for the faithful who frequent the winery on the eastern edge of the property, redemption is more easily found in a nice bottle of Revelation, a Bordeaux-style blend. For a truly divine experience, reserve a wine and cheese tasting ($35 per person) on the terrace that includes a private hostess, sampling of all wines, and an artisanal cheese, bread, fruit, and chocolate plate. ✉ *3011 E. U.S. 50, Cañon City* ☎ *719/276–5191, 877/422–9463* 🌐 *www.abbeywinery.com.*

Restaurants

Cañon City Brews & Bikes

$ | **AMERICAN** | Centrally located on Main Street, Cañon City Brews & Bikes offers an extensive craft beer menu and pub food that attracts hikers, bikers, and locals alike. The massive outdoor space, with tables and a beer garden, offers a perfect place to wind down from outdoor activities. **Known for:** extensive craft beer menu; outdoor beer garden; casual atmosphere. 💲 *Average main: $8* ✉ *224 Main St., Cañon City* ☎ *719/275–2472* 🌐 *www.canoncitybrewsandbikes.com* 🕒 *Closed Mon. and Tues.*

Pizza Madness

$ | **PIZZA** | **FAMILY** | There is no shortage of fun or food at family-friendly Pizza Madness. Arcade games keep kids and adults entertained while you wait for your hand-tossed pie. **Known for:** central location; noisy and family-friendly atmosphere; speciality pizzas. 💲 *Average main: $10* ✉ *509 Main St., Cañon City* ☎ *719/276–3088* 🌐 *www.mypizzamadness.com.*

Hotels

★ **Royal Gorge Cabins and Glamping Tents**

$$$$ | **RENTAL** | With views of the Sangre de Cristo Mountains, these rustic but cozy cabins offer a comfy spot to rest your head without leaving the outdoor setting that brings visitors to the region. **Pros:** spectacular views; modern decor; spacious cabins. **Cons:** less expensive glamping tents lack restrooms; several miles from downtown restaurants; limited availability. 💲 *Rooms from: $435* ✉ *45054 W. U.S. 50, Cañon City* ☎ *800/748–2953* 🌐 *www.royalgorgecabins.com* 🕒 *Glamping tents closed Nov.–Mar.* 🛏 *9 cabins, 8 glamping tents* 🍽 *No meals.*

Activities

HIKING

Tunnel Drive Trail

HIKING/WALKING | **FAMILY** | This mild and flat section of the Arkansas Riverwalk Trail is less than 4 miles round-trip and features views of the Arkansas River and a series of tunnels that once housed the city's water delivery pipeline. ✉ *205 Tunnel Dr., Cañon City* 🌐 *www.royalgorgeregion.com/tunnel-drive-2.*

Red Canyon Park

HIKING/WALKING | Cañon City–owned Red Canyon Park, 12 miles north of town, offers splendid easy to moderate hiking among the rose-color sandstone spires. The easy-to-find park features towering red-rock formations and fossils. ✉ *Red Canyon Rd. and Field Ave., Cañon City* 🌐 *www.royalgorgeregion.com/red-canyon-park-trail-map.*

BIKING

South Cañon Trails

BICYCLING | Nearly 12 miles of single-track trails offering the challenging "Great Escape" section and the more moderate "Mutton Bustin'" are located closer to town. Trails are accessed at the Riverwalk Trail near Centennial Park downtown. ✉ *221 Griffin Ave., Cañon City* 🌐 *www.singletracks.com/bike-trails/south-canon-trails.html.*

JEEP TOURS

Colorado Jeep Tours

DRIVING TOURS | **FAMILY** | See the Royal Gorge from a new perspective with a Jeep ride over the 956-foot-high suspension bridge with knowledgeable guides pointing out fun facts along the way. ✉ *2320 E. Main St., Cañon City* ☎ *719/275—6339* 🌐 *coloradojeeptours.com.*

RAFTING

TOURS AND OUTFITTERS

★ **Royal Gorge Rafting and Zip Line Tours**

WHITE-WATER RAFTING | This outfitter is truly a one stop shop for adventure tours in the Royal Gorge Region. Combine rafting with ziplining, ropes courses, and helicopter tours over the Royal Gorge available at the base on U.S. 50 for a full day of fun. Most packages include lunch at White Water Bar & Grill, which serves large portions of barbecue, smothered spuds, burgers, and libations for refueling. ✉ *45045 W. U.S. 50, Cañon City* ☎ *719/275–7238* 🌐 *www.royalgorgerafting.net.*

Salida

25 miles south of Buena Vista; 102 miles southwest of Colorado Springs.

Imposing peaks, including 14,000-plus-foot Mount Shavano, dominate the town of Salida, which is on the Arkansas River. This small but artsy town is host to 20 art galleries and draws some of the musicians who appear at the Aspen Music Festival—classical pianists, brass ensembles, and the like—for its Salida–Aspen Concerts in July and August. The town's other big event is an annual white-water rafting rodeo in June, on a section of river that cuts right through downtown. It's been taking place since 1949.

GETTING HERE AND AROUND

You need a private car to explore this area. There's a compact, walkable downtown area, but you'll need to drive to most lodgings, rivers, attractions, and the trailheads in the mountains.

VISITOR INFORMATION

CONTACTS Salida Colorado Chamber of Commerce. ✉ *406 W. U.S. 50, Salida* ☎ *719/539–2068, 877/772–5432* 🌐 *www.salidachamber.org.*

Restaurants

Amicas Pizza and Microbrewery
$ | **PIZZA** | The wood-fired pizzas and craft brews at this downtown grub hub come highly recommended by locals. Families stop in for a giant pie that can easily feed a family of four while white-water rafters, hikers, and bikers unwind at the next table with one of the brewery's well-known chili beers. **Known for:** the Michelangelo, a goat cheese pizza with sausage, pesto, green chilies, and caramelized onion; on-site microbrewery; downtown location. *Average main: $11* *127 F St., Salida* *719/539–5219* *amicassalida.com* *No credit cards.*

The Fritz
$$ | **MODERN AMERICAN** | This hip small-plates restaurant is as trendy as Salida dining gets. The intimate bar and expansive patio are some of the region's best spaces for socializing. **Known for:** creative small plates; central location; trendy scene. *Average main: $15* *113 E. Sackett St., Salida* *719/539–0364* *www.thefritzsalida.com.*

Hotels

Tudor Rose
$$ | **B&B/INN** | With beautiful furnishings and an idyllic setting, this rustic mountain lodge sits on a 37-acre spread of pine forest and mountain ridges. **Pros:** owners will stable horses in their barn; perfect rustic retreat; beautiful deck with mountain views. **Cons:** not for guests with young children; no pool; a bit outside of town. *Rooms from: $125* *6720 County Rd. 104, Salida* *719/539–2002, 800/379–0889* *www.thetudorrose.com* *6 rooms, 5 chalets* *Free Breakfast.*

Activities

BIKING

Absolute Bikes
BICYCLING | This downtown shop rents cruisers starting at $25 per day and mountain bikes starting at $65 per day, and provides repair service, maps, and good advice. *330 W. Sackett Ave., Salida* *719/539–9295* *www.absolutebikes.com.*

DOWNHILL SKIING

Monarch Mountain
SKIING/SNOWBOARDING | A small, independently owned ski resort that tops out on the Continental Divide, Monarch Mountain is a family-friendly place with moderate pricing and discounts for advanced online purchases. The resort also offers 1,635 acres of snowcat skiing on steep runs off the divide, plus the 130 acres of hike-to skiing on extreme terrain in Mirkwood Basin. **Facilities:** 58 trails; 800 acres; 1,162-foot vertical drop; 7 lifts. *22720 U.S. 50, Salida* *18 miles west of Salida* *719/530–5000, 888/996–7669* *www.skimonarch.com* *Lift ticket $99.*

FISHING

The Arkansas River, as it spills out of the central Colorado Rockies on its course through the south central part of the state, reputedly supports a brown-trout population exceeding 5,000 fish per mile. Some of the river's canyons are deep, and some of the best fishing locations are difficult to access, making a guide or outfitter a near necessity. See *cpw.state.co.us/thingstodo/Pages/Fishing.aspx* for more information.

OUTFITTERS

ArkAnglers
FISHING | A good fly shop with an experienced staff, ArkAnglers offers guided float and wade trips, fly-fishing lessons, and equipment rentals. *7500 W. U.S. 50, Salida* *719/539–4223* *www.arkanglers.com.*

RAFTING

The Salida area is a magnet for rafting aficionados, and there are dozens of outfitters. Salida jockeys with Buena Vista for the title of "Colorado's White-Water Capital."

Independent Whitewater
WHITE-WATER RAFTING | This family-owned company has been running the Arkansas River since the 1980s. Groups are small, and the take-out is at a private area after running Seidel's Suckhole and Twin Falls on regular half-day trips. ✉ *10830 County Rd. 165, Salida* ☎ *800/428–1479, 719/539–7737* 🌐 *www.independentrafting.com.*

SNOWMOBILING

All Season Adventures Inc.
SNOW SPORTS | Leisurely rides and snow-throwing thrills are both offered by this snowmobile outfitter. You can ride the Continental Divide with tours starting at $120 for a single and $165 for doubles. ✉ *10238 U.S. 50, Poncha Springs, Salida* ☎ *719/530–0651* 🌐 *www.allseasonrentals.com.*

Trinidad

85 miles south of Pueblo and 13 miles north of New Mexico border.

If you're traveling on I–25 and want to stop for a night in a historic town with character instead of a motel on the outskirts of a bigger city, check out Trinidad. Walk around Corazon de Trinidad, the downtown creative district area where some of the streets still have the original bricks—instead of pavement—and visit a few of the town's superb museums, a remarkably large number for a town of barely more than 8,000 residents.

Trinidad was founded in 1862 as a rest-and-repair station along the Santa Fe Trail. Starting in 1878 with the construction of the railroad and the development of the coal industry, the town grew and expanded, but the advent of natural gas, coupled with the Depression, led to a gradual decline in population. Since the 1990s there's been a modest increase, though, and a major interest in the upkeep of the city's rich cultural heritage.

GETTING HERE AND AROUND

Amtrak stops here. You'll need a private car or you can take the free Trinidad Trolley between shops, restaurants, and museums downtown.

VISITOR INFORMATION

CONTACTS Trinidad & Las Animas Chamber of Commerce. ✉ *137 N. Commercial St., Suite 204, Trinidad* ☎ *719/846–9285* 🌐 *www.tlacchamber.org.*

Sights

Corazon de Trinidad (*Heart of Trinidad*)
HISTORIC SITE | Downtown Trinidad, called the Corazon de Trinidad, is a National Historic District, mixing historic original brick-paved streets and architecture with modern concerts, restaurants, shops, and festivals. Residents and officials recently launched a bit of a revival here with big plans for the creative district. ✉ *Trinidad* 🌐 *www.corazondetrinidad.org.*

Louden-Henritze Archaeology Museum
MUSEUM | On the other side of the Purgatoire River, this museum at Trinidad State Junior College takes viewers back millions of years to examine the true origins of the region, including early geological formations, plant and marine-animal fossils, and prehistoric artifacts. ✉ *Trinidad State Junior College, 600 Prospect St., Trinidad* ☎ *719/846–5508* 🌐 *trinidadstate.edu/archaeology-museum/index.html* 🎫 *Free* 🕒 *Closed Fri.–Sun.*

Trinidad History Museum
GARDEN | This complex with three separate museums and a garden is a place to learn about the town's history. The first museum is **Baca House,** the 1870s residence of Felipe Baca, a prominent Hispanic farmer and businessman. Displays

convey a mix of Anglo (clothes, furniture) and Hispanic (santos, textiles) influences. Next door, the 1882 **Bloom Mansion** was built by Frank Bloom, who made his money through ranching and banking. He filled his ornate Second Empire–style Victorian with fine furnishings and fabrics brought from the East Coast and abroad. The adjacent **Santa Fe Trail Museum** is dedicated to the effects of the trail and railroad on the community. Inside are exhibits covering Trinidad's heyday as a commercial and cultural center. Finish up with a stop in the **Historic Gardens,** which are open year-round and filled with native plants and grapevines similar to those tended by the pioneers. ✉ *312 E. Main St., Trinidad* ☎ *719/846–7217* 🌐 *www.trinidadhistorymuseum.org* 🎫 *$5* 🕒 *Closed Sun. and Mon.*

Restaurants

Nana and Nano's Pasta House

$ | ITALIAN | The aroma of garlic and tomato sauce saturates this tiny, unpretentious eatery. Pastas, including standards like ravioli with homemade sauce and rigatoni with luscious meatballs, are consistently excellent. **Known for:** authentic Italian pasta dishes; deli with sandwiches and imported cheeses; informal and welcoming atmosphere. $ *Average main: $10* ✉ *418 E. Main St., Trinidad* ☎ *719/846–2696* 🕒 *Closed Sun.–Tues.*

Hotels

Tarabino Inn

$$ | B&B/INN | This Italianate–Victorian B&B sits in the middle of the Corazon de Trinidad National Historic District. **Pros:** decorated with works by local artists; within walking distance of museums; historical building. **Cons:** not much privacy; decor a little old-fashioned; not suitable for young children. $ *Rooms from: $129* ✉ *310 E. 2nd St., Trinidad* ☎ *719/846–2115, 866/846–8808* 🌐 *www.tarabinoinn.com* 🛏 *4 rooms* 🍽 *Free Breakfast.*

Activities

Trinidad Lake State Park

PARK—SPORTS-OUTDOORS | There's hiking, fishing, horseback riding, and camping at this park in the Purgatoire River Valley. ✉ *Hwy. 12, Trinidad* ✣ *3 miles west of Trinidad* ☎ *719/846–6951* 🌐 *cpw.state.co.us/placestogo/parks/TrinidadLake.*

Great Sand Dunes National Park and Preserve

Created by winds that sweep the San Luis Valley floor, the enormous sand dunes that form the heart of Great Sand Dunes National Park and Preserve are an improbable, unforgettable sight. The dunes stretch for more than 30 square miles, solid enough to have withstood 440,000 years of Mother Nature.

Nomadic hunters followed herds of mammoths and prehistoric bison into the San Luis Valley, making them some of the first people to visit the dunes. The hills of sand marked a common route for Native American tribes and explorers who traveled between the plains and Santa Fe. Speculation that gold was hiding under the sand attracted droves of miners in the 19th and 20th centuries. By the 1920s, operations had sprung up along the seasonal Medano Creek at the eastern base of the dunes alarming residents of the nearby Alamosa and Monte Vista communities. Members of the Ladies Philanthropic Educational Organization lobbied politicians to protect the landmark and in 1932 it was designated a national monument. Seventy years later, it was discovered that a large inland lake once covered the San Luis Valley, but had dried up due to climate change. Residents again rallied to protect the local resource, wildlife and unique

The landspaces of Great Sand Dunes National Park are some of the country's most beautiful.

ecosystems and the area was expanded into a national park and preserve in 2004.

Today, more than half a million visitors flock to the region annually to gawk at and play on the vast mountains of sand framed by the low grasslands and high-reaching Sangre de Cristo peaks. The tallest sand dunes in North America are nestled among diverse ecosystems of wetlands, grasslands, forests and a towering mountain range where visitors can fish alpine lakes, walk among wildflowers, listen to songbirds and climb the soft sand in a single day. Pronghorn, elk, and bighorn sheep call the area home while sandhill cranes flood the area twice a year during spring and fall migrations. From star designs to sharp defined edges, the shape of the dunes are as disparate as the geography surrounding them. Warmed by the sun or coated in snow, the sand hills, which tower as high as 750 feet, offer opportunities for sledding or climbing year-round. Adding to the awe of the unusual landscape, avalanches of sand can create a rare humming sound that inspired Bing Crosby's musical hit "The Singing Sands of Alamosa." Intrigue and inspiration continues to attract visitors from all around.

WHEN TO GO

More than half a million visitors come to the park each year, most on summer weekends; they tend to congregate around the main parking area and Medano Creek. To avoid the crowds, hike away from the main area up to the High Dune. Or come in the winter, when the park is a place for contemplation and repose—as well as skiing and sledding.

Fall and spring are the prettiest times to visit, with the surrounding mountains still capped with snow in May, and leaves on the aspen trees turning gold in September and early October. In summer, the surface temperature of the sand can climb to 150°F in the afternoon, so climbing the dunes is best in the morning or late afternoon. Since you're at a high altitude—about 8,200 feet at the visitor center—the air temperatures in the park itself remain in the 70s most of the summer.

GETTING HERE AND AROUND

Great Sand Dunes National Park and Preserve is about 240 miles from both Denver and Albuquerque, and roughly 180 miles from Colorado Springs and Santa Fe. The fastest route from Denver is Interstate 25 south to U.S. 160, heading west to just past Blanca, to Highway 150 north, which goes right to the park's main entrance. For a more scenic route, take U.S. 285 over Kenosha, Red Hill, and Poncha Passes, turn onto Highway 17 just south of Villa Grove, then take County Lane 6 to the park (watch for signs just south of Hooper). From Albuquerque, go north on Interstate 25 to Santa Fe, then north on U.S. 285 to Alamosa, then U.S. 160 east to Highway 150. From the west, Highway 17 and County Lane 6 take you to the park. The park entrance station is about 3 miles from the park boundary, and it's about a mile from there to the visitor center; the main parking lot is about a mile farther.

PARK ESSENTIALS

Entrance fees are $25 per vehicle and are valid for one week from date of purchase. Pick up camping permits ($20 per night per site at Pinyon Flats Campground) and backpacking permits (free) online at 🌐 *www.recreation.gov.*

The park is open 24/7. It is in the mountain time zone.

Cell-phone reception in the park is sporadic.

VISITOR INFORMATION

CONTACTS Great Sand Dunes National Park and Preserve. ✉ *11999 Hwy. 150, Mosca* ☎ *719/378–6395* 🌐 *www.nps.gov/grsa.*

Sights

SCENIC STOPS

High Dune

TRAIL | This isn't the park's highest dune, but it's high enough in the dune field to provide a view of all the dunes from its summit. It's on the first ridge of dunes you see from the main parking area. ✉ *Great Sand Dunes National Park.*

VISITOR CENTERS

Great Sand Dunes Visitor Center

INFO CENTER | View exhibits and artwork, browse in the bookstore, and watch a 20-minute film with an overview of the dunes. Rangers are on hand to answer questions. Facilities include restrooms and a vending machine stocked with soft drinks and snacks, but no other food. (The Great Sand Dunes Oasis, just outside the park boundary, has a café that is open generally late April through early October.) ✉ *Near the park entrance, Great Sand Dunes National Park* ☎ *719/378–6395* 🌐 *www.nps.gov/grsa/planyourvisit/visitor-center.htm.*

Activities

BIRD-WATCHING

The San Luis Valley is famous for its migratory birds, many of which stop in the park. Great Sand Dunes also has many permanent feathered residents. In the wetlands, you might see American white pelicans and the American avocet. On the forested sections of the mountains there are goshawks, northern harriers, gray jays, and Steller's jays. And in the alpine tundra there are golden eagles, hawks, horned larks, and white-tailed ptarmigan.

CAMPING

Great Sand Dunes has one campground, open April through October. During weekends in the summer, it can fill up with RVs and tents by midafternoon. Black bears live in the preserve, so when camping there, keep your food, trash, and toiletries in the trunk of your car (or use bear-proof containers). There is one campground and RV park near the entrance to Great Sand Dunes, and several others in the area.

Pinyon Flats Campground. Set in a pine forest about a mile past the visitor center, this campground has a trail leading to the dunes. Sites must be reserved online; RVs are allowed, but there are no hookups. ✉ *On the main park road, near the visitor center* 🌐 *www.recreation.gov* ☎ *719/378–6399.*

FISHING

Fly fishermen can angle for Rio Grande cutthroat trout in the upper reaches of Medano Creek, which is accessible by four-wheel-drive vehicle. It's catch-and-release only, and a Colorado license is required (☎ *800/244–5613*). There's also fishing in Upper and Lower Sand Creek Lakes, but it's a very long hike (3 or 4 miles from the Music Pass trailhead, located on the far side of the park in the San Isabel National Forest).

HIKING

Visitors can walk just about anywhere on the sand dunes in the heart of the park. The best view of all the dunes is from the top of High Dune. There are no formal trails because the sand keeps shifting, but you don't really need them: it's extremely difficult to get lost out here.

■ **TIP→ Before taking any of the trails in the preserve, rangers recommend stopping at the visitor center and picking up the handout that lists the trails, including their degree of difficulty.** The dunes can get very hot in the summer, reaching up to 150°F in the afternoon. If you're hiking, carry plenty of water; if you're going into the backcountry to camp overnight, carry even more water and a water filtration system. A free permit is required to backpack in the park. Also, watch for weather changes. If there's a thunderstorm and lightning, get off the dunes or trail immediately, and seek shelter. Before hiking, leave word with someone indicating where you're going to hike and when you expect to be back. Tell that contact to call 911 if you don't show up when expected.

EASY

Hike to High Dune

TRAIL | **FAMILY** | Get a panoramic view of all the surrounding dunes from the top of High Dune. Since there's no formal path, the smartest approach is to zigzag up the dune ridgelines traversing about 2½ miles round-trip. High Dune is 699 feet high, and to get there and back takes about two hours, or longer if there's been no rain for some time and the sand is soft. If you add on the walk to the 750-foot Star Dune, plan on another two or three hours and a strenuous workout up and down the dunes. *Easy–Moderate.* ✉ *Great Sand Dunes National Park* ✣ *Start from main dune field.*

MODERATE

★ Mosca Pass Trail

TRAIL | This moderately challenging route follows the Montville Trail laid out centuries ago by Native Americans, which became the Mosca Pass toll road used in the late 1800s and early 1900s. This is a good afternoon hike, because the trail rises through the trees and subalpine meadows, often following Mosca Creek. Watch for grouse and turkey along the route and listen for songbirds and owls cooing at dusk. It is 3½ miles one way, with a 1,400-foot gain in elevation. Hiking time is about two hours each way. *Moderate.* ✉ *Great Sand Dunes National Park* ✣ *Trailhead: Lower end of trail begins at Montville Trailhead, just north of visitor center.*

Alamosa

35 miles southwest of Great Sand Dunes via U.S. 160 and Rte. 150; 163 miles southwest of Colorado Springs.

The San Luis Valley's major city is a casual, central base from which to explore the region and visit the Great Sand Dunes.

VISITOR INFORMATION

CONTACTS Alamosa Convention & Visitors Bureau. ✉ *610 State Ave., Alamosa* ☎ *800/258–7597, 719/589–4840* 🌐 *www.alamosa.org.*

Sights

Adams State University

COLLEGE | The campus here contains several superlative examples of 1930s WPA-commissioned murals in its administrative building. The college's **Luther Bean Museum and Art Gallery** displays European porcelain and furniture collections, and exhibits of regional arts and crafts. ✉ *Richardson Hall, Richardson and 3rd Sts., Alamosa* ☎ *719/587–7151* 🌐 *www.adams.edu/lutherbean* 🎫 *Free* 🕒 *Closed weekends.*

Alamosa National Wildlife Refuge

NATURE PRESERVE | **FAMILY** | Less than an hour's drive southwest of Great Sand Dunes is a sanctuary for songbirds, waterbirds, and raptors (it's also home to many other types of birds, along with mule deer, beavers, and coyotes). The Rio Grande runs through the park comprising more than 11,000 acres of natural and man-made wetlands. You can take a 4-mile hike round-trip along the river or a 3½-mile wildlife drive on the park's western side or a drive along Bluff Road to an overlook on the park's eastern side. The refuge office is staffed by volunteers sporadically from March through November and closed in winter, but a self-service kiosk provides visitor information year-round. ✉ *9383 El Rancho La., off U.S. 160, Alamosa* ☎ *719/589–4021* 🌐 *www.fws.gov/refuge/alamosa* 🎫 *Free.*

The Greenhouse at Sand Dunes Pool

HOT SPRINGS | After a long day of hiking the dunes, take a dip in the soothing soaking tubs inside the 10,000-square-foot greenhouse at the Sand Dunes Pool. Just 30 minutes northwest of the park is a sanctuary that offers 70°F comfort year-round. Visitors 21 and older can soak in three hot tubs ranging from 103°F to 110°F, or take a dip in the large, 98°F swimming pool surrounded by lush gardens. A bar offers cocktails and sweet and savory small plates. For families, a giant outdoor pool with views of the Sangre de Cristo mountains is a popular amenity. ✉ *1991 County Rd. 63, Mosca* ☎ *719/378–2807* 🌐 *www.sanddunespool.com/greenhouse* 🎫 *$20 for adults* 🕒 *Closed Thurs.*

Monte Vista National Wildlife Refuge

NATURE PRESERVE | **FAMILY** | Just west of the Alamosa wildlife refuge is its sister sanctuary, the Monte Vista National Wildlife Refuge, a 15,000-acre park that's a stopping point for more than 20,000 migrating cranes in the spring and fall. It hosts an annual Crane Festival, held one weekend in mid-March in the nearby town of Monte Vista, and a children's Crane Festival in mid-October at the park with kid-friendly activities. You can see the sanctuary by foot, bike, or car via the 4-mile Wildlife Drive. ✉ *6120 Hwy. 15, Monte Vista* ☎ *719/589–4021* 🌐 *www.fws.gov/refuge/monte_vista* 🎫 *Free.*

Restaurants

Milagros Coffeehouse

$ | **CAFÉ** | The coffee is full-bodied at this coffeehouse and café where all profits go to local charities. Amish baked goods reign on the menu where local food dominates, which includes plenty of vegetarian and gluten-free options. **Known for:** vegetarian options; charitable donations; excellent coffee. 💲 *Average main: $7* ✉ *529 Main St., Alamosa* ☎ *719/589–9299.*

Hotels

Best Western Alamosa Inn

$ | **HOTEL** | This sprawling, well-maintained complex is your best bet for reasonably priced lodgings. **Pros:** reliable accommodations; easy to find; good base for area activities. **Cons:** noisy street; nothing but fast food nearby; basic rooms. *Rooms from: $110 ✉ 2005 Main St., Alamosa ☎ 719/589–2567, 800/459–5123 🌐 www.bestwestern.com 53 rooms Free Breakfast.*

San Luis and Fort Garland Loop

San Luis is 40 miles from Alamosa, 45 miles from Great Sand Dunes National Park; Fort Garland is 16 miles from San Luis, 30 miles from Great San Dunes National Park.

To get a real feel for this area, take an easy driving loop from Alamosa that includes San Luis and Fort Garland. In summer, take a few hours to ride one of the scenic railroads that take you into wilderness areas in this region.

Sights

Cumbres & Toltec Scenic Railroad

TRANSPORTATION SITE (AIRPORT/BUS/FERRY/TRAIN) | **FAMILY** | Take a day trip on the Cumbres & Toltec Scenic Railroad, an 1880s steam locomotive that chugs through portions of Colorado's and northern New Mexico's rugged mountains that you can't reach via roads. It's the country's longest and highest steam-operated railroad. The company offers round-trip train routes, several bus-and-train combinations, one-way trips, and themed rides. *✉ 5234 U.S. 285, Antonito ☎ 888/286–2737 🌐 www.cumbrestoltec.com $110–$216.*

Fort Garland

MILITARY SITE | One of Colorado's first military posts, Fort Garland was established in 1858 to protect settlers. It lies in the shadow of the Sangre de Cristo Mountains. The mountains were named for the "Blood of Christ" because of their ruddy color, especially at dawn. The legendary Kit Carson commanded the outfit, and some of the original adobe structures are still standing. The **Fort Garland Museum** features a re-creation of the commandant's quarters and period military displays. The museum is 16 miles north of San Luis via Highway 159 and 24 miles east of Alamosa via U.S. 160. *✉ U.S. 160 and Hwy. 159, Fort Garland ☎ 719/379–3512 🌐 www.museumtrail.org/fortgarlandmuseum.asp $5.*

Manassa, San Luis, and Fort Garland Loop

SCENIC DRIVE | To get a real feel for this area, take an easy driving loop from Alamosa through much of the San Luis Valley (the whole trip is about 95 miles). Head east on U.S. 160 to Fort Garland, south on Highway 159 to San Luis, west on highways 159 and 142 to Manassa, then north on U.S. 285 back to Alamosa. More than half of the route is part of the Los Caminos Antiguos Drive, one of Colorado's Scenic Byways.

San Luis

TOWN | Founded in 1851, San Luis is the oldest incorporated town in Colorado. Murals depicting famous stories and legends of the area adorn several buildings in the town. A latter-day masterpiece is the **Stations of the Cross Shrine,** created by renowned local sculptor Huberto Maestas. The shrine is formally known as La Mesa de la Piedad y de la Misericordia (Hill of Piety and Mercy), and its 15 stations with bronze statutes illustrate the last hours of Christ's life. The trail leads up to a chapel called La Capilla de Todos Los Santos. *✉ San Luis.*

Hotels

Mountain View Motor Inn
$ | **HOTEL** | This cheerful, squeaky-clean motel is just a few miles south of the Great Sand Dunes, in the tiny town of Fort Garland, and makes a great base from which to visit the park and other San Luis Valley attractions. **Pros:** spotless, comfortable rooms; 20 minutes from park. **Cons:** no pool or other recreational amenities in hotel; no great eating options nearby. *Rooms from: $96* *411 U.S. 160, Fort Garland* *719/379–2993* *22 rooms* *No meals.*

Chapter 17

THE ROCKY MOUNTAIN SKI RESORTS

Updated by
Whitney Bryen,
Lindsey Galloway,
Kyle Wagner

Sights ★★★★★ | Restaurants ★★★★★ | Hotels ★★★★★ | Shopping ★★★☆☆ | Nightlife ★★★☆☆

WELCOME TO THE ROCKY MOUNTAIN SKI RESORTS

TOP REASONS TO GO

★ **Hot springs:** Glenwood Springs has been a therapeutic retreat since the Ute Indians called the local hot springs "healing waters."

★ **The Aspen scene:** You'll see it all in Aspen—Hollywood celebs, high-heeled Brazilians, tanned European ski instructors, and fascinating and friendly locals.

★ **Mining heritage:** It was gold that built Colorado in the 1800s, and this legacy is alive and well in Frisco and Dillon.

★ **Summit County Skiing:** You won't find more choices to ski and ride within a mere hour's drive from the Denver Metro Area.

★ **Summer festivals:** Check out some of Vail's many cultural activities—summer is full of music, culinary, and dance festivals.

1 **Aspen.** One of the world's most glamorous ski towns.

2 **Snowmass.** Aspen's more down-to-earth counterpart.

3 **Glenwood Springs.** A famed spa town home to the world's largest outdoor natural hot-springs pool.

4 **Vail.** European-style cafés and beautifully cobbled streets lined with boutiques are more than just window dressing—Vail is no longer just known for its serious skiing.

5 **Keystone.** A laid-back mountain town with the state's largest night skiing operation.

6 **Dillon.** Home to one of the state's largest manmade reservoirs.

7 **Frisco.** One of the area's more affordable towns.

8 **Breckenridge.** A mining town turned skiing and snowboarding destination.

9 **Steamboat Springs.** A mountain village famous for its hot springs and its Olympic skiers.

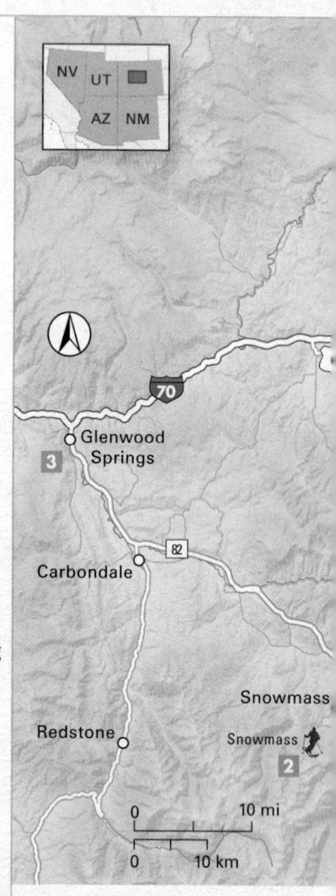

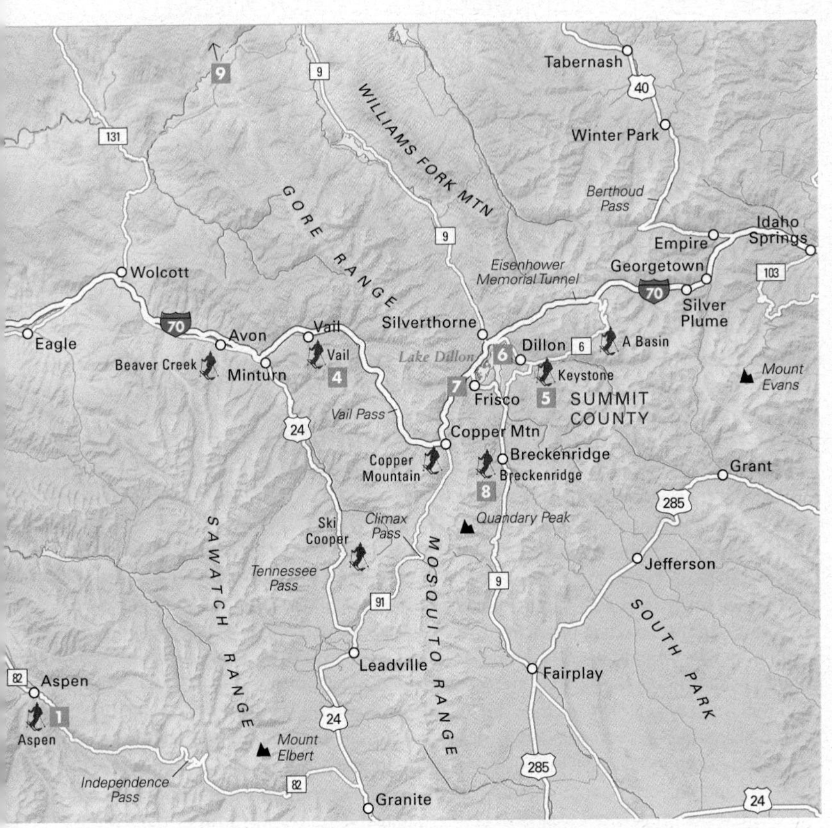

Tabernash
Winter Park
Berthoud Pass
Idaho Springs
Empire
Georgetown
Silver Plume
Eisenhower Memorial Tunnel
WILLIAMS FORK MTN
GORE RANGE
Wolcott
Eagle
Avon
Beaver Creek
Minturn
Vail
Vail Pass
Silverthorne
Lake Dillon
Dillon
A Basin
Keystone
Frisco
SUMMIT COUNTY
Mount Evans
Copper Mtn
Copper Mountain
Breckenridge
Grant
Quandary Peak
Climax Pass
Ski Cooper
Tennessee Pass
SAWATCH RANGE
MOSQUITO RANGE
Jefferson
SOUTH PARK
Leadville
Fairplay
Aspen
Mount Elbert
Independence Pass
Granite

Colorado has the best-rated ski resorts in the United States, many of which are clustered in the southern Rockies in Central Colorado. From the resorts of Summit County, immediately west of Denver, to Aspen and the Roaring Fork Valley in Central Colorado, American skiiers find a dozen popular resorts to fulfill their every skiing need.

Summit County resorts such as Keystone (in the Arapahoe Basin) and Breckinridge, an old mining town now more popular for skiing and snowboarding, offer skiing close to the state capital.Keystone is an intimate resort just 90 minutes west of Denver, while Breckenridge, Summit County's largest resort area, has a healthy dose of authentic Colorado character to balance its flashy resorts and high-end condo developments. Further west, Vail is known these days for more than its superb skiing (though you will find excellent skiing here); today it's also a lovely place to hang out, with good restaurants and charming stores. More exclusive is Aspen, one of Colorado's most glamorous spots to both ski and be seen, and its more down-to-earth neighbor Snowmass, which is more popular with families.

The Rockies aren't just about skiing. There are hot springs to soak in (Glenwood Springs is a famous spa town); charming historic towns like Frisco and Dillon to explore; farther north is Steamboat Springs, a mountain resort offering the best of both worlds: skiing and hot springs. Throughout the year, the spectacular scenery draws people for hiking and other outdoor pursuits when skiing isn't on the table.

Planning

When to Go

Although most of the ski areas of the Rockies are year-round destinations, they are particularly busy in winter. If it's skiing you're after, February and March historically have the best snow (deepest base and most terrain open) plus the warmest winter weather. Summers are legendary for their food, music, and art festivals, and Steamboat Springs in particular is busier in summer than winter. June and early July are best for rafting (snowmelt makes for high-octane rapids). Most high-country biking and hiking trails are cleared of snowdrift by mid-June, when brilliant wildflowers emerge and remain in bloom through early August. Mid-September brings hotel-room deals, cooler days, photogenic snow dustings on the mountains. But Breckinridge is so high that the ski season often dawns here weeks before it does in the rest of the state (it can also snow at any time during the year).

Getting Here and Around

AIR

Aspen/Pitkin County Airport (ASE) is 3 miles from downtown Aspen and 7 miles from Snowmass Village. Airline schedules vary seasonally, but, during ski season, you can count on several daily nonstop flights to and from Denver and regular nonstop flights to and from Dallas, Houston, Chicago, Miami, and Los Angeles.

Denver International Airport (DEN), the gateway to the High Rockies and Summit County, is 119 miles east of Vail and about an hour from Breckenridge. It's a 90-minute drive from Vail, but ski traffic can double the time. The Vail Valley is served by Eagle County Airport (EGE), 34 miles west of Vail.

Steamboat Springs is remote. Yampa Valley Regional Airport (HDN) is in Hayden, 22 miles away. United flies nonstop year-round from various gateways during ski season, while Alaska, American, JetBlue, and Southwest fly here from mid-December to March.

AIRPORT TRANSFERS

If you aren't renting a car, there are some options for transfers from Denver (except for Steamboat Springs). Colorado Mountain Express serves Aspen and Vail. Epic Mountain Express serves Breckinridge.

CONTACTS Colorado Mountain Express. ☎ *970/754–7433* 🌐 *www.coloradomountainexpress.com.* **Epic Mountain Express.** ☎ *970/754–7433, 800/525–6363* 🌐 *www.epicmountainexpress.com.*

CAR

Most ski resort areas have some kind of bus or shuttle transportation during the winter. Unless you need a car, it may be better to use that if your main goal is just skiing, especially if you are staying in a well-connected resort area, the main exception being Steamboat Springs, where it's much more advantageous to have a car.

Although it is often severely overcrowded, I–70 is still the quickest and most direct route from Denver to Aspen, Vail, or Breckinridge.

The hardest part about driving in the High Rockies is keeping your eyes on the road. A glacier-carved canyon off to your left, a soaring mountain ridge to your right, and there, standing on the shoulder, a bull elk. Some of the most scenic routes aren't necessarily the most direct. The Eisenhower Tunnel sweeps thousands of cars daily beneath the mantle of the Continental Divide, whereas only several hundred drivers choose the slower, but more spectacular, Loveland Pass. Some of the most beautiful byways, like the Mount Evans Scenic and Historic Drive, are one-way roads. Breckenridge is south of I–70 on Highway 9.

From Denver, Steamboat Springs is about a three-hour drive northwest via I–70 and U.S. 40. The route traverses some high-mountain passes, so it's a good idea to check road conditions before you travel.

Hotels

There's no shortage of lodging in any of the major ski areas. Aspen and the Roaring Fork have fabulous hotels and resorts, but you'll pay the highest rates in the state; Glenwood Springs is more attractive for budget hunters—but you'll face heavy traffic when commuting to Aspen. Before booking down-valley, however, look for special deals that might include lift tickets and parking.

Vail and Beaver Creek are purpose-built resorts, so you won't find any quaint historic Victorians converted into bed-and-breakfasts here as you will in Breckenridge and Aspen. Instead, Vail lodgings come in three flavors—European chalets that blend with the Bavarian architecture, posh chain resorts up side canyons, and loads of small but serviceable condominiums perfect for families.

Summit County is a great place for history buffs looking for redone Victorian mining mansions–cum–bed-and-breakfasts, and budget hunters who want affordable rooms close to the slopes. Note that many accommodations do not have air-conditioning—beware that rooms with southern exposures warm up quickly. Summer nights, however, are often cool enough in the mountains that opening the windows will do the trick.

Steamboat Springs is unique in the state because it has high-end dude ranches and ranch resorts, which are less abundant in resort areas like Aspen, Summit County, and Vail.

Restaurants

Colorado's culinary repertoire is at its broadest in Aspen. With all the Hummers and designer handbags come an equal number of menus with high-end ingredients and showy preparations. Plates can be pricey in the area, but many eateries have at least a few moderately priced entrées and a bar menu as a nod to the budget-conscious.

Vail has a distinctly European dining style. For the most romantic options, look into a slope-side restaurants where the fixed-course menus and unique transportation (horses in summer and sleighs in winter) make the experience more than just a meal. The farther down-valley you move, the more the prices drop.

Summit County eateries specialize in pub food and Mexican cuisine for calorie-hungry hikers, skiers, and boaters, with the exception of a few more urbane spots in Breckenridge. You won't find much sushi here, but you will find fish tacos, shepherd's pies, and burgers with every imaginable topping.

The town of Steamboat Springs, in the heart of cattle country, has far more carnivorous delights—including elk, deer, and bison—than you're likely to find in the trendier resorts of Aspen, Telluride, and Vail. The Steamboat ski resort, separated geographically from town, is more eclectic, with small sushi bars and Mediterranean cafés hidden among the boutiques.

HOTEL AND RESTAURANT PRICES

Hotel reviews have been shortened. For full information, visit Fodors.com. Restaurant prices are the average cost of a main course at dinner or, if dinner is not served, at lunch, excluding 8.2%–8.6% tax. Hotel prices are the lowest cost of a standard double room in high season, excluding service charges and 8.6%–10.7% tax.

What It Costs

	$	$$	$$$	$$$$
RESTAURANTS				
	under $15	$15–$22	$23–$30	over $30
HOTELS				
	under $125	$125–$200	$201–$300	over $300

Aspen

200 miles west of Denver via I–70 and Hwy. 82.

One of the world's fabled resorts, Aspen practically defines glitz, glamour, and glorious skiing. To the uninitiated, Aspen and Vail might be synonymous. Between the galleries, museums, music festivals, and other glittering social events, however, there's so much going on in Aspen that even in winter many people come simply to "do the scene," and never make it to the slopes. Many hotels and restaurants host lively après-ski events.

At the same time, Aspen is a place where some people live everyday lives, sending their children to school and working at jobs that may or may not have to do with skiing. It is also, arguably, America's original ski-bum destination,

At the base of the Maroon Bells is the lovely Maroon Lake, which attracts lots of wildlife.

a fact that continues to give the town's glamorous facade an underlying layer of humor and texture.

GETTING HERE AND AROUND

The rich arrive by private planes, but almost everyone else arrives in Aspen by car or shuttle bus. Parking is a pricey pain, and traffic, especially on weekends, clogs the streets. The Roaring Fork Transportation Authority has bus service connecting the resort with the rest of the valley. The easiest way to get around Aspen is on foot or by bike. For longer trips, hop aboard the free Aspen Skiing Company shuttles, which connect the Aspen, Buttermilk, and Snowmass base areas.

TOURS

Aspen Carriage and Sleigh

CARRIAGE TOURS | A romantic (albeit pricey) way to get acquainted with the backcountry is by taking a private sleigh ride with Aspen Carriage and Sleigh. They also have more affordable carriage tours around downtown and the historic West End. ✉ *Aspen* ☎ *970/925–3394* 🌐 *www.aspencarriage.com* 🎫 *From $325 an hour.*

VISITOR INFORMATION

CONTACTS Aspen Chamber Resort Association. ✉ *590 N. Mill St., Aspen* ☎ *970/925–1940, 877/702–7736* 🌐 *aspenchamber.org.*

Sights

Aspen Art Museum

MUSEUM | Known for its rotating contemporary exhibits and woven-look exterior design, this non-collecting museum exhibits mainly new pieces from top national and international artists, often commissioned by the museum. Designed by Shigeru Ban, the 33,000-square-foot facility is a three-story glass cube encased in a woven, wood-veneer exterior screen that gives passersby glimpses of the exhibitions. Inside, a glass elevator and an open-plan design create a bright space, and the rooftop sculpture garden and SO Café offer prime views of Aspen Mountain. ✉ *637 E. Hyman Ave., Aspen* ☎ *970/925–8050* 🌐 *www.aspenartmuseum.org* 🎫 *Free* ⏲ *Closed Mon.*

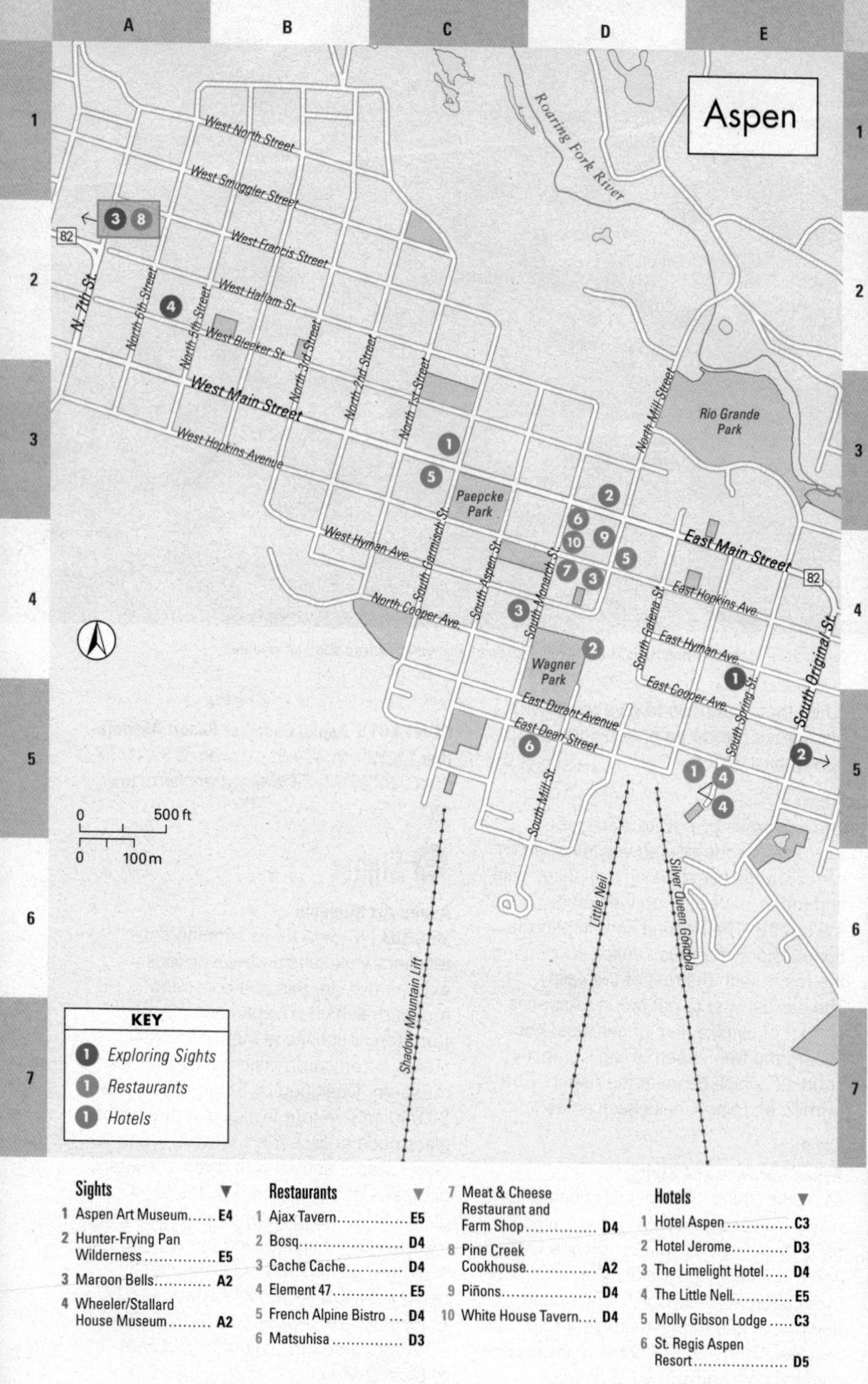

Sights	
1 Aspen Art Museum	E4
2 Hunter-Frying Pan Wilderness	E5
3 Maroon Bells	A2
4 Wheeler/Stallard House Museum	A2

Restaurants	
1 Ajax Tavern	E5
2 Bosq	D4
3 Cache Cache	D4
4 Element 47	E5
5 French Alpine Bistro	D4
6 Matsuhisa	D3
7 Meat & Cheese Restaurant and Farm Shop	D4
8 Pine Creek Cookhouse	A2
9 Piñons	D4
10 White House Tavern	D4

Hotels	
1 Hotel Aspen	C3
2 Hotel Jerome	D3
3 The Limelight Hotel	D4
4 The Little Nell	E5
5 Molly Gibson Lodge	C3
6 St. Regis Aspen Resort	D5

Hunter-Frying Pan Wilderness

NATURE PRESERVE | East of Aspen, in the Williams Mountains and lining a stretch of the Roaring Fork River, is an often-forgotten section of the White River National Forest. Overshadowed by the popular Maroon Bells to the west and the Colorado Wilderness of the Holy Cross to the north, the more than 82,000 acres of the Hunter-Fryingpan Wilderness offer 65 miles of hiking trails, excellent trout fishing, and unparalleled seclusion. Elk and mule deer call the area home, and wildflowers abound in July and August. ✉ *Aspen Ranger Station, 806 W. Hallam, Aspen* ☎ *970/925–3445* 🌐 *www.fs.usda.gov/recarea/whiteriver/recarea/?recid=81105.*

★ Maroon Bells

NATURE SITE | **FAMILY** | The majestic Maroon Bells, twin peaks more than 14,000 feet high, are so colorful, thanks to mineral streaking, that you'd swear they were blanketed with primrose and Indian paintbrush. It's one of the most photographed spots in the country. Before 8 am and after 5 pm in the summer, cars can drive all the way up to Maroon Lake (though vehicles with children in car seats or people with disabilities are allowed to do so at any time). Otherwise, parking is available at the Aspen Highlands garage, where guided bus tours and shuttles leave regularly in summer months. ✉ *White River National Forest, Maroon Creek Rd., Aspen* ✣ *10 miles southwest of Aspen.*

Wheeler/Stallard House Museum

MUSEUM | You can get a taste of Victorian high life at the Queen Anne–style Wheeler/Stallard House Museum, which displays memorabilia collected by the Aspen Historical Society and features revolving historical exhibits. Your admission fee also covers entrance to the Holden/Marolt Ranching and Mining Museum (open summer only), a hands-on exploration of Aspen's past housed in an old ore-processing building on the western edge of town. ✉ *620 W. Bleeker St., Aspen* ☎ *970/925–3721* 🌐 *www.aspenhistory.org* 🎫 *$10* ⏲ *Closed Sun. and Mon.*

Restaurants

Ajax Tavern

$$$ | **AMERICAN** | So close to the gondola you can keep your boots on while dining, this upbeat restaurant in The Little Nell hotel has big glass windows and a spacious patio with slope-side views. Large wooden beams, red booths, and sleek furnishings define this spot, which is popular both for its location and its hearty surf-n-turf dishes. **Known for:** slope-side patio; Parmesan truffle fries; double cheeseburger made with locally raised Wagyu beef. $ *Average main: $27* ✉ *685 E. Durant St., Aspen* ☎ *970/920–4600* 🌐 *www.thelittlenell.com.*

★ Bosq

$$$$ | **AMERICAN** | The dining room at Bosq is small and intimate with a rustic-chic setting that's bright in the daytime and dimly lit for a romantic experience at night. The food is equally impressive, melding root vegetables and local meats and fish with bold, and sometimes spicy, surprises like sweet-and-sour eggplant. **Known for:** Peking duck; romantic dining room; lively patio scene. $ *Average main: $42* ✉ *312 S. Mill St., Aspen* ☎ *970/710–7299* 🌐 *www.bosqaspen.com.*

Cache Cache

$$$$ | **MODERN AMERICAN** | With a focus on locally raised meats, Cache Cache brings a Continental influence to sophisticated yet filling entrées that are served on the patio or in the dimly lit room, with its white tablecloths and black chairs. In warmer months, the chic bistro's vegetable accompaniments reflect whatever is freshest from area farms. **Known for:** excellent wine selection; Russian caviar; sensational rotisserie items and desserts. $ *Average main: $38* ✉ *205 S. Mill St., Aspen* ☎ *970/925–3835* 🌐 *www.cachecache.com* ⏲ *No lunch.*

★ **Element 47**

$$$$ | **MODERN AMERICAN** | Aspen's elite book tables at this swanky, highly regarded restaurant in The Little Nell hotel not only for the beautifully presented entrées but also for the glass, ceiling-height wine cases stocked by knowledgeable sommeliers who also make tableside recommendations. The seasonal menu highlights locally sourced produce and game, as well as meat raised on Colorado ranches. **Known for:** 20,000-plus bottle wine cellar; local Wagyu beef and rack of lamb; impeccable service. *Average main: $40 ✉ 675 E. Durant Ave., Aspen ☎ 970/920–6330 🌐 www.element47aspen.com.*

★ **French Alpine Bistro**

$$$$ | **FRENCH** | Candlelight makes this bistro romantic, and decorative items such as fur pelts, wooden skis, and European antiques evoke the Swiss chalet where owner and retired pro skier, Raphael Derly, vacationed as a child. The divine, prix-fixe, seasonal menu—with such traditional dishes as escargots, foie gras, boeuf bourguignon, and dessert crepes—is a nod to Derly's upbringing in the south of France. **Known for:** intimate ambience; excellent wine selection; decadent French cuisine. *Average main: $120 ✉ 400 E. Hopkins Ave., Aspen ☎ 970/925–1566 🌐 www.frenchalpinebistro.com ⏲ No lunch.*

Matsuhisa

$$$$ | **JAPANESE** | Although you shouldn't expect to see celebrity chef Nobu Matsuhisa in the kitchen of his hopping restaurant in an 1887 Victorian house with an elegant downstairs room and a more casual, limited-menu upstairs space, his recipes and techniques are unmistakable. Nobu's sushi rolls and his new-style sashimi are marvelous, his hot dishes delectable, and his prices astronomical. **Known for:** off-menu specialty sushi rolls; caviar-topped seafood tartare; spectacular sake selection. *Average main: $35 ✉ 303 E. Main St., Aspen ☎ 970/544–6628 🌐 www.matsuhisarestaurants.com/aspen ⏲ No lunch.*

Meat & Cheese Restaurant and Farm Shop

$$ | **AMERICAN** | This shop is the perfect spot for grab-and-go lunches or for creating your own picnic lunch from an array of specialty meats, cheeses, seafood, and produce. The restaurant, with rustic wooden tables and vibrant painted flowers decorating the dark walls, features seasonal, locally sourced dishes made from scratch, with impressive charcuterie boards, sandwiches, and salads that occasionally have an Asian twist. **Known for:** seasonal charcuterie boards; specialty market; kombucha on draft. *Average main: $18 ✉ 319 E. Hopkins Ave., Aspen ☎ 970/710–7120 🌐 meatcheese.avalancheaspen.com.*

Pine Creek Cookhouse

$$$$ | **MODERN AMERICAN** | In winter, the only way to get to this homey log cabin with breathtaking views of the Elk Mountains is via snowshoe, cross-country ski, or horse-drawn sleigh. In summer, you can drive to the front door, but you should consider hiking here to compensate for the filling American alpine fare. **Known for:** floor-to-ceiling windows with views of the woods; wild game dishes; adventure activities. *Average main: $65 ✉ 12500 Castle Creek Rd., Aspen ☎ 970/925–1044 🌐 www.pinecreekcookhouse.com ⏲ Closed Tues.*

Piñons

$$$$ | **MODERN AMERICAN** | The open, modern dining room at Piñons combines Old West touches (a rustic-wood decor and a faux-tin ceiling) with a contemporary menu that goes beyond American-style entrées by incorporating selections like sashimi tuna tacos and Russian caviar. The interior fills up fast, but you can eat at the bar, with its budget-friendly, two-course, prix-fixe menu. **Known for:** creative cocktail menu; impeccable service; caviar selection. *Average main: $40 ✉ 105 S. Mill St., Aspen ☎ 970/920–2021 🌐 www.pinons.net ⏲ No lunch.*

White House Tavern

$$ | **AMERICAN** | The patio outside this cute, white, Victorian house in the heart of Aspen is a fun, lively place to see and be seen. Locals rave about the sandwiches here, and a great beer, wine, and cocktail menu makes the cozy wood-paneled interior perfect on chilly afternoons or evenings. **Known for:** crispy chicken sandwich with spicy slaw; signature margaritas; sceney patio. *$ Average main: $20 ✉ 302 E. Hopkins Ave., Aspen ☎ 970/925–1007 🌐 aspenwhitehouse.com.*

Hotels

Hotel Aspen

$$$ | **HOTEL** | Just a few minutes from the mall and the mountain, this contemporary hotel on the town's main drag takes full advantage of the spectacular view, with huge windows covering its modern exterior. **Pros:** private ski lockers; free parking; hot tubs with mountain views in some rooms. **Cons:** busy Main Street location; no restaurant; no spa or fitness center. *$ Rooms from: $208 ✉ 110 W. Main St., Aspen ☎ 970/925–3441 🌐 www.hotelaspen.com ⇆ 45 rooms 🍴 Free Breakfast.*

★ Hotel Jerome

$$$$ | **HOTEL** | The luxurious Hotel Jerome, first opened in 1889, has an upbeat, private club–like decor that retains the stately hotel's historic integrity but gives it a sumptuous sheen. **Pros:** historic property with modern amenities; central location; top-notch service. **Cons:** small spa and fitness center; very expensive, with rates that do not include the resort fee; located on busy main drag. *$ Rooms from: $725 ✉ 330 E. Main St., Aspen ☎ 970/920–1000, 800/367–7625 🌐 hoteljerome.aubergeresorts.com ⇆ 93 rooms 🍴 No meals.*

The Limelight Hotel

$$$$ | **HOTEL** | **FAMILY** | This classic is perfect for families who want a taste of luxury without tip-heavy service (guest services such as bellhops are available upon request). **Pros:** family- and pet-friendly; downtown location; complimentary snowshoes. **Cons:** busy and loud, with constant lobby traffic in ski season; often fully booked in high season; self-parking in paid garage. *$ Rooms from: $450 ✉ 355 S. Monarch St., Aspen ☎ 970/925–3025, 855/925–3025 🌐 www.limelighthotel.com ⇆ 126 rooms 🍴 Free Breakfast.*

★ The Little Nell

$$$$ | **HOTEL** | Right at the base of the gondola, Aspen's oldest ski-in ski-out hotel features luxurious, modern rooms and superior staff. **Pros:** best location in town; unmatched service; spacious rooms. **Cons:** expensive; difficult to get a room in high season; no spa. *$ Rooms from: $750 ✉ 675 E. Durant Ave., Aspen ☎ 970/920–4600, 888/843–6355 🌐 www.thelittlenell.com ⇆ 92 rooms 🍴 No meals.*

Molly Gibson Lodge

$$$ | **HOTEL** | One of the only hotels in Aspen with traditional wood-burning fireplaces, the reasonably priced Molly Gibson feels and smells like a European ski lodge, and its stacks of freshly cut cedar and rustic furniture keep the hotel grounded. **Pros:** central downtown location; lovely outdoor pool area; plush bedding. **Cons:** hotel parking is limited; few rooms with patios; lacks amenities like fitness center and spa. *$ Rooms from: $229 ✉ 101 W. Main St., Aspen ☎ 970/925–3434 🌐 www.mollygibson.com ⇆ 53 rooms 🍴 Free Breakfast.*

★ St. Regis Aspen Resort

$$$$ | **HOTEL** | The well-established St. Regis Aspen resembles a mountain chalet that's both stately and contemporary: the lobby and library have rich wood paneling and modern furnishings; the gray-and-brown guest rooms have hardwood floors and large, leather-frame beds; and the elegant bathrooms feature gray marble tile and polished silver fixtures. **Pros:** one of Aspen's most luxurious properties; close to the slopes; ultraposh spa. **Cons:** very expensive; only

valet parking; difficult to get a room. *Rooms from: $1101* *315 E. Dean St., Aspen* *970/920–3300, 888/627–7198* *www.stregisaspen.com* *179 rooms* *No meals.*

Nightlife

BARS AND LOUNGES

Downtown's East Hyman Avenue is an ideal place for barhopping, with a cluster of nightspots sharing the same street address and additional options for drinking and dancing on the Hyman Avenue Mall.

Aspen Tap

BREWPUBS/BEER GARDENS | Home to Aspen Brewing Company, Aspen Tap serves a small menu of pub food, liquor, wine, and, of course, microbrews from the city's only brewery. The centrally located bar includes a patio that's great for people-watching and sipping an Ajax Pilsner. *121 S. Galena St., Aspen* *970/710–2461* *www.aspenbrewingcompany.com.*

Eric's Bar

BARS/PUBS | Whiskey—and lots of it—is the claim to fame of Eric's Bar, a hip little watering hole that attracts a rowdy crowd. There's also a varied lineup of at least a dozen microbrews and other beers on tap. *315 E. Hyman Ave., Aspen* *970/920–6707* *www.sucasaaspen.com/erics-bar.*

J-Bar

BARS/PUBS | You can't say you've seen Aspen until you've set foot in the historic Hotel Jerome's lively J-Bar, with its textured leather walls and decorative tin ceilings. The centerpiece is the wooden, original, (circa1889) bar, where the Aspen Crud, a bourbon milkshake, was invented during Prohibition. *Hotel Jerome, 330 E. Main St., Aspen* *970/920–1000* *www.hoteljerome.com.*

Shopping

ART GALLERIES

Baldwin Gallery

ART GALLERIES | This modern gallery is the place to see and be seen at receptions for nationally known artists. *209 S. Galena St., Aspen* *970/920–9797* *www.baldwingallery.com.*

Galerie Maximillian

ART GALLERIES | You can find 19th- and 20th-century prints, sculpture, and paintings here—including original Picassos and Chagalls. *602 E. Cooper Ave., Aspen* *970/925–6100* *www.galeriemax.com.*

BOOKS

Explore Booksellers

BOOKS/STATIONERY | Located in a Victorian house, this independent store stocks more than 20,000 books in its multiple rooms and is especially strong in politics, travel, and literature. The upstairs, vegetarian-friendly Pyramid Bistro is the perfect place for a light meal or snack. *221 E. Main St., Aspen* *970/925–5336 bookstore, 970/925–5338 bistro* *www.explorebooksellers.com.*

CLOTHES

Pitkin County Dry Goods

CLOTHING | Founded in 1969, Pitkin County Dry Goods may be one of Aspen's oldest clothing stores, but it carries contemporary, casual apparel for men and women, as well as fun and funky belts, scarves, and jewelry. *520 E. Cooper Ave., Aspen* *970/925–1681* *www.pitkincountydrygoods.com.*

MARKETS

★ **Aspen Saturday Market**

OUTDOOR/FLEA/GREEN MARKETS | Show up in downtown Aspen any Saturday from mid-June to mid-October, and you can enjoy the Aspen Saturday Market, a sort of farmers' market–meets–arts fair. Tents cluster along the corner of Galena and Hopkins and then extend to the intersection of Hyman and Galena. Everything here is Colorado made (or grown), from pottery and paintings to peppers and peaches. Enjoy live music and ready-made foods to eat on the spot. ✉ *Aspen* 🌐 *www.aspen-saturdaymarket.com.*

SPORTING GOODS

Ute Mountaineer

SPORTING GOODS | This sporting-goods store sells and rents a variety of back-country gear and also carries outdoor clothing and guidebooks. ✉ *210 S. Galena St., Aspen* ☎ *970/925–2849* 🌐 *www.utemountaineer.com.*

Activities

BACKCOUNTRY SKIING

Alfred A. Braun Hut System

SKIING/SNOWBOARDING | The Alfred A. Braun Hut System is one of Aspen's major backcountry networks, with seven huts that sleep 7 to 14 people located near the tree line in the Elk Mountains. They're open in winter only, and reservations for nonmembers can be made beginning in early May through the 10th Mountain Division Hut Association. Take the usual precautions, because the trails cover terrain that's prone to avalanche. ☎ *970/925–5775* 🌐 *www.huts.org* 🎫 *From $250 for an entire cabin.*

Aspen Alpine Guides

SKIING/SNOWBOARDING | If you're unfamiliar with the hut system in Aspen or are inexperienced in backcountry travel, you should hire a guide. This is a highly reputable company for guiding services. The cost is from $545 per day. ✉ *Aspen* ☎ *970/925–6618* 🌐 *www.aspenalpine.com.*

10th Mountain Division Hut Association

SKIING/SNOWBOARDING | Named in honor of the U.S. Army's 10th Mountain Division, whose troops trained in the central Colorado mountains, this nonprofit organization maintains nearly three dozen backcountry huts, including a handful that are just a few miles from Aspen. You must be in good shape and have some backcountry skiing experience to reach the huts in winter. There is a fair amount of terrain along tree-lined trails, as well as a good bit of high-alpine ups and downs. Accommodations in the huts, which sleep 6 to 20 people vary, but you can count on mattresses and pillows, wood-burning stoves, and utensils for cooking. ✉ *1280 Ute Ave., Suite 21, Aspen* ☎ *970/925–5775* 🌐 *www.huts.org* 🎫 *From $37 per person per night; full huts from $270.*

DOWNHILL SKIING AND SNOWBOARDING

Aspen is really four ski areas rolled into one resort. Aspen Highlands, Aspen Mountain (Ajax, to locals), Buttermilk, and Snowmass can all be skied with the same ticket. Three are clustered close to downtown Aspen, but Snowmass is down the valley in Snowmass Village. A free shuttle system connects the four.

★ **Aspen Highlands**

SKIING/SNOWBOARDING | Locals' favorite Aspen Highlands is essentially one long ridge with trails dropping off either side, with thrilling descents at Golden Horn and Olympic Bowl and hike-in runs at Highland Bowl. The steep and often bumpy cluster of trails around Steeplechase and Highland Bowl makes this mountain one of the best places to be on a good-powder day. Aspen Highlands has a wide-open bowl called Thunder Bowl that's popular with intermediate skiers, as well as plenty of lower-mountain blue runs. The best overall downhill run is Highland Bowl. Besides the comparatively short lift lines and some heart-pounding runs, a highlight of Aspen Highlands is your first trip to the 12,392-foot summit. The view, which includes the Maroon Bells and Pyramid Peak, is the area's most dramatic and one of the best in the country. **Facilities:** 117 trails; 1,040 acres; 3,635-foot vertical drop; 5 lifts. ✉ *Maroon Creek Rd., Aspen* ☎ *970/925–1220, 800/525–6200* 🌐 *www.aspensnowmass.com* 🎫 *Lift ticket $179.*

Aspen Mountain

SKIING/SNOWBOARDING | Open since 1946, Aspen Mountain is a dream destination for mogul and steep skiers. Bell Mountain provides some of the best bump skiing anywhere, followed by Walsh's (also a favorite for snowboarders), Hyrup's, and Kristi's. Those wanting long cruisers head to the ridges or valleys: Ruthie's Run and International are the classics. There are no novice-level runs here: this is a resort where nearly half the trails are rated advanced or expert, and a black-diamond trail here might rank as a double black diamond elsewhere. The narrow ski area is laid out on a series of steep, unforgiving ridges with little room for error. Most skiers spend much of the morning on intermediate trails off the upper-mountain quad. Then they head for lunch on the deck of Bonnie's, the popular mid-mountain restaurant. After a big storm, there's snowcat skiing on the back side of the mountain. Many trails funnel into Spar Gulch, so it can be quite crowded late in the day. For an alternate route, head down the west side of the mountain below the Ruthie's chair, and take the road back to the main base area. **Facilities:** 76 trails; 675 acres; 3,267-foot vertical drop; 8 lifts. ✉ *E. Durant Ave., Aspen* ☎ *970/925–1220, 800/525–6200* 🌐 *www.aspensnowmass.com* 🎫 *Lift ticket $179.*

★ Buttermilk

SKIING/SNOWBOARDING | **FAMILY** | If you're looking for an escape from the hustle and bustle of Aspen, spend a day at Buttermilk—a family-friendly place where it's virtually impossible to get into trouble. Buttermilk is terrific for novices, intermediates, and freestylers, thanks to the superpipe and Buttermilk Park (which has more than 100 features). A low-key, lighthearted sort of place, it's an antidote to the kind of hotdogging you might encounter at Aspen Mountain. Red's Rover on West Buttermilk is a mellow long run for beginners, while Racer's Edge appeals to speed demons. Among the featured attractions is a hangout for children named The Hideout. The Tiehack section to the east, with sweeping views of Maroon Creek valley, has several advanced runs (though nothing truly expert). It also has superb powder, and the deep snow sticks around longer because many serious skiers overlook this mountain. Buttermilk's allure hasn't been lost on pros, however: it's the longtime host of the Winter X Games. **Facilities:** 44 trails; 470 acres; 2,030-foot vertical drop; 5 lifts. ✉ *W. Buttermilk Rd., Aspen* ☎ *970/925–1220, 800/525–6200* 🌐 *www.aspensnowmass.com* 🎫 *Lift ticket $179.*

LESSONS AND PROGRAMS

Aspen Mountain Powder Tours

SKIING/SNOWBOARDING | This company provides access to 1,100 acres (or up to 12 untracked runs) on the back side of Aspen Mountain via a 12-person snowcat. Most of the backcountry terrain can be handled by confident intermediates, with about 10,000 vertical feet constituting a typical day's skiing. Reservations are required and should be made as early as possible beginning October 1. Full-day trips include a hearty lunch served in a cabin with a woodstove, snacks, wine, chair massages, two guides, and all the skiing you want. ✉ *Aspen* ☎ *970/920–0720* 🌐 *www.aspensnowmass.com* 🎫 *From $600.*

Aspen Skiing Company

SKIING/SNOWBOARDING | Aspen Skiing Company gives lessons at all four mountains. Full-day adult group lessons start at $248 for advance purchase; a private full-day lesson for up to five other people is another option. Beginner's Magic is a package for first-time adult skiers and snowboarders that includes a full-day lesson, lift ticket, and gear rental. Aspen Skiing Company also offers women-only clinics, children's lessons, and freestyle camps just for teens; check availability in advance. ✉ *Aspen* ☎ *970/925–1220, 800/525–6200* 🌐 *www.aspensnowmass.com* 🎫 *From $248.*

RENTALS

Numerous ski shops in Aspen rent equipment. Ski and snowboard rental packages start at around $60 per day and rise to $75 or more for the latest and greatest equipment. Reserve your gear online before you arrive in town to save 10%–20%. For convenience, consider ski-rental delivery to your hotel or condo.

Aspen Sports

SKIING/SNOWBOARDING | This sporting-goods store has a huge inventory of winter gear to choose from. There are three locations in Aspen and three in Snowmass. ✉ *408 E. Cooper Ave., Aspen* ☎ *970/925–6331* 🌐 *www.aspensports.com.*

Black Tie Ski Rentals

SKIING/SNOWBOARDING | Reserve your ski or snowboard package online or over the phone, and Black Tie Ski Rentals will deliver your gear directly to your condominium or hotel room. ✉ *Aspen* ☎ *970/925–8544, 800/925–8544* 🌐 *www.blacktieskis.com.*

Four Mountain Sports

SKIING/SNOWBOARDING | Owned by Aspen Skiing Company, Four Mountain Sports has an impressive inventory of ski and snowboard rental equipment and an equally impressive fleet of stores; there are nine locations, including one at the base of all four mountains. ✉ *520 E. Durant Ave., Aspen* ☎ *970/920–2337* 🌐 *www.aspensnowmass.com.*

FISHING

★ Aspen Outfitting Company

FISHING | Friendly, expert guides lead rafting, horseback riding, and clay-target shooting adventures, but Aspen Outfitting Company, located inside the St. Regis Aspen, is best known for fly-fishing excursions that provide access to miles of private land just outside of town. Trips include boots and waders, but fish are not guaranteed—they call it fishing, not catching, after all. ✉ *315 E. Dean St., Aspen* ☎ *970/925–3406* 🌐 *aspenoutfitting.com* 🎫 *Fly-fishing trips from $325.*

Aspen Trout Guides

FISHING | This company, which is in the Hamilton Sports Shop, runs guided fly-fishing tours of local waterways in Aspen. Half-day trips start at $250. ✉ *520 E. Durant Ave., Aspen* ☎ *970/379–7963* 🌐 *aspentroutguides.com.*

Roaring Fork River

FISHING | Fast, deep, and uninterrupted by dams from its headwaters to its junction with the Colorado, the Roaring Fork River is one of the last free-flowing rivers in the state. The healthy populations of rainbow and brown trout—of the hefty, 12- to 18-inch variety—make the Roaring Fork a favorite with anglers. From the headwaters at Independence Pass to within 3 miles of Aspen, most of the river access is on public lands and is best fished in summer and early fall. Downstream from Aspen, the river crosses through a checkerboard pattern of private and public land; it's fishable year-round. 🌐 *cpw.state.co.us/thingstodo/Pages/Fishing.aspx.*

GOLF

Aspen Golf Club

GOLF | Water is featured on nearly every hole at this 18-hole championship course with long greens and views of the Rocky Mountains. Designed by Frank Hummel, Aspen Golf Club is a challenging, parkland-style, municipal course only 2 miles from downtown. The course has a pro shop and a full-service restaurant and bar. It closes December through March and April, depending on the weather. ✉ *39551 Hwy. 82, Aspen* ☎ *970/429–1949* 🌐 *www.aspengolf.com* 🎫 *$68–$104 for 9 holes; $69–$170 for 18 holes* ⛳ *18 holes, 7114 yards, par 71.*

HORSEBACK RIDING

Maroon Bells Guide & Outfitters

HORSEBACK RIDING | For day or overnight horseback tours into the spectacular Maroon Bells, try Maroon Bells Guide & Outfitters. Two-hour dinner rides (from

$195) culminate with steak or lobster prepared over a campfire. ✉ *3133 Maroon Creek Rd., Aspen* ☎ *970/920–4677* 🌐 *www.maroonbellsaspen.com.*

KAYAKING

Aspen Kayak & SUP Academy

KAYAKING | Longtime Aspen paddler Charlie MacArthur runs the Aspen Kayak & SUP Academy, where you can learn to roll and drop in on a wave in a kayak. You can also sample stand-up paddling. Group clinics start at $105, and private lessons are $365. ✉ *315 Oak Ln., Aspen* ☎ *970/618–2295* 🌐 *www.aspenkayakacademy.com.*

MOUNTAIN BIKING

Aspen Sports

BICYCLING | This store has a wide selection of rental bikes, as well as trail-a-bikes and trailers for kids. ✉ *408 E. Cooper Ave., Aspen* ☎ *877/945–7386* 🌐 *www.aspensports.com.*

Hub of Aspen

BICYCLING | Here you can rent high-performance mountain and road bikes and get tips on the best rides in the valley from the passionate local staffers. ✉ *616 E. Hyman Ave., Aspen* ☎ *970/925–7970* 🌐 *www.hubofaspen.com.*

RAFTING

Blazing Adventures

WHITE-WATER RAFTING | For the truly adventurous, Blazing Adventures runs mild to wild rafting excursions (prices start at $103) on the Roaring Fork, Colorado, and Arkansas rivers. This outfitter also offers hiking, biking, and Jeep tours. ✉ *555 E. Durant Ave., Aspen* ☎ *970/923–4544, 800/282–7238* 🌐 *www.blazingadventures.com.*

TRACK SKIING

Ashcroft Ski Touring

SKIING/SNOWBOARDING | About 12 miles from Aspen, Ashcroft Ski Touring is sequestered in the high-alpine Castle Creek Valley. The 21 miles of groomed trails are surrounded by the high peaks of the Maroon Bells–Snowmass Wilderness, and a novice section passes by the old ghost town of Ashcroft. Rental gear and guided tours are available. ✉ *11399 Castle Creek Rd., Aspen* ☎ *970/925–1044* 🌐 *www.pinecreekcookhouse.com/ashcroft-adventures.*

Aspen Cross-Country Center

SKIING/SNOWBOARDING | Lessons and rentals for track skiing are offered at the center, which acts as a hub for nearly 60 miles of trails maintained by the Aspen/Snowmass Nordic Council. Subsidized by local taxes, the trails are free, making this one of the largest free, groomed, Nordic-trail systems in North America. For a longer ski, try the Owl Creek Trail, connecting the Aspen Cross-Country Center trails with the Snowmass Club trail system. More than 10 miles long, the trail leads through some lovely scenery. Diagonal, skating, and racing setups are available for a fee. ✉ *39551 Hwy. 82, Aspen* ☎ *970/925–2145* 🌐 *www.aspennordic.com/trails/aspen-cross-country-center.*

Snowmass

9 miles northwest of Aspen via Hwy. 82.

One of four ski mountains operated by Aspen Skiing Company, and one of the best intermediate hills in the country, Snowmass Village has more ski-in ski-out lodgings and a slower pace than Aspen. Snowmass was built in 1967 as Aspen's answer to Vail—a ski-specific resort—and although it has never quite matched Vail's panache or popularity, it has gained stature with age, finding its identity as a resort destination with year-round community activities that inject a village feel.

GETTING HERE AND AROUND

Heading east along Highway 82 toward Aspen, you'll spot the turnoffs (Brush Creek and Owl Creek roads) to the Snowmass ski area. Snowmass is best navigated with your own car or the free Village Shuttle system. All parking in Snowmass is free during the summer, but there's usually a fee in the winter season.

WHEN TO GO

Snowmass Village is a year-round resort, though the peak times are June through September for hiking and biking and November through April for skiing.

Sights

Treehouse Kids' Adventure Center

LOCAL SPORTS | **FAMILY** | Interactive, age-appropriate play areas for young children and a full menu of activities for older children and teens make the Treehouse Kids' Adventure Center in the Snowmass Base Village a good headquarters for family fun. Summer camp activities include mountain biking, skateboarding, and mountain boarding. When winter comes, the center serves as an upbeat base camp for ski lessons. *40 Carriage Way, Snowmass Village 970/923–8733 www.aspensnowmass.com/plan-your-stay/kids-programs-child-care.*

Restaurants

New Belgium Ranger Station

$ | **AMERICAN** | It's best to arrive when this place opens for lunch on sunny winter days, since the light-wood tables at this tiny, casual, slope-side restaurant fill up fast with hungry skiers. Patrons squeeze in for soft pretzel rolls with dipping sauces, sandwiches, and snacks, as well as the several beers on tap from Fort Collins–based New Belgium Brewing. **Known for:** Colorado-brewed beer; beer-and-cheese fondue sauce and hazelnut cocoa spread; chili nachos. *Average main: $10 100 Elbert Ln., M-115, Snowmass Village 970/236–6277 www.rangerstation.org No credit cards.*

★ TORO Kitchen & Lounge

$$$$ | **LATIN AMERICAN** | Inside the Viceroy Snowmass hotel, TORO warms up the night after a day of skiing with its craft cocktails, Latin American cuisine, and dining room decorated with wood accents and a fireplace with nearby couches that are the perfect spots for sipping drinks. This spacious restaurant has a daring menu focusing on creative seafood and chops; spicy, smoky flavors pop in many dishes, with milder options for those who can't take the heat. **Known for:** grilled Spanish octopus; chipotle-miso Alaskan black cod; spectacular views of Snowmass. *Average main: $36 Viceroy Snowmass, 130 Wood Rd., Snowmass Village 970/923–8008 www.viceroyhotelsandresorts.com/en/snowmass/dining_and_nightlife/toro.*

Hotels

Stonebridge Inn

$$$ | **HOTEL** | Slightly removed from the busy Snowmass Village Mall, this hotel has a lobby and bar that are streamlined and elegant—with mood lighting, art that reflects the region's ski history, and rustic lodge furniture—as well as contemporary mountain-style rooms that have rough-hewn paneling, rustic wooden furnishings, and stone-colored fabrics. **Pros:** quiet location; good on-site restaurant; bus stop outside. **Cons:** not ski-in ski-out; minimal service; small fitness center. *Rooms from: $295 300 Carriage Way, Snowmass Village 970/923–2420, 866/939–2471 www.destinationhotels.com/stonebridge-inn 90 rooms No meals.*

★ Viceroy Snowmass

$$$$ | **HOTEL** | Perched like a palace atop the hill at the base of the slopes and overlooking the Roaring Fork Valley, the Viceroy Snowmass is the undisputed king of the village in terms of luxury, service, and location. **Pros:** ski-in ski-out; stellar spa; ski valet. **Cons:** a short walk or gondola ride to the main village; small gym; often busy with visitors to the spa and restaurant. *Rooms from: $599 130 Wood Rd., Snowmass Village 970/923–8000, 888/235–7577 www.viceroyhotelsandresorts.com/snowmass 168 rooms No meals.*

Snowmass offers great skiing and one of the most comprehensive snowboarding programs in the country.

The Westin Snowmass Resort

$$$ | **HOTEL** | **FAMILY** | The modern, airy Westin has the best location in Snowmass, right on top of Fanny Hill. **Pros:** ski-in ski-out; on-site gourmet restaurant; big, year-round outdoor pool area. **Cons:** no-frills spa; outdoor furniture worn and dated; small balconies. *Rooms from: $299* *100 Elbert Ln., Snowmass Village* *970/923–8200* *www.westinsnowmass.com* *254 rooms* *No meals.*

Shopping

Anderson Ranch Arts Center

ART GALLERIES | Pottery, jewelry, and art supplies are sold at ArtWorks, the museum-style gift shop at the Anderson Ranch Arts Center. The center also hosts visiting artists, summer workshops, and art sales. The on-site Cafe Konbini serves grab-and-go noodle bowls and specialty teas inspired by the offerings at Japanese convenience stores. *5263 Owl Creek Rd., Snowmass Village* *970/923–3181* *www.andersonranch.org.*

Activities

DOWNHILL SKIING AND SNOWBOARDING

★ **Snowmass**

SKIING/SNOWBOARDING | This sprawling ski area is the biggest of the four Aspen-area mountains (Aspen Highlands, Aspen Mountain, Buttermilk, and Snowmass), all of which are connected by a free shuttle system and can be skied with the same ticket. Snowmass includes shops and restaurants, the Elk Camp Gondola, and The Lost Forest activity center. There are six major chairlifts: Elk Camp, High Alpine–Alpine Springs, Big Burn, Sam's Knob, Two Creeks, and Campground. Except for the last two, all these sectors funnel into the pedestrian mall at the base. Snowmass is probably best known for Big Burn, itself a great sprawl of wide-open, intermediate skiing. Experts head to such areas as Hanging Valley Wall and the Cirque for the best turns. For powder stashes among the trees, head to the glades on Burnt Mountain (to the east of Longshot), Hanging Valley, Sneaky's, and Powerline.

At Snowmass nearly 50% of the skiable acres are designated for intermediate-level skiers. The novice and beginning-intermediate terrain on the lower part of the mountain makes it a terrific place for younger children.

Snowmass is four times the size of Aspen Mountain and has triple the black- and double-black-diamond terrain, including several fearsomely precipitous gullies at Hanging Valley. Although only 30% of the terrain is rated expert, this huge mountain has enough difficult runs, including the challenging Powderhorn and the more relaxed Sneaky's Run, to satisfy skilled skiers.

This mountain has one of the most comprehensive snowboarding programs in the country, with the heart of the action in the Headwall Cirque. The terrain map points out the snowboard-friendly trails and terrain parks while steering riders away from flat spots. You'll want to visit Snowmass Park's halfpipe in the Coney Glade area, also known as Makaha Park. **Facilities:** 98 trails; 3,339 acres; 4,406-foot vertical drop; 23 lifts. ✉ *West of Aspen via Brush Creek Rd. or Owl Creek Rd., Snowmass Village* ☎ *970/925–1220, 800/525–6200* 🌐 *www.aspensnowmass.com* 🎫 *Lift ticket $179.*

LESSONS AND PROGRAMS

Aspen Skiing Company

SKIING/SNOWBOARDING | The company runs a top-notch Ski & Snowboard School at Snowmass and Aspen's other mountains. ✉ *Lower Snowmass Village Mall, Snowmass Village* ☎ *970/925–1220, 800/525–6200* 🌐 *www.aspensnowmass.com.*

RENTALS

Numerous ski shops in Snowmass rent equipment. Ski and snowboard rental packages start at around $60 per day and rise to $75 or more for the latest and greatest equipment. Reserve your package online before you arrive in town to save 10%–20%. For convenience, consider ski-rental delivery to your hotel or condo.

Aspen Sports Westin

SKIING/SNOWBOARDING | This sporting-goods store is one of the best-known ski outfitters in Snowmass with three locations in the village, including one inside the Westin Snowmass Resort adjacent to the slopes of Fanny Hill. ✉ *100 Elbert La., Unit M1153, Snowmass Village* ☎ *970/923–6111* 🌐 *www.aspensports.com.*

Four Mountain Sports

SKIING/SNOWBOARDING | Owned by the Aspen Skiing Company, Four Mountain Sports has an impressive rental inventory of premium skis and snowboards and five locations in Snowmass village. ✉ *Snowmass Village Mall, 45 Village Sq., Snowmass Village* ☎ *970/920–2337* 🌐 *www.aspensnowmass.com.*

Incline Ski & Board Shop

SKIING/SNOWBOARDING | Locally owned and operated, Incline Ski & Board Shop is steps from the shuttle-bus stop. Staffers here know the mountains well and offer personalized recommendations based on snowfall and experience. ✉ *1 Village Mall, Snowmass Village* ☎ *800/314–3355* 🌐 *www.inclineski.com.*

MOUNTAIN BIKING

Four Mountain Sports

BICYCLING | Cruiser, street, mountain, downhill, and electric bikes are available along with trail maps and lift tickets so you won't have to ride uphill. For a small fee, you can opt for a one-way journey by dropping your equipment at one of the shop's four valley locations, Woody Creek Tavern, or Tipsy Trout. ✉ *61 Wood Rd., Snowmass Village* ☎ *970/923–0430* 🌐 *www.aspensnowmass.com.*

TRACK SKIING

Aspen Snowmass Nordic Trail System

SKIING/SNOWBOARDING | The Aspen Nordic Council maintains more than 60 miles of trails in the Roaring Fork Valley. Probably the most varied, in terms of scenery and terrain, is Trail 60 at the Snowmass Golf Course. For a longer ski, try the Owl Creek Trail, connecting the Snowmass Village trail system and the Aspen Cross-Country Center trails. More than 8 miles long, the trail provides both a good workout and a dose of woodsy beauty, with many ups and downs across meadows and aspen-gladed hillsides. You can take the bus back to Snowmass Village when you're finished. ✉ *Snowmass Village* ☎ *970/429–2039* 🌐 *www.aspennordic.com.*

Vail

100 miles west of Denver via I–70.

Consistently ranked as one of North America's leading ski destinations, Vail has a reputation few can match. The four-letter word means Valhalla for skiers of all skill levels. Vail has plenty of open areas where novices can learn the ropes. It can also be an ego-building mountain for intermediate and advanced skiers who hit the slopes only a week or two a season. Some areas, like Blue Sky Basin, can make you feel like a pro.

Although Vail is a long, thin town spread for several miles along the Eagle River and comprising East Vail, Vail Village, Lionshead in the center, and West Vail, the hub of activity in winter and summer revolves around Vail Village as well as the recently redone Lionshead, which has shops, restaurants, a heated gondola, and even a glockenspiel tower. Vail Village is also a hub of retail and dining with direct lift access to the mountain.

With the blooming of summer columbines come the culture crowds for music and culinary festivals. While the valley teems with visitors, hikers and mountain bikers stream up the steep slopes on foot and via the Eagle Bahn Gondola to head into the network of trails that web the seemingly endless backcountry.

GETTING HERE AND AROUND

The best way to get to the Vail Valley is with a rental car. Once in the valley, a free shuttle makes it easy to get around town, and inexpensive bus service runs between Vail and Beaver Creek.

TOURS

Nova Guides

ADVENTURE TOURS | Vail's Nova Guides runs Jeep and all-terrain-vehicle tours, as well as fishing and snowmobiling expeditions. ✉ *7088 U.S. 24, Vail* ☎ *719/486–2656* 🌐 *www.novaguides.com.*

Timberline Tours

ADVENTURE TOURS | One of the oldest outfitters in the state, Timberline offers guided Jeep and rafting excursions in Vail Valley for every experience and adrenaline level. ✉ *1432 Chambers Ave., Eagle* ☎ *970/476–1414* 🌐 *www.timberlinetours.com.*

VISITOR INFORMATION

VISITOR INFORMATION Vail Snow Report. ☎ *970/754–4888* 🌐 *www.snow.com.*

Betty Ford Alpine Gardens

GARDEN | At 8,200 feet above sea level, the Betty Ford Alpine Gardens are the highest botanical gardens in the world. This oasis of columbines, alpine plants, colorful perennials, and wild roses offers stunning views of the Rocky Mountains from meandering pathways that pass beside streams and waterfalls. The gardens are free to the public and open year-round; peak flower season is June through August. Guided tours are available. ✉ *Ford Park, 522 S. Frontage Rd., Vail* ☎ *970/476–0103* 🌐 *www.bettyfordalpinegardens.org* 🎫 *$5 suggested donation.*

Colorado Snowsports Museum and Hall of Fame

MUSEUM | The Colorado Snowsports Museum and Hall of Fame traces the development of skiing and snowboarding throughout the world, with an emphasis

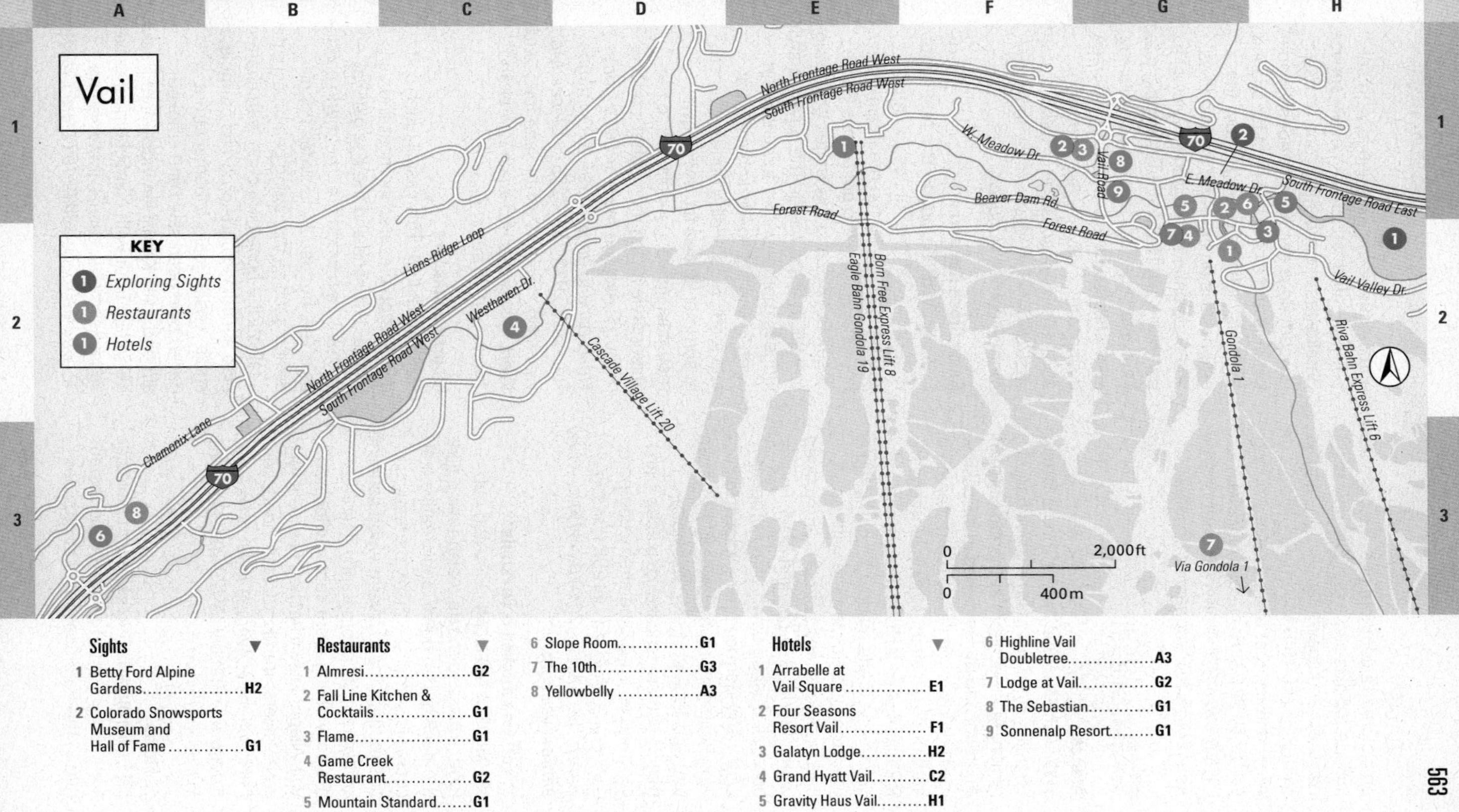

Sights

1 Betty Ford Alpine Gardens H2
2 Colorado Snowsports Museum and Hall of Fame G1

Restaurants

1 Almresi G2
2 Fall Line Kitchen & Cocktails G1
3 Flame G1
4 Game Creek Restaurant G2
5 Mountain Standard G1
6 Slope Room G1
7 The 10th G3
8 Yellowbelly A3

Hotels

1 Arrabelle at Vail Square E1
2 Four Seasons Resort Vail F1
3 Galatyn Lodge H2
4 Grand Hyatt Vail C2
5 Gravity Haus Vail H1
6 Highline Vail Doubletree A3
7 Lodge at Vail G2
8 The Sebastian G1
9 Sonnenalp Resort G1

on Colorado's contributions. Six galleries include old skis and tows, Olympic displays, ski and snowboard history, and an exhibit on the 10th Mountain Division, an Army division that trained nearby during WWII. ✉ *231 S. Frontage Rd. E, Vail* ☎ *970/476–1876* 🌐 *www.snowsportsmuseum.org* *$5 suggested donation.*

Restaurants

Almresi

$$$$ | GERMAN | Run by the Thoma family, originally from Germany's Black Forest region, Almresi offers authentic German, Austrian, and Swiss dishes in a Rockies-meets-Alps rustic dining room, served by staff outfitted charmingly in lederhosen. Popular dishes include the *griebenschmalz* (a bread made with pork), Alpler macaroni (a Swiss favorite with pasta, bacon, onions, and potatoes and topped with cheddar cheese), and Black Forest cake, all washed down with European wines and German beers. **Known for:** cozy wood cabin dining room; hearty German fare and large portions; kaiserschmarr, Austrian pancakelike pieces with caramelized sugar and cherry compote. *Average main: $31* ✉ *298 Hanson Ranch Rd., Vail* ☎ *970/470—4174* 🌐 *www.almresi-vail.com.*

★ Fall Line Kitchen & Cocktails

$$ | MODERN AMERICAN | Elevated pub food, rotisserie meats, Asian-fusion (like the duck ramen bowl), and creative craft cocktails somehow marry perfectly on this modern menu. Warm wood paneling and vibrant ski photography decorate the cozy dining room centrally located in Vail Village. **Known for:** hearty meals for après-skiers; trendy cocktail menu; central location. *Average main: $18* ✉ *232 Bridge St., Vail* ☎ *970/470–4803* 🌐 *www.falllinevail.com.*

★ Flame

$$$$ | AMERICAN | Steaks carved tableside are the highlight of this high-end restaurant in the Four Seasons that provides a luxurious dining experience with surprisingly informal, family-friendly service. Small bites like the spicy tuna tacos or elk corn dogs served with house-made ketchup and aioli are perfect for sharing, which is highly encouraged, but the emphasis is on big here: big windows and a big patio with mountain views; a bar with a big (165-inch) TV; and big bites. **Known for:** aged steaks carved tableside; sophisticated dining room; large terrace dining with a view. *Average main: $65* ✉ *Four Seasons Vail, 1 Vail Rd., Vail* ☎ *970/477–8650* 🌐 *www.flamerestaurantvail.com* *No lunch.*

Game Creek Restaurant

$$$$ | FRENCH | Getting to this restaurant is certainly half the fun, as you must catch a gondola up the mountain, then hop on a snowcat to get across Game Creek Bowl during the winter, or shuttle or walk in the summer. The Bavarian-style lodge is members-only for lunch, but open to the public for dinner all year and for an outstanding Sunday brunch in summer. **Known for:** spectacular mountain views; gondola ride to the chalet-style dining room; chef's tasting menu. *Average main: $109* ✉ *Lion's Head parking garage, 395 S. Frontage Rd., Vail* ☎ *970/754–4275* *Closed Mon. year-round, Sun. in winter, and Tues. and Wed. in summer. No lunch winter and Thurs.–Sat. in summer.*

Mountain Standard

$$$$ | AMERICAN | This casual lunch and dinner stop prepares its meat and fish with a deft hand and the age-old way—over an open wood fire. The menu changes often, but usually includes popular dishes such as the spring pea bruschetta, a fall-off-the-bone pork chop with charred okra succotash and cornbread crumble, and a whole Rocky Mountain trout with grilled pole bean salad and smoked almond milk. **Known for:** wood-fired Rocky Mountain trout with chimichurri; creative, seasonal menu; casual, lively setting. *Average main: $34* ✉ *193 Gore Creek*

Dr., Vail ☎ 970/476–0123 ⊕ www.mtn-standard.com ▭ No credit cards.

Slope Room

$$$$ | **MODERN AMERICAN** | With spacious glass windows, this sleek, sophisticated space in Gravity Haus looks as if it belongs in a big city, with only the fireplace reminding you that this is Vail. The menu puts a modern spin on the classic steak house, featuring food from Rocky Mountain ranchers and farmers. **Known for:** central location in Vail Village; modern dining room; excellent local steaks. [$] *Average main: $36 ✉ Gravity Haus, 352 E. Meadow Dr., Vail ☎ 970/476–6836 ⊕ www.sloperoom.com ⊙ No lunch.*

The 10th

$$$$ | **AMERICAN** | Find respite from the usual mountain fare at this high-end, high-up restaurant at the base of Look Ma run. A favorite lunch spot for skiers, there are spectacular views of the Gore Range, a cozy bar and lounge with fireplace, a south-facing outdoor deck with heated tables, and hearty pasta and popular meat dishes. **Known for:** on-mountain location; luxury amenities like slippers and hair dryers cater to cold skiers; very popular so can be packed. [$] *Average main: $38 ✉ At the base of Look Ma run, Mid-Vail, Vail ☎ 970/754–1010 ⊙ Closed Mon.–Thurs. No dinner.*

Yellowbelly

$ | **AMERICAN** | **FAMILY** | Fried-chicken joints usually require several napkins to mop up the grease and a long workout the next day to make up for the indulgence—not so at Yellowbelly. Order the fried white or fried dark plate—this gluten-free recipe is as tasty as it gets without weighing you down. **Known for:** gluten-free fried chicken; delivery and to-go options; affordable eats. [$] *Average main: $8 ✉ 2161 N. Frontage Rd. W., No. 14, Vail ☎ 970/343–4340 ⊕ www.yellowbellychicken.com.*

Hotels

Arrabelle at Vail Square

$$$$ | **RESORT** | Surrounded by shops, restaurants, and galleries, and just steps away from the Eagle Bahn Gondola (which runs right to the top of Vail Mountain), the Arrabelle is a star in Lionshead Village. **Pros:** ski valet and complimentary GoPros to document your adventures; great location; fabulous on-site spa. **Cons:** the valet parking entrance is hard to find; expensive rates; steep service charges added to most purchases. [$] *Rooms from: $1,000 ✉ 675 Lionshead Pl., Vail ☎ 970/754–7777, 866/662–7625 ⊕ www.arrabelle.rockresorts.com ⇒ 69 rooms, 29 condos ¶ No meals.*

Highline Vail Doubletree

$$$$ | **HOTEL** | **FAMILY** | Located just off I–70 in West Vail, this family-friendly property features large, standard rooms and suites with kitchens and lofts. **Pros:** warm cookies served upon arrival; on-site bar and restaurants; a convenient hub for families. **Cons:** rooms include standard hotel decor; location is 2 miles from skiing and main village; fitness center is crowded with people entering and exiting the pool area. [$] *Rooms from: $516 ✉ 2211 N. Frontage Rd., Vail ☎ 970/476–2739 ⊕ www.highline-vail.com ⇒ 116 rooms ¶ No meals.*

★ **Four Seasons Resort Vail**

$$$$ | **RESORT** | **FAMILY** | Rooms at the Four Seasons are large and attractive, in a contemporary alpine style (with warm hickory-wood and limestone accents); every room has at least one gas-burning fireplace and a balcony. **Pros:** large guest rooms with luxurious bathrooms; dedicated ski concierge located right at the Gondola One chairlift; popular on-site dining. **Cons:** a slight walk from slopes; valet and resort fees not included in room rates; some rooms look onto unappealing buildings or parking structures. [$] *Rooms from: $565 ✉ 1 Vail Rd., Vail ☎ 970/477–8600, 800/819–5053 ⊕ www.fourseasons.com/vail ⇒ 121 rooms ¶ No meals.*

Galatyn Lodge

$$$$ | **RENTAL** | This luxury lodge in a quiet part of Vail Village maintains a low profile, which is just the approach its hard-core skiing regulars prefer. **Pros:** outdoor heated pool; quiet getaway from the lively Vail scene; apartment style lodgings. **Cons:** no children's programs; no restaurant or bar; no fitness center or spa. *Rooms from: $375 365 Vail Valley Dr., Vail 970/479–2418, 800/943–7322 www.thegalatynlodge.com 19 rooms No meals.*

Grand Hyatt Vail

$$$$ | **HOTEL** | With its setting in the quieter west part of town and its dedicated chairlift, the Grand Hyatt Vail suits those more focused on the slopes than the social scene. **Pros:** sleek and polished decor; mountain- and creek-side setting; ski-in ski-out luxury. **Cons:** lobby can be crowded during conferences and events; pricey resort fees and parking; small spa. *Rooms from: $699 1300 Westhaven Dr., Vail 970/476–1234 www.hyatt.com 285 rooms No meals.*

★ **Gravity Haus Vail**

$$$$ | **HOTEL** | This upscale boutique hotel on Gore Creek is perfectly located for outdoor enthusiasts, but its private fireplaces and feather beds, as well as the sprawling spa and fitness center, may tempt guests to spend the entire stay indoors. **Pros:** spacious rooms; great fitness club; easy access to town. **Cons:** no hotel-specific parking but valet available; rooms cannot be booked more than six months out; winter valet fee starts at $60 per day. *Rooms from: $599 352 E. Meadow Dr., Vail 970/476–0700, 888/794–0410 www.gravityhaus.com/locations/vail-haus 20 rooms, 7 condos Free Breakfast.*

Lodge at Vail

$$$$ | **HOTEL** | One of the first hotels to open in Vail, in 1962, the sprawling lodge is popular with skiers and families because of its fabulous location only 150 feet from the village's main lift, the Gondola One. Ski valets ready your skis every morning and collect your gear for drying in the evening. **Pros:** located near main ski lift; popular steak house, Elway's, on-site; great spa. **Cons:** pricey; quality of rooms varies; some rooms are small and outdated. *Rooms from: $669 174 E. Gore Creek Dr., Vail 970/754–7800, 877/528–7625 www.lodgeatvail.rockresorts.com 160 rooms No meals.*

★ **The Sebastian**

$$$$ | **HOTEL** | **FAMILY** | Manhattan chic meets Colorado ski lodge at this boutique hotel where you will find the work of Mexican abstract artist Manuel Felguérez throughout, and the lively Lounge at Leonora with its craft cocktails and street-fare–style bites. **Pros:** great location; attention to detail and top-notch service; family-friendly, with pop-up tents in room, a camp, and playroom. **Cons:** many rooms overlook the freeway; some of the town's higher room rates; on-site amenities can be crowded during ski season. *Rooms from: $995 16 Vail Rd., Vail 970/477–8000, 800/354–6908 www.thesebastianvail.com 107 rooms No meals.*

Sonnenalp Resort

$$$$ | **HOTEL** | It's the sense of family tradition and European elegance that makes the Sonnenalp Resort the most romantic of all hotels in the faux-Tyrolean village of Vail. **Pros:** classic alpine ambience; romantic atmosphere; spa and beautiful indoor-outdoor pool. **Cons:** removed from lifts; wooden beams can make ceilings feel low; some rooms are small. *Rooms from: $699 20 Vail Rd., Vail 970/476–5656, 800/654–8312 www.sonnenalp.com 127 rooms No meals.*

Activities

ADVENTURE PARKS

Adventure Ridge

LOCAL SPORTS | FAMILY | In summer ride the gondola from Lionshead up to Adventure Ridge at Eagle's Nest, the hub of Vail Mountain activities offered through the Epic Discovery park. It's cool and high, and it has the views, especially from the zipline and ropes course. It also has tons of activities like Friday Afternoon Club, live bands, beer, sunset watching, a climbing wall, tubing, an alpine coaster, and scenic hiking and biking trails. Winter activities at Adventure Ridge include snow tubing, kids snowmobiling, and (free) snowshoe tours. ✉ *Atop Front Side of Vail Mountain, Eagle's Nest, Vail* ☎ *970/476–9090* 🌐 *www.vail.com.*

BACKCOUNTRY SKIING

★ Paragon Guides

SKIING/SNOWBOARDING | It's a good idea to hire a guide if you're unfamiliar with the area's backcountry trails. Paragon's capable guides can lead you along 300 different trails on snowshoes and skis, including overnight hut trips. ✉ *210 Edwards Village Blvd., Edwards* ☎ *970/827–5363* 🌐 *www.paragonguides.com.*

★ 10th Mountain Division Hut and Trail System

SKIING/SNOWBOARDING | This famed network is one of Colorado's outdoor gems. Its 34 huts are in the mountains near Camp Hale, where the decorated namesake World War II division trained. Skiers and snowshoers in winter (snowmobiles are not permitted to approach the huts) and hikers and mountain bikers in summer tackle sections of the more than 350 miles of trails linking new and rustic cabins on day trips or weeklong expeditions. Apart from the joy of a self-reliant adventure among rugged mountains, travelers enjoy the camaraderie of communal living (there are very few private rooms in the huts), and evenings spent swapping stories by the glow of a wood-burning stove or the twinkle of summer stars. Hut reservations should be made at least a month in advance. ✉ *Vail* ☎ *970/925–5775 for hut reservations* 🌐 *www.huts.org.*

BIKING

A popular summer destination for both road bikers and mountain bikers, Vail has a variety of paved bike paths (including one that leads up to Vail Pass), plus dozens of miles of dirt mountain-bike trails. You can take bikes on lifts heading uphill, then head downhill on an array of routes.

Vail Bike Tech

BICYCLING | Known as Vail Ski Tech in the winter, this shop rents and repairs bikes the rest of the year. Best of all, they are only steps from the Eagle Bahn Gondola, a summer gateway to the ski-slope trails. They also offer shuttle service to Vail Pass for downhill mountain biking. ✉ *555 E. Lionshead Circle, Vail* ☎ *800/525–5995* 🌐 *www.vailbiketech.com.*

DOWNHILL SKIING AND SNOWBOARDING

★ Vail

SKIING/SNOWBOARDING | Year after year, Vail logs more than a million "skier days" (the ski industry's measure of ticket sales), perpetuating its ranking as one of the most popular resorts in North America. From the top of China Bowl to the base of the Eagle Bahn Gondola at Lionshead, the resort is more than 7 miles across. The vast acreage is roughly divided into three sections: the Front Side, the Back Bowls, and Blue Sky Basin. Snowboarders will find plenty of steeps on the Front Side, and technical challenges at the Golden Peak or Bwana terrain parks, but they should avoid the Back Bowls, where long catwalks can get slow in the afternoon sun.

Vail's Gondola One is one of the fastest 10-passenger gondolas in the world, clocking in at 1,200 feet per minute. The heated gondola with Wi-Fi and cushioned seats replaced the Vista Bahn. From

With its excellent slopes and great restaurants, Vail is one of the most popular ski resorts in the United States.

Mid-Vail, the Mountaintop Express Lift has also been upgraded from a high-speed quad to a high-speed six-passenger chairlift.

Vail is perhaps best known for its legendary **Back Bowls,** more than 3,000 acres of wide-open spaces that are sensational on sunny days. The terrain ranges from wide, groomed swatches for intermediate skiers to seemingly endless bump fields to glades so tight that only an expert boarder can slither between the trees. When there's fresh powder, these bowls beckon skiers intermediate and above.

The **Front Side** of Vail Mountain delivers a markedly different experience. Here there's lots of wide-trail skiing, heavily skewed toward groomed intermediate runs, especially off the Northwood Express, Mountaintop Express, and Avanti Express lifts, as well as the slopes reachable via the Eagle Bahn Gondola. The upper parts of Riva and the top of Look Ma are just a few of the places you'll find skilled skiers. The best show in town is on Highline (you can see it while riding Chair 10), where the experts groove through the moguls and those with a bit less experience careen around the bumps. The other two extremely difficult double-black-diamond trails off this slow lift are the best cruisers on the mountain for skilled skiers.

It takes time (as long as 45 minutes depending on conditions and skier level) to reach **Blue Sky Basin,** made up of three more bowls, but it's worth the effort. Intermediate skiers will find a few open trails with spectacular views of rugged mountain peaks. For advanced and expert skiers, the real fun is playing in glades and terrain with names such as Heavy Metal, Lovers Leap, the Divide, and Champagne Glade. **Facilities:** 195 trails; 5,317 acres; 3,450-foot vertical drop; 31 lifts. ✉ *Vail* ☎ *970/476–5601* 🌐 *www.vail.com* 🎫 *Lift ticket $199.*

LESSONS AND PROGRAMS

Vail Ski & Snowboard School

SKIING/SNOWBOARDING | **FAMILY** | This respected operation runs classes, workshops, and clinics for skiers of all levels. Beginners can take three-day courses that include equipment rental and lift passes. Workshops for women, teen sessions, and telemark courses are among the programs targeting specific groups. Family lessons keep your group together and provide individualized instruction. ✉ *250 Vail Rd., Vail* ☎ *970/754–8245* 🌐 *www.vail.com* 🎫 *From $210* ⏲ *Closed in summer.*

RENTALS

Vail Sports

SKIING/SNOWBOARDING | Within steps of the lifts and with 13 locations along the mountainside in Vail Village and Lionshead, this shop rents a wide range of ski gear, including high-end equipment. Prices for skis start at $57. Book online for discounts. ✉ *151 Vail La., Vail* ☎ *970/477–5740* 🌐 *www.vailsports.com.*

FISHING

★ Minturn Anglers

FISHING | **FAMILY** | Minturn Anglers offers excellent guided fly-fishing, combo horseback and fly-fishing outings, float trips, and cast-and-taste trips (a fly-fishing outing followed by a catered outdoor dining experience) for all experience levels in various locations throughout the Vail Valley. Experienced instructors share their passion for fly-fishing and love of the outdoors (especially fun for novices or families looking for a unique day trip), and the store rents and sells a wide array of gear and bait. ✉ *106 N. Main St., Minturn* ☎ *970/827–9500* 🌐 *www.minturnanglers.com.*

GOLF

Golfers who love to play mountain courses know that some of the best are in Vail Valley. These courses meander through the valleys dividing the area's soaring peaks. The region is home to more than a dozen courses, and there are another half dozen within easy driving distance. It's all just a matter of where you're staying and how much you want to spend. Some courses are only open to members and to guests at certain lodges.

Know Your Snow

Vail is known for its "powder": slopes puffed with light, fluffy flakes that make you feel that you are gliding on silk. Ungroomed runs, however, can quickly turn to "crud" as they get "tracked out" (scarred with deep tracks). That's when it's time to hunt up the "corduroy"—freshly groomed runs.

Vail Golf Club

GOLF | The area's municipal course is situated in the White River National Forest with views of the Gore mountains. ✉ *1775 Sunburst Dr., Vail* ☎ *970/479–2260* 🌐 *www.vailclubhouse.com* 🎫 *$105; $75 for 9 holes* ⛳ *18 holes, 6281 yards, par 71* ✍ *Reservations essential.*

HIKING

★ Booth Lake

HIKING/WALKING | This is one of Vail's most popular hikes, so get on the trail early or pick a weekday during the summer high season. It's a sustained 4-mile one-way climb with more than 3,000 feet in elevation gain to Booth Lake at 11,500 feet, right above the tree line. Fit hikers can do this in about seven hours. En route, you can cool off at the 60-foot waterfall; at only 2 miles in, this is also a great spot to turn around if you're seeking an easier hike. The reward for pushing on is a nice view of Booth Lake cradled among the alpine tundra. ✉ *Trailhead: Take Exit 180 from I–70 to end of Booth Falls Rd., Vail.*

Eagle's Loop

HIKING/WALKING | **FAMILY** | This trail starts from atop the Eagle Bahn Gondola at 10,350 feet, but it's a mellow, 1-mile stroll along the mountaintop ridge with panoramic views of the Mount of the

Holy Cross. Allow about half an hour. A one-day lift ticket for the 14-minute gondola ride is $39 for adults. Adventurous types may prefer to skip the gondola (and the fee) and hike the intermediate, often steep, 4½-mile trail through aspen trees and wildflowers to the beginning of the Eagle Loop trail. ✉ *Trailhead: Top of Eagle Bahn Gondola, Vail.*

OUTFITTERS AND EXPEDITIONS

★ Paragon Guides

HIKING/WALKING | In summer, hiking with llamas is a highlight of this backcountry adventure company's offerings. Llamas carry food, wine, and water on lunch hikes or wine and cheese excursions, and help with overnight packs on hut trips. Paragon Guides also offer rock climbing, mountain biking, and fly-fishing trips in and around Vail Valley. ✉ *210 Edwards Village Blvd., Edwards* ☎ *970/926–5299* 🌐 *www.paragonguides.com.*

Frisco

9 miles north of Breckenridge via Hwy. 9.

Keep going past the hodgepodge of strip malls near the interstate and you'll find that low-key Frisco has a downtown district trimmed with restored B&Bs. The town is removed from the ski lifts, but is a low-cost lodging alternative to pricier resorts in the surrounding communities.

GETTING HERE AND AROUND

Private car is the best way to arrive in Frisco, but the town is compact enough for walking or biking.

Sights

Historic Park & Museum

MUSEUM VILLAGE | **FAMILY** | This sprawling museum re-creates Frisco's boom days. Stroll through 11 buildings dating from the 1880s, including a fully outfitted one-room schoolhouse, a trapper's cabin with snowshoes and pelts, the town's original log chapel, and a jail with an exhibit on mining. ✉ *120 Main St., Frisco* ☎ *970/668–3428* 🌐 *www.townoffrisco.com* 🎟 *Free.*

Restaurants

Butterhorn Bakery & Café

$ | **AMERICAN** | There's usually a wait at this popular breakfast and lunch spot, where meals are cheap, portions are large, and the coffee is perfect. Snag a seat on the patio on weekends when the restaurant can get packed and loud. **Known for:** eggy bread; homemade cakes and baked goods to go; lively spot. $ *Average main: $10* ✉ *408 Main St., Frisco* ☎ *970/668–3997* 🌐 *www.butterhornbakery.com* ⏲ *No dinner.*

Hotels

Frisco Lodge

$$ | **B&B/INN** | This 1885 stagecoach stop has morphed into a European-style boutique hotel complete with a chalet facade and a garden courtyard. **Pros:** great location on Main Street; outdoor hot tub and fireplace; courtyard garden. **Cons:** street noise audible; thin walls; some rooms have shared baths. $ *Rooms from: $159* ✉ *321 Main St., Frisco* ☎ *800/279–6000* 🌐 *www.friscolodge.com* 🛏 *18 rooms* 🍴 *Free Breakfast.*

Hotel Frisco

$$ | **B&B/INN** | This Main Street hostelry is a great home base for skiers wanting to hit Breckenridge, Copper, Keystone, and Arapahoe Basin. **Pros:** centrally located; quaint, charming decor; friendly staff. **Cons:** small bathrooms; no elevator; fees for parking. $ *Rooms from: $169* ✉ *308 Main St., Frisco* ☎ *970/668–5009* 🌐 *www.hotelfrisco.com* 🛏 *20 rooms* 🍴 *No meals.*

Activities

FISHING

Trouts Fly Fishing

FISHING | Float, wade, or shore fish the Colorado or Arkansas River on guided fly-fishing trips on private and public lands with this outfitter. If you're lucky, you may catch 10- to 20-inch rainbow and brown trout. ✉ *309 B Main St., Frisco* ☎ *888/453–9171, 970/668–2583* 🌐 *www.troutsflyfishing.com.*

Dillon

73 miles west of Denver via I–70.

Dillon can't seem to sit still. Founded in 1883 as a stagecoach stop and trading post for men working in the mines, Dillon has had to pack up and move three times since. It was first relocated to be closer to the Utah and Northern Railroad, and then to take advantage of the nearby rivers. Finally, in 1955, bigwigs in Denver drew up plans to dam the Blue River so they could quench the capital's growing thirst. The reservoir would submerge Dillon under more than 150 feet of water. Once again the town was dismantled and moved, this time to pine-blanketed hills mirrored in sapphire water. Residents agreed that no building in the new location would be taller than 30 feet, so as not to obstruct the view of the reservoir, which is appropriately called Lake Dillon.

Dillon now blends with neighboring Silverthorne, where dozens of factory outlets are frequented by locals and travelers vying for bargains. Combined, the two towns have hotels, restaurants, and stores galore.

GETTING HERE AND AROUND

Private car is the best way to explore Dillon, although in summer a network of bicycle trails around the reservoir makes pedaling an attractive option.

VISITOR INFORMATION

CONTACTS Summit Chamber of Commerce. ☎ *970/668–2051* 🌐 *www.summitchamber.org.*

WHEN TO GO

Dillon is a hub for all seasons. In winter, during ski season, Dillon is the place to get gas, groceries, and directions before heading to Keystone, Arapahoe Basin, Breckenridge, or Copper. Beginning with the snowmelt in May, Dillon unfolds as a center for hiking, biking, and water sports. Dillon also is home to Summit County's largest farmers' market every Friday in warmer weather.

Sights

★ Lake Dillon

BODY OF WATER | Resting in the heart of Summit County at 9,017 feet is the Front Range's answer to a day at the beach—beautiful Lake Dillon and her two ports, Dillon, just off I–70 on the south, and Frisco, off I–70 and Highway 9 on the west. The lake is actually backed up by a 231-foot earth-filled dam that fills the valley where Dillon once sat. During the frequent Western droughts, when water levels can drop dramatically, collectors wander along the exposed shores hunting for artifacts from this Rocky Mountain Atlantis. Below the mile-long dam the Blue River babbles past the outlet shopping haven and turns into miles of gold-medal fly-fishing waters on its journey north. There are more than 27 miles of gravel beaches, marshes, peninsulas, and wooded islets for picnickers to enjoy, many accessible from a 7½-mile paved trail along the northern shores, or from the informal dirt paths elsewhere. Gaze out at the deep blue waters from **Sapphire Point Lookout** (a short ½-mile hike on the south side of the lake) any nice day, and you'll see a flotilla of motorboats, sailboats, canoes, kayaks, and sailboarders dancing in the waves. In winter the frozen waters are enjoyed by ice anglers and cross-country skiers. Because the

While swimming in Lake Dillon is not permitted, boating, canoeing, and kayaking are allowed.

lake is a drinking-water source, swimming is not permitted, and the lake is patrolled vigorously by Summit County sheriffs. ✉ *Dillon.*

Restaurants

★ Dillon Dam Brewery

$$ | **AMERICAN** | At this popular brewery, one of the largest brewpubs in the Rockies, you can belly up to the horseshoe-shaped bar and sample ales and lagers while you munch on burgers, sandwiches, or pub grub. The menu is steps above average bar food with plenty of vegetarian and gluten-free options. **Known for:** house-brewed beers; customizable, piled-high nachos (make sure to top with pork green chile); large, two-story dining room anchored by the bar. *$ Average main: $16 ✉ 100 Little Dam St., Dillon ☎ 970/262–7777 🌐 www.dambrewery.com.*

Red Mountain Grill

$$ | **SOUTHWESTERN** | **FAMILY** | The colorful decor of this American Southwest joint is something you'll remember. High-backed chairs ring the tables, stone buttresses arch toward vaulted ceilings, and mobiles of round- and star-shaped metal lights dangle above. **Known for:** outdoor patio with funky decor; bistro burger with blue cheese mousse, fig jam, bacon, and port wine reduction; secret southwestern flair in most dishes. *$ Average main: $15 ✉ 703 E. Anemone Trail, Dillon ☎ 970/468–1010 🌐 www.redmountaingrill.com.*

Activities

BIKING

Summit County attracts cyclists with its 55 miles of paved bike paths and extensive network of backcountry trails. There are dozens of trailheads from which you can travel through gentle rolling terrain, up the sides of mountains, and along ridges for spectacular views. Starting in Dillon, you could bike around the reservoir to Frisco. From there you could ride the Blue River Pathway, largely along the river, to Breckenridge. Or you could ride through beautiful Tenmile Canyon all the way to Copper Mountain. If you're really fit, you could even continue your ride over Vail Pass and down into Vail Village.

BOATING

Boats rented from the Frisco Bay and Dillon marinas are not permitted to beach; the aluminum pontoons are easily damaged on the rock and gravel shores.

Dillon Marina

BOATING | At Dillon Marina you can rent a kayak, stand-up paddleboard, sailboat, pontoon boat, or runabout to play on the water, or take sailing lessons at the on-site school. Reserve ahead in high season. ✉ *Take I–70 Exit 205 to U.S. 6, and follow signs to the marina, 150 Marina Dr., Dillon* ☎ *970/468–5100* 🌐 *www.townofdillon.com/marina.*

Frisco Bay Marina

BOATING | **FAMILY** | This marina is less crowded than Dillon and has quick access to the numerous pine-cloaked islands along the western shores. Here you can rent pontoon boats, fishing boats, canoes, and kayaks. ✉ *267 Marina Rd., Frisco* ☎ *970/668–4334* 🌐 *www.townoffrisco.com/things-to-do/frisco-bay-marina.*

FISHING

Cutthroat Anglers

FISHING | A favorite with locals, Cutthroat Anglers has a pro shop chock-full of gear for avid fly-fishermen. Their wade trips are good for beginners; full-day float-trip adventures are a favorite for those with a bit more experience. The wade trip is available in half-day and full-day versions. ✉ *400 Blue River Pkwy., Silverthorne* ☎ *970/262–2878* 🌐 *www.fishcolorado.com.*

GOLF

Raven Golf Club at Three Peaks

GOLF | A technically challenging layout and rich, natural beauty, including stands of pine and aspen trees and visiting elk and deer herds, make this one of the state's best mountain courses. All 18 holes have dramatic views of the Gore Mountain range. ✉ *2929 Golden Eagle Rd., Silverthorne* ☎ *970/262–3636* 🌐 *www.ravenatthreepeaks.com* 🎫 *$169* ⛳ *18 holes, 6386 yards, par 72.*

Keystone

8 miles southeast of Dillon via U.S. 6; 69 miles west of Denver.

One of the region's most laid-back destinations, Keystone is understandably popular with families and, as the state's largest night skiing operation (with lifts running until 8 pm), has long been a local favorite. Its trails are spread across three adjoining peaks: Dercum Mountain, North Peak, and the Outback. Through the years, as the resort added more runs, it morphed from a beginner's paradise on Keystone Mountain to an early-season training stop for the national ski teams that practice on the tougher and bumpier terrain on North Peak. Keystone also has full-day guided snowcat tours. Today it's a resort for all types of skiers and riders, whether they prefer gentle slopes, cruising, or high-adrenaline challenges on the Outback's steep bowls.

The planners were sensitive to the environment, favoring colors and materials that blend inconspicuously with the natural surroundings. Lodging, shops, and restaurants are in Lakeside Village, the older part of the resort, and in River Run, a newer area at the base of the gondola that has become the heart of Keystone. Everything here is operated by Keystone, which makes planning a vacation one-stop shopping.

GETTING HERE AND AROUND

The easiest way to travel to and around Summit County is to rent a car at Denver International Airport. Catching one of the numerous shuttles up to the ski areas and then taking advantage of the free transportation by Summit Stage (taxi service is also available) is a more economical route, but requires patience and a good timetable. You'll want a car to reach both resorts, but once there both Keystone and A-Basin are easily navigated on foot.

VISITOR INFORMATION

CONTACTS Keystone Snow Report. ☎ *970/496–4111 Press 1* 🌐 *www.keystoneresort.com/the-mountain/mountain-conditions/snow-and-weather-report.aspx.*

WHEN TO GO

From late October to late April winter sports rule. But Keystone is quickly becoming a magnet in summer as well, with a small lake for water sports, mountain biking and hiking trails, two highly respected golf courses, and outdoor concerts and special events.

Restaurants

★ Alpenglow Stube

$$$$ | EUROPEAN | The competition has heated up in recent years, but Alpenglow Stube remains among the finest mountaintop restaurants in Colorado. The exposed wood beams, a stone fireplace, and floral upholstery make it elegant and cozy. **Known for:** outstanding wine list; ragout of blue crab; weekend brunch with complimentary mimosas. 💲 *Average main: $46* ✉ *100 Dercum Sq., Keystone* ☎ *970/496–4386* 🌐 *www.keystoneresort.com* ⏲ *Closed late Apr.–early June and mid-Sept.–late Nov.*

Inxpot

$ | AMERICAN | A blend of books, coffee, martinis, and some of the best breakfast and lunch sandwiches you can get your hands on make this cozy shop a local favorite. Collages covering ceiling tiles and worn couches give this spot its character, and the après-ski rehashing over hot buttered rum and wine samplings bring in the community. **Known for:** lively atmosphere; smoked salmon breakfast sandwich; warm cocktails for the après-ski crowd. 💲 *Average main: $10* ✉ *195 River Run Rd., Keystone* ☎ *970/262–3707* 🌐 *www.inxpot.com.*

Keystone Ranch

$$$$ | AMERICAN | This 1930s homestead was once part of a working cattle ranch, and cowboy memorabilia is strewn throughout, nicely blending with stylish throw rugs, antler chandeliers, and a trophy mount. The gorgeous and massive stone fireplace is a cozy backdrop for dessert, or sipping an aperitif or after-dinner coffee. **Known for:** Colorado cheese and charcuterie board; seared pheasant; signature Grand Marnier soufflé. 💲 *Average main: $48* ✉ *Keystone Ranch Golf Course, 1239 Keystone Ranch Rd., Keystone* ☎ *970/496–4386* 🌐 *www.keystoneresort.com* ⏲ *Closed Sun. and Mon.*

Kickapoo Tavern

$$ | AMERICAN | This rustic bar and grill has local microbrews on tap and big portions of home-style dishes like piled-high burgers, sandwiches, and giant, stuffed burritos perfect for skiers, hikers, or cyclists recovering from a day on the mountain. The central location, pleasant outdoor patio, and live music keep the place hopping both après-ski and après–night ski. **Known for:** outdoor patio scene; live music and events; hearty portions of pub food. 💲 *Average main: $18* ✉ *129 River Run Rd., Keystone* ☎ *970/468–0922* 🌐 *kickapootavern.com.*

Ski Tip Lodge Restaurant

$$$$ | MODERN AMERICAN | In this ski lodge dating from the 1880s, the four-course, prix-fixe dinner is a favorite for its Colorado-spun American cuisine. Main courses have included whiskey sage–glazed Muscovy duck, peppered bacon-wrapped buffalo tenderloin, and thyme-seared wild Alaskan halibut. **Known for:** homemade bread and soup; seasonal venison; creme brûlée. *Average main: $80 ✉ 0764 Montezuma Rd., Keystone ☎ 970/496–4950, 800/354–4386 🌐 www.keystoneresort.com ⊗ No lunch.*

Hotels

Keystone Lodge & Spa

$$ | **RESORT** | The cinderblock structure gives no hint of the gracious, pampered living just inside the door. **Pros:** one of the larger properties in the resort; lovely on-site spa; dog-friendly. **Cons:** rooms are small; hot tubs get crowded; limited housekeeping. *Rooms from: $150 ✉ 22101 U.S. 6, Keystone ☎ 877/753–9786, 970/496–4500 🌐 www.keystoneresort.com 152 rooms No meals.*

Ski Tip Lodge

$$$ | **B&B/INN** | Opened as a stop along the stagecoach route back in the 1880s, this property was turned into the state's first ski lodge in the 1940s by skiing pioneers Max and Edna Dercum. **Pros:** updated rooms; on-site restaurant; cozy and romantic. **Cons:** small rooms; not near the lifts; some rooms are noisy. *Rooms from: $260 ✉ 0764 Montezuma Rd., Keystone ☎ 970/496–4950, 877/753–9786 🌐 www.keystoneresort.com 10 rooms Free Breakfast.*

Activities

DOWNHILL SKIING AND SNOWBOARDING

★ Keystone Resort

SKIING/SNOWBOARDING | **FAMILY** | What you see from the base of the mountain is only a fraction of the terrain you can enjoy when you ski or snowboard at Keystone. There's plenty more to Keystone Mountain, and much of it is geared to novice and intermediate skiers, but full-day guided snowcat tours cater to higher-level skiers on some of the state's steepest terrain. Its trails are spread across three adjoining peaks: Dercum Mountain, North Peak, and the Outback. The Schoolmarm Trail has 3½ miles of runs where you can practice turns. Dercum Mountain is easily reached from the base via high-speed chairs or the River Run gondola. You can ski or ride down the back side of Dercum Mountain to reach North Peak, a mix of groomed cruising trails and ungroomed bump runs. A family ski trail with green/blue trails through the woods and kid-friendly features, like tunnels and bridges, is a mountain favorite.

If you prefer to bypass North Peak, the River Run gondola is a short walk from the Outpost gondola, which takes you to the Outpost Lodge (home to the Alpenglow Stube, which, at 11,444 feet above sea level, is advertised as the "highest gourmet restaurant in the country"). From here there are two easy downhill runs to the third mountain, appropriately named the Outback because of its wilderness setting. Some glades have trees thinned just enough for skiers and riders who are learning to explore gladed terrain; other sections are reserved for advanced skiers.

One of the most popular non-skiing or -boarding sports at Keystone is tubing at Adventure Point.

Rental packages (skis, boots, and poles, or snowboards and boots) start at around $50 per day for a basic package but increase quickly for high-performance gear. **Facilities:** 128 trails; 3,149 acres; 3,128-foot vertical drop; 20 lifts. *✉ Keystone ☎ 800/239–1639 🌐 www.keystoneresort.com Lift ticket $159.*

GOLF

Keystone Golf

GOLF | With 36 challenging holes spread across two 18-hole courses situated at 9,300 feet, Keystone lures golfers as soon as the snow melts. **Keystone Ranch,** designed by Robert Trent Jones Jr., has a links-style front nine; the back nine has a traditional mountain-valley layout. Holes play past lodgepole pines, meander around sage meadows, and include some carries across water. **The River Course** is a par-71 stunner designed by Michael Hurdzan and Dana Fry. The front nine runs around the Snake River, whereas the back nine threads through a stand of lodgepole pines. Dramatic elevation changes, magnificent views, bunkers, and water hazards combine to test golfers of all abilities. Add magnificent views of the Continental Divide and Lake Dillon, and it's easy to see why this course is so popular. ✉ *1239 Keystone Ranch Rd., Keystone* ☎ *800/464–3494* 🌐 *www.keystonegolf.com* 🎫 *Keystone Ranch, $160; The River Course, $180* ⛳ *Keystone Ranch: 18 holes, 7017 yards, par 72; The River Course: 18 holes, 6886 yards, par 71* ⏲ *Closed mid-Oct.–mid-May.*

NORDIC SKIING

Keystone Nordic Center

SKIING/SNOWBOARDING | This center has more than 9 miles of groomed trails and access to more than 35 miles of packed trails available for skiing and snowshoeing through the White River National Forest. Cross-country, skating, snowshoeing, family tubing, and telemark lessons and rentals are available. ✉ *155 River Course Dr., Keystone* ☎ *970/496–4275* 🌐 *www.keystoneresort.com.*

Breckenridge

22 miles southwest of Keystone via U.S. 6, I–70, and Hwy. 9.

Breckenridge was founded in 1859, when gold was discovered in the surrounding hills. For the next several decades the town's fortunes rose and fell as its lodes of gold and silver were discovered and exhausted. Throughout the latter half of the 19th century and the early 20th century, Breckenridge was famous as a mining camp that "turned out more gold with less work than any camp in Colorado," according to the *Denver Post.* Dredging gold out of the rivers continued until World War II. Visitors today can still see evidence of gold-dredging operations in the surrounding streams.

At 9,603 feet above sea level and surrounded by higher peaks, Breckenridge is the oldest continuously occupied town on the western slope. Much of the town's architectural legacy from the mining era remains, so you'll find stores occupying authentic Victorian storefronts, and restaurants and bed-and-breakfasts in Victorian homes. Surrounding the town's historic core, condos and hotels are packed into the woods and along the roads threading the mountainsides toward the base of Peak 8.

GETTING HERE AND AROUND

Most people arrive by car or a shuttle from Denver International Airport. Getting around is easiest by car, but can also be done by local shuttles and taxis.

CONTACTS Breckenridge Free Ride. ☎ *970/547–3140* 🌐 *www.breckfreeride.com.*

VISITOR INFORMATION

CONTACTS Breckenridge Tourism Office. ✉ *111 Ski Hill Rd., Breckenridge* ☎ *970/453–2913* 🌐 *www.gobreck.com.* **Breckenridge Snow Report.** ☎ *970/496–4111* 🌐 *www.breckenridge.com.*

TOURS

Breckenridge Heritage Alliance

GUIDED TOURS | FAMILY | The Breckenridge Heritage Alliance leads lively tours of downtown Breckenridge, one of the largest National Historic Districts in the state. ✉ *203 S. Main St., Breckenridge* ☎ *970/453–9767* 🌐 *www.breckheritage.com* 🎫 *From $5.*

WHEN TO GO

The ski season runs from November to April, but festivals and warm-weather activities attract visitors year-round.

Festivals run rampant here, and it's rare to show up when locals aren't celebrating. Among the best festivals are the annual tribute to the Norse god of Winter, Ullr Fest (usually in December or January), and the International Snow Sculpture championships in winter (usually January). Summer events include the Breckenridge Summer Beer Festival (July), the Breckenridge Food and Wine Festival (late July), and the National Repertory Orchestra (*www.nromusic.com*) performances at the Riverwalk Center near the center of town.

Sights

★ Breckenridge Downtown Historic District

HISTORIC SITE | Downtown Breckenridge's Historic District is one of Colorado's largest, with about 250 buildings on the National Register of Historic Places. The district is roughly a compact 12 square blocks, bounded by Main, High, and Washington streets and Wellington Road. There are some 171 buildings with points of historical interest, from simple log cabins to Victorians with lacy gingerbread trim. *Breckenridge* *www.townofbreckenridge.com.*

Country Boy Mine

MINE | **FAMILY** | When gold was discovered here in 1887, the Country Boy Mine became one of the region's top producers—lead and zinc, which were vital for U.S. efforts in World War I and World War II, were big here, too. The gold mine tour takes visitors more than 1000 feet deep into the mountain. Visitors can pet the donkeys that roam the area, pan for keepable gold, or go on a treasure hunt with a metal detector. The mine has a 55-foot ore chute slide, historic buildings, and plenty of mining artifacts. *0542 French Gulch Rd., Breckenridge* *970/453–4405* *www.countryboymine.com* *Gold panning $20; tours $35* *Closed Wed. and Thurs. in fall and winter.*

Edwin Carter Discovery Center

MUSEUM | **FAMILY** | The Edwin Carter Discovery Center is dedicated to the 19th century miner-turned-environmentalist who helped to create Denver's Museum of Nature and Science. Look for realistic stuffed animals and interactive exhibits like the hands-on taxidermy workbench. *111 N. Ridge St., Breckenridge* *970/453–9767* *www.breckheritage.com/museums* *Free, or $5 donation.*

Restaurants

Blue Moose

$ | **AMERICAN** | Locals flock here for the hearty breakfasts of eggs, oatmeal, pancakes, and much more, so you can expect a wait unless you get there early. Neither the food nor the decor is fancy, and the service—while friendly—can be slow. **Known for:** popular so there's often a wait; hearty breakfasts; cash only. *Average main: $10* *540 S. Main St., Breckenridge* *970/453–4859* *No credit cards* *No dinner.*

Downstairs at Eric's

$ | **AMERICAN** | **FAMILY** | Loud and fun best describes this place, which is popular among locals and visitors of all ages. Kids hang out in the arcade while their folks watch sports on the big-screen TVs. **Known for:** sporting events bring in huge crowds; arcade games; wings. *Average main: $13* *111 S. Main St., Breckenridge* *970/453–1401* *www.downstairsaterics.com.*

Sancho Tacos

$ | **MEXICAN** | The tacos, house salsa and guac, frozen margaritas, and tequila are everything you hope for when you spot the Day-of-the-Dead skull on the sign of this lively dining room in central Breck. Locals rave about happy hour and visitors dig the funky toppings and unique tacos like fried chicken, duck confit, and sweet potato. **Known for:** happy hour drink specials; duck confit taco; central location on La Cima Mall. *Average main: $4* *500*

S. Main St., Breckenridge ☎ *970/453–9493* 🌐 *www.sanchotaco.com.*

Hotels

Grand Colorado on Peak 8

$$$$ | **RESORT** | **FAMILY** | Breckenridge's newest crown jewel, the Grand Colorado sprawls the base of Peak 8, with walk-out access to the Rocky Mountain and Colorado Superchair lifts. **Pros:** huge aquatics area with hot tubs and pools; rooftop bar with great views; shuttle service to town. **Cons:** some rooms can be loud; time-share offers are plentiful and pricey; resort signage lacking in spots. $ *Rooms from: $329* ✉ *1627 Ski Hill Rd, Breckenridge* ☎ *970/547–8788* 🌐 *www.grandcolorado.com* *253 condos* *No meals.*

Lodge at Breckenridge

$$$$ | **HOTEL** | This lodge more than compensates for its location on a mountainside beyond the downtown area with breathtaking views of the Tenmile Range from nearly every angle. **Pros:** great mountain views; complimentary shuttle service; plush bedding. **Cons:** no room service; limited shuttle service in summer; not all rooms include kitchens. $ *Rooms from: $329* ✉ *112 Overlook Dr., Breckenridge* ☎ *800/736–1607* 🌐 *www.thelodgeatbreckenridge.com* *45 rooms, 2 houses* *Free Breakfast.*

Activities

BACKCOUNTRY SKIING

They don't call this place Summit County for nothing—mountain passes above 10,000 feet allow relatively easy access to high-country terrain and some of the area's best snow. But remember: avalanche-related deaths are all too common in Summit County. Don't judge an area solely on appearances or the fact that other skiers or snowmobilers have been there before, as even slopes that look gentle may slide. Never head into the backcountry without checking weather conditions, letting someone know where you're going, and wearing appropriate clothing. Always carry survival gear and travel with a buddy.

Dillon Ranger District Office of the White River National Forest

SKIING/SNOWBOARDING | For information on snow conditions and avalanche dangers, contact the Dillon Ranger District Office of the White River National Forest. ✉ *Breckenridge* ☎ *970/468–5400* 🌐 *www.dillonrangerdistrict.com.*

CROSS-COUNTRY SKIING

Breckenridge Nordic Center

SKIING/SNOWBOARDING | This center has more than 18 miles of cross-country ski trails and more than 12 miles of snowshoe trails starting at 9,800 feet. They also offer lessons and guided tours. ✉ *9 Grandview Dr., Breckenridge* ☎ *970/453–6855* 🌐 *www.breckenridgenordic.com.*

DOWNHILL SKIING AND SNOWBOARDING

★ **Breckenridge**

SKIING/SNOWBOARDING | Affectionately known as "Breck," this mountain attracts skiers and snowboarders with equal fervor, with its terrain parks and an area where you can learn to freeride. The resort's slopes are spread across five interconnected mountains in the Tenmile Range, named Peaks 6, 7, 8, 9, and 10. Peak 6 includes 543 acres, three bowls (two at an intermediate level), and 21 trails to the ski area. The highest chairlift in North America—a high-speed quad lift called Imperial Express SuperChair on Peak 8—tops out at an air-gulping 12,840 feet. Peaks 6, 7, and 8 have above-the-timberline bowls and chutes. The lower reaches of Peak 7 have some of the country's prettiest intermediate-level terrain accessible by a lift. Peak 8 and Peak 9 have trails for all skill levels. Peak 10 has some of the best expert terrain including groomed steeps, challenging moguls, and technical tree chutes.

The slopes at Breckenridge are spread across five interconnected mountains.

In line with the town's proud heritage, some runs are named for old mines, including Bonanza, Cashier, Gold King, and Wellington.

Rental packages (skis, boots, and poles; snowboards and boots) start around $45 per day. Save on rentals and find discounted lift tickets by purchasing online at least a week in advance. **Facilities:** 187 trails; 2,908 acres; 3,398-foot vertical drop; 34 lifts. ✉ *1599 Ski Hill Rd., Breckenridge* ☎ *970/453–5000* 🌐 *www.breckenridge.com* 🎫 *Lift ticket $169.*

LESSONS AND PROGRAMS

Breckenridge Ski & Snowboard School

SKIING/SNOWBOARDING | Specialty clinics, traditional lessons, guided sessions, and programs geared to women and children are among the multitude of offerings from Breckenridge Ski & Snowboard School. Ski Girls Rock caters to girls ages 7 to 14 and Elevate teaches groups to conquer steeps, bumps, and park terrain. ✉ *Breckenridge* ☎ *888/576–2754* 🌐 *www.breckenridge.com.*

FISHING

Mountain Angler

FISHING | This company organizes fishing trips on the Colorado, Eagle, Arkansas, Blue, and South Platte rivers year-round. ✉ *311 S. Main St., Breckenridge* ☎ *800/453–4669* 🌐 *www.mountainangler.com.*

GOLF

Breckenridge Golf Club

GOLF | This is the world's only municipally owned course designed by Jack Nicklaus. You may play any combination of the three 9-hole sets: the Bear, the Beaver (with beaver ponds lining many of the fairways), or the Elk. The course resembles a nature reserve as it flows through mountainous terrain and fields full of wildflowers. ✉ *200 Clubhouse Dr., Breckenridge* ☎ *970/453–9104* 🌐 *www.breckenridgegolfclub.com* 🎫 *$117; $59 for 9 holes* ⛳ *The Bear, 9 holes, 3385 yards, par 36; The Beaver, 9 holes, 2945 yards, par 36; The Elk, 9 holes, 3312 yards, par 36.*

KAYAKING

Breckenridge Kayak Park

KAYAKING | FAMILY | With splash rocks, eddy pools, and S-curves, the 1,800-foot Breckenridge Kayak Park is a playground for kayakers. This public park on the Blue River has 15 water features, is free, and generally open from May through August. ✉ *880 Airport Rd., Breckenridge* ☎ *970/453–1734* 🌐 *www.breckenridgerecreation.com/locations/parks-fields/kayak-park.*

RAFTING

Breckenridge Whitewater Rafting

WHITE-WATER RAFTING | This outfitter runs white-water rafting trips on stretches of the Colorado, Arkansas, Eagle, and Blue rivers in Summit County, and Clear Creek on the Front Range. They also offer zipline, rock climbing, fly-fishing, hiking, and horseback tours. ✉ *411 S. Main St., Breckenridge* ☎ *877/723—8464* 🌐 *www.breckenridgewhitewater.com.*

Steamboat Springs

42 miles east of Craig; 160 miles west of Denver.

Steamboat got its name from French trappers who, after hearing the bubbling and churning hot springs, mistakenly thought a steamboat was chugging up the Yampa River. Here Stetson hats are sold for shade and not for souvenirs, and the Victorian-era buildings, most of them fronting the main drag of Lincoln Avenue, were built to be functional, not ornamental.

Steamboat Springs is aptly nicknamed Ski Town, U.S.A., because it has sent more athletes to the Winter Olympics than any other town in the nation (and also more than some small countries). When sizing up the mountain, keep in mind that the part that's visible from below is only the tip of the iceberg—much more terrain lies concealed in back. Steamboat is famed for its eiderdown-soft snow; in fact, the term "champagne powder" was coined (and amusingly enough registered as a trademark) here to describe the area's unique feathery drifts, the result of Steamboat's fortuitous position between the arid desert to the west and the moisture-magnet of the Continental Divide to the east, where storm fronts duke it out.

The mountain village, with its maze of upscale condos, boutiques, and nightclubs, is certainly attractive, but spread out and a little lacking in character. To its credit, though, this increasingly trendy destination has retained much of its down-home friendliness.

GETTING HERE AND AROUND

Yampa Valley Regional Airport (HDN) is in Hayden, 22 miles from Steamboat Springs. Go Alpine and Storm Mountain Express provide door-to-door service to Steamboat Springs from Yampa Valley Regional Airport. A one-way trip with either starts at $36.

Steamboat Springs Transit (SST) provides free shuttle service between the ski area and downtown Steamboat year-round. Most of the major properties also provide shuttles between the two areas for their guests.

From Denver, Steamboat Springs is about a three-hour drive northwest via I–70 and U.S. 40. The route traverses some high-mountain passes, so it's a good idea to check road conditions before you travel.

TOURS

Sweet Pea Tours

BOAT TOURS | Steamboat's Sweet Pea Tours visits nearby hot springs. The ride takes about 25 minutes each way, and rates are higher in winter and on weekends. ✉ *Steamboat Springs* ☎ *970/879–5820* 🌐 *www.sweetpeatours.com* 🎫 *From $30.*

VISITOR INFORMATION

CONTACTS Steamboat Ski & Resort Corporation. ✉ *2305 Mount Werner Circle, Steamboat Springs* ☎ *970/879–7300, 800/922–2722* 🌐 *www.steamboat.com.* **Steamboat Springs Chamber Resort Associationcom.** ✉ *125 Anglers Dr., Steamboat Springs* ☎ *970/879–0880* 🌐 *www.steamboat-chamber.com.* **Steamboat Springs Snow Report.** ☎ *970/879–7300* 🌐 *www.steamboat.com/the-mountain/daily-snow.*

Sights

Medicine Bow/Routt National Forests
NATURE PRESERVE | In summer Steamboat serves as the gateway to the magnificent Medicine Bow/Routt National Forests, with a wealth of activities from hiking to mountain biking to fishing. Among the nearby attractions are the 283-foot **Fish Creek Falls** and the splendidly rugged **Mount Zirkel Wilderness Area.** To the north, two sparkling man-made lakes, **Steamboat** and **Pearl,** each in its own state park, are a draw for those into fishing and sailing. In winter the area is just as popular. Snowshoers and backcountry skiers are permitted to use the west side of Rabbit Ears Pass, whereas snowmobilers are confined to the east side. ✉ *Hahns Peak–Bears Ears Ranger District Office, Steamboat Springs* ☎ *970/870–2187* 🌐 *www.fs.usda.gov/mbr.*

Old Town Hot Springs
HOT SPRINGS | **FAMILY** | There are more than 150 mineral springs of varying temperatures in the Steamboat Springs area, including this one, in the middle of town. Old Town Hot Springs gets its waters from the all-natural Heart Spring. The modern facility has a lap pool, relaxation pool, climbing wall, and health club. Two waterslides are open noon to 6 pm in summer and 4 to 8 pm in winter; they require an additional $7 fee. The inflatable playground called The Wibit is open Friday to Sunday from noon to 6 pm between June and September, and also requires an additional $7 fee. ✉ *136 Lincoln Ave., Steamboat Springs* ☎ *970/879–1828* 🌐 *www.steamboathotsprings.org* 🎫 *$25.*

★ **Strawberry Park Hot Springs**
HOT SPRINGS | About 7 miles west of town, the Strawberry Park Hot Springs is a bit remote and rustic, although only the winter drive on the gravel portion on the road is challenging. The way the pool is set up to offer semi-privacy makes for an intimate setting and relaxation. It's family-oriented during the day, but after dark clothing is optional, and no one under 18 is admitted. Feel free to bring food to eat in the picnic areas. A variety of massages, including aquatic-style, are offered next to the pools. ✉ *Strawberry Park Rd., 44200 County Rd. #36, Steamboat Springs* ☎ *970/879–0342* 🌐 *www.strawberryhotsprings.com* 🎫 *$20, cash or check only.*

Tread of Pioneers Museum
MUSEUM | In a restored Queen Anne–style house, the Tread of Pioneers Museum is an excellent spot to bone up on local history on Fridays and Saturdays. It includes ski memorabilia dating to the turn of the 20th century, when Carl Howelsen opened Howelsen Hill, still the country's preeminent ski-jumping facility. ✉ *800 Oak St., Steamboat Springs* ☎ *970/879–2214* 🌐 *www.treadofpioneers.org* 🎫 *$6* ⏲ *Closed Sun.–Thurs.*

Restaurants

★ **Aurum Food & Wine**
$$$$ | **MODERN AMERICAN** | Situated along the Yampa River, with an expansive deck and couch seating that juts out over the water, Aurum serves seasonal modern American fare made from locally sourced ingredients. Inside, the pretty space features dark woods, lots of fresh flowers, and expansive windows to showcase the view. **Known for:** stunning views; good happy hour; jumbo lump crab cakes. $ *Average main: $41* ✉ *811 Yampa St., Steamboat Springs* ☎ *970/879–9500* 🌐 *aurumsteamboat.com* ⏲ *No lunch.*

A visit to Strawberry Park Hot Springs is charming in all four seasons.

★ Cafe Diva

$$$$ | **MODERN AMERICAN** | A pretty, egg-yolk yellow but unfussy dining room is an ideal backdrop for fresh, locally sourced modern American dishes. The menu lists a significant number of vegan and gluten-free options that put some effort into their creation, such as quinoa risotto with butternut squash and mushroom jus. **Known for:** by-the-glass wine list; venison tenderloin; elegant atmosphere that's not fussy. *Average main: $43* ✉ *1855 Ski Time Square Dr., Steamboat Springs* ☎ *970/871–0508* 🌐 *www.cafediva.com* ⏲ *No lunch.*

Carl's Tavern

$$ | **AMERICAN** | Named after Karl Hovelsen, the Norwegian ski jumper who brought the sport to Colorado in the early 1900s and who also lent his name to Steamboat's Howelsen Hill, this modern tavern serves updated takes on comfort food, with an emphasis on locally sourced ingredients and as many items produced in-house as possible. Local favorites include chicken-fried steak, three-cheese mac, and lemon icebox pie, but it's also tough to pass up the pot roast made from Angus beef or the banana-chocolate bread pudding. **Known for:** half-price happy hour; Tuesday night prime rib; well-crafted cocktails. *Average main: $18* ✉ *700 Yampa Ave., Steamboat Springs* ☎ *970/761–2060* 🌐 *www.carlstavern.com* ⏲ *Closed Mon. and Tues.*

Creekside Café & Grill

$$ | **AMERICAN** | **FAMILY** | This café's hearty breakfasts and lunches, which are crafted to get folks through a day of skiing or biking, are served in a casual atmosphere that's family—and group—friendly. The most popular item on the menu, and for good reason, is the roster of a dozen eggs Benedict choices, including "the Mountain Man," with smoked bacon, ham, and chorizo. **Known for:** bustling atmosphere; rotating local art; "the Mountain Man" eggs Benedict with smoked bacon, ham, and chorizo. *Average main: $16* ✉ *131 11th St.,*

Steamboat Springs ☎ *970/879–4925* 🌐 *www.creekside-cafe.com* ⏲ *No dinner.*

★ Harwigs

$$$$ | FRENCH | Steamboat's most intimate restaurant is in a building that once housed Harwig's Saddlery and Western Wear. The classic French cuisine, with subtle Asian influences, is well crafted, and the menu changes monthly. **Known for:** wine cellar with more than 10,000 bottles; lamb sliders; duck and seafood dishes. 💲 *Average main: $49* ✉ *911 Lincoln Ave., Steamboat Springs* ☎ *970/879–1919* 🌐 *www.harwigs.com* ⏲ *Closed Sun. and Mon. No lunch.*

Johnny B. Good's Diner

$ | AMERICAN | FAMILY | Between the appealing kids' menu and the memorabilia that suggests Elvis has not left the building, Johnny's is all about fun and family. Breakfast (until 2 pm), lunch, and dinner are served daily, and they are all budget minded and large portioned. **Known for:** kid-friendly locals hangout; reasonable prices; burgers and milkshakes. 💲 *Average main: $13* ✉ *738 Lincoln Ave., Steamboat Springs* ☎ *970/870–8400* 🌐 *www.johnnybgoodsdiner.com.*

★ Laundry Kitchen & Cocktails

$$$$ | MODERN AMERICAN | Small plates are the way to go in this convivial, casual setting, which was indeed the Steamboat Laundry from 1910 to 1977 but now serves tasty modern American tidbits such as fried shoestring potatoes sprinkled with duck-fat powder and house-smoked trout with goat cheese in a jar (the "jar" offering routinely changes). The dining room is rustic and cozy—exposed brick and original wood—and the service is spot-on. **Known for:** house-cured meats; inviting bar; specialty cocktails. 💲 *Average main: $40* ✉ *127 11th St., Steamboat Springs* ☎ *970/870–0681* 🌐 *www.thelaundryrestaurant.com* ⏲ *No lunch.*

Hotels

Hotel Bristol

$$$ | HOTEL | FAMILY | A delightful small hotel nestled in a 1948 building, the Bristol—which is now owned by the Magnuson Hotels chain—not only has its location working for it, but also old-fashioned personalized service. **Pros:** families and groups can stay comfortably for a little bit extra; convenient location; ski lockers. **Cons:** rooms may seem uncomfortably small, bathrooms even more so; thin walls; in-house restaurant noise can be heard from some rooms. 💲 *Rooms from: $217* ✉ *917 Lincoln Ave., Steamboat Springs* ☎ *970/879–3083* 🌐 *www.steamboathotelbristol.com* *24 rooms* *No meals.*

Inn at Steamboat

$$$ | B&B/INN | Rustic knotty pine, leather furniture, comfortable linens, and panoramic views of the Yampa Valley make this inn a good choice for visitors looking to stay somewhere that feels like a mountain lodge at lower-than-ski-resort prices. **Pros:** magnificent views, even from the heated pool and particularly in fall; spacious rooms; house-baked cookies and pastries. **Cons:** not ski-in ski-out; not walking distance to downtown; property feels dated. 💲 *Rooms from: $229* ✉ *3070 Columbine Dr., Steamboat Springs* ☎ *970/879–2600* 🌐 *www.innatsteamboat.com* *33 rooms* *Free Breakfast.*

Mountain Resorts

$$$ | RENTAL | This vacation rental company manages condominiums at more than two dozen locations. **Pros:** some properties are very upscale; some have pools and fitness facilities; accommodating staff. **Cons:** properties vary wildly in price and decor; some properties are dated; some are relatively far from slopes or town. 💲 *Rooms from: $280* ✉ *2145 Resort Dr., Suite 100, Steamboat Springs* ☎ *888/686–8075* 🌐 *www.mtn-resorts.com* *378 condos* *No meals.*

Ptarmigan Inn

$$$ | **HOTEL** | **FAMILY** | Situated on the slopes, this laid-back lodging couldn't have a more convenient location. **Pros:** great location; ski-in ski-out; mountain views. **Cons:** chain-hotel vibes; decor feels dated; late-night slope grooming can be noisy. *Rooms from: $221 ✉ 2304 Après Ski Way, Steamboat Springs ☎ 888/236–2163 www.theptarmigan.com 77 rooms No meals.*

Rabbit Ears Motel

$$ | **HOTEL** | **FAMILY** | The playful, pink-neon bunny sign outside this motel has been a local landmark since 1952, making it an unofficial gateway to Steamboat Springs. **Pros:** great location; family- and pet-friendly; huge rooms. **Cons:** beds may be uncomfortable; kitschy and nothing fancy; it can be noisy along the main drag. *Rooms from: $169 ✉ 201 Lincoln Ave., Steamboat Springs ☎ 970/879–1150, 800/828–7702 www.rabbitearsmotel.com 65 rooms Free Breakfast.*

★ **Sheraton Steamboat Resort & Villas**

$$$$ | **HOTEL** | **FAMILY** | This bustling high-rise is one of Steamboat's few ski-in ski-out properties; the amenities are classic resort-town, with a ski shop, golf course, an outdoor heated pool, and four rooftop hot tubs with sweeping views of the surrounding ski slopes. **Pros:** convenient location, with the slopes, three restaurants and a market, and town right there; large size means lots of amenities; cozy hangout areas. **Cons:** lobby areas can be chaotic; prices now on par with major ski areas; decor a bit bland. *Rooms from: $417 ✉ 2200 Village End Ct., Steamboat Springs ☎ 970/879–2220 www.marriott.com 281 rooms No meals.*

Steamboat Mountain Lodge

$$ | **B&B/INN** | **FAMILY** | River or mountain views await at this budget-minded spot, which counts a river-rock fireplace surrounded by cozy couches and a Jacuzzi on the deck among its charms. **Pros:** great views; spacious rooms; bargain prices. **Cons:** very simple decor; breakfast is nothing special; property feels dated. *Rooms from: $170 ✉ 3155 S. Lincoln St., Steamboat Springs ☎ 970/871–9121 www.steamboatmountainlodge.com 38 rooms Free Breakfast.*

★ **Vista Verde Guest Ranch**

$$$$ | **B&B/INN** | On a working ranch, the luxurious Vista Verde provides city slickers with an authentic Western experience; lodge rooms are huge and beautifully appointed, with lace curtains, Western art, and lodgepole furniture, while the spacious cabins are more rustic, with pine paneling and old-fashioned wood-burning stoves, plus refrigerators, coffeemakers, and porches. **Pros:** authentic dude ranch experience; lots of amenities; good packages available. **Cons:** pricey compared to other area lodging; remote location; can be snowed-in during winter. *Rooms from: $632 ✉ 31100 County Rd. 64, Clark, Steamboat Springs ☎ 970/879–3858 www.vistaverde.com Closed late Mar.–early June and mid-Oct.–mid-Dec. 12 rooms All-inclusive.*

Wyndham Vacation Rentals

$$$ | **RENTAL** | Torian Plum slope-side is just one of the properties managed by Wyndham Vacation Rentals (now the clearinghouse for most of the rental condos in the area); properties include elegant one- to six-bedroom units in a ski-in ski-out location and units sprinkled around town. **Pros:** secure rooms for ski storage; free shuttles to town; some rentals have hot tubs. **Cons:** properties vary in comfort and style; often completely booked during ski season; units can be cramped. *Rooms from: $276 ✉ 1855 Ski Time Sq., Steamboat Springs ☎ 800/467–3529 www.wyndhamvacationrentals.com 347 condos No meals.*

Nightlife

Mahogany Ridge Brewery & Grill
BREWPUBS/BEER GARDENS | Mahogany Ridge Brewery & Grill serves superior pub grub and pours an assortment of its own ales, lagers, porters, and stouts. Live music is a nice bonus on weekends. ✉ *435 Lincoln Ave., Steamboat Springs* ☎ *970/879–3773* 🌐 *www.mahoganyridgesteamboat.com.*

Old Town Pub
BARS/PUBS | Located in a 1904 building, this pub serves juicy burgers and fiery wings accompanied by music from some great bands. A limited bar menu and homemade pizza is served until 1 am. ✉ *600 Lincoln Ave., Steamboat Springs* ☎ *970/879–2101* 🌐 *www.theoldtownpub.com.*

Shopping

At the base of the ski area are three expansive shopping centers—Ski Time Square, Torian Plum Plaza, and Gondola Square.

BOOKSTORES

Off the Beaten Path
BOOKS/STATIONERY | Off the Beaten Path is a throwback to the Beat Generation, with poetry readings, lectures, and concerts. It has an excellent selection of New Age works, in addition to the usual best sellers and travel guides. The on-site coffee shop is the best in town, with fresh baked goods and sandwiches. Hours vary by season so call ahead to confirm. ✉ *68 9th St., Steamboat Springs* ☎ *970/879–6830* 🌐 *www.steamboatbooks.com.*

BOUTIQUES AND GALLERIES

Jace Romick Gallery
LOCAL SPECIALTIES | A former member of the U.S. Ski Team and a veteran of the rodeo circuit, Jace Romick has shifted from crafting splendid textured lodgepole furniture at his now-closed Into the West shop and focuses instead solely on his photography there, which features contemporary Western images for sale. ✉ *837 Lincoln Ave., Steamboat Springs* ☎ *970/879–8377* 🌐 *www.jaceromickgallery.com.*

Silver Lining
CRAFTS | This shop displays beautifully designed jewelry from around the world, such as Peruvian opal necklaces, as well as locally crafted Western pieces using turquoise and silver. They carry an extensive and well-organized selection of beads and found objects for making your own, which you can do on a small scale at one end of the tiny store. They also offer jewelry repair and pearl knotting. ✉ *Torian Plum Plaza, 1865 Ski Time Sq. Dr., Steamboat Springs* ☎ *970/879–7474* 🌐 *www.steamboatmountainvillage.com.*

Wild Horse Gallery
ART GALLERIES | Native American images, local landscapes, and wildlife adorn the walls of the Wild Horse Gallery. This shop across from the Steamboat Art Museum is the place to buy artwork, jewelry, and blown glass. ✉ *802 Lincoln Ave., Steamboat Springs* ☎ *970/879–5515* 🌐 *www.wildhorsegallery.com.*

SPORTING GOODS

Ski Haus
SPORTING GOODS | If you need to be outfitted for the slopes, look no further than Ski Haus, which has a full line of winter gear and also offers rentals. The Ski Haus Bike Shop rents bikes directly across the street. ✉ *1457 Pine Grove Rd., Steamboat Springs* ☎ *844/878–0385* 🌐 *www.skihaussteamboat.com.*

Straightline Sports
SPORTING GOODS | This sporting-goods store is a good bet for downhill necessities. ✉ *744 Lincoln Ave., Steamboat Springs* ☎ *970/879–7568* 🌐 *www.straightlinesports.com.*

WESTERN WEAR

F. M. Light and Sons
CLOTHING | Owned by the same family for four generations, F. M. Light and Sons caters to the cowpoke in all of us. If you're lucky you'll find a bargain on Western wear here. ✉ *830 Lincoln Ave.,*

Steamboat Springs ☎ *970/879–1822* 🌐 *www.fmlight.com.*

Activities

BACKCOUNTRY SKIING

The most popular area for backcountry skiing around Steamboat Springs is Rabbit Ears Pass, southeast of town. It's the last pass you cross if you're driving from Denver to Steamboat. Much of the appeal is its easy access to high-country trails from U.S. 40. There are plenty of routes you can take.

Hahns Peak Ranger Office

SKIING/SNOWBOARDING | A popular backcountry spot is Seedhouse Road, about 26 miles north of Steamboat, near the town of Clark. A marked network of trails across the rolling hills has good views of distant peaks. For maps and information on snow conditions, contact the Hahns Peak Ranger Office. ✉ *400 Seedhouse Rd., Steamboat Springs* ☎ *970/870–2299* 🌐 *www.steamboatchamber.com.*

Ski Haus

SKIING/SNOWBOARDING | Touring and telemarking rentals are available at ski shops in the Steamboat area. One of the best is the Ski Haus. ✉ *1457 Pine Grove Rd., Steamboat Springs* ☎ *844/878–0385* 🌐 *www.skihaussteamboat.com.*

Steamboat Ski Touring Center

SKIING/SNOWBOARDING | Arrangements for backcountry tours can be made through Steamboat Ski Touring Center. Trail passes cost $23. ✉ *Steamboat Springs* ✣ *Left on Steamboat Blvd. from Mt. Werner Rd.; second right at Steamboat Ski Touring Center sign* ☎ *970/879–8180* 🌐 *www.nordicski.net.*

DOWNHILL SKIING AND SNOWBOARDING

Howelsen Hill Ski Area

SKIING/SNOWBOARDING | The tiny Howelsen Hill Ski Area, in the heart of Steamboat Springs, is the oldest ski area still open in Colorado. Howelsen, with 4 lifts, 17 trails, 9 Nordic trails, 1 terrain park, and a 440-foot vertical drop, is home to the Steamboat Springs Winter Sports Club, which has more than 800 members. The ski area not only has an awesome terrain park, but has night skiing as well. It's the largest ski-jumping complex in America and a major Olympic training ground. **Facilities:** 17 trails; 50 acres; 440-foot vertical drop; 4 lifts. ✉ *845 Howelsen Pkwy., Steamboat Springs* ☎ *970/879–4300* 🌐 *www.steamboatsprings.net/ski* 🎫 *Lift ticket $35.*

★ Steamboat Springs Ski Area

SKIING/SNOWBOARDING | The Steamboat Springs Ski Area is perhaps best known for its tree skiing and "cruising" terrain—the latter term referring to wide, groomed runs perfect for intermediate-level skiers. The abundance of cruising terrain has made Steamboat immensely popular with those who ski once or twice a year and who aren't looking to tax their abilities. On a predominantly western exposure—most ski areas sit on north-facing exposures—the resort benefits from intense sun, which contributes to the mellow atmosphere. In addition, one of the most extensive lift systems in the region allows skiers to get in lots of runs without having to spend much time waiting in line. The Storm Peak and Sundown high-speed quads, for example, each send you about 2,000 vertical feet in less than seven minutes. Do the math: a day of more than 60,000 vertical feet is entirely within the realm of possibility.

All this is not to suggest, however, that Steamboat is a piece of cake for more experienced skiers. Pioneer Ridge encompasses advanced and intermediate terrain. Steamboat is renowned as a breeding ground for top mogul skiers, and for good reason. There are numerous mogul runs, but most are not particularly steep. The few with a vertical challenge, such as Chute One, are not especially long. If you're looking for challenging skiing at Steamboat, take on the trees. The ski area has done an admirable job of clearing many gladed areas of such nuisances as saplings, underbrush, and fallen timber, making Steamboat tree skiing much less hazardous than at other areas. The trees are also where advanced skiers—as well as, in some places, confident intermediates—can find the best of Steamboat's much-ballyhooed powder. Statistically, Steamboat doesn't report significantly more snowfall than other Colorado resorts, but somehow snow piles up here better than at the others. Ask well-traveled Colorado skiers, and they'll confirm that when it comes to consistently good, deep snow, Steamboat is hard to beat. Also, when conditions permit, the ski area opens up for night skiing. **Facilities:** 165 trails; 2,965 acres; 3,668-foot vertical drop; 21 lifts. ✉ *2305 Mount Werner Circle, Steamboat Springs* ☎ *877/783–2628* 🌐 *www.steamboat.com* 🎫 *Lift ticket $145.*

LESSONS AND PROGRAMS

Half-day group lessons begin at $199; all-day lessons are $299. Clinics in moguls, powder, snowboarding, and "hyper-carving"—made possible by the design of shaped skis—are available.

Snow-cat skiing—where a vehicle delivers you to hard-to-reach slopes—has been called the poor man's version of helicopter skiing, although at $525 a day that's probably a misnomer. It's true that snow-cat users don't have to worry about landing, and can get to places that would be inaccessible by helicopter.

Kids' Vacation Center

SKIING/SNOWBOARDING | **FAMILY** | Programs for children from two years, six months to kindergarten age are offered through the Kids' Vacation Center. Day care is also available. ✉ *Steamboat Springs* ☎ *800/922–2722.*

Steamboat Powder Cats

SKIING/SNOWBOARDING | Buffalo Pass, northeast of Steamboat, is one of the snowiest spots in Colorado, and that's why it's the base for Steamboat Powder Cats. There's a maximum of 12 skiers per group, so the open-meadow skiing is never crowded. ✉ *1724 Mt. Werner Circle, Steamboat Springs* ☎ *970/879–5188* 🌐 *www.steamboatpowdercats.com* 🎫 *From $625.*

Steamboat Ski and Resort Corporation

SKIING/SNOWBOARDING | General information about the Steamboat Springs ski areas is available through the Steamboat Ski and Resort Corporation. ✉ *Steamboat Springs* ☎ *970/879–6111, 877/783–2628 reservations* 🌐 *www.steamboat.com.*

RENTALS

Steamboat Central Reservations

SKIING/SNOWBOARDING | Equipment packages are available at the gondola base as well as at ski shops in town. Packages (skis, boots, and poles) average about $55 a day, less for multiday and advance online rentals. Call Steamboat Central Reservations for rental information. ✉ *Steamboat Springs* ☎ *800/922–2722* 🌐 *www.steamboat.com.*

GOLF

Haymaker Golf Course

GOLF | Three miles south of Steamboat Springs, this public-access 18-hole Keith Foster course has a pro shop and café, the Haymaker Patio Grill ($$). The challenging, rolling course has hills, streams, and native grasses, as well as exceptional views. The course is noted for being well maintained, with large greens and a 10,000-square-foot putting green. ✉ *34855 U.S. 40, Steamboat Springs* ☎ *970/870–1846* 🌐 *www.haymakergolf.com* 🎫 *$135* ⛳ *Silver course: 18 holes, 7308 yards, par 72; Blue course: 18 holes, 5059 yards, par 72; Gold course: 18 holes, 6728 yards, par 72; White course: 18 holes, 6151 yards, par 72* ✍ *Reservations essential.*

Rollingstone Ranch Golf Club at the Sheraton Steamboat Resort

GOLF | Expect to see plenty of wildlife on this 18-hole championship course, which was designed by the legendary Robert Trent Jones Jr. The extensive practice facilities include a driving range, a bunker, and a putting green. The Fish Creek Grille ($$) serves lunch daily. ✉ *1230 Steamboat Blvd., Steamboat Springs* ☎ *970/879–1391* 🌐 *www.rollingstoneranchgolf.com* 🎫 *$129* ⛳ *Black course: 18 holes, 6902 yards, par 72; Green course: 18 holes, 5205 yards, par 72* ✍ *Reservations essential.*

HORSEBACK RIDING

Because of the ranches surrounding the Yampa and Elk rivers, Steamboat is full of real cowboys as well as visitors trying to act the part. Horseback riding is popular here for good reason: Seeing the area on horseback is not only easier on the legs, but it also allows riders to get deeper into the backcountry—which is crisscrossed by a web of deer and elk trails—and sometimes closer to wildlife than is possible on foot.

Del's Triangle 3 Ranch

HORSEBACK RIDING | This facility can organize rides from hour-long tours to journeys lasting several days. It's about 20 miles north of Steamboat via Highway 129. ✉ *55675 County Rd. 62, Clark* ☎ *970/879–3495* 🌐 *www.steamboathorses.com.*

Howelsen Rodeo Grounds

HORSEBACK RIDING | Every Friday and Saturday evening in summer, rodeos are held at the Howelsen Rodeo Grounds. ✉ *5th St. and Howelsen Pkwy., Steamboat Springs* ☎ *970/879–1818* 🌐 *steamboatprorodeo.com* 🎫 *$20.*

MOUNTAIN BIKING

Steamboat Springs' rolling mountains, endless aspen glades, mellow valleys, and miles and miles of Jeep trails and single-track make for great mountain biking. In summer, when Front Range trails are baking in the harsh summer sun and cluttered with mountain bikers, horse riders, and hikers, you can pedal some of the cool backcountry trails in Steamboat without passing a single cyclist.

Gore Pass Loop

BICYCLING | The 27½-mile Gore Pass Loop takes you through aspen and pine forests, with gradual hill climbs and long, sweet descents. ✉ *Hwy. 134 and Forest Rd. 185, Steamboat Springs* ✥ *Trailhead: Follow Hwy. 134 to Gore Pass Park.*

Orange Peel Bicycle Service

BICYCLING | This bike shop offers a sweet line of demos that cost about double the regular rental rates, which start at $60 for a half day. It's a good deal if you're in the market for a new bike. ✉ *1136 Yampa St., Steamboat Springs* ☎ *970/879–2957* 🌐 *www.orangepeelbikes.com.*

RAFTING

Bucking Rainbow Outfitters

WHITE-WATER RAFTING | This outfitter runs rafting excursions to the Yampa, Elk, Colorado, North Platte, and Eagle rivers. Half-day to two-day trips are available for all levels. ✉ *730 Lincoln Ave., Steamboat Springs* ☎ *970/879–8747* 🌐 *www.buckingrainbow.com* 🎫 *From $50.*

TRACK SKIING

Steamboat Ski Touring Center

SKIING/SNOWBOARDING | Laid out on and along the Sheraton Steamboat Golf Club, Steamboat Ski Touring Center has a relatively gentle 18½-mile trail network. A good option for a relaxed afternoon of skiing is to pick up some vittles at the Picnic Basket in the main building and enjoy a picnic along Fish Creek Trail, a 3-mile-long loop that winds through pine and aspen groves. Rental packages (skis, boots, and poles) are available. ✉ *1230 Steamboat Blvd., Steamboat Springs* ☎ *970/879–8180* 🌐 *www.steamboatnordiccenter.com* 🎫 *Trail fee $23.*

Vista Verde Guest Ranch

SKIING/SNOWBOARDING | This guest ranch has a well-groomed network of tracks (about 9 miles), as well as access to the adjacent national forest. ✉ *58000 Cowboy Way, Clark* ☎ *970/879–3858* 🌐 *www.vistaverde.com.*

Chapter 18

WESTERN COLORADO

WITH MESA VERDE NATIONAL PARK

Updated by
Aimee Heckel,
Kellee Katagi, and
Kyle Wagner

Sights	Restaurants	Hotels	Shopping	Nightlife
★★★★☆	★★★☆☆	★★☆☆☆	★★☆☆☆	★★★☆☆

WELCOME TO WESTERN COLORADO

TOP REASONS TO GO

★ **Skiing and snowboarding in Telluride:** Take a lift up to the sweeping, groomed trails and challenging tree and mogul runs at this world-famous ski area.

★ **Exploring Black Canyon of the Gunnison:** Play it safe, but edge as close to the rim of this 2,700-feet deep abyss as you dare.

★ **Riding the Durango & Silverton Narrow Gauge Railroad:** This six-hour round-trip journey along the Animas River will take you back in time in trains mostly powered by coal-fired locomotives.

★ **Dinosaur National Monument:** Wander among thousands of fossilized skeletons that remain embedded in the rugged hillsides or take a raft trip down the Green or Yampa River.

★ **Visiting Mesa Verde National Park:** Built atop the pinyon-covered mesa tops and hidden in the park's valleys are 600 ancient dwellings, some carved directly into the sandstone cliffs.

1 **Grand Junction.** The meeting place of the Colorado and Gunnison rivers.

2 **Dinosaur National Monument.** One of the country's best collection of fossils that you can actually touch.

3 **Gunnison.** A hub for outdoor lovers.

4 **Black Canyon of the Gunnison National Park.** An awe-inspiring canyon.

5 **Telluride.** A mining town turned celebrity ski resort.

6 **Silverton.** An old historic mining town.

7 **Durango.** Once a cultural crossroads in the Old West.

8 **Mesa Verde National Park.** National park known for its ancient cliff dwellings.

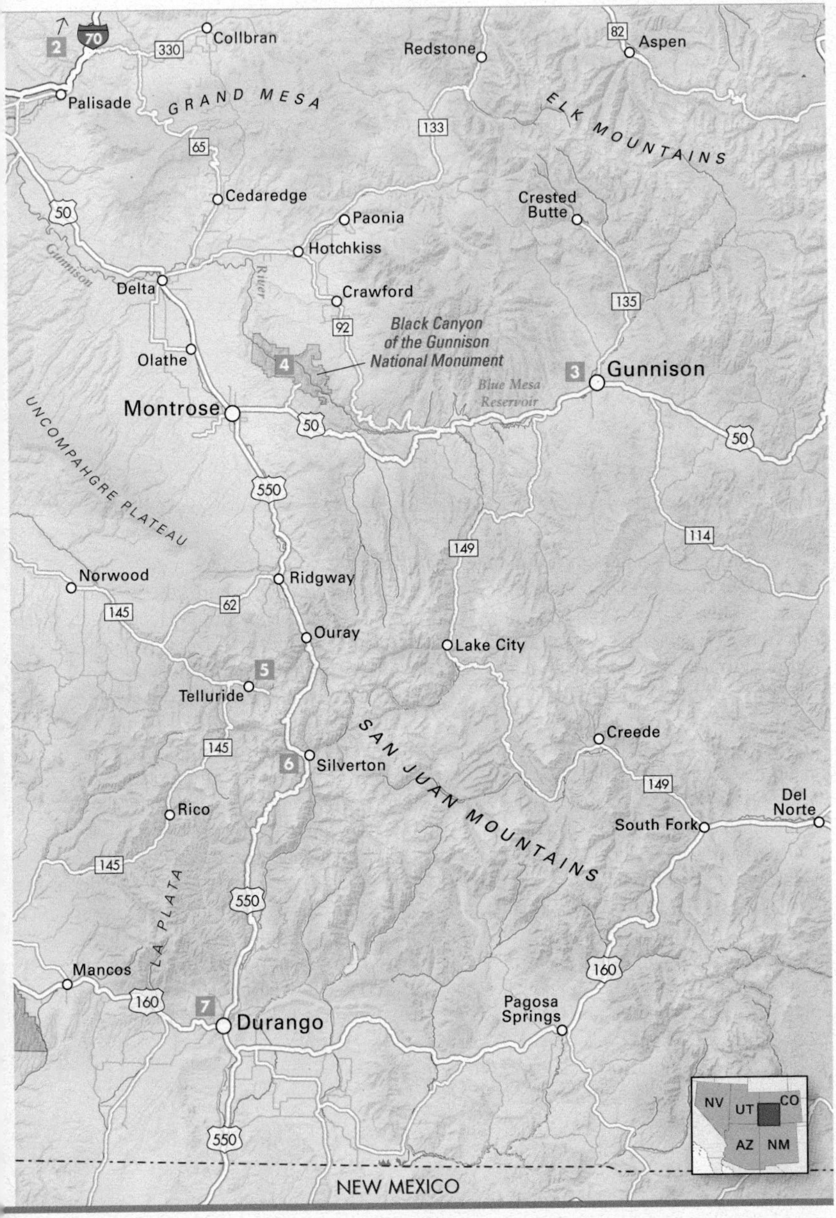

2
70
330
Collbran
Redstone
82
Aspen
Palisade
GRAND MESA
133
ELK MOUNTAINS
65
Cedaredge
50
Paonia
Crested Butte
Hotchkiss
Gunnison
River
Delta
Crawford
135
92
Black Canyon of the Gunnison National Monument
Olathe
4
3
Gunnison
Blue Mesa Reservoir
Montrose
50
50
UNCOMPAHGRE PLATEAU
550
114
149
Norwood
Ridgway
145
62
Ouray
Lake City
5
Telluride
SAN JUAN MOUNTAINS
Creede
145
6
Silverton
149
Del Norte
Rico
South Fork
145
LA PLATA
550
160
Mancos
160
7
Durango
Pagosa Springs
NV
UT
CO
AZ
NM
550
NEW MEXICO

The reddish rocks found in much of the state, particularly in the southwest, give Colorado its name. The region's terrain varies widely—from yawning black canyons and desolate moonscapes to pastel deserts and mesas, glistening sapphire lakes, and wide expanses of those stunning red rocks. It's so rugged in the southwest that a four-wheel-drive vehicle or a pair of sturdy hiker's legs is necessary to explore much of the wild and beautiful backcountry.

The region's history and people are as colorful as the landscape. Southwestern Colorado, as well as the "Four Corners" neighbors of northwestern New Mexico, northeastern Arizona, and southeastern Utah, was home to the Ancestral Pueblos formerly known as Anasazi, meaning "ancient ones." These people, ancestors of today's Pueblo peoples (including the Zuni and Hopi tribes) constructed impressive cliff dwellings in what are now Mesa Verde National Park, Ute Mountain Ute Tribal Park, and other nearby sites. This wild and woolly region, dotted with rowdy mining camps and boomtowns, also witnessed the antics of such notorious outlaws as Butch Cassidy, who embarked on his storied career by robbing the San Miguel Valley Bank in Telluride in 1889, and Robert "Bob" Ford, who hid out in Creede after shooting Jesse James in 1882.

Western Colorado has such diversity that, depending on where you go, you can have radically different vacations. You can spiral from the towering peaks of the San Juan range to the plunging Black Canyon of the Gunnison, taking in alpine scenery along the way, as well as the eerie remains of old mining camps, before winding through striking desert landscapes and Old West railroad towns. If you go further north, you can explore dinosaur fossils in the state's northwestern corner at Dinosaur National Monument, perhaps stopping in Grand Junction along the way. Even if you're not here to ski or golf in the resorts of Durango or Telluride, you'll still find plenty to experience in this part of the state.

Planning

When to Go

Northwestern Colorado has four distinct seasons. The heaviest concentration of tourists is in summer, when school is out and families hit the road for a little together time. Temperatures in summer frequently reach into the high 80s and 90s, although the mercury has been known to top triple digits on occasion. You might have a hard time finding a hotel room during late May and late June thanks to the National Junior College World Series and Country Jam music festival, both in Grand Junction.

Southwestern Colorado is intensely seasonal. Snow typically begins falling in the high country in late September or early October, and by Halloween seasonal closures turn some unpaved alpine roads into routes for snowmobiles. The San Juan Mountains see average annual snowfalls approaching 400 inches in the highest spots. Winter lingers well into the season that the calendar calls spring—the greatest snowfalls generally occur in March and April.

Getting Here and Around

AIR

Grand Junction Regional Airport (GJT), the only major airport in northwestern Colorado.

The closest regional airport to the Black Canyon of the Gunnison National Park is Montrose Regional Airport (MTJ).

The Durango–La Plata County Airport (DRO) is your closest option for Silverton, Durango, Mesa Verde National Park, and the Four Corners region. **■ TIP→ Depending on your final destination in the Four Corners region and airline schedules, you might want to consider flying to Albuquerque instead of Denver. The Albuquerque International Sunport (ABQ) is host to many of the major airlines and is closer than Denver.**

CAR

You'll be able to rent a car at any of the region's airports, and having one is essential in being able to explore (unless all you're here for is to ski, in which case you might be better off with a resort shuttle).

In northwestern Colorado, I–70 (U.S. 6) is the major thoroughfare, accessing Grand Junction and Grand Mesa (via Route 65, which runs to Delta). Rangely and Dinosaur are reached via Route 64. U.S. 40 east from Utah is the best way to reach Dinosaur National Monument and Craig.

In southwestern Colorado, the main roads in the region are Highway 135 between Crested Butte and Gunnison; U.S. 50 linking Gunnison, Montrose, and Delta; Route 149 between Gunnison, Lake City, and Creede; U.S. 550 from Montrose to Ridgway, Ouray, Silverton, and Durango; Highway 62 and Route 145 linking Ridgway with Telluride, Dolores, and Cortez; and U.S. 160, which passes from Cortez to Durango to Pagosa Springs via Mesa Verde National Park. None of these roads officially close for winter, but be prepared at any time during snowy months for portions of the roads to be closed or down to one lane for avalanche control or to clear ice or snowdrifts.

Hotels

No matter what you're looking for in vacation lodging—luxurious slope-side condominium, landmark inn in a historic town, riverside cabin, guest ranch, country inn, budget motel, or chock-full-of-RVs campground—western Colorado has it in abundance. Rates vary season to season, particularly in the resort towns. Some properties close in fall once the aspens have shed their golden leaves, open in winter when the lifts begin running, close in spring after the snow melts, and open again in mid-May or early June.

Restaurants

With dining options ranging from creative international cuisine in the resort towns of Telluride and Durango to no-frills American fare in down-home communities, no one has any excuse to visit a chain restaurant here (though they predominate in Grand Junction). The leading chefs are tapping into the region's local bounty, so you can find innovative recipes for ranch-raised game, lamb, and trout. Many serve only locally raised, grass-fed meats. Olathe sweet corn is a delicacy enjoyed across the state (and found in grocery stores and roadside stands as well as restaurants). Seasonal produce is highlighted on the best menus.

HOTEL AND RESTAURANT PRICES

Restaurant and hotel reviews have been shortened. For full information, visit Fodors.com. Restaurant prices are the average cost of a main course at dinner or, if dinner is not served, at lunch, excluding 5.9%–8.1% tax. Hotel prices are the lowest cost of a standard double room in high season, excluding service charges and 7.6%–9.9% tax.

What It Costs

$	$$	$$$	$$$$
RESTAURANTS			
under $15	$15–$22	$23–$30	over $30
HOTELS			
under $125	$125–$200	$201–$300	over $300

Grand Junction

255 miles west of Denver via I–70.

Grand Junction is where the mountains and desert meet at the confluence of the mighty Colorado and Gunnison rivers—a grand junction indeed. No matter which direction you look, there's an adventure waiting to happen. The city, with a population of more than 59,000, is nestled between the picturesque Grand Mesa to the south and the towering Book Cliffs to the north. It's a great base camp for a vacation—whether you're into art galleries, boutiques, hiking, horseback riding, rafting, mountain biking, or winery tours.

The Art on the Corner exhibit showcases leading regional sculptors, whose latest works are installed on the Main Street Mall. Passersby may find their faces reflected in an enormous chrome buffalo (titled *Chrome on the Range II*) or, a few streets down, encounter an enormous cactus made entirely of rusted (but still prickly) chainsaw chains.

GETTING HERE AND AROUND

A Touch With Class has regular limo service into Grand Junction and outlying communities. Sunshine Taxi serves Grand Junction. Amtrak runs the *California Zephyr* round-trip from San Francisco to Chicago, which stops in Grand Junction, Glenwood Springs, Winter Park, and Denver. Grand Valley Transit operates 11 public bus routes that are geared to commuters between Grand Junction, Palisade, Clifton, Orchard Mesa, and Fruita.

CONTACTS A Touch With Class. ☎ *970/245–5466* 🌐 *www.colorado-limo.com.* **Grand Valley Transit.** ☎ *970/256–7433* 🌐 *www.gvt.mesacounty.us.* **Sunshine Taxi.** ✉ *1321 Ute Ave.* ☎ *970/245–8294* 🌐 *sunshinetaxigj.com.*

TOURS

Dino Digs

ARCHAEOLOGICAL SITE | FAMILY | Ever wonder what it's like to be on a dinosaur expedition? Here's your chance. The Museums of Western Colorado sponsors one- to five-day Dino Digs all over northwestern Colorado, and folks find fresh fossils all the time. The area includes some rich Late Jurassic soil, Morrison Formation sites, and other well-preserved zones that make for impressive discoveries. You never know what might be unearthed. ✉ *Grand Junction* ☎ *888/488–3466, 970/242–0971* 🌐 *www.dinodigs.org* 🎫 *From $75.*

Dinosaur Journey

SPECIAL-INTEREST | This company leads one- to five-day paleontological treks that include work in a dinosaur quarry. ✉ *550 Jurassic Ct., Fruita* ☎ *970/858–7282* 🌐 *www.dinosaurjourney.org* 🎫 *From $9.*

VISITOR INFORMATION

CONTACTS Grand Junction Visitor & Convention Bureau. ✉ *740 Horizon Dr.* ☎ *800/962–2547, 970/244–1480* 🌐 *www.visitgrandjunction.com.*

Sights

The Art Center

MUSEUM | This center rotates a fine permanent collection of Native American tapestries and Western contemporary art, including the only complete series of lithographs by noted printmaker Paul Pletka. The fantastically carved doors—done by a WPA artist in the 1930s—alone are worth the visit. Take time to view the elegant historic homes along North 7th Street afterward. Admission is always free for children under 12; it's also free on Tuesdays for everyone. ✉ *1803 N. 7th St.* ☎ *970/243–7337* 🌐 *www.gjartcenter.org* 🎫 *$3* ⏲ *Closed Sun. and Mon.*

★ **Little Book Cliffs Wild Horse Range**

NATURE PRESERVE | One of just three ranges in the United States set aside for wild horses, this range encompasses 36,113 acres of rugged canyons and plateaus in the Book Cliffs. Between 90 and 150 wild horses roam the sagebrush-covered hills. Most years new foals can be spotted with their mothers in spring and early summer on the hillsides just off the main trails. Local favorites for riding include the Coal Canyon Trail and Main Canyon Trail, where the herd often goes in winter. Vehicles are permitted on designated trails. ✉ *Grand Junction* ✥ *About 8 miles northeast of Grand Junction* ☎ *970/244–3000, 800/417–9647* 🌐 *www.co.blm.gov* 🎫 *Free.*

Museum of the West

MINE | The Museum of the West relates the history of the area since the 1880s, with a time line, a firearms display, and a Southwest pottery collection. The area's rich mining heritage is perfectly captured in the uranium mine that educates with interactive sound and exhibit stations, and the museum also oversees paleontological excavations. The museums of the Grand Junction area have banded together as the Museums of Western Colorado, which comprises the Museum of the West (this one), the **Dinosaur Journey Museum** (550 Jurassic Court in Fruita), and the **Cross Orchards Living History Farm** (3073 F Rd. in Grand Junction). ✉ *462 Ute Ave.* ☎ *970/242–0971* 🌐 *www.museumofwesternco.com* 🎫 *$7* ⏲ *Closed Sun. and Mon.*

Restaurants

Dos Hombres

$$ | MEXICAN | FAMILY | Casual and colorful, Dos Hombres serves the usual variety of combination platters and Mexican specialties, and loads up the plates for low prices. The fajitas and enchiladas are particularly well made, with quality meats and a noticeable lack of grease, and they have an unusually large menu of interesting salads (check out the Cancun version, with pineapple and fried tortilla strips). **Known for:** sangria brunch; freshly fried, salt-free chips; margarita happy hour.

$ Average main: $15 ✉ 421 Brach Dr. ☎ 970/434–5078 🌐 www.go2dos.com.

Il Bistro Italiano

$$$ | **ITALIAN** | With a chef hailing from the birthplace of Parmigiano-Reggiano, this restaurant's authenticity is assured, down to that perfectly delivered final shredded topping. Diners are greeted by a case of pasta made fresh daily and assisted by a staff that knows the origins of each home-style dish. **Known for:** signature "Rosetta" noodle and ham dish; wine from Italy and Colorado; menu that changes weekly. *$ Average main: $29 ✉ 400 Main St. ☎ 970/243–8622 🌐 www.ilbistroitaliano.com ⏲ Closed Sun. and Mon. No lunch.*

★ Pablo's Pizza

$ | **PIZZA** | **FAMILY** | Drawing inspiration from Pablo Picasso's artwork, the pizzas at this funky joint make for a diverse palette of flavors and fun. Specialties include creations such as Popeye's Passion (featuring spinach and "olive oyl") or Dracula's Nemesis (studded with roasted garlic). **Known for:** locally sourced ingredients; party atmosphere; local wines and beers. *$ Average main: $10 ✉ 319 Main St. ☎ 970/255–8879 🌐 www.pablospizza.com.*

The Winery

$$$$ | **AMERICAN** | This is *the* place for that big night out and other special occasions in the area. The menu isn't terribly adventuresome, but the kitchen does turn out fresh-fish specials and top-notch steak, chicken, prime rib, and shrimp in simple, flavorful sauces. **Known for:** obscure, rare wines; top-notch steak; inviting wood-lined bar. *$ Average main: $40 ✉ 642 Main St. ☎ 970/242–4100 🌐 www.winery-restaurant.com ⏲ No lunch.*

Hotels

DoubleTree by Hilton

$$ | **HOTEL** | **FAMILY** | At this sprawling full-service property, service begins with a warm cookie at check-in, and the attention to detail continues from there; many of the large rooms have vast mountain views, along with a long list of amenities. **Pros:** outdoor heated pool and hot tub; kid-friendly atmosphere; sports facilities. **Cons:** restaurant and room service food is so-so; feels like a chain; big groups can make it noisy. *$ Rooms from: $136 ✉ 743 Horizon Dr. ☎ 970/241–8888, 800/222–8733 🌐 www.doubletreegrandjunction.com 273 rooms No meals.*

Fairfield Inn & Suites Grand Junction

$$ | **HOTEL** | Well situated in the middle of the downtown shopping district, this Marriott-owned property is ideal for business travelers, with spacious rooms that sport small sitting areas and large desks. **Pros:** downtown locale; cavernous rooms; quiet at night. **Cons:** chain-hotel atmosphere; extra $7 charge for parking; breakfast is average. *$ Rooms from: $130 ✉ 225 Main St. ☎ 970/242–2525 🌐 www.marriott.com 70 rooms Free Breakfast.*

Grand Vista Hotel

$ | **HOTEL** | **FAMILY** | Plush high-back chairs invite visitors to relax in the spacious lobby of this hotel that lives up to its name. **Pros:** unbeatable views; complimentary bike storage; low price. **Cons:** mediocre breakfast buffet; service is patchy; rooms feel dated. *$ Rooms from: $80 ✉ 2790 Crossroads Blvd. ☎ 970/241–8411, 800/800–7796 🌐 www.grandvistahotel.com 158 rooms Free Breakfast.*

Two Rivers Winery & Chateau

$ | **B&B/INN** | Open a bottle of wine inside the vineyard where it was created at this rustic French-styled inn set among acres of vines. **Pros:** idyllic locale; tasty wines always at hand; expansive continental breakfast. **Cons:** winery and functions make this noisier than the usual B&B; rooms are chilly in winter; walls are thin. *Rooms from: $92* *2087 Broadway* *970/241–3155, 866/312–9463* *www.tworiverswinery.com* *10 rooms* *Free Breakfast.*

Nightlife

Bistro 743 Lounge
BARS/PUBS | This lounge inside the DoubleTree by Hilton serves beverages, appetizers, and light snacks. On weekends, entertainers perform in the bar, and occasionally outside on the beer-garden stage. *743 Horizon Dr.* *970/241–8888* *doubletreegrandjunction.com.*

Blue Moon Bar and Grille
BARS/PUBS | This local bar, which serves decent wings, sandwiches, and other typical (albeit above-average) pub grub, is a popular spot for patrons to nurse their favorite brew while catching up with colleagues and friends. *120 N. 7th St.* *970/242–4506* *www.bluemoongj.com.*

Rockslide Brewery
BREWPUBS/BEER GARDENS | This brewery has won awards for its ales, porters, and stouts. The menu of burgers and other sandwiches, steaks, and pastas has something for just about everyone. The patio is open in summer. *401 Main St.* *970/245–2111* *www.rockslidebrewpub.com.*

Shopping

Enstrom Candies
FOOD/CANDY | **FAMILY** | The sweetest deal in town, Enstrom Candies is known for its scrumptious candy and renowned toffee. *701 Colorado Ave.* *970/683–1000* *enstrom.com.*

Heirlooms for Hospice
CLOTHING | The cute but upscale boutique Heirlooms for Hospice has great secondhand designer clothing and shabby-chic furniture. *635 Main St.* *970/254–8556, 866/310–8900* *www.heirloomsforhospice.com.*

Working Artists Studio and Gallery
ART GALLERIES | This studio and gallery carries prints, pottery, stained glass, and unique gifts. *520 Main St.* *970/256–9952* *www.workingartistsgallery.com.*

Activities

GOLF

The Golf Club at Redlands Mesa
GOLF | The 18-hole, Jim Engh–designed championship course sits in a natural desert setting at an elevation of 4,600 feet in the shadows of the Colorado National Monument, just minutes from downtown. Sunset across the monument is spectacular, and the game is a challenge of red-rock walls and sloping stone formations. *2325 W. Ridges Blvd.* *970/255–7400, 866/863–9270* *www.redlandsmesa.com* *$79* *Monument Course: 18 holes, 7007 yards, par 72; Redlands Course: 18 holes, 6486 yards, par 72; Canyon Course: 18 holes, 5281 yards, par 72; Desert Course: 18 holes, 4890 yards, par 72* *Reservations essential.*

MOUNTAIN BIKING

Several routes through Grand Junction are well suited to bicycle use. The city also has designated bike lanes in some areas. You can bike along the Colorado Riverfront Trails, a network that winds along the Colorado River, stretching from the Redlands Parkway to Palisade.

Colorado Plateau Mountain Bike Trail Association
BICYCLING | Those interested in bike tours should contact the Colorado Plateau Mountain Bike Trail Association. *Grand Junction* *970/901–4121* *www.copmoba.org.*

Kokopelli's Trail
BICYCLING | This trail links Grand Junction with the famed Slickrock Trail outside Moab, Utah. The 142-mile stretch winds through high desert and the Colorado

River Valley before climbing La Sal Mountains. ✉ *Loma.*

OUTFITTERS

Brown Cycles

BICYCLING | This company rents road, mountain, and hybrid bikes that start around $60 a day. It also sells and fixes bikes, and offers a full line of tandems for families, with expanded kid options for rent and sale, as well. Aficionados should allow some extra time to check out the interesting bike museum, with models from as early as the 1860s. ✉ *549 Main St.* ☎ *970/245–7939* 🌐 *www.browncycles.com.*

Over the Edge Sports

BICYCLING | Over the Edge Sports offers mountain-biking lessons and half- or full-day customized bike tours. ✉ *202 E. Aspen Ave., Fruita* ☎ *970/858–7220* 🌐 *www.otesports.com.*

Ruby Canyon Cycles

BICYCLING | This outfitter rents high-end, 29-inch, full-suspension mountain bikes for $80 the first day and $65 on subsequent days. The cycle shop also sponsors weekly evening rides around the area. ✉ *301 Main St.* ☎ *970/241–0141* 🌐 *www.rubycanyoncycles.com.*

Dinosaur National Monument

90 miles west of Craig via U.S. 40.

Overlapping the border between Colorado and Utah, Dinosaur National Monument offers river runners and dinosaur enthusiasts a remote and magnificent attraction that more than rewards the effort to get here. Colorful canyons and endless opportunities to examine fossils and bones make the monument a unique destination, and the Yampa and Green rivers provide cooling relief from what is much of the year a hot and dry desert landscape.

GETTING HERE AND AROUND

U.S. 40 west from Denver or east from Utah is the best way to reach Dinosaur National Monument. You also can take Highway 139 and Route 64 from Grand Junction. The town of Dinosaur, with a few somewhat dilapidated concrete dinosaur statues watching over their namesake town, merits only a brief stop on the way to the real thing: the bones at Dinosaur National Monument.

Sights

★ **Dinosaur National Monument**

NATURE SITE | **FAMILY** | Straddling the Colorado–Utah border, Dinosaur National Monument is a must for any dinosaur enthusiast. A two-story hill teeming with fossils—many still in the complete skeletal shapes of the dinosaurs—greets visitors at one of the few places in the world where you can touch a dinosaur bone still embedded in the earth. The Colorado side of the park offers some of the best hiking in the West, along the Harpers Corner and Echo Park Drive routes and the ominous-sounding Canyon of Lodore (where the Green River rapids buffet rafts). The drive is accessible only in summer—even then, four-wheel drive is preferable—and some of the most breathtaking overlooks are well off the beaten path. ✉ *4545 E. Hwy. 40, Dinosaur* ☎ *435/781–7700* 🌐 *www.nps.gov/dino* 🎫 *$25 per vehicle; $15 per individual.*

Dinosaur Quarry

NATURE SITE | The Dinosaur Quarry Exhibit Hall showcases an estimated 1,500 dinosaur bones that date to the late Jurassic Period still embedded in the clay. Open daily, the Exhibit Hall is ranger-guided only in the winter; check the website or call ahead for shuttle hours and access availability. Fossils are visible only from the Utah side of the monument, not the Colorado side. A half mile away is a massive 7,595-square-foot visitor center. *Visitor center: 7 miles north of Jensen, Utah, on Rte. 139, Dinosaur 970/374–3000 Canyon Visitor Center in Colorado, 435/781–7700 Quarry Visitor Center in Utah nps.gov/dino $25 per vehicle; $15 per individual.*

Restaurants

BedRock Depot

$ | **AMERICAN** | **FAMILY** | New batches of homemade ice cream show up almost every day at this roadside shop, where the walls are a gallery for the owners' photography and artwork. The shop sells fresh sandwiches—including a terrific roast beef on house-baked rolls—and specialty coffees, bottled root beer, cream soda, and ginger ale. **Known for:** "Mochasaurus" coffee; convivial atmosphere; kitschy souvenir gift shop. *Average main: $8 214 W. Brontosaurus Blvd., Dinosaur 970/374–2336 www.bedrockdepot.com Closed Thurs. No dinner Sun.*

Massadona Tavern & Steak House

$$ | **AMERICAN** | A restaurant and bar, Massadona is small, homey, and rustic, with a smattering of Western decor items and a mixture of tables and booths. It's also a casual, inviting, and relaxing place to stop after a day of digging around in dinosaur dirt, even if it's kind of in the middle of nowhere (20 minutes east of Dinosaur and a half-hour drive from the monument). **Known for:** bacon cheeseburger; weekly fish taco special; friendly owners. *Average main: $16 22927 Hwy. 40, Dinosaur 970/374–2324 Closed Mon. year-round and Sun.–Thurs. in Nov.–Mar. No lunch weekdays Apr.–Oct.*

Activities

HIKING

Desert Voices Nature Trail

HIKING/WALKING | **FAMILY** | This nature trail is near the Dinosaur Quarry. The 1½-mile loop is moderate in difficulty and has a series of trail signs produced for kids by kids. *Split Mountain area, across from boat ramp, Dinosaur nps.gov/dino.*

RAFTING

Adventure Bound River Expeditions

WHITE-WATER RAFTING | One of the best ways to experience the rugged beauty of the park is on a white-water raft trip. Adventure Bound River Expeditions runs two- to five-day excursions on the Colorado, Yampa, and Green rivers. *Grand Junction 800/423–4668, 970/247–4789 www.adventureboundusa.com.*

Black Canyon of the Gunnison National Park

South Rim: 15 miles east of Montrose, via U.S. 50 and Rte. 347. North Rim: 11 miles south of Crawford, via Rte. 92 and North Rim Rd.

The Black Canyon of the Gunnison River is one of Colorado's most awe-inspiring places—a vivid testament to the powers of erosion, the canyon is roughly 2,000 feet deep. The steep angles of the cliffs allow little sunlight, and ever-present shadows blanket the canyon walls, leaving some of it in almost perpetual darkness and inspiring the canyon's name. And while this dramatic landscape makes the gorge a remarkable place to visit, it also has prevented any permanent occupation—there's no evidence that humans have ever taken up residence within the canyon's walls.

Spanish explorers encountered the formidable chasm in 1765 and 1776, and several other expeditions surveyed it from the mid-1800s to the early 1900s.

The early groups hoped to find a route suitable for trains to transport the West's rich resources and the people extracting them. One such train—the Denver and Rio Grande narrow-gauge railroad, completed in 1882—did succeed in constructing a line through the far eastern reaches of the canyon, from Gunnison to Cimmaron, but ultimately concluded that the steepest and deepest part of the canyon, which is now the national park, was "impenetrable." Even so, the rail line's views were majestic enough and the passages narrow enough to earn it the moniker "Scenic Line of the World."

In the late 1800s Black Canyon explorers had another goal in mind: building a tunnel through the side of the canyon to divert water from the Gunnison River into the nearby Uncompahgre Valley, to nurture crops and sustain settlements, such as Montrose. To this day, water still flows through the tunnel, located at the Black Canyon's East Portal, to irrigate the valley's rich farmland.

Once the tunnel was complete, the focus shifted from esteeming the canyon for its resources to appreciating its aesthetic and recreational value. In 1933, Black Canyon of the Gunnison was designated a national monument, and from 1933–35, Civilian Conservation Corps crews built the North Rim Road, under the direction of the National Park Service. More than 60 years later, in 1999, the canyon was redesignated as a national park. Today, the canyon is far enough removed from civilization that its unspoiled depths continue, as an 1883 explorer wrote, to "arouse the wondering and reverent amazement of one's being."

GETTING ORIENTED

East Portal. The only way you can get down to the river via automobile in Black Canyon is on the steep East Portal Road. There's a campground and picnic area here, as well as fishing and trail access. Check the park website before you go, however; a repaving project will be closing the road for an extended time.

North Rim. If you want to access this side of the canyon from the South Rim, you will have to leave the park and wend around it to either the west (through Montrose and Delta) or to the east (via Hwy. 92); expect a drive of at least two hours. The area's remoteness and difficult location mean the North Rim is rarely crowded; the road is partially unpaved and closes in the winter. There's also a small ranger station here.

South Rim. This is the main area of the park. The park's only visitor center is here, along with a campground, a few picnic areas, and many hiking trails. The South Rim Road closes at Gunnison Point in the winter, when skiers and snowshoers take over.

WHEN TO GO

Summer is the busiest season, with July experiencing the greatest crowds. However, a spring or fall visit gives you two advantages: fewer people and cooler temperatures. In summer, especially in years with little rainfall, daytime temperatures can reach into the 90s. Winter brings even more solitude, as all but one section of campsites are shut down and only about 2 miles of South Rim Road, the park's main road, are plowed.

November through March is when the snow hits, with an average of about 3 to 8 inches of it monthly. March through April and July and August are the rainiest, with about an inch of precipitation each month. June is generally the driest month. Temperatures at the bottom of the canyon are about 8 degrees warmer than at the rim.

GETTING HERE AND AROUND

AIR

The Black Canyon of the Gunnison lies between the cities of Gunnison and Montrose, both with small regional airports.

CAR

The park has three roads. South Rim Road, reached by Route 347, is the primary thoroughfare and winds along the canyon's South Rim. From about late November to early April, the road is not plowed past the visitor center at Gunnison Point. North Rim Road, reached by Route 92, is usually open from April through Thanksgiving; in winter, the road is unplowed. On the park's south side, the serpentine East Portal Road descends abruptly to the Gunnison River below. The road is usually open from April through the end of November. Because of the grade, vehicles or vehicle-trailer combinations longer than 22 feet are not permitted. The park has no public transportation.

PARK ESSENTIALS

ACCESSIBILITY

South Rim Visitor Center is accessible to people with mobility impairments, as are most of the sites at South Rim Campground. Drive-to overlooks on the South Rim include Tomichi Point, the alternate gravel viewpoint at Pulpit Rock (the main one is not accessible), Chasm View (gravel), Sunset View, and High Point. Balanced Rock (gravel) is the only drive-to viewpoint on the North Rim. None of the park's hiking trails are accessible by car.

PARK FEES AND PERMITS

Entrance fees are $25 per week per vehicle. Visitors entering on bicycle, motorcycle, or on foot pay $15 for a weekly pass. To access the inner canyon, you must pick up a wilderness permit (no fee).

PARK HOURS

The park is open 24/7 year-round. It's in the mountain time zone.

CELL-PHONE RECEPTION

Cell-phone reception in the park is unreliable and sporadic. There are public telephones at South Rim Visitor Center and South Rim Campground.

VISITOR INFORMATION

Black Canyon of the Gunnison National Park
Montrose ✢ *7 miles north of U.S. 50 on CO Hwy. 347* ☎ *970/641–2337* *www.nps.gov/blca.*

Sights

SCENIC DRIVES

The scenic South and North Rim roads offer deep and distant views into the canyon. Both also offer several lookout points and short hiking trails along the rim. The trails that go down into the canyon are steep and strenuous, and essentially unmarked, and so are reserved for experienced (and very fit) hikers.

East Portal Road

SCENIC DRIVE | The only way to access the Gunnison River from the park by car is via this paved route, which drops approximately 2,000 feet down to the water in only 5 miles, giving it an extremely steep grade. Vehicles longer than 22 feet are not allowed on the road. If you're towing a trailer, you can unhitch it near the entrance to South Rim campground. The bottom of the road is actually in the adjacent Curecanti National Recreation Area. There you'll find a picnic area, a campground, a primitive riverside trail, and beautiful scenery. A tour of East Portal Road, with a brief stop at the bottom, takes about 45 minutes. Immediately after arrival through the park's South entrance, take a right on East Portal Road. *Closed mid-Nov.–mid.-Apr.*

South Rim Road

SCENIC DRIVE | This paved 7-mile stretch from Tomichi Point to High Point is the park's main road. The drive follows the canyon's level South Rim; 12 overlooks are accessible from the road, most via short gravel trails. Several short hikes along the rim also begin roadside. Allow between two and three hours round-trip.

SCENIC SIGHTS

The vast depths that draw thousands of visitors each year to Black Canyon have also historically prevented any extensive human habitation from taking root, so cultural attractions are largely absent here. But what the park lacks in historic sites it more than makes up for in scenery.

Chasm and Painted Wall Views

VIEWPOINT | At the heart-in-your-throat Chasm viewpoint, the canyon walls plummet 1,820 feet to the river, but are only 1,100 feet apart at the top. As you peer down into the depths, keep in mind that this section is where the Gunnison River descends at its steepest rate, dropping 240 feet within the span of a mile. A few hundred yards farther is the best place from which to see Painted Wall, Colorado's tallest cliff. Pinkish swaths of pegmatite (a crystalline, granitelike rock) give the wall its colorful, marbled appearance. ✉ *Black Canyon of the Gunnison National Park* ✣ *Approximately 3½ miles from the visitor center on South Rim Rd.*

Narrows View

VIEWPOINT | Look upriver from this North Rim viewing spot and you'll be able to see into the canyon's narrowest section, just a slot really, with only 40 feet between the walls at the bottom. The canyon is also taller (1,725 feet) here than it is wide at the rim (1,150 feet). ✉ *North Rim Rd., first overlook along the left fork of the North Rim Rd., Black Canyon of the Gunnison National Park.*

Warner Point

NATURE SITE | This viewpoint, at the end of the Warner Point Nature Trail, delivers awesome views of the canyon's deepest point (2,722 feet), plus the nearby San Juan and West Elk mountain ranges. ✉ *End of Warner Point Nature Trail, westernmost end of South Rim Rd., Black Canyon of the Gunnison National Park.*

VISITOR CENTERS

North Rim Ranger Station

INFO CENTER | This small facility on the park's North Rim is open sporadically and only in summer. Rangers can provide information and assistance and can issue permits for wilderness use and rock climbing. If rangers are out in the field, which they often are, guests can find directions for obtaining permits posted in the station. ✉ *North Rim Rd., 11 miles from Rte. 92 turnoff, Black Canyon of the Gunnison National Park* ☎ *970/641–2337.*

South Rim Visitor Center

INFO CENTER | The park's only visitor center offers interactive exhibits and an introductory film detailing the park's geology and wildlife. Inquire at the center about free informational ranger programs. ✉ *Black Canyon of the Gunnison National Park* ✣ *1½ mile from the entrance station on South Rim Rd.* ☎ *970/249–1914.*

Restaurants

There's no food service in the park. The closest restaurants are in Montrose, 14 miles west of the park.

Camp Robber

$$ | SOUTHWESTERN | This simply decorated restaurant serves some of Montrose's most creative cuisine, such as its famous green-chile chicken and potato soup or shrimp, avocado, and prosciutto pasta (gluten-free options available too). At lunch, salads with house-made dressings, hearty sandwiches, and blue-corn enchiladas fuel hungry hikers. **Known for:** New Mexican dishes; house-made salsa and desserts; shaded patio. $ *Average main: $15* ✉ *1515 Ogden Rd., Montrose* ☎ *970/240–1590* 🌐 *www.camprobber.com* ⏲ *No dinner Sun.*

Colorado Boy Pizzeria & Brewery

$ | PIZZA | The dough is house-made (with Italian-imported flour) and the beer is home-brewed at this trendy downtown pizzeria with high ceilings, brick walls, and contemporary decor. Sit at the pizza bar in the back and enjoy an English-style ale while you watch the chefs craft your tasty pie. **Known for:** home-brewed ales; growlers and cans to go; house-made sausage. *Average main: $10 ✉ 320 E. Main St., Montrose ☎ 970/240–2790 🌐 www.coloradoboy.com ⏲ No lunch weekdays.*

Hotels

Besides three developed campgrounds within the park boundaries, you'll need to travel 14 miles west to Montrose (or 72 miles to Grand Junction) to find lodging near the park.

Country Lodge

$ | **HOTEL** | A log cabin–style building and rooms ringing a pretty garden and pool make this hotel feel remote even though it's on Montrose's main drag. **Pros:** great value; intimate feel; nice pool and hot tub. **Cons:** small bathrooms and TVs; on main highway, so it can sometimes be noisy; breakfast is basic. *Rooms from: $90 ✉ 1624 E. Main St., Montrose ☎ 970/249–4567 🌐 www.country-lodgecolorado.com 23 rooms Free Breakfast.*

Red Arrow Inn & Suites

$$ | **HOTEL** | This low-key establishment offers reasonable prices for one of the nicest lodgings in the area, mainly because of the large, pretty rooms filled with handsome wood furnishings. **Pros:** good breakfast; outdoor firepit; pleasant outdoor pool. **Cons:** motel-style entrances; next to busy street; decor doesn't offer much local flavor. *Rooms from: $140 ✉ 1702 E. Main St., Montrose ☎ 970/249–9641 🌐 www.redarrowinn.com 59 rooms Free Breakfast.*

Activities

BOATING AND KAYAKING

With Class V rapids, the Gunnison River is one of the premier kayak challenges in North America. The spectacular 14-mile stretch of the river that passes through the park is so narrow in some sections that the rim seems to be closing up above your head. Once you're downstream from the rapids (and out of the park), the canyon opens up into what is called the Gunnison Gorge National Conservation Area. The rapids ease considerably, and the trip becomes more of a quiet float on Class I to Class IV water. Access to the Gunnison Gorge is only by foot or horseback. However, several outfitters offer guided raft and kayak trips in the Gunnison Gorge and other sections of the Gunnison River.

Kayaking the river through the park requires a wilderness use permit (and lots of expertise); rafting is not allowed. You can, however, take a guided pontoon-boat trip into the eastern end of the canyon via Morrow Point Boat Tours, which launch from the Curecanti National Recreation Area, east of the park.

Lake Fork Marina

BOATING | Located on the western end of Blue Mesa Reservoir off U.S. 92, the Lake Fork Marina rents all types of boats. If you have your own, there's a ramp at the marina and slips for rent. Guided fishing excursions can also be booked here. *✉ Off U.S. 92, near Lake Fork Campground, Gunnison ☎ 970/641–3048 🌐 www.thebluemesa.com.*

Morrow Point Boat Tours

BOATING | Starting in neighboring Curecanti National Recreation Area, these guided tours run twice daily (except Tuesday) in the summer, at 10 am and 1 pm. Morrow Point Boat Tours take passengers on a 90-minute trip into the Black Canyon via pontoon boat. Passengers must walk 1 mile in each direction to and from the boat dock (includes quite a few stairs), and reservations are required. *✉ Pine Creek Trail and Boat Dock, U.S. 50, milepost 130, 25 miles west of Gunnison, Gunnison ☎ 970/641–2337 🌐 www.nps.gov/cure $25 ⏲ Closed mid-Sept.–May.*

CAMPING

There are three campgrounds in Black Canyon National Park. The small North Rim Campground is first come, first served, and is closed in the winter. Vehicles longer than 35 feet are discouraged from this campground. South Rim Campground is considerably larger, and has a loop that's open year-round. Reservations are accepted in South Rim Loops A and B. Power hookups only exist in Loop B. The East Portal campground is at the bottom of the steep East Portal Road and is open whenever the road is open. It offers 15 first-come, first-served tent sites in a pretty, riverside setting. Water has to be trucked up to the campgrounds, so use it in moderation; it's shut off in mid-to-late September. Generators are not allowed at South Rim and are highly discouraged on the North Rim.

East Portal Campground. Its location next to the Gunnison River makes it perfect for fishing. ✉ *East Portal Rd., 5 miles from the main entrance.*

North Rim Campground. This small campground, nestled amid pine trees, offers the basics along the quiet North Rim. ✉ *North Rim Rd., 11¼ miles from Rte. 92.*

South Rim Campground. Stay on the canyon rim at this main campground right inside the park entrance. Loops A and C have tent sites only. The RV hookups are in Loop B, and those sites are priced higher than those in other parts of the campground. It's possible to camp here year-round (Loop A stays open all winter), but the loops are not plowed, so you'll have to hike in with your tent. ✉ *South Rim Rd., 1 mile from the visitor center.*

HIKING

All trails can be hot in summer and most don't receive much shade, so bring water, a hat, and plenty of sunscreen. Dogs are permitted, on leash, on Rim Rock, Cedar Point Nature, and Chasm View Nature trails, and at any overlook. Venturing into the inner canyon, while doable, is not for the faint of heart—or slight of step. Six named routes lead down to the river, but they are not maintained or marked, and they require a wilderness permit. In fact, the park staff won't even call them trails; they refer to them as "Class III scrambles" These supersteep, rocky routes vary in one-way distance from 1 to 2¾ miles, and the descent can be anywhere from 1,800 to 2,722 feet. Your reward, of course, is a rare look at the bottom of the canyon and the fast-flowing Gunnison. **■TIP→ Don't attempt an inner-canyon excursion without plenty of water (the park's recommendation is one gallon per person, per day).** For descriptions of the routes and the necessary permit to hike them, stop at the visitor center at the South Rim or the North Rim ranger station. Dogs are not permitted in the inner canyon.

Wildlife in Black Canyon

You may spot peregrine falcons nesting in May and June. Other raptors (red-tailed hawks, Cooper's hawks, golden eagles) circle above year round. In summer, turkey vultures join the flying corps, and in winter, bald eagles. Mule deer, elk, and the very shy bobcat also call the park home. In spring and fall, look for porcupines among pinyon pines on the rims. Listen for the chirp of the yellow-bellied marmot on sunny, rocky outcrops. Though rarely seen, mountain lions and black bears also live in the park.

EASY

Cedar Point Overlook Trail

TRAIL | FAMILY | This 0.4-mile round-trip interpretive trail leads out from South Rim Road to two overlooks. It's an easy stroll, and signs along the way detail the surrounding plants. *Easy.* ✉ *Black Canyon of the Gunnison National Park* ✣ *Trailhead: Off South Rim Rd., 4¼ miles from South Rim Visitor Center.*

Deadhorse Trail

TRAIL | Despite its name, the 6-mile Deadhorse Trail is actually a pleasant hike, starting on an old service road from the Kneeling Camel view on the North Rim Road. The trail's farthest point provides the park's easternmost viewpoint. From this overlook, the canyon is much more open, with pinnacles and spires rising along its sides. *Easy.* ✉ *Black Canyon of the Gunnison National Park* ✣ *Trailhead: At the southernmost end of North Rim Rd.*

MODERATE

Chasm View Nature Trail

TRAIL | The park's shortest trail (0.3 mile round-trip) starts at North Rim Campground and offers an impressive 50-yard walk right along the canyon rim as well as an eye-popping view of Painted Wall and Serpent Point. This is also an excellent place to spot raptors, swifts, and other birds. *Moderate.* ✉ *Black Canyon of the Gunnison National Park* ✣ *Trailhead: At North Rim Campground, 11¼ miles from Rte. 92.*

North Vista Trail

TRAIL | The round-trip hike to Exclamation Point is 3 miles; a more difficult foray to the top of 8,563-foot Green Mountain (a mesa, really) is 7 miles. The trail leads you along the North Rim; keep an eye out for especially gnarled pinyon pines—the North Rim is the site of some of the oldest groves of pinyons in North America, between 700 and 900 years old. *Moderate.* ✉ *Black Canyon of the Gunnison National Park* ✣ *Trailhead: at North Rim ranger station, off North Rim Rd., 11 miles from Rte. 92 turnoff.*

★ Warner Point Nature Trail

TRAIL | The 1½-mile round-trip hike starts from High Point. It provides fabulous vistas of the San Juan and West Elk mountains and Uncompahgre Valley. Warner Point, at trail's end, has the steepest drop-off from rim to river: a dizzying 2,722 feet. *Moderate.* ✉ *Black Canyon of the Gunnison National Park* ✣ *Trailhead: At the end of South Rim Rd.*

HORSEBACK RIDING

Although its name might indicate otherwise, Deadhorse Trail is actually the only trail in the park where horses are allowed. Although no permit is required, the park has no riding facilities.

Elk Ridge Trail Rides

HORSEBACK RIDING | You can take 90-minute trail rides at this ranch just outside the Black Canyon National Park. ✉ *10203 Bostwick Park Rd., Montrose* ☎ *970/240–6007* 🌐 *www.elkridgeranchinc.com* 🎫 *$75. Reservations required.*

ROCK CLIMBING

Rock climbing in the park is for experts only, but you can do some bouldering at the Marmot Rocks area, about 100 feet south of South Rim Road between Painted Wall and Cedar Point overlooks (park at Painted Wall). Four boulder groupings offer a variety of routes rated from easy to very difficult; a pamphlet with a diagrammed map of the area is available at the South Rim Visitor Center.

Irwin Guides

CLIMBING/MOUNTAINEERING | Intermediate and expert climbers can take full-day rock-climbing guided tours in the Black Canyon on routes rated from 5.8 to 5.13. ✉ *330 Belleview Ave., Crested Butte* ☎ *970/349–5430* 🌐 *www.irwinguides.com* 🎫 *$550 for one person; $500 for two or more.*

A drive on the spectacular San Juan Skyway takes you past several mountains.

Telluride

66 miles south of Montrose via U.S. 550 and Hwy. 62; 111 miles north of Durango via U.S. 160 and Rtes. 184 and 145.

Tucked away between the azure sky and the gunmetal mountains is Telluride, the colorful mining town–turned–ski resort famous for its celebrity visitors (Oprah Winfrey, Tom Cruise, and Oliver Stone spend time here).

Telluride's first mines were established in the 1870s, and by the early 1890s the town was booming. The allure of the place was such that Butch Cassidy robbed his first bank here in 1889. These days the savage but beautiful San Juan range attracts mountain people of a different sort—skiers, snowboarders, mountain bikers, and four-wheelers—who attack any incline, up or down, with abandon.

GETTING HERE AND AROUND

Although Telluride and the ski resort town of Mountain Village are two distinct areas, you can travel between them via a 2½-mile, over-the-mountain gondola ride, arguably one of the most beautiful commutes in Colorado. The gondola makes a car unnecessary, as both the village and the town are ski- and pedestrian-friendly, assuming you aren't going anywhere else.

The free Galloping Goose shuttle loops around Telluride every 10 minutes in winter, 20 minutes in summer, and less often in the off-season. The Dial-a-Ride shuttle, also free, serves the Mountain Village area during high season. Telluride Express, a private taxi company, serves Telluride Regional Airport and the rest of the surrounding area, including other regional airports.

CONTACTS Dial-a-Ride. ✉ *Telluride Ski Resort, Telluride* ☎ *970/728–8888.* **Galloping Goose.** ☎ *970/728–5700.* **Telluride Express.** ☎ *970/728–6000, 888/212–8294* 🌐 *telluride.letsride.co.*

Telluride Bluegrass Festival

Bluegrass may have evolved from country's "Appalachian mountain music," but Telluride's Bluegrass Festival has added a distinctive Rocky Mountain note to the mix.

Since its inception in 1973, the festival has featured traditional bluegrass bands from across the nation, but when contemporary Colorado bands started adding the quintessential bluegrass instruments—mandolin, fiddle, guitar, upright bass, and banjo—to their lineups, their version of the "high lonesome sound" garnered national attention. It forced bluegrass to undergo several transformations, sometimes right before the Telluride audience's eyes, as the crowd's enthusiasm prompted more and more on-stage experimentation.

As the festival gained in popularity, it brought more bluegrass artists to Colorado, and crossover between bluegrass and other musical styles became more common. The festival earned the moniker "Woodstock of the West." Colorado bands such as String Cheese Incident, Leftover Salmon, and Yonder Mountain String Band performed regularly at the event, appealing to a younger audience and encouraging more experimentation.

Now the Telluride Bluegrass Festival often draws such popular acts as Emmylou Harris, Alison Krauss, Bonnie Raitt, Robert Plant, Janelle Monáe, Mumford & Sons, Brandi Carlile, and Counting Crows—not exactly bluegrass purists. It has also boosted the popularity of other bluegrass gatherings around the state, including a sister festival held each July at Planet Bluegrass Ranch in Lyons, Colorado, a town of about 1,600 that has become a bluegrass artists' colony.

VISITOR INFORMATION

CONTACTS Telluride Visitors Center. ✉ *236 W. Colorado Ave., Telluride* ☎ *970/728–3041, 800/525–3455* 🌐 *www.telluride.com.*

Sights

★ San Juan Skyway

SCENIC DRIVE | One of the country's most stupendously scenic drives, the 236-mile San Juan Skyway weaves through an impressive series of Fourteeners (peaks reaching more than 14,000 feet). From Telluride, it heads north on Route 145 to Placerville, where it turns east on Highway 62. On U.S. 550 it continues south to historic Ouray and over Red Mountain Pass to Silverton and then on to Durango, Mancos, and Cortez via U.S. 160. From Cortez, Route 145 heads north, passing through Rico and over lovely Lizard Head Pass before heading back into Telluride. In late September and early October, this route has some of the state's most spectacular aspen viewing. ✉ *Telluride.*

★ Telluride Historical Museum

MUSEUM | Housed in the 1896 Miner's Hospital, the Telluride Historical Museum hosts exhibits on the town's past, including work in the nearby mines, techniques used by local doctors, and an 860-year-old Native American blanket. It is one of only six Smithsonian-affiliated museums in Colorado. ✉ *201 W. Gregory Ave., Telluride* ☎ *970/728–3344* 🌐 *www.telluridemuseum.org* 🎟 *$7.*

Restaurants

★ Allred's

$$$$ | **MODERN AMERICAN** | Unless you're planning some serious hiking, the town-to-mountain gondola is the only way to reach this high-end, sky-high eatery with a stone-walled dining room and panoramic windows. Locally inspired fare such as elk, bison, and lamb feature prominently on the menu. **Known for:** après-ski drinks and apps; excellent meats and fish; incredible views that make the high prices worth it. *Average main: $42* *Top of St. Sophia gondola station, Telluride* *970/728–7474* *www.allredsrestaurant.com* *No lunch.*

Baked in Telluride

$ | **CAFÉ** | This Telluride institution turns out heavenly bagels, sandwiches made with baked-in-house bread, pizzas, hearty soups, and house-made pastas (try the Alfredo), as well as huge salads. Order your meal to go or grab a seat at one of the communal-style tables, where you can enjoy displays from a local art school. **Known for:** front porch with views; delicious breakfasts; reasonable prices. *Average main: $11* *127 S. Fir St., Telluride* *970/728–4775* *bakedintel.com.*

Brown Dog Pizza

$ | **PIZZA** | This local hangout serves a mean pizza in a pub-style atmosphere, and is one of the few places in town that will feed your family for less than the cost of a lift ticket. Brown Dog specializes in Detroit-style square pizza (an international award winner), but it also offers gluten-free, classic American, and Roman-style pies. **Known for:** Detroit-style pizza; always-hopping atmosphere; gluten-free menu. *Average main: $13* *110 E. Colorado Ave., Telluride* *970/728–8046* *www.browndogpizza.com.*

The Butcher & The Baker

$$ | **CAFÉ** | Fresh farm-to-table fare and a modern-farmhouse feel define The Butcher & The Baker, a bustling café on the town's main strip where locals gather. The delectable baked goods and sandwiches, scrumptious salads, and house-made desserts do not disappoint. **Known for:** cocktail and espresso bar; pay-by-the-scoop deli salads; house-made soups. *Average main: $18* *201 E. Colorado Ave., Telluride* *970/728–2899* *www.butcherandbakercafe.com* *No dinner Sun.*

★ La Marmotte

$$$$ | **CONTEMPORARY** | It may be housed in one of Telluride's oldest buildings, but La Marmotte provides one of the city's most modern dining experiences, with menu offerings that expertly intertwine French and local influences. The candlelight-and-white-tablecloth atmosphere and simple, contemporary decor is, like the cuisine, sophisticated without being snooty. **Known for:** divine outdoor-patio seating; inspired wine list; romantic ambience. *Average main: $35* *150 W. San Juan Ave., Telluride* *970/728–6232* *www.lamarmotte.com* *No lunch.*

New Sheridan Chop House

$$$$ | **STEAKHOUSE** | This upscale steak house is arguably Telluride's best. Here you can choose your meat (sirloin, filet mignon, and succulent bison rib eye are among the choices), then your topping (think caramelized onions, blue cheese, or glazed wild mushrooms), and then your sauce (anything from béarnaise to chimichurri). **Known for:** high-quality beef and game; hearty daily brunch options; popular wine bar. *Average main: $100* *New Sheridan Hotel, 231 W. Colorado Ave., Telluride* *970/728–9100* *www.newsheridan.com* *Closed mid-Apr.–mid-May and mid-Oct.–late Nov.*

221 South Oak

$$$$ | **EUROPEAN** | Housed in a beautifully restored Victorian, this classy bistro entices you to linger with its colorful artwork, two lovely garden patios, and scrumptious meals. The dinner menu changes frequently but always includes dishes made with locally sourced fish

(like Rocky Mountain trout or Colorado striped bass) and meat (elk, lamb, or bison). **Known for:** Sunday brunch in summer; full vegetarian menu; seasonal live music. *Average main: $70 221 S. Oak St., Telluride 970/728–9507 www.221southoak.com Closed mid-Apr.–May and mid-Oct.–mid-Dec. No lunch.*

Hotels

Camel's Garden

$$$ | **HOTEL** | An ultramodern lodge that's all sharp lines, sleek surfaces, and colorful, contemporary art is just steps from the gondola and features huge rooms and suites. **Pros:** ski-in, ski-out location; full-service Aveda day spa; creek-side views. **Cons:** breakfast is generic; no amenities for kids; parking is $15 per day. *Rooms from: $295 250 W. San Juan Ave., Telluride 970/728–9300, 888/772–2635 www.camelsgarden.com 35 rooms Free Breakfast.*

Hotel Columbia Telluride

$$$$ | **HOTEL** | Conveniently located at the base of the gondola, this hotel has a crisp and contemporary vibe. **Pros:** spacious rooms with heated bathroom floors; steps from gondola; stunning views. **Cons:** expensive; some rooms can be noisy; valet parking is $35 per day. *Rooms from: $400 301 W. San Juan Ave., Telluride 970/728–0660, 855/318–7604 www.hotelcolumbiatelluride.com 21 rooms Free Breakfast.*

The Hotel Telluride

$$$ | **HOTEL** | With luxurious rooms, tasteful Western-style decor, and dramatic views from private patios or balconies, the Hotel Telluride is an ideal place to immerse yourself in mountain culture. **Pros:** free shuttle to the gondola; lots of amenities, including complimentary bikes; great views. **Cons:** $20 parking fee; a few blocks from downtown; restaurant not open for lunch. *Rooms from: $239 199 N. Cornet St., Telluride 970/369–1188 www.thehoteltelluride.com 59 rooms No meals.*

Inn at Lost Creek

$$ | **HOTEL** | A grand stone-and-wood structure, this luxury ski-in ski-out hotel in the Mountain Village resembles an alpine lodge with contemporary furnishings. **Pros:** tasty breakfast; upscale but friendly atmosphere; rooftop hot tubs. **Cons:** some bathrooms on the small side; $20 nightly fee for parking; hot tubs require reservations. *Rooms from: $200 119 Lost Creek La., Mountain Village 970/728–5678, 888/601–5678 www.innatlostcreek.com Closed mid-Apr.–mid-May 32 rooms Free Breakfast.*

Madeline Hotel and Residences

$$$$ | **HOTEL** | This spot blends the drama of a grand European hotel with the warmth of a mountain chalet. **Pros:** air-conditioning (rare for this region); ample amenities; incredible views from pool deck. **Cons:** $40 parking fee; no meals included; additional resort fee. *Rooms from: $550 568 Mountain Village Blvd., Telluride 970/369–0880 www.aubergeresorts.com/madeline Closed mid-Oct.–mid-May 137 rooms No meals.*

New Sheridan Hotel

$$$$ | **HOTEL** | Contemporary furnishings and historic black-and-white photos adorn this beautifully restored century-old landmark on Telluride's main drag. **Pros:** rooftop bar has great views; secure ski storage with boot warmers; guests receive a discount on breakfast and lunch and a permit for street parking. **Cons:** no hot tub; noise from the bar can drift upstairs at night; no fridge or microwave in rooms. *Rooms from: $350 231 W. Colorado Ave., Telluride 970/728–4351, 800/200–1891 www.newsheridan.com Closed mid-Apr.–mid-May and mid-Oct.–mid-Nov. 26 rooms No meals.*

Last Dollar Saloon

BARS/PUBS | A favorite après-ski destination, the Last Dollar (locals know it as "The Buck") has lots of beers, great margaritas, and a rooftop bar with phenomenal views. ✉ *100 E. Colorado Ave., Telluride* ☎ *970/728–4800* 🌐 *www.lastdollarsaloon.com.*

SideWork Speakeasy

BARS/PUBS | Classy cocktails, champagne, wine, and gourmet small and large plates in a refined mid-century American–style lounge make SideWork an ideal place for a nightcap. ✉ *225 S. Pine St., Telluride* ☎ *970/728–5618* 🌐 *www.sideworkspeakeasy.com.*

There

BARS/PUBS | Tucked off the main strip, this tiny bar serves eclectic small plates, family-style entrées to share, and killer cocktails in a speakeasy atmosphere (complete with a blacklist drink menu delivered in a book). It's packed from 4:30 until 11:30 pm, so reserve a table in advance online. ✉ *627 W. Pacific Ave., Telluride* ☎ *970/728–1213* 🌐 *www.experiencethere.com.*

BOOKS

Between the Covers Bookstore

BOOKS/STATIONERY | This locally owned bookstore is perfect for browsing through the latest releases while sipping a foam-capped cappuccino from the coffee bar at the back of the shop. You'll also find a good selection of field guides and books on local history. ✉ *224 W. Colorado Ave., Telluride* ☎ *970/728–4504* 🌐 *www.between-the-covers.com.*

CLOTHING

Telluride Trappings & Toggery

CLOTHING | Check The Toggery—the town's longest-standing retail store—for stylish Telluride and Colorado souvenir tees and sweatshirts. You'll also find a large selection of men's, women's, and children's clothing and shoes. ✉ *109 E. Colorado Ave., Telluride* ☎ *970/728–3338* 🌐 *www.thetellurideToggery.com.*

Activities

DOWNHILL SKIING AND SNOWBOARDING

★ Telluride Ski Resort

SKIING/SNOWBOARDING | Dubbed "the most beautiful place you'll ever ski," Telluride Ski Resort once was known as an experts-only ski area. Indeed, the north-facing trails are impressively steep and long, and the moguls can be massive. Chairlift 9 services primarily expert terrain, including the famed Spiral Stairs and the Plunge, while Gold Hill, Bald Mountain, Black Iron Bowl, and Palmyra Peak provide challenging chutes and other double-diamond runs, as well as hiking options for expert skiers.

But then there is the other side—literally—of the ski area, the gently sloping valley called the Gorrono Basin, with long groomed runs excellent for intermediates and beginners. On the ridge that wraps around the ski area's core is the aptly named See Forever, a long cruiser that starts at 12,570 feet and delivers views over the San Juan Mountains and into Utah's La Sal mountain range. The best areas for beginners are the Meadows, off Lift 1, and Galloping Goose, a long winding trail off Lift 12 or 10. Near Gorrono Basin, off Lift 4 (the ski area's main artery), is another section that includes supersteep, double-diamond tree runs on one side and glorious cruisers on the other.

Midmountain, Lift 5 accesses a wealth of intermediate runs. From there, slide through a Western-style gate and you come to Prospect Bowl, a 733-acre area with a network of runs cut around islands of trees. Prospect Express (Lift 12) appeases not only experts—who can navigate double-diamond chutes, cliff bands, and open glades—but also beginners and intermediates, who can ski some of the highest green and blue terrain in North America.

Telluride also has three terrain parks for skiers and snowboarders of all levels. **Facilities:** 127 trails; 2,000 acres; 4,425-foot vertical drop; 16 lifts. ✉ *565 Mountain Village Blvd., Telluride* ☎ *800/778–8581* 🌐 *www.tellurideskiresort.com* 🎟 *Lift ticket $140.*

LESSONS AND PROGRAMS

Telluride Ski & Snowboard School

SKIING/SNOWBOARDING | At this well-regarded school, adult group lessons start at $160. Lessons are available for alpine and telemark skiers as well as snowboarders. Children's programs are $220 per day and include a lift ticket, lesson, and lunch. The school also offers Women's Week programs, which include three or five days of skills-building classes with female instructors. ✉ *565 Mountain Village Blvd., Telluride* ☎ *970/728–7540* 🌐 *www.tellurideskiresort.com.*

RENTALS

Bootdoctors

SKIING/SNOWBOARDING | Despite its name, Bootdoctors services go way beyond boots, renting all manner of skis, boots, and snowboards, along with backcountry gear and snowshoes. It also offers ski tuning, boot fitting, and repairs. It has two sister locations: one in Mountain Village and another on the city's main street that also serves as a year-round bike and paddleboard shop. ✉ *236 S. Oak St., Telluride* ☎ *970/728–4581* 🌐 *www.bootdoctors.com.*

Telluride Sports

SKIING/SNOWBOARDING | All manner of ski and snowboard rentals are available from the ubiquitous Telluride Sports, with 10 locations in Telluride and Mountain Village. The shop will deliver everything to your hotel for no extra charge via 🌐 *www.epicmountainrentals.com* 🌐. The Camel's Garden location has a ski valet. ✉ *150 W. Colorado Ave., Telluride* ☎ *970/728–4477* 🌐 *www.telluridesports.com.*

FOUR-WHEELING

For a short but very sweet four-wheel-drive trip, start at the east end of Colorado Avenue, where a 1¾-mile road from the old Pandora Mill leads to spectacular Bridal Veil Falls, which, at 365 feet, tumbles lavishly from the top of the box canyon. At the northern end of town, off of Oak Street, you'll find Tomboy Road, also known as Imogene Pass Road, which leads to one of the country's most interesting mining districts. The road has fabulous views of Bridal Veil Falls and Ingram Falls. After about 7 miles, it crests over 13,114-foot-high Imogene Pass, the highest pass road in the San Juans. If you continue down the other side, you end up in Yankee Boy Basin, near Ouray.

GOLF

Telluride Ski & Golf Club

GOLF | The soul-stirring, 360-degree mountain views at Telluride Golf Club may just elevate your game. Ease into play on the front nine, which includes downhill holes and a few par 3s. On the back nine, the holes lengthen, stretch uphill, and bend around doglegs for an invigorating challenge. Guests can also take advantage of a greatly expanded practice facility. The club is designated an Audubon Cooperative Sanctuary for its wildlife-habitat protection and water and biodiversity conservation efforts. Green fees include cart rental. ✉ *The Peaks Resort & Spa, 136 Country Club Dr., Mountain Village* ☎ *970/728–2606* 🌐 *www.tellurideski-andgolfclub.com* 🎟 *$210* 🏌 *18 holes, 6574 yards, par 70.*

HIKING

The peaks of the rugged San Juan Mountains around Telluride require some scrambling, occasionally bordering on real climbing, to get to the top. A local favorite is Wilson Peak, which is one of the easier Fourteeners to climb if you take the Navajo Lake Approach. July and August are the most popular months on this 9½-mile round-trip hike.

Bear Creek Falls

HIKING/WALKING | An immensely popular trail leads to Bear Creek Falls, 2½ miles from the trailhead. It's a steady climb, but the destination is worth it. The route is also used by mountain bikers. ✉ *Telluride* ✣ *Trailhead at end of S. Pine St.*

Jud Wiebe Trail

HIKING/WALKING | This 3-mile loop is an excellent hike that is generally passable from spring until late fall. The first segment of the trail is fairly steep, so this is not the best choice for novices. It links with the Sneffels Highline Trail, a 13-mile loop that leads through wildflower-covered meadows. ✉ *Telluride* ✣ *Trailhead at north end of Aspen St.*

HORSEBACK RIDING

Telluride Horseback Adventures

HORSEBACK RIDING | Roudy Roudebush is a cowboy straight out of central casting (he starred in a television commercial and in Disney's 2004 film *America's Heart and Soul*). His company, Telluride Horseback Adventures, offers ultrascenic trail rides departing from his ranch in Norwood, 33 miles northwest of Telluride. You can also book sleigh rides in the winter. ✉ *4019 County Rd. 43ZS, Telluride* ☎ *970/728–9611* 🌐 *www.ridewithroudy.com.*

MULTI-TOUR OPERATORS

Telluride Outside

FISHING | Telluride's longest-running outfitter, this service offers a wealth of ways to experience the outdoors. Options include rafting trips, four-wheel-drive tours, paddleboarding tours, snowmobile trips, and guided fly-fishing outings from its store, the Telluride Angler. You can also buy fly-fishing gear here. ✉ *121 W. Colorado Ave., Telluride* ☎ *970/728–3895, 800/831–6230* 🌐 *www.tellurideoutside.com.*

TRACK SKIING

Telluride Nordic Center

SKIING/SNOWBOARDING | Operated by the Telluride Nordic Association, the center offers cross-country ski lessons and a wealth of trail information. It also rents ski equipment, ice skates, snowshoes, and sleds for adults and children. ✉ *500 E. Colorado Ave., Telluride* ☎ *970/728–1144* 🌐 *www.telluridenordic.com* 🎫 *Group lessons start at $65 per person.*

TopAten Snowshoe and Nordic Area

SKIING/SNOWBOARDING | There are 6 miles of rolling trails groomed for cross-country skiing and snowshoeing, as well as a warming teepee, a picnic deck, and restroom facilities. To access TopAten, you'll need to buy a "foot passenger" lift ticket for $25. ✉ *Telluride Ski Resort, Telluride* ✣ *Located near the unloading area for Chair 10* ☎ *970/728–7517* 🌐 *www.tellurideskiresort.com.*

Durango

47 miles south of Silverton via U.S. 550; 45 miles east of Cortez via U.S. 160; 60 miles west of Pagosa Springs via U.S. 160.

Wisecracking Will Rogers had this to say about Durango: "It's out of the way and glad of it." His statement is a bit unfair, considering that as a railroad town Durango has always been a cultural crossroads and melting pot (as well as a place to raise hell). Resting at 6,500 feet along the winding Animas River, with the San Juan Mountains as backdrop, the town was founded in 1879 by General William Palmer, president of the all-powerful Denver & Rio Grande Railroad, at a time when nearby Animas City haughtily refused to donate land for a depot. Within a decade, Durango had completely absorbed its rival. The booming town quickly became the region's main metropolis and a gateway to the Southwest.

A walking tour of the historic downtown offers ample proof of Durango's prosperity during the late 19th century, although the northern end of Main Avenue has the usual assortment of cheap motels and fast-food outlets.

About 27 miles north of town, the down-home ski resort of Purgatory welcomes a clientele that includes cowboys, families, and college students. The mountain is named for the nearby Purgatory Creek, a tributary of the River of Lost Souls.

GETTING HERE AND AROUND

Durango Transit operates regular trolleys and bus service throughout town. Purgatory Resort runs a $10 skier shuttle between the town and the mountain on weekends and holidays during the winter. Buck Horn Limousine is your best bet for airport transfers.

CONTACTS Buck Horn Limousine. ☎ *970/769–0933* 🌐 *www.buckhornlimousine.com.* **Durango Transit.** ☎ *970/259–5438* 🌐 *www.durangotransit.com.* **Purgatory Resort Skier Shuttle.** ☎ *970/426–7282* 🌐 *www.purgatoryresort.com.*

VISITOR INFORMATION

CONTACTS Durango Welcome Center. ✉ *802 Main Ave.* ☎ *970/247–3500, 800/525–8855* 🌐 *www.durango.org.*

Sights

★ Durango & Silverton Narrow Gauge Railroad

TRANSPORTATION SITE (AIRPORT/BUS/FERRY/TRAIN) | FAMILY | The most entertaining way to relive the Old West is to take a ride on the Durango & Silverton Narrow Gauge Railroad, a nine-hour round-trip journey along the 45-mile railway to Silverton. Travel in comfort in restored coaches or in the open-air cars called gondolas as you listen to the train's shrill whistle. A shorter excursion to Cascade Canyon in heated coaches is available in winter. The train departs from the Durango Depot, constructed in 1882 and beautifully restored. Next door is the Durango & Silverton Narrow Gauge Railroad Museum, which is free and well worth your time. ✉ *479 Main Ave.* ☎ *970/247–2733, 877/872–4607* 🌐 *www.durangotrain.com* 🎟 *$91–$199.*

Durango Hot Springs Resort & Spa

HOT SPRINGS | FAMILY | Come to this newly renovated, luxurious hot springs resort to soak your aching bones after a day of hiking or skiing. The complex includes an Olympic-size, saltwater swimming pool infused with aquagen, and 27 total natural mineral pools ranging from 98°F to 110°F; all are open year-round. The pools are outdoors, perched at the base of the mountain and thoughtfully designed to blend in with nature. The grounds also feature a spa, sauna, reflexology path, food carts and firepit, stage for live music, stream, separate adults-only area, and a hydrotherapy "yin-yang" pool. ✉ *6475 County Rd. 203* ✥ *About 5 miles north of Durango* ☎ *970/247–0111* 🌐 *www.durangohotspringsresortandspa.com* 🎟 *$20.*

Main Avenue National Historic District

HISTORIC SITE | The intersection of 13th Street and Main Avenue marks the northern edge of Durango's Main Avenue National Historic District. Old-fashioned streetlamps line the streets, casting a warm glow on the elegant buildings filled with upscale galleries, restaurants, and shops. Dating from 1887, the Strater Hotel is a reminder of the time when this town was a stop for many people headed west. ✉ *Main Ave., between 13th St. and 12th St.* 🌐 *www.durango.org.*

★ Purgatory Resort

AMUSEMENT PARK/WATER PARK | FAMILY | Purgatory does summer better than just about any Colorado ski resort, especially for kids. In the past, activities have

Durango's Purgatory Resort offers activities for all four seasons.

included a new mountain coaster, an off-road go-kart track, an alpine slide, a family-friendly ropes course, a short zipline, pony rides, bungee trampolines, an airbag jump, lift-served hiking and biking, and, of course, the obligatory climbing wall and minigolf course. ✉ *1 Skier Pl., Purgatory* ☎ *970/247–9000* 🌐 *www.purgatoryresort.com* 🎫 *$79 for 10 activities, $59 for 5, or choose à la carte pricing. Subject to change.*

Restaurants

Carver Brewing Co.

$$ | **AMERICAN** | The "Brews Brothers," Bill and Jim Carver, have about 12 beers on tap at any given time at this Durango favorite. If you're hungry, try one of the signature handmade bread bowls filled with green chile, soup, or chicken stew. **Known for:** hearty, creative breakfasts; lovely shaded patio out back; elevated pub cuisine. $ *Average main: $15* ✉ *1022 Main Ave.* ☎ *970/259–2545* 🌐 *www.carverbrewing.com.*

East by Southwest

$$$ | **ASIAN FUSION** | Asian food gets a bit of a Latin treatment in this inviting space. The menu has a strong Japanese bent, with sushi and sashimi, tempura, beef, and other traditional dishes elegantly presented and layered with complementary, often Southwest-inspired flavors. **Known for:** vegan and vegetarian options; bento boxes and poke bowls for lunch; sake, beer, wine, and tea lists. $ *Average main: $23* ✉ *160 E. College Dr.* ☎ *970/247–5533* 🌐 *www.eastbysouthwest.com* ⏲ *No lunch Sun.*

11th Street Station

$ | **FAST FOOD** | Seven locally owned food trucks, serving cuisine from Thailand to breakfast burritos to pizza to sushi, surround an outdoor courtyard with picnic-table seating. Ernie's Bar anchors the eating collective and offers craft beers, tap cocktails, and a wide tequila and mezcal selection. **Known for:** moderately priced eats; variety; fresh, contemporary vibes. $ *Average main: $12* ✉ *1101 Main*

Ave. ☎ 970/422–8482 🌐 www.11thstreet-station.com.

Ken & Sue's

$$ | **MODERN AMERICAN** | Plates are big and the selection is creative at Ken & Sue's, one of Durango's favorite restaurants. Locals are wild for the contemporary American cuisine with an Asian flair, served in an intimate space. **Known for:** large, pretty patio out back; worth-it desserts; pistachio-crusted grouper with vanilla-rum butter. *Ⓢ Average main: $18 ✉ 636 Main Ave. ☎ 970/385–1810 🌐 www.kenandsues.com ⏲ No lunch weekends.*

★ Ore House

$$$$ | **STEAKHOUSE** | Durango is a meat-and-potatoes kind of town, and the rustic Ore House is a splurge-worthy place to indulge (just ask the locals). The steaks are fantastic, and there are plenty of expertly prepared seafood and vegetarian selections as well. **Known for:** chateaubriand; cornbread with bacon butter; deep whiskey and wine lists. *Ⓢ Average main: $39 ✉ 147 E. College Dr. ☎ 970/247–5707 🌐 www.orehouserestaurant.com.*

★ Sow's Ear

$$$ | **STEAKHOUSE** | This airy eatery in Silverpick Lodge is known for providing "the best steaks on the mountain," topped with incredible au poivre, which it does with aplomb. It also serves up the best views of thick aspen groves. **Known for:** lovely views of mountains and cliffs; three-season alfresco patio open nightly, weather permitting; steak au poivre. *Ⓢ Average main: $30 ✉ 48475 U.S. 550 ☎ 970/247–3527 🌐 www.sowseardurango.com ⏲ No lunch. Closed Mon. and Tues.*

Steamworks Brewing Co.

$$ | **AMERICAN** | Widely acclaimed craft brews and above-standard sandwiches, burgers, pizzas, and salads raise Steamworks beyond usual pub grub. It's no surprise that the large, high-ceilinged venue is nearly always overflowing and has been a Durango favorite for more than two decades. **Known for:** skillfully brewed beer; daily drink specials ($3 pints, $11 pitchers, and more); back patio with mountain views. *Ⓢ Average main: $16 ✉ 801 E. 2nd Ave. ☎ 970/259–9200 🌐 www.steamworksbrewing.com.*

Hotels

Apple Orchard Inn

$$ | **B&B/INN** | This quiet B&B sits on five acres in the lush Animas Valley with an apple orchard, flower gardens, and trout ponds on the grounds. **Pros:** beautiful views; peaceful and quiet setting; cottages are intimate and romantic. **Cons:** no dinner on-site; several miles from town; rooms in the house are all upstairs (no elevator). *Ⓢ Rooms from: $160 ✉ 7758 County Rd. 203 ✣ About 8 miles north of downtown Durango ☎ 970/247–0751, 800/426–0751 🌐 www.appleorchardinn.com 🛏 4 rooms, 6 cottages 🍽 Free Breakfast.*

General Palmer Hotel

$$ | **HOTEL** | The General Palmer Hotel is a faithfully restored historic property in downtown Durango with a clean, bright look, as well as period furniture and Victorian touches that reinforce an old-timey feel. **Pros:** central location; some rooms have balconies; free off-street parking. **Cons:** no restaurant or bar; cramped elevator; pricey in season. *Ⓢ Rooms from: $200 ✉ 567 Main Ave. ☎ 970/247–4747 🌐 generalpalmerhotel.com 🛏 39 rooms 🍽 Free Breakfast.*

Purgatory Lodge

$$$$ | **HOTEL** | **FAMILY** | This mountain-luxe slope-side hotel provides an upscale retreat at a down-home resort, featuring roomy two- to four-bedroom suites decorated with contemporary furnishings. **Pros:** slope-side location; good restaurants; ample amenities. **Cons:** can be pricey; far from town; no meals included. *Ⓢ Rooms from: $350 ✉ Purgatory Resort, 24 Sheol St. ☎ 970/385–2100,*

800/525–0892 ⊕ www.purgatoryresort.com ⇆ 37 suites ¶○I No meals.

Rochester Hotel & Leland House

$$ | **B&B/INN** | The Rochester Hotel is a historic, boutique hotel that features paraphernalia and posters from movies filmed in the Durango area. **Pros:** free guest parking; amazing outdoor space; close to the action, yet off the main drag. **Cons:** no on-site food; no counter space in bathrooms; no pool or hot tub. *$ Rooms from: $199 ✉ 726 E. 2nd Ave. ☎ 970/385–1920, 800/664–1920 ⊕ www.rochesterhotel.com ⇆ 27 rooms ¶○I Free Breakfast.*

★ **Strater Hotel**

$$$ | **HOTEL** | Still the hottest spot in town, this Western grande dame opened for business in 1887 and has been visited by Butch Cassidy, Louis L'Amour (he wrote many of the *Sacketts* novels here), Francis Ford Coppola, John Kennedy, and Marilyn Monroe (the latter two stayed here at separate times). **Pros:** right in the thick of things; free guest parking; filled with gorgeous antiques. **Cons:** breakfast not included in all rates; noisy bar; Wi-Fi is spotty. *$ Rooms from: $220 ✉ 699 Main Ave. ☎ 970/247–4431, 800/247–4431 ⊕ www.strater.com ⇆ 88 rooms ¶○I No meals.*

Activities

BIKING

With a healthy college population and a generally mild climate, Durango is extremely bike-friendly and a popular destination for single-track enthusiasts. Many locals consider bikes to be their main form of transportation. The bike lobby is active, the trail system is well developed, and mountain biking is a particularly popular recreational activity.

Animas River Trail

BICYCLING | This 7-mile paved path parallels the river from Animas City Park south to Dallabetta Park in one smooth stroke. It's the main artery, linking up with several of the town's other trail systems. *✉ Durango.*

Durango Mountain Bike Tours

BICYCLING | Take a guided, private ride tailored to your skill level and interests with Durango Mountain Bike Tours. Rides range from a two-hour "Town & Trails" tour for beginners, complete with riding instruction, to full-day excursions on the area's most challenging single-track. Ask about guided tours at Phil's World, the famous single-track trail network a few miles outside of Mesa Verde. If you don't have a bike, you can rent one here. *✉ Durango ☎ 970/367–7653 ⊕ www.durangobiketours.com 🎟 From $90.*

Hermosa Creek Trail

BICYCLING | This single-track trail travels roughly 19 miles from Purgatory Resort to the lower Hermosa parking area. It's an intermediate-to-difficult ride with a couple of steep spots and switchbacks along with mellow rolls through open meadows and towering aspen and pine forests. The trail hugs the steep riverbank at a few places and there are a few creek crossings, so you shouldn't try it too early in the season, while the snow is still melting (the water can be waist-high in the spring and early summer). To minimize the fight against gravity, you can leave your car at the lower trailhead and catch a shuttle to the top—even so, there will still be plenty of climbing. *✉ Durango ✣ Trailhead: 2 miles from Purgatory's upper parking lot.*

GOLF

Hillcrest Golf Club

GOLF | Since 1969, a relaxed atmosphere, affordable rates, and gorgeous views have attracted golfers to this 18-hole public course, perched on a mesa near the campus of Fort Lewis College. Carts are $16 per person for 18 holes, but the tee-to-green distance is relatively short, so most patrons opt to walk. *✉ 2300 Rim Dr. ☎ 970/247–1499 ⊕ www.golfhillcrest.com 🎟 $48 for 18 holes late May–early Sept. midweek only and $50 weekends;*

$37/$39 early Sept.–late May ⛳ *18 holes, 6727 yards, par 71* ⏲ *Closed Dec.–Mar.* ✍ *Reservations essential.*

HIKING

Hiking trails are everywhere in and around Durango. Many trailheads at the edges of town lead to backcountry settings, and the San Juan Forest has plenty of mind-boggling walks and trails for those with the urge to explore.

Across from the Fort Lewis College Recreation Complex is a kid-friendly hike called **Lion's Den Trail.** It connects with the **Chapman Hill Trail** for a nice moderate hike, climbing switchbacks that take you away from town and hook up with the **Rim Trail.**

HORSEBACK RIDING

Rapp Corral

HORSEBACK RIDING | At the entrance to Haviland Lake, about 20 miles north of town, Rapp Corrall offers a variety of trail rides into San Juan National Forest. Trips range from one-hour jaunts to daylong treks to above-timberline trails on Engineer Mountain, or you can combine horseback riding with cave exploration. In winter, they offer sleigh rides. ✉ *51 Haviland Lake Rd.* ☎ *970/247–8454* 🌐 *www.rappcorral.com* 🎫 *From $75.*

RAFTING

Durango Rivertrippers and Adventure Tours

WHITE-WATER RAFTING | This outfitter runs day trips down the Animas River and other multiday options around the area. You can up your adrenaline output by swapping the raft for an inflatable kayak when the river conditions are right. Or ask about discount packages that combine rafting with Jeep tours or other rentals. ✉ *724 Main Ave.* ☎ *970/259–0289* 🌐 *www.durangorivertrippers.com.*

Mild to Wild Rafting and Jeep Tours

WHITE-WATER RAFTING | FAMILY | The Lower Animas is a mostly mellow stretch of river, with a few livelier rapids thrown in, making it a good choice for families. Mild to Wild offers trips of various lengths, and also rents out inflatable kayaks. You can book Jeep tours here as well. ✉ *50 Animas View Dr.* ☎ *800/567–6745, 970/247–4789* 🌐 *www.mild2wildrafting.com* 🎫 *Raft trips start at $33. Jeep tours start at $76 for a half day.*

SKIING AND SNOWBOARDING

★ Purgatory Resort

SKIING/SNOWBOARDING | This unpretentious ski resort 27 miles north of Durango has plenty of intermediate runs and gladed tree skiing, but what's unique about it is its stepped terrain: lots of humps and dips and steep pitches followed by virtual flats. Purgatory is just plain fun, and return visitors like it that way. It's not all old-school, however: A high-speed quad on the back side (Lift 8) conveys skiers to the top of the mountain in five minutes and accesses three advanced trails. The ski area is perfect for families and those who are open to other diversions, such as horse-drawn sleigh rides, snowshoeing, cross-country skiing, and snowmobiling. **Facilities:** 105 trails; 1,635 acres; 2,029-foot vertical drop; 12 lifts. ✉ *1 Skier Pl., Purgatory* ☎ *970/247–9000, 800/525–0892* 🌐 *www.purgatoryresort.com* 🎫 *Lift ticket $109.*

RENTALS

Expert Edge

SKIING/SNOWBOARDING | This is the go-to shop at the base village for demos, retail, and repair. It features top-of-the-line men's and women's skis, boots, bindings, poles, and more from top brands. Expert Edge also does custom boot fitting, ski tuning, and equipment repair. ✉ *Village Center, Purgatory* ☎ *970/385–2181* 🌐 *www.purgatoryresort.com.*

Mesa Verde National Park

Unlike the other national parks, Mesa Verde earned its status from its ancient cultural history rather than its geological treasures. President Theodore Roosevelt established it in 1906 as the first national park to "preserve the works of man," in this case that of the Ancestral Pueblo, previously known as the Anasazi.

They lived in the region from roughly 550 to 1300; they left behind more than 4,000 archaeological sites spread out over 80 square miles. Their ancient dwellings, set high into the sandstone cliffs, are the heart of the park. Mesa Verde (which in Spanish means, literally, "Green Table," but translates more accurately to something like "green flat-topped plateau") is much more than an archaeologist's dreamland, however. It's one of those windswept places where man's footprints and nature's paintbrush—some would say chisel—meet. Rising dramatically from the San Juan Basin, the jutting cliffs are cut by a series of complex canyons and covered in several shades of green, from pines in the higher elevations down to sage and other mountain brush on the desert floor. From the tops of the smaller mesas, you can look across to the cliff dwellings in the opposite rock faces. Dwarfed by the towering cliffs, the sand-color dwellings look almost like a natural occurrence in the midst of the desert's harsh beauty.

GETTING HERE AND AROUND

Durango (36 miles east of the park entrance) has an airport. The park has just one entrance, off U.S. 160, between Cortez and Durango in what's known as the Four Corners area (which spans the intersection of Colorado, New Mexico, Arizona, and Utah). Most of the roads at Mesa Verde involve steep grades and hairpin turns, particularly on Wetherill Mesa. Vehicles over 8,000 pounds or 25 feet are prohibited on this road. Trailers and towed vehicles are prohibited past Morefield Campground. Check the condition of your vehicle's brakes before driving the road to Wetherill Mesa. For the latest road information, tune to 1610 AM, or call ☎ *970/529–4461*. Off-road vehicles are prohibited in the park. At less-visited Wetherill Mesa, you must leave your car behind and hike or bike to the Long House, Kodak House, and Badger House Community.

PARK ESSENTIALS

PARK FEES AND PERMITS

Admission is $25 per vehicle for a seven-day permit. An annual pass is $40. Ranger-led tours of Cliff Palace, Long House, and Balcony House are $5 per person. You can also take ranger-guided bus tours from the Far View Lodge, which last between 3½ and 4 hours and cost $55 ($33 for kids; under five free). Backcountry hiking and fishing are not permitted at Mesa Verde.

PARK HOURS

Mesa Verde's facilities each operate on their own schedule, but most are open daily, from Memorial Day through Labor Day, between about 8 am and sunset. The rest of the year, they open at 9. In winter, the Spruce Tree House is open only to offer a few scheduled tours each day. Wetherill Mesa (and all the sites it services) is open from May through October, weather depending. Far View Center, Far View Terrace, and Far View Lodge are open between April and October. Morefield Campground and the sites nearby are open from mid-April through mid-October (and until early November for limited camping with no services). Specific hours are subject to change, so check with the visitor center upon arrival.

CELL-PHONE RECEPTION AND INTERNET

You can get patchy cell service in the park. Best service is typically at the Morefield Campground area, which is the closest to the neighboring towns of Cortez and Mancos. Public telephones can be found at all the major visitor areas (Morefield, Far View, and Spruce Tree). You can get free Wi-Fi throughout the Far View Lodge and at the Morefield Campground store.

TOURS

BUS TOURS

Aramark Tours

GUIDED TOURS | FAMILY | If you want a well-rounded visit to Mesa Verde's most popular sites, consider a group tour. The park concessionaire provides all-day and half-day guided tours of the Chapin Mesa and Far View sites, departing in buses from either Morefield Campground or Far View Lodge. Tours are led by Aramark guides or park rangers, who share information about the park's history, geology, and excavation processes. Cold water is provided, but you'll need to bring your own snacks. Buy tickets at Far View Lodge, the Morefield Campground, or online. Tours sell out, so reserve in advance. ✉ *Far View Lodge, 1 Navajo Hill, mile marker 15* ☎ *970/529–4422 Far View Lodge, 800/449–2288 Aramark* 🌐 *www.visitmesaverde.com* 🎫 *From $41* ⏲ *700 Years Tour closed late Oct.–mid-Apr. Far View Explorer Tour closed mid-Aug.–late May.*

GUIDED TOURS

Ranger-Led Tours

GUIDED TOURS | The cliff dwellings known as Balcony House, Cliff Palace, and Long House can be explored only on ranger-led tours; the first two last about an hour, the third is 90 minutes. Buy tickets at the Mesa Verde Visitor and Research Center. These are active tours and may not be suitable for some children; each requires climbing ladders without handrails and squeezing through tight spaces. Be sure to bring water and sunscreen. Site schedules vary so check ahead. ✉ *Mesa Verde National Park* ☎ *970/529–4465* 🌐 *www.nps.gov/meve/planyourvisit/tour_tickets.htm* 🎫 *$5 per site* ⏲ *Closed: Cliff Palace: Oct./Nov.–late May. Balcony House: early Oct.–late Apr. Long House: mid-Oct.–mid-May.*

Morefield

Sights

SCENIC DRIVES

Park Entrance Road

NATIONAL/STATE PARK | The main park road, also known as SH 10, leads you from the entrance off U.S. 160 into the park. As a break from the switchbacks, you can stop at a couple of pretty overlooks along the way, but hold out for Park Point, which, at the mesa's highest elevation (8,572 feet), gives you unobstructed, 360-degree views. Note that trailers and towed vehicles are not permitted beyond Morefield Campground. ✉ *Mesa Verde National Park.*

TRAILS

Knife Edge Trail

TRAIL | Perfect for a sunset stroll, this easy 2-mile (round-trip) walk around the north rim of the park leads to an overlook of the Montezuma Valley. If you stop at all the flora identification points that the trail pamphlet suggests, the hike takes about 1½ to 2 hours. The patches of asphalt you spot along the way are leftovers from old Knife Edge Road, built in 1914 as the main entryway into the park. *Easy.* ✉ *Mesa Verde National Park* ✥ *Trailhead: Morefield Campground, 4 miles from park entrance.*

Prater Ridge Trail

TRAIL | This 7.8-mile round-trip loop, which starts and finishes at Morefield Campground, is the longest hike you can take inside the park. It provides fine views of Morefield Canyon to the south and the San Juan Mountains to the north. About halfway through the hike, you'll see a cutoff trail that you can take, which shortens the trip to 5 miles. *Difficult.* ✉ *Mesa Verde National Park* ✥ *Trailhead: West end of Morefield Campground, 4 miles from park entrance.*

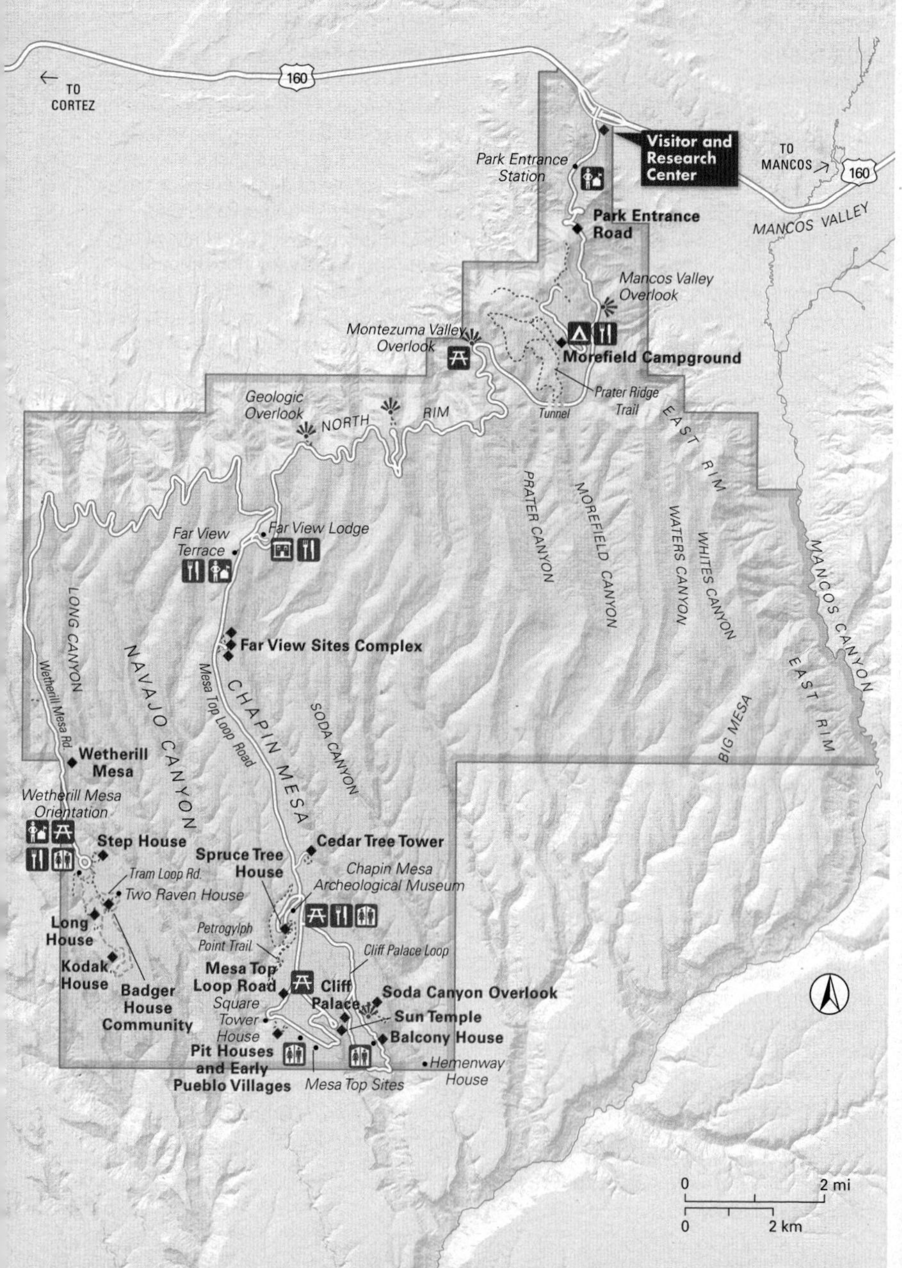

Mesa Verde National Park
TO CORTEZ
160
TO MANCOS
Visitor and Research Center
Park Entrance Station
Park Entrance Road
MANCOS VALLEY
Mancos Valley Overlook
Montezuma Valley Overlook
Morefield Campground
Prater Ridge Trail
Tunnel
Geologic Overlook
NORTH RIM
EAST RIM
PRATER CANYON
MOREFIELD CANYON
WATERS CANYON
WHITES CANYON
MANCOS CANYON
Far View Terrace
Far View Lodge
Far View Sites Complex
LONG CANYON
NAVAJO CANYON
Wetherill Mesa Rd.
Mesa Top Loop Road
CHAPIN MESA
SODA CANYON
BIG MESA
Wetherill Mesa
Wetherill Mesa Orientation
Step House
Tram Loop Rd.
Two Raven House
Long House
Kodak House
Badger House Community
Spruce Tree House
Cedar Tree Tower
Chapin Mesa Archeological Museum
Petroglyph Point Trail
Cliff Palace Loop
Mesa Top Loop Road
Square Tower House
Cliff Palace
Soda Canyon Overlook
Sun Temple
Balcony House
Pit Houses and Early Pueblo Villages
Mesa Top Sites
Hemenway House
0
2 mi
0
2 km

VISITOR CENTERS

Mesa Verde Visitor and Research Center

INFO CENTER | FAMILY | The visitor center is the best place to go to sign up for tours, get the information you need to plan a successful trip, and buy tickets for the Cliff Palace, Balcony House, and Long House ranger-led tours. The sleek, energy-efficient research center is filled with more than 3 million artifacts and archives. The center features indoor and outdoor exhibits, a gift shop, picnic tables, and a museum. Find books, maps, and videos on the history of the park. ✉ *Park entrance on the left, 35853 Rd H.5, Mancos* ☎ *970/529–4465* 🌐 *www.nps.gov/meve/planyourvisit/meve_vc.htm.*

Restaurants

Knife Edge Cafe

$ | CAFÉ | FAMILY | Located in the Morefield Campground, this simple restaurant in a covered outdoor terrace with picnic tables serves a hearty all-you-can-eat pancake breakfast with sausage every morning. Coffee and beverages are also available. **Known for:** lively gathering spot; breakfast burritos; large coffees with free refills all day. $ *Average main: $10* ✉ *4 miles south of park entrance* ☎ *970/565–2133* 🌐 *www.nps.gov/meve/planyourvisit/restaurants.htm* ⏲ *Closed mid-Sept.–late Apr.*

Far View

Sights

HISTORIC SITES

Far View Sites Complex

ARCHAEOLOGICAL SITE | FAMILY | This was probably one of the most densely populated areas in Mesa Verde, comprising as many as 50 villages in a ½-square-mile area at the top of Chapin Mesa. Most of the sites here were built between 900 and 1300. Begin the self-guided tour at the interpretive panels in the parking lot, then proceed down a ½-mile, level trail. ✉ *Park entrance road, near the Chapin Mesa area* 🌐 *www.nps.gov/meve* 🎟 *Free* ☞ *In winter, access by parking at the gate and walking in.*

TRAILS

Farming Terrace Trail

TRAIL | FAMILY | This 30-minute, ½-mile loop begins and ends on the spur road to Cedar Tree Tower, about 1 mile north of the Chapin Mesa area. It meanders through a series of check dams, which the Ancestral Pueblo built to create farming terraces. *Easy.* ✉ *Mesa Verde National Park* ✣ *Trailhead: Park entrance road, 4 miles south of Far View Center.*

Restaurants

Far View Terrace Café

$ | AMERICAN | This full-service cafeteria offers great views, but it's nothing fancy. Grab a simple coffee here or head across the dining room to Mesa Mocha for a latte. **Known for:** beautiful views; lattes; great gift shop. $ *Average main: $12* ✉ *Across from Far View Center* 🌐 *www.visitmesaverde.com/lodging-camping/dining/far-view-terrace-cafe* ⏲ *Closed late Oct.–mid-Apr.*

Metate Room Restaurant

$$$ | AMERICAN | The park's rugged terrain contrasts with this relaxing space just off the lobby of the Far View Lodge. The well-regarded dining room is upscale, but the atmosphere remains casual. **Known for:** Native American artwork; cheese and cured meats board; great views. $ *Average main: $25* ✉ *Far View Lodge, 1 Navajo Rd., across from Far View Center, 15 miles southwest of park entrance* ☎ *970/529–4422* 🌐 *www.visitmesaverde.com/lodging-camping/dining/metate-room-restaurant* ⏲ *Closed late Oct.–mid-Apr. No lunch.*

Hotels

★ Far View Lodge

$$ | HOTEL | Talk about a view—all rooms have a private balcony, from which you can admire views of the neighboring states of Arizona, Utah, and New Mexico up to 100 miles in the distance. **Pros:** close to the key sites; views are spectacular; small on-site fitness center. **Cons:** simple rooms and amenities, with no TV; walls are thin and less than soundproof; no cell-phone service. *Rooms from: $151 ✉ Across from Far View Center, 1 Navajo Rd., 15 miles southwest of park entrance ☎ 800/449–2288 🌐 www.visitmesaverde.com ⏲ Closed late Oct.–mid-Apr. 150 rooms No meals.*

Shopping

Far View Terrace Shop

CLOTHING | In the same building as the Far View Terrace Café, this is the largest gift shop in the park, with gifts, souvenirs, Native American art, toys, and T-shirts galore. *✉ Mesa Top Loop Rd., 15 miles south of park entrance ☎ 800/449–2288 Aramark.*

Chapin Mesa

Sights

HISTORIC SIGHTS

★ Balcony House

ARCHAEOLOGICAL SITE | The stonework of this 40-room cliff dwelling is impressive, but you're likely to be even more awed by the skill it must have taken to reach this place. Perched in a sandstone cove 600 feet above the floor of Soda Canyon, Balcony House seems suspended in space. Even with modern passageways and trails, today's visitors must climb a 32-foot ladder and crawl through a narrow tunnel. Look for the intact balcony for which the house is named. The dwelling is accessible only on a ranger-led tour. *✉ Cliff Palace/Balcony House Rd., 10 miles south of Far View Center, Cliff Palace Loop 🌐 www.nps.gov/meve/learn/historyculture/cd_balcony_house.htm $5 ⏲ Closed early Oct.–late Apr.*

★ Cliff Palace

ARCHAEOLOGICAL SITE | This was the first major Mesa Verde dwelling seen by cowboys Charlie Mason and Richard Wetherill in 1888. It is also the largest, containing about 150 rooms and 23 kivas on three levels. Getting there involves a steep downhill hike and three ladders. **■ TIP→ You may enter Balcony House or Cliff Palace by ranger-guided tour only so purchase tickets in advance.** The 90-minute, small-group "twilight tours" at sunset present this archaeological treasure with dramatic sunset lighting. Tour tickets are only available in advance at the Visitor and Research Center, Morefield Ranger Station, Durango Welcome Center, and online at *🌐 www.recreation.gov. ✉ Mesa Verde National Park ✥ Cliff Palace Overlook, about 2½ miles south of Chapin Mesa Archeological Museum 🌐 www.nps.gov/meve/learn/historyculture/cd_cliff_palace.htm Regular tickets $5; twilight tours $20 ⏲ Closed Oct./Nov.–late May; loop closes at sunset.*

Pit Houses and Early Pueblo Villages

ARCHAEOLOGICAL SITE | Three dwellings, built on top of each other from 700 to 950, at first look like a mass of jumbled walls, but an informational panel helps identify the dwellings—and the stories behind them are fascinating. The 325-foot trail from the walking area is paved, wheelchair accessible, and near a restroom. *✉ Mesa Top Loop Rd., about 2½ miles south of Chapin Mesa Archeological Museum Free.*

Spruce Tree House

ARCHAEOLOGICAL SITE | FAMILY | This 138-room complex is the best-preserved site in the park; however, the alcove surrounding Spruce Tree House became unstable in 2015 and was closed to visitors. Until alcove arch support is added, visitors can view but not enter this site.

The landscapes of Mesa Verde are beautiful no matter the season.

You can still hike down a trail that starts behind the Chapin Mesa Archeological Museum and leads you 100 feet down into the canyon to view the site from a distance. Because of its location in the heart of the Chapin Mesa area, the Spruce Tree House trail and area can resemble a crowded playground during busy periods. When allowed inside the site, tours are self-guided (allow 45 minutes to an hour), but a park ranger is on-site to answer questions. ✉ *Mesa Verde National Park* ✣ *At the Chapin Mesa Archeological Museum, 5 miles south of Far View Center* 🌐 *www.nps.gov/meve/learn/historyculture/cd_spruce_tree_house.htm* 🎫 *Free* ⏲ *Tours closed for reconstruction.*

Sun Temple

ARCHAEOLOGICAL SITE | Although researchers assume it was probably a ceremonial structure, they're unsure of the exact purpose of this complex, which has no doors or windows in most of its chambers. Because the building was not quite half finished when it was left in 1276, some researchers surmise it might have been constructed to stave off whatever disaster caused its builders—and the other inhabitants of Mesa Verde—to leave. ✉ *Mesa Top Loop Rd., about 2 miles south of Chapin Mesa Archeological Museum* 🌐 *www.nps.gov/meve/historyculture/mt_sun_temple.htm* 🎫 *Free.*

SCENIC DRIVES

Mesa Top Loop Road

SCENIC DRIVE | This 6-mile drive skirts the scenic rim of Chapin Mesa and takes you to several overlooks and short, paved trails. You'll get great views of Sun Temple and Square Tower, as well as Cliff Palace, Sunset House, and several other cliff dwellings visible from the Sun Point Overlook. ✉ *Mesa Verde National Park.*

SCENIC STOPS

Cedar Tree Tower

ARCHAEOLOGICAL SITE | A self-guided tour takes you to, but not through, a tower and kiva built between 1100 and 1300 and connected by a tunnel. The tower-and-kiva combinations in the park are thought to have been either religious structures or signal towers. ✉ *Mesa Verde National Park* ✣ *Near the 4-way intersection on Chapin Mesa; park entrance road, 1½ miles north of Chapin Mesa Archeological Museum* 🌐 *www.nps.gov/meve/learn/historyculture/mt_cedar_tree_tower.htm* 🎫 *Free.*

Soda Canyon Overlook

CANYON | Get your best view of Balcony House here. You can also read interpretive panels about the site and the surrounding canyon geology. ✉ *Cliff Palace Loop Rd., about 1 mile north of Balcony House parking area* ☞ *Access in winter by walking the Cliff Palace Loop.*

TRAILS

★ Petroglyph Point Trail

TRAIL | Scramble along a narrow canyon wall to reach the largest and best-known petroglyphs in Mesa Verde. If you pose for a photo just right, you can manage to block out the gigantic "don't touch" sign next to the rock art. A map—available at any ranger station—points out three dozen points of interest along the trail. However, the trail is not open while Spruce Tree House is closed; check with a ranger for more information. *Moderate.* ✉ *Mesa Verde National Park* ✣ *Trailhead: At Spruce Tree House, next to Chapin Mesa Archeological Museum.*

Soda Canyon Overlook Trail

TRAIL | FAMILY | One of the easiest and most rewarding hikes in the park, this little trail travels 1½ miles round-trip through the forest on almost completely level ground. The overlook is an excellent point from which to photograph the Chapin Mesa–area cliff dwellings. *Easy.* ✉ *Mesa Verde National Park* ✣ *Trailhead: Cliff Palace Loop Rd., about 1 mile north of Balcony House parking area* ☞ *Access in winter via Cliff Palace Loop.*

Spruce Canyon Trail

TRAIL | While Petroglyph Point Trail takes you along the side of the canyon, this trail ventures down into its depths. It's only 2.4 miles long, but you descend about 600 feet in elevation. Remember to save your strength; what goes down must come up again. The trail is open even while Spruce Tree House is closed. Still, check with a ranger. *Moderate.* ✉ *Mesa Verde National Park* ✣ *Trailhead: At Spruce Tree House, next to Chapin Mesa Archeological Museum* ☞ *Registration required at trailhead.*

VISITOR CENTERS

Chapin Mesa Archeological Museum

MUSEUM | This is an excellent first stop for an introduction to Ancestral Pueblo culture, as well as the area's development into a national park. Exhibits showcase original textiles and other artifacts, and a theater plays an informative film every 30 minutes. Rangers are available to answer your questions. The shop focuses on educational materials, but you can also find park-themed souvenirs. The museum sits at the south end of the park entrance road and overlooks Spruce Tree House. Nearby, you'll find park headquarters, a gift shop, a post office, snack bar, and bathrooms. ✉ *Park entrance road, 5 miles south of Far View Center, 20 miles from park entrance* ☎ *970/529–4465 General information line* 🌐 *www.nps.gov/meve/planyourvisit/museum.htm* 🎫 *Free.*

Restaurants

Spruce Tree Terrace Café

$ | AMERICAN | This small cafeteria has a limited selection of hot food, coffee, salads, burgers, and sandwiches. The patio is pleasant, and it's conveniently located across the street from the museum. **Known for:** Southwest specialties; soup of the day specials; Navajo tacos. $ *Average main: $10* ✉ *Near Chapin Mesa Archeological Museum, 5 miles south of the Far View Center* ☎ *970/529–4465* 🌐 *www.visitmesaverde.com/lodging-camping/dining/spruce-tree-terrace-cafe* ⏲ *No dinner in off-season.*

You'll find ancient petroglyphs in many places throughout the park.

Shopping

Chapin Mesa Archeological Museum Shop

BOOKS/STATIONERY | Books and videos are the primary offering here, with more than 400 titles on Ancestral Pueblo and Southwestern topics. You can also find a selection of touristy T-shirts and hats. Hours vary throughout the year. ✉ *Spruce Tree Terrace, near Chapin Mesa Archeological Museum, 5 miles from Far View Center* ☎ *970/529–4445* 🌐 *www.nps.gov/meve/planyourvisit/museum.htm.*

Wetherill Mesa

Sights

HISTORIC SIGHTS

Badger House Community

ARCHAEOLOGICAL SITE | A self-guided walk along paved and gravel trails takes you through a group of four mesa-top dwellings. The community, which covers nearly 7 acres, dates back to the year 650, the Basketmaker Period, and includes a primitive, semisubterranean pit house and what's left of a multistory stone pueblo. Allow about 45 minutes to see the sites. The trail is 2.4 miles round-trip. ✉ *Wetherill Mesa Rd., 12 miles from Far View Center* 🌐 *www.nps.gov/meve/historyculture/mt_badger_house.htm* 🎟 *Free* 🕓 *Closed late Oct.–early May; road closes at 6 pm.*

Long House

ARCHAEOLOGICAL SITE | This Wetherill Mesa cliff dwelling is the second largest in Mesa Verde. It is believed that about 150 people lived in Long House, so named because of the size of its cliff alcove. The spring at the back of the cave is still active today. The in-depth, ranger-led tour begins a short distance from the parking lot and takes about 90 minutes. You hike about 2 miles, including two 15-foot ladders. ✉ *On Wetherill Mesa, 29 miles past the visitor center, near mile marker 15* 🌐 *www.nps.gov/meve/learn/historyculture/cd_long_house.htm* 🎟 *Tours $5* 🕓 *Closed mid-Oct.–mid-May.*

Step House

ARCHAEOLOGICAL SITE | So named because of a crumbling prehistoric stairway leading up from the dwelling, Step House is reached via a paved (but steep) trail that's ¾ mile long. The house is unique in that it shows clear evidence of two separate occupations: the first around 626, the second a full 600 years later. The self-guided tour takes about 45 minutes. ✉ *Wetherill Mesa Rd., 12 miles from Far View Center* 🌐 *www.nps.gov/meve/learn/historyculture/step_house.htm* 🎫 *Free* ⏲ *Closed mid-May–mid-Oct.; hrs vary seasonally.*

SCENIC DRIVES

Wetherill Mesa Road

SCENIC DRIVE | This 12-mile mountain road, stretching from the Far View Center to the Wetherill Mesa, has sharp curves and steep grades (and is restricted to vehicles less than 25 feet long and 8,000 pounds). Roadside pull-outs offer unobstructed views of the Four Corners region. At the end of the road, you can access Step House, Long House, and Badger House. ✉ *Mesa Verde National Park* ⏲ *Closed late Oct.–early May.*

SCENIC STOPS

Kodak House Overlook

VIEWPOINT | Get an impressive view into the 60-room Kodak House and its several small kivas from here. The house, closed to the public, was named for a Swedish researcher who absentmindedly left his Kodak camera behind here in 1891. ✉ *Wetherill Mesa Rd.* 🌐 *www.nps.gov/meve* ⏲ *Closed late Oct.–May.*

Index

H

I

J

K

Photo Credits

Front Cover: Sarah Bossert [Description: The last few rays of sun on Sedona's Cathedral Rock as seen from the middle of Oak Creek.]. **Back cover, from left to right:** The World in HDR/Shutterstock, Sean Pavone/Shutterstock, Traveller70/Shutterstock. **Spine:** TRphotos/Shutterstock. Interior, from left to right: RomanSlavik.com/Shutterstock (1). Sean Pavone/iStockphoto (2). **Chapter 1: Experience the Southwest:** Sandra Salvas/Visit Utah (8-9). Anton Foltin/Shutterstock (10). Utah Office of Tourism (11). f11photo/Shutterstock (11). Zach Maraziti/Aspen Chamber Resort Association (12). Courtesy of Deer Valley Resort (12). Douglas Pulsipher/Visit Salt Lake City (12). imageBROKER / Alamy (12). Evgeny Moerman/Dreamstime (13). Carolina Arroyo/Unsplash (13). Ffooter | Dreamstime.com (13). The Springs Resort & Spa, Pagosa Springs, CO (13). f11photo/Shutterstock (14). Andriy Blokhin/Shutterstock (14). Ian Dagnall / Alamy (14). Tashka | Dreamstime.com (14). Jakub Zajic/Shutterstock (15). RRuntsch/Shutterstock (15). Sepavo | Dreamstime.com (15). Greg Gard / Alamy (15). Crackerclips/Dreamstime (16). Steve Lagreca/Shutterstock (16). Eric Limon/Shutterstock (16). stuinaz/Flickr, [CC BY-ND-ND 2.0] (16). bjul/Shutterstock (17). Luckyphotographer/Dreamstime (17). Johnny Adolphson/Shutterstock (20). DnDavis/Shutterstock (20). RWShea Photography/Flickr, [CC BY-NC 2.0] (20). Benkrut | Dreamstime.com (20). Patrick Myers/NPS (21). Danica Bona - Sweet Tea Studios (21). Zack Frank/Shutterstock (21). Zack Frank/Shutterstock (21). Gimas/Shutterstock (22). Sopotnicki/Shutterstock (22). Nick Fox/Shutterstock (22). Zack Frank/Shutterstock (23). Crackerclips/Dreamstime (23). Roschetzky Photography/Shutterstock (24). Joshua Resnick/Shutterstock (24). Jeremy Janus/Shutterstock (24). kavram/Shutterstock (24). jdross75/Shutterstock (25). Courtesy of WeldWerks (26). Courtesy of Visit Mesa, AZ wine (26). Esantacruz/Shutterstock (26). carlosrojas20/iStockphoto (26). Brent Hofacker/Shutterstock (27). StudioGShock/Shutterstock (27). Top Photo Corporation/Shutterstock (27). azhighwaystv from Crowdriff (27). **Chapter 3: Las Vegas and Vicinity:** Courtesy of MGM Resorts International (51). Photoquest | Dreamstime.com (77). **Chapter 4: Great Basin National Park:** Dennis Frates / Alamy (81). Heeb Christian / age fotostock (89). **Chapter 5: Salt Lake City:** f11photo/Shutterstock (97). Sopotnicki/Shutterstock (106). Nagel Photography/Shutterstock (108). Chris Curtis/Shutterstock (114). Kristi Blokhin/Shutterstock (120). **Chapter 6: Park City and Vicinity:** johnnya123/iStockphoto (123). Sean Pavone/iStockphoto (129). johnnya123/iStockphoto (139). Johnny Adolphson/Shutterstock (144). Layne V. Naylor/Shutterstock (148). **Chapter 7: Southwestern Utah with Zion, Bryce Canyon, and Capitol Reef National Parks:** Dmitry Pichugin/Shutterstock (151). bjul/Shutterstock (173). Inc/Shutterstock (186). Edmund Lowe Photography/Shutterstock (197). **Chapter 8: Moab and Southeastern Utah with Arches and Canyonlands National Parks:** Evan Spiler (203). Lukas Urwyler/Shutterstock (221). Alex Grichenko/Dreamstime (231). Colin D. Young/Shutterstock (237). **Chapter 9: Phoenix, Scottsdale, and Tempe:** David Liu (239). Jeremy Janus/Shutterstock (248). Kerrick James (252). Raeann Davies/Shutterstock (255). Kerrick James (263). DCA88/Shutterstock (265). Anton Foltin/Shutterstock (272). **Chapter 10: Tucson and Southern Arizona:** Sean Pavone/Shutterstock (275). luchschenF/Shutterstock (281). Underawesternsky/Shutterstock (286). csfotoimages/iStockphoto (289). Johnny Coate/Shutterstock (291). Kyle Benne/Shutterstock (294). Timrobertsaerial | Dreamstime.com (300). Adeliepenguin | Dreamstime.com (302). wikipedia.org (311). **Chapter 11: Northern Arizona with Sedona, the Grand Canyon, and Monument Valley:** Traveller70/Shutterstock (321). Michael Landrum/Shutterstock (328). JUAN CARLOS MUÑOZ (333). Allnaturalbeth/Dreamstime (335). Anton Foltin/Shutterstock (337). shutterupeire/Shutterstock (340). Kerrick James (349). kavram/Shutterstock (355). CAN BALCIOGLU/Shutterstock (358). Dz1958 | Dreamstime.com (367). Spargo | Dreamstime.com (369). **Chapter 12: Santa Fe, Taos, and Albuquerque:** Swdesertlover/Dreamstime (373). Swdesertlover/Dreamstime (382). Nagel Photography/Shutterstock (384). William Cushman/Shutterstock (388). Genevieve Russell/ StoryPortrait Media 2014 (390). Gimas/Shutterstock (402). **Chapter 13: Southeastern New Mexico with Carlsbad Caverns:** zrfphoto/iStockphoto (415). ehrlif/Shutterstock (422). Doug Meek//Shutterstock (438). **Chapter 14: Southwestern New Mexico with White Sands National Park:** sunsinger/Shutterstock (441). Michael Rosebrock/Shutterstock (452). Richter MachThunder/Shutterstock (458). **Chapter 15: Denver and North-Central Colorado with Rocky Mountain National Park:** Zhu_zhu | Dreamstime.com (471). Reedcody | Dreamstime.com (482). Arina P Habich/Shutterstock (484). Kitleong | Dreamstime.com (487). Mikle15 | Dreamstime.com (496). Brendalynn6769 | Dreamstime.com (503). Mudwalker | Dreamstime.com (506). Virrage Images/Shutterstock (509). **Chapter 16: Colorado Springs and Vicinity with Great Sand Dunes National Park:** ABDESIGN/iStockphoto (513). Pixelview Media/Shutterstock (522). Neil Podoll/Shutterstock (524). F11photo | Dreamstime.com (537). **Chapter 17: The Rocky Mountain Ski Resorts:** Jonathan Ross/iStockphoto (543). SeanXu/iStockphoto (549). David A Litman/Shutterstock (560). Margaret619 | Dreamstime.com (568). marekuliasz/iStockphoto (572). Margaret.Wiktor/Shutterstock (579). Teri Virbickis/Shutterstock (582). **Chapter 18: Western Colorado with Mesa Verde National Park:** Rob Crandall/Shutterstock (589). Tristanbnz | Dreamstime.com (606). KaraGrubis/iStockphoto (614). John De Bord/Shutterstock (623). Dominic Gentilcore PhD/Shutterstock (625).

*Every effort has been made to trace the copyright holders, and we apologize in advance for any accidental errors. We would be happy to apply the corrections in the following edition of this publication.

Fodor's ESSENTIAL SOUTHWEST

Publisher: Stephen Horowitz, *General Manager*

Editorial: Douglas Stallings, *Editorial Director*; Jill Fergus, Amanda Sadlowski, Caroline Trefler, *Senior Editors*; Kayla Becker, Alexis Kelly, *Editors*

Design: Tina Malaney, *Director of Design and Production*; Jessica Gonzalez, *Graphic Designer;* Mariana Tabares, *Design and Production Intern*

Production: Jennifer DePrima, *Editorial Production Manager*; Elyse Rozelle, *Senior Production Editor;* Monica White, *Production Editor*

Maps: Rebecca Baer, *Senior Map Editor*; Mark Stroud (Moon Street Cartography), *Cartographer*

Photography: Viviane Teles, *Senior Photo Editor;* Namrata Aggarwal, Ashok Kumar, *Photo Editors;* Rebecca Rimmer, *Photo Intern*

Business and Operations: Chuck Hoover, *Chief Marketing Officer*; Robert Ames, *Group General Manager*; Devin Duckworth, *Director of Print Publishing*; Amber Zhou, *Business Analyst*

Public Relations and Marketing: Joe Ewaskiw, *Senior Director of Communications and Public Relations*

Fodors.com: Jeremy Tarr, *Editorial Director;* Rachael Levitt, *Managing Editor*

Technology: Jon Atkinson, *Director of Technology;* Rudresh Teotia, *Lead Developer*; Jacob Ashpis, *Content Operations Manager*

Writer: Eric Peterson

Editor: Douglas Stallings

Production Editor: Jennifer DePrima

First Edition

ISBN 978-1-64097-455-5

ISSN 2768-4539

PRINTED IN THE UNITED STATES OF AMERICA

10 9 8 7 6 5 4 3 2 1

About Our Writers

THE SOUTHWEST

Eric Peterson has written travel guides on Yellowstone and Yosemite, as well as newspaper and magazine stories covering the business of gateway towns, education within the parks, and other issues. Eric lives in Denver, Colorado, with his wife, Jamie. His website is 🌐 *www.ramblecolorado.com*. As our primary coordinating writer, he created the Experience and Southwest chapters and oversaw the development of all the New Mexico chapters.

Many other writers contributed to this book by updating and writing content for the books from which it was derived.

NEW MEXICO

Lynne Arany: Albuquerque

Andrew Collins: Southeastern New Mexico, Southwestern New Mexico

Yvonne Pesquera: Day Trips from Santa Fe

Zibby Wilder: Santa Fe

UTAH

Shelley Arenas: Zion National Park, Bryce Canyon National Park

Andrew Collins: Salt Lake City, Southwestern Utah

Jenie Skoy: Park City & Vicinity

Stina Sieg: Arches National Park, Canyonlands National Park, Moab

ARIZONA

Teresa Bitler: Northeast Arizona

Mara Levin: Grand Canyon National Park, North-Central Arizona, Tucson & Southern Arizona

Elise Riley: Petrified Forest National Park, Phoenix, Scottsdale & Tempe

COLORADO

Whitney Bryen: Aspen, Colorado Springs & South-Central Colorado

Lindsey Galloway: Rocky Mountain National Park, Summit County, Vail

Aimee Heckel: Mesa Verde National Park, North-Central Colorado, Telluride & Southwestern Colorado

Kellee Katagi: Telluride & Southwestern Colorado

Kyle Wagner: Denver & Vicinity, Steamboat Springs & Northwestern Colorado

NEVADA

Stina Sieg: Great Basin National Park

Mike Weatherford: Las Vegas & Vicinity